ENGRAVED FROM A BUST BY EDWARD V. VALENTINE.

THE LIFE

OF

GEN. ALBERT SIDNEY JOHNSTON,

EMBRACING

*HIS SERVICES IN THE ARMIES OF THE UNITED STATES,
THE REPUBLIC OF TEXAS, AND THE
CONFEDERATE STATES.*

BY

WILLIAM PRESTON JOHNSTON.

NEW INTRODUCTION BY T. MICHAEL PARRISH

WITH ILLUSTRATIONS ON STEEL AND WOOD.

DA CAPO PRESS • NEW YORK

Library of Congress Cataloging-in-Publication Data

Johnston, William Preston, 1831–1899.
   The life of Gen. Albert Sidney Johnston: embracing his services in the
armies of the United States, the Republic of Texas, and the Confederate
States / by William Preston Johnston.
      p.   cm.
   Originally published: New York: D. Appleton, 1879.
   Includes index.
   ISBN 0-306-80791-2 (alk. paper)
   1. Johnston, Albert Sidney, 1803–1862. 2. Generals—Confederate
States of America—Biography. 3. Generals—United States—Biography.
4. Confederate States of America. Army—Biography. 5. United States.
Army—Biography. 6. Texas—History—Republic, 1836–1846. I. Title.
E467.1.J73J7   1997
973.7′ 3′ 092—dc21   97-8742
[B]   CIP

First Da Capo Press edition 1997

This Da Capo Press paperback edition of *The Life of General Albert Sidney
Johnston* is an unabridged republication of the edition published in New York
in 1879, here supplemented with a new introduction by T. Michael Parrish.

Published by Da Capo Press, Inc.
A Subsidiary of Plenum Publishing Corporation
233 Spring Street, New York, N.Y. 10013

THIS BOOK

IS

D E D I C A T E D

TO

G O O D S O L D I E R S E V E R Y W H E R E ;

BUT ESPECIALLY TO

THE SOLDIERS OF THE SOUTH,

AND

T O T H E S O N S O F T H E M E N

WHO SUFFERED IN ITS CAUSE.

INTRODUCTION

HAD ALBERT SIDNEY JOHNSTON survived the Civil War, would the South have won its independence? Many Southerners at the time fervently believed so, and many have reasserted the argument ever since. When Johnston fell mortally wounded at Shiloh in the spring of 1862, the Confederacy lost its shining star, a man widely considered far superior in military ability to any commander, North or South. Robert E. Lee and Thomas J. "Stonewall" Jackson would not seize the limelight for several more months, while Ulysses S. Grant and William T. Sherman, Johnston's adversaries at Shiloh, would remain mired in controversy for many months and seemed ordinary by comparison. Clearly, neither did Joseph E. Johnston or P. G. T. Beauregard, the two heroes of Manassas, claim as much of the Southern people's passionate hopes for victory, nor did these generals enjoy the sheer respect and affection President Jefferson Davis felt for Albert Sidney Johnston as a close friend, honorable career army officer, and natural leader of men. Confederate General Richard Taylor's forthright appraisal in his Civil War memoir *Destruction and Reconstruction* (1879; Da Capo Press reprint, 1995) underscores Johnston's Herculean reputation among his host of admirers:

> His character was lofty and pure, his presence and demeanor dignified and courteous, with the simplicity of a child; and he at once inspired the respect and gained the confidence of cultivated gentlemen and rugged frontiersmen. . . . Like pure gold, he came forth . . . the foremost man of all the South; and had it been possible for one heart, one mind, and one arm to save her cause, she lost them when Albert Sidney Johnston fell on the field of Shiloh.

Albert Sidney Johnston was born in 1803 in Washington, Kentucky. As a young man he attended Transylvania University, where fellow student Jefferson Davis befriended him. In 1822 he gained admission to the United States Military Academy at West Point, where he and cadet Davis perfected their enduring friendship. At West Point, Johnston emerged as the senior adjutant of the Corps of Cadets and ranked eighth in his graduating class in 1826. He married twice, first in 1829 to Henrietta Preston, the mother of two children (including William Preston Johnston), and, after her death, again in 1843 to Eliza Griffin, the mother of five.

Albert Sidney Johnston's varied military career reflected an era of unprecedented national expansion and sectional upheaval. He served in the Black Hawk War in 1832, but resigned his army commission in 1834. After Henrietta's death he started a new life in the fledgling Republic of Texas in 1836 and soon became the revolutionary army's senior brigadier general in the Republic's fight to secure independence from Mexico. Afterwards, he served as the Texan nation's secretary of war from 1838 to 1840. After suffering a gunshot wound in a duel with a military rival, as well as sustaining various political injuries, he embarked on a rather disappointing career as a gentleman planter in Brazoria County, Texas.

The Mexican War rejuvenated Johnston, who served with General Zachary Taylor and displayed particular bravery and resourcefulness during the siege of Monterrey—even saving the life of his old friend Jefferson Davis. According to the general's son, Richard Taylor, "General Taylor . . . declared [Johnston] to be the best soldier he had ever commanded. More than once I have heard General Taylor express this opinion." After the Mexican War, again unable to succeed as a planter, Johnston rejoined the United States Army in 1849 upon appointment from President Zachary Taylor and became a paymaster on the Texas frontier.

Thanks to his old friend, Secretary of War Jefferson Davis, in 1855 Johnston was promoted to colonel and given command of the prominent new Indian-fighting unit, the Second Cavalry, whose subordinate officers included Robert E. Lee, William J. Hardee, George H. Thomas, Edmund Kirby Smith, and Earl Van Dorn. Under Johnston's leadership the Second Cavalry forged a successful record along the frontier of Texas. In 1857 he accepted

the delicate assignment of leading an armed expedition into Utah
Territory to subdue the Mormon Rebellion. A difficult but peaceful conclusion brought him promotion to brevet brigadier general.
By 1860 he commanded the huge Department of the Pacific,
headquartered in San Francisco; his professional reputation had
reached its apex. Rumors implied that aging army commander
Winfield Scott spoke of Johnston, along with Robert E. Lee, as
his possible successor as the nation's top military officer. William
Preston Johnston pinpoints his father's merit for such a role in
his natural abilities as a commander and in his forceful personal
presence:

> He was six feet and an inch in height, weighing about 180 pounds, straight as
> an arrow, with broad and square shoulders and a massive chest. . . . His bearing
> was essentially military, and dignified rather than graceful. . . . He was, indeed, in
> appearance a model for the soldier. . . . He was a graceful and excellent rider, and
> no man presented a grander and more martial appearance on horseback. It was
> remarked of him by Jefferson Davis . . . that "in combat he had the most inspiring
> presence" he ever witnessed. . . . There were in his actions a certain vigor and de-
> cision, in his manner a winning frankness and kindness, and in his whole thought
> and life a simplicity and directness, that were generally irresistible.

Although, like so many other Southerners, he was opposed to
the political tactics and radicalism of the secession movement,
Albert Sidney Johnston abhorred the apparent danger to the
South embodied in the latent abolitionism of President-elect
Abraham Lincoln and the Republican Party. Soon after Texas seceded from the Union in early 1861, Johnston journeyed across
the country from California to Virginia, arrived in Richmond, and
went immediately to see Confederate President Jefferson Davis.
"Suddenly I heard footsteps in the hall," Davis later recalled,
"and I exclaimed, 'There's Sidney Johnston.'" Davis had already
given Johnston the rank of full general, placing him second in
seniority only to the Confederacy's chief military bureaucrat, Adjutant General Samuel Cooper. At Davis's behest Johnston took
command of the immense region called "Confederate Department
No. 2," which embraced a large portion of the western theater of
war. His supreme responsibility would be the protection and control of Kentucky, Tennessee, Missouri, and the heart of the Mississippi River Valley.

Inspired by his new duties, Johnston wrote to his wife, "Never before have I had so many probabilities of success and better grounds for the belief that my star will continue to be in the ascendant." He took command in the West in mid-September 1861, but from the beginning he faced chronic shortages in military manpower and had to depend on poor and untried subordinate officers to shore up a defensive line stretching for more than five hundred miles. In early 1862 Fort Henry on the Tennessee River and Fort Donelson on the Cumberland fell to General Ulysses S. Grant's invading army, forcing Johnston to abandon Kentucky and most of Tennessee. Despite a bitter public outcry against the general, President Davis was confident that Johnston could redeem himself by concentrating his remaining forces and drawing thousands more from other points in the Confederacy. Johnston accepted the public ridicule and mounting expectations, affirming flatly, "The test of merit in my profession with the people is success." Davis asserted openly that if Johnston could not succeed as a general, "we had better give up the war, for we have no generals."

By April 1, 1862, Johnston had gathered about 40,000 men—the Army of the Mississippi—at the northern Mississippi town of Corinth, a vital railroad crossing that represented the strategic key to defending the Mississippi River Valley. Along with his second in command, the flamboyant and nervous General P. G. T. Beauregard, who had come west to advise him and to help organize his thousands of green Confederate troops, Johnston faced one all-important task. He had to move quickly to strike Grant's army (also totaling about 40,000 men) and deliver a mortal blow before 35,000 Union reinforcements marching from central Tennessee under the command of General Don Carlos Buell arrived. With Grant already pushing deep into southwestern Tennessee and encamped only twenty miles from Corinth at Pittsburg Landing on the Tennessee River, Johnston determined to launch a surprise attack on April 4. "I am going to hit Grant, and hit him hard," he vowed to a staff officer. But confusion in the ranks, heavy rains, and muddy roads prevented the Confederates from approaching the enemy until April 5.

Late that day Johnston held a dramatic impromptu meeting with his senior generals. Appalled by the delays and sure that all hope of surprising the Federals had been lost, Beauregard urged his superior to call off the battle. But Johnston had decided to stick with his plan, even on the slightest chance of catching Grant off guard before Buell could arrive. "I would fight them if they were a million," he calmly informed a staff officer. The next morning, April 6, just before dawn, several of his officers were still debating the wisdom of an offensive. When the first flurry of shots rang out along the front lines, Johnston remarked brusquely, "Gentlemen, the ball has opened; no time for argument now."

The first wave of Confederate attacks proved disjointed but effective nonetheless. The Rebels swarmed haphazardly through Grant's unprepared outposts and most remote camps, catching the Yankees completely by surprise. Many of Johnston's triumphant soldiers considered the battle already won, stopping to loot the camps of the fleeing enemy. Thousands of Federals, hysterical with panic, rushed to the banks of the Tennessee River. Other Confederate units often stalled as they struggled through the thick underbrush and dense pine forests, gradually pushing back those blue-clad units still brave enough to resist the onslaught. By noon several thousand Federals had managed to establish a stout defensive line, forming a compact semi-circle supported by some artillery—a death trap the Confederates called the "Hornet's Nest."

When repeated assaults against the "Hornet's Nest" proved futile, Johnston rode forward on his splendid horse "Fire-eater" to urge his men onward. General John B. Breckinridge confessed to being unable to prompt a bloodied Tennessee regiment to renew the attack; Johnston replied earnestly, "Then I will help you." Riding along the line in front of the Tennesseans, he appealed to their notions of duty, devotion to family, and Southern patriotism, stirring them into a frenzy by his confident voice and mere presence. Urging them to "use the bayonet," Johnston finally yelled out, "I will lead you!" Inspired by his courage, the Tennesseans rushed toward the "Hornet's Nest."

Johnston followed for a short distance and turned back, his horse nicked badly by two bullets and the entire sole of his left boot nearly ripped off by another. "They came very near putting me *hors de combat* in that charge," he commented to his staff officers. Suddenly an intense barrage of Federal artillery and musketry spewed forth from the "Hornet's Nest." Most likely, at that moment a bullet wounded Johnston, entering his right leg behind the knee, although in the heat of battle he did not even realize it. A few minutes later his aides saw him reel slightly in the saddle. "General, are you wounded?" one of them asked. "Yes," Johnston replied, "and I fear seriously." His aides carried him to a nearby ravine and stretched him out on the ground, but they could not locate the wound. The bullet had struck an artery, and by now Johnston was already rapidly bleeding to death. Overcome by the loss of blood, he could not think to use the tourniquet in his pocket that could have saved his life. Worst of all, there was no attending physician on hand because while crossing the battlefield earlier Johnston had instructed his personal surgeon, Dr. David Yandell, to assist some badly wounded Yankees. "They were our enemies, but are fellow sufferers now," the general had insisted.

After learning of Johnston's death, Beauregard took command, finally overwhelming the awful "Hornet's Nest." He sent word to Richmond of his "complete victory." But in the long shadows of late afternoon he considered his army nearly exhausted. Grant had established another compact line of desperate troops, this time supported by heavy artillery and the booming firepower of shells from gigantic mortars on two gunboats a short distance away on the Tennessee River. Believing that Buell's reinforcements would not help Grant anytime soon, and confident of crushing the Federals completely the following morning, Beauregard withdrew his troops from the field. But the advance units of Buell's forces had already begun to arrive. Outnumbered by so many fresh troops, the Confederacy's battered Army of the Mississippi was slowly driven from the field the next day.

Still assuming Shiloh to have been a glorious victory, Jefferson Davis issued an official statement to the Confederate Congress, noting Johnston's tragic death: "My long and close friendship with this departed chieftain and patriot forbids me to trust myself in giving vent to the feelings which this sad intelligence has evoked. . . . Our loss is irreparable. . . . There exists no purer spirit, no more heroic soul than that of the illustrious man whose death I join you in lamenting. . . . His last breath cheered his comrades to victory. The last sound he heard was their shout of triumph."

Johnston was buried in New Orleans, but in 1867, in accordance with his wish that his body rest in the soil of his beloved adopted state, the Texas Legislature arranged for reburial in the Texas State Cemetery in Austin. According to Texas historian John H. Jenkins: "When General Johnston's remains arrived at the docks in Galveston, United States General Charles Griffin refused to permit its unloading until the mayor pledged not to allow public mourning. . . . Federal occupation troops prevented the planned solemnities, but virtually the entire populations of Galveston, Houston, and Austin lined the road for miles, silently, in Johnston's honor and dared the troops to act." This mute outpouring of affection from the people of Texas made the event unforgettable for the thousands who witnessed the procession. By 1900 the United Daughters of the Confederacy had commissioned the renowned sculptress Elizabeth Ney to create a white marble recumbent statue of Johnston as she imagined him dying on the field at Shiloh. This magnificent statue adorns his grave in Austin.

William Preston, the oldest son of Albert Sidney Johnston, boasted a distinguished professional career of his own. He was born in Louisville, Kentucky in 1831. After his mother's death when he was four years old, he grew up with maternal relatives. Bright and ambitious, he attended the Western Military Institute in Georgetown, Kentucky and then gained admission to Yale College, graduating in 1852. A year later he earned a law degree at the University of Louisville Law School, and soon afterward married Rosa Elizabeth Duncan, with whom he would have six children. He practiced law for several years in Louisville and in New York City.

At the outbreak of the Civil War, William Preston Johnston was commissioned a major in the Second Kentucky Artillery, later transferring to the Third Kentucky Infantry. Promoted to lieutenant colonel in August 1861, he was assigned to the First Kentucky Infantry in the Army of Northern Virginia, but in early 1862 he fell ill with pneumonia and typhoid fever. Still in precarious health after recovering, he gladly accepted Jefferson Davis's offer to have him serve as an aide-de-camp with the rank of colonel. During the rest of the war William Preston rendered valuable service to Davis by personally inspecting and investigating troops and commanders throughout the Confederacy, thus gaining extensive knowledge of military, political, and social conditions. He was captured along with Davis near Irwinville, Georgia in May 1865, took the oath of allegiance to the United States on July 19, and was released from prison at Fort Delaware in early August. After briefly taking his family to Canada, he returned to Louisville in the spring of 1866 to practice law again.

In 1867 he accepted a call to teach English and history at Washington College (later renamed Washington and Lee) in Lexington, Virginia, where Robert E. Lee served as president. Shortly afterwards, he determined to write a full biography of his father Albert Sidney Johnston. Despite the continual challenge of supporting his family, he began organizing and studying his father's large collection of personal papers (saved and protected during the war), and interviewed dozens of persons who had known the general. Taking leave from most of his teaching duties, he began writing in 1872 and completed his biography five years later. In 1878 the book was published in a large, impressive volume titled *The Life of General Albert Sidney Johnston*. In the meantime, William Preston had joined the faculty of the Law School at Washington and Lee in 1876. Four years later he became the first president of Louisiana State University in Baton Rouge, serving until 1899. He died that same year on July 16 while in Lexington, Virginia and was buried in Louisville.

William Preston considered himself the only author capable of writing the definitive biography of his father, the one able to offer a rich and compelling description of the general's life, career, character, and tragic death. A contemporary review of the book in the *Southern Historical Society Papers* affirmed this view: "With a loving but delicate touch the author tells the story of the life of a great man and illustrates it with anecdote, reminiscence, and private letters in such a style as to rivet the attention of the reader from the beginning to the end of the book." His massive and detailed biography fully deserves renewed attention from all Civil War scholars and readers. Even at a glance, the book's merits are obvious, manifold, and even startling.

Only a son like William Preston, himself a prominent Confederate officer, could have written such a book. His intimate knowledge of private family life and of countless details about his father's personal habits, pivotal experiences, decisions, and actions, and his profound understanding of his father's remarkable character emerge on nearly every page of the narrative. The son was also a superb scholar who not only utilized his father's large collection of personal manuscripts, but tracked down dozens of the general's friends, comrades-in-arms, and former antagonists, all of whom contributed colorful anecdotes and insights. Scores of these excellent letters and reminiscences, available in no other printed source or otherwise lost to the ages, are quoted, often in full, throughout the book. Finally, William Preston Johnston was a fine writer. His prose is clear, steady, and piercing. He effectively weaves hundreds of telling facts and vignettes into the narrative. And, most importantly, his critical judgment is surprisingly free of overt defensiveness about his father's skill and reputation as a military officer. "Hostile criticism can always begin its argument with the charge that it is impossible for a son to be fair," he admits in the preface. "But it is not necessary to be impartial in order to be truthful; and, without love, there can be no correct interpretation of character.... General Johnston was so truthful and simple in all he said and did that the fittest tribute to his memory is absolute accuracy in whatever relates to him."

William Preston devotes more than two-thirds of his book to describing his father's experiences during the last two years of his life. He argues unflinchingly that Albert Sidney Johnston would have carried the day at Shiloh and would have achieved far more than any of his successors, if only his life had been spared. Jefferson Davis, of course, agreed completely, later asserting, "His plans at Shiloh were perfect.... Up to the moment of his death every step in that plan of battle had been successfully taken. Had he lived, Buell never would have crossed the Tennessee River; Grant would have been driven into the river ... and Sidney Johnston would have marched to the Ohio."

The general's former opponents, as expected, were typically far less lavish and even guarded in their praise. When asked about Johnston's "greatness" as a commander, Ulysses S. Grant replied:

> I knew Albert Sidney Johnston before the war. I had a high opinion of his talents. When the war broke out he was regarded as the coming man of the Confederacy. I shared that opinion, because I knew and esteemed him and because I felt as we all did in the old army, where there was a public opinion among the officers as to who would come out ahead.... Johnston might have risen in fame, and we all had confidence in his doing so, but he died too soon, as Stonewall Jackson died, too soon for us to say what he would have done under the later and altered conditions of the war.

Without question, prior to the Shiloh campaign, Johnston had proved unequal to his new responsibilities because he failed to formulate, much less execute, a viable plan for defending the vast Western theater of the Confederacy. "Yet in the Shiloh campaign," notes his modern biographer, Charles P. Roland, "Johnston succeeded in achieving what Napoleon said was one of the most difficult feats in warfare, that of turning a general retreat into an advance." In other words, Johnston quickly seized the initiative from Grant. "Johnston clearly outdid Grant in bringing together the wings of his army under Grant's very eyes and in staging against him one of the most remarkable surprise assaults in military history," Roland argues convincingly. "Johnston stood above Beauregard also when at the last moment—Carl von Clausewitz's 'moment of truth'—Johnston ordered the attack to proceed over the objection of his unnerved second-in-command."

Might Johnston have made all the difference in the Confederacy's quest for independence? Because his successors in the Western theater—Beauregard, Braxton Bragg, and Joseph Johnston—

proved so erratic and ineffective, it is tempting to claim that surely Albert Sidney Johnston would have done better. Had he been given the time to develop fully—as Robert E. Lee had the time to develop as commander in the East—Johnston probably would have become a tremendous asset, perhaps an even greater asset than Lee, to the Southern cause. Historian Albert E. Castel has made this assertion most forcefully:

> Johnston possessed many of the same attributes that made Lee a great commander: aggressiveness, willingness to take great risks, resolution and persistence in overcoming obstacles, composure and decisiveness when faced with a crisis, and an intellect and personal character that inspired trust, even devotion, in others. . . . But whether Albert Sidney Johnston could have equaled Lee's performance is another matter. Johnston had a much larger and more vulnerable area to defend than did Lee, and he had fewer men and resources. His opponents would have been Grant, George H. Thomas, William S. Rosecrans, and William T. Sherman [commanders greatly superior in abilities to Lee's opponents]. . . . Johnston could, conceivably, have prevailed in spite of these handicaps, but probably the most he could have done was to prolong effective Confederate resistance in the West by avoiding the disasters of his successors. This might not seem like much, but it might have been enough. After all, in 1864 the South . . . came close to winning the war by causing the North to lose the will to continue fighting.

Because the war was finally lost in the West, the Confederate Army of Tennessee slowly giving ground to the increasingly powerful forces of Grant and Sherman, the South desperately needed a commander comparable to Lee in the task of staving off defeat. Had he lived, Albert Sidney Johnston most likely would have succeeded in preventing what the habitually carping and unaggressive Joseph Johnston could not: the fall of Atlanta in September 1864, the single most disastrous defeat of the war and a catastrophe that effectively sealed Abraham Lincoln's re-election in November by reinvigorating the Northern public's will to push the war to a victorious conclusion, regardless the cost. Albert Sidney Johnston had demonstrated convincingly at Shiloh that he, like Robert E. Lee, was determined to resist the Union army's formidable power by seizing the initiative and pressing the attack. With Lee thwarting the Yankees for three years in the East, Johnston could have done the same in the West, especially given the invading enemy's immense logistical problems—the need to protect supply lines and to defend occupied territory—and the huge strategic risks that confronted Union forces at Vicksburg, Port Hudson, Chattanooga, and Atlanta.

Most of all, like Robert E. Lee, Albert Sidney Johnston enjoyed the complete respect and friendship of President Jefferson Davis. It is entirely reasonable to argue that Davis and Johnston would have evolved into a powerfully effective team, just as Davis and Lee did, and that enough battlefield victories—at least enough to aggravate and ultimately to stall Union forces in the West—would have proved the inevitable result. But at Shiloh that great hope bled to death. For this reason alone, it is easy to accept the lament that Jefferson Davis repeated so often after the war—that Albert Sidney Johnston's fatal wounding signified "the turning of our fate."

T. MICHAEL PARRISH
Austin, Texas
March 1997

T. Michael Parrish is the author of Richard Taylor: Soldier Prince of Dixie. *A graduate of Baylor University, with a doctorate from the University of Texas, he is on the staff of the Lyndon B. Johnson Library.*

FOR ADDITIONAL INFORMATION READERS CAN CONSULT THE FOLLOWING WORKS:

Castel, Albert. "Dead on Arrival: The Life and Sudden Death of General Albert Sidney Johnston." *Civil War Times Illustrated*, 36 (March 1997), pp. 30–37.

Castel, Albert. "Savior of the South? Was Albert Sidney Johnston the 'Robert E. Lee of the West'—the Missing Ingredient for Southern Victory?" *Civil War Times Illustrated*, 36 (March 1997), pp. 38–40.

Connelly, Thomas L. *Army of the Heartland: The Army of Tennessee, 1861–1862*. Baton Rouge: Louisiana State University Press, 1967.

Crist, Lynda Lasswell, Mary Seaton Dix, and Kenneth H. Williams, eds. *The Papers of Jefferson Davis*. 9 vols. Baton Rouge: Louisiana State University Press, 1971–1997.

Davis, Jefferson. *The Rise and Fall of the Confederate Government*. 2 vols. New York: 1881; reprinted by Da Capo Press, 1990.

Davis, Jefferson; Hudson Strode, ed. *Jefferson Davis: Private Letters, 1823–1889*. New York: Harcourt, Brace & World, 1966; reprinted by Da Capo Press, 1995.

Daniel, Larry J. *Shiloh: The Battle that Changed the Civil War*. New York: Simon & Schuster, 1997.

McDonough, James Lee. *Shiloh: In Hell Before Night*. Knoxville: University of Tennessee Press, 1977.

Roland, Charles P. *Albert Sidney Johnston: Jefferson Davis's Greatest General?* Fort Worth: Ryan Place Publishers, 1997.

Roland, Charles P. *Albert Sidney Johnston: Soldier of Three Republics*. Austin: University of Texas Press, 1964.

Roman, Alfred. *The Military Operations of General Beauregard in the War Between the States, 1861 to 1865*. 2 vols. New York: Harper & Brothers, 1884; reprinted by Da Capo Press, 1994.

Shaw, Arthur Marvin. *William Preston Johnston: A Transitional Figure of the Confederacy*. Baton Rouge: Louisiana State University Press, 1943.

Sword, Wiley. *Shiloh: Bloody April*. New York: William Morrow, 1974.

Taylor, Richard. *Destruction and Reconstruction: Personal Reminiscences of the Civil War*. New York: D. Appleton and Company, 1879; reprinted by Da Capo Press, 1995.

Thompson, Jerry D., ed. *Into the Far, Wild Country: True Tales of the Old Southwest by George Wythe Baylor.* El Paso: Texas Western Press, University of Texas at El Paso, 1996.

Woodworth, Steven E. *Jefferson Davis and His Generals: The Failure of Confederate Command in the West.* Lawrence: University Press of Kansas, 1990.

PREFACE.

A BIOGRAPHY of ALBERT SIDNEY JOHNSTON will need no apology with a large class of his countrymen. Many discreet men have urged upon the writer that his duty, both as son and citizen, required him to do this work. They believed that the omission of a picture of this heroic life would leave unfilled an important panel in the gallery of American history, in which the Civil War occupies so large a space. In response to such demand this memoir has been written.

The writer would gladly have devolved his task on some more competent and disinterested hand. He has felt keenly the restrictions and obligations imposed by the filial relation. Hostile criticism can always begin its argument with the charge that it is impossible for a son to be fair; and the writer's own heart teaches him how difficult it is to be always and perfectly just. A writer who strives to delineate a dear, dead father will not mar the picture by a portrait below his own ideal, though it may well fall short of the heroic proportions of the original. But it is not necessary to be impartial, in order to be truthful; and, without love, there can be no correct interpretation of character. Knowing that he has made an honest effort to find out and relate the truth in every particular in this volume, the writer trusts that much will be pardoned to him.

If a friend could have been found fitted by preparation, leisure, and literary enthusiasm, for so heavy a charge, it would have been consigned to him with a feeling of immeasurable relief. But this was not to be. The labor promised and proved to be very great. The very sources of information had often to be discovered, and the material employed has been gathered from quarters remote and obscure; siftings of the memories of the aged or the unwilling, for many of those best qualified to speak of the events of the Civil War are often the most averse to recall its painful experiences. Then, too, the verification of the facts involved processes too tedious for any one not animated by the strongest sense of personal interest and responsibility. Hence it came to pass that the writer was himself compelled to discharge this duty.

In spite of these serious obstacles, the writer has had some peculiar facilities for the successful achievement of his purpose. A strong call from within and from without has urged him on. The friendship of eminent Confederates and the sympathy of a multitude of worthy people have encouraged him in his design and furnished him with valuable information. General Johnston's own papers have been preserved almost entire since 1836; and these, including his Confederate archives, complete, have supplied ampler and more perfect materials than most biographers enjoy. Gentlemen who were opposed to him in the late Civil War have been both courteous and generous in affording all proper information; and, in this respect, he is especially indebted to the Honorable George W. McCrary, the present Secretary of War, to General D. C. Buell, General Fitz-John Porter, and Colonel George H. Elliott, of the Engineers, and to other gentlemen to whom acknowledgments are made in the course of the narrative.

Such frequent and important services have been rendered in the preparation of this book by so many friends that their recognition can be made appropriately only in the same way; and, indeed, a large part of the value of this work is due to their unselfish aid. But the writer cannot omit to express here his deep obligations to the Honorable Jefferson Davis, ex-President of the Confederate States; to the late General Braxton Bragg; to Governors I. G. Harris, John C. Brown, and James D. Porter, of Tennessee; to Colonel Edward W. Munford, General William Preston, General W. C. Whitthorne, General William J. Hamby, Dr. William M. Polk, Colonel A. Ridley, Captain G. W. Gift, and Captain N. J. Eaton. His late colleagues, Prof. Edward S. Joynes, now of Vanderbilt University, and Prof. Carter J. Harris, of Washington and Lee University, have given him most acceptable literary assistance.

In addition to the writer's unusual opportunities for arriving at the truth, there were certain exceptional features in his relations to

General Johnston, not often found between father and son. There was the utmost confidence and intimacy in their intercourse, and yet General Johnston sedulously cultivated the independent development of his children. Further, the writer's lines of life and habits of thought have been widely remote from his father's. Hence he believes that, thus unfettered by his authority yet conversant with his ideas and affairs, he can often explain better than any one else the bearing of obscure transactions.

Nevertheless, the close tie between the biographer and his subject has to some extent marred the artistic effect of this book. Not only delicacy but a sense of duty to the intelligent reader has dictated that it was better in all personal matters to speak in the language of others, wherever it was possible; and yet this could only be done at some sacrifice of brevity and of apparent unity. Then, too, in the discussion of controverted points, where a bias might be presumed to exist, he has thought it proper, while frankly stating his own conclusions, to give the evidence on which they rest. Some original documents and tables of military statistics, pertinent to the narrative, have been published with it, for the sake of their historical value.

There has been no effort to make General Johnston the central figure of his times, or to drag into his biography matters extraneous to his career. But where any phase of life, or series of events, was interwoven with it, the reader is not assumed to be acquainted with unfamiliar or forgotten facts. Such facts are recounted as succinctly as the matter will admit, but not, it is hoped, at the expense of accuracy. But, though he has been diligent in seeking to be exact, he knows the difficulties, and, so far from deprecating judicious criticism, he invites it, in the interest of historical truth.

General Johnston was singularly tolerant of others, though himself severe in principles and circumspect in conduct. Hence it has not been thought necessary, for the most part, to vindicate his opinions or actions; since, if the tenor of his life was noble and good, its errors and mistakes may well be left standing for such warning or censure as the moralist shall feel compelled to employ. Such would have been his own wish. But the integrity and sincerity of the man permit the writer to use an uncommon frankness in detailing not only the events of his public career, but such incidents of his domestic life as may serve for instruction or illustration. The *facts* of a life are the best—perhaps, the only—apology for writing it ; and General Johnston was so truthful and simple in all he said and did that the fittest tribute to his memory is absolute accuracy in whatever relates to him. No ideal of what a hero ought to be has been framed herein ; but the story of a life has been told, just as it was lived. Sympathetic spirits, however wide the differences of circumstance, creed, or opinion, may learn, in its adversities and its consolations, some lessons of fortitude and magnanimity.

This biography recounts a stirring theme. The most casual reader must be struck with the dramatic interest of the career of a man who, with small share of wealth, patronage, or political arts, filled so large a sphere by mere moral and intellectual force. It is something in this material age to find a man almost wholly above the accidents of fortune. In some respects he was a man representative and typical of his times, his country, his section and his profession ; in others he stood apart with an individuality so marked that Marcus Aurelius might have welcomed him as a brother-stoic, or the Chevalier Bayard as a knightly peer. In Albert Sidney Johnston's long life he mingled in many great and memorable events, and in some of the greatest he acted the chief and most conspicuous part. In all of them, his countrymen accounted him a fine example of civic and military virtues. His death was not only the decorous and becoming end to a grand life, but many of the wisest and ablest leaders believed that in his fall a national tragedy culminated, which ever after declined toward its final catastrophe. Many of the most judicious have declared that on his arm rested the fortunes of the Confederate cause. It cannot be well that such a figure should pass into utter oblivion.

CONTENTS.

CHAPTER I.

CHAPTER II.

CHAPTER III.

CHAPTER IV.

CHAPTER V.

CHAPTER VI.

CHAPTER VII.

CHAPTER VIII.

CHAPTER IX.

CHAPTER X.

CHAPTER XI.

CHAPTER XII.

CHAPTER XIII.

CHAPTER XIV.

PAGE

Federal Policy toward the Mormons. Expedition to sustain Civil Officers. General Harney appointed to command it. General Johnston succeeds him. Army Orders. Start. Celerity. Journey. Mormon Hostilities. South Pass. Concentration. Movements of Troops. Winter. Efforts to reach Winter-Quarters. In the Snow-Drifts. His Defense by Mr. Davis. General Johnston's Letters detailing the Circumstances. Rescue of the Army. Arrival at Bridger. The Tests of Soldiership. In Winter-Quarters. Fort Bridger. Major Porter's Diary. Brigham's Salt Embassy. Ornithology. Conflicting Policies. Colonel Kane the Diplomatist. Senatorial Criticism on General Johnston. Trouble with Governor Cumming. An Icy Spring. Peace Commissioners. Submission of the Mormons. General Johnston's Reply to Peace Commissioners. His Proclamation. Governor Cumming's Protest. Army Matters and Orders. Brevet Brigadier-General. Commendation and Criticism. General Johnston's Review of Strictures on Himself.

CHAPTER XV.

Location. Duties. Disbanded Volunteers. Winter-Quarters. Indian Affairs. Mormon Slanders. Issue with Governor Cumming. Conflicts of Authority. Governor's Proclamation. Ambiguous Policy of the Government. General Johnston's Administration of Utah. Relieved. Letter in regard to *personnel* of the Army. Family Affections. Parting with his Army. A Gift declined. Attempt to bring him forward for the Presidency. His Letters on the Subject. His Valuation of his Citizenship. A Fleet-footed Indian. The Japanese. A Quartermaster-General appointed. Reunion with his Family. 1860. The Crisis of American Destiny. Assignment to Command in California.

CHAPTER XVI.

Origin of the Troubles. Standpoint of the Southern People. The Slavery Question. Views of the Constitution. Mr. Lincoln's Election. Confederate Government organized. Its Policy. Opinion in the South. Virginia. Lincoln calls for Troops. Revulsion and Secession of Border States. War. Bethel. Manassas. Its Results. Comparative Strength of the Sections. Kentucky, Missouri, Maryland, West Virginia.

CHAPTER XVII.

General Johnston's Ideas of Government. The Right of Resistance. The Alternative presented. Resigns and is relieved. Imaginary Plot. Slander refuted. General Buell's Letter. Governor Downey's Statement. General Mackall's Letter. Incidents of Resignation. Attempted Reparation by the Administration. Hon. Montgomery Blair's Letter. Los Angeles. Advice to Citizens. Writer's Recollections. General Johnston's Correspondence.

CHAPTER XVIII.

Resignation accepted. Impending War. A Dread Alternative. Cherished Gift. Surveillance and Escape. On the Road. The Desert. The Comet. Tucson. The Pimos Indians. Anecdote. Federal Troops. Running the Gantlet. An Indian Massacre. The Rio Grande. Anecdote. Escape of Moore and Lord. Lynde's Surrender. Through Texas. Anecdotes. The Journey summed up. A Nation's Suspense and Joy. Arrival at Richmond.

CHAPTER XIX.

CHAPTER XX.

CHAPTER XXI.

CHAPTER XXII.

CHAPTER XXIII.

CHAPTER XXIV.

CHAPTER XXIX.

CHAPTER XXX.

CHAPTER XXXI.

CHAPTER XXXII.

CHAPTER XXXIII.

LIFE

GENERAL ALBERT SIDNEY JOHNSTON.

CHAPTER I.

FAMILY AND BOYHOOD.

ALBERT SIDNEY JOHNSTON was born on the 2d of February, 1803, in the village of Washington, Mason County, Kentucky. He was the youngest son of Dr. John Johnston, a physician, and one of the early settlers of that town. Dr. Johnston's father, Archibald Johnston, was a native of Salisbury, Connecticut, and descended from a Scotch family of some property and local influence, settled in Salisbury. John Johnston, having received a liberal education at New Haven, and at the medical school at Litchfield, began the practice of his profession in his native town. In 1783, at the age of twenty-one, he married Mary Stoddard, by whom he had three sons, Josiah Stoddard, Darius, and Orramel. In 1788 he removed to Kentucky, and settled at Washington, where he remained until his death in 1831.

Mason County, which then included all the northern and eastern portion of Kentucky, in 1790 contained only 2,729 inhabitants, while the whole population of the Territory of Kentucky was less than 74,000. The country still suffered from Indian incursions across the Ohio, and was indeed the very frontier of civilization. But, although an outpost, this beautiful and fertile neighborhood already enjoyed the benefits of social order, and was fast filling up with substantial and educated families, principally from Virginia and Maryland. Dr. Johnston's skill and worth soon secured him not only a large practice, but the warm friendship of the best people, with whom he continued in the kindest relations during his whole life.

Having lost his first wife in 1793, in the following year he married Abigail Harris, the daughter of Edward Harris, an old settler, who, with his wife, had emigrated from Newburyport, Massachusetts, and whom a venerable citizen describes as "the old John Knox Presbyterian of the place ;" adding, "anecdotes are still told of the spirit and courage with which he defended his Church." One of General Johnston's earliest recollections was of his grandfather giving him money to buy a catechism. Edward Harris had been a Revolutionary soldier, and was appointed military storekeeper and postmaster at Washington, Kentucky, by President Washington. A letter to the Postmaster-General is still extant in which he resigns the latter office, because some new postal arrangement required him to open the mail on Sunday, which he could not conscientiously do. The letter is a candid expression of very decided religious convictions, and is evidently the production of an educated and thoughtful man. Edward Harris died in 1825, aged eightyfour years. He, at one time, owned a large body of land in Ohio, but lost it by the intrusion of squatters. Dr. Johnston's second wife lived about twelve years after her marriage, and died, leaving him six children—John Harris, Lucius, Anna Maria, Clarissa, Albert Sidney, and Eliza. Anna Maria married Mr. James Byers, Clarissa remained unmarried, and Eliza married John A. McClung, distinguished first as a lawyer and afterward as a Presbyterian minister. Dr. Johnston subsequently married Mrs. Byers, a widow with a large family of children, but there was no issue from this marriage. He died in 1831. Wonder was often expressed that he did not remove to a city, where his acknowledged skill would have secured adequate reward ; but it may be presumed that he fairly estimated his advantages, and was satisfied to be able to maintain and properly educate so large a family. This he did, giving all his children the best education that the times afforded. Though diligent and conscientious in his profession, he was not anxious to accumulate money, and late in life became poor from the payment of security debts. To discharge these he voluntarily gave up all his property; his home was sold at public sale, but it was bought and restored to him by his eldest son, who had then become eminent and prosperous. Mr. J. S. Chambers, from whom these facts were obtained, adds :

I always thought General Johnston inherited his frank, manly nature from his father. His mother was a gentle, quiet woman; while the old doctor was bold and blunt to a remarkable degree. He had no concealments, and was physically energetic, and mentally bold and independent. He had a large practice, and was often called into consultation in difficult, or rather in desperate, cases.

All the old citizens of Washington bear witness to his industry, skill, talents, and probity, and to his kind and genial temper. General Johnston's mother is spoken of by others as a woman of handsome person, fine intellect, and sterling worth ; but, whatever traits her children inherited from her, she died too young to have done much toward moulding their character.

The boyhood of Albert Sidney Johnston was a fit prelude to his after-life. Though his father's means were narrow, yet the education which he had, at whatever personal inconvenience, bestowed upon all his children, could not fail to exercise a liberalizing influence on his household. The habits of all classes at that time were plain and unostentatious ; but this family was necessarily trained to a Spartan simplicity that was ever after the rule and habit of life most congenial to the subject of this memoir. Captain Wilson Duke, United States Navy, one of the choice friends of his youth, used laughingly to tell how he tore off his ruffled shirt-collar and hid his shoes on the road to school, from fear of Albert Johnston's ridicule. His intimate friends in those early days nearly all obtained more than ordinary positions in after-life. Among them were : Captain Wilson Duke, the father of the gallant General Basil W. Duke ; Captain William Smith, also of the United States Navy; Captain William Bickley, of the United States Army ; Hon. John D. Taylor, well known in the politics and jurisprudence of Kentucky; Mr. Charles Marshall (known as Black Dan), Mr. John Green, and John A. McClung.

Albert Sidney Johnston was endowed by nature with an ardent and enthusiastic temperament ; but to this were joined a solidity of judgment and a power of self-control, that early held it in check, and eventually so regulated it that it was only displayed in resolutions and actions requiring uncommon loftiness of soul. The feature of his character most remarked by his contemporaries was, in his early boyhood, an energy that made him an acknowledged leader among his comrades ; later, it was a self-contained dignity and reserved power that subjected affections, will, and passions, to the performance of duty.

His eldest sister says of him that, when he was a boy, he was fearless and impetuous ; but kind, affectionate, and just; amenable to reason, and deferential to age.

Mr. J. G. Hickman, of Maysville, writing in 1869, "after consulting all the old folk," says :

My aunt and Mr. Lashbrooke remember General Johnston from his infancy; and they say, as indeed all say, that there was great promise about him from his childhood. He was a handsome, proud, manly, earnest, and self-reliant boy; and his success and distinction in after-life were only what were expected of him by those who knew him in his boyhood. Mr. Lashbrooke says he went to the same school with him, in 1811, to Mann Butler, a teacher of some distinction in his day. He was distinguished, too, for his courage in boyhood and early manhood. While he was a born gentleman, as they all say, and as far from being a bully as any boy in the world, yet he was one whom the bullies left undisturbed. Colonel C. A. Marshall told me of one fellow about Washington who was proud of playing the bully, but who, to the amusement of the town, always skipped Albert Johnston and Black Dan Marshall.

General Johnston sometimes told an anecdote of his early boyhood, from which he was wont to draw many a valuable moral. Playing marbles "for keeps"—a species of boyish gaming—was a favorite sport of his schoolboy days; and he was so skillful and successful a marble-player that at one time he had won a whole jar full of white alleys, taws, potters, etc. It was then that the design entered his breast of winning all the marbles in the town, in the State, and eventually in the world. Filled with enthusiasm at the vastness of his project, he cast about for the means; and finally concluded, as the first step, to secure his acquisitions by burying them. He buried his jar very secretly, reserving only marbles enough "to begin life on." Purpose lent steadiness to his aim, so that again he beat all his rivals "in the ring," and added daily to his store. Only one competitor stood against him, whose resources seemed to consist not so much in skill as in an exhaustless supply of marbles, that were sacrificed with a recklessness arguing unlimited pocket-money. At last he, too, succumbed, and the victor went with a jar larger than the first, to add it to his spoils. To his dismay, however, he found *his hoard plundered and his treasure gone.* The inferior, but desperate, marble-player had furtively watched him, robbed him, and then staked and lost his ill-gotten gains. The second jar contained the same marbles as the first, and larceny had contended for empire with ambition. General Johnston said that he felt the lesson as a distinct rebuke to his avarice and rapacity; the plans he had built upon success vanished; and he learned that world-wide renown as a marble-player was merely "vanity and vexation of spirit."

Mr. J. S. Chambers, writing in January, 1873, says:

He was six or seven years my senior, yet I remember him with great distinctness. He was my *beau-idéal* of a manly, handsome boy. He went to school for several years to James Grant, about one mile and a half west of Washington. He was active and energetic in the athletic games of the period, and fond of hunting on Saturdays, and always stood well in his classes, having a special talent for mathematics. He was grave and thoughtful in his deportment, but, when drawn out, talked well, and was considered by his associates and teachers as a boy of fine capacity.

When he was nearly fifteen years of age his father yielded to his wishes, and sent him to a school in Western Virginia; but he was disappointed in its character, and remained only one session. He was afterward, for a short time, in the drug-store of Mr. Thomas Duke; but, whether with the intention of adopting trade or medicine as a line of life, we are not informed. Throughout life he showed an uncommon knowledge of physiology, and acquaintance with medical practice ; due in part, perhaps, to this apprenticeship, but probably still more to the informal instruction of his father.

Colonel C. Marshall, writing with reference to this period of his life, says :

> His dignified bearing, his reserved and quiet manners, even at that time, I can recall. The influence he always possessed with the young men of his own age, and his habitual interference for the protection of the smaller and weaker boys, are well remembered.

He was then sent to Transylvania, where he remained a session, the room-mate of his townsman, John D. Taylor, who was of his own age, and who wrote concerning him :

> Nature had endowed him with a genius and fondness for mathematics, which enabled him to hold a high position in his class at Transylvania.

He studied hard, but at the end of the term became restless, from a desire to enter the navy. The gallant achievements of the American Navy in the war against Great Britain, and the subsequent daring exploits of Decatur at Algiers, had doubtless inspired him with the desire to emulate these high examples. His friends Duke and Smith, under the same impulse, sought and obtained warrants as midshipmen. But this project received no favor at home. His father and family opposed it ; and, in order to divert his mind from brooding over a plan on which he had set his heart, it was proposed that he should accompany his sister, Mrs. Byers, and her husband, who were going to Louisiana. In the autumn of 1819 he went with them to the parish of Rapides, whither all his brothers had preceded him, and made a visit to his eldest brother, Josiah Stoddard Johnston. This visit was attended with important consequences to the adventurous youth, changing the theatre of his ambition from sea to land. Indeed, as the youngest son, the Benjamin of the household, sent to this new land of plenty by the old man, his father, he was received with a double portion of kindness by the elder brother, who, now in middle life, had already achieved a conspicuous position.

It will not be inappropriate here to give a brief account of the brothers of Albert Sidney Johnston, since a strong family likeness to "the old man, their father," and to each other, serves in some measure to throw light upon his character. It has been already mentioned that the immigration to Mason County had brought with it a degree of wealth, culture, and social order, unusual in new communities, to which was joined the enterprise that had peopled the wilderness. The intellectual vigor of the settlers is evinced in the "Kentucky Law Reports" of an early period, which show legal ability and acumen rare in any country. Nowhere were the characteristic traits of Kentucky people more fully displayed than in Mason County, from whose pioneer families proceeded many noted men ; but from under no roof-tree went forth a hardier brood than from that which sheltered the boyhood of Albert Sidney Johnston. First among his brothers in age and eminence was Josiah Stoddard Johnston. The following facts, obtained from a sketch of him by Hon. Henry D. Gilpin, of Philadelphia, and from other sources, will give some idea of his career.

Born in Salisbury, Connecticut, November 24, 1784, he was taken to Kentucky by his father at an early age. When twelve years old his father carried him to New Haven, Connecticut, to school, where he remained some years ; but he completed his academic education at Transylvania University, Lexington, Kentucky, and then studied law with the famous George Nicholas. His acquirements were solid, and his reading choice and various. In 1805 he emigrated to the Territory of Louisiana, lately acquired from the French, and then sparsely settled by a rude population. Settling at Alexandria, at that time a frontier village, he devoted himself to the practice of law, and rapidly gained wealth and distinction. His firm yet gentle temper and strong sense of justice kept him free from the personal collisions that marked the period and region, and, indeed, enabled him to maintain the honorable character of an umpire in an unorganized society, so that he was called "the Peacemaker," while his education and talents placed him in the front rank of the leaders of public opinion. He was elected to the first Territorial Legislature, and continued a member of that body until Louisiana became a State in 1812. He held the position of district judge from 1812 to 1821. Toward the close of the war, when Louisiana was invaded by the British, he was elected to the command of a regiment of volunteers, which he had aided in raising, and to equip which he had from his own means bought a large quantity of arms and ammunition ; but, though they joined General Jackson, it was too late to share in the decisive victory of January 8, 1815. In 1814 he married Miss Eliza Sibley, the daughter of Dr. John Sibley, of Natchitoches, a lady of rare personal and intellectual attractions. In 1821 he was elected to the Seventeenth Congress, and in 1823 to the Senate of the United States; in 1825 he was reëlected ; and in 1831 he was chosen again by a Legislature opposed to him in political opinion. These successive trusts were justified by the fidelity and success with which they were discharged; and his last election was due to the conviction that his continuance in the Senate was necessary to the welfare of the State. As a member of that body, though he did not decline to take part in the exciting political contests then waged, his chief attention was directed to the advancement of the material interests of the country. Although not a brilliant orator, he was a clear and forcible speaker, and always commanded the ear of the Senate. As chairman of the Committee on Commerce, and as a member of the Committee on Finance, he brought to bear an untiring industry that mastered the details, while it grasped the principles of whatever subjects came before him; and this not only by the study of books, but by conference with practical men and by severe, independent thought. Hence his reports and speeches, which were marked by the directness of his mind and the unselfishness of his political character, were listened to with respect even by his opponents, while his amiability and forbearance secured him a large personal influence. He enjoyed a very close friendship with Mr. Clay, with whom he was in political affiliation. He opposed the doctrine of Nullification, and was a leading advocate for a carefully-guarded protective tariff which, by a judicious adjustment of duties, should advance American industry. But, while he was a close student of the history and Constitution of the United States, and a representative diligent in the protection of his constituents, his position in reference to the commerce of the country called his attention to questions of even wider range. It is to his credit that, with an enlightened benevolence and enlarged view of international law, he strenuously pressed upon the Government the duty of seeking a mitigation of the laws of maritime war. To this end he urged especially that neutral vessels should protect the goods on board to whomsoever they might belong; and that articles contraband of war should be limited to the smallest possible number of such as are of direct use and essential in their operations.

Mr. Johnston was somewhat below middle size, of graceful person, handsome countenance, and most winning manners. The testimony of his contemporaries represents him as a firm yet moderate partisan; a statesman of singularly disinterested views; a most steadfast and loyal friend ; and a man of warm, pure affections, cheerful, generous, and honorable. The happy influence of such a character and career upon a band of younger brothers cannot be over-estimated, especially when they saw virtue crowned with a success which met neither check nor reverse from its beginning in 1805 to the close of an honored life in 1833. He was a man well beloved, and well deserving the love of his fellow-men. His conduct toward his brothers not only illustrates the warmth of his affections, but exerted a powerful influence over the destinies of his family. As they approached man's estate he directed and aided in their education, invited them to his home, and advanced them in their professions.

Darius was graduated at Transylvania, and studied law with Hon. William T. Barry, afterward Postmaster-General. Orramel and Harris were thoroughly trained, under the eye of their eldest brother, by private tutors ; the former completing the study of medicine in New Orleans, and the latter studying law with Judge Alexander Porter, an eminent jurist. Darius and Orramel, however, took part in the Mexican War of Independence ; and, although they survived to return, it was with constitutions ruined by hardship, fever, and imprisonment, so that the former soon died, and the latter survived only a few years. Lucius, who was said to possess fine oratorical powers, went to Louisiana with the view of becoming a planter; but in the second year of his residence succumbed to a prevalent malignant fever, when only twenty-four years old. These were all remembered as young men of much promise. John Harris Johnston, with better fortune, at once made his way at the bar, and was also several times elected to the State Legislature. He was then chosen district judge ; which position, after some years, he resigned, to take the place of parish judge, which he held until his death in 1838. He was a remarkably handsome man, with fine legal abilities and great industry, and with the same amiability that characterized his brothers. As Josiah S. Johnston showed to his brothers of the half-blood the same affection and kindness as to his own brothers, so to him and his memory were returned a gratitude and devotion that lost none of their warmth by lapse of years. Not many years before his own death, General Johnston said to the writer, with great feeling, " I am more indebted to my brother Stoddard for whatever I am, than to any other man." He taught his children to love and revere the memory of this generous brother and his good wife.

In the course of a winter passed most pleasantly in Louisiana, Albert Sidney Johnston yielded his purpose to enter the navy, in deference to his brother's advice, and consented to return to Transylvania University. Once resolved, he reëntered with ardor and steady industry on his collegiate course at Lexington, where he remained two years. Transylvania University, though planted almost in the wilderness, had the good fortune to be under able direction, and had thus acquired great reputation as a seat of learning. It was the Alma Mater of many illustrious men, among whom is Jefferson Davis. In his own reminiscences of his college-life, General Johnston spoke with great respect of the eminent talents and distinguished urbanity of Dr. Holley, the president; and with affectionate remembrance of Mr. and Mrs. Deweese, the amiable friends with whom he boarded, and by whom he was treated like a kinsman. He not only advanced himself in his mathematics during his stay at Transylvania, but obtained a very thorough training in the Latin classics, and an acquaintance with other branches of learning that were useful to him later in life. Twenty-five years afterward he read and construed Sallust with considerable facility. But his preference was for mathematics and the natural sciences. Mr. John P. Morton, of Louisville, who sat next him in class, says, " He was conspicuous for always knowing his lessons."

He was undoubtedly a hard student, and he met his reward in the form he most desired. After the check given to his wish to enter the navy, the desire to become a soldier had entirely supplanted it; and in this hope his eldest brother had indulged him. In 1822 Josiah S. Johnston, being then a member of Congress from Louisiana, procured for him an appointment to the Military Academy at West Point; and he entered on his preparation for the military career with an enthusiasm that had in it almost the spirit of consecration. His sister, Mrs. Byers, supplies a little anecdote that may be related here. He had a beautiful riding-horse, which he thought of selling; but, as the time approached for his departure, he would turn his favorite out of the stable, and watch his graceful movements as he enjoyed the freedom of the pasture. When about to go, he gave him to his sister, saying: "I cannot sell that horse; he might fall into hands where he would be badly treated; but you will use him well." Mrs. Byers says: "His dog and his horse he always treated with the kindest consideration. I have often known him to walk, and lead his horse, when it had become fatigued." This trait grew upon him with years, and his comrades and followers can attest the benevolence that noted and regarded every sign of fatigue or suffering in animals under his control.

The writer recalls many lessons from his father to impress upon him that a man has no right to inflict upon any creature of God unnecessary pain. He would habitually turn aside from treading upon a worm in his path; but there was no morbid sentimentality in this, as he enjoyed field-sports moderately. He preferred, however, not to injure the most insignificant beings. It may not be amiss to give here another little anecdote, that shows in part how his habits of self-control were formed. The same sister tells how, when he was a lad fourteen years old, on one occasion, "though not in the habit of giving way to anger," he entirely lost patience, after having repeatedly tried in vain to pull on a tight boot, and at last threw it violently out of the window. She gave him a gentle and rather playful rebuke, at which he left the room with a look of quiet defiance, but soon returned with the boot, and silently set it against the wall. No further allusion was made to it. When ten years later he visited his family, Mr. Byers presented him with a fine rifle. He loaded the rifle to try it; but, on attempting to shoot, it snapped. He examined it, and tried again; again it snapped; and so on for several times. At last, he quietly put it down, saying, "This is a very fine rifle, but it needs oiling." His sister, who had been admiring his patience and calmness, said, "I wonder you did not strike it across the railing." He laughed, and replied: "You remember *the boot.* I have not forgotten it; but I have learned that a soldier should have perfect control of himself, to be able to control others." That this was not a young man's idle boast, subsequent events will show.

Poets, wits, and men of letters, often exhibit precocious signs of coming greatness; "Pope lisped in numbers," and "Poor Goldsmith" jested as a boy; but the youth of men of action is usually spent in uneventful preparation for the work before them, and their early record is generally unmarked by interesting incidents, or wise and witty sayings. The chief value of what little can be gathered of the youth of Albert Sidney Johnston lies in its entire consistency with his after-life. It is in this view that such glimpses of his boyhood, and life at West Point, as can be collected, are here given. On his way to West Point he first met Nathaniel J. Eaton, with whom he formed a friendship that subsisted for nearly forty years. The steadiness and loyalty of this attachment will receive ample illustration in these pages; but Captain Eaton's own account manifests both his enthusiasm and the deep and earnest nature of, his friend. In a letter of January 1, 1873, he says :

I first met Albert Sidney Johnston in June, 1822, on board the little steamer Fire-Fly, on the North River, as we were going to West Point to be examined for admission as cadets in the Military Academy. He was a full-grown man, of commanding figure and imposing presence. He was then a little over nineteen years old; and I was a stripling of a boy, not quite fifteen years old, and as green as I was young. The notice your father took of me, and his kindness of manner toward me, made a deep impression on my heart; and now, after the lapse of more than half a century, I often think of it very pleasantly. We arrived at West Point on Saturday evening; and the next morning, which was bright and beautiful, as your father and I stood on the veranda on the north side of the old " South Barracks," looking at the parade and inspection of the corps of cadets, and listening to the music of the band, he laid his hand on my head and said kindly, " Well, my young friend, what do you think of that ? " His manner was most kind, and filled the measure of youthful love, respect, and, I may say, reverence, that I had for him ; and to this day it remains as fresh, as bright, and as pleasant to me as it was then. But it was many years after that before I dared to hope that the warm regard I had for him was reciprocated. He was a reticent man, as you know, and was undemonstrative. Besides, he was five years my senior, and was even then a man of a good deal of culture. Hence there was but little social intercourse between us while we were together at the Academy. But on joining my regiment in 1827, at Jefferson Barracks, the gallant old Sixth Infantry of glorious memory, I was cordially greeted by your father, who had been assigned to that regiment. We were on very pleasant terms, but his reticence and dignity of manners prevented me from knowing exactly how I stood with him ; and it was not until I took leave of him, when about to start on furlough in the fall of 1828, that I was able to penetrate beneath his reserve of manner. But his cordial grasp, as I shook hands with him and bade him good-by, and his hearty " God bless you, Eaton ! " revealed what I had for years yearned to know, that my warm feelings for him were reciprocated ; and I think those feelings were never for a moment alienated ; so that, when he fell at Shiloh, I felt as if I had lost a brother.

That the friend so cherished had desired and valued this boyish devotion is proved by a letter of General Johnston's from Utah, in 1858. He writes to Captain Eaton :

I have known you long ; more than the lifetime of a generation. I remember when I first saw you on North River. The son of a noble patriot could not fail to attract my attention ; and, although you were much my junior, I felt a desire for your friendship, which in the course of time I acquired. I need not say that it was reciprocal, and in all that time not one incident has occurred to mar a friendship purely disinterested.

To many a veteran soldier, this little episode will serve to recall like friendships, prompted by the same scenes and similar emotions, and cemented by sincere esteem ; and to none, indeed, can the spectacle be altogether indifferent of the honorable sympathy of young and ardent souls ripening into enduring regard.

Colonel N. C. Macrae, who was his classmate, says:

His whole career at West Point was marked by a staid firmness, not always found among young gentlemen. He commanded the respect of all who knew him.

Colonel William H. C. Bartlett says :

No one of his large class at the Academy enjoyed more than he the respect of all who knew him, and none had a larger share of the affectionate regards of his classmates. His nature was truly noble, and untainted by anything small or contracted.

Colonel Edward B. White says :

During our few years at West Point, he was esteemed by us all as a high-minded, honorable gentleman and soldier, for whom we entertained much affection, and whose death was unaffectedly mourned by the few of us who survive. He was, as a mark of his good conduct and soldierly bearing, a non-commissioned and commissioned officer of the corps of cadets, I think, during his whole term ; a distinction much valued and desired by all of us; and, during the last or graduating year, was adjutant of the corps, which he preferred to a captaincy, which my contemporary Bartlett says was at his option.

Hon. Jefferson Davis says :

He was sergeant-major, and afterward was selected by the commandant for the adjutancy, then the most esteemed office in the corps.

And adds :

He was not a hard student, though a fair one. His quickness supplied this defect. He did not have an enemy in the corps, or an unkind feeling to any one, though he was select in his associates.

The testimony of others might be adduced to the same purport ; suffice it to say, however, that he pursued the prescribed course at the Military Academy with diligence and success.

The struggles of the South American republics for independence, and
the revolt of Greece against Turkey, had excited the warmest interest
in the United States ; and the poetry of Byron and the eloquence of
Clay found an echo in the feelings and opinions of the young men at the
Military Academy.   Johnston and some others were approached by the
agents of the revolutionary governments.   The era of profound peace
that was evidently opening before the United States was contrasted with
other arenas which seemed to offer the most splendid prizes to military
talent and ambition ; and it was seriously discussed among the more
adventurous cadets whether aid to the nationalities striving for liberty
against oppression was not a more pressing call than the routine service
of the United States Army.   Fortunately, prudent counsels prevailed ;
but General Johnston, many years after, spoke of it to the writer as a
strong temptation wisely resisted.   He stated that this incident had
directed his attention to the careers of men who had enlisted in a foreign army, and that his observation was that the greater the services
rendered by them the more jealously were they regarded by the native
rulers, and that this prejudice against the foreigner was sure to thwart
their ablest efforts.   I think he cited, as one instance, General Woll,
of the Mexican Army, a Belgian, whom he esteemed as its best soldier.

The circumstances attending the graduation of Albert Sidney Johnston were somewhat unusual.   He had won his way by hard labor to a
grade in mathematical attainment only excelled by W. H. C. Bartlett,
afterward distinguished as a professor of the institution, to whom he
accorded an easy eminence ; and by Mr. Twiss, who was inferior to
Bartlett only.   Mr. Davis says :

Johnston did not highly value *class-standing*, but was anxious for a thorough
knowledge of the course.

He devoted himself earnestly to the preparation for the examination, and was satisfied with his mastery of the whole course except two
problems ; but, when he was called upon to come forward, the subject
presented to him for discussion was one of these very problems.   He
was compelled to decline, hoping for better fortune next time ; but,
to his dismay, by a coincidence not included in his doctrine of chances,
the professor gave him the other neglected problem.   He was again
obliged to say that he was unprepared.   He was ordered to take his
seat ; but, feeling that his reputation and future standing were at
stake, he briefly yet forcibly stated the fact that these were the only
two exceptions to his knowledge of the course.   The superintendent
sternly ordered him to take his seat, which he did.   If the matter had
ended here, he would probably have lost his commission as well as his
grade ; but, as soon as the class was dismissed, he sent a written communication to the examiners, stating the facts, and *challenging* the

most rigorous examination. There was some indisposition to grant the reëxamination ; but it was finally accorded to him, through the friendly intervention of General Worth, then commandant of the Corps of Cadets, who had been greatly pleased with his bearing under such difficult circumstances, as well as with his previous conduct as a cadet. It was a most trying ordeal. The board took him at his word, and gave him a long and most searching examination ; after which, however, in spite of a reduction on account of his misadventure, and of a want of skill in drawing, he was graded eighth in his class. He was not only grateful to Worth for this good turn, but always retained an admiration for him as a dashing soldier. Worth had a large measure of knowledge and experience, and was full of martial spirit and generosity, which, with his handsome person and gallant bearing, made him a model for these young soldiers. He always treated Johnston with marked consideration ; and, after the Mexican War, recommended him as leader for a difficult enterprise.

When Albert Sidney Johnston was graduated, in June, 1826, he was entitled, by virtue of his rank in his class, to select which arm of the service he preferred. Had a cavalry corps then existed, his tastes would have led him to enter it ; but as between the artillery, then generally stationed in the seaboard fortresses, usually considered preferable, and the infantry, which was employed in more active service on the frontier, he chose the latter. He was accordingly assigned to the Second Infantry, with the rank of brevet second-lieutenant, to take date from July 1, 1826, with a furlough until the 1st of November. He left the Military Academy with very kind feelings to his classmates, and with a high regard for the institution, which he retained through life. His recollections of Prof. McIlvaine, then chaplain at West Point, and afterward Bishop of Ohio, were especially kindly. Hon. Jefferson Davis says :

Johnston valued one feature of cadet-life very much, the opportunity to select one's own acquaintance from congeniality of tastes, which was denied to the officer in barracks.

The subsequent careers of his friends is the best justification of his discrimination. Leonidas Polk, of Tennessee, subsequently Bishop of Louisiana, and a lieutenant-general in the Confederate service, was his room-mate and intimate friend ; and General Johnston never slackened in his affection for him, which was based upon a perfect confidence in his nobility of soul. He confirmed the reasonable opinion that Polk's religious development was the natural outgrowth of habits and beliefs cherished as a cadet. A single letter, written him in 1827, by Polk, who was still a cadet, remains. It is that of one intimate friend to another, on topics personal or pertaining to the Academy. Robert

Anderson, afterward famous for his defense of Fort Sumter, was another close friend at West Point. Some of their correspondence yet remains.

Among his friends at the Military Academy were William Bickley, his townsman, Daniel S. Donelson, of Tennessee, afterward a gallant general in the Confederate service ; Berrien, of Georgia ; the veteran Maynadier; Bradford, a grandson of the first printer in Kentucky; W. H. C. Bartlett, already mentioned; and Lucien Bibb, the son of Hon. George M. Bibb, and a noble, graceful man of genius.

His most intimate friend was Bennett H. Henderson, some time assistant professor at West Point, a man of brilliant talents, who resigned and began the practice of the law in St. Louis, but met an early and accidental death. Jefferson Davis, who was two classes below Johnston in the Academy, formed with him a fast friendship, that grew and strengthened, and knew neither decay nor end. There were others for whom Albert Sidney Johnston entertained a warm and lasting regard, and to whom, it is hoped, these pages may recall pleasant passages of youthful fellowship and happiness ; but we refrain from further detail. It was a society of young, ardent, and generous spirits, in which prevailed general good feeling and little bitterness—a generation of brave spirits, steadfast and reflective, but beyond comparison ardent and generous.

CHAPTER II.

EARLY ARMY-LIFE.

LITTLE of general interest remains, either in documentary form or in the memories of men, respecting the early years of Albert Sidney Johnston's army-life. He passed the furlough granted after graduation in Kentucky with his father. The following incident of this visit is related in a letter from a friend, some five years General Johnston's junior, and still living in Kentucky, highly respected :

Our intercourse was always pleasant, and to me instructive and highly valued and sought after. At that time the social life of young men in Kentucky, more I think than at present, was stained with the vice of gaming, which threw them into associations at other times unwillingly acknowledged. I did not escape. Your father on one occasion, as I was quitting one of the dens, at that day open at all hours, joined me, and, proposing a walk, introduced the subject of games and gaming, not as a mentor or moral lecturer—for against such a one I might have rebelled—but with many anecdotes of his early friends, whose lives had been marred, and in some instances disgraced, by the habit. He turned to me: " Come, my friend, I wish to teach you a game more intellectual than whist or any game of cards. It needs no betting to make it interesting; and, indeed, the interest would be spoiled by a bet." With that, we went to his room at your grandfather's, and, for the first time, he introduced me to the chess-board, and taught me the game. I shall never forget the patience with which he, an accomplished player, instructed me in the moves and principles of the game; and frequently in after-life I have felt that nothing but a desire to save and reform me, which to a great extent was effectual, could have prompted his action.

This kind of personal effort for the good of others is commonly given more grudgingly than advice, or even than money ; but it does more good than either, because it evinces sympathy, and not merely benevolence.

In explaining to the writer that he had divested himself of all claim to some land in which he was supposed to be interested, General Johnston wrote, December 20, 1858 :

My grandfather, Edward Harris, gave to my brother, J. H. Johnston, my sisters, and myself, 640 acres of land in Ohio. When I came of age I gave to Mr. Byers my interest in this land, and whatever else I inherited from my father, being a share in a small farm, a few negroes, and a homestead of small value. It was not much, but, whatever it was, I gave it all for the benefit of my sisters.

My recollection is, that my father told me that his brothers united in this action.

During the fall of 1826 Lieutenant Johnston accepted an invitation from his brother, then in the United States Senate, to visit him at Washington City. Senator Johnston at that time occupied an enviable position, socially and politically, at the seat of government. As the trusted friend of Mr. Clay, then Secretary of State, he gave an independent support to President Adams's Administration; while he enjoyed, nevertheless, very cordial relations with the best people of all parties. Mrs. Johnston was a person of great vivacity and amiability, and her grace of manner and social tact made their house one of the most attractive at the capital. In a letter written to Lieutenant Johnston that winter she says :

Our street is filled with members and their families, and we are all gay. Our house has already the name of " The Neutral Ground," where all parties meet, and must, of course, be polite to each other. Parties innumerable, weddings, and grand dinners, fill up all the evening; visits and visitors, all the morning.

In this brilliant and polished society, in which moved Clay and Calhoun, Webster, Benton, Everett, and Scott, Lieutenant Johnston had his first experience of the great world ; but it made slight impression on a soul bent upon martial enterprise, and impatient for strenuous action. Mrs. Johnston exerted herself to make his stay agreeable, and he shared in all the pleasures of the cultivated society in which she was an acknowledged leader.

The following popular piece of verse, written in her honor by the Hon. Warren R. Davis, of South Carolina, a wit and a poet, as well as a politician, is here correctly reproduced, because it has been the subject of considerable literary controversy:

A FAMOUS OLD SONG.

Air—" Roy's Wife of Aldivalloch."

> Johnston's wife of Louisiana!
> Johnston's wife of Louisiana!
> The fairest flower that ever bloomed
>   In Southern sun or gay savanna;
> The Inca's blood flows in her veins,
>   The Inca's soul her bright eyes lighten;
> Child of the Sun, like him she reigns
>   To cheer our hopes, and sorrows brighten.
>   Johnston's wife of Louisiana!
>   Johnston's wife of Louisiana!
>   The fairest flower that ever bloomed
>   In Southern sun or gay savanna.
>
> Johnston's wife of Louisiana!
> Johnston's wife of Louisiana!
> She hath a way to win all hearts,
>   And bow them to the shrine of Anna;
> Her mind is radiant with the lore
>   Of ancient and of modern story;
> And native wit in richer store
>   Bedecks her with its rainbow glory.
>   Johnston's wife of Louisiana!
>   Johnston's wife of Louisiana!
>   She hath a way to charm all hearts,
>   And bow them to the shrine of Anna.
>
> Johnston's wife of Louisiana!
> Johnston's wife of Louisiana!
> The hapless bard who sings her praise
>   Now worhips at the shrine of Anna!
> 'Twas such a vision, bright but brief,
>   In early youth his true heart rended;
> Then left it, like a fallen leaf,
>   On life's most rugged thorn suspended.
>   Johnston's wife of Louisiana!
>   Johnston's wife of Louisiana!
>   The hapless bard who sings her praise
>   Wept tears of blood for such as Anna!

Lieutenant Johnston was a guest at the White House and at Mr. Clay's, and a favorite in the gayer circle of fashionable life, where his handsome person and winning address made him always acceptable. Mr. and Mrs. Johnston's indulgent partiality sought to make their house his permanent home, confident that, at the centre of political favor, their influence and his own merits would rapidly advance his fortunes. A way was unexpectedly opened by an offer from General Scott to make him his aide-de-camp, a proposal very flattering in itself, and opening as brilliant a career as could be desired had he possessed the temper of the courtier. The temptation of rapid promotion and graceful pleasures would have proved irresistible to many minds, and perhaps most men would have acted judiciously in accepting the friendly offer. Senator Johnston and his wife anxiously wished him to accept ; the latter wrote in 1870 as follows :

I well remember my disappointment when, as a very young and handsome man, he was offered the position of aide to General Scott, and, from his own judgment, refused it, saying that, " although much gratified to have been mentioned by General Scott, he felt that the life of inactivity in a large city did not accord with his views, and that he preferred to go off to the far West, and enter at once upon the duties of his profession." His brother did not think it right to oppose his inclination, although General Scott was our particular friend. As for myself, I fairly scolded and wept at this determination.

But nothing could deter him from his resolution to enter at once on the rugged duties of his chosen career, and to owe his advancement to meritorious service, not patronage. General Johnston always believed and regretted that his seeming indifference to an overture that was intended as a kindness, and certainly was a compliment, had prejudiced him in the good opinion of General Scott. That eminent soldier regarded him for more than a generation with a certain coolness, and opposed to his advancement the most fatal check to rising merit— official reluctance and the discountenance of the great. There was no intentional injustice, however, only this distrust and neglect ; and it is creditable to General Johnston's soundness of judgment and sobriety of mind that he felt no resentment at conduct so natural, and was always able to do full justice to the military abilities of General Scott. When, in his later years, he had, through other agencies, attained an exalted position, and had, by his services, compelled the entire respect of the commander-in-chief, that respect was exhibited in a cordial and unreserved manner, and with the largest measure of official approbation, evincing that it was want of confidence, not of magnanimity, that moved General Scott. The question of Lieutenant Johnston's wisdom in declining General Scott's tender may be left to the verdict of others ; but the incident illustrates both his theory of life at that time and a certain independence of spirit and unwillingness to owe aught to favor, which characterized him throughout life. He certainly chose the more rugged path, in which, however, he was sustained by his self-reliance and by a contempt for mere rank and place, except as the evidences of achievement.

Lieutenant Johnston did not leave without regret the hospitable house where he had been treated with such fraternal affection. His sister-in-law kept up a correspondence with him for several years ; and, although they did not meet often in after-life, he always gratefully remembered the sisterly interest she had shown toward him as a youth. He left the capital, not to visit it again for thirty years, except in passing through it rapidly on two or three journeys. In an era when office-seeking was a national vice, extending even to the army, he felt a pardonable pride in holding aloof from the source of preferment.

His formal orders to proceed to Sackett's Harbor, on Lake Ontario, are dated December 22d ; but he had probably preceded them a month or more, as Mrs. Johnston, writing to him at that point on the 26th, says :

" We are pleased to hear that you like your situation, and are determined to spend your time usefully and agreeably." And adds : " I heard General Brown speak of you in high terms to a young military gentleman last night."

From a letter of his friend Polk's it appears that his chief employment at the little frontier post was " in books ; " but what he read and what he did there are things forgotten.

But a single incident is preserved of General Johnston's winter at Sackett's Harbor. This he sometimes cited as an illustration of the recklessness of youth. He was engaged with some fellow-officers in artillery-practice on the ice of Lake Ontario, when a wild party of sleighers kept dashing across the line of fire, near the target. Meaning to rebuke this bravado with a good scare, he waited for the rush of their Canadian ponies near his target, and then fired. He succeeded so well that, for an instant, the whole party was enveloped in snow and splintered ice, and seemed to be blotted out. A moment after they emerged from the frosty spray with wild yells and affrighted gestures, and returned no more. He felt during the instant of suspense that murder had been done, and the relief of the revelers at their escape was not greater than his own. He accepted the adventure, however, as a lesson in something more than artillery-practice.

The President, John Quincy Adams, signed his commission April 4, 1827, as second-lieutenant of the Sixth Regiment of Infantry, to take date from July 1, 1826. "The Sixth," commanded by brevet Brigadier-General Henry Atkinson, was then esteemed the "crack" regiment ; so that at once he proceeded rejoicing to its headquarters at Jefferson Barracks, where he arrived on the 1st of June.

This post, famous in the traditions and cherished in the affections of the old Army, was his home for the next six or seven years. It was situated on the bank of the Mississippi, nine miles from St. Louis, then an inconsiderable but promising town of 5,000 inhabitants. Lieutenant Johnston says, in a letter to his friend Bickley :

The position is a good one, and particularly excellent in a military point of view, because of the facility of transporting troops to any other position in the West. The celerity of the recent movement of the First and Sixth Regiments up the Mississippi and Wisconsin sufficiently attests that. . . . The site of the barracks rises gradually from the river and swells to a beautiful bluff, covered with oak and hickory trees, almost far enough apart to permit military manœuvres, and with no undergrowth to interrupt a ride on horseback in any direction.

The most notable event with which Lieutenant Johnston was connected in the year 1827 was the expedition to compel the Winnebago Indians to atone for outrages upon the white settlers. This tribe occupied the country about Lake Winnebago and along the banks of the Wisconsin River, with the Menomonees for their neighbors on the north ; the Pottawattamies dwelt about the head-waters of Lake Michigan, and the Sacs and Foxes on both banks of the Mississippi in Northern Illinois, Southern Wisconsin, and Iowa. On the 24th of June the Winnebagoes had suddenly put to death some white people ; and seemed disposed to break out into open war, in which also they endeavored to enlist the Pottawattamies. As the Winnebagoes numbered some 600 or 700 warriors, were physically large, well formed, and strong, and were the most indomitable and irreclaimable savages on that frontier, great apprehensions were felt of a cruel warfare. They refused to negotiate with General Cass, who thereupon turned the matter over to General Atkinson. The expedition left Prairie du Chien on the 29th of August, and returned to Jefferson Barracks September 27th. The letter to Bickley, already quoted, describing the movement of troops to preserve peace on the Northwestern frontier, continues as follows :

The detachment of the Sixth Regiment which left this place was accompanied by two companies of the Fifth Regiment from St. Peter's, up the Wisconsin River as far as the portage, where it was met by a detachment of the Second Regiment from Green Bay, under the command of Major Whistler. The Winnebagoes, in council, agreed to deliver up the leading men in the several outrages committed against the whites. Accordingly, Red Bird, Le Soleil, and two others, the son and brother-in-law of Red Bird, were given up, there ; and two more, afterward, at Prairie du Chien, belonging to the Prairie La Crosse band. They bound themselves to hold a council in the spring for the determination of the boundary-line ; and to permit the miners of Fever River to proceed peaceably in their " diggings," till the true boundary was determined.

Although, after seeing the Sacs and Foxes, Menomonees, Sioux, etc., my romantic ideas of the Indian character had vanished, I must confess that I consider Red Bird one of the noblest and most dignified men I ever saw. When he gave himself up, he was dressed, after the manner of the Sioux of the Missouri, in a perfectly white hunting-shirt of deer-skin, and leggins and moccasins of the same, with an elegant head-dress of birds' feathers; he held a white flag in his right hand, and a beautifully-ornamented pipe in the other. He said: "I have offended. I sacrifice myself to save my country," etc. He displayed that stoic indifference which is wrongfully attributed to the Indian character alone. I'll stop. I am not going to write a whole letter about a rascally Indian.

We have been encamped here since June, but expect to get into quarters before winter sets in. I could say a great deal more, but I am almost converted into bacon, already, by the smoke from a big log-fire before my tent. I am on guard.   Yours truly,   JOHNSTON.

Six companies of the First, six of the Third, and the Sixth Regiment, to which I belong, are stationed here. Plenty of sport. I am in excellent health and fine spirits. Present my respects to Marshall, Taliaferro, R. and J. Taylor, Hannegan, Green, and Beattie.   Yours truly,   J.

Brown, in his " History of Illinois " (New York, 1844), says :

Red Bird died in prison. A part of those arrested were convicted, and a part acquitted. Those convicted were executed on the 26th of December, in the following year (1828). Black Hawk and Kanonekan, or the Youngest of the Thunders, and a son of Red Bird, all of whom had been charged with attacking the boats, were acquitted. Black Hawk was confined for more than a year before he could be brought to trial; and imprisonment to him was more intolererable than any punishment which could have been inflicted. . . . Black Hawk was discharged merely for want of proof, not for want of guilt. Although doubts on the subject were once entertained, there was none afterward. His confessions, which he had sense enough to withhold till after his acquittal, were conclusive.

From this time, probably, dated Black Hawk's effort to organize a league that should unite all the Western tribes from the lakes to Mexico in war against the encroaching whites.

The remains of Lieutenant Johnston's correspondence, belonging to this period, are meagre. This is due, in part, to his destruction of his papers after the death of his wife in 1835, and in part to his repugnance to mere friendly letter-writing. His relations and friends reproached him with a neglect which he deprecated, but did not amend. He shrank from the platitudes of ordinary correspondence, and professions and protestations of every kind were distasteful to him. He was a man of powerful affections ; yet he believed in, and exercised, self-restraint in their expression. He had a very exalted ideal of friendship, and a great contempt for mere lip-service ; and, although he was aware that there was another side to the question, yet he could never fully overcome his aversion to writing, without a special object, and unless he had something important to say. But this aversion did not extend to official or business correspondence, in which he was prompt, exact, and full; and, indeed, it is doubtful whether an instance can be pointed out where he was in default in a duty of this sort.

To those who knew the grand composure, resulting from long years of self-control, which characterized the latter years of General Johnston, a little anecdote, that he used humorously to relate of the impetuosity of his hot youth, may serve to illustrate the power of will that wrought the change. During his sojourn as a bachelor at Jefferson Barracks, being fond of music, he tried to learn to play the flute. A wide difference of opinion existed between himself and his friends as to his musical aptitudes. He persevered in spite of their jests; until these, and the resulting doubts in his own mind, rendered him somewhat irritable on the score of his skill. One day, as he was practising in his room, he heard a tapping on the floor above, occupied by a fellow-officer. Instantly referring this to his music, and regarding it as an indecorum, he nevertheless continued the air; but, when it occurred again, he stopped—and the tapping stopped. Waiting a moment to restrain his rising anger, he resumed the tune, and the tapping began again. This was too much for the outraged patience of the angry musician, who, dashing down his flute, sprang up the stairs, determined to exact satisfaction. To a thundering knock at the door, a friendly voice replied, inviting him to come in ; and, when he strode in, he found his neighbor, with a look of mild inquiry at his evident excitement, unsuspiciously *cracking walnuts on the hearth.* With a brief apology for his intrusion, he rushed down-stairs again, mortified at his own hastiness and loss of temper. He at once gave up the flute ; for, said he, " I did not think that a man so sensitive about his skill was fit for a flute-player."

In 1828 Lieutenant Johnston was selected as adjutant of the regiment by Brevet-General Henry Atkinson, the colonel commanding. Atkinson was an officer of fair military capacity and experience, of a bright and social temper, and of popular manners. General Scott, in his autobiography, calls him " an excellent man and fine soldier ; " and this opinion expresses fairly the army estimate of him. His wife was a daughter of Alexander Bullitt, one of the original settlers of Louisville, Kentucky, and the eldest of a family celebrated for beauty, wit, and charm of manner. Mrs. Atkinson, aided, after the lapse of some years, by her brilliant and beautiful sisters, made Jefferson Barracks something more than a mere military post ; it was a delightful and elegant home for the gay and gallant young soldiers serving here their apprenticeship in arms. There was at this period of his life no officer more highly regarded in the regiment than the adjutant. Captain Eaton says of him that, " while no man was more approachable, no one could remain unimpressed by his dignity ; " and Colonel Thomas L. Alexander, who joined the regiment in 1830, says that, " possessing in an extraordinary degree the confidence, esteem, and admiration of the whole regiment, he was the very *beau-idéal* of a soldier and an officer." How early he began to exercise that forbearance in judging his fellow-men which afterward became so characteristic, may be seen in a letter to Eaton, written in this period:

Our friend and fellow-soldier has destroyed himself. Being entirely unprepared for such an event, you may well judge that we were greatly shocked and grieved on hearing it. Notwithstanding the manner of his death, let us mourn the loss of a chivalric companion. Let us not, in the vigor of health and intellect, reproach his memory for committing an act which the paramount control of reason alone can prevent.

Every humane and fearless nature which clearly perceives the ills of others—the afflictions of feebleness, sin, and pain—must feel tenderly toward the frailty which gives way before the temptation of a great agony. General Johnston, for himself, however, seems early to have adopted the theory that, while we are irresistibly swayed by an over-ruling destiny, yet it is the duty of a man manfully to oppose to adverse circumstances or fate all the resources he can command—a somewhat Promethean philosophy, but not unfruitful of mental steadfastness and, sometimes, of large results. He quoted, with approbation, the argument against suicide, attributed to Napoleon, that "suicide is never justifiable while hope remains; but that, while there is life, there is always hope." His beliefs ripened in after-years into a profound faith in the Supreme God, his providence and his mercy.

Jefferson Barracks was near enough to St. Louis to allow the young officers to mingle freely in its gay and hospitable society, in which the influence of the old French element was still predominant. The descendants of the first settlers had preserved in their colonial isolation some of the best features of the old *régime*, lost even in France itself through the Revolution. To innocent sprightliness was joined decorum, and the inherent grace and polish of the French race were united to the cordiality and generous freedom of intercourse which mark a young and prosperous community. The benefits and enjoyment of such a society were very great to the young officers, whose commissions, in that happy day of the republic, accredited them to the best society everywhere. Lieutenant Johnston, without allowing himself to fall into fashionable dissipation for which he had no taste, did not withdraw himself from the pleasures and amusements of the city, and found in St. Louis attachments which lasted all his life. The Gratiots, the Chouteaus, the Mullanphys, the O'Fallons, the Clarks, the Bentons, and other noted and estimable families, were among his chosen and remembered friends.

At a ball at Mr. Chouteau's, Lieutenant Johnston met for the first time Miss Henrietta Preston. She was the eldest child of Major William Preston, a member of the Virginia family of that name, and an officer of Wayne's army, who had resigned, and settled at Louisville, Kentucky. He was remarkable for his extraordinary size and strength, and likewise for his wit. He is yet remembered by old people for these traits. He died, leaving a large family and an embarrassed estate to the care of his widow. Mrs. Caroline Hancock Preston was the daughter of Colonel George Hancock, of Fincastle, Virginia (an aide to Pulaski, a colonel in the Revolutionary War, and a member of the Fourth Congress), and belonged to a family distinguished for beauty and talents. By her ability in business and indomitable courage, she relieved the estate from its incumbrances, and successfully defended it from all the legal assaults so common in the early history of Kentucky. At the same time she gave her children the best education then to be had. Her best monument is the grateful remembrance of the poor of Louisville.

Mrs. Preston's youngest sister had married Governor William Clark, of Missouri, and her husband's niece was the wife of Thomas H. Benton. Governor William Clark was one of the foremost men of the West; a younger brother of the great George Rogers Clark, he shared his boldness and sagacity without his infirmities, and reaped the legitimate rewards of energy and intellect from which unthrift debarred the hero. He had early in life obtained great celebrity by his explorations, in conjunction with Lewis, of the sources of the Columbia River and in the Far West. He was Governor of Missouri for many years, and, as Indian agent, enjoyed justly the confidence of his Government and of the Indian tribes. With wealth, intelligence, virtue, and popular manners, he was well fitted for his place as a leader in a young republic. His first wife, Miss Julia Hancock, was a woman of eminent graces and singular beauty: after her death he married her cousin, Mrs. Radford. His descendants and collaterals are prominent citizens of St. Louis and Louisville. Thomas H. Benton belongs to history. Counted among the first, when Jackson, Webster, Calhoun, and Clay were his competitors, his name reopens a page illustrious in American annals. His wife was a daughter of Colonel James McDowell, of Rockbridge County, Virginia, and sister of the eloquent Governor of Virginia, of the same name. She was the niece and favorite kinswoman of Major Preston and spent four or five years in his house, devoting herself for the most part, as a matter of choice, to the education of his daughter Henrietta, then a little girl. As she was a woman of fine accomplishments and uncommon literary culture, as well as of a sprightly temper and vigorous intellect, she not only taught her pupil the rudiments, but advanced her well in French and other studies, and imbued her especially with a love of the best literature. Henrietta, and her sisters also, received instruction from a private tutor, Mr.

Quinan, a scholar versed in the classics and devoted to his occupation. After this, in the hospitable house of her aunt's husband, Colonel Nathaniel Hart, at Spring Hill, in Woodford County, Kentucky, she was well taught by Mr. Ruggles, afterward a United States Senator. As years passed, the kinswomen exchanged the relation of preceptor and pupil for that of dear friends, which was severed only by death.

In the customary interchange of hospitalities, Miss Preston was on a visit to these relations when she met Lieutenant Johnston, and the interest that she at once inspired was reciprocated. This mutual attachment was thorough and unbroken; and Lieutenant Johnston, being sent for a great part of the year 1828 on recruiting service to Louisville, Kentucky, Miss Preston's home, became engaged to her. They were married January 20, 1829. There were many points of resemblance between Albert Sidney Johnston and his wife; and a friend, who knew them both well, has told me that he never knew two people more alike in character. Another, a relation, says they were often mistaken for brother and sister. But this was true rather as to the outcome of character in similar sentiments, and the same philosophy of life, than in their original traits or acquired habits of mind. The affinity was one of sympathy in feelings and aspiration; and the usual law of attraction, based upon contrast of character and community of tastes, was reversed. As they were both persons of most loyal natures, these coincidences increased. Mrs. Johnston was above middle size—five feet six inches in height—and of agreeable person, with a full form, a brilliant color, hazel eyes, dark hair, and somewhat irregular but pleasing features. Her voice had wonderful harmony in its modulations. Her manner was full of dignity and ease, but vivacious and engaging, and her conversation has been variously characterized as piquant, graceful, and eloquent. Mrs. Johnston was a woman of firm yet gentle temper, and, as the eldest daughter of a struggling family, the confidante and counselor of her mother, had been trained to a severe self-discipline. She was eminently benevolent and forbearing. Gifted with a poetic temperament, and very fond of verse, she wrote it with facility and feeling; while her husband, rigorously schooled in a training almost exclusively mathematical, and loving unrefracted truth, jocularly called it good prose spoiled. With these traits, with high literary culture, and with strong religious impulses, she had formed a lofty ideal of the aims and duties of life; and this ideal, she thoroughly believed, was realized by her husband. She was much beloved by her family and friends, and the feeling she awoke in her husband was one of chivalric devotion. He told me that "it was impossible to have felt her influence, and afterward to cherish low views; that to her he owed the wish to be truly great." This portraiture will show that she was a worthy helpmate for the man of whom I write.

The married life of this happy couple was the simple and uneventful one of an officer's family. Their home was at Jefferson Barracks, where their plain quarters, furniture, and mode of life, are evidenced by their household accounts as well as by tradition. Some cut glass seems to have represented the splendor of their little establishment. They made occasional visits to Mrs. Johnston's mother, at Louisville, and Lieutenant Johnston, writing from that city, October 3, 1830, says, "The last two months I have spent pleasantly and quietly in the country, reading, shooting the rifle," etc.

On January 5, 1831, his eldest son was born at Louisville, and, immediately afterward, Lieutenant Johnston was obliged to return to Jefferson Barracks. His family rejoined him in May, and remained there until the fall of 1832. In the tranquil flow of these years, he enjoyed the easy routine of a peace establishment, agreeable social intercourse, and the happiness of perfect domestic concord, unbroken except by the two dire episodes of the Black-Hawk War and the cholera plague. Suffice it to say, that these were halcyon days, when youth and hope, as well as peace, abode with them. But they were soon to be disturbed by the rude note of war, whose expectation keeps the professional soldier ever on the alert even in the profoundest calm.

CHAPTER III.

BLACK-HAWK WAR.

THE Black-Hawk War, which occurred in 1832, following a profound peace of many years, agitated not only the Northwestern frontier but the whole country. The causes and conduct of the war were, in its day, severely criticised both by partisan politicians and philanthropists. The motives of the latter entitle them to a respectful hearing; but the common-sense of the people has always sustained the practical view that the first duty of the Government in its relations with the Indians is to protect its citizens from the horrors of savage warfare, after which it should accord the most generous and considerate treatment to the aborigines.

Unfortunately, the Government has sometimes, from mistaken views of economy, chosen to forget the half-paternal position it had assumed toward the Indians, and has, for trifling sums, obtained title to vast tracts of country. Unfortunately, too, among the brave and good men who go to the frontier as pioneers there are never wanting so many unprincipled persons and outlaws, who, from selfish greed of gain, are willing to brutalize with whiskey, or to cheat, oppress, and kill the Indian, that the latter has always suffered demoralization from contact with the vanguard of civilization, and has had only too just grounds of complaint against both individuals and the Government. A further source of discord has arisen from the inability of the Indians to distinguish between the loose verbal promises of commissioners, anxious to secure a treaty, and the provisions of the treaty itself. The Indians remember and claim the benefit of all that is said or done by the agents that can be construed to their advantage ; while the Government, not knowing or recognizing these things, merely executes the treaty on its face. Hence mutual distrust and collision have been almost inevitable.

The higher tribes of Indians were formerly full of the martial virtues—courage, enterprise, fortitude, sagacity, scorn of servitude, with an occasional though unfrequent loftiness of soul and heroic generosity; but they were restless, prone to war, cruel, and perfidious. In the contact of a civilized race with these sons of the forest, a wiser and more liberal treatment by the Government might have averted many evils and much mutual wrong ; but with these wild and intractable savages no kindness or forbearance could have prevented quarrels and violence ending in war.

Yet, wheresoever the responsibility may originally have rested, no blame can properly be laid on such military officers as, being charged with the peace of the frontier, have been faithful in carrying out the orders and instructions of the Government, and have restrained predatory bands of Indians from inflicting injury on the whites and on each other. This duty was always, with very rare exceptions, honestly discharged ; and force was only used in the last resort, after every measure of conciliation had failed. The best proof that peace, on the basis of justice, was earnestly sought by the officers of Government is that it lasted so long, although the Indians had serious causes of dissatisfaction, which were said to have been fomented by British agents on the frontier. That the Indians had confidence in the equity and friendship of the military is evinced by the respect they paid to soldiers, even at a time when they were engaged in actual though secret warfare against the white settlers. They had some notion that the soldiers and citizens were different though allied tribes ; and a blue uniform was a safe-conduct, even when a white settler's life was not worth a pin's fee with them. The Hon. Jefferson Davis related to the writer how, at such a time, with only three men, he passed from Rock Island to Chicago without molestation, and with only a single threatening demonstration from the Indians he met. It was properly the first care of the commanding general to see to the safety of the white settlers ; and he was compelled to act upon each case, as it arose, from a practical standpoint. Hence, whether the Black-Hawk War was a necessary consequence of the policy of the Government, or of Indian fickleness, it is believed that the events herein narrated will show that the military commander pursued the only course open to him.

A brief sketch of the Black-Hawk War is here needful, as it was directly connected with Lieutenant Johnston's apprenticeship in the field. But a more extended narrative of this military episode seems fully warranted, since not only are all the official documents in regard to the campaign based upon Lieutenant Johnston's report, as assistant adjutant-general of General Atkinson, but his private journal furnished the most exact and authentic account of the transactions against Black Hawk. Moreover, although his military rank did not give him a conspicuous place, yet his office and his personal position, as the confidential friend of the commanding general, gave him a certain influence over affairs. Mr. Chambers, in a letter heretofore quoted, says: "I remember hearing an officer of the army tell my father that Johnston had more influence with the general in command than anybody else in the army, and that he really directed the movements of the army in that war." Although this was the opinion of a highly-zealous friend, yet it is evidence that his part was one that called for an unusual amount of energy and discretion. Without indulging the popular delusion that the chief of staff is necessarily keeper of his commander's conscience, it is plain that where he enjoys his confidence, and has fidelity and justness of perception, he is eminently fitted to be the historian of a campaign. General Atkinson's own opinion of the value of the journal may be inferred from the following extracts from a letter of his to Lieutenant Johnston, written in December, 1833, after the close of the war, in reference to the proposition of a gentleman named Russell to write a history of the war:

As this history is to be written, I could but feel, as you may readily imagine, a deep interest in its faithfulness. . . . To enable me to give him the best information as to dates and facts, I have to request that you will send me the journal you kept of the campaign.

It is this journal which forms the groundwork of the present summary, and as copious extracts are given from it as space permits.

Before proceeding to narrate the transactions of the Black-Hawk campaign, which, however small in perspective, shook the United States with excitement at the time, it will be necessary to make a rapid survey of the relations of the United States Government to the Sac and Fox nation, and of the condition of the frontier at the beginning of the outbreak. In the eighteenth century, a number of tribes, of common origin, occupied the present limits of Illinois, and were united in a league, known as the Minneway, Linneway, or Illinois. This confederacy is said to have numbered, in 1745, four thousand warriors,

noted for martial prowess and inhuman cruelty. In a great war, said
to have originated in the murder of the Sac chieftain, Pontiac, the
Illinois tribes were overthrown and nearly exterminated by a rival
confederacy, composed of Sacs and Foxes, Sioux, Kickapoos, Chippewas, Ottawas, and Pottawattamies, from the North, and Cherokees
and Choctaws from the South. This overthrow occurred between 1767
and 1780 ; and in 1826 a miserable remnant of less than five hundred
souls was all that was left of the great Illinois nation.

In the victorious league, the Sacs or Osaukies, and the Foxes or
Outagamies, appear to have been the leaders and principal gainers.
These kindred branches of the great Algonquin nation are said to have
been driven from their homes on the St. Lawrence by the Iroquois
before the year 1680, and to have settled at Green Bay, where their
weakness compelled them to unite, so as to form one people with only
a nominal distinction between its two members. After the destruction
of the Illinois, the Sacs and Foxes took possession of their most desirable hunting-grounds, and occupied the country on both sides of the
Mississippi, from the present southern boundary of Iowa to the present northern boundary of Illinois, with their most populous village at
Rock Island.

Other tribes of Algonquin or Dakota descent—Chippewas, Ottawas, Pottawattamies, Kickapoos, Menomonees, and Winnebagoes,[1]
pressed upon the eastern and northern limits of the hunting-grounds
of the Sacs and Foxes ; while the Sioux, a powerful nation of fierce
and skillful horsemen, flanked them on the west and northwest. In
1779 the Sacs and Foxes, with their allies, attacked St. Louis, then a
village of less than five hundred people ; and, encouraged by the treachery of the commandant of the Spanish garrison, would have destroyed
it, but for the gallant defense of the French inhabitants and its timely
relief by George Rogers Clark with an American force.

After this, the Sacs and Foxes were engaged in wars with the
Osages and other tribes, but especially with the Sioux, against whom
they waged a deadly feud. Nevertheless they were prosperous, and a
leading tribe in numbers; while in warlike spirit, sagacity, polity, and
general intelligence, they were excelled by none of the tribes of the
Northwest. In 1805 Lieutenant Pike represented their numbers at
4,600, of whom 1,100 were warriors; but Lewis and Clark compute
that they were 3,200 strong, of whom 800 were warriors, which was
probably nearer the truth. In 1825, the Secretary of War, adopting
the estimate of Governor William Clark, reckoned their entire strength
at 6,600, with a force of 1,200 or 1,400 warriors ; thus showing a rapid
gain in strength in twenty years.

[1] Winnebago is a term of reproach, signifying "Dirty-Water-People;" they call
themselves "Hochongalas, or Trout Tribe."

General St. Clair, Governor of the Northwest Territory, made the first treaty with the Sacs and Foxes in 1789. General William Henry Harrison concluded another treaty with them, November 3, 1804, by which, for an immediate payment of $2,234.50, and an annuity of $1,000, they relinquished all their lands outside certain prescribed limits.

In 1810, when war was impending between the United States and Great Britain, the emissaries of the latter power induced a hundred or a hundred and fifty Sacs to visit the British agent on the island of St. Joseph, in Lake Huron, where they received arms, ammunition, and other presents, and most probably made engagements to adhere to the British cause in the event of war. In 1811, however, another deputation from the tribe visited Washington City, and offered their services in the impending war, but were requested by the President to remain neutral.

In 1812 they again offered to assist the Americans, but were told to stay peaceably at home, to which command the greater part of the tribe reluctantly submitted. About two hundred of the more restless braves, eager for blood and plunder, joined the British, and shared in the military operations on the northwestern frontier. In this contingent, known as "the British band," was Black Hawk. In September, 1815, the United States commissioners made a treaty with the friendly bands of Sacs and Foxes, confirming the treaty of 1804, and granting amnesty for all offenses committed during the war; and, on May 13, 1816, they made a like treaty with the British band. On the 24th of August, 1824, General William Clark, Indian Agent, purchased for the United States all the lands claimed by this tribe in Missouri. In July, 1829, in furtherance of a provisional agreement made the year before, the United States commissioners bought from the deputies of the Winnebagoes, Chippewas, Ottawas, Pottawattamies, Sioux, Menomonees, and Sacs and Foxes, about 8,000,000 acres, extending from Lake Michigan to the Mississippi River. At this treaty, Keokuk and Morgan, with about two hundred Sac warriors, were present and forwarded the negotiation.

While such had been the treaty relations with the Sacs and Foxes, two rival war-chiefs divided the double tribe by their counsels, and contended for the first place in authority and influence. These were Keokuk, who was said to be of Fox descent, though chief of the Sac village on the Des Moines River; and Black Hawk, chief of the Sac village near Rock Island. Each had risen to his position by courage and talents. Keokuk, born about 1780, acquired very young a skill in horsemanship which enabled him, at fifteen years of age, to slay a Sioux warrior, and thereafter to be accounted a brave. In the wars with the Sioux he was distinguished for audacious courage and military stratagem. He was called to the leadership of his village, when about thirty-three years of age, in a public emergency ; and gradually won the confidence of the tribe by his prudent administration and persuasive eloquence. His conduct was firm yet conciliatory, both in the internal management of the tribe and in his relations to other tribes and to the white people. By fidelity to his engagements and steadfastness of purpose, he was able to preserve a peaceful policy, so difficult with such a restless people, and to save his followers from much of the suffering which fell upon others. He was an accomplished warrior, and an orator of rare tact, grace, and vigor. Keokuk's temper was naturally amiable and kind, as well as politic. He was somewhat luxurious for an Indian, fond of pomp, and given to the use of ardent spirits, which finally destroyed him.

Black Hawk was thirteen years his senior, and belonged to a darker and more savage type of the Indian character. He, too, at the early age of fifteen, won the rank of brave by killing an Osage warrior, and was soon noted for his boldness and success in war. In 1786, at the head of two hundred braves, he defeated the Osages with equal numbers, killing one hundred of the enemy, and only losing nineteen of his own men. He was a leader in the wars against the Cherokees, Chippewas, Kaskaskias, and Osages, in many battles, and truthfully claimed that he had killed many foes with his own hand. He seems from the first to have had an aversion to the Americans, and to have cherished an hereditary friendship for the British. In the War of 1812 he had led to their aid about two hundred of his own tribe, and commanded a band numbering in all about five hundred warriors. He shared in the hostilities against the Americans in that war, though without special distinction ; but, at its close, was again received under the protection of the United States, according to the provisions of the Treaty of Ghent, and of the treaty of 1816 with the British band.

From 1816 to 1832 Black Hawk was not engaged in open war against the United States, but was almost certainly an accomplice in the Red Bird outrage, and in other secret forays on the white people. He frequently visited the British commander at Malden to renew the allegiance of the past, and to receive presents for himself and band. His early prejudices against the Americans gradually settled into an inveterate rancor ; the continually-increasing contention between his own people and the whites aroused his fierce passions ; and enforced peace galled his unquiet soul like a fetter. In the gloom of his seclusion, superstition stirred his wrath to frenzy ; and, as he saw the shadows of the dead summoning him to vengeance upon the race that had dispossessed them of the land, he brooded over vast schemes that should rival the conspiracies of Pontiac and Tecumseh. In these projects he was encouraged by the counsels of the Prophet Wabokieshiek, or White Cloud, a chief of mixed Sac and Winnebago blood, who had a village on Rock River, and possessed a wide influence among the Indian tribes. This savage charlatan, who combined great cunning with a love of intrigue, was the evil genius of Black Hawk, and lent the sanction of his omens and auguries to attempts which had no other assurance of success.

Black Hawk advocated a hostile policy, in opposition to the pacific course of Keokuk, because he was thus enabled to divide the suffrages of the tribe, and to allure from his peaceable rival to himself a following of the more feverish spirits. He is said, too, to have suffered personal insults and wrongs in the feuds and quarrels that arose between his village and its white neighbors, and to have once been beaten with sticks by white men, which indignity ever after rankled in his breast. Most of the anecdotes told of him, however, have all the indication of mythical origin ; and his own stories were always exaggerated, and often evidently false. He was undoubtedly a man of lofty and unquenchable spirit. In his old age, after his defeat, he was in the house of a man with whom he frequently dined ; a captain in the army came to dinner, and the host intimated to Black Hawk that he should *come to the second table.* Black Hawk's eye glistened with anger as he answered him, raising the forefinger of one hand to his breast to represent the officer : "I know the white man is a chief ; but *I*," elevating the finger of the other hand far above his head, "was a chief, and led my warriors to the fight, long before his mother knew him ! *Your meat—my dogs should not eat it !*" [1] He was the husband of one wife for forty years, and was affectionate to her and his children. In this haughty warrior we see some of the best and worst traits of the savage character—intense devotion to friends, and pitiless cruelty to foes.

As the tide of emigration poured westward, the rich lands ceded by the Sacs and Foxes in the treaty of 1829 were a principal point of attraction to the pioneers. Keokuk and all the tribe, except the band under Black Hawk at the Rock Island village, removed to the west bank of the Mississippi River ; but these Indians remained deaf to the advice of the agents and the solicitations of Keokuk. The Government, assuming that it had acquired a valid title to the land east of the Mississippi, threw it open to entry and purchase by the settlers, who, naturally looking no further for a foundation for their own rights, selected the most fertile spots for their locations. Among these was the land on which stood Black Hawk's village. The angry chief viewed their intrusion as alike an injury and an insult. Of all those broad acres, why select the site of his wigwam ? A contest began for the actual occupation of the soil, with the usual consequences of

4   [1] Drake's "Life of Black Hawk."

mutual depredation, violence, and strife. To put an end to this state
of affairs, the United States Government ordered the Indians of the
Rock Island village to comply with the treaty of 1829, surrender the
disputed lands, and cross the Mississippi River.

Black Hawk and his party denied the binding force of the treaties
to which he himself had assented, and also the construction placed
upon them by the United States Government, and induced the Sacs
on Rock River not to remove from their village. The quarrel between
the white people and the Indians reached such a point that in May,
1831, Governor Reynolds, on an appeal from the settlers, called out
700 Illinois militia "to repel the invasion of the State," as he styled
the refusal to move. General Gaines, likewise, at his request,
assembled ten companies of United States troops at Fort Armstrong,
where, on the 7th of June, he held a council with the chiefs of
the Sacs and Foxes. At this council Black Hawk denied that they
had sold their lands, and refused to move. General Gaines, to avoid
bloodshed, and hoping to effect his object by mere show of force,
assembled 1,600 mounted militiamen to coöperate with his troops ;
and, on the 25th of June, took possession of the Sac village without resistance. During the previous night the Indians, perceiving the hope-
lessness of resistance, had left their village, and encamped near by
under the protection of a white flag. Black Hawk and the other chiefs
then came into a council with General Gaines, in which, after claiming
that the land could not have been ceded in 1829, because it belonged
to an old squaw, whom he called his "mother," [1] he declared that he
yielded to force. Nevertheless, on the 30th of June they signed a
treaty, agreeing to submit to the authority of the United States, and
to remain on the west side of the Mississippi.

It is almost certain that Black Hawk had been trying for some
years to unite the Northwestern Indians in a league against the whites,
and that he believed that he had secured the adhesion of nine bands
of different tribes; while the Prophet also promised him the aid of
the British. When he found himself compelled to submit, through
the failure of his allies, he readily attributed the miscarriage to their
fickleness, their unreadiness, and their want of organization, and postponed his plan until the difficulties could be removed. Black Hawk
probably made the treaty of 1831 as a mere blind, with no intention of
remaining on the west side of the Mississippi. The treaty was scarcely
concluded before his people were crossing the river to take corn from
their former fields, while his emissaries were busy stirring up discontent in his own and other tribes. But for the quiet yet resolute
resistance of Keokuk, and the resulting apathy of the majority of the
Sacs and Foxes, he would have succeeded in organizing a wide-spread

[1] This title was tribal, not domestic.

and formidable insurrection; as it was, it is almost certain that he had many allies, who only waited for success to crown his earlier efforts before joining him. That he was not altogether unsuccessful in his diplomacy is best evinced by General Scott's statement that at least eight lodges of Winnebagoes, and many Kickapoos, Pottawattamies, and other Indians, were present with the British band in the campaign of 1832. The contest with Black Hawk, however, was finally precipitated before the maturity of his conspiracy—not by direct collision between the white men and Indians, but by one of those bloody outrages of one tribe upon another, so frequent in savage annals, which the United States Government, as supreme conservator of the peace, and by virtue of its treaty obligations, was compelled to punish.

The following is Lieutenant Johnston's account of the occurrences of the war:

On the 1st of April, 1832, Brigadier-General Atkinson, then commanding the right wing, Western Department, received an order, dated 17th of March, from the headquarters of the army, announcing that the Sacs and Foxes, in violation of the Treaty of Prairie du Chien of 1830, had attacked the Menomonees near Fort Crawford, and killed twenty-five of that tribe, and that the Menomonees meditated a retaliation. To preserve the pledged faith of the Government unbroken, and keep peace and amity among those tribes, he was instructed to prevent any movement, on the part of the Menomonees, against the Sacs and Foxes, and to demand of the Sac and Fox nation eight or ten of the party engaged in the murder of the Menomonees, including some of the principal men. For these purposes he was empowered to employ the regular force on the Mississippi, or so much as could be dispensed with after providing for the security of the several posts. The remote position of Fort Snelling, at the Falls of St. Anthony, surrounded as it was by powerful bands of Indians, precluded the possibility of drawing any portion of the force from that point. The force then to be relied on, to carry into effect the views of the Government, was such of the troops as could be spared from the slender force at Prairie du Chien, the troops at Fort Winnebago at the portage of the Fox and Wisconsin Rivers and Fort Armstrong at Rock Island, and the companies of the Sixth Regiment at Jefferson Barracks, amounting in all to about 420 men.

April 8th.—In obedience to the above-mentioned order, General Atkinson set off for the Upper Mississippi, with six companies of the Sixth Infantry (220 men), which were embarked at Jefferson Barracks, Missouri, in the steamboats Enterprise and Chieftain.

April 10th.—Arrived at the rapids of the Des Moines about 2 P. M. Here the commanding officer was informed that the British band of Indians, under Mucatah-mich-i-ca-Kaik[1] (Black Hawk), had crossed the Mississippi to the east bank, near the mouth of the Lower Iowa River. This band consisted of four or five hundred well-appointed horsemen, besides men and boys, employed in transporting the canoes, capable of bearing arms, making an active and efficient force of between five and six hundred: the whole—men, women, and children—amounting to above two thousand souls. The ultimate intentions of Black Hawk were unknown; this movement, however, was in direct contraven-

---

[1] Spelled, by McKenny and Hall, Ma-ka-tai-she-kia-kiak. ("Indian Tribes," vol. ii.)

tion of a compact made and entered into, the year previous, by the Sacs and Foxes and the United States.

The troops had to be disembarked and marched to the head of the rapids, on account of shallow water, and, going on board again next day, arrived at Rock Island on the 12th.

April 13th.—Black Hawk's band was reported this morning to be passing up on the east side of Rock River; some canoes were also seen passing up Rock River. Several white men were sent among these Indians to obtain information of their designs. They learned nothing of their destination; their course indicates that their movement is upon the Prophet's village. At 10 A. M. General Atkinson met the Sacs and some of the Fox chiefs in council.

The minutes of the council, in Lieutenant Johnston's handwriting, give the speech of General Atkinson, stating the treaty obligations of the parties and their violation, and demanding eight or ten of the murderers of the Menomonees. He also warned them to stay away from Black Hawk, whom he intended to compel to recross the river. The chiefs, after withdrawing to the plain to deliberate, returned, prepared to reply. Keokuk admitted all that General Atkinson said to be true, but declared his inability to control or surrender the murderers, who were with Black Hawk. He concluded:

You wish us to keep at peace, and have nothing to do with the Rock River Indians. We will do so. In token of our intentions, you see we have laid our spears there together. While you are gone to Prairie du Chien, we will endeavor to speak to Black Hawk's band, and try to persuade them to go back. If we do not succeed, I can do no more; then we will go home and try to keep our village at peace. The one who has raised all this trouble is a Winnebago, called the Prophet.

Prince (Wapello), the chief of the Foxes, spoke to the same effect. General Atkinson then told them that, in justice to the Menomonees, he must require hostages of them. Keokuk declared that he and his friends would be the first to be killed by Black Hawk if he had the power. The speakers also informed General Atkinson that Black Hawk was eight or nine miles up Rock River, with 500 warriors. The council was then adjourned to the 19th of April.

General Atkinson then proceeded up the river, and made arrangements with the commander at Prairie du Chien, and with General Dodge at Galena, relative to the protection of their districts, and the prevention of hostilities by the Menomonees and Sioux against the friendly Sacs and Foxes.

On his return to Fort Armstrong, General Atkinson again met the friendly Sacs and Foxes on the 19th. They brought in three young men who had been engaged in the murder of the Menomonees. In delivering them up, Wapello said : " There are the young men, who have taken pity on the women and children. There are three of them. These are my chiefs. These are the men who went into the braves' lodge to give themselves up. Father, I have received these young men; I now deliver them to you." Keokuk spoke to the same effect. General Atkinson expressed himself satisfied, and promised generous treatment to the young men who had given themselves up. He also promised protection to the friendly Sacs and Foxes, and threatened punishment to Black Hawk's band. The journal continues:

April 24th.—General Atkinson, having sent several persons to the British band of Indians, and hearing nothing of them, resolved to dispatch two young Sacs with a *mild talk.*

April 26th.—The two young Sacs returned to day from the British band, bringing Black Hawk's answer, which was, that "his heart was bad, and that he was determined not to turn back."

On April 27th Mr. Gratiot brought word from the Prophet's village that Black Hawk's band had run up the British flag, and was decidedly hostile. General Atkinson now made arrangements to secure the co-operation of the Illinois volunteers with the regular troops, but they were not concentrated at Rock River Rapids before the 9th of May. In the mean time emissaries had been sent to the Winnebagoes, and other measures taken to secure the peace of the frontier. On May 10th the movement up Rock River was begun.

The mounted volunteers, under General Whitesides, marched for Dixon's Ferry. The United States and Illinois infantry moved by water to the same point, under the command of Colonel Taylor, First Infantry. The provisions, etc., for the troops were transported in *keels* by the infantry.

On the 14th the troops arrived at and burned the Prophet's and Witticoe's villages, and on the next day received the news of Stillman's defeat at Kishwarkee (or Sycamore) Creek. It appears that Major Stillman, with his battalion of mounted volunteers from the command of General Whitesides, who was in advance, had volunteered for a scouting expedition. This battalion presented the unfortunate combination of an incompetent leader and an armed, disorderly mob. Proceeding without due caution about thirty miles in advance, they fell in with some Indian scouts, who, according to Black Hawk, carried a white flag, but whom the whites represent as defying them with a red flag. The militia killed two, and pursued another party incautiously. Before they were aware they found themselves in the presence of the enemy, when the commander ordered an immediate retreat. A disgraceful flight ensued, which lasted for thirty miles, and only terminated at Dixon's Ferry. The next morning fifty-two men were reported missing; and the fugitives represented that they had been overpowered by 1,500 or 2,000 Indian warriors, after a desperate conflict.

Lieutenant Johnston remarks in his journal :

The truth is, there was no action, or engagement, between the troops of General Stillman and the Indians. From the incapacity of their leader, the total absence of discipline in his battalion, and consequently a want of confidence in each other, these troops, that might under different circumstances have contended successfully against any enemy, had not the courage to face the Indians at Kishwarkee. Facts speak for themselves: only one man was killed near the ground where they met the Indians, the remainder were killed in flight six miles below, at or below a small, deep creek, now called Stillman's Run. The whole number killed was eleven. The Indians lost three or four, who were probably killed before the main body was discovered.

The Hon. Jefferson Davis told the writer that the Indians now became very insolent. They said contemptuously "they wanted more saddle-bags," Stillman's men having thrown away a good many.

The Indians then spread their scouts over the country, who killed and plundered the settlers, while the main body retired up Rock River to the Four Lakes. In the mean time, Governor Reynolds was obliged to yield to the clamors of Whitesides's militia, and disbanded them on the 26th of May, which put a stop for a time to the campaign. Abraham Lincoln was a captain in Whitesides's command, and is said, by his biographer, Lamon, in his queer narrative, to have reënlisted as a private in an independent spy company. Jefferson Davis, who was with General Gaines in his operations in 1831, was absent on furlough in Mississippi when the Black-Hawk War broke out, but gave up his furlough, and, joining his company, served in the campaign. Thus, in early life and with small rank, met as co-workers in this remote field, three men, who, forty years later, measured arms on an arena whose contest shook the world. Lieutenants Johnston, Eaton, and Robert Anderson, received commissions as colonels on the staff of the Governor of Illinois, dated May 9th. This militia rank was given, in order to secure the ready obedience of the Illinois officers, who refused to obey orders received through staff-officers of less rank than their own, and it proved a successful device.

On May 29th, Governor Reynolds, upon the requisition of General Atkinson, ordered 3,000 militia to assemble June 10th. To provide for and expedite their arming, equipment, and subsistence, General Atkinson dispatched his staff-officers to points where they were required. Lieutenant Johnston was sent to Jefferson Barracks, where, during his absence, his eldest daughter, Henrietta Preston, had been born. After passing a few days at home, between the 1st and 10th of June, he was at his post in time to assist in the organization of the militia, for whom General Atkinson, by extraordinary diligence, had prepared whatever was necessary to begin the campaign. Three brigades were organized at the Rapids of the Illinois, under the command of Generals Posey, Alexander, and Henry ; but it was not until the 25th of June that they were able to move from Dixon's Ferry. General Posey marched toward Galena, to coöperate with General Dodge. General Alexander was detached in the direction of the Plum River, to cut off the retreat of the enemy, who were reported to be marching toward the Mississippi. The rest of the command, under General Brady, United States Army, moved up Rock River, with seventy-five Pottawattamies, under their chief Cháboni, as guides. The time will not appear long in which these levies were assembled, organized, equipped, and moved to the scene of action, if we consider the condition of the country at that day, the want of facilities for transportation, and the distance from which supplies were drawn. In the mean time, however, every express brought intelligence of new outrages and disaster, the slaughter and scalping of citizens, and the defeat of small bodies of soldiers.

Lieutenant Johnston, in his private journal, after complimenting the zeal and energy of the quartermaster's and commissary departments, says :

No time was to be lost. An active and cruel enemy was now busy in the work of death and devastation, since the last levy was disbanded. Their mode of warfare is such that, while you keep a sufficient force in motion against them to contend with their main body, you must necessarily keep troops at every assailable point on the frontier to hold in check small parties, which it is their custom to detach to a great distance. Thus military men, acquainted only with the warfare of civilized nations, are surprised that so many troops are called into the field to subdue a comparatively small body of savages. Great allowance, in estimating for a militia force, must be made for the probable daily diminution, or actual loss of strength, from a variety of causes, which do not affect a regular force in the least; this, in addition to what is said of the enemy, will explain the reason why so large a militia force is usually called out.

The journal relates a number of instances in which marauding bands of Indians surprised and butchered solitary families and small parties. It also gives a detailed account of " General Dodge's affair with the Sacs on the Peketolica ; in which, with the loss of one killed and two dangerously wounded, he succeeded in destroying the whole party, thirteen in number." This was a very gallant skirmish with a ravaging band. Dodge, with eighteen men, attacked the Indians in a swamp. Under cover of the high bank of a small lake they wounded two of his men ; but the rest charged them, and, in a hand-to-hand encounter, in a space scarcely forty feet square, killed all the Indians except two, who were shot trying to swim the lake.

On the 2d and 3d of July the main body encamped one and a half mile from Lake Cosconong, where the Indians had evidently remained some time. Fresh signs were discovered of small parties ; but the main trail was toward the head of Rock River. General Brady was here obliged, by sickness, to turn over the command to General Atkinson. By the 6th of July, Generals Dodge, Alexander, Posey, and Henry, were brought into concert on both banks of Rock River, near the mouth of White Water Creek, with an almost impassable country before them. Reconnoitring parties of soldiers and friendly Indians advanced many miles, and reported access as very difficult, by reason of undergrowth and swamps.

Lieutenant Johnston says in his journal :

The volunteers having been for several days in great need of provisions, and not knowing when supplies would arrive, the commanding general ordered Alexander's and Henry's brigades and Dodge's battalion, to march to Fort Winnebago (a distance of thirty-six miles), and Posey to Fort Hamilton (a distance of forty-five miles). He directed General Posey to remain with his brigade at Fort Hamilton. Alexander, Henry, and Dodge, were to return to Fort Cosconong, as soon as provisions were procured. He gave verbal instructions to pursue the trail of the enemy, if it was met with in going or returning.

The troops were now in a country almost totally unknown, and in great want of provisions. Hence the necessity of sending this heavy detachment to procure them. The Indians were supposed to be at "the Four Lakes," now the site of the flourishing town of Madison, Wisconsin, and to be about to move westward for the Mississippi River. The line of march of the volunteers to Fort Winnebago left the Four Lakes to the right ; and, therefore, in going or returning, would necessarily cross the trail of the Indians, if they had moved as was expected. In returning from Fort Winnebago the detachment fell in with the trail of the Indians ; and General Henry, in obedience to his verbal instructions, sent forward his provisions with a small guard, and pursued the Indians with his main body. He overtook them on July 21, 1832, and successfully engaged them at what was known as Wisconsin Heights, a crossing of the Wisconsin River, twenty miles below Fort Winnebago.

A letter from Mrs. Johnston to her mother gives the following account of the fight, as received from her husband :

Generals Dodge and Henry, with their mounted men, overtook the retreating Indians at a point on the Wisconsin River fifteen miles above Blue Mounds. The Indians rose the crest of a hill on horseback, set up a yell, and fired, when they discovered the whites. The mounted men formed, *yelled* as dreadfully as the enemy, dismounted, and charged on them. There was one man killed, and eight wounded, but none badly. Between thirty-five and forty Indians were killed, and it was supposed that numbers were wounded. They were pursued till night, when they escaped, much shattered, to an island in the Wisconsin; leaving (as Captain Smith writes) many old men, and sick and dead children, on their march. They also abandoned all their heavy baggage. The whites had but one day's provisions, and were, consequently, compelled to return for more.

Though the volunteers had marched that day forty miles, and were drenched with a six hours' rain, they attacked the Indians with great spirit. Black Hawk, however, made a gallant stand, to enable his women and children to get across the river, which they succeeded in doing; and his band made their escape during the night in bark canoes. He was said to have lost sixty-eight men, but this number probably included those fugitives killed and captured by Lieutenant Ritner. The volunteers fell back to Blue Mounds, where they arrived on the evening of the 23d, and were joined next day by the main body.

During the campaign, Black Hawk's people had suffered much from want of provisions ; many subsisted on the roots and bark of trees, and some starved to death. On the 14th of July several families of Winnebagoes came into camp, much in need of provisions. July 16th, General Atkinson received dispatches from General Scott. He speaks of "the deplorable condition of his command of regular troops at Chicago and elsewhere on the lakes, as far as Detroit, produced by Asiatic cholera." So formidable was the outbreak of the British band considered by the Government, and so imminent seemed an insurrection of the Northwestern tribes, that all the available forces on the seaboard were hurried toward the scene of action, under the command of General Scott. But, in their progress across the lakes, the cholera broke out ; and, of the 1,500 regular soldiers in his command, over 200 died, many were prostrated by disease, a large number deserted, and nearly all were demoralized. Under these circumstances, and for fear of spreading the infection, General Scott prudently and properly held aloof from the campaign. As it turned out, his contingent was not needed to finish the pursuit of the starving Indians, who were now, in reality, fugitives.

The troops having received provisions, and many of the volunteers being dismounted and broken down, the main body was moved back to Lake Cosconong on July 20th ; but, in consequence of information received from Generals Henry and Dodge, the command was marched, on July 21st, toward Blue Mounds, one hundred miles distant, where a junction was effected on the 24th with General Henry, who had fallen back there for provisions. In their forced march along a ridge, through a swampy and flooded country, the troops suffered from storms, want of drinking-water, and dysentery, caused by the raw pork and dough, which was their only food. On the 25th, the regulars, with Alexander's and Henry's brigades, moved to within three miles of the Wisconsin River.

In Mrs. Johnston's letter, already quoted, occurs the following :

We got letters again last night, dated the 27th. Our men had hurried on to the scene of action, as soon as the express arrived, leaving their sick and bag-

gage at Blue Mounds. They were constructing rafts, to cross the Wisconsin at
that point, for it was much swollen with late rains. They expected to get over
that day. Captain Rogers [Sixth Infantry] thought it impossible for foot-
soldiers to overtake the mounted Indians; but Mr. Johnston was more sanguine.
His letter is not here. I was requested to send it to town, or I could be even
more particular, certainly much more graphical than I am. He hoped for a
speedy termination of these affairs, as the enemy are now making for the Chip-
pewa country, or will try to cross the Mississippi at Prairie du Chien. Mr.
Johnston thinks they will be overtaken before they reach either place. They
are nearly starved, subsisting on the bark of trees, dogs, and their horses.

Lieutenant Johnston's journal contains the following record :

July 27th.—Many of the horses having failed through fatigue and insufficiency of proper food, General Atkinson selected about 900 of the best mounted
volunteers to cross the Wisconsin and pursue the enemy, in conjunction with
the regular troops. The remainder of the several volunteer corps was ordered
to Fort Hamilton. Generals Henry, Posey, Alexander, and Dodge, commanded
the volunteers, whom they had selected from their several commands for this
duty. Colonel Zachary Taylor, First Infantry, commanded the regular troops,
about 400 infantry.

July 28th.—The troops, having all passed the river, moved up the Wisconsin ;
and, having advanced three or four miles, the trail of the enemy was discovered,
bearing in the direction of the Ocooch Mountains. The columns were turned
to the left, and pursued, *on the trail*, ten or twelve miles, and encamped. At
this point the trail turned up a deep creek. The same kind of ancient fortifications were observed at this gap of the hills as we had noticed on Rock River.

July 29th.—The trails of the enemy were pursued with activity to-day. We
passed several of the Sac encampments ; they are hard pressed for provisions,
and forced to kill their horses for subsistence. The country is rough and
mountainous, with a rich soil ; dense forests, with thick underwood, cover the
whole country, which affords no grass. The troops encamped on a high hill ;
the horses were tied up without food.

July 30th.—The march was continued to-day. The face of the country
bears the same character as that passed yesterday. The general course of the
trail is northwest. Encamped this evening in a deep, narrow valley, near a
small stream running westward ; the water was remarkably cold. Small sap-
lings of maple and elm were cut down for the horses to feed on ; they had suffered much for want of grass.

July 31st.—After a hard day's march, the troops encamped near the Kickapoo
River—a small stream flowing into the Wisconsin.

August 1st.—Passed the Kickapoo to-day at a shallow ford. Here com-
mences a prairie country, with scattering groves of oak, quite as rough as that
we had passed over. This was a long day's march for the infantry, who found
no difficulty, however, in keeping pace with the mounted men, whose horses
were exhausted for want of food. The troops encamped after dark. The appearance of the trail indicated the proximity of the enemy, who were supposed
to be at the Mississippi, which was conjectured to be within a short march.
The commanders of the several corps were directed to hold them in readiness to
march at two o'clock the following morning. This order was not communicated

to the brigades of Generals Alexander and Henry before their horses were turned out to graze.

August 2d.—At two o'clock this morning the troops turned out; and, having made hasty preparation, were on the route of the enemy before sunrise, except Henry's and Alexander's brigades, for reasons before mentioned. About one hour after sunrise, a small body of spies, under the command of Captain Dixon, thrown in advance from Dodge's battalion, brought information that the enemy were drawn up in position on the route, and near at hand. We had previous notice of our proximity to the Mississippi, from having seen the fog over it, distant probably five or six miles.

General Dodge instructed his spies to reconnoitre the enemy, and occupy his attention; the spies advanced as ordered, and succeeded in killing eight Indians, while they retired through the woods. In the mean time, General Dodge's battalion was drawn up in line, and a report was made to the commanding general. The regulars and mounted volunteers were ordered forward. The regulars, being immediately in rear of Dodge's battalion, moved forward and formed in extended order on his right; Dodge's battalion, having dismounted, was also formed in extended order; the whole advanced in this order for some minutes before General Posey's command came up. Generals Henry and Alexander promptly obeyed the order to advance, and came up in good time to take the position assigned to them by the commanding general.

General Posey was posted on the right of the regulars, and General Alexander on the right of General Posey. The troops by this time, in following the movements of the retiring enemy, had been drawn considerably to the right of the trail. The commanding general, apprehending this to be a feint intended to divert him from his purpose and to gain time, ordered General Henry to pursue the trail quite to the river. At the same time, General Alexander was ordered to move down a deep ravine to the river.

The centre passed down a steep declivity and ravine. In taking possession of these only accessible approaches to the plain, or rather swamp lying below, the right and left were necessarily two miles or more apart. General Henry in pursuing the trail, which followed the easiest descent, was brought in contact with the position of the enemy sooner than either of the other corps. He reached the plain in advance of the centre, and attacked the enemy.

The regulars and Dodge's and part of Posey's command promptly moved to the support of the left. The enemy then retired, disputing the ground step by step, which they had done from the beginning. Many of them, men, women, and children, fled to the river, and endeavored to escape by swimming. In this situation our troops arrived on the bank, and threw in a heavy fire, which killed great numbers, unfortunately some women and children among the warriors, an event deeply deplored by the soldiers. The enemy, in retiring, had taken some strong positions at the foot of an island, from which they were driven by the repeated charges of the regulars, and the volunteers under Dodge.

They were now completely overthrown and beaten, with the loss of one hundred and fifty killed, forty women and children taken prisoners, their baggage captured, and about one hundred horses killed or captured. The loss on our part was five regulars killed and four wounded; six of Henry's wounded, one mortally; and one of Posey's brigade. This action was decisive; the remnant of the band fled to the west of the Mississippi, and, after having suffered almost beyond endurance, reached their own country, and were given up by Keokuk and other influential friendly Sacs to the whites.

The losses of the campaign in encounters and skirmishes, and in the heavy fight at Wisconsin Heights, had greatly weakened Black Hawk's force, which had been further diminished by the desertion of his Indian allies, as the tide of war turned against him. Moreover, after the affair at Wisconsin Heights too, a detachment, under Lieutenant Ritner, sent from Prairie du Chien, intercepted a party of the Sacs attempting to descend the Wisconsin, and killed fifteen men and captured four men and thirty-two women and children.

When Black Hawk reached the Mississippi, and was preparing to effect its passage on the 1st of August, he found the steamboat Warrior ready to dispute the crossing. This boat, with a detachment of troops and a cannon, had been interposed, under orders from General Atkinson, to cut off his retreat; and a sharp skirmish ensued, with the effect, at least, of retarding his flight until the assault of the main body on August 2d.

The fight on that day, known as the battle of the Bad Axe, from a stream near by, effectually crushed the power of the British band. The exhausted condition of the victors, but still more the desire to stop the effusion of blood, induced General Atkinson to desist from the pursuit of the miserable remnant who fled across the Mississippi. But the pursuit, which was thus abandoned by the whites, was taken up by the Indians in alliance with the United States so eagerly that it is believed that not one of the fugitives escaped death or capture. Those who reached the west bank of the river were attacked by their foes, the Sioux, and were either killed, or taken prisoners and surrendered to the United States authorities. Among those thus given up was Naopope, Black Hawk's second in command.

Black Hawk, with the Prophet and other chiefs, escaped from the combat, and took refuge on some islands above Prairie du Chien, whence they were routed by a detachment of regulars under Lieutenant Jefferson Davis. In despair they gave themselves up to two Winnebago Indians, Decorie the one-eyed and Chaetar, who claimed to have captured them, and delivered them to Colonel Taylor and the Indian agent, General Street, at Prairie du Chien, with a false and fulsome speech. The other captives were released; but Black Hawk and his two sons, the Prophet, Naopope, and nine other chiefs of the hostile band, were retained as hostages.

Four or five hundred Indians and about two hundred white people had lost their lives in the Black-Hawk War, and an expenditure of $2,000,000 had been incurred. Whether the war might not have been averted by foresight and timely generosity on the part of the Government is a question; but, when the savage chief and his band were once upon the war-path, any other than the promptest and severest measures of repression would have been construed by these rude warriors as an evidence of timidity, and any partial display of military strength as a confession of weakness. The Winnebagoes, Pottawattamies, and other disaffected tribes, would probably have seized the opportunity and bathed the frontier in blood. Hence the necessity for a large force and for decisive action. Indeed, but for the unfortunate defeat of Stillman, which was precipitated by the rashness and disorganization of his command, it is quite possible that Black Hawk might have submitted, in the presence of an overpowering force, to General Atkinson, as he had yielded to General Gaines the year previous. But, after this first act of overt war, the cruel atrocities of the Indians upon the white settlers made impossible any other solution than such swift and heavy retribution as would punish the guilty, warn the wavering, and thenceforth deter the discontented from similar attempts.

The whole country felt great relief at the termination of a war which threatened to assume such proportions ; but in the border settlements, where the lives of the women and children were at stake, there was heart-felt rejoicing.

The Secretary of War addressed the following letter to General Atkinson :

DEPARTMENT OF WAR, *October* 24, 1832.

SIR: The return of the President to the seat of government enables me to communicate to you his sentiments in relation to the operations and results of the campaign, recently conducted under your orders, against the hostile Indians; and it is with great pleasure I have received his instructions to inform you that he appreciates the difficulties you had to encounter, and that he has been highly gratified at the termination of your arduous and responsible duties. Great privations and embarrassments necessarily attend such a warfare, and particularly in the difficult country occupied by the enemy. The arrangements which led to the defeat of the Indians were adopted with judgment and pursued with decision, and the result was honorable to yourself, and to the officers and men acting under orders. I will thank you to communicate to the forces that served with you, both regulars and militia, the feelings of the President upon this occasion. I have the honor to be, very respectfully, your obedient servant,

LEWIS CASS.

To General H. ATKINSON, Jefferson Barracks, Mo.

The favorable opinions of the President, General Jackson, and of General Cass, on the conduct of the war, carry more weight than the ordinary bestowal of official compliments, as they were both well acquainted with the nature of the service from actual experience.

The Secretary of War, in his report for 1832, says :

The arrangements of the commanding general, as well in the pursuit as in the action, were prompt and judicious, and the conduct of the officers and men was exemplary.

President Jackson, in his annual message, approves of the action of the military authorities, thus :

> The hostile incursions of the Sac and Fox Indians necessarily led to the inter-position of the Government. A portion of the troops under Generals Scott and Atkinson, and of the militia of the State of Illinois, were called into the field. After a harassing warfare, prolonged by the nature of the country and by the difficulty of procuring subsistence, the Indians were entirely defeated, and the disaffected band dispersed or destroyed. The result has been creditable to the troops engaged in the service. Severe as is the lesson to the Indians, it was ren-dered necessary by their unprovoked aggressions; and it is to be hoped that its impression will be permanent and salutary. This campaign has evinced the effi-cient organization of the army, and its capacity for prompt and active service. Its several departments have performed their functions with energy and dis-patch, and the general movement was satisfactory.

The best proof of the influence of the Black-Hawk campaign is to be found in the quiet acquiescence of the Indian tribes in the measures taken immediately thereafter by the Government for their removal westward, and in the permanent peace established on that frontier.

Black Hawk and his associates were treated with generosity by the Government. They were retained in mild captivity at Jefferson Barracks long enough to break their power and destroy their prestige with their tribe, and to allow their own heated passions to cool under the genial influence of kindly intercourse with their captors. They were then carried through the principal cities of the East, that they might view the numbers, wealth, and resources, of their recent antag-onist, and realize the folly of such an unequal struggle; after which they were released and dismissed to their homes. In the tour among the Atlantic cities Black Hawk was treated more like a popular favorite than a merciless foe ; and a respect was paid him that was measured rather by the trouble he had given than by the greatness of his talents. The Indians who had followed him in his last campaign represented the Prophet as the mover of the strife and the most cunning in counsel; to Naopope was given the credit of the highest military skill; while the preëminence of Black Hawk was ascribed not so much to sagacity or warlike genius as to the force of his relentless will, the intensity of his passions, and the singleness of his purpose.

Hon. Jefferson Davis informed the writer that Black Hawk told him, while he was in his custody at Jefferson Barracks, that he crossed the Mississippi to join the Prophet ; that his engagement was to give up Rock Island village ; and that there was no engagement not to join the Prophet. Mr. Davis said Keokuk was a politic man ; but that

Black Hawk was a proud, silent savage. He bore himself with dignity in his confinement, and thanked Mr. Davis for his kindness to him.

Black Hawk saw his power pass to his rival; but he could scarcely envy the self-indulgence enjoyed by Keokuk as the pensioner and placeman of a people whom he had himself defied in arms. The short remnant of his old age was worn out in sullen submission to the conqueror; his enemy, Keokuk, became the slave of drink, died, and is almost forgotten; and now no trace of the stern warrior, of his more politic opponent, or of the red clansmen who followed them in war or in the chase, is found in all their broad domain, except in a few isolated geographical names. Perhaps the most striking commentary on the events which supplanted roaming savages with a civilized people is seen in the change that less than half a century has wrought in the theatre of war. The very region where a moving column of less than 3,000 soldiers was compelled to carry its provisions, and 1,000 Indians endured the pangs of famine, is now one of the greatest grain-producing centres in the world; while the territory east of the Mississippi, within a hundred and fifty miles of Rock Island, for which the British band contended, now supports an intelligent and prosperous population, numbering more than 1,250,000 souls.

CHAPTER IV.

JEFFERSON BARRACKS.

As soon as it was manifest that Black Hawk and the British band were utterly crushed, General Atkinson disbanded the volunteers, and distributed the regulars according to the exigencies of the service. That officer had concluded the campaign, which was really creditable to him, with an enhanced military reputation. Colonel Zachary Taylor, who, after the departure of General Brady, was the second in command, now belongs to history as a victorious general in the Mexican War, and as the twelfth President of the United States. His character and deeds have been weighed and recorded; and, in this connection, therefore, it is only necessary to state the impression he made upon the subject of this memoir. It is true that circumstances contributed to a very favorable estimate of Colonel Taylor by Lieutenant Johnston; but, as a life-long acquaintance and his matured judgment confirmed this, it may not be without interest as one soldier's opinion of another. Lieutenant Johnston was probably, from the first, kindly disposed to Colonel Taylor, because he was a kinsman of Mrs. Johnston's mother; which tie had been strengthened by long acquaintance, good neighborhood, and mutual kind offices. Colonel Taylor had shown an earnest and active friendship for Mrs. Preston and her family, when circumstances rendered it peculiarly acceptable, especially as surety in settling Major Preston's estate. Moreover, he was always cordial and appreciative to Lieutenant Johnston, both in social and military intercourse ; and this conduct had the more weight as he was a bold, open man, whose offices outran his professions. His popular title of "Rough and Ready" only did him half justice ; for his ruggedness was that of the oak, and he was as ready to help a friend as to strike a foe. Under blunt manners he concealed a warm heart. He was an expert in the practical routine of his profession, and handled his army like a machine with which he was perfectly familiar. He was well acquainted with English history ; Hume was his favorite author. General Johnston's sincere and lasting attachment for General Taylor was based upon genuine esteem. He had a high opinion of General Taylor's military ability ; and told the writer, when the battle of Buena Vista was impending, that no man had better military instincts, or a more stubborn resolution under adverse circumstances. He saw in him a strong, single-minded, faithful, upright man. General Taylor lacked power of verbal expression, and was impatient of homage and conventionalities. He was tenacious of opinions, purposes, and affections ; clear in his perceptions of familiar subjects ; and prompt, decided, and thorough, in his actions. Lieutenant Johnston was greatly drawn toward a character so perfect in its massiveness, integrity, and simplicity.

In the Black-Hawk War Lieutenant Johnston was thrown into the intimate relations of camp-life with his brother officers ; and the favor in which he was before held by them was increased by his share in the campaign. In a letter to the writer, from Major-General George H. Crosman, United States Army (retired), written in 1873, occurs the following, giving voice to this opinion: "Your father acquired a very high reputation for his wise and successful conduct during the Black-Hawk War."

Captain Eaton relates a little anecdote of the Black-Hawk War, which it may not be amiss to give in his own language :

On the same campaign an incident happened, illustrating Lieutenant Johnston's keen sense of propriety, his respect for female virtue, and his power of rebuke. One evening, as a group of officers were talking in the tent of one of them, a Lieutenant ——, who was of a coarse and vulgar nature, and who was eventually dismissed from the service, said he did not believe in female virtue. Lieutenant Johnston at once arose and said: "Mr. ——, you have a mother : and, I believe, you have a sister." He made no other remark ; but the rebuke silenced Lieutenant ——, and, vulgar as he was, he hung his head in shame and confusion. I never knew a man who could give a rebuke with more crushing effect than Albert Sidney Johnston.

His power of rebuke lay in his serenity and benignity. It was clearly seen that it was the sentiment, not the person, that was condemned.

General Atkinson dropped down the river to Prairie du Chien, on August 3d ; and, having delayed there until the 25th, proceeded to Rock Island. In consequence of the movement of cholera-infected troops from Chicago to that point the pestilence broke out there, and carried off a number of victims. Lieutenant Johnston was attacked, but recovered after severe suffering. Lying upon the floor, he was wrapped in heavy blankets, drenched with vinegar and salt, and then dosed with brandy and Cayenne pepper; the Faculty must decide whether he recovered in consequence or in spite of the treatment. The doctors yet disagree as to the mode of cholera propagation. Lieutenant Johnston, from his own observation, inclined to the belief that cholera might be averted, from isolated places at least, by strict quarantine.

Lieutenant Johnston, on his return to Jefferson Barracks, found that the absence which had proved so fruitful to him in professional experience had been a season of sore trial to his wife, whose delicate nervous organization had been too severely taxed for her strength. An infant daughter, born in April, was, as the mother's record has it, "on June 28th, supposed to be dead, but was, by God's mercy, restored to us." The child was in her coffin ; but Mrs. Benton, thinking she detected signs of life, by a hot bath and other remedies brought her to life, and she still lives. The following extract, from a letter to her mother, explains how the seeds of the malady that cost Mrs. Johnston's life were sown :

I am still afflicted with the sickness of both my children. Between physical fatigue and mental anxiety for my children, for you, and for my good husband, I am scarcely myself. I try to be cheerful. God alone knows how it will all terminate! I have been busy to-day, making up flannel for my husband, and writing to him. I have so bad a cold that I can't be heard when I speak, and I am often fatigued and sick.

Her husband's return, safe from the war and the epidemic, the recovery of her children, and the soothing hope of a less exciting life, relaxed this grievous mental strain. Mrs. Johnston's constitution was naturally good ; but, in the change from the mountains of Virginia, where she was born and passed a good deal of her girlhood, to the neighborhood of Louisville, then in bad repute for malarial fevers, her health had been injured, and again still more by a three years' residence on the banks of the Mississippi. But, although her enfeebled system was thus laid open to the inroads of disease, its approaches were so insidious that the apprehensions which had been aroused were lulled into a fatal security. In the happy illusions of the moment her

imagination pictured a long and tranquil existence, in which the alarms
of war should be exchanged for the peaceful delights of a country-
home. She urged her husband to resign from the army ; and her
lively and affectionate representations would easily have effected their
purpose but for a conflict of duties and sentiments that alternately
swayed him. No traits were more strongly marked in the character of
Albert Sidney Johnston than his powerful domestic affections and his
love for Nature in all her aspects, but especially as seen through the
coloring of a rural life. On the other hand—so strangely are our qualities mingled—he felt the desire, the power, and the call, to achieve
something great, useful, and memorable. Never was a man more
deeply conscious that he was born into the world not for himself, but
for others; and that, whosoever else might fail, on *him*, at least, lay an
obligation of public duty, to which self must be sacrificed. He recognized the duty to return in service the gift of an education received at
West Point. He saw, too, that the habits of life and thought, the
associations, studies, and aspirations of ten years, would be difficult to
lay aside. As no public emergency required his services, and as the
call of domestic duties seemed, therefore, the more urgent, his conclusion was to yield to the wishes of his wife, and choose some other
occupation, in which he would not be separated from her. Yet, con-
senting, he delayed, for it was hard to abandon his chosen career. In
this state of mind he took counsel with his eldest brother, on whose
prudence and good feeling he knew that he could rely.

The reply of Senator Johnston is written in the most affectionate
strain, and discusses the subject in all its bearings, but space permits
only a few extracts, which, as indications of the writer's character, as
well as for their general value, may prove interesting :

WASHINGTON, *January* 12, 1833.

MY DEAR BROTHER : I received your letter with great pleasure, since it re-
news a correspondence that had been, on your part, for a considerable time neglected.

I am very happy to hear of your wife, and the interesting family growing
up around you, and of the fortunate circumstances of your life. You have no
reason to regret your profession, or the military career you have run, since you
have been entirely successful, and as useful and distinguished as the nature of
the service permits. It has, besides, led you to a happy union, and has given a
fortunate direction to your pursuits.

If you should retire now, as you may do under the most favorable and flattering circumstances, you will carry with you your military character and services, which will always be a source of pride and pleasure, as well as of proper
consideration, among your friends and countrymen. In the event of war, which
is not, however, probable at present, you will be called into service with much
higher rank. If you should aspire to political life, your past career will be the
highest claim to public confidence and favor. Wherever you go and whatever

you do, you will find that it will exert a favorable influence in your intercourse with society.

In all these respects you have gained more than you would in any other profession in the same time ; and, taking all the chances of life, you are eminently successful in all that constitutes our happiness here.

After suggesting the various inducements to different occupations, Mr. Johnston advises farming, and adds :

You might connect this with some other pursuits, such as those of a literary or political kind. The former is full of interest and pleasure, but the country-life lacks excitement to keep it up ; as to the latter, it is replete with disgust and disappointment.

This last sentence is remarkable, as the utterance of a man of cheerful temper, who, from early manhood to the day of his death, continually advanced in popular favor without a single reverse.

After discussing the advantages and disadvantages of planting in Louisiana, the strong fraternal feeling and confident spirit of the man break out thus :

I can only say I shall be most happy to render you any assistance ; and that, with the support of Harris and myself, you could not fail in any enterprise.

He continues :

You think you are too old to study a profession. That is a mistake ; you could never read with greater advantage. If you could devote all your leisure to law, history, and literature, it would not only give you excellent habits, good taste, and much valuable information, but would qualify you for any duty to which you may be called. I can, from my own experience, say that books are the source of the purest and most rational pleasures. They are the most durable, and, unlike almost all others, increase with age, as the taste for others diminishes. To a gentleman this taste is essential ; in the country it is necessary, to avoid *ennui* and tedium of life ; and this is equally true of both sexes. . . . Military talents are held in high estimation all over the world, less perhaps than they deserve in this country ; but no one knows how long we shall be peaceful neighbors. *You may live to see not only war among the States, but civil and perhaps servile war*, in which all your military skill and experience may be put in requisition.

This seems written in the spirit of prophecy, but it was only the calm reading of the signs of the times by the experienced eye of a veteran statesman.

There are several other letters indicating Mr. Johnston's natural desire that his brother should cast his lot in the community where he himself had been so fortunate and so much honored ; still this is not urged upon him unduly. The following extracts are from his last letter to Lieutenant Johnston :

April 25, 1833.

My DEAR BROTHER: I am now on board the Homer on my way to Louisiana, with my son William. The indisposition of my wife detained me until the 13th, when she was so far recovered as to permit me to leave her.

Since the pacification, all parties seem reconciled to the terms of the compromise. The South is content, and the manufacturers are perfectly satisfied. The country enjoys at this moment an unexampled degree of prosperity, and we can foresee nothing likely to interrupt it for many years. Everything is appreciating in value—stocks of all kinds, lands, lots, houses, manufactures, rents, etc. Property in cities and towns is rising in value. I was glad to see Louisville partaking of the general prosperity; it gives indications of considerable improvement, and will doubtless become a flourishing place. . . . It is impossible for one person to advise another wisely with regard to his vocation and pursuits in life. We cannot enter fully into each other's views and feelings. If money was your chief object, you would accomplish your purpose most rapidly in Louisiana; but the climate and slave-property are objections. . . .

I duly received the account of General Atkinson's expedition. He pursued a wise and prudent policy. If he had hurried on and been defeated, the whole frontier would have been exposed, while the timid and wavering Indians would have joined Black Hawk, and gained possession of the country. It would then have required another year, a more formidable force, and a greater expenditure of money, to conquer them.

I had a conversation with the President, at the meeting of Congress. He was, I believe, satisfied with the final results. He thought the general might, in the first instance, have felt the force of the Indians, and, having done so, he would have found himself able to defeat them. Caution is no part of his policy. The general was placed in a position either to suffer defeat by a prompt movement, or censure by a prudent one. The country is entirely satisfied. It must have been a very arduous service, in which you had your share of labor and responsibility.

You will please make my affectionate regards to your wife. Affectionately,

J. S. JOHNSTON.

The next tidings brought the distressing intelligence of this brother's sudden death, by the explosion of the steamboat Lioness. The following extracts from a letter of Judge John Harris Johnston to Albert Sidney Johnston sufficiently narrate the sad event :

My DEAR BROTHER: Detailed accounts of the dreadful disaster on board the Lioness, in Red River, will have reached you before this time, confirming the melancholy loss of life. The explosion occurred on May 19th, at 5 A. M., at the Recollet Bon Dieu, on Red River. Among others who perished was our much-beloved brother, who, with William,[1] had taken passage the evening before for Natchitoches. In one instant, when all on board were unsuspecting, the boat was, by some unaccountable accident, blown to atoms by gunpowder, and between fifteen and twenty-five persons were destroyed. Our brother was instantly killed, and his body was not found for several days. William, who occupied the upper berth in the same state-room, was thrown to the middle of

[1] Senator Johnston's only son.

the river, and saved himself on a plank or door. He was severely injured, and confined to his bed for twelve or fifteen days. He is now restored, and able to walk out.

Thus perished, in the fullness of his honors and usefulness, a man who was, in his generation, a diligent and unselfish public servant, and who left a name without reproach. From a notice of his death in the *New Orleans Argus*, the following is a brief extract :

Those who only knew him as a public man will *regret* his loss; those who knew him intimately will *mourn* it. It will be long again before they can meet with the same warm heart and cool head; the same absence of and contempt for profession and pretense; and the same ready performance of all the duties which friendship imposes.

Niles's Register says that he was—

An able statesman and one of the most useful members of the Senate. He was a gentleman of rare accomplishments—generous, faithful, and kind, of very courteous manners, and possessed of the most liberal feelings ; a fast friend, and an honorable opponent.

His son William, mentioned in the foregoing, was graduated at Yale College ; and, having begun to practise law at Alexandria, was, at the age of twenty-two, selected for the lucrative office of parish judge, vacated by the death of his uncle, John Harris Johnston. A year later he fell a victim to the climate, leaving a widow and one son. In talents, character, and industry, his promise was worthy of his father. Seven years after Josiah Stoddard Johnston's death, and thirty-five years after his first settlement in Louisiana, not a single scion of all his hardy race remained upon the soil of that State. Death and emigration had done the work.

If Albert Sidney Johnston entertained any serious purpose of making a home in Louisiana, the shock of his brother's untimely end turned him from it. In the winter of 1832–'33 great commercial distress in Louisville would have prevented the sale of real estate for such investment. Mrs. Johnston seemed to be recovering her wonted health, and the spring and summer of 1833 were passed happily at Jefferson Barracks, with no greater anxiety than " a little cholera in St. Louis," of which Lieutenant Johnston writes to his friend, E. D. Hobbs, of Louisville, " As we have seen it before in its worst form, we will meet it now with a steady front." This brief and touching minute, in Mrs. Johnston's handwriting, records the beginning of her final malady :

I was taken ill on September 19, 1833, at Jefferson Barracks, Missouri. Came to Louisville October 4th. Maria Preston Johnston was born October 28, 1833, and returned to her Maker the 10th of the following August. " The Lord gave and the Lord hath taken away. Blessed be the name of the Lord."

In Louisville the physicians pronounced Mrs. Johnston's lungs affected, and, according to the prevailing practice, bled her freely and often, and confined her diet to such insufficient nourishment as goat's-milk and Iceland moss. Of course, no more effectual way could have been adopted to produce pulmonary consumption in an enfeebled constitution. She was carefully and tenderly nursed by her mother and friends in Louisville, and her husband deceived himself with the hope that travel and a change of climate, and his own untiring care, might restore her. Accordingly, on March 4, 1834, they made a journey to New Orleans, from which they returned the 8th of May. During their stay in New Orleans they were the guests of Dr. Davidson, an eminent physician. While in New Orleans, Lieutenant Johnston took the step at which he had hesitated for eighteen months, and on April 24, 1834, forwarded his resignation of his commission as second-lieutenant in the United States Army. Mrs. Johnston's failing health made her long for the secure quiet of a permanent home; and her husband, anxious to soothe and encourage her, in order to gratify the cherished wish of her heart, bought a farm near St. Louis, with the purpose of engaging in its cultivation. That he did not quit the army without a severe struggle is evident from his letters and actions. He writes to Eaton:

I have this day mailed my resignation, the acceptance of which will be notified to you almost as soon as this will reach you. That I felt some little pain at seeing my letter glide into the letter-box you may judge. I hope, although we shall be separated, we shall not be estranged. I quit my profession and my regiment with lively interest for the welfare of *all*, and the recollection of strong friendship for very many of the officers of the regiment.

Dr. John Pintard Davidson, who was then living with his father, says the letter of resignation was reluctantly written and placed in his hands "to mail at noon, if not recalled before that hour," and that Lieutenant Johnston showed all the signs of great regret in performing this act.

On their return to Louisville, in obedience to medical advice they undertook a journey to the Virginia Springs and the seaboard. On July 15th they embarked on the steamboat Hunter for Guyandotte, with their son, a nurse, a driver, and a carriage and pair of stout horses. From Guyandotte the journey was pursued in the carriage. After visiting the Red Sulphur Springs, esteemed salutary in lung-diseases, they made the round of the watering-places in the mountains, relying more upon exercise in the open air than upon the mineral waters. They also visited some of Mrs. Johnston's relations in that region, especially Colonel James McDowell, in Rockbridge County. During this distant tour he paid a visit to Mrs. Edmonia Preston, at Lexington. The writer then visited a house which forty years later he occupied as a residence for a time. Lieutenant Johnston visited the Peaks of Otter with John T. L. Preston, who later in life was of Stonewall Jackson's staff.

Leaving Cherry Grove, the residence of Colonel McDowell, on the 8th of September, they traveled by carriage, passing through Fredericksburg on the 11th, and reaching Baltimore on the 14th. They spent several days in Philadelphia, in order to consult the eminent Dr. Physick; and, after visiting New York, returned to Louisville, where they arrived on the 21st of October. During their absence their youngest child had died. Mrs. Johnston says : " After much traveling and fatigue I am here again. My babe is in her place of rest, and my dear grandmother [1] living long enough to bless us once more—and die."

Mr. Johnston devoted the autumn and winter to the care of his invalid wife, whom he tenderly nursed through an almost painless decline. In the spring they removed to Hayfield, about five miles from Louisville, the country-home of Mr. George Hancock, Mrs. Johnston's uncle. Mr. Hancock and his newly-wedded wife did all in their power to cheer these last sad hours. In this kind home, soothed by the unwearying affection of her husband, by her confident religious hopes, and by the ministrations of the Episcopal Church, and invoking blessings on all her loved ones, Henrietta Preston Johnston gradually passed away. She died on the 12th of August, 1835.

The introduction of the following letter from Mrs. Hancock, who was a daughter of Dr. Davidson, and a very constant and cherished friend of General Johnston, needs no apology. As a skillful chess-player and an enthusiastic florist, she naturally touches upon those points of sympathy :

The long and intimate acquaintance with your father, dating back to my girlhood, and the double tie of kinship (his brother, Judge Johnston, having married my sister), gave me an opportunity to know him well, and to study the many noble qualities of his nature. I am glad the history of one so noble will be given to the world ; and I wish I could do justice to the many beauties of his character, that you might place my impression of them on record.

I saw him for the first time in the spring of 1834, when he came to New Orleans with your mother for the benefit of the climate to her feeble health. While the guest of my father, I was struck with his tender devotion to his wife, which caused him soon to resign his position in the army, that he might the better add to her comfort for the few remaining months allotted her on earth ; the fulfillment of which I saw most devotedly carried out, for she died at my house in the August of the following year.

He impressed me at first as an austere man, but I found him the kindest and gentlest of friends ; a stoic, yet he had the tenderest nature, so mindful of others' feelings, so fearful of saying aught that might offend. In bringing one's duties

---

[1] Mrs. Margaret Strother Hancock, who died about this time, at a very advanced age.

before a person, it was done in such a way as to make him feel that it was suggested by his own sense of right. He was a close observer of Nature—no one
loved its beauties more than he did. His love for flowers was remarkable—the
tiniest one did not escape his observation and admiration. I owe much of my
knowledge of them to him, and it is now a pleasant thought with me to have
him connected in my memory with what I so admire and enjoy. We often
played chess together—his knowledge of the game was very thorough. Whenever I was so fortunate as to be the winner, he would fight on to the last, though
perhaps the fate of the game might have been long decided, saying, "While I
have a man left I will not despair." Doubtless so he felt in the sacrifice of his
life for his country. I feel assured it was not given without due reflection and
knowledge of right; for, in all his actions, *right* prompted him, and they were
the result of deep reflection. In the smallest as in the greatest affairs of his
life, he took time to deliberate before acting. I was struck with an observation
of his (which goes to prove this), when I remarked that he took a good while
to write a letter. "Yes," said he, "I do, for I never put on paper what I am not
willing to answer for with my life." So also, in conversation, he considered
well before he spoke.

After the death of his wife, Mr. Johnston first went to his farm near
St. Louis, making the home he had prepared in anticipation of happiness his refuge in affliction. He was a man who, alike from temperament and philosophy, shrank from the exhibition or indulgence of great
emotion; and to such, in the season of grief, solitude is the most acceptable friend. General Crosman, who was as much in his confidence
as any man, says that he was in great distress of mind. He had left
his children, who were so young as to require female care, in charge of
their grandmother, Mrs. Preston, at Louisville, with a vague intention
of carrying out, at whatever cost of feeling, designs formed under such
different auspices. But though his habits of self-restraint enabled him
to enter mechanically upon this career, they could not counteract the
restlessness that urged him toward a life in which activity would produce oblivion. In October, he wrote that he was thinking of building,
but that he believed that it would suit him better to go farther West;
indeed, he seems to have contemplated establishing, with the consent
of the Government, a colony in the country of the Sioux. The next
spring this consent was refused, and the project finally abandoned. His
wife's family, with kindly solicitude, tried to induce him to return to
Louisville and engage in business, and friends proposed various occupations there. He yielded at last to their representations, and went to
Louisville in the early part of 1836. His farm, which had served as a
retreat, had become distasteful to him as a home and painful as a residence. His plan of life was shattered, and he cast about him for some
new avenue for energies that would not be repressed. Had reëntrance
into the United States Army been possible, his way was plain ; but the
only method of reinstatement open to him was by the use of political

influence, of which he would not avail himself. His friends urged upon him various commercial or manufacturing employments, and his desire to be with his children induced him to weigh well their arguments and schemes, but he concluded that he was unsuited to such a life. He felt that his education, habits, and native qualities, fitted him for a soldier; and, in default of that career, he was inclined to pursue whatever most nearly resembled it. In April he made a journey to Washington City to obtain the consent of the Government to his enterprise in the Sioux country. He spent two or three days in Washington; but, as has been stated, his request was refused. In a letter to his brother-in-law, William Preston, he says:

I had the good fortune on Monday to hear many of our most distinguished Senators address the Senate on the expediency of employing railroads for the transportation of the mail, etc., under the provisions of the bill reported by Mr. Grundy, who supported it in a speech of some length. The remarks of Messrs. Webster, Clay, Calhoun, and Buchanan, of Pennsylvania, were brief, but long enough for a stranger, who only wished to gratify a curiosity with regard to their different styles. . . . The more I see of great men, the more I am convinced that they owe their eminence to a fortunate combination of circumstances, rather than to any peculiar adaptation or fitness for their stations. There is not that wide difference in mental endowment that most persons are apt to conceive; and hence every young man of *moderate* ability may hope for the same distinction, and should struggle to attain it.

Mr. Johnston returned to Louisville still doubtful as to his future, when an opportunity offered that seemed to open to him such a career as he desired. In March, Stephen F. Austin, commissioner from Texas to the United States, had arrived in Louisville, and made there his great speech, which served as the key-note for the appeals in behalf of Texas. Through him General Johnston's interest was first fully awakened. Subsequently Mr. Dangerfield, the agent of the young republic of Texas, and an enthusiast in that cause, approached him with representations of the heroism and sufferings of the emigrants from the United States to that country, and speedily enlisted his sympathies. He gave freely from his means to assist the revolutionary party in that republic, and, after debating with himself the whole matter, resolved to throw his sword into the cause of Texan independence, in which the stake was the destiny of a people struggling for their birthright of freedom.

CHAPTER V.

THE TEXAN REVOLUTION.

On February 18, 1685, the adventurous La Salle, looking for a mouth of the Mississippi, which he had discovered in 1682, landed in Matagorda Bay. Six miles up the Lavaca River he built Fort St. Louis. This was the first settlement in Texas. Two years afterward, in attempting to pass by land from Lavaca to the French colony in Illinois, he was murdered near the river Neches by his own men ; and in a few years the little post on the Lavaca was destroyed by disease, Indian assaults, and Spanish hostility. The claim to this territory was disputed between France and Spain, but the latter power practically settled the question in 1715 by founding the missions, which were the first permanent colonies in the country. Called at first the New Philippines, it took its name, Texas, from *Tejas*, a word meaning *friends*. In 1744, and again in 1765, the Spanish population was estimated at 750, and the domiciliated Indians at the same number. On September 3, 1762, France ceded Louisiana to Spain. After this, though the seaports of Texas were closed by Spanish jealousy, the trade across the country between Mexico and Louisiana, possessions of the same power, gave some impulse to the settlement and growth of the country, though these again were retarded by the increased hostility of the Indians.

In 1800 Philip Nolan, with twenty men, made an expedition into Texas, as is said, in the interests of Burr and Wilkinson. He claimed to be in search of horses. He was attacked by 150 Spaniards, who killed him and some of his men, and made prisoners of the others. Ellis Bean, the second in command, was held a prisoner eleven years.

In 1800 Louisiana was restored by Spain to France, and in 1803 ceded by France to the United States. Under this cession the United States set up some claim to Texas, and the boundary-line itself between Texas and Louisiana was left undetermined. Hostilities seemed impending in 1806, but were averted by compromise. In the same year Lieutenant Pike explored Red River and the Arkansas, evading the Spaniards sent to capture him, until he was arrested on the Rio Grande and sent prisoner to Chihuahua. The population of Texas was at that time estimated at 7,000, of whom 2,000 were at San Antonio and 500 at Nacogdoches, including a good many Americans.

The first revolutionary movements in Mexico were in 1808. When Joseph Bonaparte took the throne of Spain in that year, the Spaniards in Mexico, adhering to their hereditary sovereign, established a regency.

Availing themselves of the confusion arising from these events, the natives, who had long groaned under the despotism of the Spaniards, tried to throw off the yoke. The patriot cause, led by Miguel Hidalgo, was at first eminently successful ; but, having suffered some defeats, Hidalgo was betrayed to the enemy in March, and executed on July 27, 1811.

In 1812 Don Bernardo Gutierrez organized an attempt to revolutionize Texas and establish an independent government, in conjunction with Lieutenant Augustus W. Magee, a native of Massachusetts and graduate of West Point, who resigned from the United States Army to take military command of the expedition. The forces were mainly composed of restless young men of good families in Kentucky and Louisiana, but a body of outlaws, who infested the neutral ground, were accepted as auxiliaries. The movement was made in sympathy, though not in concert, with Morales, the patriot chief west of the Rio Grande. Magee invaded Texas with 365 men, and defeated very superior forces of the Spaniards wherever he met them. He was a man of military capacity and daring. He died of consumption during the expedition ; but his successor, Colonel Samuel Kemper, completed the conquest of the country, taking prisoner, at San Antonio, General Salcedo and many others of note. Gutierrez, under some plea of retaliation, had General Salcedo and thirteen other prisoners put to death in cold blood, which caused part of the Americans to withdraw, and the remainder to depose Gutierrez and select as his successor General Toledo, a Spanish republican exile.

After victory had been secured, the inherent difficulties of all such enterprises came in to disconcert the plans of the adventurers and prevent a successful issue. Mexican jealousy of their Spanish leader and Anglo-American allies, American distrust of Mexican valor and fidelity, insubordination, discord, collision of authority, and other causes, led to the defeat, on the banks of the Medina, of 400 Americans and 700 Mexicans, by General Arredondo with 10,000 royalists. The revolution was disastrously crushed, and the unfortunate adventurers who survived expiated their temerity by all the sufferings that Spanish arrogance and vindictiveness could inflict. Albert Sidney Johnston's brothers, Darius and Orramel, shared in the hazards, the hardships, the victories, and the calamitous consequences of this expedition. Fever, privation, and Spanish prisons, brought them to early graves.

In 1817 General Mina, a Spanish republican, made another gallant but unsuccesful attempt to revolutionize Texas, but was finally captured and shot. Again, in 1819, Colonel Long with 200 or 300 Americans made two attempts, which ended in their own destruction. After the separation of Mexico from Spain, in 1821, the changes in the Central Government merely changed the masters who oppressed this distant and suspected province, until 1823–'24, when the constituent Cortes created the Federal Union of the Mexican Republic, and constitutional liberty seemed about to dawn on that unhappy land.

In the mean time, however, Texas had taken a step forward that rapidly led to unforeseen results. The establishment of the boundary of the Sabine had removed a constant source of suspicion against the United States, and the increasing hostility of the Comanches and other Indians required the interposed barrier of a hardy people, who would withstand and chastise their incursions. Hence ensued a change in the policy of the Government, which had hitherto sought to keep Texas a desert.

In 1821 Moses Austin, a native of Connecticut and resident of Missouri, obtained from the Mexican Government a contract for the introduction of a colony of 300 families into Texas. Each family was to receive an allotment of land, and the *empresario*, or contractor, was to receive a large premium, also in land. He died, however, before completing his arrangements, leaving the execution of his scheme to his son, Stephen F. Austin.

Stephen Austin, like his father, was a man of large designs and excellent administrative ability. Though an enthusiast, he was prudent, moderate, benevolent, and unselfish, and devoted himself to his work with an eye single to its success. It was only after all the delays incident to Mexican law and legislation, and a year's residence at Mexico, that he obtained a confirmation of his contract. The large civil powers granted to *empresarios* were exercised by Austin in the interests of the colonists, and his high qualities as a man gave to his enterprise a success not achieved by others. Nevertheless, others, following his example, introduced a large number of excellent people into Texas. Though most of the colonists were poor, some were persons of substance, and very many were of high character and superior talents. This is evidenced by the stability with which many of the original families have maintained their respectability and influence through the vicissitudes of more than half a century. Of course, many men of stained reputation found refuge in that vast and sparsely-settled territory ; but malefactors, when known, were expelled by the colonists, and the foundations of the future republic were solidly laid. In June, 1825, Mr. Austin contracted for the introduction of 500 families; and Texas seemed destined to advance rapidly in her career of progress.

In 1826 an abortive insurrection, known as the Fredonian War, occurred at Nacogdoches, in which Austin and his colony did not sympathize. It had, however, the effect of arousing the suspicions of the Mexican Government, which gradually set on foot a more rigorous course of policy. Indeed, the growing wealth and numbers of an Anglo-American State on her borders were enough to excite the narrow jealousy of that republic. The eagerness of the United States Government to purchase the Territory still further stimulated this feeling. When the Mexican States had, in 1824, adopted a Federal Constitution, based on that of the United States, Texas alone, of all the constituent members, thoroughly understood, heartily embraced, and really meant to fulfill the solemn pledge engrafted in the Constitution, "to obey and sustain, at all hazards, the Supreme Federal powers, and its own union with the rest of the States, and *the constitutional independence of all and each of them.*" Whatever was meant by others, the American settlers were in dead earnest, and intended to adhere to a Constitution that guaranteed self-government. Coahuila and Texas were temporarily united under the terms of this compact. In the vicissitudes of Mexican politics, which usually, however, did not affect greatly "the men between the plough-handles" who were settling Texas, General Bustamante, a vainglorious despot, attained the Executive power of Mexico by force, and tried to establish a centralized government by proscription and terror. Texas naturally fell under his displeasure ; and, by a decree of April 6, 1830, he initiated measures for the complete subjection of that State. He suspended the colonization contracts, prohibited immigration from the United States, and prepared to make a penal colony of Texas by the transportation thither of convicts. The custom-house regulations were also made more stringent and onerous, and in the administration of the laws the Mexican officials practised the most invidious discrimination between citizens of Mexican and of American birth. To enforce these rigorous measures, the garrisons were reënforced with the lowest and most debauched of the mercenaries who propped the despotism on their bayonets. Immigration from the United States had raised the number of the colonists to 20,000 ; and it is not to be supposed that men born free, of the high-spirited Anglo-Saxon race, and not the most tractable of that race, who had faced the perils of an Indian frontier and an untried wilderness, would patiently submit to spoliation and oppression.

The first collision between the military forces and the colonists was brought about by the arbitrary acts of Colonel Bradburn, commandant at Anahuac, an American in the service of the Central Government. In 1830 Bradburn undertook to govern the country by military law, arresting citizens, abolishing the municipalities by force, and otherwise overriding the law of the land, in a way *then* deemed intolerable by men of Anglo-American descent. Finally, in 1832, a struggle ensued which has passed into the annals of the country under the name of the Anahuac Campaign. Bradburn arrested William B. Travis, Patrick C. Jack, and other leading citizens, under various pretexts, without warrant of law, and refused to release them, or allow them a trial. But those were days when life without liberty was disdained by Americans.

An armed force of colonists was collected and besieged his fort, when he agreed, if they would retire, to release the prisoners. Perfidiously availing himself of their compliance, he brought in a quantity of military stores, and then retracted his promise. He was again besieged; and a force was sent, under Captain John Austin, to prevent Colonel Ugartechea, commandant at Velasco, from assisting him. The conference with Ugartechea resulted in an assault on his fort by the Texans. After a hot fight of one day, the garrison, 125 strong, having lost half their strength, capitulated. The Texan loss was 23 killed and mortally wounded, and 40 wounded, out of a force of 112 men. The loss attests the valor of both parties.

In the mean time, the colonists, 300 strong, intercepted Colonel Piedras, advancing from Nacogdoches to aid Anahuac; and he was glad to compromise, by superseding Bradburn and releasing the prisoners. In order to give legal color to proceedings that might appear revolutionary to the Mexicans, and to secure the aid of one of the rival factions, the colonists declared their adhesion to the Plan of Vera Cruz, a movement, projected by General Santa Anna, in favor of the Constitution of 1824, against the despotic system of Bustamante. General Mejia, Santa Anna's lieutenant, was glad to accept the explanation, and withdraw such soldiers as would go with him, the colonists expelling the remainder.

In 1832 Texas suffered under the double calamity of Indian aggressions and cholera. In October, 1832, the people assembled in convention at San Felipe, and memorialized the Central Government for the separation of Texas from Coahuila, and for the repeal of the invidious law of April 6, 1830. The request for a separate government was not unreasonable, as the State capital was 500 miles beyond its limits. The convention adjourned, to assemble again the 1st of April, 1833, for the formation of a constitution, and to pray for the admission of Texas into the Mexican Union as a State. This was done in April, 1833; and Stephen F. Austin, Erasmo Seguin, and John B. Miller, were delegated to represent their grievances and urge their requests. Austin, though not strictly in harmony with this movement, recognized its essential justice, and faithfully performed the duties of his trust.

Apparently, no time could have been more propitious for his mission, as the inauguration of Santa Anna, as President, on May 15, 1833, seemed to be the triumph of the federal system over the centralized despotism of Bustamante. But Austin found that these plans and platforms had no real meaning in Mexican politics, and were but the war-cries of ambitious leaders. Mexico was in revolutionary turmoil: Santa Anna, the legal President, intriguing for a dictatorship; Gomez Farias, the acting President, projecting radical reforms; and various military chiefs in open revolt; but in all he found a like jealousy, hatred, and ignorant contempt for the frontier, half-Americanized province of Texas. After waiting in vain from April till October, he wrote to the municipality of Bexar, advising the organization of a local State government, " even should the Supreme Government of Mexico refuse its consent." This letter led to his arrest and strict imprisonment for many months; and, indeed, his detention did not end until September, 1835, when he returned to Texas after an absence of two years and a half.

On May 13, 1834, Santa Anna dissolved Congress by force and assumed dictatorial powers, and in January, 1835, assembled a Congress which destroyed the Federal Constitution and erected a central government on its ruins. The colonists of Texas, though greatly disturbed by the refusal of their request, and by the anarchy arising from the failure to elect State officers, remained at peace, not wishing to involve themselves in Mexican politics, unless their own rights were trampled upon.

Colonel Almonte, special commissioner to inspect Texas in 1834, estimated its whole population at 21,000 civilized inhabitants and 15,300 Indians, of whom 10,800 were hostile nomads. Kennedy places the civilized population at 30,000 whites and 2,000 negroes.

The northern States of Mexico were strongly republican; and the people of Puebla, Oaxaca, Jalisco, and other States, were also opposed to a change of government; but Santa Anna easily put down all opposition by force. Garcia, Governor of Zacatecas, tried the issue with arms, and was defeated with a loss of 2,700 men. A feeble and irresolute attempt at resistance was made by the State authorities of Coahuila, under their Governor, Viesca; but he was defeated by Santa Anna's brother-in-law, General Cos, captured and imprisoned. The Legislature was then deposed, and Santa Anna's authority fully established.

As the State government of Coahuila had corruptly and lavishly alienated the public domain of Texas, the people of Texas disregarded Viesca's appeals, and refused to make common cause with him.

Though Santa Anna tried to soothe the Texans with friendly declarations, they could not be deceived, as his theory of government was avowed, and he continued to assemble troops to carry it out. Austin, whose familiarity with Mexican affairs enabled him to penetrate the designs of its rulers, threw off his habitual caution, and submitted to the people the question whether they would, by assenting to the change from a federal to a central government, surrender the vested rights and State sovereignty secured to them by the Constitution of 1824; and he recommended a general consultation of the people of Texas to decide this question. In this movement he had the advice and countenance of Don Lorenzo de Zavala, a sincere republican, who had been Governor of Mexico, Secretary of Finance, and minister to France. Santa Anna issued orders for their arrest, and for the disarming of the citizens; and General Cos moved toward San Antonio, declaring his intention to establish military rule in Texas.

The issue between military despotism and constitutional government was now squarely made. Committees of safety were organized, which determined to repel invasion by force. The first shock of arms occurred on the banks of the river Guadalupe on the 20th of September, 1835. Eighteen Texans of Gonzales, under Captain Martin, repulsed a body of 200 Mexican cavalry, who attempted a passage of the river. On the 1st of October, 168 volunteers from the Guadalupe, under Colonel John H. Moore, without loss, defeated General Castañeda and a large Mexican force. This success inspirited the colonists ; and Austin took command in the west, and Sam Houston at Nacogdoches.

On October 8th Captain Collinsworth captured Goliad with $10,000 worth of stores, and 300 stand of arms. Benjamin R. Milam, who had just escaped from Mexico, shared in this assault as a volunteer. On October 28th Colonel James Bowie, with 92 men, having approached within a mile and a half of San Antonio, found his little troop surrounded at the Conception Mission by a large force of Mexicans, which had moved out under cover of a dense fog. He engaged the enemy briskly, captured a cannon, and killed and wounded 100 Mexicans, with the loss of only one man. A number of other engagements resulted favorably to the colonists. General Cos had strongly fortified San Antonio, and intrenched himself there with an army of about 2,000 men. General Burleson, who then had command in the west, permitted Colonel Milam to lead 300 volunteers to the assault of this position on December 5th. The Texans effected a lodgment, and fought their way from house to house until they got possession of the public square. On the 9th Cos sent in a flag of truce, and on the 11th capitulated, his force being allowed to retire beyond the Rio Grande, on condition that they should not again serve against Texas. In the third day's fight, Milam fell, with a rifle-ball through his head. His death was a great loss, as he was a man of resources, daring, and experience. The first campaign thus ended with the complete success of the colonists.

The General Consultation of Texas met on the 3d of November, 1835, and chose Branch S. Archer as president. This body put forth a declaration stating that the people of Texas had armed in defense of their just rights and liberties, and of the republican principles of 1824. A provisional government was formed, and Henry Smith was elected Governor, with ample executive powers. Sam Houston was chosen commander-in-chief ; and Stephen F. Austin, Branch S. Archer, and William H. Wharton, were appointed commissioners to the United States, with authority to borrow $1,000,000. Arrangements were made for an army and navy, and for all the functions of civil government, and inducements were offered to volunteers to join their standard. In January, 1836, Austin wrote, advising a declaration of independence; and, on the 1st of February, delegates in favor of that measure were elected to a national convention, which, on the 2d day of March, 1836, declared Texas a free, sovereign, and independent republic. On the 17th of March a constitution was adopted, and an executive government, *ad interim*, appointed—of which David G. Burnet was President; Lorenzo de Zavala, Vice-President; Thomas J. Rusk, Secretary of War; and other distinguished Texans chiefs of the usual bureaux. The President was a man of noble character—temperate but firm in opinion, tenacious of principles, diligent in business, pure, patriotic, and enlightened. He was a native of New Jersey, the son of a Revolutionary patriot, and had long been a resident of Texas. Yet, such was his sensibility that he felt a slight as if it were a stain, and this rendered him, even when most useful, most unhappy. His colleagues were men of like patriotism and fine abilities.

In the mean time events had moved rapidly. Santa Anna had set out on the 1st of February from Saltillo, with his grand army of invasion, computed at 7,500 men. On the 16th he crossed the Rio Grande, and on the 23d appeared before San Antonio. Instead of finding this stronghold of the west fortified, garrisoned, and provisioned against his advance, it was occupied by a small detachment, which, at his approach, retired to the Alamo, a mission which had been turned into a barrack. Two months and a half had completely changed the condition of affairs in Texas. The colonists, present at the fall of San Antonio, had retired to their homes immediately after that event; and the volunteers, who remained, weary of inaction, eagerly entered upon an expedition, projected against Matamoras, and said to have been approved by the Government and General Houston. Some 400 started, leaving only about sixty men as a garrison.

The civil Government had split into two hostile factions; the Council on one side, and Governor Smith and General Houston on the other: and the defenders of the frontier were perplexed, and eventually sacrificed, by the contradictory orders and neglect of preparation of these opposing heads. Clothing and munitions came in from friends in the United States, and a considerable number of volunteers also arrived; but, directed by no competent common authority, the energies of these valiant and enthusiastic men were wasted for the purposes of defense, and their blood served only to immortalize their own heroism, and to consecrate the cause to which it was devoted.

Thus, while Santa Anna was assembling his army, and making his preparations for invasion, the hardy but undisciplined militia remained at home. If a man with the true instincts of leadership had been at this juncture at the head of affairs, he could have confronted Santa Anna at San Antonio, or on the banks of the Colorado, with 3,000 or 4,000 men, defeated him, and carried the Texan arms far enough into Mexico to have settled the question of independence forever. As it was, massacre and wide-spread desolation, from the Rio Grande to the Brazos, marked the path of the invader. While the main force of Santa Anna marched on San Antonio, a column under General Urrea swept up the coast-lands, laying waste the country, and surprising and destroying several detachments of volunteers. Urrea slaughtered his prisoners, and omitted no circumstance of outrage and cruelty.

Santa Anna entered San Antonio without resistance ; the commandant, Colonel William B. Travis, retiring with a little band to the untenable position of the Alamo. He sent several appeals for relief, and reenforcements. On the 24th of February he sent "an address to the people of Texas." He says : " I am besieged by a thousand or more Mexicans. . . . I shall never surrender, or retreat. . . . Victory or death ! " He received no aid, except 33 men from Gonzales, who broke through the enemy, to die with him. From the 23d of February to the 6th of March, 156 resolute men kept at bay 4,000 Mexican troops, of whom at least 500 were killed and wounded. When the final assault was made, the defenders, worn down in strength, but erect in spirit, met it with unshrinking front. They perished with their slain around them—Travis, Bowie, Crockett, Bonham, and all that heroic band. It is said that one man escaped in the smoke of the fray, but no other sought to do so ; they were a willing sacrifice. The bodies of the dead were savagely mutilated, thrown into a heap, and burned. This was the fall of the Alamo.

Another calamity, more destructive still, soon after befell the unfortunate volunteers. Fannin had collected at Goliad about 500 men ; from whom he detached Lieutenant King, with 14 men, to remove the families at Refugio. King sent an express to say that he was surrounded ; and Fannin dispatched 120 men, under Lieutenant-Colonel Ward, to his succor. Both detachments fell into the hands of the enemy, and were savagely butchered. Fannin, having received orders from General Houston, on March 14th, to retreat, delayed until the 18th, with the generous hope that he might be able to render aid to his detachments. At last, when he left Goliad, it was too late. He was overtaken and surrounded on the open prairie by Urrea's army, 1,700 strong. Three charges of the Mexicans were repulsed, with heavy loss to the assailants. After nightfall, the Indian skirmishers of the enemy killed and wounded 54 of the Texans. Daylight showed that Urrea had been largely reënforced with artillery and infantry. After some negotiation, Fannin surrendered his command as prisoners of war. Out of 365 prisoners captured with Fannin, 27 escaped, eight surgeons and attendants were spared, and 330 were led out and shot, in cold blood, on Palm-Sunday. Fannin, wounded as he was, put aside the hand that would have blindfolded him, and received, like a soldier, the death-shots in his breast.

Santa Anna now regarded the conquest of Texas as complete, and was with difficulty dissuaded from returning to Mexico and leaving the occupation of the country to his subordinates. Having finally resolved to finish his work, he proceeded to it with that celerity which was his sole military virtue. With presumptuous infatuation, he detached from his army three columns of about 800 men each, directing Gaona to move by Bastrop across the country to Nacogdoches, Urrea to march by Matagorda along the coast, and Sesma to precede the main body in the direction of San Felipe; thus exposing his force to be destroyed in detail. General Houston remained from March 18th to March 27th at Beeson's Ferry on the Colorado, with a force of over 1,500 volunteers, eager for combat; and it has never been satisfactorily explained why he did not attack and crush Sesma's inferior force within easy striking distance, and follow up the advantage by giving battle to Santa Anna's main body. His army was rapidly augmenting by the arrival of considerable bodies of men, anxious to protect their homes, and avenge the inhuman butchery of their comrades. Nevertheless, he retreated precipitately, without an avowed policy, leaving the Colorado and Brazos countries open to the ravages of the enemy. His army melted away; so that, notwithstanding considerable accessions, it only numbered 783 men at the battle of San Jacinto. The colonists could not leave their families at the mercy of a ruthless invader, who spared neither age nor sex.

General Houston's conduct and motives have been severely censured by eminent and honorable men ; but it is a sufficient explanation to say that his talents were essentially popular, not military. His apology for his retreat was, that it drew the enemy from his base, and would, if continued farther, have enabled reënforcements from the United States to join the Texan army. That this is not a sufficient reply is evident, because the Mexican army was living on the country, while the Texans grew weaker daily by desertion. One all-sufficient answer, however, was held as an ample justification in all his subsequent political contests and personal controversies—the result of the battle of San Jacinto ; the splendid success of the Texan army condoning any previous mistakes or subsequent errors of the commander. Houston, though destitute of military capacity and the knowledge which sometimes makes partial amends for it, and, in the opinion of the writer, slenderly endowed with administrative talents or political wisdom, had all the qualities that go to make a popular leader. He was a man of imposing presence, an agreeable orator, with an uncommon gift of political tact. His manners were free and persuasive, and he possessed that self-assertion so impressive to the multitude. He was a friendly man, too, when there was no possible chance of a conflict of interests ; but vigilant and far-seeing to prevent the rise of any who would not subserve his ends. He really believed himself born to command, and was imperious in the exercise of power. Altogether, if neither a wise nor a great man, he was an able politician.

On the 28th of March Houston reached San Felipe ; and, on the 29th, Groce's Ferry on the Brazos. Santa Anna pushed forward Sesma's column, followed by Filisola with the main body. On the 13th of April he crossed the Brazos with Sesma's division and arrived at Harrisburg on the 15th, and at Lynchburg on the 16th. Filisola was now low down the Brazos, the lowlands of which were flooded and nearly impassable ; and Santa Anna was within the reach of a force of Texans not much inferior to his own. General Houston seemed to entertain a design to retreat beyond the Trinity, where he expected to receive reenforcements ; but the voice of his army compelled him to confront the enemy, which he did on the 19th, on the San Jacinto River. On the 20th the cavalry, under Colonel Sherman, engaged the enemy ; but the ardor of the Texan army was restrained by their commander until the afternoon of the 21st of April. On that morning the enemy were reënforced by 500 men under General Cos. At half-past three, the Texans moved forward in line of battle. Colonel Burleson commanded the centre ; Colonel Sherman, the left ; Colonel Hockley, the artillery on the right ; and, on his flank, Colonel M. B. Lamar, a troop of 61 cavalry. Sherman first encountered the enemy ; and then the whole line burst impetuously upon the slight intrenchments thrown up by the Mexicans, with the war-cry : "Remember the Alamo ! Goliad and the Alamo !" The combat lasted only eighteen minutes. It was a rout, not a battle. The Texans lost two killed and 21 wounded, six of them mortally. The Mexican loss was 630 killed, 208 wounded, and 730 prisoners, among whom were Santa Anna, Cos, Almonte, and others of note. General Houston was wounded in the ankle.

The opinion of the army favored the execution of the butcher of the Alamo and of Fannin's men ; and, surely, he had forfeited his right to mercy by these crimes and by the devastation of the land. It was thought more politic, as well as more humane, to spare his life ; in consideration of which he agreed to a convention, by which Filisola and Gaona were to retire to San Antonio, and Urrea to Victoria. According to Filisola, such was the condition of his army, from the weather, starvation, dysentery, and demoralization, that, but for this convention, it would have fallen an easy prey to the victorious Texans. As it was, the Mexican army gladly retreated not only to the points stipulated, but beyond the Rio Grande; not, however, without a violation of the articles of the convention, by dismantling the Alamo. On the 14th of May the Government, by General Houston's advice, agreed to release Santa Anna and the Mexican prisoners, on condition that the Texas prisoners should be released and that hostilities should cease. Santa Anna also stipulated secretly for the reception of a mission from Texas, for a treaty of amity and commerce, and for the Rio Grande as the boundary between the two republics. On June 1st Santa Anna was embarked, but on the 3d the Government was compelled by the soldiers to bring him ashore again, and his execution was strongly urged. The hope was soon dispelled that his release would effect anything favorable to Texas. Already, on the 20th of May, the Mexican Senate had annulled his stipulations, and preparations were begun for a more formidable invasion of Texas. It was not until December, 1836, that Santa Anna was dismissed to the United States, when he illustrated his perfidy by solemnly denying and repudiating all the engagements he had made while in captivity.

The massacre of Fannin's men, the fall of the Alamo, and the other crimes of the Mexicans against humanity, had aroused the warmest sympathy for Texas in the people of the United States. The appeals of the agents of Texas stirred the heart of the South, and volunteers poured in, singly and in companies, to aid the cause of independence. San Jacinto virtually settled that question; but this was not then apparent, in view of the threatening attitude of Mexico with its 8,000,000 inhabitants.

Mr. Clay made a brilliant speech in favor of the independence of Texas, and on June 18th made a report in the United States Senate in favor of its recognition, to which effect both Houses of Congress passed resolutions. On June 27th the Senate, on motion of Mr. William C. Preston, of South Carolina, adopted a resolution for sending a commissioner to Texas; and the President, General Jackson, was known to be favorable to its annexation to the United States.

In September, General Houston was elected President over Stephen F. Austin, the known friendship of General Jackson contributing not less powerfully than the *éclat* of San Jacinto to his success. General Mirabeau B. Lamar was elected Vice-President. The constitution was ratified, and a declaration given in favor of annexation to the United States by a vote of the people. Congress met on October 3d.

Albert Sidney Johnston shared in the general sympathy with the Texan cause, but there were personal reasons which increased the intensity of his own feelings. In early youth, as has been mentioned, he had spent some time in Alexandria, Louisiana, then a border village, and consequently had familiar recollections of many from that region who were now earnest actors in the events of the revolution. His brothers, too, had taken part in Magee's expedition in 1812, and the remembrance of their extraordinary sufferings may have further influenced him. It is now difficult to estimate how far mental disquietude and the spirit of adventure may have entered into his motives. He was unhappy, he was unemployed, and here was a field open alike to his energies, his patriotism, and his philanthropy.

It was the cause of a community struggling for self-government against a central despotism, for the maintenance of guaranteed and vested rights against a military usurpation, for constitutional freedom against chronic anarchy. It was a contest between 20,000 Americans, kindred in race and sentiment, who had been invited by Mexico tq take possession of the soil, and 8,000,000 alien Mexicans, incapable of stable government. It was the weak against the strong, order against political confusion, Americans against a foreign enemy. The men of that day had been bred in republican ideas and nurtured with visions of the greatness and the expansive force of our people, and they were willing to lay down fortune and life to forward these mighty ends.

Albert Sidney Johnston was a republican from the bottom of his heart, and, though not a propagandist in either temper or sentiment, he was a sincere believer in the blessings of regulated liberty and the supremacy of law. With these ideas of public right, and with the conviction of his call to render public service, he thought his talents could not be put to better use than in aiding to secure their liberties to men of his own race, who were ready to sacrifice all else to achieve them. Originally, however, the most potent motive that urged him to enlist in this enterprise was the hope that, Texas having been freed, he might promote its annexation to the United States; and, since readmission into the army was impossible, that he might employ the sword, for which his country deemed she had no need, in laying an empire at her feet. Of course, after he had devoted himself to the cause of Texas, her interests became paramount; but he frequently admitted that, in the first instance, he was in large measure animated by the desire of assisting to add another star to the American constellation. Indeed, strong as were his feelings in behalf of the infant nation, he did not consummate his resolution to enter its service until the Government of the United States had recognized its independence. With this sanction he felt no further hesitation, and threw himself into the cause with all the ardor of his nature.

CHAPTER VI.

AS TEXAN SOLDIER.

In spite of the brilliant victory of San Jacinto, it was soon apparent that Mexico had not abandoned her plans of subjugation, and that Texas needed every man she could draw to her standard. Mr. Johnston, leaving Louisville, proceeded by way of New Orleans to Alexandria, Louisiana. After staying a few days with his brother, Judge Johnston, he started on horseback for the camp of the defenders. His companions were Leonard Groce and brother, and Major Bynum, of Rapides. Crossing the Sabine on the 13th of July, he arrived on the 15th at Nacogdoches, where he met General Sam Houston, the commander-in-chief, then in the full flush of his popularity. From Nacogdoches he went with Leonard Groce to his plantation, on the river Brazos, where an adventure befell him that has been told in various ways, but of which the following is the true version. Hearing a great uproar near the house, Mr. Johnston seized his gun and hurried with Mr. Groce to the spot, where they found the dogs fighting a puma or American lion. The lion was playing havoc with the dogs, scalping one, crippling another, and disemboweling a third. Mr. Johnston immediately shot the puma, the ball breaking the jaw, but not disabling the animal, which continued the slaughter of the pack with the tearing wounds of its terrible claws. Mr. Groce, much excited at the loss of his favorites, cried out, "Save the dogs! save the dogs!" Mr. Johnston then clubbed his gun, which was a heavy German Yager rifle, and, springing into the *mêlée*, dispatched the beast by blows over the head. His rifle-stock was splintered, and the barrel much bent. He escaped without a scratch, but no one could tell how. The puma was one of the largest of its kind, and very fierce. Mr. Groce had the skin stuffed, and long kept it as a memento of the event. He was ever afterward a warm friend of General Johnston. From Mr. Groce's Mr. Johnston proceeded to the headquarters of the army, which were then on the river Coleto, about fifteen miles east of Goliad.

Although Mr. Johnston bore with him the highest testimonials to his personal worth and military ability, in the form of letters of introduction from persons of distinction in the United States to the leading men of Texas, he forbore to deliver them. General Atkinson had sent him a letter to Stephen F. Austin, couched in language of the highest eulogy; and personal friends of Houston, Rusk, and others, had also given him letters that would have secured him a cordial welcome at

their hands ; but, with that peculiar combination of pride and conscientiousness which made him unwilling to receive advancement as a favor,
and, it may be, somewhat in the spirit of knight-errantry, he preferred
to reach his destination unannounced, and then enlisted as a private in
the ranks.

The Texan army was at that time under the command of General
Thomas J. Rusk, who was distinguished both in council and in the
field during the republic, and afterward as a United States Senator,
and whose career belongs to the history of the country.   When Mr.
Johnston reached the Texan camp he found himself in a situation sufficiently novel to one who had been trained in and accustomed to the
exact discipline and routine of a regular army.   The call of Texan
independence, the liberal bounty of land to the soldiers, the prospect
of booty or license, the realization of political theories or philanthropic
aspirations, all the motives that impel men to desperate enterprises, had
assembled a mixed multitude of restless spirits under the banner of the
Lone Star.   Here were gathered those indomitable men of battle whom
Santa Anna pointedly characterized as the *tumultuario* of the Mississippi Valley ; the ardent youth of the South, burning for glory and
military enterprise.   Here enthusiasts of constitutional freedom were
mingled with adventurous soldiers from Europe ; and souls as knightly,
generous, and unstained as Bayard's, with outlaws and men of broken
and desperate fortunes.   Some of the best and some of the worst people in the world were thrown into contact ; but in one quality all were
alike, a hardihood that no danger could check.

Never was an army collected in which the spirit of combat was
more supreme.   Manhood and personal prowess were the standards of
superiority among these men, and they followed their chosen leaders
with a fidelity and reckless devotion that had neither stint nor measure.   They would have marched unmurmuringly into the open jaws of
death, rather than yield a point of pride, or of their idea of honor.   It
was a handful that a soldier might have rejoiced to lead against a host.
But they were without discipline, subordination, or effective organization, so that obedience was a mere matter of choice.   Released from
such necessary restraints, these fiery bands were easily stirred to turbulence and mutiny by the demagogues of the camp.

Republican habits of self-government and the conservative influence of an instinctive tendency toward order have a powerful hold on
the American intellect ; but this little army, for lack of an organizing
mind, seemed destitute of all coherence, and threatened to become
more terrible to the republic than to its enemies.   It had wrested
Santa Anna from the custody of the Executive, and put him in irons,
thus furnishing him with a pretext for his perfidy ; and it had even
sent a body of men to seize the person of President Burnet in order to

compel compliance with the army sentiment, thereby indicating a purpose of military revolution.

After the battle of San Jacinto General Rusk had assumed command of the army in the absence of General Sam Houston, who had taken a furlough on account of his wound. About the 1st of July the contending factions in the army had reached such a point that the Government thought the best way to reconcile them was to appoint as major-general the gallant and eloquent Lamar, who had won distinction at San Jacinto, and was popular with both soldiers and citizens. On his arrival at the army he found it greatly excited and a strong opposition organized against him. He made a persuasive speech to the soldiers, and then appealed to a vote, which, proving largely against his taking the command, he was constrained to retire, General Rusk remaining in command.

Rusk soon found that Felix Huston, who had been chairman of the organization that resisted and finally rejected Lamar, had superseded him in the suffrages of the army; and, though brave and able, yet being an easy-tempered man, he readily yielded the point, and recommended that Huston should be appointed major-general, and receive the chief command. The expectation of an expedition against Matamoras about this time, however, occupied the attention and thus allayed the discontents of the camp; and, General Huston having been temporarily detached with his command to San Patricio on the Nueces, Rusk's recommendation was not favorably considered by the Government. In the mean time Rusk was anxious to avail himself of any opportunity to bring his mutinous troops into some sort of order and discipline. It was at this juncture that Mr. Johnston arrived at the camp on the Coleto ; and, being the fortunate possessor of a horse, joined as a private trooper the little body of mounted men that represented the cavalry of the army.

Mr. Johnston's appearance at this period of his life is described as both commanding and attractive. In some respects the bust of Alexander Hamilton is the best extant likeness of him, a resemblance very frequently remarked. His cheek-bones were rather high, and his nose somewhat irregular, which, with his clear, white-and-red complexion, gave him a very Scotch look. His chin was delicate and handsome ; his teeth white and regular ; and his mouth square and firm. In the portrait by Bush, taken about this time, his lips seem rather full ; but, as he is best remembered, they were somewhat thin and very firmly set. Brown hair clustered over a noble forehead, and from under heavy brows his deep-set but clear, steady eyes looked straight at you with a regard kind and sincere, yet penetrating. With those eyes upon him any man would have scrupled to tell a lie. In repose his eyes were as blue as the sky, but in excitement they flashed to a steel-gray, and exerted a wonderful power over men. He was six feet and an inch in height, weighing about 180 pounds, straight as an arrow, with broad, square shoulders and a massive chest. He was strong and active, but his endurance and vital power seemed the result rather of nervous than of muscular energy, and drew their exhaustless resources from the mind more than the body. His bearing was essentially military, and dignified rather than graceful; and his movements were prompt, but easy and firm. He was, indeed, in appearance a model for the soldier.

Sidney Johnston's skill in arms was but moderate, for, though his eye was quick and his hand steady, yet he lacked the dexterity that comes from predilection and practice. He was not only cautious himself in handling fire-arms, but often recommended the same carefulness to others, playfully quoting a saying of John Rowan, the dead-shot of Kentucky, "Never point a pistol at a man unless you intend to shoot him." He was a graceful and excellent rider, and no man presented a grander or more martial appearance on horseback. It was remarked of him by Mr. Jefferson Davis, who saw him at the battle of Monterey, that "in combat he had the most inspiring presence he ever saw."

Substantially the same remark was many times made by others. There were in his action a certain vigor and decision, in his manner a winning frankness and kindness, and in his whole thought and life a simplicity and directness, that were generally irresistible. His deference to and dignified sympathy with women, his tenderness to children, his reverence for old age, and his forbearance with every form of weakness, were genuine and unvarying—habits as well as principles. A sensitive interest and the finest judgment were united in his intercourse with children. His indulgence seemed unlimited, and yet they rarely abused it. He observed toward them a careful respect; and many younger friends will remember the benign and ennobling influence of Albert Sidney Johnston on their lives.

General Rusk told Mr. Jefferson Davis that he was first attracted to Mr. Johnston, a few days after he joined his army, by his bearing as a soldier and the way he sat his horse. He made inquiries about him, and, learning that he had been an officer of experience and high reputation, he was glad to seek him out. He called on him, and, after a brief interview, offered him the place of adjutant-general of the army. He told him, however, that there were several aspirants who thought themselves entitled to the office, and who would probably require him to fight if he took the position. Mr. Johnston said he felt qualified for the office ; and, if General Rusk appointed him, he was not concerned as to how these young gentlemen might regard it. General Rusk appointed him, and the young gentlemen concluded not to trouble him.

On the same day, the 5th of August, on which Rusk appointed him adjutant-general of the army, with the rank of colonel, President

Burnet, who had learned through other sources of his arrival in the country, appointed him a colonel in the regular army, and assigned to him the duties of adjutant-general of the republic. General Sam Houston, the commander-in-chief, who had seen him as he passed through Nacogdoches, also sent to him from that point, on the 9th of August, a commission as aide-de-camp, with the rank of major. These repeated marks of confidence show the interest created in all quarters by his arrival in the country. Colonel Johnston at once undertook the organization and tactical instruction of the army, with an address that gained the good-will of the troops, and a success that secured the gratitude and friendship of General Rusk, which were afterward evinced on all proper occasions.

The following incidents go to illustrate the life of the camp. The first is a reminiscence told by General Johnston ; the names are suppressed in both, for obvious reasons: He used to relate that, one day as he was resting on his blanket, a colonel, a very fine fellow, stepped up to him, with a cocked pistol in his hand, and said: " Colonel, my friend here, Major ——, and I, have had a difference. Will you oblige us by observing that its settlement is entirely fair ? " Before he could rise to expostulate, one of the duelists gave the word, " Are you ready ? " the other replied, " Ready ! " Both fired, and one fell severely wounded. This was hot blood, indeed.

The second incident is here given in the words of a letter written to General Johnston twenty-five years after the occurrence :

It has been so many years since I had the pleasure of seeing you that I am almost afraid you have forgotten me altogether. Do you remember the judge-advocate of the army in Texas, when you were in command as colonel on the Lavaca River in 1836 ? If you do not, I can possibly recall myself to your remembrance by mentioning a circumstance that may not have entirely escaped you. One morning, at General Green's tent, Major V—— and I got into an accidental quarrel. He insulted me and I struck him, whereupon he drew out a bowie-knife upon me and I a pistol upon him, which Major D——, who was standing by my side, wrenched suddenly out of my hand. V—— then drew a pistol upon me, and, just as he was in the act of shooting me, you came thundering by, with your spurs in your horse's sides, and, with a tremendous grab, jerked his pistol out of his hand, which was all that saved my life. But for *you*, I should long ago have been eaten up by worms on the banks of the Lavaca. Can you wonder, therefore, that I have since retained the most grateful remembrance of you, and rejoiced at all calculated to promote your happiness as well as your fame ?

Colonel Johnston's success in organizing and disciplining the army was so great that he received the highest commendations in every quarter. But he was not permitted to remain long enough to perfect the work he had begun. What he did accomplish was under the most disadvantageous circumstances, as he suffered from the fever of the country, and was greatly reduced in strength. The Government felt the need of his services at the capital; and the Hon. John A. Wharton, Secretary of War, summoned him thither by an order, dated September 17, 1836, requiring him to discharge the duties of his office at that place. The Secretary's letter represents the greatest confusion as existing in the bureau, and relies upon Colonel Johnston's efforts to introduce better system and method. Proceeding with General Rusk, early in October, to Columbia, where the Congress was assembling, he entered upon his duties shortly before the inauguration of General Sam Houston as President of the Republic. Here he exercised the functions of his office satisfactorily until the 16th of November, when he went to New Orleans, on a nominal furlough of three months, but really in the interests of the Texan Government. On December 22d President Houston wrote him that he had put him in nomination as senior brigadier-general of the army, and his commission bears that date. He was notified of this, January 11th, but was detained in New Orleans by business; so that it was not until January 31st that he was ordered to assume command of the army. General James Hamilton, of South Carolina, had, on December 22d, been tendered the post of major-general and the command of the army, but had declined on account of private business.

General Johnston's appointment to command led to an affair that resulted in great suffering to himself; but, fortunately, in no injurious consequences to the republic. About the time Johnston withdrew from the army, Rusk, having grown tired of the mingled sedition and intrigue that continually annoyed him, had abandoned the command to Felix Huston, who has already been mentioned. Huston was a Kentuckian, who had emigrated to Mississippi, where he had practised law and engaged largely in politics. He was a large, fine-looking man, of great personal gallantry, a good speaker, and endowed with popular qualities. He was extremely ambitious and self-confident, and overbearing and turbulent, though not ungenerous, in temper. Without military education or experience, though not without good military instincts, he had, nevertheless, so often seen civilians employ a brief military career as the stepping-stone to political preferment that he was justified in hoping to win this double distinction on so fair a field as Texas. He had been disappointed in arriving too late to share in any of the combats of the revolution; but he thought, nevertheless, that the contingent recruits that he brought to the defense of the frontier entitled him to the command of the army. The force Huston brought to the army is usually put at 500 men. Colonel Charles De Morse, then the adjutant-general, informs the writer, in a letter of January 25, 1875, that Huston did not bring more than 100 or 125 men. He says he recollects only three officers, none of them of the rank of captain, and that none of the men were specifically organized in companies. It was enough, however, to found a claim upon; and, as he soon won the suffrages of the soldiers by his audacity and popular manners, it was not long before he spoke of the troops as "my army," and really felt that such was the case.

After the rejection of Lamar by the army vote, and the resignation of Rusk, he felt indisposed to allow the command that Fortune had placed in his hands to pass to another; and his public declarations that the officer who attempted to supersede him in the command of his army would do so at his peril, as well as his notoriety as a skillful duelist, were not without effect in checking the pretensions of a certain class of aspirants. So restless and uncompromising a politician was little likely to be acceptable to the leaders of any party; and, in view of the formidable invasion then threatened, it was natural enough for the President to prefer, as commander, a trained soldier, like Johnston, whose ambition was solely military, and to whom the army was indebted for all the organization and discipline it had. Accordingly, he was appointed senior brigadier-general, with command of the army; and Felix Huston was appointed junior brigadier-general, and assigned the second place. Whatever were the motives that led to his appointment, General Johnston, who had held aloof from all political complications, regarded it from a purely military point of view ; and, though duly informed of General Huston's threats, was, of course, not deterred thereby from accepting the command.

Mr. Norvall, who was then in the Texan army there, gives some entertaining reminiscences in an article in the New York *Sun*, March 7, 1877; and, in correspondence with the writer, Norvall says General Johnston's appointment was bitterly resented by Huston's adherents, who now made a large majority of it. The supersedure of "Old Longshanks," or "Old Leather-Breeches," as Huston was affectionately nicknamed, roused the anger of his friends, and this feeling was fanned until there was a dangerous state of mind in the camp.

On General Johnston's arrival at camp, February 4th, he was received civilly by General Huston, who, however, thought proper on the same day to address him the following letter:

HEADQUARTERS CAMP INDEPENDENCE, *February* 4, 1837.

SIR: From the acquaintance I have had with you, and your high reputation, I wish to tender you my regards as a gentleman and soldier.

Your assuming the command of the army would have excited in me no feelings but those of respect and obedience to you, as my superior officer, were it not for the fact that your appointment was connected with a tissue of treachery and misrepresentation, which was intended to degrade me and blast my prospects in the Texian [army].

You, in assuming the command under an appointment connected with the attempt to ruin my reputation and inflict a stigma on my character, of course stand in an attitude of opposition to myself.

This situation might not, in ordinary cases, lead to serious results. But as I have not made up my mind to leave the service, and cannot, consistently with honor, submit to be overslaughed under humiliating circumstances, I prefer taking a plain and direct course, to one which would lead to a similar result from the mere force of circumstances.

I do this, as I really esteem your character, and know that you must be sensible of the delicacy of my situation.

I therefore propose a meeting between us, in as short a period as you can make convenient. My friend Major Ross has authority to make all necessary arrangements. Reiterating my respects and regards, I am

Your most obedient, humble servant,

FELIX HUSTON.

To General A. S. JOHNSTON.

General Johnston's reply was as follows :

HEADQUARTERS CAMP INDEPENDENCE, *February 4th.*

SIR: I have had the honor of receiving your note of this evening. After reciprocating the sentiments of respect and esteem which you have been pleased to express toward me, it only remains to accord to you the meeting proposed. I have designated 7 o'clock, A. M., to-morrow. My friend Colonel Morehouse is authorized to make the necessary arrangements.

Your most obedient servant,   A. SIDNEY JOHNSTON.

To Brigadier-General FELIX HUSTON.

It was found that no dueling-pistols were to be had in camp, and it was proposed to use General Huston's horse-pistols. Hon. Jefferson Davis calls them " crook-handled pistols, twelve inches in the barrel." Mr. Davis says General Johnston was a very good shot with ordinary pistols, and the writer knows that such was the case subsequently ; but Captain Eaton says he had been quite disused to them for several years, and was a poor shot with them, though a skillful marksman with the rifle.

Mr. Norvall says Huston's unrivaled skill with the pistol was so well known that astonishment was expressed that Johnston did not choose rapiers, with which he would have had an advantage. This was probably the reason he did *not* choose them. The advantage he was striving for was a moral one. Mr. Norvall gives the following version of the report set afloat at the time :

General Johnston arrived a few days after his appointment was announced. He at once, without communicating with General Huston, directed the adjutant-general to have the army paraded and the general order read. This was too much for Huston, already boiling over with rage. He sat down, wrote a peremptory challenge to mortal combat, and handed it to his friend Colonel Rogers, with instructions to deliver it at once and accept of no delay.

It so happened that this was a matter discussed by both parties with the Hon. Jefferson Davis, who makes the following statement to the writer: He says that Huston told him that "General Johnston came on the drill-ground and had the order read superseding him, and that *that was pretext enough for him;* that he could not fight the President, Sam Houston, and he was glad to have a gentleman to hold responsible."

General Johnston told Mr. Davis that "it was true that the order was read by the adjutant-general of the army, but not by his direction or intention; that he was present merely to observe the drill."

My father made the same statement to me. It must be observed that Huston does not base his challenge upon this ground, which, even if not an after-thought, did not really amount to an offense.

Mr. Norvall, in a letter to the writer, says: "Everybody understood the real cause of the trouble to be the fact that Huston had been superseded." Mr. Norvall also says that an arrangement was made between the seconds, at the suggestion of General Johnston's friend, to fire with the butt of the pistol resting against the hip, in order to equalize the skill of the parties ; and that General Johnston responded on learning this, " I am not sure I could hit the side of a house in firing from the hip;" and that the duel was thus fought.

The writer doubts the accuracy of the anecdote ; but, if true, it gave the expert an additional advantage over the novice. Norvall says that, accompanied by their friends, they forded the Lavaca on horseback, and, after passing through the forest, met on an open, grassy spot, on the edge of the prairie.

Colonel Morehouse objected that General Huston was familiar with, and expert in the use of, these weapons, and that General Johnston had never handled one in his life. But the latter, willing to yield every advantage to his adversary, waived the objection. Mr. Norvall thinks there were very few witnesses. The writer believes from other information there were a considerable number present, to which, for obvious reasons, neither party was averse. The contest, though deadly in intention, was chiefly one for the moral control of these very men; and their presence was, therefore, equally desired by the antagonists.

If General Johnston, for the sake of dramatic effect, deviated somewhat from that perfect simplicity so eminently his characteristic, it is believed to be the only juncture of which this can be recorded; and allowance must be made for the character of the witnesses, the antagonist, and the occasion that brought him to the field.

General Huston, according to the custom of practised duelists, who wish to present as inconspicuous a mark as possible to the aim of an opponent, closely buttoned his coat as he took his position. General Johnston, on the contrary, laid aside his coat and vest, and bound his sash around his waist, thus offering his body, clad in a white shirt, as an almost certain target. When Huston perceived this, not wishing to be outdone in audacity, he somewhat angrily followed his example. Mr. Norvall says in a letter, with the *naïveté* of an old Texan, "It was quite natural that he should do so, as the morning was warm enough for such an act."

General Johnston was perfectly aware of the disadvantage at which he stood, and had calmly resolved on a course of action which would lessen his disparity with his opponent. He knew he stood no chance with the weapons employed if General Huston was ever able to take aim at him. It is known, to those familiar with the use of the hair-trigger, that, if the finger is allowed to touch it, the report of another pistol will almost always produce a sufficient involuntary muscular contraction of the finger to cause a premature discharge. Availing himself of this fact, General Johnston raised his pistol quickly, and, with his eye on his opponent's finger, just anticipated him enough to succeed in "drawing his fire" before he could cover him with his pistol. He repeated this five times with the same result, much to Huston's discomfiture, whose reputation as a "dead-shot" was at stake. Huston declared years afterward that he did not wish to kill Johnston; but that a shot, through his hair and grazing his ear, admonished him that it was necessary in order to save himself. This is not probable, as he had the privilege at any time to express himself satisfied, and end the contest, a right not accorded to the challenged. At the sixth shot Huston's superior skill prevailed, and General Johnston fell, with a ball through his hip.[1]

Huston at once asked leave to approach him, and expressed his regret, and his willingness to serve under him. Mr. Norvall makes the following statement, as of his own knowledge:

The surgeon declared the wound so dangerous as to leave little hope of recovery, and the injured man was removed to the little hamlet of Texana, where he lay for weeks at the point of death. Huston mounted his horse and rode back to camp with a pale, agitated face. A thousand soldiers rushed forward to congratulate him as he crossed the lines, but he waved them off sadly, and rode straight to his quarters. That afternoon I saw him pacing up and down in the *chaparral*, and looking so miserable that, even at this distant day, I cannot think of him without pity.

He adds: "One circumstance I remember distinctly, which surprised me, a mere boy at the time, and occasioned remark. This was that

---

[1] There is a question whether there were five or six shots. The writer believes the above account to be correct.

a ration of whiskey, a most unusual thing, was issued that morning. I believe to this day that, if Huston had been killed or seriously wounded, there would have been an irrepressible riot in the camp." This act meant mischief; but the writer has no idea that General Huston was aware of it.

While he remained with the army, Huston acted in good faith as a subordinate officer; but the combined loss of command and influence soon rendered his situation distasteful to him. His loss of influence was the natural sequence of the events mentioned. General Johnston tried to mitigate his discomfort, by detaching him with a command toward the Nueces, to observe the enemy; but, not having cavalry to support him, was compelled to reunite his detachment with the main army. General Huston, after a time, withdrew from the army, and eventually returned to the United States.

It is characteristic of General Johnston that he never felt any resentment toward Huston, as is evident from his correspondence and from all subsequent references to him in conversation. Huston, in like manner, confiding entirely in General Johnston's magnanimity, was writing to him in a most unreserved and confidential strain only a few weeks after the duel.

It is stated, and, I believe, on good authority, that when the surgeons announced their fears that General Johnston's wound was mortal, "his friend and second, thinking that he was dying, muttered that the matter should not rest, for that he would avenge it. Johnston turned to him and said, 'It is my request, in the event of my death, that you shall yield obedience to my second in command, General Huston, and I trust you will not by such conduct promote a spirit of insubordination.'" I remember, when I was a little boy, asking my father "if he did not hate Felix Huston." He replied, "No," and then I asked him what he would do if he were to meet him then. He laughed, and answered, amusedly, "As he would be a stranger here, I would ask him to dinner." I thought a good deal about this before I could reconcile it to my sense of right.

The aim of this memoir is biographical, not apologetic, and a mere statement of the facts may probably be deemed sufficient; yet, since General Johnston's motives are entitled to be considered, it may be well to state the grounds of his action. In every society there are persons who, in their judgment of human conduct, hold the rules of action to be so inflexible as to admit of no modification, and who, hence, make no allowance for the conditions by which a man is surrounded and the circumstances in which he is placed. But people in general recognize their constraining influence. Such will appreciate the change of sentiment in regard to dueling in the last forty years, and the absence of legal restraint and protection, at the time and place mentioned, which compelled a man to abandon his rights, or to protect them himself by wager of battle.

Captain Eaton says: "The first time I saw General Johnston after the duel I asked him how he came to fight Huston; and he answered that he did it as a public duty. . . . He had but little respect for the practice of dueling." His view, as detailed to the author, was that the safety of the republic depended upon the efficiency of the army; and that, again, upon the good discipline and subordination of the troops, which could only be secured by their obedience to their legal commander. General Huston embodied the lawless spirit in the army, which had to be met and controlled at whatever personal peril. Independent of personal feeling, the point was a vital one to the country; and, whatever the issue of the duel, General Huston would be rendered harmless in consequence of it. Moreover, he could not have held the command an hour, if he had shown the least hesitation in meeting General Huston's challenge. In view of the character of the army, it was necessary to allow neither time, nor obstacle, nor military subordination, nor any disadvantage, to prevent him from fighting at once. While quite willing to admit that, in an organized society, dueling was not defensible in ethics, in this case he saw no alternative, except to surrender his military efficiency and career, and the interests of the country.

The effect of the duel was a complete revolution in the sentiment of the army; and the excitable feelings of the troops were warmly enlisted for his recovery. Huston then, and always afterward, declared that "he was the coolest and the bravest man he had ever known." At first, his wound was pronounced mortal; the ball passed through the orifices of the pelvis, not breaking the bone, but so as to injure the sciatic nerve severely. His recovery was slow and painful; and his suffering was increased by the performance of his duties, which it did not suit him to devolve upon another. He bore great torture with the stoicism that he regarded as essential to the soldierly character, and did not permit his pain to interfere with measures of preparation against the threatened invasion. Though he could soon walk, he was not able to mount his horse for a long time. Yet, meanwhile, he made a marked improvement in the condition of the troops; so that the Secretary of War, Colonel William S. Fisher, wrote him March 28th, "The President is much gratified at the favorable report made, on my return, of the state of the army."

General Johnston received from the President and Secretary of War official reprimands of a somewhat perfunctory character for fighting a duel, together with assurances of complete confidence and esteem; and the President sent the surgeon-general and Dr. Jones to afford him the best medical aid. It was not in the power of the surgeons, however, to give him relief, which, they informed him, could only be obtained by rest.

The situation of Texas at this time was very critical. Confidential communications to the President, from Matamoras, through Mr. John Ricord, confirmed for the most part by Colonel Seguin at San Antonio, reported with certainty the enemy's force, January 26th : in Matamoras, 2,855 men ; and with Bravo, at Saltillo, 2,500 men ; amounting, including detachments, to 5,500 soldiers, with 28 cannon and two mortars. This force was augmented, until, in March, it was estimated at 8,000 Mexicans and a large body of Indian auxiliaries, who occupied the country between the Nueces and the Rio Grande. A combined attack by sea and land was intended ; and a naval blockade was, in fact, established, which inflicted several severe blows on the republic by the capture of vessels and supplies. But, though an invasion at one time seemed imminent, civil commotions at home soon divided the attention and dispersed the armies of Mexico.

How far they were checked in their enterprise by the resolute attitude of the little army of 1,800 men in their front it is needless now to consider ; it is certain, however, that their advance would have been welcomed equally by the Texan army, eager for combat, and by its wounded leader. Inaction, a source of disorganization in any army, was especially injurious to men so adventurous. General Johnston believed that safety lay in boldness, and that the true policy to secure peace was to inflict rather than to suffer invasion. Felix Huston, who agreed with him in this view, wrote to him, March 28th, from the seat of Government :

I hope little from the war policy of the Administration. The facility of arriving at the same conclusions from the most opposite states of fact renders it entirely useless to argue or reason with the President on this subject. . . . As to our waging active war, he will not hear of it. I am in very low spirits as to our prospects, and deem Texas in a very critical situation.

Huston was then on his way to New Orleans to try to raise men and supplies. Though the best-informed of his contemporaries denied his fitness for command, he had a certain audacity that, under proper direction, might have gained him the distinction which he craved almost morbidly. Though somewhat " splenetive and rash," his character was broad and manly.

From the time he took command, General Johnston tried with good results to improve the discipline of the army by drill and occupation in other military duties; and the troops were kept as much in motion as was safe and practicable. The army was increased from 1,500 to nearly 2,000 men by the arrival of recruits, for whose enlistment

General Johnston had provided while in New Orleans. Under the in-structions of the Government, with insufficient munitions, transporta-tion, and supplies, and with scarcely any cavalry, the army was neces-sarily merely one of observation. The consequent dissatisfaction was increased by want of proper rations. The troops soon consumed the scanty supplies of the country, reducing the sparse inhabitants to ab-solute want. The army was fed from hand to mouth ; and often only two or three days' supplies remained in depot. At times, half-rations of beans and flour only were issued on alternate days, and frequently the men were without meat. The most rigid economy and system were practised, however, so that no actual suffering occurred.

General Johnston was aware of the difficulties of the Government ; but, nevertheless, felt that its energy was not commensurate with the importance of the issues at stake. Another serious embarrassment arose from want of sufficient cavalry. General Johnston urged the expediency of employing a larger force of mounted men to watch the enemy, guard against forays by the Indians, and aid in collecting pro-visions. The President frequently promised him this aid ; but, on the 31st of March, wrote, " All my efforts to get you cavalry appear to be in vain." The small force of this arm at General Johnston's disposal was kept actively employed watching the roads. Wells, Seguin, Cook, and Karnes, with small parties of rangers, reconnoitred the frontiers with vigilance and secrecy ; and that daring partisan, Deaf Smith, pene-trated to the Rio Grande with twenty men, and defeated a superior force of the enemy near Laredo.

A secret traffic in ardent spirits added greatly to the difficulty of enforcing discipline. President Houston was very uneasy on this point, and issued stringent orders for the destruction of liquor intended for the camps. General Johnston shared in the President's solicitude, and wrote that he would enforce his orders *to the letter.* Having appre-hended and confined some men, while they were attempting to intro-duce liquor into the camp, a mutiny arose; and about fifty men rushed upon the guard at midnight, and rescued the prisoners, so that the camp became the scene of riot and confusion. The next day seven of the ringleaders were arrested, and quiet was restored. Not long after, Colonel Teal, a gallant and useful officer, was assassinated; and both public opinion and the suspicions of the President pointed to an officer of high rank as the instigator of the deed.

All these circumstances indicate the difficulties of General Johnston's position ; but, sustained by the hope of meeting the enemy with these valiant though unruly warriors, he endured the pain of his wound and the vexations of his command, and continued to perform the duties devolving on him. As this hope gradually vanished, and the torment from the injured nerve became more acute with the increasing heat, he was forced to consider the question of his resignation. He wrote from Texana, April 22d, to the Secretary of War, as follows:

DEAR SIR: The state of my health has been a source of great embarrassment and anxiety to me. During the first period of my confinement I was buoyed up with the hope of soon being able to resume the active duties of my station, believing that the healing of my wound would be the period of relief from pain and of my restoration. But I have been greatly disappointed; my attempts to take exercise on horseback have proved exceedingly injurious, and I am compelled to refrain; and, of course, am greatly discouraged, as my suffering is without intermission.

My situation requires repose and suspension from fatigue. I do not ask it, nor do I wish it, at this time, but the public interest requires that *all the duties* of the commander should be energetically performed by a competent officer; to do which, his presence at every point is necessary. The office of major-general is vacant. Let an appointment be made. I should be wanting in honor were I to conceal from you that I am unable to discharge all my duties, and have been restrained until this time from reporting it by the hope of recovery, which I do not now believe will be soon. My physicians commend my case to time.

I have recommended the appointment of a major-general. Should any other arrangement be deemed more conducive to the public interest, let no motive of consideration for me interfere. I feel the most ardent desire to serve the country, and whatever ability I may have shall be devoted to it.

The President and Secretary earnestly opposed any change, and urged General Johnston to retain command. He did so until May 7th, when, worn down by care, fatigue, and physical suffering, he took the advice of his physicians, and turned over the command to Colonel Rogers. On the 18th of the same month, the President furloughed about two-thirds of the men, thus virtually disbanding the army; while the Mexican navy swept triumphantly along the coast, and the Indians pursued their cruel warfare upon the border with but faint resistance.

As President Houston and General Johnston subsequently became unfriendly, it is proper to state that there is no evidence of such a feeling during this period.

The President's letters on public affairs are full and frank. Occasionally, his language is imperious; and he conveys rudimentary instruction in the military art after a fashion that might have wounded the self-love of a trained soldier less tolerant of human foibles than General Johnston; but he accepted all proper suggestions with cheerfulness, and responded to others with calmness and dignity. In a letter of April 4th General Johnston, in view of the possibility of a forced retreat, says:

I agree with you that the Colorado is the proper line of defense, having more strength than any other, and affording more facility of coöperation with the militia, and of supply.

To a rebuke from the President for writing to him in general terms, and an order requiring him to conform to the regulations in making returns, etc., he replies that all that the President conceives to have been omitted has been done, and that "the detailed information he desires is on the files of the War Department."

These, however, were minor matters, and led to no personal ill-feeling. But the conduct of affairs by the Administration certainly impaired General Johnston's confidence in its wisdom and energy. The President, from his antecedents, was naturally inclined to attach undue importance to treaties with the Indians, and to depend upon them for succor in emergencies. General Johnston, on the other hand, though quite ready to treat with or subsidize them, regarded them as utterly faithless, and placed no reliance upon their promises. In accordance with the tenor of his instructions, he made a treaty with the Comanches on the 25th of April. President Houston was satisfied with a do-nothing policy toward Mexico. He was content to allow an annual invasion from that country, if the independence of Texas was not put in too imminent peril thereby.

The time has passed for party-feeling about these matters; the actors are in their graves, and new issues have arisen of more vital importance to this generation; but, as the subject belongs to history, it seems appropriate to state the objections to this policy which for the most part controlled Texas, until it drifted into annexation. It was not *defensive*, as claimed; because it took no adequate steps to resist or punish aggression by Mexico or her Indian allies, who harassed the frontier. But, if it had been able to resist this aggression, still it fell short of measures essential to the security of Texas. Annexation to the United States was the general wish; and, if this could not be obtained, then independence, guaranteed by England or France. In either case a large immigration was desired by all Texans.

Before any of these results could be calculated upon, it was necessary for Texas to prove herself able to protect her own borders. General Johnston, with the more energetic spirits, believed that Texas had the men for an army of invasion, and could dictate a peace better within the boundaries of Mexico than beyond them; and that these men, admirable for offensive warfare, were a burden while idle. Five times as many men would have been required to guard the frontier securely as to invade. He thought a forward movement would attract a large number of adventurers, and that the removal of the pressure upon the frontier would invite an immigration of hardy colonists, who, in time, would form a sufficient bulwark. With the men of the border, he resented the idea that Mexico should be allowed annually to assert her eminent domain by an incursion of *rancheros* and convicts, while the pioneer was to be left unaided to the mercy of the savage.

That these sentiments were not his alone is manifest from the letter, already quoted, of General Felix Huston. Colonel W. S. Fisher, after retiring from the War Department, writes February 6, 1838 : "The people have lost faith in the Administration. They consider that the tendency of the whole of its measures is to prolong the war to an indefinite period, and they cry aloud for action and decided measures that will put an end to the harassing state of incertitude in which they now stand." Other testimony might be cited.

General Johnston did not feel it incumbent on him to arraign the Administration for inefficiency, though he chafed under what he considered lost opportunities for the country. These adverse views gradually led to a bitter hostility in the breast of the President, who eventually came to regard him as a man to be crushed, at whatever cost. The vehemence of this dislike was the more singular, as General Johnston at no time in his life, even to his intimate friends, allowed himself to show resentment at the ill offices done him, and generally forbore to speak when he could not commend. At this time, however, there was no rupture of friendly relations, and none would have occurred had others shown the same reserve in criticism of General Johnston that he exhibited toward them.

After General Johnston left the army, a meeting of officers voted him an address of confidence and regard. He received a furlough, May 17th, to visit the United States, and proceeded to New Orleans to consult his friend Dr. Davidson, and Dr. Luzenberg, an eminent surgeon of that city. These skillful medical authorities, after a month's attention to his case, confirmed the view of the army-surgeons, and recommended absolute repose. They also laid down a course of treatment which, in time, almost entirely restored him. In later life he was troubled with a slight lameness after any severe fatigue, and with numbness and occasional pain in one foot; there was also some shrinkage of the muscles. He was so much discouraged by the disbanding of the army, and by the opinions of his physicians as to his wound, that on the 27th of June he wrote to the Secretary of War, again tendering his resignation, which was again declined.

By the advice of his surgeons, General Johnston spent the summer and fall in Kentucky. His correspondence shows that the friends of Texas deemed his services of the first importance to the republic. Colonel Hockley, eminent in the struggle for independence, whom General Johnston characterizes as "one of the best officers and patriots in the army," writes from Nashville, November 5, 1837: "I have just returned from the Hermitage, where I spent all last week, and have had many and long conversations with the old chief in relation to the next campaign. He will be pleased to see you, if you can make it convenient to pass this way."

Hon. Henry D. Gilpin, the Attorney-General, and a confidential friend of President Van Buren, had married the widow of Senator Johnston. He wrote to General Johnston, August 13th, kindly urging him to visit him at Washington. He says: "It is very evident the annexation of Texas to our Union is to form a subject of importance and of contest too; I am sure your presence and information might often, very often, be of service." He adds: "When we saw you at the head of the army, we began to think of Cortes and De Soto; and conjectured that you would have as many toils among swamps, mountains, and prairies, as the one, to end in your putting a new flag on the same walls, as the other." In view of the intimate relations between the writer and the President, there is *suggestion* at least in the foregoing. From traits in General Johnston's character, already sufficiently manifest, including a certain impatience of patronage not altogether judicious, he declined to avail himself of these favorable opportunities of introduction to powerful party chiefs, and of familiar intercourse with them. Having spent his furlough with his children and friends in Louisville, he returned, as soon as he was able, in December, to Texas.

His naturally buoyant temper had aided in his recovery, and he now reëntered upon the scene of his former labors with high and cheerful purpose. The following extract is given not only as an index of his own spirit, but of that of the Texan people; and, also, as exhibiting the condition of the country, at the mercy, not only of invasion, but even of the rumor of invasion. It is from a letter to Mr. Edward D. Hobbs, of Louisville:

CITY OF HOUSTON, *December* 31, 1837.

MY DEAR SIR: A few hours after my arrival at this place, news reached us from San Antonio of the approach and investment of that devoted town by a large body of the enemy's cavalry. Immediate measures were taken by the people, here and elsewhere, to organize the whole available force of the country, and aid the Government in every possible manner. The greatest enthusiasm was manifested in our public meetings, and a determination to meet the enemy and drive him from our country. Our scanty means were fully known to all, being almost destitute of munitions and provisions; yet this did not abate the ardor of their devotion to the cause. Yesterday an express arrived from San Antonio, which informs us that the rumor was caused by the sudden irruption of a marauding party of fifty Mexicans for the purpose of stealing horses, in which they partly succeeded. The alarm, I hope, will act as a solemn admonition to the Government to commence preparations for the renewal of the war in the most energetic manner. The commander of San Antonio says that "things bear a threatening aspect in that region;" and information from different sources confirms the reported movements of the enemy; indeed, we may say that a heavy column has already crossed the Rio Grande. It is now too late to lament that ample preparation has not been made; we must be up and doing, with such force and such means as we have. Texas is now free, and will always be, while her citizens are faithful; and in this they will never be found wanting.

I shall leave this evening for the west. I will take charge of 200 mounted men at the Colorado, and proceed with them for the purpose of making a reconnaissance. The information I shall gain will enable the Government to act promptly and energetically, if need be. I am ordered to take charge of the military operations. I hope to render a good account if the war goes on.

A letter to the same gentleman explains the conclusion of this affair :

MERCER'S FERRY, COLORADO RIVER, *January* 17, 1838.

DEAR SIR : I wrote you in my last of my intention of going to San Antonio de Bexar with a small force, for the purpose of reconnaissance on the frontier, with the view of ascertaining the strength and composition of the enemy's forces, and how far they have been pushed on this side of the Rio Grande. Thus far I have been unable to raise the force I anticipated, the excitement of the false report of the investment of Bexar having subsided. I think it probable I shall have to advance with one company of forty men, or relinquish the undertaking, which I would not do were all the powers of Mexico in full array on our territory. [*Confidential.*—Our Government wants energy and prudent foresight, which those intrusted with the liberties of a people should possess.]

I leave to-morrow for the Navidad, thence for Bexar, thence—I will determine when I get there. Salutations to all friends, Prentice in particular.

Very truly your friend,

A. SIDNEY JOHNSTON.

The sentence marked " Confidential," in this letter, will not be considered incautious, or censorious, when it is remembered that it was addressed to a most intimate and trustworthy friend, not in Texas. It is given to show the drift of General Johnston's opinions at that time. A little later, if he had chosen to give expression to them, they would have been more emphatic in tone.

On the 20th of January the Secretary of War, Barnard E. Bee, remarks in a friendly letter, that it would be useless to get men together without supplies; and adds, " The nakedness of the land you will be struck with." On the 27th of January he informs General Johnston that the President is opposed to his making his headquarters beyond San Antonio. On February 26th H. McLeod writes very emphatically, " The President will *not* change the frontier line, or reënforce General Johnston with militia." On the same day the Secretary of War writes, " As we have not a dollar in the Treasury, we must be content to fold our arms;" and again, on another occasion, he says: " The Treasury is drained. Not a dollar is to be had."

As the winter and spring dragged on, it became evident that Mexico, busied with her own civil wars, would not attempt the conquest of Texas, but would limit her attacks to predatory raids and the stirring up of Indian hostilities ; and Texas was again saved more by the faults of the enemy than by her own vigor. On the 13th of March General

Johnston addressed a letter to the Secretary of War, in which he says: "Although, from the distracted condition of Mexico, which is confirmed by reports from every source, it will not be possible for that Government to carry on the war this year against the republic ; and although the enemy is unable to make any serious movement against this country, we should not forget that our frontier is in a most feeble situation, and incapable of defense against even predatory parties. It is unnecessary for me to say to you that on the northern frontier there is no force whatever, and on the western there will not be a mounted man after the 3d of April." The letter goes on to urge not only the duty but the expediency of protecting the settlers, and recommends the organization of a regiment of cavalry for frontier defense. The Government, however, took no measures, except to advise a renewal of the treaty with the Comanches, the preliminaries of which General Johnston, after much negotiation, finally arranged.

In 1854 I took notes of some conversations with General Johnston, among which I find the following account of these transactions. The Comanches had committed great depredations, but now sent in word that they were willing to treat for peace. General Johnston knew that there could be no satisfactory peace until the limits of the two races were definitively settled, and each was restrained within its own territory ; but the difficulty was, that the Spanish law had recognized no right to the soil in the Indians, and Texas still held to this doctrine. Could a territory, then, be marked out for the Comanches ? As General Johnston's authority to assign a territory to them was at least doubtful, and he was unwilling to transcend his legitimate powers, he sent an officer to the President to inquire how this question should be disposed of; but Houston made no reply. General Johnston determined, therefore, merely to hold a friendly talk with the Indians, avoiding all disputed points.

After a delay of some two months a band of about 150 Comanches, led by two chiefs, Essowakkenny and Essomanny, came in to hold the "talk." The chiefs were about twenty-seven or twenty-eight years old, and about five feet eight inches in height; Essomanny was rather a bull-headed fellow, with a firm and sensible expression ; Essowakkenny had a more intelligent countenance.

It had been the immemorial custom of the Comanches, after plundering the country, to ride down at their pleasure to San Antonio to trade, receive presents, and offer prisoners for ransom. On such occasions, to relieve themselves from the care of their horses, these fierce warriors condescendingly committed their *caballado* to the custody of the commandant, from whom they required a scrupulous return of their chattels when they should be ready to leave. On this occasion, Essowakkenny, on meeting General Johnston, waved his hand with a lordly

Indian Council at San Antonio, Texas.

gesture toward his horses, saying: " There is our *caballado*. Take care of it." " Yes," replied General Johnston, looking at him steadily, " I see your *caballado*. You ride good ponies. I advise you to watch them well. All white men are not honest. I take good care of my own horses. Take care of yours." General Johnston told the writer that he meant to teach the Comanches that he was not " a Mexican hostler in uniform." The chief understood the irony, and that he had to deal with a warrior ; he smiled grimly, and detailed some of his own men to watch the grazing herd.

A " big talk " was held. General Johnston told them of the great advantages of peace, and that the Texans wished to be friendly with them ; to which they replied that they also wished for peace. General Johnston told them that, if they were better acquainted with the white people, they might like them better ; and that, if they desired it, trading-posts would be established in their country. Essowakkenny rose, and said that the Comanches had noticed that trading-posts always seemed to frighten the buffalo away, so that they did not want any in their country ; but that they did not object to a line of posts along the *border* of their country—drawing an imaginary line with his hand, so as to indicate a distance of about three miles from San Antonio. Not caring to discuss the delicate subject of the boundary, General Johnston, without alluding to the trading-posts again, dilated upon the benefits of peace. Essowakkenny rejoined that his people had made peace with the Mexicans. General Johnston said that he was glad of it ; although the Mexicans were not his friends, it was good for the Comanches to be at peace with *everybody*. Essowakkenny added, with a humorous look, that he did not make peace with the Mexicans until he had stolen all their horses ! To General Johnston's request that he would visit the President at Houston, Essowakkenny replied that he could not go, but that his brother, Essomanny, who was a braver man than himself, would go. He then declared sentiments of the strongest friendship. General Johnston gave them presents of considerable value, and dismissed them, not only well pleased, but delighted, with their reception.

Karnes, on the strength of this talk, took a quantity of goods and traded with them. He was well treated, and made much money. Encouraged by these results, a party of thirteen men started with goods to trade with them ; but, as they were never heard of again, it was supposed that they were treacherously murdered by the Comanches. President Houston concluded a treaty with them in May, 1838, which they observed with their usual bad faith ; and we find them, during the summer and fall, raiding, robbing, and scalping ; so that, in the language of Yoakum, " the frontier was lighted up with the flames of savage war." This author ascribes these outrages to the opening of the land-office;

but they should rather be imputed to the secret negotiations between Mexico and the Indians, and to the defenseless condition of the frontier.

General Johnston used to relate that, while pursuing, with friendly Tonkaways, some Lipan horse-thieves, they came upon a gigantic brave, who, on foot, long outstripped his pursuers. At length, finding his enemies closing round him, he turned, confronted them, and defiantly shouting, "Lipan!" rushed among them to certain death. General Johnston said he would gladly have saved him, but was unable to do so. Next day, his Indian allies told him they had cooked the Lipan, and asked him to dinner ; nor could they be made to understand his abhorrence at feasting on the flesh of an enemy. This is mentioned because it has been doubted whether the Texas Indians were cannibals.

On another occasion, he was following the trail of some hostile Indians, when he found, among other tracks in the sand, the footprint of a little child. He halted his men, pointed it out to them, and told them they must spare the party for the sake of the little child. The rude frontiersmen, equally open to emotions of revenge or generosity, readily agreed to forego the pursuit. He had a great reverence for the innocence of childhood.

During the spring General Johnston was much urged to allow himself to be nominated for President of the Republic ; and it was stated that Rusk would allow his name to be used as a candidate for Vice-President, on this condition, but on no other. He, however, steadily rejected all overtures, in which course he was fully confirmed, when General Mirabeau B. Lamar and Hon. Peter W. Grayson, both personal friends, appeared as rival candidates.

On the 8th of April the Government was startled by information, five days only from Matamoras, that a heavy column of invasion was already in motion in the direction of San Antonio. The dispatch from the Secretary of War, conveying this intelligence to General Johnston, concludes :

I communicate with you by express, and at the instance of the President, who has but just returned. He wishes you to avail yourself of every possible means of defense ; and, if necessary, consult with the Comanches, who will doubtless render you every assistance ; your force is so inadequate that I can scarcely do more than say I know all that bravery can achieve will be accomplished.

As the Mexican force was reported at 1,500 or 2,000 men, and General Johnston had only forty men at his disposal, he might well have disregarded an order the tenor of which, in its plain construction, seemed to require him to contest the advance of the invaders with the force at his command. Though he did not suspect any deliberate purpose to sacrifice him, he felt a deep indignation at the terms in which the order was drawn, which, according to his construction, left him no liberty of action. The next day he replied:

You are aware of the very limited means of defense at my disposal; but, such as they are, you may rely upon their being employed to the best advantage.

The direction to call upon the Indians for aid was a proposition not to be considered. It is probable that the Administration only meant that he must run away judiciously; but he was hardly of a temper so to construe "*all that bravery can achieve.*" He resolved that he would not retreat, and that, if a Thermopylæ or an Alamo were required of him, he would not involve San Antonio in his destruction. He therefore advanced to meet the enemy and contest with him the passage of the streams. The result proved the wisdom of his action, the safety of which lay in its boldness. The Mexicans, apprehending that his little troop was but the advance-guard of an army, hastily recrossed the Rio Grande; and, in furtherance of some other political project, were soon diverted into distant quarters, thus freeing the frontier from present danger. Thus was this official death-warrant annulled by Providence. The coast of Texas was about the same time relieved from the depredations of the enemy by the French blockade of the ports of Mexico.

General Johnston, having no troops to command and no present occupation, again wished to resign, but was so strongly dissuaded that, in June, he accepted a furlough and went to Kentucky. Colonel Hockley, who had succeeded Mr. Bee as Secretary of War, informed General Johnston, August 21st, of Cordova's revolt, which ended in smoke, however; and, apprising him that he was authorized to retain such officers as were necessary, added, "*You hold your rank, and are wanted.*"

Most of the emigrants to Texas had gone thither with the hope of seeing it ultimately admitted as a State into the Federal Union. When they saw the possibilities of greatness in its vast territory and wonderful natural advantages, they felt assured that in its annexation the United States would gain even more than Texas. When, then, in the Northern States the opposition to annexation found vent in a torrent of insult and invective, a great revulsion of feeling occurred in Texas. President Houston withdrew the offer of annexation, and public attention was directed toward the maintenance of independence, with free trade and closer relations with England.

In letters to General Johnston from prominent Texans, former enthusiasts for annexation, the opinion prevails that "perhaps it is better thus." Others went further, disappointment adding bitterness to alienation. President Lamar, in his inaugural address, says with his usual fervor: "The step, once taken, would produce a lasting regret, and ultimately prove as disastrous to our liberties and hopes as the triumphant sword of the enemy." General Johnston shared the common sentiment that national dignity and manifest policy both demanded the withdrawal of the offer of annexation. It was evidently unfair to

Texas to leave the option open to a hesitating suitor; and, indeed, the shortest road to annexation was to compel the United States to consider the alternative of a European protectorate. A few years' delay enabled Texas' to make a much better bargain, and the United States reënacted the purchase of the sibylline books. It is a curious problem how a final rejection of Texas by the United States might have affected the events of the last twenty years—possibly not as the opponents of annexation would have wished.

Mirabeau B. Lamar was elected President, and David G. Burnet Vice-President, September 3, 1838, and they were inaugurated on the 9th of December. On December 22d General Johnston was appointed Secretary of War. Louis P. Cook was made Secretary of the Navy, and Dr. James H. Starr Secretary of the Treasury; and the Department of State was filled in rapid succession by Hon. Barnard E. Bee, Hon. James Webb, and Judge Abner S. Lipscomb; Judge Webb becoming Attorney-General. General Johnston lived on terms of great harmony and kindness with his colleagues.

CHAPTER VII.

SECRETARY OF WAR.

THE outlook of Texas seemed anything but bright at the beginning of Lamar's administration. Fortune, which at first appeared to smile upon the rising republic, finding her favors neglected, had now begun to turn away her face. Nearly three years had passed since San Jacinto, and yet no government, except the United States, had acknowledged the independence of Texas. The European powers refused recognition, and pointed to the claim of title maintained by Mexico, with an annual invasion that disputed possession of the soil and pretended to imperil the national existence. The navy, created by the Texan Congress in 1836, had disappeared in 1837: of its four vessels, two had gone down at sea, one had been sold, and one captured. The army had been disbanded, and Mexican machinations had been allowed to mature, drawing the wild tribes and the Cherokees into an alliance which was drenching the defenseless border in blood, and now loomed up into the larger proportions of a general war. The whole policy of President Houston had been to postpone the evil day, and to evade difficulties instead of meeting them. Time is so important an element in setting straight the crooked things of this world, and was, especially, of such moment in the affairs of Texas, that the President's procrastination appears pardonable; but its sole advantage turned out to be the personal one of shifting the accumulated burden upon his successor. Yet Providence had supplied the defects of human foresight, and stood friend to the struggling young nation.

In 1837 the Mexican army of invasion, after surveying the attitude of the Texan force on the Coleto under General Johnston, concluded to retire; and in 1838 it retreated, as has been narrated, before a shadow. In the same year the French blockade of the Mexican ports ended the Mexican blockade of the coast of Texas, and supplied the loss of the fleet; but on the 9th of March, 1839, the French blockade was raised by the peace between France and Mexico. The Treasury was empty, the paper-money much depreciated, and public credit gone. No army, no navy, no money, no credit, and no national recognition; with Mexico relieved of French invasion, and an Indian war ready to burst upon the country—what was left? Hope, God's gift to the young—men or nations—hope, destined to many disappointments, but still buoying them up.

The youthful statesmen who now guided the republic fortunately felt an enthusiasm that was neither turned aside by obstacles nor dismayed by dangers. The future greatness of the country inspired them, and they opposed to the odds against them the intrepidity, the energy, and the intellectual resources, of the martial race they represented. Imagination, displaying itself in action, lent a certain grandeur to the designs of the President and cabinet—heroic wills grappling with an adverse fate.

General Johnston, writing to Mr. George Hancock, from Houston, April 21, 1839, says, "There is now nothing doubtful in the stability of our institutions or in our ultimate success in the establishment of the independence of the country upon a most auspicious basis."

Mirabeau B. Lamar was born in Jefferson County, Georgia, August 16, 1798. He was of Huguenot stock, and of a family which has produced men of note as orators and statesmen. He was already distinguished for eloquence when he came to Texas, in 1835, to aid the constitutional cause; and is said to have been the first to declare publicly for independence. He was not less ardent as a soldier than as a speaker; and, in the cavalry-skirmish on the day before the battle of San Jacinto, saved the life of General Rusk by a free exposure of his own. He was conspicuous for gallantry at San Jacinto, was soon after appointed Secretary of War by President Burnet, and was elected Vice-President in 1836. His impetuous valor, enthusiastic temper, and unselfish aspirations for the honor and welfare of his country, made him the fit choice of Texas as her President. Lamar was a man of high, unbending honor; his native gifts were fine—largeness and brilliancy of conception, fancy, eloquence, readiness, and courage. Though ardent, impulsive, and open to present impressions, sometimes, especially in seasons of ill-health, he gave way to the reaction that displays itself in waywardness, dejection, and lassitude.   But he was brave, affectionate, open as the day, lofty, and magnanimous.   Among his chosen friends and counselors were men of purpose as high as his own, and of more exact modes of thought.   Judge Lipscomb and Mr. Webb were able lawyers, Cook was a man of fine talents, and Dr. Starr has through a long life justified both his financial ability and his perfect uprightness.

The Administration accepted the trust imposed upon it, with the full purpose and reasonable expectation of carrying out a broad plan for the security and greatness of the country.   It achieved much; and even where it fell short of the design, as is apt to be the case in a free government whose legislation is based upon compromise, it laid the foundation of future power and progress for the State.   The financial policy proposed by the President was rejected by Congress. While, of course, it cannot be asserted that a national bank, which he recommended, with its credit based upon the public domain and the public deposits, would have created financial confidence and maintained values in those distressed times, still the adherence to a system of unlimited, unguaranteed, irredeemable issues was not the device nor the choice of this Administration.   Bankruptcy could not be arrested by it, and indeed was certain under it.   It is doubtful, however, whether any prudence or wisdom could have averted the result.   The recommendation of a national bank was, however, used as a handle of prejudice among those who, under entirely different circumstances, had learned to distrust the United States Bank.

To the eloquent appeals of Lamar are due the foundation of the educational system of Texas, and the consecration of noble grants of public lands to the School and University Funds.   By him, too, a great tide of corruption and public plunder was suddenly stopped.   An Auditorial Court had been established, which by some legislative inadvertence was almost compelled to approve all claims presented, on the flimsiest proof.   The court was overwhelmed with fabricated claims against the Government, when it was suspended by the President until the meeting of Congress, which ratified his action and corrected the evil.   The existence of an organized system of public robbery was discovered, by which a vast number of fraudulent land-certificates had been issued and circulated, evidently through the collusion of dishonest local land commissioners.   The President again interposed to check this manufacture, and end the reign of bribery, perjury, and forgery ; and, on his recommendation, Congress took such action as broke up the system and saved the republic from enormous losses.   The land-pirates and bogus-claim swindlers, forming a numerous and adroit class, were roused into an active and bitter hostility, which was not without effect in hampering the measures of the Administration.

The foreign relations of Texas were now put upon an entirely new footing. Her independence was acknowledged by France, England, Belgium, and Holland; treaties of amity and commerce were made, and diplomatic relations were established which, by alternately piquing the pride and the interest of the great powers, eventually led to annexation to the United States. The two subjects most pressing, however, were the defense of the frontier and the settlement of the Indian question. A navy was put upon the Gulf, which not only secured the coast of Texas but annoyed that of Mexico, lent aid to her rebels, and helped to embarrass her counsels. By judicious encouragement to the Federalists, and by letting loose upon her the more restless spirits of the border, Mexico was kept busy in defense of her own soil, so that, during this Administration, Texas was not invaded by land or sea—the best justification of its foreign policy. This energetic line of action was stigmatized as a war policy; but it was, in fact, the only true peace policy, since it transferred the theatre of war to the enemy's territory, gave to foreign countries an assurance of strength, and by an exhibition of internal security, unknown before, invited capital and population. Moreover, Texas showed an earnest desire for peace, seeking the mediation of friendly nations, and sending Mr. Bee as envoy to Vera Cruz to try to open negotiations. Though spurned by Mexico, these overtures, seconded by warlike preparations, helped to gain the respect of civilized peoples.

The conduct of military affairs was intrusted by the President to the Secretary of War, whose wish was to raise a small regular force, which, thoroughly armed, drilled, and disciplined, would serve as the nucleus and example for a volunteer army. General Johnston's views to this effect were laid before the President in the following letter:

WAR DEPARTMENT, *December* 18, 1838.

I have the honor herewith to submit for your consideration views with reference to the measures which, in my opinion, should be adopted to maintain the attitude assumed by this republic, and lead to a prompt adjustment of the difficulties existing with the Government of Mexico, and to more amicable relations with the Indians on the northern frontier. Menaced by powerful, vindictive, and unrelenting enemies, the wisdom of experience dictates that the preparations should be ample and adequate in all respects to meet all emergencies. In the previous invasions by the enemy this country presented everywhere abundant resources for the subsistence of troops and for mounting and equipping them, which do not now exist. They have long since been exhausted, and it is believed that they do not exceed the wants of the inhabitants. In former emergencies the vast means always available facilitated the rapid concentration of the force of the country, and enabled it to meet the enemy with promptitude in advance of the frontier. With the same patriotic devotion and zeal for the cause, with the same eager desire to turn out for defense with which they were inspired on former occasions, is it not manifest that, without depots of pro-

visions and military stores, without means of transportation of any kind, the call for aid in defense must be feebly responded to? There is another consideration which will contribute powerfully to render this resource for defense precarious, which should under favorable circumstances constitute the main dependence of the Government. It is the apprehension of attack from hostile Indians, founded in evidence which they cannot reject. The advance of a Mexican army would be the signal for the active coöperation of the unfriendly tribes; and, whether it took place or not, the anticipation of such an event among a sparse population, feeling the necessity of the utmost vigilance and activity for their own protection, would produce the same result—a strong diversion in favor of the enemy, which our knowledge of the Indian character inclines us to believe would not be the case if we had an army in position on the border. If this be the true condition of things, and I think no one informed on the subject will differ with me, I should ill discharge the high obligations of duty were I to delay making them known, or deserve the confidence of the intelligent, bold, and patriotic population of the republic, who do not desire to be flattered with deceptive accounts of their power where circumstances prevent its efficient application, or with illusive hopes of peace founded on no just expectations. We cannot conceal from ourselves that we are at war with a powerful nation, however much leisure his supineness has left us for the pursuits of peace. The example of all nations teaches the necessity of active, vigorous and unremitted preparation till the termination of the contest; the greatest and most powerful nations do not disdain it. I do not hesitate, therefore, from the conviction that peace will be most easily and readily obtained by making ample preparations for war, to recommend that, besides the measures in progress for the defense of the coast, the force authorized by the act to fix and establish the military force of the republic, of November, 1836, be raised and equipped for immediate service, with such additional force as may be found necessary. I also recommend that the officers and soldiers now on the rolls of the army, except those of the regiment recently authorized for the protection of the frontier and of the advance corps, be disbanded in anticipation of the new organization which I have the honor to suggest. I have the honor to be, with great respect, your Excellency's obedient servant,   A. SIDNEY JOHNSTON,
                                                    Secretary of War.

To his Excellency MIRABEAU B. LAMAR, President of the Republic of Texas.

It was proposed then to cross the Rio Grande in aid of the Federalists, who sought the alliance, until that party prevailed throughout Mexico, or at least established an independent republic of its northern States, which would interpose a friendly nation as a barrier to centralist aggression. This hope does not seem chimerical, when we recollect how near the Federalists were to success ; nor does there seem much reason why such an army, under an able leader, might not in such an undertaking have dictated the terms of peace in the city of Mexico. There was no wish or intention, however, to form any political union with any Mexican State. When this was strongly urged by General Anaya, the Federalist envoy, upon the consideration of General Johnston, on the ground that *all* republics ought to be federal in their organization, General Johnston replied that " every nation ought to choose its own form of government, and be a good neighbor; that Texas could exist alongside a monarchy if it treated her well."

To carry out so large a plan as the invasion of Mexico would have required great unanimity of sentiment among the people in favor of aggressive war; in fact, a vigorous and undivided national feeling. Without this, it was vain to hope that the Government could obtain the men and means at home, or the credit abroad, necessary to prosecute it with energy. But for the first time an opposition was organized against the Administration. President Houston had been able to tide over his two years of office without encountering one. Though he had his embarrassments, it was from independent resistance to particular measures, and not in the desire to thwart or impede his executive action. There was at that time neither the material nor the temper for an opposition. Everybody wished to make the best of what happened; errors and faults were condoned; and the power of patriotism and good feeling in the first flush of victory, together with the prestige of San Jacinto, prevented any combination to thwart the Executive. A negative policy, if it effected nothing, at least offered nothing tangible to resist; so that, if there was much to complain of, there was little to undo or overthrow, and dissatisfaction effervesced in grumbling. Now, however, it was different. Opinions had crystallized, and politics was becoming a profession. The elements of party, personal, local, and sectional considerations, as well as those springing from honest differences of opinion, only waited the call of a leader to marshal in strong array. Such a leader was soon found in the late President. Whatever view may be taken of General Houston in other respects, it is idle to deny him superior talents in the management of men. His temper was not such as to be satisfied with a subordinate position ; and he beheld with impatience and anger a course of proceeding which, reversing his own, seemed a tacit rebuke to him, which, if successful, would eclipse San Jacinto, and if it failed would injure the country. With such alternatives, he was unwilling it should be tried. He soon gathered all the discontented into a well-knit party, who made his name its watchword. All who differed with the Administration were taught where they would find sympathy for their opinions and their grievances ; and following these was a mighty contingent of the inert, the timid, and the short-sighted, who were willing to trust all to chance, to whom was added the compact phalanx of land-swindlers and claim-forgers, eager for revenge. Of course the body of the party was honest; but, whatever its material, or motives, it hung with such a dead weight upon the measures of the Administration as to prevent the realization of its plans.

But the event which gave General Houston the deepest offense, and

most sorely wounded at once his self-love and his affections, was the
Cherokee War. After that, reconciliation was impossible; and he always
cherished the bitterest hostility to the authors and principal actors in
it. Whoever else made their peace with him, he never forgave General
Johnston. It was natural, and not discreditable to General Houston,
that he should resent a line of conduct which reversed his Indian policy, and treated as enemies a tribe to which he was under the deepest
personal obligations. It was not in his nature to discriminate between
his personal relations and the public policy, and there can be no doubt
that he felt the warmest indignation at the repudiation of his acts,
which he identified with those of the republic.

The causes which led to the Cherokee War, as well as an outline of
the events, will be related here; not only because General Johnston,
as Secretary of War, made the issue with the Indians and superintended
the conduct of the campaign, but because it is necessary to the vindication of a whole people, to whom it has been imputed as a national
crime, to be pardoned, however, in view of the strong temptations to
which they were subjected. This seems to be the view of Yoakum,
their most elaborate historian, who, representing the opinions and justifying the action of General Houston, has so recorded the events, and
with such inferences as to lead to the most erroneous conclusions. As
the whole matter is a question of *good faith*, which must be kept sacred
with savages as well as with others, the reader will pardon a complete
though succinct statement of all the facts, cleared from the confusion
of outside considerations.

A small band of Cherokees, led by Richard Fields, a half-breed, emigrated from the United States to Texas in 1822. They easily extorted
a permission to settle from the Mexicans of Nacogdoches, who had been
dispersed and cowed by the recent invasions of Colonel Long. Fields
is said to have visited the city of Mexico to obtain a grant of lands, and
to have returned satisfied with some vague and illusory promises. In
1825 he was joined to John Hunter, a white man, who, whether fanatic
or impostor, had varied experience and much address, and who went to
Mexico on the same mission. The constitutional right to make such a
grant residing in the State, and not in the Federal Government, his request was refused. Fields and Hunter made a treaty with the "Fredonian" insurgents, in the winter of 1826; but a rival faction of the
Cherokees murdered Hunter, and, led by Bowles, aided in putting down
the revolt. Bowles became the war-chief of the Cherokees, and the
leading spirit of the Texas Indians.

The first concession by the Government to the Cherokees was an
order, made August 15, 1831, to the local authorities, to offer them an
establishment on a fixed tract of land, which the Political Chief at Bexar
afterward reported that they had selected. When it is borne in mind

that the chief motive of Mexico, in the colonization of Texas, had been to oppose the organization and valor of white men as a barrier between the restless and predatory Indians and interior Mexico, it seems a curious coincidence that the Government should begin to accord rights and privileges to savages, just when it was denying them to white men. The usurping Central Administration of Bustamante had, on April 6, 1830, absolutely forbidden the immigration of citizens of the United States, and was then trying to carry out its plan of arbitrary government in Texas.

On the 22d of March, 1832, Colonel Piedras was commissioned " to put the Cherokee families into individual possession of the lands they possessed ; " so natural is it for despotism to ally itself with barbarism, and to seek to depress its intelligent opponents by the aid of an inferior race. That the order to Piedras was obeyed, either technically or substantially, is not probable, as the Indians would not have been satisfied with an allotment of lands in severalty in lieu of the range of country which they hunted over. It served the purpose intended, however ; and 50 or 100 Shawnees and Cherokees followed Piedras, the next June, to aid Bradburn, at Anahuac, against Austin's colonists. In the Declaration of Grievances, by the Ayuntamiento of Nacogdoches, the colonists complained that " Colonel Piedras had called in and employed Indians, in his meditated warfare on their rights ; " and " had insulted them by saying that he held Americans and Indians in the same estimation, and as standing on the same footing." [1]

The Colonization Act of March 24, 1825, admitted Indians as settlers, " when any of them, after having first declared themselves in favor of our religion and institutions, wish to establish themselves in any settlements that are forming." It has been pretended that the emigrant United States Indians were entitled to lands as colonists under this act ; but, when we consider that its intention was to induce white men to come in for the purpose of keeping Indians out, it cannot be considered an invitation, but a conditional permission, to a certain class of Indians. It was framed in a spirit of equity, and plainly intends the case of Indians willing to become civilized and to settle in the colonies of Austin and other *empresarios*. The Cherokees did not comply with either the legal formalities or other prescribed conditions ; nor, indeed, did they wish to acquire any rights under the law. In point of fact, the republic of Texas, in 1839, would not have denied reasonable allotments of land to any resident Indians wishing in good faith to try the experiment of civilization.

Up to 1832 the intruding Indians had been stragglers or discontented bands, which had broken away from the great tribes in the United States. Now, however, under the aggressive policy of that Govern-

[1] "Texas Almanac," 1869, p. 39.

ment, forcing them westward, the emigration assumed a new phase. In spite of treaty stipulations to the contrary between the United States and Mexico, a formidable body of Cherokees, Shawnees, Kickapoos, Delawares, and Quapaws, numbering 1,530 warriors and five times as many souls, entered Texas in the winter of 1832–'33—about the time of General Houston's arrival in the State.

No people could suffer such an invasion without disquietude; and accordingly we find that the *empresarios*, Messrs. Austin, Milam, and Burnet, early in 1833, addressed a memorial to General Bustamante, calling attention to the facts. Colonel Bean, too, commanding the Eastern Department, made a similar complaint to General Cass, United States Secretary of War, remonstrating against this breach of the treaty of 1831, by which "both parties bind themselves expressly to restrain by force all hostilities and incursions on the part of the Indians living within their respective boundaries." It is hard to see how any rights accrued to these Indians, constituting fifteen-sixteenths of the intruding bands, from their incursion, when colonists and authorities alike attempted to prevent it. The centralists wanted a sprinkling of savages, not a deluge; the colonists objected to their neighborhood altogether.

Here the matter seems to have rested until September 11, 1835, when Colonel Bean addressed another letter to the President of the United States, referring to his former communication, and the frequent breaches of the treaty already mentioned ; adding, "The annoyance to the community, as well as the danger, which has resulted from the fact of their incursion, was clearly anticipated at the time of my letter to the Secretary of War." He then requests that the Government will prevent the execution of a contract for the introduction of 24,000 Creeks into Texas.

On the same day, the Committee of Vigilance for Nacogdoches also wrote to President Jackson, giving the details of the aforesaid contract, pointing to its violation of the treaty of 1831, and soliciting the interference of the United States Government; praying that " a sparse and defenseless population be protected from the evils that were so tragically manifested on the frontiers of Georgia and Alabama." [1] This letter was signed by Sam Houston and five others. Mr. Castello, Mexican *chargé d'affaires*, offered the same remonstrance, October 14, 1835. President Jackson took the steps necessary to prevent the threatened irruption.

In the beginning of the Texan Revolution, the Consultation, a provisional government, representing the municipalities, met November 3, 1835. On November 13th, on the motion of Sam Houston, it made a " solemn declaration " to the Indians, "that we will guarantee to

---

[1] " Niles's Register," vol. xlix., p. 160.

them the peaceable enjoyment of their rights to their lands, as we do our own. We solemnly declare that all grants, surveys, or locations of lands, within the bounds hereinbefore mentioned, made after the settlement of said Indians, are, and of right ought to be, utterly null and void." Lieutenant-Governor Robinson, a member of the committee that reported this declaration, says that General Houston assured the committee that he had himself seen the grant from the Mexican Government to the Cherokees, and that it was in the hands of Captain Rogers, at Fort Smith, in Arkansas; and avers that these assurances constrained the committee to unite in, and the Consultation to adopt, the report. Judge Waller, another member, confirms Lieutenant-Governor Robinson's statement. It is not now pretended that there was any such grant extant.[1]

Sam Houston, John Forbes, and John Cameron, were appointed commissioners to negotiate with the Cherokees. But the Legislative Council, apparently distrusting this action, passed a resolution, December 26th, instructing the commissioners "in no wise to transcend the declaration, made by the Consultation in November, in any of their articles of treaty ; . . . . and to take such steps as might secure their" (the Indians') "effective coöperation when it should be necessary to summon the force of Texas into the field."[2] Houston and Forbes made a treaty, February 23, 1836, ceding to the Indians a large territory.

It has been objected to the Declaration that "it was an ill-advised, disingenuous, if not subtle and sinister measure, null and void for want of fundamental authority, of no moral or political obligation, and only calculated to embarrass any future transactions with these obtruding savages."[3] Vice-President Burnet, acting Secretary of State, says that the provisional government was acting outside the sphere of its legitimate power, "and could not, in a matter so extraneous to the avowed purposes of its creation, impose any moral or political obligation upon the independent and separate Government of Texas."[4] It will be observed that the Consultation, by its very name, was provisional, and professed to act under the Mexican Federal Constitution of 1824. That its powers were *considered* merely *provisional* seems evident from the action of General Houston, who, having been appointed commander-in-chief by it, demanded another election when the convention met in the following March.

It was also charged that the commissioners transcended their powers, ceding a vast and undefined territory to the Indians, "without securing their effective coöperation," according to the restriction of the Council in their instructions to the agents. Vice-President Burnet fur-

[1] "Texas Almanac," 1860, p. 44.   [2] Kennedy, "History of Texas," vol. ii., p. 159.
[3] "Texas Almanac," 1859, p. 18.
[4] Dispatch, May 30, 1839, to General Dunlap, Texan minister to the United States.

ther says :[1] "That pretended treaty was never ratified by any competent authority on the part of Texas. On the contrary, when it was submitted to the Senate of the republic, which was the only power authorized to confirm, it was rejected by a decisive vote of that body, and no subsequent action of the Government has been had upon it."

General Houston tried once and again to secure the constitutional approval to his action ; but even his great personal popularity and political power failed in this. It is not improbable that his peculiar relations to the Cherokees had something to do with the rejection of the treaty by the Senate. A friendly biographer says that he passed "the moulding period of his life," between fourteen and eighteen, with the Cherokees. When he abandoned his family, his home, his high office, in Tennessee, and the habits of civilized life, in 1829, it was to seek a refuge in this tribe, which adopted him into full citizenship. He lived with them, as an Indian, three years, and is supposed to have entered Texas on some mission connected with their interests. He then located himself at Nacogdoches, near the Texas branch of the Cherokees, and always showed for them an interest and affection which, if it clouded his judgment, was at least creditable to his heart.

When this treaty was made Texas was still nominally a State of Mexico, and Houston was still a Cherokee, if indeed he ever renounced that affiliation. Such complicated relations unfitted him to act as agent where the parties had conflicting interests ; but he, nevertheless, showed an eagerness to complete this negotiation, that induced him, while commander-in-chief, to leave Refugio for that purpose, as the enemy was advancing. Thus the same day witnessed the conclusion of the treaty and the appearance of Santa Anna before San Antonio; and this ill-omened, futile, and wasteful compact was linked with the fall of the Alamo and the massacre of Fannin's men. Thus, too, it came to be regarded as General Houston's personal act, and as an agreement not binding on the State.

The treaty, which was to have engaged the effective coöperation of the Indians, is claimed by Yoakum to have secured their neutrality at least, thus imposing a moral obligation upon Texas to perform it; but his own pages dispel this slender claim. J. H. Sheppard says [2] that on the retreat in April, 1836, he was sent by General Houston to summon the Coshatties to his aid. Though long domiciled in Texas, and the most friendly of all the tribes, they would not even consider the request. It may be assumed that General Houston did not spare even more strenuous efforts to enlist the powerful Cherokees, with whom he was familiar. Though the Coshatties stood aloof and were sometimes

---

[1] Dispatch, May 30, 1839, to General Dunlap, Texan minister to the United States.
[2] "Texas Almanac," 1872, p. 101.

implicated in acts of hostility, yet, because their rights were prescriptive, they were treated with indulgence and allowed to retain their foothold when the immigrant Indians were expelled.

Of the Cherokees, Shawnees, Kickapoos, etc., "recent intruders," it is said "they were restless and discontented," and in 1836 "they gave unmistakable signs of hostility to the colonists by acts of depredation and murder." [1] Yoakum says that the Indians were kept quiet by the assurances of the committees of San Augustine and Nacogdoches, September 18, 1835, that their just and legal rights would be respected, and that "no white man should interrupt them on their lands." [2] Yet a different inference might be drawn from one of his anecdotes. He says that (in October or November, 1835) "the appearance of Breese's company at Nacogdoches had a fine effect on the Cherokee Indians, a large number of whom were then in town. Their fine uniform caps and coats attracted the notice of the chief Bolles. He inquired if they were *Jackson's* men. 'Certainly they are,' said Stern. 'Are there more coming?' 'Yes,' was the reply. 'How many more?' asked Bolles. Stern told him to count the hairs on his head and he would know. In twenty minutes the Indians had all left town." [3]

It is quite evident indeed from Yoakum's own account that the Indians were not restrained by treaty obligations, but by the presence of a competent force, and that the cause of Texan independence was put to the utmost hazard from the necessity of retaining troops to watch them. Both Texans and Indians knew, in April, 1836, that General Gaona, one of Santa Anna's lieutenants, with a well-appointed column, was moving on Nacogdoches under orders to kill or drive out the colonists.

Yoakum says: "The country through which he marched was thronged with Indians, already stirred up by the emissaries of the Mexicans, and naturally disposed to join them. . . . The people of Eastern Texas then felt that their danger was imminent. This apparent danger was increased by the threats and movements of the Indians. To ascertain the facts, the Committee of Vigilance at Nacogdoches dispatched agents to the Indians. C. H. Sims and William Sims, who were sent to the Cherokees, reported them to be hostile and making preparations for war; that they were drying beef and preparing meal, and said they were about sending off their women and children; that they had murdered Brooks Williams, an American trader among them; that they said a large body of Indians, composed of Caddoes, Keechies, Ionies, Tawacanies, Wacoes, and Comanches, were expected to attack the American settlements; that the Cherokees gave every

---

[1] "Texas Almanac," 1858, p. 174.   [2] Yoakum, "History of Texas," vol. i., p. 358.
[3] Ibid., vol. ii., p. 23.

indication of joining them; that the number of warriors embodied on the Trinity was estimated at 1,700; and that Bolles, the principal Cherokee chief, advised the agents to leave the country, as there was danger. M. B. Menard, who was sent to the Shawnee, Delaware, and Kickapoo tribes, reported that, while these tribes were friendly, they had been visited by Bolles, who urged them to take up arms against the Americans." [1]

In consequence, three companies, numbering 220 men, were detained, and three more were delayed in completing their organization, until it was too late to aid the retreating army under Houston. The women and children were hurried across the Sabine, and a panic paralyzed the action of these hardy men. The detention of the volunteers, General Gaona's change of route and failure of support, and especially the presence and attitude of United States troops, repressed the rising of Bowles and his followers. General Gaines, with fourteen companies of United States troops, took position on the Sabine, under orders to execute the treaty of 1831, and prevent hostilities by the emigrant United States Indians. A hearty sympathizer with Texas, he used with energy his influence and power to keep the Indians peaceable. He sent Lieutenant Bonnell to inform them of his instructions, and of his intention to use force if necessary to carry them out. Bonnell found that Manuel Flores, a Mexican agent, had been among them, exerting every effort to induce them to declare war on Texas. [2]

"General Gaona, at the head of a motley host of Mexicans and Indians, did not debouch from the forests of the Upper Trinity, but was making his way from Bastrop to San Felipe. Bolles, the Cherokee chief, indignant at the supposed suspicion of his good faith and pacific intentions, sent in his denial." [3]   Yoakum adds (vol. ii., page 170): "There is no doubt but that the savages were collected in large numbers on the frontier, were greatly excited, and *that nothing but the defeat of the Mexicans prevented them from making an attack upon the settlements.* As it was, they did not disperse without committing an act of barbarism." He then narrates the massacre of the settlement at Fort Parker, May 19, 1836. This plain summary shows that the treaty was entered into by the Indians with no intention of performing it, and while they were under conflicting engagements with the Mexicans; that it served merely as a cloak to cover their hostile designs, and was perfidiously violated in letter and spirit; and hence that it was not binding in conscience on the people or Government of Texas.

[1] Yoakum, "History of Texas," vol. ii., pp. 125-127.
[2] Ibid., vol. ii., p. 167.   [3] Ibid., vol. ii., p. 157.

The Indians continued in this hostile disposition. Yoakum says: "The frontiers of Texas, during the winter and spring of 1837, had been unsettled. The Indians, actuated by the persuasions of Mexican agents, and the imprudence of many white people living near them, kept up a very annoying predatory warfare. They began their depredations by the murder of three men on the Trinity at Fort Houston; then by the murder of two more on the Neches; and these were followed by numbers of others along the frontier. Besides these outrages, many horses were stolen. The Government did what it could to make treaties with the savages, and to keep up a vigilant ranging service, but still, while the Mexican emissaries were among them, they could not be quieted." [1] Though these outrages were attributed to the prairie Indians, they were committed on the edge of the Cherokee district, and pointed suspicion to that tribe. "Every day or two, during the year 1837, some murdered citizen or stolen property attested their hostile feeling." [2] The Mexican emissaries promised the Indians "arms, ammunition, and the plunder and prisoners—women and children included—taken during the war; also the peaceable possession of the country then held by them."

In August, 1838, "Cordova's Rebellion" occurred. In this abortive insurrection the Mexicans about Nacogdoches disclaimed their allegiance to Texas, and collected a force reported 600 strong, three-fourths of whom were Indians; but on the approach of the Texan volunteers under Rusk they retreated to the Cherokee country, and thence, when pressed by him, to the Upper Trinity, whence they dispersed. The Indians continued their hostilities, and later in the season, October 16th, General Rusk had a sharp combat with them at Kickapoo Town. Yoakum says the Mexican Government had commenced a system whose "object was to turn loose upon Texas all the Indian tribes upon her borders from the Rio Grande to Red River. Of this fact the Texan Government had undoubted evidence." [3] This secret league against the Texans seems to have existed at least as early as 1835, and to have continued unbroken.

The United States Government received information from Colonel Mason, at Fort Leavenworth, in July, 1838, confirmed by General Gaines, that the Cherokees were arranging for a council of all the tribes on the frontier, "preparatory to striking a simultaneous blow upon the settlements of Arkansas and Missouri, from Red River to the Upper Mississippi," instigated and organized by the agents of Mexico. One of these emissaries, Don Pedro Julian Miracle, was killed near the Cross Timbers, in Texas; and his journal also confirmed the suspicions of the conspiracy against Texas at least. The Cherokees and Caddoes visited

[1] Yoakum, "History of Texas," vol. ii., p. 213.   [2] Ibid., vol. ii., p. 228.
[3] Ibid., vol. ii., p. 257.

Matamoras in June, and obtained large quantities of ammunition from the authorities there.[1]

On November 26, 1838, Mr. Jones, Texan minister, complained to the United States Government of the continual removal of discontented Indians from Arkansas to Texas, and of their marauding war. Under instructions from the Administration of President Houston, he represented that "murders and other hostile aggressions were committed by these Indians, and that a combination is now formed between most of these tribes . . . . for the purpose of commencing a general warfare. For this object large numbers of Caddoes, Kickapoos, Choctaws, Coshatties, Cherokees, Tawacanies, and a few from several other tribes, are now collected upon the river Trinity, from which point they are preparing to assail the settlements of the whites." In November, 1838, General Rusk felt obliged to raise a force in Eastern Texas, disarm the Caddoes, numbering about 300 warriors, and force them to return to the United States.

Nevertheless, in spite of the rejection of the treaty by the Senate, and the Indian havoc on the border, President Houston, in the fall of 1838, directed Colonel Alexander Horton to run the lines he had designated in the treaty. As it was an act of arbitrary authority on the part of the Executive, and in defiance of legislative action, it was clearly null.[2]

Affairs stood thus when Lamar was inaugurated. The Hon. James Webb, Secretary of State, writing to the Texan minister at Washington, March 13, 1839, says: "The report of Major-General Rusk, together with the accompanying affidavit of Mr. Elias Vansickles, will show that the Cherokees, Delawares, Shawnees, Choctaws, Coshatties, Boluxies, and Hawanies, have all either been directly engaged in committing murders and other depredations in Texas, or are contemplating a war on the country and making preparations for it." Early in January a series of butcheries on the border called attention to the Indians. General Johnston, who was now Secretary of War, at once undertook a more thorough organization of the frontier troops, and new vigor was imparted to their operations. The prairie Indians were severely punished in a series of combats, in the most memorable of which Burleson, Moore, Bird, and Rice, were the leaders.

General Edward Burleson was born in North Carolina, in 1798. He married at seventeen, tried farming in several States, and finally removed to Texas in 1830. Though a farmer, his tastes and aptitudes were all for military life; and he was constantly called to high command in repelling the Mexicans and Indians, in which service he always acquitted himself well. He had the qualities that make a successful

---

[1] Report of the Secretary of State (Texas), November, 1839, p. 22.
[2] Ibid., November, 1839, Document A, p. 13.

partisan leader—promptness, activity, endurance, enterprise, and heroic courage. His manners and habits were simple and unpretending, yet marked by native dignity. He filled many important stations, and in 1841 was elected Vice-President of Texas.

In the active campaign under Burleson against the prairie Indians the line of communication was cut between Mexico and the Cherokees, and the noted emissary Manuel Flores was killed and his papers captured. These contained convincing proofs of the alliance between the Mexicans and Cherokees. Yoakum infers that the acquaintance between them was slight, because General Canalizo addresses Big Mush as the "Chief *Vixg Mas*," and Bowles as "Lieutenant-Colonel *Vul*," when Bowles, as war-chief, was so much more important than the civil chief. But the Mexican spelling and pronunciation of the names count for nothing as an argument ; and General Douglass, the Texan commander, styles the Cherokee chief *Colonel* Bowles. Then, too, among nations with crude ideas of civil liberty, there is no inconsistency in the supreme power being lodged in some military underling, the chief civil functionary being subordinated in fact to a lieutenant-colonel or a lieutenant-general, as the case may be.

The case, then, stands thus : The Cherokees, originally intruders, show no evidence of title prior to General Houston's treaty, except certain promises by Centralist commanders, as inducement or reward for services *against* the Texan colonists. They themselves were in no sense colonists, but a host of invading savages, who entered the Territory against the wishes and remonstrances of the inhabitants, and maintained possession by the show of force. They had no equity of long residence, for, with the exception of the pioneer band under Fields, far the greater part had immigrated since 1832, against the protests of the inhabitants. The treaty of 1836 was held void for want of authority in the Consultation, for want of verity in the "Solemn Declaration," for want of propriety, want of consideration, and overstepping of the powers delegated, in the execution of its articles. It was rejected by the Senate, the constitutional tribunal for its ratification. But, had it been valid, the steadfast friendship of the Indians was its condition, and this condition was broken as soon as made. Indeed, the treaty was used as a mere cover for warlike preparation and a secret league with the enemy. Instead of adhering to Texas, they were, at the crisis of San Jacinto, the clandestine ally of the foe, only awaiting his appearance to strike, and requiring the whole strength of Eastern Texas and the interference of the United States Army to keep them in check. Afterward, with a settled purpose of eventual war, they had continually instigated and often enacted hostilities and outrages against the whites. They now laid claim to exclusive political sovereignty over Northern and Central Texas, and prepared to maintain it by force of arms. Had the treaty been ratified with the most solemn sanctions known to international law, the failure of every consideration, the breach of every condition, and the utter disregard by the Indians of its letter and spirit, would have absolved Texas from its performance. But it was a dead letter from the beginning. The "legal and equitable title" of the Cherokees to the heart of Texas, summoned into being by General Houston, and incorporated into history by Yoakum, vanishes into thin air.

President Lamar's Administration found a host of haughty and cunning savages, occupying and claiming the best part of the republic, engaged in actual hostilities against Texas, and threatening a devastating war. Whatever might have been their original rights, the law of necessity and self-preservation must finally have led to their expulsion; but, in truth, they were treated with forbearance, though with firmness; and, if the present possessors of the soil have a title adjudicated by the sword, yet this remedy was tried only when all others failed. How the Cherokee question was met will, perhaps, be best explained in the report of the Secretary of War, November, 1839 :

The reason for the adoption of more summary measures in the settlement of the Cherokee question, than was originally intended, is found in the knowledge of the facts (displaying their settled hostility and treachery toward this Government) acquired since the mild course intended to be pursued toward them was fixed upon.

During the summer and fall of 1838 many of the inhabitants residing among and in the vicinity of the Cherokee settlements were murdered and plundered, and in one instance a family of eighteen persons, consisting of men, women, and children, was barbarously massacred by them, which, by their cunning representations, were supposed to be the acts of the Indians of the prairies and malcontent Mexican citizens; but circumstances have since been made known which leave no doubt that the Cherokees themselves were the perpetrators of these atrocities. Also, early in December last, evidence of an undoubted character was placed on file in the War Department that the Cherokees had held constant correspondence with the Mexican Government since the commencement of our revolution, and during that time had made treaties, offensive and defensive, with that Government. With a knowledge of these things, it became the duty of the Government to watch narrowly the movements of the Cherokees, and to preserve, if possible, peaceable relations with them, and to prevent the destruction of the lives and property of the citizens living in their neighborhood, until the wisdom of Congress should devise the best method of relieving them from their annoying and dangerous proximity. Accordingly, under your instructions, in the month of February last, Martin Lacy was appointed agent for the Cherokees and other tribes of that district of country, with instructions to preserve friendly relations between the Cherokees and whites until the peculiar situation of the Cherokees could be brought under the consideration of Congress.

In furtherance of these intentions Major Walters was authorized to raise two companies of six-months' men to occupy the Saline of the Neches. At this point it was thought that all intercourse might be cut off between the Cherokees and the Indians of the prairies, who were known to be hostile; and that the adoption of this measure would give protection to that portion of the frontier, and leave no pretext for attributing any depredations committed to the Indians of the prairies, while it would be no inconvenience to the Cherokees. Having raised one company, Major Walters marched to the Saline. On his arrival he was informed by Bowles, through the agent, that any attempt to establish the post in obedience to his orders would be repelled by force. Under the advice of the agent, as he conceived his force too small to make the attempt, he crossed to the west bank of the Neches and there established his post. This assertion of claim to exclusive jurisdiction could not be disregarded, when considered in connection with the abundant evidence in possession of the Department of the treacherous and unfriendly designs of that tribe and their associate bands. Colonel Burleson, who was then organizing a force on the Colorado to march against the hostile Indians on the Brazos and Trinity, was therefore ordered to direct his march lower down the country, after crossing the Brazos, so as to be in position to enter the territory claimed by the Cherokees on the shortest notice. A few days after these orders were transmitted a dispatch was received from Colonel Burleson announcing the interception of letters from General Canalizo, commander of the Central forces at Matamoras, to the chiefs of the Seminoles, Caddoes, Biloxies, Kickapoos, and to Bowles and others, with instructions for them and the plan of operations to be pursued against the Texans, which intercepted letters were at the same time forwarded to the Department.

On their reception, Colonel Burleson was instructed to raise his force to 400 men, and to march into the Cherokee district. He was advised at the same time that a volunteer force had been called for in the eastern counties to act with him. Some greater delay took place before the troops under the command of Colonel Burleson took the route for the Cherokee district than was anticipated by him, which it is scarcely necessary to mention, as no embarrassment was occasioned by it in the subsequent operations. He was not able, however, to cross the Neches until about the 14th of July; about which time the regiment of Landrum arrived from the counties of Harrison, Shelby, Sabine, and San Augustine. The regiment from Nacogdoches, which was under the command of General Rusk, had arrived some days before and taken a position near the camp of the Cherokees. The promptitude with which these movements were executed at that season of the year (early in July), and the spirit manifested on all occasions by the troops, claim the greatest praise. On the arrival of the regiments of Burleson and Landrum, the whole force was placed under the orders of Brigadier-General Douglass.

Pending these movements, Commissioners Hon. David G. Burnet, Thomas J. Rusk, J. W. Burton, James S. Mayfield, and myself, appointed at the instance of Bowles, had been engaged for several days in endeavoring to bring about an arrangement, under your instructions, on an equitable basis for the peaceable removal of the Cherokees. We had been instructed to allow a fair compensation for their improvements, to be ascertained by appraisement, and to be paid for in silver and goods before their removal. The commissioners, in several talks held with them, essayed every means to effect a friendly negotiation, but without success, and at noon on the 15th of July announced their failure.

Orders were immediately given by me to General Douglass to put the troops in motion and to march against the camp of the Cherokees, but not to attack them until they had been summoned to submit to the terms proposed by the Government for their removal, and had refused. On the arrival of the troops at their camp it was found that they had retreated from it some hours previous. Their route was taken, and in the evening they were discovered in a strong position near a Delaware village, from which they fired on the advanced guard. They were immediately attacked and beaten. The next morning, July 16th, the troops were marched in pursuit, and near the Neches another conflict ensued in which the Cherokees and their allies were again defeated and driven from the field; for the particulars of which engagements I refer you to the extracts from the official reports of the commanding general, marked 8 and 16. After the affair of the Neches the Cherokees made no stand against our troops, but fled with great precipitation from the country, thus terminating this vexed question of claims to soil and sovereignty, which our laws do not in any wise concede to any Indian tribe within the limits of the republic.

The Hon. Thomas J. Rusk and James S. Mayfield, Esq., were appointed commissioners to arrange for the removal of the Shawnees. Stipulations on the same just basis as those made to the Cherokees were agreed upon, and they have received the compensation for their improvements and have been removed in accordance with the agreement entered into between the commissioners and their chiefs.

Dr. Starr, explaining these transactions, says:

The Government at once resolved to remove them. To this end means were provided to purchase from these Indians whatever personal property they might wish to dispose of, and troops were assembled to enforce, if need be, the measures of the Government. To insure success, and at the same time avoid harshness in the character of the proceedings, General Johnston, aided by Vice-President Burnet, took personal supervision of their removal and proceeded to the Indian country with the Government forces. In a friendly but firm manner he made known to the chiefs the object of his visit. . . . The Cherokees attempted diplomacy, with a view to procrastination and ultimate resistance. Their civil chief, Big Mush, favored removal; but Bowles, a halfbreed, who had long held the first position of his tribe as war-chief, a cunning, bad man, relying upon expected aid from Mexico and the Indians of the prairies, to whom he had sent runners, prevaricated and resorted to many ingenious excuses and devices to gain time. The magnanimity of the Secretary of War indulged the chiefs for a few days, hoping to avoid bloodshed; but this lenity was probably construed into timidity by Bowles, and it soon became apparent that he must be undeceived. A peremptory demand for immediate removal was made; no response came, and our troops moved forward.

In the rough draft of the report of the commissioners, part of which is now in the writer's possession, it is stated that on the morning of the 9th of July they dispatched from Kickapoo Town Colonel McLeod, John N. Hensford, Jacob Snively, David Rusk, Colonel Len Williams, Moses L. Patton, and —— Robinson, with a communication to Bowles. The party was directed to carry a white flag and proceed to the Indian camp, fifteen or twenty miles distant ; but, " about five miles from the Indian encampment they met Bowles and twenty-one of his warriors, who came up, whooping and painted, and surrounded the messengers." While Bowles and his warriors were conversing with the messengers, six more Indians joined them and announced the advance of General Rusk's regiment—"upon which the whole party of Indians rallied around our messengers in a hostile attitude, and deliberated some time whether they would or would not kill them. The result of the interview, however, was that Bowles and his head-men would meet the Indian commissioners next day at a creek about two miles above Debard's." When the commissioners arrived at the place appointed to hold the talk, they were met by a message that Bowles could not come that day, but would meet them next day at a creek five miles from their general encampment. " At the appointed hour the commissioners proceeded to the place appointed, sending James Durst and Colonel Williams in advance to notify the Indians of their approach. On their arriving in sight Bowles and some of his men were discovered on the bank of the creek, and twenty-five warriors painted, armed with guns, war-clubs, etc., posted behind trees, with their arms in readiness." Durst rode back and informed the commissioner of these facts, and " that the whole body of Indians was posted back of a hill some three hundred yards from the place for holding the talk." Rusk's regiment was immediately ordered up, and posted about a quarter of a mile off. " The commissioners invited Bowles, Spy Back, and a Delaware who represented the Delawares, to take seats. General Johnston opened the talk." The hostile feelings of the Indians were clearly indicated in this conduct.

In the detailed report of General K. H. Douglass it appears that, on the failure of the negotiation, the whole force was put in motion, under orders from General Johnston, toward the encampment of Bowles on the Neches ; Landrum moving up the west bank. The regiments of Burleson and Rusk found the Indians about six miles beyond their abandoned village, occupying a ravine and thicket. The Texans charged these, and after a sharp skirmish drove the enemy from the field. The Indians left eighteen dead upon the field, carrying off their wounded. They abandoned their baggage and much property, ammunition, horses, cattle, and corn.

The engagement, having taken place late in the afternoon, was not resumed until the next day. On the 16th the troops took up the trail about ten o'clock, and pursued it some five miles, when the Indians were again encountered. As soon as the enemy was discovered, the following order of battle was adopted : " Burleson, with one battalion of his command, was ordered to move forward and sustain the spy company in the event the enemy made a stand; and Rusk, with one bat-

talion of his regiment, to move up and sustain in like manner Burleson
and the spy company if the enemy engaged and made a stand against
them ; one battalion of each regiment to be kept in reserve, to act as
occasion might require." This order was handsomely obeyed. Burleson,
leading two of his companies against the Indians, drove them back upon
the main body, which was strongly posted in a ravine and thicket. The
rest of the troops were brought into action in good order, and were
briskly engaged for about an hour and a half, when upon a concerted
signal a charge was made which drove the enemy from their stronghold.
The Indians retreated precipitately to a swamp and thicket in the
"bottom" of the Neches, about half a mile distant, from which they
were again driven by a general charge. About 500 Texans and 700 or
800 Indians were engaged. The loss of the former was two killed and
thirty wounded—three mortally; of the latter, about 100 killed and
wounded, according to their own report. Among those left dead on
the field was the noted war-chief Bowles, the arch-enemy of Texas,
and the central figure of the Indian conspiracy.

The army followed the Indians for a week, destroying their villages
and cornfields, capturing cattle, and killing a few warriors who were
overtaken. At last it was discovered from the trails that the organized
Cherokees and their allies had scattered, and, as no resisting force was
left, further pursuit was unavailing. The troops were immediately
turned against the Shawnees, who, disheartened by the defeat of their
brethren, submitted to the terms imposed upon them. They were
promptly returned "from whence they came"—the United States—
having been fairly paid "a full and just compensation for their improvements, crops, and all such property as they left through necessity
or choice."

"This single measure," says Dr. Starr, "relieved the frontier of the
entire east, carried forward the settlements at least one hundred miles,
and gave to our citizens permanent occupancy of a region not surpassed
in fertility and all the elements for successful agriculture by any portion of the State. The counties of Rusk, Cherokee, Anderson, Smith,
Henderson, Van Zandt, Wood, Upshur, Hunt, Kaufman, Dallas, and
others, were subsequently formed from territory which could not be
safely peopled by whites till these treacherous Indians were expelled."
The counties named above contained in 1870 a population of 116,370,
with property assessed at $15,857,191. The faults charged against the
white race in its dealings with inferior races must, in this case, be laid
at the door of the United States, if anywhere, and not of Texas. The
savages were subject to the United States, which, contrary to natural
right and treaty stipulations, permitted them to invade a weaker neighbor, and did not, on proper remonstrance, compel them to return.[1]

[1] Report of the Secretary of State of Texas, 1839, Documents A and B.

Texas communicated to the United States her intention to protect herself from the active hostilities and dangerous neighborhood of these savages by their expulsion,[1] and drove them back to the territory of the United States, without protest from that Government, which thus tacitly admitted the propriety of these transactions.

General Douglass's report of the battle of the Neches presents the odd feature of a return of thanks to the Vice-President and Secretary of War for "active exertions on the field in both engagements," and for having "behaved in such manner as reflected great credit upon themselves." Honorable mention by this gallant soldier was grateful to both the gentlemen named.

General Johnston mentioned to the writer his seeing a boy, who was shot through the face, riding about on the next day attending to his duties. His hardy life, and the dry, wholesome air, prevented any further inconvenience than the healing of the wound. General Johnston also related the following: In the main charge, as he was riding a little behind the line of battle, he encountered a young man retreating and evidently panic-stricken. He stopped him, and asked where he was going. The young man, much confused, replied that he was looking for his horse. "My young friend," said General Johnston, calmly, "you are going the wrong way. Think a moment. Rejoin your command and do your duty." The soldier hastily answered, "You are right, sir," and, turning, ran forward until he overtook his comrades. After the battle, as General Johnston was retracing his steps, he came upon a squad of wounded, and among them this youth. He dismounted and said a few kind words to him. The soldier smiled, and pointed to his wound. I asked General Johnston if he knew the man. "No," replied he. "I was glad not to know his name. There would have been a painful association with it. I avoided learning it. I only knew him as a young man who had retrieved himself."

The joy and relief of the people of Eastern Texas were very great, and General Johnston was welcomed everywhere as a public benefactor. Public dinners were tendered him, most of which he was compelled to decline because the duties of his office required his presence at the capital.

Congress passed an act, January 14, 1839, appointing five commissioners to select a site for the capital of the republic. They fixed upon its present location—a position central to the boundaries of the country, secure in all the conditions of health and growth, and marked by picturesque beauty. The Government obtained the title, laid out a city, and named it Austin, in honor of the "Father of the Republic."

To the situation there were objections not to be disregarded, except by men mindful not of themselves but of posterity only. It was an

[1] Report of the Secretary of State of Texas, letter of March 10, 1839.

outpost, within the range of the fierce Comanches, 35 miles beyond Bastrop, the extreme settlement in that direction. Houston was 200 miles to the east; San Antonio, 80 miles southwest; the Gulf, 150 miles distant, with only two intervening stations; and Red River, the only inhabited frontier, 400 miles away. General Johnston wrote, May 9, 1839, to a friend in Kentucky, " The agent has gone forth with his workmen *armed*, under the protection of a company of riflemen, to begin the new city of Austin." The commissioners, truly representing the spirit of the people, put aside all considerations of personal discomfort, privation and social isolation, the actual distribution of population, and the danger of Indian and Mexican enemies upon a long and exposed frontier, and looked only to what an accomplished destiny would require as the proper conditions of the capital of a great republic. Their wisdom has been justified by the event; but what buoyancy of hope, what confidence in the future and in themselves, must have inspired these men ! General Johnston, who was a citizen of Austin in the first month of its existence, said to the writer fifteen years afterward: " I believe the foundation of this town has no precedent in history. The Government placed itself on a frontier open to its foes, and fixed there the centre of its future dominion. By doing so it secured the desired result. Where the American has planted his foot he will not go back."

In August, 1839, the new capital was laid out ; in September the government offices were removed from Houston; on the 1st of October the officers of government resumed their duties, " as directed by law, with very little inconvenience to themselves and no derangement of the public business beyond its temporary suspension." [1] The venerable Dr. Starr, then Secretary of the Treasury, writing to the author, in 1869, says : " We there took position on the very verge of the territory in our actual possession, the Comanches disputing our advance by frequent raids into the immediate vicinity of the capital. There your father and I had our rooms in the same double log-cabin down to the time of his resignation in the spring of 1840; and, though the claims of the offices we filled allowed no relaxation, and our time and energies were taxed to the utmost extent, my memory rests upon the incidents of that period as among the most interesting reminiscences it is capable of recalling." In 1840 a stockade was placed around the capital.

It has been seen that General Johnston, while never an aggressor in his dealings with the Indians, believed in such a policy as would protect the white people and compel the savages to observe peace by severely punishing its infraction. This decisive treatment led to a short but bloody struggle with the Comanches, ending in their severe chastisement and in comparative security to the harassed frontier. In May, 1839, Charles Mason, Assistant Secretary of War, writing to Gen-

---

[1] President Lamar's message, 1839.

eral Johnston, says: "Colonel Karnes gives a deplorable account of the west; and I believe thinks, of the two, the marauding parties of the Americans are worse than the Mexicans or Indians. This, of course, will be relieved by the command of Captain Ross." While the brigands were readily put down, the prairie warriors called for more vigorous measures of repression.

The Comanches, the fiercest and most cruel of the savage tribes, take no adult male prisoners, and subject captive women to every hardship and outrage. They are not excelled in the world as horsemen, and such is their skill with the bow that they can shoot their arrows unerringly and more rapidly than a dragoon can discharge his revolver. The Lipans probably belong to the same race, but were finer men physically, and were generally at war with the Comanches. Hence they were often used by the Texans as scouts. The Tonkaways, the best warriors of all, and much feared by the other tribes, were friendly to the whites. Their chief, Placidor, had a handsome, peaceful face, and was much trusted.

The Comanches had always been the scourge of neighboring peoples. General Houston, who was extremely solicitous for the alliance of the Indian tribes, had made several treaties with them. Under his instructions General Johnston had in February, 1838, arranged the preliminaries of a treaty with them, and in May they had come into the town of Houston, under protection of a white flag, at the President's invitation, had made a treaty and received presents. Nevertheless, as they retired, still under the white flag, they killed two men in sight of the town, and while passing Gonzales carried off Bird Lockhart's daughter, a girl fourteen years old. Shortly afterward they killed a party of six men near San Antonio.

Louis P. Cooke, one of the commissioners to select the site of the capital, writing to General Johnston from the frontier, March 12, 1839, says: "The people of both the Brazos and the Colorado sections of country are in a continual state of alarm; and I am convinced that speedy relief must be had, or depopulation will necessarily soon ensue. The whole country is literally swarming with red-skins. I received an order at Bastrop, directing the organization of the militia, which I delivered to Judge Cunningham. He commenced his duty immediately. The people, so far as I have had an opportunity of observing, appear quite willing to comply with anything that may be desired of them for the defense of their frontier, or the systematizing of the militia." Though the militia organization was necessarily imperfect, yet its increased efficiency led to satisfactory results.

In the autumn of 1839 some Comanches came to San Antonio and informed Colonel Karnes that all the bands had held a grand council and wished to make a treaty. Karnes informed them, by General

Johnston's orders, that no further treaty would be made with them until they brought in all their white prisoners, and that they must not come again to San Antonio without them. Colonel Fisher, who succeeded Karnes as commandant, received the same orders, and was also told not to give presents or pay any ransom, which only encouraged the Comanches to renewed depredations. Colonel Fisher conveyed his warning to them in February, 1840, on which they agreed to bring in their prisoners, and "talk." Colonel Hugh McLeod and Colonel William G. Cooke were appointed commissioners to assist Fisher at the meeting ; and Captain Thomas Howard, with five companies of rangers, was sent to protect the commissioners.

The narrative herein given of the occurrences at San Antonio is somewhat different from, and more detailed than, any account given elsewhere, and is derived from notes of conversations held with General Johnston twenty years ago, and taken down at the time. General Johnston had resigned before the catastrophe ; but there was no caution which could have effectually prevented the result, precipitated as it was by the perfidy and ferocity of the savage character. On March 19th a party of thirty-two warriors and thirty-three women and children entered San Antonio. Major Howard arrived at the same time, rather unexpectedly to the Comanches. Twelve chiefs met the commissioners in the stone council-house ; and the "talk" was opened by the surrender of Lockhart's daughter, the only prisoner they had brought in. This poor child bore every mark of brutal treatment ; all her hair had been singed off, and she had suffered cruelly from other ill-usage.

Colonel Fisher began by reminding them that he had forbidden them to come to San Antonio without their prisoners, thirteen of whom they were holding back, and asked why they had disobeyed this positive order. They replied that they had brought in the only prisoner they had, and that the others were with other bands whom they could not control. They were told that they were known to have thirteen other prisoners ; and Miss Lockhart, being confronted with them, stated that she had within the last few days seen several of these in camp who were held back to extort a larger ransom by bringing them in one at a time. Fisher, who was a patriot and a good soldier, and likewise of a kind and generous though high temper, was moved with indignation at this conduct, and also at the treatment Miss Lockhart had endured. He reproached them with these things, and with their perfidy in former treaties, and asked if they recollected murdering two men and stealing Miss Lockhart while under a white flag. A Comanche chief arose, and, with an insolence of manner and tone scarcely conceivable by those who have not witnessed their audacity, replied, "No, we do not recollect!" He then seated himself after the Indian fashion, but again rose up and asked, with an air at once contemptuous and threatening, "How do you like our answer?" Fisher said: "I do *not* like your answer. I told you not to come here again without bringing in the prisoners. You have come against my orders. Your women and children may depart in peace, and your braves may go and tell your people to send in the prisoners. When those prisoners are returned, your chiefs here present may likewise go free. Until then we will hold you as hostages."

Besides the commissioners and the chiefs, there was present in the room a crowd of by-standers, drawn together by curiosity; and at this moment Captain Howard marched in a company of soldiers. But, if the commissioners hoped to overawe these indomitable savages by a show of force, they were mistaken. If the Comanches do not spare, neither do they ask mercy nor submit to captivity. When they had heard Fisher's speech, they strung their bows, gave the war-whoop, and sprang for the door. Howard tried to halt them, motioning them back with a gesture of his hand. The reply was a knife-thrust, stabbing him seriously, and the sentinel was also cut down. He then ordered the soldiers to fire, and immediately a desperate conflict ensued, in which all the chiefs were killed.

When the Comanches outside the building heard the war-whoop within, they at once attacked the people ; but Captain Redd's company coming up promptly, they retreated, fighting, toward a stone house, which only one of them succeeded in reaching. All the other warriors, except one renegade Mexican, were killed. Wishing to spare the warrior in the house, the commissioners sent in an Indian woman to tell him to retire peaceably. This he refused to do ; and, as he could not be safely left where he was, holes were picked in the cement roof, and burning pitch thrown in until he was forced to leave the house. He stepped out with his bow strung and arrow ready, but, before he could aim it, was shot down. Three women and two boys, who, as is their custom, took part in the fray, were also slain. One of the lads was amusing some idlers, shooting at small silver coins which rewarded his skill, when the war-whoop was raised. Quick as thought, the arrow upon his string was sent through the heart of the nearest white man— a very mild and peaceable citizen. Seven Texans were killed and eight wounded. Twenty-eight Indian women and children were detained as prisoners until the Comanches brought in their captives in exchange.

This sudden affray, ending in such a massacre, was a heavy blow to the Comanches. They made extensive preparations to avenge it, and in August 400 warriors swept down to Lavaca Bay, butchering and plundering as they went. Twenty or thirty persons were killed, and great booty taken. But the time was gone when these forays could be made with impunity. A militia as hardy, as daring, and more intelligent than themselves, was on their track. It rallied, following and attacking whenever it could overtake them. While they contended with the rangers who were harassing their flanks and rear, they were intercepted at Plum Creek by other militia, under Felix Huston and Burleson, and routed with heavy loss. In the raid they lost about eighty warriors and most of their booty.

In October severe retaliation was meted out to the Comanches by Colonel Moore, with a force of ninety Texans and twelve Lipans. He fell upon their village on the Red Fork of the Colorado, 300 miles above Austin, and killed 130 Indians and captured thirty-four, together with about 500 horses. This was the end of Comanche incursions for a long time. Finding war with the Texans so unprofitable, they turned their arms against their late allies of Mexico, and thus became to all intents the unpaid auxiliaries of Texas. Judge Love, writing June 4, 1840, says, " The situation of the frontier proves the correctness of the Indian policy." This was the general sentiment, which was strengthened by the Plum Creek victory and Moore's reprisal. Though all the combats with the Comanches herein narrated took place after General Johnston's resignation, their success was the direct result of his more efficient organization of the militia, and the active policy he had inaugurated. General Johnston resigned the War office about the 1st of March, 1840.

<hr/>

CHAPTER VIII.

1840–1845.

THE four years that General Johnston had given to the public service of Texas had been years of sacrifice, but of sacrifice that brought its own reward. His activity, which had chafed against enforced idleness, there found employment as good as the times afforded. He had gone there heavy-hearted; but, having become warmly enlisted in the cause of Texas, his nature, which could not rest satisfied with merely selfish aims, had fixed itself upon an idea that thereafter was its pole-star—the welfare and honor of his adopted State. His ambition, always well regulated, had been gratified by the general recognition of his merits and services. It was conceded that he had never failed to accomplish whatever was possible with the means at his command, and, if the results were not splendid, they were at least substantial. Such was the public confidence that all Texas looked to him as its fittest leader in case of active war with Mexico.

On the other hand, General Johnston's health had suffered, from his wound, from the privations of a frontier life in a devastated country, and from exposure to malaria and to the extreme alternations of the climate. But his rigid temperance in both food and drink preserved him from evils that proved fatal to so many of his contemporaries, and, as he was not apt to complain of minor ills, he seems to have been rather inclined to exult in the blessings he retained than to grieve over what he had lost in this respect.

When he first went to Texas he owned a handsome estate, in part devised by his wife, and in part purchased at St. Louis. But his property, though rising in value, was unproductive and had become embarrassed from neglect, from sales for reinvestments in Texas, and from the drain of a large personal expenditure. The neglect was inevitable; the reinvestments, often made rather upon feeling than judgment, had proved unprofitable; and the expenditure was a natural consequence of his position. His fortune at that time nevertheless promised, if carefully husbanded, to make him rich; and when he found it impaired and his independence in danger, he was forced to consider the propriety of retiring to private life. Some of his friends thought him heedless about money. Heedless he was not, and, no man was ever more sensitive about debt, or more scrupulous in payment; among all the many burdens that he bore during his life none was so hard as that of a debt under which for a time he labored. As I shall soon be obliged to recur to this subject, it may be just as well now to state the reasons why he was not successful in money-matters.

Men usually succeed best in the things that absorb most completely their interest and enlist most strongly their desires. The education and life of a United States officer at that time, professional but not mercenary, while it taught method, economy, and other useful rules of life, discountenanced commercial transactions of all kinds. While in that army he had been accustomed to regular pay, by which he had accurately measured his expenses; and, with no taste for luxury or display, and no avidity for fortune, he had never acquired habits of either making or saving money. The salary was meagre, but a man who possessed the means of paying all his debts was within the limits of safety and honor. Such was his education. When he was in Texas, his children had already been provided for, and he was not responsible to a family for the accumulation or even the preservation of wealth. On his own part, a certain sense of superiority to common wants, and a confidence in his ability as a soldier to supply his simple needs, took away the stimulus to lay up riches. But it was not all education or habit. He was by nature a cheerful giver, of a generous spirit, and openhanded to the distressed. He thought every man's necessity greater than his own, and was ever graceful in giving, because he loved to give better than to receive.

When it is stated that his expenditure in Texas was large, it is not intended to imply any prodigality. His salary, paid in a depreciated currency, was little more than nominal, so that he was compelled to draw upon his private resources for subsistence, and to maintain the wide though primitive hospitality entailed by his position. Though not otherwise profuse in his personal expenses, he prized and ordinarily owned handsome horses and serviceable arms ; but he valued these for use, not show, and if a friend needed them he bestowed them willingly. He felt that what he had was not his exclusively, to hoard against the proverbial "rainy day," but a trust for those who lacked; so that he was literally a man "who would share his last crust with a friend," or even with a stranger in want. In a poor and struggling country he could not refuse a demand upon his purse any more than upon his time, his toil, or his blood, if it was directly or indirectly for the public good. So, too, if a friend or a useful soldier required a blanket, a pistol, a gun, or a horse, he did not hesitate to present him his own, without anxiety as to future necessities. General Johnston was not a rare example of these traits. There were many like him; so that in after-days it came to pass that, when he was making ready to go out to battle, friends contended which should have the right to arm and equip him. In view of what has been said, it is easy to see why he should have been growing poorer, and should desire to look to his private affairs.

But, a stronger motive for leaving public life than impaired health and wealth, was a great distaste for the routine of civil office. General Johnston felt a strong impulse and entire fitness for military command. He had taken his place in the War Department with the hope of organizing an army, at the head of which he knew Lamar would place him if Mexico were invaded. But Texas, which during the republic alternated between the white heat of warlike rage and a frigid apathy, was now sinking into the latter condition. The President's continued ill-health and enforced absences from duty had so strengthened the opposition that it was now able effectually to thwart the progressive policy of the Administration, and General Johnston saw no hope of such a concentration of resources and power as would enable him to punish the insolence of Mexico. His motive for remaining in office therefore failed.

The details of party management and the ordinary conduct of American politics were something more than repugnant to him ; they were odious. In spite of much earnest solicitation, he was never a candidate for election to a civil office, and but once in his life for a military position. His correspondence is full of the efforts of those who loved or admired him to draw him into active contention for the highest places. The presidency and vice-presidency are constantly mentioned as the proper objects of his ambition, but the inducement does not seem to have dazzled him. In January, 1840, Colonel Love (a very partial friend, it is true) wrote, "The reason I have for saying you ought not to retire just now is, that your position is better than any man's in the country, and not to be abandoned hastily." And again in May, addressing him at Louisville, he says, "If you desire the presidency, your chance is good."

But he felt no inclination for the pursuit of politics. He shrank from the concessions of personal independence so often demanded ; and the fence of words and dexterity in conduct that delight the legal and political mind displeased him. He was not at all an advocate, and sought only to see facts in the cold, clear light of truth. The personalities of controversy were regarded seriously by him ; and, although forgiving of injuries, he was resentful of insult. Indeed, he did not leave office without a disagreeable occurrence, which, though adjusted for the time, probably rankled in the breast of the other party, as afterward appeared. It was reported to him by gentlemen of unimpeached veracity that General Houston had spoken of him in violent and disrespectful terms. The following correspondence ensued, upon which comment is needless:

CITY OF AUSTIN, *January* 5, 1840.

SIR: I have just been informed that on last evening, and also on this morning, you thought it necessary to use the most vituperative language with regard to me, for what cause I know not. In doing so you bore in mind the responsibility you incurred, and you will not be surprised that I inform you that *immediately* after the termination of the present session of Congress I will hold you accountable. A. SIDNEY JOHNSTON.

To General SAM HOUSTON.

Memorandum by General Johnston :

General Houston, on this note being presented by my friend the Hon. S. M. Williams, disclaimed having at any time spoken in disrespectful terms of me, and gave a list of the names of the persons present at the time specified who could be referred to. He said to Mr. Williams he would write to me to that effect. On being told so by Mr. Williams, I said he (General Houston) would not consider my note before him in writing to me, and it might be returned with the general's answer, which, if in accordance with his verbal statement, I will consider satisfactory.

HALL OF REPRESENTATIVES, *January* 7, 1840.

DEAR SIR: The conversations which I have had with you relative to expressions said to have been used by me, vituperative of the character or standing of General A. Sidney Johnston, Secretary of War, having produced a conviction on my mind that there is no hostile feeling existing with General Johnston toward me which should cause me to refrain from declarations respecting the rumors which have been said to exist, I take pleasure in assuring you in this note, as I have done on previous occasions verbally, that the reported expressions said to have been used, evenings since, *never* were used by me, nor has anything transpired within my knowledge which could change the estimation which I have always entertained of the high and honorable bearing of General Johnston and his character.

In presenting this to you, I add my authority that, if you deem proper, you may show it to the gentleman interested, as also the document inclosed. I am as ever yours, cordially and fraternally,   SAM HOUSTON.
To Hon. SAMUEL M. WILLIAMS.

Active men are apt to indulge in dreams of rural peace and quiet ; and, in General Johnston's case, this fancy was based, as has been heretofore related, upon genuine impulses and tastes. He had for some time sought to gratify this wish for the tranquillity of domestic life ; but the call of public duty had still held him to his post. The following letter, written under these emotions, will serve to explain this phase of feeling :

CITY OF AUSTIN, TEXAN REPUBLIC, *October* 24, 1839.

DEAR FRIEND : I am very sorry to learn that you have suffered so much from sickness this summer. We have, the most sagacious of us, but little ken of the future. When we went together to Galveston, you expressed great concern for me when I announced my determination to remain in Texas during the summer. Yet I have escaped unscathed, although exposed for more than forty days to the burning heat of a vertical sun, with no other comfort than camp-fare; while, with all the probabilities in your favor, you have suffered much. Such is destiny. You and your family are, I hope, in the enjoyment of health and happiness now.

I would be much pleased to hear that you will settle here. Standing alone without a relative in the country, I feel like an exile. What more should a man desire than the countenance of kind and devoted friends to sustain him ? These are mine, in the finest climate and most beautiful and lovely country that the "blazing eye" of the sun looks upon in his journey from the east to the west. Yet I am not contented. I sometimes fancy myself most miserable. I stand alone. But here I have cast my lot; and here, come weal or woe, I shall, unless Fate has otherwise decreed, spin out the thread of life.

. . . . I hope you will make up your mind to come to this fine country. You are now shivering with cold ; here all is verdant as spring. In a gallop over the hills this morning, I frequently noticed the beauty of the flowers. Here you will live ten years longer, which is a consideration with most persons. For myself, I look to the *end* with more concern than to the length of life. If that be decorous and honorable, I feel that I can encounter the grim monster unflinchingly whenever he may present himself. . . .

I do not know when I shall be able to go out of office. I hope soon ; though I cannot calculate on it with any certainty. I am anxious to see the roof of my cedar cabin peering among the live-oaks. When shall it be ? I am most anxious to see Will and Hennie ; but this cannot be yet. Present my kind regards to your family, and believe me to be very truly your friend,

A. SIDNEY JOHNSTON.
To GEORGE HANCOCK.

Under all these circumstances General Johnston felt that the time had come for him to retire from the cares of office. The foreign policy pursued protected the country from immediate invasion, the organization of the militia made it a safeguard of the Indian frontier, and the honor and independence of the country seemed for the present secure; all this, however, without any prospect of active service. Accordingly, he resigned in February, 1840.

In order to give definite shape to his purpose of establishing himself as a farmer in Texas, it was necessary for General Johnston to raise the means by selling his real estate elsewhere. After his resignation he went to Louisville for this purpose, but came back to Galveston during the summer on business. In November, 1840, he returned to Kentucky, and was absent from Texas a year. Part of the summer of 1841 he spent at Newport, Rhode Island, and other agreeable places on the Atlantic coast, in charge of some young relations.

During General Johnston's absence in December, 1841, President Lamar's health became so bad that he vacated his office, leaving the Administration in the hands of Vice-President Burnet. In the following spring the names of a good many gentlemen were canvassed in view of the presidency, but finally the struggle was narrowed down to a contest between Houston and Burnet. Judge Burnet, in spite of his exalted character, was not popular; and it soon became evident that he would be signally defeated. General Johnston had been strongly urged by his friends to remain in Texas and enter the canvass for the presidency. He was now as strongly solicited to return and make the contest "as the only man around whom all the opposition (to Houston) would be willing to rally." He was assured by his friends that he could beat Houston. General Johnston, however, in addition to other objections, would not permit his name to be used in opposition to Judge Burnet. He thought this much was due to the loyalty of friendship. In May, Love, Mayfield, and other mutual friends of Burnet and himself, tried to induce the former to withdraw in favor of General Johnston, as his cause was hopeless. General Johnston was not apprised of this negotiation until it had failed. He was not a party to it, and did not approve of the proposition; nor, indeed, did he return to Texas until after the election. This resulted in the success of General Houston by a large majority; and the only consequence of the connection of General Johnston's name with the canvass was to imbitter the animosity of the new President toward him.

On the 5th of March, 1842, General Vasquez, with a column of 700 men, appeared before San Antonio. As the force there consisted of only 100 men, under Colonel John C. Hays, it withdrew, and the town fell into the hands of the Mexicans. The enemy only remained two days, but carried off all the valuables and a number of Mexican citizens who voluntarily accompanied them. Eight days later 3,500 Texan volunteers had assembled at San Antonio under Burleson, and they impatiently demanded to be led in pursuit of the retreating foe. Their commander was equally ready to retaliate upon the Mexicans, but they were restrained by one Executive order after another, until on April 2d they were disbanded. On the 6th of April General Burleson published an address, in which he says:

I feel no hesitation in believing that if my orders had permitted me to cross the Rio Grande and retaliate upon our enemy his oft-repeated outrages, by this time 5,000 brave men would have been west of said river, inflicting a chastisement upon him that would result in an honorable peace. But President Houston's order of the 22d of March—in which he says that ' one hundred and twenty days will be necessary before we can make a move against the enemy '— was a finishing stroke to all our present prospects of redress.[1]

General Johnston was one of those who started for the rendezvous, and it was understood that Burleson concurred in the intention of the volunteers to choose him as their commander. It was probably this fact that led to their discharge by the Executive.

The President, in the first excitement of the invasion, professed an intention to pursue and punish the enemy, and hastily dispatched agents to the United States to enlist volunteers and solicit contributions of money, clothing, and provisions " for the munitions of an invading army" and "for a military chest." Some recruits, unarmed, unequipped, and unprovisioned, were pushed forward, and left without care until they were starved into mutiny, when they were discharged. The agencies resulted in nothing; and the whole conduct of the Government in these transactions was such a burlesque on administration, and had awakened such general resentment against the President, that it was considered necessary to mislead the public mind by directing its attention to false issues. The more excitable Texans were threatening a raid across the Rio Grande, and would gladly have availed themselves of General Johnston's leadership if he would have consented; indeed, all Texas looked to him as its general in case of war, and this was General Johnston's real offense with the President. While General Johnston would gladly have led an army properly authorized and organized by his Government, all his habits of thought precluded the idea of his heading an expedition not covered by a national flag. Without his denial even, such a charge would have been incredible.

Yoakum's account is as follows, being, in fact, General Houston's version of the matter:

In fact, it was reported ·that an army would be raised and march into Mexico on its own account, and that for this purpose agents, other than those appointed by the Government, were collecting troops and means in the United States. To counteract these lawless proceedings, President Houston issued his

---

[1] Yoakum, " History of Texas," vol. ii., p. 354.

proclamation on the 25th of April, declaring such agents as acting without the authority of the republic; that the war with Mexico was national, and would be conducted by the nation; and that such conduct on the part of such pretended agents was calculated to embarrass the republic.[1]

But the proclamation went on to allege that "said agents have offered commissions to gentlemen about to emigrate, as they say, by the authority of General A. Sidney Johnston, whom they represent as in command of the army of Texas, etc." Whether General Houston's own agents had transcended their authority and used General Johnston's name where he was favorably known in order to commend their cause to popular confidence, or whether impostors had availed themselves of the looseness with which the commissions had been issued to pursue a like course, or indeed whether the rumor ever had existence except in the proclamation itself, is matter of surmise merely. But this is certain: General Johnston was in no sense a party to the transactions, had given no such authority, and had countenanced no such course.

General Johnston being at the time in Galveston, the President could have ascertained the truth, but he preferred to use his high official position to deal a vindictive blow at the reputation of an honorable opponent. Though it was made clear to him that the charge was baseless and unjustifiable, he evaded all real redress. The following documents are laid before the reader in full, as the best explanation of the entire affair:

TO THE PEOPLE OF TEXAS.

GALVESTON, *May* 6, 1842.

My name having been used in a proclamation issued by the President on the 27th ult., which I conceived might be interpreted as a charge against me of the commission of illegal acts against the Government, I addressed a communication to the President, disclaiming any knowledge of the transactions, and transmitted to him a statement from Dr. Turner, upon whose representations the proclamation was issued.

These, with the reply of the President, are at the present deemed sufficient to disabuse the public mind, if an opinion has been produced prejudicial to me, and to show, if any such opinion existed, there was no foundation for it in fact.

A. SIDNEY JOHNSTON.

CITY OF GALVESTON, *May* 1, 1842.

SIR: Your proclamation, which appeared in the *Civilian* of the 27th ult., alleges that it has been represented to the President that "certain individuals are passing through various parts of the United States, and claiming to be agents of certain 'committees of vigilance and safety,' and receiving contributions and

---

[1] Yoakum, " History of Texas," vol. ii., p. 353.

aids to assist in forwarding and sustaining with suitable implements immigrants to Texas, and who represent the preparation in this republic of a warlike character as the work of such committees, and not originating with the Executive; and whereas said agents have offered commissions to gentlemen who were about to immigrate, as they say, by the authority of General A. Sidney Johnston, whom they represent as in command of the army of Texas, etc."

Now, these representations, if true—and you must have thought them true when you deemed it necessary to counteract them by a proclamation—clearly implicate me before the world, as far as the expression of your opinion goes, as in the commission of illegal acts against this Government; which being untrue, so far as regards myself (for I have given no authority, either verbally or in writing, to grant commissions, raise means, or to take any measures to raise troops in my name), your proclamation does me injustice, which I request may be remedied in such manner as may serve to relieve me from imputations so injurious. I beg leave to furnish you, in addition to my disavowal of all knowledge of the transactions alleged, the written statement of Dr. Turner, upon whose representations the proclamation was issued.

Very respectfully, your obedient servant,   A. Sidney Johnston.

To his Excellency General Sam Houston, President of the Republic of Texas.

DR. TURNER'S STATEMENT.

Texas, *April* 27, 1842.

Should any apprehension in regard to the statement that I made to the President of the Republic of Texas, concerning the appointing power as emanating from General Johnston as proffered by the Texas commissioners in the United States, have a tendency to cast blame on them, it was foreign from my design.

The only power that they seemed to convey was recommendation for promotion, and my impression was that it was by the Government authority.

Yours, respectfully,
William C. Turner.

To General A. S. Johnston.

George B. Jones, } *Witnesses.*
J. S. Sydnor,   }

Executive Department, Galveston, *May* 2, 1842.

Sir: Your note of yesterday's date, disclaiming any illegal acts against this Government, or any participation in or knowledge of the conduct of certain persons who, in the United States, are representing themselves as the agents of certain "committees of vigilance" in this country, acting in entire independency of the constituted authorities of the country, and who, it has been represented to the Executive, are offering to grant commissions in an army to be commanded by yourself, has just been handed to me.

Although my proclamation of the 27th ult. did not implicate you as being concerned in the illegal and disorganizing acts of the agents spoken of, and was intended as a rebuke to such persons alone as were concerned in them, it gives me great pleasure to learn from yourself that you had no participancy in or knowledge of such unpatriotic and mischievous acts of insubordination to the laws and constitution of our country. The letter of Dr. Turner (a copy of which you inclose me) has no relevancy to the facts so far as you may be concerned.

It will give me great pleasure in this trying crisis of our national existence to receive the coöperation of all true patriots who are capable of rendering effectual service to our common country.   Your obedient servant,

SAM HOUSTON.

To General A. S. JOHNSTON.

President Houston had adopted the policy of undoing whatever had been attempted by his predecessor. Yucatan, which, aided by the Texan navy, had employed so much of the energies of Mexico, was abandoned to the conquering sword of Santa Anna. Treaties were substituted for militia as a defense against the Indians, who had, however, been too severely punished to be troublesome for some time, and were glad of a breathing-spell. The transportation of the mails had entirely ceased; and the revenue derived from direct taxation scarcely paid the expense of collection. The volunteers, who were scouting along the Rio Grande, were disbanded; so that the frontier was now left not only without the means of protection but of warning.

The consequences of this "masterly inactivity" were soon realized, and the dream of security rudely broken by another Mexican invasion, repeating that led by Vasquez in March. On September 11th General Adrian Woll entered San Antonio with a force of 1,200 men. Congress, warned, by Vasquez's invasion, of the inefficiency of the President in providing for the public defense, had passed a bill for that purpose just before its adjournment in July, in which the President was *required* to hold an election for major-general on the 1st of September. There is no doubt that General Johnston would have been chosen almost by acclamation; but the President, not signing the bill, defeated it by what is called "a pocket-veto."

The want of an organized force and a competent commander was felt when Woll burst suddenly upon San Antonio with his *rancheros*. He captured the judge and bar of the district court, and other prisoners, fifty-three in all. The Texan minute-men made a gallant fight at the crossing of the Salado with part of Woll's force, but suffered a heavy blow in the loss of Captain Dawson and fifty-three men, who were surrounded and massacred by the Mexicans. After a week's occupation of San Antonio, Woll retreated with his prisoners and plunder unmolested, having attained the object of the expedition—"to contradict the argument, advanced by the annexationists in the United States, that the war was *in fact* at an end" (Yoakum). On November 18th General Somerville, under instructions from the Government, set out with 750 men against Mexico, on an expedition of retaliation which culminated in the disaster at Mier.

General Johnston's friends continued to urge him to reënter public life. During his absence from Texas, in 1843, he was continually assured by his correspondents that, if he would come forward for the presidency, Rusk, Burleson, and Lipscomb, then the three most prominent candidates, would unite their influence for him. Dr. Starr, in 1844, spoke of him "as the only man suited for the presidency." Clay Davis wrote that nine-tenths of the voters of the west wanted him for President. The narrowness of his private fortune forced him to refuse to enter the lists. Love, urging him strongly to return to Texas, in 1844, he replied : "My fortunes are such that I am determined to remain in Kentucky for the present, or until my affairs wear a brighter complexion, *unless the men of Texas are needed for her defense. In that event I will not, if alive, fail to be with you.*" Seventeen years later he crossed the continent to keep this promise, and sealed it with his blood.

Although General Johnston took no further part in the public affairs of Texas, yet the annexation of that country to the United States was so important an event to all its citizens that a recapitulation of the chief facts that led to it seems necessary and proper. Though not politically connected with these events, General Johnston was a deeply-interested spectator, and rendered all the aid he could in producing the result. The liberties which Texas had achieved by the sword had received the sanction of time, and were now rendered secure by the large immigration of a warlike and wealthy population. Her increased power and productive capacity gave her importance in the eyes of the great powers which, having at first stood selfishly aloof, now jealously contended for the control of the councils of the rising republic. Finally, the United States, actuated less by sympathy with Texas than by jealousy of Great Britain, offered such terms as Texas could accept; and the free republic exchanged her independence for sisterhood in the family of States from which her people had sprung.

In the United States, annexation, which seemed impending in 1836, was not accomplished until after a series of severe political struggles. The President, Mr. Tyler, and the people of the South and West, favored it strongly; but Mr. Clay, Mr. Van Buren, and the more prominent leaders of both parties, were anxious to ignore it, as a question fraught with peril to its advocates and opponents alike. Under some sort of understanding, they all declared against it. In 1844 President Tyler forwarded the plan of annexation by treaty; but the Whigs, under the discipline of Mr. Clay, voting against it, it was defeated. "The question," however, was stronger than the politicians, and at the Democratic Convention in 1844 a new man, Mr. Polk, was nominated for President, and annexation made the main issue in the canvass. His election practically settled the question, and Congress passed a joint resolution March 1, 1845, admitting Texas into the Union. Whether justly or unjustly, it was feared in Texas that the Texan Administration was averse to annexation, and would throw obstacles in its way. The popular enthusiasm, however, overrode all opposition; and, on the 23d of June, 1845, the Texan Congress consented to the terms of annexation, and Texas became a State of the American Union.

It is now necessary to recur to General Johnston's private life. During his visits to Kentucky he had formed an attachment for a young lady of great beauty, talents, and accomplishments, Miss Eliza Griffin. Miss Griffin was the sister of Captain George H. Griffin, U. S. A., an aide of General Taylor, who died in the Florida War; of Lieutenant William P. Griffin, who died in the navy; and of Dr. John S. Griffin, long an army-surgeon, but now for many years a resident of Los Angeles, California. They were all men of mark, physically, mentally, and morally. Miss Griffin was cousin to General Johnston's first wife, and the niece and ward of Mr. George Hancock, in whose family he had long enjoyed entire intimacy. There was some disparity of years, but his uncommon youthfulness of temperament and appearance diminished the inequality. After some delay, principally on account of the unsettled state of his business, they were married October 3, 1843, at Lynch's Station, near Shelbyville, Kentucky, the home of Mr. Hancock.

It may be remembered that, when General Johnston retired from the War Office, it was his intention to engage in agricultural pursuits. In partnership with a friend, he purchased the China Grove plantation, in Brazoria County, Texas. General Johnston describes it thus: "It consists of 1,500 acres of cotton-land, between 300 and 400 acres cleared, with gin, fences, etc.; and 4,128 acres of rich prairie, affording fine grass for stock, and every way more suitable for the production of sugar-cane than richer bottom-lands. The location is very convenient to the market, being about thirty-five miles from Galveston by land, and twelve miles from the navigable waters of the bay." The estate was undoubtedly valuable, but the price, nearly $16,000, was too great; and the purchase proved to be injudicious and disastrous. The purchase was originally a joint one with a personal friend, who was largely engaged both in planting and in mercantile pursuits. It was supposed that his command of credit would enable them to buy the slaves and supply the machinery requisite for a sugar-plantation. General Johnston performed his part of the contract, realizing the necessary funds by the sale of real estate at a considerable sacrifice. In the mean time his partner had become so involved as to be in danger of bankruptcy, and appealed to General Johnston to relieve him from his share of the transaction, resting his request upon the ground that he had in the first instance suggested the arrangement more with a view to General Johnston's advantage than his own, which probably was to some extent true. General Johnston, with a sense of obligation perhaps too scrupulous, at once assumed the whole responsibility, thus incurring a load of debt from which he was not freed for ten years. His friend was saved, but he sacrificed himself; the same act by which he encumbered himself depriving him of the means and credit for stocking the plantation.

The years between 1842 and 1846 were spent in the vain effort to pay for the plantation, either by its sale or by that of other property. General Johnston saw the proceeds of the sales of his farm near St. Louis and of his handsome property in Louisville gradually swallowed up by the expenses of living and the interest on his debt, without diminishing its principal. He spent a good deal of time in Kentucky, occupied with futile attempts to sell or stock his place. But these unavailing efforts hastened rather than retarded his financial ruin by putting him to additional expense. He preserved throughout, however, his independence, meeting his obligations at whatever sacrifice.

After the annexation of Texas, in 1845, his friends sought to have him appointed colonel of one of the new regiments. Love, writing in reference to the Constitutional Convention, of which he was a member, says: "There were many inquiries made for you in the most friendly manner, and almost every one expressed for you sincere friendship. There is scarcely anything Texas would not do for you if you would place yourself in a position to permit it. The general wish prevails that you may be colonel of the new regiment which it is supposed will be raised. All the prominent men have told me if you wished the office they would urge your appointment. The aspirants in Texas yield their claims to yours." General Johnston himself took no part in this application; but his friends presented his name, knowing how acceptable the appointment would be to him. When the selections were finally made by Mr. Polk, the adverse influence of General Houston, who had become Senator, was believed to have decided the President against him.

At last General Johnston, seeing no other resource, resolved to retreat to his plantation, and there, by economy and industry, to repair his broken fortunes, or at least to prevent ruinous outlay until opportunity offered to carry out his plans. But this design was deferred on the very eve of its consummation in consequence of the outbreak of the Mexican War.

Before entering on this topic a word must be said of the men whose steadfast friendship continued constant and active through these years. Among these were his kinsmen, Hancock and Preston, and Albert T. Burnley, James S. Mayfield, Judge B. C. Franklin, and others. General James Hamilton was his frequent and confidential correspondent and zealous friend. The following sentence is selected from a mass of his correspondence as supplying the key-note to the whole: "Be assured I cherish your unabated kindness and friendship to me with the most sincere and cordial gratitude." The man whom General Johnston wore nearest to his heart was Colonel James Love, of Galveston. Love was six or eight years his senior, and had been a Whig member of Congress from the mountains of Kentucky, whence he removed to Galveston soon after the Revolution of 1836. He was a man of quick perceptions, strong intellect, and powerful will. Impetuous in temper, free in the expression of his opinions, open, brave, and affectionate, he attached himself to General Johnston with all the ardor of his nature. General Johnston, writing of him in 1846 to one who did not like him, says, "I have experienced at his hands many acts of disinterested kindness, perhaps more than from any living man." This sense of obligation was increased by subsequent events, and to the day of his death General Johnston cherished the strongest attachment to this friend.

CHAPTER IX.

THE MEXICAN WAR.

As soon as the annexation of Texas was consummated, the United States Government ordered General Zachary Taylor, commanding the Southwestern Department, to put troops in motion to protect the frontier against the invasion threatened by Mexico. As Mexico not only asserted a general right to the sovereignty of Texas, but also set up a special claim to the country between the Rio Grande and the Nueces, as belonging to Tamaulipas, General Taylor, pending negotiations, established himself at Corpus Christi, near the mouth of the Nueces, where he remained until March 8, 1846.

Love, writing to General Johnston in September, 1845, says:

General Taylor has 4,000 soldiers at Corpus Christi. Six companies of Texan Rangers, under Hays, have been mustered into service. They are teaching the United States officers and soldiers how to ride. The feats of horsemanship of our frontier-men are most extraordinary. I saw one of them pick up from the ground three dollars, each fifty yards apart, at full speed, and pass under the horse's neck at a pace not much short of full speed.

On the 8th of March, 1846, General Taylor made a forward movement to Point Isabel, which commanded the mouth of the Rio Grande. In spite of a protest and some acts of hostility committed by the Mexicans, a fortification was erected opposite Matamoras, afterward known as Fort Brown. On the 12th of April General Ampudia addressed a letter to General Taylor, requiring him to withdraw to the left bank of the Nueces, or "that arms alone must decide the question." A little later, the Mexicans captured Captain Thornton and 60 men, and committed other overt acts of war; and, finally, threatened General Taylor's communications with Point Isabel, his base of supply. To reëstablish his communications and secure his base, General Taylor marched with his army to Point Isabel, leaving a small but sufficient garrison in the fort. The Mexicans opened upon the fort with a heavy bombardment, by which the commander, Major Brown, was killed ; but the garrison held out until relieved by the successes of the American troops.

General Taylor started on his return from Point Isabel, on May 7th, with 2,300 soldiers, and, on the next day at noon, found the Mexican army, under General Ampudia, drawn up on the plain of Palo Alto to dispute his advance. An engagement ensued, in which the artillery acted a conspicuous part, ending in the retreat of the Mexicans with a loss of 600 men. The American loss was nine killed and 44 wounded.

On the next day the American army again encountered the Mexicans, strongly posted in a shallow ravine called Resaca de la Palma. It was a hotly-contested fight with 6,000 Mexicans, who showed a stout courage ; but they were driven from the field with the loss of 1,000 men. The American loss was 110. The war had begun.

Volunteers were called for, and came pouring in from all quarters. The martial enthusiasm of the people of the United States was only equaled by the imbecility of the Government in its preparations for the conflict. It was a political *régime* merely, and nowise adapted to organize or carry on a successful war ; but the ability of the commanders and the splendid valor of the troops supplied all defects, and made the Mexican War an heroic episode in our annals. General Taylor, having initiated the struggle by two brilliant victories, was condemned to idleness until September by the Carthaginian policy of the Government, which failed to supply stores, equipment, and transportation.

General Taylor, early in 1846, sent the following reply to a letter from Mr. Hancock, requesting his recommendation of General Johnston as colonel of one of the new regiments :

CORPUS CHRISTI, TEXAS, *February* 8, 1846.

DEAR SIR: Your esteemed favor of the 17th ult., from Galveston, reached me on the 2d inst., and let me assure you I was much gratified at hearing from you, and should have been more so to have had the pleasure of taking you by the hand at my tent at this place.

The day after the receipt of your letter, I addressed a communication to the Secretary of War, recommending General Johnston to the favorable consideration of the President of the United States, in the strongest terms possible, for the appointment in question, which I did with a clear conscience and hearty good-will, as I know of but few as well, and none better, qualified for the situation, and can truly say that no one desires his success more than myself. At the same time, I regret to learn that General Houston is unfriendly to General Johnston, as I am disposed to believe if he exercises his influence with Mr. Polk, he will prevent his succeeding, as most, if not all, of the appointments made or selected from Texas will be on the recommendation of General Houston.

I have, this moment, received orders from Washington to take possession of the country to the Rio Grande, and establish myself on the left bank of that river, as soon as I could make the preparations necessary for doing so (which will occupy some three weeks, principally in collecting transportation, etc.); but not to cross the Rio Grande unless Mexico should make or declare war, in which case I would act on the offensive. Whether war will grow out of this movement, time must determine; but I, for one, hope that all difficulties between the two countries will be settled without an appeal to the sword; but, if war must come, I trust we will not only be prepared to meet it, but to bring it to a speedy and honorable termination. With sincere regards,

I remain, yours truly,

Z. TAYLOR.

To Mr. GEORGE HANCOCK, Louisville, Ky.

When General Taylor found that he would have to contend with a greatly superior force of Mexicans, he called for volunteers to sustain his movement. The Texan Legislature promptly passed a bill raising the quota of that State. It was proposed to confer upon the Governor, who was himself requested to take chief command, the appointment of field and staff officers ; and, under this supposition, Governor Henderson wrote, May 8th, urging General Johnston to meet him at Point Isabel, and again, through their mutual friend, Thomas F. McKinney, assuring him that he should receive rank next to himself in the Texan contingent. A messenger from General Taylor had arrived in Galveston on the 28th of April, with a request to General Johnston to join him at once. As, unfortunately, no vessel could be obtained to proceed by sea, he started on horseback, with a squad of gallant young men, for the scene of action. The time required for a land-journey brought him to Point Isabel too late for a share in the actions at Palo Alto and Resaca. His wife and infant son were left at Galveston under the care of Colonel Love and his good wife.

Leonard Groce, for many years General Johnston's friend, knowing his military ardor, promptly sent him a fine war-horse, which bore him nobly through the campaign. On the road to Point Isabel, General Johnston saw the tarantula for the first time. He had been ten years in Texas, and much in the field, without seeing one; but after passing Corpus Christi they appeared in great numbers, fiercely rearing themselves up and offering battle to an approaching horse and rider.

The Texans were gathering in hot haste at Point Isabel to defend their border, and their organization was rapidly effected. As General Johnston's extant letters give a clear and succinct account of the campaign and his connection with it, they may be allowed to tell their own story:

POINT ISABEL, *July* 10, 1846.

DEAR HANCOCK: I suppose some time since you have stricken me from the roll of your friends, and, seemingly to yourself, with great justice; but things are not all that they seem. About the time I should have written to you I felt myself obliged, by the request of the Governor, who desired to give me rank next himself in the Texas quota of four regiments, to go by land to Corpus Christi. Once away from Galveston there was no opportunity of writing until I should reach this point, and since my arrival here I have been so occupied that I have only taken time to write to my wife. The Governor was not allowed to make the appointments as he desired. The Legislature referred the appointments to the troops; so that, on my arrival here, I had to stand a canvass. I was elected by the First Regiment of Foot Riflemen of Texas colonel of the regiment, which gave me the rank I expected of the Governor. I have now encamped near this fort a regiment of ten companies, numbering 650 fine riflemen, ready and anxious to take the field. We are losing no time by waiting. They are daily undergoing instruction, which will make them the more efficient. General Taylor is making most strenuous efforts to prosecute the campaign with vigor, though I must say that his exertions are not sustained as they should be by the Government. There has been great deficiency of supply in the quartermaster's department. We understand that this will be speedily remedied both in means of transportation and equipment, and we have already seen a good many steamboats, adapted to river navigation, passing up the Rio Grande. The advanced guard has been pushed to Reynosa, about 60 miles above Matamoras, and several regiments are marching upon the same point; but, on account of the great quantity of rain which fell last month, their progress is necessarily slow. I am daily expecting my regiment to march. The troops are occupying Point Isabel, Brazos Santiago, Burita on the Rio Grande, Matamoras, and Reynosa, but we have no means of ascertaining the number—say 14,000. I visited the camp of the Louisville Legion on Brazos Island; they are a fine body of men; they are now at Burita. Rogers [1] was quite well.

Very truly, your friend,   A. SIDNEY JOHNSTON.

POINT ISABEL, TEXAS, July 30, 1846.

DEAR HANCOCK: When I last wrote to you we knew nothing of our destination. The discharge of all the Louisiana regiments created great uneasiness among the Texas regiments, lest they, being six months' men, should also be discharged. It was, however, decided otherwise. I have received orders to march, and will be en route this evening with my regiment, a fine body of riflemen, capable, from the instruction received here, of manœuvring with great rapidity and precision; and I do not doubt that they will acquire distinction. The commanding general is concentrating upon Camargo as rapidly as possible with the very limited means of transportation at his disposition; and we suppose we will march immediately upon that point. The war should be conducted directly against the city of Mexico, the seat of vitality and strength. Apart from all science, a mere animal instinct would inculcate that.

The desire of a speedy termination, as well as economy, points out Alvarado, or some place south of Vera Cruz (at the proper season), as the initial point of operation, retaining an army corps at Monterey, or on the route thence to Mexico. These movements would compel a concentration of the strength of Mexico at the capital, where a decisive engagement would soon be fought with adequate force and the war terminated. Mexico is to that republic what Paris is to France.

---

[1] Lieutenant-Colonel Jason Rogers, of the Louisville Legion—General Johnston's brother-in-law.

If Mexico falls, her dependencies fall with her. Why, then, waste a cartridge on the castle of St. Juan d'Ulloa, or throw away the public treasure in a war of marches against a country without population comparatively, as Santa Fé, Chihuahua, or California? These are portions of country which Mexico does not pretend to defend against the Indians.

Your friend,   A. SIDNEY JOHNSTON.

A letter to Hancock, written August 11th, near Camargo, informs him of the movement of the troops from Matamoras to that point, and describes what he saw in his voyage up the Rio Grande. He portrays the six days' journey up the tortuous channel of that river, its alluvial banks with their teeming crops, and the half-barbarous population gathered there, together with their houses, dress, and manners. General Johnston felt gratification that, while a good deal of sickness prevailed among the volunteers, only three men of his regiment had died; and those not with the command, but in a company of unacclimated Germans, and on detached service. The health of the regiment was due to its discipline, and to regard for sanitary precautions not usually observed.

The letter states: "General Taylor is rapidly concentrating his force at Camargo. The regular troops are nearly all there, and the volunteers are all in motion. My regiment was the first ordered to advance. The next movement, I suppose in fifteen or twenty days, will be for Monterey."

General Johnston had taken great pride in his regiment, and such were their drill and discipline that General Taylor had given him the advance of the army. A question having been raised whether the six months' volunteers were to be disbanded immediately, unless they reenlisted for an additional six months, a deputation of discontented soldiers called upon General Taylor during General Johnston's absence. The soldiers found " Old Rough and Ready," in his shirt-sleeves, shaving. They began to state their grievance, when the old general, divining the purpose of their visit, half-turned and bluntly said: "I suppose you want to go home. Well, I don't want anybody about me who don't want to stay. I wouldn't give one willing man for a dozen that wanted to go home." He went on shaving, and the committee left. The general had spoken the truth; but to some it gave offense as an implied insult, to others it afforded a pretext to get away from the hardships of a severe service. The agitators availed themselves of these circumstances ; and on General Johnston's arrival pleaded General Taylor's promise that they might go home. On finding the state of the case, General Johnston assembled the regiment and put to the vote the question of returning home or reënlistment : 318 voted to disband, and 224 to reënlist. The majority was due in great part to the German company, which had been on detached service and had suffered from sickness, and which voted as a unit 77 votes to disband. General Johnston sometimes told, as an illustration of his want of effectiveness as an orator, that after the adverse vote was given he told the men he could not believe that such was their deliberate purpose, and made an appeal to them in terms which he thought could not fail to move them, but only *one man* changed his vote. The regiment was disbanded, but a number reënlisted in the company of Captain Shivers and won distinction at Monterey.

Thus was General Johnston again compelled to see the labor of months undone in an hour, and his hopes of honorable distinction dissipated, without fault of his, by the instability of others. He was deeply chagrined; but he determined not to return home until his six months of service had expired, and he had shared with the army in the impending battle. General Taylor relieved him from the awkwardness of a subordinate position by assigning him as inspector-general to Butler's division, in which capacity he served until after the battle of Monterey.

When the regiment was disbanded, a good many young men, who subsequently reëntered the service, availed themselves of the opportunity to visit their homes, and thus enjoy a furlough at least. One of them, a brave but easy young fellow, the son of a noble Texan patriot and gentleman, useful and famous in the history and career of the republic, came back with the rest. As he joyfully hastened from the beach at Galveston to his father's house, he saw his father sternly regarding him from his front porch. When he came within speaking distance the old gentleman halted him by inquiring, in no tender tones, "What are you doing here, sir? Your six months are not up!" "The regiment is disbanded, father, and the men have gone home; and I thought I would come to see you, and then go back." "*Has General Johnston come home?*" "No, sir." "Then go back; you cannot come in here!" The son hurried back to the beach, got aboard a schooner, and was with the army in time to share with his comrades under Shivers in the attack on Monterey.

The following letter, written soon after the battle of Monterey, gives a sufficient view of the campaign, terminating in that fine feat of arms:

MONTEREY, MEXICO, *September* 28, 1846.

MY DEAR SON: My regiment was disbanded at Camargo on the 24th of August, under the construction of the law given by the War Department in reference to six months' volunteers. Soon after, General Taylor offered me the appointment of inspector-general of the field division of volunteers under Major-General Butler, which I accepted, as I was desirous of participating in the campaign which was about to commence. The army moved from Camargo, and was concentrated at Ceralvo on the 12th; and marched thence to Monterey, successively in divisions, on the 13th, 14th, and 15th, as follows: Twiggs's division on the 13th, Worth's on the 14th, and Butler's on the 15th.   They were again united at Marin on the 17th, and arrived together at the forest of St. Domingo, three miles from Monterey, on the 19th.   The 19th and 20th were passed in reconnoitring the position of the enemy's defenses and making the necessary disposition for the attack.   These arrangements having been made, and General Worth's division having occupied the gorge of the mountain above the city on the Saltillo road, the attack was commenced by General Worth, who had by his position taken all their defenses in reverse, and pressed by him on the 21st until he had captured two of their batteries.   At daylight, on the 22d, he took the height which commanded a strong work on the slope of the hill in the direction of the city, at the bishop's palace, and on Wednesday entered the city, fighting from house to house with his infantry (regulars and dismounted Texans), and along the streets with his light artillery.   In coöperation with the attack of General Worth, General Taylor ordered Twiggs's division to attack their admirably arranged and powerful system of defense at the lower end of the city; here was the means of greatest resistance.   This attack was supported by Butler's division, with the exception of the Louisville Legion, which was ordered to take a position near the mortar which was throwing shells into the main fort near the upper end of the city.   These divisions approached the city under a tremendous shower of artillery and musketry from the fort and numerous batteries, suffering great loss.   Twiggs's division attacked the batteries, and afterward filed off by the right flank toward a *téte-de-pont* (a species of fort), across a branch of the St. Juan, which runs through the city.   The Tennesseans and Mississippians of Butler's division and a few regulars under Captain Backus, moving rapidly in support, attacked the first battery or redoubt, a strong work armed with artillery and *escopetas* or muskets, and bravely carried the work (Alexander McClung, at the head of the Mississippians of his wing of the regiment, being the first to enter), driving the enemy from it with considerable loss.   The Ohio regiment, under Colonel Mitchell, entered the town more to the right, and attacked the works with great courage and spirit; but here was concentrated the fire of all their works.   From this point, or a little in the rear, the regulars had been forced back with great loss of officers and men, after keeping up the attack for more than an hour, and after having lost in killed and wounded a great number.   Having been ordered to retire, the Ohio regiment did so in tolerably good order. As it debouched from the streets of the city, believing that it was routed, the lancers of the enemy charged the Ohio regiment; but it had none of the *vim* of an American charge, and was easily repulsed with some loss to them.   On the night of the 22d the enemy abandoned their strong line of defense at the lower end of the city, and retired to the plazas and barricades.

During these operations the light artillery and howitzers kept up a terrible fire of shot and shells against the enemy.   On Wednesday, the 23d, the Texans and Mississippians were ordered to attack in the streets, and fight and work their way through the houses to the plaza.   These orders were faithfully executed, so that at night they had arrived as near the public square (plaza) at the lower part as Worth had at the upper part of the city.[1]   On Thursday the Mexicans sent in,

---

[1] It is probable, as was subsequently ascertained, that at the time mentioned Worth's command had not got beyond the Plazuela del Carne. The Mississippians and Tennesseans on the east had forced their way to within 100 yards of the Grand Plaza.

early in the morning, a white flag; and during the day articles of capitulation were agreed to, by which the city, its defenses, public property, munitions of war, etc., were surrendered to the United States army, except their army, which is allowed to march beyond designated limits, viz.: Rinconada (the main pass of the mountains), Linares, and St. Fernando—a line passing through these points being the boundary. Within these limits the armies will remain for eight weeks, or until their respective governments can be heard from. Thus, after a series of brilliant and sanguinary actions, we have possession of this beautiful and strongly-fortified place. Butler's division sustained about half the loss of the army, say 250 killed and wounded, not less and perhaps many more. General Butler was wounded in the leg, while I, finely mounted throughout, escaped with my huge frame without a scratch. I endeavored to do my duty well, and I presume my conduct will be spoken of approvingly. Send a copy of this to Henny, and my love to your uncles George and Will, and to Aunt Mary and Margaret. Your affectionate father,

A. SIDNEY JOHNSTON.

To WILLIAM PRESTON JOHNSTON.

To this clear and succinct account of the storming of Monterey I add the following interesting description of the desperate assault of the Mississippians, given me in a letter from the Hon. Jefferson Davis, who commanded them, with other incidents of the battle :

The first attack was made on Fort Taneria, a stone building covered by a low and hastily-constructed redoubt. Twiggs's brigade, led by Colonel Garland, was in advance, and after a brief attempt was moved off to the right into a cornfield. Then the Tennesseans and Mississippians moved up; the former were brought into line to the left of the redoubt, the Mississippians on their right and in front of the work. The firing commenced on our side, and was continued on that of the enemy. In the redoubt, musketeers lined the breast-work between the pieces of artillery, and on the flat roof of the Taneria musketeers in large numbers fired over the heads of the men in the redoubt. After firing a few minutes, it was perceptibly our best policy to storm the covering work, and I ordered my men to advance. Lieutenant-Colonel McClung had been the captain of the company raised in the Tombigbee Valley, and which was on the left of the centre. He sprang before it, and called out, "Tombigbee boys, follow me!" The whole regiment moved forward—that company most rapidly—and Lieutenant-Colonel McClung and Lieutenant Patterson first sprang upon the breastwork. The Mexicans ran hastily out of the redoubt to the stone building in the rear, and we pursued them so closely that I reached the gate as they were closing it, and, jumping against it, forced it open. The cry immediately went up of surrender, and the officer supposed to be in command advanced and delivered his sword.

After the capture of the redoubt and the Fort Taneria, I followed the flying Mexicans with a large part of my regiment to attack the Fort el Diablo, and when near to it was ordered back by General Quitman, the brigade commander, and directed to join our division. It was behind a long wall, and under cross-fire of the artillery of the enemy's salients on our left. I approached General Johnston, and told him I had been recalled when about to take the salient on our left, that we were uselessly exposed where we were, and said, "If not the left, then let the right salient be attacked." He answered, with his usual calm manner and quick perception, "We cannot get any orders, but if you will move your regiment to the right place the rest may follow you."

I moved off across a small stream, and through a field to the front of the *tête-de-pont*, which covered the front of the Purissima Bridge, where I met Captain Field, of the United States Infantry, with his company, and Colonel Mansfield, of the United States Engineers. Under their advice, a plan was formed for immediate attack; and, while we were making the needful dispositions, General Hamer, who had in the mean time succeeded to the command of the division, General Butler having been wounded, came up with his command and ordered me to retire. Both Colonel Mansfield and I remonstrated with him, and endeavored to show him the importance of our position. He was not convinced, but persisted in his own view. My men were withdrawn from the several posts assigned to them; but before this could be done the division had gone a considerable distance. Captain Field withdrew with me, and was killed while crossing the open field, by fire from the main fort. This field was inclosed by a high fence made of chaparral-bushes beaten down between upright posts.

My regiment (the First Mississippi) was following the movement of the division, and some distance in the rear, when the Mexican Lancers, seeing the movement from off the field of battle, came from the direction of the Black Fort, and, passing behind the column to a place where the fence was old and low, leaped into the cornfield and commenced slaughtering stragglers and wounded men. I halted my regiment, formed line to the rear, and advanced on the enemy, firing. The effect of this attack was the sudden flight of the lancers, leaving a number of killed and wounded, their leader being of the former. General Johnston afterward spoke of it as a remarkable event in war.

During the passage through the cornfield, General Hamer moved on until he reached a point where the fence was too high to be crossed by horsemen; a deep irrigating ditch was before them, and the lancers in their rear. Your father told me that the signs were such as precede a rout, and he felt that his hour was near. His only weapon was a sword I had received from the commanding officer when we burst open the gate of Fort Taneria, and received the surrender of the garrison, and which subsequently I had handed to him. Other reliance he had none. Just then, he said he heard some one giving orders in tones welcome and familiar to his ear, and saw the Mississippi Riflemen formed and advancing on the enemy. He told me he called General Hamer's attention to it.

During the assault upon the city, General Johnston accompanied Hamer's brigade of Butler's division, remaining for the most part with Colonel Mitchell's First Ohio Regiment. He was near that officer when he fell wounded in the streets of Monterey, at the point mentioned by Mr. Davis as the place where he met General Johnston, under the converging fires of the salients. General Butler was wounded at the same point. General Johnston's horse was thrice wounded; but, though he offered a conspicuous mark, he would not dismount when all the officers around him were dismounted or disabled. He told me that his reason for incurring this extraordinary hazard was, "that he was unwilling to risk separation from his horse, as his efficiency would be greatly impaired if left on foot." "There is a friend that sticketh closer than a brother."

In following the Ohio Regiment from the city, when he came to the irrigating ditch mentioned by Mr. Davis, he found it too wide for his horse to clear at a leap. He dismounted, and, forcing his horse into the canal, crossed on a narrow plank, which he fortunately found. He then discovered that his horse was swimming about, unable to clamber up the perpendicular walls of the canal. He called to his horse, who, obeying his master's voice, immediately swam to him. Leading the good steed to the lowest point in the wall, he braced himself, and, lifting him with both hands by the bit, encouraged him to come out. The spirited animal made a desperate effort, planted his forefeet on the bank, and, with his master's aid, struggled out. The docility and intelligence of his gallant charger probably saved General Johnston's life on this occasion, as he was left alone not far from the enemy.

General Joseph Hooker, who has subsequently attained eminence in the United States Army, has, in a letter dated June 3, 1875, furnished the following description and generous estimate of General Johnston's conduct at Monterey:

In approaching the subject of your letter, I may premise with stating that the episode in the battle of Monterey to which you allude was the only real service in which I had an opportunity to participate with your father. A few days before the battle of Monterey, his regiment returned to Texas, and your father accepted the appointment of inspector-general on the staff of Major-General Butler. At that time, General Taylor's army was encamped at Walnut Spring, four or five miles in advance of Monterey.

On Sunday morning, September 21, 1846, Major-General Worth was dispatched with his division to take possession of some high ground a few miles to the north of Monterey, and to threaten the city *via* the Bishop's Palace; and the following morning Garland's brigade was advanced to cover a reconnaissance in front of the city, and at the same time to create a diversion in favor of the column. Soon after they left camp, we learned that Garland's troops were engaged with the enemy, and General Butler's division was at once marched out in support. As the firing became brisk, our step was quickened, and by the most direct route. This took us within point-blank range of a formidable battery in the Black Fort, standing about a mile in front of the city in an open and level country. By a short *détour* this work might have been avoided, but, in our haste to join our comrades, we took the shortest route, and did not discover our mistake until after we had lost a number of men from the enemy's batteries. Our men became confused, and, just at that moment, the enemy's lancers were seen to sally out from behind the fort, and to make toward us.

From causes, which I do not now remember, our troops, from the moment we left the Rio Grande, had invested the enemy's lancers with a good deal of prowess; and, as soon as it was announced, all organization was lost, and our men were flying to the left in the direction of a cornfield a few hundred yards off. This was inclosed by a strong chaparral-fence, formed by piling in chaparral-branches between posts driven six or eight inches apart, and the fence itself was so substantial that it was as good as a stone-wall of corresponding height for defensive purposes against cavalry. It was no discredit to new troops, in my opinion, to break under the circumstances, as it was the first time they had been exposed to fire from artillery, where they had no opportunity to return it with their own weapons.

It was thought by myself that, when they had gotten over the fence, they would stop and receive the enemy, it being a perfectly safe place; but, when I rode up to the fence, I found that the men had not stopped, but were continuing to run to the rear through the corn. As they had nowhere thrown down the fence in climbing over it, and as it was too high to leap, I dismounted, and made into the corn on foot, when I first met your father in trying to bring and keep the men up to their work. The artillery of the enemy was playing on us all the time, and appeared to be much more severe, I suppose, than it really was. The shots made more fuss in the corn-leaves in their flight than if uninterrupted in the open air. We succeeded in keeping about 150 or 200 men up to the fence; and, after a discharge or two of our pieces, emptying many saddles, the lancers retired and gave us no further annoyance.

It was all the work of a few moments, but was long enough to satisfy me of the character of your father. It was through his agency, mainly, that our division was saved from a cruel slaughter; and the effect on the part of the army, serving on that side of the town, would have been almost, if not quite, irreparable. The coolness and magnificent presence your father displayed on this field, brief as it was, left an impression on my mind that I have never forgotten. They prepared me for the stirring accounts related to me by his companions on the Utah campaign, and for his almost godlike deeds on the field on which he fell, at Shiloh.

General Johnston probably entered the cornfield a few minutes later than General Hooker, or at a different point, as he told the writer that the rush of the men in retreat broke down a space in the fence, through which he easily rode. He alluded in complimentary terms to General (then Captain) Hooker's bearing and efforts. He cited the quickness of the Ohioans to avail themselves of the chaparral-fence as a barrier against cavalry so soon as it was pointed out to them, as a proof of the intelligence of the American soldier, even when a recruit.

Some days before the battle, there had been an unpleasant official difference, reaching high words, between General Johnston and Brigadier-General Hamer. This officer had been a member of Congress, and was appointed by President Polk, because of his political importance. He was not a soldier, but he was a very gallant and estimable gentleman. On the field he found the counsel and assistance of General Johnston of the utmost value to him. He was a man of quick and generous emotions; and, that night, after the fight was done, he came to General Johnston, and, with tears standing in his eyes, took him by both hands, and told him he wished henceforth to be accounted his friend. General Johnston felt a deep regret when Hamer, shortly after, fell a victim to the climate. It was believed that, had he survived, he would have been the next Governor of Ohio.

General Butler and General Taylor certified on General Johnston's pay-account that, as inspector-general, " he performed the duties of the office on the march from Camargo, and during the operations before Monterey, resulting in its capture, with zeal, efficiency, and courage ; and that his services were eminently important to the public interest." General Butler also complimented him in his report; and both he and General Taylor recommended him for the position of brigadier-general. But military recommendations counted for little at that time, when generals were neither born nor made, but manufactured to order. He was even refused pay by the Government for this month in which he had done such good service, on the ground that his assignment by the commanding general gave him no legal status. He was thus thrust, as it were, from the United States service. Happy and fortunate the people who can afford to cast aside as superfluous a soldier so willing and capable !

It was a great pleasure to General Johnston to meet again in this campaign his early comrade-in-arms, Jefferson Davis. Mr. Davis had resigned from the army in 1835, and retired to his plantation near Vicksburg, Mississippi, where he lived in seclusion until 1844. He then appeared in political life as presidential elector, and the next year was elected to Congress. At the breaking out of the Mexican War he was elected colonel of the First Mississippi Rifles, which under his command won great distinction at Monterey, and subsequently at Buena Vista performed exploits which made the Union ring with applause.

Colonel Davis was selected by General Taylor as one of the commissioners to negotiate for the capitulation of Monterey. In speaking of these events, Mr. Davis has frequently related a circumstance illustrative of General Johnston's character. He said that General Johnston excelled all the men he had ever known, in consistency of conduct and in equanimity and decisiveness. Every action seemed weighed beforehand. The smaller as well as the greater acts of his life showed these traits. If he met a man in the street, whose uncertainty of movement indicated that he would blunder against him, he would calmly stop and allow the man to take his choice on the path, thus avoiding the unseemly jostling that sometimes occurs. No apology is necessary for offering the following incident of the capitulation, which I have heard from the lips of both Mr. Davis and General Johnston, in the language of the former. He writes as follows :

When the commissioners had completed their labors, and written out the terms of capitulation in English and Spanish, each to be signed by both of the commanding generals, there was a manifest purpose on the part of General Ampudia to delay and to chaffer. I left him, after an unpleasant interview, with a promise on his part to give me General Taylor's draft with his (Ampudia's) signature, as early in the morning as I would call for it. At dawn of day, I mounted my horse and started for the town, about three miles distant. General Taylor, always an early riser, heard the horse's feet as I passed by his tent, and called to me, asking where I was going, then inviting me to take a cup of coffee with him. The question was answered, and the invitation declined, having already had coffee. Your father, seeing me on horseback, came from his tent to learn the cause of it, and proposed to go with me. General Taylor promptly said he wished he would do so; and, as soon as his horse could be saddled, he joined me, and we rode on for General Ampudia's headquarters, at the Grand Plaza of Monterey.

As we approached the entrance to the plaza, the flat roofs of the houses were seen to be occupied by infantry in line and under arms. The barricade across the street, behind which was artillery, showed the gunners in place, and the port-fires blazing. It may well be asked, Why should they fire on us? The only answer is, the indications were strong that they intended to do so. We were riding at a walk, and continued to advance at the same gait. Your father suggested we should raise our white handkerchiefs; and thus we rode up to the battery. Addressing the captain, I told him that I was there by appointment to meet General Ampudia, and wished to pass. He sent a soldier to the rear, with orders which we could not hear. After waiting a due time, the wish to pass was stated as before. Again the captain sent off a soldier; and a third time was this repeated, none of the soldiers returning. In this state of affairs we saw the adjutant-general of Ampudia coming on horseback. We knew that he spoke English, and that, as the chief of the commander's staff, he was aware of my appointment and could relieve us of our detention. There was a narrow space between the end of the breastwork and the wall of the house, barely sufficient for one horse to pass at a time. We were quite near to this passage, and as the adjutant-general advanced, evidently with the intention to ride through, I addressed him, stating my case, and remonstrated on the discourtesy with which we had been treated. He turned to the captain, and, speaking in Spanish, and with such rapid utterance that we could not comprehend the meaning, he put his horse in motion to go through. Quick and daring in action, as slow and mild in speech, your father said, "Had we not better keep him with us?" We squared our horses so as to prevent his passing, and told him it would much oblige us if he would accompany us to the quarters of General Ampudia. He appreciated both his necessity and our own; and, feigning great pleasure in attending us, he turned back and conducted us to his chief.

Whether the danger of being fired on was as great as it seemed, cannot be determined; but the advantage of having the well-known chief of staff exposed to any fire which should be aimed at us will be readily perceived. On this, as on many other occasions, during our long acquaintance, your father exhibited that quick perception and decision which characterize the military genius. The occasion may seem small to others; it was great to us. Together we had seen the sun rise; and the chances seemed to both, many to one, that neither of us would ever see it set. Ampudia received us with the extravagant demonstrations of his nation, ordered our horses to be taken care of, and invited us to breakfast with him. Declining the invitation, he was reminded of the object of our visit, and of the desire to avoid further delay in the exchange of the articles of capitulation. He promptly delivered the duplicate left with him, which he had signed; and we took formal leave of him.

A little incident occurred during our brief visit, which illustrates one aspect of the Mexican character. In the "Black-Hawk" campaign, your father had given me one of a pair of pistols, and it was in my holster when our horses were in charge of Ampudia's orderly. After we had ridden, perhaps a mile, out of Monterey, on our way to General Taylor's headquarters, in leaping a ditch the flap of my holster flew up, and I discovered that the pistol had been stolen while we were holding an official interview with the general-in-chief. It was the loss of a weapon valued more for its associations than its intrinsic worth, though it was the best one I ever owned; and the petty pillage was in bold contrast with the grandiloquent professions with which we had been entertained, and the rich appointments of the headquarters where we were received.

Great in small things as in large ones, measuring matters with the exactness of cold calculation, yet keenly alive to every demand of honor or of courtesy, or of personal or official obligation, General Johnston was a friend to whom one could go for counsel in the most delicate affair of life, and equally rely on where personal hazards were to be taken, or values in business transactions to be balanced. Viewing him, as I did, through the medium of ardent affection, my estimate might seem the result of bias were it not sustained by all who knew him intimately. General Z. Taylor, whose judgment of soldiers was wellnigh unerring, gave full evidence of his high appreciation of your father, both as an officer and as a man. But this is a theme on which I feel so warmly and know so much, that even to his son there is danger of my becoming prolix in speaking of your father; therefore I desist.

General Johnston told the author that his only embarrassment in accompanying Colonel Davis was his dress. By an accident at Point Isabel, his uniform had been soaked with sea-water, and shrunken out of shape; and hence his garb was, *per force*, a red-flannel shirt, blue-jean pants, a torn check coat, and a wide-awake hat; a costume picturesque, but undiplomatic. Colonel Davis made light of the difficulty, and so he waived it. This trifling circumstance led, however, to a little incident which, though in itself grotesque, increased the danger of the situation already described in Mr. Davis's letter. While they were waiting at the barricade, with the dark faces of the Mexican soldiers glowering at them over the parapet, a rabble gathered around them with menacing gestures. One old hag, darting from the mob, thrust out her skinny finger toward General Johnston and hissed out, "Tejano!" Her divination of his nationality was probably due to his uncouth attire. But such was the hatred of the lower Mexicans to the Texans, that immediately the aspect of the mob became more threatening; and they were probably saved from violence only by the opportune arrival of Ampudia's adjutant-general.

As it was evident that the capitulation and armistice closed active operations for some time, General Johnston, having no fixed rank or employment recognized by the Government, thought it right to retire until there should be some call for his services.

CHAPTER X.

PLANTATION-LIFE.

GENERAL JOHNSTON returned to Galveston in October, and was received with enthusiasm by its citizens, with whom he was always a favorite. A public dinner was tendered him, which his business, however, compelled him to decline. A question of the utmost importance to himself now came before General Johnston for decision. When he had gone to General Taylor's assistance in May, he had promised his wife, who strongly opposed his volunteering, that he would not reënlist at the expiration of his term of service without her consent. He knew that she was too high-spirited to insist on his retirement while in the line of either duty or distinction. But he had come back from the army with a heavy heart. When the war broke out, rank and celebrity seemed to await him, and the opportunity had apparently arrived when his abilities would find a fair field for their display; but his brief career had ended in disappointment. He had seen the regiment, which he had converted into a powerful engine of war, dissolved before his eyes by a stroke of the pen. Though he had done all that a man could do under the circumstances, and had won the approbation and esteem of his commanders and fellow-soldiers, his services were not such as his Government chose to acknowledge. It was almost an avowed policy to confer military command as the reward of political activity; and party notables, transformed into generals and accompanied by special correspondents for the manufacture of glory, became the centres of faction and the ephemeral heroes of the press. Such methods and appliances were not only discouraging to merit and distasteful to real soldiers, but, detected at last by the newspapers and people, recoiled on the pretenders. Still, for the time, confounding spurious and genuine reputation, they repelled many good soldiers from the service.

General Johnston was not without sufficient influence to have arrested the attention of the Administration and enforced some sort of recognition of his claims; but such a course of procedure was altogether foreign to his nature and principles, and rank or power thus attained would have afforded him no gratification. He valued these as the symbols of accorded merit and the opportunity of more useful services. His inclination was to return to the army as a volunteer, and do whatever work came to his hand. It was the natural desire of a professional soldier, unwilling to rust while others mingled in the fray. On the other hand, he was no mere military adventurer, and there was no call of patriotic duty upon him when there was an excess of soldiers impatient for the same service, and a Government that did not want his sword. His wife, moreover, insisted upon a fulfillment of his promise not to rejoin the army against her consent. Untrammeled, he would probably have followed professional instincts and returned to the field; but the claims of his family upon him were very strong, and he finally determined to yield to the wishes of his wife, abandon the military profession forever, and enter upon the peaceful pursuits of agriculture. This step was not taken without a severe mental struggle; but, when once taken, all the force of a resolute will was exerted to banish vain regrets, and conform his mental habits to the mode of life adopted.

The author takes pleasure, as an act of gratitude and of filial duty, in recording an instance of General Johnston's self-abnegation and generosity. As tenant by the courtesy, he possessed a life-estate in the property inherited from his first wife by her children. Considering the avails not more than sufficient for their education, maintenance, and start in life, he divested himself of his life-estate, and surrendered it for the benefit of these children.

With the small means now at his command he bought the simple furniture, utensils, and supplies, required in the humble home to which he was retiring, and such stock, farm-implements, and seed, as were absolutely necessary. His housekeeping was in a style as primitive as any of the pioneers. A double log-cabin, covered with clapboards, and fronted with a wide porch, gave a rude shelter; and the pine tables, hickory chairs, and other household effects, might have suited a camp better than a permanent establishment. Such as they were, they sufficed for his wants.

The China Grove plantation, to which he removed, was situated partly in the alluvial bottom-lands of Oyster Creek, a stream nearly parallel with the Brazos River, and partly in the flat and rather sandy prairie that stretched away toward Galveston Bay. Three or four hundred acres, constituting "the plantation" proper, had been cleared of the dense timber and undergrowth of the primeval forest, which still shaded nearly a thousand acres more; while toward the south and east a square league of prairie, waving with the luxuriant grasses of the coast-lands, afforded ample pasture for herds of cattle which ranged at will. A belt of thick woods, eight or ten miles wide, almost pathless, filled with all manner of wild beasts and game, thick set with jungle, and concealing miasmatic swamps caused by the annual overflow of the river, reached almost to the doors. A fever-breeding malaria exhaled from these marshes and crept toward the prairie, where it was met by the salt sea-breeze, which, sweeping steadily across the broad savanna, mastered it with a doubtful victory. The open friend was always gladly welcomed; the secret foe sometimes laid its poisonous finger on an unsuspecting household.

From the front porch the view extended as far as the eye could reach over a grassy plain, unbroken except by an occasional fringe or *mot* of distant timber. To a lover of Nature in all her moods, like General Johnston, this vast amphitheatre was a source of continual pleasure. Everywhere were the evidences of fertility; and Nature offered to the observant eye all the beauty that a level surface, unaided by art, could afford.

In early spring an emerald sward, embroidered with the blue lupin, the crimson phlox, the fragrant and flossy mimosa, and a thousand flowers of varied perfume and hue, invited great herds of deer to browse upon the tender grass, while the long-horned cattle, scarcely less wild, watched with startled eyes the unfrequent traveler. Innumerable flights of wild-fowl circled and settled in the shallow pools left by the winter rains. Cranes, herons, wild-geese, brants, ducks, and sea-birds, gulls, curlews, and others, made this their feeding-ground. Summer saw the tall, yellow grass waving like a sea of gold, and the transforming power of a Southern sun and moist atmosphere working the marvels of the mirage. In winter came the long rains driving slant, or the air cleared by the bracing norther, or the midnight sky lit by a distant or nearer circle of flame that marked the movement of the prairie-fire. Over all was solitude with its narrowing, strengthening influences, its lessons of self-reliance and self-denial, and its invitations to self-communion and the study of Nature.

General Johnston's family, when he settled on the China Grove plantation, consisted of his wife and infant son, a negro man and his wife, two negro boys and a girl. Of course, he did not expect to be able to work the place with this force, but merely to find shelter and food until he could either sell the land and obtain a less costly home, or secure labor sufficient to work it. He preferred this latter course, by means of which he could easily have extricated himself from debt and derived a handsome revenue. But, although, in view of the large immigration of planters to Texas, he had just grounds for believing this plan feasible, he was, from causes not necessary to enter into here, continually disappointed in his hopes. By the application of the rent to repairs he had managed to keep the plantation in tolerable order and cultivation from its purchase until his own arrival there; and now, by his personal supervision and labor, he made it a desirable home.

In this secluded spot he was buried for three years. His chief business was to make a crop of Indian-corn, for bread for his family and forage for his work-animals; a crop of cotton, for the purchase of supplies; a small crop of sugar-cane; and an ample supply of all sorts of vegetables. To these ends he gave a good deal of hard labor in the field and garden, but he did not neglect the simple but delightful recreation of the flower-garden. His house was shaded by a grove of the fragrant pride of China, and the spacious yard contained towering live-oaks, pecans, and other beautiful native forest-trees. A hedge of Cherokee rose with its snowy bloom protected the inclosure; and an ample orchard of figs and peaches furnished its fruits for the table. When General Johnston went there, he was told leeks were the only vegetable that would thrive, but he soon proved that hardly any vegetable known to American gardens would fail under ordinary care. It is true that he was careful, patient, industrious, and skillful in plant-nurture; but all this is necessary to the best success anywhere.

The frequent allusions in his correspondence to his own share in the labor of the plantation sprang from an honest pride in doing well in every part of the work he had undertaken. I remember that some years after, when he had changed his occupation, a wealthy and cultivated friend with whom we were dining very ingeniously maintained the theory that manual labor unfitted a man for the higher reaches of thought and spheres of action. "What you say," replied General Johnston, "seems very plausible, but self-love forbids me to agree with you. I have ploughed, and planted, and gathered the harvest. The spade, the hoe, the plough, and the axe, are familiar to my hands, and that not for recreation, but for bread."

He had but one near neighbor, Colonel Warren D. C. Hall, who, with his wife, rendered General Johnston's family every friendly office that kind hearts could suggest. Colonel Hall was one of Austin's colonists, and prominent in the earlier conflicts of the revolutionary struggle. He was elderly, and had not been fortunate; so that his large estate was laboring under embarrassments, from which I believe it was subsequently relieved. He was a bold, warm-hearted, hospitable planter. He and his wife were childless, but their affections went out to cheer all about them. As almost the only family that General and Mrs. Johnston saw in their years of plantation-life, this notice seems to me brief; but the record of the amenities that sweeten life are written elsewhere than in printed books.

I trust that some recollections of the earlier part of my father's stay at China Grove will not be considered an obtrusive introduction of my own personality into this memoir. But as his treatment of me illustrates not only many of his views but some of his characteristics, what might otherwise seem an unnecessary self-display will, I hope, be pardoned. Soon after establishing himself on the plantation, my father sent for me to visit him, and I spent about three months from New-Year's

(1847) there. It is proper to say that he had always treated me with a confidence and consideration proportioned not at all to my merits, nor probably even to his conception of them, but to the ideal which he set before me as worthy of imitation. His rule with children was to give them a character, that they would try to live up to it. He was an indulgent husband, father, and master. He viewed the conduct of others with charitable eye, and made their opportunities the measure of their responsibilities. While he did not expect in slaves the virtues of freemen, he incited them to well-doing by kindness, and tried hard to raise their moral tone by a ready recognition of their good traits. Few people wished or attempted to resist his authority. He had the gift of command. Though his sway was gentle, I, at least, felt that its constraint was absolute. He was no believer in the rod, or in any form of terror, which he said made cowards and liars. His appeal was always to the reason and moral nature, and was made with irresistible force and persuasiveness. His children were his companions and friends, and this without sacrifice of his dignity or of their filial relation. The sympathy was very deep and tender ; but it was accompanied by a sense of grateful obligation and the perception that they had been lifted to his moral plane, from which an unworthy act would hopelessly banish them.

When I went to Brazoria County I was a lad of sixteen, with health and strength somewhat impaired by too rapid growth, and, as my father imagined, by too much study. To remedy my defect of vigor, he set me to hunting, riding, digging, planting, and other kinds of exercise, on which I entered with the same enthusiasm I had given to books, and from which I derived great benefit in many ways.

For some months I was his companion in the labors of the farm and garden. I was allowed to rive out, sharpen, and nail on the pickets of a long line of fence, and to dig a trench a quarter of a mile long and two feet or more in width and depth, on the embankment of which I planted a hedge of the Cherokee rose. In this last venture my instructor was our Irish ditcher, named John. John, in personal appearance, might have passed for a doctor of divinity, and, barring an occasional spree, was an honest fellow, with a rich vein of Irish humor. Once having returned from a fortnight's frolic, sick, sober, and penitent, he was groaning rheumatically over his spade, when, desiring " to improve the occasion " for his benefit, I opened up a lecture on temperance and thrift. Probably not wishing to discuss delicate questions, John silenced me by this assurance: "You misconsthrue the whole matter intirely, Misther William. It is *gout* I have. I am sufferin' for another man's sins, you see. It all comes of me father drinking claret at a guinea a bottle ! "

After I left Texas my father wrote me : " Old John has greatly lamented your absence. Mr. Will is still the subject of the greatest

laudation with him. He has finished his ditch, greatly to his own delight and to my praise as a judicious farmer, and to the disgrace of
other farmers who have neglected such means of improvement, 'though
so long *stoppin' in the counthry.'"

My father encouraged me to hunt, and sometimes accompanied me.
His deliberation and steadiness of hand made him a very successful
shot; though at other times he limited his destructiveness by the needs
of the larder, and said that he was "not a true sportsman, but a mere
butcher, who hunted for meat."

There was a great variety of game in the neighborhood. Besides the
water-fowl which have been mentioned, wild-turkeys, grouse, and quail,
were plentiful ; a single shot supplied a dinner of robins or rice-birds ;
hares and squirrels were a nuisance to the crops, and there was no lack
of the larger game. On the prairie grazed long lines of deer, marshaled
like the open files of a cavalry brigade ; and in the woods a fat bear was
a frequent victim. Panthers and wild-cats were often met with. I remember my father's shooting a wild-goose feeding on the prairie at the
measured distance of 140 yards. Though shot through the liver with a
half-ounce ball, it rose and flew several hundred yards. In a healed
wound were found several long slugs, which he recognized as Canadian
in manufacture. On another occasion, seeing three wild-turkeys approaching him *en echelon*, he waited till he had them all in range, when
he fired. A twenty-pound gobbler dropped, one flew off, and the third
escaped, evidently wounded. An hour later Colonel Hall came over,
and mentioned that a wounded wild-turkey had run into his blacksmith-
shop at full speed and dropped dead. It ran half a mile after being shot
entirely through.

General Johnston took pleasure in observing the habits of animals.
He once called my attention to a woodcock, which was imitating the
actions of a wounded bird, as the lapwing does ; and, on going to the
spot from which it rose, we found its nest with the unfledged young.
We took the nest of a beautiful crested wood-duck from a hollow tree,
and hatched the eggs, seventeen in number, under a hen. The young
ducks could not be kept in confinement, but would even climb up the
perpendicular sides of a barrel. Nevertheless, with a good deal of
pains, we managed to rear four or five ; but they did not lose their
wild nature, and eventually escaped to the woods.

General Johnston brought down, at long range, an eagle, which was
threatening the poultry-yard. His wing was broken, and he was chained
to a log. Some large turkey-gobblers became very indignant at his
presence, and gave expression to their feelings by strutting around him
with uncouth antics of rage. The captive sat in silent majesty, seemingly unconscious of their existence. At last, one of these dons of the
poultry-yard, a foolhardy blusterer, went too near ; when, quick as a

flash, the eagle's talons tore his head off. My father pointed to the human analogies and obvious moral in this scene.

His clearness of mental vision and steadiness of purpose enabled General Johnston to govern his life by a few simple, general principles. With these his own life was consistent, and he wished for those he loved that their lives also should accord with the fixed standards of right. He felt the duty and necessity of walking by such lights as he had and the strength to do so; but, conscious of his fallibility, he viewed his own conduct and opinions severely, and those of others with the utmost toleration, not enforcing his views or opinions even upon his children. In dealing with the writer, he was solicitous to impress the idea that life should be conformed to the principles of virtue and right—that truth, justice, mercy, honor, the decorous and the beautiful, should, in harmony, control our thoughts and actions; but he was likewise careful that moral and intellectual growth should be, by processes of self-development, under the concurrent operation of these quickening powers, uninfluenced by his own individuality. The writer has often regretted that such was the case, as there never was a man he would rather have chosen to resemble. But General Johnston, perceiving that, though principles are eternal, opinions are modified by our surroundings, was unwilling to transmit his prejudices, and imposed upon himself great reserve of censure, especially in personal matters. In relating the variances between General Sam Houston and himself, in reply to my questions, he stated the facts clearly, but with a total absence of coloring. He used no resentful or derogatory epithets, and was always willing to cover his injuries with silence. It was the same in other cases. Petty wrongs he considered as beneath a wise man's concern, and greater ones as demanding either prompt punishment or magnanimous oblivion.

General Johnston was little disposed to take narrow or provincial views. In reply to boasts of the superiority of Southern hospitality, he was wont to resolve it into a habit, resulting from ample means and the easy gratification of a selfish want—the lack of society. He said:

The solitary planter, who gives a traveler supper and lodging, receives in return human intercourse, news from the outer world, and, perhaps, intelligent discourse. He is very well repaid. But in a dense population, crowded into a city, or on a poor soil, entertainment implies personal inconvenience and outlay of money, not compensated by companionship, the need of which is amply supplied. In the first case, provisions and house-room are cheap, and society scarce; in the second, provisions and house-room are dear, and society a drug in the market.

The intellectual pastime of chess was General Johnston's chief recreation. His correspondence contains many problems submitted to him by letter, with his solutions. He was as a chess-player admirable, not only for skill, but for the equanimity with which he met both victory and defeat. Although throughout life he was more of a thinker than a reader, yet he always had some book undergoing the processes of digestion and assimilation. His habit was to read slowly, weighing the matter of the book as he went along, and reflecting on it afterward. But, during this period, I recollect that he was accustomed to run rapidly over Euclid and other mathematical works with which he was familiar, reviving at a glance their trains of reasoning.

General Johnston read slowly, and not many books; but he thought much on what he read. His habit was to revolve what he read in every possible relation to practical life. He was familiar with Shakespeare; he enjoyed Dickens, and drew largely upon Gil Blas for illustration. He was fond of physical science, and Mrs. Somerville and Sir Charles Lyell were favorites with him. But, at the time of which I speak, his chief literary delight was a translation of Herodotus. He was the first to impress upon me the *veracity* of the Old Historian, and to point out the care with which he discriminated between what he saw, what he heard, and what he surmised or inferred.

While I was with him, a report came that his friend, Colonel Jason Rogers, commanding at Monterey, was cooped up in the Black Fort, with a small garrison—the Louisville Legion—by an overwhelming force of Mexicans, to whom he must surrender. He said to me: "They don't know Rogers, if they think he will surrender. He will hold the citadel to the last man, and then blow it up, before he will surrender. But I am glad he is there. He will beat the Mexicans, and has now a chance to win renown." Unfortunately, the Mexicans did not make the attempt.

When the battle of Buena Vista was impending, it was said that "Old Zach" had made a mistake in his movements, and would be destroyed by Santa Anna. General Johnston reviewed the campaign, explaining the reasons that made General Taylor's strategy the best under the circumstances, and confidently predicted his success. He had faith in Taylor's military capacity and soldierly qualities.

Though cut off from a participation in the exciting events of the Mexican War, General Johnston took a lively interest in the operations of the American army. His correspondence shows a full appreciation of the valor and skill of our officers and soldiers, but no very high estimate of the superintending wisdom of the Government. There is no real discrepancy between his opinion of the propriety of employing a larger attacking army against Mexico, and his own willingness at an earlier period to invade that country with a force so much inferior. The circumstances had changed. In the present case, the Mexicans were united against what they fancied was an army of subjugation; in the former instance, the Texans were to act as auxiliaries of one of the two parties into which Mexico was almost equally divided. General Johnston so rarely indulged in personal criticism that his judgment as to General Taylor will not be found the least interesting part of his letters. His reflections on the waste of war are commended to those who are used to look only at its scenic and splendid side.

General Johnston, writing in regard to a kinsman, who had volunteered to go to Mexico, says:

It is a game upon which there is, in his case, too much staked. The die, however, is cast; and, I have no doubt, he will play it out nobly. Few comprehend the ravages and perils of war. They are not to be found in the reports of the battle-field, which account for but a small portion of the waste of life or the dangers encountered. The unaccustomed life of a soldier, privations without number, and hard marches under a vertical sun, or in the chilly hours of the night, make up a bill of mortality treble that of the fiercest warfare. This was the case with the British army in the Peninsular War. It has been peculiarly so with ours in this war; and, I have no doubt, if any one would take the trouble to examine, it would be found the history of all warfare. . . .

War, like any other business, cannot progress prosperously unless with means adequate to the end. Our Government had them, but, instead of concentrating its power with the paralyzing shock of the thunderbolt on some vital point, it has wasted its momentum by breaking up the force into army corps, which, from the vast extent of the country they operate in, have in every instance been isolated and placed *en prise*, from which positions the indomitable courage of our gallant soldiers has alone extricated them. This is peculiarly the case with that noble column in possession of the Mexican capital. A foreign army so placed in our midst could never extricate itself. Our armies, whenever employed, have acquitted themselves admirably ; but, being separated, their efforts have produced no results. The simplest knowledge of mechanical power would indicate the folly of dividing our forces. But enough of this ; our officers and soldiers, notwithstanding everything opposing, have added the greatest lustre to our arms.

The following testimonial to the great abilities and solid character of the hero of Monterey and Buena Vista is inserted as one soldier's estimate of another, whom he had known under trying and widely-varying circumstances :

August 3, 1847.

DEAR PRESTON : . . . I will effect all or more than I expected in coming here, without encountering the dangers from the climate, with which the apprehensions of our friends threatened us. If by any good fortune I can obtain the capital to cultivate my plantation in sugar-cane, I feel sure that I will accumulate wealth. Like the poor, imprisoned abbé of the Castle d'If, I am sure that, in the ownership of this beautiful estate, I possess a great treasure ; but I fear I shall not be able to make it manifest to any capitalist.

Fifteen years ago yesterday we fought the Sacs and Foxes, and defeated them at Bad Axe on the Upper Mississippi. Old Zach, as lieutenant-colonel, commanded the First Regiment there. His conduct on that occasion established in my mind an unshaken confidence in his great courage and loyal devotion to his country, as well as a high opinion of his good sense and excellent judgment; but no one imagined that in that honest and faithful brain there were, even latent, those great principles of strategy which the events of last year have so splendidly illustrated. My memory now recalls the expression of the most vigorous thoughts connected with military operations, and I am convinced that he then possessed all the high powers of mind which he has lately displayed; that his capacity is no sudden endowment; that the great strategic problems solved by him have often undergone the severest scrutiny of close investigation.

These things are true of all minds which are accounted great on any subject. The vast conceptions of Hannibal, Cæsar, Napoleon, Newton, Cicero, Homer, Angelo, Wren, Davy, etc., following the analogies of Nature, were embodiments which were developed by the active and toilsome labors of the mind. Hence the confidence, energy, and readiness, when the emergency arises. They are no sudden inspirations. We tread with rapidity and confidence the path we have often traveled over, all others with tardy doubtfulness.

We hear nothing of the progress of the war. There is too much to be done with too little means. An acknowledged principle of war is that, when the line of operations is pierced or even interrupted, the army is in danger. How far this applies to the condition of things in Mexico I do not know, or from what jeopardy the heroism of our troops can extricate themselves—we believe a very great one, but who can calculate it? The glory of the American arms ought not to depend upon the hazard of the die. The United States can play a sure game. It is therefore *foolishness* to run the risks they have done from the beginning of the war. The magnitude of the object is now apparent, though it was not in the beginning. Let the means be adequate to the object, a proposition perfectly simple, and comprehended and acted upon by all who can. Let the Government in this matter imitate the conduct of men in private life. No sensible citizen believes that less than 50,000 men ought to invade by way of Vera Cruz. With a less number the operations will be *tardy and expensive.*

Your friend,
A. Sidney Johnston.

While the writer is aware that on some accounts a summary of incidents and opinions is preferable to the method by which a man's life is exhibited in his letters, yet there are also cogent reasons why in this case as much as possible of the record should be presented in General Johnston's own language. Drusus wished so to live that all his actions might be open to the eyes of all men. The subject of this memoir did so live that all the world might share his thoughts with his bosom friends. He was eminently sincere, so that the unconscious autobiography set down in his correspondence has a value above " confessions " written for the public eye. Though frank where frankness was proper, he had a certain delicacy of feeling and a proud reserve that prevented him from laying bare his private griefs. His religion was one of thankfulness, endurance, and self-restraint ; and it was alike his instinct and his philosophy to offer a cheerful front to whatever ills befell him. Hence, as the blasts of penury and disappointment blew more chill, he drew his mantle closer around a wounded breast and lifted his brow a little higher toward the sunlight ; and it may be pardoned him if he pictured to infrequent friends the bright side only of his Arcadia.

It must be borne in mind, in reading the letters that follow, that they were written under great mental strain. Those were years of a new and severe discipline of spirit. A heavy, increasing, and seemingly hopeless burden of debt taxed his energies, his pride, and his patience. He heard the sound of arms afar off, and the echoes of fame pronouncing the names of companions and rivals in arms ; but he had turned his back upon glory, and the arena where he had felt sure of success was for others—to him it was closed. Rare greetings came from old friends, and in the mighty sweep of events he was passing out of memory. His life was, in a manner, condemned to prison-bounds, and Poverty and Oblivion were the jailers. There was no escape except through solicitation, from which his soul recoiled as from the worst of humiliations. Yet he never dreamed of succumbing to poverty, privation, debt, and solitude. It was a campaign in which he might die struggling, but in which he did not intend to surrender manhood, cheerfulness, or hope.

General Johnston's strongly domestic nature found a stay in his family. His two infant boys, one born on the plantation, were a great comfort to him, delighting as he did in the company of little children ; and his wife not only bore privations, and managed her household with contentment and good-humor, but whiled away the weary hours by her resources in music and painting. If friends were few they were steadfast. Colonel Love came to see him whenever he could, and wrote often ; and General Hamilton occasionally. Colonel Samuel M. Williams wrote him, when his fortunes were lowest, to draw on his bank at Galveston according to his necessities. Hancock, Preston, Burnley, and some others, retained their interest, and manifested it as occasion offered. The letters appended present a fair record of his plantation-life and current of thought, and illustrate the facts and characteristics already mentioned. The first extract is from a letter written by General Johnston in the spring of 1847 to the author, who had recently left him :

Sid is a fine boy, grows well, and talks a great deal about brother Willie. Like all healthy children, he is considered a prodigy, physically and mentally. His mother will give you the facts sustaining this opinion, and can do it better than I can. With the exception of the loss of Newman Noggs,[1] whom no skill could save, everything continues to thrive with us ; the dairy, the piggery, the

---

[1] A horse, whose name was considered characteristic.

poultry-yard—and a well-filled poultry-yard, with no market at hand to tempt the cupidity of owners, is no contemptible thing in the opinion of a person in robust health. We have bushels of figs, and wish you were here to enjoy them. We have also a fine patch of sweet-potatoes.

A few letters are given from a large correspondence with Mr. Hancock and the writer:

CHINA GROVE, *February* 28, 1847.

DEAR HANCOCK: You have long since, I fear, condemned me for neglect, and appearances are so much against me that I would not blame you; but I had a reasonable excuse in the unremitted labor I had to encounter in repairing my farm and preparing for a crop. I may say with truth that I have scarcely taken time to rest since we came here. The plantation has quite a renovated appearance, and I hope by next winter to have it in complete reparation, with a comfortable house to live in, and everything farmer-like about it. I hoped to be able to return in the autumn in time to make you a visit, but I was detained so much later than I expected that I was compelled to come here at once and go to work. This I believed to be the best course to pursue, whether I sold the place or kept it; and I have no doubt that what I have already done would make the place sell for two thousand dollars more. You would be surprised, I think, at what I have achieved in three months with my limited means. If a good opportunity to sell occurs, I will not let it pass. . . .

The successful cultivation of the cane here is no longer a problem. Everywhere it has been tried in this neighborhood it has succeeded excellently well. The yield has been great; and the quality Mr. Kenner, I understand, says equal, if not superior, to Louisiana sugar made by the most improved means. Mr. Caldwell, fifteen miles from here, on the same kind of soil as mine (peach-land[1]), made 104 hogsheads (or thousands of pounds) of sugar, besides molasses, with sixteen hands, which is selling from eight to ten cents per pound. Sweeney has been quite as successful, and others that I have heard from.

Your kind invitation and offers to us will be long gratefully remembered. It is at the *dead* point that aid is most valued and most seldom offered; and, therefore, when it is, it ought never to be forgotten.

Writing to Mr. Hancock, October 21, 1847, General Johnston says:

We have been blessed with excellent health since we came here, and everything has prospered with us better than we had any right to anticipate. I have *cribbed* 900 bushels of corn, and will send enough cotton to market to pay all of our expenses of every kind, besides considerable repairs and improvements. This, I think, is as much as could have been expected from so small a force. I esteem it also of great importance to me to have acquired some practical knowledge as a farmer; and mine has been truly so, for I have often lent a hand in the work.

My object in coming here with a force so inadequate was to repair the dilapidations which rented property always suffers, and to keep the place until I could sell it, or make such an arrangement for the cultivation of the whole of

---

[1] The wild-peach, a kind of laurel, grows on the low ridges and drier spots of the alluvion.

the cleared land as to enable me to pay the remainder of my debt. The latter arrangement I would prefer, as I still regard this as a splendid estate, which, if possible, I would like to hold. If I had it paid for, I would be satisfied to live here with the little force I have, with the confidence of supporting myself; but it would be a pity to let so large a place lie idle, when its cultivation in sugar-cane would, without doubt, produce abundant wealth in a few years. . . .

I promised my wife last year that, if she would patiently submit to my volunteering for six months' service, I would then, if she desired, abandon military life forever. I found her, upon my return, more obstinately bent upon my withdrawal than ever; so much so that, although I told her it might result in daily labor for support, she said she would cheerfully encounter every trial rather than I should return. I therefore yielded up all the hopes and aspirations of a soldier, and with them has vanished all regret. I made no effort to obtain a post in the army, nor did I request any friend to do it; nor would I, after that, have accepted any offer. I have had the firmness to resist the most powerful impulse of Nature and education; and, no doubt, for the best, at least so far as my family is concerned.

You will oblige me by presenting my most friendly regards to General Butler. His soldierly and gallant bearing commanded the admiration of every one, and I would be glad to know that he will lead an effective force to the aid of Scott; for, truly, the situation of our army is precarious. The force to have accomplished the work given to him, promptly and economically both with regard to blood and treasure, should not have been less than 50,000 men. With that amount of force he could have controlled the resources of the country for the support of his army, and saved all further expense to his own Government after his outfit. A force so small as his present one, and so isolated in the midst of any other people than Mexicans, would never receive from home another biscuit, nor the succor of another detachment. It would be inextricably compromised. But we cannot reason with regard to Mexicans as with regard to any other people.

General Johnston wrote as follows on the 22d of March, 1848, to Mr. Hancock:

We like our residence here, although entirely secluded from the world and from all society whatever. If we lose the pleasures and sweets of society, we are free from all the drawbacks, which themselves form a numerous catalogue. Happy contentment reigns under our humble roof. We both industriously endeavor to do our part in our own sphere, and the result of our efforts is never the subject of complaint. We have been married nearly five years and the first unkind word or look has never passed between us. If this is true—and it is so, *for I have said it*—have we not sufficient indemnity for the loss of society and the absence of wealth? There are those who, not comprehending the object of life, would sneer at our humble and satisfied views of it, but experience will in the end convince. . . .

After apologizing for not accepting a kind invitation to visit his friend in Kentucky, he continues:

Our little crop will need my constant supervision, and the expense of the journey would go far toward building a comfortable residence for us. Our expense is very little, for we manage to raise almost everything we want.

We are now in the midst of spring. Everything is very beautiful around us. The grounds around our cabin are filled with China-trees in full bloom; large monthly roses, also blooming; the Cherokee-rose hedge, its dark green spangled with large white roses; the Ouasatchee, a species of acacia, "waving its yellow hair;" and the air redolent of sweets. Tell Aunt Mary I am reaping the fruits of my apprenticeship under her as a gardener; my horticultural knowledge is very respectable. We have fine strawberries and Irish potatoes, tomatoes in bloom, and many other vegetables. My corn all came up in February, and the stand is excellent and growing finely. I had a time of it to save it from the birds. "The price of *corn* is eternal vigilance" here.

In a letter of May 16, 1849, to the writer, General Johnston says:

My crops are small, but since I have become a farmer I have the gratification of success in everything I have attempted; and in gardening I have succeeded as well. We have had a great abundance of strawberries; and at this time we have a good variety of excellent vegetables—artichokes, pie-plant, fine heads of early York cabbage, squash, tomatoes, Irish potatoes, and your favorite yams of last year's crop, which we have never been without since we came here. Our cantelupes will soon be ripe, and in a short time we will have plenty of figs and watermelons.

The statistics of the poultry-yard and dairy are still more creditable to the industry and attention of your mother. She boasts of her flock of 100 turkeys, with prospects of as many more, besides swarms of chickens and ducks, and as many eggs as we want; this latter remark applies to Sid and Hancock, too. All these things, with butter and milk, and a good appetite gained by some toil, enable us to live, so far as these matters are concerned, as well as rich folk; and these are the things within the reach of the industrious poor from the St. Lawrence to San Francisco. This is the mystery which foreigners cannot unveil. They do not perceive that the well-being of our population flows from a fostering government, which does not meddle much with private pursuits, and taxes with great moderation—always excepting the municipal tyrannies of our land. The patriotism of our people is founded in the advantages derived from their institutions; hence its ardor; hence it is " a constant quantity," never short of the exigency.

General Johnston regretted deeply that distance, poverty, and the requirements of their education, separated his elder children from him. In expressing this feeling to his daughter, in 1848, he says:

It is a great disappointment to me; but we have learned to repine at nothing, believing that there is a Power that orders all things for the best—that even those things that are seemingly to our finite mental vision a chastisement are ultimately for some good beyond our ken.

In a letter dated June 10, 1849, replying to some good-humored reproaches from Mr. Edward Hobbs for not writing to him, General Johnston says:

The life of seclusion and obscurity in which I have lived accounts for your not having heard from me. On my return from Mexico after the campaign of Monterey, I found that all the proceeds of the Louisville property would scarcely suffice for the education of Will and his sister, and that it was necessary to go to work at once with small means for the support of my family. It was a question of bread. I immediately carried my resolution into effect. My own personal labor (this is no figure of speech—I don't mean head-work) was necessary in conducting my small farming operations; and I have yielded it with cheerfulness, and have thus, after three years' toil, become a rugged farmer, with good habits.

We have been away from home but about three or four times to visit a neighbor since we came here. So you see our habits conform to the humbleness of our position; and, as for correspondence, a man in my situation is not likely to be overburdened by his friends. In this "battle of life" such ammunition so aimed would be uselessly expended. A series of adverse circumstances have, with me, disappointed expectations most justly founded; and, although I am still confident of a final extrication, the effect has been to throw me beyond the sphere of motion of friends and acquaintances to a distance, I fear, at which sympathy languishes. But, as this is the result of a natural law of our organization, I do not complain. I feel satisfied that I have not deserved to forfeit their *esteem*. It ought to be held as honorable to battle with adversity with unquailing front as to lead the way to the deadly breach amid the roar of cannon and the din of mortal combat. Thus much I have said in vindication. Do not believe that silence is forgetfulness; nor that the scenes with which I am surrounded engender any but cheerful feelings, and kindly thoughts and charitable. Even the bitterness of ancient enmity is softened down or forgotten.

The writer ventures to introduce at some length a number of extracts from General Johnston's letters, touching topics connected with the education of his son. Writing with the freedom of private correspondence, it is not to be expected that the subjects discussed should be elaborately treated, and his opinions are marked rather by wisdom than novelty. Still, as the result of wide experience and deliberate, independent thought and not of borrowed lore, they are eminently characteristic, and may deserve the attention even of educators. Doubtless the same subjects may be found handled in a more skillful and striking manner in the systematic essays of professed teachers; but, nevertheless, the absolute sincerity and practical nature of his conclusions will probably give them a certain value to a large class of readers.

In a letter to Colonel William Preston, who had kindly interested himself in the education of General Johnston's children, he says:

Your letter in reference to the education of my children has received my most grateful attention. It has long been with me an object of deep solicitude. They both have superior mental endowments, which will bear all the culture that the most liberal education can bestow. . . .

With regard to a foreign education my judgment is opposed to yours. I would greatly prefer that my son should be educated in one of our own schools, and that my daughter should be educated as near her grandmother as possible. I do not wish her to cross the mountains. Your mind will at once cite our excellent wives as examples of the superiority of Eastern schools. They are only exceptions. Thousands are made worthless by them.

As I place the American people above all others, so I place their institutions. In their schools only will our children learn to comprehend the essence and spirit of those institutions in a liberal and enlightened manner, and to love and admire them. You are aware of the value, to one who looks forward to political preferment, of the great advantages to be derived from the friendships and general acquaintance formed in our public schools. Their influence is incalculable; and, if it is granted that a superior education can be had abroad, we must still claim for our own a better adaptation for this particular arena. To seek an education abroad seems to me like groping in the dark in search of those things which are here everywhere exposed to view. Acknowledged truths with us are yet subjects of doubt and investigation with them. They are ages behind us in the science of government—the well-being of the many. I know of no great man of any country who was educated away from his people. An important part of education is the study of the temper and tendencies of our own race—of the people, in units and in mass, among whom we are to act—without a knowledge of which no one need ever hope to wield power in a free country. One educated at home is recognized and received as a man of the people; he is of them; there is no disruption of those strong bonds of sympathy, without the power to arouse which the greatest mind would be impotent. Besides all this and many more reasons I could give, did I not fear to fatigue and annoy you, I oppose an instinctive dread of a foreign influence. European opinions, manners, notions, and habits differ, *in toto cœlo*, from ours; I fear he would unconsciously imbibe them. If my son could stand in the midst of any assembly in Europe and think or believe that there was present any nobler or bolder spirit than his own, I would scorn him; yet, did he not, they would deem him a fool. This illustrates the difference between them and us. Let us rear our children among equals, and let them take such eminence as genius and merit may command. We will not bow down their honest pride of manhood by placing them among acknowledged classes, where they are never *esteemed* first, whatever may be said to the contrary. I have perfect confidence in your judgment with regard to our own institutions, and have already referred William to you for your advice.

Truly, your friend,   A. SIDNEY JOHNSTON.

It may not be amiss to state here that, when General Johnston was Secretary of War of Texas in 1839, Admiral Baudin, of the French Navy, then visiting Texas on diplomatic business, was pleased to express great esteem for General Johnston, and tendered him an appointment for his son in the Polytechnic School. General Johnston, though much gratified at this mark of respect, felt constrained to decline it. He also dissuaded his son at a later date from taking an appointment at West Point, his own experience pointing to so many evils and discouragements in the career of a professional soldier in America as to render it most undesirable. He sent his son to Yale College, and wished him to travel and study in Europe, after his principles and habits were established; but circumstances prevented this. The following brief extract in regard to parental duty in the matter of education, and the dignity of labor, is from a letter to the writer :

Education in the present age is a positive right. It would be criminal in a parent to withhold it, if any sacrifice or privation on his part could procure it. In my opinion, there is no excuse in this country for neglect in this matter. If there be not ready and available means, then the parent is bound to labor for them. With a resolute heart and a right way of thinking about it, this is neither a humiliation nor a hardship; it is a labor of love. Labor does not degrade the mind of an educated man; if he has talents, they are invigorated; if he has honor, it becomes more steadfast. He regards his brawny hands as the guarantee of his independence; a view of them brings no shame to his proud heart; he sees in them nothing more than the evidence of honorable exertion. The opinions of those whose opinions are worth anything sustain him. They would intrust him with the transaction of important business, or with power, if there was need. They who affect to despise those of whom circumstances demand personal exertion, and exult in their own exemption as an evidence of their superiority, are the moths of society, who, after a few giddy gyrations, usually have their wings clipped and fall, to struggle in impotency. Their foolishness has prevented many a thoughtless, but noble, spirit from pursuing the course pointed out by duty, while their miserable fate seems to have taught but few that they ought to have despised rather than feared them.

The writer, having been selected by his comrades as the orator in a college celebration of the birthday of Washington, received the following letter of encouragement from his father. There are in it some old-fashioned lessons of patriotism that will bear revival:

BRAZORIA COUNTY, *January* 4, 1848.

I have the opportunity, my dear Will, of writing a few lines to you, and I seize it with great pleasure, as it affords me the gratification of acknowledging the receipt of your letter since you were installed as a member of the Military Institute, by which we learn that you are agreeably situated, and have been greatly honored by the good opinion of your comrades in their selection of you as their speaker for the 22d of February. It is said to be a difficult theme, on account of the immense number of speeches that have been made in commemoration of the birth of Washington ; that all has been said that can be ; that the subject is trite. The same might be said of all the most sublime virtues ; of whatever is great, good, or beautiful ; of fortitude, courage, patriotism ; but it would be no more true than the remark with regard to the birthday of Washington. Do we not see that everything in Nature, in every new light in which it is viewed, presents new beauties ? Every position gives a different light, and, as these positions are infinite, there cannot be any limit to the beauties of whatever is beautiful. It is the same in the moral world as in the physical. Does a man possess great goodness, great courage, great patriotism, the coloring of language may be so skillfully applied as to make their representation charming to the mind, although the thoughts in reference to them might be familiar to all. We all have some conception of the infinite attributes of Deity, and we are awed and delighted in the ratio of its strength; yet there are those who can so finely describe these subjects of familiar contemplation as greatly to enhance our awe, admiration, and pleasure.

The Father of his Country imbued the minds of the people with his own great qualities, and great occasions invariably draw them forth. Let the noble enthusiasm and devotion of the soldiery to the cause of the country serve for an illustration. Remember the last 22d and 23d; the day had its inspiration.[1] There is a holy inspiration in the memory of Washington's great services that would make any American willingly risk the sacrifice of his life in emulation of them. You ought not, therefore, to be discouraged. Your subject will find sympathy in the minds and hearts of your audience if they be American. . . .

Your affectionate father,
A. Sidney Johnston.

The following letters and extracts are offered without further apology :

May 9, 1848.

Neglect none of the subordinate means for the attainment of a superior knowledge of law. A limited acquaintance with mathematical science is one of those means. The course you mentioned will be sufficient; proficiency in algebra, the elements of geometry, trigonometry, and surveying, will give you the art of developing truth by the skillful use of the reasoning powers, and, besides, store your mind with a species of knowledge of daily practical utility to a lawyer. The art of reasoning employed by the mathematician is beautifully synthetic and analytic; and this method, not limited by the restrictions exacted by rigid science, but aided by the conceptions of a mind fertile in its ingenuity, must give him who employs it a decided advantage over one not so guided. It is the helm of the mind, steering it over the shortest route from the point of departure to the destination—from cause to effect.

But inasmuch as in mathematical reasoning the arguments (or proof) are furnished, the facility with which a correct conclusion is reached is determined by the skillful use of axioms and truths founded upon them. The mind, therefore, long employed in the investigation of mathematical propositions becomes impoverished in ingenuity and worldly comprehensiveness. Many moral truths, illustrations, etc., which convince the minds of men are not admitted by the mathematician, and therefore not employed. His language takes the form of his reasoning; it is stiff, rigid, exact, without ornament. His argument is sound and incontrovertible; it is a solid, granite structure, without a bunch of ivy or straggling flower to please the eye, and with its fragrance charm the senses. But the skillful speaker conjures up every fascination to hold his audience, while they listen to his reasoning and concur in its truth.

The science of law, as I understand it, consists in the reasons of the law and their applications. These reasons are not always founded in abstract justice, but are derived from the wants of society, dependent upon a multitude of causes; and the acquirement of a knowledge of the science calls into requisition the whole circle of human knowledge. The knowledge you have and what

---

[1] The battle of Buena Vista was fought February 22 and 23, 1847.

you will acquire are so many degrees in the noble profession you are about to adopt.

In your commencement, do not plunge *in medias res.* Begin at the beginning. Learn well the axioms and principles of the law as a first step; your progress afterward will be easy and pleasing. In your debating society, venture on no subject that has not been well considered beforehand, and do not be much upon your legs. Be courteous and calm, and endeavor to convince by the earnest exhibition of your argument, and do not employ personalities. Above all, do not try to show your superiority: if you have it, it will be felt and silently acknowledged; if exacted by words or bearing, it will be withheld. With the consciousness of having deserved well be content. If you deserve well, the merit of it will usually be accorded to you. But no one must try to find out what people think of actions he himself may approve. At the same time that the good opinion of those by whom we are surrounded is to be highly valued, those who fish for it usually catch minnows. Avoid in your speaking what Macaulay calls "*carmagnoles*" (puns, jests, rant, interjections); but few conditions of society admit their use.

Your own good sense, my dear son, has already suggested to you better counsel than I can give you; but it is the privilege of age to make youth suffer in that way, and you perceive I use my privilege.

Your affectionate father,

A. SIDNEY JOHNSTON.

BRAZORIA COUNTY, TEXAS, *December* 11, 1848.

MY DEAR WILL: Your last letter, giving renewed assurance of the satisfactory progress and improvement in your studies, was received with all the gratification the most solicitous parent must naturally experience for a son whose conduct has always commanded his highest respect as well as unbounded affection.

You express the determination to make great efforts, and if necessary great sacrifices, for the attainment of the first honor. While I would inculcate all the diligence compatible with good health and a full development of physical power, I would most assuredly deprecate and regret any exertion beyond that, if it endangered the loss of the one or checked the other.

You are, I hope, preparing for a long career. In that case, our experience teaches us that the powers, physical and mental, should be husbanded, or used moderately and economically; otherwise the goal can never be reached with distinction. If our experience is correct, it would be unwise to waste our strength in a first effort. The untaught pedestrian who is trained for a ten-mile race knows this; he wins his race by at no time in the course attaining the highest speed of which he is capable. What would you think of the judgment of a race-rider who would give his horse the highest speed at the start, or who, all other things being equal, would agree to carry ten pounds more than his opponent? Now, this latter view embraces your case; you have one more study than your rival. You may possibly beat him; so may the horse that carries undue weight win, but in most cases he never wins again—all his powers have been sacrificed for a single object.

Would it not be thought insane if a man should agree to give his left arm for a full knowledge of integral and differential calculus? If so, to use the language of mathematics, how much more insane would he be who would risk the loss of all his physical powers for a less object, or for *any* object! Mind and matter are dependent upon each other for effective action; if one is sick or debilitated, the other will sympathize. Cæsar with the ague whines like a sick girl. An effective mind can spare nothing from the physical organization—not even its shadow. Cultivate the mind; but with the same sedulous care cultivate the body. Learn if you can; but learn nothing at the risk—I do not say loss—at the *risk* of health. Neither wealth, nor power, nor human admiration, if gained in exchange, could compensate for its loss.

Higher honors await moderation than any qualities you may possess. "Bide your time." Study moderately; exercise moderately; eat moderately; in fine, let this be your rule. I say these things for your sister as well as yourself, for I know no difference in my feelings toward you. You are both my pride and hope. I believe I am very honest, and I would maintain my honor at the risk of my life; but I do not think there is anything else in my character worthy of imitation: your own good sense will inform you of whatever is defective; that, of course, you will avoid. So, if I give you advice not in harmony with my own course, it is to warn you off the shoals upon which my own little bark has been stranded.

My judgment is that, after you have taken your degree at Georgetown, you will be qualified to begin the study of the law. Those who do not begin early rarely succeed in law. If you like mathematics, you will like law more. Whatever of ingenuity your mind may possess will be brought into play in the solution of its entangled and difficult problems. It is often said that descriptive geometry is the poetry of mathematics; if so, its imaginings are stereotyped. The science furnishes the arguments and the imagination. Not so the law; here more is required of mind. Give my love to Henrietta.

Your affectionate father,

A. SIDNEY JOHNSTON.

Again, in the same strain, he says :

Take exercise regularly and moderately, and rest, and so of study; and you will be able to continue your exertions in the acquirement of knowledge even to old age. Infinite magnitudes may be the accretion of infinitely small increments. Great learning may be the result of the daily acquirement of small items of knowledge. Be patient, therefore, and be satisfied with moderate progress. Go to bed early; rise early; read three or four hours a day. Turn your reading over in your mind well and frequently, and be sure to talk about it with some one able to illustrate and explain it.

I have occasionally offered you a little of my experience, of which I have a large stock, purchased at high prices (which men of strong will have always to pay), to save you expense; but I doubt if it is a transferable article. It does not do to deal too much in such expenditures; the means will not hold out. Caution and reflection are a cheap and safe substitute. It is better to make a survey, and sound where you intend to dive, than buy the same information by heedlessly plunging in and breaking your head.

Every step taken by the man who would acquire fame or fortune must receive the sanction of his own judgment, unwarped by passion and unbiased by prejudice. Facts and information from friends you will find valuable; but their advice as to the use to be made of them, or as to the course you ought to pursue in any matter, is not so much to be depended upon as the result of your own reasoning. The one is often an off-hand shot; while the latter is usually a long, labored, and patient investigation. Upon this we ought early in life to learn to rely, rather than to catch up the hasty opinions of friends, which, however well meant, are not sufficiently elaborated. If, then, acting from a judgment so well guarded against extraneous influences, we should fail, there is left behind no mortification or stings of conscience, and we have only to deplore that our mental endowments have not sufficient scope. The love of approbation or the urgency of friends, generally well intended, sometimes precipitates us on a course which we have greatly to regret. Be careful, therefore, not to mistake these influences for a decision of your own judgment. I have now nearly torn this subject to tatters, and turn over the letter to your mother.

From what has been said, and from General Johnston's own utterances, it is manifest that under the humble roof of his frontier cabin a lofty philosophy made its home. Though luxuriant Nature had poured out so much of beauty upon this teeming spot, it was, nevertheless, a monotonous plain ; and ever lurking near was the insidious, fever-breeding malaria, which saps the health and strength and energies of its victims. Although General Johnston and his family did not suffer the worst consequences of a residence so near the swamp, yet when they left the plantation they were sallow, gaunt, and ague-stricken in appearance. But the causes that wore down the edge of his spirit were moral rather than physical. This was not the country-home that his fancy had portrayed when Fortune seemed ready to provide him a field and ample returns for all his energies, together with such delights and recreations as taste and culture might suggest. Gradually, too, the conviction must have forced itself upon him that he had mistaken his vocation; and that, though his occupation was endurable, and had its own stock of simple, rational pleasures, yet it was in arms alone that he found full play for all his faculties and for the exercise of his special talents. Then, too, he saw the interest on his debt steadily swelling the burden that galled his neck like an iron yoke.

Mrs. Johnston says, in one letter : "He is almost in despair, and often says he feels like a drowning man with his hands tied; but he tries to keep up his spirits." And again, writing in October, 1849, she says : "Our home is now a beautiful place, and I have become so attached to it that I shall grieve a great deal when we must leave it. Your father looks care-worn and sad. You would be astonished at the great change in him since you last saw him (April, 1847). From a fleshy, stout man he has grown quite thin, and, considering his frame, slender."

It would not have been strange if disappointment had tinged with bitterness a nature so aspiring ; but, if it was so, it took the form of an almost silent self-reproach, which accepted with stoical firmness both the consequences of his own mistakes and the hard decrees of a seemingly inexorable destiny. It is proof of the strength of his principles and the sweetness of his temper, as well as of the practical soundness of his philosophy, that he came out of this trial with a nature enlarged and ennobled. He had a great share of magnanimity; and his soul, exalted above the jealousies and littlenesses of small minds, learned in solitude to correct, in many important points, its standard of the world.

While General Johnston was planting in Brazoria County, a political revolution occurred which again changed the current of his fate. The Whig party, thoroughly vanquished by its opposition to the annexation of Texas and its adhesion to a narrow commercial policy, was seeking to rally its forces on a broader platform, under the leadership of a candidate available and uncncumbered with the weight of political disaster. Though Clay, Webster, and other political chiefs, had each a following of devoted adherents, the most obtuse felt that without some new and more popular name the fate of the Whig party was sealed; and presently attention was turned to the victor of Resaca and Monterey. General Taylor promptly and bluntly put aside the glittering temptation; but the over-astute policy of the Government in its further employment of him gave color to the popular notion that his services were to be depreciated, and perhaps, even, that himself and his army were to be sacrificed for political considerations. The prevalence of such an opinion, whether just or unjust, was at once fatal to the organization charged with such conduct, and an augury of triumph to the supposed victim. Already a popular favorite, General Taylor became a popular idol; and the evident sincerity with which he at first resisted all manifestations on his behalf swelled the tide of enthusiasm, which finally bore him into the White House over all opposition, and almost against his own protest. There is no doubt that General Taylor felt a real disquietude on account of his inexperience in political affairs, and committed himself too entirely to a clique unequal to the greatness of the situation. Had he lived, it is not improbable that his strong sense and courage would have asserted themselves by casting off the trammels of party management, and that he would have vindicated his ability in civil as in military affairs; but his presidential career was so brief as to furnish no sufficient criterion of what he might have been.

General Johnston shared in the popular sentiment that raised General Taylor to the chief magistracy, and entertained the liveliest hopes of reform as a consequence of the defeat of the old organized parties; but he contributed to it no more than his vote. It is somewhat remarkable that this was the first vote he ever cast, and I believe the only one. Officers of the United States Army formerly regarded partisanship in political struggles as indecorous; and, after his removal to Texas, his position had either been similar, or circumstances prevented the exercise of this right.

When General Taylor was elected, General Johnston's friends confidently expected his appointment to some position of trust or honor which would relieve him from his unsuitable situation. Though the legitimate use of influence would seem quite natural under the circumstances, his friends, knowing his proud sensibility, did not propose that he should employ-it, but only that he would indicate for their guidance in what direction his wishes inclined. Hancock and Burnley, who were intimate personal friends of the President, were especially zealous. General Johnston, however, looked at the matter in an unexpected light, as will be seen in the correspondence presented herewith ; so that, but for the voluntary efforts of these and other friends, and still more the personal interest of the President and his brother, Colonel Joseph P. Taylor, it is likely he would have been forgotten in the eager press of aspirants. As it was, his appointment was delayed until December, 1849. General Taylor then conferred upon him the place of paymaster in the army, a *quasi*-military office, which was permanent, with a living salary, and gave him a footing in the regular army establishment, from which he might hope, by possible promotion or transfer, to reënter the line. If General Taylor's death had not occurred so soon after, it was thought that at the first opportunity he would have effected this transfer to a position strictly military and entirely congenial. Regarding it as a probation, but as the only door to the regular army open to him, General Johnston accepted the post. For the fuller explanation of the foregoing statements, the following letters are now introduced:

BRAZORIA COUNTY, TEXAS, *December* 2, 1848.

DEAR HANCOCK: Your letter of the 10th November has been received, but not in time to answer you at Carrollton. In my reply, I hope you will not misunderstand me; but, on the contrary, always believe that I appreciate your kindness toward me.

With regard to appointments to office, I have notions of my own, which, if peculiar, should not be so. I think the President should be left free to select for himself. Heretofore, General Taylor's judgment has proved unerring in selections for services to be performed under his orders. It has been remarked that he has always found the right man when anything was to be done. Let the reform in this commence now. The scramble for office after a presidential election is well calculated to make the world doubt whether it is a mere contest for principle. It is time that this disgraceful feature of a great public event was done away with. It was not, I understand, the custom in the early history of the Government. No one presumed then to consume the valuable time of the President in setting forth the respective merits and claims of applicants for office. In truth, for some years past the President's audience-room has been but little better than an " intelligence office," where employment was sought for and could be found. Every one says it is a shameful evil. If it is, let it be changed. The announcement that the employment of congressional influence to obtain office would be considered a species of bribery fatal to the hopes of the applicant would do much to relieve the President from this clamor. It is said that this is the best method to obtain information. It is the worst. It is the way in which mere partisans and demagogues receive their reward. I do not, therefore, wish my friends to ask General Taylor for any office for me. He knows me well; and if it should not occur to him to offer me a place, I shall only think that he has selected others whom he believed better capable of promoting the public interest. This consideration, I believe, will alone guide him; and God grant that it may be always the only rule of action!

We now have a man for President who will administer the Government according to the Constitution construed in a liberal and enlightened spirit, whether the principles educed by him have been approved or condemned by one party or the other. The extremes of neither party will find any footing with his Administration. He will be as averse from the fanaticism that imposes high and oppressive tariffs as from that which, standing upon "54° 40'," bullies our rivals in trade and threatens the peace of the world; or from that which, as a rabid propagandist, preaches "the extension of the area of freedom." Attempt to conceal it as they may, a new and great party has arisen, which, like "the rod of Aaron, has swallowed up all the others." A. S. JOHNSTON.

DEAR GENERAL: Burnley informed me he had seen you; and showed me a letter the day he started for Washington, that he had just received from you, giving him the reasons why you could receive no office from General Taylor. I had some time before received one of a similar kind, and had followed your injunction "that no application should be made to General Taylor in your behalf." I was one of a committee sent by the city and county to escort the general to Louisville, and, being several days with him, had frequent and confidential talks with him. He asked kindly after you. I told him you were struggling along in Texas. He remarked that it was no place for you, and observed, "I had not been informed of my election long before I determined to do something for Johnston." I am convinced that it is not only his *wish*, but that it would give him great *pleasure*, to put you in a position that would be lucrative and honorable; and the only thing is to know *what place would be most agreeable to you*— Governor of Oregon, commissioner to run the Mexican boundary, Treasurer of the United States, *chargé* to Sardinia or Naples, Superintendent of the Mint in California, Surveyor-General of California or Missouri, or paymaster in the army. I will guarantee you will have the offer from General Taylor of whatever he may know it would be agreeable to you to accept. . . .

G. HANCOCK.

To General A. S. JOHNSTON.

Mr. Hancock further says, in a letter of April 22, 1849 :

You seem to have misapprehended me in relation to your *applying* for office. I agree with you fully that a gentleman ought not to ask for one, but in your case this never was asked of you. The President *of his own accord* expressed the determination to give you one, if you would take it, and your friends only wanted to learn from you what you preferred. However, the thing is now settled. Joe Taylor is now here, and tells me you will shortly be offered the place of paymaster in the army. . . . G. HANCOCK.

Mr. A. T. Burnley was in General Taylor's confidence, and had been selected by him as one of the proprietors of the Administration " organ." He wrote to General Johnston, on the 21st of May :

General Taylor intended to offer you the marshalship of Texas. I told him you would not have it. He said then, if Reynolds resigned, he intended to offer you the collectorship of Galveston. I told him you would not have it. " Then," said he, " I shall offer him a paymaster's place in the army." Not knowing your views as to that place, I replied, I expected you would take it; because I thought it was a good office, and wanted it offered to you. I have since ascertained that it is worth about $3,000 per annum, and is *permanent*.

In thus exchanging the life of the plantation for military service again, General Johnston had the encouragement of his wife, who now clearly perceived that, however faithfully he might perform the duties that fell to the lot of a farmer, his heart, his thoughts, and his aspirations, were in the profession to which he had been educated. But though he deliberately reëntered a military life, which he had thought closed upon him forever, it was through no arch of triumph, but by an obscure postern and along the hard and narrow path of petty and clerical routine. He saw in it the path of duty, and trod it manfully.

General Johnston, in conversation with the writer, said, in allusion to this appointment :

A good character has a solid value. I had tried to live blameless and to deserve well; and yet, at last, I found myself where I thought I was entirely forgotten. Now, do you think that if I had been a *sharp fellow*, General Taylor would have taken the trouble to hunt me up in the mud of the Brazos bottom to make a paymaster of me ?

CHAPTER XI.

PAYMASTER IN UNITED STATES ARMY.

GENERAL JOHNSTON was appointed paymaster, October 31, 1849. On the 2d of December, 1849, he wrote to the adjutant-general, accepting the appointment.[1] This office gave him the emoluments and the nominal rank of major in the United States Army ; but, in fact, the paymaster was a mere disbursing officer and nothing more, without authority or command. On the frontier of Texas, to which he was as-

---

[1] It is proper to state that General Johnston's legal rank while paymaster was major ; but it has not been thought necessary in this or subsequent chapters to change the title by which he was generally known.

signed, his duties were arduous and dangerous ; and, as has been suggested, General Johnston accepted the office because he regarded it "as a stepping-stone to service in the line." More than once he seemed on the point of attaining this end by exchange with a major of the line, but each time he was disappointed.

So much had his health been impaired by the malaria of the Brazos bottom, that, on the 8th of April, 1850, while waiting orders at Galveston, he was obliged, at the suggestion of his superior officers, to ask a little indulgence before reporting for duty. He availed himself of this to take his family to Kentucky. The pay district assigned to him included the military posts from the river Trinity to the Colorado. He selected Austin as his home on account of its healthfulness, natural beauty, pleasant society, and proximity to his district. Some of his old friends had settled there, which was another attraction. General Johnston, having placed his family in Kentucky for the summer, returned to Texas, and entered upon his duties. In September he proceeded to New Orleans for funds to pay the troops, when, notwithstanding his long experience in a Southern climate, he took the yellow fever on shipboard while returning. The fever, though sharp, was short, and yielded to his own treatment and simple remedies, detaining him, however, several weeks in Galveston. On November 13th he reported to the paymaster-general that he had completed the first payment of troops in his district.

At first his duty was to pay every four months the troops at Forts Croghan, Gates, Graham, and Belknap, and at Austin. This required a journey of about 500 miles each time, besides a visit to New Orleans for the funds requisite for each payment—between $40,000 and $50,000. He was usually assisted in the transportation of these funds by a clerk ; but these journeys were, nevertheless, periods of great solicitude to him. The route was by steamer to Galveston, thence by steamboat to Houston, and thence by stage, a distance of 185 miles, to Austin ; and the journey was continued day and night for about a week. In addition to perils of the sea and yellow fever, the stage-road had its dangers. Passing through the boggy Brazos bottom, through wide post-oak woods, and across broad tracts of sparsely-settled prairie, there was considerable danger of robbery, and greater still from upsets which several times happened. The money was in gold and silver coin packed in a small iron chest, and always placed between the feet of its guardians, who watched in turn from New Orleans to Austin. This exhausting vigilance was happily rewarded by exemption from loss or serious accident. In 1851 General Johnston was obliged to visit New Orleans in May, in June, and in August, to obtain extra funds to pay off the Texas volunteers of 1848-'49. This work, which required great care and circumspection to protect both the Government and the soldier, was completed that fall. In the autumn of 1852 he was enabled to discontinue his harassing visits to New Orleans by arranging for the sale of drafts in Austin, which he had been unable to do before.

General Johnston's pay district was gradually altered and enlarged in consequence of the movements of troops, until finally it embraced Forts Belknap, Chadbourne, and McKavitt, and required a journey of 695 miles for each payment. In 1854 payments were ordered to be made every two months, thus compelling the paymaster to travel annually nearly 4,200 miles. Each journey took more than a month, of which only four or five days were spent at the posts, which were occupied in paying the soldiers. General Johnston, with his clerk, negro driver John, and negro cook Randolph, rode in a covered ambulance drawn by four mules, and carried his money-chest and baggage in the same conveyance. He was accompanied by a forage-wagon and an escort of dragoons, varying from four to twelve in number, under charge of a non-commssioned officer. The escort was usually too small to guard against outlaws or Indians who constantly menaced that region ; and his escape from attack was due in great measure to his extreme wariness, and to the observance of every possible precaution against surprise.

General Johnston says, in a letter written in 1850 :

Scarcely a day has passed since my arrival that a depredation has not been committed. They (the Indians) have driven off nearly all the horses and mules from the Cibolo, Salado, and other portions of of the frontier. Parties are sent in pursuit, but without success. To give peace to the frontier, and that perfect security so necessary to the happiness and prosperity of communities, the troops ought to act offensively and carry the war to the homes of the enemy.

The continued movement of these marauding parties on the border for the next five years made each of General Johnston's pay-tours a perilous expedition.

General Johnston suffered great annoyance because the transportation furnished him was never suitable to the work to be done. He had to remonstrate often, but in vain, against the tired mules and worn-out wagons supplied to him. As his circuit was made through a wilderness, he prevented detention and its ill results only by the most heedful preparation of his outfit and the utmost attention to details, so that no bolt, buckle, or horseshoe-nail, was overlooked.

The following extracts will suggest some of his difficulties. In a letter dated October 18, 1853, to Colonel A. J. Coffee, deputy paymaster-general, he writes that if his tour were increased, as was proposed, to 925 miles, a payment would occupy forty-five days, and adds :

If, after the information I have given you as to the distances to be traveled, etc., you think the public interest would be properly subserved by my including Paymaster Hutter's district with my own, I will, as soon as notified, take upon myself the duties of the district, thus arranged, with pleasure. I think it my duty to say that the quartermaster at this place has not had the means to give a good team for the ambulance for a long time, and I would do no injustice to say that I have at no time had a sufficiently good team. . . . The team furnished at this point now has to work in the trains when not in the service of the pay department, a practice which makes a team totally unfit for ambulance service.

He adds:

There is no ambulance here; the one mentioned in my requisition became a wreck on a late trip of Major Woods from Phantom Hill. This is a small matter to trouble you with, and I hate grumblers so much that I dislike to make any complaint; but, if service is to be promptly and efficiently performed, the means should not be withheld.

In a letter addressed to Colonel B. F. Larned, paymaster-general, April 8, 1852, General Johnston says :

I have the honor to report that the district to which I have been assigned has been paid to the 29th February last. It is constituted as follows : Fort Graham, Brazos River ; Fort Worth, Clear Fork of the Trinity ; Belknap, Salt Fork of the Brazos ; and the post on the Clear Fork of the Brazos. The distance traveled in making the payment was 730 miles; time—from 29th February to 3d April—thirty-five days, under favorable circumstances. The country is elevated, the greater portion being a succession of ranges of high hills, intersected with numerous streams, the crossing of which is always troublesome, and often produces delay in the journey. The march is commenced at daylight, and continued industriously during the day, except two hours in mid-day ; and thus the journey is prosecuted without any loss of time, either on the route or at the posts. You may, therefore, fix the average time at thirty-five or forty days. This six times repeated during the year makes up an amount of travel, sleeping on the ground, privation, and exposure to heat and cold, not imagined by the framers of the law, nor encountered by a private soldier in time of war or peace, for it must be remembered that the country traversed is uninhabited.

The commanding general of this department issued an order last summer fixing the period of the payments at four months, which I thought the circumstances of the case called for, and which has been productive of no detriment whatever to the public service; since then the interior line has been established, making the travel much greater. In conclusion, I beg leave to refer you to Colonel Cooper for the best information with regard to this district, and to say that I will endeavor to execute faithfully whatever order you may deem it proper to give with regard to the period of the payment.

General Johnston, in a letter of August 10, 1854, to his daughter, gives this account of his tours of duty :

My dear Daughter : I received your beautiful letter on my return from my last tour to the military posts, and have had necessarily to defer my answer until I could get off to Washington a statement of my accounts, which is the first thing to be done after each payment, and cannot be dispensed with. The payments have to be made every two months; the distance to be traveled is near 700 miles; so you see, with traveling and making up accounts, I have but little leisure. Traveling in an uninhabited country, making from twenty-five to thirty miles a day, is no longer by me classed with trips of pleasure. With your modern improvements you accomplish as much in two days as we can in a month.

Although we do not travel far in a day, it is sufficiently fatiguing. We are, every morning, on our feet at the first peep of dawn; and, as the glorious orb of day discloses his radiant face, which in this sunny climate is almost every day, we begin our march. We continue till 11 A. M., and start again about 2 P. M., and stop for the night, about five o'clock, in some romantic spot made hospitable to us by Dame Nature; and so, on and on, as one day, so all. A first trip is delightful; all that is beautiful and charming, and much that is magnificent or sublime, in scenery, daily feasts the eye. But even this becomes tiresome and uninteresting when seen too often. I took Sid [1] with me on my last trip. It was a rich treat to him. He swam and fished in almost every stream on the route. He is a bold, intelligent boy, with a splendid *physique.*

In March, 1854, the writer made one of these rounds of duty with General Johnston, taking the place of his clerk. The journey was one of lively enjoyment, and afforded a good opportunity for noting some of General Johnston's traits. The average rate of travel was about thirty miles a day. The trail over dry and treeless plains, though hardly to be called a road, offered little interruption or detention, except at the crossings of streams, where sometimes a large part of a day was spent. General Johnston's equipage has already been described; a buffalo-robe and some blankets furnished the bed; and two daily meals of cold bread, cold ham, and black coffee, with an occasional bird or wild-duck, shot by the road-side, made our simple fare. It may be remarked that he did not use spirits on the road, though, of course, he had them in case of need.

General Johnston pointed out with interest both the geological and topographical features of the country. Our route, for the most part, lay across high, wide, rolling prairies, the rich soil of which was clothed with its earliest verdure, and spangled with hyacinth, coryopsis, verbena, pink phlox, yellow primrose, and other flowers just beginning to bloom. Of course, in a circuit of 700 miles, the aspect of the country varied greatly. From Austin to Fort Belknap, after passing for miles over swelling prairies capable of the utmost productiveness under the hand of man, but then uninhabited, we would sometimes skirt a range of low hills, covered with cedar-brake, or plunge into a belt of live-oak or post-oak forest. Emerging, we would again strike across a plain overgrown with scrubby mesquite, or wind around the base of a conical hill, the frequent landmark of the region. The soil was gener-

[1] His son, thirteen years old.

ally calcareous; and at the hill-tops a bald crown of white marl rose above the encircling sod. Though marks of volcanic action were not wanting, the strata, where visible, were commonly horizontal. In Hamilton's Valley, marble was found, pure white, pink, or drab, of fine grain and good polish. At Belknap, and along the Brazos, there was plenty of coal.

From Fort Belknap to Phantom Hill, Fort Chadbourne, Fort McKavitt, and thence to Austin, the country was bolder, wilder, more rugged and sterile. The breaks in these elevated table-lands often present the appearance of successive mountain-ranges, and the eye is often delighted with a landscape forty miles in extent, under a cloudless sky. A conical peak, sometimes called "Abercrombie's Peak," where General Johnston often camped, he named "Bleak House," after Dickens's fictitious mansion. There were manifold and unmistakable signs that the whole land had once been submerged, and had risen from the deep, by numerous successive elevations of the most gradual character. On the hill-sides the well-defined water-levels, beaches of a vanished ocean, resembled walled terraces, and were surmounted by summits which looked like the remains of embrasured strongholds; so that everywhere was presented the illusion of ancient fortifications on the most gigantic scale.

These high plains are the border-land of the desert. At Fort Chadbourne, we were told, by Captain Calhoun and Dr. Swift, that on the 9th of June, 1854, a terrible hailstorm had swept over them, which had drifted six or eight feet deep in the bed of the creek; twenty wagon-loads of hailstones were gathered, and a hundred more might have been, had it pleased them. Hailstorms followed for two weeks. In October, a flight of grasshoppers from the northeast was three days in passing over the place; and such was the multitude, and so constant the flitting of wings, that it resembled a snow-storm.

On this journey we were assailed by several "northers," the peculiar wind of a Texan winter, and the dread of the pioneer. The prevailing wind is a strong sea-breeze that blows with the regularity of a trade-wind, except when interrupted by the norther. On a day as balmy as spring, the thermometer perhaps at 80° in the shade, the weathercock suddenly veers, and without warning a fierce, dry, searching blast comes howling down from the northwest, accompanied by a change of temperature of as much, often, as 60° or 70° in two or three hours. The cattle flee to thickets; indeed, every living thing seeks shelter, and people exposed to it are often chilled to death. By General Johnston's direction I recorded observations and collected data as to the direction, progress, and phenomena, of the norther. From these, combined with his long experience of the characteristics of this wind, he arrived at the conclusion that it was a wind of propulsion; that is to say, that it began to blow at the more northerly points first, and was not a "caving-in " wind, commencing to blow at the Gulf, as some imagined ; that its rate of progress was from thirty to forty-five miles per hour ; and that it had its origin in the Rocky Mountains or on the Plains. He surmised that a great snow-fall, evolving an enormous amount of heat, produced a rising, moving column of air, with a southward tendency, which drew after it the arctic blasts that made the norther.

General Johnston's interest in animals—what might be called his friendliness to them—has been mentioned. There was along our road a tract many square miles in extent, reaching from Bluff Creek to Fort McKavitt, which was called the Prairie Dog City. Here dwelt in large communities these lively little marmots. Most of them occupied plain holes in the ground ; these, General Johnston called the plebs. Others, who seemed to enjoy consideration on account of the broad, elevated terraces around their dwellings, from which they harangued the multitude with great chatter, he said were the magistrates and orators. He speculated amusingly on the analogies here to human government, and called attention to the common lot by which they fell victims to the rattlesnakes, which in turn became the prey of the owls that infested the city.

General Johnston noted closely the habits of birds. I remember well the infinite patience with which he reared a nest of red-birds for me near Shelbyville, Kentucky, when I was a boy. They had an incessant, metallic clack, and were always hungry. The same year he brought up by hand, in like manner, two orioles which became great pets. On our frontier journey, he continually called attention to the ways of the animals that we saw. A blue, swallow-tailed hawk kept near us all one day, allowing us to flush the small birds for him. General Johnston knew not which most to admire, the poise and swoop of the aërial hunter, or the intelligence that made him avail himself of our aid in getting his dinner. "That hawk," he said, "doubtless considers himself the centre of creation, and that our place in it is to play jackal to him."

In his study of Nature, General Johnston combined scientific exactness with æsthetic gratification. A flower was viewed by him in more than one aspect. Grouped with others it was a piece of color, or a feature in the landscape; and again, as a single study, it became in turn an index of the soil, a sign of the season, or, with its wonderful arrangement of stamen and petal, an evidence of design and a symbol of order in the universe. He showed me the distinctive features and the relative practical values of the white mesquite, the curly mesquite, and half a dozen other nutritious native grasses. His acquaintance with plants was very intimate. In the cultivation of this taste, he had the aid and encouragement of his wife, who possessed remarkable talent and skill in painting flowers. In his various tours he collected for her a large number of varieties of cactus—as many as sixty, I believe.

General Johnston showed me a tract on the dividing ridge between the San Gabriel and its South Fork, where, fifteen years before, with Burleson, Tom Howard, William S. Fisher, and half a dozen others, he had hunted buffalo. Out of six that they saw they killed five. The Indians had attacked every other party that had attempted to cross the country; they, however, took the risk of meeting them, as they were all old frontiersmen; but they were not molested.

I had occasion to remark, on this visit, the great patience and unselfishness of General Johnston in attending to the wants and business of others. As he made his round from post to post, he was intrusted with a budget of commissions that might well have taxed his equanimity. To buy a horse, a gun, a pair of boots, a ribbon; to have a watch mended; to pay taxes; to adjust some entangled business—any and every sort of affair that these isolated people could not attend to in person was committed to his care and looked after with solicitude. No right or claim of a soldier was neglected; and these poor fellows little knew the amount of thought and correspondence frequently involved in enforcing their demand for some inconsiderable sum. Friends in other States availed themselves of his extended and minute topographical knowledge to obtain information in locating lands; and, ignorant that this knowledge had a fixed commercial value, accepted his services without compensation. In one instance he located for a friend 40,000 acres of land without remuneration, the fee for which would have been, according to custom, one fourth of the land. But he imparted what he knew freely and cheerfully; not seeking to engross for himself what he was aware would become a great fortune. He seemed to feel that, as a public servant, all his faculties were to be used for the benefit of others.

It has been stated that, on his tours, General Johnston's only companions were a clerk (not always congenial), negro servants, and a dragoon escort, with whom the custom of the service permitted only formal communication. Hence he was thrown much upon his own resources, and passed many days without conversation; but this was less wearisome to him than to most men, owing to a large capacity for enjoyment, to his habits of observation, and to a way he had of thinking over contingencies likely to happen. Without doubt, on these long and wellnigh solitary journeys, his meditation was fruitful. It was a study of probable, practical events, as close and compact as the solution of the difficult chess-problems for which he had so great a relish, and not at all resembling reverie, for which he felt a marked dislike. If he saw a child listlessly musing over a book, he would say: "Do not nurse your book; study it, or put it by." It was often remarked that he was never taken by surprise, or unable to come to a prompt decision as to his course of action. Though this was undoubtedly due in part to the even balance of his mind and moral nature, General Johnston explained it by saying that "what was called his presence of mind was often merely putting into action a course of conduct long determined on." His forethought surely saved him many times from surprise and unexpected situations.

Long service on the frontier, individual aptitudes, and continued exercise of the faculty, had given General Johnston that sort of topographical knowledge and insight which, when put in practice, seems almost like an instinct. He had ample woodcraft, but the habit of prairie-travel unquestionably helped to train his eye and imagination to take in at a glance the salient features of a country. An instance illustrating this occurred during his service as paymaster. The road from Austin to Belknap followed the old Indian trail, as is usual on the frontier. As this route diverged much from a direct line, and crossed the breaks of the table-lands instead of following the water-sheds to advantage, it was thought best to establish a new wagon-road. General Johnston was consulted, and gave such accurate instructions that the road was shortened twenty or thirty miles, and avoided the chief difficulties of frontier travel; yet in many parts he had never been over the ground, and in some not within ten or fifteen miles of it. He knew, however, what its profile and characteristics must be.

Whatever concerned the honor or happiness of Texas interested General Johnston deeply. The rights of her old settlers and revolutionary patriots enlisted his warmest sympathies, and he lent his voice in behalf of those claimants for reimbursement who had suffered spoliation at the hands of their own Government and army. The productive capacity and material development of the State were constant themes in his letters. He had high hopes that the manifest superiority of the Southern route to the Pacific would secure the completion of a railroad along that line which would be the beginning of an era of wonderful progress and prosperity for the State. He predicted that its cotton, its wheat, and its beef, would then successfully compete, in New York and the markets of Europe, with the most favored rivals.

General Johnston was drawn into warmer sympathy with the Democratic party by his attitude of resistance to Know-Nothingism and to the antislavery crusade that was now beginning to become formidable. The allusions in his correspondence to these questions are few and brief, but explicit: "I am glad Kentucky came so near giving a good Democratic vote. She will yet be saved." In another letter he alludes pointedly and with reprobation to the abolition movement.

In a letter to the author, dated October 19, 1854, General Johnston says:

Know-Nothingism will have its day, perhaps a brief triumph, and then will be denounced as an anti-republican heresy. The restriction of the right of suffrage to the present population and their descendants, and to the descendants of future immigrants, can now be effected without the intervention of a secret political organization of *unknown* principles—perhaps menacing religious toleration, and opposed by the secrecy of its proceedings to the genius of our institutions. If our leading men would have the boldness to meet the question openly and on the grounds of its utility alone, I do not doubt that the aid of most of our naturalized citizens could be obtained for the enactment of a law that would give every security.

In 1853 General Johnston was relieved from the burden of indebtedness he had so long borne, by the sale of his plantation on terms that paid off all incumbrances and left him a free man. But, by a cruel stroke of fortune, he had hardly got rid of the heavy load that had so long weighed down his spirits and wounded his sensibilities, when a new and more severe trial befell him from an unexpected source. He found, on counting the Government funds in his possession, a deficit of several hundred dollars; and on several other occasions in 1853 he discovered similar losses, amounting to $1,700. Such was the accuracy of his accounts and payments that robbery was the only solution. The money was kept in an iron strong-box, rarely from under the eye of himself or his clerk ; and, as no violence was used, access must have been had by false keys. Owing to various causes several persons succeeded each other in his office as clerk, all reputable men, who united with General Johnston in trying to detect the thief, but in vain. In 1854 about the same amount was abstracted by the same methods, but the utmost vigilance failed to furnish any sufficient clew. These mysterious robberies, and his inability to frustrate them, were not only impoverishing him, but so seriously threatened him with loss of property and reputation that he almost sunk under it, and determined to resign a position so perilous. In the mean time, being aware that to report these circumstances would be merely to undermine the confidence of his superiors and to draw unmerited suspicion upon himself, he made good the losses from his private means by appropriating in that way some old debts that came in providentially just then, and by a frugality in his expenditure amounting to privation.

When I accompanied him in March, 1855, he stated all the facts to me, and we counted the money just before starting. I asked him if he suspected no one, and he replied that he had "no *right* to suspect any particular person, though he did; but he wished me to watch with him, and to consider the case unbiased by his prejudice, and therefore he preferred not to state his suspicions." During the journey the strong-box was out of our sight for only a few hours at Fort McKavitt, when it was under guard. The most scrupulous exactness in payment had been observed, and yet, on the second day after our return, on counting the money, $700 was missing. The cash had been taken as usual from different bags, and this time in half-eagles with some marked coins included. My own mind had been made up before, but now I was certain of the thief. I pointed out to General Johnston that by the principle of exclusion the guilt had been narrowed down to his negro servants, and that his driver John was the man. John was a family slave, an ugly, black fellow, but handy, who had been greatly indulged. About two years before he had married a quadroon woman, whom he had supported in considerable luxury. He explained his means of extravagance by the profits of barter with the soldiers. There were certain other subtile signs of guilt that convinced my mind.

I proposed a prompt and thorough search of John's luggage, which was stowed at the house of his wife's master. General Johnston admitted that he had long suspected John, but had no proof; and he now hesitated to make the search, because, if the man was innocent, it would be a hard case indeed for such a blow to be dealt by the hand of his master, who was the one person in the world to whom he could look for protection. I insisted that where so much was at stake such extreme conscientiousness and tenderness were morbid. General Johnston yielded, and stated all the circumstances to three neighbors who made the search, the owner of the premises being one. Impunity had made the negro careless; and six hundred of the seven hundred dollars, including some of the marked coin, were found in his trunk. He afterward told me that a white gambler had furnished him the false keys.

Persons to whom the facts became known were eager to punish the crime by severely whipping the culprit, hoping thus to ascertain his accomplices, if he had any; but General Johnston would not permit it. "Such evidence is worthless," said he. "Besides, the whipping will not restore what is lost; and it will not benefit the negro, whom a lifetime of kind treatment has failed to make honest. It would be a mere act of revenge, to which I cannot consent." He agreed with the views of his friends, who urged that the negro should be sold out of the community, where, indeed, he was not safe. He was taken to Galveston, and allowed to select his own master. He was sold for $1,000, which went to make up in part what he had stolen from the United States Government.

Soon after, General Johnston was appointed colonel of the Second Cavalry. The report of the Second Auditor in the settlement of his accounts to the 9th of April, when he resigned, stated:

Balance due him per official statement $4 22
    "   "   "   his own   " 0 00

Difference in his favor $4 22

It is due to General Johnston to say that not only were his trusts as paymaster executed with scrupulous fidelity, but his accounts were kept

with rare accuracy and beauty. The Second Auditor, construing statutes under a different light, of course often disallowed small sums paid
by General Johnston; but he had in him a strenuous and punctilious
correspondent, who hardly ever failed to present an argument setting
forth the grounds on which the payment had been made. When I
asked him why he took so much trouble for so little, he said it was due
to himself to justify himself from even the appearance of carelessness.

The following was a playful reply to a letter of the author, written
when he came of age, in 1852:

You have formally announced your majority, and your right to independent
action. It only remains to me, as an act of comity, being convinced of your
ability to maintain the attitude you have assumed, to recognize you as a man, *de
facto et de jure*, and to invest you in good faith and with all solemnity with the
toga virilis. You have, therefore, the right in your sovereign capacity to make
treaties of *alliance, coin* money, regulate and control your own trade, and do
whatever else it may seem best to you in the pursuit of happiness, always keeping in view the prohibitions of the law as to other sovereigns so situated.

You are still willing to acknowledge an allegiance to me. I have no right to
demand it; and, for your own good, would not accept it. Now that you are
about to pass from the sham fights of life to its real battles, your security and
success will depend upon a high degree of *self-reliance*. It is the momentum of
great confidence, regulated by sound judgment, that crushes every obstacle.

The following letter also was written during the period of his service
as paymaster, and while he was under the shadow of doubt, loss, and
privation, already mentioned. It is another illustration of his resolute
trust and cheerfulness in trouble:

AUSTIN, TEXAS, *December* 23, 1854.

MY DEAR SON: I send you and Rosa and Hennie the best wishes of my heart
for your health and happiness always; but especially do I offer my wishes for a
" happy Christmas " and a " happy New Year," which I am reminded to do by
the happy little faces around me, impatient for the arrival of those days so
delightful to the beneficiaries of that merry little friend of good children, St.
Nicholas. Maggie implicitly believes in his advent and good works; but Sid and
Hancock are disenchanted, though the little hypocrites, like taller ones, wisely
affect a belief they do not entertain, for the accruing benefits. The children are
in fine health, and improving in their studies; each has earned a reward for
extra work. These little cheerful faces, happy in the hopes of the future, reflect
their sunshine on us; and if Brother Willie, Sister Hennie, and Sister Rosa, as
these prattlers call you, were here to throw their sunlight on us, the evening of
our days would be as beautiful and as full of exquisite repose as the close of day
in this delicious climate.

You mentioned that you had not yet had any business to do in your profession. I was glad to see that you feel no discouragement. You should feel
none. You knew well beforehand the long probation of those who are now
successful, and could not reasonably expect to be an exception. Wait patiently,
and *prepare;* your time will come. Live with economy, spend nothing for

appearance' sake, and you will be able to hold out till the harvest-time. The history of almost every successful lawyer of your State is one of hope deferred. J——, one of your very best lawyers, sat, I am told, seven long years without a case, like a huge spider spread out on his web, and like that courageous insect, in expectant attitude, waited to throw the meshes of the law around some opponent. His patience was crowned with success. Wait, but work. Do not reject business because it is not important. Be faithful over a few things, and you shall soon be steward over many. . . .

Sebastopol may possibly fall, though the science of war has had little to do, thus far, in the work. The great master of the art of war would have made preparation commensurate with the object to be accomplished. He would have seized the neck of the Crimea with a good army, and carried on the siege of the place, according to well-approved principles, undisturbed by a relieving army, to a certain success, with due regard to economy of life.

Affectionately your father,   A. SIDNEY JOHNSTON.

The following reminiscence is from the pen of the Rev. Edward Fontaine, the Episcopal minister at Austin, a gentleman of eloquence and earnestness :

I have said that he had at all times perfect self-control. I will mention some instances in which I saw his power of self-government severely tried ; but his temper stood the various tests admirably.

I was once fishing with him in the Colorado River. A large bass seized his hook, and it required all his skill to reel him to the surface of the water with a small silk line. After a contest of several minutes with the powerful fish, he succeeded in bringing his fine proportions in full view ; but just as he was about landing him, with a sharp strain upon his rod, he gave an " indignant flounce," and disappeared in the clear depths of the stream, leaving the snapped line tangled fast to a willow-limb, high above the head of the disappointed general. He gave it a gentle pull ; but finding it hung fast, he walked up the bank and cut a pole with a hook to it, and pulled down the limb very cautiously ; and then set to work very deliberately to untangle the Gordian knot into which he, the bass, and the limb together had tied the line.

After the patient labor of at least half an hour, he succeeded in righting his tackle, put on another hook and minnow, and " threw out " to tempt another bite. In the mean time, I watched his motions, very much amused at the mishap, but said nothing. He made no exclamation of impatience, and exhibited no emotion. I then remarked : " General, although you are not a member of the Church, I believe you are a better Christian than myself in one respect— you are more patient. If old Izaak Walton himself had lost that fish after such a tussle, and lost his hook with him, and tied up his tackle in that way, he might not have cursed the fish or his luck, but I think he would have said something spiteful, and have felt a little blasphemous." He replied : " I have long since learned, sir, by experience, that it is best never to get excited about anything ; for in a fit of excitement very sensible men are apt to do or say something rash or foolish, for which they may have to repent in a cooler moment.

He had a valuable Newfoundland dog, which was a very great favorite with the family. It guarded little Sidney, Hancock, and Maggie, his three youngest children, in their rambles about his premises, and I think it sometimes pulled the little girl in a toy carriage. But the dog one day went into the lot of a near neighbor to play with a "cur of low degree"—a proper dog for a master as mean and worthless as himself. This man, who had been kindly treated by the general and his family, but who envied and hated him with that sort of malice which the base and vulgar generally cherish toward the noble and refined, to distress the children, or show his spite against his distinguished neighbors, or from the promptings of some dirty motive which is only understood by the devils that got into the swine of Gennesaret, or by those who are instigated by them, threw a piece of meat poisoned with strychnine to the dog, which came home, and in a few minutes died with convulsions, in the presence of the children and their parents. The little children wept bitterly the loss of their favorite, and Mrs. Johnston shed tears. The general was deeply distressed, but said nothing in anger. Some one present declared that the villain who committed the deed ought to be prosecuted or shot. He replied that if he sued or killed him, it would make the man no better, and it would do himself and family no good ; that he would be compelled to endure the outrage, as there was no redress for it. The dog was dead, and nothing could restore him to life, and he hoped that his family would bear their loss with fortitude.

It has been mentioned that, when General Johnston was appointed paymaster, his family spent the summer in Kentucky. On their return he met them in New Orleans, only to learn that his infant daughter had recently died. The following touching letter expresses exactly the spirit in which he habitually accepted afflictions, as well as other dispensations of Providence :

NEW ORLEANS, *Saturday, December* 14, 1850.

DEAR HANCOCK : My family arrived here yesterday, and I only then learned from my wife the loss of our dear little Mary. Great as our distress is, I can still thank God that my wife and my other children are left to me. It is not right to judge of his dispensations, nor do I, but bow with humble submission to decrees the wisdom of which I cannot comprehend and the justice of which I must not question.

I received Aunt Mary's letter. I cannot write to her now. I hope she will write to my poor wife as often as she can, for she needs her sympathy.

Your friend,   A. SIDNEY JOHNSTON.

To Mr. GEORGE HANCOCK, Louisville, Ky.

He spoke little of his inner life; but once in Austin he said to the writer that a minister had been urging upon him the benefits of prayer, and added : " I did not think it necessary to tell him, but it is many years since I have closed my eyes in sleep without prayer. Indeed, I feel that I cannot thank God enough for his goodness to me. Beyond that thanksgiving I almost dread to go ; his care is so great, and my views so narrow, that I do not know how to ask God for anything better for me and mine than that his will be done." On many other occasions he said to me substantially the same thing. He delighted in the glories of the starry heavens, which led him, as they have so many other watchers in the desert, to contemplate the splendors and unfathomable mysteries of the universe and its Creator.

CHAPTER XII.

THE SECOND CAVALRY.[1]

WHEN General Franklin Pierce was elected President, he appointed General Jefferson Davis Secretary of War. Pierce's gallantry, amiability, and address, had enabled him to avoid the blunders of the other "political generals" in the Mexican War; while his actual service made him perceive clearly the necessity of positive qualifications at the head of the War Department. He had the good fortune to secure as secretary a man who combined political knowledge and administrative ability with a perfect experience in the details and requirements of the service. It is not too much to say that the department was never conducted with more intelligence and skill, or with more satisfaction to the army and the country. The secretary attempted and secured great improvements in the organization and efficiency of all branches of the service. In carrying out these plans he had to ask for an increase in the force, which resulted in a bill, passed March 3, 1855, providing for four new regiments—two of cavalry and two of infantry.

The necessity for this increase in the strength of the army will be at once apparent by reference to the President's message, and to the secretary's report of December 4, 1854. The secretary says:

We have a seaboard and foreign frontier of more than 10,000 miles; an Indian frontier and routes through the Indian country requiring constant protection of more than 8,000 miles; and an Indian population of more than 400,000, of whom probably one-half, or 40,000 warriors, are inimical, and only wait the opportunity to become active enemies. If our army should be expanded to its greatest limits it would have a force of 14,731 officers and men; but as a large allowance must always be made for absentees, invalids, etc., the effective force would probably never exceed 11,000.

The secretary also estimated the Indian frontier of Texas at nearly 2,000 miles, the lines of communication through the Indian country

---

[1] The Second Cavalry is now styled the Fifth Cavalry.

at more than 1,200 miles, and the nomadic and predatory Indians at 30,000; while the army in that department was only 2,886 officers and men, a force entirely inadequate for its protection and defense.

While the policy of the Administration was taking shape, the friends of different aspirants for appointment or promotion naturally urged their claims in the usual manner. General Johnston followed the same line of conduct which he had prescribed for himself during General Taylor's Administration, and abstained from presenting his claims. His patient performance of the duties of paymaster, however, incited the friends who witnessed it to move on his behalf. The Texas Legislature contained a number of those brave spirits who had formerly looked to him in the days of the republic as their leader in every martial enterprise; and, under this guidance, the whole Legislature united in a recommendation for General Johnston's appointment to the command of one of the proposed regiments. This memorial, dated January 8, 1854, in which the Governor, Lieutenant-Governor, and Speaker of the House united, was addressed to Senator Rusk, and urged the coöperation of himself and his colleagues in securing the object of the petition.

When the bill was passed, in 1855, General Rusk, who needed no other prompting than his own feelings in the matter, used active efforts to secure the appointment for General Johnston. His position was somewhat embarrassing, as that gallant and popular partisan leader, Major Ben McCulloch, was vehemently pressed by influential friends for the same appointment. Hon. P. H. Bell, although an advocate of the claims of McCulloch, kindly offered a testimonial to the capacity and character of General Johnston. Hon. William Preston, member of Congress from Kentucky, was in the opposition, but was able, perhaps partly on that account, to smooth the way for General Johnston's promotion. But as it had been General Johnston's good fortune previously to be personally known and appreciated by President Taylor, so he chanced again to have in the Secretary of War a friend who had known him from boyhood and who esteemed him as highly as any man living. Mr. Preston wrote: "Johnston's merits should have given him a regiment years ago, but his pride and delicacy have always prevented him from pressing his claims. Davis was truly his friend."

It had been a custom, almost passing into precedent, on the formation of new regiments, for the existing Administration to reward its supporters with important commands, so that the army was in danger of degenerating into a retired list for decayed politicians. Nothing could be more fatal to honorable ambition. But now the Secretary of War, himself a soldier of distinguished merit, was able to present the subject so strongly to the President, that he was allowed to make his selections, for the most part, from the army. The political pressure brought to bear upon Mr. Davis was very great, but no man was ever less amenable to such considerations ; and that his appointments were made with sole reference to efficiency is best evinced by the subsequent careers of the men selected.

To the Second Regiment of cavalry, which was intended for immediate service in Texas, General Johnston was appointed as colonel, with rank from March 3, 1855. Brevet Colonel Robert E. Lee was made lieutenant-colonel ; and Brevet Lieutenant-Colonel William J. Hardee and Major George H. Thomas, majors. Hardee was afterward a lieutenant-general in the Confederate army, and was always found equal to the occasion. Thomas is equally well known as a distinguished general on the Northern side. Among the captains were Earl Van Dorn, E. Kirby Smith, and N. G. Evans, who were generals in the Confederate army; and I. N. Palmer, George Stoneman, and R. W. Johnson, who held the same rank in the Union army. Among the subalterns, John B. Hood, Charles W. Field, Chambliss, and Phifer, became Southern generals ; and K. Garrard and others attained the same place in the Northern army. It is doubtful whether any other one regiment furnished an equal number of distinguished officers to the two contending armies during the great civil war.

McCulloch, in his disappointment at not receiving a colonel's commission, refused the position of major tendered him. He had been a gallant and enterprising leader of partisan troops, and deserved well of his country. His nomination was a high compliment, as he was the only field-officer selected from civil life. Long before his untimely death in battle, he had the generosity to say that Mr. Davis had acted wisely in preferring General Johnston above him.

General Scott said to Mr. Preston, who was on intimate terms with him, that the appointments were very good, but that the positions of Johnston and Lee should have been transposed. The acquaintance that had existed between these two officers ripened into mutual regard and esteem, of which some slight but decided evidences will appear in the course of this memoir. Indeed, the writer's admiration of General Lee, which has been expressed elsewhere under so many forms, had its origin in General Johnston's commendations of that soldier subsequently so illustrious. From each he has heard in regard to the other sentiments of respect and appreciation, delivered in terms of noble sincerity—an estimate that grew and strengthened to the close. Some years after, General Scott, in another conversation, with Mr. Preston, referring to his former conversation took occasion to say that no better appointment than General Johnston could have been made ; that he was equal to any position, and he would not have it otherwise. Captain Eaton informs the writer that General Scott told him in the winter of 1858 that he regarded General Johnston's appointment as "a Godsend to the army and to the country." His opinion of General Johnston's qualities had greatly improved on a better acquaintance.

Thus while General Johnston was undergoing the combined hardships, drudgery, and mental torture, arising out of his duties and losses as paymaster, a kind Providence and zealous friends advanced him to the very position which he preferred to all others. It is true that he had never held a regular cavalry command, though he had served with the rangers in Texas; but his professional knowledge was wide, and his special tastes inclined him to that arm of the service, so that he felt no difficulty in accepting the promotion. The writer was with him when he received, at Fort McKavitt, the notification of this fact ; and, though his heart's desire was gratified by it, he learned it with perfect composure, and delayed his acceptance until he had surveyed the case in every possible bearing.

The citizens of Austin tendered him a public supper and ball, "as an unostentatious display of genuine feeling and respect for a distinguished public servant." But a still more gratifying evidence of the public estimation was the confidence inspired on that whole frontier, that his presence in command there was a sufficient guarantee of its safety. On May 19th he was ordered to Louisville, Kentucky; and, by telegram, on June 29th, to report at Washington City.

When General Johnston was ordered on, it was not expected that his regiment would be filled for some time ; and both he and Colonel Lee were directed to proceed to Fort Leavenworth, to sit on a general court-martial, to be held September 24th. Recruiting for the army had been slow, and often from an undesirable class of persons. But now, owing to the increase of pay, the prospect of a life of active adventure on the Plains, and other motives, the cavalry regiments were rapidly recruited with farmers' sons and other daring young men, making its complement of men (850) about the middle of August. The recruits were rendezvoused at Jefferson Barracks, Missouri, under the command of Major Hardee, with orders to march to the frontier of Texas in October. General Johnston was troubled at being absent from his regiment at this critical period, and in a letter to the writer, dated September 29th, says: "I am much annoyed at being absent from my regiment at a time when the presence of every officer is peculiarly needed. It is really bringing form out of chaos to organize a regiment of raw recruits and prepare them for a long march. They have suffered some from cholera and other diseases, which has caused a considerable number to desert. I do not expect desertion to cease while the regiment remains at Jefferson Barracks." He was relieved, however, early in October, and proceeded to assume the command of his regiment.

Major Hardee, an officer of tact, intelligence, and professional knowledge, had been in charge of the regiment, and had accomplished all that could be expected under the circumstances ; but ague, cholera, desertion, and the other discouragements incident to novitiates in garrison, kept the regiment in an unhappy and restless condition until it moved. General Johnston began by the application of a rigid discipline, and the letter of a witness mentions that six men were on the same day drummed out of the regiment with shaven heads and other marks of degradation. The preparations were urged with all possible dispatch ; and, on the 27th of October, the column was put in motion for the frontier of Texas.

It was a happy day for General Johnston when, mounting his splendid gray charger, he led a regiment of United States regular cavalry, nearly 800 strong, on the road toward Texas. As Texas was to be their home for some years, the families of the married officers accompanied them. General Johnston's wife and family were packed into an ambulance-wagon, and occupied a tent ten feet square during the halts. They, with the other families accompanying the regiment, bore the hardships of a winter's march and a gypsy-life with uncomplaining fortitude.

The march was not eventful. Though in the earlier part of the journey the progress was slow, on account of rain, high water, and bad roads, yet the change from garrison-life to the march and active work put new life into the men. Discontent vanished, and only one desertion, I believe, occurred. Some casualties happened, of course. A drunken soldier was killed by a fall from his horse. Another soldier was killed by a kick of his horse ; and a few men died in consequence of the extreme cold weather. The strictest discipline was enforced ; and though offenses were few, they were promptly and severely punished. The rights of citizens were respected without qualification; and of this regard for law the colonel himself set a good example. In Mrs. Johnston's journal occurs the following entry : " Marched to-day eighteen miles through a well-cultivated country, but inhabited by a mean set of people. A man refused to sell me fresh milk for my sick baby at any price ; ' for,' said he, ' that milk has butter in it. After it is churned, if you will send for it, I will sell it to you.' " No further effort was made with him, not even a remonstrance. The supremacy of law over force was fully recognized. The incident is trifling in itself, but it has its value.

The route from Jefferson Barracks lay through the Ozark Mountains, in Southwestern Missouri, and passed by the way of Springfield and Neosho into the Indian Territory. Reaching Talequah, November

28th, and traveling by Fort Gibson and Fort Washita, they entered Texas at Preston on the 15th of December. From Preston the column moved to Belknap, and thence to Fort Mason, its destination, where it arrived January 14, 1856. Four companies were left on the Clear Fork of the Brazos, under Major Hardee. In this march they forded many rivers, and suffered three weeks of the coldest weather ever felt in Texas.

While still on the elevated table-lands, some sixty miles northeast of Fort Belknap, the regiment was caught by a terrible norther. General Johnston says in a letter to the writer, of January 17th:

Norther! It makes me cold to write the word. I do not believe that any of the hyperborean explorers felt the cold more intensely than did my regiment. Noble fellows! Officers and men, they will always be found at their post, wherever duty calls them. Think of a northern blast, sixty miles an hour, unceasing, unrelenting (the mercury below zero, ice six inches thick), coming suddenly down on the highest table-lands of Texas, 2,000 feet above the sea, upon a regiment only a few moments before luxuriously enjoying the balmy, bland south breeze, and dissipating in a moment the sweet, illusive hope that, having traveled far into the sunny South, we had escaped the horrors of a Northern winter!

This wonderful change of temperature occurred on the night of December 22d. I had just received and finished reading your letter, in which you mentioned the delightful weather with which you were blessed in New York. I rejoiced that the rude blasts had not visited you all too roughly, but pitied you in the future. Blind mortals that we are! I could not know that what I so dreaded for you would in a moment be inflicted upon myself. From the 22d to this time it has been severely cold, but it is moderate now. On the 23d I did not march, as we had a ration of corn on hand for our poor, benumbed horses. On the 24th we were compelled to give up the little shelter afforded by a skirt of timber, and take our route over the prairie. This was a hard day for all. I do not go much into detail, because you have with me faced a Texas norther, and you will comprehend that it was fortunate that our course was southwest. I think we could not have marched northward. On the 25th, having overtaken our supply-train the evening before, and having a ration of corn for our horses, we remained in camp, the best sheltered by timber that we could find for so large a body of troops, but not good. This bright, clear, beautiful day was the coldest of all; the ground was covered with snow, and the small quantity of water to be found was nearly all congealed, so that with great difficulty an insufficient supply was obtained for our horses. On the 26th we were compelled to take the route again and go on to our depot of corn, and there encamped without water for our horses and with very little for our men. On the 27th we reached Belknap, and encamped near the post until the 2d of January, when we marched for this place. We are now comfortable, and begin to forget the past.

During their march from Belknap they encountered hail, snow, and sleet; and both men and animals suffered severely. A train on its way from the coast to meet them lost 113 oxen. At Fort Mason, as the accommodations were insufficient for the comfort of the officers' families, General Johnston reserved only one small room for his own family. Soon after his arrival there he was attacked by a violent remittent bilious fever, brought on by the exposure of the march. The disease nearly proved fatal, but he finally rallied and seemed to recover.

Having been ordered, on the 2d of April, to proceed to San Antonio to take command of the department, he made the journey on horseback while still convalescent. He had hardly secured comfortable quarters before he suffered a relapse, which brought him to the verge of the grave. His strong constitution at last brought him safely through. Writing about the middle of May, he says: "I try my physical powers a little every day. I have been so little accustomed to sickness that I can hardly realize it, and find myself inclined constantly to jump up and go right off to work." He was gradually restored to strength and health, but did not recover his robust appearance until braced by a winter in Utah.

During the summer and fall of 1856 all other interests were subordinate to the political struggle which resulted in the election of Mr. Buchanan, the Democratic candidate, over Fremont, the nominee of the Antislavery party. The following letters are inserted, because they clearly define General Johnston's views on the subject of abolitionism and his apprehensions at that time.

On the 21st of August, writing from San Antonio to the author, he says:

The best friends of the Union begin to feel apprehensions for its permanency. A disruption is too horrid for contemplation. War and its accompaniments would be a necessary consequence; a peaceful separation is impossible. Let us make war against the world rather than against each other. Our compact of union seems to be drifting toward a lee-shore; already expectant, we stand to listen for the insolent shouts of the greedy wreckers. May Divine interposition prevent the shock!

SAN ANTONIO, TEXAS, *September* 12, 1856.

MY DEAR SON: We are all well, but good health is no novelty here; the beneficence of Providence has accorded this blessing to all the inhabitants of this beautiful region. The simplicity of our habits, from the necessity of practising a rigid economy, imposes upon us the fulfillment of the conditions which insure that blessing to us. After providing for our wants, though not many, there is nothing left for hospitality. This gives me no uneasiness. I prefer rather that my creditors (now very few) should regard me as an honest man than that the world should esteem me a generous fellow. My outfit and necessary expenses in bringing my family to this country on a long overland route will keep me under half-pay until March.

I notice with sorrow the progress of fanaticism in the North. What do they want? We want the Union with the Constitution. We want to share in its glorious, benevolent, civilizing mission, and its high and magnificent destiny.

Our whole hearts are devoted to its support and perpetuity. We want the rights and independence of the States and the security to individuals guaranteed by its Constitution; we claim immunity from intervention and interference. Do they want these things? Let them then cease to agitate a question which reaches our hearths and should be sacred, which disturbs our peace and produces a feeling of insecurity which is intolerable. With whatever sorrow, however heart-felt and agonizing, we will not hesitate to encounter separation with all its attendant horrors rather than bear the evils and degradation relentlessly heaped upon us by the heartless folly of fanaticism.

Hypochondriac persons, without a single cause of unhappiness, by cherishing insane ideas, contrive to make themselves truly miserable. So with our people of the North. A merciful and beneficent God has placed within our grasp every source of human happiness. He has given us the finest country on earth, embracing every variety of climate, soil, and production, affording the means of a perfect independence of the rest of the world; a government more free than any other, and laws whose extreme benevolence hardly restrains individual action sufficiently for public safety; and the right to worship even according to our *fancy*. Yet with all these gifts—surely divine—they cannot be happy unless their Southern brothers will consent to lie upon the Procrustean bed they have constructed for them. They must adopt some other basis for the settlement of the question in agitation than passion. Why not let reason again resume its sway?

Yours, affectionately,   A. S. JOHNSTON.

Writing on the 23d of November, he says, in allusion to the same topic, and the election of Mr. Buchanan as President :

MY DEAR WILL: We are all well, and contented with the result of the election. If our Northern brethren will give up their fanatical, idolatrous negro-worship, we can go on harmoniously, happily, and prosperously, and also gloriously, as a nation. We *hope* this, although we fear it is asking too much of poor human nature. It is more in accordance with human experience to believe that they will cherish their unhappy delusion. What a people! what a destiny! Great, almost without limit we would be, if they would employ all the energy, all the talents, all the genius, and all the resolution, to build up, beautify, adorn, and strengthen our Government, which they have used from the beginning to cripple and destroy it.

General Johnston's administration of the Department of Texas was eminently satisfactory, not only to the Government, but to the people of the frontier—a state of affairs very rare indeed. He was keenly alive to the duty intrusted to him—the defense of the frontier. It was a subject that had engaged his interest and sympathy for twenty years, and the field of operations was perfectly familiar to him. His command was a force more suitable for service than had formerly been employed, and his orders were carried out by as able and enterprising a body of officers and men as has ever been collected into one regiment in America. Enjoying, too, very fully, the confidence of the people, he received that justice at their hands which is not always accorded to commanders, even when deserving.

When General Johnston reached Fort Mason, the border was full of terror. The year 1855 had been one of unusual disaster and suffering. The Indians had murdered and pillaged as far down as the Blanco, within twenty miles of Austin, and even below San Antonio, in September. The arrival of the Second Cavalry changed the aspect of affairs ; and a vigorous warfare upon the Comanches, illustrated by many successful combats, gave an unwonted security to the settlers.

General Johnston, in allusion to this improvement in the condition of the department, says in a letter to the writer, dated August 21st :

So far, since my administration of the affairs of this department, our frontiers have been free from Indian incursions. Our troops have driven them far into the interior, and I hope they will not soon venture in again. This is, of course, only a hope; for there is nothing in the nature of the country offering any obstacle to their movements. The country, as you know, is as open as the ocean. They can come when they like, taking the chance of chastisement. If they choose, therefore, it need only be a question of legs.

In General Orders No. 14, dated November 13, 1857, the commander-in-chief compliments no less than eleven exploits of the Second Cavalry. Although these exhibit the actual conflicts of the regiment, they afford no measure of the activity, the toil, the suffering, and the useful results of its employment. In their rapid pursuit of the flying marauders, the troops were exposed to severe cold and rains in winter, and to the still more trying heat of a semi-tropical sun in summer; they endured the extremities of thirst, were often compelled to subsist on the flesh of broken-down horses, or even, in some cases, to go without food for several days ; and yet the marches performed under these circumstances were sometimes surprising ; in one case, as much as 160 miles in two days and a half. These expeditions, conducted with energy, judgment, and courage, inflicted serious loss on the enemy, and made the frontier of Texas a safe residence in comparison to what it is now.

One of their newspapers, in speaking of General Johnston, said :

We believe we express the common sentiment of our frontier people, that no predecessor has given more satisfaction to them, or inspired them with more confidence in the United States Army, than this gallant officer and well-known citizen.

And another says :

Colonel Johnston's regiment has been quite successful in operating against the Indians. They have acquired considerable character as Indian fighters. The colonel has for many years enjoyed the confidence of the Texans. They expected much from him, and he has not disappointed them. His conduct, since he has been in command of the Texas frontier, challenges the admiration and esteem of his fellow-citizens. He has shown himself an able and energetic commander."

These notices might be multiplied, but it is unnecessary. A vacancy occurring in the rank of brigadier-general, a great many of the Texas journals testified their good-will by expressing the hope that General Johnston would be appointed to it; a fact which is now mentioned merely to show their satisfaction with his administration on their frontier.

The following instance is given as an illustration of General Johnston's mode of dealing with the people of the frontier. The citizens of Hays and Comal Counties joined in a petition to General Johnston, requesting him to station a force to protect their settlements. To their spokesman, Judge William E. Jones, General Johnston sent the following reply:

SAN ANTONIO, TEXAS, *December* 1, 1856.

DEAR SIR: Your letter in relation to the exposed condition of the settlements between the Guadalupe and Pedernalis Rivers, embracing those of the Blanco, has been received.

Captain Bradfute, Second Cavalry, with the effective strength of his company, has been ordered to encamp at some suitable position between five and ten miles to the northward of Sisterdale, to keep the country up the Guadalupe, on the Pedernalis, and intermediate, constantly under observation by means of scouting parties, and also to examine the country in the direction of the Blanco.

While all that activity and zeal can accomplish may be expected from the officers and men of this company, a hearty coöperation of the people of the settlements, in the way of communicating prompt intelligence of the presence of Indians to the troops, and furnishing the latter with reliable guides, will greatly contribute to their security.

The frontier has been unremittingly watched over by the small force stationed on it; but on a frontier of such extent, presenting so many facilities of approach and concealment, small parties can elude the vigilance of their scouts, and penetrate into the settlements.

With great respect, your obedient servant,

A. S. JOHNSTON.

Hon. W. E. JONES.

Commenting upon this in grateful terms, a local journal says:

This is one of the few efforts made by regular officers to conciliate the people and secure their services. It is the first step toward producing the harmony and good feeling which ought to exist between the Texans and the United States Army. Colonel Johnston, notwithstanding he is an officer of the army, does not forget he is at the same time a citizen of the United States. This is a sentiment, it is to be feared, some officers do not entertain, or cannot sufficiently appreciate.

The people of this State were much gratified when they learned Colonel Johnston had charge of this department. His course, and the successes of his officers, have fully met their expectations, and, should he be continued, there is an abiding trust reposed in his ability to give protection to the frontier.

In a letter to the author, dated December 24, 1856, inclosing the foregoing, General Johnston remarks :

They praise or condemn on grounds equally untenable. In this case they totally misapprehend me. They believe I have a desire to conciliate, and consider it the motive of my action. The truth is, they felt unsafe. A feeling of security was due to them. According it to them was a simple act of duty, nothing more.

General Johnston's influence with young and ardent men was very great. Two illustrations of this are given by a devoted friend and admirer, whose terms of laudation I have sometimes omitted, though I have naturally accepted them as genuine and just. He was the son of a friend of General Johnston, and, having settled at San Antonio as a lawyer while the latter had his headquarters there, was at once put upon familiar terms with him and his family. He says :

I regard the hours spent with them as among the happiest and best improved of my life. I have long since recognized that his interest was purely the result of a desire to guard the son of an old friend against the temptations of youth incident to a frontier town. During the two years that I was a constant visitor under his roof, he could not have been kinder or more considerate if I had been his own son, as the incidents alluded to will go to show.

The writer goes on to narrate how, a personal altercation having arisen between an officer of the Second Cavalry and another person, he was engaged to act as the friend of the former. Unfortunately, the correspondence passed to such a point that he felt constrained to advise his principal that, in the event of an anticipated contingency, he must kill his antagonist on sight, pledging himself to do the same to any other man who should interfere.

That night between ten and twelve o'clock, General Johnston entered his room, and inquired whether he had given such advice. Before answering, my informant asked General Johnston whether he proposed to take official action in the premises. On his replying that he did not propose to avail himself of his position to interfere officiously in the affair, he was told that such had been the advice given. General Johnston then asked whether he had counted the cost and weighed the possible consequences ; and was told that he had, and that he had advised the course that he himself would have adopted if principal, though he knew it must lead to a bloody street-brawl. To General Johnston's expressed hope that he might convince him that his action was, to say the least, precipitate, he replied that he feared the task was hopeless. "But," to use the language of my informant, "he did, at length, succeed, by the mathematical argument of *honor* and the inexorable logic of 'the code,' in inducing me to withdraw my counsel and leave my friend free to act after a plan which he (General Johnston) suggested. I now know that it was the wisest and best that could have been adopted, and that by its substitution for mine I have been saved a life-long term of remorse and self-reproach. . . . Not for worlds, *now*, would I have had my advice followed. General Johnston was probably the one man in the world who could have prevented it, and his arguments were the only ones that could have proved effectual." Both of these young men attained high rank and distinction in the civil war; the writer of the above in the Confederate Army, and his principal in the Federal Army.

The other incident occurred at the crisis of the Nicaragua filibustering fever, and is narrated as follows by my informant:

A battalion was raised in and around San Antonio to go to General Walker's assistance, and I was waited upon by a committee to know whether I would accept a command. Nothing could have been more consonant to my feelings at the time; but, for some reason, I demanded until the next day before returning an answer, suggesting, in the mean time, to swell the numbers by additional recruits. While that was going on that night quite briskly in the plaza, General Johnston came along, and, taking me by the arm, asked me to accompany him out of the crowd. Then, turning to me, he desired to know whether it was true that I purposed going on such a wild-goose chase. On being told that such was my intention, he replied: "My young friend, think twice, and think seriously, before taking this step; because, in all likelihood, it is the turning-point in your life."

Admitting that in youth the impulse was natural, and referring to analogous cases in his own career, he continued: "The days of Quixotism are past, and with them the chance for name and fame in all such enterprises as this. The age is materialistic, and he who goes about in search of windmills and giants is apt to be considered a fit candidate for Bedlam. The question, however, wears a moral aspect, which should be duly weighed and considered. Is there any material difference between the filibuster and the buccaneer? Tell me not of philanthropy as a plea. I say of it as Roland's wife said of liberty: 'Alas! how many crimes are committed in thy name!' Besides, if you are pining for adventure, you will not have long to wait. *Liberty* and *philanthropy* are at work, and on a broader field than yours. Fanaticism will soon bring on a sectional collision between the States of the Union, in which every man will have to choose his side. When it comes there will be no lack of blows, and may God help the right! Then give up your present project, and wait. Go to Austin and enter on your profession there. I will give you letters which will insure you an advantageous business connection there." By these arguments, here given almost in his very words, and similar ones, he again induced me to defer my wishes to his judgment, and I have never regretted the decision. The letters I have now.

Permit me to say, in conclusion, that I have never known the man who held in such nice equipoise qualities akin and yet in a measure antagonistic—the genial and reserved, the gentle and the grand, the humane and the heroic. He would have gone a day's journey to reclaim an erring brother, and would have turned out of his path to avoid crushing a worm; and yet he would have sacrificed his life and all he held dear in it rather than deviate one hair's breadth from the strictest line of right and duty.

There was no cant in his composition, for he was a cavalier of the straitest sect; but I have never met the man who combined in himself more of the elements of a follower of the Unerring Teacher. In his company the humblest felt at ease, and yet a crowned head would not have ventured upon a freedom with him. In the course of an eventful life and extensive travel, I have come in contact with many of the historic personages of the day; and yet I scruple not to say that of them all, but *three*, to my thinking, would stand the test of the most rigid scrutiny. Of these, by a singular coincidence, the colonel and lieutenant-colonel of a cavalry regiment in the United States Army, afterward respectively the ranking officers of a hostile army, Albert Sidney Johnston and Robert E. Lee, were two; the third was Mr. Calhoun. No time-serving or self-seeking entered into their calculations. Self-abnegation at the bidding of duty was the rule of their lives. Could our much-maligned section lay no further claim to the consideration of mankind, the fact that it produced, almost in the same generation, such a triumvirate, typical of their people, is enough to place it among the foremost nations of the earth in the realms of thought, honor, patriotism, and knightly grace.

CHAPTER XIII.

THE MORMON REBELLION.

GENERAL JOHNSTON, as commander of the United States troops employed to enforce the Federal authority in Utah, was for more than two years placed in relations of either direct or indirect antagonism with the Mormon chiefs ; and, as his position was peculiarly dangerous and difficult, it is impossible clearly to understand it without some knowledge of the situation of this people and of the abnormal development of religious ideas which led to their separation into a distinct community.

The rise and spread of the Mormons, or Latter-Day Saints, is one of the most remarkable facts of this century. Observers recognize the existence in civilized society of a barbarous element, sometimes characterized as "the dangerous classes." Its manifestation is usually political and communistic, or predatory. Under the influence of religious fanaticism, it gave birth to Mormonism. Joseph Smith, an ignorant and cunning charlatan, with the aid of certain confederates animated by similar sordid motives, deliberately framed and preached and organized a system of religious imposture, which was to establish him as the prophet and vicegerent of the Most High. He pretended to announce his mission by divine revelation, and to attest it by miracles. Secretly he made it the instrument of unbounded license, and of a perfect despotism, spiritual and temporal, over his deluded followers.

Joseph Smith was a native of Vermont, where he was born in 1805. His father removed during his boyhood to near Palmyra, New York. His family was of the vagabond class, thriftless and superstitious. They were people of the lowest social grade, subsisting on the proceeds of irregular labor—hunting, trapping, well-digging, and peddling beer and cakes, together with some shiftless and ill-directed work on the farm on which they had "squatted." Their neighbors testified that they were idle, thriftless, and suspected of pilfering. The family were very ignorant and superstitious, dreaming dreams, seeing visions, and catching eagerly at all the marvels current in their circle. In the camp-meetings and revivals that formed the chief recreation of their community, they picked up an extensive Scriptural vocabulary and some ill-defined views of theology, but no impulse, apparently, to carry the word of God into the practical conduct of life. Their spiritual life was passed in that sediment of fanaticism which consists chiefly of credulity, self-deception, and imposture. Such was the school of morals in which Joseph Smith was educated in all the points of charlatanism.

Joseph Smith was himself accounted in youth a worthless, idle, lying, immoral vagabond ; though both he and his mother testified that it was religious meditation which occupied his thoughts. "He was," according to his father, "the *genus* of the family." His neighbors assert that he professed to discover hidden treasures by the use of "a peep-stone "—a large crystal through which he looked—and that he was also "a water-witch," who found wells with the hazel-rod. According to his own account, at the age of fifteen, he had a vision in which Christ appeared to him and warned him against all existing creeds and sects. He received his call as a prophet on the 23d of September, 1823, when "Nephi, a messenger of God," appeared to him in a vision, and told him that "God had a work for him to do," etc.

It is not necessary to recapitulate here the steps by which a bold imposture rose to a formidable fanaticism. Smith began his practices in 1823, at the age of eighteen, but it was seven years later before Mormonism began to take shape as a sect. His shallow pretenses of the discovery of "the book of Mormon," and of miraculous spectacles to read it with, and his other tricks, have all been laid bare. Nevertheless, he drew around him a band in which craftiness, audacity, and superstition, accompanied by an American aptitude for organization, were the marked characteristics. A sect was founded.

Converts were made rapidly, and colonies were established at Kirtland, Ohio, and Independence, Missouri. Great missionary enterprises were undertaken, and the sect was separated into a distinct body, organized for political and ecclesiastical ends, and literally, not figuratively, "at war with the world." Horse-stealing and counterfeiting were charged as effective means by which they "spoiled the Egyptians;" and so deep-seated was this belief that they were expelled from Ohio and Missouri by popular uprisings. In 1839 the exiles took refuge in Illinois, and built a handsome city on the banks of the Mississippi, named Nauvoo, which in two years contained two thousand houses. Though warmly welcomed at first, their ill name followed them, and a war seemed imminent between them and the people of the country. In the half-hostile, half-legal phases of the contest, Smith fell into the hands of his enemies, and, while in the custody of the law, was murdered in jail by a mob in June, 1844. The martyrdom of its founder gave a seal to the church. His place as "seer" and "revelator of God," after a brief contest, was usurped by a man of real ability, grasp, and steady purpose. Brigham Young, one of his earliest converts and chief counselors, a man of rude, native strength and cunning and excellent administrative power, came to the front as successor. Holding with firm hand the reins of power, he guided the destiny of the Latter-Day Saints until his death in 1877.

Brigham Young was born in Vermont, June 1, 1801, whence he was removed while an infant to New York by his father, who was a small farmer. Though brought up to farm-labor, he became a painter and glazier. He was an early proselyte in 1832, and joined Smith at Kirtland. He soon attained a high place in Smith's confidence, and in rank in the church. In 1835 he was made an apostle, and in 1836, president of the twelve apostles. He was absent in England two years on a successful mission; but, except during this absence, followed Smith's fortunes closely, and was his most trusted counselor. He owed his position to qualities of which his chief felt the need—business sense, persistence, and self-control. He had shrewdness and insight, and cloaked an imperious will under a profession of blind obedience. He is said to have managed Smith, and to have ruled as vizier before he became sultan. At first he was a poor preacher, only affecting "the gift of tongues," or talking gibberish to be translated by another. The habit of command and long practice at length made him a strong though rude speaker. Such was the successor of Joseph.

Prophecy required the completion of the temple at Nauvoo; and Brigham finished it after a fashion. In the mean time, foreseeing the conflict impending with the Gentiles, he cautiously paved the way to a removal of his people to the Rocky Mountains, and at last declared a revelation to that effect. In February, 1846, the advance-guard crossed the Mississippi, Nauvoo was abandoned, and that toilsome pilgrimage began, which ended in the valley of Salt Lake. Nauvoo was said to contain 15,000 inhabitants, and it was entirely deserted. The sudden exodus of such a population from the midst of enraged neighbors was marked by every form of hardship, privation, and affliction, and their migration across the Plains was at a heavy cost in human life. The United States Government, in order to relieve the distress of the Mormons, authorized the enlistment of a battalion of volunteers, who received $20,000 pay in advance, were marched to their destination, and dismissed with their arms. This act of sympathy, gratefully acknowledged at the time, was afterward basely misrepresented as a cruel and malignant persecution.

Brigham Young arrived at the site of Salt Lake City with a small detachment, July 24, 1847; and, leaving a colony, returned to lead forward the main body from their winter-quarters near Council Bluffs, Iowa.

On the 24th of December, 1847, by a second *coup d'état*, he had himself chosen first president of the church, and thus succeeded to the place and power of Joseph Smith. Henceforth, as prophet, priest, and king, he ruled as absolute monarch of the Mormons—a Grand Lama, or incarnate deity. In 1848 he led his people to the valley of Salt Lake. The city he built there he proclaimed the Zion of the Mountains. In his explorations, and as the pioneer leader of a mixed multitude in their passage over the desert, Brigham Young appears at his best. He showed great energy, skill, and decision, and, when he had fairly crossed the boundary into Mexican territory, he set up his standard.

The Mormons from the origin of their sect have tried to preserve every possible analogy to the Hebrews; and this memorable migration out of Egypt to the promised land has enabled them to indulge it. Utah reproduced to their imaginations a new and enlarged type of Canaan. As they emerged from the defiles of the Rocky Mountains they beheld a vast basin, in which lay a Dead Sea, with a shore-line of 290 miles, in a frame of treeless mountains, its sullen waves lapping a snow-white beach. From a second sea of Galilee—the beautiful Utah Lake—another Jordan poured down, along whose green banks the Mormon, in his mind's eye, saw set the cities of the Lord.

Brigham Young looked beyond these types, and perceived himself posted in a stronghold where he thought he could bid defiance to the armies of the world. Lofty and inaccessible mountains girdled it, to whose few and narrow gateways he would hold the key. His new city would be a Tadmor of the desert, a city of refuge, a holy place, and a prison whose door he would keep—a city of which the world had not seen the like, at once a new Rome and a new Jerusalem.

At first the Mormon colony suffered for food ; but judicious management and fortitude tided them over the danger of starvation ; and in 1849 an abundant harvest relieved them. In 1850 and thereafter a great emigration passed over the continent to California ; and, as the

Salt Lake City, from the North.

owners of the half-way station, the Mormons were enriched by legitimate commerce. Brigham showed administrative talent; and, with full command of the resources of his people, he was able to combine cooperative effectiveness with the individual energy and spontaneous industry of the population in such a way as to work marvels of achievement.

Utah was transferred, by the treaty of 1848, from Mexico to the United States. The question was thus revived, whether it were better to pursue their pilgrimage still farther, encountering Apache cruelty and Mexican bigotry, or to trust to their isolation, and " build up the kingdom " on United States territory. The Mormons chose the latter course. Early in 1849 they organized the State of " Deseret ; " but Congress ignored it, and, in September, 1850, created instead the Territory of Utah. President Fillmore appointed Brigham Young Governor ; and he took the oath of office February 3, 1851. Stenhouse says,[1] " President Fillmore appointed Brigham on the recommendation of Colonel Thomas L. Kane, and upon the assurance of that gentleman that the charges against Brigham Young's Christian morality were unfounded." A judge, the attorney, and the marshal of the district court, were also Mormons. Two of the judges were " Gentiles." Thus was impressed a Mormon policy upon the Federal relations of the Territory.

The Federal officers arrived in July, and were soon involved in trouble. Judge Brocchus reprobated polygamy in a public assembly, and was told by the Governor, " I will kick you or any other Gentile judge from this stand, if you or they again attempt to interfere with the affairs of our Zion ! " He afterward said, " If I had *crooked my finger*, the women would have torn him to pieces." Disliking such tenure of office and life, the Gentile Federal officers retreated from the Territory, and left affairs in the hands of their Mormon colleagues. Judge Shaver, who succeeded Brocchus, died, with some suspicion of foul play ; and Judge Reed, his associate, returned to New York. A third set of officials was sent out in 1854, whose relations with the Mormon chiefs became still more unpleasant. A bitter controversy sprang up between Judge Drummond and the Saints, with mutual accusations of crime. The former charged the massacre of Lieutenant Gunnison's party on the Mormons, together with many other outrages; while the latter retorted with allegations of gross immorality. Judge Drummond, having got to Carson's Valley, took care not to return.

The Secretary of State, Almon W. Babbitt, having offended Brigham Young, started across the Plains, but was murdered on the road by Indians " who spoke good English ; " or, in other words, by Mormons. Brigham's comment was : " There was Almon W. Babbitt. He undertook to quarrel with me, *and soon after was killed by the Indians.* He

[1] " Rocky Mountain Saints," p. 275.

lived like a fool, and died like a fool." This unrelenting vindictiveness of Brigham seems the worst feature of his character.

Judge Styles was a Mormon who had outgrown his faith ; and, having offended the Saints by his decision of a question of jurisdiction adversely to their wishes, he was set upon, insulted, and threatened by the Mormon bar. His records and books were stolen, and, as he supposed, burned ; though, in fact, they were hidden for subsequent use by Clawson, Brigham's son-in-law and confidential clerk. Styles escaped to complain at Washington City; but his intimate friend, a lawyer named Williams, was murdered.

Whether the immoralities charged against the Federal officials were true or not, their chief sin was the effort to punish the crimes of certain violent men, who in the name of religion had instituted a reign of terror over the Mormons themselves. The Danites, or Destroying Angels, were a secret organization, said to have originated with one Dr. Avard, in the Missouri troubles of 1838. They had their grips and passwords; and blind obedience to the Prophet was the sole article of their creed. They have had their prototypes under every aspect of despotism, such as the Kruptoi of Sparta, the stabbers of Dr. Francia, and the assassins of the Old Man of the Mountain. This secret police executed the bloody decrees of the church and the will of its president with merciless rigor, and hunted down Gentiles and apostate Saints under the combined influence of fanaticism, greed, and private vengeance.

Elder Stenhouse, in the thirty-sixth chapter of his "Rocky Mountain Saints," gives a terrible picture of the outburst of fanaticism in the "Reformation" of 1856. This was "a revival" begun by Jedediah M. Grant, in which the most dangerous dogmas of their church were pressed to their extremest consequences, and the whole population was in a ferment of religious frenzy. It has already been stated that whatever was plausible in doctrine or popular in ritual had been adopted into the Mormon Church, so that its creed was a seething mass of incongruous heresies and monstrous errors. Humanity recoiled 4,000 years with the growth of this bastard dispensation, which seemed to have exuded from the slime of the Nile, instead of drawing living waters from "Siloa's brook, that flowed fast by the oracle of God." The Godhead was dragged down to the likeness of the created, and pictured with all the appetites of humanity, while a brutal peasantry were taught that each one should become "a god " to create, populate, and reign over a new earth as his peculiar domain. This procreation, transmigration, and exaltation of souls, was to be secured by obedience and the practice of polygamy. All the worst possible phases of polygamy were practised, including incest. Heber C. Kimball, Young's associate in the first presidency, " declared to the people that Young was his God and their God." Grant said, "If President Young wants my wives, I will give them to him without a grumble, and he can take them whenever he likes." Confession was insisted on ; those who hesitated were excommunicated, and those who confessed were published and punished. Rebaptism for the remission of sins was enjoined. The wavering, the doubtful, the suspected, were seized by night, whipped, ducked, or even worse maltreated. Brigham Young taught that " to love thy neighbor as thyself " meant to prevent his apostasy by shedding his blood. Many murders and other outrages were the consequence ; and the hatred and fury against the Gentiles, engendered in these heated imaginations, had much to do with the resistance to the United States Government, and the acts of open hostility in 1857.

After the inauguration of Mr. Buchanan, he determined to put an end to the conflict of authority in Utah by the removal from office of Brigham Young, and the appointment of an entire body of Federal officers in no wise affiliated with Mormonism. Alfred Cumming, of Georgia, was made Governor; D. R. Eckles, Chief-Justice ; John Cradlebaugh and Charles E. Sinclair, Associate Justices; John Hartnett, Secretary ; and Peter K. Dotson, Marshal. A detachment of the army, under Brigadier-General Harney, was ordered to accompany the Federal appointees, to protect them from the violence shown their predecessors, and to act as a *posse comitatus* in the execution of the laws.

Brigham is said to have received this news on the 24th of July, 1857, when celebrating the tenth anniversary of his arrival in Salt Lake City. Two thousand persons were present in a camp-meeting at Big Cottonwood Lake, and their leader fired all hearts by his denunciation of the Gentiles, and his resolve to resist the authority of the United States. " God was with them, and the devil had taken him at his word. He had said ten years before, and he could but repeat it, he would ask no odds of Uncle Sam or the devil." He had said in 1853, "*I am and will be Governor, and no power can hinder it*, until the Lord Almighty says, ' Brigham, you need not be Governor any longer.' "

When the Mormons had found that the Treaty of Guadalupe Hidalgo, in 1848, made them American instead of Mexican citizens, they had submitted patiently in the belief that they would be able to build up a sovereign state on the basis of their peculiar ideas. They were satisfied with their allegiance when they only felt it in the payment of salaries by the Federal Government to officials of their own faith. The California immigration proved so lucrative to the Saints that, at first, it gave little discontent; but when it left a residuum of Gentiles in Utah, whose criticism or obduracy provoked the enmity of the Mormon leaders, the old rancor was quickly revived, and the Destroying Angels were summoned to their bloody work. Assassination was very common, and other outrages frequent, traceable to this cause. But to place the civil government in Gentile hands would, it was feared, prove the downfall of the "kingdom;" Gentiles would be protected, Danites punished, and the machinery of the church dislocated. Resistance was resolved upon.

Stenhouse says (page 353):

The Saints had no time now to lose; the enemy was approaching their homes. The leaders preached war, prayed war, taught war; while saintly poets scribbled war, and the people sang their ditties. The 'God of battles' was the deity of the hour, and his influence was everywhere seen and felt. Public works and private enterprise were alike suspended, while every artist who had sufficient genius for the manufacture of revolvers, repairing old guns, or burnishing and sharpening rusty sabres and bayonets, was pressed into the service of Zion. The sisters, too, were seized with the war-fever, and their weaving and knitting talents were fully exercised in preparation for the coming campaign. It was a great time for rejoicing in the Lord, cursing Uncle Sam, and keeping powder dry.

The Mormon outlying colonies, at San Bernardino, Carson's, Washoe, and Jack's Valleys, and elsewhere, were called in; and these Saints sold for a song property soon after worth millions. Missionaries returned in disguise. Preparations for desperate revolt were made; and the people were taught that war to the knife, even to the desolation of the land, was to be the measure of their resistance. Major Van Vliet, the quartermaster, sent to purchase lumber for quarters, forage, and subsistence, arrived on September 3d, and found to his surprise that he could buy nothing for the Government, and that the troops were to be treated as enemies. He was told by Brigham Young that " the troops now on the march for Utah should not enter Salt Lake Valley."

Major Van Vliet explained that the action in regard to Utah was exactly that taken in regard to all the other Territories, and that no hostile demonstration against the inhabitants was contemplated. But he found the president, leaders, and people, unanimous in their determination to prevent United States troops from entering the valley.

Major Van Vliet left on the 14th of September; and, on the next day, Brigham Young issued a proclamation of the most inflammatory character, beginning—

Citizens of Utah: We are invaded by a hostile force who are evidently assailing us to accomplish our overthrow and destruction.

After reciting the various supposed grounds of grievance against the United States, and declaring, "Our duty to ourselves, to our families, requires us not tamely to be driven and slain without an attempt to preserve ourselves," he concludes:

Therefore, I, Brigham Young, Governor, etc.—1. Forbid all forces of every description from coming into this Territory, under any pretense whatever.

2. That all the forces in said Territory hold themselves in readiness to march at a moment's notice to repel any and all such invasion.

3. Martial law is hereby declared to exist in this Territory from and after the publication of this proclamation, and no person shall be allowed to pass or repass into or through or from the Territory without a permit from the proper officers.

On the next day, at the Tabernacle, the spirit of enthusiasm was increased by war speeches from the leaders. Brigham broke into the following strain of denunciation and vigorous metaphor:

We have borne enough of their oppression and hellish abuse, and we will not bear any more of it, for there is no just law requiring further forbearance on our part. And I am not going to have troops here to protect the priests and hellish rabble in efforts to drive us from the land we possess; for the Lord does not want us to be driven, and has said, "If you will assert your rights, and keep my commandments, you shall never again be brought into bondage by your enemies." . . . They say that their army is legal; and I say that such a statement is as false as hell, and that they are as rotten as an old pumpkin that has been frozen seven times and melted in a harvest sun. Come on with your thousands of illegally-ordered troops, and I will promise you, in the name of Israel's God, that you shall melt away as the snow before a July sun. . . . You might as well tell me you can make hell into a powder-house as to tell me you could let an army in here and have peace; and I intend to tell them and show them this if they do not stay away. . . . And I say our enemies shall not slip the bow on old Bright's neck again. God bless you! Amen.

This declaration of independence by the Mormon Prophet was reiterated from every pulpit. It is a curious illustration of the power of fanaticism that the refutation of his fallacious revelations and the speedy failure of his prophecies did not shake the faith of his disciples.

At the same meeting of September 16th, Heber Kimball, Brigham's first councilor, abject sycophant, and a blasphemous old buffoon, preached thus:

Is there a collision between us and the United States? No; we have not collashed; that is the word that sounds nearest to what I mean. But now the thread is cut between them and us, and we will never gybe again—no, never, worlds without end (voices, "Amen!"). . . . Do as you are told, and Brigham Young will never leave the governorship of this Territory, from this time henceforth and forever. No, never. . . . The spirit that is upon me this morning is the Spirit of the Lord, that is, the Holy Ghost—though some of you may think the Holy Ghost is never cheerful. Well, let me tell you, the Holy Ghost is a man; he is one of the sons of our Father and our God, and he is that man that stood next to Jesus Christ—just as I stand by Brother Brigham. . . . You think our Father and our God is not a lively, sociable, and cheerful man; he is one of the most lively men that ever lived. . . . Brother Brigham is my leader, he is my prophet and my seer, my revelator: and whatever he says, that is for me to do, and it is not for me to question him one word, nor to question God a minute.

Such were the teachings of the heads of the church.

In the mean time the Saints were organized and drilled; and rough defenses were built in Echo Cañon, and other approaches to the valley.

The Territory of Utah, as at present constituted, extends from 109° to 114° west longitude, and from 37° to 42° north latitude, with an area of 84,476 square miles. But the kingdom which Brigham tried to set up claimed wider and undefined limits. The Wahsatch Range bisects the Territory for 400 miles in a southwesterly direction, including in its eastern section table-lands 5,000 feet above the sea-level, and on its western slopes a series of valleys of half that altitude. The air has the dryness of the desert, and the sandy, porous soil drinks up the mountain-torrents. Wherever irrigation is possible, the earth yields abundantly; and coal, iron, gold, silver, and lead, are found in the mountains; but the largest part of the country must always be devoted to pastoral purposes. Its cloudless skies, lofty mountains, and green intervales, offer grand and varied scenery to the eye and imagination. The population has generally been over-estimated. In 1870 the census reported it at 88,374; and in 1857 it may be safely computed at about 35,000 cr 40,000.

When Brigham looked up at his Alpine walls and their warders, he believed his stronghold impregnable. Its defiles were guarded by hardy mountaineers, trained to blind obedience and pitiless zeal by ten years in the wilderness; and the Indian tribes, the intervening desert, and an almost arctic winter, were counted on as sure and cruel allies. He had seen the unopposed emigrant fall their victim; and the prophecy seemed safe that, great as were the odds, he could foil an invading army. In spite of his undoubted ability, and well-organized people, he was without intelligent military advice, and but repeating the policy of Schamyl and other barbarian chiefs, to whom he was little superior in information. He therefore indulged himself in the dream of successful revolt and complete independence.

The following are his orders, issued through Daniel H. Wells, his commander-in-chief, on the 4th of October, 1856:

On ascertaining the locality or route of the troops, proceed at once to annoy them in every possible way. Use every exertion to stampede their animals and set fire to their trains. Burn the whole country before them and on their flanks. Keep them from sleeping by night-surprises. Blockade the road by felling trees, or destroying the fords when you can. Watch for opportunities to set fire to the grass on their windward, so as, if possible, to envelop their trains. Leave no grass before them that can be burned. Keep your men concealed as much as possible, and guard against surprise. Keep scouts out at all times, and communication open with Colonel Burton, Major McAllister, and O. P. Rockwell, who are operating in the same way. Keep me advised daily of your movements, and every step the troops take, and in which direction.

God bless you, and give you success.

Your brother in Christ,

(Signed)   DANIEL H. WELLS.

These judicious instructions for partisan warfare, though not executed with much vigor, met some success, as will appear hereafter. It
were well for humanity and the Mormon name had their hostility been
restricted to legitimate war ; but who shall set bounds to religious
hate ? The chronic rancor against the Gentiles had been envenomed
by the delirious " reformation " of the year before, and by the killing of
the apostle Perley Pratt, in Arkansas. Pratt had seduced the wife
and abducted the children of a man named McLean, who followed him
from San Francisco to Arkansas, where he overtook and slew him in
combat. Though Mormon "common law" justifies homicide as the
penalty of adultery, the Gentile has not the benefit of the rule, and vengeance was denounced against the people of Arkansas. The new access
of fury, stimulated by the approach of the troops, culminated in September, 1857, in an unparalleled atrocity. Robbery, outrage, and murder, had been the ordinary fate of the alien and the waverer, but the
climax of religious rage was reached in the massacre at Mountain
Meadows.

A band of emigrants, about 135 in number, quietly traveling from
Arkansas to Southern California, arrived in Utah. This company was
made up of farmers' families, allied by blood or friendship, and far above
the average in wealth, intelligence, and orderly conduct. They were
Methodists, and had religious service regularly morning and evening.
They expected, according to custom, to refit their teams in Utah, and
buy food and forage sufficient to pass the California Desert ; but, to
their horror, this reasonable traffic was everywhere refused. When they
stopped at the Jordan to rest, they were ordered to move on ; and
Brigham sent a courier ahead to forbid all intercourse with the weary
and terror-stricken band. Pity or covetousness evaded the decree so far
as to permit the purchase of thirty bushels of corn at Fillmore, and
fifty bushels of flour at Cedar City. But so exhausted did the emigrants become, that they made but thirty-five miles in their last four
days of travel.

As they were thus crawling along, " the decree was passed, devoting said company to destruction ; " and the militia was regularly called
out under orders from a military council at Parowan. The authorities
were Colonel W. H. Dame, Lieutenant-Colonel Isaac C. Haight, President and High-Priest of Southern Utah, and Major John D. Lee, a
bishop of the church. Their orders were to "kill the entire company,
except the little children." The Mormon regiment, with some Indian
auxiliaries, attacked the emigrants soon after they broke up camp on
September 12th. The travelers quickly rallied, corraled their wagons,
and kept up such a fire that the assailants were afraid to come to close
quarters. Reënforcements were sent for, and arrived ; but still the
Mormons did not venture to assault the desperate men, who were fight-

ing for their wives and little ones. At last, on the 15th, the fourth day of the siege, Lee sent in a flag of truce, offering, " if the emigrants would lay down their arms, to protect them." They complied, laid down their arms, and half an hour afterward the massacre began. All were killed except seventeen little children. Every atrocity accompanied the slaughter, and the corpses were mutilated and left naked on the ground. " Three men got out of the valley, two of whom were soon overtaken and killed ; the other reached Muddy Creek, fifty miles off, and was overtaken and killed by several white men and one Indian." Eighteen months afterward the surviving children were rescued and restored to their friends in Arkansas, by Jacob Forney, Superintendent of Indian Affairs. Thirty thousand dollars' worth of plunder was distributed ; and Beadle, in his " Life in Utah," says : " Much of it was sold in Cedar City at *public auction ;* it was there facetiously styled ' property taken at the siege of Sebastopol.' " But it is needless to dwell upon the details of this foul crime; though at first denied by the Mormons, proofs of their guilt accumulated as the years rolled on, and the evidence that it was a cold-blooded affair of state is now complete. It was asserted, at the time, that the order of extermination came from headquarters ; Lee was a son by adoption of Brigham Young, and was always protected by him. Brigham's word was law in church and state, and such a deed would not have been done without his approbation, and scarcely except by his orders. It was in accordance with the letter and spirit of his teaching at the time ; and his subsequent conduct proving him an accessory after the fact also implicates him with the perpetration of the crime. He availed himself of his official position, as Governor and Superintendent of Indian Affairs, to bury in oblivion this dreadful crime, and throw the mantle of the Prophet around the shedders of innocent blood. According to his works let him be judged.

John D. Lee enjoyed twenty years of impunity, but he was at last brought to justice, convicted of and executed for this crime in 1877. Soon afterward the hand which had shielded him so long yielded the reins of power to the conqueror Death.

The words and deeds of the Mormons, which have been given, are illustrations of the temper of that people and their chief toward the United States, in 1857. A violent revolt was in motion, and we shall now see how this hostile population was brought back to its allegiance.

CHAPTER XIV.

UTAH CAMPAIGN.

THOUGH the troubles in Utah had been so long brewing, their nature seems to have been imperfectly understood by the people and Government of the United States. The Mormons made occasional public and formal professions of loyalty to the Government and of adhesion to the principles of American liberty; and their complaints were nominally against particular acts and persons. Hence it was not unreasonable to suppose that the remedy of particular grievances and the punishment of particular offenders would insure the peace of the Territory. This inference, though natural, was a mistake; because the grounds of variance were general and radical, and not special, as pretended.

The Mormons alleged national persecution, when, in fact, the religious freedom of the country had allowed them to preach a pagan doctrine and a barbarous code of ethics, to proselytize, and to develop their heresy into a system. Where the strong hand of an arbitrary government would have repressed their extravagances, American faith in the power of truth to triumph over error by moral forces permitted them to occupy an almost impregnable stronghold on the established road across the continent for commerce and immigration, where they were encouraged to levy a peaceful tribute as farmers and traders. But the Government went even beyond this; and, in the spirit of conciliation, aided the union of church and state in the hands of the Prophet by making him Governor and Superintendent of Indian Affairs, and by giving him the virtual control of the Territory. This policy had worked badly; Brigham Young and his coadjutors had abused the trust reposed in them ; life, liberty, and property, were all made unsafe by his machinations. It was, therefore, found necessary to supersede him; but this was done in no hostile spirit.

The general conduct of our Government toward all dependencies had been fostering; and this could not be otherwise with the Administration of Mr. Buchanan, which, moulded by the character of its chief, was essentially bureaucratic, conservative, and pacific. The Secretary of War, Mr. Floyd, expresses this sentiment in his report for 1857-'58: "It has always been the policy and desire of the Federal Government to avoid collision with the Mormon community. It has borne with the insubordination they have exhibited under circumstances where respect for its own authority has frequently counseled harsh measures of discipline." The Secretary adds that this forbearance might have been prolonged but for their attitude—"a lion in the path"—across the line of commerce and emigration, defying the Federal authority, and exciting the Indians to pillage and massacre.

To sustain the newly-appointed civil functionaries, and protect the line of travel, it was determined to send a small force of troops to Utah and establish a military department there similar to others on the frontier; but every measure was taken to avoid offense to the self-love and prejudices of the people. The force sent was small, and the orders given were strict. Though the intended commander, General Harney, was informed that he must not be unprepared for general, organized, and formidable obstruction, still it was not really expected that the local authorities, or Mormon Church as such, would array themselves in open opposition to the United States; but that embarrassments from popular disorder, mob violence, and secret combinations, fomented by priestcraft, would require management and a show of force. Indeed, the state of affairs in Utah was entirely unforeseen at Washington. The Government expected turbulence—it found armed and open hostility; it provided against sedition, and had to meet a rebellion; it sent a *posse comitatus* where it needed an army of occupation.

When the expedition to Utah was determined on General Harney was selected to command it. In his orders of May 28th the Fifth and Tenth Regiments of Infantry, the Second Regiment of Dragoons, and Phelps's light artillery, were designated as the force to be sent forward, with supplies for 2,500 men. Reno's battery was afterward added. As no active opposition was expected, and the season was already advanced, the troops and supply-trains marched as soon as they could be put in motion, in July, in a somewhat irregular manner. General Scott suggested to General Harney, on the 26th of June, to send part of his horse in advance to Fort Laramie to recruit in strength before the main body came up; but, unfortunately, this was not done. The Second Dragoons were detained in Kansas in consequence of the political troubles there; and, finally, at the request of Governor Walker, and probably in accordance with his own wishes, General Harney was himself retained in command of that department.

From information received, it began to be feared that the dissension might end in a rupture with the Mormons, and apprehensions were awakened that, owing to the lateness of the season and the desultory character of the movement, some disaster might ensue. As cold weather approached these fears increased, and the public shared with the Government in the most painful surmises as to the result. Finally, General Johnston was selected to succeed General Harney, and, on the 28th of August, received orders to repair to Fort Leavenworth and assume command, governing himself by the orders and instructions already issued to General Harney. The following extract contains the most important points in these, and is inserted to show the scope of the intended movement, and also the nature of General Johnston's duties, which subsequently became matter of controversy between Governor Cumming and himself:

HEADQUARTERS OF THE ARMY, *June* 29, 1857.

. . . . The community and, in part, the civil government of Utah Territory are in a state of substantial rebellion against the laws and authority of the United States. A new civil Governor is about to be designated, and to be charged with the establishment and maintenance of law and order. Your able and energetic aid, with that of the troops to be placed under your command, is relied upon to insure the success of his mission. The principles by which you should be guided have been already indicated in a somewhat similar case, and are here substantially repeated.

If the Governor of the Territory, finding the ordinary course of judicial proceedings, and the power vested in the United States marshals and other proper officers, inadequate for the preservation of the public peace and the due execution of the laws, should make requisition upon you for a military force to aid him as a *posse comitatus* in the performance of that official duty, you are hereby directed to employ for that purpose the whole or such part of your command as may be required; or should the Governor, the judges, or marshals of the Territory find it necessary directly to summon a part of your troops to aid either in the performance of his duties, you will take care that the summons be promptly obeyed; and in no case will you, your officers, or men, attack any body of citizens whatever except on such requisition or summons, or in sheer self-defense. In executing this delicate function of the military power of the United States the civil responsibility will be upon the Governor, the judges, and marshals of the Territory. While you are not to be, and cannot be, subjected to the orders, strictly speaking, of the Governor, you will be responsible for a zealous, harmonious, and thorough coöperation with him, on frequent and full consultation, and will conform your action to his request and views in all cases where your military judgment and prudence do not forbid, nor compel you to modify in execution the movements he may suggest. No doubt is entertained that your conduct will fully meet the moral and professional responsibilities of your trust, and justify the high confidence already reposed in you by the Government.

The lateness of the season, the dispersed condition of the troops, and the smallness of the numbers available, have seemed to present elements of difficulty, if not hazard, in this expedition. But it is believed that these may be compensated by unusual care in its outfit and great prudence in its conduct. . . .

GEORGE W. LAY,
Lieutenant-Colonel, Aide-de-Camp to General Scott.

General Johnston arrived at Fort Leavenworth, September 11th, and remained one week to complete arrangements for the expedition. The Second Dragoons were called in, and, such was the diligence of preparation, were on the road to Salt Lake on the 17th. Six companies of this cavalry were assigned as an escort to Governor Cumming and the civil officers of Utah ; but General Johnston in person waited on the Governor, and offered him his choice between the escort and accompanying himself to Utah. The Governor chose the former. General Johnston allowed great discretion in the movements of the escort to the commander, Lieutenant-Colonel Philip St. George Cooke, whom he mentions as " a cavalry-officer of great experience, and well acquainted with frontier service."

So much was General Johnston impressed with the necessity of celerity that, leaving Fort Leavenworth on the 18th of September, with an escort of forty dragoons, he made the journey to camp, near South Pass, 920 miles, over bad and muddy roads in twenty-seven days, arriving there October 15th. But this speed was not at the expense of any important interest, as he availed himself of every opportunity on the route to further the ends of the expedition, by providing for the safe and rapid movement of mails, trains, and troops. Learning that the grass ahead was bad, he arranged to have thirty-one extra wagons of corn with strong teams waiting for Colonel Cooke at Fort Kearny, and attended to many details not necessary to specify here. The journey across the Plains has been so often and so well described that its incidents are familiar to all who take an interest in the subject. There was nothing unusual in General Johnston's progress, except its speed, which was great, considering the absence of relays, and the condition of the roads, softened by the fall rains.

General Fitz-John Porter, then major and assistant-adjutant-general, who accompanied General Johnston on this expedition, rendering him valuable aid, has placed the writer under great obligations by memoranda, of which he has freely availed himself. General Porter says :

Colonel Johnston entered upon no ordinary task. His command and their subsistence, clothing, and means of erecting shelter, were stretched over nearly 1,000 miles of almost desert road between Fort Kearny and Salt Lake. So late in the season had the troops started on their march that fears were entertained that, if they succeeded in reaching their destination, it would be only by abandoning the greater part of their supplies and endangering the lives of many men amid the snows of the Rocky Mountains. Colonel Johnston felt and accepted the responsibility, determined, if possible, to reach his destination and to secure the expedition against ·disaster and perhaps destruction, which the rapidly-approaching winter threatened. So much was a terrible disaster feared by those well acquainted with the rigors of a winter life in the Rocky Mountains, that General Harney was said to have predicted it, and to have induced Governor Walker (of Kansas) to ask for his retention. The route was not then, as now, lined with settlements and ranches, which would afford some comfort to man and beast.

The narrow valleys, already grazed over by thousands of animals, yielded a scanty subsistence for his horses; yet he pushed on at the rate of from thirty to sixty miles a day, stopping at Forts Kearny and Laramie only time enough to rest his teams—a day at each.

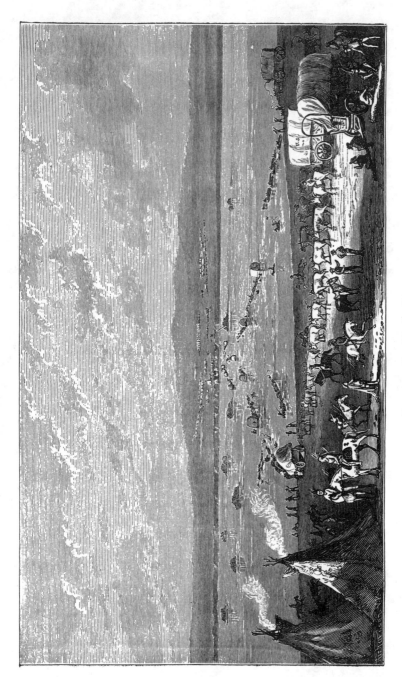

Crossing the Platte River.

On the 29th of September, on the South Fork of the Platte, General Johnston received Captain Van Vliet's report of his journey to Salt Lake City, which was his first authentic information that actual organized resistance by the Mormons might be expected. General Johnston gathered some 200 mounted men on the route, with whom he reënforced Lieutenant-Colonel C. F. Smith, and gave support to the supply-trains. General Porter says:

Beyond Fort Laramie, rumors of trains destroyed and troops attacked reached Colonel Johnston. Van Vliet's return with ill reports only tended to increase the alarm along the route. Conductors of trains hesitated, and teamsters shirked duty and delayed progress. Colonel Johnston's anxiety increased, yet his speed could be no greater; but, experienced on the Plains and of established reputation for energy, courage, and resources, his presence restored confidence at all points, and encouraged the weak-hearted and panic-stricken multitude. The long chain of wagons, kinked, tangled, and hard to move, uncoiled and went forward smoothly. Near the Rocky Mountains snow-storms began to overtake us, but Bridger, the faithful and experienced guide, ever on the alert, would point in time to the "snow-boats," which, like balloons, sailing from the snow-capped mountains, warned us of storms, and would hasten to a good and early camp in time for shelter before the tempest broke upon us. At the South Pass a cold and driving snow-storm barred progress for a few days, but permitted the gathering of trains, which, assured of protection and of intelligent control, and encouraged by the cheerful words and bearing of our commander, moved on with renewed life.

When General Johnston arrived in the neighborhood of the South Pass, October 15th, his first endeavor was to concentrate his trains at Pacific Springs, five miles beyond, and to assemble and organize a sufficient force for their protection. To this end he hastened the march of Lieutenant Smith and Colonel Cooke by all means possible, and enrolled in military companies all unemployed teamsters and camp-followers. He also interdicted all communication with the Mormons, and took measures for the arrest of spies and unknown persons approaching the camps. On the 2d of October the Mormons had moved to the rear of Colonel Alexander's command and burned three trains, including seventy-five wagons loaded with provisions and quartermaster's stores, and driven off the draught-animals to Salt Lake Valley. This occurred on Green River, near the Sandy, before General Johnston arrived at Laramie. They were greatly elated with this successful stroke; but it is evidence of great want of enterprise, or of intelligence, that they did not pursue their advantage and burn all the trains, which they might easily have done without risk, as they were well mounted, and the infantry too far off to interfere, while the cavalry was 700 miles in the rear.

The infantry and artillery of the expedition, about 1,100 men, were assembled on October 4th, on Ham's Fork, at a camp some thirty miles from Fort Bridger and 130 miles from South Pass. Next day Colonel Alexander, having assumed command, determined, after counsel with his senior officers, that the Fort Bridger route to Salt Lake Valley was impracticable on account of the defenses in Echo Cañon, and that the more circuitous route by the most northern bend of Bear River Valley offered the best chance of safely wintering the troops. This movement was begun without knowledge of the mishap to the supply-trains in his rear.

General Johnston, having satisfied himself by those mental processes so much like intuition to the observer that Bear River Valley was impracticable, and Fort Bridger the only point of concentration where the army could be wintered, acted with his usual decision. He took every means to this end, and ordered Colonel Alexander to withdraw his command, so as to effect a junction, and "to treat as enemies all who might appear in arms or in any way annoy him." In the mean time he advanced the trains as fast as he could under escort.

But General Johnston found his efforts to concentrate opposed by a foe more potent than the Mormons. Winter fell suddenly upon his unprepared men and animals. On the night of the 17th there was a snow-storm, and the thermometer fell to 16°. Colonel Smith lost eleven mules by cold, and as many more in the next few days, and the trains suffered severely. General Johnston had passed about 200 wagons, belonging to contractors and merchant-trains, near the Three Crossings of the Sweetwater, on the 13th. It was nine days before the rear of these trains came up with Lieutenant Smith's command, so much were the draught-animals reduced by want of grass. These trains were necessary to the march of the troops, as they contained the winter clothing and Sibley tents, besides subsistence, ordnance, and medical stores, to a large amount, indispensable to the comfort and efficiency of the men. Without them no advance could be made, except with great suffering, and perhaps loss of life. Still, go forward they must, in order to effect the junction with Colonel Alexander on Ham's Fork, ninety miles distant. Colonel Alexander in the mean time, on account of the heavy snows and to secure supplies, had fortunately begun to retrace his steps before receiving General Johnston's orders. A few days of delay would have rendered a junction impossible. General Johnston, convinced by the destruction of the army-trains, and by their hostile language and attitude, of the warlike purpose of the Mormon leaders and people, wrote to the adjutant-general on November 5th, reciting the facts. He adds :

The state of things now existing has not been brought about by the movement of troops in this direction, for these people understand the relation of the military to the civil power of the Government as well as any other portion of the inhabitants of the Union, and that the arms of our soldiers are designed for the preservation of the peaceful condition of society, and not for its disturbance. Their conduct, as I have before stated as my opinion, results from a settled determination on their part not to submit to the authority of the United States, or any other outside of their church.

These views of General Johnston, though sustained theoretically by the Administration, Congress, and the country, were the subject of severe animadversion by some members of Congress, who perhaps misunderstood and certainly misapplied his language, representing him as breathing slaughter and vengeance against the Saints. The following is from a reply made to these strictures, in the Senate, by the Hon. Jefferson Davis:

Moreover, I would say, as the question of the expedition to Utah has been touched, that I hold that the country is indebted to the Administration for having selected the man who is at the head of the expedition; who, as a soldier, has not his superior in the army nor out of it, and whose judgment, whose art, whose knowledge are equal to this or any other emergency; a man of such decision, such resolution, that his country's honor can never be tarnished in his hands; a man of such calmness, such kindness, that a deluded people can never suffer by harshness from him.

General Johnston, writing February 5, 1858, from Fort Bridger, to Captain N. J. Eaton, of St. Louis, gives an account of the progress and extrication of the army, as follows:

The country over the distance to be traversed, and, in fact, to this place—125 miles—presents the appearance of a great desert, including the whole space between the Rocky Mountains and the range in front of us. There is neither tree nor bush anywhere, except in the water-courses. They are sparsely fringed with stunted willows, cottonwood, and aspen. The upland is everywhere covered with wild-sage and its varieties and with grass in bunches in season. Grass is found on all the water-courses in abundance in summer. The bad condition of our animals, and the country before us almost destitute of subsistence, offered but little encouragement to the hope of reaching our destination this winter, and I had already had under consideration the most suitable position to pass the winter. On our march from the South Pass we had fine roads and fine weather, and effected the march in eight days, uniting the troops and supplies on the 3d of November, with the exception of Cooke's command. Two days were occupied in distributing clothing and making arrangements to resume our march. On the 6th of November it was resumed, and then commenced the storm and wintry cold, racking the bones of our men and starving our oxen, and mules, and horses, already half starved. They died on the road and at our camps by hundreds, and so diminished were their numbers that from camp to camp, only four or five miles, as many days were required to bring them all up, as it was necessary to give time to rest the animals, now incapable of protracted efforts, and to hunt for food. In this way fifteen days were consumed in making thirty-five miles to this place, the nearest and best place for shelter and fuel for the troops, and for shelter and grass for the animals. The struggle then amid snow and arctic cold (the thermometer 16° below zero) was for a place of safety. If any doubt existed before this storm of the propriety of risking the troops on the mountains before us before spring, or of the ability to accomplish the march, the destruction among our draught-animals, the necessity of saving all the oxen left for food, even if capable of further exertion, now dispelled that doubt and solved the question.

Colonel Cooke's command arrived here with the rear of the main body on the 19th of November. The storm which he encountered on the Sweetwater, and on through the South Pass, destroyed more than half of his horses and a large number of his mules, although he had corn for them. In that high region, much higher than where we were, the cold must have been much more intense than experienced by us, and his animals, I presume, perished mainly from cold. I have the satisfaction to say that the privations of the march were endured by officers and men without complaint, or, perhaps, I might more justly say, with cheerfulness. The troops are in fine health and condition. The winter, thus far, has not been so rigorous as to prevent often the daily instruction of the troops. They have proved themselves to be hardy enough for any service; a few only—as many as thirty or less—have been frost-bitten, but now our scouts bivouac, when necessary, in the passes without suffering.

The horses and mules, and the cattle left, after slaughtering as many as would serve until April, have been distributed on Smith's and Henry's Forks, and most of them will get through the winter. We have, of course, a large number yet, and hope many of them will be fit for service after they have the spring grass a while. I have not, however, trusted to that, but, soon after I established my camp here, I dispatched Captain Marcy to New Mexico for draught-mules, and a remount for dragoons and batteries, and expect him to return before the 1st of May. If I get the spring supplies from Laramie in time I will be able to advance as soon as the route is practicable, in May, with an effective force, much improved by drilling the recruits.

The Mormons have declared, as fully as words and actions can manifest intentions, that they will no longer submit to the Government, or to any government but their own. The people of the Union must now submit to a usurpation of their territory—to have a government erected in their midst, not loyal to, or rather not acknowledging any dependence upon, or allegiance to the Federal Government—and what is not less impolitic and entirely incompatible with our institutions, must allow them to ingraft their social organization upon ours and make it a part of our system, or they must act with the vigor and force to compel them to submit. This is due to the dignity and honor of the Government.

In a subsequent explanatory letter, he says :

The march was resumed on the 6th of November, amid snow, intense cold, and every circumstance of privation to men and animals, and with enormous mortality to the latter, as long as it was possible to take another step, and long after any one believed a passage of the mountains at all possible for an army, encumbered with a train. This continued effort to advance was a struggle for fuel, and grass, and shelter, which we knew were near Fort Bridger. The army under my command took the last possible step forward at Bridger, in the condition of the animals then alive. These dying and half-dead animals were my only dependence for meat six days out of seven; and every day's work reduced fearfully the probability of my being able to feed the troops—a terrible risk with a six months' winter before us. The country being covered with snow, there was no subsistence for animals to be found in the mountains. I do not, of course, speak of small parties; a few men can go anywhere generally.

Describing this march, General Porter says:

That night (November 5th) a great storm covered the ground with six inches of snow, and the next day the march was for thirteen miles against a driving snow, threatening every hour to arrest the march. Many trains did not break camp for several days, and some, whose animals had been killed by intense cold and starvation, were not moved for weeks. Maintaining a cheerful and confident bearing, Colonel Johnston footed along at the head of the command, setting an example of endurance that checked complaint, and turned these trials into matter for jest and good-humor. The following day (November 7th) was one of a series of stormy days for nearly a month, and few can appreciate it who have not experienced a Rocky Mountain winter. All remained in the temporary shelter obtained the previous night. A driving snow-storm and intense cold prevailed all day. Sage-brush and "grease-wood" were the only fuel, and that very scarce. The burden was to be borne; the question was one of self-preservation; there must be no confusion, no grumbling, no demoralization. Officers and men were accommodated alike, and the former, taking their cue from the bearing of their commander, maintained a cheerful tone and assured their men. The snow covered the ground to about a foot in depth; there was no food for animals, and the streams were frozen by cold 16° below zero. Unshod, the oxen slipped to rise no more; hundreds died, and the mules would cluster around the abandoned night-fires to waste away with hunger and cold. Whenever the weather would permit, the troops would march, going three to five miles a day, till they reached Fort Bridger, near which camp was pitched for the winter. The trains were about twenty days making the last fifteen miles. The great loss and weakened condition of the animals required many trips to bring up each train.

Colonel Cooke, in his report, says:

The assurances you gave me of confidence in my commander have been more than realized, and he now has, I believe, the unbounded confidence of the army. You will see from his letters and orders how he grappled with the difficulties in his path, and I hope the spring will see him the conqueror. This little army is in fine health and cheerful spirits. The men have borne their trials without a murmur. Duty is severe upon the men, but not a word of complaint have I heard. We have all endured alike, and the fact that Colonel Johnston has on the march "footed it," as did the men, suffers the same exposure, and will not permit the officer to receive more than the soldier, has endeared him to all.

The arrival at Fort Bridger marked one distinct phase of the expedition. It was rescue from sudden and impending death under the pitiless pelting of the winter storms. It was present safety.

It is hardly necessary to point out the severe tests of soldiership to which General Johnston was subjected in this extraordinary march. He had, in the face of an unexpected enemy and of an unprecedented season, gathered the disjointed fragments of his army into a compact body, and, in the midst of the snow-clad and mountain-girdled desert, had secured it in a place of shelter and safety. In a Moscow campaign he had won a victory over the elements ; and his little command rose from its frozen couch in the desert, not only without demoralization, but fully inspired with confidence in themselves and their commander. A great result had been achieved ; but the arrival at Fort Bridger was but the beginning of new cares and responsibilities. If, in carrying out his plans, he was untrammeled by Government, he was likewise unassisted. He did not receive one word of orders or advice from headquarters from the middle of September to the middle of March. The problem was so to apply existing resources as to maintain the army without suffering until the next May, when belated trains at Fort Laramie could bring up supplies, and then have it in condition to force the passes to Salt Lake City. This hope and intention he expressed in decided terms to the Government ; but, at the same time, he pointed out that, in case of vigorous resistance by the Mormons, a coöperating force sent from the side of California would prove the most effective means of crushing resistance with the least delay, expense, and loss of life. Arrangements were made to carry this plan into effect, but were subsequently abandoned.

General Johnston mustered into service for nine months, at Fort Bridger, a battalion of four full companies of volunteers, 325 men, the discharged employés of army contractors and others, of whom he says : "They are young, active, and hardy men, generally good shots; and, with such instruction as they will receive, will make most excellent light troops." These auxiliaries, with the cavalry, raised the force to about 2,000 men.

The Mormons, before retiring, had burned the buildings at Fort Bridger and Fort Supply, twelve miles distant, and had destroyed the grain and crops round about. Fort Bridger was situated on Black's Fork of Green River, near the foot of the Uintah Mountains, in latitude 41° 20', and longitude 110° 30', at an altitude said to be 7,254 feet above the sea. The basin, in the southwest corner of which it is placed, is bounded far away to the east by the Black Hills and other flanking ranges of the Rocky Mountains, on the northeast by the Wind River Mountains, on the south by the Uintah Mountains, and on the west by the mighty Wahsatch range. These mountain-ranges tower with a crest-line of from 10,000 to 12,000 feet in height, broken by peaks that are often over 13,000 feet high, sometimes snow-clad in August. In the valleys and cañons, whose narrow bottoms are threaded by Alpine torrents, the precipitous walls rise from 800 to 1,000 feet perpendicular; and here gather the winter snows to the depth, sometimes, of fifty feet, forming, too, in favorable sites, avalanches and land-slides of great extent. The Uintah Mountains break down in terraces to the foot-hills; and they, to the wide, arid, sterile plateau, over which the troops had toiled from the South Pass. The soil of this table-land, like that of many other deserts, contains the elements of fertility, but is unproductive from want of water.

From the ravines of the mountains pour down the streams that form Henry's, Black's, Smith's, Muddy, and Sandy Fork, and other tributaries of Green River. These small rivers, bordered by sunken valleys, rich, alluvial, and teeming, traverse the Desert Basin. The valley of Henry's Fork is from one to five miles wide, and thirty miles long, abounding in luxuriant grass; that of Black's Fork is nearly a mile wide, and composed of rich, black mould; and others have similar characteristics. These valleys were, in the summer-time, oases, where wood, water, and fine pasturage, invited and rejoiced the first pioneers. But it was only by comparison with the surrounding region that such a nook as Fort Bridger could be considered a favored spot. In their dire need, however, the storm-pressed wayfarers looked toward it as a city of refuge in a solitude of snow.

Fort Bridger itself was only the ruins of a trading-post, belonging to the adventurous and large-hearted James Bridger. "Major" Bridger, as he was called, was a fine specimen of his class, the early pioneer, who was at once hunter, trapper, herdsman, and trader. It was located in the comparatively warm, wooded, and well-watered valley of Black's Fork, and consisted of a high, well-built, strong stone-wall, inclosing a square of 100 feet. General Johnston fortified it by the addition of two lunettes, which made it defensible by a small force, and a safe place for the storage of supplies and for a guarded depot when the army should advance. The army was put into winter quarters close by, at Camp Scott.

The diary of Major Porter, assistant adjutant-general, kindly put at the disposal of the writer, has this entry:

November 17*th.*—Marched and camped on Black's Fork, about one mile and three-quarters above Fort Bridger, and established winter-quarters. The arrangements for a permanent camp were entered upon immediately. Nothing seems to have been neglected by our chief for the health and comfort of our men, the security of the camp, provisions, animals for the winter, and to insure movement as early as spring will permit.

General Porter, in a letter to the writer, says:

Horses and mules, followed by such oxen as would survive the trip, were sent to the neighboring valleys where the grazing was ample. The starving oxen, now almost skeletons, were butchered to prevent dying, and their meat smoked, or dried, or packed in ice. The provision was carefully estimated, and the ration so proportioned that there should be no suffering. Officers and men fared alike, and there was no deviation from the rule for any one's benefit. The bulk of the ration was poor beef six days in the week, and bacon one day, and thirteen ounces of flour daily, made into bread; but the other component parts of the ration were served out in quantity sufficient for health.

General Porter continues:

No idleness was permitted in camp. There was no time or mercy for gamblers. The hundreds of citizen teamsters were not permitted to become an element of trouble. They had either to enroll as volunteers in the United States service, or return to the States. No permission to remain would be given them otherwise. Every one had an occupation; and an effective police, under a provost-marshal, responsible to the colonel, was established.

Captain Randolph B. Marcy, an accomplished, energetic officer and experienced explorer, was selected, with a small body of volunteering soldiers, to make their way across the Uintah Mountains into New Mexico, make known to General Garland our dangers and wants, and bring relief by way of Bridger's Pass early in the spring. Dispatches *via* Fort Laramie went to the Government, and an expedition through Bridger's Pass and along Lodge-Pole Creek was also sent with letters, with the view of testing the practicability and utility of this route, which was some seventy miles shorter. An expedition was also sent into the Snake Indian country to quiet the Indians, and prevent their employment by the Mormons, and to induce traders to bring cattle and horses to camp. These expeditions were all fruitful in good results. Captain Marcy's command, deemed a forlorn hope when it started, after many struggles against storms and starvation in the mountains, finally reached Fort Union, New Mexico, safe, but greatly weakened. Early in the spring Captain Marcy returned with numerous head of sheep and horses, escorted by cavalry under Colonel Loring, to guard against a threatened movement of the Mormons. The success of these expeditions through Bridger's Pass led in the spring to the opening by the Sixth Infantry of the route up Lodge-Pole Creek, through Bridger's Pass and down Bitter Creek; and that summer, as the road was shorter, easier, and better for grass, the Overland Stage Line and Pony Express were transferred to it from the Laramie route. Thus was opened the route afterward adopted by the Union Pacific Railroad. General Johnston made constant representations and strenuous efforts to have this route opened, feeling sure that it must be the route for a railroad, if one was ever made through the Salt Lake region.

As the army was bound to Salt Lake Valley, the Government regarded sending salt for rations as unnecessary—"coals to Newcastle." General Johnston took prompt steps to get a supply from Laramie; but, when none was to be had at Fort Bridger, grumbling began at the insipid food, and maledictions were hurled on the Subsistence Department at Washington. In the midst of one of the heaviest snow-storms of the season the picket-guard brought in three men bearing letters from Mormon officials to General Johnston. When admitted to his presence they stated that they bore letters from Adjutant-General Wells and were messengers from Governor Young, bringing several mule-loads of salt, which "he understood the army had none of, and that there was enough to last until spring, *when the army should retrace its steps to the United States*, as enter the Mormon settlement it should not."

After carefully reading the letter, and reëxamining parts of it, General Johnston, in an impressive manner, said:

"I will not accept of this salt sent by Brigham Young, not for the reason hinted in his letter, but I can accept of nothing from him so long as he and his people maintain a hostile position to my Government. I regret he has insinuated the probability of its refusal on account of its deleterious property. There is no portion of the American people who would be guilty of so base an act, and none to suspect it. So far as poison is concerned, I would freely partake of Brigham Young's hospitality, but I can accept of no present, nor interchange courtesies so long as he continues his present course. I have no answer to send. I can hold no intercourse with Brigham Young and his people. I have nothing to do with him or them. The Governor of the Territory is here, and his proclamation you have seen. To him Brigham Young must send his communications. When he returns to his allegiance I will be happy to interchange courtesies with him. I have been sent here by my Government, and I shall advance. His insinuation of this army returning in the spring, I assure you, is not to be relied upon; an American army never retrogrades, and I intend to advance in the spring. If he and his people oppose me with an army, I shall meet it and offer the same resistance. Peace or war is in their hands, and if they have war it will be of their own making.

Your people must know that an army entering this Territory comes to it in the same manner as to any other, and I tell you I have no more to do with your people than I would with the inhabitants of New York if going there. All persons who stay at home, when I advance, and mind their own business, will be undisturbed; but all who oppose my march I shall treat as enemies. Those who have been molesting my trains and cattle I shall regard and treat as robbers; and I wish Brigham Young, if he has anything to send to me (but I cannot imagine the occasion), I wish him to send it by a flag, that I may know who to treat as messengers as distinct from robbers. I wish to hold no intercourse with him now, but when he and his people express their willingness to return to their allegiance—and that must be done through the proper channel—I will be pleased to acknowledge his courtesies. Till then I must treat them as enemies if they offer resistance to my advance. I hope you will remember what I have said. I have no written answer to this letter. It requires none from my hands, as I tell you I cannot recognize him in any manner. Your salt you will take back with you; not, as I tell you, because I suspect its purity, but I will not accept a present from an enemy of my Government."

The mission of these men was soon known in camp, and much rejoicing was expressed at the prospect of a little salt; so that the disappointment was grievous when it became known that they were to return with their burden. When the stand the general had taken and his reply were also learned, they were not merely approved, but applauded. The course he had taken gave the army an insight into the character of the man, whose every step increased their confidence and respect. The salt soon arrived from Fort Laramie.

General Johnston found in the rigors and necessities of the situation the means to enforce a more exact instead of laxer discipline. The volunteers, instead of constituting a disorderly element, when organized vied with the regulars in all the duties of the soldier. Drill and instruction brought the troops to a high state of military efficiency, and the monotony of camp-life was relieved and the health of the men improved by the character of the tasks imposed. The vigilance requisite for an active campaign in the presence of an enemy was observed by pickets and outposts; and, owing to the weakness of the draught-animals, the men had to haul by hand from the mountains all the fire-wood used. These toilsome tasks were cheerfully performed, because the men knew that they were necessary to safety and comfort, and not imposed simply to occupy time. Very few and slight punishments were inflicted, and there has rarely been a military force where less harshness was exercised toward the soldier.

Nor did the pressure of large cares and heavy responsibilities prevent him from forwarding those scientific researches to which he attached so much importance. Mr. C. Drexler, the ornithologist, who started in 1857 with Magraw's wagon-train, but did not reach Fort Bridger before March, was enabled, through the assistance afforded him by General Johnston, to catalogue 106 species of birds near Fort Bridger in the next three months, as is mentioned in his report published in the Pacific Railroad explorations. If space allowed, it could be shown from the order-books that in the minutest details the safety and comfort of the soldier were provided for by the same mind which, grasping the important features of the campaign in its large strategic generalizations, waited calmly and sternly the proper moment to close with the enemy.[1] General Johnston's view of the policy to be pursued toward the Mormons, as already shown, was to hold no terms with armed resistance, and to do all for law and obedience to the Federal authority, nothing for vengeance.

In a letter to army headquarters, January 20, 1858, General Johnston says:

MAJOR: I have nothing material to report since my last communication. Accompanying that I sent a file of the *Deseret News*, containing the message of Brigham Young to the Legislature of Utah. You have in that message and the resolutions of the Legislature a full confirmation of the charge of their disloyalty to the Union heretofore made against this people. My information respecting their conduct since is that their troops are organized to resist the establishment of a Territorial government by the United States, and, in furtherance of that object, they have erected works of defense in the mountain-passes and near Salt Lake City.

---

[1] The reader who desires to know in fuller and more detailed form the interesting particulars of this winter's work will find the most of them in "Executive Documents," first session, Thirty-fifth Congress, vol. ii., part ii., and in second session, Thirty-fifth Congress, vol. ii., part ii.

Knowing how repugnant it would be to the policy and interest of the Government to do any act that would force these people into unpleasant relations with the Federal Government, I would, in conformity with the views also of the commanding general, on all proper occasions have manifested in my intercourse with them a spirit of conciliation; but I do not believe that such consideration for them would be properly appreciated now, or rather it would be wrongly interpreted: and, in view of the treasonable temper and feeling now pervading the leaders and a great portion of the Mormons, I think that neither the honor nor the dignity of the Government will allow of the slightest concession being made to them. They should be made to submit to the constitutional and legal demands of the Government unconditionally. An adjustment of existing differences on any other basis would be nugatory.

Their threat to oppose the march of the troops in the spring will not have the slightest influence in delaying it; and, if they desire to join issue, I believe that it is for the interest of the Government that they should have the opportunity.

President Buchanan, by temperament and education, and from all his habits of life and thought, a diplomatist, naturally took a different view of the situation. The prospect of civil strife and a large budget for war expenditure during his chief magistracy was utterly repugnant to his notions of a successful Administration, and he cast about to postpone the present trouble. There is a wisdom in avoiding dangers, and a wisdom in meeting them; no general rule can be established to fit every case, and the result alone can decide where lay the true line of action. The decided policy proposed by General Johnston would have definitively settled the Mormon question, which remains unsettled to the present day. Brigham Young must have submitted unconditionally, with a loss of prestige and power among his people; or he must have fought and been subdued, with the disorganization and new arrangements consequent upon reconstruction; or he must have fled the country with his followers, and thus relieved the United States from further consideration of the embarrassing question. Mr. Buchanan, on the contrary, finding that the mere show of force had irritated instead of subduing the Mormons, was quite willing to return to the *statu quo*, nominal submission and real independence, in which the Federal Government should be represented by an array of civil and military functionaries with hands tied—a pageant not unlike that Byzantine supremacy which commanded and trembled before its Gothic vassals.

Most opportunely for the inauguration of this policy, an agent presented himself in every way fitted for the office of such negotiation. Colonel Thomas L. Kane was a son of Judge Kane, of Philadelphia, and a brother of the arctic explorer—of a family connected with the President by ties of friendship. He was a man of talents and restless energy, but of an intriguing and erratic temper. He was supposed to have been baptized into the Mormon Church; but, however that may be, he always manifested the deepest interest in carrying out their policy. When they were expelled from Nauvoo he had delivered lectures to excite popular sympathy on their behalf; he is said to have procured Brigham Young's first appointment as Governor from Mr. Fillmore on the representation that he was not a polygamist, and he now offered himself as a volunteer agent to secure the submission of the Mormons. The President gave him a guarded letter of recommendation, sufficient, however, to accredit him unofficially to both Brigham Young and the United States officers. Armed with this he started about New Year, and made his way through California to Salt Lake City, where he arrived early in March.

When Colonel Kane arrived, Brigham Young was already virtually conquered. The army, which his prophecies had doomed to certain destruction, had neither been overwhelmed by avalanches, nor starved with hunger and cold, nor entrapped in the cañons and scattered by the sword of Gideon. On the contrary, it lay in its mountain-lair silent, stern, and collected. The enthusiasm of the saints had cooled, and their courage had waned in the long season of inaction, and in the presence of a power that made no mistakes. Brigham Young, for the first time, felt himself opposed by moral forces with which he could not cope. He was already suggesting flight as a possible contingency. Colonel Kane's arrival, therefore, was a godsend to him as a means to abate his high pretensions, and to avail himself of some decent pretext for submission. So far it may have been fortunate for both the Government and the Mormons; but it was not a happy conception in Mr. Buchanan to intrust, in any manner, the interests or honor of the United States to the hands of a person so closely identified with the enemy.

Colonel Kane, after receiving the inspiration for his mission in a full consultation with the Prophet, appeared suddenly in camp. He affected a certain mystery in his movements, and left his escort of Mormons in such an equivocal position that he was under apprehensions, unfounded but not unreasonable, that they had been fired on by the picket.

Brigham Young, whether as a measure of diplomacy and conciliation or as an act of insolence, having "just learned," as he said, "through the southern Indians that the troops are very destitute of provisions," offered through Colonel Kane to send in 200 head of cattle and 15,000 or 20,000 pounds of flour, "to which they will be made perfectly welcome, or pay for, just as they choose." General Johnston replied to Colonel Kane, March 15th:

SIR: President Young is not correctly informed with regard to the state of the supply of provisions of this army. There has been no deficiency, nor is there any now. We have abundance to last until the Government can renew the supply. Whatever might be the need of the army under my command for food, we would neither ask nor receive from President Young and his confederates any supplies while they continue to be the enemies of the Government. . . However unfortunate the position now occupied by that portion of the citizens of Utah belonging to the sect of Mormons, it is of their own seeking, and it is one from which they can be relieved by the mere act of obedience to the proclamation of Governor Cumming. Having the question of peace or war under his own control, President Young would, should he choose the latter, be responsible for all the consequences.

Colonel Kane tried to induce General Johnston to change this action. He wrote:

SIR: At the request of his Excellency Governor Cumming, I consent to bear the reply which you request me to communicate to President Brigham Young. I fear it must greatly prejudice the public interest to refuse Mr. Young's proposal in such a manner at the present time. Permit me, therefore, to entreat you, most respectfully, to reconsider it.

This diplomatic trick failed. Had any part of the provisions been received, it would have been claimed by the Mormons that the army was rescued by them from starvation, and yet was ready to smite the hand that fed it.

Colonel Kane, having asked an interview, had a conference with General Johnston, in which he urged a modification of General Johnston's reply to him. He said his object was peace; that in Utah there was a war party and a peace party, and that Brigham Young belonged to the latter. General Johnston then said to him:

I have nothing whatever to do with the political question between the Government and the Mormons. I am here in the fullfillment of special instructions from the Government, and I have on another occasion informed Brigham Young of that fact, and that peace or war is in his hands. I told Mr. Earle (the man who brought the salt) to inform him that I had nothing to do with him or his people, and that when I advance, if the people stay at home and behave themselves, and do not molest me, they will not be troubled. The army is to protect, not oppress; but if my advance is opposed with force I shall meet it with force. It becomes Brigham Young to consider before he so acts as to bring on the horrors of war. The officers under me do not want war, but fear not its results if forced upon them. Brigham Young should consider the calamities he is bringing upon his people in pursuing a course of open opposition.

No new result was arrived at, nor was Brigham Young without friends and allies at Washington. While General Johnston lay hemmed in by the avalanches of the Rocky Mountains, and nearly all Americans were anxious as to his fate, the ancient animosity of General Houston still pursued him. That veteran politician, from his place in the United States Senate, on the 25th of February,[1] made the following remarks in allusion to the "salt" embassy, declaring at the same time that the Mormons expected extermination at the hands of the army.

An act of civility was tendered by Brigham Young, and you might, if you please, construe it under the circumstances rather as an act of submission. He sent salt to the troops, understanding it was scarce there, and was selling at seven dollars a pint. As an act of humanity, thinking at least that it could not be regarded as discourteous, he sent a supply of salt for the relief of the encampment, intimating to the commander that he could pay for it, if he would not accept it as a present. What was the message the military officer sent him back? I believe that the substance of it was, that he would have no intercourse with a rebel, and that when they met they would fight. They will fight; and, if they fight, he will get miserably whipped.

That was a time to make peace with Brigham Young; because there is something potent in salt. With the Turk, who has similar habits and religion with the Mormons, it is the sacrament of perpetual friendship. Why may not the Mormons have incorporated that into their creed? But, instead of that, he sent him a taunt and a defiance.

But this fine spurt of senatorial rhetoric, for a wonder, culminated in cabals that merely hampered without overthrowing the officer assailed.

Brigham Young renewed his effort to patronize the army by making his offer anew through Governor Cumming, after a month's interval, but without effect. Though unsuccessful in his diplomacy with General Johnston, the Prophet accomplished more through his friend Colonel Kane with Governor Cumming than he had a right to hope.

But let General Porter tell the story, of which he had personal knowledge in all its details:

The presence of Governor Cumming and some of the judiciary in camp relieved Colonel Johnston of all concern in regard to civil affairs. His command was, of course, independent of the civil authorities, except to fill a requisition to suppress insurrection, and to support the United States marshal in executing the decrees of the court.

Governor Cumming was a guest in his camp, and dependent for everything upon the courtesy of Colonel Johnston, who made him as independent and comfortable as was possible under the forlorn circumstances, without the slightest indication of obligation. His dependence, however, seemed to annoy him; and being a Governor without anything to govern, he showed a continual irritation and petulance, which Colonel Johnston forbore to notice.

The arrival of Colonel Kane, a self-imposed embassador, caused a slight breach in the intercourse between the Governor and the colonel. Kane's ante-

[1] *Congressional Globe*, vol. xxxvi., part i., p. 874.

cedents, his mode of proceeding, and his uncivil behavior on entering camp, confirmed the belief that he was connected with the Mormons. Yet he was at once taken to his heart by Governor Cumming, and no emissary to foment trouble and stir up Governor Cumming against Colonel Johnston could have been better chosen. Fortunately, Colonel Johnston was above petty quarrels; and such were his dignity and bearing in all matters as to force Governor Cumming and every one else to respect him and his position. His staff entered into his feelings, and bore themselves so as not to compromise him by act or word.

Colonel Johnston's orderly, happening to be in personal attendance upon Colonel Kane for a short time, said, of his own motion, to another sent to relieve him, to "keep an eye on the d——d Mormon." Colonel Kane, though in-doors, and the orderly outside, overheard the remark, and fired Governor Cumming's heart. The Governor chose to construe it as an intentional insult by Colonel Johnston to his guest, and hence to himself, and proposed to resort to a challenge. As Colonel Johnston had nothing to do with the instructions given the orderly, his adjutant-general assumed whatever responsibility existed, and the absurdity of the Governor's position was finally made plain to him, and the matter ended.

Conduct so captious, however, put Colonel Johnston on his guard, and destroyed all possibility of any cordial or confidential relations between himself and the Governor. While it did not diminish the courtesy that he practised as due the Executive of the Territory, yet the Governor, on his part, retained and exhibited a rankling irritation and jealousy that proved injurious to the public interests.

The army was well drilled and thoroughly disciplined during the winter, at Fort Bridger, and was prepared in every respect to carry out whatever might be required to secure an entrance into Salt Lake Valley. The idea of open resistance by the Mormons now became absurd. The chief anxiety was so to maintain discipline that it should not be broken by the insults of an ignorant community, excited by its leaders to acts and expressions of hostility.

The advance of spring in this ice-bound desert was very slow. Major Porter's diary says, on March 19th :

Stormed all day severely. This is the worst storm we have had since we have been here; snowing and blowing hard; no wood, no fire, except for the cooks, and very cold.

April 1st.—Clear and warm. Thermometer 64° at 12 M.

2d.—About 3 A. M. a violent storm of wind arose, threatening to carry away tents and all habitations. So violent a storm I never felt. At reveille, snow mixed with hail in large quantities fell, covering the ground till noon. Squalls of snow were passing over all day. The storm is severe upon the animals; but the moisture is good for the grass. If our animals do not improve shortly, I fear we will have to resort to mule-meat, though the ration of beef is diminished to avoid such a contingency.

3d.—Still blowing, and very cold. Streams were frozen last night. Thermometer, at sunrise, 20°.

7th and 8th.—Snow and hail, and very cold.

9th.—Snow about two inches deep fell last night.

18th.—Stormed again last night, covering the mountains with as white a mantle as as they have had the past winter.

29th.—Commenced snowing after dark.

30th.—Cold and severe storm of snow from the east.

May 1st.—Cold and storming.

These extracts are sufficient to show why no earlier advance could be made in these mountains, as well as to illustrate the hardships of the command. It is difficult for the resident of a city or favored rural community to appreciate the intense interest of the frontiersman in the phases of the weather. General Johnston used to praise his rather frail cabin in Brazoria to the writer. "Civilization," he would say, "destroys our habits of observation. What does a man care for the weather who has brick walls and a tight shelter overhead? Your true meteorologist is the man with a leaky roof."

The arrival of Governor Powell and Colonel McCulloch, as embassadors of peace from Mr. Buchanan, with power to declare a general amnesty for all offenses, etc., soon led to a semblance of peace. In all their deliberations for the settlement of troubles with Brigham, General Johnston was fully consulted, and the decisions were generally founded on his counsel. General Johnston, feeling that any check or delay to the army after it was ready to move would diminish its future utility, insisted that no promise or agreement should be made that would in the slightest trammel his movements. It is true that Governor Cumming tried in his correspondence to produce an opposite impression; but the commissioners sustained General Johnston in his view that he was left free to move when and where he chose. General Porter says:

Governor Cumming was placed in his chair, and became Governor without power and without the respect or obedience of the community he presided over. The semblance of peace thus restored was really due not to negotiation, but to the moral effect of the presence of the army, commanded by an honest, brave, and accomplished soldier and statesman.

Colonel Kane had in some manner satisfied Governor Cumming that not only would he be personally welcomed, as the Executive of the Territory, at Salt Lake, but that such submission would satisfy every requirement of the situation, without the advance of the army into Salt Lake Valley. Governor Cumming left camp on the 5th of April, and arrived at Salt Lake City on the 12th, after having been fully impressed with the formidable nature of the warlike preparations on the route, and also of the respect felt for himself. He seemed to fall at once into the views of the Mormon leaders; and, although the populace were dangerously excited, and could scarcely be restrained by the leaders who had aroused them, he regarded his reception as the "auspicious issue of our difficulties." The Mormon troops, in the mean time, continued to occupy the approaches to the valley, and it was not until the 21st of May that General Johnston was notified that they were disbanded. In accordance with the command of Brigham Young, the people of Utah, most of them reluctantly, abandoned their homes, and began another exodus, destined, it was said, to Sonora. After the people had been congregated at Provo, they were allowed to return to their homes. Neither the motives for the removal, nor for the return, have been satisfactorily explained.

The commissioners from the President arrived in camp June 2d, and in Salt Lake City on the 7th. They accepted the submission of Brigham and the Mormons, and issued the President's proclamation of pardon. The army, having received its reënforcements and supplies, advanced June 13th, and arrived without opposition, June 26th, near Salt Lake City. The commissioners suggested that a proclamation would relieve the inhabitants from fear of injury by the army. General Johnston's reply and proclamation were as follows :

GENERAL JOHNSTON'S REPLY TO THE PEACE COMMISSIONERS.

HEADQUARTERS DEPARTMENT OF UTAH,
CAMP ON BEAR RIVER, *June* 14, 1858.

GENTLEMEN : Your communication from Salt Lake City was received to-day. The accomplishment of the object of your mission entirely in accordance with the instructions of the President, and the wisdom and forbearance which you have so ably displayed to the people of the Territory, will, I hope, lead to a more just appreciation of their relations to the General Government and the establishment of the supremacy of the laws. I learn with surprise that uneasiness is felt by the people as to the treatment that they may receive from the army. Acting under the twofold obligations of citizens and soldiers, we may be supposed to comprehend the rights of the people and to be sufficiently mindful of the obligations of our oaths not to disregard the laws which govern us as a military body. A reference to them will show with what jealous care the General Government has guarded the rights of citizens against any encroachment. The army has duties to perform here in execution of orders of the Department of War, which, from the nature of them, cannot lead to interference with the people in their various pursuits ; and, if no obstruction is presented to the discharge of those duties, there need not be the slightest apprehension that any person whatever will have cause of complaint against it.

The army will continue its march from this position on Thursday, 17th inst., and reach the valley in five days. I desire to encamp beyond the Jordan on the day of arrival in the valley.

With great respect, your obedient servant,

A. S. JOHNSTON,
Colonel Second Cavalry and Brevet Brigadier-General United States Army, commanding.

To the Hon. L. W. POWELL and Major BEN McCULLOCH, United States Commissioners to Utah.

GENERAL JOHNSTON'S PROCLAMATION TO THE PEOPLE OF UTAH.

The commissioners of the United States, deputed by the President to urge upon the people of this Territory the necessity of obedience to the Constitution and laws, as enjoined by his proclamation, have this day informed me that there will be no obstruction to the administration and execution of the laws of the Federal Government, nor any opposition on the part of the people of this Territory to the military force of the Government in the execution of their orders. I therefore feel it incumbent on me, and have great satisfaction in doing so, to assure those citizens of the Territory who, I learn, apprehend from the army illtreatment, that no person whatever will be in anywise interfered with or molested in his person or rights, or in the peaceful pursuit of his avocation; and, should protection be needed, that they will find the army (always faithful to the obligations of duty) as ready now to assist and protect them as it was to oppose them while it was believed they were resisting the laws of their Government.

A. S. JOHNSTON,
Colonel Second Cavalry and Brevet Brigadier-General, commanding.

Such utterances from a calm, intelligent, and patriotic soldier would, in these days of loose construction, form a better guide to the young officer than more recent precedents drawn from Cossack rule in Poland and the dragonnades of Louis XIV. Nor were they mere words; such was the rule of conduct for officers and men, and no people ever had less right to complain of injuries to person and property.

The commissioners in all their reports to the Secretary of War mention General Johnston's hearty aid in furtherance of their mission, and in their letter of July 3d say: " Brevet Brigadier-General Johnston has continued cordially to coöperate with us in carrying out the wishes of the President. He has discharged the important and delicate duties intrusted to him with eminent prudence and distinguished ability."

It may be remembered that Ben McCulloch, one of the commissioners, had been disappointed in not receiving the colonelcy of the Second Cavalry when General Johnston was appointed to it. His magnanimity was evinced not only in his correspondence with General Johnston, but in his conversation with others. Colonel Love, writing to General Johnston from Washington City, June 11, 1860, says:

Ben McCulloch told me yesterday that he was rejoiced that you had been appointed, instead of himself, colonel of the regiment, as, from close observation in Utah, he believed you were the best man that could have been sent there, and that he yielded to you in everything in the line of your duty, as you had nobly performed it.

As the army approached Salt Lake City, Governor Cumming wrote to General Johnston, June 17th:

The present excited condition of the public mind demands the utmost caution on your part. . . . It is my duty to protest against your occupancy of posi-

Triumphal Passage of United States Troops through Salt Lake City.

tions in the immediate vicinity of this city or other dense settlements of the population. Should you resolve to act in opposition to my solemn protest, you may rest assured that it will result in disastrous consequences, such as cannot be approved by our Government.

General Johnston had no intention of fixing his headquarters in any such location; and, for the obvious advantages of commanding situation, isolation, grass, water, wood, and shelter, had selected the north end of Cedar Valley as a proper site. Nevertheless, it was evident that the Mormons ought to feel that the Federal authority extended *everywhere;* and, therefore, General Johnston marched his command in perfect order through the chief streets of the sacred city. After thus formally asserting the Federal authority, he moved his troops to Cedar Valley, and made his headquarters at Camp Floyd.

Early in January, while the Government and the country alike were in suspense and anxiety as to the fate of the expedition, it was determined that reënforcements to the number of 4,000 soldiers should be sent to the aid of the little command of 1,700 regulars, buried in the snows of the Wahsatch range. General Scott at first intended to proceed to the Pacific coast to direct the movements of the coöperating force, but gave up that part of the movement in February. When the public mind had been relieved in regard to the safety of the army, General Johnston's conduct was the subject of general commendation, and the military authorities gave him every assurance of approval. General Scott wrote, on the 23d of January:

Your conduct in command, as set forth in the reports, meets with full and hearty approval, united with sympathy for those difficulties you have so manfully conquered, and which it is clearly perceived no act or omission of yours had any part in creating.

Early in April General Scott sent renewed assurances of his confidence, and on the 10th of April General Johnston was notified by the adjutant-general of his appointment as brevet brigadier-general. A few days later, April 15th, it was announced, in General Orders No. 8, that Brevet Major-General Persifer F. Smith and Brevet Brigadier-General William S. Harney were assigned to the Department of Utah, thus superseding General Johnston and placing him third in command. Notwithstanding the compliments paid him, this was a practical way of saying that, though he was good enough for a winter campaign, the Government preferred some one else to do its summer fighting.

General Johnston, on the 8th of July, having placed the army in a commanding position at Camp Floyd, addressed a communication to headquarters, which closes thus, without any allusion to what he might naturally have considered a grievance :

On the arrival of General Harney or Colonel Sumner I desire to be ordered to join my regiment. If that cannot be granted, I request that the general will grant me a furlough for four months, with leave to apply for an extension. I have had no relaxation from duty—not for a day—for more than nine years.

His request was refused; but, as there was no longer danger of war in Utah, and a general was not needed there, he was retained to administer the duties of the department nearly two years longer.

The adjutant-general, however, after declining his request, and informing him that he was not to be superseded, writes, August 28, 1858:

I am further instructed to add that General Johnston's measures in the management of affairs in Utah, from time to time reported by him, are fully approved by the War Department.

The commanding general was kind enough to issue the following order, summing up the conduct and character of the expedition:

(General Orders No. 19.)   HEADQUARTERS OF THE ARMY,
WEST POINT, NEW YORK, *August* 10, 1858.

The general-in-chief, learning of the arrival of the troops under Brevet Brigadier-General Johnston at their destination in the Salt Lake country, after their detention in the valley of Green River during the last winter, takes occasion to commend them in general orders—as he has already done through their commander—for their exemplary conduct under the trying circumstances in which they have been placed.

Detained, after a long and wearisome march of over a thousand miles, by causes over which their commander had no control, in a most barren and inhospitable region; subjected—by the rigors of the season, which destroyed or paralyzed their draught-animals—to toils of no ordinary nature; and, on account of the destruction of part of their supplies, obliged to labor with insufficient clothing; indifferent, and often restricted, rations of food—this fine body of men, instead of giving way to insubordination, irregularities, or murmurs even, went on improving in discipline and instruction, and discharging their accumulating duties with the utmost alacrity and cheerfulness; and, at the order of their commander, not showing the inhabitants of Salt Lake Valley, as they passed through their settlements, either by act, word, or gesture, that they had recently stood toward them in a hostile attitude.

The march—in the depths of winter—of Lieutenant-Colonel (now Colonel) P. St. George Cooke, commanding the Second Dragoons, from Fort Laramie through the South Pass to Green River; and that of Captain R. B. Marcy, Fifth Infantry, from Camp Scott over the mountains to New Mexico, deserve, as they have already received, special commendation.

Brevet Brigadier-General Johnston has had the honor to be supported by officers of great intelligence, zeal, and experience. Yet it is not to be doubted that to his own high soldierly qualities, untiring exertions, tact, and sound judgment, the credit for the condition and high tone of his army is preëminently due.

By command of Brevet Lieutenant-General SCOTT :

IRVIN McDOWELL,
Assistant Adjutant-General.

The Secretary of War in his report, December 6, 1858, made the following mention of the conduct of General Johnston, after discussing the causes that led to the expedition:

The conduct of both officers and men has been worthy of all praise. The commander, Brevet Brigadier-General A. S. Johnston, who joined his command at a time of great trial and embarrassment, with a calm and lofty bearing, with a true and manly sympathy for all around him, infused into his command a spirit of serenity and contentment which amounted to cheerfulness, amid uncommon hardships and privations which were unabated throughout the tedious and inclement season of the winter.

The correspondent of the *New York Times*, Mr. Simonton, I believe, writing from Camp Scott, under date of May 28th, says:

I called on General Johnston to-day. He is, apparently, something over fifty years of age, and a plain, frank, whole-hearted soldier, equal to any emergency, and always prepared for it. In simple, honest directness of manner, coolness of purpose, readiness of action, and practical common-sense, he reminds me much of the lamented General Taylor. During the time I spent in his tent I had no difficulty in understanding the magnetism which attracts to him the respect and love of his command. I am told that amid all the privations of winter the men never thought of complaining, even among themselves, of their commander, whom they saw sharing equally with themselves in the inconvenience of short rations, and struggling, with the aid of an excellent commissary department, to defeat the Mormon design of starving the army—a design which the destruction of the supply-trains in October last would have rendered easy of accomplishment except for General Johnston's efforts.

It is not to be supposed, however, that in the general applause which greeted General Johnston's conduct of the Utah campaign he altogether escaped criticism. By whatever motive actuated, a writer in the *St. Louis Democrat*, in August, 1858, made a violent assault upon him, which elicited a full and conclusive answer from the friendly pen of Captain N. J. Eaton. These articles are not here inserted, because it is believed that the events of the campaign as narrated are a sufficient reply to cavil. It is, indeed, alluded to only because it drew from General Johnston a letter to Captain Eaton, already quoted, of October 11, 1858, from which it is thought proper to make further extracts in response to the following charge by his critic:

We propose directing attention to the claims of an individual who has won rank and, perhaps, reputation by the exhibition of unparalleled inactivity. General Johnston has gained his brevet by no deed of heroism or display of generalship, but by obstinate immobility for eight or nine months.

General Johnston contented himself with a simple statement of the circumstances as the best refutation of the strictures of the letter-writer. The rest of his letter is as follows:

MY DEAR EATON: I received your letter of the 3d inst., and have now the pleasure to acknowledge the great obligations under which you have placed me, and to express my grateful sense of your generous conduct in defending an absent friend from an unjust and unfair attack by a person wholly unknown to him, but I hope not so prejudiced as to condemn upon an *ex parte* hearing.

Connecting as he does a criticism of my course as a commander with an assault upon the Administration, he evidently imagines that I am the recipient of political favor, and that the patronage of the Government placed me in command of the Utah army. On this point it is easy to disabuse the minds of any who entertain such a notion.

If I were much of a favorite it would very naturally be supposed that I was personally known to the party whose patronage I am supposed to enjoy. It so happens that I have never had the opportunity to be introduced to the President, and of course have never spoken to him, and am personally unknown to him. I was called to the command of this department, I understand, at the request of the commander-in-chief. The command was unsolicited by me, and not desirable on account of the inconvenience to my family and the unprotected situation in which I was obliged to leave them. The notice was sudden and unexpected; and, moreover, I was sick and in need of surgical aid: the notice, however, was promptly responded to. I am sure the service was repugnant to the wishes of every one, as it must always be where it involves the enforcement of the laws upon any portion of our citizens, be they good or bad. No one so employed can escape censure; though to the honor of the army be it said that, with this foreknowledge, there has never been a want of zeal in the execution of such, or any, orders. . . .

The brevet rank conferred upon me was not at my solicitation; it was voluntarily offered, and of course accepted. I did not consider whether I deserved it or not; and I know I would be unable to determine that question. With regard to the service performed by me, I felt that it was done with a loyal, hearty good-will, and regretted that more could not be done.

It is, of course, painful to any gentleman to speak of himself; but I think I can say without vanity that the brevet rank conferred upon me was the discharge of a debt of twelve years' standing, during nearly ten of which, as a public servant, I have not had one day's relaxation from duty, and more than half of which time, from the nature of my duties, I have not slept in a house. I say it was an old debt in this wise. At the storming of Monterey I was a volunteer, acting as inspector-general with the rank of colonel. By reference to official reports you will see that favorable mention was made of my name with others. Those belonging to the regular army were brevetted for this notice. I could not be, but received in lieu, what was very precious to me, the thanks of General Taylor in special orders. This being so, is it too much to say that the brevet was won twelve years since, and for the same grade as that now given?

It is quite ridiculous, especially as connected with a person so obscure, without political influence, and unsustained by the patronage of any party, to attribute a motive of interest to our venerated Chief Magistrate or commander-in-chief, standing, as they do, each in his own sphere the first man of his day.

I am by some pointed out as a *novus homo*—a person but a short time in the service. My experience in the service runs back more than thirty years. I claim that my life and my means (not small) have been devoted to the service of my country. It is true that I was out of the army for some years, but I was not idle. I was laboring on another field; the benefits, not less than an empire in extent, enured to the Government. To this result I contributed my humble aid. It was not my good fortune to be present at the battle at which was won the independence of Texas by a band of heroic men; but I served long and faithfully, assisting to maintain that independence, and, in so doing, I think, the interest of the United States was well subserved. . . .

Your friend and obedient servant,
A. S. JOHNSTON.

CHAPTER XV.

CAMP FLOYD.

CAMP FLOYD, the headquarters of the Army of Utah, was situated at the north end of Cedar Valley, midway between Salt Lake City and Provo, about thirty-six miles distant from each. The valley was about eight miles wide and twenty-five miles long, and situated three miles west of Utah Lake, with a low range of mountains intervening. The population of the Territory was located chiefly at the western base of the Wahsatch range, and along the eastern rim of the Great Salt Lake Basin. The position selected for the camp was a commanding one, as the valley debouched in the direction of Salt Lake City by two routes, toward Provo by two, and also into Tintic Valley in the direction of Fillmore City. The grass of Cedar Valley, and of Tintic and Rush Valleys, which communicated with it, was the main reliance for the subsistence of the horses, mules, and beef-cattle. The grass, though nutritious, was bunchy and sparse, so that a large space of country was required to support the animals, about 8,000 head in number. To guard this stock from both Indians and white robbers was an important and troublesome duty, but successfully performed.

When the army had been established at Camp Floyd, three duties devolved upon General Johnston : first, to secure the troops under his command against the hardships and privations of the preceding winter ; second, to control the Indians, at least so far as to prevent or punish depredations upon the inhabitants ; and third, to aid the civil authorities in executing the laws, by furnishing troops to act as a *posse*, on the requisition of the Executive or judicial officers of the Territory. To these might be added the auxiliary work of exploration and road-making.

His first care was so to disband the volunteers as to avoid turning loose a large body of strangers " who might," as he remarks, " produce disturbance in the communities, although it may be truly said of them that the Government never had a better regiment of volunteers." The battalion was ordered to Leavenworth to be disbanded, so as to afford them transportation and subsistence home, except where they preferred to take employment in Utah or go to California. Similar precautions were taken with the employés discharged by the quartermaster's department and contractors, some 500 in number. Those who would emigrate to California or return home were allowed to purchase arms and outfits from the Government, and those who wished employment in Utah were hired as wood-choppers and herdsmen. No confusion or trouble ensued.

General Porter says:

General Johnston's attention was now successfully turned to establishing his command in comfort for the coming winter, to securing the necessary supplies for the support of men and animals, and to protecting provisions from the effects of the climate. Before winter set in, the men were all comfortably housed, the provisions under shelter, and the mules and cattle distributed to proper grazing-grounds.

Quarters were built of *adobe*, and covered with plank and earth; and, with such comforts as could be added, the troops were wintered in health and contentment.

In a letter to the writer, September 23, 1858, General Johnston says:

Although nothing has been changed in the Mormon polity, quiet prevails. The people take employment at our camp, when they are needed. Large numbers are employed making *adobes* and in the various mechanical pursuits. They bring in freely their surplus grain and vegetables. Our winter-quarters will be comfortable; we are building a great many houses to shelter the men, and large storehouses for our supplies. The walls of our houses are eight feet high; the roofs are covered with plank, which is again covered with three or four inches of clay. Small windows, rough doors, and well-pounded clay floors complete the building. To put up buildings, even of rude structure, for 3,000 or 4,000 men, is a work of immense labor, where the materials are to be brought from a distance.

Congress has made no appropriations for sheltering the troops here, and all this considerable outlay of money is on my own responsibility. Congress, I do not doubt, will make the appropriation; yet it is not pleasant to have to incur weighty responsibilities. At this distance from the seat of government much responsibility has at all times to be assumed, and I shall not shrink from it. As I will do no one thing which my conscience does not approve as beneficial to my country, I shall always be without fear, and, I hope, without reproach.

The arrival, in October, of Colonel Crosman, who had been assigned as his chief quartermaster, was a source of great relief to General Johnston. His predecessor had done his part well, but Crosman was an old and tried friend, in whose experience, good sense, and loyalty of heart, he placed an unbounded trust, which was never impaired.

It is sufficient to say that this well-administered army passed the winter not only contentedly but cheerfully, bringing to their aid the recreations and amusements of civilized life without relaxation of discipline, or of the vigilance necessary to a strict performance of their duties. General Johnston applied again for a leave of absence, to take effect in the spring, but without success.

In regard to the relations established by General Johnston with the Indians, General Porter makes these remarks:

While journeying to Utah, and while at Fort Bridger, Colonel Johnston took every occasion to bring the Indians within knowledge and influence of the army, and induced numerous chiefs to come to his camp. There is nothing so civilizing to an Indian as the display of power, and the appearance of the troops insured respect and quietude. Colonel Johnston was ever kind, but firm and dignified, to them; and he was respected and feared as the "Great Chief."

Washki, the chief of the Snakes, the white man's friend, was invited by the colonel, when near South Pass, into camp, and feasted and smoked for a talk. This resulted in the disclosure that Brigham Young had sent to him and his young men, to induce them to make war on the United States army; and that he (Washki) had turned the Mormons from his country, telling them that his tribe did not meddle in white men's quarrels, and never against the United States; that they knew no difference between white men, and were as apt in war to slay Mormons as Americans. How much Colonel Johnston's impressive presence and the manifestations of power had to do with Washki's attitude cannot be known; but it is to his credit that he maintained it, holding his men under control on trying occasions, when unworthy white men had deservedly earned the enmity of the Snake tribe.

The Utes, Pi-Utes, Bannocks, and other tribes, visited Colonel Johnston, and all went away expressing themselves pleased, assuring him that so long as he remained they would prove his friends, which the colonel told them would be best for them. Thus he effectually destroyed all influence of the Mormons over them, and insured friendly treatment to travelers to and from California and Oregon.

General Johnston, while using every means to secure the friendship of the Indians, was most careful to warn them to keep clear of the impending conflict. This did not, however, prevent malicious attacks by those who had often found unscrupulous detraction a powerful engine against opponents. Governor Cumming's first communication from Salt Lake City to General Johnston, written within three days after his arrival, while the Mormons were yet confronting the troops in arms, was to apprise him of charges made by William H. Hooper, the Mormon Secretary of State, against United States officers, as advising the Indians to murder and pillage, and of insinuations against General Johnston himself. The *Deseret News* also made similar statements. These were fit fabrications to emanate from the conclave which had instigated the Mountain Meadows massacre. As General Johnston's "talks" with the Indians had been in the presence of others, he had no difficulty in placing on record the false and slanderous character of these statements ; and those who are curious in such matters will find them set forth in "Executive Documents," second session, Thirty-fifth Congress, vol. ii., part ii., 1858–'59, pp. 71–87.

During General Johnston's administration of that military department, the Indians behaved very well. A few outrages only were perpetrated by bands of "vagabond" Indians, who were promptly punished ; and California and Oregon emigrants will remember that their wagon-trains received escorts of dragoons over the dangerous parts of the route.

In the spring of 1859 an issue arose between General Johnston and Governor Cumming, in which the latter was evidently misled by his feelings. The documents and correspondence will be found in the executive document just quoted above, and may be summarized as follows : Governor Cumming, from the time of his association with Colonel Kane, imagined that his civil functions were to protect the Mormons from the military, who were seeking their destruction ; a very praiseworthy and magnanimous state of mind, if it had been founded upon facts. His error was, I presume, of the head rather than of the heart ; and it is not probable that he could have so misconceived General Johnston, if he had allowed himself to become better acquainted with him. He indulged another fancy, that his office, somehow, clothed him with military authority ; while, in fact, his sole function in this direction was to obtain, by requisition upon the commander, troops who should act as a *posse* to enforce the laws or protect citizens in their rights of person or property. It will be remembered that General Johnston's orders (page 209) directed him to obey the requisition of the judges, as well as of the Governor ; but this fact the Governor did not choose to recognize.

Judge Cradlebaugh, who had charge of the southern district of Utah, determined, if possible, to bring to justice the leaders in the Mountain Meadows massacre, and, on proper information, had John D. Lee, Isaac Haight, and six others, committed for trial at a term of the district court, held on the 8th of March at Provo. In accordance with his authority, he made a requisition for troops to protect the court and witnesses, and hold the prisoners securely, there being no jail. A company was sent to Provo, and later a regiment put within supporting distance ; and an examination of all the facts will show that the instructions from the commanding general, and their execution by his subordinate, were clearly within the letter and the spirit of the law, and scrupulous in their conformity to technical observances as well as to the necessities of the case. Not only were the officers firm and discreet, but the soldiers avoided even the appearance of incivility. Nevertheless, the mayor and council protested against " the military occupation " of their town, to " the annoyance and intimidation " of citizens. Judge Cradlebaugh replied politely, pointing out the necessity of his action; and a controversy ensued in which the Mormons dwelt upon the dangers of military despotism, and offered to provide for the security of the prisoners. This, of course, would have been a mere mockery of justice.

At this juncture, March 20th, Governor Cumming appeared upon the scene, and requested General Johnston promptly to withdraw the guard from Provo, adding, "I am satisfied that the presence of the military force in this vicinity is unnecessary, and for this and other reasons I desire to impress upon you the propriety of the immediate disposition of the troops as above indicated." He also complained that the detachment commander, Captain Heth, had not reported to him.

General Johnston returned a courteous reply to this letter, declining to obey the Governor's commands, and reciting his own orders, Judge Cradlebaugh's requisition, the want of a jail or any other means of detaining the prisoners, except by the guard, and his care to avoid giving just offense to well-disposed persons. He says, also :

I beg most respectfully to suggest that, under the circumstances, there would have been a manifest impropriety in Captain Heth's reporting to you; such an act would be an acknowledgment of military supremacy on your part, which does not exist. To prevent any misunderstanding hereafter, I desire to say to your excellency that I am under no obligations whatever to conform to your suggestions with regard to the military disposition of the troops of this department, except only when it may be expedient to employ them in their civil capacity as a *posse;* in which case, should the emergency arise, your requisition for any portion of the troops under my command will be complied with, and they will be instructed to discharge the duty pointed out.

In transmitting the correspondence to the general-in-chief, March 24, 1859, General Johnston writes :

I regret that his instructions should have impressed upon him (Governor Cumming) a view of his powers so inconsistent with the well-understood theory of military organization; and so much the more do I regret it, because this discrepancy of view between the Executive of the Territory and the commander of the department cannot fail to entail all the evil consequences of want of harmony and of unity of purpose. . . .

By my instructions I am equally bound to respond to the call of the judiciary as of the Executive ; and, if I had complied with his command, to make any other disposition of the force acting in aid of the administration of justice than as requested by the judge, without his consent, I should have been accessory to an executive interference with a coördinate branch of the Territorial government.

Governor Cumming issued the following proclamation, denouncing the action of General Johnston, and placing him before the people of the Territory in an entirely false light:

By Alfred Cumming, Governor of Utah Territory.

A PROCLAMATION.

Whereas, One company of the United States Infantry, under the command of Captain Heth, is now stationed around the court-house at Provo, where the Hon. Judge Cradlebaugh is now holding court, and eight additional companies of infantry, one of artillery, and one of cavalry, under the command of Major Paul, are stationed within sight of the court-house; and—

Whereas, The presence of soldiers has a tendency not only to terrify the inhabitants and disturb the peace of the Territory, but also to subvert the ends of justice, by causing the intimidation of witnesses and jurors; and—

Whereas, This movement of troops has been made without consultation with me, and, as I believe, is in opposition to both the letter and spirit of my instructions; and—

Whereas, General Johnston, commander of the military department of Utah, has refused my request, that he would issue the necessary orders for the removal of the above-mentioned troops:

Now, therefore, I, Alfred Cumming, Governor of the Territory of Utah, do hereby publish this my solemn protest against this present military movement, and also against all movements of troops, incompatible with the letter and spirit of the annexed extract from the instruction received by me from Government, for my guidance while Governor of the Territory of Utah.

       In testimony whereof, I have hereunto set my hand, and caused
...... the seal of the Territory to be affixed. Done at Great Salt Lake City,
: L. S.: this twenty-seventh day of March, A. D. eighteen hundred and fifty-
     nine, and of the independence of the United States the eighty-third.

ALFRED CUMMING.

By the Governor: (Signed)   JOHN HARTNETT,
Secretary of State.

With whatever accuracy Governor Cumming may have interpreted his instructions from the State Department, it was manifestly unreasonable in him to expect General Johnston to conform to them in disobedience of his own orders. But, however that might be, the issue having been made and referred to competent authority for decision, should have rested there. His proclamation was erroneous in law and in fact, and calculated to exasperate an already excited people, unless they had been restrained by leaders who now felt the folly of open war.

In the mean time the Mormon county court impaneled a grand-jury, in which sat some of the men implicated in the massacre and in other murders which were to be investigated. Nevertheless, a considerable number of witnesses appeared before them, testified to the most conclusive facts, and then sought the protection of the military from an "intimidated" people. The grand-jury having sat two weeks, and failed to make a presentment, was finally discharged by the judge. It was evident that the local authorities and the people, with the countenance of the Territorial Executive, were able to arrest the course of justice, so that the functions of the judiciary were virtually at an end, unless other modes of trial were adopted by Congress. Judge Cradlebaugh was able, however, as a committing magistrate, to place on record a mass of testimony that fixes on the Mormon leaders the indelible stigma of atrocious deeds, which will cling to the church until it perishes.

Closer contact with the Mormons, and continued observation of their system, gave General Johnston no better opinion of them than he had held at Fort Bridger. In commenting upon his own official reports, he wrote to General Scott, March 31, 1859:

I have refrained from speaking of the horrible crimes that have been perpetrated in this Territory—crimes of a magnitude and of an apparently studied refinement in atrocity hardly to be conceived of, and which have gone unwhipped of justice. These, if the judges are sustained, they will endeavor to bring to light.

General Johnston was not at all satisfied with the measure of support he received from the Administration, which, for many obvious reasons, was anxious simply to tide over the troubles in Utah. He had obeyed his orders scrupulously in letter and in spirit, and yet he found himself left in a somewhat ambiguous attitude before the country. Moreover, he had become convinced that proper laws should regulate the Territorial relations to the General Government; yet he found that these were drifting at the mercy of events.

The Government could not disapprove of General Johnston's course, but tried to obviate the difficulty by modifying his orders, as will be seen by the following letter from the Secretary of War. The letter is the key to the subsequent policy at Washington. It ties the hands of the judiciary, and leaves Utah to ferment into whatever it may—living waters or a hell-broth, as the case may be:

WAR DEPARTMENT, WASHINGTON, *May* 6, 1859.

SIR: The change which seems to have taken place in the condition of things in Utah Territory since the date of your former instructions renders some modification of these instructions necessary.

Peace being now restored to the Territory, the judicial administration of the laws will require no help from the army under your command. If the services of the United States troops should be needed under any circumstances it could only be to assist the executive authority in executing the sentence of law or the judicial decrees of the court; and that necessity could only arise when the services of a civil *posse* were found to be insufficient. You will therefore only order the troops under your command to assist as a *posse comitatus* in the execution of the laws, upon the written application of the Governor of the Territory, and not otherwise.

The fidelity with which you have obeyed the instructions of this department heretofore given you is the fullest guarantee that you will with the same zeal and efficiency conform to these.

I am, general, very respectfully, your obedient servant,

(Signed)   JOHN B. FLOYD,
Secretary of War.

Brevet Brigadier-General A. S. JOHNSTON, commanding Department of Utah, Camp Floyd, U. T.

General Johnston, in a letter to the author, June 10th, comments upon the modification of his orders thus:

This, in view of the premises *assumed* by the Secretary, is rightly done; but these are not the law-abiding people the Administration believes them to be, and he will find that henceforward the law here is a nullity.

I suppose the Secretary found it difficult to sustain me at all, so I ought to be satisfied with him, for I do not doubt that he had to combat the foregone conclusion of the President and most of the cabinet that this question is finally settled, or their predetermination so to view it. I have conscientiously discharged my duty in sustaining the judiciary, and the people will applaud me for it; for the time is not far distant when they will know the utter incompatibility of Mormon institutions and those that our own people are pledged by every obligation of duty and honor to establish and cherish in every part of our broad territory.

During the remainder of my sojourn here I shall not be called upon in the discharge of my duty to make any comment upon events transpiring here not purely of a military character. I now hope I may be granted a leave of absence.

It would seem proper, in view of the want of harmony in sentiment and personal relations between the Governor and the military commander, that the Government should have removed one of them. The Administration thought otherwise; and, although General Johnston requested to be relieved, he was obliged to retain his unpleasant post another year. The motive for adopting this sort of middle ground, so characteristic of Mr. Buchanan, was not an unkind one. To relieve General Johnston, under the circumstances, might have the semblance of condemning him for obedience to orders; to appoint another Governor would look like an intent to pursue a decisive policy instead of the *laissez-faire* course represented by Governor Cumming. So he let things drift.

Though the transaction of business with a population trained to annoy and pillage the Government was always disagreeable to its representatives, yet such were General Johnston's exact justice and circumspection of conduct that no commander has held this department with less detraction.

General Porter says in his letter to the writer:

The army had now nothing to do but to maintain discipline and efficiency, and be ready for any emergency. Yet General Johnston availed himself of every occasion to display force where its presence would have a good influence.

He sent Colonel Loring to New Mexico by a new route directly across the mountains, through the Ute tribes. He dispatched a force to the southern part of the Territory to the scene of the Mountain Meadows massacre, that the guilty might feel that a power was close at hand to prevent or punish such crimes in future. He sent a large and well-provided force to Oregon, and another to California, taking care they should pass through the regions least frequented by troops. He had the country south of Salt Lake explored to Carson's Valley, and opened a mail route and emigrant trail to California, 300 miles shorter than the old road. He opened the route up Provo River to Fort Bridger, which, with the route through Bridger's Pass to the east, and to California west, established the easiest, best, and shortest route across the continent.

These explorations had in view not only the display of force and the opening of as many avenues as possible into the country so as to counteract as far as possible the policy of isolation on which the priesthood relied for its absolute control, but information which would render easier the location of a railroad route to the Pacific.

The Union Pacific Railroad now runs some distance east and west of Fort Bridger over the route laid down, and much of it opened, by Colonel Johnston; and, had not the local interests of Brigham Young prevailed over the interests of the road and of the Government, its better location would have carried it down the Provo River to the bench-lands of the valley, and thence with the main trunk south of the lake, and with a branch to Salt Lake City.

General Johnston bore with some impatience the political arrangements that kept him in Utah. He found the climate healthful but disagreeable, and the separation from his family and social isolation very irksome. Though he could not express these feelings to his superiors, he did to the writer occasionally. Writing August 5, 1858, he says: "I shall be obliged to remain here another winter, at least. We cannot avoid our destiny; so I will try to be contented, and hope always. This is the most sterile country I have ever seen or imagined." Again, September 15th, he says: "I bear my exile here badly. My philosophy sometimes gives way. I try to be content, and hope for better times." Finally his request to be relieved was granted, and on February 29, 1860, he turned over his command to Colonel Smith. Gladly obeying his orders, he proceeded to San Francisco, and thence by sea to New York.

The army of Utah was, for the most part, withdrawn from the Territory, and the Saints were left to their own devices. As soon as the pressure of the troops was removed, the voice of the Prophet resumed its earlier tone of truculent defiance, blackguardism, and blasphemy.

The following from an officer at Camp Floyd, August 11, 1860, gives
the changed aspect of affairs:

The same game has commenced on the part of the Mormons that was played
before the army came here as regards the Gentiles. Brigham preached a very
inflammatory sermon last Sunday. He cursed the Government, the President,
and the Gentiles. He said "he would wipe them all—*every one*—out, d—n them!
that he would let the Government know that he was still here; that he would
send every Gentile to hell *with wooden legs*, and that they had better be supplying themselves now while lumber was cheap."

With the further history of events in Utah this memoir has no concern, and hence it may be dismissed with the remark that the vexed
question is still an open one, under the changed conditions, however,
that eighteen years make in all human affairs.

The following letter will not be without interest to those who feel a
concern about the United States army:

CAMP FLOYD, UTAH, June 22, 1859.

MY DEAR SON: Your letter of May 14th, ult., concerning the nephew of Dr.
L—— B——, has been received. I have made inquiry respecting him, and am
glad to learn that he is regarded as a worthy soldier. I have the power by the
articles of war to discharge soldiers from the service, but it is an authority never
exercised for private reasons. Great length of service, disability from physical
or mental causes, etc., are some of the motives which would justify a department commander in exercising this power. If B—— is ambitious he can be gratified; the door is open to all in the ranks. Having the prerequisite of a good
moral character, the other qualifications can be obtained by proper industry. If
he prepares himself for the examinations which must be gone through, I feel
sure he will find no difficulty in procuring the recommendations of his company
and regimental commanders to be allowed to be examined. The quality of the
enlisted men of the army, morally and physically, is not well understood by the
citizens. There exists so deep-rooted a prejudice against the soldiery that I
must believe that, some time or other in our history as a nation or as provin-
cials, they must have been intolerably bad. I think this is likely. Within my
own knowledge of the reputation of this class of men, which runs back more
than thirty years, they were very objectionable. I am glad to say that since my
first acquaintance with them there has been a vast improvement, morally and
physically. They were then said to be broken-down drunkards; now, physically, they are literally without blemish. After several minute inspections of the
naked *corpus* by surgeons, they, if found perfect in their *physique*, are accepted;
and, all being very young men, very few, if any, of them can have been injured
by previous habits. A large majority of them write their names; so that there
can be claimed for them, *for their class*, a high degree of intelligence. It is said
many of them are foreigners; this is true, and in that they represent very perfectly the population of the country. Their pay, though nominally less than
laborers', with all the advantages of clothing and food and physicians' bills free,
with good care in the hospitals when they are sick, makes it appreciated by
many as more desirable than the precarious wages of the laborer who may lose

all his earnings through the grasping cupidity of the doctors. Soldiers cannot be associates for refined persons; but they ought now to be as much respected as it is the custom to despise them. When called upon for duty they do not count the cost.

Numerous illustrations might be given of General Johnston's deep and tender feeling for his family—an affection that never failed in any act of self-sacrifice, and was manifested rather by a constant course of gracious and forbearing conduct than by extravagant demonstration. These are for the most part omitted, as no public end would be served by their introduction ; but the following extract from one of his letters to his daughters, with its personal allusions, is given because it truly represents his relations to his children :

The thermometer has fallen once to 22° below zero, and often to 10° below. I do not mind the cold now. I ride on horseback or walk every day without an overcoat. My mustache soon becomes an icicle; yet I do not suffer from cold, or have the dread of it that every one feels for a Texas norther. I am in robust health. Every symptom of liver-complaint has vanished, and I am now as active and strong as I have ever been. You may know that my fare is not meagre when I tell you I weigh 194 pounds.

Will has a charming family, and I am delighted with your account of my dear little granddaughters. I am sure he deserves all the blessings with which he is surrounded, and that your presence gives additional sunlight to the happy scene. I wish I could be with you more, that I might manifest the love I bear for you and him and all my children, and the pride I feel in the high tone and honorable principles of each. Destiny has otherwise decreed. I do not repine, for in a great measure we make our own destiny, and ought to submit without murmuring; but I hope the future has many good gifts in store for us. *I trust in God;* in that consists the sum of my religion. No hour passes without my thoughts reverting to you and each one of my family.

When General Johnston relinquished his command in Utah, it was with that mingled feeling of regret and relief that accompanies the severance of ties binding us to comrades with whom we have shared arduous duties, to enter on a more attractive field. Mutual confidence, affection, and esteem, bound together the army and its commander. General Henry Heth told the writer that the most touching scene he ever witnessed, except the surrender at Appomattox Court-House, was General Johnston's departure from the army of Utah. As he rode along the line of soldiers, drawn up to bid him farewell, there was not a dry eye.

During General Johnston's official career in Utah, as elsewhere, it was his wish so to conduct the affairs of his command that every citizen might feel that the Government he represented was ready to accord him the most generous treatment. When the snow-storms broke upon him in the valleys of the Wahsatch, he made common cause with the army contractors against the elements, and, in serving the Government and providing for his army, he was able to place the army contractors and merchants with trains for Utah under heavy obligations. One of the wealthiest and most powerful of these merchant princes of the desert sent General Johnston a New-Year's gift that gave rise to the following correspondence:

CAMP SCOTT, January 1, 1858.

DEAR SIR: Accept the articles sent you on the inclosed memorandum as a New-Year's gift from your humble servant,   —— ——

General Johnston sent a polite note of thanks, but on opening the package next day discovered the character of the present, and at once returned it with the following note:

CAMP SCOTT, January 2, 1858.

To —— ——, Esq.

DEAR SIR: In my note to you yesterday evening, accepting your New-Year's gift, I thought it was some trifle in value, offered in a spirit of kindness, which I might properly receive; but, on examination of the packages, finding that it is a splendid and costly service of plate, I feel constrained by our official relations to decline the acceptance of it, which I do with the utmost respect for you, and with grateful acknowledgment of the friendly sentiment which dictated the offer.

I beg that you will believe that, in declining to receive this token of your regard (but which will also be considered as an evidence of your approbation of my conduct as commander), I am actuated by no other feeling than a sense of military propriety.

In the turmoil of parties preceding a presidential election, prominent citizens not unfrequently endeavor to find some new man, with such elements of popularity and usefulness as will render his name acceptable to the people. Polk and Taylor, Pierce and Lincoln, have all been selections of this sort. While General Johnston was in Utah, some leading gentlemen in the West, of conservative views, and doubtless moved by a friendship that overlooked all obstacles, fixed on his name in conference as a proper one to be introduced into the canvass for the presidency. They believed that he combined certain popular features that would make him strong before the people in an uprising against faction and fanaticism, and with this view they communicated with him to learn his feelings on the subject.

General Johnston made the following reply to one of them, who united in himself a warm and loyal friendship with an ardent patriotism:

"I have no ambition for the high place you mention in your letter; or, I might better say, I have no taste for political life. You describe a state of things for which there is no cure, and which it would be wholly beyond the power of any man, no matter how honest or how able, to remedy. It must run its course. When the moral basis of political action has become corrupt, it is a disease which cannot be arrested. It is like some diseases of the human body, which men wise and learned in medicine abstain from treating. We must imitate them. We must watch and sustain the patient when he sinks, and trust to the medicinal power of Nature. Time will, I trust, restore to us a sound and healthy basis of moral action, such as we set out with as a people in the days of Washington and the elder Adams.

In another letter, to the same friend, he says:

I have known you long, more than the lifetime of a generation. . . . It must be believed from our personal antecedents that, with you (if such a course on my part were possible with any one) I would not feign a reluctance to take that which I ardently desired. You will know that my opinions, expressed in reference to so important a matter, are candid and sincere, and that my decision as to my own course is final.

I have given the subject full consideration, for it has been before me for some time, and I have been ruled by a sense of duty in the conclusion I have arrived at, and not by desire. I well comprehend that, to be thought worthy of so high a trust is an honor, and at the same time a testimonial, than which there is none higher; but, while entertaining toward my friends, should they proffer a nomination, a grateful sense of their kindness and good opinion, in order to prove myself worthy of such regard, I should feel it my patriotic duty to commend to their choice some other citizen more competent for the discharge of the duties appertaining to that eminent station.

Your partiality, my friend, would draw me from a vocation and duties for which, from my education and taste, I have I believe some qualification, to place me upon an arena which, with my views of it, would seem to demand a life-long familiarity with the objects and operations of our institutions to do justice to the requirements of so responsible a position. I will not consent, but will rather imitate your own example when civic honors were offered to you.

In a letter to the present writer, adverting to the foregoing, General Johnston says:

My friends, some of them, in the States, say that a glittering prize is within my grasp, in their opinion. If I had you to write my answer, declining the proffered honor, if by any chance it should be offered, I could, by displaying the folly of our people in selecting men for public office without any regard to their fitness by education and training for the particular duties they are called upon to perform, more entitle myself to their good opinion than by accepting. My education, my taste, and my ambition, if I have any, would find nothing congenial in the performance of the duties of a civil office. If success were certain. I still have honor and patriotism enough to say that there are others much more capable and more fit for the station who ought to have precedence. A friend of mine used to say that there is nothing in which we so well display our judgment as to stop speaking when we have said enough. I suppose it must be the same in writing. I therefore dismiss the subject.

When General Johnston first went to Texas, he bought a league of land, which was afterward "squatted" upon, and thus became the subject of litigation. This suit wore on for many years, the local claimants obtaining all those advantages which the elective system gives the voter over the non-resident. The precedents in the State courts pointed to a final decision adverse to General Johnston, while in the Federal courts the adjudications were in his favor. For this reason, and to remove the cases from the sphere of local influence, the attorneys for General Johnston wished to bring them before the United States tribunals. It was therefore proposed to him, through the present writer, that, as he had been so long an officer of the army, and for some years absent from the State, he should renounce his citizenship for this purpose. The following was his reply, from Camp Floyd, August 27, 1859 :

> My citizenship in Texas was obtained at the cost of the bloom of health and the prime of life spent in the service of the State, and of property, which, if I had it now, would constitute a princely estate. I will not give it up now, though I should lose in consequence every foot of land I have in the State. This I would regard as a mere mess of pottage in comparison with my citizenship.

General Johnston returned to the Atlantic coast by way of California and the Isthmus, as it was too cold to cross the Plains. In Southern Utah, an Indian chief, to prove his friendship and warn off prowling clansmen, ran on foot for several days beside his wagon, keeping pace with the trot of the mules. General Johnston on parting gave him among other presents, to his extravagant delight, "a coat of many colors"—a gay patchwork quilt that had served through the campaign. He said it was a prudent gift, as its *bizarre* brightness was fascinating enough to an Indian to stir up a border war, or, at least, induce a massacre.

At San Francisco he saw the first Japanese embassy to this country. He was much interested in the Japs, and observed them, both then and afterward at Washington, with friendly curiosity. He remarked to the writer in regard to them :

> How apt we are to undervalue what is unfamiliar! We call the Japanese barbarians. Yet compare their skill and perfectness in all handicraft with our own. Look at their cutlery and lacquer-ware, their fabrics of paper and silk, and the cunning joinery of one of their little cabinets; and then consider how few men in America can make a bureau-drawer that will open without a jerk. Then, too, they are brave, aspiring, and sensitively honorable. We call them barbarians; but such a people ought to have a great future.

No important incidents occurred on his voyage or after his arrival in the East. General Scott received him with the utmost kindness, approved heartily of all his acts, and spoke of him publicly in the most unqualified terms of commendation. The office of quartermaster-general, with the assimilated rank of brigadier-general, became vacant in the summer of 1860, and was conferred by Secretary Floyd on Lieutenant-Colonel Joseph E. Johnston. It was said at the time that General Scott urged the name of General A. S. Johnston for the appointment; and a rumor was prevalent that he had also filed a paper in the War Department, recommending him as commander-in-chief in case of his own decease. Without means of verifying the correctness of these reports, they evince, nevertheless, the estimate that General Scott was commonly supposed to place upon him.

General Johnston was greatly rejoiced to be reunited to his family after two years and a half of separation. His wife and children had resided in Louisville under the protection of kind friends during his absence; and, now that he was again in a home of his own for a brief season, its happiness was the brighter by the contrast with the clouds that lowered over the world without. His health had been completely restored by three winters in Utah; and, such was his vigor that, at fifty-eight years of age, he might have been mistaken for forty-five. He spent most of the summer and fall in Louisville, except when called to Washington on army business. In Kentucky and wherever he went the greatest respect and consideration were shown him.

The year 1860 was the crisis of American destiny. The presidential election that resulted in the triumph of the antislavery Republican party was a season of tremendous political excitement, and every passion that sways a popular government was aroused to the utmost. General Johnston beheld the scene with gloomy forebodings, and yet with a calmness which did not condescend to discussion even. His opinion, his voice, his utmost energies, would have no effect in stilling the storm which he had done nothing to stir. The angry passions of men seemed to be moved by an unseen power, as the waves of the sea are lifted by the breath of the tempest. Though far from feeling indifference, yet, as he had no power for active good, he maintained that attitude which he thought most becoming in an army-officer of his rank —the utmost reticence. He saw the wisdom, the eloquence, the political skill, of powerful and patriotic statesmen set at naught in the elemental strife; and to him—a man of action, not of words—silence seemed the only proper course.

During the summer, prominent Texans at Washington had been soliciting the secretary to assign General Johnston to command the Southwestern Department. Finally, on the 1st of November, the adjutant-general informed General Johnston that the secretary had given orders to that effect, and wished to see him as soon as convenient. He was at the same time apprised, by telegram and letter, of October 30th, that General Scott desired to send him to California to take command of the Pacific coast. On November 2d General Scott addressed an official communication to the adjutant-general to that effect.

When General Johnston reported to the Secretary of War, he had made up his mind, as he subsequently informed the writer, *not* to go to Texas.   If the State seceded, and the Federal Government did not promptly accommodate the questions thus started, a collision would probably occur.   In this event, General Johnston took the view that he could only surrender the charge committed to him to the authority from which he had received it.   He would thus be forced either to fail in his duty to the power which had confided in him and to which he owed service, or in his duty to the Commonwealth to which he owed allegiance; to violate the trust reposed in him, or resist the State which had a paramount claim upon him.   He said that it was impossible for him to do the former; and he would not be so placed as to be compelled to encounter his State.   With this dilemma before him, he preferred to resign rather than accept the command of the Department of Texas.   The alternative was not forced upon him.   He placed his preferences for California before Mr. Floyd in so strong a light, though without touching the above-named difficulty, that, with General Scott's backing in the matter, he was assigned to the Department of the Pacific.

General Johnston, before leaving for California, manumitted his body-servant, Randolph, a slave born in his family in 1832.   Randolph had served him faithfully in Texas and Utah, and wished to go with him to California.   He was employed on wages, and followed his master's fortunes to California, and afterward to the Confederacy.   He was with him at Shiloh, remained in the Southern army till the close of the war, and yet lives a humble but honorable remembrancer of the loyal attachment which could subsist between master and slave.

General Johnston sailed from New York on the 21st of December, with his family, by way of the Panama route, reaching San Francisco about the middle of January.   During the three months that he administered the department no military events occurred, except some movements of troops against the Indians, for the management of which he received the approbation of the press and people at the time.   It may be here mentioned, in advance, that he resigned his commission April 10th, and was relieved by General Sumner April 25, 1861.

CHAPTER XVI.

THE SOUTHERN CONFEDERACY.

As the purpose of this biography is to set forth, not to justify, the acts and opinions of its subject, a discussion of the causes of the civil war would here be out of place. Success gives strong ground for self-complacency, and so does martyrdom. Hence the very conclusiveness of such an argument, while not needed to confirm the faith of its believers, would only serve to arouse anew the prejudices of adversaries. Nor is it necessary to the truth of history ; since all the phases of that famous controversy, though settled at last by the arbitrament of the sword, had been thoroughly sifted and debated, before this final appeal, by orators, statesmen, and jurists—and by an innumerable throng of politicians, preachers, philanthropists, editors, writers, and talkers.

Nevertheless, it seems necessary here to state briefly the standpoint of the Southern people, as an historical fact. In a struggle so momentous and so unequal, it is impossible to understand the motives that influenced the best men of the South to maintain her cause with such unexampled unanimity and devotion, without knowing the beliefs and opinions upon which their action was based.

In 1861 long-pending disputes between the slaveholding and non-slaveholding States came to an issue. Springing primarily, doubtless, from the difference in social organization, the more immediate causes of strife were certain real or imaginary collisions of material interests, a different mode of interpreting the Constitution, and the agitation for the abolition of negro-slavery. Of the first, there were none so vital as to be incapable of adjustment, as had been shown in the tariff compromise with South Carolina in 1832–'33. Nor would theoretical differences about the Constitution have assumed so dangerous a form, unless they had been embodied in a sectional or revolutionary movement. But, at the South, it was the Northern method of dealing with the slavery question which was considered not only sectional and revolutionary, but unjust and dangerous to its property and liberties.

The material interests and social and political difficulties involved in the slavery question rendered it impossible for the South to consider it dispassionately. On the other hand, the sentimental and philanthropic origin of the slavery agitation in the North made it impossible to fix any legal or constitutional limits to the abolition crusade. At the South the Constitution was regarded as an historical document. It was a charter conveying to the Federal Government, as the agent of the States, certain well-defined powers for certain specific purposes ; all powers not thus explicitly granted being reserved to the several States. The instrument was to be strictly construed ; and a breach of the covenant entitled the aggrieved party to redress, the measure of which the State must fix, as no common tribunal had been established for that purpose. This involved the right of withdrawal from the Union, either by peaceable secession or by revolution. In the extreme South the former was regarded as the legitimate method. When the emergency arose, those States attempted thus to exercise their right.

In the North these primitive views of the Constitution were changed by an immense influx of European immigrants, who, controlled by speculative republicans, regarded the Constitution as a mere Bill of Rights, and the mission of the republic to be the emancipation and illumination of the world. A modern national, or rather an *imperial*, theory of the nature of our Government prevailed there. Legalists gave form and color of authority to attacks on slavery, which were regarded in the South as willful, dangerous, and manifest infractions of the Constitution.

The irritations of the controversy were great and growing. The loss of $1,000,000 worth of slaves annually ; aids to their escape and incitements to their insurrection ; resistance to their rendition when fugitives, by mobs, or by nullifying State laws ; appeals to the "higher law" of conscience as overruling the Constitution ; and the intemperate invectives of the abolitionists, engendered a bitter and unmeasured resentment in the South. This was evinced in words and acts.

It is true that, when Mr. Lincoln was elected President in 1860, the Republican party made the basis of its creed the exclusion of slavery from the Territories of the Union by act of Congress. But this will hardly be regarded now as more than a mere phase of the antislavery agitation. It was so considered in the South then. It was there held to be a gross violation of the Constitution. The success of this party opened to the South a vista of unnumbered ills. The Gulf States resolved on immediate separation : South Carolina began by seceding December 20, 1860 ; the others quickly followed ; and the government of the Confederate States was formed.

The Confederate Government was organized February 8, 1861, by South Carolina, Georgia, Florida, Alabama, Mississippi, and Louisiana, which adopted a Constitution not differing materially from the old one. It was not of the provisions of the Constitution that they complained, but of their infraction. The Convention of Texas passed an ordinance of secession February 1st, which was ratified by a vote of the people February 23d, and went into effect March 2d. Thus, the seven most southern States presented a compact front to the Union, from the Rio

Grande to the Atlantic. The party in those States which had preferred coöperation to separate State action found in the prompt organization of the new Confederacy a more practical solution of their policy than in prolonged and indecisive deliberation, and at once coalesced with their opponents.

The Provisional Congress, which met at Montgomery, Alabama, elected Jefferson Davis, of Mississippi, President, and Alexander H. Stephens, of Georgia, Vice-President ; and the new government fell into shape, and went into operation, with as little friction as if it had stood the tests of a decade. All of its utterances were pacific ; and, though the President did not share the expectation, many of the leaders and a large part of the people confidently believed that they would be permitted to separate without war. .This delusion, and a kindred one indulged in by certain dreamy statisticians and turgid orators, and formulated in the phrase "Cotton is king," encouraged a vainglorious apathy in the masses, and enabled their representatives to paralyze in many essential points the policy of preparation which the President undoubtedly desired to inaugurate. Still, the fervid condition of the public mind enabled him to secure appropriate legislation on most matters of the first importance. An instance of the inadequacy of the provision for war is to be found in the appropriation by the Mississippi Legislature, after the act of secession, of $150,000 for armament, when Mr. Davis recommended $3,000,000. The language and acts of the "cotton" fanatics lent plausibility to the idea that union with the border States was scarcely desired by the extreme South.

The establishment of the Confederate Government had the effect, in the other Southern States, of drawing more sharply the lines which divided opinion. Scarcely anybody in them had wished for disunion, though many believed it inevitable ; and, on the other hand, there were few willing to avow themselves unconditional submissionists to Federal decrees. Those hopeless of compromise and peace now began to urge measures that would place their States in a position for defense, and thus give weight to their voice in the final settlement. They advocated either an alliance with the Confederacy, or such prompt and simultaneous action as would secure sufficient constitutional guarantees, or at least convince the North that war was not expedient. On the other hand, the unconditional Union men were able to point out to the rich, the timid, and the indifferent, that a disruption along the line between the free and slave States exposed the border States to great peril and damage ; and that the precipitate action of the cotton States, without proper delay for conference or coöperation, was derogatory to their dignity, and with the selfish view of interposing them as a barrier to Northern aggression, or of coercing them "to follow South Carolina." The reply to this was, that the Unionists had prevented that coöperation whose failure they now resented ; that the danger was to all, and resistance to be effectual must be united, and hence that punctilio as to forms was absurd; and that complete armament and a solid front would be the strongest arguments for peace, and the only way to restore the Union as it was.

Between these extremes halted the body of the people.   They were indignant at the conduct of the Republican party, but unconvinced that secession would afford a safe remedy for their grievances.   If they should abide in the Union, their liberties and property were at the mercy of hostile legislation; if they went with the South, they were in danger of subjugation by the sword.   Hence the final decisions and actions of persons were governed more by their circumstances and characters than by their abstract opinions.   While the Unionists condemned all preparation for war, as leading to that result, the State-rights men denounced vacillation and apathy as the prelude to submission to tyranny and political death.   To a community in doubt, inaction is the natural policy; and it only needed moderation and a *pacific purpose* on the part of the Administration to have preserved the Union intact in seven Southern States, and to have inaugurated measures of peaceful reconstruction with the others.   But this would not have accorded with the designs of its leaders ; and, though President Buchanan is reviled for permitting the peaceful withdrawal of half the Southern States, President Lincoln is applauded for driving the other half into armed resistance.   A survey of the whole field evinces the fact that the border States, though averse to disunion, and not satisfied with the prospect of the Confederacy, were resolved to maintain their own rights, as they understood them, and to resist the coercion of the seceding States.

The voice of Virginia had all along been for conciliation, but without sacrifice of principle.   Her traditions, her moderation, and her unwavering courage, gave her the right to be heard, but her counsels were drowned in the tumult of passion.

The Virginia Convention, in spite of the failure of many well-meant efforts to save the Union by compromise, as late as the 4th of April, rejected, by a vote of eighty-nine to forty-five, a motion to submit an ordinance of secession to the popular vote.   Fort Sumter surrendered on April 13th, after thirty-four hours' resistance ; and on the 15th of April President Lincoln issued a proclamation, under the pretended authority of an act of Congress of 1795, calling on the Governors of the several States for militia—75,000 in the aggregate—to suppress certain "combinations" in the seceding States.   Governor Letcher, a sturdy patriot, replied on the 17th :

I have only to say that the militia of Virginia will not be furnished to the powers at Washington for any such use or purpose as they have in view.   Your object is to subjugate the Southern States, and a requisition made upon me for such an object—an object, in my judgment, not within the province of the Constitution or the act of 1795—will not be complied with. *You have chosen to inaugurate civil war, and, having done so, we will meet it in a spirit as determined as the Administration has exhibited toward the South.*

On the same day Virginia passed an ordinance of secession, subject to a ratification by the vote of the people on the fourth Thursday of May following.

The decisive step taken by Virginia, in placing herself in the breach, is among the most heroic acts in history. The issue was not of her choosing, but was forced upon her; she did not seek it, neither did she shrink from or evade it. Detached from the Confederacy by States still passive, she was, even with their support, a salient, inviting attack; an advanced post with no natural barriers, no other defenses than her indomitable sons. But she counted upon the derided chivalric instinct of the South to come to her rescue, and she was not disappointed. The responses of the Southern Governors were in a like spirit with Letcher's. Jackson, of Missouri, replied, "Your requisition is illegal, unconstitutional, diabolical, and cannot be complied with." Harris, of Tennessee, said, "Tennessee will not furnish a single man for coercion, but 50,000, if necessary, for the defense of our rights or those of our Southern brethren." All *acted* with vigor, except in Kentucky and Maryland. Arkansas and Tennessee seceded May 6th, and North Carolina May 20th. The popular vote, to which the several ordinances were submitted, ratified them by overwhelming majorities. In Tennessee, which had a little before refused by a large popular majority even to call a convention, the ordinance of secession was now passed by a vote of 104,913 *for*, to 47,238 *against* it. In Virginia, the vote was 125,950 *for*, and 20,273 *against* secession. There was a similar revulsion of feeling in the other States; and the change was due, not as Greeley and other Northern writers allege, to fraud and intimidation, but to despair of justice and peace, and a resolution to resist coercion.

Most of the Union leaders gave in their adhesion to the new government with more or less frankness and zeal, and notably the Hon. John Bell, of Tennessee, the late Union candidate for the presidency; and party distinctions were lost in patriotic emulation. The only marked exception was in the mountain-region of Western Virginia and East Tennessee, in which prevailed the spirit of unconditional submission. This sentiment, and its vulnerability, enabled Mr. Lincoln, with the aid of ambitious local leaders, to effect the schism of West Virginia, and, by a proceeding totally unconstitutional and revolutionary, to establish it as a State. In East Tennessee, a sedition was organized by Andrew Johnson, T. A. R. Nelson, and William G. Brownlow, which proved a constant source of weakness and danger to the Confederacy.

Passing by, for the present, transactions in Maryland, Kentucky, and Missouri, brief mention will suffice, in this connection, of the military events which happened before General Johnston's arrival at Richmond. The reduction of Fort Sumter and President Lincoln's call for 75,000 men for "the irrepressible conflict" were met with tumultuous fervor at the North as the signal for war. The North gave its men and money without stint to the work of "putting down the rebellion." Three months time was set apart for the work, and troops were hurried to Washington, ostensibly to protect the capital, but, in fact, as the advance-guard of the army of invasion.

As "the defense of the capital" made Washington the first and most important base of the Federal army, so the adoption of Richmond as the Confederate seat of government made that city the objective point of attack. As Virginia had placed herself in the fore-front of battle, and must bear its brunt, a magnanimous wisdom led the Confederates to plant their standard on her border, "point to point opposing." The Confederate Government was established at Richmond, June 1st.

When the Southern States seceded, they seized the Federal fortifications within their limits, as a precautionary measure, offering, however, at the same time, to adjust their claims thereto by negotiation. Of all the Federal fortresses in those States, Fort Pickens, near Pensacola, Florida, and Fortress Monroe, near Norfolk, Virginia, alone remained in the hands of the United States. In retiring from the navy-yards at Pensacola and Norfolk, and the arsenal at Harper's Ferry, the United States troops had wrought all the damage and destruction they could; but, still, enough arms and material of war fell into Confederate hands to perform an important part in the resistance of the South, unprepared as it was for the struggle.

The war opened with a slight skirmish at Bethel, near Fortress Monroe, June 10th, in which the Federals were repulsed with loss by a smaller force of Confederates. The effect of Bethel and some other skirmishes was to exalt, perhaps unduly, the confidence of the Southern troops; but this was chastened by reverses in West Virginia, which seemed about to admit the enemy by a postern to the citadel. The Federal plan of campaign, apparently, was to envelop the shores and frontiers with its armies and navies, and test every joint in the armor of defense; but its main attack was directed from Washington—"on to Richmond."

It is not necessary to narrate here the campaign in Virginia. The battle of Manassas, or Bull Run, fought July 21, 1861, began and ended it. Its story is well known.

The immediate advantages of the victory were very great. The effect abroad was enormous. Time had been gained, so valuable an element of success in revolutions, and prestige, so valuable in every contest. There was a reverse to the picture, however. The North, suddenly checked in its vainglorious boast of subjugating the South in ninety days, sobered itself down to a steadier prosecution of its deadly purpose. Scott and McDowell went into eclipse, and McClellan was called to the work of organization and command. Nevertheless, operations were closed on that line for nearly a year, and the activity of preparation was transferred to the West. In the South an undue and ignorant exultation blinded the masses of the people to the dangers ahead. They could not be made to believe that preparation was necessary to meet the formidable armaments gathering for their destruction. The effects of this fatuous apathy at such a season extended themselves to the close of the war; but the first stunning result was felt by the subject of this memoir, in his efforts to create an army for the defense of the West. This will be seen more fully hereafter.

The map of the Southern States and the distribution of population there evince the odds encountered in the vain struggle for independence. The eleven seceding States, including the present State of Virginia, contained a little more than 5,000,000 whites, and about 3,700,000 negroes, of whom 130,000 were free. The aggregate population of Maryland, West Virginia, Kentucky, and Missouri, was about 3,400,000; of whom 2,850,000 were white, 446,000 slaves, and 100,000 free negroes. Nearly one-sixth of their population was black; a fourth belonged to families from Europe or the North; and a twelfth is not a large estimate for persons influenced by party or other considerations to side with the North. Thus, a half of the aggregate population may be counted as in sympathy with the North; but, of the voters and of the rich and intelligent, a great majority were in favor of the South, and the existing local State governments were all in the hands of the State-rights party. But it is one thing to believe in ideas, and another to fight for them; and the troops furnished by these States to the Confederate army—say 40,000 men—were not more than an offset in numbers to the counter-current of Union refugees from East Tennessee and other disaffected localities. Deducting, then, 5,000,000 for the population that supplied the Confederate army with troops, and 4,000,000 for negroes, etc., from the 31,500,000 total population, 22,500,000 represent the available force for men and tribute on which the United States drew, without counting foreign enlistments and negro recruits. But, if Kentucky, Missouri, Maryland, and West Virginia, are excluded from the calculation altogether, the result still leaves in the South only 5,100,000 whites and 3,700,000 blacks, representing the resisting force, against 19,000,000 of the North.

A brief explanation is necessary to show how these border Commonwealths were so easily transferred from their natural alliance with the South to the side of her adversary. The situation was different in each ; yet all were alike in being exposed to direct and flank attacks, in suffering from a divided sentiment, and in earnestly desiring peace. Geographically, Maryland was a mere fringe to the Southern border. The ocean, Chesapeake Bay, and the Potomac, laid open all her homes to attacks by water; while the Baltimore & Ohio Railroad and the railroads from Philadelphia and Harrisburg were channels along which poured the living tide to Washington. In a word, the State was defenseless ; and, unless her people could have been brought to act with unanimity and promptness in some early coöperative movement, her resources would necessarily be counted in the scale of the North. Her voice was raised in indignant protest and her hand in unavailing defiance against the Northern host that overran her and trampled out her liberties ; but the voice was soon silenced in the dungeon, and the hand manacled by martial law. Henceforth, Maryland's quota to the South was paid in suffering, exile, and martyrdom. When the Federal troops occupied Alexandria, Virginia (May 24, 1861), the Potomac became the boundary.

In West Virginia, though the State was occupied by large Federal armies, and its severance accomplished as a political fact, the State-rights men maintained their allegiance to the " Old Dominion " by stubborn warfare until the close of the contest ; and its eastern border was at all times a " debatable ground." On this field General McClellan gained his first distinction, which raised him, as the successor of Scott, for a time to the chief command of the United States Army. The movements in this quarter from the Ohio River Valley as a base, though well contested in many a bloody combat, resulted on the whole advantageously to the North.

CHAPTER XVII.

CALIFORNIA.

GENERAL JOHNSTON had never been a politician or party-man. He had cast but one vote in his life, and that had been for General Taylor, who, he thought, would rise above party. He never forgot, however, that he was the citizen of a republic. Deeply interested in its welfare, conversant with its history, well acquainted with its practical working, long associated with its leading men, and himself a thinker and a leader in his own particular sphere, he could not fail to have decided opinions on the greater questions that divided the country. Though little bound by prejudice, his opinions were, of course, much influenced by his associations and circumstances. A recapitulation of these will exhibit the conditions under which his ideas took form.

His family affiliations, his early associations, and some of his warmest friendships, inclined him, while young, to the principles of the Whig party, then in its best days. The constitutional text-book at West Point in his cadetship was, I believe, Rawle's " Commentaries," a book of wholesome doctrine. The military education there had a natural and necessary tendency to inspire affection for the union of the States, and exalt the Federal authority in the youthful mind ; and continued service in the army increased the feeling. On the other hand, the temporary severance of his allegiance, and his service under the independent government of Texas, and its formal voluntary annexation to the United States, must have compelled him to define the nature of Federal relations in a clearer way than did most army-officers. In the latter half of his life he saw the Democratic party as the champion, interpreter, and representative of conservative ideas, especially in the South. This, with other causes, contributed to draw him nearer to it. At once strongly Southern and strongly Unionist, he regarded with aversion the Republican party, which was anti-Southern, and, in its inception and tendency, disunionist.

To a soldier, that government commonly seems the best which is best administered ; and the nurture and protection of liberty are less apt to engage his admiration than the display of certain other virtues. Order, justice, and vigor, are more apparent agencies than the spirit of freedom which gives them the breath of life. Power, exercised with decision, and restrained only by a sense of responsibility, appears as the model of government ; and fetters upon the hands of authority seem the evidence of blind jealousy and unreasoning suspicion. Though General Johnston was something more than a mere soldier, this military ideal was not without its influence on his conception of government. A powerful, stable, energetic government, careful of the interests of the people, presents so many excellences that it is hard not to wish to see it realized. Such a vision influenced to some extent his imagination, the more so, as he deemed the spirit of personal independence the only effectual check upon the tendency to despotism present in all government. Devotion to the Union, fostered by the conviction of its unnumbered blessings, and by his military service, made him unwilling to consider it otherwise than as " perpetual." In Utah, as the exponent of the military power of the Government, he was intrusted with the execution of its orders ; its honor and dignity were in his custody; its welfare was the constant motive of his acts; and in his hands the mere symbols of its power had triumphed over the causeless rebellion of that disaffected yet dependent population.

But his life had not been passed altogether in the service of the

United States. He had been the soldier of Anglo-Saxon freedom, the cabinet officer of a constitutional and independent republic, and a planter who had earned his bread in the sweat of his brow. He understood the delicate and complicated mechanism of our Government; and, much as he desired to see its hands strengthened within its legitimate sphere, he knew that the sovereignty of the States was the palladium of our liberties, and was to be respected and defended with jealous care. It is true that he thought that the rights of the States could be better secured by many concessions even than by arms; but he had no doubts as to which party was the aggressor, and his convictions, as well as his sympathies, were with his own State and section. Moreover, he had learned from the patriots of 1776 the inherent right of every people to select their own form of government, and to maintain their independence by revolution.

General Johnston's views in regard to slavery were those generally held in the South, where he was born and brought up, and with whose social structure he had been identified. Right or wrong, they were the beliefs of eight millions of people, who have shown as high traits, as pure a morality, as lofty a courage, and as intelligent a statesmanship, as any who ever lived. With no great respect for political abstractions, and perceiving clearly the differences that mark race and condition, he rejected with intellectual scorn the generalizations which overlook all existing facts, and confound all the relations of life. He recognized our common humanity, no man more distinctly; and acted upon it, no man no more fully. But he could not ignore that the manifest inferiority of the negro fitted him for the place he held, and that time alone could fit him for any other. The slaves had been bought with a price, under the strongest legal sanctions, and all arguments for their forcible emancipation applied equally well to the confiscation of every other species of wealth or property. The destructive consequences of the abolition of slavery had been proved in the West Indies, and were as certain as any future event could be. Hence he shared the resentment, though not the expression of it, universal in the South, against the domineering philanthropy that assailed its institutions. His views in regard to the nature and polity of the United States Government, on the whole, fairly represented the ideas of the army-officers as a class, but enlarged and modified by a wider experience. If they could be summed up in a single word, it would be—*conservative.*

General Johnston had been so long the stanch soldier of the United States that he was unwilling to contemplate the picture of its majestic fabric shattered and in ruins. If the States were to be severed, it mattered little to him under what class of rights the act was to be consummated. Whether called secession, or revolution, or rebellion, it was the prostration of that governmental ideal for whose exaltation his life had been spent. Like Mr. Madison, he had "veiled" the possibility, but the rude hand of fanaticism had rent the veil asunder. Ah! was it wise for the mighty North to force such faithful servants, such loyal hearts as this, as Jackson, as Lee, into resistance and the final argument of the battle-field. Lip-service and the hireling sword are everywhere at the command of power; but men like these, at their need, the generations must wait for. They are the product of wisdom, and justice, and beneficence, in the country which possesses them. Besotted is the people who believe that their place can be supplied by able adventurers. The splendid military genius of Hannibal could not sustain itself with mercenary spears against the moderate talents of Fabius and the unequal inspiration of Scipio, animated by patriotic fervor.

But, devoted as General Johnston was to the Union, he could not forget that he was also the citizen of a State. To Texas he had sworn allegiance; his estate and his best years had been spent in shielding her; he had aided to merge her autonomy and to limit her independent sovereignty by annexation, and he knew that when she entered the Union it was *by treaty, as an equal*, and that the Constitution was the bond to which she had consented. She had performed her covenant faithfully; it was the North by which it had been trampled into the dust. She had, therefore, the right to renounce the broken contract, or to try to enforce it, as she deemed most expedient. If she elected to secure her liberties by withdrawing from a Union in which they were assailed, her action would be justified by either the letter of the bond, or by the "inalienable right," as the Declaration of Independence has it, of a people to choose their own form of government. It was an act of sovereignty, for which the State was responsible to whatever other community should choose to dispute it; but not to its own citizens, who were bound to adhere to it the more closely the more it was endangered.

Now, though General Johnston was satisfied that Texas and the other Southern States had ample grounds for resistance or withdrawal, and the right to take the extremest measures to secure themselves, he did not believe the means adopted were wise or expedient. His mind was too sternly practical to allow him to suppose, when the clearest guarantees of the Constitution had failed to restrain partisan zeal and the lust of dominion, that these passions would be arrested now by the assertion of a disputed right. He was sure that peaceable secession was impossible, and therefore thought that it was a remedy to be tried only when all others had been exhausted, and not until every effort at conciliation had failed, and every sacrifice had been made to preserve the Union. Nor was he without hopes that, if an interval were left for returning reason to resume its sway, fanaticism might be dethroned, and the people would demand equity and peace. But, if resistance was to be made, he thought it should be attempted on no doubtful issue, but only after radical tactics had fully laid bare the purposes of that party. Such delay would unite the South, justify its action, and give the opportunity for coöperation, organization, and the accumulation of adequate means of defense. Delusive as were these hopes, they were those of a patriot, and had much to do in shaping General Johnston's conduct in the opening of the war.

He knew that no man's voice or influence could control the tempest of human passions which was driving the republic on the breakers ; yet such was his faith in its destiny that he could still trust that a good Providence would rescue it, even if by a miracle. In such a state of affairs, there was nothing left for a man in his position but to drift, standing at his post. His temper was of a cast so cheerful, his philosophy so bracing, and his code of duty so exacting, that he felt able to perform the minutest detail of service required of him with perfect fidelity of spirit and unshaken by the tumult, until a conflict of duties should arise. He would not anticipate the painful hour, for " sufficient unto the day is the evil thereof ; " but, when the moment for decision came, he would obey that conscience which had been his constant monitor.

When Texas seceded, the alternative was presented him. On one side was the grand nationality, whose flag he had borne, whose authority he had upheld, to whose glory he had consecrated his career, and in whose service were embarked all his plans for power, prosperity, and worldly advancement. On the other were his feeble State and her concurring sisters, as yet not united even in a defensive league, rent by faction, unprepared for war, and making no definite call upon his services. Had he listened to the voice of ambition, the tempter would have told him that, in the United States Army, he stood at the head of the list of active officers, and that above him were none except those whom age or meagre ability excluded from rivalry, and that the large resources and commanding position of the established Government offered every advantage a soldier could wish, while its rewards would accord with its imperial designs. Whatever others may have thought, he was not deceived as to the comparative strength of the opponents. He knew the facts only too well. When, therefore, he made his choice, it was the easy triumph of duty over interest, and of affection for his own people over all the allurements that ambition can hold out.

Until Texas seceded he went forward unswervingly in the service of his employer the General Government; but, when that event presented a definite issue, he promptly took his choice of evils. The United States Army was no longer the place for him, when, at any moment, he might be called upon to aid in the work of subjugation. He had resolved never to lift his hand against " his people ; " and, since Texas had left the Union, in the army he could not remain. He therefore resigned. Still, as secession was not war, and Texas ardently desired peace, he indulged the hope that the mercy which had so often saved the country from the consequences of its own sins and follies might even yet avert impending disasters. In this event he would retire to some small farm, near Los Angeles, California, and, among congenial friends, far from the strife of faction, would pass the evening of his days in tranquillity. His age and services might claim exemption from contests for which he had no heart ; and, in the balmy air of that garden of the West, he would nurture his children in scenes unvisited by civil discord.

He tendered his resignation, and asked that a successor might be sent to relieve him. He was very anxious to fulfill strictly and satisfactorily the trust committed to him, and to be relieved from it before the jar of civil war should complicate his position. Lest the knowledge of his resignation might weaken the moral hold he had over the soldiers, or promote disaffection and a revolutionary spirit among the numerous Southerners resident in California, he kept the fact concealed. His adjutant-general (Major Mackall) and Mrs. Johnston were aware of the fact, which he also communicated to Dr. Griffin, and Mr. and Mrs. H. P. Hepburn, his kinsfolk, under the seal of secrecy. This was so well observed that San Francisco was taken by surprise when his resignation was announced a fortnight later.

About this time, General Johnston was told, by some Republicans of San Francisco, that a plot existed to seize Alcatraz, the fortress which commands the entrance to the bay and harbor of that key of California, in order to set up a Pacific republic. General Johnston replied that he hoped they were mistaken, but that precautions would be taken to prevent the success of such an enterprise. He proceeded quietly to remove several thousand stand of arms from the arsenal at Benicia, where they were exposed, to Alcatraz, which was virtually impregnable, and informed the Governor that, in case of any outbreak or insurrection, they could be employed by the militia to repress it. He also took other measures to insure peace. The writer does not believe that any plot or design was made by the Southerners, or others in California, to take the State out of the Union; but there is no doubt that, if the large element of restless and revolutionary men on that coast had imagined they would receive the aid or countenance of the military commander in such an undertaking, they had the hardihood to make the attempt. A friend, long domiciled there, who would have known if anybody in that country knew, told the writer that there were prominent men in California who *wished* such a result, and, knowing his long intimacy, asked him to sound General Johnston as to the feasibility of a Pacific republic, and as to his wishes and intentions. " But," said he, " I did not dare to approach him on the subject. He told me, however, of his own accord, that as long as he held his commission he would maintain the authority of the United States to the last extremity; and we knew he would do it."

While he was waiting, in suspense and much inward sorrow, the action of the authorities at Washington, General E. V. Sumner suddenly arrived unannounced at San Francisco, with orders to supersede him in the command of the department. As the circumstances of General Sumner's arrival have been greatly falsified by some of the baser sort of party journals, and the more careless sort of partisan histories, it is necessary to mention them here with more detail than would otherwise be called for. General Sumner sailed from New York about the 1st of April, secretly, and perhaps, as was stated at the time, under an assumed name. His name was not in the list of passengers forwarded by the Pony Express, which reached San Francisco a week in advance of the steamer. He had hardly taken command, before the Administration organs from ocean to ocean began to hint darkly of a deep-laid conspiracy nipped in the bud by this wonderful *coup-d'état*. With that fertility of fancy which characterizes a certain class of journalists, the story grew by embellishment. This was the manner, as published by one of them:

> There came one day to our good President a message that caused his cheek to pale, and his great heart to beat quick with apprehension. This was the message—short, as it was ominous—" There is treason on Alcatraz!" Alcatraz is the name of the island and fort, etc.

Then follows a long description of the situation, with full details of an imaginary plot, evidently evolved from the inner consciousness of this political romancer:

> To insure the success of the scheme, Albert Sidney Johnston was placed in command at Fort Alcatraz. It was arranged that the leaders in San Francisco, with a force of picked men sufficient for the purpose, should surprise and capture the fort. The details were all arranged. They were waiting only for orders from the rebel government to strike the fatal blow. The birds of the air carried whisperings of this treason to loyal ears, etc.

General Sumner's secret appointment and transit are then given, with this *dénoûment:*

> The eager thousands who thronged the streets hardly noticed the momentary pause of the steamer when passing Fort Alcatraz, nor did they note the little boat that shot out from her side toward the island; yet that tiny boat bore more to them "than Cæsar and his fortunes." It bore General Sumner, who, in a few minutes, stood before the commander, and, as his superior in rank, and under special orders from the President, assumed command of Fort Alcatraz. California was saved to the Union.

This is a pretty fair sample of a story that has since been frequently reproduced with variations in Northern prints. On its face it bears the marks of a mythical origin—signs of improbability—circumstantial details, resting on the evidence of "the birds of the air"—a metaphor, probably, for that vile brood of troubled times, the paid informers. It would not be worth while to notice such a rumor, had it not been suggested by the conduct of the Administration, and, most probably, from its source and prevalence, by official inspiration. The truth was, that General Sumner landed at the wharf with the other passengers, and did not see General Johnston till the next day at noon. When the command was turned over to him, he expressed an approval of all his predecessor's acts, and much gratification at the condition of the department, also asking his advice as to future arrangements, the disposition of troops, etc. He stated that he would make a favorable report to the War Department.

The following extract from his report of April 28, 1861, to the adjutant-general, gives all that he says in regard to General Johnston; but, in so far as it goes, it confirms what has been said:

I have the honor to report that I arrived here on the 24th inst., and on the 25th relieved General Johnston in command of this department. My departure from New York was not known here till the night before my arrival. It gives me pleasure to state that the command was turned over to me in good order. General Johnston had forwarded his resignation before I arrived, but he continued to hold the command, and was carrying out the orders of the Government.

Having applied for information on this topic to General Buell, who was Sumner's chief of staff, in California, he replied, in a letter of April 2, 1873:

I did not accompany General Sumner to California in the spring of 1861, and was not there when your father turned over the command to him. I arrived, however, very soon after. I do remember that a report had some currency about that time to the effect that your father desired, or had it in contemplation, to surrender California to the cause of the Southern Confederacy. Those were days of a good deal of distrust and bitterness; but I do not believe that any well-informed person ever gave credence to the report. For, besides the intrinsic absurdity of such a proposition, and its utter inconsistency with your father's character, there was no foundation whatever for such a report. No man who knew your father well could ever believe him capable of a base action.

This slander having been lately revived in California, possibly for some political motive, has called forth a letter from Governor Downey. The article from the *Los Angeles Express* and the reply of Governor Downey are here given.

All old residents of the Pacific coast know that at the time of the breaking out of the rebellion a plot was formed by A. S. Johnston, then the military commander of this department, in connection with a number of prominent leaders (some of whom are still prominent in that party), to seize the United States Arsenal, distribute the arms to their partisans, and hand the State of California over to the Southern Confederacy. Unfortunately for the success of this precious scheme, it by some means leaked out, and the Government at Washington, comprehending the danger, lost no time in dispatching General Sumner to supersede Johnston, and save the State to the Union. General Sumner arrived here *incognito*, and immediately proceeded to Benicia, where he presented the order assigning him to the command, and demanded possession of the department. Sumner's appearance was like a thunder-clap to the conspirators, who had not anticipated such prompt action, and were not prepared to resist, so there was nothing for Johnston to do but submit, and turn over the command to Sumner, which he did, and himself left a few days after for the South, where he fell on the field of Shiloh.

To the Editor of the *Express:*

The above is taken from an article in the *Los Angeles Daily Republican*, and is written to subserve the local campaign ; but it is at great sacrifice of the truths of history. During the term of General Albert Sidney Johnston I had constant intercourse with him on official business. Up to my term of office we had yearly wars with the Indians, in which the State annually incurred great expense. I took the ground that this was all wrong, that it was a Federal matter purely, and that the Federal troops on this coast were ample, at all times, for every Indian emergency. The executive office was flooded with petitions to call out troops. I applied to General Johnston for relief, which he immediately granted, and assured me that he had all the force and material required to quell the Indian disturbances, and that this service was about all that himself, officers, and men, had to perform on this coast. It was suggested by several citizens to me that there were 75,000 stand of arms at Benicia that might, in those disturbed times, fall into hands that would use them against the Government. I called on General Johnston in relation to these arms. He said, in the most impressive manner : " Governor, I have spent the greater part of my life in the service of my country, and while I hold her commission I shall serve her honorably and faithfully. I shall protect her public property, and not a cartridge or a percussion-cap shall pass to any enemy while I am here as her representative. There is," he said, " no man in the Union more sorely afflicted than I am at the occurrences now taking place. I do not know yet what position Texas may take. I have been long identified with Texas, her interests and public men, and her action may control my future destiny, but in any event I shall give due notice, and turn over intact my department to my successor." Now, I say it is not true that there was any plot to carry this State out of the Union. I was in constant communication with Mr. Seward and the Secretary of War. I raised all the troops that were required, without an expense of twenty-five cents to the State. The railroad was no factor in this question. No troops came here from the East. I raised them and sent them forward East, all under Democratic officers—the Arizona column, under Generals Carleton and West, and the Utah column, under Generals Conner, Evans, O'Neal, and others. General

Johnston did not leave the State in a few days after the arrival of Sumner. He remained in San Francisco a long time, and his house was the centre to which the army-officers tended in a social way. Long after his replacement by General Sumner I met the most of the Federal officers at his house, many of them men who distinguished themselves afterward during the war. It was long after this occurrence that General Johnston was in Los Angeles, and I believe still undetermined what course to pursue. So it is plain that the *Republican* is badly informed. I have the kindest letters from General Sumner and General Wright, his successors, thanking me for my aid in helping them to discharge their duties at this very critical period. Neither of these gentlemen believed that General Johnston had any knowledge of any plot on this coast; nor that there was any necessity for the unusual and precipitous manner which the War Department pursued. It is plain that, if the Department of War thought there was any danger, they would not have shipped the arms at Benicia East by way of Panama. They would have kept them here for us to put down rebellion.

JOHN G. DOWNEY.

This chapter having been submitted by letter to General W. W. Mackall, Assistant Adjutant-General of the Department of California in 1861, he replied January 7, 1876. The following is an extract from the letter of General Mackall:

That your father exercised his command honestly for the Government he served in California is thoroughly known to me; but, as a matter of course, my evidence can have no weight with those inclined to doubt it. When Texas seceded, he told me that he had sent in his resignation. I was surprised, and said, "I always thought you were a Kentuckian." He replied, "I adopted Texas, and its people have been my fast friends and are entitled to my best services." In reply, some days after, to a remark of mine (not, however, in reference to himself), that I thought an officer inexcusable in negotiating with another government for position, while holding a United States commission, he said, "Major, I assure you that I have never written one word to any one on such a subject."

The morning General Sumner arrived, General Johnston and I were in the office with some other officers, when my clerk announced Sumner's arrival. General Johnston turned to me and, smiling, said, "Major, you and I know how welcome he is." Neither of us suspected that it had any other significance than the natural answer to his resignation, or a command given to Sumner on his promotion. I am satisfied that no officer, Northern or Southern, had up to this time thought that General Johnston would act otherwise than as a gentleman true to his trust. Nor do I believe that he, much as his character commanded the respect of all, had he attempted to make use of his position to injure the Government he then served, could have called to his side a single Southern officer. Sure am I that none of those who afterward, with great sorrow, felt themselves obliged to leave the service and go to the defense of their own people, for whom many of them gave up their lives, would have been found among the number. The only complaint I ever heard from General Sumner as to the condition of the command as he received it was, that he was not assured of the loyalty of the commander of Alcatraz Island. I do not remember whether or no he superseded him. This, however, is known, that the officer continued to serve the United States during the war; and so Sumner must have learned that, even in this instance, General Johnston had been true. General Johnston, however, had acted from no special knowledge of the officer's politics, but from his own honest instincts, which brought the conviction that a gentleman would not accept a trust which he might be induced to betray.

The meeting was cordial on both sides. Whomsoever else that bluff soldier might suspect, he knew that the man before him was the model of spotless integrity. General Johnston mentioned the facts of his resignation to General Sumner, who then said: "General, I wish you would reconsider and recall your resignation. General Scott bade me say to you that he wished you for active service, and that you should be only second to himself." General Johnston replied, "I thank General Scott for his opinion of me, but nothing can change my determination."

When General Johnston learned how his successor had been sent forward, and the inference thus suggested to the public mind, together with the version of his conduct which had been put forth by the Administration press for some weeks previous, he felt the deepest indignation. To the officers who informed him of General Sumner's arrival, he had said with emotion at the weight of care which had been lifted from his shoulders, "Then am I doubly relieved." But, after he had so guarded his action as to keep his fair fame spotless, at the expense of feeling and interest, the iniquity of this insidious blow rankled in his bosom. Whether it was the fabrication of some malignant slanderer, or a nightmare conjured up from the tangled designs of the cabinet, he scorned the imputation upon him of conspiracy or infidelity to his duty as a United States officer. He said once and again to friends, "If I had proved faithless here, how could my own people ever trust me?"

Colonel Munford, on his staff during the civil war, made the following statement in his public address at Memphis, on General Johnston:

When his resignation of command in the army of the United States was sent from California, he kept his purpose and action a profound secret. I heard him say that he believed if he had tried he could have brought nearly or quite his entire command with him, and, remarking that we needed them very much, I asked him if he did not regret not having done so. "No sir," he replied. "That army was not mine; it belonged, with all its appointments, to the Government of the United States. My position was a trust which for myself I could relinquish, but only on condition of handing over, to those for whom I held, whatever was in my hands. I waited till I had cause to know my resignation had been received in Washington, turned over the entire command to the next ranking officer, mounted my horse and started across the Plains."

Colonel Thomas F. McKinney, his old friend, wrote in 1872, in regard to General Johnston:

One thing is very clear from what he said as he passed through Texas, that the war between the North and South distressed him exceedingly.

The whole proceeding was at once imbecile and insulting. Had the suspicion been correct, and General Johnston the arch-conspirator he was represented to be, no man who knows the boldness and decision of his character can doubt that he would have solved the problem of a Pacific republic promptly enough, by clapping his successor in irons, and turning the guns of Alcatraz upon San Francisco. As his correspondence will show, however, he was still hoping for a peaceable solution of the question, and was alternately swayed with grief at the condition of affairs and satisfaction at the Union feeling in San Francisco. The only effect upon him was to revolt his whole soul against those who had assailed his honor. His friends on the Atlantic coast, without fully comprehending the force of the thrust made at him, tried to wipe out or repair the injury as far as possible. General Scott, as soon as he heard what had been done, sent him the strongest assurances of friendship. A cadetship at the Military Academy for his son was forwarded on the 19th of April, probably through General Scott's instrumentality ; and other evidences were offered of a desire to employ him in high position, which were communicated to him through various channels more or less direct.

The Hon. Montgomery Blair, Mr. Lincoln's Postmaster-General, in a letter to the writer, shows that, at a later date, when opportunity for investigation and a correct knowledge of the facts had been afforded, the Administration entertained no such view of conspiracy as the loyal press had disseminated. Mr. Blair says :

There is a fact in regard to your father that I ought to mention. When General Ord came here from San Francisco, he called on me, and stated that great injury had been done your father by the manner in which he had been superseded, that he was opposed to the secession movement altogether, and that he had often heard him check persons using secession talk in his presence, telling them that it was not respectful to him, as a United States officer. This statement was substantiated by a letter of yours which had been intercepted and given to me. I immediately told Mr. Lincoln the facts, and recommended him to send your father a major-general's commission, and he at once executed the commission. I had it forwarded to your father at San Francisco. But a few days afterward I learned that he had started for Texas, and I directed the postmaster to retain the package for cancellation.

This must have been early in July.

So far as his merely personal attitude was concerned, the assurances he received of the disposition of the President and cabinet toward him might have been accepted as satisfactory, though it is not probable that he ever would have resumed his sword, under any circumstances,

under the orders of an Administration that had touched his honor so
nearly. But the allurements held out to him had no weight in altering
a resolution formed on entirely different grounds. From the moment
Texas seceded, his purpose was fixed, no longer to bear arms for a Government of which she was not a member.

General Johnston was now again a private citizen. He left San
Francisco on the 28th of April, and proceeded to Los Angeles, where
he became the guest of his brother-in-law, Dr. John S. Griffin. He had
made comparatively few acquaintances in California ; but, as soon as
he ceased to wear the uniform of the United States, numbers flocked to
him for advice as to what should be done in such a crisis. His habitual
reply was :

If you sympathize with either side, and feel the call of duty to take part in a
sectional war, go home, and fight there if necessary. But here there should be
peace. Strife here would be civil war—not North against South—but neighbor
against neighbor ; and no one can imagine the horrors that would ensue.

The writer does not think he is claiming too much when he says
that the exemption of the Pacific coast from the calamities of civil war,
and, in great measure, subsequently, from the bitterness engendered
elsewhere thereby, was due to General Johnston, perhaps, more than
to any other man, by reason of his firm and unshaken attitude as a
commander until relieved, and afterward by his counsels as a private
citizen.

About the first of May, the writer, hearing that it was probable that
General Johnston would be arrested if he returned to the United States
by the way of New York, determined to apprise him of his danger.
Knowing that all letters were liable to official scrutiny, he engaged
a midshipman, who had lately resigned and was highly recommended,
to bear advices to General Johnston. The messenger, with excellent
intentions, was so indiscreet as to confide his letters to a United States
consul in the West Indies, and to land in New York, where he was
arrested. This is the intercepted letter alluded to by Mr. Blair. As
General Johnston knew nothing of this attempt to warn him, it did not
influence his movements. It is mentioned now only because it was proclaimed at the time as another link in the grand chain of conspiracy
which was erroneously assumed by the excited imagination of the North
to encircle the Confederate States.

With fair opportunities of knowing the details of the secession
movement, the writer does not hesitate to say that its most salient
characteristics were spontaneous enthusiasm and reckless confidence.
The revolution was essentially popular ; and a martial democracy, in
which public measures had always been settled by oral discussion, was
not apt to practise any concealment of conduct or opinion. In fact, as

the entire State action claimed to be based on legal right, all mystery was repudiated as savoring of intrigue, and much force was spent in vehement assertion that might better have been put into preparation for the conflict. Conspiracy is alien to the genius of a free people. It requires generations of despotism to train men to the secrecy, perfect organization, and implicit obedience, necessary to success in it. There were no materials for this sort of work in the South ; and, indeed, the education that supplies them unfits a people for the liberty it seeks through them. It would, nevertheless, be well for Americans of all sections if the spirit of self-restraint were cultivated more, and if a greater reserve were studied to replace the unbridled expression of thought and feeling that is becoming so marked a national trait.

In a letter written January 17, 1861, from San Francisco to the writer, General Johnston, after describing the rough voyage by which he and his family reached their destination on the 14th of January, says :

When we get to our new home and look around a little, I shall be able to give you some account of California affairs. I think the public sentiment here is decidedly in favor of the maintenance of the Union.

Again :

SAN FRANCISCO, CALIFORNIA, *February* 25, 1861.

MY DEAR SON : We are all well, and almost as comfortable as we could desire, were it not for the unhappy condition of our country. I confess I can only expect a general disruption, for passion seems to rule. Yet, though hope has been so often disappointed, a gleam breaks upon us from the efforts of the 4th of February convention at Washington, leading us on to indulge in its illusions a little longer.

A huge Union meeting was held here on the 22d. The day was a perfect holiday for the whole population, who filled the streets, and in their best dresses seemed to enjoy the beautiful weather. The resolutions adopted testified to a devoted loyalty to the Union, declared against secession as a right, and repudiated the idea of a Pacific republic as impossible. They express fraternal feelings for all the States, and declare that their interest and honor demand every exertion on their part to bring about harmony again. I presume that the sentiments of these resolutions, which are those of the people of this city, may be set down as those of the State, with the exception of a small minority.

I send Hennie, Rosa, Mrs. Duncan, and grandpa's little pets, best love. Your affectionate father,　　　　　　　　　　　　　　　A. S. JOHNSTON.

The following letter to Major Fitz-John Porter, though in parts nearly identical with that just given, is inserted as corroborative of General Johnston's perfect frankness of dealing. While his son was acting with those in the South who were readiest to meet the issue of war, his late adjutant-general and trusted friend, looking at affairs from a Northern point of view, was gradually yielding his conservative views and entering with zeal into the idea of coercing the South. General

Johnston, agreeing with neither, did not resent in those he loved that liberty of thought and action which he claimed for himself as his dearest right :

SAN FRANCISCO, CALIFORNIA, *February* 25, 1861.

MY DEAR MAJOR : I have received your letter of 22d of January. I found my trunk at Wells, Fargo & Co.'s office. I have no news to give you from this far-off region. Everything is quiet, and the affairs of the department are being conducted quietly and without difficulty from any source; though, *without any excuse for it*, the Government has allowed every department of the staff here to fall into a state of pauperism, making the military arm as impotent for action here as the greatest enemy of the republic could desire to have it. The district of Oregon owes not less than $200,000, and no money on hand except a few thousands in the Subsistence Department; this department owes probably $100,000, and *not a cent* to pay with. Is our Government absolutely stupefied? or why overlook the fact that they can protect the public interest here at least? There is abundance of money in the Mint to pay *all* the indebtedness of the Government here, and meet any emergency, if the Secretary of the Treasury would only recognize the fact, and transfer the funds in the Sub-Treasury to the credit of the disbursing officers. Volumes have been written against the credit system and the losses to the General Government in consequence of it, when it had credit ; how much more strongly may all the arguments be urged now, when men begin to doubt its longer continuance ! The loss to the Government must be so much the greater in consequence.

There was a huge Union meeting here on the 22d. The weather was beautiful, and the day was made a perfect holiday by the whole population, who, well dressed and entirely respectable in appearance and deportment, seemed to enjoy the fine weather. The streets were filled all day, the people going to and fro in pursuit of pleasure. The resolutions adopted by the meeting were declaratory of the devoted attachment of the people to the Union, of their opposition to secession as a right, of their repudiation of the idea of a Pacific republic as impossible, and expressive of their fraternal feelings toward all the States, and their duty and interest to bring about harmony. I would that there were no other sentiments within the broad expanse of our country.

Please present my kind regards to Mrs. Porter and Mrs. Holbrook, and believe me, very truly your friend,

A. S. JOHNSTON.

To Major F. J. PORTER, No. 66 Union Place, New York City.

SAN FRANCISCO, CALIFORNIA, *April* 9, 1861.

MY DEAR SON : Yesterday the newspapers of this city announced that Texas had completed all arrangements contemplated as necessary to separate her destiny from the General Government, the final act being the taking the oath of allegiance to the new Confederacy by the Legislature and other State officers. I have hoped to the last that a reconciliation would be, by some great statesmanlike move in the right direction, effected, with such guarantees as would be satisfactory and reëstablish the tranquillity of the Southern mind and those fraternal relations which alone make our confederate system possible. Whether these acts could or could not be rightfully done under the Constitution need no longer be discussed. The people have resolved, and so declared to the world, to establish a government for themselves. A great fact thus presents itself, which must be dealt with not with technicalities, but in view of all the considerations and interests which affect the future of two great sections of our country. To continue to hold my commission after being apprised of the final action of my State, to whose partiality in a great measure I owe my position, could find no justification in my own conscience; and I have, therefore, this day forwarded the resignation of my commission for the acceptance of the President, which I hope may be promptly accepted. I have asked that my successor be appointed and ordered to relieve me as soon as practicable.

You probably have seen a paragraph in the papers to the effect that evidence is in possession of the War Department that General Johnston and other officers are conspiring to establish a Pacific republic. I say the whole charge is false in every particular, and that there is not the slightest ground for it. I am a stranger here, and have had no conversation even with any one who desires such a result or entertains such views. If the War Department has such information, why don't they order an investigation, and not give it to the letter-writers to damage the reputation of officers? My escutcheon is without a blur upon it, and never will be tarnished. I shall do my duty to the last, and when absolved take my course. I must now look out for a livelihood for my poor family; how or where to find it is not apparent, but with my courage all will not be lost. Give my love to Hennie, Rosa, Mrs. Duncan, and the children.

Your affectionate father, A. S. JOHNSTON.

You had, perhaps, better let the announcement of my resignation come from the department.

[CONFIDENTIAL.] SAN FRANCISCO, CALIFORNIA, *April* 14, 1861.

MY DEAR DOCTOR: The news reached this place on the 9th inst. that Texas had, in the most solemn and conclusive manner, taken the final step to separate her destiny from that of the Northern States, and had joined the Southern Confederacy. This extreme action is entirely consistent with the belief on their part that the unfriendly sentiment of the North, which so injuriously affected the tranquillity and security of the Southern communities, would undergo no change, and that the future, in consequence of it, would be worse than the past. For my own part, I thought differently. I believed that the joint action of the slaveholding States (if it could be brought about) would obtain from the North all the guarantees necessary for the preservation of the equality of the States, and prevent for the future the system of molestation kept up by fanaticism, and that the unfriendly sentiment (sufficiently prevalent at the North for mischief), no longer sustained by political sanctions, would die out. I thought this course would preserve the integrity of the Union, and make it compatible with the honor and interests of the whole to maintain it. But the persistent obstinacy of the Republican party, in refusing to concede anything whatever for the sake of the Union up to the hour of the adjournment of the Senate, seems to indicate that the action of the South was based upon a correct understanding of the true sentiments of the North and their unbending character.. It seems instinctively to have seized the right conclusion. The Government has now to deal with a great fact—a portion of the Confederacy in the attitude and progress of revolution. It is now immaterial whether the steps by which they have reached this point are legal or not; the question now rests upon principles which constitute the essence of our organic law, i. e., the right of revolution. A wise, straightforward, manly statesmanship may lead to a peaceful solution; but there is nothing so far to found the basis of such a hope upon. The quibbling about technicalities, which can no longer enter into the question, has only produced embarrassment so far. I felt, as soon as I learned the course adopted by my State (Texas), that it was my duty to conform to her will, and that I ought to forward *my resignation* to the President; and I have accordingly done so. I have served faithfully to the present moment, and will continue to until I am properly relieved. Until then, rest assured that I will do nothing inconsistent with my obligations to the Government as an officer. The pressure of Northern views had begun to manifest itself in the army, and therefore I felt less repugnance in severing my connection with it. You will allow that a man's convictions of the necessity must be strong to lead him to take the step I have done. I have counseled only with my wife. It brings us face to face with poverty. There is no dishonor in this; but, to serve without the proper *animus*, there would be. In the contingencies of life, we have taught ourselves to believe that all conditions of life are tolerable, without dishonor. I am willing to undertake any employment that will yield a support for my family. Your advice would assist me. I will have in cash about $1,500 to begin with.

Your friend and brother,   A. S. JOHNSTON.

Any publicity given to the fact of my having resigned would embarrass me in the proper discharge of my duty. It would be better for the notice to come from the East.

To Dr. JOHN S. GRIFFIN.

WASHINGTON CITY, April 18, 1861.

MY DEAR GENERAL: I take the greatest pleasure in assuring you, for the Secretary of War, that he has the utmost confidence in you, and will give you the most important command and trust, on your arrival here. Sidney is appointed to the Military Academy.

I hope soon to see you; and, with a heart glowing with pride and pleasure for my commander and friend, I remain, ever yours,

F. J. PORTER,
Assistant Adjutant-General.

To General A. S. JOHNSTON, San Francisco, California.

The following letter, addressed to Major Porter by an officer, then and since very prominent in the United States Army, needs no comment:

WASHINGTON, May 10, 1861.

DEAR PORTER: General Johnston has resigned. He did so, *April* 9, 1861! Sumner's orders were not known here till near that time. He left Washington April 1st. Johnston asked that a successor might be sent to relieve him! His letter did not show that he had any idea that he was suspected, or that any one was sent to relieve him—says that he has heard that Johnston has been talking, very openly, secession doctrines in San Francisco. The thing is all up. His resignation is accepted, and the feeling is so strong against those who have abandoned the country, that it would be utterly useless to say a word.

General Johnston's resignation was accepted on the 6th of May, to take effect on the 3d instant.

From his sister-in-law, Mrs. Eliza Gilpin, already mentioned as the widow of his brother, Josiah Stoddard Johnston, he received a letter, dated at Philadelphia, April 15th, breathing the excited feeling of devotion to the Union just then newly aroused by the fall of Fort Sumter. The following extract, however, contains all that is essential to this memoir :

My very dear Brother : The newspaper account of your having been superseded in your command, and without any reasons having been assigned for it, has given me much anxiety on your account, and excited much indignation, as no one alive has a right to feel for you a more natural and affectionate interest. Your elder brother, my beloved husband, having felt for you as a father, gives me a right to speak as a mother ; and I do affectionately request you not to act hastily and resign your commission. I have a letter, this moment received from Washington, from the most reliable source—an officer of rank, and a great personal friend of yours. From him I asked what it meant. His reply is : " Great astonishment prevails at the course taken with regard to your brother, General Johnston, and General Scott expresses great mortification at the course, which we all believe to be purely political. The general designs, when General Johnston arrives here, to place him in a *position at once* which will relieve him from the slightest imputation." Therefore, my dear Albert, do not think of resigning. Remember your dear brother's love for the Union, his exalted patriotism, and his many virtues. You are his representative now, and will remain by our beloved flag. . . .

God bless you, my dear brother, and direct you in the right way !

Your Sister.

The following was General Johnston's reply:

Los Angeles, California, *June* 1, 1861.

My dear Sister : I received your kind and affectionate letter of April 15th, last evening. The resignation of my commission in the army was forwarded from San Francisco, for the acceptance of the President, on the 10th of April, by the Pony Express. It should have reached Washington on the 25th of April, the day on which General Sumner, under the orders of the Secretary of War, relieved me from the command of the Pacific Department. I was directed in that order to repair to Washington to receive orders. Presuming that my resignation had been accepted by the President, to take effect on the arrival of my successor, as had been requested by me, I have awaited here the announcement of its acceptance. It may be that, having, under the influence of an unaccountable and unjustifiable distrust, ordered me to be relieved, the authorities deferred the acceptance till they received General Sumner's report, in which case I cannot receive an answer before the 23d inst.

Having faithfully administered the affairs of the department until I was relieved, there can be no reason to refuse the acceptance. As I am neither indebted to the Government, nor have done any exceptionable act, a refusal to accept would be without precedent ; and, inasmuch as themselves made it impossible for any man with a spark of honor, in my position, to serve longer, it would also be most unjust. I do not say I would have served much longer under any circumstances; but I do say that it would have been impossible for me to have done any act inconsistent with the trust reposed in me; and that trust would, under all circumstances, have been restored, as it was, to the Government, intact.

After General Sumner's promotion, I expected, as a matter of course, to be relieved by him, and was not aware when I was relieved that his being sent out was accompanied by circumstances manifesting distrust. This I learned afterward. I was astonished to see in the *San Francisco Bulletin* of the 7th of April, and I must say also disgusted, that the War Department, which should guard and protect the fame of the officer of the army, allowed itself to be the vehicle of foully slanderous imputations against me, derived no doubt from anonymous sources. If not, justice required an investigation, which would have fixed the guilt, or have acquitted. Instead of this, letter-writers were suffered to spread the charge of disloyalty against me through the wide extent of the States, though there was not a single fact to sustain it.

I have since received the assurances of the Secretary, dated April 18th, through an excellent friend, of full confidence in me, and that my son was appointed a cadet. This is better than nothing, but is a small compensation for the damage done. I have at no time thought that General Scott had anything to do with this. I still feel for him all the gratitude and kindness I have always felt.

I do not desire ever again to hold an office. No one could feel more sensibly the calamitous condition of our country than myself; and, whatever part I may take hereafter, it will always be a subject of gratulation with me that no act of mine ever contributed to bring it about. I suppose the difficulties will now only be adjusted by the sword. In my humble judgment that was not the remedy.

I hope, my dear sister, you are in good health, and that you may long live to enjoy the good things Providence has placed in your hands. Such is the prayer of your affectionate brother, A. S. JOHNSTON.

It is a pleasant thought, now that death has reunited these kindred and exalted spirits, to remember that, though differing so widely, the affection of a lifetime was not imbittered even by the events of the civil war. This venerable lady cherished a tender, sisterly recollection for the memory of the soldier to whose martial virtues her benign influence had early imparted some of the grace of her own refined and elegant character. In a letter to the writer, dated July 12, 1861, she says:

I truly grieve for the necessity of your father's resignation. Still, I cannot blame him. He has always been the soul of honor; and so he will be, in my estimation, while I live.

Years afterward these sentiments were reiterated by the trembling hand of age.

CHAPTER XVIII.

THE DESERT JOURNEY.

GENERAL JOHNSTON remained at Los Angeles from May 2d to June 16th. His letter to Mrs. Gilpin, already given (page 273), reveals in some measure his feelings at this time. The Administration, which thought the personal indignity put upon him atoned for by an offer of promotion, and the crooked policy of discrediting an upright soldier an act merely " political," left his reputation to this late vindication. The arbitrary delay, without cause or explanation, in accepting his resignation, as if to embarrass his action, evidently aroused General Johnston's indignation. The acceptance was received at last, however, before he left Los Angeles, thus completely severing the tie that bound him to military service. As has been said, the grievances that wounded his proud spirit, though sufficient to drive him from the army, were not the considerations that impelled him to his final course of action. These were totally different.

When General Johnston resigned, the elements were astir with the strife and evils brewing, but hostilities had not begun ; and he still flattered himself with a hope of peace. But he had not been long at Los Angeles before there came the news of actual conflict. The tremendous outburst of resentment in the North at the fall of Sumter made it evident that the contest would be waged within no ordinary bounds ; and the soberest minds felt the most concern. A martial people, whose wars for nearly a century had been but the pricking of a spur to their enthusiasm, finding themselves of a sudden arrayed in two hostile camps, would not sheathe their swords without a fierce and protracted struggle. To a man used to study the passions as evinced in warfare, this was plain.

The question was now forced upon General Johnston whether he was to remain neutral in this contest, submissive to the authority he could no longer serve, and alien to the land and people to which his heart called him, or resist the Government he had served so long and so devotedly. To those who have read this biography, it is needless to say that, in this supreme action of his life, General Johnston was guided by the same severe convictions of duty that had always animated him. The powerful passions of his energetic nature, by long subjection, had become the ministers, instead of the counselors, of his reason. Their dictates entered but as a slight element into his motives. Hence his course was consistent. If he would not, in his action, anticipate a painful duty, yet, when it was fully and fairly presented, there was neither hesitation in entering upon it nor vacillation in following it to its remotest consequences.

He soon came to the conclusion that the same reasons that had compelled him to resign for the sake of his State must, at its need, also constrain him to return to its soil and adhere to its fortunes. But, unaware in that isolated community of the martial tread of events or of the fury of the public mind, he had made his arrangements to return by sea to New York, and was about to put his family on the steamer, when he was warned by friends that he would be arrested if he tried to leave ; and it soon became clear that, even if he escaped this fate in California, he must submit to it on the Atlantic coast. As events thickened and the news kept pouring in, his ardent nature took fire. If he had been accustomed to ordinary self-appreciation, he might have known all along that a soldier of his temper, reputation, and position, would not be allowed to stand aloof with such interests at stake to be decided by wager of battle. He was a man who, in the piping times of peace, might be left to rust in obscurity ; but, when the fate of an empire was at poise, no one on either side believed that the sword of Albert Sidney Johnston would weigh lightly in the scale. There were mighty demands upon him now. In California there were many Southerners, Texans especially ; and the low murmur of appeal, even of remonstrance, made itself heard in behalf of the beloved land. " It looks like fate," he said to his wife ; " twice Texas makes me a rebel."

While General Johnston was at Los Angeles a beautiful set of silver was sent to him, on the salver of which was this inscription, " To General A. Sidney Johnston, from friends in San Francisco." Coming at such a time, this mark of approbation from valued friends was doubly prized. While in service, he had scrupulously regarded the obligation laid upon public officers alike by a jealous self-respect and by the Mosaic injunction : " Thou shalt take no gift ; for the gift blindeth the wise and perverteth the words of the righteous." But as a private citizen, insulted and proscribed, this proof of esteem was very grateful to him.

There were considerations to hold him back from the fray that might well have weakened the stoutest resolution. A wife and helpless family of little children looked to him for protection and support. He had saved no fortune : fifteen hundred dollars made up his available means. And now, when a great public duty demanded his talents and experience, it seemed that it must yield to the more immediate call of domestic obligations. But the very spot and people to which Providence had led him afforded to his family a retreat unequaled for security, while a generous, affectionate, and vigorous protector was raised up for their care and succor. Dr. John S. Griffin, Mrs. Johnston's brother, had the will and power to relieve General Johnston's embarrassment, by taking charge of his family. To him they were committed, and nobly was the trust redeemed. Freed from this imperious demand, General Johnston made up his mind to sacrifice all private interests for the sake of his State and of the South. Once resolved, he entered upon his line of action without reserve, and took the steps for its successful accomplishment with his accustomed sagacity.

General Johnston's position had now become one of anxiety, difficulty, and danger. The sea, thoroughly in the interest of the North, was closed to him. Soldiers had been sent to Los Angeles to watch his movements, and he was subjected to a most unpleasant surveillance. Note was taken of all his acts, and the eager hand of military power threatened each moment to seize him. He was virtually a prisoner in the department he had lately commanded. The only way of escape, by which he could reach Texas, was across an inhospitable desert, beset with hardships and perils that might well appall even a veteran campaigner. While considering the proper means for such an enterprise, he learned, to his great satisfaction, of the formation of a band of bold and enthusiastic Southerners pledged to the attempt, and he gladly joined them. The writer is largely indebted to Captain Gift, Colonel Ridley, and Colonel Hardcastle, for important details in regard to General Johnston's journey through Arizona ; and, assured that the spirited narratives of these faithful companions will be cheerfully accepted in lieu of his own, he has preferred to use their own words, except where, for the sake of conciseness, the account is abridged.

Captain Gift was a Tennesseean, and had resigned a midshipman's warrant in the United States Navy in 1849, to settle in California. He served faithfully through the war, and now resides at Napa, California. Alonso Ridley, though of Northern birth, was deeply impressed with the righteousness of the Southern cause. He will often appear in this narrative. He was captain to General Johnston's body-guard, and afterward major of the Third Arizona Regiment.

The following is Captain Gift's account of the organization and start of the expedition :

Prior to the arrival of General Johnston in Los Angeles, Captain Alonso Ridley [1] and the writer had determined to go South, and waited a favorable opportunity. Ridley favored the journey across the Plains, and I favored the route by sea, being a seaman.

On the arrival of the general from San Francisco, we had an interview, and it was determined to try to raise a party sufficiently strong to cross the Plains without fear of molestation from the Indians, then very hostile and enterprising. It was concluded that the party should consist of at least thirty men. Ridley undertook to collect the party, and to his tact and indomitable energy is due the success of the enterprise. He rode several hundred miles to consult with friends, and spent all the money needed in the outfit of nearly half the party.

---

[1] Captain Ridley is now known as Colonel Ridley.

The Federal military authorities deemed it necessary to order a force of horse and foot to Los Angeles to observe our movements; and, as the time of departure drew near, we began to suspect that arrests would be made, or attempted. The time of departure was fixed for the 20th of June; but, upon consultation, we determined to give it out that we would not leave until the 25th, and then leave on the 17th or 18th. The general left on the 16th. His outfit consisted of a strong, light, covered ambulance, drawn by two good American mules (American as distinguished from Mexican), a saddle-horse of California breed, and a small, black, Mexican pack-mule, a hardy, untamable beast. The general carried all his provisions, camp-equipage, etc., in the ambulance, and, in crossing the desert, a good quantity of barley for forage. The mule was also packed with barley.

As previously mentioned, it was given out that our starting-day had been postponed to the 25th. The general being all ready on the 16th, he started to the place of rendezvous, Warner's Ranch, or Agua Caliente, in San Diego County, which was more than a hundred miles on the road. He left Los Angeles at daybreak with Captain Ridley and his servant Ran, and went to the Chino Ranch, thirty miles from Los Angeles, whence he was accompanied by Dr. Carman Frazee. Dr. Frazee knew the country well, and acted as guide.[1] They rested at Chino during part of the day, and then moved forward, Mr. Carlisle, the proprietor of the Chino, having first picketed the road with some of his *vaqueros*, with orders to ride forward and warn the general should soldiers appear in his rear. In this event, he and Frazee would have made their way to Mexican territory on horseback. The Federals, however, had no knowledge of the general's departure, and did not follow him. About the 25th of June nearly the whole party had arrived at the rendezvous, where we found the general enjoying himself, though the weather was excessively hot. The ranch was owned by John Rains, Esq., whose major-domo had orders to kill several bullocks, and jerk the meat for our use. This necessitated several additional days of delay, and I think it was the 29th of June, or about that time, when we finally moved away, organized under command of Alonso Ridley, to whom we intrusted the order of marching, etc., etc.

The following additional particulars are from a letter of Colonel Ridley. They vary in some unimportant respects from Captain Gift's account:

It gives me great pleasure to learn that you are engaged in so laudable a labor as a memoir of that great and good man, General Albert Sidney Johnston. The simple story of his life is sufficient. It is the proudest memory of my own life to have been associated with him.

I first made the general's acquaintance on his arrival at Los Angeles, after his resignation. I was quietly engaged at the time in raising a party to proceed to Texas. In conversation one day with Dr. Griffin, who knew of my movements, I remarked that if the general desired to go South it would be a good opportunity for him. Griffin thought it would not do; the Indians were bad all along

---

[1] Frazee served as private in Colonel Jefferson Davis's First Mississippi Regiment in the Mexican War.

the route, and the general had so many friends that he could easily reach the South by way of New York. A few days after I met the general in the street, and he asked if he could see me a few minutes privately. We walked to the office of Dr. Griffin, and, being alone, he told me that he had been informed of my proposed expedition, and he thought he should like to go along. I told him at once that the party would be glad to escort him. He said, "No;" that he was no longer an officer of the army, and that if he went it would be simply as one of the party. After some further conversation relative to my movements and the proposed time of departure, he decided then and there to accompany us.

We hurried our departure, leaving some days before we intended, having learned that movements were on foot for the arrest of the general and myself, on the charge of treason. Owing to this quite a number who had proposed to accompany us were left behind. The general and I left Los Angeles at a very early hour, accompanied only by his servant Randolph. I left him at Ranch Chino, some thirty-five miles distant, where we arrived the same day, in order to collect our company, and sent Dr. Frazee to guide him to Agua Caliente, our place of rendezvous. There I joined him after a few days.

The following letter, written by General Johnston to his wife from near Warner's Ranch, June 26th, will conclude the account of the preparations:

My dear Wife: We arrived this far on our journey on Friday, 22d. I rode on my horse from Chino to this place, except a few miles which I got Ran to *do* for me. I am now pretty well seasoned, and have no apprehension of fever. I thank you for the veils. I am now well supplied with means of defense against the mosquitoes. How will Ran look with a blue veil on? He is as good a hand with mules as need be; with my backing, Ran is *sans peur*. . . . We should not borrow trouble by apprehension of dangers in the future, but nerve ourselves to meet them bravely should they come. I am happy that my family is away from the turmoil and conflicts of civil dissension, and I can, on account of their security under the protecting arm of a brave, kind brother, discharge my duty in whatever position Fortune may assign me, with equanimity and cheerfulness, and with the hope that there is much good in store for us. Can I better testify my love for you and my children than by this journey? Love and hope cheer me on to discharge a great duty. Kiss our dear children. My most ardent hope is that they may love you and each other.

The march was begun from Warner's, June 27th, and a halt made June 30th, at Vallecito. The itinerary at the end of this chapter may be found useful in elucidating the incidents of the journey.

General Johnston wrote as follows to his wife, from Vallecito:

Vallecito, 130 Miles to Yuma,
Sunday, June 30, 1861.

. . . . I received your letter of June 25th by Major Armistead, who arrived here this morning. Our party is now as large as need be desired for safety or convenience in traveling.[1] They are good men and well armed. Late of the

---

[1] Eight resigned army-officers and twenty-five citizens.

army we have Major Armistead, Lieutenants Hardcastle, Brewer, Riley, Shaaf, Mallory, and Wickliffe.[1] These young gentlemen, though accustomed to a life of comparative ease, rough it as well as the best of them; wash, cook, pack, and harness animals, etc. The party is well armed, and, by observing a good compact order of march and vigilance in camp, we will be free from any danger of attack from Indians. I think there is no need of apprehension of molestation on the part of the authorities, civil or military, unless orders come from Washington. Should there be such, I will have notice in time.

We find it very hot in some parts of the day; in others, not unpleasant. We have, tell your brother, in our mess, Captain Dillard, Mr. Jordan, and Mr. Frazee; and, with Ran as our cook and driver of my carriage, I could have no better arrangement for the most comfortable traveling the season and route will admit of. I have ridden but a few miles in the carriage since we started. . . . I have nothing to say to my boys that has not already been said. I have perfect confidence that they will be all that ought to be desired or expected. They must learn that one man by an exhibition of physical power can control but few. It is by moral power alone that numbers of minds are controlled and directed by one mind. By not preserving his equanimity a man throws away his moral power. He who cannot control himself cannot control others. He should know when to feel and to show resentment; and it is only on grave occasions that this is necessary. Napoleon knew the value of a scene; but his judgment, rather than his passion, dictated it. Be patient; be hopeful. . . .

I am writing on a barley-sack. We leave here this evening and go to Carrizo, eighteen miles; to-morrow to Indian Wells, thirty-two miles, and so on, traveling from four o'clock till late at night, till we get to a better climate. . . .

From Yuma General Johnston addressed a third letter on July 5th to Mrs. Johnston, as follows:

We arrived at this place last evening. They were firing the Federal salute of the evening in honor of the day, thirteen guns. We were near enough at 12 o'clock to hear the national salute. We passed the desert without much suffering, either among the men or animals. The heat from the sand, as well as from the direct rays of the sun, was intense, but tempered for us by gentle breezes. We started from Carrizo at 3 P. M., and arrived at Indian Wells, thirty-seven miles, at sunrise. Here the water, if clear, is good; but the well had to be cleaned out, and it was, for us, muddy and unpalatable. At this place the flies —house-flies—swarm in myriads. It was not possible to throw a veil over your face quick enough to exclude them. The scrubby mesquite afforded but little shelter from the burning heat, and on these accounts we concluded to take the route again at 12 M., and go to Alamo Well, twenty-eight miles, where we arrived at 9 P. M., worn out for want of sleep and the long time we had been in the saddle. In going from Carrizo to Indian Wells I rode by the carriage all night. Though Ran is very trustworthy, I found he would go to sleep. He kept wide awake and bright, whistling at times, till about 3 A. M., when nature, not faithful Ran, gave way. Falling fast asleep, he drove square off

[1] Of the eight, four fell in battle—Johnston, Armistead, Mallory, and Brewer.

into the desert. Of course I immediately roused him, and put him on the road again. Our march, Sunday, 30th, was far in the night. When night came on we were astonished to see a huge comet, as large as Venus, with a tail 100° long, stretching far into the milky-way. Its brightness contributed to make our route quite apparent during the march, and also favored us with great additional light during the whole of the following night. In marching through this great desert, although we have only had a cloud of dust by day, we had a pillar of flaming light by night. We regard this comet as a good omen; its tail stood to the southeast, which was our course. It seems to move with inconceivable velocity, and is already fast disappearing. I have been compelled to wait here to-day to have our carriage-tires cut.

General Johnston's letters, written to his wife on the road, do not convey a full conception of the sufferings of this midsummer march. His stoicism and the wish to relieve his wife's solicitude caused him to treat lightly annoyances that in the aggregate amounted to torture; torrid heat, swarms of flies and mosquitoes, clouds of stifling dust, brackish drinking-water, wearing vigils, prolonged night-marches, and exhausting fatigue, are but a part of the ills undergone. The route lay through one of the hottest regions in the world, where the thermometer often marked over 120° in the shade, when shade could be found. The Colorado Desert, through which their route lay, is a depressed basin, treeless, arid, and cut off from moisture and the cooling breath of the sea-breeze. One hundred and thirty miles across, sixty miles of waste stretch away without a drop of water, or a sign of animal or vegetable life. The struggling mules sometimes sank to the knee in its dry sands; and the hot blast of the sirocco lifted the loose, moving soil, in clouds and pillars of dust, that fell like the showers of ashes that buried Pompeii. Captain Gift gives the following vivid description of their passage of the desert :

On the afternoon of July 1st, after the sun had sunk low enough to permit the waters of the spring to cool so that our animals would drink, we commenced our first real desert march of forty-two miles or thereabouts, to Indian Wells. The memory of that weary night-march remains with me like a horrible nightmare. The first few miles was through sand, but the remainder over a beautiful hard road, as level as a floor and as firm as a turnpike. But it was horribly monotonous—sage-brush and barren plains. A companion with whom I rode proposed during the latter part of the night that we fall out and leave the road a hundred yards, and lie down to sleep until daylight, and then mount and gallop on to camp; urging that we would be greatly refreshed, and our horses would also be improved by the opportunity of sleeping. Each of us had begun the march with a *bota* (leather bottle) of water holding a gallon and a half. We had at no time during the night permitted ourselves to more than moisten our lips, and yet such was the evaporation that, when we lay down, we had scarcely a drink of water left. The solitude of the desert came upon me in all its force, as the rattle of the ambulances (we had four in the whole party) was lost. But the solitude was not so overpowering as the heat or rather the drying, withering breeze that blew from toward the Gulf of California. I had never met the sirocco before, and as I breathed it I felt as one confined in a burning apartment. Weariness brought sleep, and daylight found us resting. The coming sun cast his heat ahead of him, and we saddled and galloped away.

Five or six miles from the "Wells," we overtook one of our party, whose weak and jaded horses (he had a pack-horse and a saddle animal) were almost ready to fall by the way-side; and our companion had dismounted and was trudging along on foot, driving his beasts before him. He begged us to go ahead and send him some water, as he was almost famished. Within an hour we rode into camp and reported the matter to our captain, who detailed one of the messmates of the straggler to return and carry water, and otherwise assist him. The young man, who was also weary and his horse exhausted, was loath to go. Some words ensued in regard to it, which attracted the attention of the general, who approached, and desired to know what the difficulty was. Ridley stated the case, when the general begged him not to insist on the return of the young fellow, but permit him (the general) to go in his place and carry succor. This aroused the pride of a dozen, and a messenger was soon galloping away with water. This was our severest trial. Men and animals fairly wilted. The general, Ridley, and myself, stood at the well and drew water from it until it was dry, and still we did not appease the thirst of our famishing cattle. We would permit our animals to drink ten gallons of water, and then have to drag them from the spot. They were so thirsty they would eat but little. At noon we left this place, and at ten o'clock reached the Alamo Mocha Well, thirty miles farther, where the water was better. We got a little rest here, and rolled out at eight o'clock next morning, reaching our next station, Cook's Wells, in the afternoon.

We had now crossed 100 miles of desert, and were near the Colorado and Fort Yuma. It was necessary to approach this place with caution, as a trap might be set for us. A scout was sent forward, and at noon, it being July 4th, we heard the national salute. The scout returned, and reported all the officers of the garrison sick, and that we could cross the river without fear. In the afternoon we camped in sight of the post, at the village on the west bank of the river. We stationed sentinels, and preserved our military appearance. Major Armistead was the first sentinel on post, and was approached by a soldier from the garrison, who was one of the major's old regiment, and who desired a parley. He had come with a proposition from some of the soldiers to desert over to us, and then to seize the place and plunder it. But for the general's coolness on that occasion, we would in all likelihood have left Fort Yuma behind us a heap of smoking ruins. He objected to the procedure, on the ground that we were not in commission, and that an attack would be equivalent to piracy at sea. I think we remained here three days, having tires cut, horses shod, and preparing for the next stage of the journey. No effort was made to molest us.

Ridley says:

Traveling from Vallecito to Carrizo Creek, we observed a luminous appearance in the heavens resembling a comet, extending two-thirds across the heavens, its nucleus near the horizon toward the northwest. The general and I were riding together when we first observed it. He remarked that it was not strange that we should see sights and portents in the heavens, making playful allusion to events in old Rome.[1] Its appearance was so sudden that I am sure that there was not a man in the party upon whom it did not make an impression.

Captain Gift says :

At Blue Water we were met by two citizens of Tucson, who came to apprise us of the fact that the Federal forces were evacuating the Territory, and had already burned Fort Breckinridge, and, in passing through Tucson toward Fort Buchanan, had burned the town grist-mill, the only one upon which the people had to depend for their flour. Therefore, much indignation existed, and there was a general wish to join forces with us and punish the vandals. The Federal troops amounted to four companies—two infantry and two dragoon— and with our force of thirty men, the people could combine an equal number, and, by pouncing suddenly on the enemy, it was thought an easy victory could be obtained. Many of our party were eager to burn powder, and try their mettle; but the general restrained them with the same argument he had used at Yuma—we must commit no illegal act. We rested by the pure waters, and grazed our animals on the pastures near Tucson, for two days.

The country through which they passed was uninhabited, except at rare intervals. There were a few villages of Pimos Indians, a peaceable agricultural tribe ; but the country was infested by roving bands of Apache and Navajo Indians, tribes very similar to the Comanches, heretofore described in this volume. Timber was scarce ; and, on every hand, the distant landscape was broken by rugged ranges, or bald, isolated mountains. Sometimes the road passed through a region of thorns and cacti, of all forms and sizes, prickly and threatening, that pressed their spines against the unwary traveler. Then the road would ascend from these depressed valleys to high, rocky table-lands, threading the most accessible paths around the foot of detached ridges and " lost mountains," on which grew a scanty herbage of agave, salt grass, and wild-sage.

Captain Gift tells the following anecdote of their stay at Tucson :

Encamped near us was a party of Texas Unionists, bound to California. During the afternoon one of the elders of the party came over to enjoy a little

[1] " A mote it is to trouble the mind's eye.
    In the most high and palmy state of Rome,
    A little ere the mightiest Julius fell, . . .
    (Were) stars with trains of fire and dews of blood. . . .
    And even the like precurse of fierce events,
    As harbingers preceding still the fates,
    And prologue to the omen coming on,
    Have heaven and earth together demonstrated,
    Unto our climatures and countrymen."

    Hamlet, Act I., Scene 1.

conversation with us. He sat down in the general's camp, and I happened to be present. The general and his visitor soon discovered a mutual acquaintanceship as to various localities, roads, and towns, in Texas. The emigrant described a route between two certain towns ; the general disagreed with him as to some minor detail. The old fellow insisted on his point, the general as stoutly resisted, remarking that he had passed over that road daily for several years. "Indeed!" said his visitor; "stage-driving, I presume?" "No," said the general, "just traveling from home to town." And so he went on talking for an hour or more, and his guest went away, little thinking that he had mistaken the greatest general of his time for a stage-driver. When I told the joke the general begged that I should be sure and have it appear that he had not undeceived the Texan.

Colonel Hardcastle also mentions this incident as happening in his hearing.

The troops then in that part of the Territory were collected at Fort Buchanan, south of Tucson, but were preparing to evacuate the country and join the forces on the Rio Grande. Hardcastle says:

> Lieutenant Lord said to one of the citizens that he would take General Johnston's scalp, if he could catch him. The general told the citizen that we might be called foreigners passing through the country to our homes, and, if molested or hindered, we would cut our way through to the last man.

As General Johnston did not wish to encounter the United States troops, he took the road on the morning of the 22d, at 8 A. M., with the intention of reaching Dragoon Springs, where the Fort Buchanan road came into the trail from Tucson to the Rio Grande, before the United States troops should arrive there. His party marched thirty miles that day, and forty miles the next, camping without water. On the next morning they pushed forward fifteen miles to Dragoon Springs, before breakfast. A vast column of smoke from Fort Buchanan had previously warned them that the enemy had burned his depot, and was on the road. The report of the scouts that the Federal troops were near at hand compelled them, tired as they were, to go on. It was between forty and fifty miles to the next water, at Apache Pass, and it was now nine o'clock in the forenoon. But it would not do to await the advancing column, nine or ten times stronger than their little party, so they pushed on. That their precautions were well-judged is manifest from the following letter, written from El Paso some weeks later:

> MY DEAR GENERAL: Colonel Canby sent an order to Fort Buchanan to have you intercepted and made prisoner. An officer and twenty-five dragoons were sent from Buchanan to Dragoon Springs to execute the order ; but they reached the Springs, it is said, some thirty-six hours after you passed that point. All this I get from ——, who came in behind Moore's command. Of its truth there is not a question. I am sorry the dragoons did not intercept you; as, had they done so, they would have been made prisoners by your party.

It is probable that the delay occasioned by a collision with this scout would have brought the main body on them. Captain Gift says:

We saddled and harnessed, and took the road again. It was a long, weary journey. The road to the entrance of the pass lay before us all day, like a line ruled through the immense green meadow (this part of Arizona is very fertile). It was eleven o'clock at night before we reached the spring, and then we found more Texas Unionists to dispute our right to the use of the water. We were too thirsty, tired, and bad-tempered, to argue long. We had the force, and our necessities were great. We took the water. There was more ill-nature expressed here than at any other encampment on the journey. We were very sore, tired, and irritable. A proposition to await the approach of the enemy, surprise him in the pass, cut him off from the water, and force his surrender, was overruled by the general. The plan was very captivating to the younger members of the party; but we moved away during the forenoon, and gave it up. I have neglected to mention that after leaving Fort Yuma we were constantly in the country of hostile Apaches, who no doubt watched our every movement, and would have made an effort to cut us off had our watchful commander neglected any precaution in the way of guards or the order of marching. We moved always in compact order, and no one was permitted to leave the column or camp under any pretext. Between Tucson and Mesilla we saw the wrecks of two stages which had been robbed, and the guards, drivers, and passengers, some fourteen persons, murdered.

Colonel Ridley adds:

Some buzzards, wheeling about a neighboring cliff, gave evidence that one of those sickening tragedies, so common in Arizona before and since, had been enacted here. I was afterward told that the party was attacked by a large band of Indians; but, having succeeded in reaching a hill near by, they maintained themselves for several days, killing many Indians and striking terror to the others. But their gallant defense did not save them. The lost men could not reach the water, and at last succumbed to thirst and many wounds. My informant had this story from Cochise, the chief who said he led the Indians.

This massacre was between Apache Pass and Cook's Spring.

The journey from Cook's Spring to the Rio Grande, some sixty miles, was made without camping. The road led to the river at a point several miles above Mesilla, where was situated the little Mexican village of Picacho, inhabited by poor farmers, whose cornfields lay about the town. Eight miles below Mesilla was Fort Fillmore, with a strong Federal garrison, and it was probable that they would find the road picketed, and troops in the village. There was good ground for apprehension, as a cavalry scout had gone ahead of them one day, and, notwithstanding their celerity, had gained on them. They therefore halted about two miles from Picacho, to make such dispositions as prudence dictated. It was determined that, in case they were assailed by an overpowering force, their little column should amuse the enemy,

while General Johnston, accompanied by two picked men, should ride
for the Mexican frontier, forty miles distant, and to Chihuahua, if necessary. For this purpose, his riding horse and two of Ridley's had been
kept in good condition and unsaddled. He now mounted afresh, and
took his place, with Mackenzie and Ryerson, who had been selected to
accompany him ; Ryerson for his familiarity with the country, Mackenzie for his personal devotion to General Johnston, and for the possession of every quality to fit him for such an enterprise. Gift says :

> Dave Mackenzie was one of the best scouts in America, and one of the cool-
> est and bravest men in the world. As a shot he had few equals, if we except
> Ridley himself, between whom and Dave existed a friendship only found among
> men of the frontier.

After these arrangements had been made, Ridley and Bowers rode
to the village. They could get no answer to repeated calls from any of
the mud-huts, and not a soul was visible anywhere. Finally, they captured a Mexican creeping behind a hedge. Ridley says :

> He was evidently dodging us, and watching our motions. We could get
> nothing out of him at first, but, when I told him we were scouts from Lord's
> command, he replied in Spanish, " The brush is full of Texans, creeping about
> like cats in every direction." He also told us that the Texans had captured all
> the soldiers, and that they would get us also, unless we were careful. We told
> him we were not afraid, as our whole command would be up shortly. We
> learned afterward that the rascal went immediately and told the Texans of the
> good opportunity they had to catch Lord. But I forgive him. The news was
> good, though vague, and hardly to be believed. We returned and reported, and
> the general decided to go to the village.

Captain Gift gives this description of their entrance into the village :

> Ridley took the head of the column, with Stonehouse, Bower, and myself
> riding abreast with him. It was 11 o'clock at night when we entered the vil-
> lage, yet the people were out of bed, and, what was most singular, on the roofs
> of their flat-topped houses, and peeped down at us furtively and in doubt.
> Ridley, who spoke Spanish like a native, hailed and inquired the news. The
> man before answering demanded to know whether we were troops of the line
> or Texans. Ridley said, troops of the line. Then said the Mexican, " By all
> means go north at once, for the Texans only yesterday captured all the troops,
> and have all the guns, horses, and stores ! " While this colloquy was going on
> the general rode up, and Ridley interpreted the sense of what he had learned.
> The general doubted the information, as Lynde's regiment was one of the best
> in the service, and did not believe the story. It proved to be the truth, however.

Ridley continues :

> I had just laid down when I heard Hardcastle, who was posted with Poer,
> cry out, " Captain, I have got a prisoner." It proved to be a fellow called the

" Skinned Pant'er." He had crawled into camp to take observations, but could not resist his admiration for horse-flesh, and was getting away with Hardcastle's own charger, when Poer stopped him with his shot-gun. He told us he belonged to Captain C——'s spy company, and that they had all the Federals prisoners. I told Hardcastle to turn him loose, which he did reluctantly. I ordered him to tell his captain, whom I had known in California, that Mackenzie and Ridley, with a party of Californians, had just arrived, and wished to see him. The captain soon came, and we learned that Baylor had, indeed, captured all of Lynde's command.

Some days after, Captain C—— was expatiating on the astuteness of his company, and making rather vainglorious allusions to the " Skinned Pant'er " having got into our camp. The general was present, and said in his quiet way, " Yes, captain, he got in, and we took very good care of him, thanks to Hardcastle, until we found it convenient to let him go out again."

General Johnston could hardly believe the good fortune that relieved him from all danger of the United States troops on the Rio Grande. Gift says:

The next morning Colonel Baylor called, and begged to turn over the command of his troops to the general, to give him an opportunity to catch and punish the fellows who had chased us in. This command he accepted for a few days; but a Mexican scout having gone out, notified the advancing enemy of the trap set for him, when he changed his course for Santa Fé.

Ridley says:

The general was anxious to get on, but the Texans desired him to take command of them and capture Lord. Baylor asked him to do so; he complied very reluctantly, and told me privately he did not like the delay; " but that it was like being asked to dance by a lady—he could not refuse."

Ridley attributes the escape of Moore and Lord, when they burned their camp at Cook's Spring, and turned off to Fort Craig, to the negligence of the scouts, who did not report the movement for some twenty-four hours.

General Johnston's letter, written immediately after these events, gives the dispositions made by him for the capture of Lieutenants Moore and Lord, with their commands. It also contains what may be accepted as a well-weighed report of the capture of Lynde's command by the Texans under Colonel Baylor:

MESILLA, ARIZONA, *August* 7, 1861.

MY DEAR WIFE: We arrived at this place on July 28th, three days after the capture of eleven companies of United States troops by the Texan Confederate troops under the command of Colonel John R. Baylor. These troops, consisting of eight companies of the Seventh Infantry and three companies of the Rifle regiment, had been concentrated at Fort Fillmore, eight miles below this place, with the view of transferring them to the States after the arrival of four companies from Fort Buchanan, viz., two of the Seventh Infantry and two of the First Dragoons, which we preceded on the road. The audacity of the Mesilla people in keeping up a secession flag had excited the ire of the commander of the United States forces at Fort Fillmore, Major Lynde, and, after frequent threats, he resolved to chastise them. The Texan commander, hearing of the condition of affairs at Mesilla, came up, and occupied the place with about 280 Texans. Major Lynde crossed the river, marched to this place, and demanded the surrender of the Texans, who received his proposition with bitter taunts. He then made a feeble attack—perpetrating, however, a great outrage against humanity, in firing into the town filled with women and children, without any notice to have them removed.

In the attack the Mounted Rifles charged on the Texans, who with their rifles knocked a few of them from their saddles, when they turned, running over the infantry and producing great confusion in their flight. The major then withdrew. They were thus, I think, wholly demoralized, and that night commenced a disorderly retreat toward New Mexico. Next day they were overtaken by the Texans, and, without the loss of a man, surrendered themselves prisoners of war; that is, the major surrendered them. They certainly were in no condition to resist, though Captain Potter and one or two others protested, Captain —— among them. He commanded the rear-guard. Captain Hardiman, a Texan and a good soldier, says, " —— fled from his company with his squadron before he was within 600 yards of him." Six hundred United States troops, arms, transportation, etc., surrendered to 280 Texans, and are now paroled, officers and men, on their way to the States.

At the request of Colonel Baylor and the Texans I remained here with my party, and took command of the troops, to capture the United States troops from Fort Buchanan, who were coming on. I took every precaution to prevent their obtaining any information of the condition of affairs here, by the employment of experienced scouts, who gave us daily information of their movements. On the night of the 5th these assured us that the troops were coming on, though they much doubted it before. They judged from the disorderly character of their march, and their apparent unconsciousness of danger. The troops were then at Cook's Spring, fifty miles from our camp at the forks of the road to Fort Thorn, fifty miles above here on the river. Our scouts took their position to watch them during the night, and to ascertain in the morning which route they would take. On either there could have been no chance of escape, as, being advised of their taking the route to Thorn, our troops could have reached there first.

During the early part of the night Captain Moore received a dispatch from Fort Craig, notifying him of his danger. They immediately destroyed their cannon, burned their train, all but eight wagons, mounted their infantry upon the mules, and marched or rather took to flight on the route to Fort Craig, 120 miles above this, I judge, a forlorn-looking band. Thus 250 infantry and dragoons—United States soldiers—saved themselves from the terrible Texans by an ignominious flight.

It is due to the Texans to say that they accorded to the prisoners taken in their recent engagement the most honorable terms, and treated them with the greatest consideration, which was acknowledged by their officers in a handsome letter to the commander.

Our party arrived all well and animals in good condition, and the best of feeling prevailing. To-morrow we will resume our journey. Great events are transpiring, and we feel called on to hurry on. I may take the stage at El Paso, though I dread stages overland, especially as they are always crowded. Tell Dr. John that his friend Captain Potter was among the prisoners, and, it is said, would have managed better if he had been in command.

I have stood the journey well so far, and expect to get to Richmond in good health. May God preserve you, dear wife, and sustain you in your trials! Give my love to our dear children.

At Mesilla, the party disbanded, most of them taking the stage for San Antonio, and, on by land, to New Orleans. Ridley says :

There was a stage from Mesilla to San Antonio, and some of our party availed themselves of it at once. The general, after nearly two weeks' unavoidable delay, proceeded by the same conveyance, from El Paso. He did this very reluctantly, and would have remained with us, until the last of the party could start for San Antonio, but for our urging upon him the necessity of getting to Richmond as fast as possible. In his entire forgetfulness of self, he was ever ready to sacrifice himself and his own interests and desires for others.

Among the little incidents retained in the memory of his companions on this journey, Ridley relates this :

At El Paso, a small party were collected, among whom were the general and Major Armistead. The usual topic was being discussed—the Yankees and the war. Some one made the remark, "But they won't stand steel." The general, who had been a quiet listener, said: "Gentlemen, I think you are mistaken. We are a proud people. Manners and customs in the different sections make about the only difference that really exists. If we are to be successful, what we have to do must be done quickly. The longer we have them to fight, the more difficult they will be to defeat." His words were prophetic. They made a great impression on me at the time, as much, perhaps, from his manner of saying them as from the words themselves.

Colonel Hardcastle writes :

During our trip, subjected as we were to the oppressive tropical heat, scanty rations for man and beast, and scarcity of water—at one time going seventy miles without any for our stock, and supplying ourselves from canteens and kegs —I could not but remark the patience and endurance of our general, who at all times bore himself with cheerfulness and dignity, and set us an example of fortitude and self-denial. After our seventy miles' ride without water, when we reached the wells entirely spent and dry, we found them foul and noxious with dead rats. We set to work to draw out and clean them; and, after we had finished, the first cup was handed to the general. He drank, and remarked, "This water tastes like the White Sulphur Springs in Virginia." After that, no man could decline to taste of the waters, and we gladly cooled our parched throats.

On a certain night, wet and stormy, as I sat by the camp-fire of the general, I expressed my dread of water, having nothing but blankets to sleep upon.

Whereupon a most cordial invitation was given me to share his water-proof rubbers, which afforded us a most comfortable night's lodging.

The journey from Los Angeles to Mesilla was 800 miles, and thence to San Antonio, the frontier city of Texas, 700 more. It was made under the burning glare of a July sun, through wastes of shifting sand or treeless gravel, often with no fuel, grass, shade, or water. It is strange how well General Johnston, at his age, fifty-nine, bore the toils and hardships of this journey. After the wearisome march, he would lie down to sleep upon the ground, with his saddle for a pillow, and the sky as his only canopy. His abstemious habits made the poor fare a small privation, and his chief concern was a veteran's anxiety for the endurance of his younger or less hardy comrades. It needed bold hearts to seek out, at the summer solstice, the secrets of the desert. It would not be hard to weave, from such a pilgrimage of patriotism, a page of romance; but the plain truth is far better. The heroic spirit, that "scorned delights and lived laborious days," took but passing note of the dangers and distress that beset him. In the simple but sublime confidence of his creed—"in the great hand of God I stand"—he moved on to his fate.

When General Johnston plunged into the desert and was lost to the sight of men, the relays of the overland express swiftly bore the tidings East. The Washington Government sent its orders to intercept him ; and, even in that crisis of a nation's destiny, both sides watched the issue with intense interest. Weeks of suspense passed ; and his reappearance on the frontier, at the place and almost at the moment of Baylor's brilliant victory and of the fall of the Federal power in Arizona, linked his coming with auguries of victory. He had safely run the gantlet, in spite of the snares in his path.

A general burst of relief and joy throughout the South greeted General Johnston's safe arrival, and evinced the importance attached to his services. An auxiliary army could not have been welcomed with a more certain assurance of its value, or with more genuine rejoicing. It is in such times that the people are forced to count how priceless may be the services of one man who is equal to the highest command. In his rapid progress to Richmond, General Johnston could not escape a continued ovation. Popular recognition of him as a great leader was suddenly and spontaneously accorded by acclamation. This was due in part to the well-settled opinion of the officers and men of the old army, and to President Davis's frank declaration to that effect, but still more to the strong belief of the Southwest in his ability as a soldier. He had been marked for vengeance, and hunted as an outlaw for months; but he was once again among his own people. He had come to them without communication or understanding with the Confederate Government or any of its leaders, ready to take whatever post of duty might be assigned him, and he found a nation waiting for him and calling him to the front. The telegraph, of course, had announced him ; but President Davis was not aware that he had reached Richmond, when he called at the Executive mansion. The President was sick in bed; but, when he heard the bell and General Johnston's step below, he started up, and exclaimed : " That is Sidney Johnston's step. Bring him up." He said many times afterward, " I hoped and expected that I had others who would prove generals, but I knew I had *one*, and that was Sidney Johnston."

ITINERARY.

1861.
June 16.—Left Los Angeles—to Rancho Chino, thirty-five miles.
   " 22.—Arrived at Warner's Ranch. One hundred miles from Los Angeles.
   " 27.—Left Warner's. To Vallecito.
   " 30.— " Vallecito. Sunday night. Eighteen miles to Carrizo Wells. Comet seen.
July 1.— " Carrizo, 3 P. M. Thirty-seven miles to Indian Wells.
   " 2.— " Indian Wells at noon. Twenty-eight miles to Alamo Springs.
   " 3.— " Alamo Springs at 8 A. M. Thirty miles to Cook's Wells.
   " 4.— " Cook's to Yeager's Ferry. (Fort Yuma.)
   " 7.— " Yuma, up the Gila, and thence two hundred and seventy miles to Tucson.
   " 18.—Arrived at Tucson.
   " 22.—Left Tucson, 8 A. M. Thirty miles.
   " 23.—Forty miles to a dry camp.
   " 24.—Fifteen miles to Dragoon Springs, thence fifty miles to Apache Pass.
   " 25. ⎫
   " 26. ⎬ —From Apache Pass. One hundred and sixty-five miles to the Rio Grande
   " 27. ⎭   at Picacho, near Mesilla.
   " 28.—To Mesilla.

CHAPTER XIX.

SITUATION IN THE WEST.

BEFORE General Johnston's arrival at Richmond, deputations from the West had reached there, asking that he might be assigned to command on that line. General Polk had visited Richmond partly for that purpose, and had also written urgently ; a committee from Memphis, and other delegations, had made the same request, and the public expectation hopefully awaited the announcement of his appointment. But the President needed no urging. It was evident that the general direction of affairs in the West should be intrusted to one chief, and that he must be a man to whom both President and people should give their entire confidence. Men of ability commanded the small armies of observation stationed at intervals along the extended frontiers, from Virginia to Kansas ; but no general plan of defense had been adopted, and each emergency was met as best it might be. Want of coherence and coöperation, not lack of vigor or valor, prevented efficient action, and combined movement seemed impossible.

Accordingly, on the 10th of September, General Johnston was assigned to command, under the following orders:

[EXTRACT.]

ADJUTANT AND INSPECTOR-GENERAL'S OFFICE, }
RICHMOND, *September* 10, 1861. }

SPECIAL ORDERS No. 149.

14. . . . General Albert Sidney Johnston, Confederate States Army, is assigned to the command of Department No. 2, which will hereafter embrace the States of Tennessee and Arkansas, and that part of the State of Mississippi west of the New Orleans, Jackson & Great Northern and Central Railroad ; also, the military operations in Kentucky, Missouri, Kansas, and the Indian country immediately west of Missouri and Arkansas. He will repair to Memphis, Tennessee, and assume command, fixing his headquarters at such point as, in his judgment, will best secure the purposes of the command.

By command of the Secretary of War :

JOHN WITHERS,
Assistant Adjutant-General.

He was further directed to go by Nashville, confer with Governor Harris, and then decide upon the steps to be taken.

The rank of " general," the highest in the Confederate army, had been created by law, and five officers had been appointed by the President and assigned to duty with the following relative rank : 1. S. Cooper (the adjutant-general) ; 2. A. S. Johnston ; 3. R. E. Lee ; 4. J. E. Johnston ; 5. G. T. Beauregard. General J. E. Johnston regarded himself as entitled by law to the first place, and engaged in a controversy with the President relative thereto, the points of which he has perpetuated in his " Narrative " (pages 70–72). It is needless here to enter on a discussion of the merits of this question ; but it is proper to say that it was one of no concern to General A. S. Johnston. President Davis has frequently told the writer that the question of rank was never mentioned in his conversations with General A. S. Johnston. It is not probable that he ever heard of this discussion : he certainly had no share in it. His relative rank was a matter to which he ascribed no importance, and his great responsibilities occupied his full attention. The subject is alluded to only to disclaim for him all connection with it.

The command to which General Johnston was called thus embraced all the northern frontier west of the Alleghanies, and a portion of that mountain-barrier. The interests confided to him were not only vast, but often conflicting. The great Mississippi divided his department into two theatres of war with widely-separated bases, and it was penetrated by the solid wedge of the Northwest. A brief view of the situation of affairs in Kentucky and Missouri is necessary, in order to comprehend the campaign which General Johnston conducted against the powerful armies collected by the United States Government in the West.

The war in the West first fairly took shape in the State of Missouri. Here, a great debatable ground was occupied by able and well-matched antagonists, who executed a series of bold and striking enterprises, which were ended at last by the mere weight of the heaviest battalions. The lessons of this struggle would be entertaining and instructive to the student of American history, and its results were very important in determining the exact character of General Johnston's military operations; but the limits of this biography do not permit its narration here.

It may be briefly stated that Missouri was in political sentiment strongly Southern and Democratic, and, at the same time, equally opposed to a dissolution of the Union. Probably three-fourths of its citizens held these views. Though a very warlike people, they contemplated with horror the idea of civil or sectional war, and, according to preconceived opinions, looked on this or that party with aversion as the promoters of strife. When once engaged in it, however, they became relentless.

The two men who were most prominent in Missouri affairs, on the Federal side, were General Frank P. Blair and General Nathaniel Lyon. They were both Republicans, with fixed views and purposes to maintain an unconditional union of the States at all hazards, and to inaugurate a policy looking to the emancipation of the slaves. Their following was small and odious to the native white population of the State; but they were supported by the unlimited means of the Government at Washington, and, under its secret authority, Blair wielded the prerogatives of a dictator.

To this powerful and compact organization was opposed a vast majority of the people, under leaders of every shade of opinion and every degree of daring. There was no concert of views, organization, or action. The Governor, Claiborne F. Jackson, was a man of courage and capacity; but he deplored, while he recognized, the approach of war, and procrastinated when he should have struck a blow. But he was embarrassed by dissensions in the counsels of his own party. His policy might, nevertheless, have prevailed, had he been confronted by less able antagonists. General Sterling Price, subsequently so eminent as a Confederate leader, was at first a Unionist.

The Governor contemplated the capture of the St. Louis Arsenal; and the assemblage of the militia at Camp Jackson, in the suburbs of

St. Louis, was with some ulterior purpose of that sort. General D. M. Frost had established a militia camp there, some 1,200 strong, on the 3d of May. The radical secret clubs, on the other hand, had been for several months organized by Blair, into regiments, and armed with muskets from the United States Arsenal, so that Lyon was able suddenly, on the 10th of May, with these and his regulars from the arsenal, to surround Camp Jackson, which surrendered to him.

In the course of the turmoil the German volunteers fired on the people in the streets, and killed thirty-one, including women and children. This was the signal for war. The Southern party took up arms and began to organize, and Price was appointed their commander-in-chief by the State authorities. Lyon ended some fruitless negotiations, by declaring his unalterable purpose to make no terms with rebels; and, being now ready, by a rapid and aggressive movement, he took possession of the whole of Central Missouri, the heart of the Southern cause. On the 15th of June Lyon began operations by occupying Jefferson City, the seat of government. Two days later an insignificant skirmish at Boonville won him great reputation. Moving about with a few thousand men, he overawed the timid, secured the lukewarm and time-serving, and forced the unorganized Southern volunteers to seek refuge in the southwestern corner of the State.

The war had finally begun. Troops were poured in from other States by the United States Government, and recruits were enlisted in large numbers by both parties ; the Federals acting under the authority of the United States Government and of a State Convention, the Southerners under that of the Governor and Legislature. There were many skirmishes, and in the swamps of the southeast a guerrilla war was maintained by the Missourians. At Carthage there was an engagement, almost reaching the dignity of a battle in the numbers present, but in no other respect. The first occasion on which the opposing forces measured arms, under their leaders and with real purpose, was on the 10th of August, 1861, at the battle of Wilson's Creek or Oak Hills, near Springfield, Missouri.

Lyon had followed the Missourians to this remote quarter with a small, though well organized, drilled, and disciplined, army. According to the official report, he had 5,868 men, including 1,200 regulars, inured to war and strong in the mutual dependence of an exact discipline. He had sixteen guns, manned by experienced gunners. His officers were trained soldiers, and his army a compact machine.

The army confronting him was made up of 3,200 Confederate troops from Texas, Louisiana, and Arkansas, under General Ben McCulloch, 1,800 Arkansas State troops under General N. B. Pearce, and 5,000 or 6,000 Missourians under General Price. McCulloch had command. McCulloch puts his force at " 5,300 infantry, fifteen pieces of artillery, and 6,000 horsemen," poorly armed. The *personnel* of this army was excellent, and it was animated by a splendid martial enthusiasm ; but it was little more than an aggregation of bands of raw recruits. After some days of fruitless skirmishing and vacillation, Lyon's haughty and impatient spirit cast off the counsels that impeded it, and he resolved on the aggressive. Moving from Springfield in two columns by a night-march, he attacked the Confederate army at daylight on the 10th of August. An attack on the rear was led by General Sigel, with 1,500 men. He was at first successful, but was soon repulsed, routed, and pursued from the field, with the loss of his artillery. Lyon, who commanded in the front attack, had for a long time better fortune. The Confederate vanguard was surprised and routed. But now ensued a desperate conflict between Lyon's front line and the Missouri troops. It was a death-grapple of the fiercest and most relentless character. Pearce led his Arkansas troops to Price's aid, and McCulloch returned from the defeat of Sigel to join in the struggle. All of Lyon's troops were now engaged in the doubtful contest. In the crisis of the fight, Lyon, while leading a charge, was shot through the heart. The tide of battle rolled back, and after a little while the Federals sullenly left the field. The Confederates were unable to pursue. They slowly followed the Federals, who fell back to Springfield, and thence to Rolla. Major Sturgess reported the Federal loss at 1,235 men. The Southerners lost 265 killed, 800 wounded, and thirty missing ; but it was a dear-bought victory, especially in officers.

Fremont had 70,000 men in Missouri, with only some 20,000 opposed to him. But, by his harsh and arbitrary orders and conduct, he aroused such a feeling in the Southern party that it required all of his force to keep it down. Price, after a short delay, moved, with 5,000 men and seven pieces of artillery, upon Lexington, his old home, a town of about 8,000 inhabitants, on the Missouri River. General McCulloch did not accompany him, for reasons not necessary to discuss here. Price's expedition was short and brilliant. On the 4th of September he routed Lane and Montgomery's "Jayhawkers," near Fort Scott. His force swelled as he advanced, until it reached some 12,000 men, before he arrived at Lexington. The garrison of 3,500 men, under Colonel Mulligan, had made good preparations for defense. But Price attacked his fortifications on the 12th of September, and so sharp and continuous were his assaults that, on the 20th of September, the garrison, after a very gallant defense, were worn out, and compelled to surrender. They were paroled. Price captured five cannon, 3,000 muskets, and $100,000 worth of commissary stores.

In the mean time Fremont had been concentrating his large army, and, to evade him, Price moved southward on the 27th of September. He skillfully eluded the enemy, and made good his retreat to Neosho, where McCulloch held himself in reserve. Most of his new recruits returned to their homes, leaving him little stronger than when he set forward. But he had gained prestige and some material advantages, and had employed a large force of the enemy. Fremont then advanced slowly, with a numerous army, as far as Springfield, where he was relieved November 2d.

During General Price's operations, General Hardee had assembled six or seven thousand men, at Pocahontas, in Northeastern Arkansas. Some ineffectual attempts were made toward combined movements by this force with Price and with Pillow, who became otherwise employed. But virulent types of camp epidemics disabled his command, and nothing of importance was accomplished.

Thus, General Johnston had hardly assumed command when he found the Federal armies in possession of nearly the whole of Missouri, and continually menacing Columbus, the left flank of his line in Kentucky, with heavy forces massed at Cairo.

The war in Kentucky had been fought with different weapons. Here, diplomacy instead of arms had transferred a Commonwealth of strongly Southern feelings from its natural alliance with the other slaveholding States to the ranks of their invaders. Kentucky was the first State admitted to the Union by the original thirteen. Settled from Virginia, her people brought with them from that ancient Commonwealth its characteristics and traditions, with a greater vehemence and keener enterprise. The spirit of combat was fostered in the early Indian contests ; and, in the wars with Great Britain and Mexico, no troops won a more enviable distinction for steadiness and valor.

Kentucky, along with Virginia, had, in 1798–'99, taken the most advanced position in regard to the reserved rights of the States ; nor did she recede from it for more than a generation. For nearly forty years previous to 1850 her destinies were guided by the commanding talents of one man. Henry Clay, by his oratory, his imperious will, and his skill in leadership, became not only the political chief of Kentucky, but the favorite of a national party, which blindly followed his personal fortunes. In the mutations of politics, it became the policy of this party to exalt and intensify the idea of the Union.

Much of Mr. Clay's great fame had been won as a leader in compromising sectional quarrels ; and it was natural that the party which followed him should exalt the idea of the Union, even at the expense of the vital principle which gave to it its sanctity. Mr. Clay was a conservative, and it is not possible that he would have consented to the terms imposed upon their Southern adherents by the Lincoln Administration. He lived to witness the decay of his power, and the transfer of Kentucky to the Democratic party. When he died, his sceptre fell to an unlineal hand. A youth, who had gathered his honors in opposition to Mr. Clay, succeeded to his unbounded influence.

John C. Breckinridge, who drew to himself much of the enthusiasm that had attached to Mr. Clay, was a man of widely different type. Though born to narrow means, he was the son of a public man whose early death alone cut him off from high distinction. His grandfather had been President Jefferson's attorney-general ; his great-grandfather, a signer of the Declaration of Independence; and his lineage was traced to John Knox, the Reformer. Among his immediate and remoter kindred were many distinguished for oratory, in the pulpit, at the bar, and in legislative halls. Breckinridge, though never a severe student, had natural gifts that made him a vigorous writer, an agreeable talker, and a ready and impressive speaker. His person was commanding, his countenance striking, his address frank and gracious, his personal influence irresistible. His judgment and temper were calm and sober, and he had the poise of perfect moral and physical courage. Though somewhat indolent and fond of pleasure, he had the capacity for heroic deeds and under the pressure of great occasions was always found equal to them—at the bar, in the Senate, and on the battle-field. Though his genial manner awakened a contagious enthusiasm, he was singularly reticent and cautious in matters of import. He made few promises and broke none, and was truthful and magnanimous. It was difficult to move him to anger, impossible to provoke him to revenge. He did not strive for wealth or place, and, as a citizen and statesman, was stainless and incorrupt. He seemed born under a star, and greatness sought him out.

After a short military experience in Mexico, he was adopted by a State-rights coterie in Kentucky, by whom his fortunes were eagerly pushed. In 1851, and again in 1853, he was sent to Congress ; and in 1856 was elected Vice-President, when only thirty-five years of age. He presided over the Senate with fairness and dignity in very troubled times. When the rupture took place in the Democratic party, he was selected at Baltimore as the nominee of the State-rights party for President. He continued until Lincoln's inauguration to preside over the Senate, when he took his seat in that body as Senator from Kentucky.

With Breckinridge's powerful hold on all classes in Kentucky, it was in his power, at any time before June 1st, by putting himself at the head of a party of movement, to have dictated the policy of the State. Events drifted so rapidly that, after that time, it was too late. He knew the tendency of public feeling, and thought it would carry the State with him, counting at too little the hundred-handed grasp that was throttling public opinion and binding the State hand and foot. Though he afterward proved a brave and able soldier, wise in counsel, able in administration, vigorous in action, it is no discredit to him to say that his talents were not revolutionary. While his intel·lectual convictions carried him with the secessionists, his heart inclined him to peace and the hope of compromise. Thus the State-rights men of Kentucky lost the leadership of the only man then able to rally them into a compact organization. Though numerous, and ready for any enterprise, no name of acknowledged authority appeared at their head. Mr. Guthrie had renounced his place with them, and was openly acting with the unconditional submissionists. The Governor, Magoffin, was unequal to the difficulties by which he was surrounded. William Preston was absent, as minister to Spain. Humphrey Marshall, and some other men of ability, were hampered by their positions in Congress.

Under the circumstances, the situation seemed more in the hands of General Simon B. Buckner than of any other one man. Buckner was a native of Kentucky, and thirty-eight years of age. He was graduated at West Point, where he was subsequently an instructor in ethics and in tactics. In the Mexican War he was wounded at Churubusco, and brevetted for gallantry. After a varied service, he resigned in 1855, and in 1858 settled in Louisville. Though the care of a large estate occupied much of his time and attention, yet, being an enthusiast in his profession, he undertook, as a congenial pursuit, the organization of the militia of Kentucky. Of this, with the title of inspector-general and the rank of major-general, he became the virtual chief. Under his management, the old "cornstalk" militia was transformed into the State Guard; and the absurd levy *en masse*, whose reviews were a burlesque on military training, was replaced by a compact corps of 10,000 or 12,000 men, organized, uniformed, armed, drilled, and, to some extent, disciplined. It was not equaled in effectiveness by any military body in the United States, except the regular army. Composed of the flower of the people, it was a unit in its sympathy for the South, and was animated by a powerful *esprit de corps*.

Buckner obtained unbounded influence with this command by his attractive manners and by a genuine enthusiasm in military matters, shared by the young volunteers under his command. In personal appearance he was thought to bear a marked likeness to General A. S. Johnston. His decided though moderate views gave weight to his counsel; he was committed to resistance against coercion; and his course, from first to last, was open, manly, and consistent. His interests were in the North; but his heart and his sword were with the cause of constitutional liberty. With the great influence Buckner had acquired over the State Guard, he might, if he could have been induced to employ constraint, have compelled, under all the forms of law, the State government to act according to his own views. But he regarded himself as the servant of the Commonwealth; and, scrupulous by nature and education, construed his rights and duties with legal strictness.

Everything tended to fasten the Federal authority on the people of Kentucky. The established government, even when regarded as a tyranny, has mighty advantages. In Kentucky the Union seemed panoplied; and, as lingering superstition paralyzes the arm of the recent convert who would cast down the idols of ancient gods, conviction of duty could not rouse the people to action till the time for action had passed, and chains were on every limb.

The State government had been elected by the State-rights party; but the Legislature suffered from all the dissensions which had produced the schisms in that opposition which had lately been vanquished by the solid minority that elected Lincoln. Under the urgent advice of veteran leaders, like Guthrie and Crittenden, entreating time for compromise, the trimmers and waverers got possession of the government and of the public confidence. It seemed so much better to trust those who promised peace than men who called for armament, expenditure, and action! One of the most potent agencies in lulling the spirit of resistance, until Kentucky found itself bound hand and foot, was the *Louisville Journal*, which for thirty years had struck the key-note of the Whig party. Its editor, George D. Prentice, a New-Englander by birth, was a pungent wit, a poet, a man of careless and convivial habits, an effective editor, and a politician who had grown gray in the service of his party. He displayed great tact in marshaling the ranks of the Unionists, and contributed more to their success than any other man in Kentucky. The *Louisville Courier* was the advocate of the State-rights party. Its publisher, Walter N. Haldeman, was proscribed, plundered, and exiled. By a curious turn of fortune, he is now the proprietor of an establishment which unites in one concern — the *Courier-Journal*—all the interests of these two former rivals of the press; while above the main entrance, as the presiding genius of the place, sits the marble effigy of the gifted Prentice.

In the winter of 1860–'61 the feeling in Kentucky against coercion was so general and decided that there were few men bold enough to approve it openly. The writer recollects only one of any consequence, Lovell H. Rousseau, who was fearless and sincere in his unconditional Unionism. Even those who secretly favored it pretended to reprobate and to be willing to resist it. It is not necessary, in this connection, to trace the modes by which they arrived at conclusions exactly opposite to their original professions, and perhaps to their convictions. We have here to deal with events rather than motives.

On the 8th of January a convention was held at Louisville by representative Unionists, which recommended certain amendments to the Constitution, and that the States agreeing to them " shall form a separate Confederacy ; " and resolved that " we deplore the existence of a Union to be held together by the sword." This was a strange prelude to the stringent tests of later loyalty ; but opinions, about that time, were very unfixed and drifting.

The Legislature met in extra session in February, 1861. The Governor recommended the call of a State Convention; and there is little doubt that, if such an authoritative body had convened, it would have occupied a position similar to that of Virginia, adhesion to the Union, except in the event of an attempt at coercion and subjugation, and then resistance. The Legislature refused to call a convention, and recommended the abortive " Peace Conference " held at Washington, and also a National Convention. But it directed the Governor to reply to certain resolutions from Northern Legislatures :

That when those States should send armed forces to the South for the purpose indicated in said resolutions, the people of Kentucky, uniting with their brethren of the South, will, as one man, resist such invasion of the soil of the South, at all hazards, and to the last extremity.

It also resolved :

That we protest against the use of force or coercion by the General Government against the seceded States, as unwise and inexpedient, and tending to the destruction of our common country.

The Union leaders and journals denounced secession and coercion with the same breath. On the 18th of April they first shadowed forth, in a meeting at Louisville, that sham " neutrality " policy in whose tangled web the State was ensnared. It declared:

That, as we oppose the call of the President for volunteers for the purpose of coercing the seceded States, so we oppose the raising of troops in this State to coöperate with the Southern Confederacy; that the present duty of Kentucky is to maintain her present independent position, taking sides not with the *Administration*, nor with the seceding States, but with the Union against them both, declaring her soil to be sacred from the hostile tread of either, and, if necessary, to make the declaration good with her strong right arm.

It is true that no one ought to have been deceived by such fraudulent pretenses, but they answered for the moment ; and thousands willingly lent themselves to the delusion, who were unable to face the consequences of decided action in either direction. The unconditional Unionists, comparatively few, but compact, thoroughly organized, and backed by the Federal Government, wanted time to rally a following ; the Southern party, numerous, but without leaders or definite purpose, were content that time should develop a course of action for them; the uncertain multitude hailed it as a verbal breakwater for the tides and storms of an ocean. After all, this " neutrality " was a sad thing—

a false pretense that served for some months as the cloak of irresolution and all its consequent ills. Horace Greeley, in his "American Conflict," says that this " astounding drivel " " insulted the common-sense and nauseated the loyal stomach of the nation ; " but it was the opiate that stupefied both the common-sense and the moral sense, and unnerved the arm of the people of Kentucky.

When Mr. Lincoln made his first call for troops, Governor Magoffin replied in the same spirit with the other Southern Executives :

Your dispatch is received. In answer, I say emphatically, Kentucky will furnish no troops for the wicked purpose of subduing her sister Southern States.

And on the 24th of April, in a proclamation convening the General Assembly, the Governor said :

The tread of armies is the response which is being made to the measures of pacification which are being discussed before our people; while up to this moment we are comparatively in a defenseless attitude. Whatever else should be done, it is, in my judgment, the duty of Kentucky, without delay, to place herself in a complete position for defense.

On May 16th the General Assembly, which had convened May 6th,

Resolved, That this State and the citizens thereof should take no part in the civil war now waged, except as mediators and friends to the belligerent parties, and that Kentucky should, during the contest, occupy the position of strict neutrality.

Resolved, further, That the act of the Governor in refusing to furnish troops or military force, upon the call of the Executive authority of the United States, under existing circumstances, is approved.

The Unionists, however, secured the passage of an act compelling the State Guard to take the oath of allegiance to the United States, as well as to the State of Kentucky. The Governor issued a proclamation of neutrality on the 20th of May; and on the 24th of May, just before its adjournment, the Senate

Resolved, Kentucky will not sever her connection with the national Government, nor take up arms for either belligerent party; but arm herself for the preservation of peace within her borders.

It also passed laws for arming.

Garrett Davis visited Washington, and engaged Mr. Lincoln to respect this neutrality. He not only avouched the fact of Lincoln's promise, but his own belief that it would be faithfully kept. Davis was highly respected in Kentucky as an honorable man, and his declaration carried great weight ; but Mr. Lincoln subsequently denied and repudiated the arrangement.

The same issue arose between General Buckner and General McClellan, in regard to the terms of an oral agreement made between them June 8th, resulting, it is to be presumed, from such misunderstanding as all oral communications are liable to. General Buckner took active measures to carry out his part of the convention. On the 10th of June he advised Governor Magoffin of its stipulations, and, on the 11th, engaged Governor Harris, of Tennessee, to consent to the same terms, and give assurances on the part of the South that the neutrality of Kentucky should be respected. This agreement enabled General Buckner to arrest a movement of General Pillow, who was about to seize Columbus, Kentucky, with Tennessee troops. The inhabitants of this commanding site were strongly Southern in feeling, and, under a violent apprehension that their town was in danger, had induced General Pillow to consent to occupy it. He now suspended his movement, and General Buckner placed Colonel Tilghman there, with six companies of the State Guard, with orders to enforce neutrality, give protection to all citizens claiming it, and "restrain our own citizens from all acts of lawless aggression."

The active partisans on either side were not deceived by the pretense of neutrality. The Federal faction organized the "Union Club," a secret society, with ramifications throughout the State, which, backed by the money and patronage of the Government, made converts rapidly ; and, to quote Van Horne, in his "Army of the Cumberland," "was potent, if not decisive, in saving Kentucky from secession." It reached the Legislature with its influence. At the election for Congressmen, July 1st, the Union candidates were elected by an overwhelming majority, by denouncing and pretending to abhor abolitionism, Republicanism, coercion, and war. And so with those elected to the Legislature. Their commission from the people was to keep the peace. They executed it by an immediate and unconditional surrender to the war party of the North.

Immediately after Lincoln's first call for volunteers, two regiments were recruited in Ohio, near Cincinnati, known as the First and Second Kentucky Regiments. Early in June, Lovell H. Rousseau established Camp "Joe Holt," in Indiana, opposite Louisville, and began to recruit the Louisville Legion. The first overt attempt to organize Federal troops on Kentucky soil was on the 2d of July, when 2,000 men assembled at Camp "Dick Robinson," near the centre of the State. Lieutenant William Nelson, of the Navy, afterward a major-general, was the secret agent through whom the Union men were organized and armed.

Seeing the drift of public sentiment and the popularity of neutrality in Kentucky, the more ardent secessionists left the State and entered the Confederate army. Camp Boone was established in Tennessee, near the State line, not far from Clarksville. The Southern party in Kentucky were careless as to the abstract right of secession. Their distinctive struggle was for *constitutional liberty*, and, regarding the Administration as a revolutionary propaganda and the State authorities as traitors to their trust, they left the soil of the Commonwealth without hesitation, certain that the march of events and the voice of the people would speedily demand their return.

Events now began to move very rapidly. The crisis had arrived when Buckner was compelled to decide whether he would inaugurate revolution with the State Guard, or leave the solution of the tangled maze to destiny. He would not cut the Gordian knot, nor yet consent to become the tool of party managers. He resigned July 20th. The State Guard elected Colonel Thomas L. Crittenden to succeed him; but, when it was found that they could not be used to carry out the purposes of the North, they were disbanded, and their arms and equipments were turned over to the loyal " Home Guard," which harassed the State for the next four years. Most of the soldiers of the State Guard found their way into the Southern army during the first year or two of the war, singly or in squads; but all the advantages of their excellent organization were lost. Nevertheless, under other names, the heroic men who composed it made for their State a record of surpassing brilliancy, even in the peerless annals of Confederate achievement.

Governor Magoffin, on the 19th of August, addressed letters to the Presidents of the rival sections, endeavoring to secure the promised neutrality. Mr. Davis expressed a willingness to leave Kentucky untrammeled, but Mr. Lincoln's reply intimated somewhat superciliously that the farce of neutrality had ended.

While the United States Government had been secretly perfecting its military preparations in Kentucky, it had anxiously postponed a collision. On the 28th of May, Major Robert Anderson, promoted to brigadier-general, had been assigned to the " Department of Kentucky," with his headquarters at Cincinnati. He was a native of Kentucky, conservative in opinions, and had conducted himself with dignity at the surrender of Fort Sumter. He did not directly interfere with the affairs of the State, and this, together with his absence, seemed a confirmation of the neutrality policy. Meanwhile, Nelson, Rousseau, and the Union committees were secretly enlisting troops and introducing arms and ammunition.

Those who had been indulging in dreams of peace were now rudely awakened. On the 1st of September, Anderson removed his headquarters to Louisville, and Nelson was made a brigadier-general and began to organize a force at Maysville to operate in Eastern Kentucky. He was replaced at Camp Dick Robinson by Brigadier-General George H. Thomas, a soldier of ability, vigor, and experience. Thomas was a native of Southampton County, Virginia, a West-Pointer, and a man of mark in the old army. He was the junior major of the Second Cavalry, General Johnston's regiment ; and, having decided to adhere to the Federal cause in the civil war, was rapidly promoted to the rank of brigadier-general. His position at Camp Dick Robinson was central and important. The country east of him was friendly to the Union; and that in his rear, Northwestern Kentucky, greatly divided in sentiment, was now nearly surrounded by a cordon of Federal encampments, ready, at any moment, to be drawn in upon it. Camp Dick Robinson, which had until now been regarded as a threat rather than a real peril, at once assumed its true character of a military stronghold. It dominated the political centre at Frankfort, where an obsequious Legislature eagerly registered the decrees of the military commander, while the State sank to the condition of a subjugated province.

The reproach which fell upon Kentucky that it suffered such a body to make sport of its destiny was due to the division of sentiment in the State, and to a laudable unwillingness to begin a civil war. The consequent hesitation accrued to the advantage of the party in actual possession of the government, and the United States used this advantage with energy and skill.

An examination of the map will show the great peril of the situation to the Southern sympathizers in the State. The people of its eastern section, from the Ohio River to the Tennessee line, Democratic at the opening of the contest, and Southern in their sympathies, though non-slaveholding like their neighbors of West Virginia and East Tennessee, had been won over to the Unionists. Hence the Southern party was chiefly prevalent in the western half of the State, in a district projecting like a peninsula, and surrounded by non-slaveholding and hostile regions. It may, also, be said in a word, what might be proved in a volume, that, while the centralizing Lincoln Administration spared no efforts or means of influence to control the action of the State, the Confederate Government, either from inability to assist, or on some extreme theory of independent State action, or regarding Kentucky, for political reasons, as a better boundary than the Ohio River, did not turn its hand either for aid or counsel to the secessionists in that Commonwealth. Without the power to revolutionize the State, they were compelled to stand fast and see her bound to the car of conquest. Henceforth her people were treated as a conquered population, and pillaged, oppressed, and insulted, at the will of every lawless officer.

To rehearse the story of those times is, at best, a melancholy duty, in which no Kentuckian can find satisfaction. The humiliation of a proud people is a painful spectacle ; but it was the inevitable result of their own political folly in clinging to faithless leaders, instead of following the generous impulses that would have placed them in the van of battle. There was a time when her resolute demand for peace, in armed conjunction with the other border States, might have stayed the hand of war; but the vacillation and imbecility of her counsels reduced her to the condition of an unwilling auxiliary in the abolition crusade. Providence protected the people of Kentucky from degradation, by subjecting them to a purgation of fire; "for there was not a house where there was not one dead." But despoiled, outraged, and bewailing their sons slain in battle, they remembered the traditions of State-rights and constitutional Democracy, and have since testified thereto, through good and evil report.

This rapid sketch of the condition of Kentucky will serve to show the causes that paralyzed her action, humbled her people, and ultimately duped the leaders who were employed by the Federal Government to secure her unnatural adhesion to the side of the North.

The mock neutrality of Kentucky was ended early in September. Major-General Polk, the Confederate commander in West Tennessee, having information that the Federal force at Cairo was about to seize Columbus, a strategic point of great importance in Southwestern Kentucky, crossed the State line, occupied Hickman on the 5th of September, and on the 7th secured Columbus. General Grant, who had just taken command at Cairo, where he had arrived on the 2d of September, thus anticipated and foiled in that quarter, promptly seized Paducah, at the mouth of the Tennessee River, September 6th, with a detachment, following it with additional forces next day. General Polk made a respectful representation of the facts to Governor Magoffin, offering at the same time to withdraw the Confederate forces from Kentucky provided the Federal forces also withdrew simultaneously, with a mutual guarantee not to enter or occupy any point in Kentucky in the future. He was warned by the proclamation of the Governor, September 13th, in obedience to a resolution of the General Assembly, "that Kentucky expects the Confederate or Tennessee troops to be withdrawn from her soil unconditionally." This defiance was thrown at the Confederate general, under the dishonest pretext that "Kentucky's peace and neutrality have been wantonly violated," etc., "by the so-called Southern Confederate forces." Thus Kentucky formally threw down the gage of battle, and arrayed herself with the North.

CHAPTER XX.

MILITARY SITUATION IN KENTUCKY.

THE command intrusted to General Johnston was imperial in extent, his discretion as to military movements was unlimited, and his powers were as large as the theory of the Confederate Government permitted. He lacked nothing, except men and munitions of war, and the means of obtaining them. His army had to be enlisted, before it could be led. Subsistence could be obtained, it is true, through his commissaries ; but the country was already drained of material of war to supply its first levies. Even soldiers were to be recruited only through the machinery of the States, by requisitions on their Governors ; and to be armed and equipped, by demands on the empty arsenals of the Confederacy. The means which he adopted to carry out his purposes, and the causes that impeded his success, will be detailed as they arise.

General Johnston proceeded to Nashville, stopping in Knoxville only long enough to confer with General Felix K. Zollicoffer, who commanded in East Tennessee, and to approve of the arrangements already made by that officer for an advance into Kentucky by way of Cumberland Gap.

On the 14th of September General Johnston reached Nashville. He had been looked for with the greatest anxiety by both the people and the State authorities; and his arrival was greeted with a general and spontaneous enthusiasm. An immense multitude gathered about the precincts of the Capitol, and he was compelled to show himself to the excited concourse, and to make a brief response to their words of welcome. Although not a public speaker, his words were apt to have the ring in them that gives the key-note to popular thought. On this occasion he began :

Fellow-soldiers—I call you *soldiers*, because you all belong to the reserve corps.

The public intelligence apprehended the twofold significance of the phrase ; it was a people's war, and the whole people would be called upon to maintain it. One of the more sober journals, commenting upon it, observed :

This was a well-timed remark, and showed that, as a military man, he knew what was coming. The South will need all of her force. Every able-bodied man may as well make up his mind to it, and that soon.

The great exaltation of public sentiment on this occasion had an assuring and inspiring effect on General Johnston's hopeful temperament.

This was the last day that I ever saw my father—the only day after his return from California. I was on my way to the Army of Northern Virginia, in which I held a commission, and saw him for a few hours. He was, of course, full of the cares and business of that eventful day ; but, in a full, free, and confidential conversation, I learned the outline of much that had happened to him, and of the matters then in his mind. He was advised by friends to put me on his staff, as I had met some disappointment at the hands of the War Department. But he thought, and I agreed with him at the time, that, for my own sake, and to avoid even the semblance of partiality, it was better for me to forego the pleasure of this association, and serve in the position I had made for myself. This decision, proper as it was in its general aspects, I have often since regretted, for obvious reasons; most of all, that I was not with him in the painful season of his reverses, for such use as I might have been to him, and for the lessons I might have learned in his example. The occasion will be my apology to the generous reader for these personal remarks.

When the war began, it was at the extremities of the northern frontier of the Confederacy that the United States had massed its armies, and hither had flocked the Southern youth who had sprung to arms at the first note of the conflict. But the centre, the line of Tennessee from Cumberland Gap to the Mississippi River, had been left temporarily to such protection as the neutrality of Kentucky afforded. A few camps of instruction, in which unarmed recruits were learning the "goose-step," were magnified by the excited apprehensions of rustics into armies of invasion, and accepted as such by opposing generals. Neutrality, so long as it lasted, served well enough as a breakwater, but when this was swept away there was a gap suddenly left, and an army had to be created to fill it. Now that the pretense of neutrality was cast aside by the United States Government, it was evident that its plans were ripe for a forward movement upon some point of this line. The time had come, therefore, when the Tennessee frontier must be protected by a competent Confederate force so placed as to be most effective, and when its detached corps must be moved in unison, or be destroyed in detail.

The occupation of Columbus by General Polk has already been related. This, and the simultaneous seizure of Paducah by General Grant, opposing two hostile armies on the soil of Kentucky, had ended the supposed neutrality of that State. With a strong body at Camp Dick Robinson, and their troops in possession of all the important points on the Ohio River, an advance of the Federals seemed imminent. Although

General Johnston had no force able to cope with that in his front, a bold forward movement and the establishment of a strong line might convince his adversary that he was beginning an offensive campaign, and thus procure such delay as was required for the levy and organization of an army. The few troops under his control, ready for service, used as *a skirmish-line*, would cover his real operations; and there were both moral and material advantages, for which much might be hazarded, to be secured by striking the first blow. A fertile and populous district in Kentucky would be occupied, and the semblance even of military power might keep at arm's-length the troops designed for the invasion of Tennessee. General Johnston, therefore, determined, while in reality only acting on the defensive, to obtain as many as possible of the advantages of an aggressive movement. The result proved that he had not miscalculated the effects of his policy.

General Johnston arrived in Nashville September 14th, and on the same day determined to seize Bowling Green. He placed General S. B. Buckner in charge of the column of advance, telegraphing to Richmond for his appointment as brigadier-general, which was made next day, September 15th.

The grounds of his intended movement were given by General Johnston to the President, the day before it was made, in the following letter:

NASHVILLE, TENNESSEE, *September* 16, 1861.

MR. PRESIDENT: Your dispatch of the 13th instant was received at Chattanooga. After full conference with Governor Harris, and "after learning the facts, political and military," I am satisfied that the political bearing of the question presented for my decision has been decided by the Legislature of Kentucky. The Legislature of Kentucky has required the prompt removal of all Confederate forces from her soil, and the Governor of Kentucky has issued his proclamation to that effect. The troops *will not* be withdrawn. It is not possible to withdraw them now from Columbus in the west and from Cumberland Ford in the east, without opening the frontiers of Tennessee and the Mississippi River to the enemy; and this is regarded as essential to our present line of defense, as well as to any future operations. So far from yielding to the demand for the withdrawal of our troops, I have determined to occupy Bowling Green at once.

Information I believe to be reliable has just been received that General Polk has advanced upon Paducah with 7,500 men. The indications are distinct leading to the conclusion that the enemy design to advance on the Nashville Railroad, and will immediately occupy Bowling Green if not anticipated.

I design to-morrow (which is the earliest practicable moment) to take possession of Bowling Green with 5,000 troops, and prepare to support the movement with such force as circumstances may indicate, and the means at my command may allow.

Full reports of the forces of my department will be made at the earliest practicable moment.

But enough is already apparent, I respectfully submit, considering the intended line of our defenses, and the threatening attitude and increasing forces of the enemy in Missouri and Kentucky, to authorize and require of me the assurance to you that we have not over half the *armed* forces that are now likely to be required for our security against disaster.

I feel assured that I can command the requisite number of men, but we are deficient in arms.

By letter of the 15th instant, borne by a special messenger, I have called earnestly upon the Governors of Georgia and Alabama for arms which I am assured they possess. If I fail with them, I shall appeal to your Excellency for your support and assistance. I believe that those States have quite a number of arms, and that a portion, at least, of them ought to be spared to this line of our defenses.

Having no officer that I could place in command of the movement on Bowling Green, I have been compelled to select and appoint General Simon B. Buckner a brigadier-general, subject to your approval, which I hope it may meet.

The occupation of Bowling Green is an act of self-defense, rendered necessary by the action of the government of Kentucky, and by the evidences of intended movements of the Federal forces.

I would be glad to have the services of G. W. Smith, if it is in the power of your Excellency to assign him to my command.

Any orders of your Excellency will be executed promptly, and any suggestions you may make will be received with pleasure.

With great respect, your obedient servant,

A. S. JOHNSTON, *General C. S. A.*

Ilis Excellency JEFFERSON DAVIS.

A few days prior to Buckner's movement, General Felix K. Zollicoffer, in accordance with arrangements previously made, advanced to Cumberland Ford with about four thousand men. In the west, Feliciana, thirty miles east of Columbus, Fort Henry, Fort Donelson, and Hopkinsville, were garrisoned with small bodies of troops ; and the territory between Columbus and Bowling Green was occupied by moving detachments, which created a vague apprehension of military force and projected enterprises. These dispositions gave the Confederates, when Bowling Green was occupied, an angular base, with its extremities at Columbus and Cumberland Ford, and its salient at Bowling Green. The passes of the Cumberland Mountains into Southwest Virginia, also committed to General Johnston's care, were intrusted to about three hundred militia, enlisted in Virginia for three months for local defense. The movement upon Bowling Green was committed to General S. B. Buckner, as already stated.

Buckner, after his resignation, and after some ineffectual attempts to secure the promised neutrality of Kentucky, had gone South, but with no settled purpose of taking up arms. He had refused a commission of brigadier-general ; but, at General Johnston's request, he now threw himself into the cause, thinking the moment for action had arrived. Like many others who made great sacrifices for peace, he suffered more obloquy than fiercer spirits; but the man who questions Buckner's integrity invites doubt of his own honesty or intelligence.

General Johnston's instructions to him were as follows:

You will, in order to cover the northern line occupied by the Confederate army in this department, and threatened by the army of the United States, concentrate your command at Bowling Green, Kentucky, and secure and hold this important point in our line of defense. . . . Secrecy in preparation and promptness in execution give the best, if not the only, promise of success; and the general is confident you will be wanting in neither.

Buckner moved on the 17th of September by rail, and entered Bowling Green on the 18th, at 10 A. M. He had some 4,000 men, about 3,000 of whom were Tennessee troops from Camp Trousdale, near Nashville, and the remainder Kentuckians, composed of the Second Kentucky Regiment, Byrne's battery, and part of the Third and Fourth Kentucky Regiments, the greater part being left behind unarmed. Colonel Hawes was thrown forward with the Second Kentucky Regiment and Byrne's battery, as an outpost, to the Green River railroad bridge, where these troops staid two weeks, when they were withdrawn to Bowling Green. A train carrying some troops to Horse Cave, to reconnoitre and recruit, was thrown from the track by a displaced rail. This slight accident, of no special import, has passed into Federal history as a discomfiture that prevented the capture of Louisville, and arrested a whole plan of campaign.

Buckner's movement produced an excitement out of all proportion to his force. It had all the effect of a surprise, causing the utmost confusion among the enemy. His scouts burned the bridge over Salt River, thirty miles from Louisville, in which city the wildest rumors were afloat and his vanguard was hourly expected. His advance was significantly interpreted as an answer to the defiance launched by the Legislature one week before. General Sherman says (vol. i., page 197):

This was universally known to be the signal for action. For it we were utterly unprepared, whereas the rebels were fully prepared. General Sidney Johnston immediately crossed into Kentucky, and advanced as far as Bowling Green, which he began to fortify, and thence dispatched General Buckner *with a division* forward toward Louisville.

Van Horne, speaking of Buckner, says, " He advanced to capture Louisville."

The Comte de Paris tells us his purpose was—

To traverse the whole State of Kentucky by rail, so as to reach Louisville with a sufficient number of troops to take possession of that city, and to hoist the Confederate flag on the banks of the Ohio. . . . It failed of success. . . .

Learning that his movements were known, and that the enemy was on the watch for him, Buckner, who had already reached the suburbs of Elizabethtown, not far from the Ohio, halted, and fell back upon Bowling Green.

When it is remembered that these eminent Federal military writers published their volumes more than thirteen years after the events narrated, and that the facts could have been easily learned by inquiry, it will be seen how profound and permanent an impression the misconception of the time made upon them.

General Johnston's whole available force—4,000 men—a mere skirmish-line to mask his preparations from the enemy, was thrown forward with Buckner. About 4,000 more Tennesseeans were already in camp in Middle Tennessee, but not half of them were armed, and these with country rifles and shot-guns; they were not yet fully organized or equipped; and nearly half their number were on the sick-list with measles and other camp epidemics. One regiment (foreigners), at Fort Henry, was in open mutiny. Besides these troops there were also some unarmed Kentuckians in Tennessee.

On taking possession of Bowling Green, General Buckner, in General Order No. 2, September 19th, particularly charged his soldiers—

To respect the civil rights of every citizen of Kentucky, without regard to political sentiments. Any invasion of these rights on their part will be visited by the severest penalties.

General Buckner issued a stirring proclamation, September 18th, reciting the breaches of neutrality by the Legislature, and the despotic acts of the President of the United States, and offering to retire from the State if the Federal forces would do likewise. But, of course, this was no longer expected by anybody.

General Johnston issued the following manifesto :

PROCLAMATION.

Whereas, The armed occupation of a part of Kentucky by the United States, and the preparations which manifest the intention of their Government to invade the Confederate States through that territory, has imposed it on these last as a necessity of self-defense to enter that State and meet the invasion upon the best line for military operations;

And whereas, It is proper that the motives of the Government of the Confederate States in taking this step should be fully known to the world :

Now, therefore, I, Albert Sidney Johnston, general and commander of the Western Department of the army of the Confederate States of America, do proclaim that these States have thus marched their troops into Kentucky with no hostile intention toward its people, nor do they desire or seek to control their choice in regard to their union with either of the Confederacies, or to subjugate their State, or hold its soil against their wishes. On the contrary, they deem it to be the right of the people of Kentucky to determine their own position in regard to the belligerents. It is for them to say whether they will join either Confederacy, or maintain a separate existence as an independent and sovereign State. The armed occupation of their soil, both as to its extent and duration, will, therefore, be strictly limited by the exigencies of self-defense on the part of the Confederate States. These States intend to conform to all the requirements of public law, and international amity as between themselves and Kentucky, and accordingly I hereby command all who are subject to my orders to pay entire respect to the rights of property and the legal authorities within that State, so far as the same may be compatible with the necessities of self-defense. If it be the desire of the people of Kentucky to maintain a strict and impartial neutrality, then the effort to drive out the lawless intruders who seek to make their State the theatre of war will aid them in the attainment of their wishes. If, as it may not be unreasonable to suppose, those people desire to unite their fortunes with the Confederate States, to whom they are already bound by so many ties of interest, then the appearance and aid of Confederate troops will assist them to make an opportunity for the free and unbiased expression of their will upon the subject. But if it be true, which is not to be presumed, that a majority of those people desire to adhere to the United States and become parties to the war, then none can doubt the right of the other belligerent to meet that war whenever and wherever it may be waged. But harboring no such suspicion, I now declare, in the name of the Government which I serve, that its army shall be withdrawn from Kentucky so soon as there shall be satisfactory evidence of the existence and execution of a like intention on the part of the United States.

By order of the President of the Confederate States of America:

A. S. JOHNSTON,
General of the Western Department of the Army of the Confederate States of America.

In determining his line of operations, General Johnston had to consider the geography of the theatre of war, the political complexion of the population, and the strength and disposition of the forces opposed to him. Each of these conditions was of such a character as to put him at a disadvantage.

There were moral and political as well as physical considerations entering into the situation, which made the more advanced positions impracticable. It is true that Federal writers have constantly spoken of the ease with which the line of the Ohio River might have been taken by the Confederates, but it is always on the assumption that General Johnston had a large and well-appointed force, which was not the case. The political attitude of the Commonwealth of Kentucky gave a decided advantage to the Federal cause ; but the peculiar distribution of political sentiment by geographical strata also operated to strengthen the Unionists and to disable the Southern sympathizers. An inspection of the map will reveal how powerful this influence was, and what an element of weakness it became to the Confederacy on General Johnston's line.

The Alleghany Mountains and their western side-ranges form a huge quadrangle, extending from Pennsylvania southwestwardly into Georgia and Alabama, and embracing Western Virginia, East Tennessee, and Eastern Kentucky. Its population, the overflow by emigration of the poorer classes of Virginia and North Carolina, was rude, hardy, and ignorant. A sort of clanship, based on association and kinship, prevailed among this primitive people, who followed with blind confidence local leaders, eminent for wealth or popular arts. Hence they usually voted and acted in masses. It is sufficient to say that the United States Government, more clearly than the Confederate, appreciated the character and importance of these mountaineers, and secured the adhesion of their leaders to the Federal side. The consequence was, the loss of the whole population, from the crests of the Alleghanies to their western foot-hills, and the creation of a disloyal and hostile section, severing the East from the West, and converting the Gibraltar of the South into a stronghold for its foes.

A line from the mouth of the Big Sandy River, where West Virginia, Ohio, and Kentucky corner, to Bowling Green, roughly indicates the western edge of this Union district. But a belt of country through Western Kentucky and Tennessee, from the Ohio River to the State of Mississippi, was also full of Unionists ; and, indeed, in all Western Kentucky county was set against county, and every house was divided against itself. The whole land was become a debatable ground. The chief Confederate element, however, was contained in a narrow district along the Ohio River, fifty or sixty miles wide, almost isolated from the South, and surrounded by hostile regions. Wealthy and slaveholding, this population was much demoralized by the course of events and by Federal military occupation ; and no effectual assistance could be rendered it, without an invasion in force and a Confederate army on the banks of the Ohio. As this was not possible, the only practical question was, how much territory could be included in the Southern lines, and how far these could be advanced without rashness, and without disclosing the insufficiency of the Confederate force.

Every circumstance pointed to Cumberland Gap as a strategic point of the first importance ; and a fortified camp was established there as the right of General Johnston's line, and a barrier to the invasion of East Tennessee.

The water-lines of the West were a source of great weakness to the Confederacy. The converging currents of so many rivers, uniting at Cairo in one great flood, enabled the United States Government to collect flotillas of gunboats, which searched out every navigable stream, and overawed communities unaccustomed to war. The line of defensive works in progress at different points from Columbus to Memphis might be expected to defy this fresh-water navy ; but the river system of Kentucky itself was tributary to the North. The Cumberland and the Tennessee Rivers, rising in the Alleghanies, flow first southwest, and thence by sharp bends to the north, traversing respectively the northern and southern portions of Tennessee, and finally emptying close together into the Ohio near its mouth. The history of the attempt to defend these rivers by forts at Donelson and Henry will be given in detail hereafter. General Grant had possession of Smithland and Paducah, at their mouths. Indeed, the outlets and navigable waters of all the rivers of Kentucky, the Sandy, Licking, Kentucky, and Green, were in the hands of the Federals, and gave them the great military advantage of easy communication with their base by water-ways. Green and Barren Rivers, locked and dammed, cut the Louisville & Nashville Railroad, so as to render any point in advance of Bowling Green unsafe ; while Bowling Green itself, situated on the turnpike, railroad, and river, was a good position for defense. Thus, as Columbus and the Cumberland Mountains had become the extremities of the Confederate line by force of natural conditions, so Bowling Green, likewise, became its salient. The communications to the rear of this point by railroads and by a macadamized turnpike, and the facilities for transportation by land and water, were as good and as safe as could be expected. The line was not all that could be wished; it ran through an unfriendly or lukewarm population, and it was pierced by two great rivers, whose mouths were in the possession of the enemy ; but every other line had equal or greater disadvantages. In war, as elsewhere, we must take things as we find them, not as we would have them.

But to the other considerations already mentioned must be added the great disparity in the numbers and resources of the opponents. The Federal forces in General Johnston's front were everywhere about double the numbers he could bring to bear against them ; and their superiority in arms, equipments, transportation, organization, and discipline, was still greater. The United States troops opposed to him were over 36,000 strong, while his own available force was less than 20,000 men. General Fremont reports that he had, September 14, 1861, at and near Cairo, 12,831 men, and at Paducah, 7,791 men ; together, 20,622 men, under General U. S. Grant.[1] General Robert Anderson commanded the Central Department. The fortune of war, which gave General Johnston his former room-mate at West Point as his second in command, confronted him thus with his early friend Anderson as his antagonist. Anderson was able to oppose to Buckner,

---

[1] "Report on the Conduct of the War," part iii., p. 41. In this estimate he only puts the forces in his department at 55,000 men. General McClellan, in his "Report of the Army of the Potomac," p. 48, estimates Fremont's forces, from the best information at the War Department, at 80,000 men, or about 45 per cent. more. This rate of increase would give General Grant 30,000 men.

at the tap of the drum, Rousseau's brigade, 1,200 strong, 1,800 Home Guards from Louisville, and several companies led by Lieutenant-Colonel R. W. Johnson, under General W. T. Sherman, at Muldrough's Hill, to whom he also sent, within a week, the Sixth, Thirty-eighth, and Thirty-ninth Indiana Regiments, the Forty-ninth Ohio Regiment, and the Twenty-fourth Illinois Regiment (not less than 3,000 men), making over 6,000 effectives in all.[1] General Thomas had at Camp Dick Robinson four Kentucky, two East Tennessee, and "several" regiments from Ohio and Indiana;[2] probably 6,000 men. He had also a large auxiliary force of Home Guards, useful "to protect roads and keep the disloyal element in awe." General William Nelson had six regiments of infantry, besides cavalry and artillery, at and near Maysville, probably 4,000 men.[3] Here we have 34,000 volunteers; and, with home guards, probably over 40,000 troops.

To oppose this force General Johnston had, available under Polk, 11,000 troops (estimated); under Buckner, 4,000 men; and under Zollicoffer, 4,000 more. The whole force in Zollicoffer's district of East Tennessee consisted nominally of ten regiments of infantry, seventeen companies of cavalry, and a six-gun battery of six-pounders; but only five regiments, the artillery, and twelve companies of cavalry, were in condition to move into Kentucky—less than 4,000. There was not a quartermaster or engineer in the command, and the arms and equipments were very poor. At Pound Gap, 300 Virginia militia, enlisted for three months, constituted the sole defense. Thus, General Johnston's available force, from the Big Sandy to the Mississippi, was only about 19,000 men.

It is thus apparent that the real question to be determined was not as between an offensive and a defensive campaign; this had already been settled by the physical and political considerations mentioned, and by the preponderance in the Federal strength, organization, and resources. The real questions were, how and where to maintain the semblance of a force sufficient for defense until an army could be created.

It has been alleged that Louisville might have been captured by a bold stroke. This is possibly true; but this event, so much dreaded by the Federals, must have been followed by a concentration of their troops, by the precipitate retreat and demoralization of the Confederates, and by an exposure of weakness that must have led to disaster. It is evident that, until an adequate force could be collected, actual collision was to be avoided. The strength of the Confederate line has been recognized by their adversaries; and there can scarcely be a doubt that it was the most judicious that could have been adopted under the circumstances.

[1] "History of the Army of the Cumberland," vol. i., p. 29.
[2] Ibid., vol. i., pp. 27–37.   [3] Ibid., vol. i., pp. 74, 75.

Among General Johnston's papers are certain memoranda, intended as the basis of his reply to an inquiry instituted by the Confederate Congress as to why he did not inaugurate an offensive campaign. Though applying to his conduct at a later period, they contain substantially his reasons for the adoption and maintenance of the defensive line established by him. With the explanations already given, these ought to settle the question :

MEMORANDUM.

I took command at Bowling Green on the 28th day of October, 1861, the force being nearly 12,000 men. From the best information we could get, the forces of the enemy were estimated at nearly twice the number of our own when I assumed command. There were many reasons why Bowling Green was held and fortified. It was a good base of military operations; was a proper depot for supplies; was capable, if fortified, of being held against largely superior numbers. If the army should be such that a forward movement was practicable, it could be held by a garrison, and our effective force be left free to operate against an enemy in the field. It was in supporting distance of Tennessee, from and through which reënforcements and munitions must come, if the people of Kentucky should be either hostile or neutral. My force was too weak and too illy appointed to advance against greatly superior numbers, perfectly equipped and provided, and being much more rapidly reënforced than my own. Our advance into Kentucky had not been met by the enthusiastic uprising of friends, which we, and many in and out of that State, had believed would take place. Arms were scarce, and we had none to give them. No prudent commander would thus hazard the fate of an entire army, so much weaker than the enemy, and dependent upon support not certain to come, and wanting in arms and discipline if it should.

Muldrough's Hill possessed no strategic importance, was worthless as a base of operations, and I had ordered General Buckner, in the first place, not to advance to that position, because the Green River, flowing directly across the line between Bowling Green and Muldrough's Hill, and being navigable, gave the enemy every desirable facility to cut the line in two in the rear of any force at Muldrough's Hill. Buckner's force was small, was illy armed, had no transportation except by rail, was deficient in many necessary appointments for making a campaign, and many of his men were fresh from home and wholly undisciplined. The enemy's forces increased much more rapidly than Buckner's; and the ratio of increase was fully preserved after I took command.

In another rough memorandum, General Johnston states that Buckner's force was at first only 4,000 strong. He adds :

Arrived 14th of October; took command, 28th. Force, 17th of October, about 12,000; same on 28th. Enemy's force reported by Buckner, on 4th of October, advancing, 12,000 to 14,000; 28th of October, estimated at double our own, or about 24,000. The enemy's force increased much more rapidly than our own; so that by the last of November it numbered 50,000, and continued to increase until it ran up to between 75,000 and 100,000. Force was kept down by disease, so that it remained about 22,000.

Tennessee was threatened on four lines : by the Mississippi, the Cumberland and Tennessee, the Louisville & Nashville Railroad, and East Tennessee. These four approaches were covered, as far as possible, by the three corps already mentioned : Polk at Columbus, Buckner at Bowling Green, and Zollicoffer at Cumberland Gap. The enemy was much the stronger, and was operating on interior lines. It was desirable to strengthen the centre ; but Zollicoffer required all of his little army for the service in which he was employed, and more too. Its successes in Western Virginia and Missouri had encouraged the United States Government to plan an invasion of East Tennessee, which should cut the only Confederate line of railroad communication between Virginia and the South west of the Blue Ridge, and stir up the disaffected inhabitants to insurrection. Already two regiments of East Tennesseeans had found their way to Camp Dick Robinson; and, at that time, the presence of a United States army would have roused a numerous and warlike population in revolt against the Confederacy.

Van Horne says ("Army of the Cumberland," vol. i., page 37) :

General Thomas suggested to General Anderson the importance of concentrating for an advance to Knoxville, Tennessee, to seize the East Tennessee & Virginia Railroad, destroy all the bridges east and west from Knoxville, and then to turn upon Zollicoffer, while in the passes of the Cumberland Mountains, and, by getting between him and his supplies, effect the capture or dispersion of his army. The desirableness of this movement was enhanced by the fact that Nashville had recently been made a base of supplies for the Confederate army in Virginia. Its success would sever the most direct connection between the Confederate armies East and West, and relieve from tyranny the loyal people of East Tennessee.

The same pages show that this design was kept constantly in view, and demonstrate the necessity for a Confederate army in that quarter to guard the entrances to the land. It certainly never had force to spare.

On the 15th of September, 1861, in Orders No. 1, General Johnston assumed command of the department, and Lieutenant-Colonel W. W. Mackall was announced as assistant adjutant-general and chief of staff. A little later, Order No. 2, as follows, was issued:

> HEADQUARTERS, WESTERN DEPARTMENT, }
> COLUMBUS, KENTUCKY, *September* 26, 1861. }

Orders No. 2.

The following officers are announced as the personal and departmental staff of General Albert S. Johnston, commanding, viz. :

PERSONAL STAFF.—*Aide-de-Camp:* R. P. Hunt, lieutenant C. S. Army. *Volunteer Aides:* Colonels Robert W. Johnson, Thomas C. Reynolds, Samuel Tate; Majors George T. Howard, D. M. Haydon, and Edward W. Munford.

DEPARTMENT OF ORDERS.—*Assistant Adjutant-Generals:* Lieutenant-Colonel W. W. Mackall, Captain H. P. Brewster, First-Lieutenant N. Wickliffe (acting).

QUARTERMASTER'S DEPARTMENT.—*Principal Quartermaster:* Major Albert J. Smith.

COMMISSARY DEPARTMENT.—*Principal Commissary:* Captain Thomas K. Jackson.

ENGINEER'S CORPS.—First-Lieutenant Joseph Dixon.

By command of   General A. S. JOHNSTON.

W. W. MACKALL, Assistant Adjutant-General.

The appointments of "volunteer aides" were made chiefly to secure intelligent advice on the political affairs of the department, each State of which was represented on the staff.

CHAPTER XXI.

GENERAL POLK AND COLUMBUS, KENTUCKY.

As General Polk felt unwilling to leave his post at Columbus, just at this juncture, and as General Johnston wished to obtain as full a knowledge as possible of his line of defense, he went thither on the 18th of September. It was a great pleasure to him to meet again, after the lapse of many years, his old comrade. It was no small consideration to feel that he had in so responsible a position a friend to whose loyalty of heart and native chivalry he could trust entirely, and one who, if long unused to arms, was yet, by virtue of early training, and a bold, aggressive spirit, every inch a soldier.

General Polk's great services, his close public and private relations with the subject of this memoir, his anomalous position as bishop and general, and the wide misapprehension of his life and character by those who knew only one side or the other, warrant a more extended notice.

Leonidas Polk was descended from a family noted in our Revolutionary annals. It came from the north of Ireland about 1722, to Maryland; and about 1753, Thomas, the son of William Polk, found a congenial home in the Scotch-Irish settlement of Mecklenburg County, in the province of North Carolina. Here he married and prospered, attaining wealth and eminence among his people. It may be recollected that for Mecklenburg County is claimed the honor of making the first Declaration of Independence from the mother-country. According to the historian of these events, Colonel Thomas Polk convoked the meeting that took this first step in treason. He was a prime mover for resistance, an active patriot and soldier in the War of the Revolution, and rose to the rank of brigadier-general in the State forces.

William Polk, his eldest son, then a lad not seventeen years old, left college in April, 1775, to become a lieutenant in the South Carolina line. He was actively engaged to the end of the war, toward the close as lieutenant-colonel, and was twice desperately wounded, once in the shoulder and again in the mouth. In 1783, he was made Surveyor-General of Middle Tennessee, and removed to where Nashville now stands. He returned, however, to North Carolina, where he held various honorable and important trusts, and died at Raleigh in 1834, aged seventy-six years. Like his father, he was a fine type of that sturdy and tenacious Scotch-Irish stock which knows so well how to subdue the opposing forces of Nature and man, and to maintain its rights against all odds.

Leonidas Polk was the fourth son of Colonel William Polk, and was born in Raleigh, North Carolina, April 10, 1806. He was an ardent, energetic, athletic youth; and, after spending one year at the famous college at Chapel Hill, North Carolina, went to West Point in 1823. Here, as has been previously told, he became the room-mate of Albert Sidney Johnston, who, though one year his senior in the Academy, and several years older, regarded him with an affection that ripened into life-long friendship. He applied himself with zeal to his studies, and stood among the first for more than two years; but some neglect of duty lost him his stand, and he fell into a brief state of indifference and disappointment. Looking into the future from this gloom, he began to contemplate the mysteries of life and death, the solution of which he found in the religion of Christ. He entered on his new walk in life with enthusiasm, and it served as an incentive to every honorable deed. He even went beyond his strength, and, persevering in duty while ill, brought on an attack of pneumonia that impaired his health for years. He was graduated eighth in his class in 1827.

The young soldier, after a little delay, resigned his commission, resolving to devote himself to the ministry. At this time he engaged himself to Miss Devereaux, to whom he had been attached from early boyhood; but the marriage was postponed until he had finished his theological education at Alexandria. He was married in May, 1830, and ordained in the Monumental Church, Richmond, Virginia, by Bishop Moore, to whom he became episcopant. To those who remember the stately presence and powerful form of the warrior-bishop thirty years later, it may sound strange to hear that for years he was often disabled by ill-health, and more than once pronounced on the verge of the grave. He was ordained priest May 31, 1831, but soon betook himself, on horseback, to the Valley of Virginia and thence to Philadelphia, in search of health. He was advised by eminent physicians that a sea-voyage and rest from all labor could alone save his life, and at once sailed for Europe.

Mr. Polk remained more than a year abroad, traveling in France, Germany, Italy, and England, and returned greatly improved in health, in October, 1832. He was still warned that the open air alone would save him, and in 1834 settled as a farmer on a large tract of land in Maury County, Tennessee, which Colonel William Polk divided between four of his sons. Here these brethren dwelt in unity, as affluent farmers. His restless energy remaining unsatisfied by the management of a large estate and many slaves, he established a saw and grist mill, a steam flouring-mill, and a bagging-factory, and interested himself in other kindred enterprises. He also projected and raised the funds to build the Columbia Institute, a seminary for girls. Though Columbia was seven miles distant, he preached in the church there, and also weekly to the negroes; attending likewise the General Convention, and performing other ministerial duties. These labors brought on two attacks of illness, in May, 1836, and he was obliged to desist. But he persuaded Bishop Otey to take the church in Columbia, while he still preached to his own servants, and devoted himself to good works. He was, in very truth, a pillar of his Church; and his genial and affectionate temper cast a pleasant light over his happy and hospitable household, and throughout his neighborhood.

In 1838 he was made Missionary Bishop of the Southwest, and was consecrated on the 8th of December. Though he had embarrassed himself by a security debt for $30,000, his means were still ample, and he entered with energy upon a field embracing Louisiana, Arkansas, Texas, and the Indian Territory. Hardship, danger, and privation, were constant attendants of his missionary work; and not only his salary, but much more, went to build up the infant church. In 1841 he was elected Bishop of Louisiana, and his usefulness was increased by this concentration of effort.

A series of providential visitations, not necessary to be recounted here, had crippled Bishop Polk's large estate; but his pecuniary losses neither shook his earnest faith nor abated his hope and zeal in all good works.

The chief business of Bishop Polk's life for five or six years before the war, though not to the detriment of his duties as bishop, was in developing the plan and procuring the endowment of the University of the South, at Sewanee, on the Cumberland Mountains, in Tennessee. He secured 5,000 acres of land, and subscriptions for $400,000, and gave the start to an institution which is now doing a very useful work, and has before it a career of most excellent promise, but which he designed making second to none in this country—a place where Southern youth could obtain all those advantages of the higher university education which they were then seeking at the North or abroad. The building up of this institution had now become the great end of his life, when the war broke in upon his labors.

He was largely engaged in sugar and cotton planting, and was growing old gracefully in the beneficent exercise of two responsible functions, as a patriarchal master of many slaves, and as an overseer of part of Christ's flock, when the clangor of war called him to the field of battle. Considerable surprise was created by Bishop Polk's action in taking a military command early in the war. The circumstances were as follows, as they are detailed to the writer by Dr. William M. Polk, the bishop's son, himself a gallant soldier of the "Lost Cause:"

In June, 1861, Bishop Polk went to Virginia to visit the Louisiana troops in his episcopal capacity. Governor Harris, of Tennessee, had asked him to call upon Mr. Davis, and urged upon him prompt measures for the defense of the Mississippi Valley. This, together with a desire to see his old friend, induced him to call on the President. The bishop, knowing the transcendent ability of General Johnston, urged Mr. Davis to reserve that most important field for him. As it was known that the general could not reach us for some time, the question came up as to who should be sent out to take the position pending his arrival. To Bishop Polk's utter surprise, Mr. Davis urged it upon him. Suffice it to say, that, after mature deliberation, he deemed it his duty to accept the position, and he did so; it being understood that, so soon as General Johnston had assumed full control, General Polk should be allowed to resign and return to his episcopal work.

In November, 1861, General Polk, feeling that there was no longer a necessity for his remaining in the army, and anxious to be permitted to return to his episcopal work, sent in his resignation to the President. Mr. Davis declined to receive it, however, and gave such reasons, backed up by those of other members of the Government, as to convince General Polk that it was not proper, at that time, to urge the matter further. He therefore consented to hold his position until such time as the Government should feel disposed to release him. Upon two subsequent occasions he made like attempts, but with like results. Proceeding to Memphis, he assumed command of his department.

Bishop Polk, at this time, wrote to the patriarchal Meade, Bishop of Virginia, justifying his course. He said, "When I accept a commission in the Confederate army, I not only perform the duties of a good citizen, but contend for the principles which lie at the foundation of our social, political, and religious polity." He did not resign his bishopric, and always hoped to resume its functions. He said, not long before his death: "I feel like a man who has dropped his business when his house is on fire, to put it out; for, as soon as the war is over, I will return to my sacred calling." This was not to be; he died in harness. But his great work went on in his example as a soldier; for self-sacrifice is the highest consecration known to the Christian world. He had his martyrdom, which, if doubtful in the eyes of many, is yet veritable with those for whom he fought and died.

Many anecdotes are told of him, illustrating his martial energy, while he was still a missionary bishop. His tall and powerful form, his resolute gray eye, broad, square, intellectual brow, aquiline features, massive jaw, and air of command, made him a striking figure, whether in the pulpit or in the saddle. His manner combined suavity, vivacity, and resolute will. When a missionary in the Southwest, he stopped to dine at the house of Mr. McMacken, a planter. His host, addressing him as " general," was corrected, and told he was " *Bishop* Polk; " but replied, quickly, " I knew he was a commanding officer in the department to which he belonged."

He was once at church, where he heard a brother bishop preach, the subject of the discourse being principally the travels of the speaker in Europe. As they were coming out of the building, a friend asked Bishop Polk, sarcastically, " Do you call that the gospel ? " To which he replied : " Oh, no ! that is the *Acts of the Apostles !* "

The following is an illustration of the piety and earnestness of his character, as well as of the charm of his manner : After having, in the course of his travels, staid at the house of a gentleman, previously unknown to him, as the bishop drove from the gate his host remarked, " I now realize what the apostle meant when he said, 'Some have entertained angels unawares.' "

In this brief sketch and these anecdotes may be discovered the signs of an heroic nature. Polk believed that no calling gave the citizen exemption from the duty of defending his home and country. As a *priest*, he had always remembered that he was a gentleman and a *soldier* of Christ ; as a soldier, he never forgot that, though consecrated to a mission of patriotism, he was first of all a *Christian*. It certainly does not become any preaching zealot, who served as a trumpeter calling others to the fray, to condemn or censure him who took up the sword. While Cornelius, the centurion, is accounted righteous, or Abraham is justified for rescuing Lot, the Southern people will hold dear the memory of the soldier-bishop. Henceforth, General Polk was the right arm of his commander. The currents of these two lives that had so nearly touched toward their sources, and afterward had parted so widely, moved thereafter with a common purpose to a common end. Their friendship was founded upon mutual esteem. When General Polk came from Europe, he brought with him a beautiful onyx cameo— the head of Washington—which he gave to General Johnston on his return, saying : " I could find nothing so appropriate as a present for you ; for I have never known any one whose character so closely resembled Washington's in all respects as your own." A very dear friend confirms this view of General Johnston thus : " Did you ever see Jefferson's estimate of the character of Washington ? It is better than the best for General Johnston."

When General Polk took command in West Tennessee, his department extended from the mouth of the Arkansas River, on both sides of the Mississippi, to the northern limits of Confederate authority, and east as far as the Mobile & Ohio Railroad. For the following account of his services, previous to General Johnston's arrival, I am again indebted to Dr. William M. Polk:

The force which he found in his command was mainly composed of a part of the Tennessee State army, together with some few Confederate troops in Mississippi. General Pillow, as the representative of the Tennessee State forces, was in chief command at Memphis; and the credit of all that had been done prior to that time is clearly his. A man of marked energy and executive ability, he was in a position to be of signal service to General Polk in the work that lay before him. Isham G. Harris, the Governor of the State, was in truth a "war Governor." Filled with energy and of great ability, he had done much toward organizing an efficient force throughout his State. This was now transferred to the Confederate Government, that portion belonging to West Tennessee coming under General Polk's jurisdiction. He at once set himself to work to increase his army, and perfect its organization. Much had been done, but much remained to be accomplished before we could be in condition to make headway against the enemy. Everything was in embryo. Seizing upon the materials at hand, General Polk set himself to work to create out of it an efficient army, and to prepare his department for offensive or defensive operations, as occasion might require. Recruiting was pushed night and day; the entire country was ransacked for small-arms, and metal from which to manufacture field-ordnance; nitre-beds were opened; and, under the supervision of Colonel Hunt, ordnance-officer, arrangements for the manufacture of all kinds of ordnance material were completed. Thus did General Polk obtain a large proportion of the ordnance-supplies for his entire command. Under the management of Major Thomas Peters, quartermaster, aided by Major Anderson, and of Major J. J. Murphy, commissary, quartermaster and commissary supplies were abundantly accumulated. When it is remembered that this successful organization, not only of an army but of the departments necessary to equip an army, was the work of a few months, all being created from the raw material, one can afford to smile at those who pretend that the Southern people are without energy.

One of the pleasantest moments of General Polk's life was at Columbus, where General Johnston, after inspecting his department, complimented him upon what had been done. They had been talking of the affairs of the Western Department, and General Polk, in the full confidence of that friendship which he knew General Johnston entertained for him, expressed himself concerning certain criticisms of the management of the affairs of his command. General Johnston replied to him affectionately: "Never mind, old friend; I understand and appreciate what you have done, and will see that you are supported."

At a later period, when the concentration at Corinth took place, it was chiefly from the ordnance, quartermaster, and commissary supplies belonging to this department that the army was supplied. This was especially the case in regard to that all-important element of an army's success—field transportation.

The troops under General Polk's command were chiefly the State troops transferred by Tennessee to the Confederate service—the equivalent of about ten regiments of all arms, with 3,000 muskets, and a brigade of Mississippians under Brigadier-General Charles Clark. Polk

had taken command on July 13th, and, two weeks after, sent General
Pillow with 6,000 men to New Madrid, on the right bank of the Mississippi. This point was important, because its occupation prevented
any movement by the enemy on Pocahontas, by the way of Chalk
Bluffs. While it was expected to make the campaign in Tennessee
defensive, the intention was to carry on active operations in Missouri
by a combined movement of the armies of Price, McCulloch, Hardee,
and Pillow, aided by Jeff Thompson's irregular command. It has
already been seen that this plan failed through want of coöperation.
Both Generals Polk and Pillow felt the pressing necessity for the occupation of Columbus, and on August 28th Pillow wrote to Polk urging
its immediate seizure. This had been Polk's own view for some time,
but orders from the War Department had restrained him. It was only,
therefore, when an hour's delay might have proved fatal, and when it
was too late to prevent the seizure of Paducah by the Federals, that
General Polk felt justified in exceeding his instructions, and thus dis-
turbing the pretended neutrality of Kentucky. The Secretary of War
and Governor Harris both remonstrated; but President Davis replied
to his explanations, " Necessity justifies your action." Polk was rapidly
fortifying, when General Johnston arrived at Columbus. About this
time, September 10th, Grant wrote to Fremont, proposing to attack
Columbus, which, under the circumstances, seems to the writer judicious
though apparently bold; but Fremont took no notice of his application.[1]

After the failure of the campaign projected against St. Louis, in
the summer of 1861, General Polk turned his attention toward perfecting the river-defenses. Missouri and Arkansas were added to his
department, but he was unable to avail himself of these increased powers, as the defense of the Mississippi was his main object, and occupied all his resources. Dr. Polk says :

Finding in Island No. 10 a most advantageous position, works were begun
there. His design now was to make that the advanced point of defense—holding Fort Pillow as a position to fall back upon, in the event he was driven to
it. With those two points thoroughly fortified, he saw that the bulk of his
force would be left free for aggressive movements upon the enemy. While
engaged in this work, the opportunity for seizing Columbus presented itself.
He promptly availed himself of it, and held on to it until his conduct was
approved by his superiors. General Polk's plan for the defense of the river was
now this: Columbus, the advanced and most important point, was to be most
thoroughly fortified. The lines in the rear, covering the batteries commanding the river, were to be so constructed as to permit of their being held by
a fraction of his force, the larger portion remaining free to operate in the open
field. Island No. 10 was to be fortified as a reserve to Columbus; New Madrid to be fortified, so as to prevent the enemy getting possession of the Missouri shore at that point, and thus obstructing river navigation below No. 10;

¹ Badeau's " Life of Grant," vol. i., p. 13.

while Fort Pillow was to form the last stronghold in the chain. Most of the winter was spent in strengthening these positions. From the nature of the surrounding country the larger portion of the work was required upon Columbus and Pillow; and a proportionate amount was put on No. 10 and New Madrid; so that when the time came to occupy them, they, as well as Fort Pillow, were in a proper state of defense.

General Polk's share in this campaign will appear as the events arise. Of his valuable and conspicuous services after the battle of Shiloh, it is not within the scope of this work to give a detailed account. At Perryville, at Murfreesboro, at Chickamauga, in baffling Sherman in February, 1864, and in General J. E. Johnston's retreat from North Georgia, his courage and skill made him one of the main supports of the Confederate cause in the West. Whoever was at the head, it was upon Polk and Hardee, the corps commanders, as upon two massive pillars, that the weight of organization and discipline rested. General Polk was made a lieutenant-general, October 10, 1862, and was killed by a shell aimed at him, June 14, 1864, near Marietta, Georgia, while boldly reconnoitring the enemy's position.

Hon. Thomas C. Reynolds, the constitutional Lieutenant-Governor of Missouri, and, after Governor Jackson's death, its legal Governor, has given the writer his recollections of General Johnston at Columbus. Himself a gentleman of fine talents and culture, Governor Reynolds's opinions and impressions cannot fail to receive consideration :

My recollections of your illustrious father are of little or no historical interest. Soon after he arrived at Columbus, Kentucky, he did me the honor of inviting me to come upon his staff as honorary aide-de-camp, with the rank of colonel; at the same time he appointed on his staff other gentlemen holding high political offices in Kentucky, Arkansas, or in some other State within his department. He stated to me that he had made those appointments in order to have near to him gentlemen of position, who could advise him on the condition, politically and otherwise, of any State in which he might be carrying on a campaign, so that he might take it into consideration in deciding on his military operations. This was one of the many incidents which showed me that he was a *complete* general; for, while no true soldier will permit any merely political influences around him, yet an able commander should always take into consideration, and be minutely and accurately informed of, the condition, resources, etc., of the country in which he operates. At that time General Johnston contemplated a campaign in Missouri, General Price having taken Lexington about that time, and Fremont being the Federal commander in this State. I accepted the position on his staff with the understanding that I should not be expected to serve on it, except in such a campaign. We both thought my position, as Lieutenant-Governor of Missouri, might lead to misconstruction of my course, should I serve in any other State. The Missouri Unionists, we believed, would endeavor to dampen the hopes of the Confederate element in the State, by representing that the second officer of its government had so little confidence in our holding it, that he had joined a campaign in some other quarter.

The only incident at all resembling actual hostilities during General Johnston's stay at Columbus, Kentucky, occurred on October 11, 1861. A Federal gunboat commenced shelling the fortifications we were erecting on the high bluff immediately north of the town. That shelling continued only about an hour. During all of it he and his immediate staff remained near the battery of Captain Bankhead, which from the bluff was answering the fire of the gunboat. We stood close by the battery; and, after a shell had exploded near to it, Captain Bankhead came up to the general and remarked to him that the gunboat was evidently "getting its range," and he should not expose his person needlessly. The general very calmly answered, "Captain, we must all take our risks." Afterward, the manner of his death at Shiloh impressed the incident permanently on my memory. But, in fact, his conduct on that occasion was not rash, but wise. He doubtless was aware of that defect of new troops (to which General Joseph E. Johnston subsequently alluded in a conversation with Colonel Freemantle), in refusing full confidence, even to a commander-in-chief, unless they had *seen* him under fire. The rising ground back of the bluff was filled with those soldiers who were not under arms or on duty at the time, and their admiration, as they saw the tall form of the general, standing in full uniform next the battery, and in full view from the gunboat, was evidenced by loud cheers.

On one occasion only did General Johnston have a case presented to him in which my knowledge of the border States could be of any use to him. Some Unionist of local prominence (whose name I forget) had been brought in as a civilian prisoner, and, as usual in such cases, there was a local clamor for harsh treatment of him. The general advised with me concerning the policy to be pursued in such cases, frankly stating his own preference, on military grounds, for the exemption of civilians from molestation of any kind. He was evidently much gratified by my entirely agreeing with him on political grounds, and assuring him that I believed he would be sustained in such a policy by the civil authorities of Missouri and Kentucky, at least on the Confederate side.

His habit was to spend an hour or two after tea with his immediate staff, and his conversations in those social reunions gave me the very highest opinion of his profound judgment. He was a man of stately but winning courtesy, although occasionally indulging in pleasantry. At present I can recall but two of those conversations. One evening we received a St. Louis paper containing a general order of General Fremont, announcing his staff—a numerous body, composed largely of gentlemen with foreign names.[1] After the list was read over to him, the general, with an expressive smile, remarked, "There is too much tail to that kite." I believe the United States Government soon afterward came to the same conclusion. On another evening, some of his staff were discussing the question of the probable boundary-line of the Confederate States, in the final treaty of peace; none then doubted their achievement of independence. The general's opinion being requested, he answered: "In the beginning of a great war like this, I never try to prognosticate final results. I do the duty which, for the time being, lies before me, and I leave the rest to Providence."

He possessed, in an admirable degree, the habit of reticence—so essential in a commander. When he left Columbus for Bowling Green, his departure was

---

[1] As, for instance, General Asboth, Colonel De Alma, Majors Kappner and Blome, Captains Emavic Meizaras, Kalmanuezze, Zagonyi, Vanstein Kiste, Sacche, and Geister, Lieutenants Napoleon Westerburg, Addone, Kroger, etc.

conducted at night with such privacy that I doubt if any one of those he left at the former place, except the officer in command, had even a suspicion of his intention to transfer his headquarters. A few days before we left, he called me out one afternoon into the lawn, to a distance from the house, beyond the possibility of being overheard by any one, and remarked to me: "Colonel, you may desire to go to Richmond; I called you here to tell you that there is no need at present of your remaining with me; for a long time to come there will be no active operations on this line, if I can prevent them; we have no powder." We had then been so long together, and had become so well acquainted, that he knew he did not need to enjoin secrecy on me. It was accordingly arranged that I should have an indefinite leave of absence, but return to the staff should he enter on a campaign in Missouri. I accompanied him a part of the way toward Bowling Green, and then went on to Richmond, Virginia.

While he was not a martinet, his enforcement of discipline was admirable, and yet extremely quiet. When he reached Columbus, the discipline of the considerable forces assembled there had been visibly relaxed. Within a week after he had assumed command, a great change was apparent, and was noticed by every one, although few could understand precisely *how* it was effected. I presume it was done simply by calling the attention of the higher officers to the enforcement of the army regulations. Much also was due to his habit of personal inspection. He once remarked to me that he did not feel entirely well unless he rode every day about twenty miles. The figure may seem large, but I remember it perfectly. Every afternoon, in the fine October weather, he rode with some of his staff about the camps, quietly inspecting; his eye seemed to be everywhere. He had nothing whatever of the military demagogue in his composition; every one under him was quietly but firmly kept to his proper position. I remember that, from the moment I joined his staff until I left it, he invariably addressed me as "colonel," dropping the use of his previous salutation of me as "Governor." The entire army, as by some instinct, soon conceived the greatest admiration of and confidence in him; he *looked* like a great soldier, but had also a kindly face and high-bred courtesy which gained him the affection of all who came near him.

He paid great attention to the health of his troops and the sanitary condition of his camps. But a little incident made me suspect that, in his reliance on his iron constitution, he was not equally careful of his own health and comfort. The night on which we left Columbus was very cold, and the car on which we traveled had no stove in it, or a very small one. He complained of cold feet, and I at once took from my valise a pair of stout woolen socks, and put them *over* his boots. He said that he had never heard of that expedient, and, soon finding himself relieved, got me to explain how the effect was produced; of course, he was perfectly familiar with the atmospherical laws which elucidated it.

A very warm friendship grew up between General Johnston and myself; my admiration of his character and military abilities is such that I consider his death to have been *the greatest* blow which the Confederacy received. More than any other officer that I have met, he appreciated the great military fact that the occupation of Missouri, *flanking* the somewhat disaffected Northwest, might have totally changed the course of the war.

I remain, my dear colonel, sincerely your friend,

THOMAS C. REYNOLDS.

Colonel WILLIAM PRESTON JOHNSTON, Lexington, Virginia.

CHAPTER XXII.

EFFORTS TO GET ARMS AND TROOPS.

It has already been shown that, when the Confederate troops advanced into Kentucky and established their line of operations, it was with the confident hope that the people of that Commonwealth would promptly join them in large numbers, and also that a strong army, rallied in the South, would speedily follow to support them. The first illusion was soon dispelled. The causes of inaction in Kentucky, already made sufficiently plain in Chapter XIX., continued, and destroyed the hope of any considerable accession of volunteers from that quarter. But the disappointment was even more grievous at the want of appreciation of the danger, and of the means necessary for defense, exhibited by the Gulf States.

General Johnston fully foresaw the difficulties and dangers of his position, and his first steps on arriving at Nashville were to procure men and arms. It will be made manifest in this chapter that he neglected no lawful means to that end. In his address to the Memphis Historical Society, Colonel Munford, General Johnston's aide-de-camp, states the essential question, and answers it:

To those who ask why so able a man lost Kentucky and Tennessee, and *seemed* to fail, four words will answer, namely—*he had no army.*

Colonel Munford then, in a powerful and convincing statement of facts, which the writer has largely followed, shows that this failure to assemble an army equal to the emergency was not due to General Johnston. While the writer will have occasion frequently to employ this interesting historical monograph, it is thought best to produce the original correspondence, which conclusively demonstrates that in no point of vigilance, decision, or energy, was General Johnston at fault. The narrative of military operations is therefore postponed, and the facts in regard to General Johnston's efforts to obtain men and arms are here grouped together, that the reader may arrive at his own conclusion as to where the responsibility rests.

The only legal mode by which a Confederate general could raise troops or secure munitions of war was through the instrumentality of the State, or the General Government. Of his own motion he could do nothing. He had not the power to commission a lieutenant, to raise a company of soldiers, or to buy a gun, except through the intermediary channels of the civil service. Experience had taught General Johnston, what subsequent events of the war proved to other generals, that the Southern people deeply resent any breach of legality ; and, moreover, he was not the man to transcend his authority. Without compulsory power of enlistment, his only resource was to induce the Governors of States and the Confederate Administration to send him such force as he required.

Before relating his efforts to raise troops, it will be proper to show the means used by General Johnston to procure arms. This will be best done, though at the risk of some prolixity, by an exhibit of his correspondence. He arrived at Nashville on the 14th of September; on the 15th he dispatched Messrs. T. H. Hunt and D. P. Buckner, who had been prominent members of the Kentucky State Guard, and were afterward distinguished officers in the Confederate service, as special messengers to obtain arms.[1] The following letter was addressed to the Governor of Alabama, a duplicate being sent to the Governor of Georgia, and a similar communication to General Bragg, commanding at Pensacola :

NASHVILLE, TENNESSEE, *September* 15, 1861.

SIR: The condition of the defenses of our northern frontier requires every possible assistance from the South. We have men in large numbers. We are deficient in arms. I understand that your Excellency has a considerable number in your arsenal. I feel justified by the circumstances in making the strongest appeal to your Excellency's patriotism to aid me in this respect. I shall beg to rely upon your Excellency to furnish us as rapidly as possible at this point with every arm it may be in your power to provide—I mean small-arms for infantry and cavalry.

I view the matter of such urgent necessity that I send this letter by a special messenger, who will confer freely with you upon this subject.

I am, etc.,   (Signed)   A. S. JOHNSTON.

A. B. MOORE, Governor of Alabama.

EXECUTIVE DEPARTMENT,
MONTGOMERY, ALABAMA, *September* 23, 1861.

SIR: I have the honor to acknowledge the receipt of yours of the 15th inst., and, fully recognizing the necessity of speedy and energetic action in the direction contemplated by your letter, regret that it is out of the power of Alabama to afford you any assistance in the way of arms. Our own coast is threatened with invasion by the Federal forces; and within the last ten days we have been called upon to arm two regiments for the defense of this State. When this is done, I shall not have one hundred stand of muskets left which are fit for use. Our cavalry and sabre arms are entirely exhausted; and I am now waiting to forward sabres to Tennessee, which I have contracted for in Georgia.

Very respectfully,

A. B. MOORE.

General A. S. JOHNSTON, General C. S. A., Nashville.

Governor Brown made the following reply, from Atlanta, September 18th :

[1] *See* letter of September 16th to the President, p. 308.

SIR: Your letter of the 15th instant, in which you make the request that I will forward to you such arms as may be at my disposal for defense of our northern frontier, has been handed to me by Colonel Hunt and Captain Buckner. In reply, I beg leave to state, and I do so with much regret, that it is utterly impossible for me to comply with your request. There are no arms belonging to the State at my disposal; all have been exhausted arming the volunteers of the State now in the Confederate service in Virginia, at Pensacola, and on our own coast—in all some twenty-three regiments. Georgia has now to look to the shot-guns and rifles in the hands of her people for coast-defense, and to guns which her gunsmiths are slowly manufacturing. I deeply regret this state of things, for to respond to your call with the arms you need would afford me the greatest gratification.

I am, very respectfully, your obedient servant,

JOSEPH E. BROWN.

The Governors of these two great States felt that their coasts were more immediately threatened, and that the defense of them was of more vital importance than an obscure and distant danger in Kentucky, and trusted to fortune for the protection of the postern to their citadel. General Bragg's reply discusses the aspects of the situation so well, for the most part, that it is here given entire:

HEADQUARTERS, NEAR PENSACOLA, FLORIDA,
September 27, 1861.

DEAR SIR: Colonel D. P. Buckner called on me yesterday in behalf of yourself and our great cause in Kentucky. His accounts of our affairs there are by no means cheering; but, with the blessing of Providence and your exertions, we yet expect a great deal in that direction.

It is in my power to do but little for you. We have no spare arms, and are still deficient in ammunition. I have men, and can get any number; and those who have been with us some months are well-instructed, fine soldiers. Weeks ago I offered four of these regiments to the President for an equal number of new men, believing that the cause would be advanced by such a move. This was all I could do, and all I can do now; but no reply has reached me, though I learn from an officer who has been to Richmond that the department thinks the short time my men have to serve would not justify the expense. Upon hearing this, I again wrote, requesting that I might offer the alternative to them, satisfied a very large proportion will stay "for the war." To this I ought to hear very soon.

The mission of Colonel Buckner will not be successful, I fear, as our extreme southern country has been stripped of both arms and men. We started early in this matter, and have wellnigh exhausted our resources. Besides, there is a general apprehension of invasion this fall and winter, and every means in the country is being devoted to defense—some of it very injudiciously. Mobile and New Orleans are being fortified at great expense, when they should be defended in Kentucky and Missouri.

The unfortunate state of affairs which has caused our troops to fall back in the latter State is deeply to be deplored. We are bound to accept it as necessary, though we may not see the reason. It would have been a great diversion in favor of the movements in Kentucky. In both these States all depended on rapid movement, to save our friends before the enemy could disarm and disorganize them. We fear that procrastination has cost us much; but look with great confidence to the future under your control.

Deep solicitude is felt on the subject of an appointment to the War Office. The health of the President is such that he cannot give his personal attention to the details of service; and it is essential that he should have a man of the highest abilities, and of great nerve and self-reliance.

The policy of the enemy seems now to be defensive at the North, relying on the winter to check us there, while he will operate by naval expeditions throughout the South.

Wishing you full success in the arduous and responsible task before you,

I am, most respectfully, your obedient servant,

BRAXTON BRAGG.

General A. S. JOHNSTON, Nashville, Tennessee.

But, that no stone might be left unturned to effect his object, the following dispatch was addressed by telegraph to the President, September 19th, from Columbus, Kentucky, by General Johnston, giving reports received from his agents in Georgia:

A steamer has arrived at Savannah with arms from Europe. Thirty thousand stand are a necessity to my command. I beg you to order them, or as many as can be got, to be instantly procured and sent with dispatch, one-half to Nashville, and the other to Trenton, on the Mobile & Ohio Railroad.

The President replied as follows:

The steamer was a merchant-vessel. We have purchased as much of the shipment as we could get, less than a sixth of your requisition; some of the lot pledged the troops already in service. You shall have what can be sent to you. Rely not on rumor.

JEFFERSON DAVIS.

The Secretary of War replied thus, more fully, but even less satisfactorily:

WAR DEPARTMENT, CONFEDERATE STATES OF AMERICA, }
RICHMOND, *September* 27, 1861. }

SIR: The President has communicated to me your request for small-arms supposed by you to have arrived, per Bermuda, at Savannah.

The whole number received by us was 1,800, and we purchased of the owners 1,780, making in all 3,500 Enfield rifles, of which we have been compelled to allow the Governor of Georgia to have 1,000 for arming troops to repel an attack, now hourly threatened, at Brunswick, Georgia.

Of the remaining 2,500, I have ordered 1,000 sent to you, leaving us but 1,500 for arming several regiments now encamped here, and who have been awaiting their arms for several months. I state these facts to evince our solicitude to furnish you every aid in our power, and our disposition to share with you all our resources.

We are hourly in hope of hearing of the arrival of small-arms, and the arsenal here is now turning them out at the rate of 1,000 per month. We will receive the first delivery in about ten days. I have ordered 1,200 Texan

Rangers under Terry and Lubbock, fully armed and equipped, to report to you for service, understanding from them that you can furnish horses, which is out of our power.

We have not an engineer to send you. The whole Engineer Corps comprises only six captains, together with three majors, of whom one is on bureau duty. You will be compelled to employ the best material within your reach, by detailing officers from other corps, and by employing civil engineers, for whom pay will be allowed.

Your obedient servant,

J. P. Benjamin, *Acting Secretary of War.*

General A. S. Johnston, Columbus, Kentucky.

Thus, it will be seen, the only immediate result of this appeal in so many quarters for armament was 1,000 stand of arms. Late in November, 3,650 Enfield rifles were received from the War Department. The Ordnance Bureau, ably conducted by Colonel Gorgas, used energetic measures to supply munitions of war, and eventually was quite successful in the importation of siege-guns, and in the purchase and manufacture of powder and other *matériel*. The chief defect was a lack of small-arms. This was never fully supplied so far as General Johnston was concerned, though he received some on the eve of the battle of Shiloh.

The energetic steps taken by the State government of Tennessee, immediately after secession, now afforded a partial basis of supply. A percussion-cap factory had been started in Nashville by Mr. Samuel Morgan, a wealthy and patriotic citizen, and had done good work. Ordnance-shops and workshops had been established at Nashville and Memphis, which were transferred to the Confederate Government, and proved of the greatest service. Under the efficient command of Captains M. H. Wright and W. R. Hunt, everything possible, with the means at command, was accomplished. Twelve or fourteen batteries were fitted out at Memphis by the 1st of October. At the same date, the powder-mills at Nashville were making 400 pounds of powder a day, and this production was afterward largely increased.

The State government of Tennessee coöperated with the Confederate authorities with the utmost zeal; and General Johnston often cordially acknowledged the aid received from this source. The Governor of Tennessee, Isham G. Harris, was a man of courage, decision, resource, and executive ability. Backed by the Legislature, he forwarded with untiring energy all of General Johnston's designs for recruiting and equipping an army. Laws were passed and enforced to impress and pay for the private arms scattered throughout the State, and the utmost efforts were employed to collect these rude and imperfect weapons, and to adapt them to military uses. Though far below the necessities of the occasion, the success of these efforts, under all the circumstances, was admirable. The reports of Captain Wright, under whose direction the arms were altered and repaired, show the almost insuperable difficulties of equipping an improvised army. He says:

About one-fourth of the arms brought in were without lock or stock, much worn, and utterly worthless; and these weapons, generally fowling-pieces, squirrel-rifles, etc., were very poor in quality, even when put in order.

The reports and inspection returns make it evident that, during most of the autumn of 1861, fully one-half of General Johnston's troops were unarmed, and whole brigades remained without weapons for months. Terry's Texas Rangers, one of the best-equipped and most efficient regiments at the front, report, October 30th, *twenty* varieties of fire-arms in their hands—shot-guns and Colt's navy six-shooters being most numerous. Other regimental reports show a similar state of things. This one circumstance, with the resulting confusion and diversity in ammunition, will indicate to any soldier a fruitful source of inefficiency and confusion.

The Government could not arm its troops, because of the inability of its agents to procure sufficient serviceable arms in the markets of Europe. They were there before the agents of the North, but good arms were not for sale to any considerable extent. They, therefore, made contracts for their manufacture as rapidly as was practicable. They can hardly be blamed for not buying the condemned arms offered them.

The war suddenly assumed an unexpected magnitude, and the blockade interrupted this traffic. When it is considered that the South was an agricultural country, the aptness, ingenuity, and resource it displayed in the development of the means of defense, astonished friend and foe alike. But neither by importation nor manufacture was the deficiency in number or quality of fire-arms remedied in General Johnston's lifetime. It was a constant obstacle to his success, preventing not merely military operations, but even the enlistment of troops.

It has already been shown that General Johnston was confronted by a powerful force, while his own line of defense was merely masked by Buckner's and Zollicoffer's small commands. Hence, it became his first duty to organize an army for their support. The following pages will evince that he exhausted every legal means to that end. He comprehended the magnitude of the war, and the tenacity of the assailant, as well as any man on either side. His uniform utterances bore testimony to this fact. To a staff-officer, who spoke of the struggle as an affair of one campaign, he said, " It is more likely to be a seven years' war." His correspondence, his conversations, and his scheme of preparation, all prove his conviction of the formidable character of the contest. He was equally impressed with the necessity for prompt and decisive action. He felt that, to meet the enemy, he required a large number of troops, and he required them at once. It will now be shown that his measures to recruit an army were not less energetic than his attempts to obtain arms and munitions of war. The urgency of his appeals for men was in singular contrast to the apparent apathy of the people.

General Johnston's first step was to concentrate his men. Hardee's command was drawn in from Northeastern Arkansas, where it had been lying in the swamps for six months, sick and crippled, and was added to the nucleus of an army at Bowling Green. Terry's splendid regiment of Texan Rangers, which was detained in Louisiana, dismounted, was, at its own request and on General Johnston's application, allowed to report to him on condition that he would supply it with horses. It was brought to the front, and in November was on active picket-service. On Buckner's advance, about five hundred Kentuckians joined him at once ; and the Fifth, Sixth, Seventh, Eighth, and Ninth Kentucky Regiments, were gradually formed and filled up. John Morgan, too, joined Buckner with a cavalry company, the origin of that famous command which so often carried consternation within the Federal lines. But, under existing arrangements, the main reliance for recruiting an army was the machinery of the State governments.

In a letter of the same date with General Johnston's assignment to command, September 10th, the adjutant-general says to him :

You have authority to call for troops from Arkansas, Tennessee, and such portion of Mississippi as may be within the limits of your command. You have also authority to receive into the service such troops as may be offered from the States of Missouri and Kentucky, and to call on the naval service for such assistance and material of war, including boats, as may be required for the defense of the Mississippi River.

General Johnston was further directed by the President, by telegram of the 13th, "to go by Nashville, confer with Governor Harris, and then decide upon the steps to be taken."

Acting in exact conformity with these orders, he made requisitions for 50,000 men—30,000 from Tennessee, 10,000 from Mississippi, and 10,000 from Arkansas. Had they been promptly furnished, how different might have been the result! The letter to Governor Harris is here given; those to Governors Pettus and Rector were identical, except in the number of troops named, the places of rendezvous, and the clause referring to conversations about arms, which was omitted.

HEADQUARTERS, DEPARTMENT No. 2, ⎰
COLUMBUS, KENTUCKY, *September* 21, 1861. ⎱

SIR: I have the honor to inform your Excellency that, under date of September 10, 1861, I was authorized by the President of the Confederate States to call upon the Governor of Tennessee for troops for the defense of the Mississippi River, and the States included in this military department.

The defenseless condition of this department was patent, from the moment I arrived and had a hasty view of the field.

The necessity for a strong and efficient army is present and pressing. I therefore avail myself of the permission above cited, to call upon your Excellency to furnish for the service of the Confederate States 30,000 men. I would prefer volunteers for the present war, as securing better-disciplined, more skilled, and effective forces; and, if any such shall volunteer by companies, they will be gladly accepted, under the act of May 8th. But dispatch, now, is of the first importance, and therefore companies, battalions, and regiments, offering for twelve months, will be at once received.

After the full conversations I have had with your Excellency, I need say nothing more of my deficiency in arms, except that it exists to the same extent still. I beg your influence with the volunteers to induce them to bring into the field every effective arm in their possession. Rifles and shot-guns—double-barreled guns in particular—can be made effective weapons in the hands of your skilled horsemen. These arms will be replaced in the hands of the troops by uniform arms at the shortest practicable period.

I have selected the following points in your States for the rendezvous of this force, viz.: Knoxville, Nashville, Jackson, Trenton, and Memphis. At each of these places officers will be in readiness to muster in companies, battalions, and regiments, as soon as organized, for the war, or for twelve months, as they decide to serve.

At these designated places provision will be made for supplies, and the instruction of the troops will be prosecuted until they can be armed and prepared to move to the frontier. The proportion of troops to be ordered to these different points, depending upon the districts from which the volunteers are drawn, I leave to the determination of your Excellency, asking to be informed of the probable numbers you may be likely to assemble at each, in order that my preparations for their wants may be in proportion.

I am, with great respect, your obedient servant,

(Signed)   A. S. JOHNSTON, *General.*

I. G. HARRIS, Governor of Tennessee, Nashville.

The Arkansas troops were directed to be sent to the aid of McCulloch, for the defense of their own frontier. Major Howard, aide-de-camp, was sent with orders conferring on McCulloch as large powers as General Johnston himself had for mustering, organizing, equipping, and supporting troops from Arkansas and Missouri ; and he was directed to call on the supply-officers at Memphis for whatever he could not otherwise procure. All the Governors called on took steps to comply with the requisitions, but with what tardy and incomplete success will be seen hereafter.

Governor Pettus, of Mississippi, sent two regiments, armed and equipped, immediately, and two more at a later date. But this source of supply was soon closed by the following correspondence. On the 16th of October the Secretary of War wrote the following letter to

General Johnston, disapproving of his requisition on Mississippi, though it had been made in accordance with the instructions given September 10th, and heretofore quoted :

Your call for troops on Mississippi and other States will, I am informed, produce embarrassment. When General Polk was sent to take command of the department now under your orders, he was instructed that he might use his own discretion in the calls on Arkansas and Tennessee, but not to draw on Mississippi, Alabama, Louisiana, or Georgia, without the consent of this department. The reason for this was, that Arkansas and Tennessee had not yet been subjected to any considerable drain of men, whereas the other States mentioned had been furnishing largely since the beginning of the war, and it was desired to proportion the calls on the different States with a due regard to their numbers of men capable of bearing arms.

I much lament that we are still so straitened for arms. As soon as we can get any you shall have your full share. I shall order four thirty-two pounders at once to be sent to you, for the defense of your works at Bowling Green, or such other point as you may desire to fortify with heavy guns.

Rely on the active coöperation of this department to the full extent of its disposable means.

Your obedient servant,

J. P. BENJAMIN, *Acting Secretary of War.*

General A. S. JOHNSTON, Bowling Green, Kentucky.

General Johnston's reply was as follows :

In making the call for troops, I asked from the Governors of Tennessee, Mississippi, and Arkansas, respectively, as follows: Tennessee, 30,000; Mississippi, 10,000; Arkansas, 10,000—confining my call strictly to those States. The call upon Mississippi was small compared with that on Tennessee, as only a part of that State is within the limits of my department.

I had no means of ascertaining the relative proportion of troops furnished before by each State, nor was I aware that instructions had been given Major-General Polk to refrain from making further calls upon Mississippi. I was desirous that the furnishing of the quotas should operate as little onerously as possible upon the several States of this department.

The States, as far as I know, had previously furnished troops promptly to meet the exigencies of the Government, and I did not know that there had been any considerable disparity in proportion to population. I have asked for no troops from States other than those in this department. I have accepted the services of two regiments, by special authority of the War Department, and a few detached companies, without any special sanction, from (I believe) Alabama. Terry's regiment has joined; the other, De Veuve's, from Louisiana, has not. I presume it could not be spared.

Being thus excluded from Mississippi, and having ordered the Arkansas contingent to report to General McCulloch, General Johnston was confined to Tennessee as a recruiting-ground. All the departments of the State government entered zealously on the work, but the immediate results hardly corresponded with their efforts. Colonel Munford says:

Up to the middle of November, General Johnston mustered in only three regiments, *under this call.*

This, probably, does not include the men, waiting arms, in camp, when the call was made. Colonel Hamby, the Adjutant-General of Tennessee in 1876, estimated that his State contributed to that army, before the battle of Shiloh, thirty-two regiments of infantry, ten regiments of cavalry, fourteen companies of artillery, and three engineer companies—about 33,600 men, exclusive of some 6,000 men with Zollicoffer. But this estimate included the troops under General Polk. General B. R. Johnson, in charge of the organization of Tennessee troops in 1861, reported, on the 29th of November, that one hundred and twenty-seven companies had been raised under the call of 30,000 men, sixty-five of which were fully *organized,* and the remainder nearly ready. On Christmas-day he reported that 12,000 or 15,000 men had gone forward under the call. On the same day, Adjutant-General Whitthorne wrote him, estimating that fifty regiments were in the field from Tennessee. This must have included the troops in all quarters and in every stage of organization borne upon the rolls, militia as well as volunteers. On November 28th, Governor Rector, of Arkansas, reported five companies and a battalion as organized and ready to go to the support of McCulloch. About the same time, General Polk obtained, as a loan for a few weeks, from General Lovell, at New Orleans, two regiments, 1,500 strong.

But the organization, equipment, and condition of these troops were not such as at any time to afford an effective force. It was not possible for the Confederate States to improvise army establishments. It was hard to clothe the soldiers properly. Inspection-reports, official correspondence, and the memories of men, testify how these poorly-clad volunteers bore the chilling nights of autumn and the drenching storms of winter without overcoats, often with but a single blanket. This poor and insufficient clothing added to the ravages of camp epidemics, especially of the measles, which severely afflicted this army. Thousands of recruits were prostrated at once, often to the extent of one-half of a command, and of those who were furloughed as convalescents a heavy percentage did not return to their regiments. The commander at Hopkinsville reported that he had scarcely enough men well to do guard-duty. Under such circumstances, effective organization was seriously embarrassed. As it advanced, and discipline improved, many of the hardships incident to raw levies were mitigated, and a better state of things ensued; but some of the difficulties were never removed.

The enthusiasm of revolution, which had drawn together its fiercest and most eager spirits to meet the first shock of arms, had begun to subside. The victory of Manassas had begotten a vainglorious confidence ; and the people, fondly dreaming that no necessity existed for extraordinary effort, did not urge their youth to the field. Those at the head of affairs could not arouse them to the peril of the situation and the necessity for action. In 1861 the South was exultant and careless. Ignorant of the requirements of the hour, and undisciplined by suffering, it wasted the period of preparation and the opportunity for success. Calamity was needed to stir it to its depths, and to rouse that spirit of resistance which proved equal to the sublimest efforts.

A month after Buckner's advance, the army at Bowling Green numbered only 12,000 men, 4,000 of whom were obtained not from recruits, but from the transfer of Hardee's army to that point. In his letter of October 17th to the adjutant-general, given hereafter, General Johnston concludes thus :

I will use all means to increase my force, and spare no exertion to render it effective, at any point ; but I cannot assure you that this will be sufficient, and, if reënforcements from less endangered or less important points can be spared, I would be glad to receive them.

General Johnston had from the first felt the embarrassments of distant control in many minor matters. It now touched him in a point which he believed to be vital, and which proved so. On the 25th of October, more than a month after his requisitions on the Governors, the Secretary of War addressed him the following letter, laying down as the policy of the Confederate Government certain restrictions on enlistment that did as much to obstruct the organization of this army as any other assignable cause. Mr. Benjamin presents his line of action, and the reasons for it, with his accustomed force :

CONFEDERATE STATES OF AMERICA, WAR DEPARTMENT, }
RICHMOND, *October* 25, 1861.   }

MY DEAR GENERAL: . . . There is another point connected with your proclamation calling for troops, of which I was not aware at the time, and which I fear is going to give us great embarrassment.

From the beginning of the war we have been struggling against the enlistment of men for a less period than the war or three years. We were tolerably successful, although this policy was strongly combated in some of the States. This struggle lasted, however, only so long as the States had arms to furnish. When *armed* men were offered for twelve months, necessity forced their acceptance, for we were deficient in arms. But the admirable ardor of our people in defense of their rights is such, that now, when they can no longer get arms from the Governors of States, they offer us their services "for the war," if we will arm them. I have about 10,000 men now in camps of instruction awaiting arms, and am daily adding to their number; but in Mississippi and Tennessee your *unlucky* offer to receive *unarmed* men for twelve months has played the deuce with our camps.. I have just heard from Hon. Wiley P. Harris, a member of the Congress from Mississippi, that several "war" regiments, nearly completed, have been broken up, and the men are tendering themselves for twelve months.[1]

There is this unfortunate result also. We are on the eve of winter. These men will be in camp four or five months, fed and paid by us, transported at great cost, provided with clothing, and then, when fairly able to do us service, we shall have to muster them out, and transport them back home at great expense.[2] However, I need not dilate to a man of your military knowledge on the vast advantage of "war" enlistments over those for twelve months.

Now our Treasury is sorely pressed, and I want to avoid the very heavy drain that will be caused by accumulating all these twelve months men, whose term of service may possibly expire without our arming them, for we shall certainly give arms on all occasions to the "war" volunteers in preference. Of course, I want to avoid every appearance also of running counter to your measures. It occurs to me, therefore, that all further embarrassments will be best avoided by some proclamation from yourself, in which you could announce that you were now satisfied that the people of Kentucky were prepared to take up arms in defense of their liberties in much greater numbers than you had anticipated, and that it was no longer necessary to appeal to her sister States of the South, etc., etc. I beg you will act promptly in this or some other manner, as shall seem to you best, but to get rid of the twelve months *unarmed* men, and I will engage to furnish you as many for the war as you can arm. It is not men we lack, but muskets. In the mean time I inclose you a copy of a circular letter prepared by me, which will put you in possession of our policy about accepting troops, etc., so that we may preserve uniformity and regularity in all our movements. I am, with great regard, yours truly,

J. P. BENJAMIN.

General A. S. JOHNSTON, Bowling Green, Kentucky.

The circular accompanying this letter states:

1. No unarmed troops can be accepted for a less period than during the war.
2. Unarmed troops (infantry) offered for the war are accepted by companies, battalions, or regiments, and when mustered into service are ordered into camp of instruction until equipped for the field.

General Johnston, on November 2d, issued orders to all mustering-officers, and wrote to the Governors, directing them to disband the unarmed twelve months volunteers, and informed the Secretary of his action. But, on the 5th, he wrote to him to say he would suspend the order for fifteen days. This was in consequence of Governor Harris's strong hope of arming these troops.

---

[1] The writer is confident that Mr. Harris was in error. Mississippi is the only State to which it could possibly apply; and in all General Johnston's voluminous correspondence the only case of the sort is a petition of some officers there for time to arm one battalion, on the ground that they would *probably have been able* to enlist their men for the war, but for the permission to enlist for twelve months. As the object was to raise men promptly, the fact that volunteers preferred the twelve months term made rapid enlistment easier under it, and hence it was injudicious to prohibit it.

[2] The secretary ignores the necessity of drill, discipline, and service, which will be alluded to in General Johnston's letter of January 12th (p. 347).

Colonel Munford, in his historical address already mentioned, sums up the consequences of Mr. Benjamin's order as follows :

General Johnston believed the war would be protracted, and wished to call out troops to serve during the war. He was advised, however, by leading men with whom he consulted, not to call for war-men ; that the enemy had already a considerable army in the field in his immediate front, and were in such a state of forwardness with their preparations that it was all-important he should lose not a moment in getting troops ; that to volunteer for twelve months was a habit familiar to the popular mind ; that most of these men would reënlist if needed ; and that his most successful course would be to follow what seemed the established practice. . . .

The Governors of the three States promptly responded to the call, camps were established, and volunteering began. It progressed, however, much more slowly than was anticipated. It must be confessed that, after the first spasm of excitement upon the breaking out of the war, the popular ardor seemed to cool down. This fact was so clear, that General Johnston one day said to me: " I am disappointed in the state of public sentiment in the South. Our people seem to have suffered from a violent political fever, which has left them exhausted. They are *not up to the revolutionary point.*" I replied, " The logic of your remark, general, is that *you doubt our success?* " He looked at me gravely for a moment, and said, "*If the South wishes to be free, she can be free.*"

Just at this juncture (the middle of November) an order was received from the Secretary of War, Mr. Benjamin, notifying General Johnston that no more twelve months volunteers would be armed by the Confederate Government, or mustered into service, and that he must communicate this information to the Governors of Tennessee, Mississippi, and Arkansas, that they might disband such volunteers of that description as were then in camps. He obeyed the order at once, though, for obvious reasons, he deeply regretted the necessity. In Arkansas and Mississippi the camps were at once broken up; but Governor Harris, of Tennessee, refused to comply, saying: " Not a man shall be released. If the Confederate Government has no use for them, I know Tennessee will soon need every one of them, and not a camp shall be broken up." He also, through his adjutant-general, Whitthorne, addressed an energetic protest to the Government against the enforcement of the order.

Many ill effects were produced by it. It not only extinguished General Johnston's hopes of being able to assume the offensive, or of even successfully maintaining the line of defense he had chosen, but lulled the country into a false sense of security at a time when it should have been roused as with a trumpet. It also caused it to be bruited abroad, and generally believed, that General Johnston had all the troops he wanted. It went from lip to lip, " He has notified the Governors that he will receive no more men."

General Johnston, as an old soldier, as a regular officer, was fully aware of the disadvantages of accepting twelve months volunteers. In his requisition he had said :

I prefer volunteers for the war, as securing better disciplined, more skilled, and more effective forces. But *dispatch*, now, is of the first importance ; and, *therefore*, companies, battalions, and regiments, offering for twelve months will be at once received.

It was a choice of evils. There was a wide-spread prejudice against an indefinite term of service. Thousands would enlist for twelve months where hundreds only would enlist for the war. But, having once entered the service, these same volunteers were retained in it, some by reënlistment for the war at the end of their term, the others by force of the conscript act.

Even if General Johnston had made a mistake, it was one sanctioned by the practice and precedents of every State, and of every army in the field, and should have been overlooked by his superiors. The enforcement of the order annulled all of his arrangements for enlistment, unsettled the views of recruits, and delayed, and, it may even be said, prevented the organization of an army adequate to the emergency. General Johnston's hope lay in the rapid assemblage of a large army. The Administration hesitated at the expense of the force demanded, and at the difficulties of armament. It still relied on the achievement of independence through diplomacy. General Johnston trusted to the diplomacy of the sword alone.

No censure is implied in these remarks on the Secretary of War, much less on the President. No man, no cabinet of councilors, is infallible. Differences of opinion exist among the wisest. In this case, they were inevitable from the different standpoints of the parties. The writer can bear testimony to the zeal, patriotism, and versatile talents, of Mr. Benjamin. Mr. Davis's cordial affection and confidence were too often and too clearly demonstrated for a doubt to rest upon the loyalty of his friendship to General Johnston. Nevertheless, both the importance and the danger of the situation in Tennessee were underestimated by the Confederate Government. The extreme Southern States entered on the war under the idea that, as the right of peaceable secession was theirs, no serious attempt at conquest would be made, and its political leaders adhered to this opinion till the vastness of the actual war dispelled the illusion. Mr. Davis, indeed, better foresaw the magnitude of the contest, and had predicted and endeavored to prepare for a long and great war ; but at this time he was rather the chairman of a *junta* modeled for counsel instead of action, than the real ruler of the country. His marked individuality gradually asserted itself, but when he became permanent President it was too late. Hence we find the preparations for defense in 1861 by no means equal to the ability or opportunities of the South.

But, apart from these general considerations, it was natural for the Administration to regard the defense of Tennessee as of secondary importance. The political reasons for holding the capital, the early pressure upon that point, and the great host marshaling under McClellan at Washington, induced the Government to hazard every other interest for the protection of Richmond. The Gulf States would scarcely consider any other danger than that to their sea-coast, and this influence was so powerful at Richmond that troops were left in them to defend lines of no general importance. In a parliamentary and confederated government it is almost impossible to ignore local interests for the sake of the general welfare, even when all is at stake. If the President had left bare the coast to concentrate in Tennessee, he would have encountered the opposition of the State governments, alienation of sympathy in the exposed districts, and the hostility of Congress. It was a difficult problem. The Government had to conduct a great war and a political campaign at the same time. It was the error of the Administration not to have perceived that the defense of Tennessee was vital, and that it was in more immediate peril even than Virginia—that a stab in the back is as fatal as one in the breast. Still, it must be remembered that the Government was in great difficulties, and that the primary cause of want of troops was the apathy of the Southern people.

It is no more than just to Mr. Benjamin to say that his letters to General Johnston convey the constant assurance of coöperation to the extent of his means ; and, with his sanguine temper, the danger not being under his direct observation, he naturally expected these to be equal to the occasion when it should arise. Again, the fearful odds against the Confederacy required that heavy risks should be taken somewhere, and it was a matter of judgment, and to some extent of chance, where these could be best assumed.

In a letter to Mr. Benjamin, November 15th, in allusion to these matters, General Johnston says :

SIR : I have the honor to acknowledge the reception of your telegram of this date, and to express the gratification which the announcement of soon being provided with a few thousand Enfield rifles affords me.[1]

I shall endeavor, as far as practicable, in the urgency for immediate armament, to give those arms into the hands of the troops for the war, who are now in service and not efficiently armed, and then distribute the remainder among the volunteers for shorter periods.

I have not been able yet to ascertain how many men have joined the different rendezvous under the call upon the Governor of Tennessee; so far as heard from, I believe, not a large fraction of the number called, and very poorly armed. Under the belief that by proper exertions many of them might be furnished with arms, and at the request of the Governor, I suspended my order for mustering out the unarmed men, for fifteen days, in Tennessee. The call upon Mississippi not being approved, the order for the discharge of the unarmed there was not suspended ; except for those at the rendezvous, I shall further extend the time to give the opportunity of arming them if possible.

---

[1] Thirty-six hundred and fifty rifles and 112,000 pounds of ammunition were soon after received.

But this condition of affairs could not continue. The military pressure became so great, and an increase of force so urgent, that further delay was impossible. All the information received, and all other indications, pointed to a speedy advance in force by the enemy. General Johnston determined, therefore, to attempt a levy *en masse* in his department, by a method always popular in those States—subject, however, to the condition prescribed by Mr. Benjamin's order in regard to arms. Accordingly, on November 19th, he made a requisition on Governor Harris:

To call forth every loyal soldier of the militia into whose hands arms can be placed, or to provide a volunteer force large enough to use all the arms that can be procured. A volunteer force is more desirable, if it can be raised as promptly as the militia, as more economical and producing less inconvenience to the citizen; but now time is of the first importance, that I may cover the homes of your citizens, and save them from the sufferings always attending an invasion.

The same call was made on the Governors of Alabama and Mississippi.

General Johnston requested also that the troops of North Alabama, and *slave-laborers* recruited in the same region, should be sent forward to Fort Henry, on the Tennessee River; thus indicating, as clearly as it was possible, that it was to guard its own gate that the military force of the State was drawn upon.

On the 29th of November, General Johnston says to the secretary:

We are making every possible effort to meet the forces the enemy will soon array against us, both on this line and at Columbus. Had the exigency for my call for 50,000 men in September been better comprehended and responded to, our preparations for this great emergency would now be complete.

At the close of an important letter, written to the secretary on Christmas-day, General Johnston uses the following language:

Efforts have been incessantly made by me for the last four months to augment my force in the different army corps to an adequate degree of strength; but, while the Governors of States have seconded my appeals, the response has been feeble, perhaps because the people did not feel or understand the great exigency that exists.

I have again to-day urged most earnestly the Governors of Mississippi and Tennessee to send me reënforcements; for a company now is worth a regiment next year; and if our force can be increased to one-half that of the enemy, the frontier of Tennessee will be safe, and shall be successfully defended here.

In conclusion, I would respectfully request that the Government will earnestly and zealously aid me in my efforts to procure additional reënforcements, by communications addressed to the Governors of Mississippi, Tennessee, and elsewhere; and that every influence should be brought to bear to convince them and their gallant people that a decisive battle must probably be fought here for the freedom of the South, and that every man sent forward here is of importance to the Confederacy.

With great respect, your obedient servant,

(Signed) A. S. JOHNSTON, *General C. S. A.*

General Johnston did not permit the Executives of the Southern States to remain ignorant of his weakness and of the vast interests imperiled by a tardy or inadequate response to his demands. He made known to them the strength of the enemy, his own weakness, and the scope of his designs, with unreserved frankness. Under the pressure of distress, he was obliged to abandon that silence which is so important an element of military success, and disclose his entire situation in many quarters. It is proper to say, however, that no indiscretion enabled the enemy to profit by this.

The following is his letter to the Governor of Mississippi :

HEADQUARTERS, WESTERN DEPARTMENT,
BOWLING GREEN, KENTUCKY, *December* 24, 1861.

SIR: On assuming command of this department it was my chief object to collect a sufficient force to shield the valley of the Mississippi from the enemy, and assure its safety. Calls were made by me upon the Governor of Mississippi and other States of the Confederacy for troops; but, notwithstanding the patriotic efforts of the Governors, the response has not been such as the emergency demands; and, in consequence, there is not now a force at my disposition equal to the emergency of my situation.

It was apprehended by me that the enemy would attempt to assail the South, not only by boats and troops moving down the river, to be assembled during the fall and winter, but by columns marching inland threatening Tennessee, by endeavoring to turn the defenses at Columbus. Further observation confirms me in this opinion; but I think the means employed for the defense of the river will probably render it comparatively secure. The enemy will energetically push toward Nashville the heavy masses of troops now assembled between Louisville and this place. The general position of Bowling Green is good and commanding; but the peculiar topography of the place, and the length of the line of the Barren River as a line of defense, though strong, require a large force to defend it. There is no equally defensible position as this place, nor line of defense as the Barren River, between the Barren and the Cumberland at Nashville; so that this place cannot be abandoned without exposing Tennessee, and giving vastly the vantage-ground to the enemy. It is manifest that the Northern generals appreciate this; and, by withdrawing their forces from Western Virginia and East Kentucky, they have managed to add them to the new levies from Ohio, Indiana, and Illinois, and to concentrate a force in front of me variously estimated at from 60,000 to 100,000 men, and which, I believe, will number 75,000. To maintain my position, I have only about 17,000 men in this neighborhood. It is impossible for me to obtain additions to my strength from Columbus; the generals in command in that quarter consider that it would imperil that point to diminish their force, and open Tennessee to the enemy.

General Zollicoffer cannot join me, as he guards the Cumberland, and prevents the invasion and possible revolt of East Tennessee. Notwithstanding these adverse circumstances, relying upon the firm purpose that animates the hearts of my troops to maintain the cause of the country, I will not relinquish my position without a battle; and your Excellency can well conceive the momentous importance of my situation. If troops are given to me—if the people can be made to feel how much suffering and calamity would be avoided by the presence now in my camp of 10,000 or 15,000 more brave men, so that I could attack the enemy, and not, from a disparity of force, be compelled to await it— it seems to me that the same generous ardor that induced them to embark in the great struggle for our independence would give me such succors that victory would be certain. I therefore ask that, for the coming struggle, every man shall be sent forward. A *decisive* battle will probably be fought on this line; and a company on that day will be more than a regiment next year. If the enemy does not attack, the North embarrassed at home, menaced with war by England, will shrink foiled from the conflict, and the freedom of the South will be forever established. If, however, the battle of independence is to be fought here, the history of Mississippi and the character of her gallant people compel me to believe that they would be among the first and stanchest to stand by their brethren in arms.

I have intrusted this letter to the care of the Hon. the Chief-Justice of your State, Judge Smith, to deliver, with my request to inform your Excellency of all such details as are of importance, and to urge upon you the necessity of sending forward to this place every armed man that can be spared from Mississippi at the earliest moment.

With great respect, your obedient servant,
A. S. JOHNSTON, <i>General C. S. A.</i></div>

His Excellency J. J. Pettus, Governor of Mississippi.

A letter to the same purport was addressed to Governor Harris, with a full recognition of " the energetic and efficient coöperation " he had all along received from him. The following extract is from General Johnston's letter of January 5, 1862, to the secretary :

I desire to ask your attention to the vast and methodized preparation of the Northern Government to carry on the war against the Confederacy with a purpose as inflexible as malignant.

Their large and well-appointed army, only now held back till the highest point of efficiency is attained by instruction and discipline, must make every patriot contemplate its forward movement with apprehension for the safety of the country, unless, awakened to the peril that menaces it, we make a corresponding effort to meet their forces and beat them back, by an immediate development and application of all the military resources of the South, both of material and men, to that purpose. The rapid and energetic concentration of the force of the country to meet the mighty exigencies of the present movement must be brought to bear to sustain our cause, which every one feels will justify every sacrifice for its attainment.

In the great questions of liberty and national existence, the magnitude of them will, I hope, suggest to the wisdom of the representatives of the people the necessity of augmenting the Executive authority sufficiently to meet the occasion, which now urgently calls for its exercise.

If necessary, let us convert our country into one vast camp of instruction for the field, of every man able to bear arms, and fix our military establishment upon a permanent basis.

Whenever a people will make the necessary sacrifices to maintain their liberty, they need have no fear of losing it.

On the 5th of January, General Johnston was reënforced by Floyd's brigade, which, with Maney's brigade, was sent him from Western Virginia. On January 9th he dispatched Colonel Liddell, of Louisiana, of General Hardee's staff, in whom he had great confidence, with a letter of introduction to the President. He says, "Colonel Liddell is charged with a letter from me to the Secretary of War on a subject of vital importance to my command." He also commends him as thoroughly and confidentially informed on the condition of things at headquarters. Colonel Liddell's mission was conducted with energy and tact, and was beneficial. But it was too late; one blow after another was struck with intelligence and vigor by the Northern commanders, and a series of misfortunes followed that will be narrated in their place. These two letters were evidently written as the last resort against the impending disasters:

HEADQUARTERS, WESTERN DEPARTMENT, }
BOWLING GREEN, *January* 8, 1862. }

SIR: The calls made upon the Government from every assailable point on our frontier for additional force would make me hesitate to add to your embarrassment by asking for reënforcements, were the gravity of the occasion less which urges me to press upon your attention the effort about to be made by the Federal Government with a large army (estimated on reliable data at not less than 80,000) to invade the Confederacy through Central Kentucky toward Tennessee. They have justly comprehended that the seat of vitality of the Confederacy, if to be reached at all, is by this route. It is now palpable that all the resources of that Government will, if necessary, be employed to assure success on this line. The line of the Barren affords the means of a strong defense, but my force (23,000) is not sufficient to enable me to avail myself of it. I do not ask that my force shall be made equal to that of the enemy; but, if possible, it should be raised to 50,000 men.

I have hoped to be able to raise an adequate force by the aid of the Governors of the several States of this department; but, notwithstanding zealous efforts on their part, thus far I have been able to draw to this place only a force which, when compared in number to the enemy, must be regarded as insufficient. There are three or four regiments still to come forward from Tennessee, armed with guns collected from the people, and some others waiting for their arms. These men are reaching us too late for instruction; and, liable to measles, etc., they are as likely to be an element of weakness as of strength.

If the public service would permit, I beg leave to suggest that a few regiments might be detached from the several armies in the field and ordered here, to be replaced by new levies. No doubt, the strongest attack the enemy is capable of making will be made against this place; we ought not, surely, to put in jeopardy the result, by failing to meet it with a force sufficient to place success beyond hazard. With great respect, your obedient servant,

(Signed)   A. S. JOHNSTON, *General C. S. A.*

Hon. J. P. BENJAMIN, *Secretary of War.*

The stringency with which the Secretary of War enforced his order against twelve months volunteers may be inferred from the following correspondence :

HEADQUARTERS, WESTERN DEPARTMENT,
BOWLING GREEN, *January* 12, 1862.

SIR : Adjutant-General Whitthorne, of Tennessee, has inclosed me a copy of the order issued by Acting Assistant Adjutant-General Groner, directing that no twelve months volunteer company, battalion, or regiment, shall be mustered into the Confederate service, unless armed; and, also, giving notice that General Carroll has been directed to muster out of service Colonel Gillespie's regiment.

Believing as I do that the public interest requires that the department over which you preside should fully comprehend the practical operation of this order, I beg leave to state the facts in the midst of which I have had to discharge the duties of a commander in raising forces to repel the threatened invasion.

Tennessee is generally sparsely populated. For this reason, it is often impracticable to raise even whole companies in the same neighborhood; hence, squads have sometimes been transported to some common point to form a company. The people, too, are both unwilling and often unable to subsist themselves at their own expense, after they have left their homes as volunteers, and are awaiting organization and arms. Nor will volunteers long remain together unless put under the control of law; this fact is attested by every one who has commanded volunteer forces. For these reasons it has sometimes been necessary to transport, subsist, and muster into the service, volunteers as they present themselves. Neither the Confederate Government nor the State of Tennessee was in possession of public arms to put in the hands of the men, so as to make the arming and mustering coincident. Indeed, in the great scarcity of public arms, the Legislature of Tennessee found it necessary to pass an act by which the private arms in the State could be impressed and afterward paid for. The Governor of that State and myself conferred together on that subject, and both concluded there was but one mode by which it was possible to get the volunteers and arm them; and I am happy to say that both the Governor and the Legislature of that State have most zealously and patriotically coöperated with me. These arms have been, and still are being, gathered in from the people. Those fit for use are at once put in the hands of organized volunteers, and those arms requiring repairs have been, and are being, repaired as rapidly as possible.

While this was going on, the volunteers were being collected at the rendezvous, for the purpose of being organized and armed. These squads, companies, and battalions, were not brought together as independent organizations, but with the distinct understanding and for the express purpose of consolidation, organization, and arming. The Government thus secured their services. Otherwise they could not have been procured; and the time between mustering in and arming was profitably employed in giving the men all practicable instruction in their duties as soldiers. This, it will be readily perceived, was quite as necessary to their efficiency in the field as placing arms in their hands.

If the mustering in of these volunteers had been postponed in every instance till arms were ready to be placed in their hands, or such regiments as had been mustered in without arms had been, on that account, mustered out of service and disbanded, we would to-day have been without a force to check the advance of the enemy, and our borders would have been open to the invaders. In reference to Colonel Gillespie's regiment, it is proper to state that General Carroll had reported it to me as armed, and I had ordered it to this place; and it is earnestly hoped that neither this nor any other regiment will be disbanded, for the reason that the men have not, at the day of mustering, arms in their hands. The Governor of Tennessee is using every exertion to arm all the men who volunteer, and he informs me that he has every prospect of success.

In view, therefore, of these facts, and that the enemy are immediately in my front in great numbers, and that we need every man it is possible to get, I reiterate a respectful but earnest hope that the order will not be enforced by the department. I am, sir, with great respect, your obedient servant,

(Signed) A. S. JOHNSTON, *General C. S. A.*

Hon. J. P. BENJAMIN, *Secretary of War.*

It appearing in the correspondence that Colonel Gillespie's regiment had been raised under State, not Confederate authority, the secretary promptly revoked his order to disband it. His letter to Adjutant-General Whitthorne concluded as follows:

Pray present this apology to Governor Harris, and tell him that, if he knew the incessant and ingenious attempts to force by indirection the acceptance of twelve months unarmed men against the steady refusal of the department, he would not be surprised at any effort to repress promptly such disingenuous practices.

General Johnston's letter, however, evoked no reply as to the other matters involved. The secretary had probably said in a former letter, of December 22d, all that he had to say on the subject. These are his words:

Zollicoffer reports himself in almost undisputed possession of the banks of the Cumberland, from the forks near Somerset, all the way down to the Tennessee line, and seems able to guard your right flank, so that your front alone appears to be seriously threatened, and I had hoped you had sufficient force in your intrenched lines to defy almost any front attack.

I have not, unfortunately, another musket to send you. We have an immensely valuable cargo of arms and powder in Nassau, blockaded there by a Yankee gunboat, that I am trying to get out. But, if we succeed, it will be too late for your present needs, and in the interval we must put our trust in our just cause and such means as we have in hand. We know that whatever can be done will be done by you, and rest content.

Yours, etc., J. P. BENJAMIN, *Secretary of War.*

It seems evident, from the foregoing correspondence, that General Johnston had lost no opportunity to press upon the authorities, State and Confederate, the whole truth in regard to his situation. He exhausted his legal powers in trying to raise men, and, though he failed in securing a sufficient force, his efforts were not without important results. But for the steps taken by him in the fall of 1861, it is probable that many of the battalions gathered at Shiloh would not have been in time to share in that battle.

CHAPTER XXIII.

BOWLING GREEN.

GENERAL JOHNSTON's command in Kentucky consisted of three armies : Polk's on the left, at Columbus ; Buckner's in the centre, about Bowling Green ; and Zollicoffer's, on the right, at Cumberland Ford. Early in October, Polk had some 10,000 men to protect Columbus from Grant's 20,000 or 25,000 troops at and near Cairo. Buckner's force had increased to 6,000, against double that number of adversaries under Sherman ; and Zollicoffer's 4,000 men had 8,000 or 10,000 men opposed to them in Eastern Kentucky, under General Thomas. Polk had small permanent camps at Feliciana and Mayfield, to guard his flank. Similar posts were established at Fort Henry on the Tennessee River, and Fort Donelson on the Cumberland, near the State line. General J. T. Alcorn had two or three regiments, principally Mississippians, at Hopkinsville. These commands reported to Buckner. Colonel Stanton's regiment, and some companies, watched the roads to Jamestown and Jacksboro, in Central Tennessee, and reported to Zollicoffer. In Eastern Kentucky a small force was recruiting.

The transfer of Hardee's army from Arkansas to Kentucky has already been mentioned. This was not done without exciting local jealousy, and drawing forth from Arkansas politicians a vigorous remonstrance. General Johnston was not indifferent to the military situation west of the Mississippi. He was alive to its importance in a general plan of operations, as was evinced in his requisition on Arkansas for 10,000 men for McCulloch. Indeed, could he have secured the Tennessee line, it was his wish to exchange the seat of war thence for an offensive campaign in Missouri. But Fortune denied him this advantage.

Although his military necessities compelled him to withdraw Hardee from Arkansas, General Johnston refused other applications for transfer thence to Kentucky. He was, at this time, encouraged to hope something from Jeff Thompson's activity, which promised fair, but was soon after extinguished by defeat. He ordered Thompson, September 29th, to " remove his forces to the vicinity of Farmington, on the route to St. Louis, in order to relieve the pressure on Price ; and to keep the field as long as he was able to do so with safety to his command."

General Johnston remained at Columbus superintending its fortifications, and directing the movement and organization of troops, until October 12th. Early in October Buckner advised him that the enemy was about to advance against Bowling Green. He replied : " Hold on

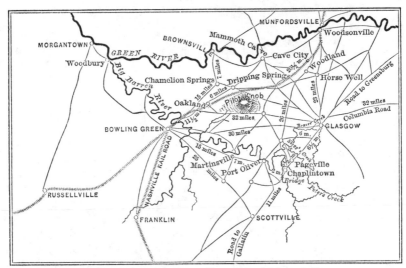

Bowling Green and its Surroundings—General Johnston's Map.

to Bowling Green.   Make your stand there.   All the troops I can raise will be with you."

To the adjutant-general he made the following report by telegraph:

COLUMBUS, *October* 12, 1861.

The troops here are still actively engaged in preparation for the defense of this point, and I hope to have the work complete soon.   I anticipate no immediate advance of the enemy on this line, but, learning they are advancing in considerable force on Bowling Green, I have ordered thither the available force without weakening this point materially, and will to-night repair there and take command in person.

General Hardee has already arrived there, and by to-night three-fifths of his command will have arrived, and the whole of the remainder will be *en route* to-morrow.   Deficiency of rolling-stock did not permit me to make his movement more compact.   Respectfully,

A. S. JOHNSTON, *General C. S. A.*

General COOPER, Adjutant-General, Richmond.

The following letter to the adjutant-general discloses more fully General Johnston's situation at this date:

HEADQUARTERS, WESTERN DIVISION, }
BOWLING GREEN, KENTUCKY, *October* 17, 1861. }

GENERAL: I informed you by telegraph, on the 12th, that, in consequence of information received from General Buckner of the advance of the enemy in considerable force, I had ordered forward all my available force to his support. Hardee's division and Terry's regiment have arrived.   Here, and in advance, our force may be estimated at 12,000 men.   Correct returns cannot be obtained until after a little organization.   Two Tennessee regiments (Stanton's from

Overton County, and one from Union City) are yet to arrive, and may reach this in two or three days, and give an increase of about 2,000 men.

I cannot expect immediately any additional force under the call of last month on the Governors of Tennessee and Mississippi. The men will doubtless present themselves promptly at the rendezvous, but I cannot suppose any considerable portion will be armed. When I made the call, I hoped that some might come armed; I cannot now conjecture how many will do so.

The call was made to save time, and in the hope that, by the time they were organized and somewhat instructed, the Confederate Government would be able to arm them. As at present informed, the best effort of the enemy will be made on this line, threatening at the same time the communications between Tennessee and Virginia covered by Zollicoffer, and Columbus from Cairo by river, and Paducah by land, and maybe a serious attack on one or the other; and for this their command of the Ohio and all the navigable waters of Kentucky, and better means of transportation, give them great facilities of concentration. As my forces at neither this nor any of the other points threatened are more than sufficient to meet the force in front, I cannot weaken either until the object of the enemy is fully pronounced.

You now know the efforts I anticipate from the enemy, and the line on which the first blow is expected to fall, and the means adopted by me with the forces at my disposal to meet him.

I will use all means to increase my force, and spare no exertions to render it effective at every point; but I cannot assure you that this will be sufficient; and, if reënforcements from less endangered or less important points can be spared, I would be glad to receive them.

I am, sir, very respectfully, your obedient servant,

A. S. JOHNSTON, *General C. S. A.*

General S. COOPER, Adjutant and Inspector-General, Richmond.

The Confederate army assembled near Bowling Green numbered, as stated, 12,000 men. This included about 6,000 under Buckner; 4,000 under Hardee, who had left 1,600 behind him, half of them sick; and some other reënforcements. The strength of the Kentucky contingent had now begun to define itself. General Johnston thus expresses his disappointment at the apathy of Kentucky, in a letter to the Secretary of War, October 22d:

We have received but little accession to our ranks since the Confederate forces crossed the line; in fact, no such demonstrations of enthusiasm as to justify any movements not warranted by our ability to maintain our own communications. It is true that I am writing from a Union county, and it is said to be different in other counties. They appear to me passive, if not apathetic. There are thousands of ardent friends of the South in the State, but there is apparently among them no concert of action. I shall, however, still hope that the love and spirit of liberty are not yet extinct in Kentucky.

General Johnston now addressed himself to the reorganization of his army, which is given in Special Order No. 51, issued at Bowling Green, October 28, 1861. It is given in full, as it not only exhibits something of the *personnel* of its officers, but assists in a verification of the strength of the army, and will elucidate its movements :

FIRST DIVISION.

Major-General HARDEE, commanding.

Cavalry.

Adams's regiment and Phifer's battalion.

Artillery.

Swett's, Twigg's, Hubbard's, and Byrne's batteries.

Infantry.

First Brigade.—Brigadier-General Hindman, commanding.
Second Arkansas Regiment, Lieutenant-Colonel Bocage.
"   "   "   Colonel A. T. Hawthorne.
Arkansas Battalion, Lieutenant-Colonel Marmaduke.

Second Brigade.—Colonel P. R. Cleburne, commanding.
First Arkansas Regiment, Colonel Cleburne.
Fifth   "   "   Colonel D. C. Cross.
Seventh Mississippi Regiment, Colonel J. J. Thornton.

Third Brigade.—Colonel R. G. Shaver, commanding.
Seventh Arkansas Regiment, Colonel Shaver.
Eighth   "   "   Colonel W. R. Patterson.
Twenty-fourth Tennessee Regiment, Colonel R. D. Allison.
Ninth Arkansas Regiment, Colonel J. J. Mason.

SECOND DIVISION.

Brigadier-General BUCKNER, commanding.

Cavalry.

Kentucky Regiment, Colonel B. H. Helm.
Tennessee   "   Major Cox.

Artillery.

Lyon's and Porter's batteries.

Infantry.

First Brigade.—Colonel Hanson, commanding.
Hanson's, Thompson's, Trabue's, Hunt's, and Lewis's Kentucky
    Regiments.

Second Brigade.—Colonel Baldwin, commanding.
Fourteenth Mississippi Regiment, Colonel Baldwin.
Twenty-sixth Tennessee   "   Colonel Lillard.

Third Brigade.—Colonel J. C. Brown, commanding.
Third Tennessee Regiment, Colonel Brown.
Twenty-third Tennessee Regiment, Colonel Martin.
Eighteenth   "   "   Colonel Palmer.

Texas Regiment of Cavalry, Colonel B. F. Terry.
Artillery—Harper's and Spencer's batteries.
Infantry—Tennessee Regiment, Colonel Stanton.

By command of General JOHNSTON:

W. W. MACKALL, *Assistant Adjutant-General.*

General Johnston assumed the chief command at Bowling Green, devolving the active duties of the field upon his two division-commanders. Buckner has already been spoken of. But, though Hardee has been mentioned more than once, his relations to General Johnston entitle him to fuller notice. William Joseph Hardee was of a good Georgia family, and was born in 1815. He was graduated at West Point in 1838, when he was commissioned second-lieutenant in the Second Dragoons. He also attended the cavalry-school of Saumur, in France. He served in Florida and on the Plains; he was with Taylor at Monterey, and with Scott from Vera Cruz to the city of Mexico, and was twice brevetted for "gallant and meritorious service," coming out of the Mexican War captain and brevet lieutenant-colonel. In 1855 he was made major of the Second Cavalry, and in 1856 commandant of the Corps of Cadets at West Point, where he remained until 1860. He was best known as the author of the standard book on military tactics. On the secession of Georgia, he promptly followed the fortunes of his State.

Hardee was first sent to command in Mobile Bay, but, in June, 1861, was promoted to brigadier-general, to take command in Eastern Arkansas. Here the diseases of camp and want of coöperation among the commanders prevented any valuable achievement. Under General Johnston, however, Hardee was with a superior officer, whom he knew, under whom he had served before, and who esteemed him highly. His subsequent career is that of the Army of the West, and deserves a biography from some faithful and judicious hand. The more exact, the more balanced, the more temperate in plan and tone, the better would such a work portray the man.

The writer's estimate of General Hardee, based upon both social and official intercourse, is very high. His personal appearance was striking. In form he was tall and sinewy, and his bearing was eminently military. His features were somewhat harsh in repose, but his frank and genial smile lit them with a most winning expression. He was good-tempered, friendly, and intelligent in conversation with men, and very charming with women. His deference and gallantry were of the old school. His social success belonged to his perfect poise, in which were mingled frankness, amiability, and tact—qualities which, a classmate says, already characterized him while a cadet at West Point.

Hardee was an accomplished soldier. His qualities were such as command respect. He was an excellent horseman, an impressive figure on the field. Though somewhat stern and exacting as a disciplinarian, expecting full performance of duty, he was reasonable, and his judgment was sound. He thoroughly knew the business of war in the camp and on the battle-field. He was a real teacher, disciplinarian, and organizer, with the troops of the West. While fond of recreation and social enjoyment, no delight could tempt him from the work of war.

He was a perfectly courageous man, cool and calculating in victory or defeat. His idea was to hurt the enemy and save his own men. Not anxious to push doubtful points, he was shrewd to see his own advantage, and hammered heavily on a discomfited foe. Some in the old army thought Hardee ambitious. If so, his ambition was well regulated. He doubted his own fertility of original suggestion, and certainly did not value himself more highly than he was valued by others. He did not wish independent command, and, when appointed as General Bragg's successor at Dalton, refused the honor. There was no better lieutenant-general in the Confederate army, Stonewall Jackson excepted.

Among the subordinates were many meritorious officers, and some who afterward rose to deserved distinction. Hindman, who commanded the advance, was a man of energy, audacity, and restless ambition. He had been a lawyer at Helena, Arkansas, and a member of Congress. Cleburne, who likewise practised law at Helena, was an Irishman by birth, had served in the British army, and was a man of broad, sober, noble nature. He died sword in hand at the head of his division in the assault on the Federal intrenchments at Franklin, Tennessee. Marmaduke was here as a lieutenant-colonel; and John C. Brown was a colonel, who since the war has been twice elected Governor of Tennessee in successive terms, and President of the Constitutional Convention which relieved the people from reconstruction disabilities to vote and hold office. All of these were subsequently major-generals.[1]

---

[1] The estimation in which Cleburne was held by the soldiers is illustrated in the following anecdote, told the writer by General Randal L. Gibson : When the Federal army made a stand at Franklin, Tennessee, Cleburne's and Brown's divisions were pushed forward on the turnpike, and captured the outer works and part of the second line after a desperate conflict, in which bayonet and clubbed musket were freely used. The carnage was terrible. Twelve Confederate general officers were disabled. General Gibson, in leading forward the advance next morning, stopped at early dawn where the Confederate line occupied the works. The ditch was full of the Confederate dead. Here he heard an Arkansas veteran relating to his comrades, in the cold gray of the morning, the story of yesterday's fight. The soldier ended it thus : " You see we were on this side of the works, and the enemy was on the other side of the works; and we kept getting over, but they would reënforce and drive us out. And finally we said, ' Let's pass the word along the line to keep quiet till General Cleburne gives the word to charge, so we'll all get over together ; then we know we'll drive them. And we waited, and we waited, and we waited.

General Zollicoffer entered Kentucky with orders to fortify Cumberland Gap, Cumberland Ford, and the intervening passes, so as to render them tenable by the smallest practicable force. It was General Johnston's intention that he should then be moved to where he could act in coöperation with Buckner. Zollicoffer was deficient in facilities for effective fortification, and was prompted by an ardent and enterprising temper to more active operations. In the centre of a hostile population, and of a poor, mountainous country, he was urged both by the want of supplies and the necessity for vigilance to send out frequent expeditions. One of these brought on the first hostile collision in Kentucky.

General Zollicoffer sent out Colonel J. A. Battle, who, with about 800 men, on the 17th of September, attacked and dispersed a camp of 300 Home Guards at Barboursville, eighteen miles distant from the position of the main body of the Confederates. The Confederates lost two killed and three wounded, and reported the known loss of the enemy as twelve killed and two prisoners. Having captured twenty fire-arms, and destroyed " Camp Andrew Johnson," they returned to Cumberland Ford.

On September 26th an expedition, sent by Zollicoffer to get salt, broke up a large encampment at Laurel Bridge, capturing its baggage, a few prisoners, 8,000 rounds of ammunition, and 200 barrels of salt. Zollicoffer reported that some plundering occurred on this expedition, which he regretted, and would punish. It was alike his interest and his desire to conciliate the population. Captain Bledsoe, with a company of Tennessee cavalry stationed near Jamestown, Tennessee, on September 30th, attacked and routed a camp of Federals near Albany, Kentucky, capturing some sixty muskets. Zollicoffer was active in these minor operations, breaking up and capturing small bodies of Union recruits.

General Johnston was anxious to fortify rapidly and formidably the strategic points in his line, so as to mobilize his troops. The strong points about Cumberland Gap, thus secured, would dominate a disloyal region, arrest an invader, and release an army for service elsewhere. But Zollicoffer's enthusiastic temperament impelled him to follow up the small advantages he had gained in the field, and he obtained General Johnston's permission to fight when it seemed right to him, a discretion not to be withheld from the general of a detached army of observation.

As soon as Zollicoffer received this authority, he sought the enemy. Deficient in staff, in organization, in transportation, and in subsistence,

And the boys kept crying for the word, and they wondered why it didn't come. But, when it didn't come, I knew Pat Cleburne was *dead ;* for, if he had been living, he would have given that order.' And, sure enough, he was dead, and all his staff with him."

he moved slowly over the mountain-paths of the rugged and barren
"Wilderness" of Kentucky. Bad roads, broken wagons, and short
rations, impeded his march ; but, on the 20th of October, he found himself at Rockcastle River, eight miles from the enemy. On that same
day, General Johnston wrote him that there were probably 4,000 Federals at Rockcastle Hills, 6,000 at Dick Robinson, and a formidable reserve in Northern Kentucky. But this was too late, of course, to reach
him.

General Thomas, who had his headquarters at Dick Robinson, had
been anxious to assume the offensive. His plan was to penetrate East
Tennessee, cut the railroad communications east and west, and raise the
Unionists there in revolt.[1] It is hardly doubtful that all the arrangements for this scheme had been made. Thomas had pushed forward
his advance to Rockcastle Hills, where, on notice of Zollicoffer's approach, the commander, General Albin Schoepf, took a strong, intrenched position, known as "Wild Cat," with six regiments, numbering from 3,500 to 4,000 men. Zollicoffer had 5,500 men, but believed
that only two Federal regiments were at "Wild Cat," not knowing
that the rest of the vanguard had been concentrated there, the whole
strength of which he estimated at 3,300 men. He reported to General
Johnston that he "threw forward two regiments and a battalion to feel
the enemy." This force assaulted the Federal position on the 21st of
October, but, finding it too strong to be taken, withdrew with the loss of
eleven killed and forty-two wounded.[2] He took forty prisoners and
some arms. General Schoepf reported his loss as five killed and eleven
wounded.

As this affair has been much exaggerated, the following brief sketch
from the pen of Colonel Albert S. Marks is here given. Colonel Marks
was a thoughtful and gallant officer, and has since the war attained
distinction on the bench of Tennessee. He says :

The hill which the enemy had fortified was at the head of a gorge about one-
fourth of a mile wide. This fortified hill commanded the road over Rockcastle
Hills. The day before the enemy was reached we found the road approaching
the Hills, miles away from it, obstructed by fallen trees. A pioneer corps was
put to work to clear them away. The men were not allowed to eat or sleep
until the enemy was reached next morning. When as much as a hundred yards
was cleared away, the brigade would be moved up, and this process went on the
whole night. When the hill was reached, the road was found utterly impassable
with fallen timber.

The regiment to which I belonged, the Seventeenth Tennessee Infantry, was
put in line of battle to the right of the road. The advance was through the
woods. When the hill was reached, it was found that the face of it was a precipitous bluff. At the centre of the regiment where my company was, the hill

---

[1] Van Horne's "Army of the Cumberland," vol. i., p. 37.
[2] Howison's "History of the War."—*Southern Literary Messenger*, 1862, p. 203.

was accessible. My company, with a part of the companies on the right and left of it, could ascend the hill. We did so. As soon as the crest of the hill was reached we found the intrenchments of the enemy about sixty yards from the crest with a solid abattis in front. I pressed my company into the abattis. The firing went on for half an hour. I had six men killed, and over twenty wounded.[1] The balance of the killed were out of the fragments of the companies with me. Their officers were with me, and the men would have been there, but our line covered the whole assailable ground. There was no attempt to support us. There was no assault or attempt at assault elsewhere. Indeed, it was impossible. I was ordered to withdraw my company, and did so, and thus ended the affair. We did not have out a skirmisher. The hill could have been turned either way without trouble, and if it had been attempted the enemy would have abandoned the place.

The skirmish at "Wild Cat" was a misadventure, the ill effects of which were not measured by its magnitude. The Confederates retreated to Cumberland Ford depressed, and with loss of reputation in a region where prestige was everything. The Federals, believing, or pretending to believe, that they had repulsed Zollicoffer's whole army, took heart and exulted in their prowess. Their projects of invasion were resumed, and the angry and elated Unionism of East Tennessee broke into open revolt.

Zollicoffer, in accordance with orders from General Johnston, October 28th and November 7th, having left about 2,000 men at Cumberland Gap, moved eastward, and finally took position guarding the Jamestown and Jacksboro roads, in defense of which line he carried on his subsequent operations. From this point he advanced, slowly feeling his way, until he established himself at Mill Spring on the Cumberland. On November 24th Major-General George B. Crittenden assumed command of this military district, having been assigned thereto by the War Department.

A general attack along the whole Federal line was attempted early in November, in concert with an insurrection in East Tennessee. Although the various combats and enterprises of this movement are recorded by the Federal annalists, their simultaneous and concerted character is not alluded to, if it was observed, by any of them. When the movement proved abortive, neither General Grant nor General Sherman felt it necessary to call attention to that fact, nor to disclose their purpose in it. Yet a simple narrative of the events of the different expeditions made under these commanders will, in time, character, and relation, evince concert, as parts of a general plan.

Grant's movement, beginning on November 3d, by an expedition from Cape Girardeau into Missouri, under Oglesby, and closing with the battle of Belmont, November 7th, will be related in the next chapter. Sherman's central army gave every evidence of preparation for an

[1] About one-half the entire loss.

advance. On the Cumberland and Lower Green River the gunboats and cavalry showed unusual activity. On the 26th of October a gunboat expedition, under Major Phillips, was made against a Confederate recruiting-station, near Eddyville, Kentucky. Phillips, with three companies of the Ninth Illinois Regiment, surprised and broke up the station, where Captain Wilcox had assembled about seventy-five men, capturing, killing, or wounding, a third of their number, with slight loss to his own command. On October 28th Colonel Burbridge, with 300 men, crossed Green River at Woodbury, and Colonel McHenry, with 200, at Morgantown, and engaged some small scouting-parties in that quarter. These were inconsiderable skirmishes. On Sherman's right flank, Schoepf was pushed forward, by Thomas, to London. At the same time the Unionists of East Tennessee burned the railroad-bridges and took up arms. But this episode will be given hereafter.

While Grant was counting his losses on the day after Belmont, another contest was occurring at the other extremity of the hostile lines in Kentucky. Although the eastern part of the State had adhered with great unanimity to the Federal cause, many localities and families were favorable to the South. About 1,000 men, poorly armed and equipped, had enrolled themselves as Confederate soldiers at Piketon, near the head of the Big Sandy River. Their commander, Colonel John S. Williams, was endeavoring to supply and equip them from the resources of the neighborhood. But he was not to be left unmolested. Brigadier-General Nelson, who had advanced to Prestonburg with a Federal force, now pushed forward, and attacked Williams on the 8th of November. Nelson had four large regiments, a battalion, and two sections of artillery—nearly 4,000 men. Williams made a stand for time to get off his stores, which he did with little loss. A sharp fight ensued ; and Williams finally fell back, having suffered little. He admitted a loss of eleven killed, eighteen wounded, and some forty missing. The Federal accounts are inconsistent. One of them acknowledged a loss of thirteen killed and thirty-five wounded. Williams conducted his retreat with success; and reached Pound Gap on the 13th of November with 835 men, the rest having scattered. Here he was met by Brigadier-General Humphrey Marshall, who had lately been assigned to the command of that district. Marshall had 1,600 men, 500 of them unarmed. With these troops he took position in observation, secure in these mountain fastnesses, but without power for an advance.

It will be observed that all these events took place in the last days of October or early in November. General (then Colonel) John C. Brown informs the writer that, at this juncture, he was accompanying General Johnston on a reconnaissance, from Bowling Green, up the Big Barren River, and through the country toward Glasgow. The general was enjoying the recreation of the march, and the pleasures of the bivouac, when, late one night, while they were sitting around the camp-fire, a telegram was handed him, advising him of Grant's movement upon Belmont. After reading it carefully, he passed it round to the other officers, and remarked, "This indicates a simultaneous movement along the whole line." He at once ordered Colonel Brown to take 100 mounted men, before daylight the next morning, and proceed down the Big Barren River to Bowling Green—about fifty miles by the meanders of the river—examine every ford upon the river, and report to him that night at Bowling Green. Colonel Brown said that he would prefer not to have more than half a dozen men ; to which General Johnston replied, " Well, as my friend Captain Jack Hays used to say, on the plains of Texas, when about leaving camp of a morning, looking at his revolvers—' Perhaps I will not need you to-day ; but, if I do, I will need you damned badly '—so with you and the cavalry, Colonel Brown ; you may not need them at all ; but, if you do, you will need them quick and very badly ; so you had better take them along with you." Colonel Brown accepted the escort, examined the fords, and reported promptly at Bowling Green that night, whither General Johnston had preceded him with all speed.

Discerning the signs of a general movement against his lines before it began, General Johnston took such steps as were in his power to frustrate it. He knew that he had a force of 20,000 men opposed to him on his front,[1] and that he was threatened on both flanks ; but he felt able to repel a direct attack on Bowling Green, and considered Columbus secure. At Columbus there were some 12,000 effectives, in a commanding position, behind strong fortifications, and with sufficient heavy artillery. Indeed, not having been properly informed of the reductions in the garrison from sickness and other causes, he estimated the force there at 16,000 men, and sought to strengthen his line where most vulnerable by a detachment from it. For this purpose, he ordered Polk to send Pillow, with 5,000 men, to Clarksville, where, with the troops at Fort Donelson and Fort Henry, he could defend that section from sudden irruption. The battle of Belmont, however, intervened, delaying Pillow's removal ; after which, on the ground of an imperious necessity, all his generals concurring, Polk suspended the order. It was represented to General Johnston that but 6,000 effectives would be left at Columbus, confronted by 25,000 men, who were being largely reënforced from Missouri. In a letter to the Secretary of War, November 15th, General Johnston thus explains his situation :

I therefore revoked my order. General Polk's force is stated far below what I have estimated it ; and, with a knowledge of the case as he presents it,

---

[1] Sherman had in all, including Thomas, 40,000 men, fully organized. (*See* Appendix A, p. 364.)

I had left but the choice of difficulties—the great probability of defeat at Columbus or a successful advance of the enemy on my left.[1] I have risked the latter. The first would be a great misfortune, scarcely reparable for a long time; the latter may be prevented. I have, however, at Nolin, on my front, about twenty-seven regiments, and a large auxiliary force at Columbia, on my right. The force on my front will await the success of movements on my left. My force must soon be put in motion. I am making every preparation with that object. It has taken much time to provide transportation (which is nearly accomplished), and all else, for a force suddenly raised. A portion of my force is well armed and instructed; the remainder badly armed, but improving in all other respects. A good spirit prevails throughout.

General Zollicoffer is taking measures to suppress the uprising of the disaffected in Rhea and Hamilton Counties, Tennessee; and, if it is true that Williams has retreated through Pound Gap, Marshall could easily suppress the insurrection in Carter, Johnson, and other counties, and then unite his force with Zollicoffer. The force under Zollicoffer, as everywhere else on this line, should be reënforced; but this you know without my suggestion. The effective force here is 12,500.

It was not without cause that General Johnston regarded the left centre of his line with apprehension. A full narrative of the defenses of the Tennessee and Cumberland Rivers will be given in another chapter. Here, it is only necessary to state that there were garrisons at the forts and obstructions in the rivers, thought to be sufficient to prevent the passage of gunboats. But the country in front, between the Cumberland and Green Rivers, was a debatable ground, in which the Federals had recruited more soldiers than the Southern army. It was continually menaced by these native corps, and also by gunboat expeditions up these rivers from the Ohio. Small commands were kept at Russellville and Hopkinsville; but these, as well as the garrisons at the forts, suffered extremely from disease.

Brigadier-General J. T. Alcorn, who was stationed at Hopkinsville with two or three regiments, to protect that region from the approach and depredations of the enemy, thus describes his ill success, and the causes for it, in one of his reports:

My command, after furnishing nurses for the sick, is reduced to a battalion. It appears that every man in my camp will directly be down with the measles. The thought of a movement in my present condition is idle. I am not more than able to patrol the town. In relation to the movements of the enemy at Eddyville, I have reliable information. The gunboat steamed up to the town, and steamed back again. A company or squad of twenty-five cavalry, from Smithland, marched within four miles of Eddyville, took all the double-barreled guns they could find, robbed some women of their jewelry, seized several horses and mules, destroyed some property, insulted some women, captured one citizen as prisoner, and returned to Smithland.

He reports at Calhoun, Owensboro, and Henderson, about 3,000 Federal troops, " who shift from one post to another, and when mov-

[1] At Donelson or Henry.

ing steal everything that they meet, and take everything valuable that they can carry." This is not an unfair sample of the reported conduct of the Federal troops on this line. Brigadier-General Tilghman, who succeeded Alcorn in command at Hopkinsville, reported, November 2d, that he was threatened by a heavy body of the enemy. He adds that he had 750 sick, and only 285 for duty. To meet a scouting-party of the enemy he raked up a battalion of 400 men, but the surgeon declared that only one-half of them were *fit for duty*. Tilghman described them as "the poorest clad, shod, and armed body of men I ever saw, but full of enthusiasm." Four days later, Gregg reached him, under orders from General Johnston, with 749 Texans, after marches of almost unexampled speed from their homes. Forrest, too, passed to the front on a scout.

Such was the condition of affairs in the western district of his department when General Johnston wrote, as above, November 15th. He could trust for protection against marauders to this force and the troops at the forts. They would of course be inadequate to meet a column, but that risk he had to take. He depended a good deal on the character of the country between Columbus and the Cumberland River for its defense. It was generally covered by heavy forest and undergrowth, and intersected by numerous roads, and thus capable of defense by a force inferior to the invader.

General Johnston, desiring to improve the organization of the army, had directed its withdrawal from its advanced positions near Green River ; but, upon consideration, he countermanded this order, for the reasons given in the following letter, which also indicates his policy at the time :

HEADQUARTERS, WESTERN DEPARTMENT, }
BOWLING GREEN, KENTUCKY, *October* 21, 1861. }

SIR : I am instructed by General Johnston to say that his order to you was based on the great deficiency in, and the great necessity for, organization of this army corps. But, on further reflection, this must yield to other considerations, and be effected by other means.

The backward movement from Green River might, and probably would, be interpreted by the enemy into a retreat, and, if it did not encourage them to a move in rapid advance, would discourage our friends and elate our enemies in Kentucky. He therefore arrests it. He desires you to maintain yourself in observation of Green River, disposing of the forces now with you so as, in your judgment, will best accomplish this, and impress the enemy with an expectation of an advance by us. Secure yourself at the same time from his enterprise on your rear from the right and left.

Let that portion of your command which, for want of teams, depends for transportation on the railroad be posted at Dripping Springs.

I am, sir, very respectfully, your obedient servant,

W. W. MACKALL, *A. A. General.*

Brigadier-General W. J. HARDEE, commanding, etc.

It will be seen that the execution of these orders was effective in arresting the combined movement projected against him at this time.

General Johnston's policy from the beginning had been to keep up such an aspect of menace as would deter the enemy from an advance. A crushing blow delivered by Sherman, on any part of his line, would discover his weakness ; and his wish was to parry, rather than to meet, such a blow. It could only be averted by inspiring the enemy with an exaggerated notion of the Confederate strength, and with such expectation of immediate attack as would put him on the defensive. Having no sufficient force to make formidable demonstrations, the same result was attained by frequent rapid expeditions through a wooded and sparsely-settled country, spreading rumors that had their effect at the Federal headquarters.

These enterprises were too numerous and uneventful to enter into this narrative. Among others, may be mentioned that of Colonel Allison who, with 250 men of the Twenty-fourth Tennessee Regiment, and 120 cavalry, routed a large camp, known as Jo Underwood's, on October 24th. Besides killing and wounding some Federals, he captured fourteen prisoners and some arms.

In pursuance of this policy, on the 9th of November General Johnston sent Colonel Cleburne, with 1,200 infantry, half a section of artillery, and a squadron of Terry's Rangers, on a reconnaissance. He was to go to Jamestown, Kentucky, and Tompkinsville, while Zollicoffer was coming westward by Jacksboro and Jamestown, Tennessee. Five hundred of the enemy were reported at Jamestown, and 500 at Tompkinsville. His orders ran:

> If the enemy are there, attack and destroy them. . . . Create the impression in the country that this force is only an advanced guard.

Cleburne marched as directed, but the Federals did not wait for him. They moved off at his approach, carrying reports of an advancing host. He found the people bitterly hostile. The able-bodied men had run away or joined the enemy. The women and children, terrified by calumnies that recited the atrocities of the Southern troops, hid in the woods or collected in crowds, imploring mercy. Cleburne says:

> Everybody fled at our approach ; but two people were left in Tompkinsville: not a friend from there to Jamestown. One old woman met us with an open Bible, saying she was ready to die.

Of course, he treated every one kindly. Trunks found in the woods by the flankers were restored to the houses with labels stating the fact. A few articles were stolen by teamsters or camp-followers; but Cleburne at once paid for them out of his own pocket. This conduct reassured the people, and he found a very good feeling on his return.

This reconnaissance of Cleburne, and other movements of troops, produced the effect intended. Sherman was greatly troubled with the apprehension of an attack upon him by overwhelming numbers. The following extracts from his " Memoirs " prove conclusively that he thought exactly what General Johnston wished him to think in regard to the Confederate army. His statement, probably unintentional, is liable to convey an erroneous impression, where he says only about 18,000 men were allotted to him, if his remarks apply to this period. The Secretary of War reports that his force, November 10th, was 49,617 men,[1] and his own statements show that his force was not less.[2] General Sherman says in his " Memoirs " (vol. i., page 199):

As to a forward movement that fall, it was simply impracticable ; for we were forced to use divergent lines, leading our columns farther and farther apart ; and all I could attempt was to go on and collect force and material at the two points already chosen, viz., Dick Robinson and Elizabethtown. General George H. Thomas still continued to command the former, and on the 12th of October I dispatched Brigadier-General A. McD. McCook to command the latter, which had been moved forward to Nolin Creek, fifty-two miles out of Louisville, toward Bowling Green. . . .

I continued to strengthen the two corps forward and their routes of supply ; all the time expecting that Sidney Johnston, who was a real general, and who had as correct information of our situation as I had, would unite his force with Zollicoffer, and fall on Thomas at Dick Robinson, or McCook at Nolin. Had he done so in October, 1861, he could have walked into Louisville, and the vital part of the population would have hailed him as a deliverer. Why he did not, was to me a mystery then and is now ; for I know that he saw the move, and that his wagons loaded up at one time for a start toward Frankfort, passing between our two camps. Conscious of our weakness, I was unnecessarily unhappy, and doubtless exhibited it too much to those near me. (Page 200.)

McClellan had 100,000 men, Fremont 60,000, whereas to me had only been allotted about 18,000. I argued that, for the purpose of defense, we should have 60,000 men at once, and, for offense, would need 200,000 before we were done. . . . (Page 203.)

I complained that the new levies of Ohio and Indiana were diverted East and West, and we got scarcely anything ; that our forces at Nolin and Dick Robinson were powerless for invasion, and only tempting to a general, such as we believed Sidney Johnston to be ; that, if Johnston chose, he could march to Louisville any day. (Page 202.)

General Sherman, under the conviction that General Johnston was about to move on him in force, on the 11th of November ordered Thomas to withdraw behind the Kentucky River ; and Thomas ordered Schœpf, who was at London, to retire to Crab Orchard. Schœpf fell back, but with such precipitation as to produce all the features and consequences of a rout. The weather was inclement ; the roads very bad ; and the order of march ill preserved. Tons of ammunition and

[1] *See* Appendix A.   [2] *See* Appendix B.

vast quantities of stores were thrown away. Broken teams and other abandoned property marked the line of retreat. A Federal reporter says:

> Our march has temporarily disabled the entire brigade, and large numbers will be in hospital in a day or two. So ends the great Cumberland Gap expedition.

The men became demoralized; and the retreat degenerated into a flight. Some soldiers died of exhaustion, and many were disabled.[1] Zollicoffer's repulse at Wild Cat and this "Wild-cat stampede," as it was called, were offsets to each other in moral effect.

The conspiracy for a general insurrection in East Tennessee was rendered abortive by Schoepf's sudden retreat and Zollicoffer's possession of the Gaps. With Schoepf's column were Andrew Johnson and other civilian leaders, whose presence was expected to give a powerful impulse to a great popular uprising. As they sullenly retired, this hope faded from the minds of their followers. Nevertheless, the arrangements for revolt were too forward to be arrested without some outbreaks, as the first steps had already been taken on the day appointed. Bands and squads of the hardier and bolder spirits had assembled in arms and begun the work of bridge-burning, which was to be the first chapter in the programme of this counter-revolution.

On the night of November 8th five railroad-bridges were burned: two over Chickamauga Creek, one over Hiwassee River, on the Georgia State Railroad, one on Lick Creek, and another over Holston River, on the Virginia & East Tennessee Railroad. At Strawberry Plains a single sentinel, James Keelan, guarded the bridge. It is said that sixteen incendiaries attacked him at midnight on the platform of the trestle-work. He defended the bridge, and killed the ringleader in the act of setting fire to it. He received three bullet-wounds, and many cuts and gashes, and his hand was nearly severed from his wrist; but he fought his assailants so fiercely that at last they fled. He reached the house of the railroad agent, where, as he sank down bleeding and exhausted, he said, "*They have killed me, but I have saved the bridge.*" Happily, he recovered from his wounds.

General Johnston ordered General Carroll from Memphis with his brigade. After Carroll's arrival in East Tennessee, there were 6,000 Confederate soldiers there, and, a month later, 7,000; but only 1,000 of them were fully armed. Among 2,000 men at Knoxville, only 600 had any arms. The insurgents were said to consist of half a dozen bands, numbering from 500 to 2,000 men each. These numbers were, probably greatly exaggerated, the more so because they rose in scattered bands. Some slight skirmishes took place; but they made no effective stand.

---

[1] "Rebellion Record," vol. iii., p. 394.

Everywhere they dispersed on the approach of troops, and hid in their mountain retreats; or, following by-paths, escaped to the enemy in Kentucky. Some of the ringleaders were arrested, and a few men were captured in arms; but there was no disposition on the part of the authorities to treat them with severity, and, after a brief detention, most of them were released on taking the oath of allegiance to the Confederate States.

General W. H. Carroll, commanding at Knoxville, proclaimed martial law on the 14th of November; but, becoming satisfied that there was no longer a necessity for its enforcement, rescinded the order on the 24th of November. His order said:

It is not the purpose of the commanding general at this post to impose any restrictions or enforce any law not required by stern necessity. Those persons who remain at home, submitting to the established laws of the country, will not be molested, whatever their previous political opinions may have been.

Though there was considerable ferment and disloyalty in East Tennessee, requiring the presence of troops, its disloyalty demanded no further active measures of repression. The Governor of Tennessee, by his firm, judicious, and temperate conduct, aided greatly in restoring order to the disaffected region.

APPENDIX A.

Through the politeness of the Secretary of War, Mr. Belknap, the writer received the following statement of the strength of Sherman's command on the 10th of November:

WAR DEPARTMENT, ADJUTANT-GENERAL'S OFFICE, {
WASHINGTON, *December* 14, 1875. }

Official transcript from the return of the Department of the Cumberland, showing the strength, present and absent, on the 10th day of November, 1861, the date of the last report received at this office before Brigadier-General Sherman was relieved of that command:

No. in commands that furnished returns to department headquarters,	30,917
" " not furnishing returns, about	9,100
Regiments in process of formation, estimated	9,600
Total	49,617

E. D. TOWNSEND, *Adjutant-General.*

APPENDIX B.

General Sherman (vol. i., pp. 206–208) undertakes to give a statement of his strength, about the 3d or 4th of November. He states that General McCook had at Nolin four brigades, consisting of fourteen regiments of volunteers and some regulars, besides artillery—a force 13,000 strong. General Sherman also furnishes a tabulated list of the regiments under his command, which must have been compiled from imperfect sources. He mentions eleven regiments in easy supporting distance of McCook, and assigns seven to Thomas at Dick Robinson, with three more near by, besides seven others at different points. This makes forty-two regiments. Nelson's command, elsewhere mentioned as containing five regiments, of which three contained 2,650 men, is probably intentionally excluded from this table. But the list contains no mention of a number of Kentucky regiments then actually or nearly completed, some of which were then doing service, such as those commanded by Garrard, Pope, Ward, Hobson, Grider, McHenry, Jackson, Burbridge, Bruce, and others.

By reference to Van Horne's work, it will be found that a number of these were brigaded December 3d. Nor is any account taken of the numerous organizations of Home Guards. General Sherman estimated the Confederate force from Bowling Green to Clarksville at from 25,000 to 30,000 men—double their real numbers.

APPENDIX B (2).

General Johnston estimated the Federal force in his front at 15,000 to 20,000; in the Lower Green River country at 3,000; near Camp Dick Robinson, at 10,000; and elsewhere in Northern Kentucky, at 10,000. These figures were substantially correct.

Sherman's command, from his own account, may be tabulated thus:

Fourteen regiments at Nolin (his figures)	13,000
Twenty-eight regiments mentioned (estimated)	26,000
Nelson's command	4,000
Ten regiments not mentioned	5,000
Total	48,000

This does not include Home Guards.

CHAPTER XXIV.

THE BATTLE OF BELMONT.

On the 7th of November, 1861, a battle was fought at Belmont, Missouri, opposite Columbus, Kentucky. General Grant's reports and authorized biographies claim this as a victory, and that it was the culmination of an expedition undertaken for good strategic reasons, and justified by complete success. It is admitted that such was not the popular estimate of the time; and elaborate apologies have been framed to prove the substantial advantages gained by the fight. The merits of a hard fighter, of boldness, persistence, and coolness, will be cheerfully accorded to General Grant by friend and foe alike; and his reputation as a soldier need not rest on this battle. His first essay was a disaster to his arms. The verdict of the hour must be the verdict of history.

General Polk's dispatch, announcing the battle of Belmont, and summing up its results, was as follows :

HEADQUARTERS FIRST DIVISION, WESTERN DEPARTMENT,
COLUMBUS, KENTUCKY, November 7, 1861.

The enemy came down on the opposite side of the river to Belmont to-day, about 7,500 strong, landed under cover of gunboats, and attacked Colonel Tappan's camp. I sent over three regiments under General Pillow to his relief; then at intervals three others, then General Cheatham.

I then took over two others in person, to support a flank movement which I had directed. It was a hard-fought battle, lasting from half-past 10 A. M. to 5 P. M. They took Beltzhoover's battery, four pieces of which were recaptured. The enemy were thoroughly routed. We pursued them to their boats, seven miles, and then drove their boats before us. The road was strewed with their dead and wounded, guns, ammunition, and equipments. Our loss, considerable ; theirs, heavy.

L. POLK, Major-General commanding.

To general headquarters, through General A. S. JOHNSTON.

This report, made on the day of battle, is substantially accurate, except that the force of the enemy is over-estimated.

General Grant represents his purpose and procedure in this movement as follows, in his report from Cairo, of November 12, 1861 :

On the evening of the 6th instant I left this place with 2,850 men, of all arms, to make a reconnaissance toward Columbus. The object of the expedition was to prevent the enemy from sending out reënforcements to Price's army in Missouri, and also from cutting off columns that I had been directed to send out from this place and Cape Girardeau, in pursuit of Jeff Thompson. Knowing that Columbus was strongly garrisoned, I asked General Smith, commanding at Paducah, Kentucky, to make demonstrations in the same direction. He did so by ordering a small force to Mayfield, and another in the direction of Columbus, not to approach nearer, however, than twelve or fifteen miles. I also sent a small force on the Kentucky side, with orders not to approach nearer than Elliott's Mills, some twelve miles from Columbus.

The expedition under my immediate command was stopped about nine miles below here on the Kentucky shore, and remained until morning. All this served to distract the enemy, and led him to think he was to be attacked in his strongly-fortified position. At daylight we proceeded down the river to a point just out of range of the rebel guns and debarked on the Missouri shore. From here the troops were marched by flank for about one mile toward Belmont, and then drawn up in line of battle, a battalion also having been left as a reserve near the transports. Two companies from each regiment, five skeletons in number, were then thrown out as skirmishers, to ascertain the position of the enemy. It was but a few moments before we met him, and a general engagement ensued.

On the 3d of November Grant had sent Colonel Oglesby with four regiments (3,000 men) from Commerce, Missouri, toward Indian Ford, on the St. Francis River, by way of Sikestown. On the 6th he sent him another regiment, from Cairo, with orders to turn his column toward New Madrid, and, when he reached the nearest point to Columbus, to await orders. The ostensible purpose of this movement was to cut off reënforcements going to General Price, and to pursue Jeff Thompson. There could not have been at this time any serious apprehension of Jeff Thompson, whose band had dissolved ; and, as there were no such reënforcements going to Price, the detachment was, in these points of view, futile—as, indeed, was the entire expedition. Oglesby's position and strength might have supported Grant in case of successful lodgment, or have afforded him a secure line of retreat, in case he had been cut off from his gunboats ; but no such intentions have been admitted by General Grant. Unless the whole movement was tentative, with ulterior designs on New Madrid, it does not seem clear why so large a contingent should not rather have been massed with Grant's command in his assault on Belmont.

General Grant says his object was " to make a reconnaissance." Badeau says :

At two o'clock, on the morning of the 7th, he received intelligence that the rebels had been crossing troops from Columbus to Belmont the day before, with the purpose of cutting off Oglesby.[1] He at once determined on converting the demonstration on Belmont into an attack, as it was now necessary to be prompt in preventing any further efforts of the rebels either to reënforce Price or to interrupt Oglesby. He still, however, had no intention of remaining at Belmont, which was on low ground, and could not have been held an hour under the guns at Columbus. His idea was simply to destroy the camps, capture or disperse the enemy, and get himself away before the rebel garrison could be reënforced.

Belmont was the inappropriate name given a settlement of three houses on the western bank of the Mississippi River, opposite Columbus. It was situated in a dreary, flat " bottom-land," cut up with sloughs, heavily timbered, and approached from the river by two natural terraces or banks. On the upper bank, a clearing had been made in the forest of some 700 acres. In this clearing was the encampment of Colonel Tappan's Thirteenth Arkansas Regiment, and a light battery named " Watson's," under Colonel Beltzhoover, placed there as an outpost of the stronghold at Columbus.

General Polk had information that led him to expect an attack on Columbus. Learning, early on the morning of the 7th, of Oglesby's march, he believed the attack would be general, and this opinion was confirmed by the Federal demonstrations on the Kentucky side of the river. The approach of Grant's gunboats and transports was observed,

---

[1] If such information was conveyed to General Grant, it is sufficient to say it was without foundation.

though a bend in the river and an intervening forest concealed the landing and subsequent movements of his troops. While preparations, thought sufficient to defend the position at Belmont against Grant's column, were made, General Polk was unwilling to weaken the force at Columbus too much, lest the weight of the attack should fall there. Accordingly, he retained the greater part of his troops at Columbus, until the failure of the enemy to advance against it and the necessities of the case developed at Belmont induced him to cross over in force.

The language of General Pillow's report will best describe the opening of the battle on the Confederate side. He says:

Under instructions delivered in person by Major-General Polk, on the morning of the 7th inst., I crossed to the village of Belmont, on the Missouri shore, four regiments of my division, and, as rapidly as possible, placed them in position about four hundred yards from the river-bank, in line with Colonel Tappan's regiment and Beltzhoover's battery, to receive the large force of the enemy advancing on the small encampment at that place. These regiments, from measles and diseases incident to the Mississippi bottom, and absentees, had been reduced below 500 men for duty, as shown by the daily morning report. They were formed into line of battle, with Colonel Wright's regiment on the left of Beltzhoover's battery, and with Colonels Pickett's, Freeman's, Tappan's, and Russell's regiments (the last now under command of Lieutenant-Colonel Bell), on the right of the battery. These regiments, all told, numbered about 2,500.

General Pillow threw forward three companies of skirmishers, who disputed the ground until his alignment was hastily made. He was unacquainted with the ground and hurried for time. The Confederate line of battle was formed in somewhat crowded order, in the edge of the forest, nearly parallel with the river, with the "clearing," or open ground, behind it. The Federal column had landed around a bend of the river, and followed the road, which ran from that landing nearly parallel with the course of the river at Belmont, and a couple of miles back from it. A line of ponds and sloughs extended through the forest from the landing to Belmont, and the road turned the head of these ponds and entered the Confederate position on its extreme left. When Grant was opposite to the Confederate position, he formed line of battle, and entered the woods to attack it. The sloughs, at this season, were dry, and offered no serious obstacle. He engaged the skirmishers sent out by Pillow, at twenty minutes past nine o'clock, and at about ten o'clock encountered his line of battle.

Grant's strength was apparently greatly over-estimated by both Polk and Pillow, and by the Confederates generally, who placed it at 7,500. Grant, in his report, puts it at 2,850, and, in a letter to his father, at 3,000. Badeau says there were 3,114 men. A soldier correspondent, writing from the battle-field, states the force engaged at 3,500. General Badeau's statement, as the most deliberate, ought to be the most correct, though much below the average strength of Federal regiments at that time. The "skeleton" regiments, as General Grant calls them, were made up of picked men. The Confederate exaggeration of their numbers may well be accepted by these hardy Northwestern volunteers as a high tribute to their prowess, which on that day was very great. But it was in part due to their more open formation in line of battle. The Federal regiments were separated in their advance by the nature of the ground, and the men themselves were compelled to employ a looser order.

The Federal force was composed of five regiments of infantry, Taylor's battery of light artillery, and two squadrons of cavalry. The cavalry, following the road, in advance and skirmishing, turned the Confederate left. The infantry was arranged as follows: On the right, the Twenty-seventh Illinois, Colonel N. B. Buford; next, the Thirty-first Illinois, Colonel John A. Logan ; next, the Thirtieth Illinois, Colonel Philip B. Fouke—making a brigade, under command of Brigadier-General John A. McClernand. The rear of the column, forming the left wing, was composed of the Twenty-second Illinois, Colonel H. Dougherty, and the Seventh Iowa, Colonel Lauman, and was commanded by Colonel Dougherty. The first attack was made by the right wing ; but, as it advanced, the Twenty-seventh Illinois, in passing around the head of a pond, was separated from the command, and found itself on the left flank of the Confederates. McClernand's other two regiments struck them on the right flank and front; and Dougherty's brigade, passing behind the Thirtieth and Thirty-first Illinois to their right, occupied the interval, and thus became the centre.

Whether there was really a greater disparity of force than the Federal writers suppose, or, whatever the cause, the Federal army presented the greater front, and attacked both in front and on each flank of the Confederates at the same time. Such is Pillow's statement, and it is corroborated by the reports of the Northern generals. McClernand was disappointed that the movement of the Second Brigade was not made on the left, as originally intended, "which," he says, "would have perfected a line sufficient to inclose the enemy's camp on all sides accessible to us, thus enabling us to command the river above and below them, and prevent the crossing of reënforcements from Columbus, insuring his capture as well as defeat." Later on he says, "A combined movement was now made upon three sides of the enemy's works."

The battle opened at about half-past ten o'clock, with an assault upon the right front and flank of the Confederate line, by the Thirtieth and Thirty-first Illinois and the artillery, led by General McClernand. He says, "The struggle, which was continued for half an hour with great severity, threw our troops into temporary disorder, but they were promptly rallied." They were, in fact, repulsed by Tappan's and Russell's regiments. On the Confederate left, Buford's Twenty-seventh Illinois, aided by the cavalry, assailed Wright's regiment, which was supported by Beltzhoover's guns, and partially defended by a rough abattis. This attack was also repulsed.

Colonel Dougherty led the Second Brigade in such a direction that he encountered the Confederate centre, composed of the regiments of Pickett and Freeman. The whole Federal line advanced through rough forest and fallen timber, which, though it impeded and annoyed, gave great advantages of shelter. This applied especially to the Second Brigade. Pickett's and Freeman's regiments, being in the cleared ground, were more exposed. They were broken several times by the vigorous assault of Dougherty's men, but were as often rallied by the officers, and by General Pillow in person. Dougherty, in his report, says:

The enemy for some time obstinately resisted any advance at this point, and a storm of musketry raged along the whole line of the Second Brigade. . . . Step by step we drove them, until they reached a secondary bank, such as abound through the river-bottoms of the West, under which they were protected from our fire; and, when they made another desperate stand for about thirty minutes, our fire became so hot that they retreated to some open ground near their encampment, covered by a rude abattis of felled timber, strewing the ground as they went with guns, coats, and canteens. Our brave troops followed them with shouts, pouring volley after volley into them. Here the enemy's movements at this point gave unmistakable evidence of being panic-stricken and defeated, retreating to the river and up the river-bank behind the shelter of some brush and timber.

The resistance was, indeed, even more resolute than this Federal report concedes. The artillery-ammunition gave out, and a regiment and battalion also fell short of ammunition. Pillow ordered a bayonet-charge, which was made gallantly, driving back the Federal line. But it retired with such a deadly fire that the Confederates in turn fell back to their original position. This was repeated a second and a third time, the Federals being each time driven back, but, in the final charge, prevailing. Pillow says he ordered his line to fall back to the river-bank. Of course, raw troops could not, under such circumstances, successfully execute this manoeuvre, and his line reached the river-bank a broken and disordered mass.

The resistance to the attack on the right and left had been similar but even more stubborn. Indeed, the lines, after the first shock, were continuous, and the contest general. The Thirtieth and Thirty-first Illinois, led and encouraged by both Grant and McClernand, thrice attacked, and were thrice driven back by the bayonet. At length, the entire Federal army was united in a final combined attack, before which the Confederates gave way. · This was about two o'clock. The Federal army, emerging from the woods, captured the abandoned guns of the

Watson Battery, and entered the Confederate encampment on three sides, almost simultaneously, the honor being conceded to the Twenty-seventh Illinois of being the first to break through the obstacles, and snatch the prize of victory. Thus ended the first engagement of the day, in the apparent rout and total defeat of the Confederates.

It is very probable that the Union army would not have allowed the Confederates to escape up the river-bank without pursuit, if their on-ward career had not been sharply checked at the secondary bank. Just as the shattered Confederates took refuge behind this bank, Pillow, who had sent to Polk for an additional regiment, found Knox Walker's regiment, the Second Tennessee, coming to his support. He pushed it forward to the edge of the bank, and it sustained the attack of the Federals, until the dispersed and beaten Confederates had made their way through the timber, up the river-bank, and, with the tenacity of American soldiers, had rallied for a renewal of the contest. But, though Walker's regiment maintained itself stubbornly for a while, it could not bear the entire brunt of the contest under the deadly fire of the Federals, flushed with success. At last it retired up the bank, keeping up a steady fire as it fell back.

When the Federals had obtained possession of the whole river-front of the camps, they advanced to the bank, and opened an artillery-fire on Columbus, and on some crossing transports, which they drove back. The heavy guns at Columbus now opened on the Federals with serious purpose. So crushing was this cannonade, plunging in from the commanding heights opposite, that the Federals rapidly recoiled. It was seen that their position at Belmont was not tenable. At the same time, they learned that General Polk had been crossing reënforcements, and was landing them some distance above, with the evident design of cutting off the retreat to the transports. Badeau says,[1] Grant's troops were "plundering," while their colonels, "equally raw, shouted, and made stump-speeches for the Union." Grant was more complimentary at the time, attributing much of the gallantry of his troops "to the coolness and presence of mind of the officers, particularly the colonels." Doubtless, they were a good deal disorganized. Badeau continues:

He (Grant) was anxious to get back to his own steamers before these reënforcements could arrive, and strove to reform his men, but in vain; they behaved like so many schoolboys, until, finally, to stop the plundering, he ordered his staff-officers to set the camps on fire.

Gathering their booty and captured guns, the column began its retreat to the transports and the protection of the gunboats.

The account of this retreat is not related in the Federal reports with candor. It is hard to see the fruits of victory wrested away ; and the

---

[1] "Life of Grant," vol. i., p. 16.

disastrous rout they suffered is denied, or glozed over, in all these narratives. The facts are these : During the retreat of his beaten regiment, Pillow found at the landing, some distance above the battleground, two regiments—Marks's Eleventh Louisiana and Carroll's Fifteenth Tennessee. Pillow determined to try to retrieve the fortunes of the day, and ordered Colonel Marks to lead these two regiments in pursuit, while he would support him with the fragments of the regiments then reforming. His directions were, " to lead the advance in double quick time through the wood and to the enemy's rear, and to attack him with vigor."

The discrepancies between the Federal and Confederate accounts of this second engagement can be reconciled only by supposing that, in approaching the Federals through the woods, Marks's line of battle encountered the head of their column at such an angle that his extreme flankers on the right were interposed on the line of retreat. These, of course, offered no serious obstacle to that column going home. They were pushed aside. When the column came in collision with it, Badeau says :

It was instantly cried, " We are surrounded!" and at first some confusion prevailed. An officer of Grant's staff, lately from civil life, rode up, a little flustered, with the intelligence. " Well," said Grant, " if that is so, we must cut our way out as we cut our way in." The men were brave enough, but it had not occurred to them before that, being surrounded, there was anything to do but surrender.

Colonel Dougherty, in his report made at the time, attributes this remark to himself; and a newspaper reporter puts it in the mouth of Colonel Logan; so that, after all, there was a *consensus* here in a sentiment as old as Pelopidas—or at least as his biographer. Badeau adds:

As soon as the troops found that their leader meant to fight, the confusion was past; they promptly charged and dispersed the rebel line, which made but a faint resistance, not half so vigorous as that of the morning, and disappeared a second time over the banks.

The Confederates know nothing of this engagement, and it is not to be explained except as above, unless it was a mere stampede occasioned by the appearance of some squad of stragglers, which, lost in the woods, fired before it fled.

There was an engagement, however, which, though almost ignored by their writers, was disastrous enough to Grant's army. Pillow says :

Marks attacked the column, and the enemy after, a feeble resistance, broke and fled, in great disorder, and was hotly pursued by our troops.

In this pursuit, Marks's command was aided by the troops that had been rallied by Pillow, and by General Cheatham, who had preceded his brigade, and gave his personal assistance in this action. They assailed the Federals on both flanks, and routed them. Polk, in his report, describes this part of the field, over which he passed later, as strewed with wounded and dead.

Badeau denies any rout, and says, "The hot pursuit was after the national troops got aboard." General Grant says in his letter to his father:

There was no hasty retreating or running away. Taking into account the object of the expedition, the victory was complete.

General McClernand, with more frankness, says:

In passing through the woods, the Thirtieth, the Seventh, and the Twenty-second, encountered a heavy fire on their right and left successively, which was returned with such vigor and effect as to drive back the superior force of the enemy, and silence his firing, but not until the Seventh and Twenty-second had been thrown into temporary disorder. Here Lieutenant-Colonel Wentz, of the Seventh, and Captain Markley, of the Thirtieth, with several privates, were killed, and Colonel Dougherty, of the Twenty-second, and Major McClurken, of the Thirtieth, who was near me, were severely wounded.

General McClernand this day lost three horses.

Colonel Dougherty says :

At this time the Seventh Iowa was in rear of the Twenty-second Illinois, and was somewhat confused; all the field-officers and many of the company-officers of that brave regiment being either killed, wounded, or taken by the enemy.

Colonel Dougherty was called away ; but, after an interval, returned to this command. He continues his account thus:

On my return I found many of the Seventh Iowa considerably scattered; while cheering them up and hurrying them forward, I received a small shot in the shoulder, and one on the elbow, and shortly afterward a ball through the ankle; my horse was also shot in several places, which fell with me, and soon expired. I found myself unable to travel, and was consequently captured by the rebels, who treated me with respect and kindness.

The rear-guard of the Federals did, in fact, make a stubborn defense, and suffered severely, but were so beaten and broken that they fled into the woods. Pillow halted his men to reform, and drew them off to await the arrival of the reënforcements which had landed and were now advancing under General Polk in person. There had been delay in landing the reënforcements, and a failure to get ashore some artillery, owing to neglect of the transport to provide staging, and from the nature of the river-bank there. Polk, as soon as he got his men ashore, attempted to lead them so as to interpose them between Grant and his transports, but the haste of the retreat saved the Federal column. On coming up with Pillow, Polk ordered the pursuit to be renewed, himself taking command and directing the movement. The troops he had brought up were Smith's One Hundred and Fifty-fourth Tennessee Militia Regiment, Neeley's Fourth Tennessee, and Blythe's Mississippi Battalion. These were part of Cheatham's command. As the Confederates advanced, they found the road strewed with abandoned plunder and material of war. The hospital of the enemy was captured, with some seventy wounded. Four of the six guns lost in the morning were recovered, and one of the enemy's guns was taken. Every evidence of precipitate retreat was found.

The gunboats Taylor and Lexington, which had convoyed the transports, thrice engaged the Confederate batteries during the day, and received some shells which killed and wounded several men. The transports also found themselves within range of the batteries, and all drew off farther up the river than the point of debarkation.

When the retreating column came up, it found the small reserve already on board, and a hasty embarkation began. Before it was concluded, the whole Confederate force suddenly appeared from a cornfield, in which it had been deployed, and fronting along the river-bank, in line of battle more than a mile in length, opened a heavy fire upon the transports. The cables were cut, and the boats put off hastily, the gunboats firing, and doing what they could to cover the retreat. General Grant was one of the last on board. Sliding his horse down the bank, he went in on a plank pushed ashore for him. The boats ran the gantlet, and, when well up the river, stopped to take on board a mass of fugitives who had fled along the bank. The Confederates claimed that the slaughter on the transports was immense, and their own loss trifling. Their adversaries insisted that they themselves had met no serious loss, but that the slaughter on shore was dreadful. It is probable that the troops crowded on the transports suffered more than those in line of battle. It was sunset when the action ended.

The Confederates had on the west bank of the river that day ten regiments and a battalion, possibly 5,500 men. It has been seen that in the first engagement the Federals had the advantage of numbers and of the ground. In the second encounter, though the Confederate attack was made by only two regiments and the fragments of the routed army, and three Federal regiments were certainly engaged, yet it was upon the rear-guard of a retreating column, so that the contest was not greatly unequal. The third engagement was merely a parting salute to an escaped foe. Had Polk's force been at that landing half an hour sooner, he would probably have struck there a decisive blow.

Six hours of hard fighting had inflicted cruel losses on both sides. In Beltzhoover's battery 45 horses were killed, and all but one wounded. The Confederates lost 105 men killed, 419 wounded, and 117 missing

—total, 641 ; of whom 562 were in the five regiments originally engaged.

General Polk says in his report :

The number of prisoners taken by the enemy, as shown by their list furnished us, was 106, all of whom have returned by exchange.

After making a liberal exchange of prisoners with the enemy, 100 of their prisoners still remain in my hands, one stand of colors, and a fraction over 1,000 stand of arms, with knapsacks, ammunition, and other military stores.

The Rev. P. C. Headley, in his "Life of Grant," says, "The rebels lost 2,800 men."

Badeau says :

At Belmont, General Grant lost 485 men in killed, wounded, and missing; 125 of his wounded fell into the hands of the rebels; he carried off 175 prisoners and two guns.

General Polk, writing November 10, 1861, could not be mistaken as to the number of prisoners. The number of dead must have been much over 100 ; and, if the wounded were in any ordinary ratio to the other losses, the writer is constrained to believe that General Badeau is in error in his statement of the losses of Grant's army at Belmont. The universal testimony of those who remained masters of the field made it much greater than he sets it down.

General Grant, writing to his father soon after the battle, says:

General McClernand and myself each had our horses shot under us. Most of the field-officers met with the same loss, besides one-third of them being killed and wounded.

Pillow, in his report, says :

We buried of the enemy, 295. The enemy, under a flag of truce, were engaged at the same labor a large portion of the day. We have near 200 Federal prisoners.

Major J. D. Webster, making report to General Grant of the flag of truce sent, asking permission to bury their dead, says he had a working-party on the 9th thus employed ; and learns from the Confederate commissioner that "the number (of Federals) reported buried by them (the Confederates) on the field yesterday, was 68."

General Polk estimates the Federal loss at 1,500. Howison, a careful writer, comparing the current accounts of the day, says:

The Federal loss, as stated in their own accounts, was 607; but this is far below the truth. According to this account they had 64 killed, while it is certain more than 200 of their dead were found on the battle-field. According to the usual proportion, their total loss was probably not less than 1,200.

Those interpreters of Scripture who find in every event of their own time a fulfillment of prophecy, noted a curious verbal coincidence in the fact that the troops of Southern Illinois, popularly known as Egypt, were slain and buried by Tennessee soldiers, many of whom were recruited at Memphis: " Egypt shall gather them, and Memphis shall bury them."

Grant showed his usual bravery and coolness on the field. On the other side, Pillow displayed conspicuous gallantry, and but one of his staff escaped untouched. General Polk complimented Pillow and his officers for their courage.

A member of Taylor's battery (Federal), writing home next day,[1] tells his friend :

We returned home last night from the hardest-fought battle our troops have had since Wilson's Creek. It is the old story. We were overpowered by superior numbers and driven from the field, leaving many of our dead and dying, although we had once fairly gained the victory. . . . The whole thing was an awful " bungle."

This, possibly, may be the criticism of many a military (or non-military) reader of the varied accounts of this opening battle of the campaign.

Whatever other comment may be made, or lesson drawn from it, its story is highly honorable to the individual courage, tenacity, and intelligence, of the American soldier. Those Western troops, who, fighting forward among fallen timber, broke through a Confederate line not much weaker than their own, were no ordinary men. The shattered and routed Southerners, who, after an hour's interval, were ready to join in an irresistible charge that reversed the fortunes of the day, evinced the spirit that made them famous on so many fields. Federal and Confederate alike may look back and feel that there was nothing to be ashamed of in the fighting at Belmont.

It is, indeed, conceded by the Federal writers that the prestige of the day remained with the Confederates. Although they admit this fact, they claim that it was unjust, and that Grant and his men learned valuable lessons in warfare that day, which is doubtless true. Before the battle, General Polk, in the interests of humanity, had proposed an exchange of prisoners, to which General Grant made a haughty reply, that he recognized no " Southern Confederacy." After the battle, however, Grant had himself to send a flag of truce to reopen the negotiations he had spurned. It is believed he ever after recognized the Confederates as belligerents.

[1] " Rebellion Record," vol. iii., p. 293.

President Davis, on the 8th of November, replied to General Polk's dispatch announcing the victory of Belmont :

Your telegraph received. Accept for yourself, and the officers and men under your command, my sincere thanks for the glorious contribution you have just made to our common cause. Our countrymen must long remember gratefully the activity and skill, courage and devotion, of the army at Belmont.

J. DAVIS.

General Johnston, in General Order No. 5, after thanks and congratulations to Generals Polk and Pillow, and to the men engaged, concludes :

This was no ordinary shock of arms, it was a long and trying contest, in which our troops fought by detachments, and always against superior numbers. The 7th of November will fill a bright page in our military annals, and be remembered with gratitude by the sons and daughters of the South.

At Belmont the gallant Major Edward Butler fell mortally wounded. He was a man of splendid presence and chivalric nature, the grandson of one of " Washington's four colonels." He said to his brother, " Take my sword to my father, and tell him I died like a gentleman and a Butler."

CHAPTER XXV.

THE FALL CAMPAIGN.

IT has been seen that the early part of November was a season of hostile activity with the enemy. It was also marked by important changes in the assignment of their generals. On November 1st Major-General George B. McClellan was assigned to the chief command of the army, in place of Lieutenant-General Scott, retired. On November 9th the Department of the Cumberland was discontinued by the United States War Department, and the Department of the Ohio constituted, embracing the States of Ohio, Michigan, Indiana, Kentucky (east of the Cumberland River), and Tennessee ; and Brigadier-General D. C. Buell was assigned to its command, which he assumed November 15th.[1] At the same time General H. W. Halleck superseded Fremont in command of the Department of the West. Sherman was removed from Kentucky, and sent to report to Halleck. His memoirs evince that he left Kentucky in disappointment and bitterness of spirit, and deeply distrusted by his Government—a distrust which it required all the great political influence of his family to remove.

Buell, Sherman's successor, had sterling qualities—integrity, ability, and a high sense of the soldierly calling. He had a fine faculty for organization, improved by long training as an assistant adjutant-gen-

---

[1] "Army of the Cumberland," vol. i., p. 46.

eral. He was càlm and resolute, and a formidable antagonist for any general. Much of the subsequent efficiency of that army was due to the share Buell had in its formation.

It was to General Johnston's advantage that Buell knew him only as an officer cautious and provident in military conduct, and that he could not presume him to have taken such risks as he did. It happens to be within the writer's knowledge that General Johnston regarded what he conceived to be Buell's opinion of him as one of the considerations to be weighed in determining his own course of action.

The camp at Bowling Green was a city of refuge for Kentuckians whose sense of duty forced them to side with the South in the pending contest. When Buckner entered Kentucky, in the middle of September, the Union leaders and the United States military authorities feared greatly an immediate revolt of the State-rights party. Breckinridge was counseling the people, but with his usual prudence, to organize against encroachments on their State-rights. William Preston and Humphrey Marshall, with more vehemence, were urging them to measures of resistance. Southern sympathizers everywhere denounced the fraud which had been practised in the name of neutrality. A dangerous excitement existed, which, if left longer, might have produced serious results. But the propitious moment had long passed when successful revolt was possible in Kentucky. The time had come when the Federal Government could give the final blow to the cherished doctrine of neutrality, and it did not hesitate at stern measures of repression, altogether alien to American ideas. It took its warrant in its fears.

On September 19th Hon. Charles A. Morehead, a man eminent for character and ability, was seized at his home, near Louisville, and, without warrant of law, was hurried off to prison in Boston Harbor. Morehead had been Governor of the Commonwealth, and the intimate friend of Clay. Though a strong sympathizer with the South, he had been conservative and opposed to disunion. His arrest gave a great shock in Kentucky, in proportion to its rude lawlessness. It evinced that in war the laws are silent, and that no bulwark was left against the terrorism of brute force. On the same night, Reuben T. Durrett, formerly editor of the Louisville *Courier*, and Martin W. Barr, of the telegraph-office, were arrested; and these arrests were rapidly followed by others, of aged, wealthy, and eminent citizens, who were carried off to captivity in the free States. On the same day, September 19th, Colonel Bramlette, with his command, reached Lexington, to arrest Breckinridge, Preston, and other Southern-rights men. But these received timely intimation of their danger, and escaped. Humphrey Marshall, George B. Hodge, John S. Williams, Haldeman and McKee, of the *Courier*, and many other Southern sympathizers, warned by these events, or by secret friendly messages, also found their way to the Confederate lines.

These fugitives resorted either to Richmond or to Bowling Green, according to the direction of their escape, or for other reasons. Breckinridge, after a short stay in Richmond, went to Bowling Green, where, on October 8th, he issued a noble and stirring address to the people of Kentucky. It recites the causes that drove so many loyal and patriotic citizens into that attitude of armed resistance to the United States Government which Northern people are pleased to call rebellion. The writer would be glad to embody this address here, but space does not permit. It may be found in the " Rebellion Record," vol. iii., page 254. In concluding his address, Breckinridge used this language :

For those who, denied by the Legislature the protection due to the humblest citizen, have been delivered over to the tender mercies of foreign mercenaries, and hunted like partridges on the mountains, what remains, but imprisonment, exile, or resistance? As one of them, I intend to resist. I will avoid conflict with Kentuckians, except in necessary self-defense, but I will unite with my fellow-citizens to resist the invaders who have driven us from our homes. To this course we are impelled by the highest sense of duty and the irresistible instincts of manhood. To defend your birthright and mine, which is more precious than domestic ease, or property, or life, I exchange, with proud satisfaction, a term of six years in the Senate of the United States for the musket of a soldier.

Breckinridge returned to Richmond soon after issuing this address. He was appointed a brigadier-general, and sent to General Johnston, who assigned him to the command of the Kentucky Brigade, November 14th. We here behold a man, who had lately been Vice-President and a candidate for President, exchanging the senatorial rank for the command of a little band of exiles, in obedience to principle ; and this they call treason !

In Breckinridge's eloquent peroration, quoted above, there was an antithesis that struck agreeably on the popular ear. A friend has sent the writer a shrewd remark of General Johnston in regard to it. To one inquiring of him what had become of Breckinridge, he replied, " He has gone to Richmond *to get his musket.*"

General Johnston set a high value, however, on the talents as well as the prestige of Breckinridge. His calmness and reticence, his manly courtesy and high courage, his good judgment and tenacity, not less than more striking qualities, commended him to his commander. Hence General Johnston gave him exceptional opportunities for distinction, and on his own last great day at Shiloh gave him a corps to command, with which Breckinridge made a record that fixed his reputation as a soldier.

Besides Breckinridge and others who entered the army, many civilians had gathered at Bowling Green. Some of these were men of mark in the State ; very many had a local importance that pointed them out

to the vengeance of the Federal Government, and almost all were em-
bittered by exile, disappointment, and wounded patriotism. They saw
the recreant Legislature registering orders from military headquarters
as legislative acts against them, which, if impotent, were yet insulting
—a burlesque on law-making—statutes for divorce from their wives,
statutes threatening the penitentiary as a penalty, statutes condemning
them to death. It was suggested that a provisional government, representing the Southern outlawed element of the people, would serve as a
rallying-point for Confederate sentiment, and give color of legality to
many things necessary to be done.

The plan of a provisional government was privately proposed to
General Johnston, and the leaders of the movement were much astonished and disappointed to find that he disapproved of it. In fact, though
he could not make known to them his reasons, he already contemplated
the contingency of being driven from the State, and foresaw the aggra-
vated force with which this disappointment would react on Kentuckians,
and he did not desire the additional embarrassment of the perambulating
pageant of a State government on wheels. Hence he offered such discouragement as he could to the project, without taking any open or
active stand against it ; recognizing indeed, too, the good side of the
scheme. It was not possible to arrest the movement without an ungra-
cious thwarting of men ardent in the cause of the South and devoted
to its interests. Hence it was gradually determined, from the various
motives that control men under such circumstances, to establish the
provisional government.

A conference was held at Russellville, October 29th, in accordance
with previous notice, which was numerously attended, and over which
presided Henry C. Burnett, who had retired from the United States
Congress. Resolutions were passed, denouncing the United States
Government and the State government, and recommending that a convention should meet November 18th. Accordingly, a convention, irregularly chosen, it is true, and professedly revolutionary, met on November 18th at Russellville. Henry C. Burnett again presided, and Robert
McKee was secretary. An ordinance of secession was passed, and a
provisional government was set up, with a Governor and ten council-
men of ample powers, including authority to negotiate a treaty with
the Confederate States, and to elect Senators and Representatives to
its Congress.

The Governor elected by the convention was George W. Johnson,
of Scott County. He was a nephew of Richard M. Johnson, who had
been Vice-President under Van Buren, and belonged to a numerous,
wealthy, and powerful connection, in Kentucky and the South. George
W. Johnson was of a very lofty and noble nature. He was impetuous
and sensitive, and his impassioned temperament sometimes warped the

correctness of his judgment ; but his talents were fine, his impulses generous, and his ideas of public duty very high. He had received an excellent education, and had acted as a professor of mathematics in his youth. He was fond of reading, and had both wealth and culture. Dispensing liberal hospitality, he yet practised for himself a total abstinence from all liquors. He was a friend of General Johnston, and personally every way acceptable to him. Much beloved by the Kentuckians in life, his self-sacrifice and heroic death endeared to them his memory.

An act had been passed by the Confederate Government, August 28th, appropriating a million dollars to aid Kentucky in repelling invasion. It was five or six months too late. Employed early enough, it might have been a fair offset to the millions used in the State by the United States Government. By an act of Congress, approved December 10th, Kentucky was " admitted a member of the Confederate States of America on an equal footing with the other States of this Confederacy."

On November 11th a large Dahlgren gun burst at Columbus, killing Captain Reiter, Lieutenant Snowden, and five gunners. General Polk was injured, the shock producing deafness, sickness, and great nervous prostration, which lasted several weeks. In the mean time his duties devolved on General Pillow. Polk offered his resignation, which was declined. He wrote to General Johnston, November 28th, " I have waived my resignation, as Davis seems very much opposed to it, and shall endeavor to do my duty."

A reference to Chapter XXII. will show that General Johnston was earnestly striving to raise troops during November and December, and it was about this time, November 19th, that he called on Tennessee, Mississippi, and Alabama, to furnish him militia, using the most urgent appeals.

On the 27th of November he wrote the Secretary of War, reporting a continued increase of the enemy's force, which had augmented in his front to thirty-seven regiments. The rest of the letter is as follows :

I suppose a change of the plan of operations has been made, and that the force intended for East Tennessee will now be combined with the force on this line, making an aggregate strength of probably more than 50,000 men to be arrayed against my forces here.

If the forces of the enemy are manœuvred as I think they may be, I may be compelled to retire from this place to cover Nashville with the aid of the volunteer force now being organized, which could in that way be brought in coöperation.

It is understood that General Halleck, who will command at Columbus, and General Buell, who is in command on this line, will make a simultaneous attack.

I doubt if Buell will make a serious attack on my position here. I hope he may. I have requested General Crittenden to send a portion of his force to

Nashville, if in his judgment it can be done without weakening his force too much. . . .

We still have a great many sick, but the measles which so afflicted our troops spreads much more slowly. The workmen of the enemy are rebuilding the railroad-bridge over Green River.

At daybreak, on the 4th of December, a body of forty or fifty Federal Home Guards, under Captain Netter, attacked Whippoorwill Bridge, five or six miles from Russellville, on the railroad from Bowling Green to Memphis. It was guarded by a detail of thirteen men from the Ninth Kentucky Infantry (Confederate). All were asleep, except four on guard. These fired on the assailants, with effect, as was supposed. A volley was returned, which killed two and wounded another of the guard. The rest, being surrounded, surrendered. The enemy then set fire to the bridge, but left too hurriedly to do it much damage. Some of the prisoners escaped.

On the 6th of December Captain John H. Morgan, with 105 men, crossed Green River, near Munfordsville, and made a dash on Bacon Creek railroad-bridge, which was within the enemy's lines, and had just been rebuilt. This he burned and utterly destroyed, and then returned to his camp without loss.

John H. Morgan was the captain of a volunteer company in the Kentucky State Guard, at Lexington. His brother-in-law, Basil W. Duke, had been prominent in St. Louis as a secessionist before the discomfiture of his party there. He then came to Kentucky, and entered Morgan's company as a lieutenant. Both became brigadier-generals during the war. It was a question among Confederates which of the two was the more excellent as a partisan leader. In truth, both had the qualities that make success in this form of warfare—audacity, wariness, enterprise, and unfailing resources. Morgan lost his life in the war, and his friend and comrade became his biographer. Duke's "Life of Morgan," without any attempt at art, has the rare merit of combining truth and picturesqueness in narration. It is the work of an intelligent soldier and an honest gentleman.

When Bramlette invaded Lexington, Morgan secured his arms and got away with his company on the 20th of September. He was joined at Bardstown by Captain Wickliffe's company, and they reached Buckner in safety on the 30th of September. Morgan was soon put in command of a squadron, composed of his own company, Captain Bowles's, and Captain Allen's, and did excellent service on outpost duty, getting here the training that afterward made him famous. It has already been mentioned that seven regiments of Kentucky infantry were recruited at Bowling Green during the autumn of 1861, though some of them were feeble in numbers.

To carry out General Johnston's designs already indicated, and for the special purpose of breaking up the railroad south of Woodsonville, General Hindman moved on that place, December 17th, with 1,100 infantry, 250 cavalry, and four pieces of artillery. Woodsonville is the railroad-station on the south bank of Green River, and was occupied by Willich's Thirty-second Indiana Regiment. Willich seems to have been an officer of merit; and his regiment of Germans, commanded in this affair by Lieutenant-Colonel Von Trebra, showed soldierly qualities. Having lost some pickets a few days before, they were on the alert; and, on the approach of Hindman, threw out some companies as skirmishers. The Federal advance was in force on the north bank. The south bank was fringed with timber, in front of which were open fields, bordered by another forest. Through this Hindman advanced almost to the edge of the opening; but halted, while still concealed in the woods, three-quarters of a mile from the river.

Von Trebra's skirmishers were driven in by a volley. Hindman's purpose was to decoy the Federals up the hill, out of range of the enemy's batteries, where he could employ his infantry and artillery against them; and he gave Colonel Terry orders to that effect. The Confederate cavalry were chiefly used as flankers, watching the fords. But Terry took seventy-five of his Rangers, and fell upon a body of the enemy, said in their account to be a company, deployed as skirmishers. When he found himself in front of a foe, Terry's fierce and impetuous courage, trained in the border warfare of the West, broke through the rules of prudence. The spirit of combat was upon him; and, charging with half a dozen comrades in advance, he rushed upon the squads, or "nests," as he called them, who were rallying by fours, using his revolver with deadly effect. Bursting upon one of these "nests," he killed two Germans, when he was himself slain by a ball through the brain. A companion instantly avenged his death. The Federals fled to the shelter of their guns, and the Texans bore the dead body of their chief from the field. Thus fell a fearless leader.

McCook now began to send over troops to the support of Von Trebra; and, after some further skirmishing and artillery-practice, the firing ceased on both sides. The opponents remained awhile in observation; when Hindman, having accomplished the chief purposes of his demonstration, and finding that nothing more was to be done without drawing upon himself the whole weight of the Federal force, which he did not desire, slowly withdrew without being followed. His loss was four killed and ten wounded, all from Terry's regiment except two slightly wounded in Marmaduke's battalion. The Federal loss was ten killed, twenty-two wounded, and eight prisoners.

The Texan Rangers had been allowed, at their own request, to report to General Johnston. Terry was his personal friend. They had since been very actively and usefully employed on this front; but in this, their first engagement, they had the misfortune to lose their colonel. They left Houston 1,160 strong, and were augmented during their term of service by 500 recruits; they shared in more than one hundred engagements from first to last ; and finally surrendered, at the close of the war, 244 men in all, with but *one* deserter during that time ! This is a noble record ; but their fame was dearly bought with the blood of most of these peerless horsemen, who, following the example of their chivalric leader, rode gayly and dauntlessly down to death.

In the second week in October a cavalry battalion of eight companies was organized at Memphis, of which Nathan Bedford Forrest was elected lieutenant-colonel. It was soon after increased to a regiment. Both this command and its leader were greatly distinguished during the war. Forrest's biography[1] has been written, and his exploits are well known. He was a man whose indomitable energy and eager spirit would have won distinction in any active vocation. Without the aid of influence or education, he had achieved wealth and local power in time of peace. Without military training, or special advantages, he became famous in a four years' war as a bold and enterprising trooper, and a formidable soldier wherever he crossed swords.

Forrest was forty years of age when the war broke out. Determined to raise a cavalry command, he ventured to Louisville, Kentucky, after the battle of Manassas, and with his own money bought and brought away the arms and equipments requisite to put them in the field. His eight companies numbered 650 men, Alabamians, Tennesseeans, Kentuckians, and Texans—a mixed command. They rendezvoused at Fort Donelson late in October, and, moving thence to Hopkinsville, were thrown forward, about the middle of November, by General Tilghman, commanding there, to observe the section between the Green and Cumberland Rivers.

Major Kelly, with one squadron, traversed the country to the Ohio River, where he captured a supply-transport, well loaded. Having rejoined Forrest, they attacked the Federal gunboat Conestoga at Canton Landing. The novel sight was there witnessed of a fight between cavalry and a gunboat ; the latter belching thunders from nine heavy guns, the former rattling her iron sides with a four-pounder and showers of Minié-balls. Little damage was done on either side ; and, after six hours' firing, the gunboat retired.

Forrest was almost constantly on picket until the 28th of December, when he had a heavy skirmish at Sacramento, which further encouraged the Confederates. General T. L. Crittenden was reported at Calhoun, on the north bank of Green River, with a large force, and with designs looking to an advance. General Johnston ordered a cavalry reconnaissance, and Forrest moved, December 26th, with 300 men,

---

[1] "Life of General N. B. Forrest," by Colonel Thomas Jordan.

over muddy, icy roads, toward Greenville, which he reached on the 28th. Learning, about eight miles beyond Greenville, that some 400 or 500 Federal cavalry were not far off, Forrest went forward rapidly along the heavy roads to overtake them. Near the village of Sacramento, a young girl, full of patriotic ardor, galloped down to point out to the Southerners the enemy's position.

When Forrest overtook the rear-guard of the Federal cavalry, his dash of thirty miles had left him but 150 men. He drove the rear-guard into the village where the Federals had posted themselves. Charging up, he found the enemy too strong for his jaded and scattered command, and retired to reform it. The elated Federals took heart, and, leaving their vantage-ground, followed him. But Forrest, by this time reënforced by the arrival of many stragglers, turned upon his pursuers, routed them, and chased them pell-mell from the field for three miles. In this hot pursuit Forrest was among the foremost ; and is said, single-handed, to have engaged three adversaries at once, killing a trooper, mortally wounding Captain Bacon, and overthrowing and capturing Captain Davis. The story is not improbable, as his personal prowess was extraordinary. Forrest's report puts the Federal loss at sixty-five killed and thirty-five wounded and captured ; including a captain and lieutenant killed, and a captain and lieutenant wounded. Captain Albert Bacon was from Frankfort, Kentucky, and his courage and soldierly conduct are noticed by Forrest. On the Confederate side the chivalric Captain Meriweather and private Terry were killed, and three privates wounded.

Forrest returned to Hopkinsville, and was employed in routine duty until January 10, 1862. He then made another reconnaissance toward Green River, where he found a heavy Federal force, and, in returning, burned the bridges over Pond River, a tributary of Green River. When General Clark retired from Hopkinsville to Clarksville, February 7th, Forrest covered his retreat. Thence he went to Fort Donelson, in time to take part in the defence there.

The following letters to the Secretary of War explain the situation in Kentucky in December. It will be remembered that it was at the date of the second of these letters, Christmas-day, that General Johnston addressed his energetic appeal for aid to the Southern Governors:

HEADQUARTERS, WESTERN DEPARTMENT, }
BOWLING GREEN, *December* 8, 1861. }

SIR: The enemy, from the best information I am able to obtain, have made no material change in the disposition of their forces in front or on either flank. Their advance in front is six miles north of Bàcon Creek, near the Louisville Railroad, a large force at Nolin, and, farther north, toward Louisville, they are massed in considerable force at different points convenient for concentrating them. I do not doubt that the Federal Government is augmenting their force in Kentucky in this direction to the extent of their ability.

The inclosed letter will serve to show the disposition they are making of different army corps, which have been elsewhere employed. As to the estimate of their forces, I suppose it is a gross exaggeration. With the addition of Nelson's and Rosecrans's columns their force on this immediate line I believe ought not to be estimated over 65,000 men.

Our returns at this place show a force of between 18,000 and 19,000, of which about 5,000 are sick (about 3,600 at Nashville), and our effective force is under 13,000 men.

The volunteers, I hear, are turning out well, but the time taken up in procuring arms has thus far prevented much accession to our force from that source. . . .

To the Hon. J. P. Benjamin, Secretary of War.

HEADQUARTERS, WESTERN DEPARTMENT, }
BOWLING GREEN, *December* 25, 1861. }

SIR : The recent movement of the enemy, and the concentration of heavy masses of troops, indicated an early advance; and the weather, which has been unusually fine, resembling the fall rather than winter, rendered it probable that a battle would be fought in this vicinity.

Information from various sources shows that every effort has been made by General Buell to concentrate all his strength for a movement upon Tennessee through Central Kentucky, and that not less than 75,000 men are assembled in front of me, while I have not more than 17,000 men for active operations.

After a careful examination, I have found the line of the Barren River the only good defensible one between Green River and Nashville. Bowling Green, from its topography, is naturally a strong position, and gives command over Central Kentucky, south of Green River, and has easy communication by railroad and turnpike to Nashville. Its local advantages for defense are good, though requiring a large force for that purpose, as it is situated in an amphitheatre of some extent. The place has been strengthened by good defensive works, requiring about 4,000 men for their defense, and to be supported by a large force. I have, as a further precaution, ordered intrenchments to be thrown up, under the direction of my chief-engineer, Major Gilmer, at Nashville. These arrangements are such that they perhaps double the efficiency of my force for the defense of this line.

The enemy have recently reconstructed the bridge between Green River and Louisville, and have thrown forward a strong advance to Woodsonville, with which Terry's cavalry had a successful rencounter on the 17th instant, in which we had the misfortune to lose the gallant leader of it. These forces, in heavy masses, are stationed at Woodsonville, Bacon Creek, Nolin, etc. There is also a corps of about 6,000 men at Columbia, which is being rapidly reënforced. There is another considerable force at Lebanon, at the terminus of the Louisville Railroad, and another at Somerset. The banks of Green River from Munfordsville down are unoccupied, as the country is quite rugged, except by a force under General T. L. Crittenden.

These dispositions of their troops are in accordance with information received from various sources, and lead to the belief that a forward movement will very soon be made in this direction ; but, at present, I can only conjecture whether they will make their attack here, or turn my right, or, relying upon their superiority of numbers, attempt both at the same time. If Floyd's brigade, from Virginia, and Bowen's division, *en route* from Columbus, reach here as I expect in a few days, they will be compelled to attack me here with my force thus considerably increased. I do not think they will attempt to turn my position.

General Hindman, with his brigade of Hardee's division, is at Bell's, on the railroad and pike, with Swett's battery; his front is covered with the Texas and Arkansas Cavalry. Breckinridge, with his brigade of Buckner's division, is at Oakland, ten miles in rear of Hindman's, with Morgan's cavalry, in the direction of Brownsville. Helm, with his regiment of Kentucky Cavalry, has been ordered back to Skegg's Creek bridge and the Barren bridge, on the route from Scottsville to Glasgow. His scouts keep the country under observation toward Woodsonville and Columbia. Should the enemy move in force on this route, the bridge across the Barren and other streams toward Glasgow will be burned. The remainder of the divisions of Hardee and Buckner, and the sixty days' State troops from Mississippi, recently arrived, under the command of Major-General R. Davis, are stationed here—my whole force amounting, as before remarked, to 17,000 men.

A brigade, under General Clark, is posted at Hopkinsville, to guard against the movements of the enemy on the Lower Green River toward Clarksville, and to follow their movements should they attempt to coöperate with the movements of the enemy in my front; his force should be much greater for these purposes.

The measures adopted at Columbus render that place comparatively secure from any immediate attempt of the enemy.

The position of General Zollicoffer on the Cumberland holds in check the meditated invasion and hoped-for revolt in East Tennessee, but I can neither order Zollicoffer to join me here, nor withdraw any more force from Columbus, without imperiling our communications toward Richmond, or endangering Tennessee and the Mississippi Valley. This I have resolved not to do, but have chosen, on the contrary, to post my inadequate force in such a manner as to hold the enemy in check, guard the frontier, and hold the Barren till the winter terminates the campaign; or, if any fault in his movements is committed, or his line become exposed where his force is developed, to attack him as opportunity offers.

If the campaign closes without any striking success to their arms, and without any impression on our territory, the North must shrink disheartened from the contest, and, with embarrassed relations if not hostile attitude toward England, the first step toward our independence is gained. The contest here must be relinquished for the winter by the enemy, or a decisive blow soon struck; to make the latter is their true policy. . . .

To the Hon. J. P. BENJAMIN, Secretary of War.

On the 23d of December the office and storehouse of the Ordnance Department at Nashville were set on fire by an incendiary, and entirely consumed. "The loss was heavy: between 400 and 600 sets of artillery-harness, 10,000 to 12,000 sets of accoutrements and equipments for infantry, 300 cavalry-saddles, 2,000,000 percussion-caps, 6,000 friction-primers, besides numerous other articles of supply." [1]

[1] Report of Lieutenant-Colonel M. H. Wright, December 23, 1861.

The following little anecdote is furnished by a friend, as an illustration of General Johnston's natural fitness for command, and quiet mode of self-assertion. It was related to him by a gallant Louisiana colonel:

"In the days around Bowling Green," said ——, "I was in command of the —— Louisiana Cavalry, and was required to picket over an extensive district. The work was onerous, and I became restive under it, and made several requests and suggestions with the view to being relieved; none of which, however, were approved. Feeling myself aggrieved, and not having yet acquired even the small modicum of discipline which later on we learned, I determined to call at headquarters and state my grievances in person. As I entered the general's tent, I saw a tall, soldierly man writing, with his back to me. Full of my own consequence and fancied wrongs, I broke forth, 'I would like to know, General Johnston, why all my suggestions and recommendations are over-slaughed or treated with silent contempt?' Looking around, with due deliberation, he quietly asked, 'Was your remark addressed to me, sir?' Fortunately," added ——, "there was a camp-stool convenient, into which I dropped, *membra dejecta*, as if a Minié had struck me. The truth flashed across me, as if by intuition, that I was in the presence of the greatest man in the world, and first impressions were confirmed by subsequent intercourse. The first was the last time that ever I essayèd 'to beard the lion in his den, the Douglas in his hall.'"

Another friend has related to me the following incident as occurring at Bowling Green:

A distinguished Tennessee politician called on General Johnston, and requested him to make a contract with parties in Nashville for the manufacture of spears, with a billhook or sickle attached to the head, with which foot-soldiers could attack cavalry, the sickle to be used in cutting the bridle-reins and pulling the troopers from their horses. He also demanded General Johnston's opinion on the plan. General Johnston endeavored to avoid a discussion of the merits of the plan for which the gentleman was warmly enlisted, by assuring him that it was a matter for the Ordnance Department to decide, and by referring him to that bureau. But the petitioner would take no denial, repeating and reiterating the merits of his "plan." General Johnston could only adhere to his original suggestion. At last the gentleman made a sarcastic allusion to "red-tape," when General Johnston asked him, "What do you think the Federal horsemen would be doing with their revolvers, while our spearmen were trying to cut their bridle-reins?" But, though there was no sufficient answer to this question, gentlemen of this class are not to be satisfied with such considerations, and he left, convinced of the red-tape of headquarters.

CHAPTER XXVI.

BATTLE OF FISHING CREEK.

THE movement of the Federal army, which had been frustrated in November, was renewed with better success early in January. General Johnston was now confronted by Halleck in the West, and by Buell in Kentucky. With the exception of the army sent under Curtis against Price in Southwestern Missouri, about 12,000 strong, the whole resources of the Northwest, from Pennsylvania to the Plains, were turned against General Johnston's lines in Kentucky. Halleck, with armies at Cairo and Paducah, under Grant and C. F. Smith, threatened equally Columbus, the key of the Mississippi River, and the water-lines of the Cumberland and Tennessee, with their defenses at Forts Donelson and Henry. Buell's right wing also menaced Donelson and Henry, while his centre was directed against Bowling Green, and his left was advancing against Zollicoffer at Mill Spring on the Upper Cumberland. If this last-named position could be forced, the way seemed open to East Tennessee by either the Jacksboro or the Jamestown routes, on the one hand, and to Nashville on the other. At the northeastern corner of Kentucky there was a Federal force, under Colonel Garfield, of Ohio, opposed to Humphrey Marshall's command. Here it was that the fighting first began again.

General Johnston had requested Marshall to send him a regiment, but Marshall replied that " to send him a single man was to risk the ruin of his whole command ; " so that the matter was dropped. Marshall had nearly 3,200 men in the district under his command, including 350 enlisted for special service in Virginia, who would not leave that State, and were, therefore, retained at Pound Gap ; but all of his troops were not available. Humphrey Marshall was the grandson of one of the earliest Senators from Kentucky, a cousin of Chief-Justice Marshall. He was a graduate of West Point, and had served in the Black-Hawk War, and afterward as a colonel of Kentucky volunteer cavalry in the Mexican War, and at Buena Vista had won distinction. He was a very vigorous and able lawyer, a shrewd politician, and a man of wit, humor, acumen, and judgment. In fact, his mind was essentially judicial. The writer has rarely known any man who impressed him so strongly in this regard. But he was not a man of action. Besides, his unwieldy size, weighing as he did some 300 or 350 pounds, unfitted him for the field.

Marshall moved forward to Paintsville, on the Big Sandy River, about

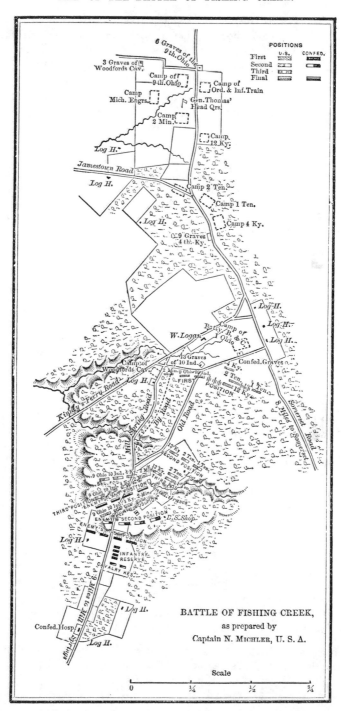

BATTLE OF FISHING CREEK,
as prepared by
Captain N. MICHLER, U. S. A.

Scale

the middle of December. This place was thirty-three miles above Louisa, and sixty from the Ohio River. At and near the mouth of the Big Sandy, and in the intervening region, were clustered some half-dozen towns of from 1,000 to 5,000 inhabitants each. The industries supporting this population were chiefly the working of coal and iron, with capital furnished by Ohio men. Hence, the people were generally hostile to the South. Marshall's force, when he reached Paintsville, was 2,240 in number; but his effectives were only 1,967 on January 3, 1862. The following is his force in detail :

Triggs's Fifty-fourth Virginia Regiment	578
Williams's Kentucky Regiment	594
Moore's Twenty-ninth Virginia Regiment	327
Simms's Mounted Battalion	360
Jeffries's battery (four guns)	58
Worsham's company	50
Total	1,967

This force was still further reduced to about 1,600 effectives, by mumps and measles, before the engagement with the enemy.

About the same time that Marshall advanced into Kentucky, Buell organized an expedition up the Big Sandy, under Colonel J. A. Garfield. This officer moved up that river, on December 22d, with the Forty-second Ohio Regiment, the Fourteenth Kentucky, and McLaughlin's battalion of Ohio Cavalry, about 1,500 strong. After delaying a week at George's Creek, he passed on to Paintsville. He was reënforced by Bolles's West Virginia Cavalry, 300 men, and by 300 men of the Twenty-second Kentucky Regiment. While this column was moving up the Big Sandy, another, consisting of the Fortieth Ohio Regiment and three battalions of Wolford's cavalry, advanced from Mount Sterling to take Marshall in the rear. To avoid this danger, Marshall fell back some fifteen miles, and took position on Middle Creek, near Preston-burg. On the 3d of January the Confederates captured a sergeant and three men of McLaughlin's cavalry, with their horses, in front of Paints-ville. On January 7th Bolles's cavalry engaged the Confederate cavalry-pickets, with a loss of two or three on each side.

On the 9th of January Garfield advanced against Marshall's position at Prestonburg, and on the next day attacked him. The engagement was not a serious one. Garfield reported that he fought all day, engaging only about 900 of his own men, inflicting a heavy loss on the Confederates, and losing only one man killed and twenty wounded. Garfield's report claimed a victory. He says :

At half-past four o'clock he (Marshall) ordered a retreat. My men drove him down the slopes of the hills, and at five o'clock he had been driven from every point.

He also claimed to have captured stores of value. On the next day, however, Garfield retired, and fell back to Paintsville.

General Marshall's report, made to General Johnston, differs radically from this. Writing from his camp in Letcher County, January 23d, he says :

GENERAL: Since I last wrote, the enemy assailed me in largely superior force, and was effectually and gallantly repulsed by the troops under my command. My loss in the action of the 10th of January is accurately stated at ten killed and fourteen wounded. The loss of the enemy was severe.

Garfield had stated that he captured one captain and twenty-five soldiers. Marshall in his report replies to this that the captain was a sick man, too ill for removal, and that the prisoners were not soldiers, but citizens—

who have been running ever since the war began like frightened hares—afraid to take arms, afraid to offer a single effort of resistance—and who, if pressed to it, would submit to have their ears cropped to show they have a master.

The report continues :

The firing was kept up, with some intervals, for about four hours, and was, occasionally, very sharp and spirited. My troops behaved remarkably well, had decided advantage in the situation, and maintained it throughout the day. . . . The enemy did not move me from any one position I assumed, and at nightfall withdrew from the field, leaving me just where I was in the morning. After he had withdrawn, I called my troops down from the hills, and pursued the march which I was executing when the enemy came in sight.

I see by the telegraphic dispatches that the enemy represents his achievement of a victory over me upon the occasion to which I am referring, and says that my troops fled in confusion, etc. I state that this is not only false, but it is an after-thought. . . . He came to attack, yet came so cautiously that my left wing never fired a shot, and he never came up sufficiently to engage my centre or left wing. His force was fired upon by the twelve-pounder howitzer, and at once cleared my front; but, concealed by a point of the hills from my artillery, confined his further efforts to assaults upon my right wing, by which he was repulsed three times.

General Marshall goes on to state that he sent forward Trigg's regiment ; but the enemy withdrew, and did not dispute the ground on which the fight had taken place :

The repulse was final. It proved final, for he has never since that day sought in any manner or form to reëngage.

Garfield is said to have fallen back fifteen miles to Paintsville ; Marshall, seven miles, where he remained two days at the foot of a lofty mountain. He then slowly pursued his retreat. He informed General

Johnston that he could not advance with less than 5,000 men; and he could not procure subsistence in the mountains for the men he had. He then fell back, through Pound Gap, into Virginia. Thus Marshall's report is a denial and a contradiction, general and specific, of Garfield's report ; and, as it is impossible to reconcile the discrepancies between them, the reader is left to draw his own conclusion.

While Garfield was at Paintsville, he was ordered by General Buell to advance, and got as far as Piketon in February. A month later, he advanced to Pound Gap, with 600 infantry and 100 cavalry ; and, having displayed himself in force there, returned down the Big Sandy, without an engagement, and was withdrawn, with his forces, to another theatre of action.

General Felix Kirk Zollicoffer, who commanded the corps in Eastern Kentucky, was the popular idol of the hour in Tennessee, and on many accounts deservedly so. He was of a Swiss family, of knightly rank, settled in North Carolina before the Revolutionary War, in which his grandfather was a captain. His father was a prosperous farmer in Maury County, Tennessee, where Zollicoffer was born May 19, 1812. He began life as a printer, and in 1835 was elected Printer for the State. After several essays in journalism, he became editor of the *Republican Banner* in 1842, and was noted as a champion of the Whig party. He was then elected Controller of the State, which position he held until 1847. In 1848 he was elected a State Senator, and in 1852 a Representative in the United States Congress, to which position he was reëlected. When war seemed almost inevitable, he was elected by the General Assembly of Tennessee as a commissioner to the Peace Congress, from which he returned dejected by its failure to accomplish any useful purpose. Governor Harris offered to appoint him a major-general ; but he would only accept the place of brigadier, on account of his inexperience.[1]

It, however, fell to General Zollicoffer's lot to command a separate army. No man could have brought a more unselfish devotion or a braver heart to the task; but talents which might have rendered the highest services on another arena were here neutralized by want of adaptation to the particular work in hand. What he might have accomplished as a commander, under more favorable circumstances, it is hard to estimate. He certainly had, however, exceptional difficulties to contend with of every possible description ; and the tests to which he was subjected might well have overborne native ability of a high order, if unversed in the habits and knowledge of the camp. But the habits of Zollicoffer's entire life and thought had been bent not only into a different, but into an opposite direction. He could not drill a squad

---

[1] These facts are taken from a spirited sketch in *Ware's Valley Monthly* (April, 1876), by General Marcus J. Wright.

himself, nor was his brigade ever drilled or put in line of battle by anybody. Though he had a splendid courage, and traits that endeared him to his troops, the cast of his mind was no more military than his training. But he was a good, brave, noble, patriotic man ; and his memory deserves well of his country.

It will be remembered that General Zollicoffer, having fortified the gaps of the Cumberland Range, had moved westward, under instructions from General Johnston, with the view of taking position where he could command the approaches toward both East Tennessee and Nashville from Central Kentucky; while, at the same time, he might, to some extent, protect the right of the position at Bowling Green. The lack of telegraphic communication, and the wretched character of the roads, made any rapid correspondence, much more any effective coöperation, almost impossible. Still, Zollicoffer could not be drawn in nearer to Bowling Green, without laying open to the enemy a choice of roads into East Tennessee. General Johnston desired to place Zollicoffer, with his limited supplies and half-disciplined troops, in observation merely, until such time as he could reënforce his army or incorporate it with the main body under his own command.

As Zollicoffer proceeded north, through Jamestown, Tennessee, and Albany, Kentucky, he reported that the country in Tennessee was sterile and unproductive ; while Wayne and Clinton Counties, and part of Pulaski County, in Kentucky, were comparatively abundant in forage and subsistence. The Cumberland River, making a big bend to the north from Cumberland Ford, describes almost a semicircle before it enters Tennessee, near Martinsburg. At one of its most advanced salients to the north is Mill Springs, on the south bank of the river. Zollicoffer describes this point as commanding the converging roads from Somerset and Columbia, as in a fertile and well-stocked country, with provisions plenty and cheap, and as possessing the advantage of a grist and saw mill, which would aid materially in supplying food for his army and lumber for huts. He stated that there was plenty of wood and water, and that the position was capable of easy defense. Already, on the 24th of November, before he reached Albany on his march, he had been warned by snow, succeeding the cold rains, that winter was at hand.

On November 30th, Zollicoffer, writing from Mill Springs, tells General Johnston that his cavalry had failed to seize the ferry-boats on the river ; but that he is " preparing to provide the means of crossing the river." He also says, " So soon as it is possible, I will cross the river in force." But it was not clear from the context whether he was going to cross for a lodgment, or merely on an expedition to harass the enemy.

General Johnston had written a letter to General Zollicoffer, on

December 4th, approving entirely of every one of his moves so far, and informing him of the steps taken to send him supplies, etc. He adds:

The most essential route to be guarded is that leading through Somerset and Monticello, as, in my opinion, most practicable for the enemy.

On the same day, General Johnson wrote again, using this language:

Mill Springs would seem to answer best to all the demands of the service; and from this point you may be able to observe the river, *without crossing it*, as far as Burkesville, which is desirable.

On the 9th of December Zollicoffer informed General Johnston that he had crossed the Cumberland that day, with five infantry regiments, seven cavalry companies, and four pieces of artillery, about two-thirds of his whole force, which in all reached less than 6,000 effectives. On December 10th he wrote again:

Your two dispatches of the 4th reached me late last night. I infer from yours that *I should not have crossed the river, but it is now too late.* My means of recrossing are so limited I could hardly accomplish it in face of the enemy.

Major-General George B. Crittenden had been assigned to the command of this district by the President. The high rank given him has been cited by Pollard, who speaks of him as a captain in the old army, as a piece of favoritism. But this is an error. He was one of the senior officers who resigned. He was a graduate of West Point, of the year 1832. He resigned, and was reappointed a captain in the Mounted Rifles in 1846, was brevetted major for "gallant and meritorious conduct in the battles of Contreras and Churubusco, Mexico," was made a major in 1848, and lieutenant-colonel in 1856. He was a Kentuckian, of a family distinguished for gallantry and talents, and known as an intelligent and intrepid officer; and it was hoped that his long service would enable him to supplement the inexperience of the gallant Zollicoffer. Crittenden took command of the district, November 24th, and made his headquarters at Knoxville. Thither General Johnston telegraphed him to dispatch without delay the supplies and intrenching-tools sent there for Zollicoffer, and to send at once a regiment and battery to his support. He added this significant intimation, sufficient for a trained soldier: "He has crossed the Cumberland at Mill Springs; *has the enemy in front and the river behind,* and is securing his front." Still, General Johnston did not contemplate any aggressive movement by Zollicoffer, after the instructions given, unless, of course, the enemy could be taken at disadvantage.

Had Zollicoffer, when he reached the Cumberland, succeeded in seizing the ferry-boats, as he attempted, and, crossing promptly, attacked Schoepf at once, he would probably have met but slight resistance. Schoepf had three regiments, a battery, and some cavalry, scattered through that neighborhood. Zollicoffer, as related above, was delayed in crossing. The movements then made by his forces revealed, to a great extent, both his strength and his purposes to his adversary. While constructing his ferries he sent some troops, on December 2d, and shelled a small force of the enemy posted on the north bank, and compelled it to move. On the 4th he threw over a small cavalry-picket, which drove back the Federal horse, and caused a precipitate retreat of the Seventeenth Ohio, which was advancing on reconnaissance. Next day the pickets wounded and captured Major Helvetti and Captain Prime, engineer-officers, and along with them a corporal. On the 7th and 8th the cavalry crossed Fishing Creek and reconnoitred the Federal camps near Somerset. On the 8th, at Fishing Creek, the cavalry was fired on by Wolford's cavalry and the Thirty-fifth Ohio Infantry, but charged these forces, killing ten and capturing sixteen, inclusive of the wounded. One Confederate was wounded, and two horses killed. On the 11th an expedition sent out by Zollicoffer attacked a small body of Federals, who were posted at Lairsville, thirty miles distant toward Columbia. It routed the Federals, killing three and capturing ten. One Confederate was drowned, the only loss sustained.

In the mean time Schoepf, overawed and put upon his guard, retired three miles behind Somerset, intrenched himself in a strong position, and called loudly in every quarter for reënforcements. General Carter, who was at London, brought two regiments to his aid, arriving on the 7th. Thomas sent him a regiment and a battery, and on the 11th another regiment. Several regiments also concentrated at Columbia under General Boyle. Zollicoffer's letters correctly estimate the force of the enemy at Somerset at seven infantry regiments and some cavalry, which agrees with Van Horne's account. He expected to be attacked, but kept his force divided, five regiments in his intrenchments, and two on the south bank to protect his communications.

General Thomas's command, occupying the country east of Lebanon, consisted at this time of a division made up of sixteen infantry regiments, a regiment and squadron of cavalry, and three batteries. The force at Columbia was not included in this estimate. On the 18th Schoepf discovered, by a reconnaissance in force, that Zollicoffer was intrenching, and justly reached the conclusion that his purpose was defensive.

On the 29th of December General Buell ordered Thomas to advance against Zollicoffer, moving by Columbia, and to attack his left so as to cut him off from his bridge, while Schoepf attacked him in front. He adds:

The result should be at least a severe blow to him, or a hasty flight across the river. But, to effect the former, the movement should be made rapidly and secretly, and the blow should be vigorous and decided. There should be no delay after your arrival.

On December 31st General Thomas started from Lebanon. His column consisted of eight and a half regiments ; namely, Manson's brigade of four regiments, three of McCook's regiments, Wolford's cavalry, a battalion of Michigan engineers, and three batteries of artillery. Rains, high water, and bad roads, impeded their progress ; so that it was the 17th of January before they reached Logan's Cross Roads, ten miles from Zollicoffer's intrenched camp.[1] Here Thomas took position to await four of his regiments that had not come up. To secure himself he communicated with Schoepf, and obtained from him a reënforcement of three regiments under General Carter, and a battery. This gave him eleven regiments, and a battalion, besides artillery. The remainder of Schoepf's force must have been near by, and in supporting distance, as they joined in the pursuit. Such was Thomas's position on the morning of the 19th of January.

About New-Year's-day General Crittenden had arrived at Zollicoffer's headquarters at Beech Grove. In his letter of December 10th Zollicoffer had written as follows :

This camp is immediately opposite to Mill Springs, one and a quarter mile distant. The river protects our rear and flanks. We have about 1,200 yards' fighting front to defend, which we are intrenching as rapidly as our few tools will allow. . . . I will endeavor to prevent the forces at Somerset and Columbia from uniting. The proximity of the terminus of the railroad at Lebanon would seem to give them the means of rapidly reënforcing my front. The position I occupy north of the river is a fine basis for operations in front. It is a much stronger natural position for defense than that on the south bank. I think it should be held at all hazards. But I ought to have a stronger force.

With further reference to this position, General Zollicoffer said :

Fishing Creek runs south into the Cumberland, five miles below[2] Mill Springs, and lies between our position and Somerset. It is more than thirty miles long, runs in a deep ravine 200 to 300 feet deep, and its summit level on the east ranges from half a mile to one and a half mile distant from that on the west. There are two crossings to Somerset, seven and eleven miles from here.

Crittenden's weekly return for January 7, 1862, of the troops at Beech Grove, shows some increase of force. He had eight infantry regiments, four battalions of cavalry (seventeen companies), and two artillery-companies ; an aggregate, present and absent, of 9,417 men,

---

[1] The particulars of Thomas's movements are from his official reports, and from Van Horne's "Army of the Cumberland."

[2] Probably a slip of the pen for *above*.

but, numbering effectives (present for duty), of 333 officers and 6,111 rank and file. As his army was composed of the same commands on the day of the battle, the above numbers give his approximate force at that time.

General Crittenden informs the writer that, as soon as he learned that Zollicoffer had crossed the river, he sent a courier post-haste ordering him to recross. When he arrived at Mill Springs he found Zollicoffer still on the north side, waiting his arrival before retiring. Crittenden immediately detailed parties to construct boats, but they were not ready when he learned of Thomas's approach.

His first intimation to General Johnston of Thomas's approach was the following letter, written January 18th:

SIR: I am threatened by a superior force of the enemy in front, and, finding it impossible to cross the river, I shall have to make the fight on the ground I now occupy. If you can do so, I would ask that a diversion be made in my favor.

A diversion was made by Hindman, on the receipt of this, but with no important consequences, as the next day decided the fate of Crittenden's army.

Crittenden's letter was inaccurately worded, and must probably have referred rather to the impossibility of removing his stores and artillery than to the feasibility of retiring with his troops from the position at Beech Grove. He had a stern-wheel steamboat sufficient for the latter purpose, though probably not available for the former. In fact, on the morning of the 18th, he did take over three regiments from the south to the north bank of the river; and between midnight and daylight on the 19th his whole army, though demoralized, and with many wounded, was carried over by it. His supplies were scanty, but not exhausted; and, though his communications with Nashville were threatened by Thomas's approach, he had time and means to retire upon supports more easily before than after a battle, though not without such loss of artillery and prestige as no general would incur except in the most desperate circumstances.

It was stated apologetically, after the battle, that the ground in front of the intrenchments gave no range for the Confederate artillery, and yet offered no formidable obstacle to an infantry assault. This would imply a serious error in the estimate of the strength of their position by the Confederate generals—in Zollicoffer's selection, and Crittenden's maintenance of it. Another statement was, that the Confederate force was insufficient to man the intrenchments. Zollicoffer states the length of his line at 1,200 yards. Six thousand men would fully man 2,000 yards, and, according to the Confederate notions, double that distance. Crittenden, however, arrived at the con-

clusion to assail Thomas after a full consultation and the unanimous
approval of his officers.

While awaiting the attack of the enemy, a heavy winter rain falling, Crittenden learned that a rise in Fishing Creek was inevitable,
and would separate Thomas from Schoepf. It was afterward alleged
that he was deceived by a treacherous guide, but this rumor is sufficiently accounted for by the ill-success of the expedition, and an
incident related by General Walthall which will be given in its place.
Crittenden, therefore, came to the sudden resolution of marching out
and attempting to take the enemy in detail, attacking Thomas first.
He called a council of officers, however, and laid the matter before
them. All of them were in favor of the movement under the circumstances, and many of them thought the attack the best thing
to be done under any circumstances. General Crittenden's special
error was not in attacking at Logan's Cross Roads, instead of defending Beech Grove; it was in being caught on the north side of the
river, and having to fight at all. General Johnston's instructions
looked to a defensive campaign by that corps, and there was nothing
in its condition to warrant an aggressive movement.

It is apparent to us now that Thomas, after thirty-six hours' delay
at Logan's Cross Roads, would be in full communication with and supporting distance of Schoepf, and that to surprise or rout him there
was almost hopeless; but such was not the information on which Crittenden acted, and we should guard our censure of the general who
leads his whole force to attack, even when he fails.

The men had been standing all day in the trenches exposed to a
constant and pelting rain, and, having been suddenly called to arms
and hourly expecting an attack, had had neither time nor opportunity to prepare food. They were now hurriedly put in motion. At
midnight, on the 18th of January, the Confederate army marched
against the enemy in this order: First, with Bledsoe's and Saunders's
independent cavalry companies as a vanguard, Zollicoffer's brigade; thus
Walthall's Fifteenth Mississippi Regiment in advance, followed by
Rutledge's battery, and Cummings's Nineteenth, Battle's Twentieth,
and Stanton's Twenty-fifth Tennessee Regiments. Then came Carroll's
brigade, as follows: Newman's Seventeenth, Murray's Twenty-eighth,
and Powell's Twenty-ninth Tennessee Regiments, with two guns under
Captain McClung, and Wood's Sixteenth Alabama Regiment in reserve.
Branner's and McClelland's battalions of cavalry were placed on the
flanks and rear.

A cold rain continued to fall upon the thinly-clad Confederates,
chilling them to the marrow, but they toiled painfully along. The
road was rough, and very heavy with the long rain following severe
freezes. Unencumbered with artillery, the infantry would have made

poor progress in the darkness, rain, and mud, but, as the guns from the first began to mire down, the foot-soldiers were called on to help them along. Hence it was six o'clock, or daylight, before the advance-guard struck the enemy's pickets, two miles in front of the Federal camps. It had been six hours getting over eight miles, and the rear was still fully three miles behind.

When the Mississippians under Walthall, followed by Battle's Tennessee Regiment, encountered the Federal pickets, they met no resistance, and, pressing rapidly forward in obedience to orders, increased the interval between themselves and the next regiment in the column to about one mile. It was thus that Walthall's and Battle's regiments came upon the first line Thomas had thrown forward to receive them.

General Thomas's troops were encamped on each side of the road, with a wood in their front from one-fourth to a half a mile through. In front of the wood were fields about 300 yards across, and beyond this, again, a low ridge parallel with the wood. The Confederates promptly crossed the ridge and fields, and found a force in the edge of the wood in their front. This consisted of the Fourth Kentucky and Tenth Indiana Regiments. General Crittenden had warned them, in the council of war, of the danger of firing into their friends, especially as many of the Southern troops wore blue uniforms, and to avoid this risk they had adopted as a password "Kentucky." The morning was dark and misty, and nothing could be seen of the opposing force except a line of armed men. The skirmishers reported to Walthall that this was Battle's command. Walthall made his regiment lie down behind a slight elevation, and, going forward to some high ground, hailed the troops in his front, "What troops are those?" The answer was, "Kentucky." He called again, "Who are you?" and the answer came as before, "Kentucky." He then went back and got his colors, and, returning, once more asked the same question, and received the same answer. He then unfurled his flag, and immediately the Federal line opened upon him with a volley. He turned to order forward his regiment, and found that Lieutenant Harrington, who had followed him without his knowledge, was lying dead by him, pierced by more than twenty balls. The flag was riddled, and the staff cut, but Colonel Walthall was untouched. It was this incident that led to the belief that the password was betrayed to the enemy by the guide; but the answer, coming from the Fourth Kentucky, was the natural and proper one.

The Mississippians drove this regiment from its cover, and, after a severe struggle, it fell back fighting. In the mean time the Tenth Indiana Regiment, coming to the aid of the Fourth Kentucky, was met by the Mississippians and Battle's Twentieth Tennessee, which had formed on their right. A strenuous combat ensued at the forks of the road, Wolford's cavalry supporting the Federal troops. The Ninth Ohio also became engaged ; but, after a desperate conflict, the whole Federal line was driven back. It now appeared as if the Southern troops, having carried the rest of the field, were about to win the crest of a hill, which was the key to the position. Just then the Second Minnesota came up, and held the ground until the beaten regiments could rally upon it, which they did with spirit. The Confederates still seemed for a good while on the point of gaining the summit, where the Federals made a desperate stand, but were unable to carry it.

In the mean time the Nineteenth Tennessee had come up on the left of the Mississippians, and found itself opposed in the woods to the Fourth Kentucky, which had returned to the conflict. In the darkness of the morning it was difficult to distinguish between the Federals and Confederates, many of the latter still wearing blue uniforms. General Zollicoffer was convinced that the regiment in his front was Confederate, and peremptorily ordered the Nineteenth Tennessee to cease firing, as they were firing upon their own troops. He then rode across toward the Federal line to put a stop to the firing there. Just as he entered the road, he met a Federal officer, Colonel Speed S. Fry, of the Fourth Kentucky, and said to him quietly, " We must not shoot our own men." General Zollicoffer wore a white gum overcoat, which concealed his uniform, and Colonel Fry, supposing him to be a Federal officer, replied, " I would not, of course, do so intentionally." Zollicoffer, then, pointing to the Nineteenth Tennessee, said, " Those are our men." Colonel Fry then started toward his regiment to stop their firing, when Major Fogg, Zollicoffer's aide, coming out of the wood at this instant, and clearly perceiving that Fry was a Federal, fired upon him, wounding his horse. Fry, riding away obliquely, saw his action, and turning, discharged his revolver. The ball passed through General Zollicoffer's heart, and he fell exactly where he had stood. Zollicoffer was near-sighted, and never knew that Fry was an enemy. His delusion was complete, as Major Fogg and others had remonstrated with him about going to the front. Major Fogg was also wounded.

The Nineteenth Tennessee now stood waiting for orders, without firing a gun, until it was flanked and broken. In the mean time the Twenty-fifth Tennessee entered the wood without direction, and engaged the enemy. Immediately its colonel was severely wounded; and, being without support on either flank, it, too, suffered and retired. The remainder of the column had come up and taken position in reserve, and toward the left of the field Murray's regiment, which last entered the fight, now experienced the same fate with the Twenty-fifth Tennessee. Rutledge's battery, which had been for some time in position in reserve, retired under orders, as is said, of General Crittenden, without having fired a gun. The Federal right, in pressing upon the front and left flank of the Tennesseeans, was able to come to very close quarters without much loss, while their adversaries suffered a good deal, owing to the disparity in arms. The Tennesseeans were armed with old flint-lock muskets, which having got wet were almost useless. Nevertheless, the Federal line was arrested at about one hundred yards' distance, and held at bay some twenty minutes. The Confederate line then gave way, and was allowed to retreat without pursuit. On the Confederate right, Walthall's regiment had continued its struggle with the Second Minnesota, and Battle's regiment had held Carter's brigade at bay, until these three regiments closed upon its flank and almost in its rear, and it, too, retired. Walthall, now finding one of these regiments almost across his path, and his command nearly surrounded, also withdrew his men, having with him in his retreat a portion of Battle's regiment, under Captain Rice.

The Mississippi Regiment and Battle's Twentieth Tennessee had borne the brunt of the day. The former had lost over 220 men out of 400 who had gone into battle. The Twentieth Tennessee lost half as many more, those two regiments thus suffering over three-fourths of all the casualties on that day. They had the advance, and were better armed than the other troops. But, had they been supported by the remainder of the column with half the valor and determination which the same troops subsequently exhibited on other fields, the result would probably have been different. Their inferior arms, want of discipline, bad handling, and fatigue, sufficiently account for their ill-success.

The defeated army was followed by the victorious Federals nearly to the intrenchments at Beech Grove. In the pursuit, if their cautious advance can be so called, checked as it was repeatedly by a rear-guard formidable even in defeat, the Fourteenth Ohio and Tenth Kentucky, with General Schoepf's whole brigade, joined. Approaching the intrenched camp at Beech Grove, General Thomas opened an artillery-fire on it, to little purpose, however. He also made his arrangements to assault it next morning.

The situation of the Confederate army was now extremely perilous. In its disorganized condition it could not have resisted the combined attack of Thomas and Schoepf. There was but one thing to be done, and that was to get away. The troops remained quietly in the intrenchments until midnight, and then between that hour and daylight escaped, by means of a steamer and some barges at the landing, without having excited the suspicions of the enemy. Crittenden got his whole force safely across the river, including all the wounded able to travel ; but he was compelled to leave behind him all of his badly wounded, all of his cannon, his supplies, and, indeed, whatever constitutes the equip-

ment of an army. Having thus saved the remnant of his command, he
burned his boats, and moved his tired army, on the Monticello road,
toward Nashville.

The condition of the Confederate army was truly deplorable. On
the night of the 18th it had marched ten miles; and on the 19th, after
a fierce battle, had retreated to its camp. That night it had stood at
the breastworks till midnight, then crossed the river; and now, without
sleep and without food, it struggled through the rain and cold of a
winter night to reach some place where it might be secure from assault. For several days the troops endured terrible hardships. The
scanty supplies of a wasted country, hastily collected and issued without system, were insufficient for the subsistence of the army; and,
though the commissary department made extraordinary efforts, many
of the troops had nothing better than parched corn to sustain life.
Crittenden marched his army through Monticello and Livingston to
Gainsboro, and, finally, by General Johnston's orders, took position at
Chestnut Mound, where he was in reach of relief from Nashville. During his retreat his army became much demoralized, and two regiments,
whose homes were in that neighborhood, almost entirely abandoned
their organization, and went every man to his own house. A multitude
deserted, and the tide of fugitives filled the country with dismay.

The battle fought at Logan's Cross Roads, also called the battle of
Fishing Creek, or of Mill Springs, was most disastrous to the Confederate arms. General Thomas lost 39 killed and 207 wounded in the
five regiments most hotly engaged. The casualties are not reported in
other organizations. General Crittenden thought the Confederate loss
was about 300. It was estimated by some as high as 500. At the time,
it was stated in the Confederate accounts that the loss was 115 killed,
116 wounded, and 45 prisoners. This could not have included many of
the wounded who escaped with the army. Van Horne says: "He lost, in
killed, wounded, and prisoners, 392 men. Of this aggregate, 192 were
killed." The writer is not aware of the data on which Van Horne
bases his statement, but is inclined to think his estimate of the aggregate loss nearly correct. In every point of view, the large number of
killed compared to the wounded is a very striking fact, and indicates
fighting at close quarters, and the superiority of the firearms of the
Federals. Van Horne also reports the capture of "twelve pieces of artillery, a heavy amount of ammunition, a large number of small-arms,
150 wagons, more than a thousand horses and mules, and abundant
quartermaster and commissary stores."

The death of Zollicoffer was a great blow to the Tennesseeans. He
was more than a mere popular leader; he was a patriot, full of noble
and generous qualities. His people felt his death as a personal bereave-
ment, and still cherish his memory with tender and reverent regret. His

fall and the Confederate slaughter were treated with indecent and ferocious exultation by camp-followers who wrote for the Northern press, and by others. But a better and more generous spirit also prevailed, which, it is to be hoped, more truly represented the feelings of the brave men who won the victory. Zollicoffer's body was borne into a tent, by Thomas's orders, and identified by Colonel Connell, of the Seventeenth Ohio, and others who knew him. An eye-witness, writing to the *Cincinnati Enquirer*, thus describes him:

A tall, rather slender man, with thin brown hair, high forehead somewhat bald, Roman nose, firm, wide mouth, and clean-shaved face. A pistol-ball had struck him in the breast, a little above the heart, killing him instantly. His face bore no expression such as is usually found on those who fall in battle—no malice, no reckless hate, not even a shadow of physical pain. It was calm, placid, noble. But I have never looked on a countenance so marked with sadness. A deep dejection had settled on it.

General Zollicoffer's body was embalmed, carried around by Lebanon, and sent by General Buell through his lines under flag of truce. A negotiation for an exchange of prisoners was begun by General Buell, during which he accepted a proposal of General Johnston to exempt from captivity surgeons in charge of the wounded. General Buell's conduct and this correspondence evince that the usages and amenities of civilized warfare had not been forgotten in these armies.

Crittenden had a lot still harder for a brave soldier than that of his dead colleague. Skulking slanderers were charging him, up and down the country, with cowardice and treasonable correspondence with the enemy. He was also charged with drunkenness; but the writer has the evidence of impartial witnesses, who saw him on that day, that he was perfectly sober. No shadow of doubt rests, in any fair mind, on his simple fidelity, his spotless integrity, and his dauntless courage. Though unfortunate, he was a stout soldier and an honorable gentleman. With most of his troops, personal devotion to a leader was almost essential to success. He was new and strange to them; and, when Zollicoffer fell, they were ready to despair.

One circumstance in connection with this battle, which has not been sufficiently pointed out, deserves consideration. It is the great disparity in arms. While the Federals were fully equipped and well supplied with good weapons, the Confederates, with the exceptions already mentioned, had but few good arms; the remainder, old squirrel-rifles and fowling-pieces. Such disparity makes an incalculable difference in effectiveness of fire ; and, with anything like equal numbers and equal prowess, such effectiveness must decide most battles. Raw troops, decimated before they can bring the enemy within range, become disheartened and demoralized, and are beaten before they strike a blow. Such was the case in this instance with most of the Southern troops.

Crittenden's attack on Thomas was as much a surprise to General Johnston as the result could have been to the defeated commander. His line was broken; his position at Bowling Green apparently turned on that flank, and an army on which he counted demolished. His correspondence, however, shows no vestige of reproach, no trace of harshness that might add to the pain of his unsuccessful subordinate. This biography has evinced that he was singularly tolerant of the faults of others, and he was too wise to treat calamity as a crime. It is true that Crittenden, stung by popular clamor, demanded a court of inquiry, which was subsequently ordered by the Secretary of War. But General Johnston's letters make no allusion to the defeat. That was past. His whole attention was turned to saving what could be saved of that army; and all his letters were directed to the *business* of restoring its efficiency—to its proper location, to its commissariat, transportation, re-armament, and reorganization.

General Johnston, in writing to General Crittenden, February 3d, after enumerating the various steps taken for his assistance, closes thus:

When Colonel Claiborne returns, I shall be informed of all the wants of your command, and take measures to have you amply provided.

Writing about the same time to the adjutant-general, he concludes his letter:

I have taken every measure necessary to reorganize and place immediately on an efficient footing the command of Major-General Crittenden.

Schoepf followed Crittenden to Monticello, and then returned. Thomas did not pursue his victory, for reasons sufficiently obvious. The season of the year, the rugged and exhausted country, drained of its supplies, the almost impassable roads, and the danger of concentration against him by forces of whose strength he was ignorant, made a further advance hazardous. Moreover, his troops could be more efficiently employed on another field, and he was recalled by General Buell to take part in a combined movement against Bowling Green. Before his command reached there, the condition of affairs had changed; and it was moved round by water, in the early days of March, to Nashville, which, by that time, had fallen into Buell's hands.

CHAPTER XXVII.

FORT HENRY.

WHEN Tennessee seceded, her authorities assembled volunteers at the most assailable points on her borders, and took measures for guarding the water-entrances to her territory. All the strong points on the Mississippi were occupied and fortified—Memphis, Randolph, Fort Pillow, and Island No. 10. The last-named place, though a low-lying island, was believed to be a very strong position. Captain Gray, the engineer in charge when General Johnston assumed command (September 18th), reported that Island No. 10 was "one of the finest strategic positions in the Mississippi Valley," and, "properly fortified, would offer the greatest resistance to the enemy;" and that "its intrenchments could not be taken by a force four or five times superior in number." It is not necessary here to enter upon a narrative of the defenses of the Mississippi River. Columbus was relied upon as the chief barrier against invasion; and was found sufficient, until, for strategic reasons, it was deemed expedient to abandon it. The defense of the points lower down the Mississippi, however important in a general history of the war, did not greatly influence the catastrophe of this biography, and hence may be here omitted.

In the location of her water-defenses, comity forbade Tennessee to invade the soil of another sovereign State under the plea of fortifying for her own defense; so that, despite the supreme value of Columbus to her security, the Southern troops did not seize that stronghold until the last shadow of neutrality vanished, and its occupation became an absolute necessity. The same consideration governed the selection of points for the defense of the Tennessee and Cumberland Rivers. Governor Harris wished to locate the forts as near the Kentucky line as he could find suitable sites for them, and sent General Daniel S. Donelson, a West Point graduate, and a man of influence and standing, to select proper situations. He reported Donelson as the strongest position on the Cumberland near the State line, and that there was no good position on the Tennessee River within the jurisdiction of the State. General Donelson wished to build a fort in Kentucky, on better ground; but, under the Governor's orders, adopted the site at Fort Henry as the best in Tennessee near the Kentucky line, and because of the convenience for mutual support between it and Fort Donelson. These locations are said to have been approved by General Bushrod R. Johnson also. Indeed, there was not time for very deliberate or well-considered engineering. Crudities, the offspring of haste and inexperience, characterized a great deal of the earlier military preparation for the conflict; and so great were the demands upon the few who had the requisite training, that they could not do their best. And this was especially the case in a branch of the military art so scientific and technical as engineering.

Hence the two forts were placed within the limits of Tennessee; Henry on the east bank of the Tennessee, Donelson on the west bank of the Cumberland, only twelve miles apart. The gates to the State were thus set as near its outer edge as was possible under the circumstances. Near their mouths, not far from Smithland and Paducah, the rivers approach within three miles of each other. Here, it is said, an intrenched camp might have commanded both streams ; but this position was on the soil of Kentucky, and Tennessee had neither the right to take nor the strength to maintain it.

A look at the map will show that the boundary between these two States is nearly a straight line westward from Virginia to the Tennessee River; it then follows this stream almost due south some twelve or fourteen miles, when it resumes its original direction and runs westward to the Mississippi River. Within a mile of the angle of this offset of Kentucky, about sixty miles above Paducah, stood Fort Henry. The Tennessee River traverses Tennessee and Kentucky by a course almost due north. The Cumberland, flowing westwardly near their dividing line, turns to the north as it approaches the Tennessee, to which it runs parallel to its mouth. At the great bend, on very good ground, Fort Donelson was established ; so that the two forts helped mutually to determine their relative locations. The governing considerations were evidently political rather than strategic, and depended more upon geography than topography. Nevertheless, even from a strategic point of view, they were exceedingly well situated. Whether the Barren River, and a line from Bowling Green to Columbus, should be adopted for defense, or that of the Cumberland and thence west to the Mississippi, these points were equally commanding. They were also near to and in front of the railroads from Bowling Green and Nashville, running west.

The topography of the two forts was not so good, though not justly amenable to the censure that the defeated generals visited upon it after its surrender. Floyd, in his reports, said of Fort Donelson :

It was ill conceived, badly executed, and still worse located. I consider the place illy chosen, out of position, and entirely indefensible by any reënforcements which could be brought there to its support.

General Tilghman spoke in his report in still more disparaging terms of the fortifications at Fort Henry :

Its wretched military position, . . . its unfortunate location, etc. *The history of military engineering records no parallel to this case.*[1] Points within a few miles of it, possessing great advantages and few disadvantages, were totally neglected; and a location fixed upon without one redeeming feature or filling one of the many requirements of a work such as Fort Henry.

The remark of General Floyd may, under the circumstances, be dismissed as a hastily-formed opinion, though it is due to him to say that he expressed great distrust of the position as soon as he arrived at Fort Donelson. But Tilghman was a graduate of West Point, and a civil engineer by profession. He had had some experience in fortification in the Mexican War and as an artillery-officer, so that, under other circumstances, his opinion would be entitled to weight. But, when it is remembered that, as an officer, he was not slow to find fault, and indeed had done so with unusual vehemence as to the ordnance, transportation, clothing, medical and other staff departments, and had been engaged in an altercation with the Engineer Department on other points, and yet had never objected to the location of the forts until after his surrender, his censure must be received with a grain of allowance.

Donelson was well enough. It was placed on high ground ; and, with the plunging fire from its batteries, was sufficiently safe on the water-side. But from the land-side it was not equally strong, and required extensive outworks and a considerable garrison for its maintenance against an attack in that quarter.

Fort Henry was on the low grounds of a river liable to great floods or "freshets," during which it was almost surrounded by water. While this was to some extent a protection against a land-assault, yet, bringing the combat to the water-level, it deprived the fort of any advantage of elevation. The engineers, following the traditions of their craft, were soon to be confronted with a problem new to them—the power of iron-clad gunboats against land-defenses. They had not estimated correctly the advantage of long-range guns, which enable the vessels to select positions for attack, so as to enfilade almost any possible line of defense, and easily to render a bastioned fort, for instance, untenable. Fort Henry was also commanded by high ground on the left flank ; but this was intended to be occupied by troops in case of a land-attack.

Fort Henry could not have been made impregnable to gunboats, except at the cost of much time, labor, and expense. But it would be unjust to hold the engineers responsible for what became manifest only in the light of subsequent events. Why it was retained will appear as we go on. Though probably not the best location, on the two rivers, each successive commander found it easier to improve them than

[1] The italics are his.

to begin anew elsewhere. But a simple narrative of facts relating to the history and progress of the river-defenses ought to give a correcter view of the case than any argument in the interest of any individual. At one time there was a profound consciousness in the Southern people that, in this campaign, the immediate commanders at these forts had not proved equal to the emergency. Doubtless time has partially effaced the conviction, but, whatever individual shortcomings may appear herein, the public dereliction is manifest. The same apathy that kept back from the field men who subsequently gave their lives to the cause, at that period withheld even the negro slaves demanded as laborers, and seemed to paralyze every arm and bring to naught the most earnest efforts and the most judicious counsel.

Not long before the battle of Shiloh, General Polk, in whose military district these events had occurred, made a report that contains a very fair summary of many important facts in relation to the defenses of Forts Henry and Donelson. It reads as follows :

HEADQUARTERS, FIRST CORPS, ARMY OF THE MISSISSIPPI, }
CORINTH, MISSISSIPPI, *April* 1, 1862. }

GENERAL : In conformity with your order to report to you on the defenses of the Tennessee and Cumberland Rivers at the time of my taking command in the West, I have to say that those defenses were at that time not included in my command, nor were they until after you assumed the charge of the Western Department. My command up to that time was limited on the north and east by the Tennessee River.

Shortly after you took command of the Western Department, Lieutenant Dixon, of the Corps of Engineers, was instructed by you to make an examination of the works at Forts Henry and Donelson, and to report upon them. These instructions were complied with, and he reported that the former fort, which was nearly completed, was built, not at the most favorable position, but that it was a strong work, and instead of abandoning it and building at another place, he advised that it should be completed, and other works constructed on the high lands just above the fort on the opposite side of the river. Measures for the accomplishment of this work were adopted as rapidly as the means at our disposal would allow. A negro force, which was offered by planters on the Tennessee in North Alabama, was employed on the work, and efforts were made to push it to completion as fast as the means at command would allow.

Lieutenant Dixon also made a similar reconnaissance on the Cumberland, and gave it as his opinion that, although a better position might have been chosen for the fortifications on that river, yet, under the circumstances then surrounding our command, it would be better to retain and strengthen the position chosen. He accordingly made surveys for additional outworks, and the service of a considerable slave-force was obtained to construct them. This work was continued and kept under the supervision of Lieutenant Dixon. Lieutenant Dixon also advised the placing of obstructions in the Cumberland at a certain point below, where there was shoal water, so as to afford protection to the operatives engaged on the fortifications against the enemy's gunboats. This was done, and it operated as a check to the navigation, so long as the water continued low.

You are aware that efforts were made to obtain heavy ordnance to arm these forts ; but, as we had to rely on supplies from the Atlantic sea-coast, they came slowly, and it became necessary to divert a number of pieces intended for Columbus to the service of those forts.

The principal difficulty in the way of a successful defense of the rivers in question was *the want of an adequate force*—a force of infantry and a force of experienced artillerists. They were applied for by you, and also by me; and the appeal was made earnestly to every quarter whence relief might be hoped for. Why it was not furnished others must say. I believe the chief reason, so far as the infantry was concerned, was the want of arms. As to experienced artillerists, they were not in the country, or, at least, to be spared from other points.

When General Tilghman was made brigadier-general, he was assigned by you to the command of the defenses on the Tennessee and Cumberland. It was at a time when the operations of the enemy had begun to be active on those rivers, and the difficulty of communicating as rapidly as the exigencies of the service required, through the circuitous route to Columbus, made it expedient for him to place himself in direct communication with the general headquarters. Nevertheless, all the support I could give him, in answer to his calls, was afforded. He received from Columbus a detachment of artillery-officers as instructors of his troops in that arm, on two several occasions, and all the infantry at my command that could be spared from the defense of Columbus.

The importance of gunboats, as an element of power in our military operations, was frequently brought to the attention of the Government. One transport-boat, the Eastport, was ordered to be purchased and converted into a gunboat on the Tennessee River, but it was, unfortunately, too late to be of any service.

Respectfully, your obedient servant,

L. POLK, *Major-General commanding.*

To General A. S. JOHNSTON, commanding Army of the Mississippi, Corinth, Mississippi.

A rigid examination of all the data confirms this report in its most important particulars. On the 17th of September General Johnston ordered Lieutenant Dixon, a young engineer of extraordinary skill, courage, and character, to report at Fort Donelson for engineer duty. Immediately afterward he applied to the adjutant-general for other engineer-officers, but for some time in vain. They were scarce, and otherwise assigned. From this time these defenses never ceased to be the subject of extreme solicitude to General Johnston. The preparations for resistance were necessarily enlarged with the magnitude of the operations directed against them.

The following extracts from his correspondence will serve to show that General Johnston not only did not lose sight of this vulnerable point, but did all that he could with the means at his command. It will be borne in mind that the points of pressure, during this period, were elsewhere, and that the Federal commanders themselves came to a very sudden and unpremeditated resolution to make this their chief point of attack.

On October 8th, Lieutenant Dixon having been temporarily employed elsewhere, Colonel Mackall, assistant adjutant-general, wrote to General Polk :

General Johnston directs you to send Lieutenant Dixon to Fort Donelson instantly, with orders to mount the guns at that place for the defense of the river.

Lieutenant - Colonel McGavock was also ordered to "remain in vigilant command." Another letter, of October 17th, says :

General Johnston orders you to hasten the armament of the works at Fort Donelson, and the obstructions below the place at which a post was intended. The operations of the enemy on the Tennessee show that the necessity of interrupting the Cumberland is urgent. . . . The general has been informed that the experiments made with the torpedoes at Memphis have been very successful. Should you, on inquiry, find this to be the case, you are authorized to employ them to any extent necessary on the Mississippi, Tennessee, and Cumberland Rivers. For the present, do not move the regiment from Fort Henry. The men are accustomed to the guns. New ones might not be so efficient.

A dispatch from Colonel Mackall to Major-General Polk, Columbus, Kentucky, October 28th, says :

General Johnston directs me to say that he wishes you to keep a vigilant eye on the Tennessee River. If possible, fortify opposite to Fort Henry, to protect it from being overlooked by the enemy. It can be held with part of the garrison of Henry. Lieutenant Dixon, who is familiar with the country, will be able to point out the proper position. No time should be lost.

General Johnston wrote to General Polk, October 31st, as follows :

Your front, *and particularly your right flank*, requires incessant watching, and may at any moment demand all the force at your disposal. The Cumberland and Tennessee Rivers afford lines of transportation by which an army may turn your right with ease and rapidity, and any surplus you may be able to spare from the left flank on the Mississippi can well be used to secure you against such movements.

In the latter part of October Major Jeremy F. Gilmer reported to General Johnston, as his chief-engineer. Gilmer was a North Carolinian, and had been graduated at the Military Academy in 1839, fourth in his class, next below H. W. Halleck. After subaltern service, he had served as captain in the Engineer Corps since 1853, and was esteemed an officer of great merit. General Johnston first knew him in California. They met next at Bowling Green. Gilmer had skill and judgment, and his military career was full of usefulness to the cause he espoused. At the close of the war he was at the head of the engineer department of the Confederate army.

General Johnston was well pleased with this assignment to him of a trained soldier, on whose scientific knowledge he could rely. After a full conference with him on the plan of defense already adopted, he promptly sent him back to establish a second defensive line along the Cumberland from Nashville to Donelson and thence to Henry, which might prove not only a secure place of retreat in case of disaster, but an effectual barrier to the invader. General Johnston gave him letters to Governor Harris at Nashville and Senator G. A. Henry at Clarksville, explaining his business and invoking their aid and influence, and suggesting the employment of slave-labor on the fortifications, to hasten their construction. Gilmer's orders were:

"To arrange the works for the defense and obstruction of the river" at Donelson, Clarksville, and Nashville, and to intrust the construction to subordinates. He was "to spare no cost, procuring barges, steamboats, and whatever else may aid in the work." His orders ran: "Arrange a plan of defensive works for Nashville, and urge them forward by all the means you can command. If you find that the work of troops will be useful, report at once here the numbers you can use, that they may be sent you."

General and specific directions were also issued to all the staff departments to furnish Major Gilmer funds, tools, materials, subsistence, transportation, and other facilities for the construction of the defenses; and Lieutenant-Colonel McGavock was ordered to work his troops day and night until the guns at Fort Donelson were protected by parapets.

The objections to the sites of the forts were quite apparent; but the purpose to maintain, instead of removing them, was not the result of a blind or careless policy, but of a deliberate weighing of difficulties and advantages. General Johnston could not give the matter his personal attention, owing to the pressure elsewhere; but, even if he had done so, his only course, as a sober-minded man, would have been to concur in the calm decision of his chief-engineer, an able and skillful officer, who, with all the lights before him, concluded to retain positions already established, in preference to attempting the construction of new forts elsewhere.

Major Gilmer, in a report of November 3d, says:

As to the defenses of the Cumberland River below Clarksville, they should be at least as low down as Fort Donelson. Our efforts for resisting gunboats should be concentrated there; and, to this end, Captain Dixon will do everything in his power to hasten forward the works at that point. Lineport, fifteen miles below Donelson, presents many advantages for defending the river; but, as the works at Fort Donelson are partially built, and the place susceptible of a good defense landward, I advised Captain Dixon to retain the position, and construct the additional defenses as rapidly as possible.

To obstruct the Cumberland at points below Donelson, old "barges" and "flats" have been sunk at Ingraham's Shoals, a few miles above Eddyville, and at Line Island, three miles below Lineport. In all ordinary stages of water the obstructions render the river impassable for gunboats, and for any other boats at this time. Such, at least, is the judgment of Captain Dixon, who superintended the sinking of the barges.

Three of the barges sunk were one hundred and twenty-seven feet long by twenty-seven feet wide and eight feet deep. These, with two smaller boats, loaded with about 1,200 tons of stone, made a sufficient obstruction for the time ; but one difficulty of these waters is, that a flood will almost always wash out a new channel.

Major Gilmer reported, November 4th, that the armament of Fort Donelson was four thirty-two-pounders and two naval guns, and recommended that it should be doubled. He added, " There are also two small iron guns and a battery of field-pieces for the land-defenses ; " and recommended an additional supply of twelve-pounder guns, mounted on siege-carriages, and some howitzers for throwing shells. General Johnston sent four more thirty-two-pounders within the next four days. Within the same period the gunboats of the enemy were stopped by the obstructions near Eddyville.

General G. A. Henry, Confederate States Senator from Tennessee, a resident of Clarksville, and deeply interested in the defense of the Cumberland, accompanied Major Gilmer on this tour of inspection. He wrote to General Johnston as follows:

Fort Henry is in fine condition for defense, the work admirably done, as Major Gilmer thinks. . . . Fort Donelson is in a very bad condition. No work has been done of any account, though Lieutenant Dixon, a young officer of great energy, will soon, I hope, have it put in a fine state of defense. Captain Harrison, an old steamboat-captain familiar with the river, concurs with Lieutenant Dixon that the work of obstruction is effectually done. They think it will be impossible for the gunboats to pass Ingraham's Shoals, even when the water is ten feet higher than it is now. Though Donelson is unfortunately located on the river, it certainly possesses great advantages against a land-attack. A succession of deep ravines nearly surrounds it, including some ten or twelve acres of land, thickly lined with trees in the right place (for an abattis).

Again, Major Gilmer wrote on the 16th of November :

At Clarksville I also employed a competent person to establish a timber-obstruction in the Cumberland River, under the range of the guns of Fort Donelson.

He adds that he had chartered " a steamer to go to Fort Donelson to be employed in placing the obstructions in the river."

Each of the forts was garrisoned by a regiment of infantry, supporting the artillery-companies stationed in them. When the movement of the Federal army was made along the lines, early in November, General Johnston, fearing an attack on the Cumberland, ordered Pillow from Columbus, with 5,000 men, to defend this line. Why this movement was not made has already been explained in a previous chapter ; but the following extract from a letter of General Johnston to the Secretary of War, November 15th, is not out of place here. He said:

I had left but the choice of difficulties—the great probability of defeat at Columbus, or a successful advance of the enemy on my left. I have risked the latter. The first would be a great misfortune, scarcely reparable for a long time ; the latter may be prevented.

On the 17th of November Brigadier-General Lloyd Tilghman, who had been in command at Hopkinsville, was ordered to turn over his command there to General Charles J. Clark, and proceed to the Cumberland River, to take charge of Forts Donelson and Henry and their defenses, and the intermediate country, under General Polk, the division commander. Tilghman's orders continue :

The utmost vigilance is enjoined, as there has been gross negligence in this respect. . . . You will push forward the completion of the works and their armament with the utmost activity, and to this end will apply to the citizens of the surrounding country for assistance in labor, for which you will give them certificates for amounts of such labor.

Authority was also given to make all needful requisitions.

General Tilghman had been assigned to General Johnston with considerable *éclat*. General Johnston, desiring a proper commander for the defenses of Columbus, had very strongly recommended for that purpose the promotion of Major A. P. Stewart to be a brigadier-general. On the 11th of October Mr. Benjamin replied as follows :

I have your letter asking for the appointment of a brigadier to command at Columbus, Kentucky, in your absence. Your recommendation of Major A. P. Stewart has been considered with the respect due to your suggestions, but there is an officer under your command whom you must have overlooked ; whose claims in point of rank and experience greatly outweigh those of Major Stewart, and whom we could not pass by, without injustice—I refer to Colonel Lloyd Tilghman, whose record shows longer and better service, and who is, besides, as a Kentuckian, specially appropriate to the command of Columbus. He has, therefore, been appointed brigadier-general, but of course you will exercise your own discretion whether to place him in command at Columbus or not.

Though General Johnston had no objection to Tilghman's promotion, knowing that Polk had previously recommended him, he accepted the secretary's letter as a rebuke. Polk urged, October 31st, that Tilghman should be assigned to the command of the defenses of the

Tennessee and Cumberland, which General Johnston ordered, as soon as the pending movements by the Federals permitted.

As soon as Tilghman took command he stopped the work of obstruction on the Cumberland, which led to a sharp remonstrance from Gilmer, and a direction from headquarters not to interfere with Gilmer. General Johnston, on November 21st, ordered Lieutenant Dixon to lay out a field-work on the commanding ground opposite Fort Henry; and on the 29th telegraphed Gilmer that " these works should not be stopped. Push them on at the same time with the obstructions at Fort Donelson." Tilghman, on the same day, wrote, pointing out the necessity of a small field-work on this eminence, and the want of a field-battery there ; but did not suggest a removal of the forts, or any other change.

As General Johnston desired the line of the Cumberland to rally on in case of retreat, he gave directions for the construction of extensive field-works, so located that they might be occupied and held by brave but undisciplined militia, without the necessity of performing tactical manœuvres in the field. But it was impossible to convince the people of their value. Their construction required a large amount of labor. The troops worked reluctantly, and the slave-owners hired their negroes grudgingly, and were continually demanding their return. Fifteen hundred laborers were needed at Nashville, as many at Clarksville, 1,000 were called for at Fort Donelson by Lieutenant Dixon, November 15th, and the same number could have been usefully employed at Fort Henry. Instead of 5,000, not 500 could be got together in all. Much of the work was done by the soldiers, at the cost of health, drill, and discipline.

The authorities of Tennessee and Alabama did what they could to obtain the labor demanded. Official action was supplemented by patriotic voluntary effort. A committee of leading citizens of North Alabama and Tishomingo County, Mississippi, headed by General Samuel D. Weakley, appealed to the people in a private circular letter, November 23d, to furnish negro-laborers and volunteers to build and defend the works at Fort Henry. They plainly said that these defenses were important and unsafe, and that no time could be lost. They said :

If our people were convinced as we are that a deadly struggle for our homes and property is impending—that the enemy in a few days will put forth his whole strength for our subjugation—they would rally en masse for the public defense.

But the American people are so used to rhetorical exaggeration, that fervor of language has ceased with them to be taken as a measure of earnestness of conviction. The response was tardy and feeble. An insufficient number of negroes reached Fort Henry early in January. Still, if their labor had then been vigorously applied, it would have made a difference in the preparation.

Governor Harris, with that inflexible courage which he ever displayed, dared to tell the Legislature and people of Tennessee, in his next message, these truths, in reference to the loss of the forts :

Many weeks before this crisis in our affairs, General Johnston sent a highly accomplished and able engineer, Major Gilmer, to Nashville, to construct fortifications for the defense of the city. Laborers were needed for their construction. I joined Major Gilmer in an earnest and urgent appeal to the people to send in their laborers for this purpose, offering full and fair compensation. This appeal was so feebly responded to, that I advised General Johnston to impress the necessary labor; but, owing to the difficulty in obtaining the laborers, the works were not completed; indeed, some of them little more than commenced, when Fort Donelson fell.

General Johnston did order the impressment of 1,500 negroes near Nashville; but not more than fifty were collected for some time, and never more than 200 in all.

It may be thought strange that, when the formidable naval preparations of the United States for operations on the Western rivers were well known to the Confederate authorities, very slight efforts were made to meet them with similar gunboats or with rams. While it is true that this application of public money was excluded by the language of the appropriation bill passed by Congress, yet the Government could have confidently relied on a deficiency bill covering any necessary expenses in this direction. The true reason was a lack of skilled labor, of docks, and of materials for construction, which could not be improvised in a beset and blockaded country.

Proposals were considered both for building gunboats and for converting the ordinary side-wheel high-pressure steamboats into gunboats. Though anxious to avail itself of this means of defense, the engineer department decided that it was not feasible. Steamboats in armor, like the ass dressed in the lion's hide, would incur more danger than they would do damage. There was not plate-iron with which to armor a single iron-clad, and even railroad-iron could not be spared. The weight of these steamboats made their draught so great that they could only be used in floods; and, unless a fleet could be built to match the enemy's, the vessels could only be used as floating batteries under the guns of the forts, where they would enjoy no advantage over the land-batteries. It was thought best to concentrate the resources on what seemed practicable. One iron-clad gunboat, however, the Eastport, was undertaken on the Tennessee River, but under so many difficulties that, after the surrender of Fort Henry, while still unfinished, it was destroyed lest it should fall into the hands of the enemy.

While these feebly-sustained attempts at defense were in progress, the mighty wealth and energy of the North were concentrating themselves for one supreme effort of invasion. All summer and fall the ring of hammer and anvil told of the toil of thousands of skilled mechanics and sturdy laborers in the great work of preparation and armament. The best talents of the country were employed in the work of construction, organization, and equipment, and in training and fighting the iron-clad fleet that was to pierce the barriers of the Western rivers.[1] As early as May 16, 1861, Commander John Rodgers had been sent West by the United States Government to provide an armed flotilla, to serve on the Western rivers. He bought steamboats, which were fitted, armored, and armed as gunboats. On the 30th of August Captain Andrew H. Foote, of the United States Navy, was ordered to take command of the naval operations upon the Western waters. When Foote took command there were three wooden vessels in commission, and nine iron-clad gunboats and thirty-eight mortar-boats in process of construction. This is not the place to relate the history of the United States Navy in the civil war ; but, as an illustration of the magnitude and celerity of its preparations, it may be stated, on the authority of Prof. Hoppin, Foote's biographer, that 600 vessels "were, in a space of time to be reckoned by months, made ready for efficient service." The fleet of gunboats on the Mississippi and its tributaries, when finally completed, " consisted of twelve gunboats, seven of them iron-clad, and able to resist all except the heaviest solid shot, and costing on an average $89,000 each. The boats were built very wide in proportion to their length, so that on the smooth river-waters they might have almost the steadiness of stationary land-batteries when discharging their heavy guns." [2] This flotilla carried 143 guns ; some sixty-four-pounders, some thirty-two pounders, and some seven-inch rifled guns carrying eighty-pound shells. Each boat had also a Dahlgren ten-inch shell-gun. Eight of the boats were powerful engines of war. They were of about " 600 tons burden each, drawing six feet, carrying thirteen heavy guns, plated with iron two and a half inches thick, and to steam nine miles per hour. They were 175 feet long, 51½ feet wide ; the hulls of wood ; their sides projected from the bottom of the boat to the water-line at an angle of about thirty-five degrees, and from the water-line the sides fell back at about the same angle to form a slanting casemate, the gun-deck being about a foot above water. This slanting casemate extended across the hull, near the bow and stern, forming a quadrilateral gun-deck. Three nine or ten inch guns were placed in the bow, four similar ones on each side, and two smaller ones astern. The casemate inclosed the wheel, which was placed in a recess on the stern of the vessel." [3] To build this powerful squadron, all the resources

---

[1] Most of the details in regard to these naval operations are from Hoppin's " Life of Admiral Foote."

[2] Ibid., p. 157.

[3] Boynton's " History of the Navy during the Rebellion."

of the forests, mines, rolling-mills, founderies, machine-shops, and dock-yards, of the Northwest were brought under full requisition.

As early as the beginning of September, the Federal gunboats were cruising on the Ohio and Mississippi, overawing and distressing the people along the banks. On the 12th of October the gunboat Conestoga, Lieutenant Phelps, ascended the Tennessee, and made a reconnaissance of Fort Henry. In November the fleet took part in the battle of Belmont, as has been related.

About the middle of January the United States forces developed an intention of moving on the Confederate lines by way of the Tennessee and Cumberland Rivers, and early in February carried out the design. This danger was one that General Johnston had foreseen, and had attempted to provide against. While this is abundantly evinced even in the allusions in his correspondence given herein to illustrate other aspects of the campaign, it will not be amiss to add some brief extracts bearing directly on this subject.

As early as October 27, 1861, he wrote the adjutant-general, pointing out the three lines in Kentucky on which " the enemy seem to design to operate:" first, against Zollicoffer; second, by the Louis-ville & Nashville Railroad; " and the other against Polk, and will per-haps endeavor to use the Tennessee in aid of the movement."

For some time after this the rivers were too low to be used by the heavy armored flotilla; and the movements of the enemy seemed to be directed from South Carrollton against Clarksville as the objective point. But as the rainfall and the advance of winter made the roads difficult and the rivers navigable, the danger evidently became more imminent at the forts and less so at Clarksville; and military move-ments and preparations were, of course, modified accordingly.

On the 10th of December General Johnston, writing to General Polk, pointed out the lines by which the enemy might attempt to turn and carry Columbus : first, by a force from Cape Girardeau to New Madrid; second, by another moving on the west bank to a point below Colum-bus, to cut off supplies ; and, third, by a movement on transports up the Tennessee to the ferry, and thence to Paris. " This movement they would probably cover by a demonstration toward Columbus."

He urged General Polk, in this last contingency, to compel the column to give him battle on ground of his own choosing, or to impede and harass it, and engage it at a disadvantage. It will be seen, by his correspondence in January, that General Johnston used every endeavor to animate his subordinates and guard against an attack by the rivers.

The respective advocates of Grant, Sherman, Foote, Halleck, and Buell, have debated with considerable heat the question, " Who is en-titled to the credit of the movements against Forts Henry and Donel-son?" The movement seems so obvious that the writer always supposed it was a long-settled purpose, deliberately carried out. Indeed, it was but part of a general plan early matured in the mind of a person who seems to have been lost sight of by the later generation of great men. It was well known at General Johnston's headquarters that General Winfield Scott told General William Preston, in August, 1861, that his plan was to bisect the Confederacy by opening and holding the Mississippi River, and then to divide its eastern half diagonally. It was now evident that the bisection by the Mississippi was effectually stopped by Columbus with its 140 guns. The diagonal movement must, therefore, be made first; but winter rendered a mountain campaign through East Tennessee clearly impracticable. It was, therefore, left to the Federal commanders to force the position at Bowling Green at great sacrifice, or to attempt to reduce the forts on the Tennessee and Cumberland. What more natural than that the Federal commanders, arrested in their advance elsewhere, and seeking a weaker point in the defensive line, should discover it on these interior rivers that marked the second line of advance laid down in General Scott's original scheme of invasion?

General Sherman gives a picturesque narrative of the origin of this movement in his "Memoirs" (vol. i., page 220). He says that, in a council between Generals Halleck, Cullom, and himself—

General Halleck had a map on his table, with a large pencil in his hand, and asked, "Where is the rebel line?" Cullom drew the pencil through Bowling Green, Forts Donelson and Henry, and Columbus, Kentucky. "That is their line," said Halleck. "Now, where is the proper place to break it?" And either Cullom or I said, "*Naturally*, the centre." Halleck drew a line perpendicular to the other near its middle, and it coincided nearly with the general course of the Tennessee River, and he said, "That is the true line of operations." This occurred more than a month before General Grant began the movement; and, as he was subject to General Halleck's orders, I have always given Halleck the full credit for that movement, which was skillful, successful, and extremely rich in military results; indeed, it was the first real success on our side in the civil war.

General H. V. Boynton, in his volume entitled "Sherman's Historical Raid" (Chapter II.), denies the justice of this claim. He gives the credit to General Grant; but also shows, from the correspondence of Buell and Halleck, that, on the 3d of January, Buell proposed a combined attack on the centre and flanks of Johnston's lines. Buell estimated the Confederate force at double its actual strength, and concluded his note, "The attack upon the centre should be made by two gunboat expeditions, with, I should say, 20,000 men on the two rivers."

Boynton also quotes a letter from Halleck to McClellan, January 20, 1862, which says:

The idea of moving down the Mississippi by steam is, in my opinion, impracticable, or at least premature. It is not the proper line of operations, at least now. A much more feasible plan is to move up the Cumberland and Tennessee, making Nashville the present objective point. This would threaten Columbus, and force the abandonment of Bowling Green. . . . This line of the Cumberland and Tennessee is the great central line of the Western theatre of the war, with the Ohio below the mouth of Green River as the base, and two great navigable rivers extending far into the theatre of operations.

These views were eminently judicious ; but Halleck, overrating General Johnston's force and means of resistance, adds, "But the plan should not be attempted without a large force—not less than 60,000 effective men."

Halleck's plan was to move against the Confederate lines with deliberation and in force. But, as this plan was slowly maturing in the brain of the chief, the conflict was precipitated by the more eager and active temper of his subordinates at the mouth of the Ohio. These were three of the ablest and boldest officers in the service of the United States: Grant, C. F. Smith, and Foote. These enterprising officers, finding by due pressure the weak point of a strong line to be on their own immediate front, were not slow to seize the advantage.

Early in January, McClellan, the general-in-chief, directed Halleck, commanding the Western Department, to make a demonstration in Western Kentucky which should prevent reënforcements being sent to Bowling Green, toward which Buell was still reaching out. Grant, under orders from Halleck, sent McClernand, with 6,000 men, from Cairo to Milburn, to menace Columbus ; and C. F. Smith, with two brigades, from Paducah toward Mayfield and Murray, threatening Fort Henry and the country from there to Columbus.

McClernand's expedition occupied the time from January 10th to January 20th, the infantry marching about seventy-five miles, the cavalry farther. Smith's movement took a little longer. These commands were moved with extraordinary precautions. Although there was no fighting, the soldiers suffered greatly from cold, and from the effects of a violent storm of rain and snow. They subsisted chiefly on plunder.[1] General Polk believed that the retreat of these columns was due to a movement toward their rear by 1,000 cavalry and some Confederate infantry regiments sent out by him. But, as the demonstration had produced its effect, impressing the garrison at Columbus with the apprehension of an advance in force on that point, besides having resulted in valuable information of the defenses of the Tennessee River, it is more probable that the columns retired because they had accomplished their objects. Their movements were too cautious and insufficiently developed to allow General Polk to follow General Johnston's instructions of December 10th, and harass or attack them. These expeditions, un-

---

[1] Badeau's "Life of Grant," vol. i., p. 25; McClellan's report, "Rebellion Record," vol. iv., p. 49.

dertaken in the depth of winter, improved the *morale* of the Federal troops, and accustomed them to the hardships of a winter campaign.

In this demonstration, C. F. Smith moved his column in concert with the gunboats, returning by the left bank of the Tennessee to Paducah. Lieutenant Phelps, of the Conestoga, after a reconnaissance as far as the Tennessee State line, made on the 7th of January, reported "the water barely sufficient to float this boat, drawing five feet five inches." He says, "Fort Henry I have examined, and the work is formidable." Again, on the 16th, he "proceeded up the river, accompanied by the transport-steamer Wilson, having on board a force of 500 —infantry and artillery—under Major Ellston, and anchored for the night near where the Tennessee line strikes the right bank of the river." The next day they proceeded up the river, shelling the banks, and fired a few shells at Fort Henry, at two and a half miles distance, without effect.[1]

The transport then landed the troops a few miles below, at Aurora, whence they proceeded to Murray, and threatened Paris. This movement, in conjunction with the demonstration against Columbus, exactly verified the prediction of General Johnston in his letter of December 10th. The columns, moving by the west bank of the Mississippi, advanced later. But the blow struck against Zollicoffer at this very date had also been pointed out, October 27th, by General Johnston, as probable.

On their return from these January expeditions, Grant telegraphed Halleck, January 28th, from Cairo:

With permission, I will take Fort Henry, on the Tennessee, and establish and hold a large camp there.

On the same day Foote telegraphed Halleck that Fort Henry could be carried with four iron-clad gunboats and troops to permanently occupy it, and for authority to move.

On January 29th Grant wrote Halleck fully, urging an immediate advance and attack on Fort Henry, and thence on Fort Donelson, Memphis, or Columbus.

Halleck gave the fullest authority, and instructions, also, for the execution of the plan. Badeau says:

On the 2d of February Grant started from Cairo with 17,000 men on transports. Foote accompanied him with seven gunboats, and on the 4th the debarkation began at Bailey's Ferry, on the east bank, three miles below Fort Henry.

The only practicable approaches to the fort by land were double this distance. Grant himself took command on the east bank, with

---

[1] Hoppin's "Life of Foote," pp. 191, 192, and Confederate archives.

the main column ; while C. F. Smith, with two brigades—some 5,000 or 6,000 men—landed on the left bank, with orders to take the earthwork opposite Fort Henry, known as Fort Heiman. During the debarkation on the 4th three of the gunboats approached the forts and tried the range of their guns, throwing solid shot and nine-inch shells at a mile's distance, and burying their shot in the fort, but doing no other damage. The fort replied with a columbiad and a rifle-gun, without effect, but had to stop firing on account of an injury to a clamp of the carriage of the columbiad. On the 5th the landing was completed, and the noon of the next day was fixed as the time of attack. Some delay had occurred while coming up the river, in fishing up the torpedoes anchored a little below the surface. Lieutenant Phelps, who had experience with river-obstructions, took up eight.

General Johnston's letters had constantly urged upon his subordinates the prompt construction, and upon the bureaus the proper armament, of the forts. But the needs of the country for ordnance were so much greater than the ability to supply it, that Columbus alone was as yet in a state of defense. The fortifications had been delayed for lack of labor, and from the difficulty of employing efficiently troops unused and unwilling to build them. The call for slaves for this purpose had been responded to slowly and feebly, as has been shown.

The condition of the Confederates in that quarter may be understood from an extract from a letter of General Polk to General Johnston, dated January 11, 1862 :

My available force is greatly reduced by sickness and absence. . . . There are many regiments in my division who are without arms, and several poorly armed. The unarmed regiments are stationed at Forts Pillow, Donelson, and Henry; at Trenton, Union City, and Henderson Station. In my return you will find embraced the brigade of Brigadier-General Alcorn. His men are sixty-day troops from Mississippi, who are armed with every variety of weapon. They are sick with measles, raw, and undisciplined. This brigade cannot be expected to be very effective.

I also send you a weekly report of the troops at this post, and am sorry to remark that they have been much reduced by sickness. My effective force is now, as you will see, only about 12,000.

On the 18th of January Colonel Munford, aide to General Johnston, received the following letter, written the day before, by the Hon. James E. Saunders :

NASHVILLE, *January* 17, 1862.

DEAR SIR: I am just starting for Fort Heiman, opposite Fort Henry, where I have been for some time. I was sent for ammunition and equipments (which I have obtained), as none of the officers could be spared.

We carried a large negro force down. They have literally done nothing, for want of the intrenchments being laid off ready to commence work as soon as the shelters were made. When the engineer, Captain Hayden, was urged to his work, the answer was that General Tilghman had not passed on the plan. A courier was sent to General Tilghman on the 3d or 4th of January, advising him that laborers were then *in transitu* from North Alabama. The general came to Fort Henry on the 15th—and then it was, when I left, debated whether it was not too late to throw up works on the west side, as contemplated by Captain Dixon and every general who knows anything of the position of the fort. All did concur in the opinion that a failure to occupy the heights would be equivalent to abandoning Fort Henry.

The Alabama troops are raw and undisciplined. In my poor opinion, a disciplined regiment should be sent to Fort Heiman, and another or two to Rickman's furnace, half-way between Forts Donelson and Henry, six miles from each, where there is a village of houses to shelter the men.

Hurriedly, your friend,   JAMES E. SAUNDERS.

P. S.—The Alabama volunteers will have finished their 100 cabins by the time I get back. Taking care of the men is of prime importance at this season of the year.

Colonel E. W. MUNFORD.

General Johnston could not neglect this warning from a zealous and intelligent citizen, and telegraphed Tilghman immediately :

Occupy and *intrench* the heights opposite Fort Henry. Do not lose a moment. Work all night.

General Johnston certainly had some right to feel disappointed at Mr. Saunders's account of the condition of things at Fort Henry. Tilghman had written him, December 28th, before the arrival of the Alabama negroes, and while as yet he had only slaves borrowed in the neighborhood, giving an encouraging account of the progress of the fortifications at Fort Donelson. The arrival of the Alabama negroes gave him the means of doing at least as much at Fort Henry. At Clarksville some 300 negroes were employed, but the works there seem not to have been pushed vigorously. Slaves, reluctantly loaned, slothful in habits, and badly organized, could not be expected to prove very efficient laborers.

The demonstrations from Cairo and Paducah, and the simulated attack on Fort Henry, January 17th, made it clear that this position was liable to attack at any moment. General Johnston telegraphed, January 19th, to the Secretary of War, an accurate account of the enemy's movements and strength. He adds :

I desire the Government, if it be possible, to send a strong force to Nashville, and another to Memphis.

On January 27th General Johnston wrote Polk, Tilghman's immediate commander :

Urge upon General Tilghman the necessity of immediate attention to the discipline and instruction of his command. A grave disaster has just befallen our arms at Mill Springs on our right, by neglect of this essential.

Next day he wrote Tilghman:

As you have now a large number of raw troops on hand, push forward their instruction as earnestly as possible.

He also authorized him to employ special instructors, and ordered him to recall all absent medical officers, and employ skillful surgeons, "as he would soon want all his medical skill at Forts Donelson and Henry."

The information received throughout January, from both Polk and Tilghman, based on intelligence received through the lines, was positive as to a projected attack on Columbus, and indicated a strong probability of a simultaneous assault on Forts Donelson and Henry. This was the plan proposed by Buell to Halleck, which the latter did not feel strong enough to attempt. At the same time, Lovell recalled to New Orleans two regiments loaned for the defense of Columbus at a critical time. Hence Polk called for reënforcements, which were collected for him from scattered recruiting-stations, and small detached commands. The same relief was sent to Henry and Donelson, and men and artillery were also drawn from Columbus to their aid.

On the 20th of January General Johnston detached 8,000 men, Floyd's brigade and part of Buckner's, from his army at Bowling Green. The infantry, artillery, and baggage, were sent to Russellville by rail, the cavalry and artillery horses moving by land. General Johnston's army at Bowling Green had numbered, December 8th, 18,000 men, including 5,000 sick. December 24th, his effective force had increased to 17,000; December 30th, to 19,000; and January 8th, by reënforcements—Bowen's brigade from Polk, and Floyd's brigade sent from Western Virginia by the War Department—his army attained the greatest strength it ever had, 23,000 effective troops. On January 20th it had fallen off to 22,000 from camp-diseases, and these numbers were again reduced, by the detachment above named, to 14,000. With this force he faced Buell's army, estimated at 80,000 men, for three weeks longer.

The following letter from General Johnston to the adjutant-general, written January 22d, gives his own conception of the situation at that time. After recounting Zollicoffer's defeat, he says:

Movements on my left, threatening Forts Henry and Donelson, and Clarksville, have, I do not doubt, for their ultimate object, the occupation of Nashville. I have already detached 8,000 men to make Clarksville secure and drive the enemy back, with the aid of the force at Clarksville and Hopkinsville; but to make another large detachment toward my right would leave this place untenable. The road through this place is indispensable to the enemy to enable them to advance with their main body. They must have river or railroad means of transportation to enable them to invade with a large force. While it is of vital importance to keep back the main body, it is palpable this great object cannot be accomplished if detachments can turn my position, and attack and occupy Nashville and the interior of the State, which it is the special object of this force to defend. A reserve at Nashville seems now absolutely necessary to enable me to maintain this position.

A successful movement of the enemy on my right would carry with it all the consequences which could be expected by the enemy here, if they could break through my defenses. If I had the force to prevent a flank movement, they would be compelled to attack this position, which we doubt not can make a successful defense.

If force cannot be spared from other army corps, the country must now be roused to make the greatest effort that it will be called upon to make during the war. No matter what the sacrifice may be, it must be made, and without loss of time. Our people do not comprehend the magnitude of the danger that threatens. Let it be impressed upon them.

The enemy will probably undertake no active operations in Missouri,[1] and may be content to hold our force fast in their position on the Potomac for the remainder of the winter; but, to suppose, with the facilities of movement by water which the well-filled rivers of the Ohio, Cumberland, and Tennessee, give for active operations, that they will suspend them in Tennessee and Kentucky during the winter months, is a delusion. All the resources of the Confederacy are now needed for the defense of Tennessee.

With great respect, etc.,

A. S. JOHNSTON.

At the time of the attack upon Fort Henry, it had been well fortified, though not strongly enough for the force brought against it. Hoppin, in his "Life of Foote," following Lossing, says:

It lay in a bend of the stream, and was at times almost surrounded by water; its guns commanded a reach of the river below, toward "Panther Island," for about two miles. It was a strong earthwork, constructed with much scientific skill, covering ten acres, with five bastions from four to six feet high, the embrasures knitted firmly together with sand-bags.

If the work was not strong, the responsibility rested chiefly with the officer in charge, General Tilghman, who had been in immediate command for two months and a half.

Lieutenant-Colonel J. F. Gilmer was ordered by General Johnston, January 29th, to proceed to Fort Henry to inspect the works and direct what was necessary to be done. He met General Tilghman there on the 31st. His report upon the defenses of Forts Henry and Donelson, made March 17, 1862, presents an intelligent and dispassionate account of these transactions. He says:

By the exertions of the commanding general, aided by Lieutenant Joseph Dixon, his engineer-officer, the main fort (a strong field-work of five-bastion

[1] General Johnston had no advices from the West, indicating an active campaign.

front) had been put in a good condition for defense, and seventeen guns mounted on substantial platforms; twelve of which were so placed as to bear well on the river. These twelve guns were of the following description : one ten-inch columbiad, one rifled-gun of twenty-four-pounder calibre (weight of ball sixty-two pounds), two forty-two-pounders, and eight thirty-two-pounders, all arranged to fire through embrasures, formed by raising the parapet between the guns with sand-bags carefully laid.

In addition to placing the main work in good defensive order, I found that extensive lines of infantry cover had been thrown up by the troops forming the garrison, with a view to hold commanding ground, that would be dangerous to the fort if possessed by the enemy. These lines and the main work were on the right bank of the river, and arranged with good defensive relations, making the place capable of offering a strong resistance against a land-attack coming from the eastward.

On the left bank of the river there was a number of hills within cannon-range, that commanded the river-batteries on the right bank. The necessity of occupying these hills was apparent to me at the time I inspected Fort Henry, early in November last; and on the 21st of that month Lieutenant Dixon, the local engineer, was ordered from Fort Donelson to Fort Henry to make the necessary surveys, and construct the additional works. . . .

The surveys were made by the engineer, and plans decided upon without delay ; but, by some unforeseen cause, the negroes were not sent until after the 1st of January last. Much valuable time was thus lost, but, under your urgent orders when informed of the delay, General Tilghman and his engineers pressed these defenses forward so rapidly night and day, that, when I reached the fort (January 31st), they were far advanced, requiring only a few days' additional labor to put them in a state of defense. But no guns had been received that could be put in these works, except a few field-pieces; and, notwithstanding every effort had been made to procure them from Richmond, Memphis, and other points, it was apprehended they would not arrive in time to anticipate the attack of the enemy, which, from the full information obtained by General Tilghman, was threatened at an early day either at Fort Henry or Fort Donelson, or possibly on both at the same time. The lines of infantry-cover, however, which had been thrown up, were capable of making a strong resistance, even without the desired artillery, should the attack be made on that (the left) bank of the river. A defect was found in the carriage of the ten-inch columbiad, which was partially remedied. With this exception, the guns were in fair working order.

After the batteries of the main work were mounted General Tilghman found much difficulty in getting competent artillerists to man them, and he was not supplied with a sufficient number of artillery-officers.

It is proper to state that an Alabama regiment of 300 artillerists was ordered from Tuscumbia, Alabama, January 18th, but, for some reason, probably a deficiency in organization and equipment, did not go to Fort Henry.

Impressed with the great deficiency in the preparations for defending the passage of the river, the commanding officer expressed to me his fears that it might cause disaster if the place were vigorously attacked by the enemy's gunboats. This he thought his greatest danger. In conjunction with General Tilghman, I made every effort during the three days I remained at Fort Henry to get all the works and batteries in as good condition for defense as the means at hand would permit. The 3d of February we went over to Fort Donelson to do the same.

On the 4th General Tilghman was startled by heavy firing at Fort Henry, at 10½ A. M., and by a message from Colonel Heiman, received at 3½ P. M., that the enemy were landing. He and Gilmer returned to Fort Henry that night, arriving there at midnight. The 5th of February and the morning of the 6th were spent in preparations and dispositions for defense, and in the instruction of the various commands in the duties assigned them. Tilghman seemed, up to this time, to have feared the effects of the overflow on the mud walls of his fort more than the gunboats, and the gunboats more than Grant's army.

General Tilghman says in his report in one place that his force was 2,734 effective troops at Fort Henry, in another that it was 2,610 ; and General Gilmer puts it at about 3,200. A careful examination of the returns satisfies the writer that the latter statement is nearly correct, and that Tilghman had about 3,400 men present at Fort Henry, and 2,300 or 2,400 more at Fort Donelson. On January 31st he had 3,033 effectives at Henry, and 1,956 at Donelson. The Fiftieth Tennessee, numbering 386, was transferred from Henry to Donelson, leaving 2,647 at the former and 2,342 at the latter. Subsequently, there arrived at Fort Henry reënforcements from General Polk, the Forty-eighth and Fifty-first Tennessee, and the Fifteenth Arkansas, which added some 700 or 800 effectives to his numbers, and gave him at the two forts about 5,750 men.

In his report of the bombardment of Fort Henry General Tilghman says :

Had I been reënforced, so as to have justified my meeting the enemy at the advanced works, I might have made good the land-defense on the east bank.

In his supplemental report he says :

The failure of adequate support, doubtless from sufficient cause, cast me on my own resources.

All the telegrams from Colonel Heiman, commanding at Fort Henry, and from General Tilghman, during the 4th and 5th of February, breathe a confident spirit. In transmitting Colonel Heiman's dispatch, General Tilghman telegraphed, 4 P. M., February 4th, to Colonel Mackall :

Better send two regiments to Danville, subject to my orders.

An hour later he telegraphed :

The landing of the enemy is between rivers, perhaps from both rivers. Give me all the help you can, light battery included. Off for Henry.

On the 5th, at 8 A. M., General Tilghman telegraphed from Fort Henry :

My force in good spirits, but badly armed. I will hold my position to the last, but should be reënforced amply, at once, if possible.

At midnight, before his surrender, General Tilghman again telegraphed :

Our scouts engaged advanced posts of the enemy yesterday afternoon. Our cavalry retired. I reënforced, and enemy retired. We lost one man. Enemy fortifying three miles below. They were reënforced yesterday. I hope not to lose the chance proposed to the general yesterday. I must have reënforcements and with well-drilled troops. The green men with me are wellnigh worthless. More of them would be in my way. The high water threatens us seriously. Enemy evidently intend to prevent us landing troops or supplies at fort, and they can do it. If you can reënforce strongly and quickly, we have a glorious chance to overwhelm the enemy. Move by Clarksville to Donelson, and across to Danville,[1] where transports will be ready. Enemy said to be intrenching below. My plans are to concentrate closely in and under Henry.

This dispatch was received on February 6th by General Johnston. A few hours later Fort Henry surrendered.

General Tilghman's requests were not neglected ; indeed, they were anticipated, but too late to save Fort Henry. There was a delay of three or four hours in transmitting dispatches by courier from Fort Henry to Donelson, and a further delay thence to the nearest telegraph-office. On the 5th General Johnston ordered a regiment, just armed, from Nashville to Donelson, and on the 6th Colonel Smith's regiment from Tuscumbia, Alabama. He also ordered Floyd, on the 6th, to proceed with his command from Russellville to Clarksville, without a moment's delay, and at the same time sent all the rolling-stock he could command to take the troops. Before any concentration could possibly have been made, Tilghman had surrendered.

On leaving Fort Donelson Tilghman ordered Colonel Head to hold his own and Sugg's regiment, together about 750 strong, ready to move at a moment's notice, with two pieces of artillery ; and on the morning of the 5th he ordered him, if no advance had been made against Fort Donelson, to take position at the Furnace, half-way on the road to Fort Henry. This gave him more than 4,000 men confronting Grant with his column of 12,000 men, on the east bank of the Tennessee ; though, of course, it was in Grant's power to draw reënforcements from

---

[1] Tennessee River railroad-crossing, twenty miles above Henry.

Smith, who was on the west bank. The Confederate force was raw, badly armed, and imperfectly disciplined ; but it is not improbable that, if well handled, they could have held the assailants at bay on the narrow approaches of that overflowed country, and with the advantage of breastworks to retire to. Even when not meeting a show of resistance, Grant advanced slowly, cautiously, and painfully, making no attempt even to carry the intrenchments until after the surrender. Indeed, he could not have done so without exposing himself to a fire from the five heavy guns of the fort mounted landward.

General Tilghman complained that the small force at his command did not enable him to avail himself of his line of defenses. Nevertheless, he drew in all his troops from the west bank, and placed his whole command in the rifle-pits. He says, " Minute instructions were given, not only to brigades, but to regiments and companies, as to the exact ground each was to occupy." It is evident that, on the 5th, Tilghman meant to dispute Grant's advance. But on the 6th, just before the attack by the gunboats, he changed his purpose, abandoned all hope of a successful defense, and made arrangements for the escape of his main body to Fort Donelson, while the guns of Fort Henry should return the fire of the gunboats.

There had been some inconsiderable skirmishing on the 5th, and on the morning of the 6th it was plain that a combined attack was impending. Tilghman ordered Colonel Heiman to withdraw the command to Fort Donelson, while he himself would obtain the necessary delay for the movement by standing a bombardment in Fort Henry. For this purpose, he retained his heavy artillery company—seventy-five men—to work the guns ; a number quite unequal to the strain and labor of the defense, as was demonstrated. It was probably impossible to repair the oversight of not having more men who had been trained at the guns, but the presence of mere laborers would have helped the tired and discouraged artillerists.

Whatever may have been Tilghman's want of earnestness in preparation during the two months and a half he held command at Fort Henry, and of judgment and steadiness of purpose in the final hours before the attack, he perfectly vindicated his personal gallantry and self-devotion in the hour of imminent peril.

Noon was fixed as the time of attack ; but Grant, impeded by the overflow, and unwilling to expose his men to the heavy guns of the fort, held back his troops in the wet woods until the result of the gunboat attack should develop some point of weakness in the defense. In the mean time the Confederate troops were in retreat.

On February 6th, at 11 A. M., the fleet set forward in two divisions. The first, under Captain Foote, consisted of the flagship Cincinnati, the Carondelet, and the St. Louis, each carrying thirteen guns, and the Essex of nine guns, all iron-plated gunboats. The second, under Lieutenant Phelps, three unarmored gunboats, each with nine guns, followed at the distance of about half a mile. At 11.45 A. M. the main division opened fire, at 1,700 yards, with their bow-guns, and kept firing as they slowly steamed up, until within 600 yards. Here they took position abreast, firing with all their might, to dismount the guns of the fort. The unarmored boats, at safer distance, kept up a bombardment of shells that fell within the works. The firing, which had increased in rapidity and precision on both sides, now became terrible indeed. The armored boats, each carrying three ten-inch guns in its bow, sent their formidable missiles, at short range, five or six a minute, some 400 in all, into the fort. This heavy cannonading, besides the bursting of shells, taxed the utmost energy of officers and men inside the fort. They were not slow to respond, and as many as fifty-nine of their shot were counted by the Federal officers as striking the gunboats. Where these hit the iron armor they bounded harmless from the surface. One thirty-two-pound shot, entering at the bow of the flagship, ranged its whole length, killing one seaman. In the course of the action, nine more seamen were wounded on this vessel. One man was killed on the Essex by a cannon-ball ; and a shot through the boiler caused an explosion that scalded Commander Porter, twenty-eight seamen, and nineteen soldiers, many of whom died. The Essex was thus forced to retire.

Five minutes after the fight began in earnest, that is, at twenty-five minutes before one o'clock, the twenty-four-pounder rifle-gun, one of the most prized in the fort, burst, disabling every man at the piece. Then a shell, entering the embrasure, exploded at the muzzle of one of the thirty-two-pounders, ruining the gun, and killing or wounding all the men at the piece. About the same moment, a premature discharge occurred at one of the forty-two-pounder guns, killing three men and seriously injuring others. But now occurred a still greater loss. A priming wire was jammed and broken in the vent of the ten-inch columbiad, the only gun able to match the artillery of the assailants. An heroic blacksmith labored for a long time, with great coolness, to remove it, under the full fire of the enemy, but in vain.

The men had fought with courage and enthusiasm; but they now became both weary and discouraged. They lost confidence in their guns, and some of them ceased to work the thirty-two-pounders, thinking them useless against the invulnerable mail of the gunboats. Seeing this, Tilghman did what was possible to encourage the men, serving himself at a thirty-two-pounder some fifteen minutes. Only four guns were now replying to the rapid fire of the enemy, which was telling with powerful effect. The men were exhausted, they lost all hope, and there were none to replace them. Tilghman's spirit rose with the danger.   To a suggestion to surrender, he answered, "I shall not give up the works."   He sent out to try to get volunteers from his retreating forces, to replace his exhausted artillerists at the deserted guns. But it was too late.   The retiring troops already felt the demoralization of a retreat.

Tilghman struggled on, but there is a limit to human endurance. Though but four of his guns were disabled, six stood idle for want of artillerists, and but two guns were replying to the enemy.   At five minutes before two o'clock, after an engagement of two hours and ten minutes, he ceased firing and lowered his flag.   He had certainly done all that was necessary to vindicate his personal prowess and honor, and to cover the retreat of his command; but the fort was gone, the Tennessee River was open, and a base by short lines was established against Fort Donelson.

Tilghman's casualties were five killed and sixteen wounded; those of the enemy were sixty-three of all kinds.   Twelve officers and sixty-six non-commissioned officers and privates were surrendered with the fort.   Captain Foote treated his prisoners with courtesy, though the contrary has sometimes been alleged.   In a letter written to General Pillow, February 10th, Colonel Gilmer expressed the opinion that the comparatively small damage done to the gunboats "was due in great measure to the want of skill in the men who served the guns, and not to the invulnerability of the boats themselves."

When the surrender was determined on, Colonel Gilmer and a few others, unwilling to be included in it, escaped, and made their way on foot to Fort Donelson.   The troops retreating to Fort Donelson lost twenty or thirty stragglers, captured by the Federal cavalry, and left some guns on the road, on account of the mud.   Their precipitate retreat demoralized these brave but undisciplined soldiers, and prepared them to accept a greater disaster.   On the other hand, the unexpected rapidity and brilliancy of their naval success at Fort Henry filled the Northern troops with exultation, and inspired them with an eager desire to surpass it with still brighter achievements.   This signal victory gave great prestige to the gunboats, and added to their assault at Fort Donelson, under entirely different circumstances, a moral weight far beyond their real power.

Foote, with his usual vigor, ordered Phelps to push up the Tennessee River with his three gunboats, while he himself returned to Paducah with his iron-armored gunboats to make ready for the attack on Fort Donelson.   The Tennessee River was open to the keels of Phelps's flotilla, and he ascended that stream, destroying whatever could be useful to the Confederate defense, and spreading as much terror among the simple inhabitants as any marauding viking a thousand years before along the coast of France.   General Johnston telegraphed to the authorities of the principal towns on the Tennessee River, on the day of the fall of Fort Henry, warning them to send all boats up the river, and to take other proper precautions; but the disaster seemed to paralyze the faculties and energies of the most patriotic, so that the gunboats swept the Tennessee River with impunity.

CHAPTER XXVIII.

FORT DONELSON.

THE fall of Fort Henry made it manifest that a combined attack on Donelson by land and water would soon follow. Such attack could not be otherwise than formidable. Indeed, the success of the gunboats at Henry had produced an exaggerated impression of their power; while the real strength of the Northern armies was too well known at General Johnston's headquarters to leave any doubt of their ability to move overwhelming forces on both Bowling Green and Donelson. Still, if the line of the Cumberland could be maintained from Nashville to Donelson for even a few weeks, General Johnston hoped that the awakened spirit of the country would supply him with the long-demanded reenforcements. Grant's movable column at Fort Henry, stated by his biographer, Badeau, at 15,000 men, was receiving accessions from Halleck, while Buell was also reënforcing him.

Forrest had reported the enemy concentrating 10,000 men at South Carrollton for a forward movement toward Russellville; and, to meet this movement, General Johnston detached Floyd, on January 20th, with his own brigade and part of Buckner's—8,000 men in all. General Johnston retained 14,000 men to restrain the advance of Buell. Floyd was sent to Russellville, with orders to protect the railroad line from Bowling Green to Clarksville. It was added:

He must judge from after-information whether he shall march straight upon the enemy, now reported at South Carrollton, or wait for further developments of his intention. It is sufficient to say, he must get the best information of the movements of the enemy southward from the river, and beat them at the earliest favorable opportunity.

Toward the close of January, General Pillow, who had been for some time sick in Nashville, was placed in command at Clarksville. On February 6th Brigadier-General Bushrod R. Johnson was placed in command at Fort Donelson. Next day, on account of the attack at Fort Henry, Pillow was ordered to move from Clarksville, with all the troops there, to Donelson, and assume command. Brigadier-General

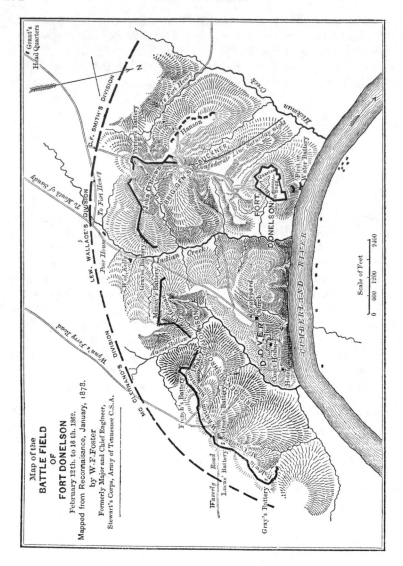

Map of the
BATTLE FIELD
OF
FORT DONELSON.
February 12th. to 16th. 1862.
Mapped from Reconnaisance, January, 1878.
by W. F. Foster
Formerly Major and Chief Engineer,
Stewart's Corps, Army of Tennessee C.S.A.

Clark was also charged to move at once from Hopkinsville to Clarksville with his command, something over 2,000 men; and Floyd was
directed to take his force from Russellville to Clarksville without a
moment's delay. Floyd was given authority to determine his movements as he might think judicious; at the same time it was indicated
to him that he should concentrate his forces at Clarksville, and move to
the support of Donelson. He was directed to encamp on the left bank
of the Cumberland, so as to leave open the route to Nashville in case

of the loss of the fort. Suggestions were also made for obstructions and submarine batteries, which, however, the engineers found them-selves unable to carry out. All these dispositions were made as soon as General Johnston heard of the advance upon Fort Henry, and before he had learned of its fall.

Events were moving so rapidly, and proper military action was so dependent on accurate information of the enemy, that it was necessary to leave the immediate commander untrammeled. Floyd was, there-fore, invested with the fullest authority. Pillow reported that the troops at Donelson were much demoralized by the transactions at Henry, and this was true. They were the rawest militia, reduced by disease and disheartened by retreat. Pillow wrote that a naval officer, who had witnessed the surrender, told him (February 7th) "that we had troops enough at Donelson, and that they are powerless to resist the gunboats."

General Johnston, presuming that Grant would follow up his suc-cess at Fort Henry by an immediate attack on Donelson, took his measures on the supposition that Donelson was no longer tenable, and already virtually lost. But, though his advices gave him little con-fidence of the ability of the batteries to prevent the passage of the gunboats, General Johnston said what he could by way of encourage-ment. He telegraphed to Pillow:

Your report of the effect of shots at Fort Henry should encourage the troops, and insure our success. If, at long range, we could do so much damage, with the necessary short range on the Cumberland, we should destroy their boats."

Gilmer, after his escape from Henry, stopped at Donelson ; and, with General Johnston's authority, engaged actively in preparations for its defense. Pillow arrived on the 9th, and pressed forward the works. Additional lines of infantry cover were constructed, to embrace the town of Dover ; and two heavy guns were mounted—the only guns there effective against the armor of the gunboats. All this was accom-plished by the night of the 12th.

Pillow says that, at the time of his arrival—

Deep gloom was hanging over the command, and the troops were greatly depressed and demoralized by the .circumstances attending the fall of Fort Henry, and the manner of retiring from that place. . . . I imparted to the work all the energy which it was possible to do, working day and night with the whole command.

But Pillow, bold and sanguine in temper, saw difficulties vanishing, and gave assurances of an improved and improving condition of affairs. Senator Bailey of Tennessee, then colonel of the Forty-ninth Ten-nessee Regiment, informs the writer that the restoration of confidence among the men in the power of the garrison to resist the passage of the gunboats was chiefly due to Lieutenant Dixon, who lost his life during the siege. On February 8th Buckner conveyed to General Johnston information, derived from friends in Louisville, that there were not more than 12,000 Federals on the Cumberland and Tennessee Rivers. In fact, the strength of the movement against Donelson was not developed. To meet it, General Johnston sent a force, which he estimated moderately at 17,000 men, reserving for himself only 14,000 men to perform the more delicate task of retiring before a larger army, ably commanded. Even after reënforcing Grant with thirteen regiments, General Buell, had left seventy regiments of infantry, besides artillery and cavalry—fully 55,000 men. Certain is it, therefore, that General Johnston took himself the place of greater hazard, and left to his subordinates the opportunity of glory. If it terminated otherwise, it was no fault of his. He had sent all the troops he could possibly spare, with abundance of ammunition and supplies. Under the circumstances, the army at Donelson might well be thought sufficient. At all events, General Johnston felt that he had done all that he could do ; and he awaited the issue with composure.

The criticism has been made that General Johnston should have concentrated his forces, and made an aggressive campaign. The foregoing facts show that this could not properly have been done at Donelson; and they make it almost as plain that the attempt would have been equally as futile at Bowling Green. This subject will be briefly considered, however, in its proper place.

But there was no reason for General Johnston to feel that he had fallen short of the requirements of the occasion. Pillow telegraphed him on the 10th, the day after his arrival:

My position undisturbed by enemy. Am pushing my work day and night. Will make my batteries bomb-proof, if allowed a little time. Have my guns mounted, and satisfactory trial of all my guns.

Pillow wrote to Floyd to the same effect. He stated that he was apprehensive that the enemy might cross the country south of him, and cut his communication by river, though the country was so rough and broken as to be nearly impracticable. He believed that the difficulty of procuring supplies insured his safety. He says:

The conflict of yesterday between our cavalry and that of the enemy resulted in three of ours wounded, and twenty taken prisoners by being thrown from their horses; and in three of the enemy killed and six mortally wounded. . . . I hope you will order forward at once the tents and baggage of General Buckner's command, as they are suffering very much this cold weather.

Writing to General Johnston the same day, the 10th, Colonel Gilmer says :

The attack expected here is a combined one—gunboats by water, and a land-force in their rear. The greatest danger is, in my opinion, from the gunboats, which appear to be well protected from our shot. The effect of our shot at Fort Henry was not sufficient to disable them, or any one of them, so far as I can ascertain. This was due, I think, in a great measure, to the want of skill in the men who served the guns, and not to the invulnerability of the boats themselves. . . .

With the preparations that are now being made here, I feel much confidence that we can make a successful resistance against a land-attack. The attack by water will be more difficult to meet. Still, I hope for success here also. . . . We are making Herculean efforts to strengthen our parapets, making narrow embrasures with sand-bags.

He also announced the landing of troops. Pillow wrote at the same time:

This position can be made stronger than Columbus is now, by water, if we had more heavy artillery. The advantage is in the narrowness of the stream, and the necessity of the boats approaching our works by a straight and narrow channel for one and a half mile. No more than three boats could possibly bring their guns to bear upon our position at once; thus admitting the construction of very narrow embrasures.

A difference of opinion arose between Pillow and Floyd as to the proper disposition of the troops, Buckner concurring with Floyd. Pillow believed that the defense of the river should and could be made at Donelson; the other two seem to have given up the idea of a successful defense of the river before the enemy appeared. Floyd proposed to withdraw Buckner's troops from Donelson to Cumberland City, where the railroad diverged from the river, whence a retreat might be easily made to Nashville. He intended to leave Pillow to defend the fort. But Pillow thought if the whole of Floyd's army could not defend Donelson, half of it could not, and that such a course must involve his capture. So, when Buckner arrived, on the night of the 11th, to carry off his division, Pillow refused to allow it, and appealed to General Johnston by telegraph. He also went by steamer to Floyd at Cumberland, leaving Buckner temporarily in command, and persuaded Floyd to concentrate all his troops at Donelson. Floyd consented, though probably with hesitation. General Johnston, that night, telegraphed Floyd to go to Donelson; and he replied that he had anticipated the order.

General Pillow, in a letter dated March 28, 1877, gives the present writer the following information:

The orders of General Johnston at Bowling Green, delivered personally, were for me to proceed directly to Donelson, to assume command of the forces there, to do all that was possible to protect his rear by holding that place; that he would give me all the force it was possible for him to spare from his position; when it was no longer possible to hold that place, to evacuate the position and march the army by way of Charlotte to Nashville.

General Pillow's recollection of his verbal orders is sustained by the correspondence, telegraphic and by letter, between General Johnston and his subordinates on the Cumberland. These matters will be made clearer by reference to the correspondence here following.

On the 12th, Pillow, being still in command, telegraphed :

If I can retain my present force, I can hold my position. . . . Let me retain Buckner for the present. If now withdrawn, will invite an attack. Enemy cannot pass this place without exposing himself to flank-attack. If I am strong enough to take field, he cannot ever reach here; nor is it possible for him to subsist on anything in the country to pass over, nor can he possibly bring his subsistence with him. With Buckner's force, I can hold my position. Without it, cannot long.

General Johnston, at three o'clock that day, communicated the above dispatch to General Floyd, adding :

I do not know the wants of General Pillow, nor yours, nor the position of General Buckner. You do. You have the dispatch. Decide. Answer.

Floyd replied :

I am moving all my troops except two Tennessee regiments, as fast as it is possible with the means at command. The force, except what is absolutely necessary for the fort, I think (General Buckner concurs), ought to be at Cumberland City, whither we go from all directions.

At 10.30 P. M., February 12th, General Johnston again telegraphed General Floyd :

My information from Donelson is that a battle will be fought in the morning. Leave a small force at Clarksville, and take the remainder, if possible, to Donelson to-night. Take all the ammunition that can be spared from Clarksville. The force at Elkton and Whippoorwill Bridge has been ordered to Clarksville.

Three hours later, Floyd replied from Cumberland :

I *anticipated your order*, which overtook me here shipping the balance of the troops from this point to Fort Donelson. I will reach there before day, leaving a small guard here.

On the 13th, at 9.50 A. M., Floyd telegraphed from Fort Donelson :

The enemy's gunboats are advancing. They are in force around our entire works. Our field-defenses are good. I think we can sustain ourselves against the land-forces. I reached here this morning at daylight.

It is sufficient to say in this connection that the telegrams continued favorable until the 16th, when, at the hour of the surrender, General Johnston was suddenly apprised of that great reverse.

When Floyd was subsequently hard pressed by public indignation for the fatal issue of Donelson, he published a letter written by him on the 12th to General Johnston, as explanatory of his plans. In the rush of events, he probably forgot their sequence. In this letter he says :

The best disposition to make of the troops on this line was to concentrate the main force at Cumberland City—leaving at Fort Donelson enough to make all possible resistance to any attack which may be made *upon the fort*, but no more. The character of the country in the rear and to the left of the fort is such as to make it dangerous to concentrate our whole force there ; for, if their gunboats should pass the fort and command the river, our troops would be in danger of being cut off by a force from the Tennessee. In this event, their road would be open to Nashville, without any obstruction whatever.

He proposed, therefore, to concentrate at Cumberland City, and threaten the flank of any force attacking the fort ; while, as the railroad diverged from the river at Cumberland, he could effect a retreat to Nashville without molestation from gunboats.

The radical defect of this plan was that it assumed that no resistance could be offered to the approach from Henry, and that Donelson must be yielded without resistance, or with a mere show of resistance. The loss of Donelson involved the surrender of the whole Cumberland Valley ; and, moreover, the plan was based upon an apprehension of dangers which did not cause the fall of the fort. The boats did not pass the fort, and Floyd's army was not called upon to meet any flanking army, but only Grant's direct attack and investment.

But as Floyd's letter was written previous to his conference with Pillow, and was not received by General Johnston until after Floyd's movement, and as he changed his plan before hearing from General Johnston, *whose order he anticipated*, he ought not to have claimed credit for this vacillation, which impeded, instead of fully carrying out, General Johnston's conception of *defending Nashville at Donelson*—the only armed barrier on the Cumberland. It seems plain enough that the duty of the hour was to concentrate rapidly at Donelson, dispute vigorously the roads from Henry, fortify as strongly and speedily as possible, secure a transit across the Cumberland, and a line of retreat along its south bank, and then fight for Donelson as became men who held the gateway to the land—in a word, *to defend Nashville at Donelson*.

General Floyd said in his report : "The position of the fort . . . . was by no means commanding, nor was the least military significance attached to the position."

General Floyd could not have meant that it had no strategic importance, but merely that it was not judiciously located ; for Gilmer says in his report what was quite evident, "The surrender of Fort Donelson made Nashville untenable."

Fort Donelson, it must be recollected, was situated on the left bank of the Cumberland, near its great bend, and about forty miles from the mouth of the river. It was about one mile north of the village of Dover, where the commissary and quartermaster's supplies were in depot, on a commanding bluff, at a bend of the river. The fort consisted of two water-batteries on the hill-side, protected on the rear, or land-side, by a bastioned earthwork of irregular outline, on the summit of the hill, inclosing about one hundred acres. The water-batteries were admirably placed to sweep the river-approaches, with an armament of thirteen guns; eight thirty-two-pounders, three thirty-two-pound carronades, one ten-inch columbiad, and one rifled-gun of thirty-two-pound calibre. The field-work, which was intended for infantry-supports, occupied a plateau about 100 feet above the river, commanding and protecting the water-batteries at close musket-range. These works afforded a fair defense against gunboats and marauding-parties ; but they were not designed or adapted for resistance to a land-attack or investment by an army.

The field-work at Donelson, elevated as it was, was commanded by a series of eminences, the crests of a range of hills three-quarters of a mile farther inland. On the fall of Fort Henry, this was selected as a line of defense for the Confederate troops, arriving hourly, and was continually strengthened by the labors of the soldiers, until Donelson itself was surrendered. Gilmer laid off the works with his accustomed judgment and skill; and, although rudely and tardily executed, owing to the bad weather and scanty supply of tools, they were really formidable when well defended. Buckner says :

The defenses were in a very imperfect condition. The space to be defended by the army was quadrangular in shape, being limited on the north by the Cumberland River, on the east and west by small streams, now converted into deep sloughs by the high water; and on the south by our line of defense. The river-line exceeded a mile in length; the line of defense was about two miles and a half long, and its distance from the river varied from one-fourth to three-fourths of a mile. The line of intrenchments consisted of a few logs rolled together, and but slightly covered with earth, forming an insufficient protection even against field-artillery. Not more than one-third of the line was completed on the morning of the 12th. It had been located under the direction of that able engineer-officer, Major Gilmer, near the crests of a series of ridges which sloped backward to the river, and were again commanded in several places by other ridges at a still greater distance from the river. This chain of heights was intersected by deep valleys and ravines, which materially interfered with communications between different parts of the line. Between the village of Dover and the water-batteries, a broad and deep valley extending directly back from the river, and flooded by the high water, intersected the quadrangular area occupied by the army, and almost completely isolated the right wing. That part of the line which covered the land-approach to the water-batteries and constituted our right wing was assigned to me with a portion of my division.

Pillow describes these defensive works as "consisting of rifle-pits and abattis for infantry, detached on our right, but continuous on our left, with defenses for light artillery." The artillery-defenses were slight and incomplete; but the abattis was difficult, and offered serious obstruction to an assailant. The hill-sides were cleared by simply felling the trees; but time did not allow the chopping to be carried far enough to the front, and the assailants had ample cover in the woods on the opposite hills. Unfortunately, a similar abattis had been made around the inclosed field-work, so that, when the new line of intrenchments was made, the inclosed area was partly filled with this felled and tangled timber, and the movements of the defenders were greatly retarded and embarrassed by it. This obstruction, with the back-water in the sloughs, destroyed the means of rapid communication, and impeded manœuvres inside the works.

When the Confederate army had assembled at Donelson, on the 13th of February, Buckner commanded the right wing and Pillow the left.[1]

That part of the line which covered the land-approach to the water-batteries—the right front—was assigned to Buckner's division, whose right flank was protected by an impassable stream, called Hickman Creek. Buckner had with him Brown's brigade and part of Baldwin's, the rest of that brigade being detached to the left under its commander. Those of his regiments which remained were attached to Brown's brigade. Buckner gave his presence and supervision to these troops. Buckner says:

The work on my lines was prosecuted with energy, and was urged forward as rapidly as the limited number of tools would permit, so that by the morning of the 13th my position was in a respectable state of defense. My disposition of the troops was as follows: Hanson's regiment on the extreme right; Palmer's regiment, with its reserve, in position to reënforce Hanson; Porter's battery occupying the advanced salient, sweeping the road which led to the front, and flanking the intrenchments both to the right and to the left. The reserve of the Fourteenth Mississippi was held as its support; Brown's, Cook's, and Farquharson's regiments were on the left; Graves's battery occupied a position near the extreme left of the intrenchments on the declivity of the hill, whence it swept the valley with its fire, and flanked the position of Colonel Heiman to the east of the valley. From three to five companies of each regiment were deployed as skirmishers in the rifle-pits. The other companies of each regiment were massed in columns, sheltered from the enemy's fire behind the irregularities of the ground, and held in convenient positions to reënforce any portion of the line that might be seriously threatened.

[1] Certain regiments were held more or less in reserve, and others were advanced or retired according to the outline of the trenches, which conformed to the undulations of the ground. Many interesting particulars in regard to these regiments will be found in the tables in the appendix to this chapter.

To Buckner's left, and separating him from the left wing, was a broad and deep valley, 500 yards wide, extending back from the river, and flooded by the high water. Pillow commanded the left wing, containing about two-thirds of the army, organized in seven brigades. He was assisted by Brigadier-General B. R. Johnson, whom he had superseded. The right of Pillow's line was held by the brigade of Colonel Heiman, about 1,700 strong. Heiman's position, as he himself describes it, was as follows :

A hill, somewhat in the shape of a V, with the apex at the angle, which was the advance point as well as the centre of my command, and nearly the centre of the whole line of defense. From this point the ground descended abruptly on each side to a valley. The valley on my right was about 500 yards in width, and divided my command from General Buckner's left wing. The one on my left was about half that width, and ran between my left wing and the brigade commanded by Colonel Drake. These two valleys united about half a mile in the rear. The ground in front of my line (2,600 feet in length) was sloping down to a ravine, and was heavily timbered.[1]

The Forty-ninth Tennessee, Colonel Bailey, and the Fiftieth, Colonel Sugg, with Colms's Tennessee Battalion, were assigned as a garrison to the fort—in all, some 700 or 800 strong. The heavy artillery was served by details from the infantry regiments[2] and light artillery.[3] Forrest commanded all the cavalry—his own regiment, Gantt's Tennessee Battalion, and three or four small companies—altogether 800 or

[1] Heiman's brigade was arranged as follows, from right to left : Tenth Tennessee, Lieutenant-Colonel McGavock ; Fifty-third Tennessee, Colonel Abernethy ; battery light artillery, Captain Frank Maney ; eight companies of the Forty-eighth Tennessee, Colonel Voorhies ; eight companies of the Twenty-seventh Alabama, Colonel Hughes. Quarles's regiment, the Forty-second Tennessee, came up, in reserve to this brigade. To the left of Heiman, in the valley, was the Thirtieth Tennessee, Colonel Head ; and to his left, on the adjoining eminence, Drake's brigade was posted in the following order : Fourth Mississippi, Major Adair ; four pieces of light artillery, Captain French ; Fifteenth Arkansas, Colonel Gee ; two companies of Alabama Battalion, Major Garvin ; and the Tennessee Battalion, Colonel Browder. The brigade organization was not preserved regularly beyond this point. The next commands in order were the Fifty-first Virginia, Lieutenant-Colonel Massie ; Third Mississippi, Lieutenant-Colonel Wells ; first division of Green's battery, Captain Green ; four pieces of light artillery, Captain Guy ; Eighth Kentucky, Lieutenant-Colonel Lyon ; Seventh Texas, Colonel Gregg ; Fifty-sixth Virginia, Captain Daviess ; First Mississippi, Lieutenant-Colonel Hamilton ; second division of Green's battery, Lieutenant Perkins ; Twenty-sixth Mississippi, Colonel Reynolds. Besides the Forty-second Tennessee, already mentioned, the Twentieth Mississippi, Thirty-sixth Virginia, and Twenty-sixth Tennessee, were also held in reserve. The Fiftieth Virginia was also in position on the left ; as was Browder's battalion (Fifty-first Tennessee).

[2] Bidwell's company of the Thirtieth Tennessee, and Beaumont's of the Fiftieth Tennessee.

[3] Ross's company, 116 strong. Captain Stankiewitz had about twenty-five men in the field-work, with some light pieces.

1,000 strong. He had arrived with his regiment only on the 10th. Scott's Louisiana Cavalry Regiment was in observation on the right bank of the Cumberland.

The aggregate of this force has been variously stated. General Johnston estimated it at 17,000, thus:

Garrisons of Henry and Donelson	5,000
Floyd's and Buckner's command	8,000
Pilllow's, from Clarksville	2,000
Clark's, " Hopkinsville	2,000
	17,000

To these must be added Polk's reënforcements, not included in Tilghman's returns—1,600 men—making 18,600 men. The generals commanding at Donelson estimated the force there at from 12,000 to 15,000 men. General Brown, General Palmer, and some other intelligent Tennesseeans present in the battle, put the effectives at 13,500, and some as low as 11,000. General Johnston accounted for this shrinkage by the prevalence of camp-diseases and the losses incident to winter campaigning. He found that, in the retreat from Bowling Green to Nashville, his own army fell off from 14,000 to 10,000 effectives. At Donelson there were other causes also at work, usual among raw and demoralized recruits. Three of Tilghman's regiments decreased, from January 14th to January 31st, from 2,199 effectives to 1,421, principally from measles ; and in many commands the effective strength after the fall of Fort Henry continued to diminish. An investigation of the tables in Appendix A to this chapter will enable any clear-headed person to arrive at an approximate calculation of the Confederate strength. The writer furnishes all the data accessible to him, and offers, as his own opinion, from careful computation and comparison of such data, that the *effective* force of the Confederates during the siege of Donelson was from 14,500 to 15,000.

Let us now turn to the Federal army at Henry. Grant, elated by success, telegraphed Halleck : " I shall take and destroy Fort Donelson on the 8th, and return to Fort Henry." Badeau says, " This was the first mention of Fort Donelson, whether in conversation or dispatches, between the two commanders." This statement is erroneous. Halleck telegraphed Buell, January 31st: " I have ordered an advance on Fort Henry and *Dover*. It will be made immediately." He frequently calls Fort Donelson Dover. He also says, February 2d, " It is only proposed to take and occupy Fort Henry and Dover," etc. Buell, however, had recommended the same movement to Halleck, as early as January 3d, and had already voluntarily started thirteen regiments to aid Grant in it. Halleck was also sending reënforcements, and he replied to Grant on the 8th :

Some of the gunboats from Fort Holt will be sent up. Reënforcements will reach you daily. Hold on to Fort Henry at all hazards. Impress slaves, if necessary, to strengthen your position as rapidly as possible.

On the 10th he again promised " large reënforcements." Grant was not able to make good his promise. His biographer attributes his delay to the impassable condition of the roads. The rains must have made them very bad in the marshy country immediately around Fort Henry; but, after the first mile or two, they were excellent for the season ; so that it is probable he was awaiting the promised reënforcements. But Grant and Foote, learning that the Confederates were reënforcing Donelson, hurried their preparations for attack; and, as soon as the first reënforcements arrived, began their expedition against Donelson.

Foote started on the 11th, with his fleet, and transports carrying six regiments of reënforcements. Near Paducah they were met by eight more transports loaded with troops, which accompanied them to Donelson. Federal writers place this force at 10,000 men. They were to land near Donelson, and coöperate with the army that marched across the country from Henry.

On the same day Grant sent forward his vanguard, under McClernand, three or four miles, and, early on the morning of the 12th, moved with his main column. His force was 15,000 strong, with eight light batteries ; and he left a garrison of 2,500 men at Henry. He marched unincumbered with tents or baggage, with but few wagons, and " no rations save those in the haversacks. . . . No obstacle was opposed to the march, although nothing would have been easier than to prepare obstructions." [1]

The column which marched from Henry was composed of two divisions, commanded by Generals McClernand and C. F. Smith, each of three brigades.[2]

Surgeon Stearn [3] reports the infantry strength of Oglesby at 3,130, and of McArthur at 1,395. Colonel Wallace reported 3,400 effectives of all arms. Add to this, for Oglesby, cavalry and artillery, 500, and we have the strength of this division, 8,425 men (*see* Appendix B to

---

[1] Badeau's "Life of Grant," vol. i., p. 36.

[2] McClernand's first brigade, commanded by Colonel Oglesby, was formed of the Eighth, Eighteenth, Twenty-ninth, Thirtieth, and Thirty-first Illinois Regiments, Swartz's and Dresser's batteries, and four cavalry-companies. The Second Brigade, Colonel W. H. L. Wallace, included the Eleventh, Twentieth, Forty-fifth, and Forty-eighth Illinois Regiments; the Fourth Illinois Cavalry ; the First Illinois Artillery, and McAllister's battery. The Third Brigade, Colonel McArthur, contained only the Seventeenth and Forty-ninth Illinois.

[3] " Medical History of the War," Part I., medical volume, Appendix, p. 34.

this chapter). Smith's brigades were commanded by Colonels J. G. Lauman, Morgan L. Smith, and J. Cook.[1]

To these divisions were soon added the Third, commanded by General Lew Wallace, with Colonels Cruft and Thayer as brigade commanders, composed of troops sent forward from Henry, and others transported by way of the Cumberland River.[2]

When all these troops were arrayed in front of Donelson, McClernand occupied the Federal right, Smith the left, and Wallace the centre.

It is extremely difficult to arrive at a correct conclusion as to the actual force of an army by any system of estimate, or indeed by any other means than investigation of the returns of commands. As these were not accessible to the writer when this memoir was prepared, he has no means of verifying the statements made by Federal writers. He gives such data as he has.

In a memorandum furnished Hon. Montgomery Blair by the War Department, for the information of the writer, General Grant's effective force at Donelson is placed at "about 24,400." In a memorandum furnished the writer by the War Department (see Appendix, Chapter XXXI.), it is placed at 27,113. General Buell, in his letter of August 31, 1865, published in the New York *World*, September 5, 1865, estimates the reënforcements sent by him to Grant at 10,000 men, and Grant's force at from 30,000 to 35,000.

Badeau says :

On the last day of the fight Grant had 27,000 men, whom he could have put into battle; some few regiments of these were not engaged. Other reënforcements arrived on the 16th, after the surrender, swelling his number still further.

In this estimate no account is taken of the coöperating naval forces, nor of troops landed and supporting, but not engaged. There was no doubt in the mind of any Southerner engaged in the defense that the Federal force was much greater than this. The conviction of all the Confederate leaders that they fought 50,000 men was probably exaggerated by the circumstances of the case ; but General Badeau's figures will prove, on a rigid investigation, below the mark.[3]

[1] Lauman had the Second, Seventh, and Fourteenth Iowa; the Twenty-fifth and Fifty-sixth Indiana ; Birge's regiment of sharp-shooters, and Stone's Missouri Battery. M. L. Smith had the Eighth Missouri and Eleventh Indiana; and Cook had the Seventh and Fiftieth Illinois, the Twelfth Iowa, the Fifty-second Indiana, and the Thirteenth Missouri.

[2] His first brigade, commanded by Colonel Charles Cruft, comprised the Thirty-first and Forty-fourth Indiana Regiments, and the Seventeenth and Twenty-fifth Kentucky Regiments. Colonel John M. Thayer commanded a double brigade ; the second, made up of the Forty-sixth, Fifty-seventh, and Fifty-eighth Illinois Regiments, and his own, the third, composed of the First Nebraska, and the Fifty-eighth, Sixty-eighth, and Seventy-sixth Ohio.

[3] Badeau's "Life of Grant," vol. i., p. 36.

After leaving the bottom-lands around Fort Henry, a broad, good road, built by Tilghman, passed through a country of hill and valley, thickly wooded, to Donelson. It was sandy, and now dry; and the troops moved swiftly over it in the bracing air of a warm winter day. Forrest, with all the Southern cavalry, had posted himself about two miles in front of the intrenchments, where the Eighth Illinois, Lieutenant-Colonel Rhodes, of Oglesby's brigade, advancing in line of battle, encountered him, and drove in the Confederate outposts, with little loss on either side. It was certainly unfortunate that the few roads to Henry were not obstructed and vigorously disputed, as a short detention would have caught the Federal army on the march in exceedingly severe weather, and might have broken up the expedition.

Oglesby's brigade was deployed and moved forward through the oak-woods until it found itself opposite Heiman's position, near the Confederate centre. His artillery, Swartz's and Dresser's batteries, opened; and Graves's and Maney's replied from the trenches. This artillery duel did little damage; but it was sufficient, with the fire of the sharp-shooters, to interrupt the work on the trenches. The advanced brigades worked their way to the right, harassing with a continuous fire the fatigue-parties of the Confederates, who, with some loss, had to suspend their labor until night. No resistance was offered to the investment; and, before the dusk of a winter's day, the army which had left Henry in the morning unfolded itself along the entire Confederate front at Donelson. McClernand's division was on the Federal right, opposite Pillow, and reaching nearly around to Dover. Smith's brigades, as they came up, drew off to the left, and rested with their flank on Hickman's Creek, facing Buckner. Grant's headquarters were in the rear of Smith's line. Such was the situation on the night of February 12th. The opposing hosts, that night, lay on their arms. The bivouac was under the shadow of the oaks and pines. A bright moon was overhead; and the still, mild air had in it scarcely a breath of winter. The Federals rested; the Confederates plied shovel and mattock to build a barrier against the next day's storm of lead and iron. Saving the random shot of some startled picket, all was quiet—the seemingly peaceful prelude to days and nights of deadly struggle.

"THE BATTLE OF THE TRENCHES," as Pillow styles it, began at dawn on the 13th. Floyd arrived before daylight with the troops from Cumberland City; but, before they had taken position, the fighting had begun.

Thursday morning, the 13th, was clear and mild; and, at earliest dawn, the Federal skirmishers came down from the hills, where they had slept, into the valley between the lines, and commenced firing; while their artillery opened from every hill along the front. Oglesby's brigade on the right, and W. H. L. Wallace's, next to it, moved to the right, along the road to Dover, keeping up a constant cannonade as they advanced. Birge's sharp-shooters, a picked corps, deployed as skirmishers, annoyed the Confederates greatly, compelling them to lie low behind their intrenchments. But skillful Southern marksmen volunteered to occupy their attention, and finally forced them to retire. Jordan says that two of Forrest's companies were thus engaged.

About half-past eight o'clock the Twelfth Iowa, of Cook's brigade, made a reconnaissance against the centre, as if about to assault, but retired before a few well-directed shots from Graves's battery. About ten o'clock in the morning, Smith made an attack on Hanson's position, but was repulsed with heavy loss. Hanson had built rapidly and roughly some rifle-pits to the right and in front of the original line of defense. Here he was again attacked, this time by three strong regiments ; but the Second Kentucky, now aided by Palmer's Eighteenth Tennessee, again repulsed the assault. A third time the Federals came to the charge, with the same result. Porter's battery played a conspicuous part in the defense. Buckner says in his report :

The fire of the enemy's artillery and riflemen was incessant throughout the day ; but was responded to by a well-directed fire from the intrenchments, which inflicted upon the assailant a considerable loss, and almost silenced his fire late in the afternoon. My loss during the day was thirty-nine in killed and wounded.

Heiman's position has already been described. A salient to the Confederate centre, it was the most elevated and advanced point on the line. Here was posted his brigade : the Tenth Tennessee, Lieutenant-Colonel McGavock ; the Forty-eighth Tennessee, Colonel Voorhies; the Fifty-third Tennessee, Lieutenant-Colonel Winston; the Twenty-seventh Alabama, Colonel Hughes ; and Maney's light battery—in all about 1,700 strong. Badeau says of the Federal operations:

Skirmishers were thrown out actively in front, and several smart fights occurred, but with no result of importance. They were in no case intended for real assaults, but simply as attempts to discover the force and position of the enemy, and to establish the national line. An attempt was made by McClernand to capture the ridge-road on which Grant moved, but this was without orders, and unsuccessful, though gallantly made ; three regiments were engaged in the affair. On the first two days Grant lost about 300 men in killed and wounded.

The assault by Smith on Buckner was one of these " smart fights; " that of McClernand on Heiman was another. The facts are these :

As Wallace was moving to the right, McClernand detached Colonel Hayne, with his regiment, the Forty-eighth Illinois, to support McAllister's battery, and giving him, in addition, the Seventeenth Illinois, Major Smith, and the Forty-ninth Illinois, Colonel Morrison, ordered him to storm Heiman's position. The approach to Heiman's left was along a ridge, obstructed with abattis ; against his right, it was through a dense wood, across a valley, and up a hill-side. The advance of this column was first discovered by Colonel John C. Brown, who notified Colonel Heiman. Brown ordered the batteries of Graves and Porter to open upon the column, which they did with great effect, contributing materially to the repulse. The Federal regiments came to the charge right gallantly, mounting the acclivity on every side. Maney's battery now opened a rapid fire on them ; but his position on the point of the hill was an exposed one, and their sharp-shooters brought down the men at his guns with deadly aim. Both of his lieutenants fell. Still, the Illinoisians rushed on almost up to the breastworks, and until they met, at close quarters, the blaze of musketry from the trenches. Entangled in the felled timber, they wavered, and, after a struggle of some fifteen minutes, gave way. The Forty-fifth Illinois, Colonel Smith, was brought up to their support, and again they attempted to assault. But Quarles's Forty-second Tennessee had arrived on the ground, in the mean time, to Heiman's assistance; and a destructive fire drove back the Federals. They made a third ineffectual assault, when Colonel Morrison, who had bravely led his men, having been severely wounded, they finally retired, after a combat of two hours, during nearly an hour of which "the entire line had been held under a brisk, galling fire." The Federals lost 200 killed and wounded, while the Confederates lost not more than thirty or forty. These were chiefly in Maney's battery and the Fifty-third Tennessee. The dry leaves on the ground caught fire from the cannonading. The Confederates rescued the wounded as far as they could venture out from the rifle-pits; but, unhappily, some of the Federal wounded perished in the flames. After the retreat, Heiman's pickets collected sixty muskets and other equipments left on the field.

The artillery-firing continued all day, and, at intervals, during the night. Nearly every Confederate regiment reported a few casualties from the shot and shell, which came incessantly ; and, doubtless, the other side suffered equally. Though the attack on Heiman was so severely repulsed, it was, in the end, fortunate for the Federals. Their determined attitude concealed the inadequacy of their force ; and, while but a small part of their army was engaged, they interrupted the Confederate fortification, and put the whole line of defense upon a strain. Badeau comments on the fact that there was—

no effort to molest Grant, allowing him to continue the investment at his leisure—a blunder almost equal to that of opposing no obstacle to the march from Fort Henry.

While these operations were going on at the trenches on Thursday, the Carondelet, Captain Walke, a thirteen-gun vessel, preceding

Foote's flotilla, arrived at Donelson early in the morning, and opened the siege by water. Taking position behind a headland, she threw 138 shots, until a 128-pound shot came crashing through one of her ports, injuring her machinery, and sending her off crippled. No damage was done to the fort, except that a shot disabled a gun, and killed Captain Joseph H. Dixon, a valuable young engineer, whose name has been mentioned in connection with the fortification of the place. Educated, enthusiastic, and full of talents and purpose, his loss was generally deplored.

Thus far the weather had been warm for the season; but, on Thursday afternoon, it turned cold and began to rain heavily, and that night a great and sudden change occurred. The thermometer fell to 10° above zero; and a driving storm of snow, hail, and sleet, set in. An icy wind came howling from the north, beating with uninterrupted fury upon the two armies. They were both fully exposed to the tempest, and both ill-prepared to meet it. The Federals were bivouacking in the woods; but, though they were comparatively well clothed, many of them had thrown away their blankets during the previous genial weather. The Southerners, poorly clad, and less fitted in constitution to endure the buffetings of a winter's storm, were kept in the trenches to guard against surprise; though, indeed, there were no quarters or other refuge for them. Many of them were working on the trenches; and the Forty-second Tennessee built a redoubt to protect the point where Maney's battery had suffered so much. No fires could be built, lest they should serve as targets for the sharp-shooters, crouching in easy range. But, in the dark, and cold, and storm, the work of death went on; and more than one struggle between the combatants mingled the noises of battle with the turmoil of the tempest. Some of the soldiers were frozen; and the wounded between the lines suffered the extremest pangs that belong to our mortal lot. Those thus stricken down lay with raw and gaping wounds, perhaps scorched in the blaze of the conflagration that had swept through the fallen timber, and aching from the frozen rain and icy wind. On that fearful night they endured isolation, hunger, pain, and exhaustion, so that death brought a blessed relief. These are some of the horrors of war; and yet it is to the sentimental philanthropists that the occasions of war are oftenest due.

During the evening of the 13th Commodore Foote's flotilla arrived, with the reënforcements, 10,000 strong or more. These were assigned to General Lew Wallace, who had also brought over the troops from Fort Henry. Part of them were landed before daylight; and Friday, the 14th, was spent in putting them in position on the centre, between Smith and McClernand. These arrangements occupied the whole day. The snow lay more than two inches deep, and the north wind still blew with chilly breath. The torpor of cold and fatigue seemed to cling to both antagonists. Nevertheless, though no assault was made, a rambling and ineffective fire was kept up. But, though the land-forces were thus paralyzed by the rigor of the season, Donelson was not permitted to enjoy a day of rest. Foote, exultant with his easy triumph at Henry, rushed in, hoping to crush the defenders with his heavy guns, and crown the navy with another victory. But the audacious policy which has once succeeded may, when essayed again, recoil with ruin on its author. It was so with Foote.

"THE BATTLE OF THE GUNBOATS"[1] began about 3 P. M., on Friday, the 14th of February. The United States flotilla consisted of the four heavy-armored iron-clad gunboats St. Louis, Carondelet, Pittsburg, and Louisville, thirteen guns each, and the gunboats Conestoga, Taylor, and Lexington, nine guns each. Any one of these boats was more than a match for the fort in armament. They were armed with eight, nine, and ten inch guns, three in the bow of each. The Carondelet had three nine inch and four eight inch smooth-bore and two 100-pounder rifled guns. In the fort the columbiad and the rifled gun were the only two pieces effective against the armor of the gunboats. The Confederates could merely pepper them with their lighter guns, ten in number, whose missiles, for the most part, rattled harmlessly against the iron sheathing.

The four iron-clads, followed by two gunboats, made the attack. They drove directly toward the water-batteries, firing with great weight of metal. Foote's purpose was to silence these batteries, pass by, and take a position where he could enfilade the faces of the fort with broadsides.[2] The gunboats opened at a mile and a half distance, and advanced until within three or four hundred yards. Colonel J. E. Bailey, of the Forty-ninth Tennessee, now United States Senator from Tennessee, commanded the garrison. It was in bad plight from cold, hunger, and protracted watching, but was resolute in spirit. Captain Culbertson, a West Point graduate, commanded the artillery after the death of Dixon. Under him were Captains Ross, Bidwell, and Beaumont, who commanded the batteries. Stankiewitz, a gallant Pole, had two six-pounders and an eight-inch howitzer on the hill. They held their fire, under Pillow's orders, until the boats came within about 1,000 yards; then, at a given signal, they delivered the fire of the heavy guns with accuracy and effect; and, at about 750 yards, the lighter guns opened also. Stankiewitz likewise helped to divert the enemy's fire by a few discharges of his pieces.

---

[1] Boynton's "History of the United States Navy," and Hoppin's "Life of Foote," give the Federal version of this conflict. Colonel Jordan shows conclusively, in his Life of Forrest," pages 67–69, the Federal superiority in armament.

[2] Hoppin's "Life of Foote," p. 222.

The boats steamed up with great confidence, based on their experience at Fort Henry ; but, although the number of guns opposed to them was the same, a brief contest taught them a woful lesson. Their shot and shell roared, and tore up the earthworks, but did no further injury. On the other hand, the Confederate guns, aimed from an elevation of not less than thirty feet, by cool and careful hands, fell with destructive power on the decks of the gunboats. The thirty-two-pound shot generally rebounded from the plated armor ; but even these, entering the port-holes, or striking at favorable angles, or on unprotected parts of the roof, shook loose the fastenings, and aided in the work of demolition. While the iron-clads could use grape and canister against the Confederates on the parapets, and their gunboats were throwing shells at long range, which burst in the fort with novel terrors to the untried soldiers there, nothing but solid shot told against the sides of the vessels. But the furious cannonade of the fleet, while terrific, was harmless, though each moment it seemed that it must sweep away gunners and batteries together. Soldiers and generals alike looked with apprehension for the catastrophe, when their guns should be silenced, and the fleet, steaming by, take them in reverse. Still, the fascination of the scene riveted to the spot, as spectators, hundreds who witnessed it with breathless suspense and anxiety. As the heavy metal smote the iron mail of the water-monsters, it rang with a mighty and strange sound—a new music in the horrid orchestra of strife and death, unheard before, and terrible to the hearer. Old fables seemed to live again; in which giants, with clash of hammer on linked scales, fought the dragons of the great deep.

But the elevation of the batteries, and the courage and coolness of their gunners, overcame all the Federal advantages in number and weight of guns. The bolts of their two heavy guns went crashing through iron and massive timbers with resistless force, and scattering slaughter and destruction through the fleet.

In the hottest of the engagement a priming-wire became lodged in the vent of the rifle-gun, through the inexperience of the artillerists, who had seen but two days' service at the guns. Sergeant Robert Cobb mounted the piece and vainly endeavored to extract it. He continued his efforts under a fire of grape at point-blank range, until the close of the action. He was afterward distinguished as a captain of artillery.

A Northern writer, who was on board the Louisville, thus describes what he saw :

We were within point-blank range, and the destruction to our fleet was really terrible. One huge solid shot struck our boat just at the angle of the upper deck and pilot-house, perforated the iron plating, passed through the heavy timbers, and buried itself in a pile of hammocks just in front and in a direct line with the boilers. Another, a shell, raked us from bow to stern, passed through the wheel-house, emerged, dropped, and exploded in the river just at our stern. Then a ten-inch solid shot entered our starboard bow-port, demolished a gun-carriage, killed three men and wounded four others, traversed the entire length of the boat, and sank into the river in our wake. Then a shell came shrieking through the air, striking fair into our forward starboard-port, killing one man, wounding two, and then passed aft, sundering our rudder-chains, and rendering the boat unmanageable. We were compelled to drop astern and leave the scene of action, and, so far as we were concerned, the battle was over.

One of their shells entered and exploded directly in the pilot-house of the St. Louis, killing the pilot, and wounding Flag-Officer Foote severely in the leg. Two of the shots entered the Pittsburg below the guards, causing her to leak badly, and it is probable she will sink before morning. Another entered the Carondelet, killing four men and wounding eight others.

Commodore Foote tells me that he has commanded at the taking of six forts, and has been in several naval engagements, but he never was under so severe a firé before. Fifty-seven shots struck his vessel, his upper works were riddled, and his lower decks strewed with the dead and wounded.[1]

Hoppin says (page 223) :

The Louisville was disabled by a shot, which cut away her rudder-chains, making her totally unmanageable, so that she drifted with the current out of action. Very soon the St. Louis was disabled by a shot through her pilot-house, rendering her steering impossible, so that she also floated down the river. The other two armored vessels were also terribly struck, and a rifled cannon on the Carondelet burst, so that these two could no longer sustain the action ; and, after fighting for more than an hour, the little fleet was forced to withdraw. . . . Foote, it is said, wept like a child when the order to withdraw was given.

The St. Louis was struck fifty-nine times, the Louisville thirty-six times, the Carondelet twenty-six, the Pittsburg twenty, and four vessels receiving no less than 141 wounds. The fleet, gathering itself together, and rendering mutual help to its disabled members, proceeded to Cairo to repair damages, intending to return immediately with a stronger naval force to continue the siege.

We learn also, from Hoppin's narrative, that Foote was twice wounded, once in the arm and once in the leg ; and, from Foote's report, that his loss was fifty-four killed and wounded. The fight lasted an hour and ten minutes. Foote believed he could have taken the fort in fifteen minutes more ; but he was mistaken—further contest would have insured the destruction of his fleet. Gilmer's report tells us :

Our batteries were uninjured, and not a man in them killed. The repulse of the gunboats closed the operations of the day, except a few scattering shots along the land-defenses.

---

[1] Howison's " History " (*Southern Literary Messenger*, 1862), p. 323.

Pillow telegraphed to General Johnston to the same effect. But the Confederates did not derive all the encouragement from the action that their successful valor and skill deserved, for they were not aware of the full extent of the damage to the fleet ; and, in fact, expected a renewal of the attack. Nevertheless, they took heart. The gunboats were neither invulnerable nor invincible, and congratulations and rejoicings went through the camps.

On the 13th Floyd and Pillow each sent several dispatches to General Johnston. Pillow's breathed a very confident spirit: "I have the utmost confidence of success;" and, at the close of the day, "The men are in fine spirits." Floyd details the events of the day very calmly; but no great subtilty of interpretation is required to perceive his distrust of the situation, in such words as the following : "We will endeavor to hold our position, if we are capable of doing so."

Whether prompted by this dispatch or not—it is now impossible to say—General Johnston on the next day sent him the following telegram, which is in effect a final summing up of all his previous instructions, and in exact accordance with them :

If you lose the fort, bring your troops to Nashville if possible.

How far this dispatch may have influenced the counsels of the generals the writer is not able to say, as no mention is made of it in their reports; but, on the morning of that day, as appears from General Buckner's report, they came to the conclusion to cut their way out, and retreat to Nashville. General Johnston's plan was general in its scope, and perfectly simple. He wished Donelson defended if possible, but he did not wish the army to be sacrificed in the attempt. Something must be dared for the maintenance of a position so important, doubtful though he felt the issue must be ; but there did not seem any imminent peril to a vigilant and able commander of not being able to extricate his army from Donelson. There was nothing in the nature of "a trap" in the situation, if the commander kept his resources well in hand, and his communications attended to. General Johnston's orders were in effect: "Do not lose the fortress, if it can be helped; but do not lose the army anyhow." For so much he is responsible. To be more specific would have been to embarrass, not to help, his subordinates. Throughout his whole life, General Johnston's only demand for himself had been that he should have the means to accomplish an end, with full responsibility for their use. He could not apply a different rule to men intrusted with these vast interests. He had no right to consider them unequal to their charge. The general who manages a battle at a distance from the scene of action plays the game of war blindfold. An Aulic Council is proverbially a curse to a campaign. Human foresight and calculation may provide for many of the contingencies of war ; but the distant control of details must ignore many of the actual conditions of a contest. Strategists who, whether a week or a year beforehand and leagues away, plan other people's battles for them, may engage in the business of prophecy, whose issues are soon forgotten, but not safely or successfully in the responsible work of high military command. General Johnston's ability to divest himself of this propensity to intermeddle with matters that belonged strictly to his subordinates, even though they were unlucky, will be recognized as a merit by any soldier who has had the misfortune to serve with his hands tied, under a superior who imagined himself omniscient.

Buckner says :

The enemy were comparatively quiet in front of my position during the 14th. On the morning of that day I was summoned to a council of general officers, in which it was decided unanimously, in view of the arrival of heavy reënforcements of the enemy below, to make an immediate attack upon their right, in order to open our communications with Charlotte in the direction of Nashville. It was urged that this attack should be made at once, before the disembarkation of the enemy's reënforcements—supposed to be about 15,000 men. I proposed with my division to cover the retreat of the army, should the sortie prove successful. I made the necessary dispositions preparatory to executing the movement; but early in the afternoon the order was countermanded by General Floyd, at the instance, as I afterward learned, of General Pillow, who, after drawing out his troops for the attack, thought it too late for the attempt.

Neither General Floyd nor General Pillow alludes to this council ; but it is evident that the foregoing statement is substantially correct, as General Pillow, having arranged the preliminaries for an attack, actually led his men out, and afterward withdrew them. Colonel W. E. Baldwin, commanding the Second Brigade, says in his report, March 12, 1862 :

About noon, General Pillow directed the left wing to be formed in the open ground to the left and rear of our position in the lines, for the purpose, apparently, of attacking the enemy's right. My command, to which the Twentieth Mississippi, Major Brown, was temporarily attached, constituted the advance, in the following order: first, the Twenty-sixth Mississippi ; second, the Twenty-sixth Tennessee ; third, the Twentieth Mississippi. Formed in column by platoon, we advanced in a road leading from a point about two hundred yards from the left of our trenches, and approaching nearly perpendicularly the enemy's right. We had proceeded not more than one-fourth of a mile, when General Pillow ordered a countermarch, saying it was too late in the day to accomplish anything, and we returned to our former position in the lines.

Major William M. Brown, who commanded the Twentieth Mississippi in this brigade, mentions ten o'clock as the hour when he received the order to form his regiment. He says :

By the time we had advanced one hundred yards, a private of Company D was shot down, showing that the enemy was close at hand. We continued the march two hundred yards more, when the order to halt was given, said to come from General Floyd, with the explanation that we did not have time to accomplish what we wanted.

We have here, in the abandonment of this projected sortie, an illustration of that vacillation and of those divided counsels which brought about the loss of the army at Fort Donelson. There is no need to pursue with unmerited blame any of the generals in command. While the springs of human action remain unchanged, such calamities will result from unforeseen combinations. Floyd was of a bold and impetuous temper, but he was a mountaineer ; and, except a few months' experience in warfare among the Alleghanies, a novice in military operations. The moment he felt himself cooped up within intrenchments, his active spirit lost its spring. The correspondence already quoted shows the reluctance with which he came to Fort Donelson. When he went behind breastworks, he was already half beaten. On any other arena than that of war, Floyd would have been esteemed at least the equal of his associates. In a charge, he would not have fallen behind them in gallantry. But he was a very sympathetic man; and, standing between them, as the commander of both, he gave ear first to one and then to the other. There was a strong antagonism of character and feeling between Buckner and Pillow ; and the influence of each swayed Floyd, as he came within its atmosphere. Buckner, measuring the power of resistance by military precedents, and his knowledge of the resources of the United States Government, apprehended the worst. He wished to escape from what might become a trap. He therefore proposed to cut his way out. This agreed with all of Floyd's preconceptions, and he eagerly embraced the proposal ; the more readily, too, as he deferred to Buckner's military education and reputation, and had, in a close association with him during the month previous, learned to appreciate his many high qualities. Now, why was this movement suddenly arrested and put off till the next day? The writer offers the following solution as an hypothesis merely : Pillow, more sanguine than the other two, believed he could hold the fort; and, when he pointed out to Floyd the immense consequences of its loss, no less than a surrender of the State of Tennessee, Floyd, perceiving that to stand still was a bolder policy than to attack and retreat, probably consented to defer the sortie and defend the trenches. If they could be held, the losses of a sortie seemed an unavailing sacrifice. Hence, the order was countermanded, or at least deferred.

The day wore away. Reports, greatly exaggerated, came of heavy reënforcements : according to Grant's statements, they were 12,000 or 15,000 men ; according to the estimates of the besieged, from 30,000 to 50,000.

Floyd says, in his report:

We were aware of the fact that extremely heavy reënforcements had been continually arriving, day and night, for three days and nights; and I had no doubt whatever that their whole available force on the Western waters could and would be concentrated here, if it was deemed necessary, to reduce our position. I had already seen the impossibility of holding out for any length of time, with our inadequate number and indefensible position. There was no place within our intrenchments but could be reached by the enemy's artillery, from their boats or their batteries. It was but fair to infer that, while they kept up a sufficient fire upon our intrenchments to keep our men from sleep and prevent repose, their object was merely to give time to pass a column above us on the river, both on the right and left banks, and thus to cut off all our communication, and to prevent the possibility of egress.

This theory of investment is based upon the hypothesis of the successful coöperation of the gunboats, which were already vanquished, and on a degree of strength and activity in the Federal army scarcely credible. Knowing General Johnston's want of troops and poverty in means, the Confederate generals assumed, perhaps properly, that, if applied to, he could not afford any relief in their desperate straits. Floyd was backed, in this view of the situation, by both Pillow and Buckner.

Floyd continues, in his report :

I thus saw clearly that but one course was left, by which a rational hope could be entertained of saving the garrison, or a part of it: that was, to dislodge the enemy from the position on our left, and thus to pass our people into the open country lying southward toward Nashville. I called for a consultation of the officers of divisions and brigades, to take place after dark, when this plan was laid before them, approved, and adopted ; and, at which time, it was determined to move from the trenches at an early hour on the next morning, and attack the enemy in his position. It was agreed that the attack should commence upon our extreme left, and this duty was assigned to Brigadier-General Pillow, assisted by Brigadier-General Johnson.

The conclusion was reached and the specific adjustment of the details of the plan of battle settled about midnight. The whole left wing of the Confederate army, except eight regiments, was to move out of the trenches, attack, turn, and drive the Federal right until the Wynn's Ferry road which led to Charlotte, through a good country, was cleared, and an exit thus secured. In this movement, Buckner was to assist, by bringing his command to the left of Heiman's position, and thence attacking the right of the Federal centre. If successful, he was to take up a position in advance of the works on the Wynn's Ferry road, cover the retreat of the whole army, and then employ his division as a rear-guard. While the combined attack was going on, Heiman was to hold his own position with his brigade and the Forty-second Tennessee. Head's regiment, the Thirtieth Tennessee, was to replace

Buckner in the trenches; and the Forty-ninth and Fiftieth Tennessee were to act as a garrison to the fort. The only essentially vicious feature of this plan was the insufficient force left in Buckner's lines. Most of the garrison of the Fort, also, might well have been posted in the rifle-pits. Head's position was the shortest and weakest line of approach to the fort, and in more immediate danger even than the water-batteries. A slight concentration at that point would probably have prevented or repulsed the Federal assault.

The Confederates passed another bitter cold night in the trenches, waiting for the morrow's conflict. The troops, moving in the small hours of the night, over the icy and broken roads, which wound through the obstructed area of defense, made slow progress, and delayed the projected operations. Before daybreak the skirmishers had opened along the line. Morning was to see bloody work.

Pillow occupied himself chiefly with the right brigades of his command, where Baldwin led the attack, the two small Virginia brigades supporting. His left, composed of Simonton's and Drake's brigades and Forrest's cavalry, was confided to Bushrod Johnson, who here first proved himself a hard-hitter—a character he bore throughout the war. At 4 A. M., on Saturday, the 15th of February, Pillow's troops were ready, except one brigade, which came into action late.

" THE BATTLE OF DOVER " was so called by General Pillow from its initial point. Baldwin's brigade began it. Moving out, in the order of the day before, by six o'clock he was engaged with the enemy, only two or three hundred yards from his lines. His three regiments, the Twentieth and Twenty-sixth Mississippi and the Twenty-sixth Tennessee, mustered 1,358 strong. Starting by the flank, along a narrow and obstructed by-road, they came suddenly and unexpectedly upon the enemy in force—Oglesby's stout brigade. While two companies of skirmishers tried to sustain the fire of the enemy, the column was formed by company, and the leading regiment, the Twenty-sixth Mississippi, Colonel Reynolds, attempted to deploy into line to the right. Three times it was thrown into confusion by the close and rapid fire of the enemy, but was rallied and formed fifty yards to the rear. The Twenty-sixth Tennessee, Colonel Lillard, formed on its left, across the road ; and the Twentieth Mississippi advanced on the left of the Twenty-sixth Tennessee, through an open field, where it was exposed to a destructive fire, which it could not return. McCausland, supporting Baldwin, perceived the emergency, and led forward his troops, the Thirty-sixth Virginia, Lieutenant-Colonel Reid, and the Fiftieth Virginia, Major Thorburn, and formed on Baldwin's right. Wharton's brigade, the Fifty-first Virginia, Lieutenant-Colonel Massie, and the Fifty-sixth Virginia, Captain Daviess, also moved up to the left, on very bad ground, which they held tenaciously. These brigades were just in time to check the Illinois troops, who, encouraged by the confusion in the Southern line, and hoping to profit by it, were now advancing.

In the mean time, Brigadier General Johnson was leading into action still farther to the left, and consequently over greater spaces, Simonton's and Drake's brigades, while Forrest's cavalry covered their flank, and forced their horses through the thick undergrowth. Simonton pushed in between McCausland and Wharton, arrayed in the following order from right to left: the Third Mississippi, Lieutenant-Colonel Webb; Eighth Kentucky, Lieutenant-Colonel Lyon; Seventh Texas, Colonel Gregg ; and First Mississippi, Lieutenant-Colonel Hamilton. To the left of Wharton, Drake put into action his brigade—the Fourth Mississippi, Major Adair ; Fifteenth Arkansas, Colonel Gee; two companies of the Twenty-sixth Alabama, under Major Garvin ; and a Tennessee battalion, under Colonel Browder. As was said, Forrest supported the extreme left flank. In this disposition of the forces, the right of Pillow's wing rested on the trenches ; and, as each command took its position to the left, it was by a larger circuit, and with a proportionate loss of time.

On the Federal side, McClernand's whole division engaged this line as it advanced. Oglesby's brigade—the Eighth, Eighteenth, Twentyninth, Thirtieth, and Thirty-first Illinois, two batteries, and four companies of cavalry—received the first shock, on its left. McArthur's brigade—the Seventeenth and Forty-ninth Illinois—next became engaged; and, finally, W. H. Wallace's brigade—the Eleventh, Twentieth, Forty-fifth, and Forty-eighth Illinois, the Fourth Illinois Cavalry, Taylor's First Illinois Artillery, and McAllister's battery—on Oglesby's left. According to the data of Appendix B to this chapter, McClernand's division was about 8,500 strong of all arms. The attacking Confederate left wing, according to the writer's estimate, was composed of five small brigades of infantry, 5,360 strong, and about 1,000 cavalry. Jordan, in his " Life of Forrest," puts the cavalry at 800. Appendix A will show the grounds for this estimate.

The antagonists were well matched in courage, confidence, and pride of prowess. Usually one or the other of two opponents promptly perceives to which side the scales of victory incline. In extreme peril, all the senses and perceptions of brave men are quickened ; and, as the Greeks at Salamis saw their guardian goddess hovering over them, so some subtile instinct seems to say to men, " This is the moment of your fate—press on "—or—" yield." As *Macbeth* says of *Banquo :*

> ". . . . There is none but he
> Whose being I do fear : and under him
> My genius is rebuked ; as, it is said,
> Mark Antony's was by Cæsar."

Fort Donelson.

But these hardy soldiers, kindred in blood, equally emulous of glory, and, like the Roman twins, jealous of the birthright and preëminence of valor, saw nothing in any foe to quell the hope of final triumph. Each side believed that the fierce assault or stubborn stand was proof that the weight of numbers was with the foe; but, nothing daunted, trusted to manhood for success.

As has been seen, when Baldwin first struck the enemy, instead of encountering pickets or skirmishers, he found the Federals in line of battle, on the alert, and ready for the fray. As other brigades came to his aid, or entered on the combat, he was crowded off to the right, and had the hard measure of continually meeting new regiments eager to receive him—most probably the men of W. H. L. Wallace's brigade, who became engaged about seven o'clock.

Every attempt of the Confederate line to advance was met by a heavy raking fire from an enemy who seemed animated by desperate resolution. Overhead was the lowering sky of a damp, cold, and cheerless day; under foot the trampled and blood-stained snow. The air was foul with mists and sulphurous smoke. Entangled in the thick oak-woods, whose dense undergrowth shook from its brown leaves the wet snow that spoiled the priming of their flint-locks, the Southerners pressed forward blindly and at disadvantage. As they struggled, with irregular and spasmodic charges, up a slope, to assault an unseen enemy, who stubbornly held the ground, it looked for a long time as if the effort would prove abortive.

In carrying the first hill, Simonton's brigade, separated from the troops on its right, received the full force of the Federal fire. Robert Slaughter's company, of the Eighth Kentucky, charged straight up on two pieces of artillery and suffered severely, but the guns were taken. Gregg's Texans met heavy losses near the top of the same hill. Here fell the brave Lieutenant-Colonel Clough and Lieutenant Nowland near together. The First Mississippi greatly distinguished itself; and the Virginians to their left planted their colors on the crest, which they carried by the most unflinching resolution.

At length, however, the Confederate left so established its line as to turn the right flank of the Federals, and, by an almost simultaneous assault along its whole length, between nine and ten o'clock, forced the position that had been so well maintained by an enveloping movement, and crushed McClernand's front back and toward his left. But the brave Illinoisans, though broken, were not routed. They fell back, fighting by companies and squads, and every step had to be won from them at the price of blood.

When McClernand found the crushing process beginning on his right flank, about eight o'clock, he sent for aid. Grant was absent, at the river, with Foote; and as McClernand's messages became more urgent, General Lew Wallace, commanding the central division, finding himself unoccupied in front, moved Cruft's brigade up to the right, in support of the retreating Federals. Cruft's brigade was composed of four regiments—the Thirty-first Indiana, Lieutenant-Colonel Osborn ; Seventeenth Kentucky, Colonel McHenry ; Twenty-fifth Kentucky, Colonel Shackleford ; and Forty-fourth Indiana, Colonel Reed—in all about 2,300 strong. They came into position about ten o'clock, and found W. H. L. Wallace retiring in comparatively good order. But the regiments farther to their right were badly broken. The Twenty-fifth Kentucky, which was carried forward rather heedlessly, on the extreme right, and attempted to stem the tide of battle, was broken into fragments by the onset, and became hopelessly involved in the crowd of fugitives. Cruft bore the brunt of battle for some time ; but, at length, he, too, had to give back, which he did somewhat broken, but in good order.

General Lew Wallace says, in his report :

Soon fugitives from the battle came crowding up the hill, in rear of my own line, bringing unmistakable signs of disaster. Captain Rawlins was conversing with me at the time, when a mounted officer galloped down the road, shouting : ' We are cut to pieces !' The effect was very perceptible. To prevent a panic among the regiments of my Third Brigade, I ordered Colonel Thayer to move on by the right flank. He promptly obeyed.

General Wallace acted with vigor and decision. Meeting McClernand's whole division in full retreat, with Cruft also falling back, he threw forward Thayer's strong brigade, to receive the combined attack of Pillow and Buckner, who now entered on the contest. The direction of the Confederate advance was now parallel with their intrenchments; so that, when Thayer's brigade was put in position, it stood at right angles to its former line of battle, with its left nearly opposite the centre of the Confederate trenches. Here it awaited the final assault.

While Pillow and B. R. Johnson were conducting these operations, breaking and driving the Federals by steady pressure, Buckner also shared in the assault. Head's regiment did not reach him at the appointed time, thus detaining him in his rifle-pits ; and the icy roads still further delayed his movements. His advance regiment, the Third Tennessee, however, was in the trenches out of which Pillow's troops had marched, an hour before daylight and the last regiment soon after daylight. As those regiments came up, he formed them, under cover, partly in line and partly in column. In his front was massed W. H. L. Wallace's brigade, with two heavy batteries. Between these and Graves's battery, with other artillery, a severe fire was kept up.

Pillow sent messages urging Buckner to attack ; and about nine o'clock Colonel Brown ordered the Fourteenth Mississippi to deploy as skirmishers under direction of Major Alexander Casseday, of Buckner's staff. The Third Tennessee, Lieutenant-Colonel Gordon, and the Eighteenth Tennessee, Colonel Palmer, both of Brown's brigade, advanced from the point where the Wynn's Ferry road crosses the trenches. Passing the valley in front, through fallen timber and open ground, under heavy fire, they attacked the Federals and drove them from their position, but not without considerable loss. The Confederate artillery, directed over their heads, embarrassed them. The snow on the bushes wet the priming of their flint-locks; and, as they penetrated the thick undergrowth, where the Federals had been posted, the heavy fire of the retiring foe threw them into some disorder. They were also told they were firing on their own men. Finally, their colonels withdrew them to the trenches.

About noon, as the tide of battle bore back the Federal army along and across the Wynn's Ferry road, General Buckner organized another attack to the right of that road, up a valley to the left of Heiman's position. Colonel Brown led his brigade, the Third and Eighteenth Tennessee, and the Thirty-second Tennessee, supported by the Forty-first Tennessee, against a battery on the road, which was supported by a very heavy infantry-force. Brown's brigade, sheltered by the ravine, advanced until within one or two hundred yards, when with a murderous fire it drove back the supports. Opening at the same time upon the Federal battery with a cross-fire from Maney's, Porter's, and Graves's batteries, it was soon disabled. The guns fell into the hands of the infantry, and Graves galloped forward on the road with his battery, and again opened at close quarters with grape and canister. Thus aided, Brown's brigade advanced, delivering well-directed volleys.

Here W. H. L. Wallace's brigade still clung to their second position, which they had retained firmly against Baldwin's and McCausland's attacks. All to the right of them had given way. Pillow's line was pressing upon their right and front, and Buckner on their left. By the retreat of Oglesby and McArthur, they had become the salient of the Federal line. Still, they fought so well that Baldwin and McCausland, who were attacking their front, called for reënforcements and ammunition from Roger Hanson, who with the Second Kentucky stood next to them, on Buckner's right. Forrest was there, too, with his cavalry, and had made two gallant but unsuccessful charges. Hanson had no orders, but, seeing them sorely pressed—a hard-headed, combative man —he gave them what they wanted. To render the needed service, he had to charge across an open field, some two hundred yards in width, against an enemy posted in the woods and brush beyond. Forrest, with his cavalry, joined in the assault; and, while Hanson attacked the infantry-supports, Forrest charged and took the battery, killing the gunners, and recovering some Confederate prisoners. Hanson says :

I directed the regiment, when the command was given, to march at quick-time across this space, and not to fire a gun until they reached the woods in which the enemy were posted. The order was admirably executed, and although we lost fifty men in killed and wounded, in crossing this space, not a gun was fired until the woods were reached. The enemy stood their ground until we were within forty yards of them, when they fled in great confusion under a most destructive fire. This was not, strictly speaking, a charge bayonets, but it would have been one if the enemy had not fled.

While Hanson was thus assailing Wallace's front, Buckner continued the movement against his left. Brown's brigade, charging up the hill, through a dense wood, had been met with grape and canister and a heavy musketry-fire, much of which passed over their heads, as the men lay down to escape the missiles. Lieutenant-Colonel Gordon, of the Third Tennessee, and Lieutenant-Colonel Moore, of the Thirty-second Tennessee, fell wounded, the latter mortally, with some fifty men killed and wounded. These regiments, reënforced at this moment by the Four-teenth Mississippi, renewed the charge, drove the Federal force from its position, and captured the guns. The batteries, and Farquharson's Forty-first Tennessee, followed the movement. In all this fighting, Graves's battery was splendid in its gallantry and efficiency. Rice E. Graves was a model soldier; inflexible and fervent in duty, a noble Christian and patriot. He left West Point to enlist in the Southern cause, and no man of his years and rank aided it more. He died at his guns at Chickamauga, as Breckinridge's chief of artillery.

It was then, at last, that Wallace's brigade, isolated by Buckner's movement on its right and toward its rear, fell back upon its supports, beaten, cut up, and much disordered, but undismayed. Indeed, not only Wallace's command, but squads from all the others, rallied on Thayer's brigade, and, with Cruft's brigade and these fresh troops, interposed another stout barrier to a further Confederate advance.

Thayer's brigade formed, under the direction of General Lew Wallace, as described, at right angles to the intrenchments. The First Nebraska, Lieutenant-Colonel McCord, and the Fifty-eighth Illinois, were on the right; Wood's battery in the centre; and to the left, a de-tached company and the Fifty-eighth Ohio, Colonel Steadman, the left of the line being obliquely retired so as to front an approach from the trenches. The line of reserve consisted of the Seventy-sixth Ohio, Colonel Woods; the Forty-sixth Illinois, Colonel Davis; and the Fifty-seventh Illinois, Colonel Baldwin. Cruft reëstablished his line on the right of Thayer.

It was now one o'clock. The Federal right was doubled back. The Wynn's Ferry road was cleared, and it only remained for the Confeder-ates to do one of two things. The first was, to seize the golden moment, and, adhering to the original purpose and plan of the sortie, move off rapidly by the route laid open by such strenuous efforts and so much bloodshed. The other depended upon the inspiration of a master-mind, equal to the effort of grasping every element of the combat, and which should complete the partial victory by the utter rout and destruction of the enemy. It is idle now to discuss whether the mind, the inspiration, or the occasion, was the one thing lacking.

It is hardly fair now to say what could or should have been done then; but it would seem that had Floyd seized this critical moment—the hour of fate—and, gathering all his forces for a final assault, hurled Pillow, Buckner, Heiman, the garrison—all—upon the crowded front and flanks of the foe, the end would have been the annihilation of the Federal army, or a sacrifice so costly and glorious that censure would have been drowned in tears. While we cannot blame a commander who does not choose such courses, we must also remember that the heavy price of victory is human blood. General Grant never forgot this, at Donelson or elsewhere, and he got what he paid for.

While, to us, one or the other alternative seems now to have been the only possible safe solution, the Confederate commander tried neither. A fatal middle policy was suddenly but dubiously adopted, and not carried out. The fate which seemed always to arrest the best endeavors of the Confederate arms, and render fruitless their victories, interposed at this juncture. The spirit of vacillation and divided counsels again prevented that unity of action which is essential to success. Circumstances were largely responsible for this. The point of view has much to do with such determinations. For seven hours the Confederate battalions had been pushing over rough ground and through thick timber, at each step meeting fresh troops massed, where the discomfited regiments manfully rallied. Hence, the fervor of assault naturally slackened, though the wearied troops were still ready and competent to continue their onward movement. Ten fresh regiments, over 3,000 men, had not fired a musket. But in the turmoil of battle no one knew the relations of any command to the next, or indeed whether his neighbor was friend or foe.

Buckner had halted, according to the preconcerted plan, to allow the army to pass out by the opened road, and to cover their retreat. Bushrod Johnson was following up the tactics of the morning, which had so far proved successful, and was pressing Cruft fiercely. At this point of the fight, Pillow, finding himself at Heiman's position, heard of (or saw) preparations by C. F. Smith for an assault on the Confederate right, where Head had replaced Buckner. But whether he understood this to be their purpose, or construed the movement as the signs of flight, was left uncertain by his language at the time. In either case, the writer is not prepared to explain why the garrison of the fort was not promptly called to the defense of this point to which it was nearest, nor why Heiman's command was not dispatched to Head's support or put into the fight. What occurred was this: Pillow ordered the regiments which had been engaged to return to the trenches, and instructed Buckner to hasten to defend the imperiled point. Buckner, not recognizing him as a superior authorized to change the plan of battle, or the propriety of such change, refused to obey, and, after receiving reiterated orders, started to find Floyd, who at that moment joined him. He urged upon Floyd the necessity of carrying out the original plan of evacuation. Floyd assented to this view, and told Buckner to stand fast until he could see Pillow. He then rode back and saw Pillow, and, hearing his arguments, yielded to them.

Pillow says, in his supplemental report:

I knew that the enemy had twenty gunboats of fresh troops at his landing, then only about three miles distant; I knew, from the great loss my command had sustained during the protracted fight of over seven hours, my command was in no condition to meet a large body of fresh troops, who I had every reason to believe were then rapidly approaching the field. General Buckner's command, so far as labor was concerned, was comparatively fresh, but its disorganization, from being repulsed by the battery, had unfitted it to meet a large body of fresh troops. I therefore called off the pursuit, explaining my reasons to General Floyd, who approved the order.

Floyd simply says that he found the movement so nearly executed that it was necessary to complete it. Accordingly, Buckner was recalled. In the mean time, Pillow's right brigades were retiring to their places in the trenches, under orders from the commanders.

B. R. Johnson, finding himself alone with Drake's brigade and some cavalry, and unsupported on the right, sent an aide for reënforcements, but received instead an order to report in person within the intrenchments. Johnson then went and asked leave to attack, but, after a conference, Floyd directed him to display Drake's brigade for a time before the enemy, while the other troops took their positions in the rifle-pits. This was done with the aid of Forrest's cavalry. The Federal accounts describe assaults and fierce struggles led by Grant in person. They are mistaken. General Grant's order of advance was decisive, because it was an *advance*, and revealed the absence of the Confederates from the battle-field; but the contest must have been slight, for Drake's brigade and Forrest's cavalry alone remained on the field, and, after holding at bay for an hour or two Wallace's division, with the remnants of McClernand's, slowly retired, under orders, over some 800 yards of intervening ground to the breastworks, not losing a man while falling back. This ended the conflict on the left. Three hundred prisoners, 5,000 stand of small-arms, six guns, and other spoils of victory, had been picked up by the Confederates. But the Federals, cautiously advancing, gradually recovered most of their lost ground.

In the combats at Donelson, Forrest, with his cavalry, showed his usual vigor and dash, although he had an unusually difficult part to perform with his troopers in the dense and tangled woods. The artillery could not have done better. Porter, Graves, and Maney, in particular, displayed in splendid manner their soldierly qualities ; and the men were worthy of their officers. Their losses were heavy, and Captain Porter was himself wounded.

As General Grant was returning, on the morning of the 15th, from his conference with the wounded commodore, he gave little heed to the heavy firing on his right, which, like Lew Wallace, he mistook for an attack by McClernand. As he rode leisurely to camp, between nine and ten o'clock, he met an aide galloping furiously from the right to tell him of McClernand's straits. Grant, being near C. F. Smith, found him, and bade him hold himself in readiness to attack the Confederate right.

Grant then rode to his right wing, where all was confusion and dismay. After examining the condition of things there, he rode back to C. F. Smith, whose pupil he had been, and who was a man from whom no soldier need feel ashamed to take counsel. It was determined to assault the advanced work on the extreme right of the Confederate line. Grant also sent word to Foote that part of his army was demoralized, and begged him to make an immediate demonstration with his gunboats. He adds, "I must order a charge, to save appearances." "Two of the fleet accordingly ran up the river, and threw a few shells at long range" (Badeau).

Though it might have been apparent to the Confederates, possibly by two or three o'clock, that an assault was meditated on their right, the unfortunate conflict of opinion and action among the generals, the confusion in their commands, and the icy and impeded roads, so delayed the movement of troops that they arrived in position too late for the purpose of their recall. It was four o'clock before the assault on the right was made by Smith; and then Hanson, who, under Pillow's direct orders, preceded the rest of Buckner's command, had the mortification of witnessing, but not sharing in, the combat, when the Federal column carried the advanced work he had constructed.

The manner of the assault was this : Grant, in consultation with C. F. Smith, determined on it, and assigned the duty to that fine old soldier. Whose suggestion it was, Grant's or Smith's, has been made subject of dispute. No matter : the inspiration was a good one. C. F. Smith was a soldier of the old school ; a graduate of 1825 from West Point, where he was afterward commandant of the corps when Grant was a cadet. He was frequently brevetted in Mexico ; and got promotion, as lieutenant-colonel of the Tenth Infantry, from Mr. Davis, when he was Secretary of War. The vicissitudes of life found him, at this early stage of the civil war, the subordinate of his former pupil.   His own career in it was brief but brilliant.

Smith's assaulting column consisted of the six regiments that composed Lauman's brigade : the Second Iowa, Colonel Tuttle ; Twenty-fifth Indiana, Colonel Veatch ; Seventh Iowa, Colonel Parrott; Fourteenth Iowa, Colonel Shaw ; Fifty-second Indiana, and Birge's regiment of sharp-shooters.   The Second Iowa led the assault.

Smith formed the regiment in two lines, with a front of five companies each, thirty paces apart.   He told the men what they had to do, and took his position between those two lines.   The attack was made with great vigor and success. The ground was broken and difficult, impeded with underbrush, as well as extremely exposed.[1]

The veteran Smith led the charge with desperate purpose.   As the Federals rushed up the hill, pushing through the abattis, Turner's little battalion poured on them a deadly fire, which would have repulsed a less numerous and determined foe.   The rest of Buckner's corps had got into position ; but when Hanson's regiment, coming from the extreme left to the extreme right, was hurrying in loose order to its aid, but had not reached the ground, a torrent of blue-coats poured over the breastworks, driving the defenders before them.   Then it fell upon Hanson's regiment as it approached, so that it recoiled with the other fugitives.   A few minutes' delay by the Federals would have saved the day ; on such trifles does the fate of armies and nations hang.

Buckner says of the Second Kentucky :

This gallant regiment was necessarily thrown back in confusion upon the position of the Eighteenth Tennessee.   At this period I reached that position ; and, aided by a number of officers, I succeeded in hastily forming a line behind the crest of the hill which overlooked the detached works, which had been seized by the enemy before Hanson had been able to throw his regiment into them.   The enemy advanced gallantly upon this new position, but was repulsed with heavy loss.   I reënforced this position by other regiments as they successively arrived, and by a section of Graves's battery, while a section of Porter's battery was placed in its former position.   During a contest of more than two hours the enemy threatened my left with a heavy column, and made repeated attempts to storm my line on the right; but the well-directed fire of Porter's and Graves's artillery and the musketry-fire of the infantry repelled the attempts, and finally drove him to seek shelter behind the works he had taken and amid the irregularities of the ground.   There was probably no period of the action when his strength was not from three to five times the strength of mine. Toward the close of the action I was reënforced by the regiments of Colonels Quarles, and Sugg, and Bailey.[2]   Generals Floyd and Pillow also visited the position about the close of the action.

[1] Badeau's " Life of Grant," vol. i., p. 46.

[2] The Forty-second, Forty-ninth, and Fiftieth Tennessee ; the two latter had been in the fort.

Head's regiment, the Thirtieth Tennessee, occupied Buckner's line, three-quarters of a mile long. In the advanced work he had placed Major Turner with three companies. Head says in his report that his regiment numbered only 450 men. This was the number in line, excluding Bidwell's company of sixty men in the batteries. The men were very raw, mere militia, and had been at Fort Henry. Colonel Head was patriotic and able in civil affairs, but in no sense a military man.

Colonel Bailey saw the Second Kentucky retreating in great disorder, and moved Sugg's regiment to the face of the works, fronting the enemy ; his own regiment was drawn up near the western sally-port, and prepared for a sally, under the impression that the enemy would follow up the dispersion of the Confederate right by a movement against the river or water batteries. These dispositions were scarcely completed, when Colonel Head in person galloped into the fort, and directed the Forty-ninth Tennessee to move to the front, which was done at a double-quick. The regiment was formed to the right of Brown's Third Tennessee, and, moving forward, met the enemy's skirmishers, now advanced nearly to the crest of the hill on which the Confederate line was being established. One or two volleys forced the enemy to retreat to the line captured from Head and the Second Kentucky. A brisk fire was kept up until sunset, when the firing ceased. A battalion of Sugg's regiment reached the field just before the close of the fight, and deployed to the right of the Forty-ninth. The right wing was likewise reënforced by Major Colms's battalion. Quarles's regiment, the Forty-second Tennessee, also came up from Heiman's position, and helped Hanson defend the second line.

In this last engagement, while Smith was attacking with Lauman's brigade, the Twelfth Iowa, Colonel Wood, and the Fiftieth Illinois, Colonel Bane, of Cook's brigade, also joined in the attack on his immediate right ; and Morgan L. Smith's brigade farther still to the right. These were all fresh troops. Besides these, Cruft's brigade, part of Thayer's, and other commands, joined in the attack on the intrenchments, or in demonstrations that occupied the Confederate regiments in their positions at the breastworks.

This assault was met by a determined resistance from Brown's brigade. The writer has been kindly supplied with a statement of this combat carefully prepared in conference by a number of the gallant participants. The following extract gives its essential features :

Within a short time after Brown's command reoccupied this line, and about 4 P. M., the extreme right of the line resting on Hickman Creek, and which had been occupied by Hanson, was suddenly attacked. That part of the line was occupied by a small part of Head's regiment, under command of Major Turner. Hanson's regiment had not then reached the works, because of the greater length of march and roughness of the road. As soon as the assault was discovered, Captain Porter opened an enfilade fire on the advancing column with grape and canister. Colonel Palmer, with the Eighteenth Tennessee, posted on Brown's extreme right, without awaiting the dangerous delay of orders, moved immediately to relieve Hanson, who was about going into position when the assault began. Colonel Brown moved the Third Tennessee at double-quick to extend Palmer's line already formed on the only practicable position for defense, so as to form a secondary line to Hanson's works, which were then already in possession of a force five or six times outnumbering any opposing troops at hand. Hanson rallied on this interior line, the stubborn resistance of which, aided by the well-directed guns of Porter's battery, saved the line and prevented the water-batteries from falling into the hands of the Federals that evening. This interior line had timely reënforcements in the arrival of Bailey's, Quarles's, Sugg's, and the balance of Head's regiments, all of which arrived after the forward movement of the Federal column was checked, but before the fortunes of the day were decided. One section of Graves's battery, which had been delayed in reaching its original position, with the other pieces, was brought up rapidly to the intersection of the new with the main line, and did most effective service under the personal direction of Captain Graves. At the same time that this section came up, the remaining section of Porter's battery, delayed in the same way, was brought into position by Lieutenant Morton, under a very heavy fire, and with the other guns continued firing until nightfall. It was in this engagement that the gallant Captain Thomas R. Porter was disabled by a very severe and dangerous wound, and was borne from the field. Captain Porter's marked coolness and dash, and the efficient and intelligent manner in which he handled his guns, elicited the unbounded admiration of all who saw him; and when he was being carried, bleeding, from the field, he exclaimed, as Jordan has it, to the only unwounded officer left with his battery, Lieutenant John W. Morton, a mere lad of nineteen, "Don't let them have the guns, Morton!" Lieutenant Morton replied, "No, captain, not while I have one man left!"

This battery, from its advanced and exposed position, lost eight men killed outright, and twenty-five wounded, out of forty-eight officers, non-commissioned officers, and men, actively engaged ; the balance of the company, forty-two men, were drivers, teamsters, and artificers, protected in a ravine at some distance from the battery.

Captain Porter was educated at Annapolis, and was an officer in the United States Navy up to the breaking out of the war, when he resigned his position in the navy and returned to his native State, Tennessee, to offer his services in her behalf. He served during the war as chief of artillery to Buckner, and afterward to Cleburne, and was wounded at Hoover's Gap. He subsequently entered the Confederate Navy as executive officer of the Florida. After the war he commanded a California merchant-steamer, and died in 1869. He was a kind and cultivated gentleman, and a gallant soldier. His young lieutenant, Morton, before the close of the war became chief of artillery to General Forrest.

Darkness separated the combatants. Jordan, in his "Life of Forrest" (page 86), calls the works gained, "the mere narrow foothold seized on the extreme right of the trenches." Buckner, however, considered it the key to his position, which it probably was.

The loss of Lauman's brigade, exclusive of the Fifty-second Indiana, temporarily attached and not reported, was 61 killed and 321 wounded ; the Second Iowa alone lost 198 men. In five Federal brigades, reported, out of ten, the loss during the siege was 1,403 men. Badeau, speaking of Grant, says: "His entire losses during the siege were 2,041 in killed, wounded, and missing ; of these, 425 were killed." Medical Director Brinton says the loss, " as stated officially, amounted to 400 killed and 1,785 wounded." [1] If to these are added the 300 prisoners captured and sent to Nashville by the Confederates, the loss would amount to over 2,500, inclusive of the fleet—fifty-six more.

In the subsequent confusion it was difficult to obtain accurate data of the Confederate loss, in killed and wounded, during the siege. Floyd estimated it at 1,500. Pillow, in his supplemental report, put it at 2,000. In two tables in the appendix, the loss is summed up respectively at 1,348 and 1,222. The writer's estimate, from all the sources of information at his command, is 325 killed and 1,097 wounded. Besides these, several hundred were missing before the surrender, of whom, excluding fugitives and prisoners, probably a hundred or more perished; so that the actual loss by death and wounds was about 1,500.

At the close of the day, Floyd and Pillow telegraphed General Johnston that they had won a victory. After nightfall, they met in consultation with Buckner. Buckner says :

It was unanimously resolved that, if the enemy had not reoccupied, in strength, the position in front of General Pillow, the army should effect its retreat ; and orders to assemble the regiments for that purpose were given by General Floyd.

Forrest was ordered to make a reconnaissance to ascertain the position of the enemy. Floyd thus states the situation :

There were but two roads by which it was possible to retire. If they went by the upper road, they would certainly have a strong position of the enemy to cut through ; . . . and if they retired by the lower road they would have to wade through water three feet deep—which ordeal the medical director stated would be death to more than one-half of the command, on account of the severity of the weather and their physical prostration.

About midnight it was determined to carry out at daybreak the plan of the day before, on the supposition that the upper road was clear. But rumors having reached the generals that the Federals had reoccupied their positions, two sets of scouts, one after the other, were sent out to ascertain the facts. General Forrest is confident that the report of the scouts was that they saw no Federals, only fires in the woods. The reports of the three generals, however, concur that all the

[1] "Medical and Surgical History of the War," Part I., med. volume, Appendix, p. 28.

information received confirmed the complete reinvestment of their lines. These discrepancies readily occur among honest witnesses. Inferences are easily mistaken for the statements from which they were drawn; and, in the mutations of opinion, the actual sequence is often lost. The scouts, who examined the river road, reported the overflowed valley about a quarter of a mile wide and half leg deep in mire, and the water in the slough one hundred yards wide and up to the saddle-skirts, and the crossing impracticable for infantry. From subsequent developments, it is probable that the investment was not so complete, nor escape so hazardous, as was reported and believed. The soldiers did escape in large numbers, many on that side of the river. The people of the vicinage came to the battle-field, some from curiosity, but generally with the more laudable motive of helping the wounded; so that the moving lights carried, and the fires kindled, by friends proved false signals, and were accepted as indications of the presence of the enemy.

The question now arose, What should be done? Buckner says in his report:

Both officers have correctly stated that I regarded the position of the army as desperate, and that the attempt to extricate it by another battle, in the suffering and exhausted condition of the troops, was almost hopeless. The troops had been worn down with watching, with labor, with fighting. Many of them were frosted by the intensity of the cold; all of them were suffering and exhausted by their incessant labors. There had been no regular issue of rations for a number of days, and scarcely any means of cooking. Their ammunition was nearly expended. We were completely invested by a force fully four times the strength of our own. In their exhausted condition they could not have made a march. An attempt to make a sortie would have been resisted by a superior force of fresh troops; and that attempt would have been the signal for the fall of the water-batteries, and the presence of the enemy's gunboats sweeping with their fire at close range the positions of our troops, who would thus have been assailed on their front, rear, and right flank, at the same instant.[1] The result would have been a virtual massacre of the troops, more disheartening in its effects than a surrender.

In this opinion General Floyd coincided; and I am certain that both he and I were convinced that General Pillow agreed with us in opinion. General Pillow then asked our opinion as to the practicability of holding out another day. I replied that my right was already turned, a portion of my intrenchments in the enemy's possession; they were in a position successfully to assail my position and the water-batteries; and that, with my weakened and exhausted force, I could not successfully resist the assault which would be made at daylight by a vastly superior force.

There is no doubt that Pillow proposed to repeat the onslaught of the day before, and cut their way out; though he seems to have con-

[1] The force of the enemy is here over-estimated; and, so far as the gunboats are concerned, it is apparent that this was an error, but the damage done the fleet was not known to the Confederates.

curred with the others in the view that it was a desperate remedy and could succeed only with great loss of men. Floyd seems also to have held this opinion at first, but to have deferred to Buckner's representation of the condition of the men, and the inevitable sacrifice of a large part of the command, the responsibility of which he would not assume. Pillow probably adhered to his opinion, but did not insist strongly upon it, in view of the opposition. At least he presented no plan of extrication. The roads were thought to be thoroughly impracticable, and the steamers, which might have been used as ferries, had been sent up the river with the prisoners and wounded; though two were expected to arrive at daylight.

General Pillow states that he proposed to make the attempt to hold out another day. The matter was discussed; and, certainly, if it could have been done, this was the best possible counsel. It was an occasion for a supreme effort. War has its chances of weal as well as of woe. No man can tell what a day may bring forth. Success so often crowns mere tenacity of purpose and stubborn endurance, that despair is scarcely a word for the soldier's vocabulary. At the same time, it has to be confessed that there is a limit to the ability of troops for resistance, and that it is the part of good sense to know when this point has been reached. Buckner was satisfied that it had been reached. He was a man of good judgment, conversant with the troops, and, if his opinion was not formed upon his observation of too small a part of the army, it may well be accepted as conclusive; as, indeed, it was by Floyd. He was sustained in his view by that resolute fighter, Roger Hanson, who, however, had seen his own regiment, the Second Kentucky, suffer very severely. Buckner believed that his command would not hold out for an hour against an assault; and that a sortie would result in a massacre. From this point of view, humanity required a surrender.

It is true that another view might well be taken of the situation. The entire loss was not more than one in nine or ten; the heaviest in any particular command was not more than one in four or five, while later in the war these same troops would undergo a loss of one-third without a shudder. Heiman's entire brigade, at the least 1,575 strong, though more probably 1,700 in number, had not been engaged in the battle of Saturday, and had the prestige of Thursday's success with the loss of only ten men killed and thirty-six wounded. In addition, the Forty-second Tennessee, 498 strong, had met but eleven casualties. The Forty-ninth and Fiftieth Tennessee, numbering 1,022 for action, had lost but nine killed and eighteen wounded. The Forty-first Tennessee, 575 men, had two killed and six wounded. Three or four batteries had had no casualties at all. Here was a force of some 3,700 men, fresh as to mere combat, having lost but ninety-two men. Other troops were coming, and 400 did arrive at daylight, making a body over 4,000 strong. What could be got out of these men of course depended on a multitude of conditions, many of which cannot now be stated, much less estimated. Pillow, who was the most sanguine of these leaders, and to whose division these troops belonged, said he could not aid Buckner at the point of expected assault on the right, because he would have as much to do as he could attend to in defending his own lines.

It should, however, be remembered that these troops were not veterans, but many of them raw levies, not only undisciplined, but ignorant of drill, armed with very inferior weapons that failed them in the hour of greatest need, and often commanded by officers as inexperienced as themselves. They had been from three to eight days at work in the trenches, almost without sleep or rest, in the wet and cold, and many were frost-bitten. The men were so worn out with watching, cold, and fatigue, that they fell asleep standing on their feet, under a heavy fire from the enemy. Three days of battle had disabled many and demoralized more. Opposed to them was an army, superior in numbers and in all the appointments of war, continually augmented by reënforcements, and thus able to fight by relays and to rest. Many other considerations present themselves to the mind now, as they did then to the leaders of the besieged; but it is useless to dwell upon them. Suffice it to say that it was finally decided that a surrender was inevitable, and that, to accomplish its objects, it must be made before the assault, which was expected at daylight.

But when it came to the question of who should make the surrender, Floyd and Pillow both declared they would not surrender; they would die first. Buckner said that after the resistance that had been made the army could be honorably surrendered. "General Pillow said he never would surrender. General Floyd said that he would suffer any fate before he would surrender or fall into the hands of the enemy alive." Floyd says in his report:

I felt that in this contingency, while it might be questioned whether I should, as commander of the army, lead it to certain destruction in an unavailing fight, yet I had a right individually to determine that I would not survive a surrender there. To satisfy both propositions I agreed to hand over the command to Brigadier-General Buckner through Brigadier-General Pillow, and to make an effort for my own extrication by any and every means that might present themselves to me. I therefore directed Colonel Forrest, a daring and determined officer, at the head of an efficient regiment of cavalry, to be present for the purpose of accompanying me in what I supposed would be an effort to pass through the enemy's lines.

To Floyd's declaration that he would not be taken alive, General Buckner responded that such considerations were personal, intimating, at least, that they should not influence a commander. Floyd replied : " I would not permit such reasons to cause me to sacrifice my command ; but, personal or not, such is my determination." General Buckner then said that, being satisfied that nothing else could be done, if the command was devolved on him he would surrender the army, and that his sense of duty required him to share its fate. Floyd immediately asked him : " General Buckner, if I place you in command, will you allow me to draw out my brigade ? " General Buckner promptly replied, " Yes, provided you do so before the enemy act upon my communication." Floyd said, " General Pillow, I turn over the command." Pillow, regarding this as a mere technical form by which the command was to be conveyed to Buckner, then said, " I pass it." Buckner assumed the command, sent for a bugler, pen, ink, and paper, and opened the negotiations for surrender.

Pillow advised Forrest to cut his way out, and let all escape who could. Taking with him his staff and Colonel Gilmer, he crossed the river in a small skiff, and escaped by land. Floyd says in his supplemental report:

One of the reasons that induced me to make this transfer to General Buckner was, in order that I might be untrammeled in the effort I was determined to make to extricate as many of the command as possible from the fort, to which object I devoted myself during the night of the 15th. . . . I supposed it to be an unquestionable principle of military action that, in case of disaster, it is better to save part of a command than to lose the whole. The alternative proposition which I adopted in preference to surrendering the entire army was, to make my way out of the beleaguered camp with such men as were still able to make another struggle, if it could be accomplished; and if it could not be, then to take any consequences that did not involve a surrender. . . . Late at night it was ascertained that two steamboats would probably reach the landing before daylight. Then I determined to let Colonel Forrest's cavalry proceed on their march by the river-road, which was impassable for anything but cavalry on account of the back-water and overflow, while I would remain behind and endeavor to get away as many men as possible by the boats. The boats came a short time before daylight, when I hastened to the river and began to ferry the men over to the opposite shore as rapidly as possible.

Floyd's brigade, which had been drawn up near the river-bank, possibly with this intent, was nearest the landing. Hence they were the first to enter the boats, but none were excluded. All who came were taken on board, and great numbers crossed and made their escape: 1,175 men of the Virginia regiments were reported at the siege, and 982 reported at Murfreesboro ten days later, accounting thereby for all except the killed and wounded.

When it was determined to cut their way out, orders had been sent to General B. R. Johnson, and between one and two o'clock he drew up the left wing, including Heiman's brigade, for the sally. By 3 A. M. it was paraded outside the intrenchments by column of regiments. A little later, the Virginia regiments were withdrawn by Floyd ; and Johnson, sending an aide to state that he was ready to move, learned from Buckner that the command had devolved upon him, and that he was negotiating a capitulation.

Many of the men had slept or rested, in order to be able to renew the contest of the day before, and their victory had made them sanguine of success. When they learned that an immediate surrender was in store for them, there was a terrible revulsion of feeling, which affected individuals according to temperament, physical condition, and other circumstances. Those favored by proximity to the boats, endowed with extraordinary enterprise and decision of character, or cognizant of the actualities of prison-life and resolute not to become captives, availed themselves of the boats to cross over, or escaped by land that night or on the following days. Floyd says :

All who came were taken on board until some time after daylight, when I received a message from General Buckner that any further delay at the wharf would certainly cause the loss of the boat, with all on board. Such was the want of all order and discipline by this time on shore, that a wild rush was made at the boat, which the captain said would swamp her, unless he pushed off immediately. This was done; and, about sunrise, the boat on which I was (the other having gone) left the shore, and steered up the river.

The boats employed as ferries enabled some 300 men to escape. Forrest carried off by the river-road 500 of his own cavalry, who could ford the slough, and some 200 of other commands on artillery-horses, or aided with a friendly "lift " by the mounted men. A great number threw themselves into the icy waters of the slough, and waded over, waist-deep, at the hazard and often with the sacrifice of health or life. Many others, trusting themselves to the devious by-paths of the forest through which they had fought, made their way to the open country beyond. Little more than one-half of the defenders of Fort Donelson went into Northern prisons. Badeau, in estimating the results of the victory, says : "Sixty-five guns, 17,600 small-arms, and nearly 15,000 troops fell into the hands of the victor." This must be an error. For, even including the six guns and 5,000 small-arms recaptured, and the thirteen heavy guns in the fort, the total artillery would fall a good deal short of his estimate. He says, "Rations were issued at Cairo to 14,623 prisoners." Very likely this was the quartermaster's return ; but, if so, it was based on muster-rolls, not men. The actual number of captives did not exceed 7,000 or 8,000.

To Buckner's proposition for capitulation, Grant replied : " No terms, except unconditional and immediate surrender, can be accepted. I pro-

pose to move immediately upon your works." Buckner somewhat re-
sentfully submitted, and Grant allowed commissioned officers to retain
their side-arms, and privates their clothing and blankets. The correspondence is given in Appendix A to this chapter. The Federal soldiers, suddenly lifted from the borders of despair, and, after all their
toils and sufferings, exulting in a first great victory, gave way to most
unseemly license. Discipline was relaxed, and the Confederate camps
became the scene of almost indiscriminate pillage. It was this demoralization that permitted so many fugitives to evade their captors.

The escape of Brigadier-General B. R. Johnson illustrates this very
well, as one example among many. He had taken no part in the council,
but determined at the time of the surrender to remain with his troops.
He says that after the officers were separated from the men—

> I concluded that it was unlikely that I could be of any more service to them.
> I, however, formed no purpose or plan to escape. In the afternoon, toward sun-
> set of the 18th of February,[1] I walked out with a Confederate officer, and took
> my course toward the rifle-pits on the hill formerly occupied by Colonel Heiman,
> and, finding no sentinels to obstruct me, I passed on and was soon beyond the
> Federal encampments. I had taken no part in the surrender, had received no
> orders or instructions from the Federal authorities, had not been recognized or
> even seen by any of the general officers, had given no parole, and made no
> promises.

Whatever opinions may have been held as to the correctness of General Buckner's judgment as to the necessity of surrender, no question
could be made as to the manliness and propriety of his conduct, if it
was inevitable. His military education and well-balanced character
stood him in good stead in his difficult situation. General Grant personally treated Buckner with the decency due to an honorable foe ; but,
as his captivity is not especially pertinent to this narrative, it suffices to
say that the details of it were not creditable to the great Government
into whose hands he had fallen as a prisoner. On their release from
captivity, Colonels Brown, Hanson, Baldwin, and Heiman, were promoted
to be brigadier-generals, for their conduct at Fort Donelson.

Floyd and Pillow, however, did not pass uncensured. Their escape
was bitterly resented by the prisoners and their friends. The Twentieth
Mississippi, who had acted as a guard during the embarkation, and
most of whom were left behind in the precipitate departure of the boat,
naturally felt very keenly their disappointment. Federal writers generally seem to feel that the United States Government had suffered some
special grievance in the escape of Floyd and Pillow, and denounce very
vigorously their perfidy and cowardice. What was of more concern to
them, the Confederate Government held them to a rigid accountability,
more of which will appear hereafter.

---

[1] Two days and a half after the surrender.

It is difficult to over-estimate the consequences to the Federal arms of the surrender of Donelson. The material results were great; but, great as they were, the moral effects were still greater. An army was demolished; nearly one-half of the Confederate soldiers in Tennessee were killed, captured, or scattered; the line of defense was broken, so as to open the whole of Kentucky, and a great part of Tennessee, to the Federal arms; Bowling Green, Nashville, Columbus—all were turned; and the valley of the Cumberland was rendered untenable. But, mighty as was the disaster, its consequences on the minds of the parties to the civil strife were still more ominous to the Confederate cause. Where now were the impregnable fortifications, said to be guarded by 100,000 desperate Southerners; where now the boasted prowess of troops, who were to quail at no odds; where the inexhaustible resources that were to defy all methods of approach? The screen was thrown down; the inherent weakness and poverty of the South were made manifest to all eyes; its vaunted valor was quelled, it was claimed, by inferior numbers and superior courage, and the prestige of the Confederate arms was transferred to their antagonists.

An immense stride had been taken toward conquest. The North rang with self-gratulations and with plaudits to the triumphing general and army. President Lincoln at once nominated Grant as a major-general, and the Senate confirmed him; and, though some cabals and military rivalries interposed themselves timidly, there can be no doubt that his promotion was honestly won; for, by decision, force of will, and tenacity of purpose, he had held up the sinking courage of a beaten army. If Fortune helped him, his case was not different from that of many others who have thus become famous.

As for the soldiers, there were no more flings or jeers on either side at the courage of the other. Each was compelled to testify to the valor of its antagonist. The combats in the shadows of the dark woods of Donelson, and in those bosky valleys, where the snows were trampled and blood-stained in the doubtful struggle, bore impartial witness to a like fearlessness in assault, stubborn resolution in resistance, and indomitable spirit in retreat. Mutual respect grew up from the horrors and strife of that field of carnage. This is not a compensation for the awful suffering and sorrow of war; but it is *something*. Any generous or elevated feeling may be paid for by a nation at heavy cost.

APPENDIX A.

HEADQUARTERS, FORT DONELSON,
February 16, 1862.

SIR: In consideration of all the circumstances governing the present situation of affairs at this station, I propose to the commanding officer of the Federal forces the appointment of commissioners to agree upon terms of capitulation of the forces and post under my command, and in that view suggest an armistice until twelve o'clock to-day.

I am, sir, very respectfully, your obedient servant,

S. B. BUCKNER,
Brigadier-General C. S. A.

To Brigadier-General U. S. GRANT, commanding United States forces near Fort Donelson.

GENERAL GRANT TO GENERAL BUCKNER.

HEADQUARTERS, ARMY IN THE FIELD,
FORT DONELSON, *February* 16, 1862.

SIR: Yours of this date, proposing armistice and appointment of commissioners to settle terms of capitulation, is just received. No terms except unconditional and immediate surrender can be accepted. I propose to move immediately upon your works.

I am, sir, very respectfully, your obedient servant,

U. S. GRANT,
Brigadier-General commanding.

General S. B. BUCKNER, Confederate Army.

GENERAL BUCKNER TO GENERAL GRANT.

HEADQUARTERS, DOVER, TENNESSEE,
February 16, 1862.

SIR: The distribution of the forces under my command, incident to an unexpected change of commanders, and the overwhelming force under your command, compel me, notwithstanding the brilliant success of the Confederate arms yesterday, to accept the ungenerous and unchivalrous terms which you propose.

I am, sir, your very obedient servant,

S. B. BUCKNER,
Brigadier-General commanding, C. S. A.

To Brigadier-General U. S. GRANT, United States Army.

APPENDIX B.

TABLE I.

Confederate Killed and Wounded at Fort Donelson.

The *Nashville Patriot* gives the following as a corrected copy of its list of Confederate losses at Fort Donelson:

REGIMENT.	Colonel.	Acting Commander.	Number engaged.	Killed.	Wounded.
Forty-eighth Tennessee	Voorhies.....	....	230	....	1
Forty-second "	Quarles.....	....	498	....	11
Fifty-third "	Abernethy...	....	280	6	12
Forty-ninth "	Bailey......	....	300	4	13
Thirtieth "	Head........	....	654	11	80
Eighteenth "	Palmer......	....	615	4	40
Tenth "	Heiman......	....	750	1	5
Twenty-sixth "	Lillard	....	400	11	85
Forty-first "	Farquharson.	....	450	2	6
Thirty-second "	Cooke.......	....	558	8	85
Third "	Brown	....	650	12	75
Fifty-first "	Clark.......	....	80	....	....
Fiftieth "	Sugg........	....	650	2	4
Second Kentucky..........	Hanson......	....	618	13	57
Eighth "	Burnett......	Lieutenant-Colonel Lyon.	300	19	60
Seventh Texas............	Gregg	....	300	20	80
Fifteenth Arkansas.........	Gee.........	....	270	7	17
Twenty-seventh Alabama....	Hughes	....	216	....	1
First Mississippi............	Simonton....	Lieutenant-Col. Hamilton.	280	17	76
Third "	Davidson....	Lieutenant-Colonel Wells.	560	5	19
Fourth "	Drake.......	....	5'5	8	88
Fourteenth Mississippi.....	Baldwin....	Major Doss.	475	17	84
Twentieth "	Russell.....	" Brown...........	562	19	59
Twenty-sixth "	Reynolds....	Lieutenant-Colonel Boone	434	12	71
Fiftieth Virginia	....	Major Thorburn........	400	8	68
Fifty-first "	Wharton	....	275	5	45
Fifty-sixth "	Stewart	....	850	....	....
Thirty-sixth "	McCausland..	....	250	....[1]	....[1]
Tennessee Battalion........	....	Major Colms.........	270	....	....
" "	....	" Gowan...........	60	8	8
" " Cavalry..	....	Gantt...............	227	....	1
" " " ..	....	Captain Milton	15	....	....
" " " ..	....	Forrest	600	8	15
Artillery.................	....	Murray	80	....	2
"	....	Porter................	113	....	9
"	....	Graves................	50	....	4
"	....	Maney................	100	5	9
"	....	Jackson...............	84	....	....
"	....	Guy...................	58	....	....
"	....	Ross..................	166	2	2
"	....	Green.................	76	....	1
Total..................	....	....	13,829	281	1,007
By error..............	McCausland..	Thirty-sixth Virginia	......	14	66
	Stewart......	....	......	8	87
			13,829	248	1,100

[1] Loss not known, but severe.

TABLE II.

From Surgeon-General's Report, Part I., Volume I., Appendix, page 35.

"XXXIII. Report of the regiments constituting the garrison at Fort Donelson, February, 1862. [This statement of the killed, wounded, missing, and prisoners, in the engagements of February 12–15, 1862, at Fort Donelson, Stewart County, Tennessee, was forwarded to the Surgeon-General's office, on March 13, 1866, by Surgeon H. V. Gill, U. S. V., with the following indorsement:]

"This is an exact copy of a report, in my possession, made by Major Johnson, First Mississippi Regiment. I procured the report at the house of Dr. Jeter, the father-in-law of Major Johnson, in the spring of 1864, and believe it to be correct. There is a remarkable item in it. In the Fourth Mississippi Regiment there were forty killed and but thirty-eight wounded, the only instance of the kind I have known."

REGIMENT.	Commander.	Engaged.	Killed.	Wounded.	Surrendered.	Missing and escaped.
Third Tennessee.................	Colonel Brown..........	650	12	76	558	4
Tenth "	" Heiman........	750	1	5	700	44
Eighteenth Tennessee..........	" Palmer.........	685	4	40	615	26
Thirtieth "	" Head..........	751	9	10	730	2
Thirty-second "	" Cooke.........	586	3	25	557	1
Twenth-sixth "	" Lillard........	400	11	85	301	3
Forty-first "	" Farquharson..	575	2	1	552	20
Forty-second "	" Quarles.......	498	2	9	465	22
Forty-eighth "	" Voorhies......	291	1	11	270	9
Forty-ninth "	" Bailey.........	372	7	14	351	....
Fiftieth "	" Sugg..........	650	2	6	547	95
Fifty-first "	" Browder......	200	....	....	185	15
Fifty-third "	" Abernethy.....	420	8	20	382	10
Second Kentucky..............	" Hanson........	618	13	57	500	48
Eighth "	" Burnett.......	350	19	41	290	....
Seventh Texas.................	" Gregg.........	385	20	34	300	31
Fifteenth Arkansas.............	" Gee..........	304	11	23	270	....
Twenty-seventh Alabama.......	" Hughes.......	280	....	1	279	....
First Mississippi...............	" Simonton.....	352	19	66	267	....
Third "	" Davidson.... ..	624	5	19	600	....
Fourth "	" Drake.........	685	40	38	550	27
Fourteenth Mississippi..........	" Baldwin.......	653	17	84	554	3
Twentieth "	" Russell.......	562	19	59	484	....
Twenty-sixth "	" Reynolds......	443	12	71	334	26
Sixtieth Virginia...............	" Stewart.......	350	....	....	....	350
Thirty-sixth Virginia............	" McCausland....	280	....	....	....	280
Fiftieth "	Major Thorburn........	400	8	68	....	324
Fifty-first "	Colonel Wharton.......	275	5	45	....	225
Battalion Tennessee Infantry	Major Colms............	270	....	....	270	....
" " " ...	Major Gowan..........	60	....	...	60	....
Company " " ...	Captain Milton.........	15	....	1	14	....
Battalion " Cavalry.....	Lieutenant-Col. Forrest.	600	8	15	100	470
" Ninth "	" " Gantt..	340	1	5	303	31
Company Tennessee Artillery....	Captain Maney.........	100	5	9	60	26
" " " ...	" Ross..........	113	2	2	110	2
" " " ...	" Porter........	113	7	4	90	12
" Kentucky " ...	" Graves........	70	....	4	50	16
" " " ...	" Green........	76	....	1	40	35
" Virginia " ...	" Jackson........	54	....	....	....	54
" " " ...	" Guy...........	58	....	....	....	58

SUMMARY.

STATE.	Engaged.	Killed.	Wounded.	Surrendered.	Missing and escaped.
Tennessee........................	8,442	85	338	7,220	799
Kentucky.........................	1,114	22	103	880	99
Texas............................	385	20	34	300	31
Arkansas.........................	304	11	23	270	....
Alabama..........................	280	...	1	279	....
Mississippi.......................	3,304	112	337	2,789	66
Virginia..........................	1,417	13	113	....	1,291
Total........................	15,246	273	949	11,738	2,286

TABLE III.

Confederate Force at Donelson.

REGIMENT.	Colonel.	Acting Commander.	Nashville Patriot.	Surgeon-Gen'l's Volume; Major Johnson's Report.	Official.	No. of Effectives at last Report.	Aggregate at last Report.
			1.	2.	3.	4.	5.
Third Tennessee	Brown	Lieutenant-Col. Gordon.	650	650	750	....	....
Tenth "	Heiman	Lieut.-Col. McGavock...	750	750	...	782	814
Eighteenth Tennessee...	Palmer		615	685	685	....	....
Twenty-sixth "	Lillard		400	400	400	....	....
Thirtieth "	Head		654	751	450	476³	812
Thirty-second "	Cooke		558	586	555	....	....
Forty-first "	Farquharson		450	575	575	....	....
Forty-second "	Quarles		498	498	498	....	....
Forty-eighth "	Voorhies		230	291	...	....	....
Forty-ninth "	Bailey		300	372	...	898⁴	773
Fiftieth "	Stacker	Lieutenant-Col. Sugg...	650	650	...	541⁵	883
Fifty-first "	Clark	Browder	80	200	...	....	....
Fifty-third "	Abernethy	Lieut.-Colonel Winston..	280	420	...	348	786
Second Kentucky	Hanson		618	618	600²	....	....
Eighth "	Burnett	Major Lyon	300	350	...	....	....
Seventh Texas	Gregg		300	385	355	....	....
Fifteenth Arkansas	Gee		270	304	...	....	....
Twenty-seventh Alabama	Hughes		216	280	...	596	805
First Mississippi	Simonton	Lieut.-Colonel Hamilton	280	352	...	...	....
Third "	Davidson	Lieutenant-Col. Webb..	500	624	...	....	....
Fourth "	Drake	Major Adair	535	665	...	584	870
Fourteenth Mississippi...	Baldwin	" Doss	475	658	650	....	....
Twentieth "	Russell	" Brown	562	562	500	....	....
Twenty-sixth "	Reynolds	Lieutenant-Col. Boone..	484	443	443	....	....
Thirty-sixth Virginia	McCausland	" " Reid....	250	280	250	....	....
Fiftieth "		Major Thorburn	400	400	...	....	....
Fifty-first "	Wharton	Lieutenant-Col. Massie..	275	275	275	....	....
Fifty-sixth "	Stewart	Captain Daviess	350	350	350	....	....
Tennessee Battalion		Major Colms	270	270	...	....	....
Alabama "		" Garvin	60	60	...	72	....
Battalion Cavalry		" Gantt	227	340	...	318	....
" "		Captain Milton	15	15	...	42	....
Ky. Batt. Cav., 5 comp's.			....	....	...	266	....
Tennessee Reg't Cavalry.	Forrest		600	600	...	....	....
Artillery¹		Porter	113	113	...	....	....
"		Graves	50	70	50	....	....
"		Maney	100	100	...	85	....
"		Jackson	84	54	...	....	....
"		Guy	58	58	...	....	....
"		Ross	166	116	...	....	....
"		Green	76	76	...	....	....
			13,809	15,246	...	....	....

[1] Scott's Louisiana Regiment of Cavalry was scouting on the right bank. Colonel Jordan ("Life of Forrest," page 61), in an intelligent account of the siege, estimates the force at 13,000 infantry and somewhat over 1,000 cavalry and artillery.

[2] About.   [3] January 14th, 883 effectives, 912 aggregate.

[4] January 14th, 680 effectives, 777 aggregate.   [5] January 14th, 686 effectives, 847 aggregate.

3. In 6,011 men in sixteen commands, the official report, column 3, falls below column 2 only forty-nine men. It agrees with column 2 in seven and with column 1 in six instances, and exceeds column 1, 497 men in the other ten.

4. In 3,565 men in nine commands, column 4 falls 498 men below column 2—4,603. It exceeds column 1, 54 men.

Column 1.—The *Nashville Patriot* list is found in "The Rebellion Record," vol. iv., p. 187.

Column 2.—Major Johnson's Report; Surgeon-General's Report, vol. i., Appendix, p. 85.

Column 3.—Official estimates and reports of men engaged, from "Battle Reports."

Column 4.—Last official return before battle in January.

Column 5.—Last official return before battle in January.

TABLE IV.

FORT DONELSON.

Right Wing.—BUCKNER.

BRIGADES.	Regiments and Commanders.	Killed.	Wounded.	Writer's estimate of Strength.
III. BROWN.	Third Tennessee, Gordon........................	12	76	....
	Eighteenth Tennessee, Palmer	10	38	....
	Thirty-second Tennessee, Cook	3	36	....
		40[1]	150	1,990
II. (Half attached to Brown's.)	Second Kentucky, Hanson[2].....................	24	50	600
	Fourteenth Mississippi, Doss...................	17	84	650
	Forty-first Tennessee, Farquharson.............	2	6	575
	Porter's battery.................................	8	25	113
	Graves's "	2	4	50
	Issaquena "	....	3	54
	Staff, etc., not included	2	15	....
		55	187	2,042

[1] The writer is informed by General Brown that the casualties in this brigade are known to exceed forty killed and one hundred and fifty wounded, and he is doubtless correct.

[2] In eight companies of the Second Kentucky, nineteen men were *known* to be killed and forty wounded. The above estimate is based on these facts.

FORT DONELSON.

Left Wing.—PILLOW.

BRIGADES.	Regiments and Commanders.	Killed.	Wounded.	Writer's estimate of Strength (effective).
I. HEIMAN.	Tenth Tennessee, McGavock......................	....	....	750
	Fifty-third Tennessee, Abernethy...............	....	....	350
	Forty-eighth Tennessee (eight companies) Voorhies	....	....	250
	Twenty-seventh Alabama, Hughes	....	....	250
	Battery, Maney.................................	....	....	100
		10	36	1,700[1]
II. SIMONTON'S.	Third Mississippi, Webb.........................	5	19	624
	Eighth Kentucky, Lyon	19	57[2]	350
	Seventh Texas, Gregg...........................	20	34	385
	First Mississippi, Hamilton.....................	19	66	352
		63	176	1,711
III. DRAKE.	Fourth Mississippi, Adair.......................	38	40	584
	Fifteenth Arkansas, Gee...	7	17	304
	Twenty-sixth Alabama (two companies) Garvin...	....	....	72
	Tennessee Battalion, Browder...................	3	2	140
		48	59	1,100
IV. HEAD.	Thirtieth Tennessee, Head.......................	11	30	654
	Forty-second Tennessee, Quarles	4	7	498
		15	37	1,152
V. WHARTON.	Fifty-first Virginia, Massie......................	9	43	275
	Fifty-sixth Virginia, Daviess....................	3	37	350
		12	80	625

FORT DONELSON.—*Left Wing*—(Continued).

BRIGADES.	Regiments and Commanders.	Killed.	Wounded.	Writer's estimate of Strength (effective).
VI. McCAUSLAND.	Thirty-sixth Virginia, Reid.........................	14	56	250
	Fiftieth Virginia, Thorburn.......................	8	63	400
	Twentieth Mississippi, Brown.....................	20	58	....
		42	182	650[3]
VII. BALDWIN.	Twenty-sixth Mississippi, Reynolds..................	12	71	....
	Twenty-sixth Tennessee, Lillard....................	11	85	....
		23	156	1,358
Not brigaded in fort.	Ross's battery..	....	....	116
	Tennessee Battalion, Colms.....................	....	....	270
	Forty-ninth Tennessee, Bailey....................	7	14	372
	Fiftieth Tennessee, Sugg.......................	2	4	650
		9	18	1,408
Cavalry.	Forrest's regiment..............................	8	15	Cavalry 1,000
	Ninth Tennessee Battalion, Gantt.................	....	1	
	Three Kentucky companies.......................	....	....	....
	Milton's company...............................	....	....	....
		8	16	....
Light Artillery batteries.	Greene's, seven guns............................	....	....	76
	French, four guns...............................	....	....	58
	Guy, four guns.................................	....	....	58
		....	....	192

[1] Colonel Heiman says about 1,600. [2] B. R. Johnson's Report.
[3] Attached on the 14th to Baldwin, who reports the Twentieth and Twenty-sixth Mississippi, and the Twenty-sixth Tennessee, 1,358 strong.

RECAPITULATION.

Killed................ 325
Wounded................................... 1,097
Total army........................ 14,923

TABLE V.

FEDERAL ARMY AT DONELSON.

First Division.—General McCLERNAND.

BRIGADES.	Regiments.	Commanders.	Strength in Action.	Killed.	Wounded.	Missing.	Aggregate.
II. W. H. L. WALLACE, Colonel commanding.	Eleventh Illinois.....	Lt.-Col. T. E. G. Ransom	579[1]	68	183	79	836
	Twentieth "	Colonel C. C. Marsh.....	753	18	109	6	133
	Forty-fifth "	" John E. Smith..	615	8	31	3	42
	Forty-eighth "	" I. N. Hayne....	512	2	20	...	22
			2,464	...	...	...	...
	Fourth Illinois Cav'ry	Colonel T. Lyle Dickey	....	...	...	...	...
	First " Artil'y	Captain Ezra Taylor..	936	1	8	...	9
	Taylor's battery...						
	McAllister..........	" E. McAllister.	....	...	2	...	2
			8,400[2]	...	...	...	...
III. McARTHUR.	Seventeenth Illinois....	Major Smith...........	750[1]	13	62	6	81
	Forty-ninth " ..	Colonel Morrison.......	645	13	46	9	68
			1,395	123	461	103	637

FEDERAL ARMY AT DONELSON.—*First Division*—(Continued).

BRIGADES.	Regiments.	Commanders.	Strength in Action.	Killed.	Wounded.	Missing.	Aggregate.
I. OGLESBY.	Eighth Illinois........	Lieut.-Colonel Rhoades.	751[3]	...	...	...	...
	Eighteenth Illinois ...	Colonel Lawler.........	671	...	...	...	...
	Twenth-ninth " ...	" Reardon	542	...	...	...	...
	Thirtieth " ...	Lieut.-Colonel Dennis ..	568	...	...	...	...
	Thirty-first " ...	Colonel John A. Logan.	598	...	...	...	...
			3,130				
	Swartz's battery.......	....	....	...	...	...	...
	Dresser's "	....	....	...	...	...	...
	Cavalry..............	Stewart, Dollin, O'Harnett, Carmichael.	500[4]	...	...	...	...

[1] Strength of these commands from Surgeon Stearns's Report, "Medical History of the War," page 1, medical vol., Appendix, p. 34. He reports the aggregate loss of this division at 1,491.

[2] The Second Brigade had 3,400 effective men of all arms. Wallace's Report.

[3] *New York Times* letter, "Rebellion Record," vol. iv., p. 173.

[4] Estimated.

Second Division.—Brigadier-General C. F. SMITH.

BRIGADES.	Regiments.	Commanders.	Killed.	Wounded.	Missing.	Aggregate.
IV. Colonel J. G. LAUMAN.	Second Iowa.................	Colonel Tuttle ...	41	157	..	198
	Twenty-fifth Indiana.........	" Veatch...	14	101	..	115
	Seventh Iowa..............	Lt.-Col. Parrot...	2	37	..	39
	Fourteenth Iowa.............	Colonel Shaw....	3	23	..	26
	First Sharp-shooters.........	Lt.-Col. Compton	1	3	..	4
	Fifty-sec'd and Fifty-sixth Ind.	(no data)	..	..	..	..
	Stone's Missouri Battery......	....	..	..	1	..
			61	321	1	383
V. Col. MORGAN L. SMITH, commanding.	Eighth Missouri.............	Col. M. L. Smith.	9	86	..	45
	Eleventh Indiana	G. F. McGinnis ..	4	20	..	24
Colonel J. COOK, commanding.	Twelfth Iowa................	Col. J. J. Woods.	1	27	..	28
	Fiftieth Illinois..............	Colonel Bane.....	..	..	..	..
	Seventh "	(no data)	..	..	..	..
	Thirteenth Missouri..........	"	..	..	..	..
	Fifty-second Indiana..........	"	..	..	..	..

Third Division.—General LEW WALLACE.

BRIGADES.	Regiments.	Commanders.	Strength.	Killed.	Wounded.	Missing.	Aggregate.
I. Col. CHAS. CRUFT, commanding.	Thirty-first Indiana.	Lieut.-Colonel Osborn..	727 [1]	13	51	5	69
	Forty-fourth "	Colonel Hugh R. Reed..	....	7	34	2	43
	Seventeenth Kent'y	Col. John H. McHenry.	510 [2]	4	33	3	40
	Twenty-fifth "	Col. Jas. M. Shackleford	....	12	60	12	84[2]
			....	36	178	22	236[3]
II., III. and IV.[4] Col. J. M. THAYER, commanding.	First Nebraska.....	Lieut.-Colonel McCord..	....	....	....	....	....
	Seventy-sixth Ohio.	Colonel Woods........	....	....	....	....	....
	Fifty-eighth Ohio	" Steadman.......	....	....	....	....	....
Second Brigade attached.	Sixty-eighth "		....	....	....	....	....
	Forty-sixth Illinois.	" Davis..........	....	....	....	....	....
	Fifty-seventh "	" Baldwin.......	....	....	....	....	....
	Fifty-eighth "	" Lynch..........	....	....	....	....	....

[1] "The Rebellion Record," vol. iv., p. 145.

[2] Regimental Report. Surgeon Keenan gives approximate strength of this brigade at 2,000.

[3] Killed and wounded—official, Cruft's Report.

[4] No data.

CHAPTER XXIX.

THE RETREAT FROM BOWLING GREEN.

FORTS Henry and Donelson had fallen, and the great water high-ways were opened to Nashville and to North Alabama. This gave access to the rear of the Confederate armies, and turned the positions both at Bowling Green and Columbus. Of course, such misfortunes could not happen in his department without subjecting General John-ston to the severest criticism, and we shall presently see to what heights of excitement and depths of bitterness the tide of feeling ran. That mighty surge of wrath belonged to the hour, but it has left its mark on the military history of the times, and in the criticism which sprang out of it. The writer believes that the plain narrative of facts he has given is a better answer to the censures of General Johnston's conduct than the most elaborate argument would be.

Without undertaking to answer, in form and controversially, the objections to General Johnston's dispositions, a brief reference to the considerations which controlled him will not be inappropriate in this connection. The reasons why he adopted a defensive instead of an offensive policy have been set forth so fully in these pages that it is not necessary to recapitulate them here. The chief were inadequate forces and armament. In Colonel Munford's pointed language, "*he had no army.*"

General Johnston's largest force present for duty at any one time on the line from Bowling Green to Columbus, and in reserve, was never more than 43,000 men. But the facts demonstrated that this was only the number capable of fighting in position, not the force available for a winter campaign. The army lost twenty-five per cent. by the mere act of moving in the well-ordered retreat from Bowling Green to Nash-ville. Suppose that these forces could have been collected into one compact body without pursuit, molestation, or other interference by the enemy—a result manifestly not in the table of probabilities—and led against either Buell or Grant, what would have been the chance of suc-cess? Buell had an army 75,000 strong. Grant could not be assailed in his fortifications on the north side of the Ohio ; and, even if his in-trenched position at Paducah had been attacked, he had his fleets and 25,000 men, with Buell and Halleck to draw upon for any required reënforcements up to 100,000 men within three or four days' call.

Nevertheless, it has been urged that these armies should have been "concentrated." To concentrate them for any merely defensive purpose strikes the writer as mere fatuity. But this aside, *at what one point* could a defense of this line have been made? At Columbus? Then must the defense of Middle Tennessee have been abandoned without an effort to save it. At Henry and Donelson? The same result would have ensued, for there was nothing to prevent Buell's advance, except the interposition of the force at Bowling Green. But, last of all, if the barrier at Columbus had been abandoned to maintain Bowling Green, or for any other consideration whatever, it opened the Mississippi River to the invader; and, if either Henry or Donelson were given up, the rear of the armies at Bowling Green and Columbus would have been uncovered. Henry had no value, except as the gateway of the Tennessee River; nor Donelson, save as an outpost of Nashville.

While it was unnecessary for the Federal armies to feel much concern about concentrating to meet any hypothetical concentration of the Confederates, inasmuch as they were sufficiently strong to repel any attack in position without it, yet, had it been desirable, their means of rapid transit were so much greater than the Confederate that they could always have opposed a superior force to any assault. The " interior lines " are not determined by a scale of miles, but by the time required to convey troops over the intervals between commands. Facilities of transportation more than distances, therefore, decide what these interior lines are. An unlimited power of water-communication enabled Halleck and Buell to coöperate fully, and practically to place what force they pleased where they pleased. Such was the concentration that actually took place. Forts Donelson and Henry were nearly twice as far from Bowling Green by land as from the Federal strongholds by water. Colonel Robert W. Woolley, in a letter written at the time, says :

The railroad was almost bare of transportation. The locomotives had not been repaired for six months, and many of them lay disabled in the depots. They could not be repaired at Bowling Green, for there is, I am informed, but one place in the South where a driving-wheel can be made, and not one where a whole locomotive can be constructed.

General Johnston did all that was possible when he placed Floyd's command at Russellville, within striking distance of both Bowling Green and Donelson, which were alike threatened. Floyd was at Donelson in time, and could have been at Henry with any reasonable warning. If there were not enough men at Donelson, it was not from defect of judgment, but from want of adequate means. The elements, too, fought for the Federals. An unprecedented flood favored their attacks by water, while it impeded the movements of the Confederates. No time was given to General Johnston, either through the sluggishness of the enemy, or by the prolonged resistance of his own troops, to repair disaster. Grant moved February 2d; in four days Henry was in his hands. Ten days only intervened between General Johnston's first information of the attack on Henry and the surrender of Donelson. He meant "to defend Nashville at Donelson," if he could, and, if not, then to reunite his corps and to fight on a more retired line.

A very astonishing statement is made by Mr. Swinton, in his "Decisive Battles of the War," page 65. He says:

In this condition, outnumbered on both lines, Johnston does not appear to have comprehended that a defensive attitude could only result fatally—that his sole ground of hope rested in taking advantage of his interior position to concentrate the gross of his force at a single point, and assume the offensive against one or the other of the two Union armies. Connected with this is a piece of secret history, revealed to me by General Beauregard since the close of the war, which will not be out of place here.

Toward the close of the first month of the year 1862, General Beauregard was transferred from Virginia to the West, to take charge, under Sidney Johnston, of the defense of the Mississippi Valley. *En route* he visited Johnston at his headquarters at Bowling Green, and between the two officers a prolonged conference ensued, touching the best method of action. It was with the liveliest concern that Beauregard, who had understood at Richmond that Johnston's force numbered 60,000 men, learned that in reality it was little over one-half that aggregate. But that officer was always essentially aggressive in his military inspiration, and he now proposed that the works at Columbus should be so reduced that their defense might be sustained by two or three thousand men; that the remaining 12,000 should be brought to Bowling Green and joined to the 22,000 there, and that with the united force a vigorous, and, if possible, a crushing blow should be dealt to Buell's army, which was regarded at the time as the most menacing, for Grant and Foote had not yet moved. Johnston fell in with this plan, and Beauregard proceeded to Columbus to put it in train of execution. Scarcely, however, had he started for Columbus when the thunder of the Union guns on the Tennessee apprised him that it was too late, and, by the time he reached the Mississippi, Fort Henry had fallen.

Without undertaking at all to solve how Mr. Swinton has fallen into such errors, a few facts will demonstrate an entirely different state of case. General Beauregard was ordered, January 26th, by letter from Richmond, to report to General Johnston, and to take command at Columbus. He did not leave Manassas for several days, and probably arrived at Bowling Green about February 5th or 6th. On the 7th he held a conference with Generals Johnston and Hardee, the minutes of which are here given.

It will be observed that, on February 4th and 5th, General Johnston was moving troops to Clarksville to support Tilghman, and on the 6th ordered Floyd's entire command thither. General Beauregard remained in Bowling Green until the 12th. His conference with General Johnston did not take place until February 7th, when they both knew of the fall of Fort Henry, and made their plans with reference to that fact.

MEMORANDUM OF CONFERENCE HELD BY GENERALS JOHNSTON, BEAUREGARD, AND HARDEE.

BOWLING GREEN, KENTUCKY, *February* 7, 1862.

At a meeting held to-day at my quarters (Covington House), by Generals Johnston, Hardee, and myself (Colonel Mackall being present part of the time), it was determined that Fort Henry, on the Tennessee River, having fallen yesterday into the hands of the enemy, and Fort Donelson, on the Cumberland River, not being tenable, *preparations* should at once be made for the removal of this army to Nashville in rear of the Cumberland River, a strong point some miles below that city being fortified forthwith to defend the river from the passage of gunboats and transports. The troops at present at Clarksville should cross over to the south side of that river, leaving only a sufficient force in that town to protect the manufactories and other property, in the saving of which the Confederate Government is interested. From Nashville, should any further retrograde movement become necessary, it will be made to Stevenson, and thence according to circumstances.

It was also determined that the possession of the Tennessee River by the enemy, resulting from the fall of Fort Henry, separates the army at Bowling Green from the one at Columbus, Kentucky, which must henceforth act independently of each other, until they can again be brought together; the first one having for object the defense of the State of Tennessee along its line of operation as already stated; and the other one, of that part of the State lying between the Tennessee River and the Mississippi. But, as the possession of the former river by the enemy renders the lines of communication of the army at Columbus liable to be cut off at any time from the Tennessee River as a base, by an overpowering force of the enemy, rapidly concentrated from various points on the Ohio, it becomes necessary, to prevent such a calamity, that the main body of that army should fall back to Humboldt, and thence, if necessary, to Grand Junction, so as to protect Memphis from either point, and still have a line of retreat to the latter place or to Grenada, Mississippi, and, if necessary, to Jackson, Mississippi.

At Columbus, Kentucky, will be left only a sufficient garrison for the defense of the works there, assisted by Hollins's gunboats, for the purpose of making a desperate defense of the river at that point. A sufficient number of transports will be kept near that place for the removal of the garrison therefrom, when no longer tenable in the opinion of the commanding officer. Island No. 10 and Fort Pillow will likewise be defended to the last extremity, aided also by Hollins's gunboats, which will then retire to the vicinity of Memphis, where another bold stand will be made.

(Signed)   G. T. BEAUREGARD,
             General C. S. A.

(Signed)   W. J. HARDEE,
             Major-General.

A true copy: S. W. FERGUSON,
     Lieutenant and Aide-de-Camp.

This plan of campaign embraced the defense of the line of the Cumberland, if possible ; or, if not, then a retreat to Stevenson. Beauregard was to fall back southward with Polk's army, leaving a small garrison at Columbus. The immediate evacuation of Bowling Green was now inevitable. His correspondence has already made manifest that General Johnston regarded his stay at Bowling Green as a mere question of time, unless he should be promptly reënforced by a strong and well-organized corps. The defenses at Bowling Green, originally slight, had been greatly enlarged by the addition of a cordon of detached forts, mounted with heavy field-guns. Though its strength had been magnified by common report, until it had become "the Gibraltar of the West," it was really only sufficiently strong to withstand an assault, which General Johnston desired, but did not expect, and which Buell was too wary to make.

General Johnston's line of retreat was safe, so long as his flanks were unbroken. If these were maintained, he hoped by a skillful defense to hold at bay the heavy odds in his front until reënforced. If anything is evinced in this biography, it is that General Johnston possessed that admirable equilibrium of judgment—boldness combined with caution—which fitted him to hold a desperate position to the last extremity, and yet to apprehend distinctly when it could be defended no longer, and retire from it in time.

Early in the autumn, the difficulties of recruiting becoming apparent, made it plain that the line of the Barren River might have to be given up, and General Johnston endeavored to provide a second line of defense on the Cumberland—with how little effect has already been seen. On this second line, if forced to retreat, he purposed to make his stand as long as possible. But when he compared the unequal preparations for aggression and resistance, and perceived that no warning could stir the Southern people to a just sense of their danger, he beheld calamity coming as the clouds gather for the burst of the hurricane, and, with almost prophetic vision, saw his army forced back to the Cumberland, and beyond to the southern frontier of Tennessee.

Colonel Frank Schaller, of the Twenty-second Mississippi, an educated soldier, who published during the war, at Columbia, South Carolina, an edition of Marmont's "Spirit of Military Institutions," with valuable annotations pertinent to the times, illustrates Chapter III. of Part IV. of that work, which describes the "picture of a general who answers to all the requirements of the command," by a review of the life and character of General Johnston.[1] He begins his brief but appreciative memoir as follows :

Two foreign officers in the service of the Confederate States were ordered to report for duty to General Albert Sidney Johnston in the month of October, 1861. When leaving his headquarters at Bowling Green, in the State of Ken-

---

[1] Colonel Schaller has for several years been Professor of Modern Languages at the University of the South, Sewanee, Tennessee.

tucky, having then seen and spoken with him for the first time, they simultaneously exclaimed, when outside of the inclosure of the unpretending quarters: "He is the very *beau-idéal* of a general." To one of these officers, who now feebly attempts to pay this humble tribute to the memory of the departed hero, this, his first impulsive exclamation, has become the basis of the greatest veneration of which he is capable.

After describing General Johnston's employment of his time at Bowling Green, Colonel Schaller adds:

The result of all this was unshaken confidence on the part of the troops in their commander. But what endeared him most to his soldiers was the great justice which was the basis of all his decisions, the promptness with which wrongs were rectified, and the facility of access to the chief commander, as well as the genuine cordiality and dignity with which every one was met by him. Heavy labors on forts in mid-winter were endured without a murmur, since every soldier knew that General Johnston would never hesitate to expose himself whenever necessary. His headquarters were a model of order, simplicity, and prompt dispatch of business. His decisions to personal applications were immediate and final. His bearing was that of a knight of the olden times. The writer will never forget the shouts which greeted the general whenever the troops passed in review. . . .

The enemy had only been awaiting the completion of the fleet of gunboats to make demonstrations by water. Long before Fort Henry fell, in view of the disappointments to which General Johnston had been subjected, he was fully aware that his line, unless it was strongly reënforced, could not be held; and in the month of January, 1862, when one day looking with Colonel Bowen upon a map, showing the course of the Tennessee River, these memorable and prophetic words fell from his lips when pointing out a spot marked "Shiloh Church:" "*Here the great battle of the Southwest will be fought.*"

The present writer, struck by this remarkable incident, applied to Colonel Schaller for more explicit information in regard to it, and received the following statement:

RICHMOND, VIRGINIA, *May 22, 1863.*

COLONEL: I give to you, according to your request, with great pleasure the following statement of facts, which occurred during the month of January, 1862, when at the headquarters of General Albert Sidney Johnston, in the town of Bowling Green, Kentucky, and in the presence of then Colonel (now General) John S. Bowen, commanding the forts and the town of Bowling Green, of which former my regiment garrisoned "Fort Buckner," a strong position on the extreme left of the fortifications.

The engineers, who had been ordered by General A. S. Johnston to survey the course of the Tennessee River as far as Florence, Alabama, where its navigation is impeded, had completed their labors and submitted a fine military map to the general commanding. In front of this map, the general and Colonel Bowen were standing, the former giving evidently an explanation of its military positions. In the course of their conversation, General Johnston directed Colonel Bowen's attention to a position upon this map, which had been marked by the engineers, "SHILOH CHURCH," and, concluding his remarks, he laid his finger upon this spot, and quietly but impressively pronounced the following words, or words to this effect : "*Here the great battle of the Southwest will be fought.*" This opinion, pronounced by so distinguished a general, could not but arrest attention at the time, but you may well imagine that it recurred to our memory in the strongest manner when Brigadier-General Bowen and myself were actually engaged in the terrible conflict, which the prophetic words of General Johnston had fully three months previously predicted.   Meeting General Bowen upon the battle-field of "Shiloh Church," shortly after he (General Bowen) had been wounded, and while my regiment was replenishing its ammunition, about two or three o'clock P. M., during the first day's battle, and before the army had any knowledge of the fall of our illustrious leader, General Bowen recalled the circumstances above cited, and they were pronounced remarkable.

I give you these facts simply as they occurred, without any addition whatsoever ; but you must permit me here to state my firm conviction that this incident in the life of General Johnston was not a singular chance, as sometimes will happen in the life of man, but gloriously illustrating the strategic genius of the lamented general.   With the information at his command, and the thorough knowledge of the strength of his line of defense, as well as of the topography of the country which he occupied, he was eminently conscious that, without a speedy accession of strength his line would become untenable, and that a new contracted line could only be obtained south of Tennessee River.   When and by whom this would be executed was, of course, beyond the bounds of human calculation ; but Corinth afterward did become the strategic point of the campaign, and Hamburg Landing was the most convenient port whereby to reach it, and from whence it could be threatened. . . .

With sentiments of the highest esteem I am, colonel, very respectfully,
            Your obedient servant,   F. SCHALLER,
                Colonel Twenty-second Mississippi Infantry, P. A. C. S.
To Colonel WILLIAM PRESTON JOHNSTON, Richmond, Virginia.

The writer is indebted to Colonel Munford's address, so frequently quoted, for the following important incident :

Not very long before the evacuation of Bowling Green, the general and myself being alone, he locked the door, and with more than his usual gravity said: "I fear I will have to evacuate this position.   I wish to talk with you on that subject."   I asked, "With or without a battle, general?"   "Oh! without a battle.   They will never come here to fight me."   Pointing westward, he continued, "They will operate on my left, by the rivers, of which their gunboats give them command."   After reflecting, I said, "It is an important step, and involves the gravest consequences to both the South and yourself."   I then sketched the connection of Kentucky with the Confederacy ; that its Governor and Council were then under the wing of his army, having already sent Representatives and Senators to our Congress; that they must flee with him, and leave Kentucky with no organized representation of the Southern cause on its soil.   I then reminded him that the very military reasons which compelled him to leave Bowling Green would make it necessary to take his new position *south* of the Tennessee River; that the Governor and Legislature would have to flee from Nashville, the enemy would occupy that capital, and thus all the resources of men and munitions in these two populous States would at one and the same time be lost. "Two States, general! It is a fearful stride toward subjugation!" I told him frankly too that I believed the effect upon his own reputation would be serious; that the public believed he had 80,000 troops then with him; that they had unbounded confidence in his success; reminded him that when he had ordered his chief-engineer, Gilmer, to fortify Nashville, the popular sense of security was such that Gilmer was laughed at for suggesting the necessity for fortifications, was called in derision "Johnston's dirt-digger," and had to abandon the attempt in despair. "Now, sir," said I, "your retreat will startle these people like a thunderbolt; the loss of positions and of States, so unlooked for, will, with as mercurial a people as ours, produce a clamor the like of which you, perhaps, have never heard, and I sincerely trust it may not strike from your grasp the sceptre of your future usefulness." He remained silent and thoughtful for several minutes, and then used words which are indelible in my memory. "This," said he, "is a step I have pondered well, and such a step as no man would take who did not *know he was right.*" After another pause he said, "I wish I had 80,000 men—I'd be to-day upon the Lakes;" and, after yet another pause, he added, with more cheerfulness: "*The popular clamor of which you speak is not unanticipated by me. But the clamor of to-day is converted into the praises of to-morrow by a simple success. All I require to rectify that is to get in position where I can fight a battle, and I think all will be well.*" The conversation was closed by his assuring me he would hold Bowling Green as long as it was safe to do so—even to the last moment. In a few weeks the enemy's plans were developed just as he had foretold, and that moment came.

General John C. Brown informs the writer that he was sent by General Buckner, between the 1st and 4th of February, from Russellville to Bowling Green, in order to have a full conversation with General Johnston touching the reorganization of the troops and some other matters. During this confidential interview, which was frank and extended, General Johnston explained to him the positions and relative strength of Buell's army and his own, and read to him a good deal of his correspondence elucidating these points. Among other things, General Johnston told him that if he should lose Henry and Donelson, he should fall back to the line of the Cumberland; but that he feared that Nashville would prove untenable, so that he might have to fall back to the line of the Tennessee; and, in that event, he looked to *Corinth,* as a convenient point for concentrating his troops. This is an explicit statement, showing that General Johnston had considered every point, and sketched, at least, in his own mind, the plan of campaign which he afterward carried out, before General Beauregard's arrival.

The memorandum quoted and the statements of General Brown and Colonels Schaller and Munford fully prove that the plan of campaign, presented in definite shape to Beauregard and Hardee, had been long maturing in General Johnston's mind. To defend the line of the Cumberland was his first intention; should that fail, to fall back to

Stevenson by the railroad from Nashville, and thence by the Charleston & Memphis Railroad to effect a junction with Polk's command at Corinth. All this was clearly foreshadowed in his conversations with Brown, Munford, Bowen, and Schaller.

The preparations for retreat were begun. But these could not be carried out, and the soil of Kentucky abandoned to the enemy, without exciting the liveliest emotions of anguish and dismay in the breasts of the Southern party at Bowling Green. The soldiers, though depressed, received the fact of retreat with that sullen resolution which the military life engenders ; but all others seemed filled with despair. The Provisional Governor, George W. Johnson, a warm friend and admirer of General Johnston, but self-confident and enthusiastic, regarded the abandonment of the soil of the Commonwealth as an act of political suicide, and all the civilians shared this opinion. He appealed to General Johnston in the most urgent and moving terms to change his purpose, and he was supported by the protests and appeals of the united voice of the Kentucky refugees. General Johnston found it hard to steel himself against these eager petitioners, who had given up their homes to follow the fortunes of his army, but he was bound to do what was right and necessary. A letter was written to him by Governor Johnson, in the very spirit of Leonidas, whom he emulated. Sometimes it is harder to do right than to hold a Thermopylæ. General Johnston was inexorable. It is sufficient here to say that this gallant and excellent man lived long enough to assure General Johnston of his approval of the strategy he then condemned.

Colonel Robert W. Woolley (now of Louisville, Kentucky), who had enjoyed exceptional advantages of observation, in a communication to the *New Orleans Picayune*, in March, 1862, in describing General Johnston's work at Bowling Green, says :

An army must be obtained, or else he must evacuate the citadel that guards Nashville. A small army was obtained ; but where, or how, it will puzzle the historian of this war to relate. By extraordinary exertions he secured a regiment here and another there ; but few with any drill, and only five of them for three months with uniforms. The army had to be built up ; and the general had not only to organize the troops, but had himself to search for them. Of transportation, without which an army cannot subsist, he had none. Eight hundred wagons were needed. He had no workshops, yet he got the wagons. Hospitals and a medical department were necessary, for the sick were never less than twenty-five per cent. The great object was to secure Bowling Green against attack, until it could be fortified and succor obtained. This was most skillfully done. The place, in front, soon became, in strength, the second fortress in America, and impregnable everywhere had infantry been sent to protect its wings. While the work was progressing, and while every effort was being made to get more troops, Johnston, by skillful manœuvres, threw his men near the river which divided the two armies, and made the forces of the North believe that he was trying to decoy them across, and then attack them, with a river in their rear; when, in fact, the last thing he wished was a battle, when the odds were four or five to one. His strategy succeeded.

General Johnston held on to Bowling Green till the last moment. But his right flank, under Crittenden, was broken. Fort Henry was lost. Donelson was about to be attacked, with a doubtful prospect of successful resistance. It was evident that the time for the evacuation of Bowling Green had come. On the 8th of February General Johnston wrote to the Secretary of War, informing him of the loss of Fort Henry, and the condition of things at Donelson. He says, further:

> The occurrence of the misfortune of losing the fort will cut off the communication of the force here under General Hardee from the south bank of the Cumberland. To avoid the disastrous consequences of such an event, I ordered General Hardee yesterday to make, as promptly as it could be done, preparations to fall back to Nashville and cross the river.

> The movements of the enemy on my right flank would have made a retrograde in that direction to confront the enemy indispensable in a short time. But the probability of having the passage of this army corps across the Cumberland intercepted by the gunboats of the enemy admits of no delay in making the movement.

> Generals Beauregard and Hardee are equally with myself impressed with the necessity of withdrawing our force from this line at once.

Every preparation for the retreat was silently made. The ordnance and army supplies were quietly moved southward ; and measures were also taken to unburden Nashville of the immense stores accumulated in depot there. The weather was wet and cold, and very trying to men unused to the hardships of a winter campaign. Only 500 were in hospital at Bowling Green; but, before the army reached Nashville, 5,400, out of the 14,000, fell under the care of the medical authorities. Medical Director D. W. Yandell, in making this report at Nashville, February 18, 1862, says this large number is to be accounted for " by the immense number of convalescents and men merely unfit for duty or unable to undertake a march."

On February 11th, everything being in readiness, the troops began their retreat, Hindman's brigade covering the rear. Breckinridge's command passed through Bowling Green on the 12th, and bivouacked on the night of the 13th two miles north of Franklin. It was on that Thursday night that the weather became so intensely cold, as was related in the siege of Fort Donelson. The next day's march brought them to Camp Trousdale, where they occupied the huts; but with little profit, as some atmospheric condition made the smoke in them intolerable. After a bad night from smoke and the bitter cold, they marched twenty-seven miles next day, and on the day after, the 16th, through Nashville, and five miles beyond. The Kentuckians retreated sullenly.[1]

---

[1] Thompson's " History of the First Kentucky Brigade," pp. 76–81.

General George B. Hodge, then Breckinridge's assistant adjutant-general, in an interesting account of that brigade, mentions that—

The spirits of the army were cheered by the accounts which General Johnston, with thoughtful care, forwarded by means of couriers daily, of the successful resistance of the army. The entire army bivouacked in line of battle on the night of the 15th, at the junction of the Gallatin and Nashville and Bowling Green and Nashville [turnpike] roads, about ten miles from Nashville. . . . . At 4 p. m., on the 16th, the head of the brigade came in sight of the bridges at Nashville, across which, in dense masses, were streaming infantry, artillery, and transportation and provision trains, but still with a regularity and order which gave promise of renewed activity and efficiency in the future. At nightfall, General Johnston, who had established his headquarters at Edgefield on the northern bank of the Cumberland, saw the last of his wearied and tired columns defile across and safely establish themselves beyond. . . . He had with promptness, unrivaled military sagacity, and yet with mingled caution and celerity, dismantled his fortifications at Bowling Green, transmitted his heavy artillery and ammunition to Nashville, and extricated his entire army from the jaws of almost certain annihilation and capture.

General Johnston left Bowling Green before daylight on the 13th, and made his headquarters at Edgefield, opposite Nashville. Colonel Woolley, in the article before mentioned, says :

The evacuation was accomplished, protected by a force so small as to make doubtful the fact. Fifteen hundred sick had to be removed. Large quantities of stores and ammunition had accumulated. The provisions were nearly all secured except a large lot of spoiled pickled beef. Not a pound of ammunition, nor a gun, was lost. The engineer who destroyed the bridge in front of the town, told me that there was not powder enough left to explode the mines, and that he succeeded only with one small gun and seven shells, the last of which did the work. The ammunition, stores, and sick, being saved, the order for retreat was given, and the first intimation the enemy had of the intended evacuation, so far as has been ascertained, was when Generals Hindman and Breckinridge, who were in advance toward his camp, were seen suddenly to retreat toward Bowling Green. The enemy pursued, and succeeded in shelling the town, while Hindman was still covering the rear. Not a man was lost, and the little army reached Nashville only in time to hear of the disaster of their comrades in arms.

While mindful of whatever might aid the commanders at Donelson, General Johnston neglected nothing to secure the retreat of his own column. He brought Crittenden's command back within ten miles of Nashville, and thence to Murfreesboro. Besides the general orders for the march, he instructed Hardee to

Let it be known that the object is to secure the crossing of the Cumberland, and no apprehension of the enemy in the rear. You will thus preserve their *morale*. This order must be communicated to the rear of the column, and cavalry must be left in rear to assist the sick and bring up stragglers.

At noon, on the 14th of February, the Federal vanguard appeared opposite Bowling Green, and opened fire from several pieces of artillery on the town, and especially on the railroad-depot, which was subsequently burned. At half-past three o'clock, General Hardee retired from the town with the last of his troops, in perfect order.

When General Johnston learned, February 15th, that a battle was raging at Donelson, he assumed that Buell might attack his rear, and placed Bowen's brigade, which had the head of column, in line of battle on each side of the road, the other brigades forming on it as they came up. Orders were issued that all stragglers should be stopped at the bridges at Nashville, and sent under guard to their proper rendezvous. This was successful for a time, but the multitudes of fugitives from Donelson who came pouring in soon overtaxed the efforts of the guards to control and organize them. Companies applying were mustered in, without hesitation, whether their organization was complete or not. These judicious arrangements prevented the demoralization of organized commands, and, though the troops were wearied, suffering, and disconcerted, they were kept well in hand for a fight, had an attack been made.

In this brief dispatch to General Beauregard, sent on the morning of the 16th, General Johnston sums up the fate of Donelson : "At 2 A. M. to-day Fort Donelson surrendered. We lost all."

Colonel Munford, who was General Johnston's aide-de-camp, in his address at Memphis, thus describes the announcement of the surrender of Donelson :

General Johnston's headquarters were in Edgefield, opposite Nashville. About midnight a dispatch was received from General Pillow, announcing a "victory complete and glorious." We were jubilant over the result. All went to bed happy, the general and myself occupying the same room. Just before daybreak, we were awakened by another messenger with "dispatches from Donelson." I lighted a candle, and at the general's request read to him the astounding official statement that the place "would capitulate at daylight, and the army be surrendered by Buckner, Floyd and Pillow having left on steamboats for Nashville ! " The general was lying on a little camp-bed in one corner; he was silent a moment, and then asked me to read the dispatch again, which I did. He then ordered the staff to be awakened, saying, "I must save *this* army ; " had runners sent to the different commands, and troops marched as fast as practicable across the river. This movement was effected without loss of anything, and headquarters established in Nashville. . . . The people of the capital were joyous over the news of the night before. The morning papers were full of the "glorious victory." In the midst of this joy came the news of the disaster. Its effects can be imagined; "confusion worse confounded," nay, a perfect panic prevailed, and people rushed here and there in a delirium of fear. In the midst of these unhappy scenes General Johnston remained calm, distributing his troops into proper positions, giving orders for the erection of batteries below the city to delay the gunboats, for the removal of public stores and property of all sorts, and receiving delegations of public functionaries and private citizens who were crowding round him for advice under the changed state of affairs. He received Generals Floyd and Pillow with the greatest courtesy, and made the former commandant of the post at Nashville. The excitement and confusion continued, and on Monday night an immense mob blocked up the street in front of his headquarters; one of them, seeming to be half drunk, mounting the steps, and exclaiming, "We have come to demand of our generals whether they intend to fight for us or not;" and, turning to the crowd, he continued: "Yes, fellow-citizens, we have a right *to know* whether our generals are going to fight for us or intend abandoning us and our wives and children to the enemy. *We will force them to tell us.*" A wild shout of approval was the response from the mob. Generals Floyd, Hardee, and myself, had to make speeches to them before they could be induced to disperse, and abandon their futile effort to extort a disclosure of plans. It was considerably after midnight before we got clear of them. Dissatisfaction was general. Its mutterings, already heard, began to break out in denunciations. The demagogues took up the cry, and hounded each other and the people on in hunting down a victim. The public press was loaded with abuse. The very Government was denounced for intrusting the public safety to hands so feeble. The Lower House of Congress appointed a select committee to inquire into the conduct of the war in the Western Department. The Senators and Representatives from Tennessee, with the exception of Judge Swann, waited upon the President, saying, "We come in the name of the people to demand the removal of Sidney Johnston from command, because he is no general." The President replied : "Gentlemen, I know Sidney Johnston well. If *he* is not a general, we had better give up the war, for we have no general."

Nashville had acquired, during the progress of the war, a high degree of importance. It was the capital of the rich, populous, and martial State of Tennessee. As the base of Bowling Green, as a depot of supplies for the armies of the East as well as of the West, as a manufactory of ordnance and army stores, as a place of refuge for thousands of Kentuckians and Tennesseeans, and as the rendezvous for volunteers for the front, it had come to be looked upon in the West as Richmond was in the East. Its original population of some 30,000 had probably been doubled, and, from a rather provincial and Union-loving town, it had become a centre of furious political agitation. The people were warlike and energetic in character, and circumstances had produced in them a blind and overweening confidence. It has been seen how impossible it was to obtain labor in order to provide defenses for the city. Even when General Johnston's army was found retiring upon Nashville, the good news from Donelson kept the public mind in a state of unnatural elation. Even as late as February 15th he found that the measures he had taken to obstruct by a raft the Cumberland River, which was falling, were thwarted by the dead weight of popular opposition, directed by the "river-men," who as a class resisted it. Reverse seemed impossible. When, therefore, the blow fell, the revulsion of feeling produced scenes the like of which were not witnessed again in the war. It was like the first crushing calamity in a family, whose traditions of honor and prosperity are unbroken. Shame, grief, rage, and terror, were mingled in the bitter draught. Every evil that marks the track of conquest was pictured to the imagination of the affrighted people. The public mind gave way first to panic, then to frenzy. Many were possessed with but one idea—that of escape ; and a frantic exodus began of all who could procure the means of flight: carriages, wagons, open carts, filled with delicate women and tender children, unprovided with ordinary comforts, set out in the gloom of a winter evening and the pelting of a pouring rain, and thronged the roads that led southward. The tramp of the tired and angry soldiers and the roll of their baggage-wagons were continuous through that dreary day and those which succeeded it.

Duke, in his "Life of Morgan" (page 113), tells what he saw, in his usual animated style. He says :

The Tennessee troops were naturally most influenced by the considerations which affected the citizens, but all shared the feeling. Some wept at the thought of abandoning the city to a fate which they esteemed as dreadful as utter destruction ; and many, infuriated, loudly advocated burning it to the ground, that the enemy might have nothing of it but its ashes.

During the first night after the army reached Nashville, when the excitement and fury were at the highest pitch, and officers and privates were alike influenced by it, it seemed as if the bonds of discipline would be cast off altogether. Crowds of soldiers were mingled with the citizens, who thronged the streets all night, and yells, curses, shots, rang on all sides. In some houses the women were pale and sobbing, and in others there was even merriment, as if in defiance of the worst. Very soon all those who had escaped from Donelson began to arrive. . . . The arrival of these disbanded soldiers, among whom it was difficult to establish and enforce order, because no immediate disposition could be made of them, increased the confusion already prevailing. Rumors, too, of the near approach of the enemy were circulated, and were believed even by officers of high rank.

Upon the second day, matters had arrived at such a state, and the excitement and disorder were so extreme, that it became necessary to take other precautions to repress the license that was prevailing, besides the establishment of guards and sentinels about the camps where the troops lay; and General Johnston ordered the establishment of a strong military police in Nashville. The First Missouri Infantry,[1] one of the finest and best-disciplined regiments in the service, was detailed for this duty, and Morgan's squadron was sent to assist it. Our duty was to patrol the city and suburbs, and we were constantly engaged at it until the city was evacuated.

Floyd had no common task in holding in check an infuriated mob, and in giving coherence to the routed fugitives of Donelson. His duty was, besides, to save from the wreck the most important supplies and

---

[1] Under Colonel Rich, a valuable officer, who lost his life at Shiloh.

stores. He impressed all means of transportation available, and employed them in saving ordnance-stores and other valuable property. Among other articles, he saved all the cannon, caissons, and battery wagons. He found all restraints of civil order not only relaxed but sundered. A mixed mob had possession of the city, and cupidity was triumphant. Floyd says, in his report to General Johnston, that when he came in view of the landing at Nashville—

The rabble on the wharf were in possession of boats loaded with government bacon, and were pitching it from these boats to the shore, and carrying what did not fall into the water, by hand or in carts, away to various places in the city.

Floyd, when put in charge, placed guards over the public stores, and made extraordinary efforts to save them, and did in fact save great quantities—all that the railroad-trains could transport from Monday morning until the evening of Thursday, the 20th of February. Of course, the removal of the sick and wounded was first attended to. Torrents of rain impeded the work, and finally the washing away of a railroad-bridge stopped it. A large amount of transportation and a great number of cattle were brought from the north side of the river before the bridges were destroyed on the night of the 19th.

Fear was replaced by greed. Duke says, in his graphic way:

Excitement and avarice seemed to stimulate the people to preternatural strength. I saw an old woman, whose appearance indicated the extremest decrepitude, staggering under a load of meat which I would have hardly thought a quartermaster's mule could carry.

This plunder of the public stores was allowed to a certain extent, where it was evident that they could not be carried off, as it was better for the poorer classes to have them than that they should fall into the hands of the enemy. But so demoralizing is the license of pillage, that the predatory instinct becomes an overpowering, unreasoning impulse ; a blind, brute appetite, only to be restrained by force or fear. Hence this permitted spoliation, when limits were overstepped, had to be kept within bounds by the sternest measures of repression. Forrest came into personal collision with mob-leaders, and his cavalry twice charged the mob with drawn sabres.

Duke speaks of Floyd's conduct in terms of the highest commendation. He says :

Nothing could have been more admirable than the fortitude, patience, and good sense, which General Floyd displayed in his arduous and unenviable task. . . . I saw a great deal of General Floyd while he was commanding at Nashville, and I was remarkably impressed by him. . . . He was evidently endowed with no common nerve, will, and judgment.

Duke illustrates his conclusions about Floyd by details of his conduct, highly creditable to that general. He continues :

At last, the evacuation was completed; the army was gotten clear of Nashville; the last straggler driven out; all the stores which could not be carried off
nor distributed to the citizens, burned; and the capital of Tennessee (although
we did not know it then) was abandoned finally to the enemy. Morgan's squadron was the last to leave, as it was required to remain in the extreme rear of the
army, and pick up all the stragglers that evaded the rear-guards of the infantry.
Our scouts, left behind when we, in our turn, departed, witnessed the arrival of
the Federals, and their occupation of the city.

Forrest's cavalry was very useful in the enforcement of order and in
facilitating the removal of stores. Their reputation and *morale* had
both been enhanced by their successful escape from Donelson; and
their commander had qualities which peculiarly fitted him for rising
above the tumult of civil commotion. His regiment remained in Nashville until Friday, and Forrest himself, with a small detachment, staid
until Sunday, the 23d of February, when the enemy's advance-guard
appeared in Edgefield. He then retired. A deputation of citizens,
headed by the mayor, went out to negotiate, and the formal surrender
of the city to Buell took place on Tuesday, the 25th. Nashville passed
under the yoke that was never to be lifted.

It is only just to say that Governor Harris gave General Johnston
all the assistance in his power, and that the measures he took were, under the circumstances, bold and judicious. The following is Colonel
Munford's account of his share in the transaction, based on his own
personal knowledge :

The Governor received the news of the disaster almost or quite as soon as
did General Johnston. Very early in the morning he rode over to the general's
headquarters in Edgefield to advise with him as to the best course under the
changed circumstances. I heard the general say to him : "Your first duty, Governor, is to the public trusts in your charge. I regard it as all-important that
the public archives should be removed to some place of safety, and for this purpose have ordered transportation to be furnished you. The Legislature can also
adjourn to some other place. You can do no further good here now, and I
think you should take the public archives under your especial charge." The
Governor said he would do so, went back, wrote a message to the Legislature,
took charge of the archives as he had promised, put them in a place of safety,
and in forty-eight hours was back at the capital, though in that time, at General
Beauregard's earnest solicitation, he had gone through Jackson, Tennessee, to
confer with him.

In putting Floyd in command at Nashville, General Johnston used
the following language, as appears by a memorandum taken at the time
by Colonel Mackall :

I give you command of the city; you will remove the stores. My only restriction is, do not fight a battle in the city.

General Johnston also telegraphed Colonel D. P. Buckner, at Clarksville, February 16th :

Do not destroy the army stores, if their destruction will endanger the city. If you can burn the army stores without destroying the city, do it.

Thus, in the hour of his own deepest distress, he was vigilant and solicitous for the welfare of citizens and non-combatants.

The following extract is from General Johnston's letter to the Secretary of War :

HEADQUARTERS, WESTERN DEPARTMENT, }
NASHVILLE, *February* 18, 1862. }

SIR: In conformity with the intention announced to the department, the corps under the command of Major-General Hardee completed the evacuation of Bowling Green on the 14th inst., and the rear-guard passed the Cumberland at this point yesterday morning in good order.

I have ordered the army to encamp to-night midway between this place and Murfreesboro. My purpose is, to place the force in such a position that the enemy cannot concentrate his superior strength against the command, and to enable me to assemble as rapidly as possible such other troops in addition as it may be in my power to collect. The complete command which their gunboats and transports give them upon the Tennessee and Cumberland renders it necessary for me to retire my line between the rivers. I entertain the hope that this disposition will enable me to hold the enemy in check; and, when my forces are sufficiently increased, to drive him back. . . .

Hon. J. P. BENJAMIN, Secretary of War, Richmond, Virginia.

A. S. JOHNSTON.

CHAPTER XXX.

FROM MURFREESBORO TO CORINTH.

IT has been seen that, in the conference of February 7th, with Beauregard, the plan adopted was substantially a division of the command, by which General Johnston should face Buell and cover East and Middle Tennessee, while General Beauregard should defend the country west of the Tennessee River. The issue at Donelson left General Johnston with little more than half his former strength in array. The whole aspect of affairs was changed by the surrender there; and hence a modification of the plan of operations was demanded by the circumstances. A contingency had happened which he had contemplated and was prepared for, though he had not expected it would occur. General Johnston's resolve was sudden, and has the appearance of a military inspiration ; but it has already been explained by General Brown's and Colonels Schaller's and Munford's reminiscences. It had evidently been matured in his mind, as an alternative. To retreat south of the Tennessee and defend that line had been his plan, with Corinth as his probable centre. He now determined to concentrate his forces there, and, uniting his own army with that which he had assigned to Beauregard, to hazard a battle.

Soon after the conference at Bowling Green, General Beauregard addressed a letter to General Johnston, dated February 12th, which shows how strong a hold General Johnston's views had taken on his mind. Though for the most part a recapitulation of those views, there are some important modifications which render proper the insertion here of the entire letter. It will be found that before the loss of Fort Donelson was known, or the capture of the army there even apprehended, General Beauregard suggests the probability that General Johnston would speedily have to retreat behind the Tennessee River. It is needless to say that it was not the purpose of General Johnston to take that step unless compelled to do so. But as soon as the army at Donelson surrendered the time had come when this move must begin, with as much celerity as was consistent with the preservation of *morale* and material of war. It must, of course, have been agreeable to him to be sustained beforehand by General Beauregard's formal approval of a retreat under much less stringent circumstances than now actually existed. The following is General Beauregard's letter:

LETTER FROM GENERAL BEAUREGARD TO GENERAL JOHNSTON.

BOWLING GREEN, KENTUCKY, *February* 12, 1862.

GENERAL: By the fall of Fort Henry the enemy having possession of the Tennessee River, which is navigable for their gunboats and transports to Florence, it becomes evident that the forces under your immediate command and those under General Polk, separated unfortunately by that river, can no longer act in concert, and will be unable to support each other until the fortune of war shall have restored the Tennessee River to our possession, or combined the movement of the two armies in the rear of it.

It also becomes evident that, by the possession of that river, the enemy can concentrate rapidly, by means of his innumerable transports, all his disposable forces, on any point along its banks, either to attack Nashville in rear, or cut off the communications of Columbus by the river with Memphis, and by the railroad with the Memphis & Charleston Railroad. Should the enemy determine on the former plan of operation, your army, threatened in front and on right flank by Buell's large army, will be in a very critical condition, and may be forced to take refuge on the south side of the Tennessee River, in Alabama and Georgia, or Eastern Tennessee. But should Halleck adopt the second plan referred to, the position at Columbus will then become no longer tenable for an army inferior in strength to that of the enemy, and it must fall back to some central point where it can guard the two main railroads to Memphis, i. e., from Louisville and from Charleston ; Jackson, Tennessee, would probably be the best position for such an object, with strong detachments at Humboldt and Corinth, and with the necessary advance-guards. The Memphis & Charleston Railroad, so important on account of its extension through Eastern Tennessee and Virginia, must be properly guarded from Iuka to Tuscumbia, and even to Decatur, if practicable. Columbus must either be left to be defended to the last extremity by its proper garrison, assisted by Hollins's fleet of gunboats, and provided with provisions and ammunition for several months, or abandoned altogether, its armament and garrison being transferred if practicable to Fort Pillow, which, I am informed, is a naturally and artificially strong position, about one hundred miles above Memphis. Island No. 10, near New Madrid, could also be held by its garrison, assisted by Hollins's fleet, until the possession of New Madrid by the enemy would compel that position to be evacuated. I am clearly of the opinion that to attempt at present to hold so advanced a position as Columbus, with the movable army under General Polk, where its communications can be so readily cut off by a superior force acting from the Tennessee River as a new base, would be to jeopardize, not only the safety of that army, but necessarily of the whole Mississippi Valley. Hence I desire, as far as practicable, specific instructions as to the future movements of the army of which I am about to assume the command ; if it be necessary for the safety of the country to make with all my forces a desperate stand at Columbus, I am ready to do so. I regret much that illness has prevented me from being already at my post, but during my stay here I believe I have made myself as well acquainted with your general views and intentions as circumstances have permitted, and which I will always be happy to carry into effect to the best of my abilities. I am general, very respectfully,

Your obedient servant,

G. T. BEAUREGARD, <i>General C. S. A.</i></div>

General A. S. JOHNSTON, commanding Western Department, Bowling Green, Kentucky.

It was the easier for General Johnston to adopt this resolution to get behind the Tennessee, as the War Department, aroused by the fall of Fort Henry, had taken steps to reënforce him. On February 8th Secretary Benjamin wrote him :

The condition of your department, in consequence of the largely superior forces of the enemy, has filled us with solicitude, and we have used every possible exertion to organize some means for your relief.

The secretary goes on to state that eight regiments had been ordered to East Tennessee, which would make the whole force there some fifteen regiments, and would leave Crittenden's command free to act with the centre. He continues :

To aid General Beauregard at Columbus, I send orders to General Lovell to forward to him at once five or six regiments of his best troops at New Orleans.

He also promises 2,800 Enfield rifles, and adds :

We have called on all the States for a levy of men for the war, and think, in a very few weeks, we shall be able to give you heavy reënforcements, although we may not be able to arm them with good weapons.

It is due to General Lovell to say that he used diligence in obeying what must have been a distasteful order to him, and in his letter to General Johnston, evinced a clear perception of the importance of Corinth as a strategic point.

To use a homely proverb, the action of the War Department looked like "locking the stable-door after the horse was stolen." But, as has already been suggested, in a popular revolution, based on the idea of State-rights or decentralization, the War Department was greatly hampered in its designs by local public opinion operating both through the State Executives and through Congress. Colonel Woolley, in the letter already quoted, says truly and forcibly:

But who is to be blamed? The answer is given by every flash of lightning that comes from the coast. I shall not be believed if I state the number of letters General Johnston wrote while at Bowling Green, urging that an indefensible coast and unimportant towns be abandoned, and that troops be sent to enable him to give battle and win a great victory. But his warning was unheeded, his requests denied. Nor was the President at fault. He knew what Johnston knew. Go to Richmond, and the truth will then be learned. Each little town on the sea-coast thought that upon its defense depended the salvation of the Southern Confederacy. Senators and Congressmen, afraid of unpopularity, demanded that the troops of their States should be kept for home protection. They formed parties against the President, and threatened him with serious opposition if he did not conduct the war as they recommended. In vain did the President remind them of the fable of the old man and the fagot of sticks—singly they could be destroyed, together no power could break them. Except a few large towns there were no points on the sea-coast of any strategic importance. The presence of garrisons at little places only invited the naval expeditions of the enemy. Had there been no troops at those points there would have been no attack.

The following letters from General Johnston to the Secretary of War give a brief but comprehensive view of his situation :

HEADQUARTERS, WESTERN DEPARTMENT, }
MURFREESBORO, TENNESSEE, *February* 27, 1862. }

SIR: The fall of Fort Donelson compelled me to withdraw the forces under my command from the north bank of the Cumberland, and to abandon the defense of Nashville, which, but for that disaster, it was my intention to protect to the utmost. Not more than 11,000 effective men were left under my command to oppose a column of General Buell's of not less than 40,000 troops moving by Bowling Green, while another superior force under General Thomas outflanked me to the east, and the armies from Fort Donelson, with the gunboats and transports, had it in their power to ascend the Cumberland, now swollen by recent floods, so as to interrupt all communications with the south.

The situation left me no alternative but to evacuate Nashville or sacrifice the army. By remaining, the place would have been unnecessarily subjected to destruction, as it is very indefensible, and no adequate force would have been left to keep the enemy in check in Tennessee.

Under the circumstances I moved the main body of my command to this place on the 17th and 18th instant, and left a brigade under General Floyd to bring on such stores and property as were at Nashville, with instructions to remain until the approach of the enemy, and then to rejoin me. This has been in a great measure effected, and nearly all the stores would have been saved, but for the heavy and unusual rains which have washed away the bridges, swept away portions of the railroad, and rendered transportation almost impossible. General Floyd has arrived here. The rear-guard left Nashville on the night of the 23d. Edgefield, on the north bank of the Cumberland, opposite the city, was occupied yesterday by the advanced pickets of the enemy. I have remained here for the purpose of augmenting my forces and securing the transportation of the public stores. By the junction of the command of General Crittenden and the fugitives from Fort Donelson, which have been reorganized as far as practicable, the force now under my command will amount to about 17,000 men. General Floyd, with a force of some 2,500 men, has been ordered to Chattanooga to defend the approaches toward North Alabama and Georgia, and the communications between the Mississippi and the Atlantic, and with the view to increase his forces by such troops as may be sent forward from the neighboring States. The quartermaster's, commissary's, and ordnance stores which are not required for immediate use have been ordered to Chattanooga, and those which will be necessary on the march have been forwarded to Huntsville and Decatur. I have ordered a depot to be established at Atlanta for the manufacture of supplies for the quartermaster's department, and also a laboratory for the manufacture of percussion-caps and ordnance-stores, and, at Chattanooga, depots for distribution of these supplies. The machinery will be immediately sent forward.

Considering the peculiar topography of this State, and the great power which the enemy's means afford them upon the Tennessee and Cumberland, it will be seen that the force under my command cannot successfully cover the whole line against the advance of the enemy. I am compelled to elect whether he shall be permitted to occupy Middle Tennessee, or turn Columbus, take Memphis, and open the valley of the Mississippi. To me the defense of the valley seems of paramount importance, and consequently I will move this corps of the army, of which I have assumed the immediate command, toward the left bank of the Tennessee, crossing the river near Decatur, in order to enable me to coöperate or unite with General Beauregard for the defense of Memphis and the Mississippi. The department has sent eight regiments to Knoxville for the defense of East Tennessee, and the protection of that region will be confided to them and such additional forces as may be hereafter sent from the adjacent States. General Buckner was ordered by the department to take command of the troops at Knoxville, but, as at that time he was in presence of the enemy, the order was not fulfilled.

As it would be almost impossible for me under present circumstances to superintend the operations at Knoxville and Chattanooga, I would respectfully suggest that the local commanders at those points should receive orders from the department directly, or be allowed to exercise their discretion.

I have the honor to remain, very respectfully, your obedient servant,

A. S. JOHNSTON, *General C. S. A.*

Hon. J. P. BENJAMIN, Secretary of War, Richmond.

HEADQUARTERS WESTERN DEPARTMENT, }
MURFREESBORO, TENNESSEE, *February* 27, 1862. }

SIR: The army supplies and stores which were forwarded to this place, having all been sent forward to Chattanooga, except what may be needed for the immediate use of the army at Huntsville and Decatur and points farther on toward Memphis, this command will commence the march to-morrow toward Decatur.

The enemy are in possession of Nashville in force—a part of which is eight miles on this side of the city.

With great respect, your obedient servant,

(Signed)   A. S. JOHNSTON, *General C. S. A.*

Hon. J. P. BENJAMIN, Secretary of War, Richmond.

Colonel (afterward Major-General) William Preston, then acting on General Johnston's staff as a volunteer aide, enjoyed as free an intercourse with him as any one could. Not long after General Johnston's death, in a letter (dated April 18, 1862) to the present writer, he gave a succinct but clear account of the campaign. The following is an extract from it:

Nashville was indefensible. General Johnston withdrew to Murfreesboro, determined to effect a junction with Beauregard, near Corinth. His two chief staff-officers, Colonels Mackall and Gilmer, deemed it impossible. Johnston persevered. He collected Crittenden and the relics of his command, with stragglers and fugitives from Donelson, and moved through Shelbyville and Fayetteville on Decatur. Halting at those points, he saved his provisions and stores, removed his depots and machine-shops, obtained new arms, and finally, at the close of March, joined Beauregard at Corinth with 20,000 men, lifting their aggregate force to 50,000.

This movement having been completed, though General Johnston fully appreciated its hazard if the enemy had interrupted him with 20,000 or 30,000 men between Decatur and Corinth, General Johnston found himself for the first time at the head of an army capable of giving battle. In the mean time, he had borne with unshaken constancy and serenity the obloquy leveled at him by ignorant assailants, consoled by the unwavering confidence reposed in him by his unalterable friend the President, and upheld by his own manly self-reliance in the midst of adversity.

General W. C. Whitthorne, then Adjutant-General of Tennessee, now a member of Congress from that State, has addressed to the writer the following communication:

After the fall of Nashville, and while General Johnston was at Murfreesboro with his troops, and while General Forrest was at Nashville superintending the removal of stores, I was at General Johnston's headquarters in Murfreesboro, having some business with his staff-officers, which being completed, I was in the act of leaving the house, when an aide of General Johnston informed me that he (General Johnston) wished to speak to me. Upon entering his room he asked if I was going to leave without calling upon him. I replied, "Yes," but excused myself upon the ground that I knew he was overwhelmed with business, etc. He at once inquired as to the feeling and views of the people of Tennessee, spoke feelingly and rapidly of the situation; informed me that he was making arrangements to move his force as rapidly as possible to Corinth, which would leave Middle Tennessee exposed; but added, or rather concluded, by saying, "General Whitthorne, go tell your people that, under the favor of Providence, I will return in less than ninety days and redeem their capital." I remember well his confident tone, his smile, and the earnestness of his manner. I had such faith and confidence in him that I believed such would be the case. And, had he lived, my conviction is, that he would have accomplished his purpose and his plan—the recovery of Nashville.

Governor Harris, on the fall of Nashville, carried the State archives to Memphis to secure them. While there, on February 20th, General Johnston telegraphed him to consult Beauregard, and call out the whole strength of the State to his aid. Governor Harris informs the writer that he received a telegram from General Beauregard asking him on his return to Nashville to come by way of Jackson, Tennessee, which he did by a special train. General Beauregard requested him to visit General Johnston at Murfreesboro, and tell him that he (General Beauregard) thought he had best concentrate at or near Jackson or Corinth, in that region. Governor Harris went to Nashville, where he remained a short time, and then proceeded to Murfreesboro. This must have been before the 23d of February, when Nashville was finally abandoned. He delivered General Beauregard's message to General Johnston, who promptly replied that such was his intention, and that he was then making preparations for that purpose.

The following statement of facts was made by Colonel Sam Tate, of Memphis, March 7, 1878, and forwarded to the writer:

MEMPHIS, *March* 8, 1878.

As soon after the fall of Donelson as practicable, I repaired to General A. S. Johnston's headquarters to confer with him as to his future probable wants in railroad transportation, my appointment on his staff having been made, as he informed me, principally with reference to this branch of duty. I met him at Murfreesboro, where he had arrived the day previous. I well remember our interview, which began by my frankly avowing no wish to inquire into his future plans, but that I thought it my duty, under the changed state of the campaign since I had seen him, to learn as far as he thought proper to inform me what provision he desired me to make, if any, in my transportation department, for the use of his army. He replied: "I have no desire to conceal my plans from you. It is my purpose to concentrate all the troops which the Government will permit at Corinth, and there, or in that vicinity, fight a decisive battle as soon as possible." He then made minute inquiry of me about the railroad-bridge over the Tennessee River at Decatur—the practicability of crossing his army over it—especially his artillery and wagon trains, and it was agreed that the bridge was to be floored for horses, troops, etc., and flats or platform-cars provided for the guns. He took a map, and also made minute inquiries as to the river below Decatur, its distance from the railroad, and the practicability of the roads lying south of the railroad leading in the direction of Corinth, suggesting that if the enemy were vigilant and enterprising they might, through their command of the river by their gunboats and their superior numbers, seriously interfere with his railroad route, and force him to take the more dilatory route south of it. It may be well enough also to state that in the course of this conversation he stated that, if for any reason he might be compelled to fall back from Corinth, his line would be from Fort Pillow with headquarters at Grand Junction, with a fixed determination at all hazards to hold the Mississippi River to Port Hudson, and keep the line of communication open between the armies east and west of that river. These are the facts. SAM TATE.

Indeed, General Johnston's letters and telegrams show quite conclusively that, from the moment of his arrival at Murfreesboro, it was his settled purpose to move his army to Corinth by the way of Shelbyville and Decatur.

As it has been suggested in certain quarters that General Johnston ought to have removed his army from Murfreesboro by the railroad to Stevenson and thence to Corinth, the writer propounded to General Gilmer the question of the practicability of such a move. The following is his reply:

Being thus occupied, I had no conversation with your father *at Nashville* as to the after-movements of his army; nor did I have on the march to Murfreesboro. I think it was at Murfreesboro that I first knew of the decision to make, if practicable, a junction with Beauregard at Corinth.

As to the movements *by rail* from Murfreesboro to Stevenson and thence to Corinth, by the Charleston & Memphis Railroad, it was simply impossible without sacrificing the supplies and munitions on which the subsistence and armament of the command depended. The entire transportation capacity of the railroads was taxed to the utmost, and even then immense quantities of meat and other commissary supplies were left at Nashville, Murfreesboro, Shelbyville, Fayetteville, and Huntsville. Again, the movement was made over the "metal" roads leading to Shelbyville, Fayetteville, and Huntsville, as expeditiously, considering the number of troops to be transported, as it could have been by rail, with the imperfect organization of the railroad, as it then existed.

The movement from Nashville, southeast by way of Murfreesboro, to a certain extent beguiled the Federal generals into the belief that General Johnston intended to retreat on Chattanooga, and masked the concentration of his troops to the west. A direct retrograde would have betrayed his purpose. Had they understood his design, with larger forces, shorter lines, and better routes, they might have anticipated him at Corinth, or even intercepted him at Decatur.

When the condition of the troops, the season of the year, the unprecedented rains and floods, and the consequent state of the roads, are taken into consideration, this retreat may well be accounted an extraordinary triumph over the greatest difficulties. The following narrative will show some of the embarrassments which had naturally caused the staff to distrust the feasibility of this circuitous route, or, indeed, of any concentration with Beauregard.

At Murfreesboro were now concentrated all the troops east of the Tennessee River and west of the mountains. It was here that General Johnston assumed command of the army on the 23d of February, thus relieving Hardee, who had thus far been holding the immediate command. As has been seen, there were fifteen regiments in East Tennessee, besides Floyd's force of 2,500 men sent back by General Johnston to Chattanooga. General Johnston reorganized his own army (now numbering about 17,000 men) at Murfreesboro. The nucleus was the force that had been posted near Bowling Green, to which was added Crittenden's command and the *débris* of Donelson. The army was reorganized in three divisions under Hardee, Crittenden, and Pillow respectively ; with a reserve brigade under Breckinridge, and the Texas Rangers and Forrest's cavalry unattached. The brigade-commanders were Hindman, Cleburne, Carroll, Statham, Wood, Bowen, and Breckinridge. There were represented in the army thirty-five regiments and five battalions of infantry, seven regiments and five battalions of cavalry, and twelve batteries of artillery. The number of organizations, as compared with the effective total, evinces that they were but skeletons.

The strictest regulations were adopted for the restoration of discipline and the *morale* of the army. Orders for the repression of straggling and of marauding under the pretext of impressment or purchase were rigid and thorough. General Johnston, always keenly alive to the rights of citizens and of their helplessness in presence of an army, warned commanders against stripping them of the " means of support even for the necessities of the army," and ordered safeguards to be granted where the means of the citizen were reduced " to the wants of his family."

The line of march from Murfreesboro through Shelbyville and Fayetteville to Decatur was a middle route between the railroad to Chattanooga and the turnpike from Nashville through Columbia and Pulaski. It was adopted so as to enable the Confederate army to intercept and give battle to Buell, in case he should advance by any of these three roads. The movement was covered by a cloud of cavalry, Helm's First Kentucky, Scott's Louisiana, Wirt Adams's Mississippi, and by Forrest's and Morgan's commands, who were bold and energetic in harassing the enemy. The incessant rains, varying from a drizzle to a torrent, flooded the roads, washed away bridges, and made encampment almost intolerable and marching nearly impossible. General Hodge, in his sketch, says of the road taken :

Lying, for the most part, through cultivated and deep bottoms, on the edge of Northern Alabama it rises abruptly to cross the great plateau thrown out from the Cumberland Mountains, here nearly a thousand feet above the surrounding country and full forty miles in width, covered with dense forests of timber, yet barren and sterile in soil, and wholly destitute of supplies for either man or beast. Two weeks of unintermitting rain had softened the earth until the surface resembled a vast swamp. . . .

During his retreat, General Johnston's movements were well covered by his cavalry, who also brought him full information of the enemy. Scott's gallant action has already been mentioned. Captain John H. Morgan here first began to win his reputation as a raider. "The raid" —a wild dash at the enemy's communications—is, of course, as old as warfare. But Morgan, and after him, Stuart, Forrest, and others, made it historic and heroic. For the raid, the torpedo, and the ram—a modified revival of the old Roman beaked vessel—legitimate modern warfare is indebted to the Confederates.

Morgan's first raid was begun on the afternoon of March 7th. With Lieutenant-Colonel Wood, ten rangers, and fifteen of his own squadron, he advanced along by-roads eighteen miles from Murfreesboro toward Nashville that day, and on the next morning marched until he came opposite the lunatic asylum, near Nashville. Here he commenced overhauling the trains as they came along, capturing and disarming the men, until he had ninety-eight prisoners, including several officers. Returning in three parties, one was pursued by the Fourth Ohio Cavalry, and obliged to abandon sixty of the prisoners. They brought in thirty-eight prisoners, however, with a large number of horses, mules, sabres, pistols, saddles, etc.

Encouraged by this essay, he and Colonel Wood, with forty men, again set out from Murfreesboro, secretly and in separate parties, on the afternoon of the 15th. They made a rapid march, reaching Gallatin, on the Louisville & Nashville Railroad, twenty-six miles north of Nashville, at 4 P. M. next day. Here he seized the telegraph-office, with several of Buell's dispatches, and burned all the rolling-stock and water-tank of the railroad at that place. He returned with five prisoners, through the enemy's lines, to Shelbyville.

On the 28th of February, the army took up the line of march, Hindman's brigade in advance, and Hardee covering the rear with all the cavalry. Orders prescribed twelve to fifteen miles a day as the march. The hardships endured have perhaps been sufficiently outlined A soldier present in the campaign says [1] of this retreat:

The difficulties attending it were great, but a more orderly and more successful one, under all the circumstances, was perhaps never accomplished. Popular indignation, even rage, blind but full of confidence and of such force as would have goaded common minds into desperation, was poured out upon the head of

---

[1] Thompson's "History of the First Kentucky Brigade," p. 79.

the commander. The wintry season, inclement, unpropitious beyond measure for such an undertaking, was calculated both to tax the skill of the general and destroy the martial ardor, even the ordinary *morale*, of the troops. Dangers menaced the retreating army as much as hardships crowded upon its course. . . .

Demoralization, almost unavoidably consequent upon the state of the public mind and the nature of a retreat, threatened to destroy the efficiency of bodies of troops who could not have been spared in case of an attack. And the state of the weather—heavy rains having set in before the command had quitted the vicinity of Nashville—foreboded evil, in retarding if not arresting the progress of the army, by swollen streams and impassable mud. But everything went on with a regularity and a degree of order that seemed to have been the result of circumstances working in entire harmony with the plans of a great general, instead of having been adverse at every step ; and he reached Corinth with so little loss of men or munition as to mark him one of the first administrative minds of his age and country.

Duke says ("Life of Morgan," page 118) :

When the line of march was taken up, and the heads of the columns were still turned southward, the dissatisfaction of the troops broke out into fresh and frequent murmurs. Discipline, somewhat restored at Murfreesboro, had been too much relaxed by the scenes witnessed at Nashville, to impose much restraint upon them. Unjust as it was, officers and men concurred in laying the whole burden of blame upon General Johnston. Many a voice was then raised to denounce him, which has since been enthusiastic in his praise, and many joined in the clamor, then almost universal against him, who, a few weeks later, when he lay dead upon the field he had so gallantly fought, would have given their own lives to recall him.

The extracts from narratives and letters, which will be quoted, give an idea of the panic and rage stirred up by the evacuation of Nashville, and the evident intention to retreat from the State. The wrath and terror, so strikingly exhibited in Nashville, spread with incredible rapidity over the whole State. Bounds could scarcely be set to the fury and despair of the people. Every hamlet resounded with denun' ciation, and every breast was filled with indignation at the author of such calamities. Those who had refused to listen to his warning voice, when it called them to arms, were loudest in their passionate outcry at what they considered a base desertion of them to the mercies of the invader. General Johnston was, of course, the special target of every accusation, including imbecility, cowardice, and treason. These rash charges were not confined to the ignorant, the malicious, or the disaffected. It is true that men with supposed grievances against the Government, the cause, or the commander, seized the occasion to vent their spleen ; and that demagogues, eager for aggrandizement at any price, joined in and directed the wild hunt for a victim. But every class helped to augment the volume of protest and appeal to the President, demanding General Johnston's removal. Indeed, the greater the stake and the more violent the revulsion of patriotic fervor, the bitterer was the disappointment, and the more vindictive the feeling. Everywhere, above, below, with louder and deeper swell, came from a whole people—noble, but mistaken, and with passions strung to the highest pitch—the terrible demand for vengeance. And the victim required by them—the man most ready, most willing to suffer as a sacrifice, if it would avail aught!

The press leveled its shafts at President Davis. One of the most rabid of the fire-eating journals in the South used this language, which is given as a sample:

Shall the cause fail because Mr. Davis is incompetent? The people of the Confederacy must answer this plain question at once, or they are lost. Tennessee, under Sidney Johnston, is likely to be lost. Mr. Davis retains him. Van Dorn writes that Missouri *must be abandoned unless the claims of Price are recognized.* Mr. Davis will not send in his nomination. A change in the cabinet is demanded instantly, to restore public confidence. Mr. Davis is motionless as a clod. Buell's proclamation to the people of Nashville has disposed the young men, already dissatisfied with Johnston, to lay down their arms, and paved the way to the campaign of invasion in the Mississippi Valley. Mr. Davis remains as cold as ice. The people must know, and feel, and be felt. The Government must be *made* to move.

A writer in one of the public prints at the time, evidently with good-will, confidence, and respect, toward General Johnston, but somewhat timidly, as if overawed by public opinion, called for "charity" to his conduct. Among other statements he says:

Special correspondents, not satisfied with charges of stupidity, must denounce him as corrupt. So complete is the revulsion of public sentiment, that soldiers, when enlisting, make it a condition that they shall not be placed under General Johnston. This precipitate and unmeasured condemnation must necessarily cripple him. Whatever ability he possesses will be rendered ineffectual through a want of confidence which will withhold from him the means of making his skill available.

Some of the telegrams addressed to the President are here given, as illustrations of the universal feeling. But it would be unjust to the writers to give their names, and thus perpetuate their mistake, for which most of them afterward felt and expressed a sincere regret. An ex-member of the United States Congress, in whose house General Johnston made his headquarters, telegraphed President Davis:

Nothing but your presence here can save Tennessee. General Johnston's army is demoralized. Your presence will reassure it, and will save Tennessee. Nothing else can. For God's sake, come!

An officer who overheard its transmission reported the fact to General Johnston, who replied: "I was aware of his distrust. Take no notice of it."

An officer, high in the staff of the army, and influential—a Mississippian—telegraphed thus:

MEMPHIS, *March* 1, 1862.

If Johnston and Hardee are not removed, the army is demoralized. President Davis must come here and take the field.

A member of the Confederate Congress telegraphed as follows:

ATLANTA, *March* 11, 1862.

I have been with and near General Johnston's army ever since he was assigned command—have been his admirer and defender—still admire him as a man; but, in my judgment, his errors of omission, commission, and delay, have been greater than any general's who ever preceded him, in any country. [He has] inexcusably and culpably lost us 12,000 men, the Mississippi Valley, and comparatively all provisions stored, by one dash of the enemy. This is the almost unanimous judgment of officers, soldiers, and citizens. Neither is it mere opinion, but is demonstrable by dates, facts, figures, and disastrous results. He never can reorganize and reënforce his army, with any confidence.

The people now look to you as their deliverer, and imploringly call upon you to come to the field of our late disasters and assume command, as you promised in a speech to take the field whenever it should become necessary. That necessity is now upon us. Such a step would be worth a hundred thousand soldiers throughout the Confederacy. Can you, then, hesitate? We cannot survive the permanent loss of Tennessee and Kentucky for the war. They must be immediately retaken, at all hazards, or great suffering for provisions and forage is the inevitable and immediate consequence. If your presence is impossible, for God's sake give immediate command to Beauregard, Bragg, or Breckinridge, or all will be irretrievably lost. Save us while it is yet time. I will be in Richmond next week.

Such was the reversal of opinion afterward in this matter that, soon after the battle of Shiloh, this gentleman voluntarily, and with tears, expressed to the writer his "remorse for this telegram, which could only be accounted for by the panic that had unhinged everybody." It is due to him to say that he but expressed the popular verdict—the public opinion with which he came in contact.

It will be seen that every one of these telegrams contains a most subtile appeal to the powerful instinct of self-love; and it is creditable to the calmness of President Davis's judgment, as well as to the constancy of his friendship, that he took them at their true value. He, almost alone, remained unmoved; and that intrepidity of intellectual conviction, characteristic of him, so often and so mistakenly called his obstinacy, saved the Confederacy, not only from a great injustice, but from a great mistake. He not only lent his moral support to General

Johnston, the weight of his great name—then a tower of strength with the Southern people—but he ordered, to reënforce him at Corinth, from the Gulf coast, Bragg's fresh, disciplined, splendid army, 10,000 strong.

All President Davis's power was needed to retain General Johnston in his position. Congress took the matter in hand; and, though the feeling there resulted merely in a committee of inquiry, it was evident that the case was prejudged.

The resolutions passed by the Confederate House of Representatives created a special committee " to inquire into the military disasters at Fort Henry and Fort Donelson, and the surrender of Nashville into the hands of the enemy," and as to the conduct, number, and disposition, of the troops under General Johnston. Great feeling was shown in the debates.

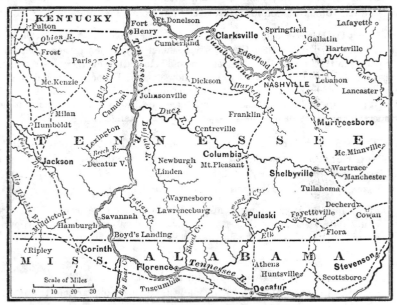

In response to the attempt of Mr. Moore, of Kentucky, to put in a plea for General Johnston, Mr. Foote, of Tennessee, asked " if the gentleman would advocate the continuance of any man in command when the soldiers under him had lost confidence in him."

The writer believes he may now safely say, without fear of contradiction among the Southern people, that General Johnston was too calm, too just, and too magnanimous, to misapprehend or resent so natural a manifestation. His whole life had been a training for this occasion. To encounter suddenly and endure calmly the obloquy of a whole nation is, to any man, a great burden. To do this with a serenity that shall not only not falter in duty, but restore confidence, obtain the best possible results, and organize victory, is conclusive proof of a greatness of soul rarely equaled.

But, while the storm of execration raged around him, the men who came into immediate contact with General Johnston never for a moment doubted his ability to perform all that was possible to man. Among these, the Kentuckians, who felt that his camp was their only ark in the revolutionary deluge, as a rule gave him their confidence. This was possibly due to State pride in his nativity ; but probably still more to the presence on his staff of several able and popular citizens of that State. The Texans, too, never faltered in their trust in him, approved by so many years of trial.

John A. Wharton, then colonel, afterward major-general, a man sagacious, able, and eloquent, wrote to him, from a sick-bed, March 14th :

I trust the Rangers will be kept as near *you* as the good of the service will permit ; and that they will not be deprived, under any circumstances, from participating in the first battle. The esteem and admiration of every honest man must be desirable to any man, no matter how exalted his position ; and, under present circumstances, I feel it is not inappropriate in me to say that I regard you as the best soldier in America, and that I desire to fight under no other leadership, and that such is the feeling of the Texas Rangers.

This was not according to regulations—a subordinate commending his superior ; but it was no time for conventionalities, as Wharton's vigorous sense clearly saw. R. Scurry, well known in the early annals of Texas, wrote from Hempstead, Texas, March 15th :

I fully approve of your movements. I have all the enthusiasm and feelings of '36 upon me. I hope for the best. With an ear deaf to popular clamor, pursue your course and follow the dictates of your own reason, and fame will be your reward.

Love and others also wrote to him in the same spirit.

Quotations have already been made from an able article from the incisive pen of Woolley ; other Kentuckians took the same view ; but one of the most gratifying testimonials was a letter, quoted hereafter, from the provisional Governor, George W. Johnson, which might properly be added as a companion-piece to his energetic protest against the evacuation of Bowling Green.

A correspondent of the *Mobile Register* said :

I remember well being with him one evening at Murfreesboro, after the retreat from Nashville, when, in the course of conversation, I urged that he should, in justice to himself, make an explanation to the people. " Ah ! my dear friend," he replied, " I cannot correspond with the people. What the people want is a battle and a victory. That is the best explanation I can make. I require no vindication. I trust that to the future." Noble, glorious, self-sacrificing heart !

He required no newspaper vindication, because he was conscious that he had taken the only course to save his little army. If there was censure deserved, the people would find out in the future where it should rest. Thus the great, magnanimous and chivalric Johnston bared his head to the storm of anathema and denunciation, without a murmur of complaint or any attempt to shield himself from its fury.

The respect due these men is that which was paid the consul who, after Cannæ, did not despair of the republic.

Colonel Munford says in his address at Memphis, heretofore quoted:

When we left Nashville for Murfreesboro the trip was made in the night, because the army, with their wagons and artillery, would then be encamped, and the road clear. About ten o'clock that night a very heavy rain commenced falling, and General Johnston called for me to exchange my horse for his driver's seat beside him, and get into a little carriage in which he was. We were alone, and the conversation soon became free and full about recent events. I told him he had begun to see and hear something of the clamor his retreat was causing. "Oh, yes," he said, "but you know I anticipated this. It will last no longer than is necessary for me to be in condition to fight a battle. As soon as I get men enough, I have no fear but that this clamor will become praise."

Thus looking for it to come, as well as facing it when in its midst, he viewed and treated it with the same philosophic calmness and just appreciation. That, as a good man, General Johnston felt the censures of his countrymen is absolutely certain; but that, as a wise man, he estimated them at their true value, and, as a manly man, deviated neither to the right hand nor to the left from the path of duty on account of them, is equally certain.

General Preston also states to the writer that General Johnston felt complete confidence in his ability to reorganize his army, and to strike such a blow as would not only restore the confidence of his compatriots, but would turn the tide of defeat into a career of victory. Whoever spoke to him, whoever saw him, went away, not so much touched with the pathos and the difficulties of his great ordeal, as sanguine of success and eager for a trial of arms with the foe. As the retreat was converted into an evident march against the enemy, the spirit of the army rose from the depths into a passionate and exultant thirst for the combat. Munford says:

He had no self-seeking. He honestly believed that the South was right, and the cause of constitutional liberty in America bound up in her fate. In joining her standard, therefore, he was actuated by such convictions of duty that he had no trouble in keeping his eye fixed singly upon her success. As illustrative of this, of his magnanimity and absolute justice, I will notice his treatment of Generals Floyd and Pillow, in the very midst of the denunciations poured out upon him for losing the army at Donelson. He received them both with the utmost kindness, and made Floyd at once commandant of the post at Nashville. After we had reached Murfreesboro, I asked him what he thought of their conduct. He replied: "The official reports are not yet before me. I do not think it would be just to those gentlemen to permit myself to form an opinion till they have stated the facts in an authentic form." At Decatur, he voluntarily said to me, "I intend to sustain Floyd and Pillow. Their conduct was irregular, but its repetition may be avoided by a simple order. They are both men of tried courage, and have had experience in the field. We have too few officers possessed of these advantages, and the country needs them. I think it my duty to sustain them, and shall do so." How rare the man, thus goaded by abuse, who, unheeding self, would do alone as *duty* bid!

On the 16th of March, however, he received a letter from the Secretary of War, dated March 11th, which closed that question. Mr. Benjamin says:

The reports of Brigadier-Generals Floyd and Pillow are unsatisfactory, and the President directs that both these generals be relieved from command until further orders. In the mean time you will request them to add to their reports such statements as they may deem proper on the following points.

The Secretary then propounded a number of interrogatories, relating to matters which have been already fully discussed. He concludes:

You are further requested to make up a report from all the sources of information accessible to you, of all the particulars connected with the unfortunate affair which can contribute to enlighten the judgment of the Executive and of Congress, and to fix the blame, if blame there be, on those who were delinquent in duty.

Out of this matter and the general situation in the West arose an unofficial correspondence, which has been published in part. General Johnston's letter of March 18th has been much admired, and comment upon it by the present writer is not called for. President Davis's letters are also given in full, and will be found to reflect equal credit on his head and heart.

[Telegram.]

HUNTSVILLE, *March* 7—11 A. M.

YOUR dispatch is just received. I sent Colonel Liddell to Richmond on the 28th ult., with the official reports of Generals Floyd and Pillow of the events at Donelson, and suppose that he must have arrived by this time. I also sent by him a dispatch, containing my purposes for the defense of the valley of the Mississippi, and for coöperating or uniting with General Beauregard, who has been urging me to come on.

The stores accumulated at Murfreesboro, the pork and provisions at Shelbyville and other points, and their necessary protection and removal, with the bad roads and inclement weather, have made the march slow and laborious, and delayed my movements. The general condition of the troops is good and effective, though their health is impaired by the usual camp disasters and a winter campaign.

The fall of Donelson disheartened some of the Tennessee troops, and caused many desertions from some of the new regiments, so that great care was required to inspire confidence. I now consider the tone of the troops restored, and that they are in good order. The enemy are about 25,000 strong at Nashville, with reënforcements arriving. My rear-guard, under General Hardee, is protecting the removal of provisions from Shelbyville. Last evening his pickets were near Murfreesboro, but gave no information of an advance by the enemy. There are no indications of an immediate movement by the enemy from Nashville. I have no fears of a movement through Tennessee on Chattanooga. West Tennessee is menaced by heavy forces. My advance will be opposite Decatur on Sunday.

(Signed)　　　　　　A. S. JOHNSTON, *General C. S. A.*

To President DAVIS, Richmond.

RICHMOND, VIRGINIA, *March* 12, 1862.

MY DEAR GENERAL: The departure of Captain Wickliffe offers an opportunity, of which I avail myself, to write you an unofficial letter. We have suffered great anxiety because of recent events in Kentucky and Tennessee; and I have been not a little disturbed by the repetitions of reflections upon yourself. I expected you to have made a full report of events precedent and consequent to the fall of Fort Donelson. In the mean time I made for you such defense as friendship prompted, and many years of acquaintance justified; but I needed facts to rebut the wholesale assertions made against you to cover others and to condemn my administration. The public, as you are aware, have no correct measure for military operations; and the journals are very reckless in their statements.

Your force has been magnified, and the movements of an army have been measured by the capacity for locomotion of an individual.

The readiness of the people among whom you are operating to aid you in every method has been constantly asserted; the purpose of your army at Bowling Green wholly misunderstood; and the absence of an effective force at Nashville ignored. You have been held responsible for the fall of Donelson and the capture of Nashville. It is charged that no effort was made to save the stores at Nashville, and that the panic of the people was caused by the army.

Such representations, with the sad forebodings naturally belonging to them, have been painful to me, and injurious to us both; but, worse than this, they have undermined public confidence, and damaged our cause. A full development of the truth is necessary for future success.

I respect the generosity which has kept you silent, but would impress upon you that the question is not personal but public in its nature; that you and I might be content to suffer, but neither of us can willingly permit detriment to the country. As soon as circumstances will permit, it is my purpose to visit the field of your present operations; not that I should expect to give you any aid in the discharge of your duties as a commander, but with the hope that my position would enable me to effect something in bringing men to your standard. With a sufficient force, the audacity which the enemy exhibits would no doubt give you the opportunity to cut some of his lines of communication, to break up his plan of campaign; and, defeating some of his columns, to drive him from the soil as well of Kentucky as of Tennessee.

We are deficient in arms, wanting in discipline, and inferior in numbers. Private arms must supply the first want; time and the presence of an enemy, with diligence on the part of commanders, will remove the second; and public confidence will overcome the third. General Bragg brings you disciplined troops, and you will find in him the highest administrative capacity. General E. K. Smith will soon have in East Tennessee a sufficient force to create a strong diversion in your favor; or, if his strength cannot be made available in that way, you will best know how to employ it otherwise. I suppose the Tennessee or Mississippi River will be the object of the enemy's next campaign, and I trust you will be able to concentrate a force which will defeat either attempt. The fleet which you will soon have on the Mississippi River, if the enemy's gunboats ascend the Tennessee, may enable you to strike an effective blow at Cairo; but, to one so well informed and vigilant, I will not assume to offer suggestions as to when and how the ends you seek may be attained. With the confidence and regard of many years, I am very truly your friend,

JEFFERSON DAVIS.

DECATUR, ALABAMA, *March* 18, 1862.

My DEAR GENERAL: I received the dispatches from Richmond, with your private letter by Captain Wickliffe, three days since; but the pressure of affairs and the necessity of getting my command across the Tennessee prevented me from sending you an earlier reply.

I anticipated all that you tell as to the censures which the fall of Fort Donelson drew upon me, and the attacks to which you might be subjected; but it was impossible for me to gather the facts for a detailed report, or spare time which was required to extricate the remainder of my troops and save the large accumulation of stores and provisions, after that disheartening disaster.

I transmitted the reports of Generals Floyd and Pillow without examining or analyzing the facts, and scarcely with time to read them.

When about to assume command of this department, the Government charged me with the duty of deciding the question of occupying Bowling Green, which involved not only military but political considerations. At the time of my arrival at Nashville, the action of the Legislature of Kentucky had put an end to the latter by sanctioning the formation of camps menacing Tennessee, by assuming the cause of the Government at Washington, and by abandoning the neutrality it professed; and in consequence of their action the occupation of Bowling Green became necessary as an act of self-defense, at least in the first step.

About the middle of September General Buckner advanced with a small force of about 4,000 men, which was increased by the 15th of October to 12,000; and, though accessions of force were received, continued at about the same strength till the end of the month of November, measles, etc., keeping down the effective force. The enemy's force then was, as reported to the War Department, 50,000, and an advance impossible. No enthusiasm, as we imagined and hoped, but hostility, was manifested in Kentucky. Believing it to be of the greatest moment to protract the campaign, as the dearth of cotton might bring strength from abroad and discourage the North, and to gain time to strengthen myself by new troops from Tennessee and other States, I magnified my forces to the enemy, but made known my true strength to the department and the Governors of States. The aid given was small. At length, when General Beauregard came out in February, he expressed his surprise at the smallness of my force, and was impressed with the danger of my position. I admitted what was so manifest, and laid before him my views for the future, in which he entirely concurred, and sent me a memorandum of our conference, a copy of which I send to you. I determined to fight for Nashville at Donelson, and gave the best part of my army to do it, retaining only 14,000 men to cover my front, and giving 16,000 to defend Donelson. The force at Donelson is stated in General Pillow's report at much less, and I do not doubt the correctness of his statement; for the force at Bowling Green, which I supposed 14,000 effective men (the medical report showing only a "little over 500 sick in hospitals"), was diminished more than 5,000 by those who were unable to stand the fatigue of a march, and made my force on reaching Nashville less than 10,000 men. I inclose medical director's report. Had I wholly uncovered my front to defend Donelson, Buell would have known it and marched directly on Nashville. There were only ten small steamers in the Cumberland in imperfect condition, only three of which were available at Nashville, while the transportation of the enemy was great. The evacuation of Bowling Green was imperatively necessary, and was ordered before and executed while the battle was being fought at Donelson. I had made every disposition for the defense of the fort my means allowed; and the troops were among the best of my forces, and the generals, Floyd, Pillow, and Buckner, were high in the opinion of officers and men for skill and courage, and among the best officers of my command; they were popular with the volunteers, and all had seen much service. No reënforcements were asked. I waited the event opposite Nashville. The result of the conflict each day was favorable. At midnight on the 15th I received the news of a glorious victory; at dawn, of a defeat. My column was during the day and night (of the 16th) thrown over the river. A battery had been established below the city to secure the passage. Nashville was incapable of defense from its position, and from the forces advancing from Bowling Green and up the Cumberland. A rear-guard was left, under General Floyd, to secure the stores and provisions, but did not completely effect the object. The people were terrified and some of the troops were disheartened. The discouragement was spreading, and I ordered the command to Murfreesboro, where I managed, by assembling Crittenden's division, and the fugitives from Donelson, to collect an army able to offer battle. The weather was inclement, the floods excessive, and the bridges were washed away; but most of the stores and provisions were saved, and conveyed to new depots. This having been accomplished, though with serious loss, in conformity with my original design I marched southward and crossed the Tennessee at this point, so as to coöperate or unite with Beauregard for the defense of the valley of the Mississippi. The passage is almost completed, and the head of my column is already with General Bragg at Corinth. The movement was deemed too hazardous by the most experienced members of my staff, but the object warranted the risk. The difficulty of effecting a junction is not wholly overcome, but it approaches completion. Day after to-morrow (22d), unless the enemy intercepts me, my force will be with Bragg—and my army nearly 50,000 strong. This must be destroyed before the enemy can attain his object.

I have given you this sketch, so that you may appreciate the embarrassments which surrounded me in my attempts to avert or remedy the disaster of Donelson, before alluding to the conduct of the generals.

When the force was detached, I was in hopes that such dispositions would have been made as would have enabled the forces to defend the fort or withdraw without sacrificing the army. On the 14th I ordered General Floyd, by telegram, "if he lost the fort to get his troops back to Nashville." It is possible this might have been done; but justice requires to look at events as they appeared at the time, and not alone by the light of subsequent information. All the facts in relation to the surrender will be transmitted to the Secretary of War as soon as they can be collected in obedience to his order. It appears from the information received, that General Buckner, being the junior officer, took the lead in advising the surrender, and General Floyd acquiesced, and they all concurred in the belief that their force could not maintain the position. All concurred that it would involve a great sacrifice of life to extricate the command. Subsequent events show that the investment was not so complete as their information from their scouts led them to believe. The conference resulted in the surrender. The command was irregularly transferred, and devolved on the junior general; but not apparently to avoid any just responsibility, or from any want of personal or moral intrepidity. The blow was most disastrous, and almost without remedy. I therefore in my first report remained silent. This silence you were kind enough to attribute to my generosity. I will not lay claim to the motive to excuse my course.

I observed silence, as it seemed to me to be the best way to serve the cause and the country. The facts were not fully known, discontent prevailed, and criticism or condemnation was more likely to augment than cure the evil. I refrained, well knowing that heavy censures would fall upon me, but convinced that it was better to endure them for the present, and defer to a more propitious time an investigation of the conduct of the generals; for, in the mean time, their services were required, and their influence was useful. For these reasons, Generals Floyd and Pillow were assigned to duty, for I still felt confidence in their gallantry, their energy, and their devotion to the Confederacy.

I have thus recurred to the motives by which I have been governed, from a deep personal sense of the friendship and confidence you have always shown me, and from the conviction that they have not been withdrawn from me in adversity. All the reports requisite for a full official investigation have been ordered. Generals Floyd and Pillow have been suspended from command.[1]

You mention that you intend to visit the field of operations here. I hope soon to see you, for your presence would encourage my troops, inspire the people, and augment the army. To me personally it would give the greatest gratification. Merely a soldier myself, and having no acquaintance with the statesmen or leaders of the South, I cannot touch springs familiar to you. Were you to assume command, it would afford me the most unfeigned pleasure, and every energy would be exerted to help you to victory, and the country to independence. Were you to decline, still your presence alone would be of inestimable advantage.

The enemy are now at Nashville, about 50,000 strong, advancing in this direction by Columbia. He has also forces, according to the report of General Bragg, landing at Pittsburg, from 25,000 to 50,000, and moving in the direction of Purdy.

This army corps, moving to join Bragg, is about 20,000 strong. Two brigades, Hindman's and Wood's, are, I suppose, at Corinth. One regiment of Har-

---

[1] This was in obedience to orders from the War Department.

dee's division (Lieutenant-Colonel Patton commanding) is moving by cars to-day (20th March), and Statham's brigade (Crittenden's division). The brigade will halt at Iuka, the regiment at Burnsville; Cleburne's brigade, Hardee's division, except regiment, at Burnsville; and Carroll's brigade, Crittenden's division, and Helm's cavalry, at Tuscumbia; Bowen's brigade at Cortland; Breckinridge's brigade, here; the regiments of cavalry of Adams and Wharton, on the opposite bank of the river; Scott's Louisiana regiment at Pulaski, sending forward supplies; Morgan's cavalry at Shelbyville, ordered on.

To-morrow, Breckinridge's brigade will go to Corinth; then Bowen's. When these pass Tuscumbia and Iuka, transportation will be ready there for the other troops to follow immediately from those points, and, if necessary, from Burnsville. The cavalry will cross and move forward as soon as their trains can be passed over the railroad-bridge.

I have troubled you with these details, as I cannot properly communicate them by telegram.

The test of merit in my profession with the people is success. It is a hard rule, but I think it right. If I join this corps to the forces of Beauregard (I confess a hazardous experiment), then those who are now declaiming against me will be without an argument. Your friend,

A. S. JOHNSTON.

P. S.—I will prepare answers to the questions propounded by General Foote, chairman of the committee to investigate the causes of the loss of the forts, as soon as practicable. But, engaged as I am in a most hazardous movement of a large force, every, the most minute, detail requiring my attention for its accomplishment, I cannot say when it will be forwarded to the Secretary of War to be handed to him, if he think proper to do so.[1]

Colonel T. M. Jack, in a letter addressed to the present writer in 1877, gives a graphic account of the circumstances under which President Davis received this letter:

Just before the battle of Shiloh your father sent me to Richmond, as bearer of dispatches to President Davis. Among these dispatches was the celebrated letter in which success is recognized as the test of merit in the soldier. My duties, of course, were merely executive—to deliver the dispatches in person, and return with the answers quietly and promptly.

Arriving at Richmond, and announcing my business to the proper officer, I was at once shown into the office of Mr. Davis and presented to him. I had never before met the President of the Confederacy. He received me with courtesy—even with kindness—asking me at once, "How is your general—my friend General Johnston?" There was an earnestness in the question which could not be misunderstood. Replying briefly, I handed him my dispatches, which he was in the act of opening, when an officer entered the room, to whom the President presented me as General Lee. This was my first meeting with him also—and the last. He had not then attained the full measure of his fame. He was not as yet the idol of the Southern people. These things came afterward, with the recognition by all fair-minded Christendom of the greatness of the Christian chieftain. There was something fascinating in his presence. His manners

---

[1] This letter was begun on March 17th, and finished March 20th.

struck me as dignified, graceful, and easy. He seated himself by my side at the window, and engaged me in conversation about the movements of our Western army, while the President read, in silence, the dispatches of your father. These two historic figures, together in the capital of the Confederacy, the one chatting pleasantly with a young and unknown officer, the other engrossed with the last formal papers of the ranking general in the field of the Confederate forces after their retreat, and on the eve of a pitched battle on chosen ground, fastened themselves on the canvass of my memory in bright and lasting colors. Listening to the pleasing tones of the general's voice, I watched, at the same time, with eager interest, the countenance of the President, as he read the clear, strong, and frank expressions of his old friend and comrade, full of facts, and breathing sentiments of the noblest spirit. There was softness then in his face; and, as his eye was raised from the paper, there seemed a tenderness in its expression, bordering on tears, surprising and pleasing at that critical juncture in the civil and military leader of a people in arms.

Next day the President handed me his dispatches, which were delivered to the general at Corinth, as he was preparing for the field.

"How did the President receive you?" he asked, in a playful way, as I handed him the dispatches. "As the aide-de-camp of his friend," was my response, in the same spirit; after which he made no further allusion to the mission.

The following was the reply borne to General Johnston by Colonel Jack:

RICHMOND, VIRGINIA, *March* 26, 1862.

MY DEAR GENERAL: Yours of the 18th inst. was this day delivered to me by your aide, Mr. Jack. I have read it with much satisfaction. So far as the past is concerned, it but confirms the conclusions at which I had already arrived. My confidence in you has never wavered, and I hope the public will soon give me credit for judgment, rather than continue to arraign me for obstinacy.

You have done wonderfully well, and now I breathe easier in the assurance that you will be able to make a junction of your two armies. If you can meet the division of the enemy moving from the Tennessee before it can make a junction with that advancing from Nashville, the future will be brighter. If this cannot be done, our only hope is that the people of the Southwest will rally *en masse* with their private arms, and thus enable you to oppose the vast army which will threaten the destruction of our country.

I have hoped to be able to leave here for a short time, and would be much gratified to confer with you, and share your responsibilities. I might aid you in obtaining troops; no one could hope to do more unless he underrated your military capacity. I write in great haste, and feel that it would be worse than useless to point out to you how much depends upon you.

May God bless you is the sincere prayer of your friend,

JEFFERSON DAVIS.[1]

On the 25th of March General Johnston completed the concentration of his troops. On that day he wrote to the President from Corinth, "My force is now united, holding Burnsville, Iuka, and Tuscumbia, with one division here."

---

[1] It will be observed that General Lee's letter (on page 551) was written the same day.

CHAPTER XXXI.

PITTSBURG LANDING.

WHILE these movements of General Johnston were in progress, a stirring campaign occurred in Missouri, and great preparations were made in the Mississippi Valley, and on the Tennessee River, to overwhelm him on that flank. The storm was gathering. It has been seen that General Johnston's efforts to raise men for the contest west of the Mississippi were as earnest and as unavailing as in Mississippi and Tennessee. Though vested with the direction of affairs both east and west of the river, so distant and distinct was the scene of operations in Missouri that he was only able to maintain a general control there.

While the armies in Kentucky, like wary swordsmen, watched every opposing movement, with only an occasional thrust and parry, until the final rush and death-grapple, the struggle in Missouri resembled those stage-combats in which many and often aimless blows are given, the antagonists exchange weapons and positions, and the situations shift with startling rapidity, until an interposing hand strikes up the weapons and leaves the contest undecided.

After the return of Price's army from the expedition to Lexington, it moved about in Southwestern Missouri until Christmas, when it advanced to Springfield, where it remained until the middle of February. McCulloch wrote to General Johnston, October 11th, that he had been able to recruit about 1,000 infantry, which did not supply his losses from sickness. McCulloch was convinced that nothing could be done until spring, except in the way of organization and preparation. Many motives impelled Price to resume the aggressive. He was flattered with the general and growing sympathy of his fellow-citizens; but he was not sustained by a corresponding accession of force, and for a long time his army remained a shifting and tumultuous throng of from 5,000 to 15,000 men. Eventually, disciplined by competent hands, sifted by hardship, and tempered in the fire of battle, it became as true, tried, and faultless, as the blade of Damascus. Dissensions arose between McCulloch and Price, which were eventually settled to the satisfaction of both parties by the assignment of Major-General Earl Van Dorn to the command west of the Mississippi River.

Van Dorn had been a captain in General Johnston's own regiment, the Second Cavalry, and was distinguished for courage, energy, and decision. On taking command, he adopted bold plans, in accordance with the views of Generals Johnston and Price. But these the enemy did not allow him to carry out. Van Dorn assumed command January 29, 1862, and was engaged in organizing the force in Northeastern Arkansas until February 22d, when, learning the Federal advance, he hastened, with only his staff, to Fayetteville, where McCulloch's army had its headquarters, and toward which Price was falling back from Springfield.

General Curtis, the Federal commander, had at Rolla, according to his report, a force of 12,095 men, and fifty pieces of artillery. He advanced February 11th, and Price retreated. He overtook Price's rear-guard at Cassville, and harassed it for four days on the retreat. Curtis pursued Price to Fayetteville, Arkansas, and then retired to Sugar Creek, where he proposed to establish himself. Leaving the main body here to fortify, he sent out heavy detachments to live upon the country and collect provisions.

As soon as Van Dorn arrived at the Confederate camps, on Boston Mountain, he made speedy preparations to attack Curtis or some one of his detachments. Learning that Sigel was at Bentonville with 7,000 men, he attempted to intercept him with his army, then about 16,000 strong. The lack of discipline and perfect methods in the Confederate army allowed Sigel to effect his escape, which he did with considerable skill. Curtis was enabled to concentrate at Sugar Creek; and, instead of taking him in detail, Van Dorn was obliged to assail his entire army.

Nevertheless, while Curtis was preparing for a front attack, Van Dorn, by a wide *détour*, led Price's army to the Federal rear, moving McCulloch against Curtis's right flank. Here, again, the want of order among the Confederate troops produced disastrous results, and so slow and embarrassed was their march that the enemy got notice of it in time to make his dispositions accordingly. Van Dorn had avoided his intrenchments, however, and fought him on fairer terms, though Curtis, posted on rugged and wooded hills, still held the stronger ground.

The battle of " Elkhorn," or " Pea Ridge," as the Federals call it, began early on the morning of March 5, 1862. The opposing armies were nearly equal in strength. Van Dorn says he had 14,000 men engaged, and Curtis puts his force at about 10,000 men and forty-nine guns. The two corps of the Confederate army were widely separated; Curtis's divisions fought back to back, and readily reënforced each other. Van Dorn, with Price's corps, encountered Carr's division, which advanced to meet it, but was driven back steadily and with heavy loss.

In the mean time, McCulloch's corps met a division under Osterhaus, and, after a sharp, quick struggle, swept it away. Pushing forward through the scrub-oak, his wide-extended line met Sigel's, Asboth's, and Davis's divisions. Here on the rugged spurs of the hills ensued one of those fearful combats in which the most determined valor is resisted by the most stubborn tenacity. In the crisis of the struggle McCulloch, dashing forward to reconnoitre, fell a victim to a lurking sharp-shooter. Almost at the same moment McIntosh, his second in command, fell while charging a Federal battery with a regiment of Texas cavalry. Without direction or head, the shattered lines of the Confederates left the field, to rally, after a wide circuit, on Price's corps.

When Van Dorn learned this sad intelligence, he urged his attack, pressing back the Federals until night closed the bloody scene. The Confederate headquarters were then at Elkhorn Tavern, where the Federal headquarters had been in the morning. Each army was now on its opponent's line of communications. Van Dorn found his troops much disorganized and exhausted, short of ammunition, and without food. He made his arrangements to retreat. The wagon-trains and all men not effective for the coming battle were started by a circuitous route to Van Buren. The effectives remained to cover the retreat. The gallant General Henry Little had the front line of battle with his own and Rives's stanch Missouri Brigades. The battle was renewed at 7 A. M. next day, and raged until 10 A. M., this stout rearguard holding off the whole Federal army. The trains, artillery, and most of the army, were by this time well on the road. The order was then given to the Missourians to withdraw. "The gallant fellows faced about with cheers," and retired steadily. They encamped ten miles from the battle-field, at three o'clock. There was no real pursuit. The attack had failed.

Van Dorn puts his losses at 600 killed and wounded, and 200 prisoners. Curtis reports his losses at 203 killed, 972 wounded, and 176 missing—total, 1,351. But the casualties did not measure the Confederate loss. McCulloch's corps was for the moment broken to pieces, though it rapidly recovered. Worse than all, a great chance was gone, and, though the Federals were badly crippled and soon left that region, Missouri was not regained, nor was the diversion effected in General Johnston's behalf which both he and Van Dorn had hoped.

Van Dorn was now called to meet General Johnston at Corinth, and was ordered to hasten his army by the quickest route to that point. Through unavoidable causes, only one of his regiments arrived in time to participate in the battle of Shiloh. Soon after, however, his army reënforced Beauregard.

Beauregard left Nashville sick, February 14th, to take charge in West Tennessee, and made his headquarters at Jackson, Tennessee, February 17th. He was still prostrated by disease, which partially disabled him throughout that entire campaign. He was, however, ably seconded by Bragg and Polk, who commanded his two grand divisions or army corps. Writing to General Johnston March 2d, he says : " General Bragg is with me. We are trying to organize every thing as rapidly as possible ; " and, again, on the 6th: " I am still unwell, but am doing the best I can. I nominally assumed the command yesterday." He directed the military operations from his sick-room, and sometimes from his sick-bed, as he informs the writer. On March 23d he went to Corinth to confer with General Johnston there, and on March 26th removed thither permanently.

Whether Columbus should be evacuated entirely or stand a siege with a small garrison, when the rest of the army retired southward, was a question which had been left by General Johnston to General Beauregard to determine on the spot, according to the exigencies of the case. On the 20th of February General Johnston telegraphed to General Beauregard :

> If not well enough to assume command, I hope that you, now having had time to study the field, will advise General Polk of your judgment as to the proper disposition of his army, in accordance with the views you entertained in our memoranda, unless you have changed your views. I cannot order him, not knowing but that you have assumed command, and our orders conflict.

Guided by these instructions from General Johnston, Beauregard directed the evacuation of Columbus, and the establishment of a new line resting on New Madrid, Island No. 10, and Humboldt. Polk issued the preliminary orders February 25th, for the evacuation, which was completed on March 2d.

General Beauregard selected Brigadier-General J. P. McCown, an old army-officer, for the command of Island No. 10, forty miles below Columbus, whither he removed his division February 27th. A. P. Stewart's brigade was also sent to New Madrid. Some 7,500 troops were assembled at these points. The remainder of the forces marched by land, under General Cheatham, to Union City. The quarters and buildings were committed to the flames ; and at 3 P. M., March 2d, General Polk followed the retiring column from the abandoned stronghold.

Polk says in his report :

> The enemy's cavalry—the first of his forces to arrive after the evacuation—reached Columbus in the afternoon next day, twenty-four hours after the last of our troops had left. In five days we moved the accumulations of six months, taking with us all our commissary and quartermaster's stores—an amount sufficient to supply my whole command for eight months—all our powder and other ammunition and ordnance stores, excepting a few shot and gun-carriages, and every heavy gun in the fort. Two thirty-two-pounders in a remote outwork were the only valuable guns left, and these, with three or four small and indifferent carronades similarly situated, were spiked and rendered useless. The whole number of pieces of artillery composing our armament was 140.

After the surrender of Fort Donelson and the first flush of satisfaction resulting in Grant's promotion, he fell under the censures of his immediate superior, Halleck, on account of the marauding and demoralization of his troops, and his own alleged neglect of duty. Grant was superseded, March 4th, but was soon after (March 13th) restored to command. It is evident, however, from Halleck's correspondence, that his own cautious and hesitating temper had as much to do with the tardy movements of the Federals as any of Grant's shortcomings. Halleck was now put in command of the whole West ; Buell, Grant, and Pope, on the west bank of the Mississippi, and Curtis in Southwest Missouri, all moving under his supreme control.

While the Confederate and Federal armies were gathering, front to front, at Corinth and Pittsburg Landing, important operations were occurring around New Madrid and Island No. 10. On the 18th of February General Halleck sent Major-General John Pope, whom he had recalled from Central Missouri, to organize an expedition against New Madrid.

His force consisted of eight divisions, made up of thirty regiments and nine batteries, in all probably 25,000 men, besides Foote's flotilla and troops with it. McCown had at first probably 7,500 men, afterward reduced to some four or five thousand by the removal of troops. General Beauregard informed him from the first that under no circumstances would his force be increased, as it was intended as a forlorn hope to hold this position until Fort Pillow was fortified. The defense at Island No. 10 was not adequate to the preparations there ; but, as its bearing on General Johnston's operations was simply to withhold from his army its garrison, which did not surrender until the day after the battle of Shiloh, an account of the transactions there may be omitted as not essential to this narrative.

While Pope was thus directed against New Madrid, a combined movement up the Tennessee by Grant's column was also projected. In orders issued March 1st, to Grant, Halleck says :

The main object of this expedition will be to destroy the railroad-bridge over Bear Creek, near Eastport, Mississippi, and also the connections at Corinth, Jackson, and Humboldt. It is thought best that these objects be attempted in the order named. Strong detachments of cavalry and light artillery, supported by infantry, may by rapid movements reach these points from the river without very serious opposition. Avoid any general engagement with strong forces. It will be better to retreat than to risk a general battle. This should be strongly impressed upon the officers sent with the expedition from the river. General C. F. Smith, or some very discreet officer, should be selected for such commands. Having accomplished these objects, or such of them as may be practicable, you will return to Danville and move on Paris.[1]

Halleck's ultimate objective point was Memphis, which he expected to reach by forcing a column down the Mississippi ; and the movement

[1] Badeau's "Life of Grant," vol. i., p. 596.

up the Tennessee was, at first, only subsidiary. It was meant to cut the
communications from Memphis east, and prevent reënforcements to the
Confederates on the Mississippi. Afterward, when the concentration
of troops at Corinth was reported to him, with wonderful exaggerations
of the Confederate strength—100,000, 200,000 men—he determined to
mass Buell and Grant against the army at that point; and Buell was
ordered, March 15th, to unite his forces with Grant's, a movement previously suggested by him.

Meanwhile, the expedition up the Tennessee was begun by C. F.
Smith, on the 10th of March, with a new division under Sherman in advance. On the 13th of March, Smith assembled four divisions—Sherman's, Hurlbut's, Lew Wallace's, and W. H. L. Wallace's, at Savannah,
on the right bank of the Tennessee, at its Great Bend. Smith at once
sent Sherman with his division, escorted by two gunboats, to land below Eastport and make a break in the Memphis & Charleston Railroad between Tuscumbia and Corinth. Sherman, finding a Confederate
battery at Eastport, disembarked below at the mouth of the Yellow
River, and started for Burnsville; but, becoming discouraged at the
continued rains, the swollen streams, the bad roads, and the resistance
he met with from the troops posted there, under G. B. Crittenden, he
retired. After consultation with Smith, he again disembarked, on the
16th, at Pittsburg Landing, on the left bank, seven miles above Savannah, and made a reconnaissance as far as Monterey, some ten miles,
nearly half-way to Corinth. On the 17th General Grant took command,
relieving Smith, who was lying ill at Savannah on his death-bed.
Smith died April 25th—a very gallant and able officer.

Two more divisions, Prentiss's and McClernand's, had joined in the
mean time, and Grant assembled the Federal army near Pittsburg Landing, which was the most advantageous base for a movement against
Corinth. Here it lay motionless until the battle of Shiloh.

The Federal army was at Shiloh, near Pittsburg Landing, in a position naturally very strong. Its selection has been censured for rashness,
on the erroneous presumption that the army there was outnumbered,
inferior in discipline to its opponents, and peculiarly exposed to attack.
The criticism is unjust, because the supposition is altogether untrue. It
cannot be denied that General Grant reported the Confederate army at
Corinth, at 60,000—80,000—100,000, and as rumored to be 200,000
strong; but we are not to suppose that his sagacity was so much at
fault as to be misled by these "old women's stories," as Sherman calls
them, especially when Buell was conveying to Halleck pretty accurate
information of the numbers there.

Grant felt safe at Shiloh, because he knew he was numerically
stronger than his adversary. His numbers and his equipment were
superior to those of his antagonist, and the discipline and *morale* of

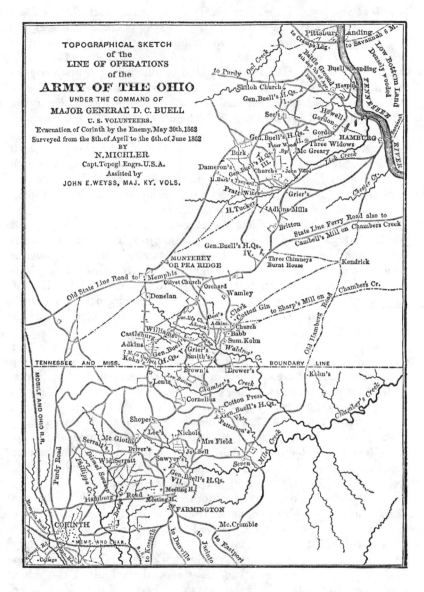

TOPOGRAPHICAL SKETCH
of the
LINE OF OPERATIONS
of the
ARMY OF THE OHIO
UNDER THE COMMAND OF
MAJOR GENERAL D. C. BUELL
U. S. VOLUNTEERS.
Evacuation of Corinth by the Enemy, May 30th, 1862
Surveyed from the 8th of April to the 6th of June 1862
BY
N. MICHLER
Capt. Topog! Engrs. U. S. A.
Assisted by
JOHN E. WEYSS, MAJ. KY. VOLS.

his army ought to have been so. The only infantry of the Confederate army which had ever seen a combat were some of Polk's men, who were at Belmont; Hindman's brigade, which was in the skirmish at Woodsonville; and the fugitives of Mill Spring. In the Federal army were the soldiers who had fought at Belmont, Fort Henry, and Donelson—

30,000 of the last. There were many raw troops on both sides. Some of the Confederates received their arms for the first time that week.

Unless these things were so, and unless Grant's army was, in whole or in part, an army of invasion, intended for the offensive, of course it was out of place on that south bank. But Sherman has distinctly asserted that it was in prosecution of an offensive movement, and hence this occupation of the south bank was a necessary preliminary to the advance projected against Corinth. There was much to foster a spirit of self-complacent security in the bosoms of the Federal generals. Not only were they the stronger, but their gunboats gave them command of the river for reënforcement or retreat; Buell was drawing near with his large army; and the character of the ground at Shiloh made it a natural stronghold. The peril to Grant's army was not in the topography, but in the want of proper precautions.

The overweening confidence that received at Shiloh so just and terrible a rebuke is inexplicable, except as the result of a natural temerity, increased by success, inexperience, and a perfect reliance on superior strength and position. Had it been otherwise, Grant would have fortified strongly, and urged to the utmost the advance and junction of Buell's army with his own, or asked for other reënforcement. We shall see he did neither. The truth is, he undervalued his adversary's celerity and daring.

The water-shed between the Mississippi and Tennessee Rivers, near the Great Bend, follows the general course of the latter stream, at the distance of some twelve or fourteen miles. The railroad system lies on its western and southern slope, and, as far east as Burnsville, passes through a poor, flat, and swampy country, covered with the primeval forest. There are twenty bridges between Corinth and Bethel, a space of some twenty-three miles. The slope toward the Tennessee is steeper, broken by short creeks, which, as they approach the river, become deep, or spread out in tangled marshes. The ridges between these creeks are considerably elevated above the river-level.

The Tennessee flows northwest for some distance, until a little west of Hamburg, a point nineteen miles from Corinth, it takes its final bend to the north. Here, two affluents, Owl and Lick Creeks, flowing nearly parallel, somewhat north of east, from three to five miles apart, empty into the Tennessee. Owl Creek, uniting with Snake Creek, takes that name below their junction. It forms the northern limit of the ridge, which Lick Creek bounds on the south. These streams, rising some ten or twelve miles back, toward Corinth, were bordered near their mouths by swamps filled with back-water, and impassable except where the roads crossed.

The inclosed space, a rude parallelogram, is a rolling table-land, about one hundred feet above the river-level, with its water-shed lying near Lick Creek, and either slope broken by deep and frequent ravines draining into the two creeks ; the side toward Lick Creek being precipitous, while that toward Owl Creek, though broken, is a gradual declivity. This plateau ends in abrupt hills, overlooking the narrow strip of river-bank ; and, the gorges near the river passing toward it, the tangle of ravines results in very broken ground. In the troughs of the ravines, brooks were running, the drainage of the recent heavy rains ; and there were boggy places hazardous for the passage of artillery, and difficult even for infantry. The acclivities were covered with forests, and often thick-set with copses and undergrowth. Indeed, the whole country was heavily timbered, except where an occasional small farm dotted the wilderness with a cultivated or abandoned field.

Pittsburg Landing, a mere hamlet of three or four log-cabins, was situated about midway between the mouths of Owl and Lick Creeks, in the narrow and swampy bottom that here fringes the Tennessee. It was three or four miles below Hamburg, six or seven above Savannah, the Federal depot on the right bank, and twenty-two miles from Corinth by the direct road. Shiloh Church, from which the battle took its name, lay two and a half miles in advance of the landing. The country between the river and Monterey, a village on the road to Corinth, is intersected by a network of roads, up to which neighborhood lead three or four roads from Corinth, cut through the forests and across the sloughs. These roads were badly made, soft with the continued rains, and not perfectly known to the Confederate leaders.

It will be perceived that the Federal position was, in fact, a formidable natural fortification. With few and difficult approaches, guarded on either flank by impassable streams and morasses, protected by a succession of ravines and acclivities, each commanded by eminences to the rear, this quadrilateral seemed a safe fastness against attack—hard to assail, easy to defend. Its selection was the dying gift of the soldierly C. F. Smith to his cause.

That the strength of Shiloh has not been overstated is evinced by the evidence of General Sherman, given then and afterward. He says, in his "Memoirs," vol. i., page 229 :

The position was naturally strong. . . . At a later period of the war, we could have rendered this position impregnable in one night, but at this time we did not do it, and it may be it is well we did not.

He says of it in a letter to Grant's adjutant-general, Rawlins, March 18, 1862 (page 232) : "Magnificent plain for camping and drilling, and a military point of great strength." On the next day (page 233), he expresses himself—

Strongly impressed with the importance of this position, both for its land advantages and its strategic position. The ground itself admits of easy defense by a small command, and yet affords admirable camping-ground for 100,000 men.

On the trial of Colonel Thomas Worthington, Forty-sixth Ohio Volunteers, who had severely criticised General Sherman, the latter testifies : [1]

I will not insult General Smith's memory by criticising his selection of a field. It was not looked to so much for defense as for ground on which an army could be organized for offense. We did not occupy too much ground. . . . But even as we were, on the 6th of April, you might search the world over and not find a more advantageous field of battle, flanks well protected and never threatened, troops in easy support; timber and broken ground giving good points to rally : and the proof is that *forty-three thousand* men, of whom at least ten thousand ran away, held their ground against sixty thousand chosen troops of the South, with their best leaders.

In a letter to the editor of the *United States Service Magazine*, published January, 1865, General Sherman says : "It was General Smith who selected that field of battle, and it was well chosen. On any other we should surely have been overwhelmed."

It cannot be said that the Federal generals availed themselves of the superior advantages of their position. Flushed with the victory at Donelson, they indulged the delusion of marching to an easy triumph whenever they might choose to advance and give battle. Sherman says ("Memoirs," vol. i., page 229) :

I always acted on the supposition that we were an invading army ; that our purpose was to move forward in force, make a lodgment on the Memphis & Charleston road, and thus repeat the grand tactics of Fort Donelson, by separating the rebels in the interior from those at Memphis and on the Mississippi River. We did not fortify our camps against an attack, because we had no orders to do so, and because such a course would have made our raw men timid.

Again, General Sherman says ("Memoirs," vol. i., page 247) :

We had no intrenchments of any sort, on the theory that as soon as Buell arrived we would march to Corinth to attack the enemy.

While the criticism, so often made, may be just, that comfortable camping-grounds for the divisions were one controlling consideration in the arrangement of the Federal army, still it would have been difficult on that ground to have selected any other than strong defensible positions.

On Colonel Worthington's trial (*vide* Boynton's volume, already quoted, page 28), Sherman testifies, under oath, thus :

---

[1] *Vide* "Sherman's Historical Raid," by Boynton, p. 29 ; also "Shiloh," p. 22, by Colonel Worthington.

He (Colonel Worthington) says, "A slight abattis might have prevented an attack." What business was it of his whether his superior officer invited an attack or not? The Army Regulations will show him that no fortification can be made, except under order of the commanding general. *To have erected forti- fications would have been an evidence of weakness, and would have invited an attack.*

Boynton says (page 31):

Immediately after the battle, General Sherman seems to have been won over to the idea that an abattis might be valuable as a protection to his camp; for, in a compilation of his orders, made under his own direction, the very first of them which appears after the engagement contains the following paragraph: "Each brigade commander will examine carefully his immediate front; fell trees to afford his men barricade, and clear away all underbrush for two hundred yards in front, so as to uncover an approaching enemy; with these precautions, we can hold our camp against any amount of force that can be brought against us." There is no indication that General Sherman considered this order either an evidence of weakness, or an invitation to attack, or as calculated to make his "raw men timid."

Sherman, in his letter to the editor of the *United States Service Magazine*, already quoted, which might by courtesy be styled his "Af- ter-thoughts," wrote as follows:

It was necessary that a combat, fierce and bitter, to test the manhood of the two armies should come off, and that was as good a place as any. It was not, then, a question of military skill and strategy, but of courage and pluck; and I am convinced that every life lost that day to us was necessary; for otherwise, at Corinth, at Memphis, at Vicksburg, we would have found harder resistance, had we not shown our enemies that, rude and untutored as we then were, we could fight as well as they.

All these excuses do not hang well together. What was the result of that test of manhood which General Sherman applies, if he did not need fortifications before the battle of Shiloh, and did need them after it? Surely, that his troops were bold before and timid after the fight —that they could not stand the test. The suggestion does injury to the brave men he commanded. It is not just.

It is perfectly evident that, if the slightest idea of an attack by Gen- eral Johnston had been foreseen, not only would defensive works have been put up, but a very different line of battle would have been estab- lished. All the controversy on the Federal side about the battle of Shiloh has arisen out of the theory that it is necessary to show that Generals Grant and Sherman are, and always have been, incapable of mistake or failure. A better theory, and more easily maintained, would be that they were capable of learning something, and at Shiloh re- ceived a lesson which rebuked their insolent contempt of an able adversary, and the perilous carelessness of their false security. These distinguished generals have since become famous; and it is not necessary to their reputations to show that they were infallible—especially, so early in their careers. If the testimony proves them somewhat at fault in wariness and sagacity, yet it shows them derelict only so far ; and they certainly exhibited on the field a gallantry and persistence worthy of commendation.

Buell seems to have advised General Halleck with very considerable accuracy and promptness of General Johnston's movements after he left Shelbyville, showing that he had greatly improved his means of information, and that the retreating army could not so effectually mask its movements as in Kentucky.

In forming a plan of campaign, there was some diversity of opinion between Halleck and Buell as to details ; but the main idea of dividing the Confederacy, by cutting the Memphis & Charleston Railroad near the Great Bend of the Tennessee, was essentially the same.

There has been controversy as to the origin of this plan of campaign. McClellan and Buell were in conference about it ; and Halleck adopted it as soon as he saw his way clear to the possession of the Tennessee River.

The original design of Halleck, as communicated to his subordinates, was a dash at the Confederate lines of communication. It had become apparent to them, however, and to his adversary, that he purposed to split the South, and that from Shiloh to Corinth was where he expected to drive his wedge.

Buell says that he and Halleck, as independent commanders, concerted the campaign against Corinth. Halleck's troops moved by water up the Tennessee—that being their only practicable route. Buell was evidently very solicitous to occupy and secure the rich region of Middle Tennessee, and for that reason preferred to move by land, and make Florence, Alabama, instead of Pittsburg or Savannah, the base of a combined movement. But Halleck, having been put in supreme command, his opinion prevailed, and the joint movement concerted against Corinth between the two commanders was set on foot.

Halleck telegraphed Buell, March 26th :

I am inclined to believe the enemy will make his stand at or near Corinth.

On the 28th :

It seems from all accounts the enemy is massing his forces in the vicinity of Corinth. You will concentrate all your available troops at Savannah, or Pittsburg, twelve miles above. Large reënforcements being sent to General Grant. We must be ready to attack the enemy as soon as the roads are passable.

On April 5th Halleck telegraphed from St. Louis :

You are right about concentrating at Waynesboro. Future movements must depend on those of the enemy. I shall not be able to leave here until the first of next week, *via* Fort Henry and Savannah.[1]

General Buell gives the following summary of his share in the campaign before Shiloh, in a letter published in the *United States Service Magazine*, to the statements of which his high character must secure entire credit :

I deemed it best that mine [my army] should march through by land, because such a movement would clear Middle Tennessee of the enemy and facilitate the occupation of the Memphis & Charleston Railroad through North Alabama, to which I had assigned General Mitchell. I believed, also, that I could effect the movement almost as promptly that way as by water, and I knew that it would bring my army upon the field of future operations in better condition. I commenced my march from Nashville on the 15th of March, with a rapid movement of cavalry, followed by McCook's division, to seize the bridges which were yet in possession of the enemy. The latter, however, succeeded in destroying the bridge over Duck River, at Columbia, forty miles distant, and another a few miles farther north. At that time our armies were not provided with pontoon-trains, and rivers had to be crossed with such means as we could make. The streams were out of their banks. Duck River was a formidable barrier, and it was not until the 31st that the army was able to cross.

He says this work was prosecuted with intelligence, energy, and diligence.

In the mean time I had been placed by the War Department under the orders of General Halleck, and he designated Savannah, on the east bank of the Tennessee, as the place for our junction. The distance from Columbia is ninety miles, and was marched at the rate of fifteen miles a day, without a halt. The distance from Nashville is 130 miles, and was marched in nine marching days, and twelve days were occupied in bridging streams. The rear divisions, in consequence of the battle, made forced marches. . . .

The assertion that I knew that General Grant was in jeopardy has no foundation in truth, and I shall show that General Halleck and General Grant themselves could not have believed that such was the case.

He says he only *casually* learned, a few days before his arrival at Savannah, that General Grant was not there, but on the west bank, adding, "And then I was told it" (the force) "was secure in the natural strength of the position." On the 18th he telegraphed General Halleck:

"I understand General Grant is on the east side of the river. Is it not so?" And the reply did not inform me to the contrary. . . . At no time did either of these officers inform me of Grant's actual position, or that he was thought to be in danger.

[1] Buell's letter to Grant, New York *World*, April 6, 1866.

On the 3d of April Buell suggested that he had better cross the Tennessee at Hamburg, and Halleck replied, directing him to halt at Waynesboro, thirty miles from Savannah—

Saying he could not leave St. Louis until the 7th to join us; but, as his dispatch did not reach me before I arrived at Waynesboro, I made no halt, but continued my march to Savannah. And further yet, the day before his arrival at Savannah, General Nelson, who commanded my leading division, advised General Grant by courier of his approach, and was informed in reply that it was unnecessary for him to hasten his march, as he could not at any rate cross the river before the following Tuesday. Nevertheless, that division and myself arrived at Savannah Saturday, as I had directed. The next morning General Grant was attacked at Pittsburg Landing.

General Buell says further that all the facts prove that Sherman shared the feeling of security.

A careful reading of the dispatches and communications of commanders sustains every statement in the foregoing summary.

General G. Ammen, in a letter dated April 5, 1871, published in the *Cincinnati Commercial*, strongly corroborates General Buell's statement that Grant delayed Nelson's march. He says Nelson told him, at Columbia, that he was not wanted at Savannah before Monday, April 7th, but, everything favoring him, he arrived there on the 5th, at noon. Thus, he anticipated in time not only the calculations of the Confederate commanders, but Buell's orders, by two days.

There is no reason for believing that General Buell disappointed any just expectation of his colleagues, or moved with less diligence and expedition than the proposed plan of campaign demanded, or the difficulties of the march permitted. If there was the error of delay, it occurred in stopping at Nashville, and arose almost inevitably from the division of the command between Halleck and Buell, and the time taken up in concerting a combined movement. It was the advance of Buell that now hastened General Johnston's resolution to attack.

The First, Second, Fourth, Fifth, and Sixth Divisions, commanded respectively by Brigadier-Generals Thomas, McCook, Nelson, Crittenden, and Wood, with a contingent force of cavalry, in all 37,000 effective men, constituted the main army, which, under the personal command of General Buell, was to join General Halleck in the projected movement against the enemy at Corinth, Mississippi.[1]

Mitchell's corps, moving against Florence, was 18,000 strong.

The writer has used every effort to ascertain with entire accuracy the forces engaged in the battle of Shiloh. He lays before the reader

[1] "Army of the Cumberland," vol. i., p. 99.

all the information he can obtain. The Hon. Mr. McCrary, Secretary of War, kindly put at his disposal all the data in possession of the War Department. These are given in the Appendix to the battle of Shiloh, showing for the first time the organization, strength, and casualties, of the Federal army, in a form which it is hoped will prove a valuable contribution to history.

The tables appended to Chapter XXXIV. (*see* summary) show that General Grant had at Pittsburg Landing—total present, 58,052 men, of whom 49,314 were present for duty. General Buell, on the information of General C. F. Smith, estimated it at 60,000 men. His aggregate on April 1st, according to a memorandum furnished the writer by Secretary Belknap, December 17, 1875, was 68,175; and Buell's aggregate was 101,051. Buell, on March 20th, reported to the adjutant-general that he had 73,472 present for duty. Thus we have present for duty in the armies of invasion opposed to General Johnston, and excluding the troops in garrison or reserve of Grant's and Halleck's commands :

Buell's troops	73,472
Grant's "	49,314
Pope's " (about)	27,000
Total	149,786

Their aggregate force reached about 200,000 men. To meet these great armies, General Johnston had about 20,000 men of his own army, 25,000 or 30,000 under Beauregard, and 9,000 or 10,000 at Island No. 10, Fort Pillow, and other garrisons; not more than 60,000 in all, of whom not more than 50,000 were effectives. The forces immediately to be encountered, exclusive of Pope's, were :

Grant	50,000
Buell	37,000
Mitchell	18,000
Total	105,000

To engage these it will be seen that he was able to get together about 40,000 available troops at Shiloh.

APPENDIX A.

(6276 A. G. O. 75.

WAR DEPARTMENT, ADJUTANT-GENERAL'S OFFICE,
WASHINGTON, *December* 17, 1875.

MEMORANDUM.

Statement showing the number of troops, present and absent, in the commands of Generals Sherman, Grant, and Buell, at the dates hereinafter specified.

GENERAL SHERMAN'S COMMAND, NOVEMBER 10, 1861.

In commands that furnished returns to department headquarters   .   30,917
"   "   not furnishing returns (about)   9,100
Regiments in process of formation (estimated)   9,600
                                                                     ————
                Total   49,617

General Grant's command, February 1, 1862   27,113
    "   Buell's   "   "   20, 1862   103,864
    "   Grant's   "   April 1, 1862   68,175
    "   Buell's   "   "   30, 1862   101,051

NOTE.—Owing to the absence of returns of a uniform date, the above figures have been taken from such returns as are on file bearing date nearest to the time desired.

DISTANCES.

By Land.	Miles.	On Tennessee River going down.	Miles.
From Corinth to Iuka . . .	23	From Chickasaw to Bear Creek . .	1¼
" " Burnsville . .	10	" Bear Creek to Eastport .	1¼
" " Chewalla . .	11½	" Eastport to Cook's Landing .	1½
" " Bethel . .	23	" Cook's Landing to Indian Creek	2½
" " Purdy . .	22	" Indian Creek to Cook's Landing .	¾
" " Eastport . .	30	" Cook's Landing to Yellow Creek	5
" " Wynn's Landing .	21	" Yellow Creek to Wynn's Landing	1¼
" " Farmington . .	5	" Wynn's Landing to Wood's .	2
" " Hamburg . .	19	" Wood's to North Bend Landing .	4½
" " Monterey . .	11	" North Bend Landing to Chambers's Creek	4
" " Pittsburg . .	23	" Chambers's Creek to Hamburg .	4
" " Savannah . .	30	" Hamburg to Lick Creek .	2
" Iuka to Eastport . . .	8	" Lick Creek to Pittsburg .	2
" Burnsville to Wynn's . .	15	" Pittsburg to Crump's Landing .	4
" Bethel to Purdy . . .	4	" Crump's Landing to Coffee .	8
" " Savannah . .	23	" Coffee to Chalk-Bluff Landing .	2
" Monterey to Purdy . . .	15	" Chalk-Bluff Landing to Saltillo .	12
" " Farmington . .	9	" Saltillo to Decatur Furnace . .	18

CHAPTER XXXII.

CONCENTRATION AT CORINTH.

GENERAL JOHNSTON had now effected the concentration of his troops at Corinth, with the intent of striking Grant before the arrival of Buell. The strategic importance of this point can scarcely be over-estimated. At Corinth, two great railway lines crossed—that running north and south from Mobile, on the Gulf, to Columbus, near the mouth of the

Ohio ; and that from Memphis to Chattanooga, running east and west, and connecting the Mississippi River with the railroad system of Georgia and East Tennessee. The Mississippi Central Railroad from New Orleans runs west of and nearly parallel with the Mobile & Ohio Railroad, gradually approaching it, and forming a junction with it at Jackson, Tennessee. Still farther west, the Memphis Railroad to Bowling Green runs northeast, crossing the Mobile & Ohio at Humboldt. With the Tennessee River as the Federal base, its Great Bend from Florence to Savannah formed a salient, to which the railway system conformed. Corinth was the central point and key of this system and its defense. Pittsburg Landing, twenty-two miles distant, was the strongest point near it on the river for a base. There was no mistake in its selection, if it had been judiciously intrenched, as has been shown.

To concentrate at Corinth, and fight the Federal armies in detail— Grant first, Buell afterward—this had been the cherished object to which, during so many weeks, General Johnston had bent every energy. That concentration was at last accomplished. Arriving at Corinth in person on the 24th of March, with his troops nearly all on the ground or at hand, he spent a week in the reorganization, armament, and array of the forces collected there from so many quarters.

It has already been seen how Polk's command was drawn back from Columbus, in accordance with the plan settled upon at Bowling Green, February 7th. It has been seen, too, that the War Department, as soon as it realized the fact of General Johnston's retreat from Bowling Green, ordered Bragg from Pensacola, with his well-disciplined army, to aid in resisting the weight of the attack. Polk had been negotiating with Lovell, in January, to spare him some troops ; and in compliance with a telegraphic request made by General Johnston from Bowling Green, February 2d, Lovell sent him Ruggles's brigade. General Johnston telegraphed, February 12th, for these troops to report, by the shortest possible route *to Corinth*, for orders from General Beauregard. Generals Chalmers and L. Pope Walker were already on the line of the Memphis & Charleston Railroad, with considerable commands.

These pages have evinced how many and how strenuous efforts had been made to raise troops in the South during that autumn and winter. Many regiments, long organized, were lying in rendezvous waiting for arms. The fall of Donelson hurried up volunteering, and these new levies were added to the others. At this juncture—at the critical moment, it may be said indeed, at the last moment—some cargoes of arms ran the blockade, and the troops were pressed to the front to receive these precious weapons, arriving, some in time, some too late, to share in the glories of Shiloh. General Beauregard issued an eloquent appeal for volunteers, and several regiments responded—a high compliment to his prestige won at Manassas.

The Comte de Paris mentions (vol. i., page 525), on what authority does not appear, that Beauregard "left Manassas with 15,000 men," and that "he had with him well-trained troops, who took with them the prestige of the Bull-Run victory, and were to inspire new ardor in the Army of the Mississippi, of which they were destined to form the nucleus."

This is an error. General Beauregard came to the Army of the West with his staff only. The troops collected under his command at Corinth were composed of Polk's corps, Bragg's corps, Ruggles's, Walker's, and Chalmers's brigades, and the new troops sent forward by the Governors. Careless writers have assumed that this considerable army was summoned into being, or concentrated at Corinth, by other than regular military methods; but they are mistaken. They were recruited, armed, disciplined, and assembled at Corinth, by the conjoint efforts of the State and Confederate governments, extending through many months, and by the slow and laborious processes already detailed in these pages.

The army now collected at Corinth consisted of Polk's corps, whom we have seen holding Columbus, and baffling Grant at Belmont; Bragg's well-disciplined troops, who had been all the fall in training at Pensacola; Ruggles's reënforcement, detached from Lovell at New Orleans; and Chalmers's and Walker's commands, as stated. To these were added such new levies as the Governors had in rendezvous, who in this emergency were sent to the front, even without arms, and a few regiments which were raised in response to General Beauregard's call.

It will be remembered that General Johnston's plan of concentration at Corinth, long contemplated, had taken shape as soon as Donelson fell.

On February 21st Mackall, adjutant-general, telegraphed to General Pillow, who was at Columbia, that General Johnston's "retreat will be toward Shelbyville." On the same day orders were given to send Cleburne's regiment to Decatur. On February 24th General Johnston telegraphed President Davis:

My movement has been delayed by a storm on the 22d, washing away pike and railroad-bridge at this place. Floyd, 2,500 strong, will march for Chattanooga to-morrow, to defend. This army will move on the 26th, by Decatur, for the valley of the Mississippi. Is in good condition and increasing in numbers.

When his arrangements at Murfreesboro were complete, he wrote to Mr. Benjamin, February 27th, that he was about to move to the defense of the Mississippi Valley, "crossing the (Tennessee) River near Decatur, in order to enable him *to coöperate or unite with General Beauregard.*" Next day he moved. This was before Halleck's orders for the movement up the Tennessee, and ten days before it began, and General Johnston was already three days on his march before Columbus was evacuated.

On the 26th of February General Beauregard asked for a brigade to assist in the defense of New Madrid, in the following terms :

Appearance of an early attack on New Madrid, in force. Position of absolute necessity to us. Cannot you send a brigade at once, by rail, to assist defense as fast as possible ?

In his report of the battle of Shiloh, he says :

General Johnston being at Murfreesboro, on the march to form junction of his forces with mine, was called on to send at least a brigade by railroad, so we might fall upon and crush the enemy should he attempt an advance from under his gunboats.

There was, in fact, no enemy there until some two weeks later, and the brigade called for was intended, as is seen above, for a different purpose—" to assist defense," not " to fall upon and crush the enemy." The correspondence between General Beauregard and General Johnston shows that the former was advised of all of General Johnston's movements.

General Beauregard wrote from Jackson, Tennessee, March 2d, to General Johnston:

I think you ought to hurry up your troops to Corinth by railroad, as soon as practicable, for *here* or thereabouts will soon be fought the great battle of this controversy.

Adjutant-General Mackall telegraphed for General Johnston to General Beauregard, March 7th :

The general understands that detachments for this army are coming east. Will you order none to pass the line of road running to Corinth ?

This, with the other circumstances already given, is conclusive that *Corinth* was the objective point of General Johnston's march. While engaged in these efforts at concentration, General Johnston fully perceived the necessity of haste in their execution, and it has been seen that all possible speed was made.

Immediately after Sherman effected his first lodgement at Pittsburg, Bragg conceived the project of striking him a blow at once, which, if it had been executed promptly, would very probably have proved successful, and might have changed the whole course of subsequent events. This bold stroke was, however, prevented by the following orders from General Beauregard, who determined to await General Johnston's arrival:

JACKSON, TENNESSEE, *March* 17, 1862.

DEAR GENERAL: I telegraphed you yesterday, *via* Corinth, my views relative to the two strategic points, *Chamberlain* and *Corinth* (according to the map). Having brigades of observation at Purdy and Iuka, the two points threatened by the enemy from the Tennessee River, I also addressed you a letter on the same subject through my adjutant-general, Colonel Jordan.

Yesterday evening, however, Captain Jordan submitted to me your intentions, formed, no doubt, before having received my communications, above referred to, relative to a proposed movement on your part, in two columns from Corinth and Bethel, to meet at Adamsville. This movement, with such troops as we have, in the presence of a determined enemy, might be dangerous, for the point of junction is too near his positions at Crump's Landing and Pittsburg. I would prefer uniting farther back, at or near Purdy, if the roads permit it. But what I wish to call your attention particularly to is, the nature of our operations. I do not think, owing to the quality of our troops, the nature of the country we would have to operate in (cut up with small streams, woods, etc.), not knowing exactly where the enemy intends to strike, and in what force, that our operations ought to be purely offensive; I would prefer the defensive-offensive—that is, to take up such a position as would compel the enemy to develop his intentions, and to attack us, before he could penetrate any distance from his base; *then*, when within striking distance of us, to take the offensive, and crush him wherever we may happen to strike him, cutting him off, if possible, from his base of operations, or the river; in that way, we would be certain not to march on Crump's Landing or Pittsburg, when, perhaps, we ought to move on or toward Iuka or Eastport. The great desideratum is to be thoroughly prepared wheresoever and whenever required, on *positive* information only of the enemy's movements, and for which purpose you must have strong advanced posts in every direction toward him, protected by a strong body of cavalry, thrown well forward, to watch the enemy and give timely notice of his approach. . . .

(Here follow directions for the disposition of the troops, not specially pertinent to this memoir.)

My health not permitting me yet to be with you, I have thought it advisable to give you these general ideas, which may be of service to you. I hope, however, to be well enough to join you when the fighting shall have commenced, not, however, to interfere with your arrangement, but merely to assist you, if I can, and prevent misunderstandings, complications, etc.

My physician tells me that I must stop talking altogether, and avoid any undue excitement. How in the world can that be done, at this critical moment? They might as well tell a drowning man that he must not catch at a straw.

Still hopeful, however, I remain, yours truly,

(Signed)   G. T. BEAUREGARD, *General commanding.*

P. S.—While I have guarded you against an uncertain offensive, I am decidedly of the opinion that we should endeavor to entice the enemy into an engagement as soon as possible, and before he shall have further increased his numbers by the large numbers which he must still have in reserve and available —that is, beat him in detail.

To Major-General B. BRAGG.

(For the information of General A. S. JOHNSTON.)

General Beauregard's report of the battle of Shiloh is given in full in the appendix to Chapter XXXV. Its statements have led to many erroneous inferences and much of the prevalent misapprehension as to the circumstances preceding and attending the battle of Shiloh. It is not the province of the present writer to deal with it controversially. It is given to the reader, not as a just or accurate view of these events, but because so important a document belongs to history. It has seemed to the writer, however, that this report ought to be looked at in the light of its intent and of the circumstances under which it was composed. It was written in the first hours of the great and sudden disappointment and reversal of the splendid dream of complete triumph opened to the Southern arms at Shiloh, and closed again by General Johnston's death. It was written, too, amid the wreck of an unavailing contest, and, unconsciously perhaps, to reconcile the results with the fair promise of its opening. Hence its standpoint is simply personal.

Its strictly personal character is readily seen, when it is observed that it contains no record of all the service of General Johnston in his last campaign and his last battle. These are attributed to an impersonal "It." The report says, "It was expected," "It was decided," "It was determined," where strong men thought the experience of a veteran and the energies of a great soldier were incorporate, vivid, and strenuous, in the person of their leader.

That the aspect of General Beauregard's report is simply personal to himself is evident from the fact that General Johnston's name appears in it but four times, and then in the following connections: 1. That he reënforced General Beauregard; 2. That General Johnston was advised that his attack conformed to the expectations of the President; 3. That he died bravely at Shiloh; 4. That he had a staff worthy of commendation. Surely, if this is a record of General Johnston's part in the battle of Shiloh, this memoir would not be worth the writing. Hence, it seems to the writer that General Beauregard's report must be taken merely as the record of General Beauregard's own services from his own point of view.

Immediately on his arrival at Corinth, March 24th, General Johnston held a conference with Generals Beauregard, Polk, and Bragg, after which General Beauregard went back to Jackson; but returned on the 26th, and lent zealous and valuable aid in spite of his malady. About the same time General Johnston had the conference with Van Dorn, in which it was determined to bring his army also to Corinth. The enemy was at this time reported in front of Monterey, almost half-way between Pittsburg and Corinth, advancing. But this was a mistake. Grant made no move of note previous to the battle. It was known that Buell was advancing, and the time taken for reorganization and armament had to be measured by his movements. If these would permit it, a little time would make the Confederate army, reënforced by Van Dorn, compact and terrible. If, however, he pressed on, the blow must be struck without waiting for Van Dorn. The Comte de Paris, in his history of the war, vol. i., page 557, attributes this delay to hesitation ; but there was no hesitation. The work of organization and armament was unavoidable and imperious. The attack was ordered within two hours after Buell's advance was reported.

This work of reorganization and armament first engaged General Johnston's attention. His personal staff was now constituted as follows :

> Colonel H. P. Brewster, assistant adjutant-general.
> Captain N. Wickliffe, assistant adjutant-general.
> Captain Theodore O'Hara, assistant inspector-general.
> Lieutenant George W. Baylor, aide-de-camp.
> Lieutenant Thomas M. Jack,   "
> Major Albert J. Smith, assistant quartermaster-general.
> Captain Wickham,   "   "   "
> Colonel William Preston, volunteer aide-de-camp.
> Major D. M. Hayden,   "   "
> Major Edward W. Munford,   "
> Major Calhoun Benham,   "

For the important work of reorganization before him, General Johnston called to his aid General Bragg, who had special qualifications for the task. At General Johnston's earnest request, General Bragg consented to act temporarily as chief of staff, with the understanding that he was to have command of his corps on the approach of a battle.

General Bragg played so conspicuous a part in the civil war that this work affords neither scope nor occasion for an account of his life, or an estimate of his character. Indeed, there is scarcely any other career that has come under the writer's personal view where there were so many questions difficult to settle fairly. In Bragg there was so much that was strong marred by most evident weaknesses, so many virtues blemished by excess or defect in temper and education, so near an approach to greatness and so manifest a failure to attain it, that his worst enemy ought to find something to admire in him, and his best friend something painful in the attempt to portray him truly. The writer saw him from many points of view and under divers lights and shadows, and as he has passed into history, gives here a brief mention of him that may serve till some abler hand performs the task of recounting his services.

Braxton Bragg was born in Warren County, North Carolina, in 1815. Members of his family attained eminence in politics and at the bar.

He was graduated at West Point, and entered the Third Artillery in 1837. He saw service in the Seminole War in Florida, and was promoted to first-lieutenant in 1838. Bragg served under General Taylor in the Mexican War, and was brevetted captain in 1846, "for gallant and distinguished conduct in the defense of Fort Brown, Texas." He was brevetted major for gallant conduct at Monterey, and lieutenant-colonel for his services at Buena Vista. The mythical order of General Taylor to him on that field, "A little more grape, Captain Bragg," made a popular catch-word, which gave him great notoriety. An attempt was made to assassinate him in camp in 1847, by the explosion of a twelve-pound shell at the foot of his bed.

After the Mexican War, he became a sugar-planter in Terre Bonne Parish, Louisiana, and his methodical habits, industry, and skillful management, gave him great success. At the opening of the war, the State of Louisiana made him commander-in-chief of her volunteer forces. When the Confederate Government was established, President Davis made him a brigadier-general, and put him in command at Pensacola. Here the people and the troops expected a great contest, and, though it did not occur, it afforded a favorable field for Bragg's excellent talents for organization, administration, and discipline. It has been seen how he was transferred with his forces to Corinth.

It is not the province of the present writer to recount his further services, but the following brief abstract from the pen of Colonel J. Stoddard Johnston, who served on his staff, will here suffice :

His first service was at Pensacola, where he distinguished himself as a disciplinarian, and whence he was transferred to Corinth shortly before the battle of Shiloh, having the rank of a major-general. He served with distinction at Shiloh, having been made by General Johnston his chief of staff, and, shortly after, being promoted to a full generalship, succeeded to the command of the Army of the Mississippi. In the succeeding summer, 1862, he transferred the main body of his command to Chattanooga, and planned and executed the Kentucky campaign of that year, being at the same time in command of the department embracing the territory between the Mississippi River and the Alleghany range. Notwithstanding the unpopularity which assailed him after the evacuation of Kentucky, he was continued in command, and transferred his army in November, 1862, to Middle Tennessee, and December 31st of that year fought with 31,000 infantry the battle of Murfreesboro or Stone River. Notwithstanding the superior numbers by which he was opposed under Rosecrans, the victory for a time was his. A bloody repulse of Hardee at the moment when the latter was thought to be giving the finishing stroke to the day, and the slaughter which befell Breckinridge's command two days after, compelled him to retreat and yield the ground to his opponent. He, however, continued to occupy a great part of Tennessee until the following September, when on the 19th and 20th he again fought Rosecrans at Chickamauga. Here his victory was decisive, as at the close of the second day's fight he occupied the battle-field, and Rosecrans retreated to Chattanooga. Failure to pursue and follow up his victory gave Rosecrans time to fortify and restore the *morale* of his shattered command, and resulted ultimately in Bragg's defeat at Missionary Ridge, November 25th, his retreat into Georgia, and his relinquishment of the command of the army to Joseph E. Johnston. His active military career may be said to have closed here, as he was assigned to staff-duty at Richmond, where he remained until shortly before the close of the war in confidential relations with President Davis, as chief of staff of the armies of the Confederacy. Not long before the surrender, he was placed in command at Wilmington, North Carolina, and was engaged in several actions.

The close of the war found him ruined in fortune, but he went to work cheerfully, following the pursuit of a civil engineer in New Orleans and Mobile, until within the past few years he removed to Galveston, where death closed his career in his sixty-first year.

General Bragg met his death at Galveston, Texas, September 27, 1876, by heart-disease. He was struck, while crossing a street, and died as suddenly as if he had met his fate on the battle-field.

Colonel Johnston continues :

The brief sketch which I have given shows that his service in the late war was large, varied, and active, and the time during which he was in command, from Shiloh to Dalton, comprises the most eventful period of the war in the West. Soldiers with whom he left Pensacola marched northward till they came in sight of Cincinnati, and fought under him at Shiloh, Perryville, Murfreesboro, Chickamauga, and Missionary Ridge; and the historian who attempts impartially to give the details of his marches and his battles will find, though the net results of his efforts were not summed up in victory, what triumphs over obstacles he achieved through the valor of his men, his skill as an organizer and disciplinarian, and his fertility of resource in matters pertaining to the quartermaster, commissary, and ordnance departments. . . .

I am not his eulogist ; but, having been personally associated with him at the most critical periods of his active service, I feel that I owe it to him to bear attestation to the unselfish and untiring devotion he always gave to the service in which he was enlisted. He was not a soldier of the first rank like Lee, lacking some of those essential grander elements which give success to a commander in the field ; but he possessed qualifications such as, rightly directed, would have made him great in the Confederate army as Moltke in the Prussian. Sidney Johnston weighed him aright when he assigned him a position hitherto unknown in American warfare, but essential to the proper organization of a great army, and so recognized by the European powers. As a commander in the field, Bragg was too much engrossed with the details of moving, disciplining, organizing, and feeding his men, to master the broader and more comprehensive duties of a great captain in time of battle. His plans of battles, and orders promulgated, as at Murfreesboro and Chickamauga, will be found to evince more ability, and to comprehend remarkable accuracy of detail as well as clearness and precision.

In both the engagements named, he attacked boldly on the flank ; at the former on the left, and the latter on the right ; but, in the supreme moment, when Lee or Jackson would have made his victory complete, he failed in the power to modify his original plan, and lost from his tendency to adhere inflexibly to his predetermined line of action. . . .

But in the matter in which General Bragg has been most criticised and held up to reproach I think injustice has been done him. That he was strict is true, and that he incited fear and alarm, by his avowed purpose to enforce discipline at all hazards, is also true, and that he may have used in some instances extreme measures we may admit ; but that his action was inspired more by a sense of the necessity of his situation as an officer charged with the safety of a great army, than by a cruel disposition, is my firm conviction. He had been bred in a strict school as a West-Pointer, and as captain of an artillery-company in actual war knew the details as well as the necessity of discipline. He was no holiday soldier, and had none of the ulterior aspirations of a volunteer to lead him to curry favor with any one. He therefore exacted of all a rigid performance of duty, a neglect of which fell heavily upon any one, whether high or low; but I was too frequently cognizant of his good deeds of mercy to the delinquents, for light offenses, and commutations, reprieves, and pardon for capital ones, to let him rest under the imputation of a heartless man, or one who wielded his great powers cruelly. In his personal habits and conduct he was thoroughly temperate, in both meat and drink, discarding the use of liquor in any form, and waging ruthless war upon all who made it or sought to supply his men with it. He was untiring in his labors, methodical and systematic in the discharge of business, an early riser, and devout in his attention to his religious duties, being a communicant of the Episcopal Church. In person he was tall and spare, but of a lithe and sinewy frame, and capable of enduring any amount of fatigue. Though in social converse he was peculiarly mild and agreeable in manner, a peculiar conformation of eyebrows, which extended continuously from eye to eye, and a cold, steel-gray eye, which exhibited much of the white when animated, gave him in his sterner moods, or when roused, a very ferocious aspect, which made him a terror to all who incurred his displeasure.

I recall with gratitude and pleasure many acts of personal kindness and friendship of which I was the recipient at his hands, and for which, despite the occurrence of the circumstances which led to severance of association, I shall ever hold him in grateful memory.

Colonel Johnston also mentions his lack of that power of conciliation so necessary to the commander of volunteer troops.

Circumstances give to Colonel J. S. Johnston's estimate of General Bragg a more than ordinary judicial character. They are inserted with such fullness, because they conform very nearly to the well-settled opinions of the present writer. While Bragg was an able man, he was too rigid and narrow to be a great one. He was very harsh and intolerant where he once imbibed a prejudice, and he was not slow, nor always just, in assuming his conclusions. He was always a partisan, and merciless toward those who resisted him, even when his acts were clearly arbitrary. He did not inspire love or reverence, but he commanded respect and fear. He trusted too much those who agreed with him, and was apt to undervalue those who held aloof from or offended him. But if this rugged outline seems too much the likeness of a military despot, it should be added that his purposes were great, pure, and unselfish, and his aspirations high.

But, whatever may have been General Bragg's defects, he was conspicuous for one trait that marks him as the worthy citizen of a republic—a profound sense of public duty. Whether wise or unwise in the means adopted, the ultimate object of his endeavors was the public good. He was a patriot, and in the poverty and trials of his latter days no temptation shook his stoical fortitude in bearing the ills of his own lot, and in maintaining the righteousness and dignity of the cause for which he had suffered. Physical studies, culture from books, and the enlarging and mellowing influences of religion and domestic happiness, gilded his latter days. It is right to give such a man his exact place in history.

Before his death, General Bragg prepared for the present writer a sketch of the battle of Shiloh, the opening of which succinctly explains the preliminaries of that event. It is as follows :

The memory of a fallen commander, however much honored and revered by his countrymen, rarely receives full justice during the excitement of war, and especially when he meets his fate in an active campaign, or on a hotly-contested and unfortunate field. Few can know the motives which influenced, the acts which distinguished, or the opposition which met him. And rules of military etiquette frequently impose silence on these few.

After the disasters incident to their dispersed condition, which naturally befell the Confederate arms, in the winter of 1861 and 1862, and which culminated in the surrender at Fort Donelson, General A. Sidney Johnston, then commanding all the Confederate forces in the Western Department, acting against the advice of some of his best and ablest commanders, wisely determined to concentrate in the valley of the Mississippi, and there risk his own fate and that of the cause he sustained.[1] This movement, directed upon Corinth—commenced early in the month of March—was not fully consummated when information of the enemy's dispositions determined Johnston to attack with the forces then available. In a period of four weeks, fragments of commands from Bowling Green, Kentucky, under Hardee ; Columbus, Kentucky, under Polk ; and Pensacola, Mobile, and New Orleans, under Bragg ; with such new levies as could be hastily raised, all badly armed and equipped, were united at and near Corinth, and for the first time organized as an army. It was an heterogeneous mass, in which there was more enthusiasm than discipline, more capacity than knowledge, and more valor than instruction. Rifles, rifled and smooth-bore muskets —some of them originally percussion, others hastily altered from flint-locks by Yankee contractors, many still with the old flint and steel—and shot-guns of all sizes and patterns, held place in the same regiments. The task of organizing such a command in four weeks, and supplying it, especially with ammunition suitable for action, was simply appalling. It was undertaken, however, with a

[1] He so stated to me at Corinth, when, as chief of staff, I advised and he ordered the troops from the Trans-Mississippi to that place, before the battle of Shiloh.

The Night before the Battle of Shiloh.

cool, quiet self-control, by calling to his aid the best knowledge and talent at his command, which not only inspired confidence, but soon yielded the natural fruits of system, order, and discipline.

This force, about 40,000 of all arms, was divided into four corps, commanded respectively by Major-Generals Polk, Bragg, and Hardee, and Brigadier-General Breckinridge, General Albert Sidney Johnston in chief command; and General Beauregard, who, having recently come out from the army in Virginia, and, being in feeble health, was assigned no special command, but was designated in orders as "second in command," and as such aided the commander-in-chief with his counsel and advice.

The difficulties mentioned by General Bragg of arming the troops were increased by the process of exchange in many instances for new weapons, some of which were put into the hands of the troops only the day before they marched against the enemy. General Beauregard likewise mentions that

want of general officers needful for the proper organization of divisions and brigades of an army brought thus suddenly together, and other difficulties in the way of an effective organization, delayed the movements until the night of the 2d inst. (April).

At this time occurred a remarkable episode, which General Beauregard gives, in the following words, in a letter to the writer:

When General Johnston first met me at Corinth, he proposed, after our staff officers had retired, to turn over the command of the united forces to me; but I positively declined, on his account and that of the "cause," telling him that I had come to *assist*, but not to *supersede* him, and offering to give him *all* the assistance in my power. He then concluded to remain in command. It was one of the most affecting scenes of my life.

Colonel William Preston, in his letter of April 18, 1862, to the writer, says:

General Beauregard was offered the immediate command of the whole force, but he declined it, as his health was bad, and General Johnston assumed it in person.

When General Johnston told his purpose to Colonel Munford, that officer remonstrated with him, saying that he appeared to have lost Tennessee and Kentucky. "This battle may regain them, and reëstablish your jeoparded fame; yet you, on such an occasion, would invite another to win the glory of redeeming what you had lost." He smiled, and said, "I think it but right to make the offer." Colonel Munford pressed upon him other considerations as to the importance of his services to the country, to which General Johnston replied, "I will be present at the battle, and will see that nothing goes wrong."

General Johnston felt constrained to make this offer, because he had brought with him the smaller fraction of the united forces, and he was on a field that he had set apart for Beauregard's control. That officer had been for some time on the ground, and he was unwilling that a subordinate should suffer by his arrival. He would make any sacrifice himself rather than take one laurel from the brow of a fellow-soldier.

It was his wish to give General Beauregard the command of the troops in the field, which would have secured to that officer whatever of glory might be won at Shiloh; but it was in no wise his intention to abdicate the supreme command, or the superintendence of affairs in the management of the department or the movements of the army. His offer to Beauregard was certainly an act of rare magnanimity. A somewhat analogous case in his career occurred at the battle of the Neches, in 1839. While Secretary of War of Texas, he attended his subordinate on the field, gave him the benefit of his military experience, and then received from his hand the report of the combat. General Johnston had no diffidence as to his fitness for command. He once said regretfully to the writer, during the Mexican War: "There is one thing I *know* I can do; I am competent to command troops." In this instance, with General Beauregard, his idea of unselfishness, even though heroic, seems somewhat overstrained; for he would chiefly have suffered in case of a failure, but would not have shared in the glories of a victory.

The rumor of this occurrence also gave rise to the following vigorous protest from Governor George W. Johnson:

BURNSVILLE, MISSISSIPPI, *March* 26, 1862.

MY DEAR SIR: A rumor has reached me that has filled me with just alarm for our cause, and which induces me again to write to you, relying on the friendship which I feel for you as my excuse. It is rumored here that you intend to yield to the senseless clamors of fools and pretenders, and to give up the command of the army at the very crisis of our fate. This, if done, will be fatal to our cause, or others will reap what ought to be the just reward of all your noble self-sacrifice for your country. I cannot sit by silent while this is being done. You did what was right; you have in your own hands ample means of self-defense against those who assail you; and, as your friend, I sincerely rejoiced when I heard that Congress had asked for explanations—because this, I knew, would at once break the seal of silence which your own noble sense of justice and mercy to others might have imposed upon you. You left Bowling Green when they would give you no reënforcements, and when it was impossible to defend Fort Donelson except by yielding that position. You had sent all to that point who could be spared from your army in the presence of Buell's army. The event showed that you had sent enough troops to that point—for we had whipped the enemy; and if the generals there commanding chose to surrender, and did so surrender, after victory and to a retreating foe, it is their fault—not yours.

From this disastrous *surrender*, and not from the defense of Donelson, have resulted the subsequent retreat and concentration of your army here. We are in the right place, at the right time, and the proudest victory of the war awaits you, unless you commit suicide, by yielding up the command of your army when it most needs energy and an active head. *You must not do this.* I beg that you will not do it, both for your own fame and the good of our country. If I hear that you are resolved upon this course, I will despair of our cause. It will sink under the curse of Heaven, upon a people, who joined *like* wolves, and *with a few wolves* in sheep's clothing, to hunt down the noblest and purest man it has been my good-fortune to know. Very truly and respectfully your friend,

GEORGE W. JOHNSON.

General A. SIDNEY JOHNSTON, headquarters, Corinth, Mississippi.

It is proper to say that General Beauregard considers himself as having inspired General Johnston with the idea of attacking Grant at Shiloh. But he must be mistaken. This was the purpose for which he had concentrated his army at Corinth. What he said to Schaller, Whitthorne, and many others, has already been stated. It was known to the President, to his own staff and generals, and to others, that his main design, in the tremendous effort by which he had transferred his army from Nashville to Corinth, was to fight the enemy in detail. In view of Grant's anticipated movement, and to be able to strike him before Buell's arrival, he had made that race of life and death. He was now within arm's-length of his enemy. While every hour of delay was important to him to augment, organize, arm, and rest his troops, it was never his intention to permit a junction of Buell with Grant. Buell's advance was to be the signal for action. As soon as the intelligence of it was received, his resolution was taken. The information reached him at eleven o'clock at night. In two hours the orders for an advance were issued. This was on the night of April 2d.

President Davis has assured the writer that he concurred in all of General Johnston's plans. They likewise received, about this time, the sanction of a name then, like General Johnston's, under the shadow of legislative disfavor and popular opposition, and supported by the almost unaided hand of the President, but since illustrious—that of General Robert E. Lee. General Lee wrote him a letter, received just before the battle of Shiloh, the text of which is here given. As General Lee was at that time in Richmond, acting as military adviser of the President, this letter may be held to convey Mr. Davis's views as well as his own.

LETTER OF GENERAL LEE TO GENERAL JOHNSTON.

RICHMOND, *March* 26, 1862.

MY DEAR GENERAL: No one has sympathized with you in the troubles with which you are surrounded more sincerely than myself. I have watched your every movement, and know the difficulties with which you have had to contend. I hope your cares will be diminished, if not removed, when your junction with the other lines of your army has been completed, which must be accomplished by this time. I need not urge you, when your army is united, to deal a blow at the enemy in your front, if possible, before his rear gets up from Nashville. You have him divided, and keep him so, if you can. Wishing you, my dear general, every success and happiness, with my earnest prayers for the safety of your whole army, and that victory may attend your movements,

                    I remain, truly and sincerely your friend,
            (Signed)   R. E. LEE.
General A. S. JOHNSTON.

General Johnston was not insensible to the perils of his aggressive movement, or to the strength of the enemy's position from the nature of the ground and the proximity of his gunboats, affording means of retreat or reënforcement ; but it was necessary to destroy that army without delay. To effect this, immediate battle must be delivered. On this General Johnston at once resolved.

The following is from Colonel Munford's address at Memphis :

When General Johnston terminated his retreat from Kentucky, at Corinth, he found General Beauregard in command of a small army, to which he united his own. All available troops were concentrated as rapidly as possible, and, before moving on the enemy at Shiloh, upward of *thirty-five thousand men* of all arms were in hand. General Beauregard's health was feeble. He was slowly recovering from a severe attack, which had given just cause for serious alarm ; but, sick as he was, he was indefatigable in duty. Much, however, devolved on the general-in-chief. Soon after his headquarters were established, General Johnston requested General Bragg, then a major-general of volunteers, to act as his adjutant-general, especially during the reorganization of the army, which was soon to take place. In a day or two he told me Bragg had consented, *but would retain his command* [as corps commander] in the approaching battle. This was my first *knowledge* that a battle was imminent. Questions have been mooted as to who projected and who planned the battle of Shiloh. I do not know. I have heard, however, from President Davis's own lips, that the concentration of troops at Corinth, for this purpose, was agreed upon between *him* and *General Johnston* beforehand ; and that, two days before the battle was fought, General Johnston sent him a despatch in cipher. But I regard these questions and their solution as wholly unimportant. The facts hereafter revealed, which took place on the field the day before the battle, demonstrate that, but for Sidney Johnston, no such battle would have been fought. As far as this question of honor between the generals is concerned, it was emphatically Sidney Johnston's battle, though this fact would never be inferred from the official report of it sent to the Government.

General Johnston was most active in his attention to all the details of reorganization and preparations for the battle. At an early stage in these proceedings, he said he could add a full brigade to his strength, if he could substitute negroes for soldiers detailed as cooks and teamsters, and asked my assistance. I advised sending out men of well-known character from the army into the counties in the rear, with authority to hire, for sixty or ninety days, such negroes as he wanted, and to give obligations binding the Government to pay their value as agreed upon, if, *on any account*, they were not returned. It was adopted, but we got less than fifty negroes, the men sent out saying, " Those people have given their sons freely enough, but it is folly to talk to them about a negro or a mule." The general said : " I regret this disappointment ; a single brigade may determine the fate of a battle. These people do not seem to be aware how valueless would be their negroes were we beaten." And on the morning of the 4th of April, our horses already waiting under saddle, I will ever remember his pause on the door-step, lost in thought, and how, looking up, he muttered, half aloud, " Yes, I believe I have overlooked nothing."

General Beauregard informs the writer :

I prepared the order of march and of battle, which were submitted by me to Generals Johnston and Bragg, in presence of Colonel Jordan, chief of staff of the whole army, and they were accepted *without one word of alteration.* They were then put in proper form by Colonel Jordan, and furnished to the corps commanders.

These orders are in Appendix C to this chapter. In a letter from General Bragg to the writer occur the following comments :

GALVESTON, TEXAS, *December* 16, 1874.

DEAR COLONEL: Yours of the 8th instant, asking for any facts in my possession as to the authorship of the plan for the battle of Shiloh, is received. The *details* of that plan, arranged after General A. Sidney Johnston decided on delivering battle and had given his instructions, were made up and published to the army in full from the adjutant-general's office. My *first knowledge of them* was derived from this general order, the authorship of which has been claimed by General Beauregard.

Conceding the arrangement of the details to Beauregard or Jordan, General Bragg continues :

In this case, as I understood then, and still believe, Johnston gave general instructions for the general movement. . . . Over his (Jordan's) signature these elaborated details reached the army.

General Bragg goes on to say that Johnston's general plan was admirable, but condemns the elaboration of the details. He continues :

When the time arrived for execution, you know well what occurred. In spite of opposition and prediction of failure, Johnston firmly and decidedly ordered and led the attack in the execution of his general plan, and, notwithstanding the faulty arrangement of troops, was eminently successful up to the moment of his fall. *The victory was won.* How it was lost the official reports will show, and history has already recorded.

Independent of General Beauregard's explicit statement, and General Bragg's recollection, nothing could be more natural than that General Johnston should confide the elaboration of the plan of advance and the orders for the movements of troops to General Beauregard. When that officer reported to him he was assigned to command at Columbus, with special reference to his distinction as a soldier and an engineer. He had now been five or six weeks in the neighborhood of Corinth studying this precise problem. What were the best arrangements for an advance against Grant was dependent on an acquaintance with the roads and the nature of the ground to be contested. This was presumably within General Beauregard's knowledge, though his adjutant-general says he had no topographical information, "which hitherto the Confederate generals had been unable to acquire of that region, and of which indeed they could learn nothing definite." [1] Governor Harris informs the writer that General Johnston seemed to understand the topography of the battle-field thoroughly, principally through information from Major Waddell, now of St. Louis, who showed peculiar talents as a scout.

General Johnston has also been censured for "miscalculating" the time it would take his troops to march from Corinth to the battle-field. General Beauregard had arranged all these details with great particularity; and though there were some mistakes and inherent defects in the order of march which led to confusion and delay, the great obstacles to the rapid movement of the troops were their own rawness and the rain and mud—obstacles which neither foresight nor skill could avert or remedy.

The Comte de Paris advances, in the following paragraph, a better-grounded charge :

We are also of the opinion that they committed a grave mistake in deploying the different corps in successive lines along the whole front of the army, instead of intrusting a part of that front to each corps, itself formed in several lines.

It will be seen by examining the orders issued, and the details of the advance given in the course of this narrative, that the Confederate army attacked the Federal position in three lines parallel to its supposed front. The Comte de Paris claims substantially that the three corps should have attacked by lines perpendicular, instead of parallel, to that front. There is force in the objection ; and that such was General Johnston's original intention is clearly evinced by the following telegram :

CORINTH, *April* 3, 1862.

General Buell in motion 30,000 strong, rapidly from Columbia by Clifton to Savannah. Mitchell behind him with 10,000. Confederate forces—40,000—ordered forward to offer battle near Pittsburg. Division from Bethel, main body from Corinth, reserve from Burnsville, converging to-morrow near Monterey on Pittsburg. Beauregard second in command, Polk the left, Bragg the centre, Hardee the right wing, Breckinridge the reserve. *Hope engagement before Buell can form junction.*

To the President, Richmond.

The words italicized are in General Johnston's own handwriting in the original dispatch.

Why this plan was changed in the orders issued the writer cannot tell. Doubtless General Johnston assented to the change in deference

[1] Jordan's "Life of Forrest," p. 110.

to General Beauregard's opinions in the matter, and for reasons which seemed sufficient at the time. It seems apparent now that much of the confusion, entanglement, and delay, that occurred on the march between Monterey and Mickey's, and of the subsequent intermingling of commands, might have been avoided by adhering to the original plan. At the same time it may be said in extenuation that the entire organization of the army was so recent and temporary in its character, that the breaking up of the corps did not greatly affect either the *morale* of the troops or the result.

But important as were the preliminaries—the maps, the roads, the methods of putting his army face to face with the enemy, which General Johnston had to take on trust—he knew that the chief *strategy* of the battle was in the decision to fight. Once in the presence of the enemy, he knew that the result would depend *on the way in which his troops were handled.* This was his part of the work, and he felt full confidence in his own ability to carry it out successfully.

APPENDIX.

HEADQUARTERS, ARMY OF THE MISSISSIPPI, }
CORINTH, MISSISSIPPI, *April* 3, 1862. }

Special Orders, No. 8.

I.—In the impending movement the corps of this army will march, assemble, and take order of battle in the following manner, it being assumed that the enemy is in position about a mile in advance of Shiloh church, with its right resting on Owl Creek, and its left on Lick Creek:

1. The *Third Corps,* under Major-General Hardee, will advance as soon as practicable on the Ridge road from Corinth to what is known as the "Bark" road, passing about half a mile northward of the Workhouse. The head of the column will bivouac if possible to-night, at Mickey's house, at the intersection of the road from Monterey to Savannah. The cavalry, thrown well forward during the march to reconnoitre and prevent surprise, will halt in front of the Mickey house on the Bark road.

2. Major Waddell, aide-de-camp to General Beauregard, with two good guides, will report for service to Major-General Hardee.

3. At 3 A. M. to-morrow the Third Corps with the left in front will continue to advance by the Bark road, until within sight of the enemy's outposts or advanced positions, when it will be deployed in line of battle according to the nature of the ground, its left resting on Owl Creek, its right toward Lick Creek, supported on that flank by half of its cavalry; the left flank being supported by the other half. The interval between the extreme right of this corps and Lick Creek will be filled by a brigade or division—according to the extent of the ground—from the Second Corps. These troops, during the battle, will also be under the command of Major-General Hardee.

He will make the proper disposition of the artillery along the line of battle, remembering that the rifled guns are of long range, and should be placed on any commanding positions in rear of his infantry to fire mainly on the reserves and second line of the enemy, but occasionally will be directed on his batteries and heads of columns.

II.—The Second Corps, under Major-General Braxton Bragg, will assemble on Monterey, and move thence as early as practicable; the right wing with left in front by the road from Monterey to Savannah, the head of column to reach the immediate vicinity of Mickey's house, at the intersection with the Bark road, before sunset.

The cavalry with this wing will take position on the road to Savannah beyond Mickey's as far as Owl Creek, having advanced guards and pickets well to the front. The left wing of this corps will advance at the same time, also, left in front, by the road from Monterey to Purdy—the head of the column to reach, by night, the intersection of that road with the Bark road. This wing will continue the movement in the morning as soon as the rear of the Third Corps shall have passed the Purdy road, and which it will then follow.

The Second Corps will form the second line of battle, about one thousand yards in rear of the first line; it will be formed, if practicable, with regiments in double columns at half distance, disposed as advantageously as the nature of the ground will admit; and, with a view to facility of deployment, the artillery placed as may seem best to Major-General Bragg.

III.—The First Corps, under Major-General Polk, with the exception of the detached division at Bethel, will take up its line of march by the Ridge road, hence to Pittsburg, half an hour after the Third Corps shall have passed Corinth, and will bivouac to-night in rear of that corps, and on to-morrow will follow the movements of said corps, with the same interval of time as to-day. When its head of column shall reach the vicinity of the Mickey house, it will be halted in column or massed on the line of the Bark road, according to the nature of the ground, as a reserve. Meanwhile, one regiment of its cavalry will be placed in observation on the road from Johnston's house to Stantonville, with advanced guards and pickets thrown out well in advance toward Stantonville. Another regiment or battalion of cavalry will be posted in the same manner on the road from Monterey to Purdy, with its rear resting on or about the intersection of that road with the Bark road, having advanced guards and pickets in the direction of Purdy.

The forces at Bethel and Purdy will defend their positions as already instructed, if attacked; otherwise they will assemble on Purdy, and thence advance with advanced guards, flankers, and all other prescribed military precautions, forming a junction with the rest of the First Corps at the intersection of that road with the Bark road, leading from Corinth.

IV.—The Reserve of the forces will be concentrated by the shortest and best route at Monterey, as soon as the rear of the Second Corps shall have moved out of that place. Its commander will take up the best position, whence to advance, either in the direction of Mickey's or Pratt's house, on the direct road to Pittsburg—if that road is found practicable—or in the direction of the Ridge road to Hamburg, throwing all its cavalry on the latter road as far as its intersection with the one to Pittsburg, passing through Grier's Ford, on Lick Creek.

This cavalry will throw well forward advanced guards and videttes toward Grier's Ford, and in the direction of Hamburg, and, during the impending battle, when called to the field of combat, will move by the Grier's Ford road.

A regiment of the infantry reserve will be thrown forward to the intersection of the Gravel Hill road with the Ridge road to Hamburg, as a support to the cavalry.

The Reserve will be formed of Breckinridge's, Bowen's, and Statham's brigades, as now organized, the whole under the command of Brigadier-General Breckinridge.

V.—General Bragg will detach the Fifty-first and Fifty-second Regiments, Tennessee Volunteers, Blount's Alabama, and Desha's Arkansas Battalions, and Bain's battery, from his corps, which, with two of Carroll's regiments, now *en route* for these headquarters, will form a garrison for the post and depot of Corinth.

VI.—Strong guards will be left at the railroad-bridges between Iuka and Corinth, to be furnished in due proportions from the commands at Iuka, Burnsville, and Corinth.

VII.—Proper guards will be left at the camps of the several regiments of the forces in the field; corps commanders will determine the strength of these guards.

VIII.—Wharton's regiment of Texas Cavalry will be ordered forward at once, to scout on the road from Monterey to Savannah, between Mickey's and its intersection with the Pittsburg-Purdy road. It will annoy and harass any force of the enemy moving by the latter way to assail Cheatham's division at Purdy.

IX.—The chief-engineer of the forces will take all due measures and precautions, and give all requisite orders for the repairs of the bridges, causeways, and roads, on which our troops may move in the execution of these orders.

X.—The troops, so individually intelligent, and with such great interests involved in the issue, are urgently enjoined to be observant of the orders of their superiors in the hour of battle. Their officers must constantly endeavor to hold them in hand, and prevent the waste of ammunition by heedless, aimless firing —the fire should be slow—always at a distinct mark. It is expected that much and effective work will be done by the bayonet.

By command of General A. S. JOHNSTON:

THOMAS JORDAN, *Assistant Adjutant-General.*

For General A. S. JOHNSTON, commanding Army of Mississippi.

HEADQUARTERS, ARMY OF THE MISSISSIPPI, }
CORINTH, *April 3*, 1862.   }

Memorandum for the Commanders of the Corps and of the Reserve.

I.—As soon as the reserve shall have taken position at Monterey, a strong working-party will be sent to repair the bridges, causeway, and road across Lick Creek, on the direct road from Monterey to Pittsburg, so that it may be used in any forward movement of the reserve.

II.—In the approaching battle every effort should be made to turn the left flank of the enemy so as to cut off his line of retreat to the Tennessee River, and throw him back on Owl Creek, where he will be obliged to surrender. Every precaution must also be taken on our part to prevent unnecessary exposure of our men to the enemy's gunboats.

By command of General A. S. JOHNSTON:

THOMAS JORDAN, *Assistant Adjutant-General.*

For the commander of the forces, Army of Mississippi, Corinth, Mississippi.

CHAPTER XXXIII.

BEFORE THE BATTLE.

ON Thursday morning, April 3d, at about one o'clock, preliminary orders were issued to hold the troops in readiness to move at a moment's notice, with five days' provisions and 100 rounds of ammunition. The orders for the march and battle were issued later in the day—in the afternoon, as it seems—after they had been elaborated by General Beauregard.

When it became apparent that the orders meant an advance and an attack upon the enemy—meant battle—the soldiers, full of ardor, were aroused to the utmost enthusiasm. With somewhat hasty preparation—for time was precious—the movement began. Hardee led the advance, the Third Corps, that afternoon. He marched from Corinth, by the northernmost route, known as the Ridge road, which, near Shiloh, led into another, known as the Bark road. Bivouacking that night on the way, he arrived next morning at Mickey's, a house seventeen or eighteen miles, by that route, from Corinth, and four or five miles from Pittsburg.

The Second Corps, under Bragg, marched by the direct road to Pittsburg, through Monterey. This road proved so narrow and bad that the head of Bragg's column did not reach Monterey until 11 A. M. on the 4th, but bivouacked that night near Mickey's, in rear of Hardee's corps, with a proper interval.

The First Corps, commanded by Polk, consisted of two divisions, under Cheatham and Clark. Clark's division was ordered to follow Hardee on the Ridge road, at an interval of half an hour, and to halt near Mickey's. This halt was to allow Bragg's corps, whose route from Monterey crossed the Ridge or Bark road at that point, to fall in behind Hardee, at 1,000 yards' interval, and form a second line of battle. Polk's corps was to form the left wing of the third line of battle; and Breckinridge's reserve the right wing.

Polk's other division, under Cheatham, was on outpost duty, at and near Bethel on the Mobile & Ohio Railroad, and was about as far from Mickey's, the point of concentration, as Corinth was. Cheatham's orders were to defend himself if attacked; otherwise, to assemble his forces at Purdy, and pursue the route to Monterey, with proper military precautions. Acting on these instructions, Cheatham did not advance until the morning of the 5th; but he effected his junction at four o'clock that afternoon, and took position, as the left wing of Polk's

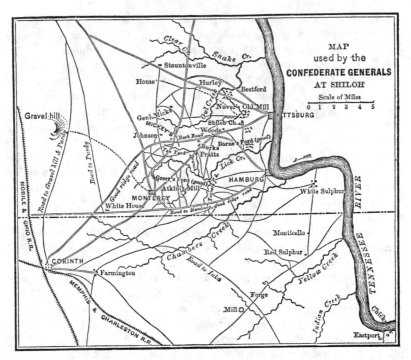

MAP
used by the
CONFEDERATE GENERALS
AT SHILOH
Scale of Miles
0 1 2 3 4 5

corps, as early as some other divisions whose presence was necessary to the attack. These movements were construed by General Lew Wallace as a reconnaissance in force against his own division at Crump's Landing, and held him in check during the 5th and the 6th, the first day of the battle.

Breckinridge's three brigades—a division, in fact, but by courtesy a reserve corps—having received their orders on the afternoon of April 3d,[1] moved from Burnsville on April 4th, at 3 A. M., by way of Farmington, toward Monterey, fourteen miles distant. "Some Enfield rifles, with accoutrements and ammunition, just received, were distributed about nightfall" to supply deficiencies, and rations were prepared during the night.[2]

The road was even worse than those from Corinth. The corps struggled painfully on, with poor progress. After a hard day's march, it bivouacked on the road. Part of the artillery was late at night reaching its position, owing to the difficulty of the road. Breckinridge had ridden forward to Monterey, and had met Generals Johnston and Bragg in consultation. He hoped, then, to be up in time, and received orders to join in the attack next morning.

[1] E. P. Thompson's " History of the First Kentucky Brigade," p. 87.   [2] Ibid.

At midnight he sent a dispatch, saying his artillery was stuck in the mud, and had stopped his train. Major Hayden says General Johnston sent him word, " Cut a new road for your column." It did not, however, effect its junction with the other corps until late Saturday afternoon, the 5th, owing to the rains on Friday and Saturday, the storm of Friday night, and other causes that delayed all the corps.

The Confederate cavalry, thrown well to the front and flanks, encountered the pickets of the enemy. In some sharp skirmishes they took a few prisoners, a major, two lieutenants, and eight privates, and wounded eight more. They lost some men, captured. Sherman says he took ten prisoners.[1] A Federal reconnaissance had been sent out under Colonel Buckland, and encountered Cleburne's brigade of Hardee's corps, but retired without ascertaining anything important, or surmising that General Johnston's army was approaching.

Bragg says[2] that, where this duty had not been previously performed, " the commanders of divisions and brigades were assembled that night, the order was read to them, and the topography of the enemy's position was explained as far as understood by us," which was imperfectly enough. They knew that in the recesses of that forest, between those creeks, 50,000 invaders were posted ; but where, or how, and with what preparation, no man could tell. Many of these soldiers, familiar with the dangerous sports of their native South, must have felt as when hunting in the dense canebrake, and, following the trail, they drew near the den of some great bear, hidden in the thicket, with whom momently they expected encounter and mortal struggle.

The order was to march at three o'clock in the morning, so as to attack the enemy early on the 5th. So far as human knowledge can reach, if this order could have been carried out, Grant and his army would have been destroyed. But man proposes, and God disposes. The same elements that had opened watery pathways up the rivers to the Federal fleet, against all expectation, by unprecedented floods, were again on the side of the strongest battalions. It may not be amiss here to remark that those people who think that " whatever is, is right," in human affairs as well as in the order of Nature, have drawn exceedingly strong and unwarrantable inferences from these and other providential dispensations as to the justice of the Federal cause.

This is no place for such argument ; but the wise Preacher, the son of David, king in Jerusalem, has answered this superstition when he said :

There is a vanity which is done upon the earth; that there be just men, unto whom it happeneth according to the work of the wicked; again, there be wicked men, to whom it happeneth according to the work of the righteous.[3]

---

[1] Sherman's " Memoirs," vol. i., p. 235.   [2] Report of the battle.   [3] Ecclesiastes viii. 14.

Again :

All things come alike to all: there is one event to the righteous, and to the wicked.

And again:

I have seen servants upon horses, and princes walking as servants upon the earth.[2]

And a greater Son of David answered the painful and perplexing question by a reply that reaches beyond the judgments of this world :

There were present at that season some that told him of the Galileans, whose blood Pilate had mingled with their sacrifices. And Jesus answering said unto them, Suppose ye that these Galileans were sinners above all the Galileans, because they suffered such things? I tell you, Nay: but, except ye repent, ye shall all likewise perish.[3]

The clouds had been sending down their showers on the 4th, to the great annoyance and detention of the moving columns. But, after midnight, they gathered for a great outburst upon the unsheltered soldiers. The leafy covert of the forest gave slight protection to the troops in bivouac. The storm broke upon them about 2 A. M.; and the drenching rain poured in torrents as they lay, without tents, exposed to its fury. The men were anxious most of all, but often in vain, "to keep their powder dry." Nevertheless, at three o'clock, the appointed hour, the whole army was put under arms, to be ready to advance. There they stood, anxious to go forward ; but it was impossible to move in the pitch-darkness, over flooded roads and swollen streams, with the cold, driving rain beating upon them.

With almost criminal recklessness, many of the soldiers discharged their small-arms, to find out the condition of the cartridges. General Johnston, as he rode along the lines on the 5th, tried to prevent the recurrence of this. Bragg alludes to it with great severity. Colonel E. L. Drake, of Fayetteville, Tennessee, who was at that time serving in Bate's Second Tennessee Regiment, of which he has furnished a valuable memoir to the writer, gives the following statement. His regiment was in Cleburne's brigade, and on the extreme left of Hardee's line. He says :

The wishes of General Johnston to move quietly were not generally regarded ; and, at one point on the march, the presence of a wild deer, which ran along the lines, evoked a yell among Hardee's men which could have been heard for miles. Hard showers fell. There was great uneasiness among the men lest their guns should fail fire ; and many pieces were discharged on the route, and on Sunday morning as the lines were forming for the attack. It seems to be

---

[1] Ecclesiastes ix. 2.   [2] Ibid., x. 7.   [3] Luke xiii. 1.

certain that our presence was disregarded by the enemy up to a late hour Saturday night. Their bands were serenading at different headquarters until after midnight. This I have since learned from a Federal officer who was present. At the time, the object of the music was misunderstood by the Confederates, being attributed to the arrival of reënforcements to take up positions for the morrow's battle. This idea was strengthened by an occasional cheer, which rang out in that direction.

It was supposed at the time that the fusillade might have aroused the enemy to a sense of their peril; and it convinced General Beauregard that a surprise was impossible. It was sufficiently distinct at the Confederate rear to keep it continually on the alert with the apprehension of an attack in front. But, whether from the direction of the wind, the noise and pelting of the tempest, the neglect and drowsiness of the Federal outpost, or their disregard of the firing in front—a prevalent practice among the pickets—no heed was taken of these hostile warnings by the Northern army. If, as has been alleged, the enemy's pickets were only half a mile out, Hardee's line was still perhaps two miles off, which might account for the failure to hear their random shots.

At daylight, on Saturday, the 5th of April, Hardee advanced, and by seven o'clock was sufficiently out of the way to allow Bragg to move his command. Before ten o'clock Hardee's corps had reached the outposts, and developed the lines of the enemy. The Confederate advance immediately deployed in line of battle, about a mile and a half west of Shiloh church, where Lick Creek and Owl Creek approach most nearly, a space of about three miles. Hardee's corps not being sufficiently strong, it had been provided that Gladden's brigade, of Bragg's corps, should occupy his right. This line extended from Owl Creek to Lick Creek. General Johnston had reached Bragg's headquarters early, and before seven o'clock his column was also put in motion; and Gladden's and Withers's other brigades were placed in line of battle, in due time, the latter about 800 yards in rear of Hardee's line. Ruggles's division did not come up promptly, and Polk's corps was held motionless by its delay.

Having recounted thus far the events of these days, let us recur briefly to General Johnston's personal movements. He left Corinth on the morning of the 4th, and arrived at Monterey at 1 P.M. Soon after, Clanton's Alabama Cavalry brought in some Federal prisoners; and it was manifest from their surprise and their conversation with the staff that the Confederate attack was wholly unexpected.

During the afternoon, General Johnston conferred with Bragg, Breckinridge, and other officers. He halted that night at Monterey. He handed to Munford and some others of his staff a small roll of papers, containing his maps and the plan of battle, with the intended positions of the different commands, and requested them to become familiar with the contents, that he might be able to use their services to the best advantage on the day of battle. Munford says:

We were to attack his army in their encampments between these creeks and that river. The military problem was so to distribute an army of a little over 30,000 men as effectually to cover our front. Its solution, involving the much-talked-of plan, was exceedingly simple. It was assumed as a postulate that no force the enemy could oppose could cut through three lines of Confederates. The army was therefore deployed into three lines.

General Johnston slept but little on the night of the 4th. He was too old a soldier not to know that the storm would delay the movement of his army. It abated about five o'clock; and, by half-past five, he was on horseback, on his way to the front, with his staff. Being joined by General Beauregard, he rode to Bragg's position; and, under his orders, by seven o'clock, Withers's division was put in motion, as has been stated. General Johnston meanwhile rode forward to Hardee's line, where some slight skirmishing seemed to be going on, which was really, however, the random firing already mentioned.

Munford tells as follows of how the morning passed:

Everything had been calculated with the utmost precision—the hour for breaking camp, the order and stages of march, and the exact time at which each separate command was to deploy into line on the field. All this was to be done by 7 A. M. on the 5th, and the battle to begin at eight. General Johnston and staff arrived on the field a little after six o'clock. Hardee's line was already formed, and the general-in-chief took position a little way in its rear. In a little while Bragg's right wing, under Withers, deployed into line, but eight, nine o'clock came, and the division on his left was nowhere to be seen. About half-past nine, General Johnston sent me to General Bragg to know "why the column on his left was not in position." Bragg replied: "Tell General Johnston the head of that column has not made its appearance. I have sent to the rear for information, and as soon as I learn the cause of its detention he shall be informed." Ten, eleven, half-past eleven o'clock came, and General Johnston began to show signs of impatience. I was again sent back to know of Bragg "*why* the column on his left was not *yet* in position." I received identically the same answer he had given earlier in the morning. At last half-past twelve o'clock came, and no appearance of the missing column, nor any report from Bragg. General Johnston, looking first at his watch, then glancing at the position of the sun, exclaimed, "This is perfectly puerile! This is not *war!*—Let us have our horses." He, Major Albert Smith, Captain Nathaniel Wickliffe, and myself, rode to the rear until we found the missing column standing stock-still, with its head some distance out in an open field. General Polk's reserves were ahead of it, with their wagons and artillery blocking up the road. General Johnston ordered them to clear the road, and the missing column to move forward. There was much chaffering among those implicated as to who should bear the blame. It was charged on General Polk; but the plucky old bishop unhorsed his accusers right on the spot. I believe their commander, General

Ruggles, was finally blamed. . . . It was about four o'clock when the lines were completely formed; too late, of course, to begin the battle then.

There was sharp controversy then and afterward as to where the fault lay. Polk's answer was sufficient—that Clark's division was ready to move at 3 A. M. His orders were to wait for the passage of Bragg's corps, and to move and form his line in rear of Ruggles's division, which composed Bragg's left wing. He could not advance or establish his line until this had passed. The road was not clear until 2 P. M.; yet he got Clark's division into line of battle by four o'clock, and Cheatham, who had come up on the left, soon after. Breckinridge's line was formed on Polk's right about the same time. Thus was the army arrayed in three lines of battle late Saturday afternoon.

The detention was unexpected; and, perhaps, will never be fully explained. The rain and storm, the mud, the passage through an unknown forest tract, over narrow dirt-roads, and the rawness of the advancing army, sufficiently account for the delay. There was, doubtless, some confusion or mistake of orders in Ruggles's division; but what would have been gross misconduct at a later period was very pardonable in a militia as uninstructed as the troops who marched out against Shiloh. Field and staff officers, fresh from the counting-house or plantation, with unaccustomed duties, ignorant of the country, must sometimes have signally failed in the performance of the most obvious duties. It is certain that one of Ruggles's brigade commanders, who was on outpost duty at Monterey, received no orders at all, and was left to surmise the meaning of the whole movement, as regiment after regiment filed by. Under the circumstances it is useless to attach censure to particular individuals or commands.

One real source of the entanglement and confusion of commands arose from the order of march and the routes by which the troops were brought upon the field. One ground of General Bragg's censure of these arrangements was probably this: After Hardee, every column was so conducted to the field that it was compelled to halt at a fork of a road until some other corps had passed by and deployed, before it could establish its own line of battle. A trained staff and better topographical information would have prevented this.

There is a letter from General Bragg, written at 10 A. M., April 4th, addressed to "General Johnston or General Beauregard," from Monterey, which has never been alluded to, and which may also throw some light on the subject of the detention. General Bragg says:

MY DEAR GENERAL: I reached here at half-past eight o'clock, ahead of my rear division. Bad roads, inefficient transportation badly managed, and the usual delays of a first move of new troops, have caused the delay. My first division is at Mickey's; and the ignorance of the guide for the second, as well as the reports I receive from people here, induces me to order my second division to move on the same road as the first. I am also influenced to do this from the information I have of General Hardee's advance. . . .

I will send a courier to notify General Polk of my change. . . .

By the first division General Bragg means Withers's ; by the second, Ruggles's.

The "special orders as to movement of troops" directed Bragg to move from Monterey to Mickey's with Withers's division, while Ruggles's division was to move from Monterey on the road to Purdy, which crossed the Bark road more than two miles in rear of Mickey's. Had Ruggles pursued this route, he could have passed to the left of Mickey's, and deployed without interference or obstruction from Hardee's or Withers's division. But Bragg's order changing Ruggles's line of march, and bringing him in rear of these commands, delayed any movement until they had cleared the way. To this cause of delay was added the confusion arising from any change of orders with raw troops as to routes in the labyrinth of roads in that vicinity.

Hardee's corps, moving on the Ridge road under its methodical commander, assisted by the ardor and energy of Hindman and Cleburne, moved with greater celerity than the other troops. But something of this was due to their apprenticeship in war, under General Johnston's own eye and inspiration, on outpost duty in Kentucky and in the long and toilsome march from Bowling Green to Corinth, which had inured them to the hardships and difficulties of this kind of service. Polk's corps was at this time superior to the others in its transportation and in its experience under fire, and Bragg's in drill and order. Each had its own excellence ; but all were soon to be welded to a common temper in the white heat of sectional war. But at this time the whole army was new, and not yet moulded into a consistent whole.

In describing his own corps, Bragg correctly portrays the whole army. He says :

But few regiments of my command had ever made a day's march. A very large proportion of the rank and file had never performed a day's labor. Our organization had been most hasty, with great deficiency in commanders, and was, therefore, very imperfect. The equipment was lamentably defective for field-service ; and our transportation, hastily impressed in the country, was deficient in quantity and very inferior in quality. With all these drawbacks, the troops marched late on the afternoon of the 3d, a day later than intended, in high spirits, and eager for the combat.

A very dear friend, who commanded a brigade in the battle, wrote as follows, in 1872, to the author:

You know I was as ignorant of the military art at that time as it was possible for a civilian to be. I had never seen a man fire a musket. I had never heard a lecture or read a line on the subject. We were all tyros—all, the rawest and greenest recruits—generals, colonels, captains, soldiers. One thing I recollect, and that was the majestic presence of General Johnston. He looked like a hero of the antique type, and his very appearance on the field was a tower of more than kingly strength. I saw him as our lines were forming, and talked and shook hands with him for the last time.

While waiting for the appearance of the various commands, detained by the storm, the mire, and the other causes already assigned—Breckinridge's, Ruggles's, and Cheatham's—General Johnston, followed by his staff, passed from one body of troops to another, encouraging the men both by his words and his presence. Major Hayden, his volunteer aide, says:

When they began to cheer his approach, he checked them, because it would call the attention of the enemy to their position. His advice to the men was brief and characteristic. He told them, "Look along your guns, and fire low."

During the intervals of the march on the 4th and 5th of April, while the men stood on their arms, the following address of the commanding general was read at the head of each regiment. It was received with exhibitions of deep feeling, and the soldiers were stirred to a still sterner resolution, which proved itself in the succeeding conflict.

HEADQUARTERS, ARMY OF THE MISSISSIPPI, }
CORINTH, MISSISSIPPI, *April 3*, 1862. }

SOLDIERS OF THE ARMY OF THE MISSISSIPPI : I have put you in motion to offer battle to the invaders of your country. With the resolution and discipline and valor becoming men fighting, as you are, for all worth living or dying for, you can but march to a decisive victory over the agrarian mercenaries sent to subjugate you and to despoil you of your liberties, your property, and your honor. Remember the precious stake involved ; remember the dependence of your mothers, your wives, your sisters, and your children, on the result ; remember the fair, broad, abounding land, and the happy homes that would be desolated by your defeat.

The eyes and hopes of eight millions of people rest upon you ; you are expected to show yourselves worthy of your lineage, worthy of the women of the South, whose noble devotion in this war has never been exceeded in any time. With such incentives to brave deeds, and with the trust that God is with us, your generals will lead you confidently to the combat—assured of success.

A. S. JOHNSTON, *General commanding.*

Between four and five o'clock on Saturday afternoon was held that famous "council of war," on the issue of which turned the question whether the battle of Shiloh should be fought at all. It has been described, with more or less picturesque effect, but under the most various forms. Some of these accounts are altogether spurious, the coinage of a lively fancy. Dismissing these romances, we shall find that the eye and ear witnesses, though differing in details, agree in all essential facts. The council was held at the cross-roads, a few hundred yards from the headquarters of the night before. Colonel Jordan's account is as follows, and is presumably to be received as General Beauregard's own statement of the matter.[1] Mentioning in a note that it occurred about four o'clock in the open air, on foot, in the road, between the generals, surrounded at a short distance by a number of staff officials, and was of short duration, he names Generals Johnston, Beauregard, Polk, Bragg, Hardee (Hardee was not present, but Gilmer was), and Breckinridge, as taking part in it, and then furnishes this narrative :

At least one division, if not the whole of Bragg's corps, was likewise inexplicably tardy in movement on Saturday, though General Johnston, through his staff, had made every effort to get his troops in position for an attack that day. Supremely chagrined that he had been balked in his just expectation, it was evidently now too late for a decisive engagement that afternoon ; so General Johnston called his corps and reserve commanders together, and a council was held within less than two miles of Shiloh Chapel, the headquarters of the Federal General Sherman.

It was now learned that many of the troops had improvidently thrown away or consumed their provisions, and at the end of three days were out of subsistence. General Bragg promised, however, to remedy this from his alleged well-stocked commissariat. But General Beauregard earnestly advised the idea of attacking the enemy should be abandoned, and that the whole force should return to Corinth, inasmuch as it was scarcely possible they would be able to take the Federals unawares, after such delay and the noisy demonstrations which had been made meanwhile. He urged the enemy would be now found formidably intrenched and ready for the attack ; that success had depended on the power to assail them unexpectedly, for they were superior in number, and in large part had been under fire. On the other hand, few comparatively of the Confederates had that advantage, while a large part were too raw and recently enrolled to make it proper to venture them in an assault upon breastworks which would now be thrown up. And this unquestionably was the view of almost all present.

General Johnston, having listened with grave attention to the views and opinions advanced, then remarked, in substance, that he recognized the weight of the objections to an attack under the circumstances involved by the unfortunate loss of time on the road. But, nevertheless, he still hoped the enemy was not looking for offensive operations, and that he would yet be able to surprise them ; and that, having put his army in motion for a battle, he would venture the hazard.

This decision being announced, the officers rapidly dispersed to their respective posts in high and hopeful spirits, notwithstanding the probabilities that all previous expectations of a surprise would fail of accomplishment.

General Polk, in his report of the battle, gives the following account of the occasion and circumstances of the meeting, which, in the

---

[1] " Life of Forrest," p. 113.

opinion of most of General Johnston's staff, was accidental so far as he was concerned. Polk says:

I had not advanced far before I came upon General Ruggles, who commanded General Bragg's left, deploying his troops. Having ascertained the direction of the line, I did not wait for him to complete it, but returned to the head of my column to give the necessary orders. By this time it was near four o'clock, and, on arriving, I was informed that General Beauregard desired to see me immediately. I rode forward to his headquarters at once, where I found General Bragg and himself in conversation. He said, with some feeling, "I am very much disappointed at the delay which has occurred in getting the troops into position." I replied: "So am I, sir; but, so far as I am concerned, my orders are to form on another line, and that line must first be established before I can form upon it." I continued: "I reached Mickey's at nightfall yesterday, whence I could not move, because of the troops which were before me, until 2 P. M. to-day. I then promptly followed the column in front of me, and have been in position to form upon it so soon as its line was established." He said he regretted the delay exceedingly, as it would make it necessary to forego the attack altogether; that our success depended upon our surprising the enemy; that this was now impossible, and we must fall back to Corinth.

Here General Johnston came up and asked what was the matter. General Beauregard repeated what he had said to me. General Johnston remarked that this would never do, and proceeded to assign reasons for that opinion. He then asked what I thought of it. I replied that my troops were in as good condition as they had ever been; that they were eager for battle; that to retire now would operate injuriously upon them; and I thought we ought to attack. General Breckinridge, whose troops were in the rear, and by this time had arrived upon the ground, here joined us; and, after some discussion, it was decided to postpone further movement until the following day, and to make the attack at daybreak.

General Bragg, in a monograph on the battle of Shiloh, prepared for the use of the writer of this memoir, says:

During the afternoon of the 5th, as the last of our troops were taking position, a casual and partly-accidental meeting of general officers occurred just in rear of our second line, near the bivouac of General Bragg. The commander-in-chief, General Beauregard, General Polk, General Bragg, and General Breckinridge, are remembered as present, and General Hardee may have been. In a discussion of the causes of the delay and its incidents, it was mentioned that some of the troops, now in their third day only, were entirely out of food, though having marched with five days' rations. General Beauregard, confident our movement had been discovered by the enemy, urged its abandonment, a return to our camps for supplies, and a general change of programme. In this opinion no other seemed fully to concur; and when it was suggested that "the enemy's supplies were much nearer, and could be had for the taking," General Johnston quietly remarked, "Gentlemen, we shall attack at daylight to-morrow." The meeting then dispersed upon an invitation of the commanding general to meet at his tent that evening. At that meeting a further discussion elicited the same views, and the same firm, decided determination.

The next morning, about dawn of day, the 6th, as the troops were being put in motion, several generals again met at the camp-fire of the general-in-chief. The discussion was renewed, General Beauregard again expressing his dissent; when, rapid firing in the front indicating that the attack had commenced, General Johnston closed the discussion by remarking: "The battle has opened, gentlemen; it is too late to change our dispositions." He proposed to move to the front, and his subordinates promptly joined their respective commands, inspired by his coolness, confidence, and determination. Few men have equaled him in the possession and display at the proper time of these great qualities of the soldier.

As far as the writer can ascertain, the meeting was, as stated by Bragg, casual. Beauregard sent for Polk. The discussion between them was conducted with some warmth. General Johnston joined the group, but not by preconcert, and Breckinridge came up afterward. General Preston says in his letter of April 18, 1862 :

General Johnston was within two miles of the chapel, and anxious to attack that evening, for fear the enemy would discover his presence, and be on the alert to receive him; but, considering the condition of the men, determined to rest them and attack in the morning. It was, moreover, discovered that some of the regiments had not brought provisions sufficient. A conference was held between Generals Johnston, Beauregard, Bragg, and Polk, at 5 P.M.; Major Gilmer being near. Some thought the long delay in the movement, of thirty-six hours, would put the enemy on the alert, and the want of provisions would endanger a failure, and that the attack was too late to be successful. I was ordered to go for General Breckinridge, to see the state of his command; but he appearing at the moment, and reporting the provisions ample, General Johnston then ordered the attack for next morning, and we bivouacked in silence for the night.

General Preston informs the writer that General Johnston said little, but closed the discussion with great decision of manner. As he moved off, he said to Preston:

I would fight them if they were a million. They can present no greater front between these two creeks than we can; and the more men they crowd in there, the worse we can make it for them. . . . Polk is a true soldier and a friend.

Governor Harris mentions the following incident, which is significant of General Johnston's train of thought during that day, and confirmatory of the above:

I was riding with him along the line of battle, which was being formed about 12 M.[1] on Saturday, when one of our scouts intercepted us, and made a report to the general which indicated the presence of a much larger Federal force than previous information had induced us to expect. For a moment after receiving this report, he appeared to be in profound thought, when he turned to me, saying: ".I will fight them if there is a million of them! I have as many men as can

---

[1] Colonel Munford thinks the hour was earlier.

be well handled on this field, and I can handle as many men as they can." He then proceeded with the inspection of his line.

The Hon. Jacob Thompson, Secretary of the Interior under Mr. Buchanan, who was present on the staff of General Beauregard, furnishes the writer with the following notes of an interview which he held with General Johnston on the way to this conference, as he thinks, but which more probably occurred soon after it:

General Johnston took my arm, and remarked, "I perceive that General Beauregard is averse to bringing on the attack on the enemy in the morning, on the ground that we have lost an opportunity by delay." I replied that I knew that such was the feeling of General Beauregard, and he seemed wonderfully depressed in spirits. "But," says General Johnston, "don't you think it is better to fight, and run the chances of defeat rather than retreat? Our troops are in high spirits, eager for the trial of arms, and confident of victory; and the effect of an order to retreat will not only disappoint them but depress their spirits, and I fear it would have the same effect as a defeat." I replied that if Buell should come up in time the odds would be greatly against us. Then General Johnston, as if wishing to draw out my opinion, said: "Don't you think we had better try and fight the two armies in detail? The junction is not yet made, and it is probable will not be made to-morrow." My reply to that was, "There are great difficulties and embarrassments, take either horn of the dilemma, and those who have the responsibility must decide it." The result of the council was an order to attack early, and General Johnston determined to lead the attack in person, and leave General Beauregard to direct the movements of troops in the rear.

General Gilmer says that Beauregard's proposition to retire without making an attack was not opposed, so far as he can remember. He adds:

General Johnston appeared much surprised at the suggestion, and held that a failure to attack would demoralize his command, which had come on the field in good spirits, expecting to give battle. I ventured to suggest that a withdrawal would certainly destroy the *morale* of the troops. General Johnston said, "We will attack the enemy in the morning." All dispositions were accordingly made, and special instructions given to the corps commanders for the engagement in the morning.

Colonel Munford, in his address at Memphis, has supplied the following interesting particulars of a conversation held with General Johnston immediately after the "council of war." He says:

The leading general officers were called together, and a short colloquy held, which General Johnston seemed to terminate a little abruptly. He turned, saw me, and, pointing to a large oak, motioned me to meet him there. It was his habit not to betray emotion. Despite this exterior calm, I saw he *was* deeply moved. His first words were: "I want to tell you something which I desire remembered. I shall tell nobody but you and Preston, but I do not wish what

I say to be forgotten, as it may become very important some day." I told him his wishes should be complied with. He then said: "They wish me to withdraw the army without a battle; what is your opinion?" My surprised reply was: "General, a defeat is preferable. This army cannot be withdrawn without a fight, and kept together. They will become disheartened and melt away. They are very raw, but are eager to meet the enemy. I have been around their camp-fires, mingled freely with them, and know, if you can ever do anything with such a number of undisciplined men, now is your time. *They are ready for the fight.*" The general said with a glowing countenance, "*I have ordered a battle for to-morrow at daylight,* and I intend to 'hammer 'em!'" I then said to him: "There is a matter well worthy of consideration. We have lost a day. We know Buell is marching an army as large as your own to this point. If he has not been inactive, he can get here to-morrow, and may be here to-night. The army you propose attacking is already much larger than your own, is better armed, and in all respects better appointed. Suppose, in the morning, instead of sixty or seventy thousand, you find yourself confronting ninety or one hundred thousand, what think you of your chances for success?" He replied: "There is Lick Creek on my right, and Owl Creek on my left. These creeks effectually protect my flanks. I have men enough to cover the front, and the more men they crowd into this small space between me and the river, the better for me and the worse for them. I think we will hammer them *beyond doubt.*" I have transcribed as much of this conversation as it is proper should now be written down—enough to shed a clear light upon this portion of the history of the battle of Shiloh. It is remarkable both for the facts it discloses and the peculiar circumstances under which it took place.

These varied presentations, in the words of the witnesses themselves, leave on the mind a vivid picture of this striking scene. The seeming disagreements in minor circumstances in the foregoing statements are easily reconcilable. They arise from the different points of view of the narrators, and are not only consistent with the strictest veracity, but are a very strong attestation of the principal facts. The substantive facts are that, on Saturday afternoon late, when the Confederate army was drawn up in battle array, within two miles of Shiloh Church, General Beauregard earnestly urged the necessity of a retreat. General Johnston, against his emphatic advice, decided to fight the battle of Shiloh. General Beauregard's counsel in this conference freed him from responsibility in case of a repulse, and compelled General Johnston to take the hazard of a doubtful and perilous contest weighted with such opposition. Success was absolutely necessary to the vindication of his military character. He was not unwilling to accept the test.

As to the soundness of General Johnston's judgment in deciding to fight contrary to the auguries of his distinguished subordinate, the writer does not pretend to offer an unbiased opinion. He rests the wisdom of General Johnston's course upon the results of the battle up to the time of his death. But, whatever may have been the weight of the reasons for and against attacking, those assigned for retreating by General Beauregard most certainly proved invalid. Contrary to his opinion of its possibility, the Federals were surprised, and they were not intrenched; and whatever disparity of military experience in the two armies existed on the evening of the 5th had also existed on the morning of the 3d, before they left Corinth. Indeed, it was a mere assumption that the enemy were on their guard and intrenched, as there was not the slightest evidence to that effect, and all the indications were to the contrary. To conclude that they were prepared because they ought to be, was a reason which applied with greater force against an advance from Corinth than against an attack on Sunday morning. The Confederate army, deployed in three lines of battle on the Federal front, ready and eager for the onset, was stronger for aggression than when it lay at Corinth. The position was almost more than its generals could have hoped for. Though the attack was not without its difficulties and dangers, every omen seemed auspicious. General Johnston, as a trained soldier, put discipline at its fullest value; but he knew what a power enthusiasm was also, and that his army was wrought up to the highest pitch. In such a state of mind, with those new levies, the demoralization of another retreat would have been worse than defeat.

Without disparagement to General Beauregard's ability, his willingness, his urgency, to retire from that field, when in the face of the enemy, evinces conclusively how little he was in sympathy with the leading idea in General Johnston's mind, that he must crush Grant before Buell joined him. This was the purpose, this was *the plan* of the battle of Shiloh.

When night fell, on the eve of battle, the following was the Confederate array: The front line, composed of the Third Corps and Gladden's brigade, was under Hardee, and extended from Owl Creek to Lick Creek, a distance of somewhat over three miles. Cleburne's brigade was on the left, with its flank resting near Owl Creek. Hindman was intrusted with a division, composed of Wood's brigade, and his own under Colonel Shaver. These occupied the centre. The interval, on his right, to Lick Creek, was occupied by Gladden's brigade, detached from Bragg, and put under Hardee's command for the battle. Hardee's three brigades numbered 6,789 effectives, and Gladden added 2,235 more—an effective total in the front line of 9,024.

Bragg commanded the second line. Withers's division formed his right wing. Jackson's brigade, 2,208 strong, was drawn up three hundred yards in rear of Gladden, its left on the Bark road. Chalmers's brigade was on Jackson's right, *en échelon* to Gladden's brigade, with its right on a fork of Lick Creek. Clanton's cavalry was in rear of Chalmers's, with pickets to the right and front. In this order the division bivouacked.

General Bragg's left wing was made up of three brigades, under General D. Ruggles. Colonel R. L. Gibson commanded the right brigade, resting with his right on the Bark road. Colonel Preston Pond commanded the left brigade, near Owl Creek, with an interval between him and Gibson. About three hundred yards in the rear of these two brigades, opposite the interval, with his right and left flanks masked by Gibson and Pond, Patton Anderson's brigade, 1,634 strong, was posted. Bragg's corps was 10,731 strong, and was drawn up in line of battle, or with the regiments in double column at half distance, according to the nature of the ground.

The third line or reserve was composed of the First Corps, under Polk, and three brigades under Breckinridge. Polk's command was massed in columns of brigades on the Bark road, near Mickey's; and Breckinridge's on the road from Monterey toward the same point. Polk was to advance on the left of the Bark road, at an interval of about eight hundred paces from Bragg's line; and Breckinridge, to the right of that road, was to give support, wherever it should become necessary.

Polk's corps, 9,136 strong in infantry and artillery, was composed of two divisions, Cheatham's on the left, made up of B. R. Johnson's and Stephens's brigades, and Clark's on his right, formed of A. P. Stewart's and Russell's brigades. It followed Bragg's line at about eight hundred yards' distance.

Breckinridge's reserve was composed of Trabue's, Bowen's, and Statham's brigades, with a total infantry and artillery of 6,439.

The cavalry, about 4,300 strong, guarded the flanks, or was detached on outpost duty; but, both from the newness and imperfections of their organization, equipment, and drill, and from the rough and wooded character of the ground, they did little service that day. The part taken by Morgan's, Forrest's, and Wharton's (Eighth Texas), will be given in its proper place.

The army, exclusive of its cavalry, was between 35,000 and 36,000 strong. Jordan, in an official report, made in July, 1862, to the writer, then on inspection-duty, gave the effective total of all arms at 38,773, who marched April 3d. In his "Life of Forrest" he makes it 39,630. Hodge, in his sketch of the First Kentucky Brigade, with a different distribution of troops, puts the total at 39,695, which he says he made up from the returns at the time. Beauregard's report of the battle gives the field return at 40,335, of which 4,382 was cavalry. This last return includes Colonel Hill's Forty-seventh Tennessee Regiment, which came up on the 7th. There are apparently some errors in the return of July, 1862. The writer believes that the figures in Jordan's "Life of Forrest" approach the truth most nearly.

It now behooves us to consider the employment of the Federal army during those fateful first days of April, when the Confederates were gathering in its front. Premising that General Grant kept his headquarters at Savannah, nine miles from Pittsburg by water and six or seven by land, and left a large discretion in the hands of General Sherman, as his friend and most experienced officer, we must turn to the "Memoirs" of General Sherman to arrive at his theory of the battle, and his account of the events preceding it. He is entitled to this consideration, since, by his position in the advance, and by the special confidence reposed in him by Grant, he shared with his chief the responsibility for whatever was done or left undone at Shiloh. We have already seen his opinion on the natural strength of the position, and the reasons he gives for not adding to it. The following is his account of the transactions ushering in the battle ("Memoirs," vol. i., p. 229):

From about the 1st of April we were conscious that the rebel cavalry in our front was getting bolder and more saucy; and on Friday, the 4th of April, it dashed down and carried off one of our picket-guards, composed of an officer and seven men, posted a couple of miles out on the Corinth road. Colonel Buckland sent a company to its relief, then followed himself with a regiment, and, fearing lest he might be worsted, I called out his whole brigade and followed some *four or five miles*, when the cavalry in advance encountered artillery. I then, after dark, drew back to our lines, and reported the fact by letter to General Grant, at Savannah; but thus far we had not positively detected the presence of infantry, for cavalry regiments generally had a couple of guns along, and I supposed the guns that opened on us on the evening of Friday, April 4th, belonged to the cavalry that was hovering along our whole front. Saturday passed in our camps without any unusual event, the weather being wet and mild, and the roads back to the steamboat-landing being heavy with mud.

It may be remarked on the foregoing, that General Sherman's reconnaissance did not advance so far as he thinks, as four or five miles, the distance named by him, did not intervene between Shiloh Church and Mickey's, in front of which Hardee's corps was deploying. Indeed, Colonel Buckland, who made the reconnaissance, says that he advanced *three*, not four or five miles.[1] Hardee was, in fact, within two miles. It will be observed that Sherman supposed the artillery belonged to the Confederate cavalry.

In his letter to Grant, dated April 5th (page 235), Sherman reports that he lost eleven men, officers and privates, taken prisoners, and eight privates wounded. He says he took ten prisoners. He continues:

I infer that the enemy is in some considerable force at Pea Ridge (Monterey), that yesterday morning they crossed a brigade of two regiments of infantry, one regiment of cavalry, and one battery of field-artillery, to the ridges on which

---

[1] "Sherman's Historical Raid," Boynton, p. 31.

the Corinth road lies. They halted the infantry at a point about five miles in my front, sent a detachment to the lane of General Meaks, on the north of Owl Creek, and the cavalry down toward our camp.

Though he did not suspect the fact, it was the whole Confederate army which was unfolding along his front.

In his report of the battle of Shiloh ("Memoirs," vol. i., p. 235), Sherman says :

On Saturday the enemy's cavalry was again very bold, coming well down to our front; *yet I did not believe they designed anything but a strong demonstration.*

General Sherman seems to deny with derision that his command was surprised on the morning of April 6th. He says ("Memoirs," vol. i., p. 244) :

Probably no single battle of the war gave rise to such wild and damaging reports. It was publicly asserted at the North that our army was taken completely by surprise, etc.

His denial is not categorical, but by inference ; but Moulton's "Criticism of Boynton's Review of Sherman" (page 11), which is virtually General Sherman's own utterance, denies any purpose or necessity "of contradicting the foolish stories about our forces being surprised by the enemy at its beginning." Moulton continues:

No matter what were the reasons for starting them originally in the newspapers or elsewhere, there is not the slightest excuse for reiterating them at this time.

He rests his defense on the ground that Sherman's *whole* line was not overthrown in the first onset, but that part of it on favorable ground formed a line of battle and fought well ; that the officers on picket—

were in a constant state of watchfulness; that the pickets were not less than two and a half miles out, and were strengthened as occasion required; that reconnaissances in force were made from time to time, and that both these and the pickets reported the presence of cavalry and infantry to the division commanders, who were on the *qui vive* in consequence, and that their troops were in line of battle on the morning of the attack.

He alleges also that they (the Confederate generals) "did not definitely fix the date of the attack until *late in the evening of the 5th,*" but this is a mere quibble, for General Johnston marched from Corinth with an unalterable resolution to attack, which nothing, not even the remonstrances of his second in command, could shake, and intended to attack on the *morning* of the 5th.

It is not necessary to consider Moulton's statements *seriatim ;* for, though all of them have some color of fact, they are not relevant to the issue. A narrative of the facts will leave a clearer impression on the reader's mind than any word-mongering or technical disputations. Whether Grant and Sherman used all requisite vigilance or not, they believed that the Confederate army was at Corinth, twenty miles away, and only a brigade at Mickey's, when that army was unfolding for an assault upon them. Whether they were "surprised" or not, the attack upon them was *unexpected*, and their own words show that a thunderbolt from a clear sky could not have astonished them more than the boom of artillery on Sunday morning.

In Badeau's "Life of Grant" (page 600) occurs the following correspondence. The first communication is a telegram from General Grant to General Halleck, his commanding officer:

SAVANNAH, *April 5,* 1862.

The main force of the enemy is at Corinth, with troops at different points east. Small garrisons are also at Bethel, Jackson, and Humboldt. The number at these places seems constantly to change. The number of the enemy at Corinth, and in supporting distance of it, cannot be far from 80,000 men. Information, obtained through deserters, places their force west at 200,000. One division of Buell's column arrived yesterday. General Buell will be here himself to-day. Some skirmishing took place between our out-guards and the enemy's yesterday and the day before.

U. S. GRANT, *Major-General.*

Major-General H. W. HALLECK, St. Louis, Missouri.

In a subsequent dispatch to Halleck, on the same day, he says that he had received notes, stating that—

our outposts had been attacked by the enemy, apparently in considerable force. I immediately went up, but found all quiet. . . . They had with them three pieces of artillery, and cavalry and infantry. How much, cannot of course be estimated. *I have scarcely the faintest idea of an attack (general one) being made upon us,* but will be prepared should such a thing take place.

General Sherman's dispatch to Grant, sent with the above to Halleck, is as follows:

PITTSBURG LANDING, *April 5,* 1862.

SIR: All is quiet along my lines now. We are in the act of exchanging cavalry, according to your orders. The enemy has cavalry in our front, and I think there are two regiments of infantry and one battery of artillery about six miles out. I will send you in ten prisoners of war and a report of last night's affair in a few minutes.

W. T. SHERMAN, *Brigadier-General.*

Your note is just received. I have no doubt that nothing will occur to-day more than some picket-firing. The enemy is saucy, but got the worst of it yesterday, and will not press our pickets far. I will not be drawn out far, unless with certainty of advantage; *and I do not apprehend anything like an attack upon our position.* SHERMAN.

To General GRANT.

In view of these quotations from Badeau's book, argument would seem entirely unnecessary in order to show that there was "scarcely the faintest idea of an attack being made," or that there was any knowledge of the Confederate movement in force. Grant and Sherman evidently expected some skirmishing on outposts, but nothing more. General Badeau's commentaries on his own text are really amusing. He dwells on Grant's letters, quoted above, which, however, speak for themselves, and adds (page 96):

It has been repeatedly asserted that Grant was surprised at Shiloh, but the evidence to the contrary is incontrovertible. The preliminary fighting of the 3d and 4th of April necessarily put division and army commanders on the alert.

The evidence he cites for this is as follows:

Prentiss had doubled his pickets the day before (the 5th), and had a reconnaissance of a regiment out at three o'clock on the morning of the 6th; he received the earliest assault outside of his camps. W. H. L. Wallace also breakfasted early, and had his horses saddled, "to be ready in case of an attack." These are not the indications of a camp that is surprised.

Badeau indulges somewhat oracularly in a piece of special pleading, very wonderful in view of the facts. He says:

Private soldiers and inferior officers very probably could not read the signs that told so plainly to their commanders the necessity of readiness; such may very likely have been surprised at what occurred; but Grant and his division generals, although of course they could not know at what hour or place the rebels might choose to assault, nor indeed that they certainly would assault at all, *although they did not really expect an attack*, yet knew the propinquity of a great army, and, so far as could be, were prepared to receive it—except in the matter of defensive intrenchments.

The translation of which into English is, that General Grant thought the Confederates were at Corinth—not two, but twenty-two miles away. The readiness for the attack consisted in what? Some colonels strengthened their pickets, one general sent a regiment on reconnaissance, and another had his horse saddled before breakfast.

Instead of the commanders having a peculiar and occult insight into the situation, unrevealed to their less-gifted subordinates, the exact reverse occurred. In the reconnaissances and cavalry-skirmishes of outposts, the ready apprehension of raw troops saw the shadow of coming danger. Like the startled stag which scents afar the perilous approach of a foe, and watches for the rustle of the leaves, and hearkens for the distant bay of hounds, these undisciplined men were touched by a vague apprehension of coming danger. They saw, in the dash of the Southern troopers at their pickets, the cloud no bigger than a man's hand that precedes the tempest. Their quick imaginations suggested

the fear that it was the vanguard of a great army threading the swamps
and thickets of the unknown forest in their front. It may even be true,
as is alleged, that the experienced eye of some veteran caught here or
there the gleam of a bayonet in the background, or detected by other
signs the massing of infantry. It is certain that a feeling of uneasiness
and mistrust pervaded the whole front line, and gradually spread from
soldiers to officers, reaching higher and higher. Every soldier knows
that "camp-rumor" has a certain undefined value, that there is something in the Greek idea of the "Pheme," the voice that addresses the
general consciousness, the voice that heralded across the Ægean the
victory of Platæa to the combatants of Mycale. Known facts, inference
and imagination, often construct in an army an hypothesis not to be
neglected. Possibly upon some such basis General Prentiss acted in
throwing to the front ten companies, under Colonel Moore, to watch the
approaches to his position.

But it is perfectly evident that Grant and Sherman considered themselves above such idle fears. The vulgar apprehension did not touch
the victor of Donelson. It never reached either Grant or Sherman.
Indeed, the latter, with bitter innuendo, points to it as proof of cowardice in certain officers with whom he was at variance. He swears in his
evidence on Worthington's trial.[1]

Therefore, on Friday, two days before the battle, when Colonel Worthington
was so apprehensive, *I knew* there was no hostile party in *six miles*,[2] though
there was reason to expect an attack. I suppose Colonel McDowell and myself
had become tired of his constant prognostications, and paid no attention to him,
especially when we were positively informed by men like Buckland, Kilby Smith,
and Major Ricker, who went to the front to look for enemies, instead of going
to the landing. . . .

On Friday, the 4th, nor officer, nor soldier, looked for an attack, as I can
prove. . . . For weeks and months we had heard all sorts of reports, just as we
do now. For weeks old women had reported that Beauregard was coming,
sometimes with 100,000, sometimes with 300,000, when, in fact, he did not leave
Corinth until after even Colonel Worthington had been alarmed for safety.

Sherman says, further on, that, after the reconnaissance on Friday
afternoon—

We knew that we had the elements of an army in our front, but did not
know its strength or destination. The guard was strengthened, and, as night
came on, we returned to camp, and not a man in camp but knew we had an
enemy to the front, before we slept that night. But even I had to guess its purpose.

Colonel Buckland, who made the reconnaissance, states that he discovered a large force of infantry and artillery, and that, when he re-

---

[1] "Sherman's Historical Raid," by Boynton, p. 29.
[2] Hardee was not more than two miles distant.

ported with his prisoners to Sherman, his manner indicated he was not pleased. He made a written report of the skirmish that night. Buckland says :

The next day, Saturday, April 5th, I visited the picket-line several times, and found the woods were swarming with rebel cavalry along the entire front of my line, and the pickets claimed to have discovered infantry and artillery. Several times during the day I reported these facts to General Sherman. Colonel Hildebrand, of the Third Brigade, and other officers, visited the picket-line with me during the day. It was well understood all that day and night, throughout Sherman's division, that there was a large rebel force immediately in our front.

Buckland strengthened his pickets, and adds, "Every officer in my brigade was fully aware of the danger, and such precautions were taken that a surprise was impossible." [1]

Concerning the same reconnaissance, Major Ricker wrote as follows: [2]

When we got back to the picket-lines we found General Sherman there with infantry and artillery, caused by the heavy firing of the enemy on us. General Sherman asked me what was up. I told him I had met and fought the advance of Beauregard's army, that he was advancing on us. *General Sherman said it could not be possible,* Beauregard was not such a fool as to leave his base of operations and attack us in ours—*mere reconnaissance in force.*

General Buell says that, "so far as preparation for battle is concerned, no army could well have been taken more by surprise than was the Army of the Tennessee on the 6th of April." [3]

Van Horne's "Army of the Cumberland," to which General Sherman's special advocate, Mr. Moulton, refers the reader, "for a fair and full history of this battle," has the following (page 105) :

While the national army was unprepared for battle, and unexpectant of such an event, and was passing the night of the 5th in fancied security, Johnston's army of 40,000 men was in close proximity, and ready for the bloody revelation of its presence and purpose on the following morning. General Johnston was already a day later in attaining position for attack than he had anticipated, and this loss of a day had brought the Army of the Ohio one day's march nearer to the conjunction with General Grant, to prevent which was the object of his advance. Usually, the indications of approaching battle are so palpable that the men in the ranks, as well as the officers of all grades, foresee the deadly struggle, and nerve themselves to meet it. But in this case the nearness of the enemy in force was not known in the national army, and there was no special preparation for the conflict.

In "Sherman and his Campaigns," by Colonels Bowman and Irwin, it is stated (page 50), "There was nothing to indicate a general attack

[1] "Sherman's Historical Raid," pp. 31, 32.　　　　[2] Ibid.
[3] Buell's letter, dated January 19, 1865, to *United States Service Magazine,* republished in the New York *World,* February 29, 1865.

until seven o'clock on Sunday morning, when the advance-guard of Sherman's front was forced in on his main line."

"Grant and his Campaigns," a book compiled by Prof. Coppee, avowedly from Grant's "Reports," and very prejudiced in its conclusions in favor of that general, says, "At the outset our troops were shamefully surprised and easily overpowered."

It is but a poor compliment to the generalship of either Grant or Sherman to believe them aware of the presence of the Confederate army in their front on the 5th. Else why was General Lew Wallace with 7,500 men kept at Crump's Landing, and Nelson and Crittenden's divisions—14,000 men—left at Savannah? Why the calm of Saturday and the confusion of Sunday? For the events of the battle, let the eulogists of Generals Grant and Sherman rather plead, than deny, the "surprise" that befell them on Sunday morning.

Boynton says (page 34):

The officers of General Thomas's army, who had charge of the pickets a few days after the battle, rode over the line from which the rebels moved to the attack. Everywhere were signs of the deliberation with which the enemy formed his forces. The routes, by which each corps and division of the first line was to march to its position in the woods, were blazed upon the trees, and the entire force of the enemy went into line for the attack wholly undisturbed, and *with as much order and precision as if forming upon markers for a grand review.* And the time that the enemy was thus forming his lines, scarcely out of rifled-cannon range, passed in our camps, says General Sherman, without any unusual event."

Such is a fair view of the situation and transactions of the Federal army before Shiloh, as taken from their own writers.

According to the general tenor of their official reports, the Federal army was disposed as follows on the night of April 5th: Sherman commanded the advance, consisting of the Fifth Division, and had his headquarters at Shiloh Church, a little wooden meeting-house, two miles and a half or more from Pittsburg Landing, on the Corinth road. The road to Purdy crosses the Corinth road, somewhat in rear of this chapel, almost at right angles, and, passing to the right and front, follows a ridge to Owl Creek, which it crosses by two bridges. This ridge was thickly set with trees and undergrowth, and fell away by a sharp declivity to a deep ravine, boggy and flooded with the storms of the past month. Sherman's First Brigade, under Colonel McDowell, was on his right, on the Purdy road as a guard to the bridges over Owl Creek. His Fourth Brigade, under Colonel Buckland, came next in his line, with its left resting on the Corinth road at Shiloh. The Third Brigade, under Colonel Hildebrand, stood with its right on the same point. His Second Brigade, under Colonel Stuart, was detached in position on the extreme left, guarding the ford over Lick Creek. Each brigade had three regiments and a battery ; and eight companies of the Fourth Illinois Cavalry were posted in an open field to the left and rear of Shiloh.

Among the multitude of roads and cross-roads, running in every direction over the broken surface of the Shiloh plateau, one principal road diverged to the left in rear of Shiloh Church from the direct Pittsburg and Corinth road, and following the ridge led into both the Bark road and the Corinth road by numerous approaches. Across this to Sherman's left, with an interval between them, Prentiss's division (the Sixth) was posted. Covering this interval, but some distance back, lay McClernand's division (the First), with its right partially masked by Sherman's left. Some two miles in rear of the front line, and about three-quarters of a mile in advance of Pittsburg, were encamped to the left, Hurlbut's (the Fourth), and to the right, Smith's (the Second) division, the latter under General W. H. L. Wallace. The Federal front was an arc or very obtuse angle extending from where the Purdy road crossed Owl Creek to the ford near the mouth of Lick Creek, which was guarded by Stuart's brigade. General Lew Wallace's division was five or six miles distant, with one brigade at Crump's Landing, and the other two on the Adamsville road, with intervals of some two miles, in observation of Cheatham's division, which he believed to be still at Purdy. The advance of Buell's army, Nelson's division, had passed through Savannah on Saturday morning, April 5th, and was distant from Pittsburg about five miles on the north bank of the river. Crittenden's division arrived there on the morning of the 6th, and the other divisions of Buell's army followed at intervals of about six miles.

The arrangement of Grant's army at Shiloh has been subjected to very severe and probably just criticism, by Federal writers, because he did not so place his troops as to make the most of his position. This may be true ; but such were the natural advantages of the ground that the attack was nevertheless almost equivalent to an assault on a strongly intrenched place. No Confederate who fought at Shiloh has ever said that he found any point on that bloody field easy to assail.

But while the Federal army, strong in the natural advantages of its position, its prestige, and its stubborn and self-reliant courage, lay unaware of its mighty peril, the Confederate army had set itself down opposite to the Federal camps, in battle array, with its flanks protected by natural barriers, ready for the onset. It had reached its positions, it is true, more slowly than could have been foreseen, but, according to all testimony, with almost the regularity of a drill or parade. More could not have been expected. More could not have been achieved under the circumstances. Thus the two armies lay face to face : the Federal host, like a wild-boar in his lair, stirred but not aroused by monitions of an unseen danger ; its foe, like a panther, hidden in the jungle, in wait to spring, tense for the deadly combat.

CHAPTER XXXIV.

BATTLE OF SHILOH.—SUNDAY.

I.—MORNING.

SATURDAY afternoon, April 5th, the sun, breaking through the mists which drifted away, set in a cloudless sky. The night was clear, calm, and beautiful. General Johnston, tired out with the vigils of the night before, slept quietly in an ambulance-wagon, his staff bivouacking by the camp-fires around him. Some of Hardee's troops having wasted their rations, he and Bragg spent a large part of the night getting up provisions for them. Before the faintest glimmer of dawn, the wide forest was alive with preparations for the mighty contest of the coming day. No bugle-note sounded, and no drum beat the reveillé; but men took their hasty morning meal, and looked with sharp attention to the arms that were to decide the fortunes of the fight. The cool, gray dawn found them in motion. Morning opened with all the delicate fragrance and beauty of the season, enhanced by the contrast of the day before. The sky was serene, the air was bracing, the dew lay heavy on the tender green of leaf and herb, and the freshness of early spring was on all around. When the sun rose it was with unclouded brilliancy; and, as it shed its glories over the coverts of the oak-woods, the advancing host, stirred by the splendor of the scene and the enthusiasm of the hour, passed the omen from lip to lip, and welcomed its rising as another "sun of Austerlitz."

The native buoyancy of General Johnston's self-repressed temper broke its barriers at the prospect of that struggle which should settle for all time by the arbitrament of arms the dispute as to his own military ability and skill and the fate of the Confederate cause in the West. He knew the hazard; but he knew, too, that he had done all that foresight, fortitude, energy, and strategy, could accomplish to secure a victory, and he welcomed with exultant joy the day that was about to decide not only these great questions, but for him all questions, solving the mysteries of life and death. Men who came within his influence on the battle-field felt and confessed the inspiration of his presence, his manner, and his words. As he gave his orders in terse sentences, every word seemed to ring with a presage of victory.

Turning to his staff, as he mounted, he exclaimed, "To-night we will water our horses in the Tennessee River." It was thus that he formulated his plan of battle. It must not stop short of entire victory.

First Position of Troops (Morning), April 6.

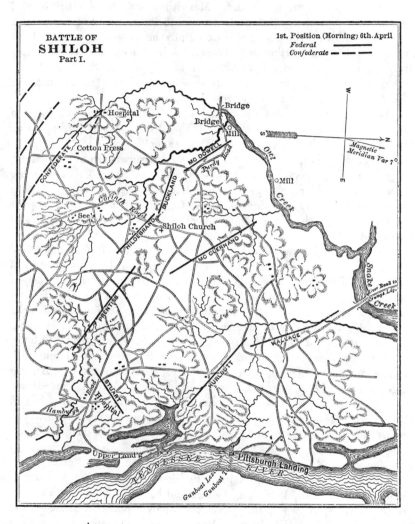

As he rode forward he encountered Colonel Randal L. Gibson, who was the intimate friend of his son. When Gibson ordered his brigade to salute, General Johnston took him warmly by the hand and said: "Randal, I never see you but I think of William. I hope you may get through safely to-day, but we must win a victory." Gibson says he felt greatly stirred by his words.

Sharp skirmishing had begun before he reached the front. Here he met Colonel John S. Marmaduke, commanding the Third Arkansas

Regiment. This officer, in reply to General Johnston's questions, explained, with some pride, that he held the *centre* of the front line, the other regiments forming on him. Marmaduke had been with General Johnston in Utah, at Bowling Green, and in the retreat to Corinth, and regarded him with the entire affection and veneration of a young soldier for his master in the art of war. General Johnston put his hand on Marmaduke's shoulder, and said to him with an earnestness that went to his heart, "*My son*, we must this day conquer or perish!" Marmaduke felt himself nerved to a tenfold resolution.

General Johnston said to the ambitious Hindman, who had been in the vanguard from the beginning: "You have *earned* your spurs as major-general. Let this day's work win them."

"Men of Arkansas!" he exclaimed to a regiment from that State, "they say you boast of your prowess with the bowie-knife. To-day you wield a nobler weapon—the bayonet. Employ it well." It was with such words, as he rode from point to point, that he raised a spirit in that host which swept away the serried lines of the conquerors of Donelson.

As he looked around on his soldiers he might well feel more like the chieftain who leads his clansmen to battle than the mere general of an army. Everywhere he beheld men bound to him by ties of ancient friendship or of service on other fields. There was Polk, his life-long friend; Hardee, for the last six years his major, for the last six months his right arm in war; Breckinridge, bound to him by many ties and marked out by him for the highest military distinctions; and Gilmer, his trusted engineer. Around him was a staff who followed him with filial reverence—Preston, Brewster, O'Hara, Jack, and others. Among the younger soldiers were many who had been his pupils in war—Hardcastle, Bowen, Rich, and many more. From the walks of civil life had come to the front a number of ardent and generous young men, without experience, but strong in native character and talent: the dashing Duke, the wily Morgan, Colonel R. A. Johnson, Colonel Ben Anderson, all sons of his early friends; Gibson, his connection, brave, faithful, and accomplished, and many more allied by blood or marriage; and a gallant band of Texans, Wharton, Ashbel Smith, and others; with a multitude besides, known to him personally or by reputation and name as the inheritors of martial virtues. But why multiply names? Regulars were there, who had wintered with him in Utah; Texans who had known him on the border, as patriot leader, statesman, citizen, soldier; the men of Monterey and the Mexican War, and the brave soldiers who had welcomed him with shouts at Columbus, or helped him to guard the line of the Barren River all winter. He regarded all these not as strangers, not as factors to be canceled in the deadly problem of successful combat, but as of his own belonging—his kith and kin by ties almost as strong as those of blood. He looked upon them with the tenderness of a patriarchal regard—of an Abraham or a Jephthah. In the dread holocaust of war, in which perish the bravest and best, he was ready to make his offering, as a sacrifice for his people and for constitutional liberty. In this spirit he sent, in this spirit he led, the sons of the South to the field of death and victory, on which he himself was to fall a victim.

Every one who witnessed the battle of Shiloh testifies to the splendid valor of the Confederate army there, rarely equaled, never surpassed, on any field of any war. It must be remembered, even by the heroes of the Army of Northern Virginia, who repulsed the multitudinous battalions of Grant in the Wilderness, and struck such blows at Chancellorsville and the Second Manassas, that these were the men who drove Grant and Sherman from an almost impregnable stronghold, and crushed one of the best armies the United States ever put in the field into a shapeless mass.

Duke, in his "Life of Morgan" (page 142), says :

Every one who witnessed that scene—the marshaling of the Confederate army for attack upon the morning of the 6th of April—must remember, more distinctly than anything else, the glowing enthusiasm of the men, their buoyancy and spirited impatience to close with the enemy. . . . When the lines began to advance, the wild cheers which arose made the woods stir as if with the rush of a mighty wind. Nowhere was there any thought of fear—everywhere were the evidences of impetuous and determined valor.

Friend and foe alike testify to the enthusiastic courage and unquenchable ardor of the soldiers that day. Bragg and many others have said that they caught their martial glow from the spirit of their commander. If it is not so, let it be denied now, while soldiers who fought there with the sword or musket yet live to tell of what they know. Would to God that every one of these might have spoken out or made his inarticulate sign of what he saw or felt that day ! It would make a record of heroism in officers and men for the ages to read with admiration.

Colonel Munford gives the following animated description of daybreak at headquarters :

Just as day was dawning I was awakened by General Johnston asking for me. I found him and the staff taking a breakfast of coffee and cold biscuit at a little fire. He told me I had better eat something, as he would move upon the enemy in a few moments. Just as I was draining my tin cup of coffee, bang—bang—bang went some muskets near the right wing of Hardee's line, and in a moment more boom went a cannon. "There," said Preston, "the first gun of the battle!" General Johnston turned to him and me, to whom he had before given blank books to note the incidents of the battle, and said, "Note the hour, if you please, gentlemen." It was precisely fourteen minutes after five o'clock. We mounted, galloped to the front, found the enemy in retreat, and our line just starting in pursuit.

Haydon says that General Johnston had ordered his horse at five o'clock. "We all got off in fine spirits. . . . The generals separated, and the general commanding made his way to where the firing was heaviest."

General Beauregard's official report of the military operations on Sunday is so brief that it is inserted here as a summary of the battle on that day :

At 5 A. M., on the 6th instant, a reconnoitring party of the enemy having become engaged with our advanced pickets, the commander of the forces gave orders to begin the movement and attack as determined upon, except that Trabue's brigade of Breckinridge's division was detached and advanced to support the left of Bragg's corps and line of battle when menaced by the enemy, and the other two brigades were directed to advance by the road to Hamburg, to support Bragg's right; and at the same time Maney's regiment, of Polk's corps, was advanced by the same road to reënforce the regiment of cavalry and battery of four pieces, already thrown forward to watch and guard Grier's, Tanner's, and Borland's Fords of Lick Creek.

Thirty minutes after 5 A. M., our lines and columns were in motion, all animated evidently by a promising spirit. The front line was engaged at once, but advanced steadily, followed in due order, with equal resolution and steadiness, by the other lines, which were brought successively into action with rare skill, judgment, and gallantry, by the several corps commanders as the enemy made a stand, with his masses rallied for the struggle for his encampments. Like an Alpine avalanche, our troops moved forward, despite the determined resistance of the enemy, until after 6 P. M., when we were in possession of all his encampments between Owl and Lick Creeks but one. Nearly all of his field-artillery, about thirty (30) flags, colors, and standards, over 3,000 prisoners, including a division commander (General Prentiss), and several brigade commanders, thousands of small-arms, an immense supply of subsistence, forage, and munitions of war, and a large amount of means of transportation—all the substantial fruits of a complete victory, such, indeed, as rarely have followed the most successful battles, for never was an army so well provided as that of our enemy.

The remnant of his army had been driven in utter disorder to the immediate vicinity of Pittsburg, under the shelter of the heavy guns of his iron-clad gunboats, and we remained undisputed masters of his well-selected, admirably-provided cantonments, after our twelve hours of obstinate conflict with his forces, who had been beaten from them and the contiguous covert, but only by a sustained onset of all the men we could bring into action.

How all this was done may now be told with more detail. But it must be premised that the writer, in spite of much diligent work among a confused tangle of obscure and contradictory reports, does not claim that his account is absolutely accurate or complete. As no artist can truly paint a skirmish even, where all is motion, so no writer can reproduce all the varying features of a great battle, where a hundred thousand combatants strove for mastery. It must be remembered that each narrator looks from a narrow point of view upon a scene which he reads in the light of every terrible passion which stirs the human breast. He has small chance to rectify errors, and many motives to perpetuate them. The easy, but unfortunate, method of the ordinary historian is to strike an average, irrespective of the credibility of witnesses or the probabilities of the conflicting testimony. But what should be sought is the absolute truth, and this he must tell without fear or favor. I have tried to tell it as I have found it.

The skirmishing began at break of day. General Prentiss, apprehensive at the near approach to his front of what he believed to be an audacious cavalry reconnaissance, had on Saturday evening sent ten companies of infantry, under Colonel David Moore, of the Twenty-first Missouri Regiment, out on the Corinth road for observation and reprisal, and had also subsequently doubled and extended his grand guards. But for these precautions the Federal army would have been taken entirely unawares. Colonel Moore advanced about three o'clock on the morning of the 6th, and cautiously feeling his way along a road that led obliquely to the right, toward Sherman's front, at early dawn encountered Hardee's skirmish-line under Major Hardcastle. The Missourians assailed it vigorously; and thus, unexpectedly to both parties, the battle was begun by the Federals. They had hoped to surprise an outpost—they found an army. The struggle was brief but spirited. The Twenty-first Missouri made a bold attack, but was held in check by Hardcastle's little battalion until relieved by the Eighth and Ninth Arkansas, when, after a sharp contest, Colonel Moore fell severely wounded, and the Federals retreated. Shaver's brigade pursued. In the horror of the recoil the Federal vanguard was swept away by the rapid onset of the Confederate skirmishers. As it fled surprised, the men caught a vision, through the dusky shadows of the forest, of a dark line of troops moving steadily upon them.

Thus it happened that, though the first collision between the two armies was with Prentiss's outpost, it occurred nearer to Sherman's camp than his own ; and, as his line was more retired than Sherman's, the first blow fell upon the left brigade of the latter, under Hildebrand. This lay in the pathway of the impetuous Hindman; and General Johnston was already with him urging him to the assault. The swiftest of the fugitives, scattering through the Federal camps, gave the alarm ; and the rattle of musketry also gave sharper notice that it was no common peril that threatened.

The long roll was beaten, the bugles sounded, and brisk volleys gave still sterner warning. There was rallying in hot haste, a sudden summoning to arms, and Sherman's division woke to find the foe pressing right upon them. Hindman, leading Wood's brigades along the direct road to Shiloh, had the advantage of a ridge and of the most favorable ground upon the field for an advance. The ardor of his troops kept pace with his own ; and, under the immediate eye of the commander-in-chief, they rushed through the woods, driving before them the Federal advance, almost without a halt, until they reached the main line where Hildebrand was posted. Sherman's advance-guards had made what resistance they could, but it was brief and fruitless.

In the mean time, Sherman and Hildebrand had hurriedly formed a line of battle in front of the camp. It was good ground for defense— a low, timbered ridge, with an open valley traversed by a small stream in front. But there was cover on the opposite hill, in which Hindman's skirmishers swarmed ; and soon his main line appeared. Sherman and Hildebrand rode to and fro encouraging the men who were firing brisk volleys. To attack them, the Southern brigades had to cross the stream and open field. Just then, General Johnston rode to the front. At that moment, he and Sherman were confronted almost within pistol-shot; the one urging the attack, the other trying in vain to hold his line. Hardee says briefly in his report: "My command advanced. Hindman's brigade engaged the enemy with great vigor in the edge of a wood, and drove him rapidly back on the field toward Pittsburg."

But the Confederate line, which had hung for a few minutes only on the crest of the hill, like a storm-cloud on the mountain's brow, now burst with a sudden impulse upon Hildebrand's camps. The "rebel yell," so inspiring to friends, so terrific to foes, rose sharp and shrill from the rushing line of Southern soldiery. Their volleys came pouring in, and the bayonet even was used on some whose heavy slumbers were broken only by the oncoming of their foes. Sherman's orderly was shot dead by his side, and he himself rode away to the right, out of the wreck. Sherman had ordered Colonel Appler, with the Fifty-third Ohio, to hold his ground at all hazards; but it could not stand the charge, and, after firing two rounds, fled, scattered, and was seen no more. Hildebrand says: "This regiment became separated from my command, and its movements throughout the day *were general.*" The Fifty-seventh Ohio soon followed, and, a little later, Hildebrand's own regiment, the Seventy-seventh Ohio. Sherman, though in error as to the hour, says, "Hildebrand's brigade had substantially disappeared from the field, though he himself bravely remained." It is due to Hildebrand to say that his discomfiture does not seem to have been due to his personal conduct on the field, which commended itself to his superiors.

While this struggle was going on, Hindman's right brigade, under Colonel Shaver, and Gladden's brigade, burst in upon Prentiss's division. Peabody's brigade, which lay upon the Bark road, was got into position. The Twenty-fifth Missouri, the Sixteenth Wisconsin, and the Twelfth Michigan, were hurriedly pushed forward into line of battle, and the remainder of the division formed in front of their camps; but they were unprepared, confused, and startled. It was not eight o'clock when Shaver's and Gladden's strong line fell fiercely upon them. Here were enacted, though in less measure, the same scenes that had occurred in Hildebrand's camps. Nevertheless, Peabody's brigade made a determined and sanguinary resistance, driving back in confusion some of the advanced regiments, which General Johnston assisted in rallying. General Preston says:

Hindman's brigade was suffering under a heavy fire. Some of the men were breaking ranks, and there were many dead and wounded. General Johnston in person rallied the stragglers, and I rode forward, where I found General Hindman animating and leading on his men. He informed me that he desired support, and, having reported this to the general, I was requested by him to order General Bragg to advance.

Bragg had already given the order. Haydon says:

Colonel Preston then carried the order to Hindman's brigade, who made a splendid and victorious charge. . . . It was while under this fire that Captain Brewster expostulated with General Johnston against his exposing his person. I was not near enough to hear his reply, but it had no effect, for he smilingly rode to the brow of the hill where we could distinctly see the enemy retreating.

There was a gap between Hildebrand and Prentiss's right, and into this poured Hindman's men. His left, too, was assailed by Chalmers's brigade, which was on Gladden's right. Here the Eighteenth Wisconsin, 1,000 strong, was attacked by the Tenth Mississippi, 360 strong, followed by the Ninth and Seventh Mississippi, which dashed at it with the bayonet, and drove it back half a mile. Chalmers was about to charge again, when General Johnston, coming up, ordered him still farther to the right, restoring his order of battle, and brought up Jackson's brigade into the interval. The conflict was severe, but not protracted. Crowded in front, to the right, to the left, by eager antagonists, Prentiss's whole division gave way, and fell back in confusion on its supports. It was not routed, but broken and very badly hammered.

In the first assault upon Prentiss's division, General Gladden, who led the attacking brigade, fell mortally wounded. He was a New Orleans merchant, who had seen service in the war with Mexico, and brought valor, experience, and enthusiasm, to the cause. He was a South Carolinian by birth, and his varied talents were applied to trade, politics, and war. His common-sense and humor were both evinced in his reply to an inquirer, who, struck by their costume, asked him " if he did not prefer *Zouaves* as soldiers." "It is very easy to make one," he replied; "you only want an Irishman and two yards of red flannel." Gladden's death was a serious loss.

It has been claimed that there was no "surprise" at Shiloh. The subject of the preparation of the Federal army for an attack has already been discussed. The following is General Sherman's own account of the opening of the battle. After mentioning the death of his orderly in front of Hildebrand's line, soon after *seven* o'clock, he says :

About 8 A. M. I saw the glistening bayonets of heavy masses of infantry to our left front, in the woods beyond the small stream alluded to, and *became satisfied for the first time that the enemy designed a determined attack on our whole camp.* All the regiments of my division were then in line of battle, at their proper posts.

The attack was made before sunrise, and by eight o'clock Hildebrand had been driven from the field. Sherman's right brigades, however, did succeed in forming and holding their ground for some time. The troops he saw were the columns moving against Prentiss. It is difficult to reconcile his admission that this was *the first time* he became satisfied that a general attack was intended, with his constant denial that he was surprised.

To appreciate the suddenness and violence of the blow that appalled and overthrew the Federal front, one must read the testimony of eye-witnesses. General Bragg says, in a sketch of "Shiloh," made for the writer :

Contrary to the views of such as urged an abandonment of the attack, the enemy was found utterly unprepared, many being surprised and captured in their tents, and others, though on the outside, in costumes better fitted to the bedchamber than to the battle-field.

Jordan says : [1]

Officers and men were killed or wounded in their beds, and large numbers had not time to clutch up arms or accoutrements. Nevertheless, few prisoners were taken, nor were many either killed or wounded in the first stage of the battle.

This is true, comparatively speaking ; but the loss in Hildebrand's brigade shows severe suffering, the greater part of it in this single onslaught. Three hundred killed and wounded, and ninety-four missing, are reported in that command.

General Preston, in his letter heretofore quoted, says :

General Johnston then went to the camp assailed, which was carried between seven and eight o'clock. The enemy were evidently surprised. The breakfasts were on the mess-tables; the baggage unpacked; the knapsacks, arms, stores, colors, and ammunition, abandoned. I took one stand of colors from the colonel's tent, which was sent by me, next morning, through Colonel Gilmer, to General Beauregard.

This, however, was one of Prentiss's camps.

[1] "Life of Forrest," p. 121.

The correspondent of the *Cincinnati Gazette*, in a letter of April 9, 1862,[1] says:

Almost at dawn, Prentiss's pickets were driven in; a very little later, Hildebrand's (in Sherman's division) were; and the enemy were in the camps almost as soon as were the pickets themselves.

Here began scenes which, let us hope, will have no parallel in our remaining annals of the war. Some, particularly among our officers, were not yet out of bed; others were dressing, others washing, others cooking, a few eating their breakfasts. Many guns were unloaded, accoutrements lying pell-mell, ammunition was ill-supplied—in short, the camps were virtually surprised—disgracefully, it might be added, unless some one can hereafter give some yet undiscovered reason to the contrary—and were taken at almost every possible disadvantage. . . .

Into the just-aroused camps thronged the rebel regiments, firing sharp volleys as they came, and springing toward our laggards with the bayonet. Some were shot down as they were running, without weapons, hatless, coatless, toward the river. The searching bullets found other poor unfortunates in their tents, and there, all unheeding now, they still slumbered, while the unseen foe rushed on.

At the first alarm, Sherman sent back to McClernand, Hurlbut, and W. H. L. Wallace, for help. McClernand hurried three Illinois regiments —the Eleventh, Twentieth, and another—to the front, which, arriving just as Hildebrand was routed, were unable long to withstand the vigorous attack of Hindman's brigades, as they pushed on in their victorious career, part of Shaver's brigade coming to Wood's assistance, breaking in on the left flank of the Illinois regiments. Assailed, beset, shivered, these gallant Northwestern troops too gave way. In their demolition, Waterhouse's battery fell into the hands of Wood's brigade. It was charged and taken by the Sixteenth Alabama and Twenty-seventh Tennessee. Colonel Williams, of the Twenty-seventh Tennessee, was killed, and Lieutenant-Colonel Brown severely wounded. Major Love was killed next day, so that this regiment lost all its field-officers. The Eighth and Ninth Arkansas, supporting, also suffered heavily, and were, moreover, fired on by the second line of advancing Confederates. What was left of Hindman's command then joined in the general assault on Sherman's heavy lines, as will be narrated hereafter. Colonel Ransom, of the Eleventh Illinois, in his report, says of the three Illinois regiments:

The enemy were immediately in front of us, in greatly superior numbers, advancing, in four ranks and in three columns, steadily upon us. When in good range we opened our fire upon them, which was responded to by a terrific fire from their lines. This fire was kept up on both sides, and told with fearful effect upon my line. My loss here in ten minutes was very heavy.

---

[1] "Rebellion Record," vol. iv., p. 388.

Among the wounded were the colonel, major, two captains, and two lieutenants, of the Eleventh Illinois. They rallied on the line which McClernand had formed.

In the mean time, Wallace had sent McArthur's brigade to support Colonel Stuart on the extreme left, and Wright's Thirteenth Missouri, 450 strong, to Sherman's aid; and Hurlbut had sent him Veatch's brigade. McClernand had also brought up Hare's brigade on his left, with Raith's next to it on the left of Sherman's line. All this time, Sherman had been maintaining well his strong position on the right. With these reënforcements interlocked with and lapping over his left, and with six batteries belching thunders upon the Confederates, Sherman made a good defense that morning. To whatever other criticism this officer may be amenable, his quickness and resource shone out conspicuously on this trying occasion. Rapid and undismayed, he rode from point to point, carrying encouragement to his volunteers, and holding hard to the vantage-ground he was on.

When Hardee's first line of battle was formed, it chanced to be at the narrowest part of the peninsula between Owl and Lick Creeks. As it advanced, gaps were left on the flanks. Chalmers occupied that on the right, near Lick Creek. Cleburne, on the extreme left, leading his brigade against Sherman's right, found such an interval between his left and Owl Creek. Nevertheless, he went at his work, sending back to Bragg for reënforcements. Sherman's strong position has already been described. The ravine that fronted it descended rapidly to Owl Creek, spreading into a marsh filled with undergrowth and tangled vines. The assailants had to cross this, under fire, and charge up a steep acclivity; though more to the right the ground was less difficult. Cleburne's gallant brigade, supported by the Second Tennessee drawn from the third line, attempted to take the heights by assault. As these bold soldiers struggled across the narrow, boggy valley, and in the jungle, and climbed the hill-side, they were exposed to the withering fire of Sherman's division and its supports, lying under cover of the crest, and of logs and trees and some extemporized defenses. Many a brave man died there disputing that ground.

Hardee thus describes the operations under Cleburne:

At the same time, Cleburne's brigade, with the Fifteenth Arkansas deployed as skirmishers, and the Second Tennessee,[1] *en échelon*, on the left, moved quickly through the fields, and, though far outflanked by the enemy on our left, rushed forward under a terrific fire from the serried ranks drawn up in front of the camp. A morass covered his front, and, being difficult to pass, caused a break in this brigade. Deadly volleys were poured upon the men from behind bales of hay and other defenses, as they advanced; and, after a series of desper-

---

[1] Of B. R. Johnson's brigade, Polk's corps.

ate charges, they were compelled to fall back. In this charge, the Sixth Mississippi, under Colonel Thornton, lost more than 300 killed and wounded out of an effective force of 425 men. It was at this point that Colonel (now Brigadier-General) Bate fell, severely wounded, while bravely leading his regiment.[1]

Supported by the arrival of the second line, Cleburne, with the remainder of his troops, again advanced, and entered the enemy's encampment, which had been forced on the centre and right by the dashing charges of Gladden's, Wood's, and Hindman's brigades.

The centre of the morass was impassable, and the brigade split into two parts: the Fifth Tennessee, under Colonel Hill, the Twenty-fourth Tennessee, under Colonel Peebles, and the Second Tennessee, under Colonel Bate, passing to the left; and the Sixth Mississippi, Colonel Thornton, and the Twenty-third Tennessee, Lieutenant-Colonel Neil, attacking on the right, with the Fifteenth Arkansas, Lieutenant-Colonel Patton, which was deployed as skirmishers, and fell back on its supports. Never was there a more gallant attack or a more stubborn resistance. Cleburne's horse bogged down and threw him, so that he got out with great difficulty. He was on the right, and Trigg's battery tried in vain there to maintain its fire against several Federal batteries opposing. Under the terrible fire from Sherman's impregnable line, the Sixth Mississippi and Twenty-third Tennessee suffered a quick and bloody repulse, though the Sixth Mississippi made charge after charge. Its two field-officers, Colonel Thornton and Major Lowry, were both wounded. The impetuous courage and tenacity of this magnificent regiment deserved a better fate. The fighting had been murderous on the left also. The Fifteenth Arkansas had lost its major, J. T. Harris, and many good men. The Twenty-fourth Tennessee had borne itself with steady valor, and the Second Tennessee had been terribly cut up by the iron storm from the hill-top.

Just as Cleburne's line first went forward with loud cheers, General Johnston came up from where he had been urging Hindman's attack. General Preston says:

General Johnston then passed to the left at a point in front of the camps, near two cabins, subsequently used as a hospital. A field of a hundred acres fringed with forest extended to the northeast. Through this General Cleburne's brigade moved in beautiful order, and with loud and inspiring cheers in the direction of the advanced camp. Heavy firing was heard as they neared it.

Finding all apparently going well in that quarter, General Johnston again pursued the track of Hindman's advance, and from there still farther to the right. He did not know the hot work Cleburne was to have, but he nevertheless sent to General Beauregard for two brigades

[1] The Second Tennessee.

to be moved to his aid.   Beauregard hearing, however, that Sherman was giving way, after beginning the movement, countermanded it, and moved the brigades to the right.   General Johnston naturally felt a greater security as to Cleburne, because General Beauregard was in this part of the field.

Colonel Drake, describing the charge of the Second Tennessee on the extreme left of Cleburne and the army, says:

With loud cheers it rose the hill and advanced on the level a short distance. . . . The fire there encountered was the worst the regiment suffered during the war, except at Richmond, Kentucky, where over two-thirds of its numbers fell killed and wounded in less than ten minutes.   The enemy, hidden behind logs and trees, delivered three volleys; when the Second Tennessee broke and retreated.   They were rallied on Bragg's line on the opposite hill.

Drake continues:

The mortification of a repulse in our first regular engagement was extreme: some wept, some cursed, and others lamented the death of some of our bravest officers and men, and not a few drifted to the rear.

The major, W. R. Doak, and Captains Tyree and Bate, and two lieutenants, were killed in the assault, besides four more officers and and nearly a hundred men wounded out of 365 men on the field.   But the regiment reformed, and the gallant Bate led them again to the charge.   As he was crossing the creek at the bottom of the valley, a Minié-ball crushed his leg-bone and wounded his horse.   He pressed on until he became too weak, when he retired.   The regiment, discouraged, fell back under a heavy fire.   Some of the men ran forward to the right and joined the Twenty-fourth Tennessee, which, on more favorable ground, clung to the advanced position it had won.   It, too, suffered heavily, losing over 200 in killed and wounded.

Pond's brigade, of Bragg's corps, came up in support, but did not attempt to cross this valley of death.   The Confederate artillery was said not to have been brought to bear with sufficient effect here ; and, though the musketry-fire was kept up, no impression was made.   The Comte de Paris thinks this ought to have been the chief point assailed by the Confederate army *en masse ;* but, as it was the strongest point on the line and virtually impregnable to a direct attack, the course pursued of turning it on the right seems incomparably more judicious. At all events, being then near that point, General Beauregard ordered to the right the two brigades sent by General Johnston to Cleburne's aid; and he acted with all the lights before him.   Cleburne's right aided in this, though with heavy loss.   When that was accomplished, the position was no longer tenable.

While Sherman was standing up so stubbornly, McClernand, on his left, had to meet the shock of Hindman's victorious troops, with Polk on their left, and Jackson's fresh brigade on their right. Gladden's brigade, which had suffered severely in its attack on Prentiss, paused after the death of its leader to gather itself up for another contest, and these brigades passed to its front. General Johnston, coming upon Gladden's brigade at this time, ordered it to charge; but, when he learned that it had just lost its leader, he countermanded the order.

General Johnston in person directed the movement of Jackson's brigade, which belonged to the second line, and was now brought up. He gave Colonel Wheeler, of the Nineteenth Alabama, afterward distinguished as a cavalry-general, his orders to charge. He also found here the Second Texas, in which were many of his friends. He threw it against the enemy, and it executed its difficult task with great dash and persistence, under his eye.

Major Haydon makes this note:

As soon as General Johnston discovered we were under the fire of the enemy, he ordered a Texas regiment to charge the camp on the opposite side of the hollow. In descending the hollow the nature of the ground somewhat disordered their lines, but they again formed at the base of the hill, and routed the camp in fine style. I was then sent for General Chalmers, who received orders to push up the road and sweep down the river, to where we heard a heavy firing, supported by Wirt Adams's regiment.

While Jackson's brigade was attacking McClernand's left flank, and Hindman his right, Anderson's brigade had got in on Hindman's left, and Gibson's brigade was trailing at his heels, adding to the momentum of the column. Indeed, Bragg's whole corps was now virtually with the front line, though not yet all actually engaged. The contest with McClernand and Sherman now grew strenuous and deadly; but so impetuous and resolute was the attack, that Hare's and Raith's brigades, sorely pressed in front and on the left flank, gave way, and fell back fighting confusedly, until they found safety in Hurlbut's and Wallace's lines. Captain Behr was shot from his horse, and his battery taken at the point of the bayonet, his gunners barely escaping.

Prentiss's division and Sherman's left were gone; and the Confederates were crowding in where they had stood. While McClernand's command was caving in under the stunning blows delivered against it, Polk led Russell's and B. R. Johnson's brigades upon Sherman's flank. As Polk's corps was advancing, Cheatham was detached, and now General A. S. Johnston himself led A. P. Stewart's brigade farther to the right, and put it into the fight. Stewart, then acting under Bragg's orders, advanced the Fourth Tennessee to take a battery. Stewart asked the gallant Lieutenant-Colonel Strahl if they could take it. "We can try," answered Strahl, and led the Fourth Tennessee to the charge at a double-quick. Giving one round at thirty paces, they rushed on with a yell, and took the battery, driving off the supports. But they lost 31 men killed and 160 wounded in this charge. The Twelfth Tennessee, Lieutenant-Colonel T. H. Bell commanding, coming up, they were able to repulse a resolute counter-charge.

In the mean time Clark, who was with Russell's brigade, received an order from Bragg to take an enfilading battery to his left. He at once led forward Marks's Eleventh Louisiana at a double-quick. The assault was gallantly made, but was repulsed with severe loss from shot and canister and the musketry-fire of a heavy infantry support. Clark and Russell then led forward the whole brigade, which charged at a double-quick, and helped to drive the enemy some five hundred yards, when pursuit was checked by the supports, and Clark fell, severely wounded in the shoulder. This was part of the simultaneous advance which drove Sherman from his first position, and in which Cleburne's, B. R. Johnson's, and Stewart's brigades joined. B. R. Johnson's brigade moved to the left of Russell's on the main road ; his right wing aiding in this attack, his left helping Cleburne to get in. They fought well ; Polk's battery, pushed to the front, was nearly disabled, and its commander wounded ; Johnson was himself finally wounded. Preston Smith then took command of the brigade. His regiment, the One Hundred and Fifty-fourth Senior Tennessee, and Blythe's Mississippi, had already captured six guns.

The whole Federal front, which had been broken here and there, and was getting ragged, gave way under this hammering process on front and flank, and fell back across a ravine to another strong position behind the Hamburg and Purdy road in rear of Shiloh. But they were not allowed to get away unmolested. The blood of their assailants was up, and they were pursued, driven, and slaughtered, as they fell back. Sherman's route of retreat was marked by the thick-strewn corpses of his soldiers.

Sherman was not allowed to remain in his new position. Polk attacked him with his two brigades, which were soon warmly engaged. Polk, summing up his work, says, "The resistance at this point was as stubborn as at any other point on the field." The Federals "fought with determined courage, and contested every inch of ground." The division commander, Brigadier-General Clark, and Brigadier-General B. R. Johnson, were severely wounded. The gallant Colonel Blythe, of Mississippi, was shot through the heart, charging a battery. The loss was severe. But the enemy was dislodged and two batteries captured.

In these attacks Anderson's and Pond's brigades joined with great vigor and severe loss, but with unequal fortune. The former blazoned its blood-stained record with one success after another ; the latter suffered a series of disasters. The blue uniforms of some of the regiments twice caused other Confederates to fire upon them, with serious effect; and the commander complained that one of Beauregard's staff, acting in Hardee's name, put the brigade into action in such a way as to subject it to a raking fire and unnecessary loss. Doubtless, however, it contributed its full share to the general result. Sherman, beaten and driven, had to go back again, with McDowell's and Veatch's brigades crushed to pieces, and to be heard of no more in the battle. But Sherman did not finally give way until General Johnston's movement had crushed in and routed the whole front line on the Federal left and was pressing back Hurlbut and Stuart.

While these furious combats, succeeding each other like well-delivered blows from the iron flail of war, were raging along the whole line, General Johnston was carrying forward the movement by which his entire right wing was swung around on the centre, Hindman's brigade, as a pivot, so that every command of the Federals was taken successively, in front and flank, and a crumbling process ensued by which the whole line went to pieces.

At last, pressed back toward both Owl Creek and the River, these broken commands found safety by the interposition on their left flank of W. H. L. Wallace's fresh division, ready to meet the thronging battalions of the South.

Colonel Drake, who was in the pursuit over this hotly-contested field with one of Cleburne's Tennessee Regiments, says:

The enemy's dead began to appear in considerable numbers on the parade-ground, in rear of General Sherman's headquarters, called by him "Shiloh Chapel." . . . From this point on, the enemy's dead lay thick, and numbers seem to have fallen in retreat.

He picked up General Sherman's order-book, which he afterward deposited with General Cleburne. He says it contained no intimation of the Confederate approach.

General Preston gives the following account of the movements on the Confederate right:

General Hardee reported his men still advancing at this camp about nine o'clock, and conferred with General Johnston, who was reconnoitring a second line of camps near the river, where the enemy were posted in force. They then commenced shelling the first camp, apparently attracted by the presence of the staff and escort, the distance being, I should think, six or eight hundred yards, and shells from the gunboats of large size were thrown. General Johnston received a report and rough draft at this time from Captain Lockett, stating that the enemy were strongly posted on the left in front of our right. Heavy musketry-firing and cannonades indicated that Bragg and Hardee were successfully advancing on our left. General Johnston rode down the hill to escape the shells, and his escort back toward the woods. This was about half-past nine. After pondering a little while, he determined to bring forward Breckinridge's reserve, and, feeling his way to the river, to turn the enemy's left.

The Hon. Jacob Thompson says, in a letter to the writer:

Sunday, 6th of April, between eight and nine o'clock, General Beauregard directed me to seek General Johnston, who was in the front, learn from him the condition of things there, and know of him what order he had to give as to the disposition of the reserves commanded by General Breckinridge. I did so, and rode with speed to the front, where I found General Johnston just as the enemy was making his last stand at the Gin-house[1] before retreating beyond their camps. The battle was then raging furiously. General Johnston was sitting on his horse where the bullets were flying like hail-stones. I galloped up to him amid the fire, and found him cool, collected, self-possessed, but still animated and in fine spirits.

After making known my errand, he said to me: "Say to General Beauregard, we are sweeping the field before us, and in less than half an hour we shall be in possession of their camps, and I think we shall press them to the river. Say, also, I have just learned from a scout, or messenger, that the enemy is moving up in force on our left, and that General Breckinridge had better move to our left to meet him." I turned my horse to leave, but he called me back, and said: "Do not say to General Beauregard that this is an order, but he must act on what additional information he may receive. The reports to him are more to be relied on than to me." When I returned, General Breckinridge, with his troops, was started to our left, but soon it was seen that the pressure was upon our right, and his direction was immediately changed, and it was fortunate that it was so ordered.

The movement to which Mr. Thompson refers was most probably that in which Trabue's brigade was detached to the left, and the remainder of the brigade was finally moved to the support of the extreme right. General Johnston had pushed Chalmers to the right and front, with Clanton's cavalry on his right flank, and thus they swept down the left bank of Lick Creek, driving in pickets, until they encountered Stuart's brigade on the Pittsburg and Hamburg road, supported by McArthur's brigade. Stuart was strongly posted on a steep hill near the river, covered with thick undergrowth, and with an open field in front. McArthur was to his right and rear in the woods. Jackson attacked McArthur, who fell back; and Chalmers went at Stuart's brigade. This command reserved its fire until Chalmers's men were within forty yards, and then delivered a heavy and destructive volley; but, after a hard fight, they were driven back down the river. Chalmers's right now rested on the Tennessee River bottom-lands, and he fought down the bank toward Pittsburg Landing. The enemy's left was completely turned, and the Federal army was now crowded on a shorter line, a mile or more to the rear of its first position. The new line of battle was established before ten o'clock. Thus far all had been successful; and, although there was at no time an absolute cessation of fighting on the line, it may be considered that the first engagement of the day had ended.

---

[1] A cotton-gin house.

The orders of the 3d of April were that "*every* effort should be made to turn the *left flank of the enemy*, so as to cut off his line of retreat to the Tennessee River, and *throw him back on Owl Creek, where he will be obliged to surrender.*" It is seen that from the first they were carried out in letter and spirit, and as long as General Johnston lived the success of this movement was complete.

The Comte de Paris, following American writers, both Northern and Southern, and their incorrect topographical descriptions, adopts the view that General Johnston should have massed his army on the Federal right, turned that flank, and driven it up the river into the angle between Lick Creek and the Tennessee. Though somewhat deficient in positive topographical knowledge as to the field, since he had no surveys, yet he had good descriptions from Major B. B. Waddell and others ; and he formed his plan of battle either on such information, which he deemed sufficient, or guided by those correct military intuitions which are the surest proofs of a genius for war. Yet that General Johnston was able to modify his strongly-preconceived ideas, if necessary, is seen in the discretion accorded to Beauregard as to the reserves under Breckinridge. *Nevertheless, the battle was fought precisely as it was planned.* The instructions delivered to his subordinates on the previous day were found sufficient for their conduct on the battle-field. General Chalmers says he received only one order on Sunday, and that was from General Johnston, and that he acted solely on his previous orders. General Johnston in person put Stewart's, Jackson's, Bowen's, and Statham's brigades into the fight, leading them to the right. The Federal left afforded the best grounds for attack. The lay of the land favored both the celerity and the success of the movement by the Confederate right. It pressed its advantage, and turned the Federal left flank with comparative ease, while it is by no means certain that the right next Owl Creek could have been carried at all by direct attack. Sherman's camp was a stronghold, yet in no sense was it the *key* to the Federal position. But it was easily turned on its left, as was proved. The point of least resistance proved, as anticipated, to be on the Federal left ; General Johnston pressed it, broke in on that flank, and piled his reserves there, till it gave way everywhere. It was this ability to see the vital point instantly, and at the exact moment to strike it a mortal blow, that so impressed his officers at Shiloh.

II.—MID-DAY.

When the battle first began, Hurlbut and W. H. L. Wallace had been apprised, and had sent forward reënforcements, as mentioned. They advanced about eight o'clock, so that Prentiss, when he was driven

Second Position (Noon), April 6th.

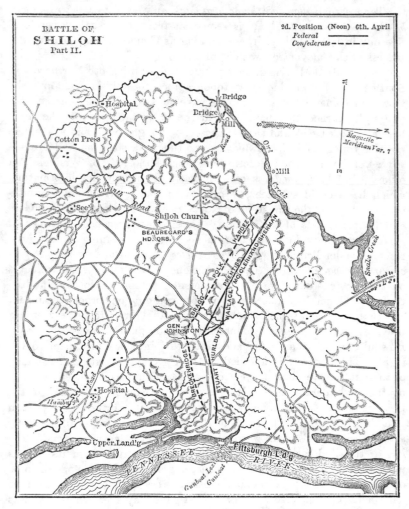

back, took refuge between them. McClernand's defense, arresting the
Confederate advance on the centre for some time, by half-past nine or
ten o'clock a new and very strong line of battle was formed, and ready
to receive the approaching Southerners. Stuart's brigade held the left,
resting on the river. Supporting Stuart, came up from Wallace the
Ninth and Twelfth Illinois, of McArthur's brigade, but they were
routed by 10½ A. M., with a loss of 250 killed and wounded. Then came
Hurlbut, with Williams's and Lauman's fresh and veteran brigades and
three batteries. On his right, Prentiss's division had rallied, reënforced

by the Twenty-third Missouri Regiment, just landed, and the Eighth Iowa. The remainder of McArthur's brigade was also in this part of the field—but probably farther to the right. Wallace had brought up Tuttle's brigade, of four veteran regiments, on his left, and Sweeney's brigade next, of three regiments. Then, to the right of Wallace, were McClernand's and Sherman's confused but unsubdued commands, which rallied and reformed as they reached their supports. The second line formed by the Federals was shorter, stronger, compacter, and more continuous, than the first. It had seized a line of wooded heights, approached only across ravines and difficult ground, and in this formidable position awaited the Confederate attack. Their line was torn, mangled, and in parts utterly routed ; but, among the fresh troops and those who stood to their colors, there was an obdurate spirit of defiance that held hard to every point of timber and broken ground.

As the first engagement was closing on the Confederate left, about ten o'clock, in desultory combats with the retreating enemy, a second engagement began on the centre and right with extreme violence. All the troops of both armies, except two of Breckinridge's brigades, were now in the front line. As the Southern army swung round to the left, by the more rapid advance of the right wing, it broke into gaps between the brigades, which were promptly occupied by the troops of the second and third lines.

General Polk says in his report:

The first order received by me was from General Johnston, who had ridden to the front to watch the opening operations, and who, as commander-in-chief, seemed deeply impressed with the responsibilities of his position. It was observed that he entered upon his work with the ardor and energy of a true soldier; and the vigor with which he pressed forward his troops gave assurance that his persistent determination would close the day with a glorious victory.

General Johnston asked Polk for a brigade, and, receiving Stewart's, led it in person and put it in position on Hindman's right. Polk sent General Cheatham with his second brigade, under Colonel William H. Stephens, to the left; but it was soon after ordered by Beauregard to the right. Polk himself advanced with Johnson's, Russell's, and Trabue's brigades down the main road toward Pittsburg. He thus had the left centre, with Pond's and Cleburne's brigades on his left, and Stewart's to his right, acting under Bragg's orders. Patton Anderson adjoined Stewart on the right, and Gibson came next, fighting in concert with Hindman's two brigades ; a little later Cheatham brought in Stephens's brigade to Gibson's right; the next was Gladden's, and then Jackson's brigade. When Breckinridge's two brigades came up, under Bowen and Statham, they occupied the ground between Jackson's and Chalmers's, which was on the extreme right. But in the rushing for-

ward of regiments to fill the gaps in the front line or to replace others
that hesitated or came limping out of the fight crippled and disheartened, the brigade organization was much broken, and, to some extent,
lost. Battles, especially of raw troops, do not present many of the
features of a parade. At Shiloh there was much dislocation of commands, but there was little loss of effective force. There was no fancy-
manœuvring; but command after command of desperate men was hurled
with overwhelming power and success against strongholds that looked
impregnable. Everybody seems to have assumed authority to command
a junior officer, whether a subordinate or not; and as the order was
"Help me!" or "Forward!" it was almost always obeyed with alacrity.
A common enthusiasm fired all hearts; a common impulse moved officers
and men alike. There was not much etiquette, but there was terrible
fighting at Shiloh.

Grant spent Saturday night at Savannah. His purpose was to meet
and confer with Buell. But the sound of hostile cannon hurried his
breakfast; and he went on board a transport, leaving a note for Buell,[1]
and an order for Nelson to march to the river opposite Pittsburg.
Grant sent this order to Nelson.[2]

Grant stopped at Crump's Landing, to order Lew Wallace to hold
himself in readiness to march on Pittsburg or defend himself, according
to circumstances. He subsequently condemned Wallace for not coming
up until night, but it does not appear that he conveyed him any orders
to that effect. Wallace took the direct road to Shiloh; but, learning
that Sherman had lost the Owl Creek crossing, he retraced his steps to
Crump's Landing, and advanced by the river road toward the Snake
Creek crossing.

Grant says he himself got to Pittsburg Landing about eight o'clock,
and was with Sherman about ten o'clock. Sherman was then in the
confusion of defeat. Commending his stubborn defense, Grant betook
himself to rallying the fugitives who were streaming to the rear. Grant
seems to have been somewhat stunned by the shock; his subordinates
make little mention of his presence on the field, and Buell found him
soon after mid-day on a steamboat with his staff. But he seems to
have retained the stolid resolution that distinguishes him. If he showed
little activity, it is certain that he had no thought of yielding.

During the morning Grant ordered General Wood, one of Buell's

---

[1] Badeau, in his "Life of Grant," vol. i., p. 75, gives this note thus: "Heavy firing is
heard up the river, indicating plainly that an attack has been made upon our most advanced positions. I have been looking for this, but did not believe the attack would be
made before Monday or Tuesday. This necessitates my joining my forces up the river,
instead of meeting you to-day as I had contemplated. I have directed General Nelson to
move to the river with his division. He can march to opposite Pittsburg."

[2] Badeau's "Life of Grant," vol. i., p. 75.

division commanders, to hasten to Pittsburg, and later sent the following significant dispatch:

COMMANDING OFFICER, Advance Forces, Buell's Army, near Pittsburg:

The attack on my forces has been very spirited from early this morning. The appearance of fresh troops in the field now would have a powerful effect, both by inspiring our men and disheartening the enemy. If you will get upon the field, leaving all your baggage on the east bank of the river, it will be more to our advantage *and possibly save the day to us.* The rebel forces are estimated at *over one hundred thousand men.* My headquarters will be in the log-building on the top of the hill, where you will be furnished with a staff officer to conduct you to your place on the field.

General Buell had arrived at Savannah on Saturday evening, the 5th, having telegraphed General Grant to meet him there. This Grant failed to do, intending to see him next day. On Sunday morning, notified by the cannonade of hot work in front, Buell went to Grant's quarters to concert measures for bringing up the troops, but Grant had just gone. Without advices, and in some perplexity, he remained until the distant din of arms made it manifest that a pitched battle was in progress. He then ordered his divisions to push forward by forced marches, while he himself hastened to Pittsburg, where he found Grant between noon and one o'clock.

While these generals were in conference on the boat, the division commanders were engaged in one of the most terrible conflicts of the war. It is difficult to give clearly the details of this gigantic contest. It commenced about the middle of the right wing, and soon raged along the whole line, lasting, with a short intermission, for six hours. It began a mile from Pittsburg. When it ended, the landing was barely covered by one flank; the other was crowded about the crossing of Snake Creek.

The battle was renewed by Gladden's gallant brigade, now commanded by Colonel Daniel W. Adams. Adams took it in with his usual mettle. There was a fierce wrestle; but it was the beating of the wave against the rock. The Confederates wilted under the scathing sheet of flame, faltered, and fell back. Jackson, too, was hammering upon this part of the line; and Chalmers, joining in the onset, turned their flank. At this critical moment, Adams seized the colors of the First Louisiana, and led his men in a desperate and successful charge. The enemy, whose flank had been turned farther to their left, fell back, but in good order. Adams, according to his wont, was wounded; and Colonel Deas took command of the brigade.

And now both armies were in the tumult of mortal endeavor. The Confederate assaults were made by rapid and often unconnected charges along the line. They were repeatedly checked, and often repulsed, by the stubborn resistance of the assailed. Sometimes counter-charges drove them back for short distances; but, whether in assault or recoil, both sides saw their bravest soldiers fall in frightful numbers. Over the blue-clad lines of the Federal troops floated the "Stars and Stripes," endeared to them by the traditions of three-quarters of a century. The Confederates came on in motley garb, varying from the favorite gray and domestic "butternut" to the blue of certain Louisiana regiments, which paid so dearly the penalty of doubtful colors. Over them were flags and pennons as various as their uniforms. Each Confederate regiment had a corps battle-flag. That of Polk's corps was a white cross on a blue field ; of Bragg's, a blue cross on a red field; of Hardee's, a white medallion on a blue field. Besides these, or in lieu of them, many of the regiments bore their State flags; and the "Lone Star" of Texas and the "Pelican flag" of Louisiana are mentioned as conspicuous among the emblems of the advancing host. On they came, their banners brightly glinting through the pale green of the foliage, but soon to be riddled, and torn, and stained with the blood of the color-bearers. At each charge there went up a wild, appalling yell, heard high above the roar of artillery; only, the Kentuckians, advancing with measured step, poured out in martial chorus the deep, full notes of their war-song : "Cheer, boys, cheer ; we'll march away to battle."

Polk and Bragg, meeting about half-past ten o'clock, agreed that Polk should direct the left centre, where part of his corps was grouped, and that Bragg should take command to his right. Bragg says:

Here we met the most obstinate resistance of the day, the enemy being strongly posted with infantry and artillery on an eminence behind a dense thicket. Hindman's command was gallantly led to the attack, but recoiled under a murderous fire.

Hindman himself was severely wounded by the explosion of a shell, and borne from the field. A. P. Stewart then took command of Hindman's brigade, with his own.

This position of the Federals was occupied by Wallace's division, and perhaps by the remains of Prentiss's and other commands. Here, behind a dense thicket on the crest of a hill, was posted a strong force of as hardy troops as ever fought, almost perfectly protected by the conformation of the ground, and by logs and other rude and hastily-prepared defenses. To assail it an open field had to be passed, enfiladed by the fire of its batteries. It was nicknamed by the Confederates, by a very mild metaphor, "The Hornets' Nest." No figure of speech would be too strong to express the deadly peril of assault upon this natural fortress, whose inaccessible barriers blazed for six hours with sheets of flame, and whose infernal gates poured forth a murderous storm of shot and shell and musket-fire which no living thing could quell or even withstand. Brigade after brigade was led against it. But valor was of no avail. Hindman's brilliant brigades, which had swept everything before them from the field, were shivered into fragments in the shock of the assault, and paralyzed for the remainder of the day. A. P. Stewart's regiments made fruitless assaults, but only to retire mangled and disheartened.

Bragg now ordered up Gibson's splendid brigade, composed of the First Arkansas, Fourth, Thirteenth, and Nineteenth Louisiana, which moved forward with alacrity. Gibson himself, a knightly soldier, as gentle and courteous as he was unflinching, was aided by colonels three of whom afterward became generals. The brigade made a gallant charge, but, like the others, recoiled from the fire it encountered. A blaze of musketry swept through it from front and flank; powerful batteries also opening upon its left. Under this cross-fire it at last fell back with very heavy loss. Allen's Fourth Louisiana was dreadfully cut up in this charge, and suffered some confusion from a misapprehension that it was fired upon by friends. Gibson asked for artillery to be sent him; but it was not at hand, and Bragg sent orders to charge again. The colonels thought it hopeless; but Gibson led them again to the attack, and they again suffered a bloody repulse.

Gibson, who, assisted by Allen and Avegno, had been leading the Fourth and Thirteenth Louisiana in the first two assaults, learning from the adjutant of Fagan that the regiments on the right had suffered equal disaster, turned over the command of his left wing to Colonel Allen, with directions to execute the orders received from General Bragg. He then proceeded to the right, and helped Fagan to lead the magnificent First Arkansas again to the assault.

"Four times the position was charged; four times the assault proved unavailing." The brigade was repulsed; but maintained its ground steadily, until Wallace's position was turned, when, again renewing its forward movement in conjunction with Cheatham's command, it helped to drive back its stout opponents. Lieutenant-Colonel Thompson, of the First Arkansas, fell pierced with seven balls. Two of its captains were killed; the major, a captain, and many officers, wounded. In the Fourth Louisiana, Colonel Allen was wounded, and three captains and three lieutenants killed or wounded. Gibson's entire staff was disabled, and his assistant adjutant-general, Lieutenant Ben King, killed. When Gibson went to Fagan, Allen, a very fearless soldier, wrung at his unavailing loss, rode back to General Bragg to repeat the need of artillery, and to ask him if he must charge again. Bragg, impatient at the check, hastily replied, "Colonel Allen, I want no faltering now." Allen, stung by the reply, said not a word, but, going back to his command, and waving his sword for his men to follow, charged once more—but again in vain. He never forgave Bragg, and the brigade thought they got hard measure in Bragg's orders and in his report.

Patton Anderson's brigade, with the Crescent Regiment, of Pond's brigade, and aided by a regiment, two battalions, and a battery from Trabue's brigade, was eventually more successful farther to the left. His ground also was very difficult, but he caught the enemy more on the flank, and clung to it, rattling them with musketry and artillery, until the movement of the Confederate right broke into this citadel, when he carried his point. But this was not until after hours of manœuvring and heavy skirmishing, with great loss, and after the enemy's left was turned. The Twentieth Louisiana was badly cut up in the underbrush, and in other regiments many companies lost all their officers. Anderson probably confronted Prentiss. The loss suffered by Pond's brigade has already been mentioned.

General Polk, with Russell's brigade, and with Johnson's under Preston Smith, and during a portion of the time with Stewart's brigade, was engaged in the same sort of heavy work, driving the enemy, and, in turn, losing the ground he had won, until it had been three times fought over. This was with McClernand's troops, and Buckland's brigade of Sherman's division.

Cheatham's division had been formed in the morning on either side of the Pittsburg road, immediately in rear of Clark's division. He was first ordered to the left, with his Second Brigade, under Colonel Stevens, by Polk, to support Bragg, and was ordered thence by Beauregard to the extreme right, to ascertain the point where the firing was heaviest, and there engage the enemy at once.

About 10 A. M. he came upon the enemy, strongly posted on the right, and engaged him in an artillery duel for an hour, when Breckinridge came up and formed on his right. At eleven o'clock, Colonel Jordan ordered Cheatham to charge, which he did across an open field. The enemy occupied an abandoned road, behind a fence, a strong position, and met the attack with a heavy fire. When Cheatham's gallant division reached the middle of the field, a murderous cross-fire from the left arrested their progress. The command fell back in good order. Cheatham, with the Second Brigade, now under Colonel Maney, again, later in the day, attacked on Breckinridge's left in Prentiss's front, when that Federal general was captured.

On the left Hardee was in charge. Here, Colonel Trabue, commanding the Kentucky Brigade, with four of his regiments, assailed part of Sherman's command, which they identified from the prisoners as McDowell's and the Thirteenth Missouri. Duke, who was with Morgan's cavalry, marching in their rear, says that as they went in, horse and foot, they struck up their battle-song, as mentioned, and that "the effect was animating beyond description." They fought for an hour and a quarter, never losing ground, and several times forcing McDowell back. Finally, bringing up the Thirty-first Alabama, which had been held in reserve, they charged at a double-quick, routing the enemy, and driving them, at a run, from the field. This defeat of the enemy was shared in by Polk's corps and Patton Anderson's brigade. Morgan's cavalry and Wharton's Eighth Texas Cavalry also pursued the routed Federals, but were checked, with loss, in the thick undergrowth. Hardee had assisted in again routing Sherman, by leading four regiments up a ravine on the extreme left, and turning the position. He also put the cavalry in pursuit of him.

After the rout of Sherman, there seems to have been not much heavy fighting on that flank. His division drifted out of the battle, clinging to the banks of Owl Creek, keeping up, however, a desultory resistance to the disconnected and indecisive skirmishing directed against it. Cleburne's brigade had lost so heavily in the morning that only a part of it remained in line. One-third of his men were killed or wounded, as his "butcher's bill" in the Appendix will show. In an assault this is one of the surest signs of honest, hard fighting. With the remnant, however, he continued to press on Sherman's right, which it kept moving, without absolutely crushing it. McClernand's line still maintained itself, and the force of the Confederate attack at the left was turned against it. General Beauregard's headquarters were about this time at Shiloh Church. The situation there seems hard to understand. An extract from Colonel Drake's sketch may throw some light on the condition of things on the left. Drake says:

It was at this juncture that the lines at this point were halted, and a lull in the battle ensued for a considerable length of time. Many supposed the fighting was ended, and scattered over the field on various errands. Entire regiments were seen marching to the rear, and then began on a large scale the pillage of the captured camps, for which our army was so harshly blamed; but the object, so far as my observation went, was not so much to gather the booty as to gratify curiosity, and pick up articles as mementos. Greenbacks were no object then, and the pockets of the dead were not rifled. Shoes, boots, and underclothes, seemed to be in more request than anything else.

Naming many other articles—patriotic envelopes, cheap pictures, caricatures, song-books, etc., he adds:

And yet the Confederate soldiers, who sought after trash, and pillaged sutler-stores, were not so much to blame as the inexperience of the times, as illustrated in field and general officers. No battle of the war—no event in Confederate history—has such a long list of "ifs" and "might have beens" as this battle of Shiloh; it is the saddest story of them all.

Colonel Munford gives the following account, which is a very good summary of the situation on the centre and right:

General Bragg was ordered to attack them at once, and here occurred the most obstinate contest of the whole day. It was full four hours of the severest fighting before the enemy gave way, and then not until General Johnston with the remainder of the active troops had driven all opposition from the entire right and centre of the field far back toward the river. Soon after our left had become so hotly engaged, other scouts brought intelligence that large bodies of the enemy were moving in the direction of Pittsburg Landing on the river. Others reported heavy masses assembled there; and, lastly, that the head of a column had started from that point up the road which turned our right in the direction of Lick Creek. When this information was received, the general looked at his watch, and continued conversing with the members of the staff for twenty or thirty minutes, when, again glancing at his watch, he remarked, "It is now time to move forward." He gave orders for the formations he desired. The troops in marching order were so arranged that, while all were compactly in hand, every man, horse, and gun-carriage, had necessary room. The beauty of the manœuvre did not escape attention even under the circumstances, and in a small way showed how justly the general had been celebrated for the ease with which he handled troops. Just then I was ordered to see that a brigade "went promptly" to the support of Brigadier-General Clark in Bragg's fight, and, in doing so, had an opportunity of witnessing a portion of the hardest fighting I have ever seen. When I overtook General Johnston, he had taken position with his right across the road, up which it was reported the enemy had begun to march, on the very verge of the ridges overlooking Pittsburg Landing. He was in the act of swinging his troops round on his left as a pivot. A brigade under Colonel (afterward Major-General) Chalmers, flanked by a battalion of Wirt Adams's cavalry, constituted the extreme right. We sat on our horses, side by side, watching that brigade as it swept over the ridge; and, as the colors dipped out of sight, the general said to me, "That checkmates them." I told him I was glad to hear him announce "checkmate," but that "he must excuse so poor a player for saying he could not see it." He laughed, and said, "Yes, sir, that mates them." The completion of this movement faced the troops at an angle of about 45° toward the left, when the forward movement became uniform. We had advanced but a few hundred yards, when we came upon a line of the enemy, strongly posted with their right in a flat covered by a dense growth of shrubs, almost a chaparral, and their centre and left along the hollow through which this flat and the hill-sides were drained. Their bodies were almost entirely protected, but their position enabled them to see the entire persons of our troops, who, when they came in sight, were within easy musket-range and wholly unprotected. They opened upon us a murderous fire. General Johnston moved forward with his staff to a depression about thirty yards behind our front line, where the bullets passed over our heads; but he could see more than half of his line, and, if an emergency arose, could meet it promptly. He fought that entire battle on the true philosophic principle which it involved. He was in command of fresh Southern volunteers. He therefore let them stand and fire, only till what is known as the "shoulder-to-shoulder" courage was developed, leaving the impetuous fire of Southern pluck unchilled. His charges were uniformly successful. I saw our line beginning to stagger, not give back, but waver along its whole length like small grain when struck by a breeze. The general passed his eye from the right of the line to his extreme point of vision in the direction of the left, and slowly back again, when he remarked to Governor Harris who was

by his side: " Those fellows are making a stubborn stand here. I'll have to put
the bayonet to them." Just then a shell from one of our batteries on the extreme right came flying over the heads of the men in line, passed just in front
of us, struck and exploded a little to our left between us and our reserve or
second line. The general asked me to correct the position of that battery.
When I returned from the discharge of this duty a charge was being executed
along the whole line, and the general was gone from the place where I had left
him.

The front on which General Johnston was now moving was almost
at right angles to his original lines and approaching a perpendicular to
the river. Chalmers's brigade, on the extreme right, next the river, was
somewhat advanced, so that it continually pressed upon and turned the
enemy's left flank. Eight hundred yards to his left and rear, Bowen's
brigade came up ; and, with a like interval to the left and rear of Bow-
en's, Statham's strong brigade. These troops advanced *en échelon* of
brigades. The batteries were in full play ; the resistance was vigorous ; the contest fierce. Chalmers pushed forward with considerable
success ; General Johnston had Bowen's brigade deployed, and it advanced with energy. Statham's brigade impinged upon what was an
angle in the Federal line, where the Northerners were collected in
heavy masses. The locality was probably that held by Hurlbut's brigades, and they opposed a desperate defense to every forward movement. The severe pressure on their left had called the Northern troops
to this point, and we find acting Brigadier-General Cruft, after having
repulsed four assaults farther to the right, strengthening it. Sweeney
also reënforced Hurlbut with three regiments.

There had been four hours of heavy fighting, during which the Federal centre had not been moved. The right had been broken ; its left
was forced back and doubled up on itself ; and Hurlbut had more than
once fallen back, retiring his left, in order to correct his alignment.
But there his command stood, dealing slaughter on every attempt at
advance. His position was evidently the key ; and it was necessary to
break down the stubborn defense that maintained it. It was for this
that Breckinridge's reserves, the only brigades which had not been
engaged, were brought forward. General Johnston's purpose was to
destroy Grant's army that day. The afternoon was upon him. The
final blow must be struck. Statham's brigade was sent in about noon.
It was made up of six fine regiments : two of them were raw, four of
them knew nothing of war, except the miserable defeat at Mill Spring.
The brigade now found itself welcomed by a fearful blaze of musketry
and artillery ; and, in getting into line, suffered enough to fall into
some confusion.

The Federals were posted in a double line of battle, protected by
the crest of a wooded hill, and the men seemed to be lying down and

firing. Opposite this strong position, one or two hundred yards distant, was another ridge, swept by the Federal fire. Behind it, Statham's troops were comparatively secure ; but, to assail the enemy, they had to cross this exposed ridge, descend one slope, and ascend another, commanded and raked by this deadly ambuscade. They stood, therefore, delivering and receiving a fire which, Governor Harris says, was as heavy as any he saw in the war ; but they could not drive the enemy from his stronghold by their fire, nor without a charge that meant death for many. Statham's brigade and even particular regiments have to some extent been held responsible for General Johnston's death. It has been held to account, as if it were the only command which on that day failed to carry a position promptly at the point of the bayonet, without first measuring its strength with the foe. But those who have read this narrative must have seen how often good and gallant troops recoiled from positions which they could not take. The measure of resistance is an element of the greatest importance, too often ignored, in estimating the value and courage of an attack.

Major (afterward General) Hodge, who was Breckinridge's adjutant-general, and on the spot, gives the following clear description of the attack :

The long slope of the ridge was here abruptly broken by a succession of small hills or undulations of about fifty feet in height, dividing the rolling country from the river-bottom, and behind the crest of the last of these the enemy was concealed; opposite them, at the distance of seventy-five yards, was another long swell or hillock, the summit of which it was necessary to attain in order to open fire; and to this elevation the reserve moved, in order of battle, at a double-quick. In an instant, the opposing height was one sheet of flame. Battle's Tennessee regiment, on the extreme right, gallantly maintained itself, pushing forward under a withering fire and establishing itself well in advance. Lytle's Tennessee regiment, next to it, delivered its fire at random and inefficiently, became disordered, and retired in confusion down the slope. Three times it was rallied by its lieutenant-colonel, assisted by Colonel T. T. Hawkins, and by the adjutant-general, and carried up the slope, only to be as often repulsed and driven back—the regiment of the enemy opposed to it, in the intervals, directing an oblique fire upon Battle's regiment, now contending against overwhelming odds. The crisis of the contest had come; there were no more reserves, and General Breckinridge determined to charge.

The Forty-fifth Tennessee was behind the crest of the hill, and thus protected. The men would advance to a rail-fence, individually, or in squads, deliver an irregular fire, and fall back; but they would not come up to their alignment, nor exhibit the purpose required for a desperate charge. They were not stampeded, but irresolute, and their conduct probably did not fall below the average of the brigade, or below what might be expected from raw troops under like circumstances. But more was required of them and of all.

The following is Governor Harris's account of the circumstances preceding the charge :

Just as day was dawning, on Sunday morning, he (General Johnston) made the attack. For some time our advance was steady and without any serious or obstinate resistance. About one o'clock, P. M., being informed that our extreme right had encountered such resistance as prevented further advance, he repaired to it at once.

We found our right wing posted upon a ridge, while upon a parallel ridge in easy musket-range the enemy was in great force. Here the firing was kept up with great energy by both armies for, perhaps, an hour, during the whole of which time the general remained upon the line, more exposed to the fire of the enemy than any soldier in the line.

After the firing had been thus continued for near an hour, the general said to me : " They are offering stubborn resistance here. I shall have to put the bayonet to them."

It was in this condition of things that Breckinridge rode up to General Johnston, and, in his preoccupation, not observing Governor Harris, said, " General, I have a Tennessee regiment that won't fight." Harris broke in energetically, " General Breckinridge, show *me* that regiment !" Breckinridge, courteously and apologetically, indicated the command, and General Johnston said, " Let the Governor go to them." Governor Harris went, and with some difficulty put the regiment in line of battle on the hill, whence they could engage in the combat effectively.

After some delay, the wavering of the line still increasing, General Johnston directed that the line be got ready for a charge. Breckinridge soon returned and said he feared that he could not get the brigade to make the charge. General Johnston replied to him cheerfully : "Oh, yes, general ; I think you can." Breckinridge, with an emotion unusual to his controlled and equable temper, told him he had tried and failed. " Then, I will help you," said General Johnston. " We can get them to make the charge." Turning to Governor Harris, who had come back to report that the Tennessee regiment was in line, he requested him to return to and encourage this regiment, then some distance to his right, but under his eye, and to aid in getting them to charge. Harris galloped to the right, and, breaking in among the soldiers with a sharp harangue, dismounted and led them on foot, pistol in hand, up to their alignment, and in the charge when it was made.

In the mean time Breckinridge, with his fine voice and manly bearing, was appealing to the soldiers, aided by his son Cabell and a very gallant staff. It was a goodly company ; and, in the charge, Breckinridge, leading and towering above them all, was the only one who escaped unscathed. Major Hodge and Cabell Breckinridge had their horses shot under them ; Major Hawkins was wounded in the face, and Captain Allen had his leg torn by a shell. Many eye-witnesses have remarked to the writer on the beautiful composure and serene fidelity with which Cabell Breckinridge, then a mere boy, rode close by his father during all this stirring scene.

General Johnston rode out in front, and slowly down the line. His hat was off. His sword rested in its scabbard. In his right hand he held a little tin cup, the memorial of an incident that had occurred earlier in the day. As they were passing through a captured camp, an officer had brought from a tent a number of valuable articles, calling General Johnston's attention to them. He answered, with some sternness : "None of that, sir ; we are not here for plunder!" And then, as if regretting the sharpness of the rebuke, for the anger of the just cuts deep, he added, taking this little tin cup, "Let this be my share of the spoils to-day." It was this plaything, which, holding it between two fingers, he employed more effectively in his natural and simple gesticulation than most men could have used a sword. His presence was full of inspiration. Many men of rank have told the writer that they never saw General Johnston's equal in battle in this respect. He sat his beautiful thorough-bred bay, "Fire-eater," with easy command —like a statue of Victory. His voice was persuasive, encouraging, and compelling. It was inviting men to death, but they obeyed it. But, most of all, it was the light in his gray eye, and his splendid presence, full of the joy of combat, that wrought upon them. His words were few. He touched their bayonets with significant gesture. "These must do the work," he said. "Men ! they are stubborn ; we must use the bayonet." When he reached the centre of the line, he turned. "I will lead you !" he cried, and moved toward the enemy. The line was already thrilling and trembling with that tremendous and irresistible ardor which in battle decides the day. Those nearest to him, as if drawn to him by some overmastering magnetic force, rushed forward around him with a mighty shout. The rest of the line took it up and echoed it with a wild yell of defiance and desperate purpose, and moved forward at a charge with rapid and resistless step. A sheet of flame burst from the Federal stronghold, and blazed along the crest of the ridge. There was a roar of cannon and musketry ; a storm of leaden and iron hail. The Confederate line withered, and the dead and dying strewed the dark valley. But there was not an instant's pause. Right up the steep they went. The crest was gained. The enemy were in flight—a few scattering shots replying to the ringing cheers of the victorious Confederates.

General Johnston had passed through the ordeal seemingly unhurt. His noble horse was shot in four places ; his clothes were pierced by missiles, his boot-sole was cut and torn by a Minié ; but if he himself had received any severe wound he did not know it. At this moment Governor Harris rode up from the right, elated with his own success

Death of General A. S. Johnston at Shiloh.

and with the vindication of his Tennesseeans. After a few words, General Johnston sent him with an order to Colonel Statham, which, having delivered, he speedily returned. In the mean time knots and groups of Federal soldiers kept up an angry discharge of fire-arms as they retreated upon their supports, and their last line, now yielding, delivered volley after volley as they sullenly retired. By the chance of war, a Minié-ball from one of these did its fatal work. As General Johnston, on horseback, sat there, knowing that he had crushed in the arch which had so long resisted the pressure of his forces, and waiting until they should collect sufficiently to give the final stroke, he received a mortal wound. It came in the moment of victory and triumph from a flying foe. It smote him at the very instant when he felt the full conviction that the day was won; that his own conduct and wisdom were justified by results, and that he held in his hand the fortunes of war and the success of the Confederate cause. If this was not to be, he fell as he would have wished to fall, and with a happier fate than those who lived to witness the overthrow and ruin of their great cause. He had often expressed to the writer a preference for this death of the soldier. It came sudden and painless. But he had so lived as neither to fear nor shun it. It came to him like an incident of an immortal life—its necessary part, but not its close.

The writer will be pardoned for adding the narrative of Governor Harris, the faithful comrade who was with him at the last. He writes as follows :

Soon thereafter our line slightly wavered with a backward tendency, when the general said, "I will go to the front, order, and lead the charge." Just as he was in the act of passing through the line to the front, he said to me, "Go to the extreme right, and lead the Tennessee regiment stationed there." I galloped to the regiment named; and when the charge was ordered, which was only a few moments after, I repeated the order on the extreme right, and moved forward with it.

The charge was successful; the Federal line gave way, and we advanced from a half to three-fourths of a mile without opposition, when we encountered the reserve line of the enemy strongly posted upon a ridge.

The general immediately established his line upon a parallel ridge in easy musket-range of the line of the enemy, and a galling fire was opened upon both sides.

Just as the line of our extreme right (with which I had moved forward) was established, casting my eye up the line to the left I saw General Johnston sitting upon his horse a few feet in rear, and about the centre of his line. He was alone. I immediately galloped to him, to ascertain if, in his new position, he wished to send orders.

I had never, in my life, seen him looking more bright, joyous, and happy, than he looked at the moment that I approached him.

The charge he had led was heroic. It had been successful, and his face expressed a soldier's joy and a patriot's hope.

As I approached him, he said "Governor, they came very near putting me *hors de combat* in that charge," holding out and pointing to his foot. Looking at it, I discovered that a musket-ball had struck the edge of the sole of his boot, cutting the sole clear across, and ripping it off to the toe. I asked eagerly: "Are you wounded? Did the ball touch your foot?" He said, "No;" and was proceeding to make other remarks, when a Federal battery opened fire from a position which enfiladed our line just established. He paused in the middle of a sentence to say, "Order Colonel Statham to wheel his regiment to the left, charge, and take that battery." I galloped to Colonel Statham, only about two hundred yards distant, gave the order, galloped back to the general where a moment before I had left him, rode up to his right side, and said, "General, your order is delivered, and Colonel Statham is in motion;" but, as I was uttering this sentence, the general reeled from me in a manner that indicated he was falling from his horse. I put my left arm around his neck, grasping the collar of his coat, and righted him up in the saddle, bending forward as I did so, and, looking him in the face, said, "General, are you wounded?" In a very deliberate and emphatic tone he answered, "Yes, and I fear seriously." At that moment I requested Captain Wickham to go with all possible speed for a surgeon, to send the first one he could find, but to proceed until he could find Dr. Yandell, the medical director, and bring him. The general's hold upon his rein relaxed, and it dropped from his hand. Supporting him with my left hand, I gathered his rein with my right, in which I held my own, and guided both horses to a valley about 150 yards in rear of our line, where I halted, dropped myself between the two horses, pulling the general over upon me, and eased him to the ground as gently as I could. When laid upon the ground, with eager anxiety I asked many questions about his wounds, to which he gave no answer, not even a look of intelligence.

Supporting his head with one hand, I untied his cravat, unbuttoned his collar and vest, and tore his shirts open with the other, for the purpose of finding the wound, feeling confident from his condition that he had a more serious wound than the one which I knew was bleeding profusely in the right leg; but I found no other, and, as I afterward ascertained, he had no other. Raising his head, I poured a little brandy into his mouth, which he swallowed, and in a few moments I repeated the brandy, but he made no effort to swallow; it gurgled in his throat in his effort to breathe, and I turned his head so as to relieve him.

In a few moments he ceased to breathe. I did not consult my watch, but my impression is that he did not live more than thirty or forty minutes from the time he received the wound.

He died calmly, and, to all appearances, free from pain—indeed, so calmly, that the only evidence I had that he had passed from life was the fact that he ceased to breathe, and the heart ceased to throb. There was not the slightest struggle, nor the contortion of a muscle; his features were as calm and as natural as at any time in life and health.

Just as he expired, General William Preston arrived, and it was agreed that he should remain with and accompany the remains of General Johnston to headquarters, and that I should proceed at once to report the fact of General Johnston's death to General Beauregard.

My own horse having run off when I dismounted, I mounted "Fire-eater," General Johnston's horse, but found him so badly crippled that I dismounted and examined him, and found upon examination that he was wounded in three legs by musket-balls. I rode him to the rear, where we had left General Johnston's orderly with two fresh horses; left Fire-eater with the orderly, and mounted one of the fresh horses and proceeded to report to General Beauregard.

Other members of the staff confirm all this, with the following slight variations:

Captain Wickham assisted Governor Harris in lifting General Johnston from his horse, and then went for a surgeon. General Preston came up before General Johnston's death. Kneeling by him, he cried passionately, "Johnston, do you know me?" General Johnston smiled faintly, but gave no other sign of recognition. They then tried to administer the brandy, but he could not swallow it. General Johnston soon became utterly unconscious, and quietly passed away. Colonel O'Hara, Major Haydon, and others of the staff, joined the group soon after.

Wrapping his body in a mantle to conceal his death from the army, some of the staff took charge of it and left the field. The others separated to inform General Beauregard and the corps commanders. Colonel Munford says:

Besides the wound which killed him, he was hit three other times: once by a spent ball on the outside and about midway of the right thigh; once by a fragment of shell just above and to the rear of the right hip; and once by a Minié-ball cutting the left boot-sole entirely in two, at which he kicked up his foot, and said, gayly, "They didn't trip me up that time." But one bullet broke the skin—and that, alas! was fatal.

The mortal wound was from a Minié-ball, which tore the popliteal artery of the right leg, where it divides into the tibial arteries, as Dr. Yandell informs the writer. He did not live more than ten or fifteen minutes after receiving it. It was not necessarily fatal. General Johnston's own knowledge of military surgery was adequate for its control by an extemporized tourniquet, had he been aware or regardful of its nature.

Dr. D. W. Yandell, his surgeon, had attended his person during most of the morning; but, finding a large number of wounded men, including many Federals, at one point, General Johnston ordered Yandell to stop there, establish a hospital, and give them his services. He said to Yandell: "These men were our enemies a moment ago, they are prisoners now; take care of them." Yandell remonstrated against leaving him, but he was peremptory, and the doctor began his work. He saw General Johnston no more. Had Yandell remained with him, he would have had little difficulty with the wound. It was this act of unselfish charity which cost him his life.

General Beauregard had told General Johnston that morning as he rode off, that, if it should be necessary to communicate with him or for him to do anything, he would be found in his ambulance in bed. Governor Harris, knowing this, and how feeble General Beauregard's health was, went first to his headquarters—just in the rear of where the army had deployed into line the evening before. Beauregard and his staff were gone on horseback in the direction of Shiloh Church. He found them there. The Governor told General Beauregard that General Johnston had been killed. Beauregard expressed regret, and then remarked, "Everything else seems to be going on well on the right." Governor Harris assented. "Then," said Beauregard, "the battle may as well go on." The Governor replied that he certainly thought it ought. He offered his services to Beauregard, and they were courteously accepted. General Beauregard then remained where he was, waiting the issue of events.

III.—AFTERNOON.

Up to the moment of the death of the commander-in-chief, the battle presented two features, at first sight incongruous and almost incompatible. The first of these was the dislocation of commands by the pushing forward of the second and third lines into the intervals of the first, and, by the shifting fortunes of the field, resulting in an effect like the shuffling of cards. The other was the most perfect regularity in the development of the plan of battle. In all the seeming confusion, there was the predominance of intelligent design; a master-mind, keeping in clear view its purpose, sought the weak point in the defense, and, finding it on the enemy's left, kept turning that flank. With the disadvantage of inferior numbers, General Johnston brought to bear a superior force on each particular point, and, by a series of consecutive blows, repeated with great rapidity and strength, broke the Federal army to pieces.

General Duke makes the following intelligent comments on the battle. He says :

The corps of Hardee, Bragg, and Polk, were now striving abreast, or mingled with each other. In reading the reports of the Confederate generals, frequent allusion will be found to regiments and brigades fighting without "head or orders." One commander would sometimes direct the movements of troops belonging to another. At this phase of the struggle, the narrative should dwell more upon "the biographies of the regiments than the history of the battle." But the wise arrangement of the lines and the instructions given subordinate commanders insured harmonious action and the desired result.

Each brigade commander was ordered, when he became disengaged, to seek and attack the nearest enemy ; to pass the flank of every stubborn hostile force

Third Position (Sunday), April 6th.

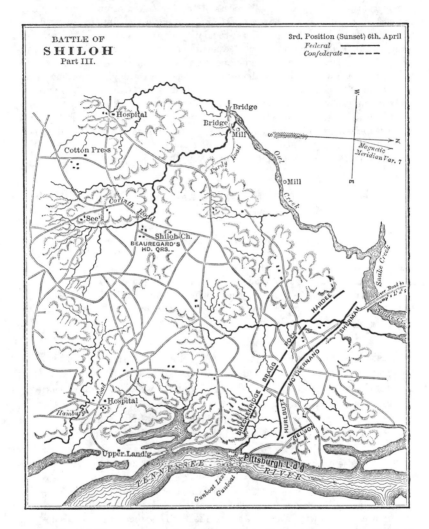

BATTLE OF
SHILOH
Part III.

3rd. Position (Sunset) 6th. April
Federal ————
Confederate – – – – –

which his neighbors could not move, and, at all hazards, to press forward. General Johnston seemed to have adopted the spirit of the motto, " When fighting in the dark, strike out straight."   He more than once assumed command of brigades which knew not what to do, and led them to where they could fight with effect.

The same remark might be made of all the higher officers.

Duke also notes as follows the systematic manner in which the troops were rapidly massed on successive points:

This disposition of the forces and the energetic conduct of the Confederate commanders explain the striking features of the battle, which have been so often remarked—the *methodical* success of the Confederates upon the first day, the certainty with which they won their way forward against the most determined resistance, the " clock-like " regularity of their advance, the desperate struggle, the Federal retreat, repeated again and again through the day. Taking into consideration the circumstances under which the collision occurred, military *savants* will some day demonstrate that success ought, with mathematical certainty, to have resulted from the tactics of General Johnston. An army moving to attack an enemy surprised and unprepared, in three lines supported by a reserve, and with its flanks perfectly protected, ought to have delivered crushing and continuous blows. Such a formation, directed by consummate skill and the finest nerve in a commander of troops who believed that to fight would be to win, promised an onset wellnigh irresistible.

Speaking elsewhere of the repeated successful assaults of the Confederates, Duke says :

Those who were in that battle will remember these successive contests, followed by short periods of apparent inaction, going on all day. To use the illustration of one well acquainted with its plans and incidents, " It went on like the regular stroke of some tremendous machine." There would be a rapid charge and fierce fight—the wild yell would announce a Confederate success— then would ensue a comparative lull, broken again in a few minutes, and the charge, struggle, and horrible din would recommence.

Just when General Johnston was stricken down, the victory seemed complete. The enemy was not merely broken, but, so close were the quarters and so rapid was the charge, that they suffered more than the usual slaughter in a defeat.

Captain Allison, who commanded the Forty-fifth Tennessee in this charge, makes the following statement to the writer :

The impulse given the Confederate line by General Johnston's presence was irresistible. The Federals were ensconced in a deep ravine, and when their assailants closed down on them for the death-struggle, they crowded for escape into a ravine which ran perpendicularly to the rear, hoping thus to avoid the line of fire, which swept the level above them. The steepness of the sides held them in a mass, into which the Forty-fifth Tennessee fired at close range with murderous effect.

Captain Allison adds that he never saw such slaughter during the whole war as took place here. He further says that, when he got orders to fall back in the afternoon, his regiment was within two hundred yards of the enemy's batteries, in fine spirits and organization. He adds some striking incidents, of which want of space prevents the insertion. The Federal reports show that, among the troops who fought here, the Twenty-fifth Kentucky (Federal), Lieutenant-Colonel Bristow, had but sixty-five men left, and Colonel McHenry reported that his regiment (the Seventeenth Kentucky) was reduced to one-half its numbers.

Now was the time for the Confederates to push their advantage, and, closing in on the rear of Prentiss and Wallace, to finish the battle. But, on the contrary, there came a lull in the conflict on the right, lasting more than an hour from half-past two, the time at which General Johnston fell. It is true that the Federals fell back and left the field, and the Confederates went forward deliberately, occupying their positions, and thus helping to envelop the Federal centre. But there was no further general direction nor concerted movements. The spring and alertness of the onset flagged; the determinate purpose to capture Grant that day was lost sight of; the strong arm was withdrawn, and the bow remained unbent. The troops who had fought under General Johnston's eye were carried forward by the impulse imparted to them, and the momentum of their own success; but with no visible or definite object. Elsewhere, there were bloody desultory combats, but tending to nothing. Indeed, it may be truly said that General Johnston's death ended the second engagement of the day.

About half-past three o'clock, the struggle at the centre, which had been going on for five hours with fitful violence, was renewed with the utmost fury. Polk's and Bragg's corps, intermingled, were engaged in a death-grapple with the sturdy commands of Wallace and Prentiss. The Federal generals had consulted, and had resolved to stand and hold their ground at all hazards, hoping thus to save the rest of the army from destruction; and there is little doubt that their manful resistance, which cost one his life and the other his liberty, so checked the Southern troops as to gain time, and prevent the capture of Grant's army.

While an ineffectual struggle was going on at the centre, General Ruggles judiciously collected all the artillery he could find, some eleven batteries in all, which he massed against Prentiss's right flank, the centre of what remained. The opening of so heavy a fire, and the simultaneous though unconcerted advance of the whole Confederate line, resulted at first in the confusion of the enemy and then in the defeat of Wallace and the surrender of Prentiss. Patton Anderson's brigade and Marshall J. Smith's Crescent Regiment were especially conspicuous in these closing scenes, the latter being so fortunate as to receive the surrender of a large number of prisoners. But, while the artillery massed by Ruggles, and his division, were so effectual in achieving this result, by hammering down the Federal front, they were not alone in the crushing coil which caught Prentiss in its folds. Polk and Hardee burst through and destroyed the troops occupying the right of Wallace's position, who were thoroughly beaten and driven from the field or captured, with the commander killed in the rout. They thus got in on Prentiss's right flank. Bragg, who had gone to the Confederate right, with Breckinridge, pushed in on Prentiss's left flank; and Chalmers on his rear—and thus intercepted his retreat.

While these movements were being executed, Prentiss determined on a bold course, afterward condemned by his more fortunate superiors, because it failed; but, in the writer's opinion, it saved both Grant and Sherman from capture. He formed his men to make an attack; but the Confederates closed in around him, and he found himself, after a struggle, cut off, encompassed, and at the mercy of his adversaries. With Hurlbut gone and Wallace gone, Prentiss was left isolated. Struck in front, in rear, and on either flank, cut off in every attempt to escape, about half-past four o'clock what was left of Prentiss's division surrendered with the Eighth, Twelfth, and Fourteenth Iowa, and the Fifty-eighth Illinois Regiments, of Wallace's division. More than 3,000 prisoners were taken, Prentiss and many officers among them. This division had received the first blow in the morning, and made the last organized resistance in the afternoon.

Each Confederate commander—division, brigade, and regimental— as his command pounced upon the prey, believed it entitled to the credit of the capture. Breckinridge's, Withers's, Ruggles's, Cheatham's, and other divisions, which helped to encircle and subdue these stubborn fighters, each imagined its own the hardest part of the work—possibly the whole of it. The capture was, in truth, due almost as much to one as to another, as it was the result of the annihilation of Grant's whole line.

A similar instance of self-deception occurs in many—indeed, most— of the Federal reports of this battle. According to these, no command ever gives way until its neighbors, on *both* flanks, have left the field. This, of course, is in the nature of things impossible. It was, as a rule, true of *one* flank; and the gaps made in the line by casualties and flight left it so ragged on the other flank as to favor, if not to create, the illusion. So many human motives concur to fortify these prejudices that we have no occasion to be astonished at them.

The following particulars of this momentous contest will not be thought out of place. In describing his share in the combat, General Polk says:

The enemy in our front was gradually and successively driven from his positions, and forced from the field back on the river-bank. About 5 P. M. my line attacked the enemy's troops—the last that were left upon the field—in an encampment on my right. The attack was made in front and flank. The resistance was sharp but short. The enemy, perceiving he was flanked and his position completely turned, hoisted the white flag and surrendered.

Commending the conduct of Bragg's troops coöperating with him, and especially of the Crescent Regiment, General Polk says:

General Prentiss delivered his sword with his command to Colonel Russell, one of my brigade commanders, who turned him over to me. The prisoners turned over were about 2,000. They were placed in charge of Lieutenant Richmond, my aide-de-camp, and, with a detachment of cavalry, sent to the rear.

Immediately after the surrender, General Polk ordered such cavalry as he had in hand to charge the fleeing enemy. A detachment under Lieutenant-Colonel Miller "dashed forward and intercepted a battery, within 150 yards of the river, the Second Michigan, and captured it before it could unlimber and open fire. It was a six-gun battery, complete in all its equipments, and was captured, men, horses, and guns. A portion of this cavalry rode to the river and watered their horses."

In this final struggle, Trabue's brigade, which was now on the left next to Cleburne's, supported by Stewart's brigade, and some fragments of Anderson's, was opposed to the remains of Sherman's and McClernand's commands, including McDowell's brigade. Hardee was giving direction to this part of the line. Trabue ordered his command to fix bayonets and charge at a double-quick, which they did in the handsomest manner, and with complete success. He says:

The enemy, unwilling and unable to stand this charge, ran through their camps into the woods in their rear, whither we followed them. They were, however, too badly routed to make a stand, and for several hundred yards I moved forward without opposition.

Embarrassed by the broken ground and thick undergrowth, by an enfilading fire from a Confederate battery on the right, and the appearance of a Louisiana regiment dressed in blue on the left, Trabue's movement was made cautiously and with some delay. Nevertheless, feeling their way with much hard fighting, and gradually drawing the lines closer, these troops from the left by a slight change of front intercepted, with volleys of musketry, the Federals flying from the impetuous charge of Breckinridge's brigades on the right. A portion of Prentiss's command which surrendered was turned over to them by Hardee, and sent to the rear in charge of Crews's battalion. Colonel Shorter, of Bragg's corps, was detached with another lot of prisoners.

Breckinridge's other brigades, advancing, soon passed to their front; and the Sixth and Ninth Kentucky Regiments availed themselves of the opportunity "hastily to exchange their guns for Enfield rifles, which the enemy had surrendered." Trabue adds:

I then moved up and rejoined General Breckinridge, who, with Statham's and Bowen's brigades, was occupying the front line, being on the crest of the hill (or high land) overlooking the narrow valley of the Tennessee River, on which, and near by, was Pittsburg Landing.

Having been halted here for more than an hour, we endured a most terrific cannonade and shelling from the enemy's gunboats.

A few of the troops were demoralized by this, and fell back ; but there was little loss.

Bragg, having found the Federal position, called "The Hornets' Nest," in front of the Confederate right centre impregnable, had ordered that the troops there, who had suffered greatly, should hold their position.   When he learned the fall of the commander-in-chief, he rode rapidly to the extreme right.   Bragg says in his report :

Here I found a strong force, consisting of three parts, without a common head : Brigadier-General Breckinridge, with his reserve division, pressing the enemy ; Brigadier-General Withers, with his splendid division, greatly exhausted and taking a temporary rest; and Major-General Cheatham, with his division of General Polk's command, to their left and rear.   These troops were soon put in motion, responding with great alacrity to the command, "Forward—let every order be forward ! "   It was now probably past four o'clock, the descending sun warning us to press our advantage, and finish the work before night should compel us to desist.

Fairly in motion, these commands again, with a common head and a common purpose, swept all before them.   Neither battery nor battalion could withstand their onslaught.   Passing through camp after camp, rich in military spoils of every kind, the enemy was driven headlong from every position, and thrown in confused masses upon the river-bank, behind his heavy artillery, and under cover of his gunboats at the landing.   He had left nearly the whole of his light artillery in our hands, and some 3,000 or more prisoners, who were cut off from their retreat by the closing in of our troops on the left under Major-General Polk, with a portion of his reserve corps, and Brigadier-General Ruggles, with Anderson's and Pond's brigades of his division.   The prisoners were dispatched to the rear under a proper guard, all else being left on the field that we might press our advantage.   The enemy had fallen back in much confusion, and was crowded in unorganized masses on the river-bank, vainly striving to cross.   They were covered by a battery of heavy guns, well served, and their two gunboats, which now poured heavy fire upon our supposed positions, for we were entirely hid by the forests.   Their fire, though terrific in sound, and producing some consternation at first, did us no damage, as the shells all passed over, and exploded far beyond our positions.

Hardee gives the following brief but spirited summary of the battle in his report :

Nothing could be more brilliant than the attack.   The fierce volleys of a hundred thousand muskets and the boom of two hundred cannon receding steadily toward the river, marked, hour by hour from dawn till night, our slow but ceaseless advance.   The captured camps, rich in the spoils of war, in arms, horses, stores, munitions, and baggage, with throngs of prisoners moving to the rear, showed the headlong fury with which our men had crushed the heavy columns of the foe."

No Federal division any longer preserved even a show of organization.   Parts of regiments, the bravest and coolest of the men, stuck to their colors and strove to rally and form a line of battle wherever they could find a nucleus. There were many such heroic spirits in the crushed and mangled mass which was huddling back into the angle between Snake Creek and the Tennessee River. Sherman in his report says: "My command had become decidedly of *a mixed character*. Buckland's brigade was the only one that retained its organization." Buckland's own report, however, does not sustain this view. He mentions that, in the combat on the Purdy road—

The fleeing mass from the left broke through our lines, and many of our men caught the infection and fled with the crowd. Colonel Cockerill became separated from Colonel Sullivan and myself, and was afterward engaged with part of his command at McClernand's camp. Colonel Sullivan and myself kept together, and made every effort to rally our men, with but poor success. They had become scattered in every direction.

They afterward formed a line of battle—what sort of a one may be imagined after reading the foregoing. Colonel Sullivan then marched to *the landing* for ammunition, and did not join Buckland till next day. This tells the story. It is difficult to see where "the organization" was.

Of the two armies, one was now an advancing, triumphant host, with arm uplifted to give the mortal blow; the other, a broken, mangled, demoralized mob, paralyzed and waiting for the stroke. While the other Confederate brigades, which had shared most actively in Prentiss's capture, were sending back the prisoners and forming again for a final attack, two brigades, under Chalmers and Jackson, on the extreme right, had cleared away all in front of them, and, moving down the river-bank, now came upon the last point where even a show of resistance was made. Two very bold and active brigadiers, they at once closed with the enemy in their front, crossing a deep ravine and difficult ground to get at him. Here Colonel Webster, of Grant's staff, had gathered all the guns he could find from batteries, whether abandoned or still coherent, and with stout-hearted men, picked up at random, had prepared a resistance. Some infantry, similarly constituted, had been got together; and Ammen's brigade, the van of Nelson's division, had landed, and was pushing its way through the throng of pallid fugitives at the landing to take up the battle where it had fallen from the hands of Grant and Sherman. It got into position in time to do its part in checking the unsupported assaults of Chalmers and Jackson.

In describing this final attack, General Chalmers says in his report:

It was then about four o'clock in the evening, and, after distributing ammunition, we received orders from General Bragg to drive the enemy into the river. My brigade, together with that of Brigadier-General Jackson, filed to the right, and formed facing the river, and endeavored to press forward to the water's edge ; but in attempting to mount the last ridge we were met by a fire from a whole line of batteries, protected by infantry and assisted by shells from the gunboats. Our men struggled vainly to ascend the hill, which was very steep, making charge after charge without success, but continued the fight until night closed the hostilities on both sides.

During this engagement, Gage's battery was brought up to our assistance, but suffered so severely that it was soon compelled to retire. This was the sixth fight in which we had been engaged during the day, and my men were too much exhausted to storm the batteries on the hill ; but they were brought off in good order, formed in line of battle, and slept on the battle-field, where I remained with them.

Brigadier-General Jackson gives this account :

My brigade was ordered to change direction again, face toward Pittsburg, where the enemy appeared to have made his last stand, and to advance upon him, General Chalmers's brigade being again on my right, and extending to the swamp of the Tennessee River. Without ammunition, and with only their bayonets to rely on, steadily my men advanced, under a heavy fire from light batteries, siege-pieces, and gunboats. Passing through the ravine, they arrived near the crest of the opposite hill, upon which the enemy's batteries were, but could not be urged further without support. Sheltering themselves against the precipitous sides of the ravine, they remained under this fire for some time. Finding an advance without support impracticable, remaining there under fire useless, and believing that any further forward movement should be made simultaneously along our whole line, I proceeded to obtain orders from General Withers ; but, before seeing him, was ordered by a staff officer to retire. This order was announced to me as coming from General Beauregard, and was promptly communicated to my command.

General Buell had reached Pittsburg Landing about one o'clock ; or, as Badeau states (page 82), "midway in the afternoon." He says :

I found Grant on his boat, with two or more of his staff, in the ladies' cabin. I proposed we should go ashore, and his horses were accordingly taken ashore.

Buell also arranged with Grant to send steamers to Savannah, to bring up Crittenden's division.

General Buell, in his official report of April 15, 1862, gives the following account of the condition of things at Pittsburg, and of the part taken by himself and his command in the battle of the 6th :

The impression existed at Savannah that the firing was only an affair of outposts, the same thing having occurred for the two or three previous days ; but, as it continued, I determined to go to the scene of action, and accordingly started with my chief of staff, Colonel Fry, on a steamer which I had ordered to get under steam. As we proceeded up the river, groups of soldiers were seen upon the west bank, and it soon became evident that they were stragglers from the army that was engaged. The groups increased in size and frequency until, as we approached the landing, they amounted to whole companies, and almost regiments; and at the landing the bank swarmed with a confused mass of men of various regiments. The number could not have been less than four or five thousand, and later in the day it became much greater. Finding General Grant at the landing, I requested him to send steamers to Savannah to bring up General Crittenden's division, which had arrived during the morning, and then went ashore with him. The throng of disorganized and demoralized troops increased continually by fresh fugitives from the battle, which steadily drew nearer the landing; and with these were mingled great numbers of teams, all striving to get as near as possible to the river. With few exceptions, all efforts to form the troops and move them forward to the fight utterly failed.

In the mean time the enemy had made such progress against our troops that his artillery and musketry began to play into the vital spot of the position, and some persons were killed on the bank at the very landing. General Nelson arrived with Colonel Ammen's brigade at this opportune moment. It was immediately posted to meet the attack at that point, and with a battery of artillery which happened to be on the ground, and was brought into action, opened fire on the enemy, and repulsed him. The action of the gunboats also contributed very much to that result. The attack at that point was not renewed, night having come on, and the firing ceased on both sides. In the mean time the remainder of General Nelson's division crossed, and General Crittenden's arrived from Savannah by steamers.

Badeau says (page 84):

A battery of artillery, well posted by Colonel Webster, of Grant's staff, did good service at this juncture, and the gunboats were also of importance, as they had been for some time previous, in checking the advance of the enemy on the extreme left. Both sides were now crippled and both fatigued, the extraordinary efforts of the day telling hard on either army. . . . It was nearly five o'clock when the head of Nelson's column crossed the river; but, after once starting his troops, this commander was prompt in marching them, and the men themselves were eager to get into battle and assist their hard-pushed comrades. Two of Nelson's regiments were put in position, on the extreme left; and, as a final spasmodic attack was made by the rebels, these regiments fired two or three volleys and lost three men; but it was too late then to affect the fortunes of the day. The exhaustion consequent upon their earlier efforts told upon the rebels as well as upon the national troops.

General Hurlbut, in a letter to the writer, says that he had " at least four thousand steady infantry in line " to the right of the artillery massed under Colonel Webster. He also thinks they could have repelled an attack upon them. But the contemporaneous reports of his subordinates lead to different conclusions.

General Nelson says in his report that, in obedience to orders from General Grant, reiterated by General Buell, he left Savannah at half-past one o'clock, and marched up the bank at Pittsburg Landing, with the head of his column, at five o'clock. He continues:

The Sixth Ohio and Thirty-sixth Indiana had hardly deployed, when the left of our artillery was completely turned by the enemy, and the gunners fled from their pieces. The gallantry of the Thirty-sixth Indiana, supported by the Sixth Ohio, under the able conduct of Colonel G. Ammen, commanding the Tenth Brigade, drove back the enemy and restored the line of battle. This was at half-past six o'clock, and soon after the enemy withdrew, owing, I suppose, to the darkness.

This repulse undoubtedly refers to some of Chalmers's later unsupported assaults.

The following, from Nelson's report, also illustrates the demoralization of the Federal army. Nelson says:

I found cowering under the river-bank when I crossed from 7,000 to 10,000 men, frantic with fright and utterly demoralized, who received my gallant division with cries that "we are whipped!" "cut to pieces!" etc. They were insensible to shame and sarcasm, for I tried both on them; and, indignant at such poltroonery, I asked permission to open fire upon the knaves.

The scene at Pittsburg is well pictured in the following extracts from the correspondence of the *Cincinnati Gazette:*

Our whole army is crowded in the region of Wallace's camps, and to a circuit of one-half to two-thirds of a mile around the landing. We have been falling back all day. We can do it no more. The next repulse puts us into the river; and there are not transports enough to cross a single division till the enemy would be upon us. . . . We have lost nearly all our camps and camp-equipage. We have lost nearly half our field-artillery. We have lost a division general, and two or three regiments of our soldiers as prisoners. We have lost —how dreadfully we are afraid to think—in killed and wounded. The hospitals are full to overflowing. A long ridge-bluff is set apart for surgical uses. It is covered with the maimed, the dead, and the dying. And our men are discouraged by prolonged defeat. . . . Meanwhile, there is a lull in the firing. For the first time since sunrise you fail to catch the angry rattle of musketry or the heavy booming of the field-guns. . . . On the bluffs above the river is a sight that may well make our cheeks tingle. There are not less than 5,000 skulkers lining the banks!

The correspondent goes on to state that Colonel Webster placed twenty-two guns in all in position, which were served by improvised artillerists. He continues:

Remember the situation. It was half-past four o'clock—perhaps a quarter later still. Every division of our army on the field had been repulsed. The enemy were in the camps of four out of five of them. We were driven to within little over half a mile of the landing. Behind us was a deep, rapid river. Before us was a victorious enemy. And still there was an hour for fighting. "Oh, that night or Blücher would come!" "Oh, that night or Lew Wallace would come!" Nelson's division of General Buell's army evidently couldn't cross in time to do us much good. We didn't yet know why Lew Wallace wasn't on the ground. In the justice of our cause, and in that semicircle of twenty-two guns in position, lay all the hope we could see.

He attributes the final repulse to the fire of these batteries, the shelling of the gunboats, and the assistance of Nelson's advance. That these combined means of resistance repulsed the assaults actually made is true. But they do not account for the failure of the Confederates to capture this position and consummate their victory, which was due to General Beauregard's premature recall of his troops at the moment of fate.

IV.—A VICTORY LOST.

General Beauregard's theory of the battle of Shiloh is so different from the writer's that it is due to him to give his version of its close, as set forth in his report and in the writings of his chief of staff, who is indorsed by him.

The following is General Beauregard's telegram to the adjutant-general:

The battle commenced on the 6th of April. We attacked the enemy in a strong position in front of Pittsburg; and, after a severe battle of ten hours' duration, thanks be to the Almighty, we gained a complete victory, driving the enemy from every position. The loss on both sides is heavy, including the commander-in-chief, General A. S. Johnston, who fell gallantly leading his troops into the thickest of the fight.

G. T. BEAUREGARD, General commanding.

To General S. COOPER, Adjutant-General.

General Beauregard's brief report of the conclusion of Sunday's battle is as follows:

The chief command then devolved upon me, though at the time I was greatly prostrated and suffering from the prolonged sickness with which I had been afflicted since early in February. The responsibility was one which, in my physical condition, I would have gladly avoided, though cast upon me when our forces were successfully pushing the enemy back upon the Tennessee River, and though supported on the immediate field by such corps commanders as Major-Generals Polk, Bragg, and Hardee, and Brigadier-General Breckinridge commanding the reserve.

It was after six o'clock, P. M., as before said, when the enemy's last position was carried, and his force finally broke and sought refuge behind a commanding eminence, covering the Pittsburg Landing, not more than half a mile distant, and under the guns of the gunboats, which opened on our eager columns a fierce and annoying fire with shot and shell of the heaviest description. Darkness was close at hand. Officers and men were exhausted by a combat of over twelve hours, without food, and jaded by the march of the preceding day through mud and water; it was, therefore, impossible to collect the rich and opportune spoils of war scattered broadcast on the field left in our possession, and impracticable to make any effective dispositions for their removal to the rear.

In accounting for the frustration of an alleged attempt of General Beauregard to consummate the victory, Colonel Jordan, General Beauregard's chief of staff, says :

Unfortunately, however, the Federal encampments were plethoric with food most tempting to hungry men, as well as with clothing and other alluring spoil; the thick woods, too, had greatly disintegrated almost every regiment, so that none of the divisions confronted in an embodied form the last position that remained between them and the deep, broad waters of the Tennessee. The superior officers present, howbeit, collected the men immediately around them of whatsoever corps. Tired, hungry, and exhausted, as were the Confederates, nevertheless a number of determined separate efforts were made by them, during the remaining hour of daylight, to wrench their last foothold from their elsewhere-beaten adversary.

He thus describes the order of withdrawal :

General Beauregard, in the mean time, observing the exhausted, widely-scattered condition of his army, directed it to be brought out of battle, collected and restored to order as far as practicable, and to occupy for the night the captured encampments of the enemy. This, however, had been done in chief part by the officers in immediate command of the troops before the order was generally distributed.

For this last allegation there is not the slightest warrant.

And if General Beauregard, as Jordan also states, after Prentiss's surrender, "urged the forward propulsion of the whole force upon the shattered fragments of the enemy," these orders must have miscarried, as a diligent search has failed to discover that any such were received by his subordinates. The only orders that reached them were to retire. The operations of the afternoon evince this, as can be seen by the field reports. There was no failure by officers or troops in their duty in this respect.

Furthermore, the final rout and surrender of Prentiss occurred much earlier than six o'clock. This is made evident in the Confederate reports ; while the correspondent of the *Cincinnati Gazette* places the rout of the Federals earlier than half-past four. As to the order of withdrawal, it was received and in part executed before six o'clock.

Colonel Jordan also says that the gunboats "were used with an effect on our troops to which all will testify who were in the advance and witnessed it." The testimony of these very people, when adduced, will show the exact reverse of this : that the roar and bursting of the shells, however terrific in the rear, at Beauregard's headquarters, were almost harmless to the troops near the river. This was one of the lamentable features of the day: that what General Beauregard saw at Shiloh Church should be mistaken for the situation at the front; that the trains of wounded and the tide of fugitives should supplant in his eyes those heroic warriors who were still marching onward.

The substance of the statements made by Colonel Jordan is, that the order of withdrawal was issued because the last position of the Federals was impregnable, because it was too late to effect anything decisive, and because the Confederate army was dispersed, disorganized, demoralized, exhausted, and incoherently managed by its superior officers. Further, he maintains that the battle ended by a sort of subsidence of the fight from inanition *before* the order of withdrawal was received by the brigades.

There is just enough of truth in all this to mislead. Among the new recruits at Shiloh there were, of course, many skulkers. There are in all armies. But there is a marked distinction between these and the reckless soldiers who, careless of the restraints of discipline and prompted by an idle and barbaric curiosity, left their ranks to gather trophies or for other purposes as vain. Big-eyed wonder, more than booty, was their motive; and, at each charge, they rallied round the nearest standard with the zest of a hunt for human game. The only effective use to be made of such men is to keep hurling them at the foe. But they are not to be confounded with those streams of fugitives which, like rivulets from the base of a glacier, trickle or pour to the rear with the refuse and *débris* of the army.

The troops were tired and hungry, it is true, and greatly weakened by casualties and straggling. But to say that they were "exhausted" in the sense that they could fight no more is abundantly disproved. It is refuted by numerous positive statements of their officers, and by the vigorous attacks by Chalmers late that evening and early next morning, after five combats and more than average marching. The troops were moving forward with enthusiasm when recalled by General Beauregard's order. To confound such men with the multitude of stragglers is to do a great act of injustice.

To illustrate the desultory nature of the "separate" attacks made by the Confederates, "abortive assaults" with "fruitless results," as he styles them, Colonel Jordan cites an unsuccessful attempt of Colonel Mouton, of the Eighteenth Louisiana, "to charge a battery on a hill" about four o'clock; when, advancing "unsupported," he was beaten back with the loss of 207 of his men. With some eighty regiments and battalions on the field, many such attacks must have occurred that day; but the particular case mentioned has no relevancy, as the time at which it was made indicates that it was one of that series of attacks by which the lines of Wallace and Prentiss were crushed, and hence, though "unsupported" and baffled, not "separate," but part of a general system of assault which was successful. Besides, no argument can be drawn as to the situation after the destruction of those divisions from a combat before that event.

Jordan also cites, as an illustration of the unconcerted movements at the front, the last assaults by Chalmers and Jackson. But these were, in fact, only parts of a well-concerted general movement, which was disconcerted, paralyzed, and brought to naught, by General Beauregard's staff officers at a critical moment withdrawing the coöperating force piecemeal. It came near being successful as it was. Had it been sustained, it would almost certainly have made the victory complete. To use it as a reason or justification for the order of withdrawal is most extraordinary.

Colonel Jordan says that "none of the divisions confronted in an embodied form the last position." This is true. It would have been an unparalleled case if, after ten hours of continual assault, in a broken and wooded country, *divisions* had been found entire. But it proves nothing. The severance of commands resulted, as already indicated, from the plan of battle, corps moving in successive parallel lines, and from the nature of the ground. But they had fought in this wise all day ; every combat on the field had been thus won ; and all the corps, except Hardee's, were *more* "embodied" after Prentiss's surrender than they had been since 10 A.M. Trabue was reunited to Breckinridge, and Cheatham to Polk, and Bragg had his men more in hand than when charging positions miles apart. The army was not demoralized, as suggested. Weakened but resolute bands of men, animated by duty, discipline, intelligent patriotism, and "the stern joy that warriors feel," still stood coherent, eager, and fired with the ardor of combat and the exultation of a marvelous success. Nothing remained except to give the finishing stroke.

The real strength and character of the attack made by Chalmers and Jackson, and the measure of the resistance possible under the circumstances by the Federal remnant, may be safely left to the intelligence of the reader who has carefully considered what has been herein recorded from the pens of both Federals and Confederates. According to the writer's view, the actual contest was between the fragments of two Confederate brigades and Webster's guns, supported by Ammen's brigade and a few infantry. What would have been achieved but for General Beauregard's order of withdrawal can only be surmised. But it will be made clear, from contemporary reports and other sources, that the state of facts did not exist on which the order was based; and that, through a total misconception of General Johnston's purposes, and a failure to carry them out, a mighty victory was allowed to glide from the hand of the conqueror. This might have been permitted to pass as a pardonable error of judgment, as indeed it seems to the writer to be, considering the ill-health of General Beauregard, his position upon the field, and the part he took in the battle of Sunday; but it would be unjust to allow to pass into history the claim set up that his order of withdrawal was an act of consummate wisdom, or anything else, indeed, than a fatal blow to the Confederate cause.

Let us see whether General Beauregard's theory, as expounded by himself and his chief of staff, or the writer's view, is verified by the evidence in the case.

Governor Harris writes as follows in a recent letter :

General Johnston's plans had been carried out with signal success up to the moment of his death; and I believed then, as I do now, that the momentum of success already achieved rendered certain a great and decisive victory.

Hardee, in his report, says :

At this moment of supreme interest it was our misfortune to lose the commanding general. . . . This disaster caused a lull in the attack on the right, and precious hours were wasted. It is, in my opinion, the candid belief of intelligent men that but for this calamity we would have achieved before sunset a triumph, signal not only in the annals of this war, but memorable in future history. . . .

Upon the death of General Johnston, the command having devolved upon General Beauregard, the conflict was continued until near sunset, and the advance divisions were within a few hundred yards of Pittsburg, where the enemy were huddled in confusion, when the order to withdraw was received. The troops were ordered to bivouac upon the field of battle.

Speaking elsewhere of Wood's brigade, he incidentally remarks :

This brigade was by my order moved forward later in the afternoon in the direction of the heavy cannonade in front, but about sunset was ordered to withdraw by a staff officer from General Beauregard.

Cleburne, in his report, says :

I again advanced until halted by an aide of General Beauregard, who informed me we were not to approach nearer to the river.

General Polk's report says :

By this time the troops under my command were joined by those of Generals Bragg and Breckinridge, and my fourth brigade, under General Cheatham, from the right. The field was clear; the rest of the forces of the enemy were driven to the river and under its bank. We had one hour or more of daylight still left, were within one hundred and fifty to four hundred yards of the enemy's position, and nothing seemed wanting to complete the most brilliant victory of the war but to press forward and make a vigorous assault on the demoralized remnant of his forces.

At this juncture, his gunboats dropped down the river near the landing, where his troops were collected, and opened a tremendous cannonade of shot and shell over the bank in the direction whence our forces were approaching. The height of the plain on which we were, above the level of the water, was about one hundred feet, so that it was necessary to give great elevation to his guns to enable him to fire over the bank. The consequence was, that shot could take effect only at points remote from the river's edge. They were comparatively harmless to our troops nearest the bank, and became increasingly so as we drew near the enemy, and placed him between us and his boats. Here the impression arose that our forces were waging an unequal contest; that they were exhausted and suffering from a murderous fire; and, by an order from the commanding general, they were withdrawn from the field.

The following is an extract from General Bragg's official report of the battle of Shiloh:

It may not be amiss to refer briefly to the causes it is believed operated to prevent the complete overthrow of the enemy, which we were so near acccm-plishing, and which would have changed the entire complexion of the war. The want of proper organization and discipline, and the inferiority in many cases of our officers to the men they were expected to command, left us often without system or order, and the large proportion of stragglers resulting weakened our forces, and kept the superior and staff officers constantly engaged in the duties of file-closers. Especially was this the case after the occupation of the enemy's camps, the spoils of which served to delay and greatly to demoralize our men. But no one cause probably contributed so greatly to our loss of time, which was the loss of success, as the fall of the commanding general. At the moment of this irreparable disaster, the plan of battle was being rapidly and successfully executed under his immediate eye and lead on the right. For want of a common superior to the different commands on that part of the field, great delay occurred after this misfortune, and that delay prevented the consummation of the work so gallantly and successfully begun and carried on, until the approach of night induced our new commander to recall the exhausted troops for rest and recuperation before a crowning effort on the next morning.

As soon as our troops could be again formed and put in motion, the order was given to move forward at all points and sweep the enemy from the field. The sun was about disappearing, so that little time was left us to finish the glorious work of the day—a day unsurpassed in the history of warfare for its daring deeds, brilliant achievements, and heavy sacrifices.

Our troops, greatly exhausted by twelve hours' incessant fighting, without food, mostly responded to the order with alacrity, and the movement commenced with every prospect of success, though a heavy battery in our front, and the gunboats on our right, seemed determined to dispute every inch of ground. Just at this time an order was received from the commanding general to withdraw the forces beyond the enemy's fire. As this was communicated in many instances direct to brigade commanders, the troops were soon in motion and the action ceased. The different commands, mixed and scattered, bivouacked at points most convenient to their positions and beyond the range of the enemy's guns. All firing, except a half-hour's shot from the gunboats, ceased, and the whole night was passed by our exhausted men in quiet. Such as had not sought shelter in the camps of the enemy were again drenched before morning by one of those heavy rain-storms which seemed to be our portion for this expedition.

But General Bragg is still more explicit in his sketch of "Shiloh," communicated to the writer. After discussing the events up to the time of General Johnston's death, which, he says, "sealed the fate of the South, and destroyed the liberties of this country," Bragg says :

The command devolved, of course, on General Beauregard, the next in rank, who, in feeble health, as previously stated, was with his carriage, where the commanding general had assigned him, far in the rear of the strife, directing the movements of the reserves. The fall of Johnston produced a sort of temporary paralysis with the troops under his immediate command on our right. But, after a short respite, which they improved to replenish their haversacks and cartridge-boxes from the enemy's rich stores, they resumed their victorious march under the direction of General Bragg, who had promptly repaired to this part of his command on receiving notice of General Johnston's death.

The troops promptly and enthusiastically responded to the command "Forward! Let every order be forward!" The rapid and near approach, at this time, of all our troops to the enemy's last stronghold, immediately on the bank of the river, where we had completely enveloped all that was left to him from five of his six divisions, indicated that the end was inevitable and near at hand. Concurring testimony, especially that of the prisoners on both sides—our captured being present and witnesses to the demoralization of the enemy, and their eagerness to escape or avoid further slaughter by surrender—left no doubt but that a persistent, energetic assault would soon have been crowned by a general yielding of his whole force. About one hour of daylight was left to us. The enemy's gunboats, his last hope, took position opposite us, in the river, and commenced a furious cannonade at our supposed position. From the elevation necessary to reach the high bluff, on which we were operating, this proved "all sound and fury signifying nothing," and did not in the slightest degree mar our prospects or our progress. Not so, however, in our rear, where these heavy shells fell among the reserves and stragglers; and, to the utter dismay of the commanders on the field, the troops were seen to abandon their inspiring work, and to retire sullenly from the contest when danger was almost past, and victory, so dearly purchased, was almost certain. . . .

What followed is a part of the sad history of the country, and need not be recapitulated. Had the first shot of the 5th, on the skirmish-line, killed Sidney Johnston, the battle of Shiloh would not have been fought and won by the Confederates. Had the fatal shot which struck him down on the 6th not been fired, Grant and his forces would have been destroyed or captured before sundown, and Buell would never have crossed the Tennessee.

A few days after our great disaster, the Secretary of War telegraphed General Bragg that the President had nominated, and the Senate had confirmed him, as general in the Confederate States Army, to fill the vacancy caused by Sidney Johnston's death. To that dispatch the following reply was sent : "I feel greatly honored at my selection by the President to succeed Sidney Johnston—no one can fill the vacancy."

Colonel Jordan, after saying that the officers in immediate command
of the troops were withdrawing before General Beauregard's order to
retire was generally distributed, adds in a note ("Life of Forrest,"
page 134) :

This was especially the case with Bragg's corps. Yet, oddly enough, General Bragg, in his own official report, ventures to state that his men, though
greatly exhausted, were about to charge with great alacrity upon the last position, and most probably would have carried it, when Beauregard's order was
received recalling them.

He says further (page 150) :

His order really was not distributed before the greater part of the Confederate troops had already given up the attempt for that day to carry the ridge at
the landing.

As it might appear from these *dicta* that Bragg's report was baseless, the following extracts are given from the reports of his subordinates.

Major-General Withers, in his official report of June 20, 1862, says :

This division was then advanced to the Pittsburg edge of the field, in which
the enemy had stacked their arms, and halted for a supply of ammunition. Most
of the regiments were supplied from the camps of the enemy. The order was
now given by General Bragg, who was present on the right during the fierce
fight which ended in the capture of Prentiss, to "sweep everything forward!"
This division was moved promptly forward, although some regiments had not
succeeded in getting a supply of ammunition, and had just entered a steep and
precipitous ravine, when the enemy opened a terrific fire upon it. Staff officers
were immediately dispatched to bring up all the reënforcements to be found, and
the order was given to brigade commanders to charge the batteries. These
orders were being obeyed, when, to my astonishment, a large portion of the
command was observed to move rapidly by the left flank from under the fire of
the enemy. Orders were immediately sent to arrest the commanding officers,
and for the troops to be promptly placed in position for charging the batteries.
Information was soon brought, however, that it was by General Beauregard's
orders, delivered thus directly to brigade commanders, that the troops were
being rapidly led from under the fire of the enemy's gunboats. Thus ended the
fight on Sunday, and thus was this command disorganized, an evil sorely felt
during the next day.

Major-General Ruggles, Bragg's other division commander, makes
the following statement in his report :

Subsequently, while advancing toward the river, I received instructions from
General Bragg to carry forward all the troops I could find, and, while assembling
a considerable force ready for immediate action, I received from Colonel Augustin notice of General Beauregard's orders to withdraw from the further pursuit ; and, finding soon afterward that the forces were falling back, I retired
with them, just as night set in, to the open field in the rear ; and, as I received

no further orders, I directed General Anderson and Colonel Gibson to hold their troops in readiness, with their arms cleaned and cartridges supplied, for service the next morning.

By reference to Jackson's report of his last charge (page 624), it will be seen that he was thus withdrawn. General R. L. Gibson, commanding one of Ruggles's brigades, commenting in an unofficial letter, writes as follows:

From all I have been able to gather, the conception, or plan of battle, was excellent. It was a complete surprise; and, at the moment of General Johnston's fall, so far as I could learn, we were successful all along the lines. The enemy was broken and routed, and in full retreat. I was riding with General Cheatham, when the news of his death was confirmed. We were moving our commands toward the river, with nothing in sight to oppose our easy march. When within a few hundred yards of the river, the gunboats opened an aimless fire in the direction we were moving. We halted and formed line of battle, and sent forward scouts and skirmishers, preparatory to attacking or resuming the march toward the river. While at this, I met my general of division, General Ruggles, and he told me *the order was to halt*. It was yet light. I am not sure the sun was down. You could see as well as at mid-day. It was before twilight. I think we had at least one good battle-hour remaining.

My conviction is that, had General Johnston survived, the victory would have been complete, and his army would have planted the standard of the Confederacy on the banks of the Ohio.

General Johnston's death was a tremendous catastrophe. There are no words adequate to express my own conception of the immensity of the loss to our country. Sometimes the hopes of millions of people depend upon one head and one arm. The West perished with Albert Sidney Johnston, and the Southern country followed.

General Gilmer, in a letter to the writer, dated September 17, 1872, gives the following statement in regard to the battle:

It is my well-considered opinion that, if your father had survived the day, he would have crushed and captured General Grant's army before the setting of the sun on the 6th. In fact, at the time your father received the mortal wound advancing with General Breckinridge's command, the day was ours. The enemy having lost all the stormed positions on that memorable field, his troops fell back in great disorder on the banks of the Tennessee. To cover the confusion, rapid fires were opened from the gunboats the enemy had placed in the river; but the shots passed entirely over our devoted men, who were exultant and eager to be led forward to the final assault, which *must* have resulted in a complete victory, owing to the confusion and general disorganization of the Federal troops. I know the condition of General Grant's army at the moment, as I had reached a high, projecting point on the bank of the river about a mile above Pittsburg Landing, and could see the hurried movements to get the disordered troops across to the right bank. Several thousand had already passed, and a confused mass of men crowded to the landing to get on the boats that were employed in crossing. I rode rapidly to General Bragg's position to report what I had seen, and suggested that if he would suspend the fire of his artillery, and marshal his infantry for a general advance, the enemy must surrender. General Bragg decided to make the advance, and authorized me and other officers to direct the commanders of the batteries to cease firing.

In the midst of these preparations, orders reached General Bragg from General Beauregard directing the troops to be withdrawn and placed in camp for the night—the intention being to resume the contest in the morning. This was fatal, as it enabled General Buell and General Wallace to arrive on the scene of action; that is, they came up in the course of the night. Had General Beauregard known the condition of the enemy, as your father knew it, when he received the fatal shot, the order for withdrawal would certainly not have been given, and, without such order, I know the enemy would have been crushed.

General Duke, in his "Life of Morgan," takes the following view of these events (page 154) :

It is a point conceded now on all sides that, had the Confederate army pursued its success on the evening of the first day, the army under General Grant would have been annihilated, and Buell never could have crossed the river. Had General Johnston survived, the battle would have been pressed vigorously to that consummation. Then, what would have been the situation? The army, remaining upon the banks of the Tennessee for a few days, would have been reorganized and recovered from the exhausting effects of the battle. The slightly wounded, returning to the ranks, would have made the muster-roll full thirty thousand effectives. Price and Van Dorn, coming with about fifteen thousand, and the levies from all quarters which were hastening to Corinth, would have given General Johnston nearly sixty thousand men.

Duke then goes on to consider the results, which he concludes must have transferred the seat of war to Kentucky, perhaps to the Northwestern States.

Finally, I shall take the liberty of quoting Colonel Jordan in reply to himself ("Life of Forrest," page 134). In giving the deeds of Forrest and his men in the fray, he says :

They assisted in the capture of General Prentiss's men, and, being mounted, as well as comparatively fresh, led the advance upon the ridge, where the battery was established. Despite the efforts of the Federal officers, such was the confusion prevalent as Forrest began to skirmish vigorously, that he sent a staff officer to report to General Polk (from whom he had last received orders), that by a strong, rapid, forward movement, the enemy might be driven into the river.

Jordan also says in a note (page 135), that Willie Forrest, a boy of fifteen—

with two other comrades of the same age, happening to get detached, made their way to the river, near which they came upon fifteen or twenty Federal soldiers. Firing upon the group with their shot-guns, these boys then charged, and captured and led away some fifteen prisoners, whom they delivered to the provost-marshal.

Could a more striking illustration be given of the demoralization of the Federal army; and this, too, under "a raking fire from the gunboats, and the artillery of both sides playing over their heads!"

Another incident of the battle, in connection with General Forrest and his son, deserves to be remembered as illustrative of the condition of our undisciplined troops after the fight, and as showing how much was lost by a failure to press forward while our men were together, and before night and the demoralization of victory, with its rich spoils, had scattered them; and it is thus told by General Chalmers:

When night put a stop to my efforts to take the last hill above Pittsburg Landing, I fell back, and found to my great surprise that our whole army had fallen back. I bivouacked my men in line on the ground where Prentiss surrendered, and about midnight was awakened by Colonel (afterward General) Forrest, who was searching for his son, whom he supposed to have been killed.

He asked me first for the headquarters of General Beauregard, then of Bragg, Polk, and Hardee; and I told him I did not know where any of them were. He asked then where my command was; and I answered, "Sleeping in line before me with their guns by their sides." He replied, "You are the first general I have found to-night who knows where his men are, and if the enemy attack us in the morning they will whip us like hell!" He said, "I will put out a picket in front of you." And he did, and gave me timely notice, before day, that the enemy was preparing to advance.

It is thus seen that, so far from General Bragg's corps withdrawing before the distribution of the order, both Jackson and Withers concur that this order came direct from General Beauregard; while Chalmers, who did not receive any order to retire, continued the fight alone until dark.

Chalmers says, in a memorandum to the writer:

One more resolute movement forward would have captured Grant and his whole army, and fulfilled to the letter the battle-plan of the great Confederate general, who died in the belief that victory was ours, and that his own reputation was fully redeemed.

General Beauregard sums up his theory of the plan of battle in his report in the following language:

By a rapid and vigorous attack on General Grant, it was expected he would be beaten back into his transports and the river, or captured in time to enable us to profit by the victory, and remove to the rear all the stores and munitions that would fall into our hands in such an event before the arrival of General Buell's army on the scene. It was never contemplated, however, to retain the position thus gained and abandon Corinth, the strategic point of the campaign.

Why, then, did he stop short in his career? Sunday evening, it was not a question of retaining, but of gaining Pittsburg Landing. On that day there was no strategic point for Confederates under all the heavens except the heart and vitals of Grant's army, which crouched throbbing, pierced, mangled, and bleeding, under the bluffs at Pittsburg Landing.

That General Beauregard's view of General Johnston's plans is fallacious, must be apparent to the reader of these pages. It is unhappily only too plain that he misinterpreted the vast purpose of his commander. What were the consequences of that mistake?

The last attack of the day was about to be made, and in sufficient force to insure its success. Most of the Confederate brigades were swarming to the front, converging their lines upon the sole point of defense. Their ability to take it seems scarcely to admit a doubt. That little screen thrown down, the Federal army lay at the absolute mercy of its antagonist. The Confederates, in possession of the heights, could have poured concentrated destruction and slaughter into the confused mass below, and compelled instant surrender. All the fruits of victory seemed within the grasp of the Confederate army, when the prize so dearly bought was suddenly snatched away. It was as in those dreams where visions of untold riches, and power, and splendor, loom before the sleeper, when a word rudely awakens him to the hard realities, it may be even to the cruel afflictions, of actual life. The Confederates *saw* Grant crushed, annihilated; Buell checked, retreating; the tide of war rolled back and pouring across the border; Kentucky, Missouri, aroused, instinct with martial fervor, and springing into the ranks with their sisters of the South; renewed prestige, restored confidence, increased credit, strength, and means of warfare; peace, prosperity, and independence; and a young and strong Confederacy, a martial virgin —a helmeted Minerva—among the nations, entering on a long and splendid career, in which liberty and order, justice and tradition, power and peace, should uphold the fabric of the state. The omen of the name was to be fulfilled. At "Shiloh," "he whose right it is" was about to prevail. But, in the sad significance of the result, the fulfillment remained as obscure as the oracle was ambiguous. After all, it was only a dream, in which bearded men and red-handed warriors saw, through the smoke of the battle-field, and the mists of blood-reeking forest-lands, an idea grow into life. But the spell was broken, the scene dissolved; all these fair promises of the future " are melted into air, thin air "—

> " And, like the baseless fabric of this vision,
> . . . . this insubstantial pageant faded,
> Leave not a rack behind."

All was shattered by one word. " On ! " would have made it history; but the commanding general said, "Retire." Oh, the power of a general-in-chief! It was all over. That bloody field was to mean nothing in all time but a slain hero, and 25,000 dauntless soldiers stretched upon a bloody field—and another day of purposeless slaughter, with broken bands of desperate men mangling and slaying to no visible end in all God's plan of setting up the right. The great forest tract was sinking into darkness, stained, trampled, and echoing with groans. But the victory—its very hope—was gone. "They had watered their horses in the Tennessee River;" but, when he fell who spoke the word, the prediction had lost its meaning.

CHAPTER XXXV.

I.

THE NIGHT OF THE 6TH.

NIGHTFALL found the victorious Confederates retiring from the front, and abandoning the vantage-ground on the bluffs, won at such a cost of blood. This gave the Federals room and opportunity to come out from their corner, and to advance and reoccupy the strong positions from which they had been driven, and dispose their troops on much more favorable ground than the crowded landing permitted. Called off from the pursuit by staff officers, who gave no specific instructions, the brigades, according to circumstances, bivouacked on the battle-field, marched to the rear, or made themselves comfortable on the profuse spoils of the enemy's encampments. Some were painfully threading the dark paths of the forest, finding or losing their way, in search of vaguely-designated positions. Others sought the sleep of exhaustion in dread of some sudden sally, not knowing how they lay toward friend or foe.

Jordan estimates the losses of the 6th ("Life of Forrest," page 138) at 6,500. There were, of course, many stragglers. He estimates the Confederate infantry, ready for battle on the morning of the 7th, at 20,000 men. Jordan also says that Polk led his troops a mile and a half to the rear of Shiloh. This is a mistake. Clark's division, now under A. P. Stewart, bivouacked on the ground. Cheatham, having become detached with one brigade, thought best to retire to his encampments of the night before ; but he held his men well in hand, and had them ready for engagement early next morning. Their withdrawal and position were reported that night by General Polk to General Beauregard, who gave no orders for their return. Polk joined them, in order to be sure of their early presence on the field, and led them back at an early hour; and their conduct was uncommonly spirited on Monday.

At regular intervals of ten minutes the gunboats threw a shell; and the boom and roar of these heavy missiles, bursting among the tired Confederates, broke their repose and added to the demoralization. At midnight, too, another heavy storm broke upon them, drenching those who had not been so fortunate as to secure shelter in the Federal encampments. There was no lack of provisions, however, and the men reveled without stint in the unwonted luxuries of the Federal sutlers' stores.

At headquarters, credence was given to a misleading dispatch from Decatur (or Florence).

Colonel Jordan, in a letter to the *Savannah Republican*, says of General Beauregard:

> Animated by the plain dictates of prudence and foresight, he sought to be ready for the coming storm, which he had anticipated and predicted as early as the afternoon of the 5th.

By this he means the arrival of Buell's reënforcements. And he says in the same letter:

> General Beauregard had the current [concurrent?] evidence of prisoners and scouts, that Buell's arrival was confidently expected. . . . It was, however, after General Beauregard had given his orders, and made his arrangements as far as practicable to meet any exigency, that I joined him and communicated the substance of a dispatch, addressed to General Johnston, that had been handed me on the battle-field, which encouraged the hope that the main part of Buell's forces had marched in the direction of Decatur.

He says (in his "Life of Forrest," page 136) that this emanated from a reliable officer, placed near Florence for observation, and adds:

> Buell's timely junction with General Grant was accordingly deemed impossible. Therefore the capture of the latter was regarded at Confederate headquarters as inevitable the next day, as soon as all the scattered Confederate reserves could be brought to bear for a concentrated effort.

Colonel Preston telegraphed to the President from Corinth, April 7th.

> General Johnston fell yesterday while leading a successful charge, turning the enemy's right, and gaining a brilliant victory. (Here follow some details already given.) Last night Colonel Gilmer informed me he saw the enemy embarking under cover of their gunboats—and no commencement of the conflict was expected by General Beauregard.

In spite of the somewhat imprudent boasts of General Prentiss that Buell's reënforcements would turn the tide of battle in the morning, it was expected, therefore, that the next day's work would be merely to pick up the spoils of victory. During the night, Forrest reported that reënforcements were arriving ; but no other steps were taken than the usual precautions against surprise by an army in the face of the enemy.

Lew Wallace's division, 8,000 strong, came marching up from Crump's Landing, a little after nightfall, and, filing over the Snake Creek crossing, was placed soon after midnight on the Federal right, covering the fragments of Sherman's and McClernand's divisions. During the night the entire divisions of Nelson and Crittenden were got across the river, and, by daylight, that of McCook began to arrive. Nelson took position on the left ; Crittenden, next to him; and then McCook. The interval between McCook and Wallace was occupied by such commands of Grant's army as the officers had been able to get into shape.

Badeau (" Life of Grant," page 86) says :

All the camps originally occupied by the national troops were in the hands of the enemy, but the rebel advance had been checked at every point. The division organization was, however, greatly broken up. Sherman had lost thousands by desertion and straggling; Prentiss had been captured, with 2,200 men; while W. H. L. Wallace's command was nearly destroyed, by casualties and the loss of its chief. The line, as constituted on Sunday night, was simply a mass of brave men, determined to hold their own against the enemy, wherever they found a commander.

General Sherman says that as early as 5 P. M., on the 6th, General Grant thought the battle could be retrieved next day, and ordered him to resume offensive operations. The inference from his letters and " Memoirs " is that these offensive movements were determined on irrespective of Buell's reënforcements ; but it is impossible to believe General Grant ignorant of Buell's movements, especially after recent conference with him. It is not hard to understand that, if he could escape capture that night, he would expect, with nearly 30,000 fresh troops coming to his reënforcement, to recover his lost ground next day. But it is evident, from the comparative sluggishness and feebleness of their next morning's operations, that Grant's troops were in no condition to attack unaided. His routed and panic-stricken army rapidly regained its courage, however, as division after division came up on its flanks, unshaken by the horrors of the day, and eager to renew the contest. The respite given by the early cessation of the combat was ably improved before night came on; and the narrow space into which the troops had been crowded, for lack of avenues of escape, now aided in their reorganization. The night was spent in this work.

Sherman estimates that 18,000 men remained, Sunday evening, fit for battle. These, with the reënforcements, would give some 46,000 Federals for the fight on Monday. But if only 18,000 remained, what a story it tells of the havoc and rout of Sunday! Two-thirds of the army dead, wounded, or missing! These statements of Grant's strength have been met by the flat contradiction of General Buell and his friends, as being absolutely inconsistent with the situation of affairs. In an interview with Major J. M. Wright, of his staff, authoritatively published in the *Louisville Courier-Journal*, General Buell speaks in reference to these matters as follows:

My own recollection has always been that General Sherman's explanations on that occasion were briefer than would ordinarily be expected from him, and that if there was much conversation it consisted mainly in my unequivocal statement to him that I should attack the enemy the next morning at daylight, and in my endeavor to get such information from him as might be useful in the execution of that design. I should not have paid much attention to his opinion with reference to what was left of the Army of the Tennessee, for I probably knew more about that than he did. I had seen its disorganized fragments about the landing and along the bank of the river, and walked pretty much the whole extent of its organized front. I have stated, on a previous occasion, that the number of troops that retained their ranks at the close of the first day did not probably exceed 10,000 men. A measurement of the ground which they occupied will show that the number could not have been more than 5,000, exclusive of Lew Wallace's division. That number may have been slightly increased the next morning from stragglers, under the encouraging effect of a large and fresh body of troops, but my belief is it did not exceed that number.

Indeed, it seems improbable that such orders were issued to Sherman that night, as the other division commanders mention *the next morning* as the time when they received them. Evidently, all depended on what Buell could do.

General Buell says, speaking of Sherman's sketch-map of the battlefield sent to the writer:

Sherman's sketch is also an interesting one, as showing the positions from which they were driven, and the dwindled front to which they were reduced. It will help to show, in connection with other circumstantial evidence, that, of the army of not less than 50,000 effective men which Grant had on the west bank of the Tennessee River, not more than 5,000 were in ranks and available on the battle-field at nightfall on the 6th, exclusive of Lew Wallace's division, say 8,500 men, that only came up during the night. The rest were either killed, wounded, captured, or scattered in inextricable and hopeless confusion for miles along the banks of the river.

II.

THE BATTLE OF MONDAY.

Buell says in his report:

Soon after five o'clock, on the morning of the 7th, General Nelson's and General Crittenden's divisions, the only ones yet arrived on the ground, moved promptly forward to meet the enemy. Nelson's division, marching in line of battle, soon came upon his pickets, drove them in, and at about six o'clock received the fire of his artillery.

Buell then pushed forward his artillery, which engaged the Confederates, while Crittenden aligned his division on Nelson's right; and McCook, whose division was beginning to arrive, took position on the right of Crittenden. The line, when formed, had a front of one mile and a half. Buell had with him, also, two fragments of Grant's army that he had picked up, each about 1,000 strong.

The forces on the Confederate right, which encountered Nelson, were extremely fragmentary. Chalmers's brigade, and the remains of Jackson's, which had fallen to pieces in the night, were there. The regiments of Gladden's brigade were represented by small bands of one or two hundred men, under various commanders. Colonel Deas, with 224 men of Gladden's brigade, was aided by the Fourth Kentucky, which had become detached from Trabue's brigade. In a charge he lost half of them. The First Tennessee from Stephens's brigade, the One Hundred and Fifty-fourth Tennessee from Johnson's, and the "Crescent" Regiment from Pond's, which had so distinguished itself on the left centre the previous afternoon, were found mingled in the confused and bloody conflict on the right. Chalmers was at one time detached from the command of his own brigade by General Withers, in order to lead one of these conglomerate commands; and Colonel Wheeler had charge of two or three regiments thrown together. General Withers strove, with great gallantry and skill, to bring order out of all this confusion; but in vain. Nelson's division encountered this line about seven o'clock, and after a contest of half an hour was driven back. The elation of yesterday would not yet permit these men to think themselves otherwise than invincible.

The battle, not only here but all along the line, consisted all the morning of a series of charges and counter-charges, in which the assailants were always beaten back with loss. The Federals suffered heavily, and the ragged front of the Southern regiments wasted away. Once or twice, during lulls in the battle, the Confederates retired, taking new and strong positions. General Chalmers tells how, after having re-

pulsed a charge of Nelson's line in force, with a double command of his
own and his temporary brigade, the Confederates were driven back some
300 yards.   Then, having been rallied, they boldly met and drove back
their pursuers in turn, and reoccupied the lost ground.   Nelson came
on again with still heavier battalions, the fight was renewed, and the
Confederates were again driven down the hill.   The One Hundred and
Fifty-fourth Tennessee and the remnant of Blythe's Mississippi coming
up, they were again rallied.   Chalmers tried once more to rouse them to
a charge ; but his appeals were unheeded by the exhausted men, till he
seized the colors of the Ninth Mississippi Regiment, and called on them
to follow.   With a wild shout, the whole brigade rushed in and drove
the enemy back, until it reoccupied its first position of the morning.
In this charge Wheeler led a regiment on foot, carrying its colors himself.   Lieutenant-Colonel Rankin, commanding the Ninth Mississippi,
fell mortally wounded ; and the major, J. E. Whitfield, who had on
Sunday led the skirmishers, was also there wounded.   The Second
Texas and Twenty-first Alabama, under Colonel Moore, while advancing, having been falsely told that the troops on their front were Breckinridge's, fell into an ambuscade and lost so heavily that they fell back
in confusion.

Equally sanguinary struggles occurred on the centre and left.   Ruggles's division was very fully engaged, both Gibson's and Anderson's
brigades charging repeatedly, and capturing batteries, which they could
not, however, bring off.   There had been an intermingling of commands
on Sunday, but on Monday all order was lost.   The positions of regiments nearly resembled a shuffled pack of cards, in which none adjoins
its next in suit except by chance.   It is not possible so to unravel the
tangled skein of narratives as correctly to assign the alignment of the
Confederate front.   Indeed, in every combat it shifted in agonized con-
tortions, as the heavy blows fell upon it from an army of double its
numbers, and largely made up of fresh troops.   It no longer fought
with the enthusiasm of the day previous, when the stake seemed empire ;
but it had been sifted of all who were physically or morally incapable
of enduring the sternest ordeals.   Its charges were made with a desperate fury from which the strongest columns recoiled.   A broken band
of heroic spirits, united by no tie but their common cause, would gather
itself for an assault, which looked impossible of achievement and fruitless of results.   As it waited the signal, looking to the right or left for
succor that would not come, it might shiver a little at the bloody jaws
of death that yawned to receive it, but it did not quail.   The word
would be given, and some martial spirit—general, colonel, or daring
subordinate impatient for glory—would seize the riddled flag, and rush
with reckless valor against the foe.   The "rebel yell"—that penetrating scream of menace and resolve—went up, and the line would hurl

Pittsburg Landing.

itself headlong, sometimes to success, sometimes to meet a storm of lead and iron, which strewed the field with the wounded and the dead. And this went on all the morning, until noon, until one, two o'clock.

This picture is not a fancy sketch. Patton Anderson says :

When one of General Cheatham's regiments had been appealed to in vain to make a charge on the advancing foe, Lieutenant Sandidge, seizing its colors and holding them high overhead, calling upon the regiment to follow him, spurred his horse to the front, and charged over the brow of the hill amid a shower of leaden hail from the enemy. The effect was electrical. The regiment moved gallantly to the support of its colors, but superior numbers soon pressed it back to its original position. Colonel Stanley, of the Ninth Texas, did the same thing with the same result.

Lieutenant-Colonel Jones, of the Seventeenth Louisiana, says that, just before the retreat, having collected some two hundred stragglers into line, General Ruggles ordered them to advance, and adds :

The general at this instant rode in front of the lines, and, seizing the flag from the hands of the color-bearer, gallantly led them to the charge. In this charge he was assisted by Colonel S. S. Heard.

Colonel Looney, Thirty-eighth Tennessee, says of Captain John C. Carter :

At one time he took the flag, and, urging his men forward, rendered me great assistance in moving forward the entire regiment.

Major Caldwell, of the Twelfth Tennessee, says in his report :

Private Fielder took charge of Companies B and G, which were left without a commissioned officer. He led these two companies all day in the thickest part of the battle.

Colonel Mouton, of the Eighteenth Louisiana, says in his report :

From 8 A. M. until half-past 1 P. M. we were constantly marching and counter-marching—the "Orleans Guards," in the mean time, having been attached to my command. About 2 P. M. we were ordered to move on the enemy—which was done without energy or life by the troops twice in succession, notwithstanding the noble and daring efforts of Generals Beauregard and Bragg to lead them on in the face of the enemy. The fact is, the men were completely exhausted from inanition and physical fatigue, many dropping in the attempt to move forward. Here I was wounded in the face.

These are but a few instances of the many acts, recorded and unrecorded, of individual heroism by which the wearied soldiers were animated and inspired. They were of no avail.

One of the most painful features resulting from the confusion was the waste of time and strength resulting from contradictory orders and purposeless manœuvres. Nearly every report mentions some fact illustrating this. Colonel Pond, whose brigade had encamped on the left, within four hundred yards of the enemy, was left some three-quarters of a mile in advance of the general line. He was attacked early in the morning by Lew Wallace's brigade, and, after a sharp engagement, fell back under cover of the artillery-fire of Captain Ketchum's battery, which was fighting within infantry-range. The artillery was managed in the most skillful and intrepid manner, and finally withdrew, covered by the Texas Rangers. Pond says of Ketchum, "The safety of my command was due to him." He continues:

Upon reaching the main line, the left of which was at the enemy's first camp on the Savannah road, I was ordered by General Ruggles to form on the extreme left, and rest my left on Owl Creek. While proceeding to execute this order, I was ordered to move by the rear of the main line to support the extreme right of General Hardee's line. I was again ordered by General Beauregard to advance and occupy the crest of a ridge in the edge of an old field. My line was just formed in this position, when General Polk ordered me forward to support his line. While moving to the support of General Polk, an order reached me from General Beauregard to report to him, with my command, at his headquarters. This was on the extreme left; where my brigade became engaged in the fight, which continued until the contest between the armies ceased.

The attack of the Federal army was well conducted, systematic, and spirited. Ammen's brigade was opposed to Chalmers, next the river; and Hazen's brigade, on Nelson's right, charged with great dash and success, until it was cut up by cross-fires from Breckinridge's command. Hazen and Ammen were driven back, but were rallied on Terrell's artillery, and on Crittenden's left brigade under Smith, and their own reserve under Bruce. The regiments in reserve of the Army of the Tennessee were also brought up. Nelson must have displayed conspicuous gallantry in this conflict. He is said to have been recognized animating his men by Kentuckians on the Confederate side.

Crittenden's division moved simultaneously with Nelson's, and with well-delivered blows; but, as has been seen, they were unavailing to break down the wall of living men opposed to it, in the main under the direction of Hardee. General Crittenden said to the writer that this was the hardest fighting he saw in the war, and was over a very narrow space.

Between eight and nine o'clock, McCook's leading brigade, under Rousseau, went in on the centre, soon followed by Gibson's, and eventu-. ally by Kirk's brigade.

General Hardee's report contains this account of Monday's battle:

On Monday, about six o'clock, portions of my command were formed upon an alignment with other troops on the left to resist the enemy, who soon opened a hot fire on our advanced lines. The battle reanimated our men, and the strong columns of the enemy were repulsed, again and again, by our tired and disordered but brave and steadfast troops. The enemy brought up fresh reënforcements, pouring them continually upon us. At times our lines recoiled, as it were, before the overwhelming physical weight of the enemy's forces; but the men rallied readily, and fought with unconquerable spirit. Many of our best regiments, signalized in the battle of Sunday by their steady valor, reeled under the sanguinary struggle on the succeeding day.

McCook's line of advance was along the road from Pittsburg to Shiloh, and through the adjacent country to the southeast. Here Breckinridge's two brigades, under Bowen and Statham, and what was left of Hindman's and Cleburne's commands, under Hardee's own eye, formed the nucleus of the defense. Cleburne, who had gone in on Sunday 2,750 strong, had but 800 men left. Half the remainder were dead or wounded; half were scattered or had fled. He advanced on Breckinridge's left, under fires and cross-fires, gallantly supported by the Washington Artillery. In a charge of the whole line, his men were mowed down and the brigade repulsed. Lieutenant-Colonel Neil, of the Twenty-third Tennessee, was shot through the body, and Acting-Major Cowley, of the Fifteenth Arkansas, killed. But, when the enemy attempted to advance, Cleburne led fifty-eight men of the Fifteenth Arkansas in a counter-charge, and repulsed them. Here fell Lieutenant-Colonel Patton, its sole surviving field officer. Hindman's troops fought near by, with almost identical results.

The Southern troops held the Federal army at bay with obstinate courage, giving back blow for blow, till the assailant reeled and called to the front all his reserves. The account already given sufficiently describes the character of the contest: stubborn combats in the woods, charges, repulses, counter-charges, surges of slaughter and fury, with lulls and pauses in the heat and motion of the fray. The Federal officers rivaled their adversaries in the display of personal bravery. Rousseau behaved with great gallantry. Colonel Kirk, commanding the Fifth Brigade, McCook's division, came upon the Thirty-fourth Illinois as it wavered, appalled, before a burst of battle-flame which had killed its commander, Major Levenway. It was Kirk's own regiment. He seized a flag, rushed forward, and steadied the line again; while doing this he was severely wounded in the shoulder.

McCook's troops deserve the more credit for their persistent attacks, as they had marched twenty-two miles the day before, and a portion of them had stood all night in the streets of Savannah without sleep. McCook says:

At Pittsburg Landing the head of my column had to force its way through thousands of panic-stricken and wounded men, before it could engage the enemy.

Sherman, in his advance toward the close of the battle, saw, from his position on McCook's right, the latter part of his contest in front of Shiloh Church. He says :

Here I saw for the first time the well-ordered and compact Kentucky forces of General Buell, whose soldierly movement gave confidence to our newer and less-disciplined forces. Here I saw Willich's regiment advance upon a point of water-oaks and thicket, behind which I knew the enemy was in great strength, and enter it in beautiful style. Then arose the *severest musketry-fire I ever heard*, and lasted twenty minutes, when this splendid regiment had to fall back.

Willich's regiment had received its "baptism of fire" from the Texan Rangers at Green River crossing, as narrated in these pages. It now accepted immersion in flame at the hands of troops under Cheatham and Gibson.

General Polk led Cheatham's division, which had probably suffered the least disorganization of any command on the field, to its position, in support of Breckinridge's left, as Cheatham says. This was, as near as can be ascertained, the left centre of the Confederate line—somewhat to the front and left of Shiloh Church. His other division, Clark's, now under A. P. Stewart, had bivouacked near the front, and got early into action. It was probably fully ten o'clock, when Cheatham, having formed his division, with Gibson's brigade, and the Thirty-third Tennessee (of Stewart's brigade), and the Twenty-seventh Tennessee (of Wood's brigade), was called on to resist the onset of Grant's reorganized forces, which were now led to the attack by Sherman. The defense was made with unblenching courage.

Sherman seems to have had a general supervision of Grant's troops. Wallace's, Prentiss's, and Hurlbut's divisions, had almost disappeared from the contest; but as their residuary legatee, and with part of his own and McClernand's men, after seventeen hours of respite, he was able to muster a formidable force. Awe of the terrible foe in front of them strove for mastery with mortification, emulation of Buell's progress, and the generous emotions of soldiers striving to recover their lost prestige. McClernand aided in leading the men, and Hurlbut was active in reorganizing the troops, and bringing them up at critical moments.[1]

This large force and Lew Wallace's division were led simultaneously against the lines held by Polk, and farther to the left by Bragg, who had here Anderson's, Pond's, and Trabue's brigades, and some remnants of Cleburne's and other commands. The odds were tremen-

---

[1] General Hurlbut informs the writer that his division was "complete in organization, every regiment in place in line of battle," both Sunday evening and Monday morning. The writer feels that it is due to General Hurlbut to give this statement, though his own inference from the Federal reports is different.

dous. It is hard to conceive how they maintained themselves. Eight or ten thousand jaded men had here to cope with twenty to twenty-five thousand of the enemy. General Beauregard was present in person directing the battle. But that gray line stood like a rock-bound coast against which the blue and silver surges beat in vain. Again and again they rushed on ; but fell back, scattered in spray, as the breaker that has spent its force. Wave after wave of Northern soldiery came pouring with deadly purpose against the Confederate front and recoiled, shattered and in dismay. It was only when the right was withdrawn, and McCook was thus allowed to press their flank, that this stout line slowly fell back in sullen defiance. Polk says :

They engaged the enemy so soon as they were formed, and fought him for four hours one of the most desperately contested conflicts of the battle. The enemy was driven gradually from his position; and, though reënforced several times during the engagement, he could make no impression on that part of the line.

Major Love, commanding the Twenty-seventh Tennessee, was mortally wounded ; and Colonel Preston Smith, commanding Johnson's brigade, was severely wounded, but retained his command.

This force maintained the position it had held for so many hours up to half-past two o'clock, the time at which orders were received from the general commanding to withdraw the troops from the field.

Cheatham's command was formed immediately in front of a large force of the enemy, then pressing forward vigorously. He gives the following report of this hard-fought field :

My engagement here commenced almost the instant I had formed, and was for four hours the most hotly contested I have witnessed. My own command fought with great gallantry and desperation, and for two hours I gradually drove the enemy from his position, and he, though constantly reënforced during the conflict, and with heavy odds in his favor at the beginning, failed utterly in accomplishing anything. . . . During the engagement here I was reënforced by Colonel Gibson with a Louisiana brigade, and by Colonel Campbell with his gallant Thirty-third Tennessee, all of whom deserve particular mention. . . . At half-past one o'clock I occupied about the same position at which I first came in collision with the enemy.

Major A. P. Avegno, commanding the Thirteenth Louisiana, of Gibson's brigade, was mortally wounded here, and many officers and men fell resisting the Federal onsets.

Being now reënforced with artillery, in which he had been deficient, Cheatham continues :

Thus strengthened, I would have had no difficulty in maintaining my position during the remainder of the day; but at half-past two o'clock, P. M., by orders from Major-General Polk, I withdrew my command slowly, and in order, in the direction of my camp, the enemy making no advance whatever.

The movement on the Federal right conducted by Lew Wallace, in conjunction with Sherman's division, was comparatively slow, as has been stated already. Wallace began skirmishing at daylight, simultaneously with Nelson. But outlying bands of Southerners promptly took up the battle, where they had left it off the night before. His skirmishers pushed these back, though not vigorously, until the Confederates on that flank, roused to the fact, rushed forward and drove his advance back for nearly a mile, thus securing a strong position " on an eminence in an open field, near Owl Creek, which we held until near the close of the conflict, against every effort the enemy could make." [1]

Wallace, making no headway in front, contented himself with trying to edge cautiously up along Owl Creek so as to turn the Confederate flank. He found this a perilous game, and at ten o'clock had made no real progress. It is evident that he was not able or willing to venture his entire strength against the Confederate left, because he did not feel secure of support from Sherman's and McClernand's beaten troops. It was ten o'clock before the combined attack was made in force. The strength of the Confederates who met it was not commensurate with the task required of them, but they made up in desperate valor for their weakness in numbers. Bragg had the chief direction here, and his force was made up, as already mentioned, of the remnants of Cleburne's brigade and other organizations and Trabue's brigade. Later in the day, part of Ruggles's division came up here and took part in the defense. About noon, this force fell back to the neighborhood of Shiloh, which it held till ordered to retreat.

On Sunday night, Trabue's Kentucky Brigade had occupied McDowell's camps between Shiloh and Owl Creek, feasting and making themselves comfortable with the spoils of war. On the other hand, Patton Anderson, for fear of demoralization, had bivouacked with his brigade in the open, resting himself under an apple-tree with a blanket over his head, while the pitiless storm once again beat upon himself and his men. Yet it would be hard to say that either brigade excelled the other in valor or in the fortitude with which it endured ten hours more of slaughter and reverse. It would seem from this— and other instances might be adduced—that the effect of the " spoils " upon the demoralization of the army has been greatly overrated, though of course they were not without their influence on the more ignorant and rapacious. The Kentucky Brigade, with Byrne's battery, got a strong position, to the left of the road from Shiloh to Pittsburg. It

---

[1] Bragg's " Report."

held this four hours. As the gradual pressure upon the right after a while brought the Federal troops upon its flank, Bragg ordered a charge by the Fourth Kentucky Regiment and the Fourth Alabama Battalion. After a contest of twenty minutes they drove back the enemy on their reserves; but were in turn driven back four or five hundred yards. Patton Anderson's brigade coming to their aid, "they again drove back the enemy; and thus, forward and backward, was the ground crossed and recrossed four times." It was a terrific combat. Lieutenant-Colonel Hines, commanding the Fourth Kentucky, was wounded; the heroic Major Thomas B. Monroe, was mortally wounded; Captain Nuckols, acting major, was badly wounded; Captains Ben Monroe, Thompson, and Fitzhenry, and four lieutenants, were wounded. Monroe died on the battle-field, bequeathing his sword to his infant son, and requesting that he might be told that "his father died in defense of his honor and of the rights of his country."

Governor George W. Johnson had gone into the battle on horseback, acting as a volunteer aide to the commander of the Kentucky Brigade. His horse was killed under him on Sunday, when he took a musket, and fought on foot in the ranks of the Fourth Kentucky. In the last repulse of that regiment he was shot through the body, and was left upon the field. He was not found until the next day, when he was taken into the Federal camp still alive, but soon died. He was a brave and patriotic citizen, who sealed his convictions with his blood.

The Sixth and Ninth Kentucky held their ground farther to the left until the close of the fight. Lieutenant-Colonel Cofer and Lieutenant Colonel R. A. Johnson and Major John W. Caldwell were wounded, and many brave men fell. In the Ninth Kentucky, four color-corporals were killed, and three color-corporals and the color-sergeant were wounded. The career of victory had, on Sunday afternoon, reunited Breckinridge's divided command with his old brigade in front of Pittsburg Landing, at the close of the battle. Separated again on Monday, they fought in opposite wings, until these were bent back, when they met again in front of Shiloh Church.

By one o'clock, it was apparent to General Beauregard that the contest was hopeless. The movement of the Federal army was that of the tide as it crawls up the beach. Each living ripple was rolled back at the musket's mouth; and yet, after seven hours of struggle, the Confederates had lost ground, and were evidently maintaining a hopeless conflict. There was no object in remaining there without a chance of victory.

Beauregard at last determined to retreat, and made his dispositions judiciously to that end. In the lull of a temporary success, he retired his right wing first, in good order, but in readiness to renew the conflict if assailed, and with such deliberation that the skirmishers were able to

contest and check the Federal advance. The retreat was by alternate
lines, and was skillfully conducted by General Beauregard. The pressure on that wing, moreover, was relieved by the direction given to
Nelson's column, which was moved toward Hamburg. General Beauregard says:

About 2 P. M. the lines in advance, which had repulsed the enemy in their
last fierce assault on our left and centre, received the orders to retire. This was
done with uncommon steadiness, and the enemy made no attempt to follow.

Before they fell back, the Kentucky Brigade, with Marmaduke's
Arkansas Regiment, and Tappan's Arkansas Regiment, had a final combat with the enemy, in which Colonel Hunt led the Ninth Kentucky in
a gallant but unavailing charge. Trabue, in his report, puts the fact
very well when he says:

The fragmentary forces of both armies had concentrated at this time around
Shiloh Church, and, worn out as were our troops, the field was here successfully
contested for two hours (i. e., from one until three o'clock); when, as if by
mutual consent, both sides desisted from the struggle.

Just as the fighting ceased, the Federals were reënforced by two
fresh brigades of Wood's division which came up.

In the mean time, under Beauregard's direction, Breckinridge had
formed Statham's brigade at the junction of the roads to Monterey
from Hamburg and from Pittsburg, about a mile and a half in the rear
of Shiloh Church, and this brigade, with the Kentucky Brigade and the
cavalry, formed the rear-guard of the retiring army. The movement
backward had been slow and well guarded. Some of the Federal accounts describe desperate charges, routing the Southerners, about this
time; but they are the vainglorious boasts of those who had done the
least real hard fighting that day. The Confederate army retired like a
lion, wounded but dauntless, that turns and checks pursuit by the grim
defiance in his face. The Federal army was well content to recover
its lost ground, and win back that field from which it had shrunk cowering and beaten the day before.

General Beauregard says:

Our artillery played upon the woods beyond for a while, but upon no visible
enemy, and without a reply. Soon satisfied that no serious pursuit was, or
would be, attempted, this last line was withdrawn, and never did troops leave
battle-field in better order.

About an hour after the Confederate troops retired, the Federal
army reoccupied its front line of April 5th. In this day's contest the
troops of McCook's division had especially signalized themselves. They
had entered the field, last of all, at a reëntrant angle, and closed the

day as the salient—the point of a wedge at Shiloh, struggling with the heaviest masses of the Southern troops.

Another rain-storm swept over the exhausted armies, the plentiful tears of Heaven shed upon a field of remorseless carnage. It brought solace to the fevered wounds of many left unheeded upon the ground by friends too eager or too hard pressed to indulge in pity. But it added to the hardships and sufferings of the Confederates as they fell back over roads thus rendered intolerably bad. The rear-guard bivouacked in the mud and rain, and next morning moved back slowly to Mickey's, about three miles, carrying off the wounded and many spoils. It remained at Mickey's, where there was a large hospital, three days, burying the dead, removing the wounded, and sending back to Corinth its captures. On Friday, Breckinridge marched the rear-guard into Corinth.

The only attempt to follow up the victory was on Tuesday. The rear-guard was covered by about 350 cavalry. Colonel Forrest was the senior officer. He had 150 men of his own; a company of Wirt Adams's regiment, under Captain Isaac F. Harrison; a squadron of Wharton's Texas Rangers; and John Morgan, with some of his men.

Sherman advanced with two brigades and the Fourth Illinois Cavalry, and, receiving the support of a column from General Wood, proceeded cautiously on a reconnaissance. Marching with Hildebrand's unfortunate Third Brigade in front, he came upon Forrest's cavalry command. He at once threw out the Seventy-seventh Ohio Regiment, supported by the Fourth Illinois Cavalry, when Forrest, perceiving the Federal infantry somewhat disordered in crossing a stream, with his quick and bold intuition took the initiative, and led a charge upon them. The ground was not favorable to him, as it was miry and covered with fallen timber; but, so sudden and fierce was the onslaught, that a panic seized the Federal infantry, and it broke and fled. The Confederate horsemen rode through it, shooting down the flying men; and, without drawing rein, rushed headlong upon the cavalry. Neither did this stand to meet the shock. As it broke in disorder, Forrest and his men burst upon the startled troopers, driving them in tumultuous rout and slaying them, until they came upon the main line of Sherman's and Wood's brigades. Forrest, carried away by the ardor of the combat, outstripped his own men and many of the enemy, and came within fifty yards of the Federal line. A volley greeted him, inflicting a severe wound in his side, and mortally wounding his horse. Nevertheless, in spite of special efforts to kill him, he got back to his men, and away. Sherman reports fifteen of Hildebrand's men killed and twenty-five wounded, which does not seem to include the cavalry, and he makes no mention of seventy-five prisoners, said by Colonel Jordan to have been captured and carried off. No steps were taken in pursuit.

There is one branch of the service to which the writer feels that his description of the battle has done scant justice—the artillery. In both armies it played a conspicuous part, and challenged the admiration of leaders and soldiers alike by its skill and the splendid gallantry with which it plunged into the foremost of the fight. The men died at their guns, and whole batteries were supplied by volunteers from the infantry, who, ignorant but ardent, made shift to hurl destruction upon their foes in this unaccustomed way. Ketchum's invaluable services have already been alluded to. Byrne's battery rendered not less useful service on Sunday, and again on Monday, to the Kentucky Brigade. When Byrne called on the Sixth Kentucky Regiment for a detail, "No detail," cried John Spurrier, springing from the ranks, "but all the volunteers you want!" and thus he was supplied.

Captain Polk lost a leg, fighting his guns well; Hodgson and Slocomb, with the Washington Artillery, are highly commended; and Bankhead's, Gage's, and Girardey's batteries; and, indeed, the record of gallant and effective service, commemorated in the battle reports, covers the entire list of batteries, so that almost any distinction seems invidious. The brigadiers and infantry commanders appear anxious to testify with generous gratitude to the obligations they were under to the artillery. A gallant soldier, Major Caldwell of the Ninth Kentucky, who afterward commanded a brigade, informed the writer that he never saw the artillery fight so audaciously on any other field as at Shiloh.

It is the same on the Federal side; and both Grant and Buell mention the good service done them by the artillery. The guns under Colonel Webster that arrested Chalmers's last charge on Sunday evening made a crisis in the day. Major Taylor is commended by Sherman, and Lieutenant Brotzman by Hurlbut; and Buell speaks in high terms of the services of Mendenhall's, Terrell's, and Bartlett's batteries.

The Rev. Robert Collyer, who went up to Pittsburg Landing with one of the first boats sent with comforts for those wounded in the battle, contributed to the *Chicago Tribune* some interesting details of what he saw and learned there. With regard to the bringing on of the first day's battle, he said :

Among these 285 (wounded) men, many of them officers of intelligence, I gathered the only clear ideas and conclusions I was able to come to, concerning the battle. I will give them as I got them. They were so evidently the true convictions of the men that I listened to them with the deepest interest, not so much because they *must* be true (though I think that is of great value), but, above all, because that is the way the *fighters* think, not individually, but in masses.

1. All who said anything about it said that the fatal surprise of Sunday morning was the result of unpardonable negligence on the part of the commanders.

The men themselves knew that the woods all about them were swarming with the enemy (I quote the exact phrases); but there was no effort made to get a clear knowledge of the real condition of things, and not even a picket-guard sent out until perhaps Saturday; and that this knowledge that a certain danger was near them, for which their officers made no provision, made the men feel unsteady and unstrung. If they could have known exactly what was hidden among the trees and ravines, they would have had better courage to grapple with it when it sprung upon them. So when the enemy came, storming down with a fierce, determined onslaught, almost without parallel in battles, they were taken at a double disadvantage. They were outnumbered and dispirited at the same time.

2. The battle on Sunday was badly managed. The men said to me: "We would have fought; we meant to fight; we wanted to fight; we will fight; but we were outflanked every time. Just as sure as we made a stand, we had to fight superior numbers, put where they could do as they liked, and we could only do as we could. We did run away, we don't deny it; we got under the bank, and staid there; we could not come out. Why? Because it was no use. If a man gives his life, he wants to get the worth of it."

3. The Tennessee River, the gunboats, and Colonel Webster, saved Grant's division on Sunday afternoon from a second Bull Run, or annihilation. The river held the troops in, and the gunboats, with the batteries skillfully placed by Colonel Webster, protected them until Buell came up. Not a man or a steamboat, probably, would have been left but for these cannon.

4. These same men who had run on Sunday went in with Buell's men on Monday. Fragments of regiments, patched together in the haste of the morning, gathered new spirit when they knew what they had to do; and the universal testimony is that they fought well—never men fought better than those that went back to fight again.

5. The battle on Monday *was a battle* on the part of the enemy, in which he apparently did his utmost before he began to retreat. He did not mean to retreat, but he had to do so because we beat him back. Still, while on the Sunday we were routed, on the Monday *he* retreated and was not routed. His retreat was well done. Such is the universal testimony.

The cavalry made very little impression on him in the retreat, for three reasons: First, his forces were well ordered; second, the roads were bad for cavalry; and, third, they could not tell what sort of a trap might be set for them in the woods. I inquired diligently after the idea of the men as to the final result, and it was that we are about where we were a week before the battle, with a loss of 8,000 in killed, wounded, and missing; yet that, with every desire to see fair, the *prestige* of the battle remains finally with our forces. As soon as we fought at all on equal terms, our men beat them without the shadow of a doubt. The men everywhere, wounded and well, are in good heart, I saw no sign of depression anywhere beyond what comes out of pain and loss of blood. The men look serious, as if they had grown older; but I did not speak to a man who did not say we can beat the enemy every time, if we get fair play.

Two battles had been fought; and each army occupied the ground which it had held before they began. A woful list of more than 20,000 killed and wounded, and 3,000 or 4,000 prisoners—many valiant dead

—many great souls blotted from the roll of the living—this was all there was left to tell of those two days of havoc.

It is true a stunning blow had been delivered to the Federal army, which arrested its progress, shattered its *morale*, and changed its tactics. But all this was as nothing, for it secured delay only. General Johnston did not mean to delay it—he meant to destroy it. This only could have secured the independence of the South.

General Beauregard reports the loss of the Confederate army :

Killed	1,728
Wounded	8,012
Missing	959
Total	10,699

After a close examination of all accessible sources of information, covering about two thirds of the army, the writer finds a possible variation of 218 more casualties, principally in missing, that might be added to General Beauregard's report, based upon the returns first sent in. The Confederate casualties may therefore be safely estimated at between 10,700 and 11,000, in killed, wounded, and missing. The missing men were the wounded left on and near the field in Monday's battle. Jordan speaks of the loss on the first day at about 6,500, which would leave over 4,000 for Monday's battle. His data are not known to the writer.

The loss of the Federal army was, according to official reports, as follows :

	Killed.	Wounded.	Captured.	Total.
Grant's army....................	1,437	5,679	2,934	10,050
Buell's army....................	263	1,816	88	2,167
Total....................	1,700	7,495	3,022	12,217

A reference to the Appendix will show that General Grant's aggregate loss was 11,220 instead of 10,050, giving a total loss, including Buell's, of 13,387. Buell's loss has not been verified, and was also probably larger than the official report. Swinton, in his "Decisive Battles," and Prof. Coppee, in his "Life of Grant" (page 96), put the Federal loss at 15,000.

It is probable that Grant's army did not lose much more than a thousand men on Monday. If this be so, it is apparent that his losses on Sunday were some 10,000, besides thousands of fugitives, at a cost of about 6,500 Confederates. On Monday the Federal loss was only some 3,000 or 4,000, with an equal or greater loss inflicted on the Southern army. In both cases, the assailant suffered less than the defensive lines. General Wallace was killed. General Grant is said to have been wounded, and Sherman was wounded in the hand, besides having three horses killed. A good many Federal officers were also killed and wounded. But among the Confederates the proportion of officers killed and wounded was much greater. Besides the commander-in-chief, and Brigadier-General Gladden, there was a great number of regimental officers killed. Bragg had two horses shot under him ; Hardee was slightly wounded, his coat cut and his horse disabled by a shell ; Breckinridge was twice slightly struck ; Cheatham was also slightly wounded, and had three horses shot under him. Brigadier-Generals Clark, Bowen, and Johnson, were severely wounded, and Hindman was injured by a shell exploding under his horse and killing it. Colonel Smith, who succeeded Bushrod Johnson in command of his brigade, was wounded ; and Colonel Dan Adams, and Colonel Deas, who in turn succeeded Gladden, were also wounded. The long list of field and company officers, and of brave soldiers, would swell too much the bulk of this volume.

The Comte de Paris says (volume i., page 542) that Sherman told him that Sunday's battle was "the most terrible that he had witnessed during his whole career." Badeau remarks (volume i., page 78) in regard to the assault on Sherman Sunday morning, that it was successful, "after several hours of as desperate fighting as was ever seen on the American Continent." He says (page 89), "With the exception of one or two severe struggles, the fighting of April 7th was light when compared with that of Sunday." Again (page 93) : "It was the fiercest fight of the war west of the Alleghanies, and, in proportion to the numbers engaged, equaled any contest during the rebellion. I have heard Sherman say that he never saw such terrible fighting afterward, and Grant compared Shiloh only with the Wilderness." He adds truly : "In the battle, each party was forced to respect the fighting qualities of the other ; the Northerners recognized the impetuous vigor and splendid enthusiasm of the rebels, and the latter found all the tenacity and determination of the North in those who opposed them."

The Federal writers have claimed that, the battles having ended in the retreat of the assailant, the moral advantages remained with them. It is true they held the field of battle, but it must be remembered that it had been for them a canvas city where, in the security of overpowering strength, they had discussed great schemes of invasion and conquest. Suddenly the bolt of war had burst over their own heads. They had seen their city taken by storm, wrapped in flames and sacked, and had been snatched from the brink of destruction only by the premature arrival of a second army and the mysterious arrest of the impending and final blow. They looked around them, and everywhere were the lamentable signs and ravages of horrid war, breathing fire and slaughter; the desolated camps, broken artillery and scattered arms; the trodden, blood-stained mire; the dead and dying; and pale, trembling fugitives creeping back to their places in the ranks. There was neither glory nor gain of any sort apparent to their eyes. There was no room for exultation anywhere. Indeed, the last combat of the field, Forrest's charge with 350 men, routing a regiment of infantry and a regiment of cavalry in the face of three brigades, which turned back from that road as if it were beset by some occult danger, is a sufficient comment on the text of the bulletins. At the close of the apologue comes the moral. The epic is ended with an epigram in cold steel, leaving no doubt as to the meaning of what had gone before.

The best proof of what conclusions were drawn from the conduct and issue of the battle is found in the entire change of Federal tactics from that day. The bayonet was exchanged for the spade; and the grand march was turned into a siege of the South. Halleck took chief command on the 9th, and Grant, though left nominally second in command, was, as his biographer, Badeau, admits, under a cloud, unconsulted, unemployed, and in disgrace. If he had not possessed excellent qualities for war, not to be disregarded in perilous times, he would have been irretrievably ruined. Sherman's family influence, with his personal conduct on the field, condoned any mistakes he had made, and he was recommended for promotion. Buell, unfortunately for himself, had done not enough to dictate his own terms, and too much to be forgiven; so that his *rescue* of Grant's army was treated almost as a failure then, and altogether as a crime afterward. He certainly had eventually to pay the penalty of it; and it is difficult to decide from the tone of the court-annalists, while Grant and Sherman were wielding the sword and purse of the country, whether Buell's delay was the cause of all the trouble, or his arrival an impertinent intrusion.

But, though the Federal plans were disarranged, their generals shocked, and their troops demoralized by the battles of Shiloh, the only satisfaction it brought to the camps of the South was pride in the prowess of her soldiers, and in the proofs she had given of power to strike a great and terrible blow. Her generals said to one another that the best, and, as it proved, the only chance to convert the wasting war of defense into one of aggression, had escaped them. This was whispered in the camps, and is yet a tradition among her people, in spite of all the glosses that factitious history has put into print. President Davis said, not once, but many times: "When Sidney Johnston fell, it was the turning-point of our fate; for we had no other hand to take up his work in the West."

The armies of the West had found in every encounter foemen worthy of their steel. But the magnitude of the contest at Shiloh, and the tremendous issues at stake, the impetuous valor and stubborn resolution of the combatants, inspired a mutual respect—a respect which it is to be hoped may do much to remove ancient prejudices and form the basis of an equal and permanent friendship.

One pleasing feature, which casts a mellow light over the dreadful carnage of the field of Shiloh, is the humanity and mutual courtesy that marked the conduct of the antagonists. It is true that General Grant refused General Beauregard's request, on April 9th, to bury the dead under a flag of truce; but he stated that he had already performed that duty. There were no complaints of "outrages"—killing of captives, mutilation of the dead, cruelty to the wounded—which made so large a part of the war news of certain correspondents. The conflict had been too serious and too grand to require or admit any merely sensational stuff in its recital.

"A participant," writing to the *Cincinnati Commercial*,[1] says:

While preparing our meal, a flag of truce, consisting of a yellow handkerchief tied to a sapling-pole, emerged from the woods beyond us. It was carried by a tall Alabamian, who brought with it the wounded lieutenant-colonel of the Fiftieth Illinois, borne on a litter. The bearers all had tied on their arms a piece of white rag, which, by questioning the wearers, I learned designated a detail for hospital duty. I am glad to be able to say something good of an army of traitors; "we will give the devil his due." No instance came to my knowledge in which our dead were treated in so diabolical a manner as they were reported to be at Manassas and Pea Ridge. They were invariably, wherever practicable, kindly cared for. A. Hickenlooper tells me that one of his corporals, who was wounded, received many attentions from them. An officer handed him a rubber blanket, saying that he himself needed it bad enough, but the wounded man needed it worse. Others brought him food and water, and wrapped him up in woolen blankets. Such instances were common; and, among the hundreds of dead and wounded I have looked upon, not one showed signs of the barbarities which the rebels are commonly supposed to practise on the patriots.

General Buell, in a letter to the present writer, says:

A circumstance occurred after the battle, which excited a good deal of interest for the moment, particularly among those who had known your father. We had heard of his death, but not the particulars of it, from prisoners taken in the course of the battle of the 7th; and, in collecting and burying the dead on the morning of the 8th, a body was found which several persons supposed to be that of your father. It was carried to the headquarters of General Nelson and laid out in a tent, where a number of persons came to see it. Several of them, acquaintances of your father, were quite confident of the identity. I

---

[1] "Rebellion Record," vol. iii., p. 416.

was not one of those who entertained that opinion, though the expression of
the face was so changed by the wound which it had received as to make it difficult to be very confident about the identity. There was the same manly form,
certainly; but that was all that I could see alike. However, the question was
determined early in the day by the information which we received from the
Confederate army, that your father was killed on the 6th, and that his body was
removed from the field at the time of his death.

It was ascertained, as the writer has been informed, that the body
was that of Colonel Thomas Preston, of Memphis, a connection by marriage of General Johnston. The writer does not know the origin of the
mistake. It is needless to say that all the respect due to his supposed
rank and personality was paid by those who had the body in charge.
It is curious to note the contrast in the conduct of these honorable
warriors, still hot from the fray, with that of Sheridan, Heintzelman,
and Griffin, which will be related in the next chapter.

But little remains to be said of what occurred after General Johnston's death. It is not the purpose of the writer to give a history of
the war, but only to tell the story of General Johnston's life, what he
did, and the great events in which he played a part. All this ended
absolutely on Sunday afternoon, April 6, 1862. Not often is there an
Elisha to catch up the mantle of the translated Elijah. When a man
dies, others take up his work to mend or mar it, and he is soon forgotten. A puff of wind, or a little pewter extinguisher, puts out the light
that shines over many a league of land and sea. No man has any
tenure of the things of this world in the grave. His power, his authority, most of his influence, die with him. There come others in his place,
and all his plans, his methods, and his informing spirit, are changed.
It was so in this case.

General Beauregard retired to Corinth, where Van Dorn reënforced
him almost immediately with 17,000 men, the strong fighters of Wilson's Creek and Elkhorn. These troops, added to the effective total
reported by Jordan after the battle of Shiloh, 32,212, give an army of
nearly 50,000 men fit for duty. Reënforcements were poured in from
every quarter. But, with an aggregate on the rolls of 112,092, the
effective total could not be gotten above a reported effective force of
52,706 men. The sick and absent numbered more than one-half the
army. No sudden epidemic had smitten the camp; the sickness was
the effect of causes evident from the hour of retreat. Halleck had taken
position at Farmington, and was advancing spade in hand; and Beauregard intrenched to resist him. Digging in the trenches among those
marshes, with consequent malaria; bad food; neglect of police duty;
impure and insufficient water, the drainage of swamps and heavily
charged with magnesia and rotten limestone; these causes, acting in
conjunction with certain moral influences, the depression of retreat and

inaction, produced obstinate types of diarrhœa and typhoid fever. The attempt to bore artesian wells failed. No sound men were left.

Beauregard twice offered Halleck battle. But he preferred regular approaches, in the mean time seizing the railroad east of Corinth, and cutting off communication with the seaboard. There was nothing to be done except to retreat, which Beauregard did, May 30th, falling back to Tupelo, on the Ohio & Mississippi Railroad. The retreat was made in good order, and with no very considerable loss in men or material of war. But the abandonment of Corinth, which was a point of the first strategic importance, involved the surrender of Memphis and the Mississippi Valley, and the loss of the campaign. General Beauregard, whose health continued bad, devolved the command of the army on General Bragg, and retired to Mobile for rest and recuperation. The President made Bragg's temporary command a permanent one.

APPENDIX.

GENERAL BEAUREGARD'S OFFICIAL REPORT.

HEADQUARTERS, ARMY OF THE MISSISSIPPI, }
CORINTH, MISSISSIPPI, *April* 11, 1862. }

GENERAL: On the 2d ultimo, having ascertained conclusively from the movements of the enemy on the Tennessee River, and from reliable sources of information, that his aim would be to cut off my communication—in West Tennessee with the Eastern and Southern States, by operating from the Tennessee River between Crump's Landing and Eastport as a base—I determined to foil his designs by concentrating all my available forces at and around Corinth.

Meanwhile, having called on the Governors of the States of Tennessee, Mississippi, Alabama, and Louisiana, to furnish additional troops, some of them (chiefly regiments from Louisiana) soon reached this vicinity, and, with two divisions of General Polk's command from Columbus, and a fine corps of troops from Mobile and Pensacola, under Major-General Bragg, constituted the Army of the Mississippi. At the same time General Johnston, being at Murfreesboro, on the march to form a junction of his forces with mine, was called on to send at least a brigade by railroad, so that we might fall on and crush the enemy should he attempt to advance from under his gunboats. The call on General Johnston was promptly complied with. His entire force was also hastened in this direction; and by the first of April our united forces were concentrated along the Mobile & Ohio Railroad from Bethel to Corinth, and on the Memphis & Charleston Railroad from Corinth to Iuka.

It was then determined to assume the offensive, and strike a sudden blow at the enemy in position, under General Grant, on the west bank of the Tennessee, at Pittsburg, and in the direction of Savannah, before he was reënforced by the army under General Buell, then known to be advancing for that purpose by rapid marches from Nashville *via* Columbia. About the same time General Johnston was advised that such an operation conformed to the expectations of the President.

By a rapid and vigorous attack on General Grant, it was expected he would be beaten back into his transports and the river, or captured, in time to enable us to profit by the victory and remove to the rear all the stores and munitions that would fall into our hands, in such an event, before the arrival of General Buell's army on the scene. It was never contemplated, however, to retain the position thus gained and abandon Corinth, the strategic point of the campaign.

Want of general officers needful for the proper organization of divisions and brigades of an army brought thus suddenly together, and other difficulties in the way of an effective organization, delayed the movement until the night of the 2d instant, when it was heard from a reliable quarter that the junction of the enemy's armies was near at hand. It was then, at a late hour, determined that the attack should be attempted at once, incomplete and imperfect as were our preparations for such a grave and momentous adventure. Accordingly, that night, at 1 A. M., the preliminary orders to the commanders of corps were issued for the movement.

On the following morning the detailed orders of movement, a copy of which is herewith, marked "A," were issued, and the movement, after some delay, commenced, the troops being in admirable spirits. It was expected we should be able to reach the enemy's lines in time to attack him early on the 5th instant. The men, however, for the most part, were unused to marching; the roads, narrow and traversing a densely-wooded country, became almost impassable after a severe rain-storm on the night of the 4th, which drenched the troops in bivouac; hence our forces did not reach the intersection of the roads from Pittsburg and Hamburg, in the immediate vicinity of the enemy, until late Saturday afternoon.

It was then decided that the attack should be made on the next morning, at the earliest hour practicable, in accordance with the orders of movement; that is, in three lines of battle, the first and second extending from Owl Creek on the left to Lick Creek on the right, a distance of about three miles, supported by the third and the reserve. The first line, under Major-General Hardee, was constituted of his corps, augmented on his right by Gladden's brigade, of Major-General Bragg's corps, deployed in line of battle, with their respective artillery following immediately by the main road to Pittsburg, and the cavalry in rear of the wings. The second line, composed of the other troops of Bragg's corps, followed the first at a distance of five hundred yards in the same order as the first. The army corps, under General Polk, followed the second line, at the distance of about eight hundred yards, in lines of brigades, deployed with their batteries in rear of each brigade, moving by the Pittsburg road, the left wing supported by cavalry. The reserve, under Brigadier-General Breckinridge, followed closely the third line, in the same order, its right wing supported by cavalry.

These two corps constituted the reserve, and were to support the front lines of battle, by being deployed when required on the right and left of the Pittsburg road, or otherwise act according to the exigencies of the battle.

At 5 A. M., on the 6th instant, a reconnoitring party of the enemy, having become engaged with our advanced pickets, the commander of the forces gave orders to begin the movement and attack as determined upon, except that Trabue's brigade of Breckinridge's division was detached and advanced to support the left of Bragg's corps and line of battle when menaced by the enemy, and the other two brigades were directed to advance by the road to Hamburg, to support Bragg's right; and, at the same time, Maney's regiment, of Polk's corps, was advanced by the same road to reënforce the regiment of cavalry and battery of four pieces already thrown forward to watch and guard Grier's, Tanner's, and Borland's Fords of Lick Creek.

Thirty minutes after 5 A. M., our lines and columns were in motion, all animated, evidently, by a promising spirit. The front line was engaged at once, but advanced steadily, followed in due order, with equal resolution and steadiness, by the other lines, which were brought successively into action with rare skill, judgment, and gallantry, by the several corps commanders, as the enemy made a stand, with his masses rallied for the struggle for his encampments. Like an Alpine avalanche our troops moved forward, despite the determined resistance of the enemy, until after 6 P. M., when we were in possession of all his encampments between Owl and Lick Creeks but one. Nearly all of his field artillery, about thirty (30) flags, colors, and standards, over 3,000 prisoners, including a division commander (General Prentiss) and several brigade commanders, thousands of small-arms, an immense supply of subsistence, forage, and munitions of war, and a large amount of means of transportation—all the substantial fruits of a complete victory, such, indeed, as rarely have followed the most successful battles, for never was an army so well provided as that of our enemy.

The remnant of his army had been driven in utter disorder to the immediate vicinity of Pittsburg, under the shelter of the heavy guns of his iron-clad gunboats, and we remained undisputed masters of his well-selected, admirably-provided cantonments, after over twelve hours of obstinate conflict with his forces, who had been beaten from them and the contiguous covert, but only by a sustained onset of all the men we could bring into action.

Our loss was heavy, as will appear from the accompanying return marked " B." Our commander-in-chief, General A. S. Johnston, fell mortally wounded, and died on the field at 2.30 P. M., after having shown the highest qualities of the commander, and a personal intrepidity that inspired all around him, and gave resistless impulsion to his columns at critical moments.

The chief command then devolved upon me, though at the time I was greatly prostrated, and suffering from the prolonged sickness with which I had been afflicted since early in February. The responsibility was one which, in my physical condition, I would have gladly avoided, though cast upon me when our forces were successfully pushing the enemy back upon the Tennessee River, and, though supported on the immediate field by such corps commanders as Major-Generals Polk, Bragg, and Hardee, and Brigadier-General Breckinridge, commanding the reserve.

It was after 6 P. M., as before said, when the enemy's last position was carried, and his forces finally broke and sought refuge behind a commanding eminence, covering the Pittsburg Landing, not more than half a mile distant, and under the guns of the gunboats, which opened on our eager columns a fierce and annoying fire with shot and shell of the heaviest description. Darkness was close at hand. Officers and men were exhausted by a combat of over twelve hours without food, and jaded by the march of the preceding day through mud and water. It was, therefore, impossible to collect the rich and opportune spoils of war scattered broadcast on the field left in our possession, and impracticable to make any effective dispositions for their removal to the rear.

I accordingly established my headquarters at the church of Shiloh, in the enemy's encampment, with Major-General Bragg, and directed our troops to sleep on their arms in such positions in advance and rear as corps commanders should determine, hoping, from news received by a special dispatch, that delays had been encountered by General Buell in his march from Columbia, and that his main force, therefore, could not reach the field of battle in time to save General Grant's shattered fugitive forces from capture or destruction on the following day.

During the night the rain fell in torrents, adding to the discomfort and harassed condition of the men; the enemy, moreover, had broken their rest by a discharge, at measured intervals, of heavy shells thrown from the gunboats; therefore, on the following morning, the troops under my command were not in a condition to cope with an equal force of fresh troops, armed and equipped like our adversary, in the immediate possession of his depots, and sheltered by such an auxiliary as the enemy's gunboats.

About six o'clock on the morning of the 7th of April, however, a hot fire of musketry and artillery, opened from the enemy's quarter on our advanced line, assured me of the junction of his forces; and soon the battle raged with a fury which satisfied me I was attacked by a largely superior force. But, from the outset, our troops, notwithstanding their fatigue and losses from the battle of the day before, exhibited the most cheering, veteran-like steadiness. On the right and centre the enemy was repulsed in every attempt he made with his heavy columns in that quarter of the field; on the left, however, and nearest to the point of arrival of his reënforcements, he drove forward line after line of his fresh troops, which were met with a resolution and courage of which our country may be proudly hopeful. Again and again our troops were brought to the charge, invariably to win the position at issue, invariably to drive back their foe. But hour by hour, thus opposed to an enemy constantly reënforced, our ranks were perceptibly thinned under the unceasing, withering fire of the enemy, and by 12 M. eighteen hours of hard fighting had sensibly exhausted a large number. My last reserves had necessarily been disposed of, and the enemy was evidently receiving fresh reënforcements after each repulse. Accordingly, about 1 P. M., I determined to withdraw from so unequal a conflict, securing such of the results of the victory of the day before as were then practicable.

Officers of my staff were immediately dispatched with the necessary orders to make the best dispositions for a deliberate, orderly withdrawal from the field, and to collect and post a reserve to meet the enemy should he attempt to push after us. In this connection I will mention particularly my adjutant-general, Colonel Jordan, who was of much assistance to me on this occasion, as he had already been on the field of battle on that and the preceding day.

About 2 P. M., the lines in advance, which had repulsed the enemy in their last fierce assault on our left and centre, received the orders to retire. This was done with uncommon steadiness, and the enemy made no attempt to follow.

The line of troops established to cover this movement had been disposed on a favorable ridge, commanding the ground of Shiloh Church. From this position our artillery played upon the woods beyond for a while, but upon no visible enemy, and without reply. Soon, satisfied that no serious pursuit would be attempted, this last line was withdrawn, and never did troops leave a battle-field in better order; even the stragglers fell into the ranks, and marched off with those who had stood more steadily by their colors. A second strong position was taken up about a mile in rear, where the approach of the enemy was awaited for nearly an hour, but no effort to follow was made, and only a small detachment of horsemen could be seen at a distance from this last position, warily observing our movements.

Arranging, through my staff officers, for the completion of the movements thus begun, Brigadier-General Breckinridge was left with his command as a rear-guard to hold the ground we had occupied the night preceding the first battle, just in front of the intersection of the Pittsburg and Hamburg roads, about four miles from the former place, while the rest of the army passed to the rear in excellent order.

On the following day General Breckinridge fell back about three miles to Mickey's, which position we continued to hold, with our cavalry thrown considerably forward in immediate proximity to the battle-field.

Unfortunately, toward night of the 7th instant, it began to rain heavily; this continued throughout the night; the roads became almost impassable in many places, and much hardship and suffering now ensued before all the regiments reached their encampments; but, despite the heavy casualties of the two eventful days of the 6th and 7th of April, this army is more confident of ultimate success than before its encounter with the enemy.

To Major-Generals Polk, Bragg, and Hardee, commanding corps, and to Brigadier-General Breckinridge, commanding the reserve, the country is greatly indebted for the zeal, intelligence, and energy, with which all orders were executed; for the foresight and military ability they displayed in the absence of instructions in the many exigencies of the battle on a field so densely wooded and broken, and for their fearless deportment as they repeatedly led their commands personally to the onset upon their powerful adversary. It was under these circumstances that General Bragg had two horses shot under him; that Major-General Hardee was slightly wounded, his coat rent by balls, and his horse disabled; and that Brigadier-General Breckinridge was twice struck by spent balls.

For the services of their gallant subordinate commanders and of other officers, as well as for the details of the battle-field, I must refer to the reports of corps, division, and brigade commanders, which shall be forwarded as soon as received.

To give more in detail the operations of the two battles resulting from the movement on Pittsburg than now attempted must have delayed this report for weeks, and interfered materially with the important duties of my position. But I may be permitted to say that not only did the obstinate conflict for twelve hours on Sunday leave the Confederate army masters of the battle-field and our adversary beaten, but we left that field on the next day only after eight hours' incessant battle with a superior army of fresh troops, whom we had repulsed in every attack on our lines—so repulsed and crippled, indeed, as to leave it unable to take the field for the campaign for which it was collected and equipped at such enormous expense, and with such profusion of all the appliances of war. These successful results were not achieved, however, as before said, without severe loss—a loss not to be measured by the number of the slain and wounded, but by the high social and personal worth of so large a number of those who were killed or disabled, including the commander of the forces, whose high qualities will be greatly missed in the momentous campaign impending.

I deeply regret to record also the death of the Hon. George M. Johnson, Provisional Governor of Kentucky, who went into action with the Kentucky troops, and continually inspired them by his words and example. Having his horse shot under him on Sunday, he entered the ranks of a Kentucky regiment on Monday, and fell mortally wounded toward the close of the day. Not his State alone, but the whole Confederacy, has sustained a great loss in the death of this brave, upright, and able man.

Another gallant and able soldier and captain was lost to the service of the country, when Brigadier-General Gladden, commanding First Brigade, Withers's division, Second Army Corps, died from a severe wound received on the 6th instant, after having been conspicuous to his whole corps and the army for courage and capacity.

Major-General Cheatham, commanding First Division, First Corps, was slightly wounded, and had three horses shot under him.

Brigadier-General Clark, commanding Second Division of the First Corps, received a severe wound also on the first day, which will deprive the army of his valuable services for some time.

Brigadier-General Hindman, engaged in the outset of the battle, was conspicuous for a cool courage efficiently employed in leading his men ever into the thickest of the fray, until his horse was shot under him, and he was unfortunately so severely injured by the fall that the army was deprived, on the following day, of his chivalrous example.

Brigadier-Generals B. R. Johnson and Bowen, most meritorious officers, were also severely wounded in the first combat, but it is hoped will soon be able to return to duty with their brigades.

To mention the many field-officers who died or were wounded while gallantly leading their commands into action, and the many brilliant instances of individual courage displayed by officers and men in the twenty hours of battle, is impossible at this time; but their names will be duly made known to their countrymen.

The immediate staff of the lamented commander-in-chief, who accompanied him to the field, rendered efficient service, and, either by his side, or in carrying his orders, shared his exposures to the casualties of a well-contested battle-field. I beg to commend their names to the notice of the War Department, namely: of Captains H. P. Brewster and N. Wickliffe, of the Adjutant and Inspector-General's Department.

Captain Theodore O'Hara, acting inspector-general.

Lieutenants George Baylor and Thomas M. Jack, aides-de-camp.

Volunteer Aides-de-Camp Colonel William Preston, Major D. M. Hayden, E. W. Munford, and Calhoun Benham.

Major Albert J. Smith and Captain Wickham, Quartermaster's Department.

To these gentlemen was assigned the last sad duty of accompanying the remains of their lamented chief from the field, except Captains Brewster and Wickliffe, who remained, and rendered valuable services as staff officers on the 7th of April.

Governor Isham G. Harris, of Tennessee, went upon the field with General Johnston, was by his side when he was shot, aided him from his horse, and received him in his arms when he died. Subsequently the Governor joined my staff, and remained with me throughout the next day, except when carrying orders or engaged in encouraging the troops of his own State, to whom he gave a conspicuous example of coolness, zeal, and intrepidity.

I am also under many obligations to my own general, personal, and volunteer staff, many of whom have been so long associated with me. I append a list of those present on the field on both days, and whose duties carried them constantly under fire, namely: Colonel Thomas Jordan, Captain Clifton H. Smith, and Lieutenant John M. Otey, Adjutant-General's Department.

Major George W. Brent, acting inspector-general; Colonel R. B. Lee, chief of subsistence, whose horse was wounded; Lieutenant-Colonel S. W. Ferguson, and Lieutenant A. R. Chisholm, aides-de-camp.

Volunteer Aides-de-Camp Colonel Jacob Thompson, Major Numa Augustin, Major H. E. Peyton, Captain Albert Ferry, Captain B. B. Waddell.

Captain W. W. Porter, of Major-General Crittenden's staff, also reported for duty, and shared the duties of my volunteer staff on Monday.

Brigadier-General Trudeau, of Louisiana Volunteers, also, for a part of the first day's conflict, was with me as a volunteer aide.

Captain E. H. Cummins, signal-officer, also, was actively employed as a staff officer on both days.

Nor must I fail to mention that Private W. E. Goolsby, Eleventh Regiment Virginia Volunteers, orderly to my headquarters since last June, repeatedly employed to carry my verbal orders to the field, discharged the duty with great zeal and intelligence.

Other members of my staff were necessarily absent from the immediate field of battle, intrusted with responsible duties at these headquarters, namely: Captain F. H. Jordan, assistant adjutant-general, in charge of general headquarters; Major Eugene E. McLean, chief quartermaster; Captain E. Deslonde, Quartermaster's Department.

Lieutenant-Colonel Ferguson, aide-de-camp, early on Monday, was assigned to command and direct the movements of a brigade of the Second Corps.

Lieutenant-Colonel Gilmer, chief-engineer, after having performed the important and various duties of his place with distinction to himself and material benefit to his country, was wounded late on Monday. I trust, however, I shall not long be deprived of his essential services.

Captain Lockett, Engineer Corps, chief assistant to Colonel Gilmer, after having been employed in the duties of his corps on Sunday, was placed by me on Monday in command of a battalion without field-officers. Captain Fremeaux, provisional engineers, and Lieutenants Steel and Helm, also rendered material and ever-dangerous service in the line of their duty.

Major-General (now General) Braxton Bragg, in addition to his duties of chief of staff, as has been before stated, commanded his corps—much the largest in the field—on both days with signal capacity and soldiership.

Surgeon Foard, medical director; Surgeons R. L. Brodie and S. Chopin, medical inspectors; and Surgeon D. W. Yandell, medical director of the Western Department, with General Johnston, were present in the discharge of their arduous and high duties, which they performed with honor to their profession.

Captain Tom Saunders, Messrs. Scales and Metcalf, and Mr. Tully, of New Orleans, were of material aid on both days; ready to give news of the enemy's positions and movements, regardless of exposure.

While thus partially making mention of some of those who rendered brilliant, gallant, or meritorious service in the field, I have aimed merely to notice those whose positions would most probably exclude the record of their services from the reports of corps or subordinate commanders.

From this agreeable duty I turn in the highest degree unpleasant—one due, however, to the brave men under me—as a contrast to the behavior of most of the army who fought so heroically. I allude to the fact that some officers, non-commissioned officers, and men, abandoned their colors early on the first day to pillage the captured encampments; others retired shamefully from the field on both days, while the thunder of cannon, and the roar and rattle of musketry, told them that their brothers were being slaughtered by the fresh legions of the enemy. I have ordered the names of the most conspicuous on this roll of laggards and cowards to be published on orders.

It remains to state that our loss in the two days in killed outright was 1,728; wounded, 8,012; missing, 959—making an aggregate of casualties of 10,699.

This sad list tells in simple language of the stout fight made by our countrymen in front of the rude log chapel of Shiloh, especially when it is known that on Monday, from exhaustion and other causes, not 20,000 men on our side could be brought into action.

Of the loss of the enemy I have no exact knowledge. Their newspapers report it as very heavy. Unquestionably it was greater, even in proportion, than our own on both days, for it was apparent to all that their dead left on the field outnumbered ours two to one.

Their casualties, therefore, cannot have fallen many short of 20,000 in killed, wounded, prisoners, and missing.

Through information derived from many sources, including the newspapers of the enemy, we engaged on Sunday the divisions of Generals Prentiss, Sherman, Hurlbut, McClernand, and Smith, of 9,000 men each, or at least 45,000 men. This force was reënforced on Sunday night by the divisions of Generals Nelson, McCook, Crittenden, and Thomas, of Major-General Buell's army, some 25,000 strong, including all arms. Also General L. Wallace's division of General Grant's army, making at least 33,000 fresh troops, which, added to the remnant of General Grant's forces, on Monday morning amounting to over 20,000, made an aggregate force of some 53,000 men, at least, arrayed against us on that day.

In connection with the results of the battle I should state that the most of our men who had inferior arms exchanged them for the improved arms of the enemy. Also, that most of the property, public and personal, in the camp from which the enemy was driven on Sunday, was rendered useless or greatly damaged, except some of the tents.

With this are transmitted certain papers, to wit:

Order of movements, marked " A."

A list of the killed and wounded, marked " B."

A list of captured flags, marked " C ; " and a map of the field of battle, marked " D."

All of which is respectfully submitted through my volunteer aide-de-camp, Colonel Jacob Thompson, of Mississippi, who has in charge the flags, standards, and colors, captured from the enemy.

I have the honor to be, general, your obedient servant,

G. T. BEAUREGARD, *General commanding.*

To General S. COOPER, Adjutant and Inspector-General Confederate States Army, Richmond, Va.

APPENDIX I.

KILLED, WOUNDED, AND MISSING.

BATTLE OF SHILOH.

COMMAND.	Commander.	Corps.	Killed.	Wounded.	Missing.	Remarks.
1st Brigade...........	Colonel Trabue..........	Reserve	151	557	92	
2d "	Brig.-General Bowen....	"	98	498	28	
3d "	Colonel Statham........	"	137	627	45	
Total.............	Brig.-Gen. Breckinridge.	Reserve	386	1,682	165	
1st Brigade...........	Brig.-General Hindman..	Third Corps...	109	546	38	
2d "	" Cleburne..	" ...	188	790	65	
3d "	" Wood.....	" ...	107	600	38	
Total	Major-General Hardee...	Third Corps ..	404	1,936	141	
1st Brigade, 1st Div....	Colonel Russell..........	First Corps...	97	512	..	Brig.-Gen. Clark &
2d " " "	Brig.-General Stewart...	" ...	93	421	3	Major-Gen. Cheat-
1st " 2d "	" Johnson...	" ...	120	607	13	ham commanding
2d " " "	Colonel Stephens........	" ...	75	413	3	div'ns in 1st Corps.
Total	Major-General Polk......	First Corps...	385	1,953	19	
1st Brigade, 1st Div....	Colonel Gibson..........	Second Corps.	97	488	97	Brig.-Gens. With-
2d " " "	Brig.-General Anderson..	"	69	313	52	ers and Ruggles
3d " " "	Colonel Pond............	"	89	336	169	commanding divis-
1st " 2d "	Brig.-General Gladden...	"	129	597	103	ions Second Corps.
2d " " "	" Chalmers..	"	83	343	19	
3d " " "	" Jackson ...	"	86	364	194	
Total	Major-General Bragg....	Second Corps.	553	2,441	634	
Grand total....	General Beauregard.....	Army Miss ...	1,728	8,012	959	

RECAPITULATION.

Killed.. 1,728

Wounded 8,012

Missing 959

Total................................. 10,699

Respectfully submitted,

JOHN M. OTEY,

Assistant Adjutant-General.

APPENDIX II. (A.)[1]

FIELD RETURN OF THE CONFEDERATE FORCES THAT MARCHED FROM CORINTH TO THE TENNESSEE RIVER.

APRIL 3, 1862. COMMAND.	PRESENT. For Duty Officers	Enlisted Men	Sick Officers	Enlisted Men	Extra Duty Officers	Enlisted Men	In Arrest Officers	Enlisted Men	Effective Total.	Total.	Aggregate.	ABSENT. Detached Duty Officers	Enlisted Men	With Leave Officers	Enlisted Men	Without Leave Officers	Enlisted Men	Sick Officers	Enlisted Men	Present and absent Total.	Aggregate.
Infantry of First Corps	561	8,440	43	1,843	18	548	5	86	9,024	10,867	10,999	26	152	73	922	30	408	9	60	11,009	12,679
" Second "	1,000	14,590	141	3,569	23	624	3	42	14,568[2]	18,435	14,564	48	432	111	2,288	9	451	3	85	22,071	23,371
" Third "	839	4,108	41	811	8	439	5	4	4,545[2]	5,365	5,750	13	159	22	281	1	255	45	942	6,988	7,462
" Reserve "	479	6,182	64	1,000	11	151	2	7	6,290	7,290	7,846	10	137	60	653	5	163	71	887	9,120	9,822
Total Infantry	2,879	33,270	294	6,723	60	1,762	15	89	34,727	41,457	44,159	97	880	276	4,144	45	1,297	128	1,974	50,088	53,334
Light Artillery of First Corps	20	331	1	94	..	10	..	5	898	492	452	..	8	2	87	1	5	..	..	480	501
" Second "	28	661	1	109	..	..	..	..	661	770	779	..	..	4	99	..	..	..	..	869	902
" Third "	16	284	1	28	2	23	..	3	310	338	457	1	1	..	1	..	5	1	37	880	405
" Reserve "	19	581	2	89	1	18	..	5	604	643	665	1	7	..	10	..	11	3	81	752	778
Total Light Artillery	83	1,857	4	210	8	51	..	18	1,973	2,158	2,353	2	11	6	147	1	21	4	118	2,481	2,586
Cavalry	125	1,884	13	712	8	187	1	2	2,078	2,735	2,932	14	359	1	57	..	16	19	466	3,653	3,854
Grand total	2,587	37,011	311	7,645	71	2,000	16	104	38,773	46,425	49,444	113	1,250	283	4,348	46	1,334	151	2,558	57,252	59,774

[1] Official returns in Appendix II. were furnished Colonel William Preston Johnston, aide-de-camp to President Davis, while inspecting the army, June 30, 1862.

[2] Part of Hardee's corps is evidently included in Bragg's by mistake.

Respectfully submitted,

JOHN M. OTEY,

Assistant Adjutant-General.

Respectfully submitted and forwarded,

BRAXTON BRAGG,

General commanding.

APPENDIX II. (B.)

FIELD RETURN OF THE ARMY OF THE MISSISSIPPI AFTER THE BATTLE OF SHILOH.

APRIL 10, 1862. COMMAND.	PRESENT											ABSENT								Present and absent	
	For Duty		Sick		Extra Duty		In Arrest		Effective Total.	Total.	Aggregate.	Detached Duty.		With Leave.		Without Leave.		Sick.		Total.	Aggregate.
	Officers.	Enlisted Men.	Officers.	Enlisted Men.	Officers.	Enlisted Men.	Officers.	Enlisted Men.				Officers.	Enlisted Men.	Officers.	Enlisted Men.	Officers.	Enlisted Men.	Officers.	Enlisted Men.		
Infantry of First Corps	461	7,198	93	1,828	2	878	4	10	7,582	9,414	9,974	34	274	122	1,224	18	544	86	1,426	12,855	13,671
" " Second "	590	8,453	277	4,748	23	628	5	35	9,118	13,866	14,761	46	455	80	1,440	9	370	67	1,065	17,196	18,298
" " Third "	425	4,805	144	2,301	9	559	2	1	4,865	7,166	7,746	27	227	56	959	5	820	47	1,363	10,475	11,190
" " Reserve	379	4,334	94	1,475	10	491	2	7	5,232	6,707	7,192	26	238	90	1,455	5	702	110	1,887	10,989	11,705
Total Infantry	1,855	24,692	608	9,752	54	2,056	13	53	26,697	37,153	39,673	129	1,194	348	5,078	37	2,436	310	5,651	51,515	54,859
Light Artillery of First Corps	18	386	1	99	:	:	:	:	390	489	504	6	2	2	39	:	20	5	58	608	636
" " Second "	19	487	4	210	1	15	:	1	504	714	738	1	5	:	13	:	3	2	70	805	882
" " Third "	8	272	8	60	:	12	1	:	284	344	356	:	1	1	7	:	:	5	47	399	417
" " Reserve	25	489	1	44	:	15	:	:	504	548	574	1	10	1	24	:	46	8	65	708	784
Total Light Artillery	70	1,634	9	413	1	43	1	1	1,682	2,095	2,172	8	18	4	83	:	69	15	240	2,515	2,619
Cavalry	259	8,554	42	1,507	5	248	2	1	8,383	5,840	5,648	33	527	48	691	3	155	17	228	6,981	7,022
Grand total	2,184	29,910	659	11,672	60	2,247	15	55	32,212	44,088	47,493	170	1,739	400	5,852	40	2,660	342	6,149	60,961	64,500

Respectfully submitted,

JOHN M. OTEY,

Assistant Adjutant-General.

Respectfully submitted and forwarded,

BRAXTON BRAGG,

General commanding.

APPENDIX III.[1]

FIELD RETURN OF THE ARMY OF THE MISSISSIPPI BEFORE AND AFTER THE BATTLE OF SHILOH.

COMMAND.	Commanders.	Effective Total before Battle.	Effective Total after Battle.	REMARKS.
1st Army Corps.	Major-General L. Polk	9,136	6,779	Casualties in battle of Shiloh : killed, 1,728; wounded, 8,012 ; missing, 959.
2d " "	General Braxton Bragg.............	13,589	9,961	
3d " "	Major-General W. J. Hardee........	6,789	4,609	
Reserve	Brigadier-General J. C. Breckinridge.	6,439	4,206	
Total Infantry and Artillery	....	35,953	25,555	
Cavalry.........	Brigadier-General F. Gardner.......	4,382	4,081	The battle-field was so thickly wooded that the cavalry was useless, and could not operate at all.
		40,335	29,636	
Difference	....	....	10,699	

Respectfully submitted,

THOMAS JORDAN,

Assistant Adjutant General.

Respectfully submitted and forwarded,

G. T. BEAUREGARD,

General commanding Army of the Mississippi.

HEADQUARTERS ARMY OF THE MISSISSIPPI,
CORINTH. MISSISSIPPI, *April* 21, 1862.

[1] Forwarded with official report.

APPENDIX IV.

ORGANIZATION AND CASUALTIES OF THE ARMY OF THE MISSISSIPPI, APRIL 6 AND 7, 1862, COMPILED FROM THE BATTLE REPORTS BY THE AUTHOR.

K., killed; m. w., mortally wounded; w., wounded.

General ALBERT SIDNEY JOHNSTON, *Commander-in-Chief.*

General G. T. BEAUREGARD, *Second in Command.*

First Corps.—Major-General LEONIDAS POLK.

First Division.—Brigadier-General CHARLES CLARK (w.).

First Brigade.—Colonel R. M. RUSSELL.

REGIMENTS.	Commanders.	Effective.	Killed.	Wounded.	Missing.	Total.
Twelfth Tennessee	Lieutenant-Colonel T. H. Bell	...	...	...	...	...
Thirteenth "	Colonel A. J. Vaughan	...	23	184	...	...
Twenty-second Tenn	(1) Colonel T. J. Freeman (w.) (2) Lieutenant-Colonel Stewart (w.)	...	...	...	...	...
Eleventh Louisiana	(1) Colonel S. F. Marks (w.) (2) Lieutenant-Colonel R. H. Barrow	550	...	...	...	...
Battery	Captain S. P. Bankhead	93	2	18	...	...

Second Brigade.—Brigadier-General ALEXANDER P. STEWART.

REGIMENTS.	Commanders.	Effectives.	Killed.	Wounded.	Missing.	Total.
Fourth Tennessee	(1) Colonel Neely (2) Lieutenant-Colonel O. F. Strahl	...	36	183	...	...
Fifth "	Lieutenant-Colonel C. D. Venable	...	...	...	...	...
Thirty-third Tennessee	Colonel A. W. Campbell	...	20	103	17	...
Thirteenth Arkansas	(1) Lieutenant-Colonel A. D. Grayson (k.) (2) Major J. A. McNeely (w.) (3) Colonel J. C. Tappan	...	25	72	8	...
Battery	Captain T. J. Stanford	131	4	14	2	...

Second Division.—Major-General B. F. CHEATHAM.

First Brigade. — { (1) Brigadier-General B. R. JOHNSON (w.).
{ (2) Colonel PRESTON SMITH (w.).

REGIMENTS.	Commanders.	Effectives.	Killed.	Wounded.	Missing.	Total.
One Hundred and Fifty-fourth Sr. Tennessee	(1) Colonel Preston Smith (w.) (2) Lieutenant-Colonel Marcus J. Wright	650	25	163	11	199
Second "	Colonel J. Knox Walker	...	...	...	...	...
Fifteenth "	(1) Lieutenant-Colonel R. C. Tyler (w.) (2) Major Hearn	...	...	...	...	...
Blythe's Mississippi	(1) Colonel A. K. Blythe (k.) (2) Lieutenant-Colonel D. Herron (k.) (3) Major Moore	...	...	...	...	...
Battery	Captain M. T. Polk (w.)	102	4	18	2	24

Second Brigade.—{ (1) Colonel WILLIAM H. STEPHENS.
{ (2) Colonel GEORGE MANEY.

REGIMENTS.	Commanders.	Effec-tives.	Killed.	Wound-ed.	Miss-ing.	Total.
First Tennessee	Colonel George Maney	...	...	...	...	...
Sixth "	Lieutenant-Colonel T. P. Jones	..	...	...	...	...
Ninth "	Colonel H. L. Douglass	...	...	...	...	...
Seventh Kentucky	" Charles Wickliffe (m. w.)	...	...	...	...	...
Battery	Captain M. Smith	120	1	13	...	...
Cheatham's report for division		3,801	...	...	...	1,213

Second Corps.—Major-General BRAXTON BRAGG.

First Division.—Brigadier-General DANIEL RUGGLES.

First Brigade.—Colonel RANDAL L. GIBSON.

REGIMENTS.	Commanders	Effec-tives.	Killed.	Wound-ed.	Miss-ing.	Total.
Fourth Louisiana	Colonel H. W. Allen (w.)	575	24	163	22	209
Thirteenth "	{ (1) Major A. P. Avegno (m. w.) { (2) Captain E. M. Dubroca	....	....	....	....	....
Nineteenth "	Colonel B. L. Hodge	..	....	....	....	....
First Arkansas	" James F. Fagan	....	....	....	....	....
Battery	Captain Bain	....	....	....	....	....

Second Brigade.—Brigadier-General PATTON ANDERSON.

REGIMENTS.	Commanders.	Effec-tives.	Killed.	Wound-ed.	Miss-ing.	Total.
Seventeenth Louisiana	Lieutenant-Colonel Charles Jones (w.)	326	....	....	....	....
Twentieth "	Colonel August Reichard	507	....	....	....	....
Ninth Texas	" W. A. Stanley	226	14	42	11	67
First Florida	{ (1) Major T. A. McDonell (w.) { (2) Captain W. G. Poole { (3) " W. C. Bird	250	....	....	....	....
Two Cos. Confederate Guards Response	Major F. H. Clack	169	10	35	1	46
Battery	Captain W. I. Hodgson	155	....	....	....	....
Anderson's report		1,634	....	....	....	434

Third Brigade.—Colonel PRESTON POND.

REGIMENTS.	Commanders.	Effec-tives.	Killed.	Wound-ed.	Miss-ing.	Total.
Sixteenth Louisiana	Major D. Gober	330	19	46	27	92
Eighteenth "	Colonel A. Mouton (w.)	....	13	80	118[1]	211
Thirty-eighth Tennessee.	" R. F. Looney	....	7	43	15	65
Crescent (Louisiana)	" M. J. Smith	....	23	84	20	127
Orleans Guards		....	17	55	18	90
Battery	Captain William H. Ketchum	....	1	12	1	14
Total		....	80	320	199	599

[1] Mostly killed and wounded.

Second Division.—Brigadier JONES M. WITHERS.

First Brigade.— { (1) Brigadier-General A. H. GLADDEN (k.).
(2) Colonel D. W. ADAMS (w.).
(3) Colonel Z. C. DEAS (w.).
(4) Colonel J. Q. LOOMIS.

REGIMENTS.	Commanders.	Effectives.	Killed.	Wounded.	Missing.	Total.
First Louisiana.........	(1) Colonel D. W. Adams (w.)......... (2) Major F. H. Farrar..............	....	....	...	....	....
Twenty-first Alabama...	Lieutenant-Colonel S. W. Cayce........	....	....	....	....	198
Twenty-second " ...	(1) Colonel Z. C. Deas (w.)........... (2) Lieutenant-Colonel J. Q. Marrast..	435	....	....	....	....
Twenty-fifth " ...	(1) Colonel Q. Loomis................ (2) Major J. D. Johnston.............	305	....	...	....	....
Twenty-sixth " ...	(1) Colonel Coltart (w.)............... (2) Lieutenant-Colonel W. D. Chadick.	440	....	....	....	....
Battery.................	Captain Robertson....................	....	....	....	....	....
Withers's report............		....	129	597	103	829

Second Brigade.—Brigadier-General JAMES R. CHALMERS.

REGIMENTS.	Commanders.	Effectives.	Killed.	Wounded.	Missing.	Total.
Fifth Mississippi........	Colonel A. E. Fant.....................	....	....	....	....	....
Seventh "	" H. Mayson.....................	....	....	....	....	....
Ninth "	" W. A. Rankin (k.)...............	....	....	....	....	....
Tenth "	" R. A. Smith....................	....	....	....	....	....
Fifty-second Tennessee..	" B. J. Lea......................	....	....	....	....	....
Battery.................	Captain Gage..........................	....	....	....	....	....
Chalmers's report............		2,039	82	343	....	425

Third Brigade.—Brigadier-General JOHN K. JACKSON.

REGIMENTS.	Commanders.	Effectives.	Killed.	Wounded.	Missing.	Total.
Seventeenth Alabama....	Colonel R. C. Favis.....................	....	....	....	....	....
Eighteenth "	" E. S. Shorter.................	....	....	....	....	....
Nineteenth "	" Joseph Wheeler................	....	....	....	....	....
Second Texas...........	" John C. Moore.................	....	....	....	....	....
Battery.................	Captain J. P. Girardy..................	....	....	....	....	....
Jackson's report............		2,208	....	....	....	....

Second Division—(Summary).

BRIGADES.	Commanders.	Effectives.	Killed.	Wounded.	Missing.	Total.
I.....................	Gladden	....	129	597	103	829
II.....................	Chalmers...................	2,039	82	343	29	454
III.....................	Jackson...................	2,208	91	364	194	649
Withers's report............		6,482	293	1,334	253	1,918
Bragg's "		6,482	....	....	....	1,880
Beauregard's report............		....	302	1,364	326	1,932

Third Corps.—Major-General WILLIAM J. HARDEE.

First Division.—Brigadier-General THOMAS C. HINDMAN.

First Brigade.—Colonel R. G. SHAVER.

REGIMENTS.	Commanders.	Effectives.	Killed.	Wounded.	Missing.	Total.
Third Confederate.......	Colonel J. S. Marmaduke.......	....	....	....	....	....
Second Arkansas........	(1) Colonel Govan.................... (2) Lieutenant-Colonel Patterson (w.).. (3) Major R. T. Harvey...............	....	....	....	....	....
Sixth "	Colonel A. T. Hawthorne.	....	....	....	....	....
Seventh "	(1) Lieut.-Colonel John M. Dean (k.).. (2) Major James T. Martin..........	....	....	....	....	....
Battery.................	Captain Swett....................	....	....	....	....	....

Third Brigade.—Brigadier-General S. A. M. WOOD.

REGIMENTS.	Commanders.	Effectives.	Killed.	Wounded.	Missing.	Total.
Sixteenth Alabama......	Lieutenant-Colonel J. W. Harris.........	325	....	....	....	....
Eighth Arkansas........	Colonel W. K. Patterson................	305	....	....	....	....
Ninth Arkansas Battalion	Major John H. Kelley..................	155	8	49	2	59
Twenty-seventh Tenn...	(1) Colonel Williams (k.)............ (2) Lieutenant-Colonel Brown (w.).... (3) Major Love (k.)....................	380	27	115	48	190
Forty-fourth " ...	Colonel C. A. McDaniel (w.)............	270	....	....	....	....
Fifty-fifth " ...	" McKoin.............	305	....	....	....	....
Third Mississippi Battal'n	Major A. M. Hardcastle................	300	....	....	....	....
Battery.................	Captain Harper (four guns)...........	....	....	....	....	....
Infantry....................................		2,040	....	....	....	....

Second Brigade (unattached).—Brigadier-General P. R. CLEBURNE.

REGIMENTS.	Commanders.	Effectives.	Killed.	Wounded.	Missing.	Total.
Second Tennessee.......	(1) Colonel William Bate (w.)........ (2) Lieutenant-Colonel D. L. Goodall...	365	....	....	....	....
Fifth "	Colonel Ben J. Hill......	369	....	....	....	....
Twenty-third Tennessee.	(1) Colonel J. F. Neil (w)............ (2) Lieutenant-Colonel R. Cantrell.....	578	....	....	....	....
Twenty-fourth "	" " Peebles...........	....	....	....	....	....
Sixth Mississippi........	(1) Colonel J. J. Thornton (w.)........ (2) Major Lowry (w.)................	....	....	....	....	....
Fifteenth Arkansas......	(1) Lieutenant-Colonel Patton (k.)..... (2) Major J. T. Harris (k.)............	....	....	....	....	....
Battery.................	Captain Trigg.......................	....	....	....	....	....
"	" Calvert......................	....	....	....	....	....
Brigade.................	Cleburne's report....................	2,750	1,000		32	1,032
Corps..................	Hardee's report......................	6,789	404	1,936	141	2,481
Corps..................	Beauregard's report	6,789	404	1,936	141	2,481

Reserve Corps.—Brigadier-General JOHN C. BRECKINRIDGE.

First Brigade.—Colonel ROBERT P. TRABUE.

REGIMENTS.	Commanders.	Effectives.	Killed.	Casualties.	Missing.	Total.
Third Kentucky	Lieutenant-Colonel Ben Anderson.......	....	....	174	....	....
Fourth "	{ (1) Lieutenant-Colonel Hynes (w.).......	431	....	213	....	....
	{ (2) Major Thomas B. Monroe (k.).......					
Sixth "	Colonel Joseph H. Lewis	....	....	108	....	....
Ninth "	" Thomas H. Hunt................	....	....	134	....	....
Thirty-first Alabama....	Lieutenant-Colonel Galbraith............	....	....	79	....	....
Fourth Alabama Battal'n	J. M. Clifton...........................	....	....	80	....	....
Crews's " "	Lieutenant-Colonel Crews...............	....	....	55	....	....
Battery................	Captain Cobb	....	....	37	....	....
Battery................	" E. P. Byrne....................	....	....	14	....	....
	Trabue's report................	2,400	....	844	....	....

Second Brigade.— { (1) Brigadier-General JOHN S. BOWEN (w.).
 { (2) Colonel JOHN D. MARTIN.

REGIMENTS.	Commanders.	Effectives.	Killed.	Wounded.	Missing.	Total.
First Missouri..........	Colonel Rich (k.).......................	....	....	....	....	....
Second Confederate	{ (1) Colonel John D. Martin.............	....	....	....	....	....
	{ (2) Major Mangum.....................					
Ninth Arkansas........	Colonel Dunlap.........................	....	....	....	....	....
Tenth "	" Merrick......................	....	....	....	....	....
Hudson's Battery.......	....	....	....	....	....	....

Third Brigade.—Colonel STATHAM.

REGIMENTS.	Commanders.	Effectives.	Killed.	Wounded.	Missing.	Total.
Nineteenth Tennessee...	Colonel Cummings..........................	....	....	....	....	....
Twentieth "	....	....	....	....	....	....
Twenty-eighth "	....	....	....	....	....	....
Forty-fifth "	....	....	....	....	....	....
Fifteenth Mississippi....	....	....	....	....	....	....
Twenty-second "	....	....	....	....	....	....
Rutledge's Battery......	....	....	....	....	....	....

Cavalry.

COMMANDS.	Commanders.	Attached to Corps.	Effectives.	Kill'd.	Wounded.	Missing.	Total.
Regiment................	Colonel N. B. Forrest (w.)	None.	...	...	....	...	...
" Mississippi.....	" A. J. Lindsay..............	Polk.	...	...	....	...	...
" Alabama......	" Clanton.................	Bragg.	...	...	....	...	...
" Texas	" John A. Wharton (w.)......	None.	...	7	56	4	67
Squadron................	Lieutenant-Colonel R. H. Brewer....	Polk.	200	2	10	1	13
" Ky. (3 comp's).	Major John H. Morgan.............	Breck.	...	...	....	...	...
Kentucky Company.....	Captain Phil Thompson.............	Breck.	...	...	....	...	...
Four companies........	Captains Jenkins, Tomlinson, Cox, } and Robins.....................	Bragg.	236	2	6	1	9

Notes.

Any official or other trustworthy information that will help to complete these tables will be gratefully received.

[1] Two regiments were known as the Second Tennessee—Bate's and J. Knox Walker's.

[2] An Alabama battalion and an Arkansas battalion had been assigned to Jackson's brigade, but were not in the battle.

[3] The Seventh Alabama Regiment was assigned to Wood's brigade, but does not appear in the battle; probably detached.

[4] The Forty-seventh Tennessee, Colonel Hill, arrived on the field on the 7th.

[5] Some of the batteries appear under different names.

APPENDIX V.

ORGANIZATION, STRENGTH, AND CASUALTIES, OF GRANT'S ARMY AT THE BATTLE OF SHILOH—*General U. S. GRANT commanding.*

Compiled from Records of the War Department.

FIRST DIVISION.

COMMANDS.	Commanders.	Present for Duty.	Total present.	Took into Action.	Killed.	Wounded.	Missing.	Aggregate.	REMARKS.
FIRST DIVISION	General John A. McClernand	6,871	7,953	7,098¹	....	....	..	1,861	
First Brigade	{(1) Colonel A. M. Hare, Eleventh Iowa.. (2) " M. M. Crocker, Thirteenth Iowa}	....	....	....	..	....	..	....	
Eighth Illinois	{(1) Captain J. M. Ashmore.......... (2) " R. H. Sturgess....}	521	582	476	23	91	8	....	
Eighteenth Illinois	{(1) Major Samuel Eaton..... (2) Captain A. J. Anderson.}	448	521	....	..	....	..	....	
Eleventh Iowa	Lieutenant-Colonel William Hall..	596	630	....	..	....	..	....	
Thirteenth Iowa	{(1) Colonel M. M. Crocker.... (2) Lieutenant-Colonel M. M. Price....}	736	801	717	24	189	9	....	
Total...........		2,301	2,534	2,552²	88	440	18	571	
Second Brigade	Colonel C. C. Marsh, Twentieth Illinois....	....	....	1,514	..	....	..	....	
Eleventh Illinois	{(1) Colonel T. E. G. Ransom... (2) Major S. Nevins....}	822	401	....	24	74	..	....	
Twentieth "	Lieutenant-Colonel E. Richards..	501	614	....	..	....	..	....	
Forty-fifth "	Colonel John E. Smith....	562	664	....	26	199	..	....	
Forty-eighth Illinois	" I. N. Haynie....	678	772	....	..	....	..	....	
Total...........		2,063	2,451	1,846²	..	....	..	....	
Third Brigade	{(1) Colonel Julius Raith, Forty-third Ill. (2) Lieutenant-Colonel A. Engelmann...}	....	....	1,650³	..	....	..	824	
Seventeenth Illinois	Lieutenant-Colonel E. P. Wood....	565	682	....	..	....	..	....	
Twenty-ninth "	" C. M. Ferrell....	364	476	500³	..	....	..	206	
Forty-third "	" A. Engelmann..	607	676	....	..	....	..	....	
Forty-ninth "	" P. Pease....	507	620	....	..	....	..	....	
Total...........		2,043	2,454	2,166²	..	....	..	....	
Cavalry Battalion	Captain Stewart....	....	....	112²	..	....	..	....	
Artillery		....	....	352²	..	....	..	....	

¹ Including 352 artillery and 112 cavalry (report).   ² McClernand's reported effective force April 5th.   ³ About.

SECOND DIVISION.

COMMANDS.	Commanders.	Present for Duty.	Total present.	Took into Action.	Killed.	Wounded.	Missing.	Aggregate.	REMARKS.
SECOND DIVISION	(1) General W. H. L. Wallace (k.)...... (2) " John McArthur (w.)...... (3) Colonel J. M. Tuttle, Second Iowa...	8,276	10,122	....	228	1,088	1,163	2,421[1]	[1] Including four batteries (McArthur's report). This does not include the Fifty-second and Fifty-eighth Illinois, which are taken from regimental records, making aggregate casualties 2,646.
First Brigade......	Colonel J. M. Tuttle, Second Iowa......								
Second Iowa......	Lieutenant-Colonel James Baker......	490	615						
Seventh "	" J. C. Parrott......	383	587						
Twelfth "	Colonel J. J. Woods......	459	639						Captured.
Fourteenth Iowa......	" W. T. Shaw......	442	511						Captured.
Total......		1,804	2,852		88	171	665		
Second Brigade......	(1) General John McA-thur... (2) Colonel Aug. Mersy, Ninth Illinois...								
Thirteenth Missouri......	Colonel Crafts J. Wright...	588	679	450	12	73	4		
Ninth Illinois......	" A. Mersy...	617	747	630	61	257	5		With Sherman.
Twelfth "	(1) Lieutenant-Colonel A. L. Chetlain...	467	619		21	86	7		
Fourteenth Missouri......	(2) Captain J. R. Hugunin...	458	611						Birge's Western Sharp-shooters.
Eighty-first Ohio......	" Thomas Morton...	463	500		2	6			
Total......		2,548	3,156		100	458	16		
Third Brigade......	(1) Colonel T. W. Sweeny... (2) " S. D. Baldwin...								
Eighth Iowa......	Colonel Jas. L. Geddes...	689	772						Captured.
Seventh Illinois......	" A. J. Babcock...	546	627						
Fiftieth "	" Moses M. Bane...	580	647						
Fifty-second Illinois...	Lieutenant-Colonel John S. Wilcox...	641	744		23	123	9	155	
Fifty-seventh "	Colonel S. D. Baldwin...	618	754		26		8		
Fifty-eighth "	" W. F. Lynch...	552	654	613	20	47		67	Regiment captured.
Total......		3,571	4,198		86	349	482		
Companies D, H, and I, First Missouri Art'y, Co. A, Firs. Illinois Artillery (Willard's)...	Major Cavender......	234	294	}	4	55	....	59	
	Lieutenant P. P. Wood...	119	122						
Total......		353	416						

THIRD DIVISION.

COMMANDS.	Commanders.	Present for Duty.	Total present.	Took Into Action.	Killed.	Wounded.	Missing.	Aggregate.	REMARKS.
THIRD DIVISION........	General Lewis Wallace.........	7,771	8,820	.....	84	485	10	579	
First Brigade.........	Colonel Morgan L. Smith, Eighth Missouri.	.....	.....	.....	.....	.....	..	.....	From regimental returns.
Eleventh Indiana..	Colonel George F. McGinnis.....	631	753	.....	11	51	..	.....	" "
Eighth Missouri....	Lieutenant-Colonel James Peckham.....	678	759	.....	2	6	..	.....	" "
Twenty-fourth Indiana..	Colonel Alvin P. Hovey.....	694	735	.....	6	45	..	.....	From General Wallace's report.
Total........		2,201	2,280	.....	21	128	..	144	
Second Brigade........	Colonel John M. Thayer, First Nebraska...	.....	.....	.....	.....	.....	..	.....	From regimental records.
First Nebraska....	Lieutenant-Colonel W. D. McCord.....	549	695	.....	2	14	1	.....	" "
Twenty-third Indiana..	Colonel W. E. Sanderson.....	688	718	.....	7	35	1	.....	On guard-duty.
Fifty-eighth Ohio....	" V. Bausenwein.....	630	736	.....	9	38	..	.....	From General Wallace's report.
Sixty-eighth Ohio....	" S. H. Steedman.....	424	646	.....	.....	.....	..	.....	
Total........		2,286	2,790	.....	20	105	5	180	
Third Brigade........	Colonel Charles Whittlesey, Twentieth Ohio.	.....	.....	.....	.....	.....	..	.....	
Twentieth Ohio....	Lieutenant-Colonel M. F. Force.....	491	600	.....	1	18	..	.....	On guard-duty.
Seventy-sixth Ohio....	Colonel Charles R. Woods.....	714	834	.....	..	4	1	.....	From General Wallace's report.
Seventy-eighth Ohio....	" M. D. Leggett.....	687	688	.....	1	8	..	.....	
Fifty-sixth Ohio....	" T. Kinney.....	701	762	.....	..	..	..	.....	
Total........		2,543	2,884	.....	43	257	5	805	
Not brigaded.		.....	.....	.....	.....	.....	..	.....	Casualties not reported.
Battery I, 1st Mo. Artil.	Lieutenant C. H. Thurber.....	118	122	.....	.....	.....	..	.....	" "
Ninth Indiana Battery..	Captain N. S. Thompson.....	114	122	.....	.....	.....	..	.....	" "
Third Bat. 5th Ohio Cav.	Major C. S. Hayes.....	283	328	.....	.....	.....	..	.....	" "
Third " 11th Ill.	" James F. Johnson.....	276	294	.....	.....	.....	..	.....	" "
Total........		791	866	.....	..	.....	..	.....	

FOURTH DIVISION.

COMMANDS.	Commanders.	Present for Duty.	Total present.	Took into Action.	Killed.	Wounded.	Missing.	Aggregate.	REMARKS.
FOURTH DIVISION	General S. A. Hurlbut	7,363	8,965	....	313	1,449	223	1,985	General Hurlbut's report of battle.
First Brigade	{(1) Colonel N. G. Williams / (2) " J. C. Pugh.								
Third Iowa	Colonel N. G. Williams	560	775	....	22	185	36	198	
Forty-first Illinois	{(1) Colonel J. C. Pugh / (2) Lieutenant-Colonel A. Tupper (k.)	553	634	....	25	88	10	123	
Twenty-eighth Illinois	Colonel A. K. Johnson	642	732	558[1]	26	151	9	186	[1] Regimental report of battle.
Thirty-second "	" John Logan	652	777	....	88	151	88	222	
Total		2,407	2,918	....	111	525	88	724	
Second Brigade	Colonel J. C. Veatch								
Twenty-fifth Indiana	Lieutenant-Colonel W. H. Morgan	651	750						
Fourteenth Illinois	Colonel Cyrus Hall	722	802						
Fifteenth "	Lieutenant-Colonel E. F. W. Ellis	689	781						
Forty-sixth "	Lieutenant-Colonel J. A. Davis	711	887						
Total		2,723	3,120						
Third Brigade	Brigadier-General J. G. Lauman								
Thirty-first Indiana	Colonel Charles Cruft	594	729						
Forty-fourth "	" H. B. Read	528	658	473[2]	34	177	1	212	[2] Colonel Read's report. [3] Colonel McHenry's report.
Seventeenth Kentucky	" J. H. McHenry	374	572	259[3]				88[3]	
Twenty-fifth "	Lieutenant-Colonel B. H. Bristow	255	898	....	6	26		32	
Total		1,751	2,867						
Fourteenth Ohio Battery	Captain J. B. Burrows	108	130	....	3	14		17	Casualties reported in McClernand's report.
Mann's Battery	Lieutenant Brotzmann	89	99						
Total		197	229						
Third Battalion Fourth Illinois Cavalry		185	175						
Thielmann's Battalion Cavalry		150	156						
Total		235	331						

FIFTH DIVISION.

COMMANDS.	Commanders.	Present for Duty.	Total present.	Took into Action.	Killed.	Wounded.	Missing.	Aggregate.	REMARKS.
FIFTH DIVISION	General W. T. Sherman	8,617	9,854¹	....	317	1,275	441	2,034	Strength taken from field returns, April 5th; casualties from General Sherman's report. ¹ Exclusive of Barrett's and Waterhouse's batteries.
First Brigade	Colonel J. A. McDowell, Sixth Iowa	....	....	....	....	....	....	....	
Sixth Iowa	{ (1) Captain John Williams (w.), (2) M. M. Walden }	632	738	....	51	120	89	....	
Forty-sixth Ohio	Colonel T. Worthington	701	875	....	84	150	52	....	
Fortieth Illinois	" S. D. Hicks	597	745	....	43	155	2	....	
Total		1,930	2,358	....	128	425	93	646	
Second Brigade	{ (1) Colonel D. Stuart, Fifty-fifth Illinois. (2) T. K. Smith, Fifty-fourth O. }	....	....	....	....	....	....	....	
Fifty-fifth Illinois	Lieutenant-Colonel O. Malmborg	657	787	....	46	191	41	....	
Fifty-fourth Ohio	Colonel T. K. Smith	616	730	....	24	188	32	....	
Seventy-first Ohio	" R. Mason	667	820	....	18	52	46	....	
Total		1,940	2,387	....	88	876	119	578	
Third Brigade	Colonel J. Hildebrand, Seventy-seventh Ohio	....	....	....	....	....	....	....	
Seventy-seventh Ohio	Lieutenant-Colonel W. De Hass	645	788	....	49	114	56	....	
Fifty-seventh " "	" A. V. Rice	542	804	....	9	83	83	....	
Fifty-third "	Colonel J. J. Appler	646	875	....	7	89	5	....	
Total		1,882	2,467	....	65	285	94	894	
Fourth Brigade	Colonel R. P. Buckland, Seventy-second O.	....	....	....	....	....	....	....	
Seventieth Ohio	" J. R. Cockerill	854	907	....	9	54	40	....	
Forty-eighth Ohio	" P. J. Sullivan	606	762	....	14	73	46	....	
Seventy-second Ohio	Lieutenant-Colonel H. Canfield (k.)	647	836	....	15	90	49	....	
Total		2,107	2,505	....	88	217	135	390	
Fifth Ohio Cavalry	Colonel W. H. H. Taylor	692	857	....	1	..	..	....	No report.
Sixth Indiana Battery	Captain F. Behr	115	130	....	1	5	..	....	
B, First Illinois Artillery	" S. E. Barrett	....	....	....	1	17	..	....	
E, " " "	" A. C. Waterhouse	....	....	....	1	..	..	....	
Total		....	....	....	8	22	....	....	

SIXTH DIVISION.

COMMANDS.	Commanders.	Present for Duty.	Total present.	Took into Action.	Killed.	Wounded.	Missing.	Aggregate.	REMARKS.
SIXTH DIVISION.........	General B. M. Prentiss......	8,855	10,211	....	260	923	946	2,184	
First Brigade...........	Colonel Everett Peabody (k.).......	....	....	....	....	....	....	....	
Twenty-fifth Missouri....	Lieutenant-Colonel R. T. Van Horn....	514	724	....	28	54	87	119	
Sixteenth Wisconsin....	Colonel B. Allen...........	827	997	....	46	176	23	245	
Twelfth Michigan......	" F. Quinn............	832	896	....	27	87	104	168	
Twenty-first Missouri...	{(1) Colonel D. Moore (w.). / (2) Lieutenant-Colonel H. M. Woodyard.}	617	889	....	17	46	64	127	
Total..........		2,790	3,506	....	118	318	228	650	
Second Brigade........	Colonel Madison Miller........	....	....	....	....	....	....	....	
Eighteenth Missouri....	Colonel Madison Miller........	552	732	....	14	82	147	243	
Sixty-first Illinois........	" Jacob Fry..........	487	701	....	12	45	18	75	
Sixteenth Iowa..........	" Alexander Chambers...	735	859	....	18	103	15	136	
Total..........		1,774	2,292	....	44	230	180	454	
Eleventh Illinois Cavalry...	Colonel R. G. Ingersoll......	622	685	....	8	8	....	6	
Fifth Ohio Battery......	Captain A. Hickenlooper......	187	147	....	1	19	....	20	
First Minnesota..........	" E. Munch...........	126	142	....	3	8	....	11	
Total..........		268	289	....	4	27	....	31	
Not brigaded...........	Colonel James S. Alban.........								
Eighteenth Wisconsin...	" D. E. Wood........	739[1]	862	....	24	524	174[4]	280	
Fourteenth Wisconsin...	{(1) Colonel J. T. Tindall / (2) Lieutenant-Colonel Q. Morton...}	738	861	720[3]	14[4]	794		98	954 aggregate; March 31, 1862.
Twenty-third Missouri...		652[2]	770[2]		31	88	356	425	Battle report.
Fifteenth Iowa..........	Colonel H. T. Reid........	827	946	....	22	156	8	180	
Total..........		2,956	8,439	....	91	355	533	994	

[1] No returns; estimated at average of non-brigaded regiments.   [2] Approximate estimate.   [3] Battle report.   [4] Report of Adjutant-General of Wisconsin, 1866.

ORGANIZATIONS NOT OTHERWISE ACCOUNTED FOR.

COMMANDS.	Commanders.	Present for Duty.	Total present.	Took into Action.	Killed.	Wounded.	Missing.	Aggregate.	REMARKS.
ARTILLERY.									
Eighth Ohio Battery.....	Captain L. Margraff.....	80	92	....	1	8	...	4	Fought in Sherman's division.
Thirteenth " "	" Meyer.....	100¹	100¹	....	1	8	...	9	Fought in Hurlbut's division. Lost its guns on Sunday; disbanded; no further record.
Second Michigan Battery	" William H. Ross.....	102²	105²	....	...	4	48	52	Fought in Hurlbut's division.
Co. H, First Ill. Artillery	" A. Silversparre	105	109	....	...	...	6	6	Fought near landing.
" I, " "	" E. Bouton.....	100¹	100¹	....	...	...	6	...	With Sherman; no record.
" B, Second "	" R. Madison.....	114	116	....	...	...	...	...	Casualties not reported.
" F, " "	" John W. Powell.....	126	142	....	...	9	8	12	With Prentiss.
Total.....		727	764						
CAVALRY.									
Cos. A and B Second Illinois.....	Captain J. R. Hotaling.....	82	120	....	...	...	...	...	No casualties.
Co. C, Second, and Co. I, Fourth U. S.....	Lieutenant James Powell.....	72	98	....	1	5	...	6	
Fourth Illinois, eight companies.....	Lieutenant-Colonel McCullough.....	400¹	400¹	....	...	...	...	...	With McClernand; no returns.
Total.....		554	618						
INFANTRY.									
Fifteenth Michigan.....	Colonel John M. Oliver.....	750¹	750¹	....	33	64	7	104	Aggregate March 27th, 869; report Adjutant-General of Michigan, 1862.
Grand total.....		2,081	2,127	....	36	98	64	198	

¹ Estimated.　　　² February report.

SUMMARY.

DIVISIONS.	Commanders.	Present for Duty.	Total present.	Took into Action.	Killed.	Wounded.	Missing.	Aggregate.	REMARKS.
I.	General John A. McClernand.	6,871	7,958	7,028	262	1,361	289	1,861	
II.	" W. H. L. Wallace.	8,276	10,122	....	228	1,033	1,163	2,424	
III.	" Lewis Wallace.	7,771	8,820	....	84	485	10	579	
IV.	" S. A. Hurlbut.	7,868	8,965	....	313	1,449	223	1,985	
V.	" W. T. Sherman.	8,617	9,854	....	317	1,275	441	2,034	
VI.	" B. M. Prentiss.	8,385	10,211	....	260	988	946	2,184	
Unorganized.	....	2,031	2,127	....	36	93	64	193	
	Total.	49,814	58,052						
	Deduct Third Division.	7,771	8,820						
	Grand total in Sunday's battle.	41,543	49,232	....	1,500	6,684	3,056	11,220	

ENGAGED IN SUNDAY AND MONDAY'S BATTLES.

Grant's effective... 49,314

Buell's reinforcements... 21,579

Total present for duty.. 70,898

APPENDIX VI.

UNITED STATES TROOPS ENGAGED AT SHILOH.

REGIMENTS, ETC.	Brigade.	Division.	Army.
Seventy-seventh Pennsylvania	5	2	Buell.
First Kentucky Infantry	22	4	Buell.
Second " "	22	4	Buell.
Fifth " "	4	2	Buell.
Sixth " "	19	4	Buell.
Ninth " "	11	5	Buell.
Eleventh " "	14	5	Buell.
Thirteenth " "	11	5	Buell.
Seventeenth " "	3	4	Grant.
Twentieth " "	22	4	Buell.
Twenty-fourth " "	21	6	Buell.
Twenty-fifth " "	3	4	Grant.
Twenty-sixth " "	14	5	Buell.
Fifth Ohio Cavalry	..	3 and 5	Grant.
G, First Ohio Light Artillery	..	5	Buell.
Fifth Ohio Battery	..	6	Grant.
Eighth " "	..	3	Grant.
Thirteenth " "	..	..	Grant.
Fourteenth " "	..	1	Grant.
First Ohio Infantry	4	2	Buell.
Sixth " "	10	4	Buell.
Thirteenth " "	14	5	Buell.
Nineteenth " "	11	5	Buell.
Twentieth " "	3	3	Grant.
Twenty-fourth " "	10	4	Buell.
Forty-first " "	19	4	Buell.
Forty-sixth " "	1	5	Grant.
Forty-eighth " "	4	5	Grant.
Forty-ninth " "	6	2	Buell.
Fifty-third " "	3	5	Grant.
Fifty-fourth " "	2	5	Grant.
Fifty-seventh " "	3	5	Grant.
Fifty-eighth " "	2	3	Grant.
Fifty-ninth " "	11	5	Buell.
Sixty-fourth " "	20	6	Buell.
Sixty-fifth " "	20	6	Buell.
Seventieth " "	4	5	Grant.
Seventy-first " "	2	5	Grant.
Seventy-second " "	4	5	Grant.
Seventy-sixth " "	3	3	Grant.
Seventy-seventh " "	3	5	Grant.
Seventy-eighth " "	3	3	Grant.
Eighty-first " "	2	2	Grant.
Second Michigan Battery	..	..	Grant.
Twelfth " Infantry	1	6	Grant.
Thirteenth " "	15	6	Buell.
Fifteenth " "	2	6	Grant.
Detachment Second Indiana Cavalry	..	4	Buell.
Sixth Indiana Battery	..	5	Grant.
Ninth " "	..	3	Grant.
Sixth Indiana Infantry	4	2	Buell.
Ninth " "	19	4	Buell.
Eleventh " "	1	3	Grant.
Fifteenth " "	21	6	Buell.
Twenty-third " "	2	3	Grant.
Twenty-fourth " "	1	3	Grant.
Twenty-fifth " "	2	4	Grant.
Twenty-ninth " "	5	2	Buell.
Thirtieth " "	5	2	Buell.
Thirty-first " "	3	4	Grant.
Thirty-second " "	6	2	Buell.
Thirty-sixth " "	10	4	Buell.
Thirty-ninth " "	6	2	Buell.
Fortieth " "	21	6	Buell.
Forty-fourth " "	3	4	Grant.
Fifty-seventh " "	21	6	Buell.
A, Second Illinois Cavalry	..	3	Grant.
B, " "	..	3	Grant.
Fourth " "	..	1 and 4	Grant.
Eleventh " "	..	6	Grant.

APPENDIX VI. (*continued*).

REGIMENTS, ETC.	Brigade.	Division.	Army.
Stewart's battalion Illinois Cavalry	..	1	Grant.
A, First Illinois Light Artillery	..	3	Grant.
B, " " " "	..	5	Grant.
D, " " " "	..	1	Grant.
E, " " " "	..	6	Grant.
H, " " " "	..	5	Grant.
I, " " " "	..	5	Grant.
B, Second " " "	..	..	....
D, " " " "	..	1	Grant.
E, " " " "	..	1	Grant.
F, " " " "	..	6	Grant.
Seventh Illinois Infantry	3	2	Grant.
Eighth " "	1	1	Grant.
Ninth " "	2	2	Grant.
Eleventh " "	2	1	Grant.
Twelfth " "	2	2	Grant.
Fourteenth " "	2	4	Grant.
Fifteenth " "	2	4	Grant.
Seventeenth " "	3	1	Grant.
Eighteenth " "	1	1	Grant.
Twentieth " "	2	1	Grant.
Twenty-eighth " "	1	4	Grant.
Twenty-ninth " "	3	1	Grant.
Thirty-second " "	1	4	Grant.
Thirty-fourth " "	5	2	Buell.
Fortieth " "	1	5	Grant.
Forty-first " "	1	4	Grant.
Forty-third " "	3	1	Grant.
Forty-fifth " "	2	1	Grant.
Forty-sixth " "	2	4	Grant.
Forty-eighth " "	2	1	Grant.
Forty-ninth " "	3	1	Grant.
Fiftieth " "	3	2	Grant.
Fifty-second " "	3	2	Grant.
Fifty-fifth " "	2	5	Grant.
Fifty-seventh " "	3	2	Grant.
Fifty-eighth " "	3	2	Grant.
Sixty-first " "	2	6	Grant.
Ram Monarch	..	..	....
C, First Missouri Light Artillery	..	4	Grant.
D, " " "	..	..	....
H, " " "	..	..	....
I, " " "	..	3	Grant.
K, " " "	..	..	....
Eighth Missouri Infantry	1	3	Grant.
Thirteenth " "	2	2	Grant.
Fourteenth " "	2	2	Grant.
Eighteenth " "	2	6	Grant.
Twenty-first " "	1	6	Grant.
Twenty-third " "	..	6	Grant.
Twenty-fifth " "	1	6	Grant.
Fourteenth Wisconsin Infantry	..	6	Grant.
Sixteenth " "	1	6	Grant.
Eighteenth " "	..	6	Grant.
Second Iowa Infantry	1	2	Grant.
Third " "	1	4	Grant.
Sixth " "	1	5	Grant.
Seventh " "	1	2	Grant.
Eighth " "	3	2	Grant.
Eleventh " "	1	1	Grant.
Twelfth " "	1	2	Grant.
Thirteenth " "	1	1	Grant.
Fourteenth " "	1	2	Grant.
Fifteenth " "	..	6	Grant.
Sixteenth " "	2	6	Grant.
First Minnesota Battery	..	6	Grant.
First Nebraska Infantry	2	3	Grant.
C, Second United States Cavalry	.	2	Grant.
I, Fourth " "	..	2	Grant.
H, Fourth United States Artillery	..	2	Buell.
M, " " "	..	2	Buell.
H, Fifth " "	..	2	Buell.
Battalion Fifteenth United States Infantry	4	2	Buell.
" Sixteenth " "	4	2	Buell.
" Nineteenth " "	4	2	Buell.

CHAPTER XXXVI.

GENERAL JOHNSTON IN THE GRAVE.

WHEN it was found that General Johnston was dead, General Preston conveyed his body from the field to the headquarters of the night before, and left it in charge of Captain Wickham and Major John W. Throckmorton. He then reported, with Majors Benham and Hayden, and Lieutenant Jack, to General Beauregard, who courteously offered them places on his staff, which were accepted, for that battle. After consultation with General Beauregard, and learning at headquarters that the victory was as complete as it probably would be, and that no attack was apprehended, the staff determined to accompany General Johnston's remains to New Orleans. Preston, Munford, O'Hara, Benham, Hayden, Jack, and Wickliffe, composed this escort. There was no cannonade, and no idea of a general engagement, when they left headquarters at 6 A. M. on Monday morning. But at eight o'clock, between Mickey's and Monterey, they were embarrassed by a stampede occasioned by *five horsemen*—one, of considerable rank. At Corinth they found the soldiers straggling through the woods, shooting squirrels. They learned, before they left that night, that Beauregard had retired.

On arriving in New Orleans, General Johnston's body was escorted to the City Hall by the Governor and staff, General Lovell and staff, and many prominent citizens. Colonel Jack, in a letter describing the scene, says :

The streets were thronged with citizens, and, as the procession moved slowly along, I saw tears silently flowing from the eyes of young, middle-aged, and old.

The body was laid in state in one of the public halls, and throngs of people of all classes, rich and poor, the lofty and the lowly, came in mournful silence to pay the last tokens of respect to the dead leader. Ladies wreathed the coffin with magnolias and other flowers.

The remains were laid in a tomb belonging to Mayor Monroe, in St. Louis Cemetery. Each year while it rested there, the writer received assurances that on All-saints'-day, there dedicated to the remembrance of the dead, friendly or admiring hands decorated his burial-place with wreaths and garlands. A visitor to the spot sent the following to the writer :

Here is the inscription, written in pencil: "General A. S. Johnston, C. S. A., Shiloh, April 6, 1862." On one corner some hand had written this: "Texas weeps over her noblest son. A Texas soldier." The tomb was decorated with flowers, some of them yet fresh. My fair companion informed me that scarcely a day had passed since his burial without fresh flowers being laid upon his grave. I have in my portfolio some of the roses that I took from the grave with no sacrilegious hand, and, if they were bedewed with tears, no true man or good woman will call it a weakness or a crime to weep at the tomb of such a man as Albert Sidney Johnston.

This constant memorial is understood to have been kept up.

When the news of General Johnston's death was spread abroad, the public heart, with that noble contrition which marks a brave and generous people, sought in self-reproach to make atonement for the wrong and injustice he had suffered. The evidences of grief were general and sincere. Not only was every official recognition given of the extent of the calamity, but the tokens of sorrow were multiplied in many a Southern household, and a great lamentation went up as if the loss of this leader was private and personal to every citizen.

GENERAL ORDER ON THE DEATH OF GENERAL A. S. JOHNSTON.

The following general order was issued from headquarters at Corinth by General Beauregard :

HEADQUARTERS, ARMY OF THE MISSISSIPPI,
CORINTH, MISSISSIPPI, April 10, 1862.

SOLDIERS: Your late commander-in-chief, General A. S. Johnston, is dead; a fearless soldier, a sagacious captain, a reproachless man, has fallen—one who, in his devotion to our cause, shrank from no sacrifice; one who, animated by a sense of duty, and sustained by a sublime courage, challenged danger, and perished gallantly for his country while leading forward his brave columns to victory. His signal example of heroism and patriotism, if imitated, would make his army invincible.

A grateful country will mourn his loss, revere his name, and cherish his many virtues.   G. T. BEAUREGARD, *General commanding*.

President Davis sent the following message to Congress :

To the Senate and House of Representatives of the Confederate States of America.
The great importance of the news just received from Tennessee induces me to depart from the established usages, and to make to you this communication in advance of official reports. From official telegraphic dispatches, received from official sources, I am able to announce to you, with entire confidence, that it has pleased Almighty God to crown the Confederate arms with a glorious and decisive victory over our invaders.

On the morning of the 6th, the converging columns of our army were combined by its commander-in-chief, General Albert Sidney Johnston, in an assault on the Federal army, then encamped near Pittsburg, on the Tennessee River.

After a hard-fought battle of ten hours, the enemy was driven in disorder from his position, and pursued to the Tennessee River, where, under the cover of the gunboats, he was at the last accounts endeavoring to effect his retreat by aid of his transports. The details of this great battle are yet too few and incomplete to enable me to distinguish with merited praise all of those who may have conspicuously earned the right to such distinction, and I prefer to delay our own gratification in recommending them to your special notice, rather than incur the risk of wounding the feelings of any by failing to include them in the list. When such a victory has been won over troops as numerous, well disciplined, armed, and appointed, as those which have been so signally routed, we may well conclude that one common spirit of unflinching bravery and devotion to our country's cause must have animated every breast, from that of the commanding general to that of the humblest patriot who served in the ranks. There is enough in the continued presence of invaders on our soil to chasten our exultation over this brilliant success, and to remind us of the grave duty of continued exertion until we shall extort from a proud and vainglorious enemy the reluctant acknowledgment of our right to self-government.

But an All-wise Creator has been pleased, while vouchsafing to us his countenance in battle, to afflict us with a severe dispensation, to which we must bow in humble submission. The last, long, lingering hope has disappeared, and it is but too true that General Albert Sidney Johnston is no more! The tale of his death is simply narrated in a dispatch from Colonel William Preston, in the following words:

"General Johnston fell yesterday, at half-past two o'clock, while leading a successful charge, turning the enemy's right, and gaining a brilliant victory. A Minié-ball cut the artery of his leg, but he rode on until, from loss of blood, he fell exhausted, and died without pain in a few moments. His body has been intrusted to me by General Beauregard, to be taken to New Orleans, and remain until instructions are received from his family."

My long and close friendship with this departed chieftain and patriot forbid me to trust myself in giving vent to the feelings which this intelligence has evoked. Without doing injustice to the living, it may safely be said that our loss is irreparable. Among the shining hosts of the great and good who now cluster around the banner of our country, there exists no purer spirit, no more heroic soul, than that of the illustrious man whose death I join you in lamenting.

In his death he has illustrated the character for which through life he was conspicuous—that of singleness of purpose and devotion to duty with his whole energies. Bent on obtaining the victory, which he deemed essential to his country's cause, he rode on to the accomplishment of his object, forgetful of self, while his very life-blood was ebbing away fast. His last breath cheered his comrades on to victory. The last sound he heard was their shout of victory. His last thought was his country, and long and deeply will his country mourn his loss.   JEFFERSON DAVIS.

The message was laid on the table, and ordered to be printed.

Mr. Barksdale moved to have 500 extra copies printed. Agreed to.

The following were the proceedings in the Confederate House of Representatives :

Monday, *April* 7, 1862.

The House met at twelve o'clock, and was opened with prayer by Rev. Mr. Crumley. Journal of Saturday read.

Mr. Wilcox, of Texas, introduced the following joint resolution :

"*Resolved*, That Congress has learned with feelings of deep joy and gratitude to the Divine Ruler of nations the news of the recent glorious victory of our arms in Tennessee.

"*Resolved*, That the death of General Albert Sidney Johnston, the commander of our forces, while leading his troops to victory, cannot but temper our exultation with a shade of sadness at the loss of so able, skillful, and gallant an officer.

"*Resolved*, That, in respect to the memory of General Johnston, the Senate concurring, Congress do now adjourn until twelve o'clock to-morrow."

Mr. Perkins, of Louisiana, thought that we could best evince our regret for the fall of our heroes by imitating their examples in discharging the duties which devolve upon us. He had no disposition to oppose the appropriate resolutions introduced by the gentleman from Texas, but there were many important matters demanding the attention of the House.

Mr. Foote : "I would ask the gentleman from Louisiana to withdraw his objection to the consideration of these resolutions.

"While I agree with the gentleman as to the necessity of speedy action upon the subject to which he refers, it seems to me that such a mark of respect to the gallant dead is peculiarly appropriate, and should be offered regardless of the consideration which the gentleman presents. Notwithstanding that we all feel rejoiced over the glorious victory which has been achieved, we cannot but feel deeply saddened at the fate of the gallant Johnston.

"It seems to me, sir, that we cannot be to-day sufficiently composed to perform our duties here, and it would, in my opinion, best comport with the feelings of respect and gratitude which we all entertain for the distinguished and patriotic chieftain, as well as the officers and soldiers who participated with him in this conflict, to adopt these resolutions, and adjourn over until to-morrow.

"I am as anxious as any man to perform the duties devolving upon us here ; but I am satisfied that we cannot do so to-day with that degree of composure which is necessary to give force and efficiency to our action.

"I trust the gentleman will withdraw his objection, and allow the resolution to pass."

Mr. Perkins : "I withdraw my objection."

Mr. McQueen, of South Carolina : "I desire to suggest to the gentleman from Texas (Mr. Wilcox) that this battle may have been fought in Mississippi. If so, it would be proper for him to change that part of his resolutions which locates the fight in Tennessee."

Mr. Davis, of Mississippi : "That battle was fought in Tennessee, very near the Mississippi line."

Mr. Moore, of Kentucky : "Mr. Speaker, I do not arise for the purpose of detaining the House by any protracted remarks in support of the resolutions offered by the gentleman from Texas, but rather to express my gratitude to that gentleman for presenting those resolutions.   I trust, however, that I may be indulged in the request that this House will unanimously adopt the resolutions, and bear their testimony of regard to the memory of that great and good man. Until our recent reverses at Forts Donelson and Henry, no cloud of darkness had rested on his fair name, no shadow had passed along to obscure the bright sunshine of his matchless military fame.   But I must not call up the memory of the past.   I do not wish to refer to any reflections which may have been indulged either here or elsewhere toward General Johnston in reference to those reverses ; but it only remains now for me to ask this tribute to his memory, since he has given the highest evidence of devotion to his country which the soldier can offer.   He has fallen at the head of his army, in the midst of the conflict, in the full tide of a glorious and brilliant victory over his country's foe.

" This crowning act of devotion to that country which he had so long loved and served has dissipated every cloud which momentarily marred the splendor of his glorious name, and his memory passes into history, undimmed by any word of condemnation, unclouded by any shadow of reproach.   Nor, indeed, Mr. Speaker, would any cloud of suspicion ever have rested upon his name had the circumstances with which he was surrounded at Bowling Green been known by the country.   No man can know the facts save those of us who were personally cognizant of his condition at that place.   I have seen and witnessed the terrible responsibility pressing upon his great heart, as, reposing on his couch of straw, he contemplated the unmeasured degree of hope and expectation with which the country looked to him, while he had an army too small to advance, and almost too small to hazard a retreat.   But, Mr. Speaker, I am happy to witness already demonstrations in this House which mark the unanimity with which the resolutions will be adopted—the unanimity with which this House, here in the Capitol, will offer a nation's gratitude as a tribute of respect to the memory of the illustrious dead.

" While I have felt justified, under all the circumstances, in alluding particularly to General Johnston, I would by no means have it understood that I feel less grateful to the memory of all the officers and soldiers who may have fallen in the same conflict.   God forbid that the humblest soldier who fell on that glorious field where victory so signally crowned our arms should fail to be remembered with the warmest affection and gratitude of our people.   In this, as in all revolutions, the officers and soldiers constitute our tower of strength. Upon their strong arms and brave hearts do we lean with all our hopes and expectations for ourselves and our country.   And now, as they have in the dread hour of sanguinary conflict laid down their lives, and thus borne the highest evidences of devotion to their country, I hope this House will unanimously adopt the resolutions, and pay that high mark of respect to those gallant soldiers who so nobly fell in defense of their country."

After the conclusion of Mr. Moore's remarks the resolutions were adopted unanimously.

They were immediately reported to the Senate ; but, that body having adjourned, Mr. Jones moved for a reconsideration of the vote by which they were adopted, with a view to passing resolutions expressive of the sorrow of this House at the intelligence of the loss of one of our distinguished chieftains.

In the course of the debate in Congress on the resolutions relative to the death of General A. S. Johnston, Mr. Barksdale, of Mississippi, said:

"I hold in my hand an unofficial letter, probably the last written by the lamented deceased to the Chief Executive of the Confederacy, to whom he had long been united by the ties of friendship, and with whom he had enlisted at an early day under the flag of a Government which together they abandoned when it became the symbol of a monstrous despotism. This letter has been given me to be used as I might think proper for the vindication of the recent acts of General Johnston, not fully understood by the public. I will, therefore, by the indulgence of the House, read this letter, that they may see the facts in the light by which his course was shaped previous and subsequent to the fall of Donelson. These facts triumphantly vindicate his fame as a true patriot and an able and skillful military leader. This letter, written under most trying circumstances, shows that no trace of passion was visible in the awful serenity of the pure, brave, and undaunted spirit in which it originated. It is a simple recital of facts in justification of his actions, before which the calumnies of the ignorant or the wicked will flee like mist before the brow of day. He has left a noble example of magnanimity in the midst of unjust complaint, and of courage and fortitude amid disaster. His fame rises brighter from the severe ordeal through which he has passed, and his name will live green and fresh forever in the hearts of a grateful people. Mr. Speaker, I will close by reading the letter to which I have referred."

Mr. Barksdale then read General Johnston's letter of March 18th, heretofore inserted (page 518).

At the conclusion of the speech of Mr. Barksdale and the reading of the letter from General Johnston—

Mr. Smith, of Virginia, offered the following resolution:

"*Resolved*, That this House, from respect to the memory of General Albert Sidney Johnston, and the officers and men who have fallen in the defense of their country in the hour of a great and glorious victory over our ruthless enemy, do now adjourn."

This resolution was adopted without opposition, and the House adjourned.

TUESDAY, *April* 8, 1862.

The Senate met at eleven o'clock. Prayer by the Rev. Mr. Kepler, of the Episcopal Church.

Mr. Haynes, of Tennessee, moved that the resolution touching the victory near Corinth, and lamenting the death of Albert Sidney Johnston, be taken up, so that he could offer resolutions in lieu. Resolutions were then presented by the Senator, expressive of the joy of Congress on hearing of the great victory of our army in Tennessee, paying a glowing tribute of respect to the memory of the commander-in-chief, and conveying the thanks of Congress to General Beauregard and the officers under his command, for their services in that memorable battle.

Mr. Haynes stated that he was one of the Tennessee delegation who requested the President to transfer General Johnston's command to some other officer, after the retreat from Nashville. Subsequently, information had caused him to alter his opinion, and he therefore felt it his duty to offer the resolutions named.

Mr. Yancey, of Alabama, moved that the resolutions be so amended as to designate the place of the battle as indicated by General Beauregard—viz., the battle-field of *Shiloh.* He moved, also, that the resolutions be so amended as to tender the thanks of Congress to General Beauregard and the surviving officers and soldiers for their gallantry and skill on that memorable field.

On October 1, 1866, the Legislature of Texas by joint resolution of both Houses, unanimously adopted, appointed a select committee to proceed to New Orleans, after the adjournment, and arrange for the removal of the remains of General Johnston to Austin, the seat of government of the State. The Hon. R. V. Cook, of the Senate, and Colonel Ashbel Smith and Colonel Jones, of Titus County, were appointed as the committee. Feeling tributes were paid to General Johnston's memory by Messrs. Cook, Smith, and F. C. Hume, of Walker County.

The following is the joint resolution concerning the removal of the remains of General Albert Sidney Johnston from the State of Louisiana, and their interment in the State Cemetery:

Whereas, The remains of General Albert Sidney Johnston, who fell at Shiloh, were stopped in New Orleans, on their way to Texas, by the capture of that city, and have never been removed thence; and, whereas, it was the desire of the deceased that he should be buried in the State of Texas; and, whereas, it is believed to be the wish of the people of the State that the dying request of one whom Texas was proud to acknowledge as one of the most illustrious of her citizens should be complied with: therefore—

Be it resolved by the Legislature of the State of Texas, That the sum of $2,000, or so much thereof as may be necessary, be appropriated, out of any money in the Treasury not otherwise appropriated by law, to defray the expenses of the removal and burial of the remains of General Albert Sidney Johnston, in the State Cemetery, in the city of Austin; and that a joint committee of the Legislature, consisting of one from the Senate, and two from the House of Representatives, be appointed, who shall proceed, in vacation, to the city of New Orleans, and carry this resolution into effect, in an appropriate manner.

Approved October 3, 1866.

(Signed)   J. W. THROCKMORTON.

The question being upon the motion to amend the joint resolution by providing that a committee of the two Houses be charged, after the adjournment of the Legislature, with carrying the object of the resolution into effect, Senator Cook said:

"Mr. President, in moving this amendment to the resolution offered by the honorable Senator from Travis, I do so from the feeling that it is but a fitting tribute to the worth and greatness of the illustrious deceased. Instead of allowing the sacred duty of his reinterment to be devolved upon some irresponsible person, let it be done by the Legislature itself. Let the body of the admirable soldier be borne to its final grave by a joint committee of the representatives of the people of Texas. General Johnston always claimed the State of Texas as his home, and was looked upon by the people as one of her citizens; and, as it was originally intended that he should be buried in our midst, and as it was only by the fall of New Orleans that his remains were stopped in that city, on their way to Texas, it is now but a just tribute to his memory that the objects of these resolutions be carried into effect.

"Mr. President, when the conflict became inevitable, and when all hope of accommodation had fled, and when the earthquake-throes of civil war began to shake the foundation of the republic, General Johnston, at that time afar off upon the shores of the Pacific, hearing the din of the approaching struggle, immediately began his journey across the howling wilderness and trackless desert that separated him from Texas, resolving to offer his sword to a cause which already had the sanction of his affections. I will not weary the Senate, sir, with a recital of his journey to the seat of government, and his final assumption of the command of the Army of the Tennessee. Nor will I attempt to follow, step by step, the disastrous events over which he had no control, and which resulted in the final retreat of the Confederate army from Bowling Green. Nor shall I advert to the detailed events which marked the progress of that army, as it swung slowly over the hills of Kentucky, and through the forests of Tennessee, amid the inclemency of wintry weather, to the memorable encampment at Corinth. But, sir, during those weeks of gloom, a burden of obloquy was heaped upon the gallant leader of the retreating army, which must have stung his proud spirit nigh unto death. No words of reproval were thought too vile with which to bring him into odium. The newspapers and the orators everywhere throughout the South denounced him as a failure, and a military empiric—a sworded and belted quack, whose movements were bringing our cause to ruin. Miserable newspaper scribblers, who never saw a 'squadron set in the field,' dared to brand the greatest soldier in the West with incompetency, if not with cowardice. Without comprehending or dreaming of the greatness of his plans, which only his death prevented from culminating in the magnificence of a crowning victory, ignorant critics imputed the retreat of our army, and all the disasters which preceded it, to his want of courage and capacity—an unjust verdict, which will excite posterity with surprise, and which an indignant sense of returning justice has already reversed.

"No marvel, sir, when our army halted amid the historic hills of Corinth, that the proud spirit of our hero chafed within him, and that he eagerly turned the heads of his columns toward the memorable field of Shiloh. I will not repeat the details of that glorious battle: how that, hour after hour, amid the shouts of advancing thousands, the eagle of the Confederacy soared to victory; how that banner after banner fluttered through smoke and storm as the foe receded; how that, while the hurrahs of victory were still ringing in his ears, Johnston died a soldier's death. Yes, sir, in the saddle, with the harness of a warrior on, the chieftain met the inevitable messenger of Fate. The pitiless musket-ball that pierced him spilled the noblest blood of the South. When he fell, all was from that moment lost! Victory no longer perched upon our flag. Less competent hands guided the strife, and a genius of lesser might ruled in his stead. What was assured success when the sun was wheeling to his zenith, became a fruitless and barren struggle ere the evening shades descended; and the shadows of night but covered the disposition for the morrow's retrograde movement. Then, sirs, was for the first time felt the priceless and inestimable loss we had sustained. Then, for the first time, men began to see, when the fruits of victory were so near being seized, the vast, gigantic, comprehensive strategy, which might have resulted in the complete overthrow of the Federal army, and the recovery of Kentucky and Tennessee. I will not say that it would have changed the result; I will not say that, had our admirable soldier been spared, the Confederacy would now be numbered with the nations of the earth. Into the counsels of Heaven let no mortal presumptuously seek to enter. But what I do say, sir, is, that from the fatal hour when the life-blood of the gallant Johnston moistened the earth—from that hour, sir, may be dated that long series of disasters, relieved, it is true, by heroic effort, and brightened from time to time by brilliant but barren victories—but reaching, nevertheless, through the darkness of successive campaigns, until the Southern Cross descended forever amid the wail of a people's agony behind the clouds upon the banks of the Appomattox.

"Fearless, honest, and loyal to principles, our hero died for what he thought was right. We know his resting-place, and we can recover his ashes. But, alas! thousands of his soldiers, the children of Texas, will never sleep in her soil. Their graves are upon the heights of Gettysburg, upon the hills of the Susquehanna, by the banks of the Potomac, and by the side of the Cumberland. They sleep in glory upon the fields of Manassas and of Sharpsburg, of Gaines's Mill, and in the trenches of Richmond, and upon the shores of Vicksburg, and upon a hundred other historic fields, afar from the land of their love. Ay, but let them sleep on in their glory. Posterity will do them justice. In the ages that are to come, when all the passions that now animate the bosom and sway the heart shall have passed away with the present generation of men, and when the teeming millions from the North and South who are to inhabit, in future centuries, the vast and fertile regions of the Mississippi Valley, shall recount, in song and story, the glorious achievements of their ancestry, and when they shall dwell, with just pride, upon the renown of their deeds, and when hoary age shall tell to kindling youth the marvelous story of a revolution, the like of which the sun has never yet gazed upon in his six thousand years of created splendor—then, sir, it will be, that our gallant dead shall live in the remembrance of mankind; then, sir, will posterity raise and build a fitting monument to perpetuate their memory.

"Perhaps the field of Shiloh will be chosen as the spot for its erection. Broad will be laid its foundation, deep down in the rock-ribbed earth. Vast will be its proportions—even vaster than the hoary Pyramids of Egypt. Upon its ascending sides, as they slowly aspire to the clouds, will be engraven the names of the great multitudes who sleep in soldiers' graves. Upon its angles, and around its broad pedestal, will be erected the bronze statues of illustrious chieftains who led the opposing hosts—while, sir, upon its lofty summit, as the crowning glory of the whole structure, a gigantic figure will be reared, girt about with a warrior's sword, while upon its head shall be wreathed a chaplet of immortal glory. The fleecy clouds will love to linger about it, and the earliest sunlight shall brighten its features. Upon the pedestal, where stands this statue, let the Muse of History inscribe in letters of everlasting fire the name of Albert Sidney Johnston!

"Sir, gentlemen who are insensible to the worth of departed greatness may declare such utterances treasonable. But I have yet to learn that admiration of true heroism and laudation of moral worth and intellectual greatness were ever regarded by an intelligent people as badges of treason. For my own part I see nothing inconsistent in honoring the worth of our departed dead, and at the same time giving our cordial support in maintaining, upholding, and defending the

Government of the United States. Sir, I love the Constitution of our fathers, and the great principles of republican government, and shall ever feel it a sacred duty to defend the same against all foes, foreign and domestic. If loyalty to the Government implies that we are to forget and execrate our dead, and are to declare by our words and acts that the glorious army of the Confederacy was only a band of outlaws and felons, and that its leaders deserved the gibbet or the dungeon—I repeat, sir, if these things must be included in the definition of 'loyalty'—then, indeed, are we all disloyal, and such will be the condition of the Southern people for generations unborn. For sooner might the stars be swept from the heavens, or the faculty of memory be eradicated from the human mind, than the recollections of the heroic and remarkable achievements of the Confederate army be forgotten by the American people. Ay, sir, while the hills exist and the mountains survive; while the Potomac continues to pour his bright waters to the broad Atlantic; while the Mississippi continues to roll his turbid flood to the delta and the Gulf of Mexico, the remembrance of the 'lost cause' shall survive, and the names of Johnston, and Jackson, and Lee, and a host of other heroes, shall live, and the glory of their endurance and their illustrious deeds shall stir the souls of future freemen, and stimulate the blood of generations yet unborn.

"Mr. President, the great Napoleon, dying on the rock-prison of St. Helena, left as his last heritage the wish that he might be buried on the banks of the Seine, among the French people that he had loved so well. For twenty years he slept beneath the rocks of the isle upon which he had died. But when at last the rage of animosity had ceased, and when human passions had subsided with the settlement of the great questions that had roused them, the voice of the great popular heart of France reached the king upon his throne, demanding that the body of the emperor should be removed and buried in the land of his love. The king heeded the voice, and sent his proud ships and the chivalry that surrounded his throne, to bring the illustrious sleeper to France.

"With a magnificence unprecedented even in that remarkable country, the remains of the chieftain were received. Millions went forth to meet the great conqueror stretched, in imperial pomp, upon his funeral-chariot. Amid tears and sobs, and the waving of banners, and the roar of cannon, and the imposing ceremonies of religion, they laid their idol to rest beneath the dome of the Invalides. We know that our hero cannot be thus received. Neither banners nor cannon can welcome his ashes to a grave in our midst. But, sir, he will be received with none the less heart-felt respect; and his sleep will be none the less sweet beside the ashes of Burleson and McCulloch, in the land of his love. And if we can lower him to his last resting-place, while the bosoms of brave men heave around him, and the tears of fair women bedew the sod that shall cover him, a sacred duty will be performed to the memory of a great, a noble, and an illustrious man:

> ' He is Freedom's now and Fame's,
> One of the few, the immortal names
> That were not born to die ! '

"Sir, I have done. I have said more than I expected to say when I arose to speak. I thank the Senate for its attention, and I trust the resolution and amendment may both be adopted."

Remarks of Ashbel Smith on moving the adoption of the resolution proposing to have the remains of General A. Sidney Johnston removed from New Orleans to the capital of Texas :

"Mr. Speaker, I rise to move that the joint resolution from the Senate which has just been read be now adopted by this House. It is fitting that the mortal remains of the great soldier therein named should repose in the bosom of this State, brought hither under the orders and auspices of the representatives of the people whom he loved so well. In moving the adoption of this resolution I perform a sad and yet not altogether unpleasant duty. To render honor and homage to worth, so great and so pure, is, sir, a pleasure. Albert Sidney Johnston was my friend—and who that ever knew him is there that was not his friend? We were fellow-soldiers, too; I served under him in the old Republic of Texas twenty-five years ago ; a quarter of a century afterward I fought under his command on the great battle-field of Shiloh—his last battle-field, where he sealed his devotion to the cause with his life's blood. I ask the privilege from the House to say a few words on this occasion. I shall not attempt any sketch of General Albert Sidney Johnston—an outline of his life, a recital of his services, a portrayal of his character, even were I adequate to this work, are too ample material to be compressed into the time allotted us on this occasion. The briefest notice must suffice." (Colonel Smith here gave a brief outline of his career.)

"It is fitting, it is profitable, to render honor and homage to great worth and great public services. We are ourselves better for this homage. Like mercy, it blesses him that gives—it makes the man, the people who render this homage, a better man, a better people. It is no superstition, it is truth, that the spirits of the mighty dead shed an influence for good over the land in which their mortal bodies repose. For, though their bodies rest in the earth, their true sepulchre is in the hearts of their countrymen. The worth of Albert Sidney Johnston is to the people of Texas, to their children and their children's children, a possession and an inheritance forever. It is fitting and due that his mortal remains be laid in this land. I move the adoption by the House of the Senate's joint resolution."

Remarks of F. Charles Hume on the joint resolution of the Senate relative to the removal of the remains of General A. Sidney Johnston to Texas :

"Mr. Speaker, I have only a few words to say in addition to the eloquent remarks of the gentleman from Harris, and I am done.

"We all know it was the dying wish of General Johnston to be buried in the bosom of his adopted State, to whose services he had given the labor of his best years, and the devotion of his great heart.

The unfortunate condition of our country has hitherto prevented the State from granting this last request ; but now that the dread scenes of war have ended, and the people enjoy an opportunity of expressing the tenderness of their memory for the irreproachable patriot who defended them and theirs 'even unto death,' it is as little as their representatives can do, in justice to the living and the dead, to ask of Louisiana the mouldering body of their warrior, that he may be buried by the waters of the Colorado, and mingle his dust with the heroes and statesmen whose names are living in the charmed numbers of undying song.

"Few names stand more prominently in our history than that of General Johnston; few memories wind around our hearts in more clinging embraces.

"Coming to Texas at an early day, and assuming at once his proper place among our wise, great, and good men, he has led our armies to battle, and identified himself in every respect with her eventful history.

"When the battle for Southern independence broke with its thunders and its threatenings upon the ears of our people, he did not hesitate to pledge to Texas and her confederated sisters the strength of his arm, and the fidelity of his heart. He did not pause before the careering waves of that Rubicon which held mirrored in its fearful depths the evils that were to come; he did not murmur in the wilderness, and curse the Moses who tried to lead his people from the savory flesh-pots and the galling bondage of Egypt; but in all, and through all, his manly heart defied the storm, and he fell 'mid its wrathful fury, still true to all the instincts of Southern manhood, and blameless in his unspotted glory.

"When the nations of Europe combined to crush the arms and the heart of the peerless Napoleon, and sent him to the barren rocks of St. Helena to sorrow, and sicken, and die, they did not dream that a day would come when France would seek the very ashes of her illustrious emperor, and bow with bleeding heart before his coffined form; but so it was, and, after the lapse of twenty years, Paris was illuminated by a thousand fires, and the whole nation bowed its head and wept as his sacred dust was laid close to the music of his own 'sunny Seine.'

"Let us do this righteous act; and, though we cannot bestrew the grave of *our* fallen chieftain with the green emblems of victory; though the floral offerings we cast upon his shrouded form are woven of the funereal cypress and the weeping-willow; though we feel and know he was the champion of a cause now lost forever—still in the deepness of our grief we may say how much we love his memory; and, while we weep for his and our country's misfortunes, whisper a prayer that God will bless his widowed wife and orphaned children."

It was known to have been the wish of General Johnston that his ashes should repose in the soil of Texas. He had so expressed himself in the presence of his staff. He had also said to Preston, "When I die, I want a handful of Texas earth on my breast."

The people of New Orleans, therefore, surrendered to the committee from Texas the body of General Johnston, which was by them escorted to Austin in January, 1867. It was the wish of the committee not to arouse the jealousy of the authorities. The chairman, in a letter to the present writer, dated January 8th, says:

In view of the strange passions which govern some persons in the United States, including some individuals in high office, the committee have deemed it in good taste and fitting the solemnity of the duty devolved on us to attract no premature and hostile attention.

This, however, they were unable to avoid, as events proved.

The following extract from the *New Orleans Picayune* of January 24, 1867, gives other interesting details of the occasion:

At the hour of three o'clock yesterday afternoon the St. Louis Cemetery was the scene of an assemblage such as never before had been witnessed within those ancient walls, which inclose the mortal remains of so many who, in their time, had been loved and revered by the population of Louisiana.

It was the occasion of the disinterment and removal of the remains of one who, though neither a native nor a resident of New Orleans, was perhaps dearer than either native or resident in the hearts of its people—General Albert Sidney Johnston, the hero chieftain of the Confederate army, the victor and victim of the bloody field of Shiloh.

The State of Texas had sent a committee for the purpose of superintending this duty, and yesterday was appointed for the exhumation. . . . It was generally known throughout the city that the disinterment and removal were to take place yesterday at three o'clock, but no formal invitation had been issued to the public to attend the ceremony.

And yet, when it was announced that the friends of the deceased and of his family were expected to be present, this simple phrase was sufficiently comprehensive to embrace a whole population, to whom the memory of the departed is even dearer than that of friend or relative. It was, therefore, not surprising that so great a number of our people assisted at the ceremony; nor that a majority should have belonged to that gentler sex who first strewed flowers upon the hero's coffin, and who ever since have tended his tomb with pious cares more precious than odorous garlands. Although the event was one which appealed directly to the sensibilities and emotions of the people of New Orleans, the ceremonies were conducted without any of the pageantry or pomp which usually characterizes such occasions. No blazonry of military rank marked the simple procession which accompanied the remains from the tomb to the steamer. No note of martial music measured the solemn tread of the long line of mourners. But grief was not less sincere because its expression in the accustomed mode was not permitted; nor was it the less intense that there was added to sorrow for the loss of one so loved sorrow for the loss of the cause for which he fought.

No stranger could have supposed that the plainly-attired pall-bearers who walked beside the hearse were generals high in rank and in reputation—men who had led armies to battle and to victory; who had defended cities, and who had organized campaigns. Among them were several who had been the friends and associates of the deceased in the old army of the United States, and some who had been his lieutenants in the recent war, and who stood beside him on that fatal but glorious day which deprived the Confederacy of his services. There was Beauregard, the favorite son of Louisiana, who immediately succeeded him in command of the army; there was Bragg, his energetic and indefatigable chief of staff; there was Buckner, who so gallantly fulfilled the chieftain's orders by the heroic but fruitless defense at Donelson.

It is remarkable, too, that, among this distinguished assemblage, there were three men—Beauregard, Bragg, and Hood—who had each in turn succeeded to the command of the army upon which the life and the death of its first leader seemed to impress a peculiar character and a strange fatality—an army whose history was illustrated by so many heroic deeds and so many signal misfortunes —an army which seemed to have inherited its heroism from his life, and its misfortunes from his death. . . .

This ceremony concluded, the coffin was lifted by the pall-bearers from the ground, and deposited in a hearse at the gate of the cemetery. Here a spontaneous procession was formed. The hearse moved slowly down the street, accompanied by the pall-bearers, and followed by a long *cortége* composed of a great number of the ladies and gentlemen of the city. Very many ladies followed immediately after the hearse, thus imparting a peculiar and touching character to the spectacle.

The line of pedestrians was many squares in length, and after these came a number of mourners in carriages. The route taken was down Conti Street to Rampart, up Rampart to Canal, up Canal to Chartres, down Chartres to St. Peter, and thence to the ferry-boat, upon which the remains were to be placed. The utmost decorum pervaded the masses of the people who were assembled on the sidewalks to witness the procession; and the feeling was manifested to such an extent that the transit of the street-cars and other vehicles was stayed along the whole route. When the coffin was transferred to the ferry-boat many persons embarked with it, and numbers of others were only prevented from doing so in consequence of the incapacity of the boat to accommodate them.

Upon the arrival of the remains at Algiers they were placed by the pall-bearers in the ladies' parlor of the depot-building of the Opelousas Railroad, where they were left in charge of Lieutenant John Crowley, who lost a hand at Belmont and an arm at Shiloh, and others who were maimed while serving under the deceased in his last great battle.

Among the pall-bearers, besides Beauregard, Bragg, Buckner, and Hood, were Generals Richard Taylor, Longstreet, Gibson, and Harry Hays.

All the papers were full of testimonials to the goodness and greatness of the deceased.

On the morning of January 24th the Texas committee, consisting of Colonel Ashbel Smith, Hon. D. W. Jones, Hon. M. G. Shelley, and Major Ochiltree, took charge of the remains of General Johnston, and conveyed them by the Opelousas Railroad to Brashear City. At Terrebonne, some fifty ladies, headed by Mrs. Bragg, strewed the coffin with fresh flowers and wreaths, and decorated it with floral emblems; and at Brashear City it was received by a large body of citizens. It was carried thence to Galveston by steamer.

Galveston had been the home of General Johnston at one time, and many of its citizens had been his personal friends—some of them among the best he had. It was proposed, therefore, and so announced, that the public honor of a solemn funeral procession should be accorded his body. When the programme was published, the United States general, commanding the district, issued an order prohibiting it. The programme is published, as the best evidence that it concealed neither treason nor sedition.

PROGRAMME FOR THE RECEPTION OF THE REMAINS OF GENERAL JOHNSTON.

The following is the programme agreed upon this morning by the committee for receiving the remains of General Johnston:

Band.
Legislative Committee.
Remains.

Pall-bearers.	Pall-bearers.
Hon. James Love,	Hon. F. H. Merriman,
Dr. Levi Jones,	Dr. N. D. Labadie,
Oscar Farish, Esq.,	Henry Journey, Esq.,
James P. Nash, Esq.,	Stephen Southwick,
Colonel Andrew Neil,	Colonel John D. Waters.

Clergy and Orator.
Mayor and Aldermen.
Reception Committee.
City and County Officers.
Judges and Officers of the Supreme Court.
Members of the Bar.
Civil, Military, and Naval officers of the General Government.
Press.
Howard Association.
German Benevolent Association.
Hibernian Benevolent Association.
St. Andrew's Society.
Galveston Literary Association.
Turners' Association.
Draymen's Benevolent Association.
Stevedores.
Fire Department.
Citizens.

The procession will form on Twentieth Street, head of column resting on Strand. To close up so soon as the reception committee reach the Strand from the wharf.

LINE OF MARCH.

Up Strand to Bath Avenue.
Bath Avenue to Broadway.
Broadway to Tremont.
Tremont to Church.
Church to Presbyterian Church.

Where appropriate religious services will be celebrated under the direction of Rev. Dr. McNair. During the time the City-Hall bell will be tolled, and it is requested that the church-bells will also be tolled.

During the progress of the ceremonies it is requested that all stores be closed and that all business be suspended.

The remains will arrive on Friday morning by the steamer Matagorda.— *Galveston Bulletin.*

This is General Griffin's order:

HEADQUARTERS DISTRICT OF TEXAS,
GALVESTON, *January* 24, 1866.

SIR: My attention has been called to the programme published in the morning papers, for the reception of the remains of General Albert Sidney Johnston, now *en route* from New Orleans to Austin.

Although there is a sacredness surrounding the remains of all deceased persons which makes it exceedingly delicate to interfere with their funeral celebrations, it becomes my duty, owing to the position that General Johnston occupied toward the United States Government, during the latter period of his life, to forbid the funeral procession.

If the body can be taken quietly, without any ringing of bells, public or popular demonstration, from the point of its arrival, direct to the point of its departure from the city, no objections will be made.

I am, very respectfully, your obedient servant,

CHARLES GRIFFIN, *Brevet Major-General commanding.*

Hon. C. H. LEONARD, Mayor of Galveston, Texas.

This order was without warrant of law. It was represented to General Griffin that no military or political significance was intended in the honors proposed; that the ashes of a great man, a soldier, a Texan, were on the way to their last resting-place, and that it was unrighteous to forbid the people to lament for their dead. It was pointed out to him that a soldier, who fell under his flag, was entitled to the honors of war. Federal officers had received them at the hands of the Confederates while the flames of civil war burned fiercest. Wainwright and Lea were so buried in Galveston. Colonel Baylor stated that he buried Colonel Mudd and Colonel Bassett with the honors of war. It was argued that a decent respect for chivalric usages could do no harm. General Thomas Green, an heroic soldier of the South, had been interred with these tokens of respect at Austin, without derogation to the Federal authority. Such arguments were in vain. General Griffin was inexorable. He affected to mistrust the statements that only a personal significance should be given to the demonstration. His sole concession was, that the body might remain at the wharf until next day. An appeal was made to General Heintzelman, who went beyond Griffin, and whose conduct is said to have been very coarse and cynical.

The mayor then appealed by telegraph to General Sheridan. The following is the correspondence:

GALVESTON, TEXAS, *January* 24, 1867.

The citizens of Galveston wish to give a civil escort, from steamer to cars, to the remains of General Johnston. General Griffin, commanding, has issued a prohibitory order. Will you give authority to the citizens here to give civil escort to his remains?

(Signed) CHARLES H. LEONARD, *Mayor.*

Major-General P. H. SHERIDAN, commanding Department of the Gulf, New Orleans, Louisiana.

Sir : I respectfully decline to grant your request.

I have too much regard for the memory of the brave men who died to pre-serve our Government, to authorize Confederate demonstrations over the re-mains of any one who attempted to destroy it.

(Signed)   P. H. SHERIDAN, *Major-General U. S. A.*

Mr. CHARLES H. LEONARD, Mayor of Galveston, Texas.

The Southern people were learning that they who have laid down their arms have no rights, and that grief may become a crime in the eyes of jealous tyranny.

In the following proclamation the Mayor of Galveston made known to the people the edict of their military master. It is well that it should be read by those who talk of beneficent despotisms :

MAYOR'S OFFICE, GALVESTON, *January* 24, 1867.

I am in receipt of a communication from brevet Major-General Charles Griffin, dated headquarters, District of Texas, Galveston, January 24, 1867, for-bidding the contemplated funeral procession in honor of the late General Albert Sidney Johnston, and directing that the remains be transported through this city without any public or popular demonstration.

I therefore hereby give notice that the proposed ceremonies will not take place.   CHARLES H. LEONARD, *Mayor.*

When the vessel arrived, and the order of the military commandant was communicated to Colonel Ashbel Smith, he directed the body to be placed upon the wharf, and, with the committee and the mayor, called on the military authorities. The result of this conference was the presentation of the following request, to which General Griffin gave a verbal assent :

MAYOR'S OFFICE, GALVESTON, *January* 13, 1867.

GENERAL : While on the part of the citizens of Galveston I would state that they did not intend, by the published programme for the reception of the re-mains of General Johnston, any political or party demonstration, I pledge that there shall be no music by bands, ringing or tolling of bells, public or private demonstrations, of any organized associations in the procession should the body be conveyed to the church in this city, and thence to the point of its departure. All persons appearing in the procession shall be invited and appear as members of the deceased's family or friends.   Respectfully, etc.,

(Signed)   CHARLES H. LEONARD, *Mayor.*

General GRIFFIN, commanding District of Texas, Galveston, Texas.

MAYOR'S OFFICE, GALVESTON, *January* 25, 1867.

The citizens of Galveston are hereby respectfully requested to implicitly con-form to the terms of the above request.   CHARLES H. LEONARD, *Mayor.*

Subsequent to the above, a meeting was called at the office of Mr. James Sorley, Mayor Leonard in the chair, when Colonel Smith moved as follows :

Out of deference to the wishes of his old personal friends, the remains of General Albert Sidney Johnston will lie in state on the Central Wharf, where they may be visited. They will be moved by the pall-bearers and committee to-morrow morning, Saturday, 26th instant, at ten o'clock A. M., from their present resting-place on Central Wharf to the depot, thence to be conveyed by special train to Houston. The friends of the family are invited to attend their removal. This was carried unanimously.

While these conferences were going on, Major McKnight says, in his letter to the *New Orleans Times:*

During the conference up-town, thousands of ladies and gentlemen went down to the wharf and exhibited the most unequivocal evidence of their respect for the memory of the deceased. I saw some thirty or thirty-five negroes, with mourning streamers upon their hats and arms, walk slowly and solemnly around the coffin, and several of them, standing near the head of the bier, freely dropped tears for the hero whose remains were before them.

The following is the account given by the *Galveston News* of the transfer of the body from the wharf to the depot, with editorial comments which reflected the sentiments of the community:

OBSEQUIES OF GENERAL ALBERT SIDNEY JOHNSTON.

The remains of the distinguished chieftain remained in state on the Central Wharf during all of Friday, where it was visited by thousands, and at night it was removed into an adjoining warehouse, where it was guarded by the following-named gentlemen: Major E. S. Bolling, Major J. W. Mangum, Messrs. S. B. Noble, J. F. Crane, Cyrus Thompson, Charles J. Jankes, M. Stoddart, A. W. Hughes, Paul Edmonds, R. W. Belo, John Adriand, Jr., A. D. McArthur, William C. Carnes, R. J. Johns, William H. Shields, P. C. Baker, A. F. French, Charles Spann, A. B. Block, J. K. Spires, William Warren, John Spann, Joseph Turner, Sidney Smith, J. P. Davis, A. P. Root, E. S. Alley, and P. P. Brotherson.

The Assembling.

Early yesterday morning, long before the time announced for the removal of the remains, thousands of our people could be seen wending their way, in the face of a stiff norther, toward the Central Wharf, while every few minutes the throng increased in numbers. About half-past nine o'clock the hearse, decorated with black plumes, and having its sides appropriately draped with mourning, pulled by four black horses, made its appearance. This was the signal for the crowd to close up together, and the coffin was removed from its resting-place to the hearse by the legislative committee and the pall-bearers, composed of our citizens.

The Start.

The hearse slowly commenced to move off, and, without any one directing, the multitude formed a column by twos, and marched behind. Along the Strand and Centre Street hundreds of ladies and children were waiting to take their places in the procession, and for a while we thought they were doomed to disappointment, so many males were moving in the line of march, and there did not appear to be any one willing to make room for them. They, however, moved on the sidewalk, parallel with those in the street. On every corner hundreds were standing, and as they saw the opportunity would take their places in the procession. The route of the *cortége* was up Centre Street, then along Market Street to the depot of the Galveston & Houston Railroad.

The Halt.

When the procession reached Tremont Street, it halted, and the ladies had a place assigned them directly behind the legislative committee, who were following the hearse. It requires no little effort to walk in the middle of our sandy streets. On plodded our fair and noble women, slowly but happily, never seeming to have a care about the fierce, cold wind blowing at the time, or the sand through which they were wading ankle-deep. Never before did Galveston witness such a scene. Ladies and children, who would not have dared to venture out in the cold on any other occasion, turned out *en masse* to pay respect and do homage to the illustrious dead. And it was a befitting tribute to departed worth. *Disheartened, crushed, oppressed,* as we are, and as we felt on this particular occasion, such a sight served to encourage every one, inasmuch as it plainly declared that, while laws and the bayonet might restrict a demonstration that would have been, these forces were utterly powerless (as they always will be) to restrain the natural feelings of the human heart, and a proper display of self-respect, always admissible on such occasions, and which will continue to be seen, in proportion to the opposition made against the wishes and rights of the people enacted by a detested military despotism.

Scenes at the Depot.

When the head of the column reached the depot, the rear of it was just turning Centre Street, and the whole width of the street, for that distance, was packed with the seething mass of human beings. We could not form an estimate of the number of persons engaged in this ovation, but we are sure we are not exaggerating when we declare that thousands participated in the sad funeral rites. The cars and engine were beautifully draped in mourning, and, as soon as the pall-bearers had placed the remains in the car, the ladies filed to the left and occupied the platform, while many passed into the car to catch a last glimpse of the remains of him who had *nobly fought, sadly bled, gloriously* and *gladly died,* for a *cause* dear to *him* and *us.* A car had been prepared especially for the ladies, and many of them accompanied the remains to Houston, also a number of prominent citizens not composing the committees. The whistle blew, and off started the train with its precious dust, while every head was uncovered. So ended the honors paid by the people of Galveston to the remains of General Albert Sidney Johnston.

A deep sense of both humiliation and indignation was aroused by General Griffin's arbitrary action. Insults cannot be offered with impunity to a free people. The excitement increased ; and when the remains of General Johnston arrived at Houston, another city where he was well known and much beloved, bitter wrath was mingled with the public sorrow. The body arrived at Houston January 26th, and remained there until the 28th.

The following account of the funeral at Houston is taken from the correspondence of the *New Orleans Times*, and was written by Major McKnight, better known as " Asa Hartz: "

The train arrived at the latter place at about one o'clock in the afternoon, when it was met by a similar committee of the city of Houston. The remains were placed in a hearse drawn by four white horses, and, followed by an immense procession of ladies and gentlemen, carried to the Houston Academy, where they were placed in state, and remained until ten o'clock on Monday morning, the 28th.

Immediately after the coffin was deposited upon the stand, Miss Moore, a poetess of no ordinary rank, and a native of the Lone-Star State, placed upon the bier a manuscript, of which the following is a copy:

ALBERT SIDNEY JOHNSTON.

Texas, like Mary, a worshiper
    Comes sorrowing!
Ha! who keeps her away from the sepulchre
    Of her shrouded king?
They strike, like cowards, her galling chains,
    And sneer that her lips are so strangely dumb!
Christ! Will the blood keep calm in our veins
    Till the end is come?

Alas, my brothers, whose brave forms moved
    In the battle-flame!
Alas, my sisters, whose hearts were proved
    When the midnight came!
He comes, whose arm was so firmly steeled!—
    O warrior, what of the hidden past?
Are you come as a messenger from the field
    Where thy sword shone last?

Oh, silent and royal, that mad day died
    In a sudden night!
But the valley was grand in the glow of thy pride!
    Is it not our right—
The laurels, thy name and thy sword have won us,
    The trust our fetterless soil will keep?
But the eyes of our masters are upon us,
    And we may not weep!

No " glorious pomp " in the guarded street—
    No roll of drums—
Naught save the echo of mournful feet
    Where our hero comes—
Silent bells in each guarded steeple!
    Met like a prisoner hanged for crime!
But a vengeance cometh, O my people—
    Let us bide our time!

The same order issued at Galveston was sent to Major Pease, commanding at Houston, but it was not strictly enforced; and the demonstration, though fervent, was entirely of a civil character, and totally devoid of political meaning. The sons and daughters of Texas wanted to honor the memory of their great citizen, and they did it.

The following extract, from a private letter from a gentleman in Houston, dated January 28, 1867, but published by the recipient, shows the feeling in that city:

It is my sad and mournful pleasure to relate to you the funeral obsequies paid to all that is left of the earthly remains of Albert Sidney Johnston, that great and good Southron, by the citizens of Houston, Texas. Excitement ran to a terrible pitch, owing to the edict issued per order of Phil Sheridan, through a "Griffin" of Galveston, that there should be no "lying in state, tolling of bells, or parading of societies," which order was not very quietly submitted to by the citizens of Galveston; but, when the remains reached the territory occupied by the pure, unadulterated Texans, the people had run mad in their sorrow, and no power could restrain them. Such a universal outburst of feeling I never saw. Early Saturday morning every house was draped in mourning from turret to foundation, with long streamers of crape and illusion; each store waved its dark plumage; no business was done, and the city presented the appearance of a vast sepulchre. On the arrival of the train from Galveston, the citizens rushed to the depot and the remains were carried to the Academy, while placards were on the street, "Our honored dead must and shall be respected." The remains lay in state until to-day on the rostrum in the Academy. From tall, silver candlesticks at the head and foot burned tapers night and day. The coffin was covered with flowers of the richest kind, and directly behind it on the wall hung the portraits of Jefferson Davis at the head, Robert E. Lee on the right, and Stonewall Jackson on the left, draped in mourning, all; and in the centre, a masterpiece—"The Weeping Confederacy;" while the coffin among the flowers was literally studded with photographs of Confederate generals of lesser grades. At ten o'clock to-day the remains were escorted by five hundred ladies on foot, and the gentlemen's procession a mile in length; then came carriages, carrying the decrepit and infirm. The hearse was of the most gorgeous manufacture and material, with six long, black plumes, arranged systematically at equal distances; six milk-white horses—the finest in Texas—draped in mourning, walked off as if conscious of the noble burden they bore. Bells were rung, and if Texas were an independent power they could not have carried matters to a greater extent.

A press telegram, among other points in regard to the funeral, says:

The bells are tolling. The solemn *cortége* is one mile in length. Five hundred ladies and little girls are on foot in the procession. No MILITARY OFFICIALS ARE SEEN ON THE STREETS.

It would do no good to reproduce the fiery denunciations of the press which were leveled at Sheridan and Griffin. The following extracts from the journals of the day are given to show the earnestness and universality of the people's grief. The *Merchants' Transcript* said :

He was received—received in Houston by the outpouring of the entire people. All joined in—mother and daughter, father and son—to swell the great anthem of grief that breaks from the popular heart when an idol is overthrown. No one cared for precedence. All were content to solemnly fall into the mournful line, and all foolish preëminences, or ideas of such, were dismissed in the presence of the solemn dead. Petty jealousies, animosities, foolish pride, disappeared, and one by one the solemn *cortége* increased its numbers at every step it took.

The bells rang from their different turrets, the houses along the road were enshrouded in mourning emblems; the young and the old participated, and the ovation of the people attested a nation's love, as well as the folly of those who would, by a military order, attempt to control the reverence and affection of a people that illuminate the sable plumes that wave solemnly over the hearse that conveys Albert Sidney Johnston to his last resting-place.

The following is from the *Telegraph :*

In the large Academy Hall of this city the honored soldier, taking his last sleep, remained Saturday evening, through Sunday, and until yesterday morning. Thousands of those who admired his wisdom, his goodness, and his courage, thronged around his bier, and gazed upon the coffin, bending under the weight of the floral offerings of Texas women and maidens. Fit shroud, these flowers, for so grand a form, for flowers are love's truest language—and it was the hand of undying love for the heroic soldier that placed them there.

On yesterday morning the streets leading to the Academy were thronged by gathering thousands of every age and condition. All thronged around the building where the cherished dead hero lay in his peaceful state of blessed repose. Soon the building was thronged to its utmost capacity, and the adjacent grounds and streets were also filled by those unable to obtain admission. A deep silence seemed to pervade all hearts, and every one was impressed with the historical sacredness and solemnity of the occasion. We noticed that tears were in the eyes of many—of the aged especially.

The bearers were composed of our best citizens. Immediately following were the delegations, etc., and after them a long array of hundreds of women and children, followed by thousands of citizens. The procession passed through the principal streets, and everywhere deep solemnity prevailed. All of the principal public and business houses were tastefully decorated with the insignias of mourning. All stores were closed, and business generally suspended. It was the grand ovation of the whole people to the "honored dead." The body was conveyed to the Central Depot, placed upon a car prepared for the purpose, and all that is mortal of this immortal man is now speeding onward, amid the grief of Texas, to its last resting-place.

The following article, from the *New Orleans Crescent* of January 27, 1867, exhibits very well the feeling of both the press and the people in relation to General Griffin's order.   It is from the pen of General S. B. Buckner:

THE REMAINS OF GENERAL JOHNSTON.

The name of Albert Sidney Johnston is consecrated in the memory and in the hearts of the Southern people.   His virtues have provoked unwilling admiration even from his foes, and the civilized world is filled with his fame.   Few men, in any age, can claim a reputation so fair as his, and there was a serenity in the greatness of his character which placed him above the petty passions of ordinary men.   He was conscientious in all his actions; and, having determined for himself what was right, he pursued the just path, regardless alike of the unjust criticisms of friends and the denunciations of his enemies.   His handsome and imposing presence, the dignity and the greatness of his character, his fine intellect and his lofty virtues, displayed

> " A combination and a form indeed,
>   Where every god did seem to set his seal,
>   To give the world assurance of a man."

It might be supposed that a character so pure would be held up, even by his former enemies, as a true type of manly virtues.   And, if, during his life, animosities may have existed against him in any ingenuous mind, we had supposed they would have been buried in his honored grave.

In some savage tribes, it is true, there once prevailed a belief that he who succeeded in slaying a great and a noble man became at once the inheritor of the virtues of the slain.   If such a belief were entertained in the present age, we might conceive of persons who, possessed of small merit themselves, might seek to acquire some nobility of soul by thus falling heir to the high virtues of Albert Sidney Johnston.   It would seem, from recent events, that some remnant of this faith still lingers upon earth, and that men who would have quailed before the fixed gaze of Sidney Johnston when living, now seek to acquire an ignoble fame by attempting an indignity to the dust of the illustrious dead.

. . . . Now, in a time of profound peace, when it has been promulgated by the highest authority in the land that civil law prevails throughout its length and breadth, a mandate has gone forth at Galveston, from a subordinate military commander, that the house of God shall be closed against the bones of Albert Sidney Johnston, and that no processions of his countrymen, whom he served so long and so faithfully, shall follow his remains to their last resting-place.

We say nothing now of the lawlessness of this usurpation of authority.   We do not ask on what pretense the officer assumes the power of closing the churches against religious ceremonies, and of attempting to stifle the sighs of sorrowing friends, and to suppress demonstrations of admiration, of love, and of esteem, for one so gifted with every quality that makes man illustrious.   The generous and the brave among all nations love to honor these qualities wherever they are found.   The envious and the ignoble alone, among men, would seek to detract from the just fame of the departed, as the wolf and the hyena, among animals, prey upon the dead.

But even if the military officer at Galveston were vested with authority to do as he has done, how impolitic, absurd, and impotent, has been his action! He may close the doors of the churches, he may disperse the assemblage of those who delight to honor the nobler virtues that dignify human nature, he may excite in ingenuous minds pity for his own weakness and scorn for his inhumanity, but he cannot detract from the fame of Albert Sidney Johnston, nor diminish in the minds of just and good men the esteem in which the memory of the illustrious hero is held. The more he seeks to suppress that feeling of reverence for so honored a name, "the bigger bulk it shows;" and, the more nearly he comes in contact with the name of the illustrious dead, the more rapidly does he dwindle into insignificance.

Despite the littlenesses that disfigure human nature, it is men like Albert Sidney Johnston who make us proud of our kind.

> " His nature was too noble for the world:
> He would not flatter Neptune for his trident,
> Or Jove for his power to thunder."

In life he possessed a serenity of soul which could have viewed with composure the dissolution of the world and a revolution in the universe. With what indifference, then, must his calm spirit view the futile attempts of petty power to disturb the remains that once held so great a soul!

At Houston there was fortunately no interference and no disturbance. In looking back at those days, good men in the North will regret that the interests and public peace of one section, and the honor of the other, were committed to such keeping. A year later, General Griffin fell a victim to the yellow fever at Galveston. No mark of disrespect was shown; but a strong public sentiment studiously withheld everything that might be construed into mourning, or the customary honors to public characters. The people refused to show an esteem which they did not feel.

The *State Gazette* gave a full account of the arrival of the committee in Austin, on the 2d instant, with the remains of General Johnston, and the ceremonies which were observed in honor of his memory. The remains were received in the hall of the House of Representatives by the Governor, his Excellency J. W. Throckmorton. On presenting the remains, Colonel Ashbel Smith, on the behalf of the committee, said :

GOVERNOR: The committee who were honored by the Legislature of Texas, on behalf of the citizens, to perform the pious duty of superintending the removal of the remains of General Albert Sidney Johnston from their temporary resting-place in the city of New Orleans, to be interred in the bosom of Texas, the land of the people whom in life he loved and served so well, and who so loved and honored him in death as in life, have to. announce to your Excellency that they have performed this duty. The committee have the honor here to present to your Excellency the remains of General Albert Sidney Johnston. The committee will, at an early time, make to your Excellency a written report in detail of their action under their appointment.

The duty of the committee, under their legislative appointment, is finished.

To this the Governor responded in the following beautiful and impressive address:

THE GOVERNOR'S ADDRESS.

GENTLEMEN OF THE COMMITTEE: The solemn duty imposed upon you by the representatives of the people of Texas, that you should repair to a neighboring State, and, in the name of Texas, receive and convey to the early home of his adoption the mortal remains of Albert Sidney Johnston, has been accomplished.

As loving friends, and as honoring countrymen, without the splendor and pageantry of public or official ceremonies, we receive his honored dust.

All that is left to us of his once manly form, wrapped in the habiliments of death—a death made glorious by lofty conduct in life—now lies lowly in the midst of mourning countrymen, who knew his worth, and who honor his memory, not alone for his achievements as a warrior, who led mighty hosts to battle, but also for the many and rare virtues that adorned his character as a citizen, and made him preëminent among the noblest of men.

His reputation as a public man belongs to history and to his country—with it to-day we have no concern.

However desirable it might be to commemorate his distinguished and useful public career, through a total misconception of the honor and fidelity of the people of Texas, we are denied the sacred and blessed privilege of testifying that homage in the manner which the people of every clime and nation, Christian or barbarian, civilized or savage, whether free or in bondage, have been wont to exhibit when consigning to the tomb the ashes of their illustrious and great men.

With truth may it be said that General Johnston lives in the hearts of the people of Texas. He is enshrined in the holiest of their affections. The showering tears, shed by thousands of our noble women and brave men, and the countless testimonials that have everywhere greeted the funeral procession on its melancholy way, attest the affectionate regard entertained for him by our people. But our tears do not alone moisten the memories that cling around the departed hero. The tears of the lovely and noble ones of other lands mingle with ours in paying holy tribute to the worth of one so pure in all the private walks of life, and so exalted in every attribute of noble manhood.

When the pen of history shall record the deeds of the fathers who made Texas a nation, the name of him whom we mourn will occupy one of the most prominent niches in that distinguished array.

When generations have passed away, and the memories of the present hour have been softened and purified by time, and the student of history lingers with admiration over the characters of the great men brought upon the stage of action by the recent war, no one name will command greater respect than that of Albert Sidney Johnston.

May the purity of his private life be an exemplar for our young men in all time to come! May the spotless integrity of his conduct as a public man be emulated by all in authority! And may his unsullied fame, as an American citizen and soldier, teach us that we cannot, and should not, share it alone! His fame, with that of his many distinguished contemporaries, whether won under the Stars and Stripes, or under the Stars and Bars, is the common heritage of the American people. It is the proud representative of American character, and is alike honorable to the North and to the South.

Many of the heroes of the late civil war grew up in arms together, and shared glories mutually won upon other fields; and, notwithstanding the follies of their fellow-citizens caused them to lead contending armies of countrymen against each other to carnage and death, yet in their hearts they were brothers in affection. Their deeds—the deeds of other heroes—the gallantry and endurance of the soldiers from every section, and the glories won by the armies of the North and the South—all, should teach us that we cannot be two people, that we should remain, as our fathers desired—one nation.

I trust in God that the afflictions we have suffered may purify us, and that the hearts of the American people may once more beat in perfect unison and accord over the prosperity and harmony of a reunited and happy people, and thrill with pride at the mention of the virtues and achievements of every American name, regardless of the section that may give it birth or prestige.

Gentlemen of the committee, you are entitled to and will receive the thanks of the people of Texas, for the very acceptable and praiseworthy manner with which you have discharged the delicate mission confided to your care.

In the next number of the *Gazette* the following account is given of the final burial of General Johnston :

The final funeral rites over the remains of General Albert Sidney Johnston were performed on last Saturday at the Capitol. All that was mortal of him now rests in the State Cemetery. There his honored dust must remain in a humble tomb, without monument or inscription, until the time shall come when it will be no crime to erect memorials, or to speak well of the illustrious dead. That it cannot now be safely done, we know, nor is it worth while, perhaps, to speak of these things. The orders of General Sheridan or General Griffin are not without precedent, and the *Telegraph* is mistaken in supposing them so. Burial-rites were refused to the remains of the mighty Montrose, and his body was drawn and quartered. A British king had the remains of Oliver Cromwell, the mightiest ruler who ever pressed the English throne, exhumed from their tomb in Westminster Abbey, and disgracefully and ignominiously buried. But history has preserved the memory of these deeds for no other purpose than to heap its curses on their authors, and hand down their names to the scorn of all the coming ages.

But now it may not be entirely safe to treat further of this subject; these things must be left for posterity. Under the present condition of things, we are forcibly reminded of the celebrated and terrible passage of Chateaubriand, when commenting on a similar state of affairs in France. He says: " In times like these the historian appears to be charged by Fate with the vengeance of the nations. It is in vain that Nero triumphs. Tacitus has been born into the empire, and already an uncompromising Providence has handed over to an obscure child of Genius the glory of the master of the world." To time, the great avenger; to history, the appointed agent of that vengeance; and to the future, in whose presence the righteous retribution will take place, we commit the case of Sidney Johnston, as against Sheridan and Griffin. He will fare no worse with posterity than has that glorious old rebel Montrose, whose bones were refused a Christian burial; or that stout old traitor Oliver Cromwell, whose remains were thrown upon a dung-hill.

After the beautiful and appropriate remarks of Governor Throckmorton, published in our last issue, the body was taken charge of by him, and lay in state in the Representative Hall of the Capitol, until Saturday, at twelve o'clock, under the charge of a guard of honor, appointed by his Excellency, and composed of the young men of Austin—soldiers who had battled bravely for the "lost cause." The bier was visited by many ladies and gentlemen, and wreaths of cedar, laurel, and fresh flowers, were strewed above it. Among the number of inscriptions placed upon the coffin, all indicative of the deep affection and even veneration in which the deceased was held by those who knew him, none was more expressive or appropriate than the following:

> " On fame's eternal camping-ground
> Their silent tents are spread,
> And glory guards, with solemn round,
> The bivouac of the dead." [1]

The pall-bearers were selected from among the oldest and most honored of our fellow-citizens. The Governor and State officers were the chief mourners.

The Episcopal burial-service was read by Rev. J. W. Phillips, Chaplain of the Senate.

The choir of ladies and gentlemen, who kindly volunteered for the occasion, sang with fine effect two sacred anthems.

Nearly all the ladies of the city were present, and the hall of the Capitol was crowded.

The procession was at least a half-mile in length, and composed of children, of ladies and gentlemen on foot, and also many others in carriages and on horseback. It proceeded from the Capitol down Congress Avenue, and then by Pecan Street to the State Cemetery, where the grave awaited its honored tenant. There was no sound of bells or of music heard during the moving of the procession, though the unheard voices of many hearts chanted the virtues and the valor of the dead. Dr. Robertson, Captain William Walsh, and Mr. Thornton, and other gentlemen, kindly assisted in forming the procession. Upon the whole, the ceremonies were exceedingly impressive, and as well calculated to paint the scene on the memory of the beholders as if there had been a parade, a programme, the tolling of bells, the sound of martial music, and a well-pronounced eulogy. Silence is sometimes more eloquent than words.

His restless life, as has been seen, was not succeeded by quiet sepulture. Borne from the field of victory and death to a distant though friendly city, when his mourning State came to ask for his ashes, her pious task was interrupted and the sacred rites broken

---

[1] From verses written on another occasion by Colonel Theodore O'Hara, one of General Johnston's staff.

in upon by an unjust and unlawful military order. Yet, for all this—

"After life's fitful fever he sleeps well."

The people of New Orleans have continued to do honor to the memory of General Johnston. On the 10th of April, 1874, the Confederate Tomb, completed by the Ladies' Benevolent Association of New Orleans in Greenwood Cemetery, was unveiled. It is a mausoleum of masonry, fifteen feet square and six feet high, with sloping sides, turfed. It is surmounted by a granite gallery, eight feet square, in the centre of which stands a marble pedestal nine feet high. On this stands the statue of a Confederate soldier, fully armed, in the attitude of an outpost sentinel. It is of Carrara marble, and is seven feet in height. It is said to be a work of rare excellence. On the four sides of the monument are placed busts : General Polk on the east side, General Lee on the south, General Jackson on the west, and General Johnston on the north. After solemn prayer by Dr. Palmer, and an eloquent oration from Mr. H. N. Ogden, the monument was unveiled. It is a great honor to be cherished in the hearts and memories of the people who erected this monument.

CHAPTER XXXVII.

THE END.

It has been the writer's aim in this biography to let a truthful narrative of facts reveal the character of its subject. He has not been prepossessed with any especial ideal to which he has striven to conform General Johnston's acts or motives. Whatsoever of error or inconsistency these facts may exhibit in a character very simple and noble —let it stand. Although the writer has made a study of General Johnston's life, in a spirit and temper which he hopes has been as nearly judicial as was possible under the circumstances, yet he is aware that his relations were too close, and his attachment too strong, to offer an impartial portrait of the man. Hence, he has chosen, often at the cost of brevity and with the sacrifice of artistic effect, to speak, where it was possible, in the words of others. Delicacy, or rather fairness, seemed to require that the *evidence* for his opinions, instead of merely his conclusions, should be laid before the reader. This has been done ; and he who has read these pages has a better conception of what General Johnston really was than the most labored characterization could give. Nevertheless, it may not be deemed amiss that he should now supplement this memoir with some incidents and anecdotes which have not fallen into place in the course of the narrative, and with some estimates of its subject which have not been included in the body of the work.

Immediately after General Johnston's death the opinion prevailed that the unjust censures of the press and people had driven him to desperation, and that he had lost his life through reckless exposure. The idea, originally suggested by popular regret, could only be held by those unacquainted with the facts and with the serene strength of his character. It is believed that it has effected no lodgment in the public mind, though it has been repeatedly published. His staff, and many of his officers, indignantly contradicted it at the time, and since. General Johnston was moved solely by a sense of duty and the requirements of the situation. He held his own life at no higher value than that of the humblest private in the ranks, where duty called. And his notion of duty was that of a soldier—that general, as well as private, ought in battle to be and to go where most effective, and that the question of danger was not to be considered.

Colonel Munford, in his address, spoke as follows:

The impression is almost universal at the South that General Johnston, stung to madness by the bitterness with which he had been denounced, recklessly exposed his life. Nothing could be further from the truth. If the narrative of simple facts already given is not sufficient, other proofs are abundant, and in justice to his memory shall be given.

After narrating an anecdote already given (page 515), illustrating General Johnston's perfect confidence in the result of the campaign, Colonel Munford continues:

Another reason why *I know* he was not "affected to recklessness" by all this clamor is, the unflinching firmness with which the President stood by him from its outbreak, and General Johnston's perfect knowledge of that fact. At Decatur, Alabama, the day before we left for Corinth, the general handed me for perusal two private letters to him from President Davis, assuring him of his continued confidence in his ultimate triumphant success, and of the resolute purpose of the Government to sustain him. He therefore had nothing to fear. It was in reply to one of these letters from the President that he used those noble words: "With the people there is but one test of merit in my profession, that of success. *It is a hard rule, but I think it right.*" Surely the man who thus felt, and thus wrote under the circumstances, was not capable of being made "reckless." It will be noted, too, that when he fell a most brilliant victory was already his, and every motive would have prompted him to live. He did not secure himself from any legitimate danger, but at no moment was he reckless, or even imprudent in unnecessarily exposing himself to injury. The pressure upon Sidney Johnston was from no selfish thought or narrow feeling, but from the *circumstances under which* he had "ordered the battle for to-morrow morning at daylight," and the disparity of his forces compared with those of the enemy. If with a thoroughly-trained army, under skillful leaders, devotedly attached to their chieftain, and accustomed to victory, the first Napoleon at Jena excused himself for taking personal risks, by saying, "I must needs *see* how things are going," surely Albert Sidney Johnston at Shiloh will not be misinterpreted. Surely, there, he "*must needs see how things were going.*" No, no, he fell in the path of duty, thinking not of self.

General Preston wrote :

I felt at Shiloh, when your father fell, that our last hope of victory perished, and that his place would never be supplied.

Major Haydon, in his "Rough Notes on Shiloh," says:

Thus fell one of the greatest generals of the age. He fell where heroes like to fall—in the arms of victory upon the battle-field. It is a mistake to suppose that the censure of ignorant men about his recent manœuvres drove him to a rash exposure of person. In this battle he was elated from the very beginning ; he knew that victory was certain, and his countenance gleamed with the enthusiasm of a great man who was conscious that he was achieving a great success, that was carrying his name down to the "latest syllable of recorded time."

His aide-de-camp, Lieutenant (afterward Colonel) T. M. Jack, writing to Judge Ballinger, from New Orleans, soon after the battle, thus closes an account of General Johnston's death :

How much of manliness, and virtue, and patriotism, and heroism, and high resolve, were cut down by that random ball ! There was no rashness or desperation in his conduct.

He regretted certain censures against him, but they did not actuate his motives, or affect his plans. He was sustained by the President. He had the approval of his military brethren. He looked with confidence to the final approbation of all his countrymen.

On the field of battle, and in the hour of trial, he seemed not forgetful that he was a Texan, remarking that Moore's regiment must have a chance at the enemy, and specially ordering it forward to the attack.

His remains lie here in state, to be placed in the vault to-morrow. He will no doubt be buried in Texas. He once remarked, in the presence of his military family, that he desired of his country six feet of Texas soil. Surely that noble State will be all the nobler with such bones resting in its bosom !

Colonel Jack, in a letter addressed to the writer in 1877, says :

The only orders, now remembered, which I carried for your father on the field, were to direct Breckinridge through the woods and to place him in line ; to order forward a Texas regiment to an effective position ; and to move a battery, on the left, so as to play on a point where the enemy offered stubborn resistance. Up to this time I had been almost constantly with him on all parts of the field. In the execution of this last order, I was separated from him; and, changing his position with the changes of the battle, when I rejoined him, he had already received the fatal ball, and his life-blood was rapidly flowing. Before this he had remarked to me, slapping his thigh and smiling, upon a spent ball which had struck and stung him.

No special incident of the battle of Shiloh survives in my memory having an important bearing on the general result. The entire scene is, of course, as vivid as of yesterday; the advance; the forward movement of troops, quick and eager; the line of battle; the shock of arms; the thundering of the gunboats; the retreating lines of the enemy; and the victorious shouts of the Confederate troops. But these are all familiar to you; and so are the conduct, bearing, action, and appearance, of your father on the field—composed, self-poised, cheerful, and confident of the devotion and courage of his men. He appears to me now, as he did then, like an inspired genius of battle and victory, lit up and glowing along his lines; a matchless example of a great man on a great occasion, and rising loftily and steadily to all the duties of that day when the fate of his flag and the cause of his country seemed to rest upon his sword.

The following extracts are taken from Colonel Munford's "Historical Address before the Confederate Association of Memphis," delivered November 21, 1871. Though an account has been elsewhere given of General Johnston's personal appearance, Colonel Munford's quick observation and graphic force entitle his remarks to reproduction. The writer thinks the description of General Johnston's eyes inaccurate. They were deep set, but not small or dull. Heavily shadowed by his brows, they were wonderfully calm and steady, and by some considered searching, in repose; but under excitement they flashed with an electric light, which changed their color from blue to gray:

In person General Johnston was tall, square-shouldered, full-chested, and muscular. He was neither lean nor fat, but healthily full, without grossness, indicating great bodily strength. His bust was superb, the neck and head mounting upward from the shoulders with majestic grace. His compact jaws terminated in a chin somewhat prominent and but slightly square, above which one of the very few really ornamental mustaches ever worn by man partly concealed, but could not render ferocious, the sweet and genial expression of his mouth. Over this stood somewhat boldly forth the clear-cut and expanded nostrils of a broad-based nose which, slightly inclining upward, grew out from beneath his prominently developed brow where thought sat as upon a throne. His full and angular though rounded forehead rose upward till its high "window's peaks" were lost under dark-brown hair a little mixed with gray, extremely fine and wavy almost to curls. His deep-set, blue-gray eyes, small, and, when unexcited, somewhat dull, were of that sort which Campbell describes as "melting in love and kindling in war." Over these features a skin naturally soft, white, and clear, though now slightly bronzed from exposure, completed a picture of more than ordinary manly beauty. Courage and modesty, intellect and goodness, cheerfully divided the empire over his expressive face.

When absorbed in thought his head leaned forward and his body slightly bent. At all other times he was strikingly erect. His soldierly port, devoid of stiffness, was characterized by a dignified and benevolent repose, at once calm, self-poised, simple, and unostentatious. I do not remember a man filling high position so utterly uncontaminated by that vulgar "divinity which doth hedge a king." There was, in both his appearance and bearing, that nameless something which, while it chastened impertinence, invited confidence, and rendered even the humblest at perfect ease in his presence. He was eminently approachable to everybody of every rank and condition in life. Neither his movement while walking, nor his manner in repose, could justly be called awkward, yet neither was light and airy; in fact, there was in both something too ponderous for grace. On horseback his appearance excited universal admiration. A cavalier by instinct and training, he sat upon a horse as if, centaur-like, he had grown up part of him. Whenever his soldiers caught sight of him in the saddle their shouts were irrepressible.

Ordinarily his conversation was grave, the style being simple, vigorous, and rigidly concise. His manner of talking was slow, measured, and thoughtful, evincing an anxious care to choose the very words which would express only his exact meaning. From this care to say just the thing he meant he never departed. Still, socially, he was one of the most interesting of men. His scholarship was ripe—his knowledge of books, of men, and of things, was extensive and varied. His views, always comprehensive and clear, never failed in their expression to rivet attention and confer pleasure. To his cheerful temper was superadded a fund of the richest humor, which not unfrequently sparkled into diamond-pointed wit. The prominent and distinguishing features of his intellect, however, were an intense perception and realization of surrounding circumstances; a power of analysis which no complication of facts could baffle; a logical accuracy of thought which could follow the most delicate clew through the mazes of any labyrinth; and a solid judgment which correctly estimated forces and values. Of the use of these faculties he was perfect master. They were thoroughly disciplined—enlightened by extensive knowledge, and perfected by a larger experience. His sound sense, therefore, was of that perfect kind which constitutes wisdom.

To strangers, his intellectual action seemed to be slow. This was a misapprehension, requiring for its correction only a better knowledge of the man. In communicating his thoughts to the outer world, in the use of the mere machinery of words, he was simply unready. Where words were not to be used, but things were to be done; where his thoughts were to be translated directly into acts, they moved with all the quickness and force of the electric flash. Of oratorical power he had none. Like Moses, he was "slow of speech," and could write better than he spoke. Some men can both speak and write greatly above their true intellectual worth. In neither could Sidney Johnston approach the very high mark of his own, and he was fully conscious of the defect. In counsel he was always great—in action, greater still; as at Shiloh, where in penetrating the designs of the enemy, and thwarting them—in seizing at a glance the decisive points of the battle-field, and concentrating upon them more troops than could be opposed to him—in grasping his army, hurling it like a thunderbolt upon the foes and scattering all opposition from before him—his genius blazed forth in all its full-orbed splendor and glory. In his short career as a Confederate general, that victory is his greatest monument. Alas! that the "proud temple he builded there" should have crumbled into dust at his death. But its memory and his will live in the bosoms of his countrymen as long as there is left on earth one true Confederate heart-beat. To these high intellectual gifts was united a large-hearted goodness of which he was "full as the dew-drop of the morning beam." Together they shed upon his name a lustre belonging of right only to the immortals. Such was Sidney Johnston—the model soldier, gentleman, and patriot. I close this sketch with a few illustrative anecdotes.

While we were at Bowling Green, a man claiming to hail from Nashville presented himself at headquarters and inquired for me. Being shown in, he said a certain friend of mine had directed him to make my acquaintance, as he had something important to communicate. I soon saw he only desired to get into communication with the general, and presented him. He was a glib talker, but had a countenance at once acute, sinister, and malignant. I saw the general fix his gaze upon him as the fellow went on to tell how "above all earthly things he had the Southern cause at heart; that he believed Andrew Johnson was the most dangerous enemy we had in Tennessee, if not in the whole South, and that his death would be a public benefaction; that he knew just where he was in Southeastern Kentucky, and that he could be easily disposed of at a trifling cost of money." The general rose up and said: "Sir, the Government which I serve meets its enemies in open and honorable warfare. It scorns alike the assassin's knife and the debased scoundrel who would suggest its use!" It is scarcely necessary to add that there was a vacant seat instantaneously in that room. The general turned to me and said, "That scoundrel wanted me to bribe him to assassinate Andrew Johnson."

On another day, while riding, we came unexpectedly upon a colonel who was a West-Pointer, and had made a most favorable impression at headquarters. He was in the midst of a portion of his regiment, cursing and d——ning the men at a furious rate. After we had passed, the general remarked: "That man has not as much sense as I had believed; he does not know how to command men. It is an error to suppose it can be done by fear. The true secret of command lies in the exercise of moderation, united with superior sense and justice. No man can command others with permanent success unless he has learned to command himself. Nor is this a regular army; these are people who have left their homes to fight for their independence. All they require is a little patient instruction." And few officers know this.

General Johnston's piety was a principle. I shall not discuss, with those who see nothing but impiety in others who do not adopt *their* cherished dogmas, whether or not his views were orthodox. I know, however, that his piety was deep and sincere, and, as illustrative of this trait, state that he and myself had been at work till long after midnight, when he proposed to me to "adjourn to his bedroom, take a drink, *say our prayers*, and go to sleep." I told him I would take that night a glass of water, and feared he would find me no better at praying than drinking. He bent on me a look of almost paternal tenderness, and said solemnly, "I never lay my head upon my pillow at night without returning thanks to God for his protecting care, and invoking his guidance in future."

The following reminiscences of General A. S. Johnston were furnished by Rev. R. M. Chapman:

I spent the first half of the year 1839 at Houston, Texas, where I boarded at the house of Colonel Gray, in company with President Lamar, General A. S. Johnston, Secretary of War in Lamar's cabinet, and several other distinguished gentlemen. The opportunity thus afforded me of seeing much of General Johnston was enhanced by his kindness in conversing with me often in a manner less public than at a large table. Of that kindness I have ever retained a most grateful remembrance, in connection with a profound admiration of the nobleness of his character. Especially do I cherish in my memory his last words to me.

When the time came for me to go away, I was undetermined whether or not I should return to make my permanent residence in Texas. In taking leave of me, General Johnston pressed my hand and said: "Come back; and, if I have only a blanket, you shall have half of it."

It was in the spring of that year that Bishop Polk, then missionary Bishop of the Southwest, made his first visitation in Texas. During his stay in Houston he was entertained at Colonel Gray's. His meeting there with General Johnston was particularly gratifying to them both, as they had been contemporaries at West Point, and for a part of the time room-mates.

Of course, at such an interview (and I believe it was the first they had had since leaving the Academy), no topic of conversation would so readily present itself as recollections of their student-life. I remember one exceedingly interesting conversation of that kind which they had one day, as we sat on the porch after dinner. They had been recalling one and another of their old comrades, and telling what each knew of their later lives and fortunes, when the bishop said, in an impulsive manner, "It is remarkable, general, that out of the three composing our staff at the Point two are in the ministry and you are left alone." General Johnston was affected by the words, and replied, with evident sensibility: "It is true, bishop, and I cannot say that it is not my fault. But I assure you it is not pride or any such thing that keeps me from confessing the same faith. If I could be convinced, I would preach from the house-tops." To this the bishop replied, warmly, "I know you would, general—I know you would."

Shortly after, General Johnston left us to go to his office; and then Bishop Polk, by way of apology for his confidence, so feelingly expressed, in his friend's sincerity even of unbelief, related to me the history of his own conversion.

While he was in the Academy a very considerable religious awakening occurred among the cadets under the ministry, as chaplain, of the Rev. C. P. McIlvaine, afterward Bishop of Ohio. Polk was one of the first to feel this new concern, and, being entirely ignorant of the first principles of Christian belief, he set to work to inform himself on the subject, beginning with the study of "Christian Evidences."

Johnston had no feeling in the matter, but, seeing his room-mate so deeply interested, he read with him such books as the chaplain put into their hands.

The event was Polk's entire satisfaction, followed by his joining the church, and determination to leave the army for the ministry, which he did.

Though General Johnston paid small attention to dogmatic theology, it has been seen that he was deeply impressed with certain fundamental religious truths, and that his religious aspirations were simple, as they were fervent and direct.

During General Johnston's residence at Austin, the Rev. Edward

Fontaine was the Episcopal minister at that place. He was a gentleman of culture, of military education (I believe), and of great zeal and enthusiasm. He saw a good deal of General Johnston, and, after his death, published some reminiscences of him in the *Jackson Mississippian*, from which the following has been clipped:

If I were selected by the South to award the palm of merit to the most worthy of all the illustrious dead who compose "the noble army of martyrs" who died in defense of our constitutional liberty, I would lay the sacred symbol of peerless excellence upon the tomb of Albert Sidney Johnston. If he were living, and in arms, with Stonewall Jackson, Robert E. Lee, Joseph E. Johnston, and Beauregard, ready to take the field again, and I had to appoint one of these illustrious heroes the generalissimo of our army, I would not hesitate a moment to give him the command of the whole, with a feeling of confidence that each one of them would obey his orders willingly, and that no master of the art of war could improve the orders he would give. In all the virtues which constitute the true patriot and chivalrous hero, these idols of the Southern States were endowed by Nature with equal measures; and whether it be attributable to blood or education, or both, although differing widely in personal appearance, they will be exhibited to future ages by history as much alike in character. Of all his living compeers among our country's defenders, General A. Sidney Johnston resembled, most in disposition and all his marked characteristics, his namesake, General Joseph Eggleston Johnston. They were not at all related by blood; but two men were never more alike in everything except personal appearance. General Joseph E. Johnston is well formed, but under the medium size. His head is unusually large; and, to a painter, it seems a little out of proportion when compared with his body. General A. Sidney Johnston was a very large man—not corpulent, but well proportioned—and weighed at least two hundred pounds. He would have been observed among a thousand good-looking men, as one formed to command others. His was

> "The lofty port, the distant mien,
>   Which seems to shun the sight, yet awes if seen;
>   The solemn aspect and the high-born eye,
>   That checks low mirth, yet lacks not courtesy."

The eyes of our living hero, I believe, are dark hazel. Those of him who fell at Shiloh, while lighting his hosts to victory, were like those of Napoleon and Washington—clear gray. They were deeply set, and the heavy shadows of the projecting brows gave them a dark-blue shade. Both possessed the same temperament—full of fire, but so smothered by perfect self-control that few of their most intimate friends have ever witnessed its flashing under any circumstances. But none could doubt that enough of it was embodied to make its possessor formidable as a sleeping lion or silent volcano. A wife, child, or servant, or intimate associate in private life, might be with General Sidney Johnston for a lifetime without ever discovering the slightest manifestation of ill-temper. It has been said that "no man appears great to his valet." This saying, which might have been true when applied to Charles XII., Frederick the Great, or the Duke of Marlborough, was not so in regard to him. He was the same great man in private and public; and it was his unselfish, generous amiability, his strict regard to truth and justice, his warm and sympathetic friendship, his tender regard for the rights and sensibilities of others, and the self-control which governed his words and actions, which made his companions love him. His profound learning, his strong common-sense, and the quickness, clearness, and the originality of his thoughts upon all subjects, excited their respect and admiration.

I will leave to the historian the task of assigning to him his just position among men as a public servant and as a general; I shall speak of him only as I saw him in private life, and mention a few circumstances which will perhaps illustrate his character.

Soon after the Mexican War, a large number of the officers of the United States Army, who had distinguished themselves and received promotion for their gallantry during that struggle, were assembled in Austin, where General Johnston was then stationed. The citizens gave these heroes a splendid ball. But, when the company met, General Johnston was absent, and his presence was considered almost indispensable on such an occasion. The committee of arrangements were much mortified when it was ascertained that, in issuing tickets of invitation to the officers of the army, they had forgotten to send one to General Johnston. They were greatly embarrassed to know how to apologize to him for their neglect. The truth was, that he had lived among them so long, and there was so little of the "pomp and circumstance" of the officer about him, that he was regarded by them as a plain citizen, and as one of themselves; but they did not know how he would be pleased with such an excuse. When he learned the difficulty he was evidently much gratified, and told them not to feel in the least unpleasant about it, as they had paid him, without intending it, a high compliment.

Rev. Mr. Fontaine also relates the following ancedotes:

I never heard Sidney Johnston make a public speech. His modesty made him averse to any display of his talents; but he was highly gifted in conversation; and, whether his companions were ladies or gentlemen, he never failed to amuse and to instruct them. He spoke fluently but deliberately, and always used the most correct and appropriate words to express his ideas. In the course of many years, in camp, in garrison, in his own parlor, and while traveling with him through the wilds of Texas, I never heard him say a rude or silly thing, or utter an expression obnoxious to the most refined Christian lady. Yet his conversation abounded with anecdotes, and was spiced with wit and humor. His knowledge of ancient and modern history, and especially that of our country, was thorough; and his acquaintance with every department of natural science was very extensive. He was particularly fond of discussing the merits of all the recent discoveries in geology, and the various branches of natural history.

I recollect an incident which will give you some idea of his humor: A clerical friend, who was often his companion in his angling-excursions in the Colorado bottom, brought upon himself a severe attack of intermittent fever by indulging too freely in this innocent amusement during the "dog-days." Wading in the cold water with an August sun burning upon his head at noon, and inhaling the miasmatic vapor from the decaying moss and aquatic plants left dead upon the sand-bars of the river, shrunk within its narrowest limits in the dry season, had given him "the chills." The general, with some other friends, called to see him during his illness. One of them asked him how he made himself sick. He replied that he could not account for the attack, unless it had been caused by getting wet in Barton's Creek and the Colorado River. General Johnston then said: "I will answer your question for my friend. I know his habits well, and I have been with him frequently lately, and but for a very strong constitution I would probably be now in his condition; but he is a clergyman, and as such he does not like to confess that he has made himself sick by frequenting too much *low places.*"

He was a regular attendant at church; but I never knew him to commune at the sacrament of the Lord's supper. His wife was a very pious and useful member of the Episcopal Church. I do not recollect ever to have heard him express his opinion upon the subject of religion but once. I dined with him Sunday after preaching a sermon upon "The Doctrine of a Special Providence," to which he listened with profound attention. After dinner, and while conversing with him and Mrs. Johnston, he remarked: "Your sermon to-day interested me very much. I believe firmly in the doctrine of a particular Providence which directs or controls the destiny of the worlds or atoms; and I will relate an incident in my own life, which, with many others of a similar character, has confirmed me in my belief, and which I think will serve to illustrate the truth of your sermon. As the paymaster of this department of our army, I have for the last four years visited Fort Croghan, Fort Worth, and other gargisons in Texas, regularly once in three months, to pay our troops. I have generally had the same escort of soldiers whom I can trust. I have had the same ambulance, the same mules, and the same driver; and, during each quarterly trip between Fort Croghan and Fort Worth, I have invariably camped about one hour before sunset under a certain post-oak tree, near a fine spring, at the end of my first day's journey from Fort Croghan. The mules were so accustomed to the spot that, whenever I reached it, they went to the oak-tree, and turned the wagon around in a position suitable for unloading and pitching the tent under it. I used the body of the tree as a support for the tent, one end of which was fastened to it. In order to reach this camping-place in proper time, I was in the habit of starting punctually at eight o'clock in the morning, and I do not remember to have deviated five minutes from that hour in four years except on one occasion. The ambulance and escort were all ready and willing for the order to march. But I sat conversing with the officers and ladies of the post one hour later than usual. I remember thinking several times that I had better be off; but I felt an aversion to starting, for which I could give no good reason. At length I found that I had idled an entire hour, and gave the order to move. One hour later than usual, traveling four miles an hour, I was at a distance of four miles from the camping-place when I met a furious storm from the northwest. The wind, rain, and hail, accompanied with tremendous thunder and incessant lightning, beat full in our faces with such violence that I was compelled to halt in the prairie, turn the front of the ambulance and the heads of the mules from the storm, and remain where we were until it was over. It continued until late in the night; and we remained upon the spot in a very uncomfortable situation until the next morning. As soon as it was light, I ordered a move to our usual camping-place, where there was plenty of wood and water, and where I intended to breakfast. In an hour we reached it. But the post-oak was gone. A flash of lightning had shivered it in fragments, and torn many of the roots of it out of the ground; and from the effects of the terrible stroke I am confident that I should have been killed, and all with me would have perished, if I had reached it at the usual time, and if the tent had been pitched where it had been once in every three months for four years. I felt truly thankful for my escape. Now, sir, I can only account for it in this way: I suppose, unconsciously to myself, the Great and all-pervading Spirit influenced my own spirit, and kept me employed or amused in conversation at Fort Croghan. It was necessary that the particular spot of earth where I usually camped should be electrified; but it was not necessary that I should then be killed. Hence a Divine Providence interrupted the regularity of my movements, and saved my life."

General Johnston's deliberation is illustrated by his remark to a precipitate friend who was about to run across a street in front of a carriage driving rapidly: "There is more room *behind* that carriage than in front of it."

Dr. D. W. Yandell, General Johnston's medical director, furnishes the following incident:

While at Corinth, the owner of a drug-store, living in Tennessee, near to Donelson, represented to the general that his entire stock of drugs had been taken by a Confederate quartermaster for the use of his command, and paid for in Confederate money, which was useless to him. He had come to ask the general if he might not be paid at least its equivalent in Tennessee funds, the difference between the two being then ten or fifteen to one. General Johnston requested me to look over the druggist's account, and see if the prices, etc., were honestly stated. He said, "Scrutinize every item." I had at the time an experienced druggist acting as clerk in my office. He examined the accounts and found them square. I so reported to the general. He directed his quartermaster to take back the Confederate money, and give instead its equivalent in Tennessee currency, remarking to me at the time, "It wouldn't be honest to pay a man in the enemy's lines in money which had no value to him."

After he had written at Tuscumbia, Alabama, his report of the operations of the army from Bowling Green, he read it to General Preston and myself. I was struck with the expression, "Success is the test of merit," and objected to its use. He said, "Well, critically perhaps it is not correct, but, as the world goes, it is true, and I am going to let it stand."

The following brief and discriminating description is an extract from an article in *Harper's Weekly*, published at the time of the Utah Expedition:

Colonel Johnston is now in the matured vigor of manhood. He is above six feet in height, strongly and powerfully formed, with a grave, dignified, and commanding presence. His features are strongly marked, showing his Scottish lineage, and denote great resolution and composure of character. His complexion, naturally fair, is, from exposure, a deep brown. His habits are abstemious and temperate, and no excess has impaired his powerful constitution. His mind is clear, strong, and well cultivated. His manner is courteous, but rather grave and silent. He has many devoted friends, but they have been won and secured rather by the native dignity and nobility of his character than by his powers of address. He is a man of strong will and ardent temper, but his whole bearing testifies the self-control he has acquired. As a soldier he stands very high in the opinion of the army. As an instance of this it may be mentioned that, in a large assembly of officers and gentlemen, the gallant and impetuous Worth, when asked who was the best soldier he had ever known, replied, "I consider Sidney Johnston the best soldier I ever knew."

Colonel Thomas F. McKinney, the Robert Morris of the Texan Revolution, in a letter from Austin, dated December 28, 1872, writes thus:

General Johnston's life will be a difficult one to write, as in his action he was always up to the full measure of purity, excellence, and high moral tone. It has often been remarked that General Albert Sidney Johnston possessed more good and high qualities, in an eminent degree, than any man we have ever known; and, though I have heard it repeatedly said where many were present, no one was ever found who did not approve the assertion.

General Johnston's ability and conduct were recognized by some persons and public journals at the North, even through the white heat of civil war. A San Francisco paper said:

THE LATE GENERAL A. S. JOHNSTON.

Elsewhere in our columns will be found the message from Jeff Davis to the Confederate Congress, notifying that body of "the irreparable loss" sustained by the South, in the death of the above-named distinguished officer.

Those of our citizens who had the pleasure of his acquaintance during his brief sojourn in our city will truly grieve for his untimely end.

From an able and dispassionate article in the *New York Times*, reviewing the career of General Johnston, we take the following extracts:

He was the man who, of all others, had been until lately looked upon in the South as a commander without a peer for active field-work—combining in himself science, skill, daring, coolness, resoluteness, experience, and whatever other characteristics or elements of success are supposed to belong to a great leader. This was the fourth war in which he had seen and done service; and in each of the previous wars he had gained only renown and achieved always success. . . . He perpetually threatened our army with assault and annihilation, kept Louisville, and even Cincinnati, for a time, in a state of perturbation, and delayed the progress of our arms until it seemed his end was on the eve of accomplishment.

Speaking of the battle of Pittsburg Landing, the *New York Times* also said:

It is clear that, while the rebel generalship of Sunday was the best, and ours of that day all but the worst ever seen on this continent, the steady valor of most of our soldiers and the gallant bearing of their officers, converted what would naturally have been a terrible Union disaster into a decided Union victory.

And, again, the *Times* declared that "the rebels, led by their very ablest General, Albert Sidney Johnston, were pressing 30,000 disorganized Unionists down a steep bluff to a deep river, in which the great mass of them must have been drowned, but for the timely arrival of two gunboats."

The writer having found among General Johnston's papers a very complimentary testimonial to the services of Colonel John N. Galleher so well and favorably known as General Buckner's chief of staff, sent it to him. Colonel Galleher, who has, since the war, entered the ministry of the Protestant Episcopal Church, replied in the following note:

BALTIMORE, *December* 12, 1872.

MY DEAR COLONEL: Your note, with the inclosure, reached me this morning. Please accept my warm acknowledgments for your thoughtful kindness. The document is one that I shall treasure always as a testimony of your honored father's kind interest in me. He was the commander to whom I first presented myself at the opening of the war, and from him I sought advice as to the selection of duty in the army. I recall distinctly the circumstances of my interview with him. He was then at Columbus, Kentucky, his headquarters, on a hill overlooking the town and the river. As I climbed the hill and approached the house, I began to feel some tremors, and was almost ready to turn back for very diffidence, and fear lest he should be annoyed. But I went on, and found him in his office, apparently at leisure. At first, I thought there was something stern and severe in his manner; but it was only the deep calmness and gravity which wrapped him round as it had been the mantle left to him by some grand old viking who knew how to rule himself and others. When I had told him that I was from Mason County, he spoke with evident interest of his birthplace and mine, asked after the people there whom he remembered, and said that the topography of the county was strangely fresh in his memory, although he had long been absent. He was extremely kind, and relieved me of my embarrassment by his manner. He advised me to repair to Bowling Green, where the Kentucky troops were, intimating his anticipation that active work with the enemy would ere long be found somewhere in that direction, and adding that he would soon be there himself. I went away, feeling that I had met a man in whose inspiring presence it would be a glorious joy to suffer any hardship. He had magnetized me; and to this hour his splendid person stands out in my thought as the incarnation of that "Confederacy" to which my heart yielded its utmost love and loyalty. He was and is to me as royal Arthur to England's brave romance. Thus reverencing him, and remembering him, the written words which connect me with his approbation and confidence are precious in my sight. I thank you for them again and again.

Respectfully yours,

Colonel WILLIAM P. JOHNSTON, Lexington, Virginia.   J. N. GALLEHER.

Some extracts from an editorial article of Colonel J. W. Avery will be pardoned, as they disclose in part the secret of General Johnston's wonderful influence over his soldiers, which stirred every man with the conviction that he was under the eye of his commander. This gentleman says:

The records of no war show a knightlier warrior than the one whose name heads this sketch. We may be pardoned for laying a leaf upon his bloody yet most honorable grave.

He was the first general to whom we reported, as the youthful leader of a cavalry band of gallant Georgians. We had raised this company, and it was unarmed, and we went to him for munitions.

Passing by some eulogy by the author on General Johnson's fortitude in the retreat from Nashville, and compliments to the affability of his staff, we come to his description of General Johnston:

General Johnston reminded us of the pictures of Washington. He was very large and massive in figure, and finely proportioned. He measured six feet two inches in height, and had flesh to give him perfect symmetry. His face was large, broad, and high, and beamed with a look of striking benignity. His features were handsomely moulded. He was very straight, and carried himself with grace and lofty and simple dignity. He dressed neatly, but always in full Confederate-gray general's uniform, that suited him admirably. His whole appearance indicated, in a marked degree, power, decision, serenity, thought, benevolence. We thought him then at first flush, and thought it unvaryingly afterward, and think now, in the hallowing memory of his noble manhood, made sacred by the consecration of his thrilling and heroic death for the Southern cause, that he was one of the sweetest and most august men we ever met. His character was entrancing in its pure nobility. We thought him an object for deep veneration; and, whenever we look at the familiar and majestic features of the great *Pater Patriæ*, we always think of Albert Sidney Johnston.

We stated our name, and presented our introductory note from General Hardee, when, greeting us courteously and kindly, General Johnston requested us to be seated. It was pretty early in the war then—in November, 1862. Old army-officers were wont to assume much pretension and style, to the great awe of civilian officers, upon whom they generally looked with very unconcealed disdain. To have been a West-Pointer was the grandest of earthly accidents; and to have grown up an unmilitary civilian was an unspeakable and ignominious misfortune. It will be remembered how many of the first class lorded it over the latter. But in Johnston there was none of it. Simple as a child, unassuming and modest as a pure woman, he affected nothing for his high rank.

We were inexperienced in tactics, and apprehensive, though ardent in the cause and eager for service. We told this to the general, and asked him to deal gently with our military ignorance in consideration of our zeal. There was something in his manner that emboldened confidence, and, when we got through, nothing could exceed the fatherly manner with which he replied, encouraging, instructing, and assuring us of his kindness. He offered to help us with his counsel, or otherwise; invited us to call on him at any time, and, giving us necessary orders, we left.

It was that gentle politeness that won everybody who approached him, and endeared him to his people. Often, afterward, we met him at his headquarters, and in the field, and he always was the same affable, considerate, fatherly gentleman, inspiring the gravest reverence, winning the fondest regard, and exciting the highest admiration.

We have not time to tell all the incidents of our experience of this rare gentleman and great captain. We never knew of any one being refused admission and a kindly hearing, and we venture that no distinguished leader ever left a tenderer personal memory than Johnston.

But we must hasten on to our last interview with him. It was at Corinth, Mississippi, a few days before the bloody battle of Shiloh. We had some important business, and rode to his headquarters. He met us with his usual cordiality, but stated that, in consequence of very pressing matters, he would be unable to give us his personal attention, and must, for once, refer us to his adjutant-general; but that we must not feel slighted, and he would always be glad to see us hereafter with the same freedom.

The consideration of his manner and remarks amid the engrossing occupation of preparing that great movement to Shiloh, upon which he depended so much to retrieve the disasters of Donelson and Nashville, prove how thorough a gentleman he was, and how kindly was his heart. He bade us good-morning with a friendly grasp of the hand, and we never spoke to him again.

That mighty struggle at Shiloh came on. We saw him once in the dread carnage, flashing across the field, the incarnation of the splendid warrior. He always rode large and magnificent horses. His favorite steed was a gray; and when he was mounted upon the noble animal he was the *beau-idéal* of a general. His firm, graceful seat in the saddle, his majestic proportions, his soldierly carriage, his handsome uniform, his noble countenance, the radiant bearing of knightly chivalry that marked every movement and feature, all leave a proud remembrance of gallant and striking manhood, for those to dwell upon who knew and loved him.

He was killed about twelve o'clock in the first day's fight. His death was kept concealed from the army, as it was feared it would dampen their ardor and chill their confidence.

But when it was known—near the close of the second day's battle—it cast a gloom that fell over every heart. And coming, as it did, with the dismal order to retreat, a sense of heavy woe pervaded every bosom. How that fight would have ended if he had lived, is a matter of speculation. That he would have pushed the first day's advantages to the bitter end no one doubts. Our cavalry were hurtling resistlessly upon the enemy's shattered fragments, huddled on the banks of the river, when we were inexplicably and unwillingly withdrawn. Night came. Reënforcements strengthened the foe. Unusual camp luxuries demoralized our men; and the next evening, crippled, worn out, decimated, our army straggled back to Corinth, and the golden chance was gone.

That stainless and imperial blood was shed only to illustrate a cause it failed to win. And, in coming days, when the historian sits to write what will be the fair chronicles of the turbulent war of those times, he will lovingly dwell upon no character more shining, illustrious, and exalted—upon no hero more luminous for chivalry, patriotism, genius, and sublime manhood—than ALBERT SIDNEY JOHNSTON.

General W. C. Whitthorne says, March, 1876:

Allow me to say, as I do from a feeling of reverence and affection for the memory of your father, that he was one of the three great men whom it has been my fortune in life to meet. His death was the severest loss the Confederacy sustained prior to its ultimate defeat.

Mr. J. M. Fairbanks writes that he was a lieutenant of engineers in the Confederate army, and sends the following anecdote :

I was chief clerk in General Hardee's adjutant-general's office, and confidential secretary for General Hardee. In common with all who came in contact with your father, I was inspired by the highest respect and veneration for his noble character.

Just before the main attack at "Shiloh," a countryman, who had been intercepted between the lines, was placed in my charge, with directions by General Hardee to conduct him to General Johnston. On reaching him, he asked a few questions of the man. "How many troops have the enemy?" "Oh, many thousands," replied the man. "Do you think they have 100,000 men?" asked the general. "Oh, yes," was the reply. "They won't be a mouthful for us!" remarked the general, smiling.

At that moment he was watching with great anxiety the progress of our line of battle, across an open field, expecting any moment when fire would be opened from the woods on the other side. This was the last time I saw him alive, and his appearance then is stamped on my memory.

Hon. Jefferson Davis told the writer that Mr. Buchanan asked him if he could advise him who was the best man to appoint to the command of the Utah Expedition. He recommended General Johnston. "But if not Johnston, who then?" inquired the President. "Persifer F. Smith, if his health will allow," answered Mr. Davis. "Whom else could you recommend, if neither of these could be sent?" asked the President. "Robert E. Lee." Mr. Buchanan then said, "Do you and General Scott ever by any possibility agree?" "I should not like to think that I did not often agree on military affairs with a man of General Scott's experience," replied Mr. Davis. "Well," said Mr. Buchanan," you have named the same persons for this service, though not in the same order."

Judge William P. Ballinger, of Galveston, Texas, writing in 1873 of General Johnston, says:

His impression on me was very strong and lasting. I was a boy of eighteen, and your father was the first great man I was ever thrown in association with. I saw a great deal of him for several years—I was his adjutant in Mexico. Since then I have met a number of the so-called great men of the day. Very few have excited in me any high degree of admiration. But I have a veneration for your father that classes him with the very loftiest historical *beau-idéals*. If I were to construct a Parthenon for perfect nobility, lofty, true, genuine, pure, undeviating—

" Standing four square
'Gainst all the winds that blow "—

his would be the statue enshrined.

Colonel Wharton J. Green, of North Carolina, some anecdotes from whose pen have already been inserted in this memoir, in a letter to the present writer says, in regard to General Johnston:

Portray him as he was—great, good, single-minded, and simple. He was the devotee of duty, but disposed to soften its asperities to others. His was a character with few counterparts in ancient or modern story. It has been said that the noblest eulogy ever written consisted of a single word—"the just." All who ever knew General Johnston will confirm that he was as well entitled to that epithet as the old Athenian, and, coupled with it, to another, "the generous." Talleyrand's saying, "No man is a hero to his valet," is true in the main; but General Johnston would have been a hero to his very shadow. Those who knew him best admired him most. His peerless, blameless life was long enough for glory; and but one brief day, perhaps one hour only, too short for liberty. One hour more for him in the saddle, and the Confederate States would have taken their place at the council-board of the nations.

Governor Harris thus notes some of the points he had observed in General Johnston in the last half-year of his life:

From the day that General Albert Sidney Johnston assumed command of the Department of the West, in September, 1861, to the moment of his death, I was in almost constant intercourse with him, either in personal consultation or correspondence by letter or telegram.

Our official positions necessarily brought us in contact, and official intercourse soon warmed into personal friendship, and, on my part, into decided admiration for the great ability, unselfish and self-sacrificing patriotism, and exalted chivalry, of the general.

I was with him when the telegram announced the surrender of the Confederate forces at Donelson, and had occasion to admire the philosophic heroism with which he met, not only the disaster, but the unjust censure and complaints of both army and people, the coolness and energy with which he set about the work of reorganizing the remnant of his army, and the establishment of a new and different line of defense. I was with him most of the time of his retreat from Nashville to Corinth, and was not unfrequently astonished at the coolness, vigilance, and untiring energy with which he struggled to overcome the numerous obstacles and difficulties which surrounded him.

The following is an extract from Dr. Craven's "Prison Life of Mr. Davis" (page 210):

Had Albert Sidney Johnston lived, Mr. Davis was of opinion our [the Federal] success down the Mississippi would have been fatally checked at Corinth. This officer best realized his ideal of a perfect commander—large in view, discreet in council, silent as to his own plans, observant and penetrative of the enemy's, sudden and impetuous in action, but of a nerve and balance of judgment which no heat of danger or complexity of manœuvre could upset or bewilder. All that Napoleon said of Dessaix and Kléber, save the slovenly habits of one of them, might be combined and truthfully said of Albert Sidney Johnston.

President Davis, in speaking of him to the writer in August, 1862, said his consistency of action and conduct differed from any other man's he ever knew. In every other man he had seen inconsistency ; in him, none. He said his was the only arm he ever felt able to lean upon with entire confidence. It was a severe struggle to let him go West—he wanted him as Secretary of War—but the West was a field vast and distant, where the chief must act without advice or aid, and he seemed the only man equal to it.

If allowance is to be made for the unlimited confidence of Mr. Davis in General Johnston, it must be remembered that the admiration was mutual, and that their friendship was founded on long and intimate acquaintance, and tried by many tests. Alfriend, in his "Life of Davis" (page 334), says:

Few of the eminent soldiers who had sought service under the banners of the Confederacy had a more brilliant record of actual service; and to the advantages of reputation General Johnston added those graces and distinctions of person with which the imagination invests the ideal commander. He was considerably past middle age, his height exceeded six feet, his frame was large and sinewy, his every movement and posture indicated vigorous and athletic manhood. The general expression of his striking face was grave and composed, but inviting rather than austere.

The arrival of General Johnston in Richmond, early in September, was a source of peculiar congratulation to President Davis. Between these illustrious men had existed for many years an endearment, born of close association, common trials and triumphs, and mutual confidence, which rendered most auspicious their coöperation in the cause of Southern independence.

The late Prof. A. T. Bledsoe, a very able and eminent writer and thinker, in one of his publications, says :

Albert Sidney Johnston, who, take him all in all, was the simplest, bravest, grandest man we have ever known, once said to the present writer, "There is no measuring such a man as Davis; " and this high tribute had a fitting counterpart in that which Davis paid Johnston, when discussing in the Federal Senate the Utah Expedition.

This tribute has been already quoted.

General Richard Taylor, in the advanced sheets of his "Reminiscences," published March, 1878, in the "Southern Historical Society Papers," says:

SHILOH.

Shiloh was a great misfortune. At the moment of his fall, Sidney Johnston, with all the energy of his nature, was pressing on the routed foe. Crouching under the bank of the Tennessee River, Grant was helpless. One short hour more of life to Johnston would have completed his destruction. The second in command—Beauregard—was on another and distant part of the field, and, before he could gather the reins of direction, darkness fell and stopped the pursuit. During the night Buell reached the northern bank of the river and crossed his troops. Wallace, with a fresh division from below, got up. Together they advanced in the morning, found the Confederates rioting in the plunder of captured camps, and drove them back with loss. But all this was as nothing compared with the calamity of Johnston's death. Educated at West Point, Johnston remained in the United States Army for eight years, and acquired a thorough knowledge of the details of military duty. Resigning to aid the cause of the infant Republic of Texas, he became her adjutant-general, senior brigadier, and Secretary at War. In the war with Mexico he raised a regiment of Texans to join General Zachary Taylor, and was greatly distinguished in the fighting around and capture of Monterey. General Taylor, with whom the early years of his service had been passed, declared him to be the best soldier he had ever commanded. More than once I have heard General Zachary Taylor express this opinion. Two cavalry regiments were added to the United States Army in 1854, and to the colonelcy of one of these Johnston was appointed. Subsequently, a brigadier by brevet, he commanded the expedition against the Mormons in Utah. Thus he brought to the Southern cause a civil and military experience far surpassing that of any other leader. Born in Kentucky, descended from an honorable colonial race, connected by marriage with influential families in the West, where his life had been passed, he was peculiarly fitted to command Western armies. With him at the helm, there would have been no Vicksburg, no Missionary Ridge, no Atlanta. His character was lofty and pure; his presence and demeanor dignified and courteous, with the simplicity of a child; and he at once inspired the respect and gained the confidence of cultivated gentlemen and rugged frontiersmen. Besides, he had passed through the furnace of ignorant newspapers, hotter than that of the Babylonian tyrant. Commanding some raw, unequipped forces at Bowling Green, Kentucky, the accustomed American exaggeration represented him as at the head of a vast army, prepared and eager for conquest. Before time was given him to organize and train his men, the absurdly-constructed works on his left flank were captured. At Fort Donelson, on the Cumberland, were certain political generals, who, with a self-abnegation worthy of Plutarch's heroes, were anxious to get away and leave the glory and renown of defense to others. Johnston was in no sense responsible for the construction of these forts, nor the assignment to their command of these self-denying warriors, but his line of communication was uncovered by their fall, and he was compelled to retire to the southern bank of the Tennessee River. From the enlighteners of public opinion a howl of wrath came forth. Johnston, who had just been Alexander, Hannibal, Cæsar, Napoleon, was now a miserable dastard and traitor, unfit to command a corporal's guard! President Davis sought to console him, and the noblest lines ever penned by man were written by Johnston in reply. They even wrung tears of repentance from the pachyderms who had attacked him, and will be a text and consolation to future commanders who serve a country tolerant of an ignorant and licentious press. As pure gold he came forth from the furnace, above the reach of slander, the foremost man of all the South; and had it been possible for one heart, one mind, and one arm, to save her cause, she lost them when Albert Sidney Johnston fell on the field of Shiloh. As soon after the war as she was permitted, the Commonwealth of Texas removed his remains from New Orleans, to inter them in a land he had long and faithfully served. I was honored by a request to accompany the coffin from the cemetery to the steamer, and as I gazed upon it there arose the feeling of the Theban who, after the downfall of the glory and independence of his country, stood by the tomb of Epaminondas.

The following has been sent to the writer from New Orleans :

No eulogy has been composed, no tribute has been rendered, giving more fitting expression to the lofty qualities that marked the illustrious dead, when living, than the following beautiful epitaph, which was found pasted on a rough board attached to the tomb, by a lady passing through the St. Louis Cemetery of this city, and which was first published in the *New Orleans Times :*

IN MEMORIAM.

BY JOHN B. S. DIMITRY, OF NEW ORLEANS.

———

BEHIND THIS STONE IS LAID, FOR A SEASON,

ALBERT SIDNEY JOHNSTON,

A GENERAL IN THE ARMY OF THE CONFEDERATE STATES,

Who fell at Shiloh, Tennessee,
On the sixth day of April,
Eighteen hundred and sixty-two.
A man tried in many high offices
And critical Enterprises,
And found faithful in all;
His life was one long Sacrifice of Interest to Conscience;
And even that life, on a woful Sabbath,
Did he yield as a Holocaust at his Country's need.
Not wholly understood was he while he lived;
But, in his death, his Greatness stands confessed
In a People's tears.
Resolute, moderate, clear of envy, yet not wanting
In that finer Ambition which makes men great and pure;
In his Honor—impregnable;
In his Simplicity—sublime;
No country e'er had a truer Son—no Cause a nobler Champion;
No People a bolder Defender—no Principle a purer Victim,
Than the dead Soldier
Who sleeps here!
The Cause for which he perished is lost—
The People for whom he fought are crushed—
The Hopes in which he trusted are shattered—
The Flag he loved guides no more the charging lines;
But his Fame, consigned to the keeping of that Time which,
Happily, is not so much the Tomb of Virtue as its Shrine,
Shall, in the years to come, fire Modest Worth to Noble Ends.
In honor, now, our great Captain rests;
A bereaved People mourn him;
Three Commonwealths proudly claim him;
And History shall cherish him
Among those Choicer Spirits, who, holding their Conscience unmixed with blame,
Have been, in all Conjunctures, true to themselves, their People, and their God.

With the apology already offered in the beginning of this chapter, and with the explanation that the writer does not profess that his delineation is unbiased, he ventures to call attention to those points in General Johnston's character which struck him most forcibly, and in the contemplation of which a young man may find his profit. Let this estimate go merely as the writer's *filial claim* for General Johnston to certain great qualities of mind and soul, unless this biography has made his title to them as clear as day. Wherein he is not justified by the facts, the reader will readily perceive that he errs, and lay it to the frailty of our common humanity.

There is, however, one relation in which he is entitled to speak with authority: General Johnston was to him not only a tender father, but a wise counselor and a safe friend. His whole conduct was marked by kindness, confidence, and unselfish devotion. In all their intercourse, memory can recall no angry word, no unkind act, not even a harsh look, to sully the untarnished record of mutual affection. Such is believed to be the experience of all his family.

He was gentle to women and children ; tender to the weak and suffering, gracious to subordinates and dependents, just and magnanimous to equals and rivals, respectful to superiors, and tolerant to all men. Not envious, jealous, or suspicious; yet so high strung was his spirit that he could ill-brook personal indignity or insult. Such was his self-respect, however, that he rarely had to check a want of respect in others. It has been seen with what patience and fortitude, indeed with what serenity, he bore private griefs and public contumely. His nature, his education, his philosophy, his religion, had so finely tempered his soul that at last he had in him no fear, except of doing wrong.

He had no love for and little need of money, and was generous and liberal in its use. In matters immaterial he was facile ; in things of import, scrupulous and just ; and his quick intelligence never failed to perceive the doubtful dividing line.

Naturally of a high, courageous, and resolute spirit, he found it difficult to swerve from a line of action he had marked out ; and the more so, because his opinions were formed after deliberation. Yet, that his mental processes were rapid is seen by the decision with which he acted. He was not proof against the love of glory; but in him it was transmuted to a fine ambition to be and to do, not simply to seem. Results he left to take care of themselves, if only he could do his duty. All this came from his love of truth, which was with him a passion. He sought the truth, striving to know it, and to live up to it in greater and smaller things. Hence, though perceiving that success is the world's test of merit, he could square his acts by another standard.

As a general, his tactics were skillful, and his strategy was bold and sagacious. In council, he was enterprising, yet wary; in assault, audacious, impetuous, and unrelenting ; in disaster, tenacious, resourceful, and composed. While he knew and regarded all the details of his profession, his skill in handling large bodies of troops was remarkable ; and he grasped with ease the broadest generalizations of war. Time will add to his reputation as a general. Above all, his life and character were self-contained, perfectly consistent, and complete in their rounded fullness.

He did many great and noble deeds, and won rank, power, and applause, without tarnish to his modesty and simplicity. He suffered much in mind, body, and estate, without repining; not only with patience, but in silence. Like some great tree, which finds in earth, and air, and storm, and sunshine, nourishment for its growth, he drew sweetness and strength from every element of Nature, and from every dispensation of Providence. He was a man to be loved, to be reverenced, and to be emulated.

General Johnston dared to say in the midst of immeasurable disasters: "The test of merit in my profession, with the people, is success. It is a hard rule, but I think it right." Perhaps, with still wider scope, *success* is the test of merit in a human life. But, even measured by this hard rule, the most adverse criticism cannot pronounce his life a failure. Rejecting patronage, standing on merit alone, inflexible in right, and devoted to duty, a whole people regard him as the very pattern of a noble citizen, an able leader, a splendid soldier, a great general, and an upright man. Millions wept for him. The ablest and the best wrote for him the proud epitaph that on his arm rested the sinking fortunes of the state. Who will, then, dare to say he did not achieve success? If money, if office, if luxury, if rank, if power, alone go to make it up, then he did live in vain. But none of these did he value highly. He won the crown for which he strove—the approval of the wise and good.

> " 'Tis only the actions of the just
> Smell sweet and blossom in the dust."

And, finally, those who loved him will find consolation for his end, in a sentiment borrowed from the civil law, that may well be a common heritage to the South in thinking on her martyrs :

> " Qui pro republica ceciderint, in perpetuum,
> Per gloriam vivere intelliguntur! "

> " We know that those who for their country die,
> Through glory live again immortally."

INDEX.

THE END.

Other titles of interest

**THE MILITARY OPERATIONS OF
GENERAL BEAUREGARD
In the War Between the States,
1861 to 1865**
Alfred Roman
New introduction by
T. Michael Parrish
Vol. I: 614 pp., 1 illus.
80546-4 $17.95
Vol. II: 715 pp., 1 illus.
80547-2 $17.95

**THE RISE AND FALL OF THE
CONFEDERATE GOVERNMENT**
Jefferson Davis
New foreword by
James M. McPherson
Vol. I: 636 pp., 10 illus.
80418-2 $17.95
Vol. II: 696 pp., 26 illus.
80419-0 $17.95

THE RISE OF U. S. GRANT
Colonel Arthur L. Conger
New introduction by
Brooks D. Simpson
432 pp., 12 photos and 14 maps
80693-2 $15.95

**SHERMAN
Soldier, Realist, American**
B. H. Liddell Hart
New foreword by Jay Luvaas
480 pp., 11 maps
80507-3 $15.95

**SINGING SOLDIERS
A History of the Civil War in Song**
Selections and historical
commentary by Paul Glass
Musical arrangement for piano
and guitar by Louis C. Singer
300 pp., 88 illus.
80021-7 $14.95

**STONEWALL JACKSON AND
THE AMERICAN CIVIL WAR**
G. F. R. Henderson
New introduction by
Thomas L. Connelly
740 pp.
80318-6 $16.95

**STONEWALL JACKSON,
ROBERT E. LEE, AND THE
ARMY OF NORTHERN
VIRGINIA, 1862**
Col. William Allan
New introduction by
Robert K. Krick
755 pp., 16 maps, 1 photo
80656-8 $19.95

**THE STORY OF THE
CONFEDERACY**
Robert Selph Henry
Foreword by
Douglas Southall Freeman
526 pp.
80370-4 $14.95

**TRAGIC YEARS 1860–1865
A Documentary History of the
American Civil War**
Paul M. Angle and
Earl Schenck Miers
1108 pp.
80462-X $23.95

**THE WARTIME PAPERS OF
ROBERT E. LEE**
Edited by Clifford Dowdey and
Louis H. Manarin
1,012 pp.
80282-1 $19.95

Available at your bookstore

OR ORDER DIRECTLY FROM

DA CAPO PRESS

1-800-321-0050